ENCYCLOPEDIA OF

U.S.-LATIN AMERICAN RELATIONS

Volume

1

ENCYCLOPEDIA OF U.S.-LATIN AMERICAN RELATIONS

Thomas M. Leonard, EDITOR IN CHIEF

Jürgen Buchenau
Kyle Longley
Graeme S. Mount
ASSOCIATE EDITORS

SAGE | CQPRESS

Los Angeles | London | New Delhi
Singapore | Washington DC

SAGE | CQ PRESS

Los Angeles | London | New Delhi
Singapore | Washington DC

FOR INFORMATION:

CQ Press
An Imprint of SAGE Publications, Inc.
2455 Teller Road
Thousand Oaks, California 91320
E-mail: order@sagepub.com

SAGE Publications Ltd.
1 Oliver's Yard
55 City Road
London, EC1Y 1SP
United Kingdom

SAGE Publications India Pvt. Ltd.
B 1/I 1 Mohan Cooperative Industrial Area
Mathura Road, New Delhi 110 044
India

SAGE Publications Asia-Pacific Pte. Ltd.
33 Pekin Street #02-01
Far East Square
Singapore 048763

Acquisitions Editor: Doug Goldenberg-Hart
Development Editor: John Martino
Production Editor: Belinda Josey
Copy Editors: Tina Hardy and Jacqueline Tash
Typesetter: C&M Digitals (P) Ltd.
Proofreaders: Barbara Johnson and Laura Webb
Indexer: Indexing Partners
Cover Designer: Anne C. Kerns, Anne Likes Red, Inc.
Maps: Vernon R. Payne
Marketing Manager: Ben Krasney

Cover photos: MONROE DOCTRINE, 1823. 'The Birth of the Monroe Doctrine.' Left to right: John Quincy Adams, William Harris Crawford, William Wirt, President James Monroe, John C. Calhoun, Daniel D. Tompkins, and John McLean. After the painting by Clyde O. DeLand. The Granger Collection, NYC—All rights reserved; PANAMA: CULEBRA CUT, 1910. Excavating the Gaillard (Culebra) Cut for the Panama Canal, c1910: contemporary engraving. The Granger Collection, NYC—All rights reserved; U.S. President Barack Obama welcomes Mexico's President Felipe Calderon at an arrival ceremony during his state visit on the South Lawn of the White House in Washington, May 19, 2010. KEVIN LAMARQUE/Reuters/Landov

Back cover photo: Antique Map of Mexico and Central America, 1890. iStockphoto Collection, Thinkstock

Encyclopedia of U.S.-Latin American relations / Thomas M. Leonard, editor in chief ; Jürgen Buchenau, Kyle Longley, Graeme S. Mount, associate editors.

v. cm.
Includes bibliographical references and index.

Contents: v. 1. A–E — v. 2. F–N — v. 3. O–Z.
ISBN 978-0-87289-762-5 (hardbound: acid-free paper)

1. Latin America—Foreign relations—United States—Encyclopedias. 2. United States—Foreign relations—Latin America—Encyclopedias. I. Leonard, Thomas M., II. Buchenau, Jürgen, III. Longley, Kyle. IV. Mount, Graeme S. (Graeme Stewart), V. Title: Encyclopedia of US-Latin American relations.

F1418.E59 2012
327.730803—dc23 2011051158

SFI Certified Sourcing
www.sfiprogram.org
SFI-00453

This book is printed on acid-free paper.
11 12 13 14 15 10 9 8 7 6 5 4 3 2 1

A special thanks to the 160 scholars and the eleven
(but two are companies) SAGE/CQ Press staff
members whose contributions made possible the
Encyclopedia of U.S.-Latin American Relations

CONTENTS

ALPHABETICAL TABLE OF CONTENTS

ABOUT THE EDITORS

Editor in Chief

Thomas M. Leonard is Distinguished University Professor Emeritus at the University of North Florida, where he served as Chair of the Department of History and Founder and Director of the International Studies Program. He has also taught at universities in Argentina, Bulgaria, Chile, China, Honduras, Mexico, and Poland. Among his eighteen books and reference works are: *A History of Honduras; Fidel Castro: A Biography; Latin America During World War II* (with John Bratzel); *Panama, the Canal and the United States; Central America and the United States; The United States and Latin America, 1850–1903;* and the *Encyclopedia of the Developing World,* chosen as an Outstanding Reference Source by the Reference and User Services Association in 2007. He has also contributed chapters and articles to numerous scholarly books and journals. Professor Leonard has been the recipient of research grants from the National Endowment for the Humanities, the Ford Foundation, the Andrew Mellon Foundation, and several presidential libraries. He has also received four Fulbright awards. In 2008 Leonard received the presidential medal for achievement from his undergraduate alma mater, Mt. St. Mary's University (Md.)

Associate Editors

Jürgen Buchenau is Professor of History and Latin American Studies at the University of North Carolina at Charlotte, where he is also chair of the Department of History. He is the author, editor, or co-editor of eight books, including the following monographs: *In the Shadow of the Giant: The Making of Mexico's Central America Policy* (1996); *Tools of Progress: A German Merchant Family in Mexico City* (2004); *Plutarco Elías Calles and the Mexican Revolution* (2006); and *The Last Caudillo: Alvaro Obregón and the Mexican Revolution.* He is currently working on a book on the Sonoran Dynasty in revolutionary Mexico. He has also published numerous articles in scholarly journals as well as book chapters in edited collections. Professor Buchenau is the founding director of the Latin American Studies program at University of North Carolina at Charlotte, and he is editor of the Viewpoints/Puntos de Vista book series published by Wiley Blackwell. He received two fellowships from the National Endowment for the Humanities (2001–2002 and 2008–2009).

Kyle Longley is the Snell Family Dean's Distinguished Professor in the School of Historical, Philosophical, and Religious Studies and School of Politics and Global Studies at Arizona State University. He is the author of *The Sparrow and the Hawk: Costa Rica and the United States during the Rise of Jose Figueres* (1997), *In the Eagle's Shadow: The United States and Latin America* (2002, second edition 2009), *Senator Albert Gore Sr.: Tennessee Maverick* (2004); editor and contributor to *Deconstructing Reagan: Conservative Mythology and America's Fortieth President* (2006), and *Grunts: The American Combat Soldier in Vietnam* (2008). He forthcoming works include *The Houses of the Purple Hearts: The Morenci Nine, Small Town America, and the Vietnam War* and *The Switzerland of the Americas? A Concise History of Costa Rica* (with Jason Colby). He has written numerous articles, essays, and reviews in journals including *The Americas* and *Diplomatic History*. Currently, he is president of the Pacific Coast Branch of the American Historical Association.

Graeme S. Mount is Professor Emeritus in the Department of History at Laurentian University, Sudbury, Ontario, Canada. He is guest editor of the thematic issue on Canada and the Caribbean in the *Revista/Review Interamericana*, VII, 1 (1977); and he is author or co-author of *Presbyterian Missions to Trinidad and Puerto Rico, 1868–1914* (Lancelot Press, 1983); *An Introduction to Canadian-American Relations* (first edition: Methuen, 1984; second edition: Nelson, 1989); *The Caribbean Basin: An International History* (Routledge, 1998); *Invisible and Inaudible in Washington: U.S.-Canadian Relations during the Cold War* (University of British Columbia Press, 1999); *Chile and the Nazis* (Black Rose, 2002). He has researched in archives in Australia, Canada, Chile, Colombia, Panama, Puerto Rico, Trinidad, the United Kingdom and the United States; and he has presented seminars or participated in conferences in Australia, Canada, China, Colombia, Jamaica, Mexico, South Korea, Trinidad and Tobago, the United Kingdom, and the United States. In 2000, he won the teaching award at Laurentian University.

LIST OF AUTHORS

Gabriel Aguilera
California State University, Chico

Omar H. Ali
University of North Carolina at Greensboro

David R. Andersen
California State University, Sacramento

Dinorah Azpuru
Wichita State University

Stephen Azzi
Carleton University

John R. Bawden
University of Montevallo

John Belohlavek
University of South Florida

Mark T. Berger
Naval Postgraduate School

Anastasia Bermúdez
Instituto de Estudios Sociales Avanzados (IESA-CSIC)); and Queen Mary, University of London

Larry Birns
Council on Hemispheric Affairs (COHA)

John F. Bratzel
Michigan State University

John A. Britton
Francis Marion University

Kendall Brown
Brigham Young University

William H. Brown
North Carolina Office of Archives and History

Alison J. Bruey
University of North Florida

Jürgen Buchenau
University of North Carolina at Charlotte

Christina Bueno
Northeastern Illinois University

Joan Caivano
Inter-American Dialogue

Peter Calvert
University of Southampton

Elaine Carey
St. John's University

David M. Carletta
The Church of St. Matthew and St. Timothy

David B. Castle
Ohio University

Miguel Centellas
University of Mississippi

Kevin Chambers
Gonzaga University

Roslyn K. Chavda
University of New Hampshire

Jack Child
American University

Joel Christenson
West Virginia University

Martin Christiansen
University of Wisconsin-Milwaukee

Lawrence Clayton
University of Alabama

Sharon C. Cobb
University of North Florida

Jason M. Colby
University of Victoria

Bradley Lynn Coleman
U.S. Southern Command

Joanne Connor Green
Texas Christian University

Christopher Conway
University of Texas at Arlington

Guadalupe Correa-Cabrera
The University of Texas at Brownsville

Gisela Cramer
Universidad Nacional de Colombia

Gregory S. Crider
Winthrop University

William W. Culver
Emeritus, State University of New York at Plattsburgh

José de Arimatéia da Cruz
Armstrong Atlantic State University

Juanita Darling
San Francisco State University

Melvin D. Davis
University of North Alabama

Fernando G. De Maio
Simon Fraser University

Gregory J. Dehler
Front Range Community College

Helen Delpar
Emerita, Emerita, University of Alabama

Arlene J. Díaz
Indiana University-Bloomington

John W. Dietrich
Bryant University

Dawn Mooney Digrius
Stevens Institute of Technology

Oliver J. Dinius
University of Mississippi

Scott Dittloff
University of the Incarnate Word

Thomas J. Dodd
Georgetown University

Michael E. Donoghue
Marquette University

Susanne Eineigel
University of Maryland

Dean Fafoutis
Salisbury University

Tamara L. Falicov
University of Kansas

José B. Fernández
University of Central Florida

Susan Fitzpatrick Behrens
California State University, Northridge

Nicola Foote
Florida Gulf Coast University

Max Paul Friedman
American University

Andrés Gallo
University of North Florida

Justin D. García
Temple University

Jolyon P. Girard
Emeritus, Cabrini College

Philippe R. Girard
McNeese State University

Ann B. González
University of North Carolina at Charlotte

Luis A. González
Indiana University-Bloomington

Alex Goodall
University of York

Peter C. Grosvenor
Pacific Lutheran University

Peter B. Gushue
Pacific Lutheran University

Paul Haber
University of Montana

Michael R. Hall
Armstrong Atlantic State University

Gina Hames
Pacific Lutheran University

William Head
Warner Robins Air Logistics Center, Office of History, US Air Force

Monica Henry
Université Paris-Est Créteil

Andrew S. Hernández III
Western New Mexico University

Sean M. Heuvel
Christopher Newport University

Jesse Hingson
Jacksonville University

James A. Holeman
Arizona State University

Imtiaz Hussain
Universidad Iberoamericana

Andrey Isérov
Institute of World History, Russian Academy of Sciences, Moscow University

Matt D. Jacobs
Ohio University

Peggy Ann James
University of Wisconsin-Parkside

Eric M. Jepsen
University of South Dakota

David Jervis
Millikin University

Blake Jones
Arizona State University

Halbert Jones
Saint Antony's College, University of Oxford

Mark S. Joy
Jamestown College

Daniel Joyce
Princeton University

William C. Kelly
Texas Christian University

Mee-Ae Kim
College of Idaho

Betsy Konefal
College of William & Mary

Glen David Kuecker
DePauw University

Jonathan Laderoute
Laurentian University

Michael LaRosa
Rhodes College

George M. Lauderbaugh
Jacksonville State University

Robert Lawless
Wichita State University

Andrew Lefebvre
University of Calgary

Thomas M. Leonard
Emeritus, University of North Florida

Daniel K. Lewis
California State Polytechnic University, Pomona

Kyle Longley
Arizona State University

Derric Ludens
Dakota Wesleyan University

Lincoln Maiztegui Casas
Instituto Preuniversitario de Montevideo

Mary Fran T. Malone
University of New Hampshire

Andrae Marak
Indiana University-Purdue University, Columbus

Daniel M. Masterson
United States Naval Academy

Gelien Matthews
University of the West Indies, St. Augustine Campus

Eugenio Matibag
Iowa State University

Rebecca Tinio McKenna
Yale University

Alan McPherson
University of Oklahoma

Carlos Meissner
University of York

Andrew P. Miller
Wilkes University

Patit Paban Mishra
Sambalpur University

Stephen D. Morris
Middle Tennessee State University

Graeme S. Mount
Emeritus, Laurentian University

Oliver Murphey
Columbia University

Greg Murphy
U.S. State Department

Todd Myers
Grossmont College

Lopita Nath
University of the Incarnate Word

Jorge Ortiz-Sotelo
Instituto Peruano de Economía y Política

Charlene T. Overturf
Independent Scholar

Steven K. Paulson
University of North Florida

Lourenço S. Paz
Syracuse University

Thomas L. Pearcy
Slippery Rock University

Luisa Peirano
Universidad de Montevideo

Ronn Pineo
Towson University

Julio Cèsar Pino
Kent State University

Ursula Prutsch
Ludwig Maximilians University Munich

Donald A. Rakestraw
Georgia Southern University

Monica Rankin
University of Texas at Dallas

Matthew A. Redinger
Montana State University Billings

Matthew L. Rhoades
University of Houston-Victoria

St. John Robinson
Montana State University Billings

Ryan Salzman
Southern Methodist University

Brinsley Samaroo
University of the West Indies, St. Augustine Campus

John Sanbrailo
Pan American Development Foundation

Lia T. Schraeder
Georgia Gwinnett College

Laura Isabel Serna
University of Southern California

David M. K. Sheinin
Trent University

James F. Siekmeier
West Virginia University

Donald C. Simmons
Dakota Wesleyan University

Cigdem V. Sirin
University of Texas at El Paso

William E. Skuban
California State University, Fresno

Joseph Smith
University of Exeter

Jeffrey W. Steagall
Weber State University

Steven L. Taylor
Troy University

Aubrey A. Thompson
Morgan State University

Ellen D. Tillman
Texas State University in San Marcos

Teruyuki Tsuji
Kwansei Gakuin University

César A. Vásquez
Independent Scholar

Ivani Vassoler
State University of New York–Fredonia

Klaus Veigel
Frankfurt, Germany

Carlos Velásquez Carrillo
York University

José D. Villalobos
University of Texas at El Paso

Miriam Elizabeth Villanueva
Texas Christian University

Christine J. Wade
Washington College

Gregory Weeks
University of North Carolina at Charlotte

W. Michael Weis
Illinois Wesleyan University

Virginia S. Williams
Winthrop University

Bruce M. Wilson
University of Central Florida

Molly M. Wood
Wittenberg University

Jasmine Noelle Yarish
University of California, Santa Barbara

Jason Zorbas
University of Saskatchewan

Cristóbal Zúñiga Espinoza
State University of New York-Stony Brook

PREFACE

Until the end of World War II, only a few universities in the United States offered a Latin American studies program, including coursework on Inter-American relations. Otherwise, a survey of Latin American history or governments was standard fare at most colleges and universities. As U.S. interest in the region's culture and history grew with Latin America's participation in global affairs since World War II and the influx of immigrants from its territories, so too has Latin American studies' place in college curriculums. Still, despite the proximity of Latin America to the United States, the average student of history and politics often misunderstood the region's due place in U.S. foreign policy. Certainly Latin America played an undeniable role in important periods in U.S. history, from westward expansion to gunboat diplomacy and above all to the Cold War against communism, but the unique trajectories of Latin American countries and the individuals who live there are not always presented or understood in their own right. Furthermore, widely available reference materials—whether the general print encyclopedias dominant until the 1980s or the Internet resources prevalent today—tend to offer limited depth and breadth about the impact of prominent U.S. figures on Latin America and vice versa. Meanwhile, owing to student reading habits, textbooks and monographs covering the subject have become more interpretative and shorter in length. A comprehensive and reliable resource that focuses specifically on the interaction between the United States and its southern neighbors has been lacking. The three-volume *Encyclopedia of U.S.–Latin American Relations* (EUSLA) is designed to fill the void.

Early surveys of U.S.–Latin American relations, such as J. Fred Rippy's *Latin America in World Politics* (1919), Samuel Flagg Bemis's *The Latin American Policy of the United States* (1947), Graham H. Stuart's *The United States and Latin America* (1955), and J. Lloyd Mecham's *The United States and Inter-American Security, 1889-1960* (1964), reflect the historical writing of the time, with attention to factual detail. More recent surveys of U.S.–Latin American relations are shorter in length and interpretative in content, as found in the works of Don M. Coever and Linda Hall, *Tangled Destinies: Latin America and the United States* (1999); Mark T. Gilderhus, *The Second Century: U.S.-Latin American Relations since 1889* (2000); and, Joseph Smith, *The United States and Latin America* (2005). Kyle Longley's *In the Eagle's Shadow: The United States and Latin America* (2002) is a blend of interpretation and historical evidence. The individual volumes of Lester Langley's widely acclaimed nineteen-volume series on relations between the United States and individual Latin American nations (except Central America, which is treated as a unit) are brief; in addition to government relations, they include discussions on culture, economics, and politics.

Fidel Castro Ruz's Cuban Revolution significantly contributed to the rapid expansion of Latin American studies in the United States, Canada, and Europe and eventually in South Korea and China. Owing to the Cold War environment, Inter-American relations received special attention. The accompanying knowledge explosion is illustrated by more than nine hundred publications dedicated to the United States and Central America during the 1980s alone. The need for a comprehensive encyclopedia became apparent.

EUSLA's A to Z format provides its users with a comprehensive set of entries that cover the historical record from 1800 to the present. Because historical events do not occur in a vacuum, EUSLA provides the users with a contextual framework. First, the encyclopedia's introduction discusses the broad parameters at play in the various historical periods. Building on this, separate entries throughout the work explain U.S. relations with the individual Latin American nations over time. Biographies of both U.S. and Latin American figures focus on their mutual interactions. Economic organizations and even the development of certain key resources (such as bananas, coffee, copper, and oil) are analyzed for their impact on Inter-American interactions. A set of cross-references at the end of each essay directs the user to related entries, and the suggested reading list steers the user to the most pertinent works related to the entry.

Several individuals are responsible for bringing EUSLA to a successful conclusion. I am grateful to Acquisitions Editor Doug Goldenberg-Hart for bringing the project to CQ Press. There, the watchful eye and skillful management style of CQ Press Development Editor John Martino brought EUSLA to a successful conclusion. John proved to be more than a most competent individual; his personal demeanor made the bumps easier to glide across. Without the efforts of the CQ Press support staff—Liza Baron, Reed Cooley—and production team of Catherine Getzie, Belinda Josey, Tina Hardy, and Jacqueline Tasch, the final product would not have been possible. Words alone fail to adequately express my appreciation to the associate editors—Jürgen Buchenau (University of North Carolina at Charlotte), Kyle Longley (Arizona State University), and Graeme S. Mount (Laurentian University–Canada)—for their continuing contributions and patience. The efforts of

Paul Mosely and Vernon R. Payne at the University of North Florida are also appreciated. Mosely, a reference librarian, appeared never to tire of the continuous calls and e-mails for assistance in verifying historical accuracy or tracking down obscure materials. Payne, a graphic artist, meticulously completed the maps that appear throughout EUSLA, no easy task as he received advice and suggestions from several individuals. All of us are indebted to the 160 scholars whose expertise, contributions, and cooperation made the EUSLA a reality. And, to my late wife, Yvonne, who cannot share the joy of this accomplishment but remains an inspiration to myself and our six children.

Thomas M. Leonard
Distinguished University Professor Emeritus
University of North Florida
Jacksonville, Florida
October 25, 2011

INTRODUCTION THE CONTEXT OF U.S.–LATIN AMERICAN RELATIONS

The United States and Latin America had vastly different colonial experiences, which affected their relationship after 1800. For their part, the British practiced *noblesse oblige* toward their North American colonies until 1763, when they finally attempted to impose British rule. The subsequent conflict resulted in the United States of America, confident of itself in both domestic and foreign affairs. In contrast, the Spanish governed their American colonies with a tight hand that left new Latin American nations in the 1820s without experience in governing at home or in conducting foreign affairs. Conventional wisdom thus concludes that the United States and Latin America carried these traditions into their mutual relations, the legacy of which remains today.

While scholars continue to debate conventional wisdom's argument, many other factors came forward to affect U.S.–Latin American relations. Nineteenth-century domestic considerations shaped the early foreign policy of each party and significantly contributed to their mutual relations during the first thirty years of the twentieth century. Latin America was motivated primarily by economic development, whereas U.S. policy became greatly influenced by the trappings of a burgeoning global power. With World War II and the Cold War confirming its role as world leader, the United States established a Latin American policy that increasingly relied on military assistance to maintain the established order. For the most part, elite civilian rulers gave way to military generals, a governmental system that lasted from the late 1960s until the early 1980s. Democracy and socioeconomic opportunity became the sacrificial lambs. During that time period, only President Jimmy Carter attempted to change U.S. policy. Starting in the 1980s, Latin America jettisoned its military rulers and returned to democratic governments, although the meaning of democracy varies from country to country. This transition resulted in a plethora of political parties, the majority of which represented deprived socioeconomic groups. At the same time, the Latin American governments accepted the neoliberal economic model, which in application meant the establishment of free markets, export expansion of primary goods, and a positive environment for direct foreign investment. By the mid-1990s, the system was in place, but the benefits thereof did not reach the downtrodden, and this played a significant role in the election of Latin America's current populist governments. The initial U.S. enthusiasm for a Free Trade Area of the Americas (FTAA) in the early 1990s gave way to greater concerns with international terrorism and a severe economic crisis. Despite presidential promises to the contrary, the United States has recently given little attention to Latin America. The vacuum led the Latin Americans to seek out other partners, notably the Chinese. One can only speculate about the future, but when Inter-American relations again are on the proverbial front burner, the United States may be dealing with a more confident Latin America.

The introduction that follows is designed to take the reader through the historical periods mentioned above and provide the ever-changing context of U.S.–Latin American relations.

A HESITANT BEGINNING: 1800–1860

In the 1820s Secretary of State John Quincy Adams instructed the U.S. ministers assigned to the newly independent Latin American nations to find out everything possible about them, including potential markets for U.S. goods. U.S. ignorance about Latin America in the 1820s can be attributed, in part, to Spanish colonial policy, which largely closed the colonies to foreigners. Only a few outsiders—among them Thomas Gage, Ravaneu de Lusan, John Cockburn, John Roach, and one North American, John Rhodes—recorded their travel experiences to Spain's New World empire. There are no indications that any North American library held any of their works. Thomas Jefferson, however, did read Alexander von Humboldt's 1808 classic, "Political Essay on the Kingdom of New Spain," which covered his travels to Venezuela, Peru, Mexico, and Cuba.

Latin America's colonial experience and isolation severely restricted its understanding of the outside world. A small number of Latin Americans may have read the works of Antonio de Aledo Bexar, Abe Renal, and Abbé Pradt, who described the U.S. economy and geography and discussed the country's revolution, constitutional government, and religious toleration. Certainly most of the early Latin American patriots had read the Declaration of Independence, U.S. Constitution, and some of Tom Paine's writings, but personal contacts between Latin Americans and U.S. citizens after the American Revolution were negligible. Most of the Latin Americans who came north were on official business seeking to enlist U.S. support for the fledgling independence movements. A few, such as Guatemalan scientist José Felipe Flores, returned home to spread their favorable impressions of the United States. Latin American liberals applauded the great extent of civil and political freedom, religious toleration, social equality, and literacy, as well as the lack of pomp and ceremony. Others understood that the societies of both hemispheres differed greatly and suggested that the federal form of government might not apply to Spanish America. In particular, Latin American elites feared that any changes in the existing institutions would destroy their orderly world and privileged position. They remained Latin America's most pessimistic group about using the United States as a political or social model.

Despite their mutual isolation and ignorance, the United States and the Latin Americans shared three foreign policy objectives: a trans-isthmian canal to facilitate shipping between the Atlantic and Pacific oceans, new markets, and opposition to the intervention of European powers in the New World. The mutual interests did not translate into common foreign policies.

Since its organization as an independent nation in 1783, the United States had pursued a foreign policy designed to protect its own interests from European and particularly British encroachments. A series of actions—refusal to support the French Crown during the French Revolution in 1792 despite treaty obligations, the Undeclared War with France from 1798 to 1800, the Louisiana Purchase in 1803, Jefferson's War with the Barbary Pirates (1801–1805), the War of 1812, and the 1819 Transcontinental Treaty—all illustrated U.S. intentions to protect its commerce and expand its territory. Thus, in December 1823, when President James Monroe declared the western hemisphere off limits to further European colonization, knowledgeable Latin Americans viewed it as another expression of anticipated U.S. economic and territorial expansion, not as a mutual protectionist declaration. Within this context, one can understand Simón Bolívar's hesitancy to invite the United States to the 1826 Panama Congress.

For the next generation, U.S. diplomats trudged to Latin America but did not find the like-minded democracies that Monroe alluded to in his 1823 declaration, nor the economic opportunity that men like Adams and Henry Clay had anticipated. Instead, they found the newly minted countries steeped in Spanish tradition: government limited to the upper class, a state-supported church, and a military ready to maintain the established order. Two political parties, conservative and liberal, represented the elite and controlled the political arena. Party philosophies differed over Church privileges and the extent of foreign trade, and they diverged widely over the power of the central government vis-à-vis the individual states within a nation's boundaries. Struggles over centralized state power often erupted into violence, as in Argentina and Mexico, and led to the destruction of the United Provinces of Central America and the splitting apart of Gran Colombia. Still, as in colonial times, social and economic mobility remained greatly limited.

The United States stood in sharp contrast to Latin America during the same generation, 1820 to 1840. Political democracy reached new heights. Property qualifications all but disappeared as a voting requirement (except for women, blacks, and those Native Americans who remained outside the U.S. political system). Publicly supported education from primary school through universities became commonplace. The federal government recognized labor unions in its construction projects, and it refused to renew the National Bank charter in 1833 so that money could be more widely distributed to the "common man." The confidence in the "American system" found expression in such terms as Jacksonian Democracy and Manifest Destiny. According to its originator, journalist John O'Sullivan, the latter term meant that God had granted the United States the right to spread its way of life from the Atlantic to the Pacific oceans. Some expansionists advocated that the United States should cast its influence as far south as the isthmus at Panama because all the nations from there north to the Rio Grande River were imprisoned by Spanish traditions and therefore denied economic, political, and social progress. President James K. Polk thought otherwise. He was persuaded by the need to incorporate Texas into the union and to take all the territory from there to the Pacific Ocean; this would expand agriculture and open Pacific coast ports to facilitate commerce with Asia. In his view, however, the United States was not yet ready to deal with large numbers of people steeped in a foreign culture. The aversion to foreign culture is illustrated by the U.S. rejection of Narciso López, a Cuban planter who, between 1849 and 1851, envisioned the island's annexation to the United States, and also by the adventures of William Walker in Central America between 1855 and 1858.

Since 1783 U.S. policymakers fixated on Great Britain as the main adversary to its western hemispheric interests, whether it was British commercial presence in Latin America, its rejection of the Monroe Doctrine, or its interest in constructing a trans-isthmian canal. The dream of a trans-isthmian canal dates to 1513, when Spanish *conquistador* Vasco de Gama Nüñez de Balboa trekked across the Panamanian isthmus. But early Spanish interest in building a passageway across Darien or Tehuantepe or dredging the San Juan River collapsed with the wars of independence. Independent Latin America and particularly Central America revived the dream just as U.S. political leaders and merchants awakened to the canal's significance for the evolution of the nation's worldwide commercial contacts. In the 1820s the Central Americans were the first to explore a possible canal, followed a decade later by a suggestion that a consortium of European banks undertake the project. Not until the conclusion of the Mexican War in 1848 did the United States take notice of the British presence in Central America and its potential influence on the trans-isthmian canal. The issue was addressed in the 1850 Clayton-Bulwer Treaty, which prevented the U.S. and Great Britain from acting alone in the construction, maintenance, or defense of such a canal anywhere in Central America. There the matter rested until the end of the nineteenth century.

While the diplomatic record and Latin American memoirs of contemporary figures along with newspapers of the time period are filled with protests and criticisms of U.S. policy, representatives of the Latin Americans governments met three times by 1865—Lima (1848 and 1864) and Santiago (1856)—to discuss possible unified reactions to U.S. expansion. Nothing came of these conclaves, but they did set a precedent for the future.

THE DEVELOPMENT OF MUTUAL INTERESTS: 1865–1900

Between 1865 and 1900, significant changes took place within Latin America and the United States that tightened their relationship. During that thirty-five-year period, liberals came to occupy presidential palaces and control national legislatures across Latin America, and they brought with them a European-rooted positivist philosophy. In application, positivism is a more formal description for what has more recently become known as the "trickle down" economic theory. Lacking funds to undertake the enormous task of economic development themselves, the Latin American liberal elite-based governments turned to the outside world, opening a door with generous benefits to foreign investors, primarily Europeans and particularly the British, who had been in Latin America since the 1810s. The foreign investors provided the money to support massive infrastructure projects from docks and wharves to railroads and highways; the extraction industries, such as nitrate, copper, and oil; and agricultural pursuits in wheat, bananas, and henequen. An informal alliance between the in-country investment managers and the ruling elite further ensured stability. Latin American legislatures enacted laws to protect those investments and to ensure labor peace. As the Latin Americans developed their export-based economies, the historically static socioeconomic structure and closed political system remained in place.

During the same thirty-five year period beginning in 1865, the United States experienced an unprecedented industrial revolution. Visitors to the world's fairs marveled at its products, from sewing machines to typewriters, from women's clothing to domestic weavings, and from farm equipment to industrial machines. In 1891, for the first time in its history, the United States exported more manufactured goods than agricultural. And at Chicago's 1898 extravaganza, Pabst beer became the first non-German beer to win a world's fair blue ribbon. During the same time period, U.S. business interests increasingly clamored for access to world markets, raw materials, and investment opportunities. All of this was justified on the liberal notion of free trade and, at home, lack of government interference in the economy. In accordance with the goodwill of U.S. nationalism, a moral crusade would follow the flag abroad to uplift the peoples of the downtrodden underdeveloped world: Democracy would follow the dollar. In this Gilded Age of American history, U.S. industrialists lived more lavishly than their Latin American counterparts, while the workers in both hemispheres suffered immense socioeconomic indignities.

With two notable exceptions—Cuba and Mexico—the United States arrived as latecomers to Latin America's open economy in the late nineteenth century. Despite its colonial status, Cuba had long-time links to the U.S. sugar market and was dependent on the United States for its consumer goods and the machinery essential for its sugar and tobacco industries. U.S.-Mexican trade dated to the latter's pre-independence period, when goods were regularly exchanged at Santa Fe in present-day New Mexico and San Antonio in present-day Texas. U.S. business interests entered President Porfirio Diaz Mori's Mexican economy on the same favorable grounds as Europeans experienced in South America and soon came to dominate its railroad, mining, cattle, and oil industries. Elsewhere, in the late nineteenth century, U.S. economic consuls reported on economic opportunities and assisted U.S. businessmen in their respective countries. Secretary of State James G. Blaine's First International Conference of American States in 1889, hosted in Washington, D.C., and paid for by the United States, did not produce the economic results that Blaine anticipated. In the weeks before the conference convened on October 2, 1889, Blaine took the representatives from thirteen Latin American states on a railroad tour of the United States industrial belt, from Boston, New York, and Philadelphia as far west as St. Louis before returning to Washington, D.C. The reciprocal trade treaties Blaine expected did not materialize. Long linked to and currently benefiting from Europe's economic investments and markets and historically distrustful of the United States, the Latin American governments were in no mood to sign U.S. trade reciprocity agreements.

THE ROAD TO IMPERIALISM: 1900–1934

The factors that long motivated U.S. policy toward Latin America—economics, security, and spreading democracy—melded together in 1898 with the Cuban War for Independence and would soon include Panama, Central America, and other Caribbean nations.

Since 1895 Cuban rebels had been fighting Spanish forces for their independence. By 1898 the conflict included attacks on civilians and the means of production, including U.S.-owned sugar plantations and mills and their supporting infrastructure. Cuban civilians were victimized in reconcentration camps. Although its forces were on the verge of defeat, the Spanish government was not about to give up its crown jewel. The sinking of the USS *Maine* in Havana harbor on February 15, 1898, served as the catalyst for U.S. entry into the war on April 22, 1898. U.S. victories led to diplomatic discussions.

The Treaty of Paris established Cuban independence from Spain in 1898 and charged the United States with establishing a functioning government. At the same time, the United States was determined to secure its own interests. U.S. officials found Cuba unprepared for the implementation of democracy, attributing this to the legacies of Spanish colonialism and the dominant numbers of uneducated Afro-Cubans. To address their concerns, the Platt Amendment, named after Senator Orville Platt (R., Conn.) was tacked on to the 1901 Cuban constitution as a condition of independence. The Platt

Amendment forbade Cuba from pursuing an independent foreign policy or incurring an international debt not approved by the U.S. government; it granted the United States the right to intervene in Cuba in cases of political instability. The model established in Cuba became the basis of U.S. policy in the circum-Caribbean region for the next generation.

While the Cubans moved toward independence, the U.S. psyche fixated on a trans-isthmian canal, owned, constructed, operated, and defended by the United States. In 1900 the U.S. Congress approved the Panama site for the canal, and U.S. naval officials argued that Cuba and Puerto Rico were essential to the security of the Panama Canal.

In addition to the indignities of Spanish colonial rule, the Panamanians had suffered politically at the hands of the Colombia government since 1821; by 1900 they had legitimate reasons to seek independence. Tension between Colombia and Panama intensified during the nineteenth century and culminated with the outbreak of war on November 3, 1903. U.S. President Theodore Roosevelt encouraged the revolt and supported the Panamanians by using U.S. naval ships to block the transportation of Colombian troops to the rebellious province. The fifteen-day conflict ended with the signing of the Hay–Bunau-Varilla Treaty on November 18. The treaty secured Panama's independence, but it also furthered U.S. interests. The treaty granted the United States the right to own, construct, maintain, and defend a canal through the center of the new country, and like the Platt Amendment in Cuba, the treaty also limited Panamanian input on foreign policy and debt and granted the United States the right to intervene in the republic to preserve political tranquility.

The Cuban and Panama examples did not apply to the entire circum-Caribbean region, as illustrated by the Venezuelan debt crisis finally settled in 1903. The refusal of Venezuelan President José Cipriano Castro to honor his government's debt obligations to European bankers led to a combined British, German, and Italian naval blockade of Venezuela from December 9, 1902, until February 19, 1903, when Castro finally succumbed to the pressure. The incident prompted U.S. President Theodore Roosevelt to declare his corollary to the Monroe Doctrine in December 1903. According to the Roosevelt Corollary, any misbehavior by Latin American nations that invited aggressive European reaction provided sufficient cause for the United States to prevent European intervention in the affairs of Latin America. In practice, over the next generation, the United States intervened in the financial affairs of several circum-Caribbean regions as a means to secure the Panama Canal from foreign threats.

U.S. policymakers also reasoned that imposing a democratic government on the former Spanish colonies in the Caribbean region would bring not only political stability, but also socioeconomic betterment to all peoples. Such changes in Central America would keep violence from spilling into Panama, they reasoned, and possibly disrupt or destroy the trans-isthmian canal operations.

In its pursuit of democracy for Central America, the United States hosted and paid for conferences in 1907 and 1923, where U.S. policymakers attempted to outlaw revolutions, control armaments, and create national guards that served governments, not the personal whims of presidents. Also during the early twentieth century, the United States administered the customs houses in Haiti, the Dominican Republic, Honduras, and Nicaragua. Part of the collected funds went to the local government for its operations, while the remainder went to repay U.S. banks that had paid off the foreign loans. With its treaty system in place, the State Department rationalized that it brought democratic political stability to the circum-Caribbean region; helped to prevent revolutions from spreading from one country to another and eventually to Panama; and established an environment that would keep Europeans from intervening in the affairs of the Caribbean nations. The Panama Canal would henceforth be secure, but democracy never came to the Caribbean nations.

For sure, the U.S. dollar followed the flag. By the mid-1920s, one could not deny that Cuba was a de facto American colony. U.S. investors controlled the sugar industry from the fields through its shipping, mostly to the United States where it received a favorable tariff preference. U.S. businesses controlled the Cuban infrastructure, including docks and warehouses, as well as the railroads that brought the sugar to port and then to market. During the same time period, Cuba's dependence on U.S. consumer goods increased. North American companies built and controlled water, sewerage, and electric systems in Cuba's main cities; U.S. firms owned and operated the banking, communications, and tourist industries. Panama's economy never prospered, except for the cattle industry, which met the demand from the Canal Zone's U.S. residents (known as Zonians). Otherwise, the Panama Canal Company's commissary operation brought in U.S. goods free of transportation costs and Panamanian import duties, to the detriment of Panamanian merchants and consumers. In Central America and in the Spanish-speaking Caribbean, U.S. companies dominated the banana, citrus, and sugar industries. In each instance, the United States was charged with responsibility for the nondiversification of local economies.

In his welcoming comments to the Sixth International Conference of American States in Havana on January 16, 1928, host Cuban President Gerardo Machado y Morales declared that the U.S. presence in Cuba benefited the country. Machado stood alone in this sentiment. Other Latin Americans, in and out of government, viewed U.S. political and economic interventions in the circum-Caribbean region as acts of political and economic imperialism that needed to be checked, and this would include the nationalization of U.S. business interests. Among the results of the Mexican Revolution (1911–1917) was the 1917 constitution, which provided the legal basis for the Mexican government's takeover of U.S. economic interests in the country. At the conclusion of World War I, most Latin American countries joined the League of Nations, seeing the institution as a vehicle to limit U.S. presence in the southern hemisphere, but they quickly became indifferent when the U.S. Congress voted against U.S. participation in the organization. Latin America's larger countries, such as Mexico, Brazil,

Argentina, Chile, and Peru, used the International Conferences of American States starting with Rio de Janeiro in 1906 to pursue legal means that would halt U.S. interference in the circum-Caribbean region. From 1927 to 1933, Nicaraguan nationalist and rebel leader Augusto César Sandino spoke for the middle sector when leading his forces against Nicaragua's elitist government and for all Caribbean workers exploited by the local elites and U.S. companies operating in the region.

In addition to Latin American protests, internal factors also came to influence a shift in U.S. policy as announced in 1933. Journalists, scholars, and politicians pointed out that Europe's military and fiscal threats to the circum-Caribbean region ended with the termination of World War I in 1919. As secretary of commerce from 1921 to 1928, Herbert Hoover asserted that a U.S. withdrawal from the Caribbean region would enhance U.S. economic opportunities in the wealthier and more advanced South American nations. In 1926 the State Department privately admitted the failure of its pursuit of democracy in the Caribbean region. Two years later, when U.S. Marine body bags started coming back from Nicaragua as the result of the latest armed incursion, the U.S. public protested against intervention abroad.

At the Seventh International Conference of American States convened in Montevideo, Uruguay, in December 1933, Secretary of State Cordell Hull announced that henceforth the United States would be a good neighbor to Latin America by no longer intervening in its internal affairs. The announcement was followed by the withdrawal of U.S. military personnel from the Dominican Republic, Haiti, and Nicaragua. The United States no longer concerned itself with the legality of a government, if it controlled the government machinery, met its international financial obligations, and apparently had the support of its people. The policy opened the door for longtime dictators such as Rafael Trujillo Molina in the Dominican Republic, Jorge Ubico y Castañeda in Guatemala, and the Duvalier and the Somoza families, respectively, in Haiti and in Nicaragua. These and other strongmen further secured their position by signing U.S.-initiated reciprocal trade agreements in the 1930s. The treaties were designed to stimulate the depressed U.S. economy by lowering trade barriers, but the Latin Americans already benefited from most-favored-nation clauses that guaranteed them the lowest tariff possible for their exports to the United States, while they lacked the means to pay for U.S. manufactured exports. The reciprocity treaties, however unintentionally, served a political purpose: how can one government deem another illegal if it has initiated a trade treaty with the other?

From 1935 until the outbreak of the European war on September 1, 1939, the Latin American nations believed that the United States used the rising war clouds in Europe and Asia as a cover to again intervene in Latin America's internal affairs. The skepticism prompted the Latin Americans to demand and receive reiterations of the 1933 Good Neighbor pledge at the Inter-American Conference for the Maintenance of Peace in Buenos Aires in 1936 and the Eighth International Conference of American States in Lima in 1938.

THE INFLUENCE OF GLOBAL AFFAIRS: 1935–1991

From 1935 to 1991 U.S.–Latin American relations felt the strong impact of global politics. For the first decade, the western hemisphere came under attack from the Nazis and Fascists, in Germany and Italy, respectively, and from the militarists in Tokyo. Thereafter, the threat of international communism dominated the world scene. In both instances, the United States came to assume the opposition's leadership.

Before its entry into World War II in 1941, the United States completed its plans for hemispheric defense, which included an examination of Latin America's capabilities to contribute to the cause. The U.S. military found their Latin American counterparts wanting in terms of training and discipline, as well as modern tactics and equipment, and concluded that, at best, the Latin Americans could provide minimal assistance should the hemisphere come under attack from abroad. Some nations, like Argentina and Chile, did not join the war effort until membership in the postwar United Nations was dangled before them. Fear of further U.S. encroachments prompted the others to join the Allied cause under terms favorable to themselves. For example, the United States established defense sites from Uruguay to Panama in preparation for a potential foreign attack, but under severe limitations. Latin American governments limited U.S. authority to the site itself and stipulated by treaty that the sites would be returned to the host country within a year after the war's end. U.S. Army training units arrived in most Latin American countries under wartime military assistance agreements, but they often found the local governments militating against the intermingling of troops. This was particularly true among the dictators, who feared for their own security should their militaries become attuned to U.S. training and tactics. Nor was Latin America flooded with U.S. military assistance. Latin America received only 10 percent of the $440 million allotment of U.S. military assistance under the wartime Lend-Lease program. The wartime experience challenges the notion that the United States contributed to strengthening of the Latin American military, as asserted by many historians.

Again, Argentina and Chile did not cooperate with U.S. anti-Axis policies, which included deportation to Germany, internment in the United States, or some form of incarceration in the host country of German, Japanese, and Italian nationals and their descendents, who were deemed a threat to hemispheric security. Over the course of the war, many foreign nationals and their descendents lost their properties to nationalization schemes or the inability to pay taxes. Axis-based companies failed to escape the net.

The war's economic impact on Latin America varied widely. Some countries benefited immensely. Cuba, for example, prospered as it became the primary source of sugar after the loss of Eastern European and South Asian sources to the Axis powers. Chile became the Allies primary source for copper, a commodity necessary for the manufacture of ammunition. Venezuelan oil fueled both U.S. wartime industries and its military. Argentine beef and wheat remained available to the highest bidder,

Allied or Axis. Mexico and Brazil also gained from U.S. largesse, which enabled them to produce needed wartime goods, such as uniforms and jeeps, and planted the seeds for postwar industrialization. These countries emerged from the war with surplus trade balances with the United States. On the other end of the spectrum, some nations emerged from the war with depressed economies; the primary products in Central America, for example—bananas and coffee—were not wartime necessities. As the United States cancelled wartime contracts with the more productive countries, the Latin American cry for a Marshall Plan-like stimulus program went unanswered. Instead, the Latin Americans were told that once the European economy recovered, those markets would again be open to Latin American goods.

The end of World War II also brought forward Latin America's "generation of rising expectations," a diverse group of middle-sector people that included doctors, lawyers, architects, small businessmen, white-collar managers, skilled labor, and teachers and students. While their wealth and social position differed, the group as a whole traced its roots to the education system introduced by the liberals in the nineteenth century; foreign-owned companies provided their jobs and exposed them to foreign ideas regarding political participation and social opportunities. Some Latin Americans were also influenced by U.S.-generated propaganda that clearly identified World War II as a fight for democracy. Near the war's end in 1944, protests from these groups brought down dictators Maximiliano Hernández-Martínez in El Salvador and Jorge Ubico in Guatemala. Elsewhere, the socioeconomic needs of the urban poor contributed to the 1945 presidential election of Juan Domingo Perón Sosa in Argentina and the appointment of communists to cabinet posts in Chile in 1946 by Gabriel González Videla.

The communization of Eastern Europe by 1948, Mao Tse-tung's 1949 victory in China, the outbreak of the Korean War in 1950, and the conclusion of President Harry S. Truman's National Security Council (NSC-68) convinced U.S. policymakers that the U.S. government had to assume the leadership role in the global struggle against communism. For the next two generations, U.S. officials targeted leftist movements in Latin America. Ignoring a caution from Assistant Secretary of State for Latin American Affairs Henry Holland that not all leftist movements were communist, the United States determined to eliminate the communist "cancer" from the hemisphere by whatever means necessary. Latin America became part of the U.S. Cold War policy.

Thus, the Central Intelligence Agency (CIA) directed a rag-tag opposition army to overthrow Guatemalan President Jacobo Arbenz Guzmán in 1954 and to organize and implement the Bay of Pigs operation in 1961, which failed in its attempt to oust Fidel Castro in Cuba. The CIA financed the presidential election of Chilean President Eduardo Frei Montalva in 1964 to ward off the possible victory of Marxist Salvador Allende Gossens. And when Allende was elected president in 1970, the CIA undertook clandestine measures to disrupt the economy, which contributed to Allende's ouster by the Chilean military in 1973. While Jimmy Carter's administration briefly shifted the focus from anticommunism to human rights, Ronald Reagan arrived at the White House in January 1981 with a conviction that the Soviets were still determined to dominate the world. Reagan directed the 1983 military invasion of Grenada to rid the small Caribbean island of alleged communists and also to prevent the construction of a Soviet air base. His support of CIA-sponsored and -directed clandestine operations against the Sandinista government in Nicaragua eventually blossomed into the Central American Wars of the 1980s, which brought Henry Holland's caution from 1955 into focus. The Latin Americans, and most of the free world, did not share Reagan's view of international communist expansion, but they accepted the argument that the Sandinistas in Nicaragua and the Farabundo Martí National Liberation Front in El Salvador represented legitimate challenges to the historic established socioeconomic and political order.

U.S. policy critics in the 1980s asserted that Latin American elites contributed to the creation of their own monster, first by snubbing the Alliance for Progress program in the 1960s because it required the elites to democratize their governments, something they would not do. The elites turned to their national military to retain order, which meant the suppression of any person or group who challenged the existing order. The United States became a willing partner by satisfying the appetite of Latin American militaries. For nearly a generation, Latin America endured military-bureaucratic governments, and the U.S. reputation as champion of liberty was further soiled.

A NEW ERA: 1992–PRESENT

A decade prior to the end of the Cold War in 1992, winds of economic change swept across the western world, including Latin America, except for Cuba. Leaders in Washington, D.C., London, Bonn, Paris, and Tokyo proselytized a new economic policy variously identified as the Washington consensus, neoliberalism, and eventually globalization. Timewise, the emergence of neoliberalism coincided with Latin America's return to democracy, a popular way of saying that Latin America was shedding itself of military governments.

Neoliberalism called for the implementation of several measures, including disciplined fiscal policy, moderate interest rates, trade liberalization, openness to direct foreign investment, privatization of state-owned enterprises, deregulation, legal security for intellectual property rights, tax reform, and the redirection of public expenditures toward education, health, and infrastructure investment. To some, it was simply supply-side economics. In other words, Latin America needed to open its doors to foreign investment, encourage domestic investment by lowering taxes on the upper class, strip away protections from domestic industries, and protect the new investments from legal challenges. Effectively, neoliberalism promised expanded economic activity, which in turn would produce increased government revenues that could be spent on roads to reach the ports and education and health care, two of the most important concerns held by the masses of people across Latin America. Many analysts drew parallels between twentieth-century neoliberalism and late nineteenth-century liberalism.

Latin America's new democratic governments implemented the program, and a decade later the business reforms were accomplished for the most part. Statistics supported the claims that direct foreign investment would increase, export trade would expand, and gross national product would grow. The promise that neoliberalism would improve the quality of life for the masses, however, failed to come true. Studies revealed that 50 percent of all Latin Americans remained in poverty; that people had little hope for their children's future; and that the middle class, along with the rural and urban poor, had lost faith in democracy. Into this malaise stepped populist-type leaders, such as Venezuela's Hugo Chávez Frías in 1999 and Bolivia's Juan Evo Morales Ayma in 2006, who branded the United States with responsibility for Latin America's plight. Even the leaders of economically successful and socially conscious governments, such as Brazil and Chile, found fault with U.S. policies. Since the year 2000 U.S. policy toward Latin America has been at a nadir and further tarnished its image south of the Rio Grande River. Promises of improved relationships may have gotten lost in the fight against terrorism and the current U.S. economic crisis. As a result, Latin Americans reached out to the world and found new partners in Europe, China, the Association of Southeast Asian Nations (ASEAN), and some African and Middle Eastern nations.

CONCLUSION

U.S.–Latin American relations had an inauspicious beginning in the early 1800s, with each party knowing little about the other. During the course of the next one hundred years, each became frustrated with the other as they established the basis for their twentieth-century relationship. For the Latin Americans, a growing mistrust of U.S. intentions was fueled by the Monroe Doctrine, the application of Manifest Destiny, and the ever-increasing late nineteenth-century search for markets and raw materials. The U.S. use of arrogant power in Cuba and Panama at the start of the twentieth century, followed by a series of interventions in the internal affairs of circum-Caribbean nations until 1934, served as reason for the Latin Americans to distance themselves from their northern neighbor. For the Latin Americans, World War II and Cold War experiences further demonstrated the dominance of U.S. interests in hemispheric affairs.

Historically, U.S. policymakers, beginning with the diplomats sent south in the early nineteenth century, held a condescending view of Latin America. Their reports and those sent by their successors during the remainder of the century described closed political systems with a lack of economic development and miniscule social mobility, which the North Americans saw as the result of Spanish colonialism. Thus, U.S. policymakers found what they considered an inept collection of nations in the circum-Caribbean region when the United States entered the world political arena in 1898 and five years later determined to construct a trans-isthmian canal at Panama. There emerged a moral crusade to uplift these backward peoples as one means to secure the canal. That the dollar followed the flag was not the government's intention, except in those instances that helped debtor nations meet their international obligations. The same can be said for World War II and the Cold War; U.S. policy was designed to meet its own needs, not those of Latin America. The self-serving nature of U.S. interests was most evident during the 1990s with its proposal for Free Trade Association of the Americas and after that with the bilateral free trade agreements concluded with many Latin American nations. One must caution that Latin American governments were not shy about using U.S. policies to meet their own purposes.

Overall, U.S.–Latin American relations remind one of a roller coaster, a series of peaks and valleys. When U.S. interests in the southern hemisphere are threatened, Washington became deeply involved but then withdrew as the crisis passed. A strong argument can be presented that Inter-American relations are receding into the valley in the early years of the twenty-first century. The United States is turning inward to address its economic and financial crisis and, at the same time, is drawing down its international commitments. For the Latin Americans, U.S. congressional delays in approving or disapproving free trade agreements illustrate the point.

When, not if, the track of Inter-American relations rises from the valley floor to reach for another peak, the United States will find a vastly different Latin America than it historically has known. The idealistic and legalistic approaches to limiting U.S. interventions in the early twentieth century gave way to more pragmatic economic paths, as seen during World War II in Brazil, Chile, and Mexico and, starting in the 1970s, with the pursuance of Japanese and European direct investments. The Brazil-led opposition to the proposed Free Trade Association of the Americas was designed to break U.S. hegemonic influence and provide Latin America with a greater freedom of action. Since 2000, as the United States focused on the war on terror, Latin America acted independently to forge economic links beyond the United States. The future maturing of those links suggests a less cooperative relationship with the United States.

Yet, many factors will continue to connect the United States with Latin America. In addition to the mutual needs for markets and raw materials, there is a mutual need to address the flow of illegal drugs northward into the United States. Since the 1920s the policies of the United States and Latin America have been poles apart. The U.S. effort focuses on eliminating drugs at the source, namely their destruction in the growing fields and the interdiction of drugs traveling north. Both policies led to the U.S. interference in the internal affairs of many nations, including Colombia, Peru, Belize, and, more recently, Mexico. In contrast, the Latin Americans charge that the U.S. demand for illegal drugs fuels the growth of them abroad. The Latin Americans assert that only a forceful effort to eliminate drug use in the United States will curtail the demand to produce the drugs abroad. While this debate continues, the use of illegal drugs within Latin America steadily increased.

Another problem of mutual concern is the migration of people to the United States, to other Latin American countries, and beyond. The movement is not confined solely to lower socioeconomic groups, who strain the social safety nets of the more advanced nations, but also the loss of highly skilled white-collar workers, whose loss severely impacts economic development at home.

Both the United States and Latin America confront the same serious domestic socioeconomic problems: government debt, educational inadequacy, health care, an aging population, housing needs, high unemployment, poverty, and aged and crumbling infrastructures. Admittedly, the depth of these challenges varies between nations, but the fundamental question confronts each: how to address them and at what cost. At the local, state, and national levels of government, the United States is in the midst of that debate. In the newly established Latin American democracies, the issue was first addressed in the election of so-called leftist politicians since 1998 and, more recently, with the newly coined term *progressive capitalism*, which promises to continue the capitalist model but with greater emphasis on social needs. In other words, it is a rejection or at least a modification of the neoliberal economic model.

The multitude of domestic issues outlined above will impact the foreign policy of each hemispheric nation in the collective relationship. Within the hemisphere, it will play out in Cuba, an economically and socially troubled nation whose military is of no real threat. The Castro brothers have admitted that the communist model has failed and have asked for the world's assistance. Where will the aid come from? The United States stands alone in its continued policy of isolating Cuba, even as the original reasons pass into history. Latin America long abandoned the U.S.-sponsored embargo of the island, while today Venezuela and China have replaced the Soviet Union as primary props of the minimal sustainability of the island nation. The opportunity for a multilateral approach stands waiting.

The world vastly changed in the two hundred years of U.S.–Latin American relations. Not only has U.S. influence in the southern hemisphere dwindled, so too has the region's elitist rule. No one can predict the future, but for sure the United States will confront multistate interests in the region, and Latin American governments will have to take into account the needs of their peoples when pursuing a foreign policy.

ENTRIES: A–E

Abrams, Elliot

(**See** *Central American Wars, 1980s*)

Accessory Transit Company

(**See** *Vanderbilt, Cornelius*)

Acción Communal

(**See** *Arias Madrid, Arnulfo*)

Acheson, Dean G.

Dean Gooderham Acheson (1893–1971) was a U.S. statesman born in Middletown, Connecticut, on April 11, 1893. In 1919, on the recommendation of his Harvard law mentor Felix Frankfurter, Acheson worked as the private secretary for Supreme Court Justice Louis Brandeis. In 1933, Franklin D. Roosevelt (FDR) appointed Acheson undersecretary of the treasury. He was briefly acting secretary but resigned in November because he opposed FDR's plan to inflate the dollar by controlling gold prices.

In 1941 Roosevelt appointed Acheson assistant secretary of state. He designed the U.S., British, and Dutch oil embargo that shut off 95 percent of Japan's oil supplies and escalated tensions. Experts argue over whether Roosevelt fully grasped the scope of the embargo, but few doubt that Acheson knew the risk of war.

In July 1944 Acheson played a key role in the Bretton Woods Conference as the lead delegate of the State Department. Representatives at this conference created the postwar international economic structure, sowing the seeds for the International Monetary Fund (IMF), the World Bank, and the General Agreement on Tariffs and Trade, which evolved into the World Trade Organization. All of these have had an impact on Latin American socioeconomic development.

As Harry S. Truman's undersecretary of state from 1945–1947, Acheson played a key role in crafting the Truman Doctrine and the European Recovery Program (ERP) (Marshall Plan), believing that working with progressive forces in developing nations was the best way to prevent the spread of communism. In January 1949 Acheson was appointed secretary of state. He and George F. Kennan developed the basic framework for what became known as the Containment Policy. Acheson was also the primary architect of the North Atlantic Treaty Organization (NATO). He was accused of making statements that showed weakness toward communism regarding both the Chinese Revolution and the North Korean invasion of South Korea, but historians have largely debunked those claims.

When President John F. Kennedy came to office in 1961, he sought Acheson's advice. During the Cuban Missile Crisis, not only did Acheson play a key role in advising the president, but he worked his many overseas contacts to prevent a nuclear holocaust. In 1964 he received the Presidential Medal of Freedom. Throughout the 1960s, he was a member of a bipartisan group of former statesmen known as "The Wise Men." Much of Kennedy's flexible response policy came from their position papers. In March 1968 they met with Johnson and recommend that he end U.S. participation in Vietnam.

In 1969, when Richard M. Nixon became president, Acheson reconciled with his old foe and quietly became a major advisor to Nixon. In 1970, he won the Pulitzer Prize in history for his memoirs, *Present at the Creation: My Years in the State Department* (1969). He also wrote *Power and Diplomacy* (1958), *Morning and Noon* (1965), and *The Korean War* (1971).

On October 12, 1971, Dean Acheson died of a massive stroke at his farm in Sandy Spring, Maryland, at the age of 78.

See also *Cuban Missile Crisis; International Monetary Fund (IMF); Kennedy, John F.; Roosevelt, Franklin D.; Truman, Harry S.*

. . . . WILLIAM HEAD

REFERENCES AND FURTHER READING

Acheson, Dean, *Present at the Creation: My Years in the State Department.* New York: Norton, 1969.

Acheson, Dean Gooderham. *Papers, 1898–1986.* MS 1087. New Haven, CT: Yale University Library and Archives.

Beisner, Robert L. *Dean Acheson: A Life in the Cold War.* New York: Oxford, 2006.

Brinkley, Douglas. *Dean Acheson: The Cold War Years, 1953-71.* New Haven, CT: Yale University Press, 1992.

Chace, James. *Acheson: The Secretary of State Who Created the American World.* New York: Simon and Schuster, 1998.

Act of Chapultepec, 1945

(**See** *Inter-American Conference on the Problems of War and Peace, Mexico City, 1945*)

Adams, John Quincy

Secretary of state of the Monroe administration (1817–1824) and sixth president of the United States (1825–1829), John Quincy Adams (1767–1848) started his long political and diplomatic career early. In 1778 he accompanied his father John Adams on a brief mission to Europe. The following year they went on a second mission as Adams's father had been commissioned to negotiate a treaty of peace with Great Britain. At fourteen John Quincy became the private secretary of Francis Dana, the U.S. representative in Russia. In 1794 George Washington appointed him minister resident to the Netherlands, where he collected valuable information on European politics. Three years later his father's administration sent him to Prussia to sign a treaty of amity and commerce. Subsequently, President James Madison named Adams minister to Russia, in 1809. During his residence in St. Petersburg he witnessed the defeat of Napoleon's army in the winter of 1812.

Adams was also a member of the negotiating commission at Ghent, which put an end to the War of 1812 between the United States and Great Britain. During the deliberations Adams had the first of many disputes with Henry Clay, a Kentucky representative, later to become a fierce critic of Adams's Spanish-American policy. Adams's last appointment as U.S. minister in Europe was to the court of St. James, in 1815. From London John Quincy wrote James Monroe, then secretary of state, that the British government was opposed to the independence of the Spanish colonies. Yet he also pointed out that the British were not unequivocally in favor of Spain. Adams claimed that Great Britain feared free commercial intercourse with Spanish America as it would promote U.S. interests in the region and injure British ones.

Adams had never shown much interest for Spanish America or its culture and institutions. His early readings about Spain, her American empire, and the Black Legend confirmed his firm belief that the United States was superior in the art of governing and political morality. Adams rejected the idea that the North American and the South American fights for independence were similar. He was thus less sympathetic to the Spanish-American revolutionaries than Monroe or Madison. Nonetheless, Adams was fully aware of the impact these revolutions would have on U.S. foreign policy in the region and hence followed closely the events in the Spanish empire.

SECRETARY OF STATE

In 1817 President Monroe nominated Adams secretary of state, a position he was fully prepared for thanks to his thorough knowledge and experience of European politics. When he took office, one of the most pressing issues was the resolution of the territorial disputes with Spain. The core of the disagreement was the western boundary of Louisiana and the possession of East and West Florida. In 1818, the Spanish minister Luis de Onís and Adams started laborious negotiations. That same year General Andrew Jackson and his troops led raids into East Florida and then captured West Florida. Despite dissension within the cabinet, the administration, in particular Adams, decided to support Jackson. The U.S. invasion of Spanish territory put additional pressure on Madrid to reach an agreement rapidly. Finally, Adams and Onís formally settled the conflict with the signing of the Transcontinental Treaty of 1819. Spain relinquished the Floridas to the United States and a new frontier line was drawn between the United States and the Spanish empire, from the Atlantic seaboard to the Pacific.

A major stumbling block to a prompt settlement between Madrid and Washington had been Spain's demand that the United States pledge not to recognize the independence of the revolutionary Spanish-American governments. Adams refused to give such a promise as the Monroe administration had adopted a policy of "impartial neutrality" vis-à-vis the crisis in the Spanish empire.

Indeed, in December 1817, an envoy of the Buenos Aires revolutionary government had requested Washington to recognize the United Provinces of the Rio de la Plata (present Argentina), yet Adams declined. He feared that the Spanish Americans would be troublesome associates. On the contrary, Henry Clay, the Speaker of the House of Representatives, supported recognition. He believed the commercial interests of the Trans-Allegheny West that he represented would benefit from a free Spanish America. Moreover, Clay suggested that his fellow citizens become real Americans and place themselves at the head of the American system. The United States would be at the center and Spanish America would act with its northern neighbors. Adams was adamantly opposed to such a project. He saw no community of interests or principles between North and South America. In fact, he claimed that the United States constituted the whole of the American system.

By 1822, however, most of the American colonies had freed themselves from the shackles of Spanish colonial rule. The Monroe administration concluded that the time had come to recognize the new republics, without departing from its policy of neutrality. Thus the United States became the first global powerworld nation to formally acknowledge the independence of Spain's American colonies. Adams rapidly instructed the U.S. plenipotentiary ministers to negotiate treaties of commerce guaranteeing mutual advantage and reciprocity with the newly independent nations. He believed that U.S. merchants should be able to trade freely. Yet Adams was fully aware that Great Britain was in a better position to supply the need of Spanish Americans for manufactured goods.

Spain and her European Allies, particularly France and Russia, also threatened the future of the Americas. Their ambition was to reconquer Spanish America, a scenario the United States was certainly not willing to tolerate. Hence, in his annual address to Congress on December 2, 1823, President Monroe warned the Europeans to keep out of western hemisphere affairs, which left the United States as potentially the strongest power in the western hemisphere. The message, later to be known as the Monroe Doctrine, was partly shaped by Secretary of State Adams, who insisted the United States act alone rather than with Great Britain. Adams contributed notably to the outlining of the noncolonization principle, which stated that the western hemisphere continent was not open to any future European colonization.

In 1824, John Quincy Adams was elected president. He appointed his former opponent Henry Clay as secretary of state. The major foreign policy issue they had to handle was the invitation to participate in the first Inter-American meeting called by Simón Bolívar. Delegates from the former Spanish colonies, Brazil, the United States, and Great Britain were to meet at the Isthmus of Panama in 1826. Adams agreed to send a mission on condition that the United States did not engage in discussion concerning the formation of a defensive and offensive alliance with the other American nations. In fact, Adams's main interest in the Panama Congress was to further promote free commercial relations with the Spanish American nations. Ultimately, the United States did not have a chance to do so as its delegates did not attend, due to various delays.

Another issue during Adams's presidency was Texas. During his term in office, he unsuccessfully tried to rectify the United States-Mexican border in order to secure Texas for the United States. Yet after his retirement from the presidency, Adams turned against such a plan as he became increasingly aware that territorial expansion also meant the expansion of slavery. Even though he was not an abolitionist, Adams feared that slavery would be introduced into the newly acquired territories in the southwest, and he rapidly understood that slavery would eventually tear the Union apart. Consequently, during his tenure as representative of Massachusetts, from 1831 to 1848, he opposed the expansionist policies of the Jackson, Tyler, and Polk administrations. He strongly criticized the annexation of Texas. His anti-expansionist stance also led him to oppose the Mexican War. He became the leader of the antislavery and antiwar faction until his death on February 23, 1848. Adams died in the House after having voted against a measure recommending the decoration of Mexican War veterans.

See also *Amistad Mutiny, 1839; Benton, Thomas Hart; Calhoun, John C.; Clay, Henry; Colombia, U.S. Relations with; Jackson, Andrew; Jefferson, Thomas; Latin American Independence, 1803–1826, U.S. Policy toward; Louisiana Purchase, 1803; Monroe Doctrine; No-Transfer Resolution, 1811; Texas, U.S. Annexation of*

. . . . MONICA HENRY

REFERENCES AND FURTHER READING

Bemis, Samuel Flagg. *John Quincy Adams and the Foundations of American Foreign Policy*. New York: Knopf, 1956.

Lewis Jr., James E. *John Quincy Adams. Policymaker for the Union*. Wilmington, DE: Scholarly Resources, 2001.

Lipsky, George A. *John Quincy Adams. His Theory and Ideas*. New York: Crowell, 1950.

Parsons, Lynn H. *John Quincy Adams*. Madison, WI: Madison House, 1998.

Weeks, William E. *John Quincy Adams and American Global Empire*. Lexington: The University Press of Kentucky, 1992.

Adams-Onís Treaty

(**See** *Transcontinental Treaty, 1819*)

Agee, Philip

Philip Agee (1935–2008) was a Central Intelligence Agency (CIA) operative who served in Latin America, but following his departure from the agency, he became notorious for exposing United States agents throughout the world. Agee graduated from the University of Notre Dame in 1956. He joined the CIA a year later and was posted as a case officer in Ecuador, Uruguay, Brazil, and Mexico before resigning in 1968.

As a CIA field agent Agee became disillusioned with its cooperation with right-wing repression in Latin America and the U.S. Vietnam War policy. Particular turning points, according to Agee, were President Lyndon Johnson's intervention in the Dominican Republic, alleged Uruguayan torture of regime opponents, and the Tlatelolco massacre in Mexico City just prior to the 1968 Olympics. Another influence appears to have been Agee's Brazilian lover at the time, a leftist who claimed she had been tortured by Brazilian security forces. Anticommunist newspaper reporter and book author John Barron offered a different version of events, subsequently claiming that Agee was forced to resign by the CIA in late 1968 for alcohol abuse and misbehavior toward embassy wives at various posts. After leaving the CIA Agee identified with leftist, oftentimes communist groups in support of social revolutions.

In the early 1970s, shortly after leaving the CIA, Agee approached Soviet KGB Committee for State Security officers in Mexico City, offering to provide sensitive information, but the Soviet intelligence service, fearing Agee was part of a CIA deception plot, turned him away. However the Cuban General Intelligence Directorate (DGI—Direccion General de Inteligencia) welcomed Agee "with open arms" (Andrew and Mitrokhin, 2005, 103–104). In Cuba Agee was provided with a house and two researchers, and for six months, he worked on his book. In a later autobiography, *On The Run*, Agee denied wanting to assist the KGB, only wishing to provide support to Cuban activities in Latin America, despite the fact that the DGI at this time was a subsidiary of the KGB and quite willingly shared Agee's information with the Soviets. Agee denied a 1992 report that he received $1 million for the passed information.

In 1975 Agee stated in an interview that "the CIA is plainly on the wrong side, that is, the capitalist side. I approve KGB activities, Communist activities in general, when they are to the advantage of the oppressed" (Rael Jean Isaac and Erich Isaac, 1983, 120). In fact Agee felt that the KGB was not doing enough and that its activities were modest.

Like other entrants into the CIA, Agee had taken an oath not to divulge classified information or to reveal the identity of fellow agents. He violated that oath with the 1975 publication of his book, *Inside The Company*, a memoir of CIA activities in his Latin American station posts, in which Agee also listed 250 CIA operatives in the region. A few retired CIA and M-16 station chiefs have nevertheless described Agee's book as providing excellent and accurate insights into the daily life of intelligence operatives working abroad.

Also in 1975 Agee founded the magazine *CounterSpy* to reveal covert operations, especially those undertaken by the U.S. government. According to Public Information Research, *CounterSpy* published thirty-two issues from 1973 to 1984, including a 1975 issue that included another list of CIA, Drug Enforcement Agency (DEA), and Britain's M-16 global operatives. Agee's list was blamed for the execution of Richard

Welch, the CIA station chief in Greece, and two British M-16 agents in Poland. For his stinging revelations Agee reported that he received several death threats and was subsequently expelled from Britain, France, West Germany, the Netherlands, and Italy.

While in Europe Agee maintained his Cuban connection. For example, in West Germany he lived at a home owned by an attorney for the Baader-Meinhoff terrorist gang where he met frequently (at least thirty meetings) with Cuban intelligence officers. Landing back in Havana in 1978, Agee announced at the World Youth Festival the formation of *Covert Action Information Bulletin,* an effort launched "on the initiative of the KGB," according to the Mitrokhin Archive from the Soviet intelligence service. Agee would serve on the editorial board. Agee also served on the editorial board of *Soberanta,* a Cuban monthly magazine devoted to denouncing imperialism and identifying CIA agents.

Two more Agee books followed: *Dirty Work: The CIA in Western Europe,* published in 1978, and *Dirty Work: The CIA in Africa,* published in 1979 to coincide with the Non-Aligned Movement conference held in Cuba that year. Two KGB agents directly handed Agee the names of alleged CIA personnel working on the African continent so that he could expose them in the latter book.

Agee, again with help from Cuba, penned a forty-six-page attack on the State Department's 1981 White Paper on El Salvador that was distributed by *Covert Action Information Bulletin.* This report became a source for negative articles on U.S. policy by Robert Kaiser in *The Washington Post* and Jonathan Kwitney in *The Wall Street Journal.*

Meanwhile the Marxist government of Maurice Bishop in Grenada granted Agee a passport in 1980. When Bishop was killed in 1983, and the Communist regime toppled shortly thereafter, Agee used a passport by the Sandinista-run government of Nicaragua.

Despite his U.S. passport being withdrawn in the 1970s, Agee traveled to New York in December 1988 to join Susan Sarandon in presenting the "Courageous Resister Awards" at a "Resist in Concert!" show headlined by Sinead O'Connor. "Resist in Concert!" was organized by Refuse and Resist, a group with close ties to the Revolutionary Communist Party USA, a group itself with ties to the Shining Path, a Peruvian terrorist group.

Among the many Agee legacies is his direct link to the 1982 Intelligence Identities Protection Act (IIPA) designed to prevent a repeat of Agee-type revelations. The law subsequently came into play with the "outing" of Valerie Plame in 2003 by the George W. Bush administration in retaliation for her husband's (Joseph Wilson) criticism of the Bush administration.

Agee died in Cuba in January 2008, one month after undergoing surgery for perforated ulcers.

See also *Central Intelligence Agency (CIA); Communism in Latin America; Non-Aligned Movement (NAM); Soviet Union, Latin American Policy*

GREG MURPHY

REFERENCES AND FURTHER READING

Barron, John. *KGB Today: The Hidden Hand.* New York: Reader's Digest Press, 1983.

Christopher, Andrew and Vasili Mitrokhin. *The World Was Going Our Way.* New York: Basic Books, 2005.

Christopher, Andrew and Vasili Mitrokhin. *The Sword and the Shield.* New York: Basic Books, 1999.

Hirson, James. *Radical Road Maps.* Nashville, TN: WND, 2006.

Isaac, Rael Jean and Erich Isaac. *The Coercive Utopians.* Chicago: Regnery Gateway, 1983.

Powell, S. Stephen. *Covert Cadre.* Ottawa, IL: Green Hill Publishers, 1987.

Tyson, James. *Target America.* Chicago: Regnery Gateway, 1981.

Agricultural Trade Development and Assistance Act

(**See** *Food for Peace*)

Alarcón de Quesada, Ricardo

Aside from the Castro brothers, one of the longest serving and most trusted officials of the Cuban government is Ricardo Alarcón de Quesada (1937–). Born in Havana on May 21, 1937, to an upper middle class family, Alarcón enrolled in the University of Havana's doctoral program in philosophy in September 1954. He became involved in the anti-Batista Federation of University Students during his freshman year, and in July 1955, he joined Fidel Castro's 26th of July Movement, a clandestine revolutionary group plotting the overthrow of Cuban President Fulgencio Batista.

Instead of joining the movement's military arm, Alarcón played a vital role in organizing its student division. As a result of his work, the Federation of University Students became the conduit by which students joined Castro's organization. Alarcón's work on Castro's behalf helped land him the Federation's vice presidency in 1959 and its presidency in 1961. When Alarcón received his doctorate in 1962, his loyalty to Castro was rewarded with a plum assignment in the Cuban Ministry of Foreign Affairs as director of the Americas division. Thus began Alarcón's diplomatic career.

ALARCÓN AT THE UNITED NATIONS AND THE NATIONAL ASSEMBLY

In 1966 Alarcón was appointed to serve as Cuba's permanent representative to the United Nations, a post he held until 1978. In that capacity, he was elevated to many high positions within the United Nations, among them, vice president of the General Assembly of the United Nations, president of the Council of Administration to the United Nations Development Program, and vice president of the United Nations Committee on the Exercise of the Inalienable Rights of the Palestinian People. Though these positions were officially attached to the United Nations, Alarcón did—where possible—interject the Castro regime's anti-American agenda into his policy decisions.

In 1978 Alarcón was recalled from New York, due to his promotion to first vice-minister of the Cuban Ministry of Foreign Affairs. Because of his long association with the Castro brothers, his advice was often sought regarding important policy decisions, especially regarding those involving Cuban-U.S.

relations. When the U.S. Special Interests Section in Havana opened (1978), it was Alarcón who was assigned the task of dealing with the section's officials. In fact, Alarcón's expertise in U.S.-Cuban Affairs made him a natural choice when it came to negotiating with those in Washington, D.C., about the thorny issues that often arose in the relationship between the two nations. Among those issues was the Mariel Boat Lift of 1980, when Castro decided to empty his prisons and insane asylums by allowing their inmates to "escape" to the United States.

By 1990 the Castro regime was ready to tap Alarcón for another term as Cuba's permanent representative to the United Nations. This time, however, Alarcón's tenure was comparatively brief, for he was appointed Cuba's minister of foreign affairs in 1992. Again, Alarcón's tenure in this post was short-lived, for it ended in February, 1993, with his election to the Cuban National Assembly and his quick elevation as that body's president. Presently, Alarcón's official capacity within the Cuban government is as president of the National Assembly. In truth, his responsibilities extend far beyond his official capacity. As a long-time "insider" within the Cuban government, Alarcón often fills many roles for the regime, especially those in the diplomatic realm.

HANDLING CRISES DIPLOMATICALLY

Alarcón's career as Cuba's top "U.S. expert" has spanned almost five decades and covered a wide range of issues. As a young diplomat, Alarcón was queried for his advice about Washington's response to the Soviet Union's installation of nuclear missiles in 1962. While some in the Castro regime expected the Kennedy administration to take a hard-line response to the missiles, Alarcón predicted the firm but diplomatic approach it took. As relations between the United States and Cuba lurched from one incident to another, Alarcón often worked behind the scenes to resolve the crises in Cuba's best interests. When thirty-eight Cuban fishermen were detained by the U.S. Coast Guard (in 1964) for fishing off Dry Tortugas, Florida, it was Alarcón who secured the fishermen's release as Castro fulminated about the incident. He also played a role in crafting the Anti-Hijacking Treaty between Cuba and the United States in 1970 as Castro welcomed the hijackers who forced U.S. commercial aircraft to land in Havana.

As Alarcón gained more experience, his role became more public, either as a lead negotiator in U.S.-Cuba talks or as a spokesperson for the Cuban government. In January 1993, for example, he accused the outgoing administration of George H.W. Bush of waging a campaign against Cuba by refusing to lift the trade embargo. He added that he did not hold out hope for improvement of U. S.-Cuban relations in the incoming Clinton administration. A year later, however, Alarcón headed the Cuban delegation for talks with the U.S. government regarding migration issues.

By 2000, Alarcón had become Cuba's public face in its relations with the United States, especially during the Elián González incident. When Elián's father pleaded for his son's return, Alarcón advised him on how to word his plea. What is more, Alarcón was the highest ranking Cuban official to greet Elián when his plane touched down at Havana's Jose Marti International Airport. When a new administration took power in Washington, Alarcón issued Cuba's public statement regarding the future of relations between Cuba and the United States. When George W. Bush ascended to office in 2001, Alarcón publicly dismissed the prospect of improved Cuban-U.S. relations. Eight years later, he issued a similar statement about the Obama administration, despite an earlier observation predicting an improvement in relations between the two nations.

CONCLUSION

As the founding members of the Castro regime start to pass from the scene, it can be expected that Alarcón will take on a larger role within the Cuban state. His current responsibilities notwithstanding, Alarcón will continue as Cuba's spokesperson to the world, especially when it comes to relations between Cuba and its northern neighbor.

See also *Castro Ruz, Fidel; Clinton, William J.; Cuba, U.S. Relations with; Cuban Missile Crisis, 1962; Operation Mongoose*

. . . . PETER B. GUSHUE

REFERENCES AND FURTHER READING

Alarcón, Ricardo and Mary Murray. *Cuba and the United States: An Interview with Cuban Foreign Minister, Ricardo Alarcón*. New York: Ocean Press, 1992.

Patterson, Thomas G. *Contesting Castro: The United States and the Triumph of the Cuban Revolution*. New York: Oxford University Press, 1994.

Quirk, Robert E. *Fidel Castro: The Full Story of His Rise to Power, His Regime, His Allies, and His Adversaries*. New York: Norton, 1993.

Smith, Gaddis: *The Last Years of the Monroe Doctrine, 1945–1993*. New York: Hill and Wang, 1994.

Albright, Madeleine

Madeleine Albright (1937–) was the first woman to serve as U.S. secretary of state. Appointed by President Bill Clinton, she served from 1997 to 2001. Albright earned a BA from Wellesley College and her master's and doctorate degrees from Columbia University's Department of Public Law and Government. She also studied at the School of Advanced International Studies at Johns Hopkins University. From 1981 to 1982, Albright served as a senior fellow in Soviet and Eastern European affairs at the Center for Strategic and International Studies. In 1982, Albright was appointed research professor of international affairs and director of the Women in Foreign Service Program at Georgetown University's School of Foreign Service. Albright served as U.S. ambassador to the United Nations during President Bill Clinton's first term (1993–1997).

As U.S. ambassador to the United Nations and U.S. secretary of state, Albright faced two major crises in Latin America, both in the Caribbean. The first began in 1996 when Cuban fighter jets shot down two aircraft belonging to the organization Brothers to the Rescue, a Cuban-exile group which had, since 1991, flown over the waters between the United States and Cuba in search of refugees fleeing the island. Immediately after the incident, Albright, who was serving at the time as president of the United Nations Security Council, called an emergency session of the Security Council. The resulting record of condemnation from the Security Council, as well as strong public criticism from Albright herself, won support from the Miami-based

Cuban exile community. Another result of this incident was the passage of the Cuban Liberty and Democratic Solidarity Act of 1996 (also known as the Helms-Burton Act), which strengthened and extended the U.S. embargo against Cuba.

In January 1998, after Albright had been named U.S. secretary of state, Pope John Paul II made a historic visit to Cuba, focusing attention once again on U.S.-Cuban relations and the possibility of changing U.S. policy of diplomatic isolation and economic sanctions. In the aftermath of the pope's visit, Albright made several recommendations to President Clinton, which he approved. Charitable organizations would be allowed to fly directly to Cuba from the United States and Americans would be allowed to send money directly to relatives in Cuba.

The other major foreign policy crisis in Latin America during Clinton's term involved ongoing turmoil in Haiti. The democratically elected president of Haiti, Jean-Bertrand Aristide, had been ousted in a coup by Lieutenant General Raoul Cedras. In July 1993 the United Nations sponsored the Governor's Island Agreement, which made provisions for Cedras to resign and Aristide to return to power. However, the Haitian military refused to cooperate, and the United Nations Security Council passed a resolution imposing economic sanctions and sending a team of human rights monitors to the island. Albright supported further United Nations action to restore Aristide to power. In 1994, she worked to convince the Security Council to authorize the use of force against Cedras and the Haitian military. The Brazilian representative, in particular, was reluctant to authorize U.S. military action in Latin America, given the long history of U.S. interventions in the region, but Albright emphasized the unique set of circumstances facing Haiti and insisted that this action would not set a precedent for further U.S. actions in the hemisphere. The Security Council finally authorized a use of force. The plan required the United States to lead the United Nations coalition to remove Cedras, establish stability on the island, and begin the groundwork for holding new elections. The Clinton administration made one last effort at diplomacy by sending former President Jimmy Carter, Senator Sam Nunn, and retired General Colin Powell to Haiti to negotiate with Cedras. Clinton also ordered the U.S. Army 82nd Airborne Division into the air, and at this point, Cedras resigned. When the U.S. military arrived in Haiti, it met with no resistance. Elections were held in June 1995, resulting in a victory for Aristide's political coalition.

Upon ending her term as U.S. secretary of state in 2001, Madeleine Albright remained in Washington, D.C., as the Mortara Distinguished Professor of Diplomacy at Georgetown University and a director on the board of the Council on Foreign Relations.

See also *Aristide, Jean-Bertrand; Brothers to the Rescue; Cuban Liberty and Democratic Solidarity Act, 1996 (United States); Helms-Burton Law, 1996; Pope John Paul II*

MOLLY M. WOOD

REFERENCES AND FURTHER READING

Albright, Madeleine. *Madam Secretary: A Memoir.* New York: Miramax Books, 2003.

Dobbs, Michael. *Madeleine Albright: A Twentieth Century Odyssey.* New York: Henry Holt, 1999.

Lippman, Thomas. *Madeleine Albright and the New American Diplomacy.* Boulder, CO: Westview Press, 2000.

Alfaro Delgado, Eloy

Eloy Alfaro Delgado (1842–1912), the *viejo luchador* (old campaigner), is one of the best known Ecuadorian presidents, closely identified as the leader of the liberal cause in the late nineteenth and early twentieth centuries. Ecuadorian liberal reformers today still see Alfaro as a national hero.

Alfaro was born in 1842 in the coastal town of Montecristi. In 1864 he began the first of his several military campaigns against various Ecuadorian governments. Over a long violent life he fought some eleven military campaigns, counting just those in Ecuador, for even during his years in exile Alfaro kept fighting, participating in wars in Central America and Cuba.

Alfaro came to power in a successful military revolt in 1895. This victory, along with his other military campaigns, relied on considerable support from the underclass, people who saw in Alfaro the hope for reform and improvement in their lives. While some historians have emphasized Alfaro's commitment to the poor, most see him as a crass opportunist. Whatever Alfaro might have intended to do, he managed to accomplish very little in the way of actual social reform. Alfaro spoke of liberalism, but in practice he could be a repressive tyrant.

One area of consistent effort was Alfaro's crusade against the Catholic clergy. The church responded in kind, bankrolling violent insurgencies against Alfaro. He answered by expelling the foreign-born clergy from Ecuador, correctly observing that they played a leading role in inciting the faithful to rise up against his authority. In 1908, Alfaro seized church land, closed monasteries and convents, initiated the practice of secular registrations of births and deaths, and removed the church from public education.

In foreign policy Alfaro saw himself as the leader of a revived spirit of pan-Americanism. He issued a call for an Inter-American Congress to be held in Mexico City in August 1896. His goal was to construct a Latin American version of the Monroe Doctrine. Alfaro also saw the conference as a chance to reopen discussions on the recreation of Gran Colombia (Colombia, Venezuela, and Ecuador). Furthermore, Alfaro wanted to use the conference to organize Latin American support for the Cuban rebels fighting for independence from Spain.

Both Spain and the United States opposed Alfaro's call for a pan-American meeting. The United States government, under Grover Cleveland (President 1893–1897), flatly rejected the idea, holding that Ecuador lacked adequate status to convene such a congress. Secretary of State Richard Olney saw Alfaro's proposal as unwelcome disruption of his ongoing and delicate negotiations with Great Britain regarding the Venezuela-British Guiana boundary issue. The United States announced that it could not attend the conference because all the U.S. states would not be there—and then worked hard to make sure that this would happen. Venezuela, Bolivia, and Uruguay, which had previously agreed to attend, backed out. In the end only Ecuador, Mexico, Guatemala, Honduras, El Salvador,

Nicaragua, and Costa Rica attended the conference, with the talks never getting beyond the most preliminary level. Alfaro's pan-American dream ended in failure.

Another Alfaro initiative was the construction of a rail line linking Ecuador's two largest cities, running 260 miles from the port of Guayaquil to the highland capital of Quito, 9,200 feet above sea level. Alfaro contracted the services of U.S. entrepreneur Archer Harman to build and operate the railway; construction began in 1899 and concluded in 1908. Sharp disputes between Ecuador and the U.S. railroad company soon developed. The railway proved very costly to build and operate, a situation made worse by Harman's questionable accounting practices. In the end this impractical railway into the sky failed to solve Ecuador's internal transportation difficulties, and the ensuing acrimony between the Ecuadorian and U.S. governments soured relations for many years.

In late 1911 Alfaro made an armed attempt to continue in office. Defeated by rival liberal leader Leonidas Plaza Gutiérrez, Alfaro and his fellow revolutionaries—General Pedro Montero and General Flavio Alfaro (Alfaro's nephew)—were taken prisoner in Guayaquil in January 1912. Montero was seized by a crowd and brutally murdered immediately after his trial and conviction. Amidst the chaos, authorities spirited the Alfaros out of town, placing them under guard and on a train to Quito. When the Alfaros arrived on January 28, 1912, a crowd pulled the ex-president and his nephew from the train and beat them mercilessly before murdering them. The crowd fell upon the bodies and mutilated them, burned them, and dragged them through the streets of the capital.

See also *Cleveland, Grover; Ecuador, U.S. Relations with; Guayaquil and Quito Railroad; Venezuela-Guiana Boundary Dispute, 1890s*

. . . . RONN PINEO

REFERENCES AND FUTURE READING

A. Kim Clark, *The Redemptive Work: Railway and Nation in Ecuador, 1895–1930*. Wilmington, DE: Scholarly Resources, 1998.

Ronn Pineo, *Ecuador and the United States: Useful Strangers*. Athens, GA: The University of Georgia Press, 2007.

Ronn Pineo, *Economic and Social Reform in Ecuador: Life and Work in Guayaquil*. Gainesville: University Press of Florida, 1996.

All Mexico Movement (United States)

In the middle decades of the nineteenth century, some citizens and politicians in the United States promoted the idea of taking over the entire national territory of Mexico. Their efforts became known as the All Mexico Movement. The thought behind the campaign was an extension of the notion of Manifest Destiny, which held that the moral imperative of the United States was to expand territorial claims throughout the North American continent. Debates around the movement reflected deep divisions in U.S. public opinion on issues of empire, race, and slavery. When the resolution of the Mexican-American War nearly fixed borders between the nations in 1848, the U.S. movement to annex all of Mexico essentially ended.

THE RISE OF THE ALL MEXICO MOVEMENT

The U.S. annexation of Texas and the Mexican-American War set the context for the rise of the All Mexico Movement. After Texas declared independence from Mexico in 1836 and the Mexican military subsequently was unable to retake the territory, the United States recognized the Republic of Texas, leading to growing tensions between Mexico and the United States. U.S. support for incorporation of Texas into the United States grew with the rise of fears of British influence in the newly formed republic, and Texans voted for annexation in 1845. As the United States was now asserting dominion over territory once claimed by Mexico, hostilities between the two nations exploded first with border skirmishes and then with the U.S. declaration of war in May 1846.

As the war wore on and the U.S. military claimed more and more Mexican territory, calls for total annexation of Mexico became louder and they came from diverse corners of the United States. Some slave owners and other investors saw total annexation as an opportunity for more slave states and more commercial gain. Senator Stephen Douglas argued the need to expand as far southward as Central America, where the United States could construct a transoceanic canal. Some "All Mexico" proponents, such as *New York Sun* editor Moses Beach, argued that annexation would liberate Mexicans from a "backward" and despotic political system, while others emphasized what they perceived to be the inherently inferior qualities of the indigenous and mestizo populations of Mexico.

All proponents shared assumptions of U.S. superiority over Mexico and its people, assumptions that were consistent with Manifest Destiny more broadly. Annexing all of Mexico was one major step to claiming dominion over the entire continent. Some opponents, including Abraham Lincoln, asserted that the war and the All Mexico Movement were initiatives driven primarily by greed and power and would only strengthen the political power of slave owners; other opponents, such as John C. Calhoun, feared that incorporation of more non-white and non-Anglo peoples would weaken the social, political, and racial fabric of the United States.

CONCLUSION

U.S. military forces forged deep into the south, invading and claiming military control of Mexico City in September 1847, prompting great optimism among "All Mexico" proponents but also compelling an end to the war. Ultimately, the need for peace, the concern of prolonged Mexican resistance, the logistical challenges of ruling distant regions, the fear of strengthening pro-slavery political forces, and racial animosities combined to limit how far south the administration of President James Polk was prepared to claim and defend. Still, the 1848 Treaty of Guadalupe Hidalgo ceded to the United States nearly one million square miles of territory, including all or part of the present-day states of California, Nevada, Arizona, Utah, Wyoming, Colorado, New Mexico, Kansas, Oklahoma, and Texas. Though the movement never regained the political momentum it had during the Mexican-American War, the All Mexico Movement had revealed historic tensions over slavery, race, and expansionism that remained unresolved through the rest of the nineteenth century.

See also *Beach, Moses Yale; Calhoun, John C.; Manifest Destiny; Mexican-American War, 1846–1848; Mexican American War: Treaty of Guadalupe Hidalgo, 1848; Polk, James K.; Texas, U.S. Annexation of*

. . . . GREGORY S. CRIDER

REFERENCES AND FURTHER READING

Haynes, Sam W., and Christopher Morris, eds. *Manifest Destiny and Empire: American Antebellum Expansion.* College Station: Texas A&M Press, 1997.
Horsman, Reginald. *Race and Manifest Destiny: The Origins of American Racial Anglo-Saxonism.* Cambridge, MA: Harvard University Press, 1981.
Pinheiro, John C. "'Religion without Restriction': Anti-Catholicism, All Mexico, and the Treaty of Guadalupe Hidalgo." *Journal of the Early Republic* 23 (Spring 2003): 69–96.
Zoraida Vázquez, Josefina and Lorenzo Meyer. *The United States and Mexico.* Chicago: University of Chicago Press, 1987.

Allende Gossens, Salvador

Salvador Allende Gossens (1908–1973) was a medical doctor, a Mason, and a member of the Socialist party. He married Hortencia Bussi in 1940 and they raised three daughters, Carmen Paz, Beatriz, and Isabel. Over the course of his lifetime Allende served as senator, deputy, cabinet minister, and president of the Republic of Chile (1970–1973) until his untimely death on September 11, 1973, during the military coup that inaugurated seventeen years of dictatorship.

ASCENT TO PRESIDENCY DESPITE ACTIVE U.S. OPPOSITION

Allende is best known for his tenure as president. He was the Popular Action Front presidential candidate on three separate occasions—1952, 1958, and 1964—before winning the national elections in 1970 as candidate for the Popular Unity coalition. Allende and the Popular Unity coalition, comprised of the Chilean Socialist party, Communist party, Radical party, Social Democrat party, Unitary Popular Action Movement, Christian Left, and Independent Popular Action party, sought to achieve socialist revolution peacefully, constitutionally, and as a member of the Non-Aligned Movement. This was known as the "Chilean Road to Socialism." On the international front, the Popular Unity government eventually established diplomatic relations with Cuba, East Germany, and North Korea.

Allende won the September 4, 1970, presidential election with a plurality of the popular vote (36.3 percent), against rival candidates Radomiro Tomic Romero of the Christian Democrat party (27.8 percent) and conservative ex-president of the Republic, Jorge Alessandri Rodríguez (34.9 percent). Congress confirmed Allende as president on October 26, 1970, despite U.S.-supported opposition and a terror plot that resulted in the murder of the army commander in chief, General René Schneider, a few days earlier.

The U.S. government had long feared Allende's election for the example that the democratic election of a Marxist could set for other countries. The CIA funded over 50 percent of Eduardo Frei Montalva's 1964 presidential campaign in what was ultimately a successful attempt to keep Allende from winning those elections. Allende's victory in 1970 incensed U.S. President Richard Nixon and Secretary of State Henry Kissinger. When the kidnapping of General René Schneider failed to avert Allende's confirmation, the United States embarked on a plan of covert action in collaboration with multinational corporations and the Chilean right to cripple the Chilean economy and destabilize the political climate. The United States denied financing and credit and pressured private investors and international lending institutions to boycott Chile. The United States sought to foment political instability through the financial support and training of actual and potential opposition organizations, including the Chilean military. Henry Kissinger served as chair of the "40 Committee," which approved in January 1971 the expenditure of $6,476,166 to support the activities of opposition groups. Over the course of the Popular Unity period, the United States funded the activities of the paramilitary organization Patria y Libertad, the national newspaper giant *El Mercurio,* and anti-government labor strikers, among others.

THE BUMPY "CHILEAN ROAD TO SOCIALISM"

The "Chilean Road to Socialism" included five major areas of governmental action: income redistribution, the expansion of social welfare programs, reactivation of the industrial sector, the nationalization of key industries, and land reform. The goal was to organize the economy into three productive sectors: the Private Area (small businesses), the Mixed Area (the state as majority stockholder in mixed-ownership enterprises), and the Area of Social Property (state-owned). In July 1971 Congress unanimously approved the nationalization of the copper industry, which provided 70 percent of Chile's foreign exchange and generated an estimated annual profit of $120 million. Previously, U.S. giants Kennecott and Anaconda had dominated 80 percent of Chile's copper industry. The government also nationalized the coal and steel industries, much of the private financial sector, part of the textile industry, Ford, Ralston Purina, and International Telephone and Telegraph.

By the end of 1971 industrial production had increased by over 14 percent, the GNP had risen by over 8 percent, unemployment had dropped nearly 5 percent, and inflation fell from 35 percent to 22 percent. However, the opposition still controlled Congress. Important sectors of the Socialist party, the MAPU (Popular Unitary Action Movement), and—from outside the ruling coalition—the Movement of the Revolutionary Left (MIR) pressured the government to radicalize its agenda and accelerate and expand its wealth-redistribution programs. Allende was hard-pressed to balance the demands emanating from Left, Right, and center, even as U.S. opposition intensified and the economic situation worsened.

The U.S. boycott and domestic economic sabotage compounded the economic instability, and by late 1972 the economy began to spiral out of control. Shops ran low on goods as demand increased and the black market proliferated. Some people feared widespread shortages and hoarded against that eventuality, while others hoarded in a deliberate effort to sabotage the economy. Scarcity led to rationing and a climate of uncertainty. The political opposition capitalized on the disarray within the production and supply chain, fomenting fear and further instability. Nevertheless, the government enjoyed the support of significant sectors of the poor and working-class population, including factory workers, rural laborers, and the urban poor. For many, this was the first time they had access to homeownership, higher education, meat, and milk for their children.

FALL OF ALLENDE

Chile entered a severe economic crisis in early 1973 as international credit and financing dried up, and the country faced runaway inflation and an overwhelming trade deficit. In an effort to appease opposition sectors and to shore up the support of constitutionalist factions of the military, Allende appointed the commander in chief of the Army, General Carlos Prats, to the post of minister of the interior. Within the armed services, however, a coup conspiracy was already underway. In late August 1973 General Prats resigned in the face of increasing pressure, and General Augusto Pinochet Ugarte replaced him as commander in chief of the Army. The Christian Democrat party joined pro-coup sectors and the political Right in support of military intervention. On September 11, 1973, the military overthrew the Popular Unity government. The Air Force bombed La Moneda (Chile's presidential palace) as well as opposition radio towers and the presidential residence. Salvador Allende refused to capitulate and defended the La Moneda until his death. His remains were buried in Viña del Mar and his family was forced into exile. In the 1990s his remains were transferred to a tomb in Santiago's General Cemetery.

See also *Castro Ruz, Fidel; Chile, U.S. Relations with; Chilean Development Corporation (CORFO); "Chileanization" of Foreign Properties; Frei Montalva, Eduardo; International Telephone & Telegraph (ITT) Corporation; Letelier de Solar, Orlando; Movement of the Revolutionary Left (MIR) (Chile); Nixon, Richard M.; Pinochet Ugarte, Augusto*

. . . . ALISON J. BRUEY

REFERENCES AND FURTHER READING

Collier, Simon, and William F. Sater. *A History of Chile, 1808-1994.* New York: Cambridge University Press, 1996.

Kornbluh, Peter. *The Pinochet File: A Declassified Dossier on Atrocity and Accountability.* New York: The New Press, 2003.

Loveman, Brian, and Elizabeth Lira. *Las ardientes cenizas del olvido: Vía chilena de Reconciliación Política 1932–1994.* Santiago, Chile: LOM, 2000.

Pinto Vallejos, Julio, ed. *Cuando hicimos historia: La experiencia de la Unidad Popular.* Santiago, Chile: LOM, 2005.

Alliance for Progress

In 1961 at a meeting of the Latin American Diplomatic Corps, President John F. Kennedy introduced the Alliance for Progress. He pledged $20 billion in public and private funding to carry out reforms that would transform social conditions in the region. The Alliance came on the heels of the 1959 Cuban Revolution. By improving social conditions through economic aid and reform, Kennedy hoped to promote democratic governance and to stave off the threat of communism. As he put it in a speech at the White House in 1962, "those who make peaceful revolution impossible, make violent revolution inevitable."

Although Kennedy announced the Alliance in 1961, it grew from efforts by Latin American leaders to encourage multilateral development. In 1958 the president of Brazil, Juscelino Kubitschek, called for an "Operation Pan-America" to promote development in the region. Kubitschek's appeal reflected the research of Raúl Prebisch, the tremendously influential economist and head of the United Nations' Economic Commission for Latin America (ECLA) who transformed ideas about Latin America's economy by emphasizing its status as a peripheral region in the world dependent on the United States.

In 1959 President Eisenhower, acting under pressure from Latin American leaders, introduced the Act of Bogotá, which in turn contributed to the creation of the Inter-American Development Bank. These initiatives provided a foundation for Kennedy's Alliance for Progress by establishing a precedent and an infrastructure through which to channel U.S. funds.

GOALS OF THE ALLIANCE FOR PROGRESS

Although the Alliance built upon early efforts to promote Inter-American development programs, it was distinct in the scale of its goals. The Charter of Punta del Este, prepared in 1961 to guide the Alliance, established nine-four specific objectives. It sought to increase economic growth to 2.5 percent per year—approximately double the rate of growth in the 1950s—and to provide "techo, trabajo, y tierra" (housing, work, and land) to the region's impoverished majority. Agrarian reform to eliminate the unjust concentration of land holdings in the hands of a small elite was central to the Alliance's goals. The Alliance also sought to reduce Latin American countries' dependence on single export crops by diversifying their economic base and promoting free trade associations within the region.

To achieve its goals of economic, social, and political transformation, the Alliance for Progress promoted economic planning initiatives. The Inter-American Committee on the Alliance for Progress (CIAP) became the foundation for an economic planning review process. Each year the economic, planning, and development ministers from member Latin American nations presented voluntarily their development plans to CIAP for review. CIAP then made an annual estimate of each country's external financial requirements that became the foundation for "country reviews" presented to multilateral funding agencies including the U.S. Agency for International Development, the Inter-American Development Bank, the World Bank, and the IMF.

Supporters of the Alliance for Progress point to this economic development model based on Latin American countries' adoption of national planning as one of its most important successes. They also observe that Alliance resources built roads, ports, railroads, telephone lines, and other infrastructure. At the same time they emphasize that the Alliance improved living conditions for most Latin Americans, claiming that infant mortality dropped, illiteracy was reduced, and educational opportunities increased with primary school enrollment up by nearly 200 percent, secondary school enrollment up by 350 percent, and higher education by 800 percent, even

President John F. Kennedy (at podium) spoke in the state dining room of the White House in Washington, D.C., on the first anniversary of the Alliance for Progress at a reception in honor of the "Committee of Nine" of the Alliance and the diplomatic corps of the Latin American Republics. Observers, including Vice President Lyndon B. Johnson, stand behind the president as he lauds "the first time in the history of Inter-American relations" that "our energies are concentrated on the central task of democratic development" (John F. Kennedy, address on the first anniversary of the Alliance for Progress, March 13, 1962).

SOURCE: Courtesy of the John F. Kennedy Presidential Library

though population increased just 70 percent. The high rate of population growth estimated at 3 percent per year was, in fact, seen as an obstacle to success because resources provided by the Alliance were absorbed by an ever increasing population.

LIMITATIONS OF THE ALLIANCE FOR PROGRESS

Critics suggest that the greatest failures of the Alliance were inherent to its goals. Although it was presented as a Marshall Plan for Latin America, the Alliance for Progress offered less aid and much of it came in the form of loans. Seventy percent of Alliance funds were loans, while 90 percent of Marshall Plan funds were outright grants. In fact, the Alliance opened Latin America to an enormous influx of loans. In the 1970s an unprecedented amount of more than $200 billion in commercial loans entered Latin America. A debt crisis followed in the 1980s. Many Latin American countries that could not repay loans received assistance from the World Bank and the IMF, which mandated that Latin American countries adopt Structural Adjustment Programs (SAPs) requiring cuts in social services that had been at the heart of Alliance for Progress.

Critics also note that while land reform was a stated goal of the Alliance for Progress, the United States did not incorporate demands for reform into its political relations with Latin America. As a result, most Alliance resources ended up in the hands of a small elite that controlled land and political positions, increasing the concentration of wealth in the region. Latin America's share of world exports during this period shrunk from 13.4 percent in 1950 to 5 percent in 1969 and disparities in distribution of income and amenities grew. Finally, the Alliance increased Latin America's dependence by granting the United States oversight of a broad range of development projects.

At the same time that the Alliance funded development and social programs to promote democracy, the Kennedy administration also increased support for the military to stave off the threat of communist-inspired revolution. Yet the military was the strongest opponent to democratic governance in the region. Only eight months after the Alliance for Progress charter, seven military coups overthrowing democratically elected presidents occurred. By 1976 only three nations in the region could be considered democratic.

LONG TERM IMPACT OF THE ALLIANCE FOR PROGRESS

The introduction of the Alliance for Progress in 1961 is clear, but its conclusion is not. Some claim the Alliance died with the assassination of John F. Kennedy in 1963. Others observe that Kennedy's successor, President Lyndon B. Johnson, continued the Alliance but took a more pragmatic approach by focusing on economic performance and eliminating the emphasis on social transformation and democracy. Finally, others argue that the Alliance ended as a result of a policy of benign neglect under President Richard Nixon's administration.

The Alliance for Progress's emphasis on economic integration, which included the creation of the Latin American Free Trade Association (LAFTA), the Central American Free Trade Agreement (CAFTA), the Andean Pact, and the Caribbean Community (CARICOM), was resurrected by President Ronald Reagan in the 1980s. The Reagan administration promoted free trade, private sector funding, and technology transfer, which all built upon Alliance precedents and relied on the generation of Latin American government and business leaders trained in the United States during the era of the Alliance. So decades after its demise, the Alliance for Progress still influenced United States relations with Latin America.

See also *Civic Action Programs; Counterinsurgency; Good Neighbor Policy; Kennedy, John F.; School of the Americas; U.S. Agency for International Development (USAID)*

. . . . SUSAN FITZPATRICK BEHRENS

REFERENCES AND FURTHER READINGS

Levinson, Jerome, and Juan de Onís. *The Alliance That Lost Its Way: A Critical Report on the Alliance for Progress*. Chicago: Quadrangle Books, 1970.

Rabe, Stephen R. *The Most Dangerous Area in the World: John F. Kennedy Confronts Communist Revolution in Latin America*. Chapel Hill: The University of North Carolina Press, 1989.

Scheman, L. Ronald, ed. *The Alliance for Progress: A Retrospective*. New York: Praeger, 1988.

Taffet, Jeffrey F. *Foreign Aid as Foreign Policy: The Alliance for Progress in Latin America*. New York: Routledge, 2007.

Amador Guerrero, Manuel

First president of the republic of Panama (1904–1908), Manuel Amador Guerrero (1833–1909) was born in Turbaco near Cartagena on the Caribbean coast of Colombia. In 1855, after studying medicine in Cartagena, he moved to Panama, then a Colombian province, where he launched his medical practice and married María de la Ossa, a member of a prominent local family. He soon became active in Panamanian politics as a leading member of the Conservative party.

After the United States committed itself to the construction of an inter-oceanic canal in Panama with the passage of the Spooner Act (1902), several local leaders formed a junta aimed at bringing about the separation of Panama from Colombia. The junta's founder was José Agustín Arango, an attorney with the Panama Railroad Company. Amador, who had long been employed as a physician by the railroad, soon joined the conspiracy.

As the Hay-Herrán Treaty (1903), which authorized the United States to build a canal in Panama, was debated in Colombia, the junta sent Amador to the United States to ascertain what action the U.S. government might take in the event of a Panamanian declaration of independence. By the time Amador arrived in New York on September 1, 1903, the Colombian Senate had defeated the treaty. In New York Amador conferred with Philippe J. Bunau-Varilla, the French engineer and canal promoter, who traveled to Washington, D.C., where he met with several high officials and reported to Amador that the United States would not oppose a revolution on the isthmus.

After Panama's successful separation from Colombia on November 3, 1903, Amador and junta member Federico Boyd were sent to the United States to negotiate a canal treaty for the young republic. Upon arriving in Washington, D.C., they were shocked to learn that Bunau-Varilla, who had been named Panama's envoy to Washington, had already signed a treaty. Bunau-Varilla tried to persuade Amador and Boyd to ratify the treaty on the spot, but they refused, whereupon it was sent to Panama and quickly approved by the provisional government.

On February 16, 1904, the assembly that had recently promulgated a constitution for Panama elected Amador president for a four-year term. The vote was unanimous as Arango had withdrawn from the race and endorsed Amador. President Amador laid the foundations of the new republic, though the government's actions were constrained by the fact that the 1903 treaty and the constitution made Panama a U.S. protectorate. In 1904 Panama adopted the gold *balboa* as the basic unit of currency, with a value equal to that of the U.S. gold dollar. The government invested most of the $10 million obtained in the canal treaty in American securities and named William Nelson Cromwell as its fiscal agent in the United States. Disputes arose over American policies in the Canal Zone, such as efforts to impose U.S. tariffs there, which would mean the exclusion of non-U.S. goods from the zone; after a visit from Secretary of War William H. Taft in 1904, the decision was reversed. Meanwhile, the Amador administration adopted a flag and national anthem for Panama, expanded the educational system, established a national museum, and built a national theater.

Amador faced political difficulties stemming from Conservative domination of his administration, though Liberals constituted the majority party. In 1904 a crisis arose when General Esteban Huertas, the army commander, exhibited political ambitions. Hailed as a hero for his role in Panamanian independence, Huertas was encouraged by Liberals to demand the resignation of certain Conservative cabinet members. With the backing of U.S. Minister John Barrett, Amador instead obtained the resignation of Huertas and disbanded the army, replacing it with a national police force.

Political tension peaked in 1908 when important municipal elections were scheduled, along with an election for a successor to Amador, who decided not to seek a second term and instead backed the candidacy of his secretary of foreign affairs, Ricardo Arias. His opponent, José Domingo de Obaldía, was nominally a Conservative but enjoyed the support of most Liberals and that of the Canal Zone governor and Secretary Taft. The U.S. government declined a Liberal request for supervision of the municipal elections on June 28 to prevent government-inspired fraud but expanded its military presence in the Canal Zone in case of disorder. The elections were peaceful, with victories for pro-Obaldía slates in Panama City and Colón. Given the strength of the Obaldía forces, Arias withdrew from the presidential race, and Obaldía was duly elected on July 12 in a contest observed by U.S. officers and Canal Zone employees. Unhappy with the outcome, Amador boycotted Obaldía's inauguration on October 1, 1908.

See also *Bunau-Varilla, Philippe J. Cromwell, William N.; Hay–Bunau-Varilla Treaty, 1903; Panama, Independence of, 1903; Panama, U.S. Relations with; Spooner Act, 1902 United States*

. . . . HELEN DELPAR

REFERENCES AND FURTHER READING

McCain, William D. *The United States and the Republic of Panama*. Durham, NC: Duke University Press, 1937.

Mellander, A. J. *The United States in Panamanian Politics*. Danville, IL: Interstate Printers & Publishers, 1971.

Amapala Agreement, 1923

The Amapala Agreement was signed on August 1, 1923, by Jorge Meléndez, Rafael López Gutiérrez, and Emiliano Chamorro Vargas, respectively the presidents of El Salvador, Honduras, and Nicaragua, upon the United States naval ship *Tacoma* anchored near Amapala in the Gulf of Fonseca. In so doing, the three presidents (a) agreed to continue the enforcement of the 1907 Treaty of Amity and Commerce, (b) promised not to permit the use of their national territories as a launching point for an invasion of another signatory, (c) promised not to permit political refugees from another country to serve in their militaries, and (d) agreed to convene a conference of the five Central American republics for the purpose of drawing them closer together.

According to the U.S. State Department's Latin American Affairs Division, the 1907 Treaty provided for political peace in Central America until 1920 when government changes took place in Costa Rica, El Salvador, Honduras, and Nicaragua. Salvadoran Carlos Meléndez, and Generals Rafael López Gutiérrez in Honduras and Diego Manuel Chamorro in Nicaragua were considered weak administrators, adversely influenced by ambitious advisors who schemed and fought among themselves and with politicians in other states. Only the newly elected Costa Rican President Julio Acosta Guardia seemed above the fray, as he promised to reassert his country's isolation from regional political affairs. The most significant change would prove to be the replacement of long-time Guatemalan dictator Manuel Estrada Cabrera with Carlos Herrera on August 16, 1920.

The new leaders' declarations on behalf of Central American unity and a federal government led to a regional conference in San José, Costa Rica, from December 4, 1920, to January 19, 1921, but only El Salvador, Honduras, and Guatemala agreed upon the resultant constitution that went into effect in October 1921. Prodded by the United States, Nicaragua subsequently joined, but Costa Rica maintained its traditionally aloof position. While the United States waited for evidence of an effectively functioning government before considering diplomatic recognition, the overthrow of the Herrera government in Guatemala on December 10, 1921, terminated efforts to implement a unity government and set off a new round of political intrigue across the isthmus. The center of the controversy was President López Gutiérrez who made Honduras a haven for Liberal exiles from El Salvador and Nicaragua with the usual implication of organized revolts against their Conservative home governments. Regional tensions increased when López Gutiérrez extended diplomatic recognition to Guatemala's Liberal government headed by Liberal General José Manuel Orellana. In May 1922 the governments in Tegucigalpa and Guatemala City also reached a secret accord to common defense interests of the Liberal party against the Conservative enemy. At the same time Salvadoran and Honduran troops skirmished at their nation's common border. The United States warned against a regional conflict and insisted upon the convening of a five nation conference under the umbrella of the 1907 Central American conference. Not until July 1922 did tension reach sufficient heights to enable the head of the State Department's Latin American Affairs Division, Francis G. White, to convince Secretary of State Charles Evans Hughes to approve the convening of a Central American conference for the purpose of bringing about regional political stability. The resultant *Tacoma* conference at Amapala paved the way for the 1923 Central American Conference that convened in December 1922 in Washington, D.C.

See also *Central American Conference, Washington, 1907; Central American Conference, Washington, 1923; United States, circum-Caribbean Interventions, 1900–1934: Honduras; United States, circum-Caribbean Interventions, 1900–1934: Nicaragua*

. . . . THOMAS M. LEONARD

REFERENCES AND FURTHER READING

Leonard, Thomas M. *U.S. Policy and Arms Limitation in Central America: The Washington Conference of 1923*. Los Angeles: Center for the Study of Armament and Disarmament, California State University, 1983.

United States Department of State. *Foreign Relations of the United States; 1922*. Washington, DC: Government Printing Office, 1938.

Amazon Cooperation Treaty, 1978 (Amazon Pact)

The Amazon Cooperation Treaty (Tratado de Cooperación Amazónica) is a treaty on economic cooperation in the Amazon basin area; the largest part of which lies in Brazil. It was signed in Brasilia on July 3, 1978, by the foreign ministers of Bolivia, Brazil, Colombia, Ecuador, Guyana, Peru, Suriname, and Venezuela. The object of the treaty was "to promote the harmonious development of their respective Amazon territories in such a way that these joint actions produce equitable and mutually beneficial results and achieve also the preservation of the environment and the conservation and rational utilization of the natural resources of those territories" (Article 1). In principle the treaty applied also to territories which are closely connected to the Amazon Basin "by virtue of its geographical, ecological or economic characteristics" (Article 2). The parties mutually agreed to "maintain complete freedom of commercial navigation on the Amazon and other international Amazonian rivers" (Article 3).

The treaty was, however, primarily the work of the Brazilian Foreign Ministry, and according to the president of Brazil, José Sarney, the pact's principal aims were to emphasize that the development and preservation of the region was the exclusive responsibility of the Amazon basin countries and to protect the area from "foreign interference." Article 4 of the treaty, therefore, declares that "the exclusive use and utilization of natural resources is a right inherent in the sovereignty of each State." This includes development of hydro resources (Article 5), actions to make rivers navigable (Article 6), improvement of road and rail links (Article 10), and the exploitation of the flora and fauna of the region (Article 7). Article 9 provides for a collaborative program of scientific investigation and communication of its results.

Initially responsibility for the implementation of the treaty (Article 21) rested with the Amazon Cooperation Council (CCA), which consisted of high level diplomatic representatives and regular meetings of ministers of foreign affairs from the member states of the Amazon Pact, who have met annually since July 1981. All decisions were to require the unanimous agreement of member countries.

It was not a coincidence that the treaty was brought forward just as environmentalists were becoming increasingly concerned about the long-term risk to the planet of unrestrained logging in the Amazon, which accounts for a fifth of the Earth's capacity to recycle CO_2 into oxygen. The Sarney administration saw the domestic political advantages of making this a nationalist issue. National sovereignty was therefore safeguarded in the treaty by a number of clauses, reserving for each signatory the sovereign right of exploitation and use of its own natural resources with no restrictions other than those established by international law. It would therefore be left to the individual states to ensure that the environmental benefits were achieved, for the preservation of species of flora and fauna and the maintenance of the ecological balance, coordination of health services to fight endemic diseases, increased scientific and technical cooperation, and the establishment of adequate transport and communications facilities. The continued destruction of the Amazon rainforest since the treaty was signed suggests that if the preservation of the environmental quality of the Amazon Basin was indeed its intended objective, it has not lived up to it. Between 1998 and 2008 the loss of forest in the Brazilian Amazon alone was estimated at some 185,000 square kilometers, and the reduction in the rate of loss since then is ascribed to improved technical methods of surveillance.

To strengthen cooperation between the parties and provide an institutional basis for monitoring the treaty, an Amendment Protocol signed in Caracas on December 14, 1998, created the Amazon Cooperation Treaty Organization—ACTO (Organizacão do Tratado do Cooperacão Amazónica/Organización del Tratado Cooperación Amazónica—OTCA). Its stated objectives are to implement the objectives of the treaty, such as improving communication in the region, studying ways of linking rivers in the Amazon Basin, coordinating the construction of ports and the adjustment of river courses, and promoting the harmonious development of the Amazon basin. The Amazon Cooperation Council became the chief organ of the new organization. A secretary general—currently Manuel Ernesto Picasso Botto of Peru (2009)—is empowered to enter into agreements on behalf of the organization and a distinct Permanent Secretariat was created, based in Brasília. A strategic plan, covering the years 2004 to 2012, was adopted on September 14, 2004, at the eighth meeting of the ministers of foreign affairs at Manaus, Brazil.

See also *Environmental Protection, U.S. Influence on Latin American Policy; Inter-American Program for Environmental Protection; United Nations Conference on Environment and Development, Rio de Janeiro, 1992*

PETER CALVERT

REFERENCES AND FURTHER READING

Calvert, Peter and Melvyn Reader. "Water Resource Management in Brazil." In *Water Resource Management: A Comparative Perspective,* edited by Dhirendra Vajpeyi, 71–92. Westport, CT: Praeger, 1998.

Protocol of Amendment of the Amazon Cooperation Treaty. http://untreaty.un.org/unts/144078_158780/19/9/9659.pdf.

Treaty for Amazonian Cooperation. www.oas.org/dsd/Events/english/PastEvents/Salvador_Bahia/Documents/Amazonannexes.pdf.

American Convention on Human Rights, 1969 (Pact of San José)

In 1959 the Declaration of Santiago proclaimed that, "Harmony among the American republics can be effective only insofar as human rights and fundamental freedoms and the exercise of representative democracy are a reality within each one of them" (Fifth Meeting of Consultation of Ministers of Foreign Affairs 1959, 5). The statement accompanied the creation of an institutional and legal framework within the Organization of American States (OAS) to promote and protect human rights and democracy in the Americas, a framework which has the American Convention on Human Rights at its center.

The American Convention on Human Rights is a treaty among OAS member states, adopted and opened for signatures on November 22, 1969, at a conference held in San José, Costa Rica. The convention entered into force as a binding agreement among those states that signed and ratified it (state parties) on July 18, 1978. Most of the thirty-five OAS member states are now party to the convention, except for the United States, Canada, Belize, Guyana, and five countries of the English-speaking Caribbean. U.S. President Jimmy Carter signed the convention in 1977, but the U.S. Senate has not ratified it.

In its preamble, the American Convention on Human Rights references principles developed in the aftermath of World War II and proclaimed in the American Declaration of the Rights and Duties of Man (1948) and the Universal Declaration of Human Rights (1948). Echoing those declarations, the American Convention sets out that "freedom from fear and want" will be achievable only if all people can enjoy a full range of human rights—economic, social, and cultural, as well as civil and political—free from discrimination of any kind.

Despite the preamble's specific reference to economic, social, and cultural rights, most of the document focuses on civil and political rights. The convention sets out the rights to a fair trial, privacy, freedom of conscience and religion, freedom of thought, right of assembly, and freedom of association. The right to property is protected, as is freedom of movement and the right of all people to participate in government. State parties to the convention pledge to desist from certain behavior: no one may be tortured or subjected to cruel, inhuman, or degrading treatment or punishment. States also have the obligation to protect individuals from slavery and forced labor. Capital punishment is not prohibited but is restricted; it may be imposed only for the "most serious" crimes and with due process. Signatories agree that capital punishment may not be reinstated in states where it has been abolished and may not be imposed for individuals under 18 or over 70 or for pregnant women.

Regarding the right to life, to be protected by law "in general, from the moment of conception" (Article 4), the convention's provisions reflect Catholic influence in the document's development. The convention does not explicitly mention abortion, and in practice a state not wanting to disallow abortion can adopt the convention with a "reservation" stating its own interpretation of Article 4 (such as the reservation by the government of Mexico). The government of Canada, on the other hand, has withheld its support for the treaty because of the "moment of conception" language of Article 4.

In the area of economic, social, and cultural rights, the American Convention is vague. Only one article (26) refers to the "economic, social, educational, scientific, and cultural standards" set out in the charter of the Organization of American States (as amended by the Protocol of Buenos Aires). Further weakening protections in this area, the Convention obliges states to achieve these provisions "progressively," as resources permit. In time, though, economic, social, and cultural rights were detailed in an optional addition to the convention, known as the "Protocol of San Salvador." Adopted in 1988, it entered into force on November 16, 1999. As of early 2011, fifteen states had ratified the optional protocol, agreeing (again, as resources allow) to work to achieve realization of the rights to work, social security, a healthy environment, food and education, and the protection of families, among other measures. Another addition to the convention, the Protocol to Abolish the Death Penalty, was approved in 1990, entered into force on August 28, 1991, and has been ratified by eleven OAS member states.

Beyond its specific rights provisions, the American Convention on Human Rights furthered protections of human rights in the region by strengthening the existing Inter-American Commission on Human Rights and by creating a new institution, the Inter-American Court of Human Rights. These two bodies share responsibility for overseeing states parties' adherence to the American Convention, and together they constitute an important system for the promotion and development of regional and international human rights law.

See also *Inter-American Commission on Human Rights; Inter-American Court of Human Rights; Ninth International Conference of American States, Bogotá, 1948; Organization of American States (OAS)*

BETSY KONEFAL

REFERENCES AND FURTHER READING

Convention Ratifications. www.cidh.org/Basicos/English/Basic4.Amer.Conv.Ratif.htm.

Fifth Meeting of Consultation of Ministers of Foreign Affairs, Santiago, Chile, August 12–18, 1959.

Naddeo, Cecilia Cristina. "The Inter-American System of Human Rights: A Research Guide," Hauser Global Law School Program, New York University School of Law, August/September 2010, www.nyulawglobal.org/Globalex/Inter_American_human_rights.htm.

Text of the American Convention on Human Rights. www.cidh.org/Basicos/English/Basic3.American%20Convention.htm.

American Declaration on the Rights and Duties of Man, 1948

(**See** *Ninth International Conference of American States, Bogotá, 1948*)

American Institute for Free Labor Development (AIFLD)

The American Federation of Labor–Congress of Industrial Organizations (AFL–CIO) created the American Institute for Free Labor Development (AIFLD) in 1962 for the purpose of carrying out its foreign policies in the Americas. AIFLD received significant financial support from the U.S. government and from major multinational corporations. Its ostensible intentions were to promote workers' rights and to stem the expansion of communism in the hemisphere, but critics charged that AIFLD was controlled by the CIA and served primarily the interests of foreign investors. AIFLD ceased to exist in 1997, when it transformed to the American Center for International Labor Solidarity.

Not long after the triumph of the Cuban Revolution in 1959, the Kennedy administration initiated the Alliance for Progress in Latin America, a set of foreign policies intended to prevent further revolution and radicalism in the region by promoting economic growth and supporting militaries that could repress social uprisings. Frustrated by the often unwieldy politics of the Inter-American Regional Organization of Workers (Organización Regional Interamericana de Trabajadores, ORIT), AFL–CIO leader George Meany quickly cooperated with the Alliance for Progress initiative and charged Jay Lovestone, Irving Brown, and Serafino Romualdi to organize an institute that would serve as a direct instrument for the U.S. labor organization's foreign policy. AIFLD sought to train and support "free" trade unionists to counter leftist and communist unions, to agitate against social reforms and legislation, and to promote conditions favorable to foreign investors in Latin America. It received significant funding from the U.S. Agency for International Development (USAID), and in the 1980s, from the U.S. National Endowment for the Humanities. Major corporations, most of which had heavy investments in Latin America, also funded AIFLD. Examples included United Fruit Company, Standard Oil, Shell Oil, International Telephone & Telegraph (IT&T), Anaconda Copper, and Kennecott Copper. In fact, AIFLD's first chairman of the board was J. P. Grace, head of W. R. Grace Corporation, which was the second largest employer in Peru at the time. Meany was the first president.

AIFLD trained and affiliated with labor organizations in virtually every nation in the hemisphere and became involved in numerous destabilization efforts against governments, politicians, or unions considered a threat to U.S. government or business interests. Some examples of these destabilization campaigns from the 1960s and 1970s include Ecuador, Uruguay, Guyana, Brazil, Dominican Republic, and Chile. In the example of Guyana, AIFLD-affiliated and CIA-funded unions began in 1962 to agitate against the reform-oriented People's

Progressive Party and in support of the more conservative People's National Congress (PNC), actions that significantly contributed to the success of the PNC in controlling the first government after national independence in 1966. In Brazil, AIFLD cooperated with CIA efforts to destabilize the elected reformist government of João Goulart, ultimately facilitating the military coup that brought down the nation's democracy in 1964. AIFLD affiliates operated to divide and weaken the strongly pro-Goulart automobile workers' unions. In another example, in 1970 Chileans elected to the presidency the Socialist party's Salvador Allende, who pushed forward a number of social reforms, including nationalization of the IT&T, the massive copper operations, and other industries. Alongside U.S. government efforts to hinder the Allende administration, AIFLD quickly accelerated its Chile operations, emphasizing promotion of trade unions that opposed the government's reforms. These efforts, alongside other U.S. government strategies to hinder Allende, created some of the conditions leading to the military coup of Chile's democracy in 1973.

AIFLD played a prominent role in the cold war conflicts in Central America in the 1980s, funding pro-military-regime unions in El Salvador and Guatemala and anti-Sandinista unions in Nicaragua. Historical examples of AIFLD cooperation with CIA and other U.S. government initiatives in Latin America abound. Some critics have suggested that AIFLD only existed as a shell for CIA activities, and rich documentation supports the notion of CIA involvement in many cases of AIFLD field operations.

AIFLD was one of four regional arms of the AFL–CIO, with similar institutes developed to promote "free labor" in Africa, Asia, and Europe. In this sense, "free labor" was understood to mean a conservative, pro-business trade unionism that countered communist or reformist labor movements. Throughout much of Latin America, AIFLD was seen as a collaborator with the CIA and as an instrument of U.S. imperialism.

See also *Allende Gossens, Salvador; Central Intelligence Agency (CIA); Inter-American Federation of Labor (CIT); Inter-American Regional Organization of Workers (ORIT); International Confederation of Free Trade Unions (ICFTU)*

. . . . GREGORY S. CRIDER

REFERENCES AND FURTHER READING

Agee, Philip. *Inside the Company: CIA Diary*. New York: Stonehill, 1975.

Scott, Jack. *Yankee Unions, Go Home! How the AFL Helped the U.S. Build an Empire in Latin America*. Vancouver: New Star Books, 1978.

Sims, Beth. *Workers of the World Undermined: American Labor's Role in U.S. Foreign Policy*. Boston: South End Press, 1992.

U.S. Senate. 94th Congress, 1st session. "Select Committee to Study Governmental Operations with Respect to Intelligence Activities." Staff Report. Washington: Government Printing Office, December 18, 1975. http://foia.state.gov/Reports/ChurchReport.asp.

American Popular Revolutionary Alliance (APRA) (Peru)

The *Alianza Popular Revolucionaria Americana* (American Popular Revolutionary Alliance) was the first mass-based political movement in Latin America, and it continues to have strong influence, particularly in Peru. Víctor Raúl Haya de la Torre, a Peruvian political activist, founded APRA on May 7th, 1924, while in exile in Mexico. He urged the party to (a) lead resistance against U.S. imperialism, (b) build Latin American unity (or more accurately "Indo-American" unity), (c) nationalize private property and industry, (d) remove the Panama Canal from U.S. control and make it international, and (e) promote an alliance of oppressed peoples everywhere. Haya proposed the name Indo-America as a substitute for Latin America as a way of escaping the region's colonial and oppressed past.

Although APRA's influence is seen in Costa Rica's National Liberation Party, Bolivia's Revolutionary Nationalist Movement, and Democratic Action in Venezuela, it was most profound in Peru, where Haya founded the Peruvian Aprista party, the country's oldest and strongest political party. On September 20, 1930, Haya established it to compete in the next year's elections. It drew on the support of students and workers from other parts of Peru, but the center of its strength came from northern Peru around Trujillo, Haya's homeland, where international investors had consolidated their hold over the region's sugar industry, to the social and economic detriment of the region's urban and rural middle class and sugar workers.

Although the party won congressional seats in the 1931 election, Haya lost the presidency. When the Apristas claimed electoral fraud, the armed forces suppressed their protests, and the party responded by launching a rebellion in Trujillo on July 7, 1932. Apristas seized and executed several army officers, which earned the party the army's long-lasting hatred. Haya was arrested and the Apristas were expelled from the Congress in 1933. In 1934 the government outlawed the party, starting a decade of clandestine activity by the Apristas. They played effectively the role of political martyrs, calling for often vague radical reforms that had a populist appeal.

Although Haya spent much of the period in exile, he continued to exert a strong influence on Aprista policy and strategy. The Peruvian oligarchy feared his radical rhetoric, but Haya was not a communist, despite cooperating with the Marxist intellectual José Carlos Mariátegui in the 1920s. Haya rejected proletarian revolution but sought reforms that served the interests of the discontented middle class. By 1945 he had moderated his program sufficiently to secure legalization of the party, and Apristas participated in the government of José Luis Bustamante y Rivero (President 1945–1948). Although Haya had grown more moderate, that was not always true of the Aprista ranks, and another violent Aprista revolt in Callao in 1948 led to further military repression of the party. In 1956 Haya reached a *convivencia* agreement with the government of Manuel Pardo y Ugarteche (1956–1962), agreeing to Pardo's offer to legalize the party in return for its responsible support of his administration. The more radical Apristas were dismayed but most fell in line behind Haya, who hoped to position himself for another run at the presidency in 1962.

The Peruvian military, however, nullified the 1962 election. Haya continued to dominate the party, and his views had moderated to the point that the United States reportedly preferred an Aprista victory in 1962. In a new election the following year, the Apristas lost to Fernando Belaúnde Terry's *Acción Popular,* another Populist party, and the Apristas in Congress obstructed the ruling party's reforms. Such tactics made effective government nearly impossible and were partly responsible for the military coup of 1968.

By the time the military turned power back to the civilians in the late 1970s, Haya was old and sick but still the dominant figure in the party. Nonetheless others had begun to maneuver to replace him. Armando Villanueva was the more radical, with Andrés Townshend sharing the elderly Haya's position. It was youthful and charismatic Alan García Pérez, however, who became the first Aprista president, with his triumph in 1985. He pursued nationalist policies and fought with the IMF over Peru's debts. Meanwhile Peru was beset with runaway inflation and economic turmoil plus a bloody insurgency spearheaded by the Marxist Shining Path. Unable to deal with the mounting crisis, APRA suffered a resounding defeat in the 1990 election. The elections of 2006, however, brought the Peruvian Apristas and García back to power in a triumph over arch-nationalist Ollanta Humala. By this time Aprista policy had become even more supportive of the market economy, private property, and globalization. García sought to reform Peru by focusing on education, health care, and elimination of poverty.

Over time U.S. attitudes toward APRA changed as Apristas shifted their rhetoric regarding the United States. Early on Haya de la Torre voiced a decidedly anti-U.S. tone, calling for Latin American resistance to U.S. imperialism and the internationalization of the Panama Canal. In 1928 he criticized U.S. intervention in Nicaragua. U.S. officials refused to allow Haya de la Torre to visit the Panama Canal Zone because of his anti-U.S. speeches. APRA rhetoric shifted, however, with the election in 1932 of Franklin Delano Roosevelt, and Haya de la Torre praised both the New Deal and the Good Neighbor policy. The Roosevelt administration sought better relations with APRA. In 1942 APRA's electoral platform decried imperialism rather than "Yankee" imperialism and moderated its demands regarding the Panama Canal. By the end of World War II in 1945, APRA had announced its support for democracy rather than Marxist totalitarianism and adopted a positive stance toward capitalism and U.S. investment in Peru. The U.S. government hosted a visit by Haya de la Torre to Washington, and he was also welcomed by the capitalists of Wall Street. Left-leaning party members criticized APRA's rapprochement with the United States, and some abandoned the movement. Nonetheless the United States increasingly saw APRA as an acceptable alternative to Peruvian military dictatorship and Marxist-inspired insurgency.

See also *Haya de la Torre, Víctor Raúl; Mariátegui, José Carlos; Peru, U. S. Relations with*

KENDALL BROWN

REFERENCES AND FURTHER READING

Graham, Carol. *Peru's APRA: Parties, Politics, and the Elusive Quest for Democracy.* Boulder, CO: Lynne Rienner, 1992.

Klarén, Peter F. *Modernization, Dislocation, and Aprismo: Origins of the Peruvian Aprista Party, 1870–1932.* Austin: University of Texas Press, 1973.

Stein, Steve. *Populism in Peru: The Emergence of the Masses and the Politics of Social Control.* Madison: University of Wisconsin Press, 1980.

American Treaty on Pacific Settlement, 1948

(**See** *Ninth International Conference of American States, Bogotá, 1948*)

Americas Barometer (Latin American Public Opinion Project—LAPOP)

The Latin American Public Opinion Project (LAPOP) was initiated in the early 1970s at the University of Pittsburgh. Currently it is hosted by Vanderbilt University in Nashville, TN. In the 1970s LAPOP began with the study of democratic values in one country, Costa Rica, at a time when much of the rest of Latin America was caught in the grip of authoritarian regimes that widely prohibited studies of public opinion (and systematically violated human rights and civil liberties). As the democratization process expanded in Latin America, so did the possibilities of conducting survey research.

The Americas Barometer, one of the many research activities of LAPOP, is the only survey of democratic public opinion and behavior that covers all independent mainland countries in North, Central, and South America (it also includes several countries in the Caribbean). Functioning as a consortium of academic partner institutions in the region, the Americas Barometer has systematically surveyed the citizens of the western hemisphere on their political views and specifically on democratic values and their behaviors related to democracy. It is an effort to measure democratic values and behaviors in the Americas using scientific national probability samples of voting-age adults. In 2004 the first round of Americas Barometer surveys was implemented with eleven participating countries; the second took place in 2006 and incorporated twenty-two countries throughout the hemisphere. In 2008 twenty-four countries throughout the Americas were included, and in 2010 the survey grew to include twenty-six countries and over 42,000 respondents.

These surveys have given rise to scores of studies and publications on various aspects of democratic values and behaviors in the Americas in English and Spanish. A sample of the topics covered in the surveys include trust in institutions, political tolerance, civil society participation, evaluations of the economy, support for democracy, electoral behavior, corruption, and crime victimization. The project regularly publishes in-depth analyses of the data collected in Spanish-language monographs on several countries. LAPOP also edits and publishes the biweekly *Insights Series* reports (in English and Spanish), each one of which examines a single facet of public opinion. The results of the surveys are also regularly disseminated in public presentations in different countries of the western hemisphere. The data produced has been utilized as well by the World Bank in its governance measures and by recipient governments, donor countries, and international organizations such as the OAS to delineate public policies in Latin America.

U.S. Agency for International Development (USAID) has provided major support for the project over the years, and recently the project has also received support from the United Nations Development Program (UNDP) as well as the Inter-American Development Bank, the U.S. National Science Foundation, the Brazilian CNPq, Princeton University, the Ford Foundation, and the Swedish International Development Cooperation Agency (SIDA).

See also *Inter-American Development Bank (IDB); Organization of American States (OAS); U.S. Agency for International Development (USAID)*

. . . . DINORAH AZPURU

REFERENCES AND FURTHER READING

Booth, John A., and Mitchell A. Seligson. *The Legitimacy Puzzle in Latin America: Democracy and Political Support in Eight Nations*. Cambridge, UK: Cambridge University Press, 2009.

Mondak, Jeffery J., Matthew V. Mondak, Damarys Canache Hibbing, Mitchell A. Seligson, and Mary R. Anderson. "Personality and Civic Engagement: An Integrative Framework for the Study of Trait Effects on Political Behavior." *American Political Science Review* 104 (2010): 1–26.

Seligson, Mitchell A. "The Impact of Corruption on Regime Legitimacy: A Comparative Study of Four Latin American Countries." *Journal of Politics* 64 (2002): 408–433.

Amistad Mutiny, 1839

The Amistad Mutiny was a successful slave insurrection that occurred on the Spanish schooner *La Amistad* in 1839, while it was transporting slaves through the coastal waters off of Cuba. The revolt highlighted the lack of Spanish enforcement of the antislavery laws and exposed the illegal slave trade in the Spanish territories. The appearance of the schooner in American waters forced the matter into the American court system, which eventually ruled in favor of the mutineers.

The Spanish schooner, *La Amistad,* was illegally transporting fifty-three slaves from Havana, Cuba, to the port of Puerto Principe, Cuba. The purchase and transportation of the slaves violated the 1817 Anglo-Spanish treaty, which outlawed slavery in the Spanish empire in 1820. In addition, false papers were created to disguise the slaves as Cuban natives to escape customs officials. On July 2, 1839, the slaves revolted on board, killed the captain and the cook, but spared the lives of two Cuban planters. They forced the two men to steer the ship back to Africa. Instead, the men steered the ship north to the American coastline. In August 1839, the *Amistad* anchored off of Long Island, New York, to obtain food, where a U.S. revenue cutter discovered the ship.

The revenue cutter captain presented the *La Amistad* and her slaves in Connecticut to collect monies for the salvage of the ship. In Connecticut, the two Cuban planters, Pedro Montez and José Ruiz, appealed to the U.S. government to return the ship and the slaves back to Cuba in accordance with Pinckney's Treaty of 1795. Northern abolitionists took up the cause of the *Amistad* mutineers by arguing that Africans were slaves illegally and that the slaves were free to return to Africa. U.S. President Martin Van Buren attempted to intervene to appease the Spanish government and the Southern slave owners.

When the U.S. District Court ruled in favor of the *Amistad* slaves, the U.S. attorney appealed the decision to the U.S. Circuit Court, which in April 1840 affirmed the decision of the lower court pro forma, thus moving the case to the U.S. Supreme Court. On February 22, 1841, the Supreme Court began to hear arguments concerning the case. John Quincy Adams, former U.S. president and U.S. representative, led the legal team advocating on behalf of the *Amistad* slaves. The U.S. government argued that the slaves were Spanish property and the legality of slavery was not on trial. Adams advocated to the Supreme Court that *Amistad* slaves were not property and would not be governed by the 1795 Pinckney's Treaty concerning the return of property to the Spanish government. In addition, he said that the intervention of President Van Buren was an unconstitutional abuse of executive power. On March 9, 1841, the Supreme Court ruled that the *Amistad* slaves should be freed and that the Pinckney's Treaty of 1795 had no bearing on the case.

After their legal victory, the freed slaves remained in Connecticut for additional education, while their abolitionist supporters raised monies for their transportation back to Mendeland, Africa. In 1842, the thirty-six remaining *Amistad* slaves were returned to Africa.

Despite public support for the freed slaves during their trials and eventual release, the United States continued to support Spanish claims for compensation for the *Amistad* and the financial loss of property by the Spanish citizens until 1860. The illegal importation of Africans as slaves into the Americas continued to be supported by slavery proponents in the United States and Spanish authorities in Cuba. This tacit support forced Great Britain to increase its efforts to curb the trafficking of humans from Africa to the Americas. The Royal Navy increased its patrols to stymie this trade across the Atlantic Ocean. In doing so, this British naval effort brought Great Britain in conflict with U.S. citizens immigrating to Latin America as filibusters looking to establish additional slave territories in the hemisphere. This conflict would eventually play a role in the defeat of filibuster groups in Latin America.

See also *Adams, John Quincy; Cuba, U.S. Relations with; Pinckney's Treaty, 1795*

. . . . WILLIAM H. BROWN

REFERENCES AND FURTHER READING

Cable, Mary. *Black Odyssey: The Case of the Slave Ship Amistad*. New York: Penguin Books, 1979.

Jones, Howard. *Mutiny on the Amistad: The Saga of a Slave Revolt and Its Impact on American Abolition, Law, and Diplomacy*. New York: Oxford University Press, 1988.

Kromer, Helen. *Amistad: The Slave Uprising aboard the Spanish Schooner*. Cleveland, OH: Pilgrim Press, 1997.

Ancón Treaty, 1883

(**See** *War of the Pacific, 1879–1883*)

Andean Pact, 1969

(**See** *Cartagena, Agreement of, 1969*)

Anglo-American Caribbean Commission

The Anglo-American Caribbean Commission (AACC), established in 1942, was created to promote agricultural and other research in the Caribbean. The AACC was further promoted as a means of enhancing social and economic cooperation between the United States and Great Britain (and their possessions) in the Caribbean and avoiding duplication of research in the area. While the United States saw the AACC as a vehicle for promoting its postwar vision in the Caribbean, Great Britain saw it as the cost of American assistance in World War II.

The United States and Great Britain set up the AACC understanding the serious social and economic problems of the Caribbean. Unemployment in the British West Indies (BWI) was high, exploitation of resources was minimal, and transportation was problematic. The two countries saw the AACC as a means to relieve the poverty of the Caribbean islands, particularly in light of the shortages brought on by World War II. However, they mandated an advisory role for the AACC to obviate U.S. interference in the domestic political affairs of the BWI colonies. Great Britain was particularly concerned about the U.S. postwar vision of the BWI, which involved free trade and political independence. Britain was not yet ready to entertain independence for the BWI and did not want to lose its position as the focal point of international trade by abandoning its imperial tariff system.

The United States had received leases for military bases in the BWI as a condition for entering into the agreement. While necessary to gain U.S. cooperation and aid, the British feared that the bases were just the beginning of an expanded U.S. role in the BWI. The AACC's first meeting confirmed the fears of the British contingent when the United States deviated from the advisory role of the commission to directly address the food shortages in the BWI. The United States saw the AACC as an institution capable of providing administrative assistance to the BWI, while Great Britain resisted American attempts to involve itself in the politics of the BWI. The United States had a much more forceful presence on the commission than did the British. In fact, the United States placed much greater emphasis on the AACC than did Great Britain.

The AACC consisted of six members: three from the Great Britain and three from the United States. One member each from the United States and the United Kingdom would serve as cochairs.

The AACC changed its name to the Caribbean Commission in October 1946 after it expanded its membership to include the French and Dutch West Indies. Despite the expanded membership, the Caribbean Commission became increasingly insignificant as postwar interests shifted away from the Caribbean. As calls for independence for the colonies increased, an organization dominated by former colonial powers and the United States seemed outdated. The Caribbean Commission was finally transformed into the Caribbean Organization in 1961 with sole Caribbean membership ending formal outside involvement in the organization.

See also *Coordinator of Inter-American Affairs, Office of, World War II; Destroyers for Bases Agreement, 1941; World War II, 1939–1945*

. . . . SCOTT DITTLOFF

REFERENCES AND FURTHER READING

Bunche, Ralph J. "The Anglo-American Caribbean Commission: An Experiment in Regional Cooperation." Paper presented at the ninth conference of the Institute of Pacific Relations, Hot Springs, VA, January 1945.

Whitham, Charlie. *Bitter Rehearsal: British and American Planning for a Post-War West Indies*. Westport, CT: Praeger, 2002.

Antarctica, Argentine, and Chilean Claims to

Argentine and Chilean claims to portions of Antarctica are deeply rooted in geopolitics, history, environmental and economic concerns, and the self-perception of these two nations as being "the southernmost countries in the world." Their claims to Antarctica are competitive, in that they overlap to a considerable degree on the key Antarctic Peninsula, and if significant resources are found in this area (possibly oil and natural gas), a serious confrontation could develop. Despite these factors, Argentina and Chile have also cooperated on Antarctica, especially when an "outside" third party establishes a competing claim (as the United Kingdom does) or even a presence, such as a scientific base or cruise ships.

In the northern hemisphere (with the exception of the UK) Antarctica is seen as a remote and relatively unimportant place due to logistical factors. For a northern hemisphere nation, sustaining human life in Antarctica can be likened to what is required in space. In South America, especially in Argentina and Chile, Antarctica is rather seen as relatively near (600 miles across the Drake Passage) and as a natural geographic and geopolitical extension of the South American homeland. Indeed, there is mention of a "South American Quadrant" where Antarctica comes closest to any other continent, from 0 degrees to 90 degrees west, which contains the peninsula. This perception of proximity helps explain the Antarctic interests of other South American nations such as Brazil, Uruguay, Peru, and Ecuador, all of which have set up temporary summer or permanent year-round bases there. The British case involves the possession of key islands (Falklands, South Georgia, South Sandwich), and its Antarctic claim overlaps to a considerable degree with Argentinian and Chilean claims.

Argentine Antarctic interest and claims are based on a number of factors, including the following:

- Inheritance from Spain under the doctrine of *uti possidetis* (as you possess)
- Early exploration and even discovery (supposedly by sealers)
- Geographic proximity (propinquity)

- Geologic continuity
- Rescue operations (mainly of European expeditions)
- Permanent occupation and presence (since 1904, the longest of any nation)
- Administrative, scientific, and technical activities

The Argentine claim is a wedge-shaped piece of Antarctica between the 25th and 74th degree west meridians and from the 60th degree parallel to the South Pole. Argentinians perceive their nation geographically as a "tri-partite or tri-continental Argentina" located on the South American mainland, Antarctica, and the chain of islands in between (Malvinas, South Georgia, South Sandwich). It is a stretch to call these islands a "continent," but the idea is deeply rooted that these islands are Argentine by right and were stolen from them by a European power (the UK, with tacit approval of the United States). There is strong emotional support for efforts to recover the islands, although the military option proved disastrous in 1982. Schools, the media, and postage stamps all contribute to the creation of a "national Antarctic conscience."

The Chilean Antarctic claim overlaps the Argentine and consists of a wedge-shaped sector limited by the 53rd and 90 degree west meridians and the South Pole. There is no stated northern limit to the claim, and the clear implication is that Chile, like Argentina, is in three parts: mainland, Antarctica, and a series of islands (most notably Cape Horn, Robinson Crusoe, and Easter Island). Chile's claim is based on the same seven factors as the Argentine, although the Argentine claim of 1904 is accepted. Chile has also rescued many European expeditions, including Ernest Shackleton's.

Cooperative aspects of Argentine-Chilean Antarctic interests are few in number. They include the 1947 Inter-American Treaty of Reciprocal Assistance (Rio Treaty), whose Southern limit was set at the South Pole due to Argentina-Chilean insistence, overcoming U.S. objections. A year later Chile and Argentina signed a bilateral treaty which recognized each others' Antarctic interests, although the contentious issue of defining the boundary line between Argentine and Chilean Antarctica was left for later, and in fact, has not yet happened. The boundary approach used to separate the mainlands (by following the highest points of the Andes) is not likely to be acceptable to Argentina since it awards Chile most of the highly valued Antarctic Peninsula. Resource issues may turn out to be an area of cooperation, although conflict over them is more likely. There is competition for the financial benefits of the quite profitable Antarctic tourism that starts out from either Ushuaia (Argentina) or Punta Arenas (Chile). The greatest possibility of competition or cooperation would be the discovery of oil in the Antarctic Peninsula in the area where Argentine, Chilean, and British claims overlap. On the other hand, since oil companies are not likely to invest heavily in a region where conflict is present or expected, it is possible a discovery would lead to collaboration between these three nations, the effective rejection of military activities contained in the Antarctic Treaty, and provision of technical expertise in cold-weather oil extraction by the United States and Canada.

See also *Antarctic Treaty; Antarctica, Argentine and Chilean Claims to; Inter-American Conference for the Maintenance of Continental Peace and Security, Rio de Janeiro, 1947 Inter-American Treaty of Reciprocal Assistance, 1982; Malvinas/Falkland Islands Controversy and War (Argentina/United Kingdom)*

. . . . JACK CHILD

REFERENCES AND FURTHER READING

Child, Jack. *Antarctica and South American Geopolitics: Frozen Lebensraum.* New York: Praeger, 1988.

Dodds, Klaus. *Pink Ice: Britain and the South Atlantic Empire.* London: I. B. Tauris, 2002.

Dodds, Klaus. *Geopolitics in Antarctica: Views from the Southern Oceanic Rim.* New York: Wiley, 1997.

Moneta, Carlos J., ed. *La Antártida en el Sistema Internacional del Futuro.* Buenos Aires: Grupo Editor Latinoamericano, 1988.

Morris, Michael A. *Great Power Relations in Argentina, Chile and Antarctica.* New York: St Martin's Press, 1990.

Antarctic Treaty, 1959

The Antarctic Treaty (drafted in 1959; in force June 23, 1961) is the principal international document governing human activities on this last place on earth without a government or agreed-upon sovereignty. Antarctica is unique among the continents since it has never had an indigenous population or agreed-upon sovereignty. Seven countries claim sovereignty over parts of Antarctica, but there is no international consensus on the validity of these claims.

The treaty has evolved from scientific cooperation during the International Geophysical Year (IGY) of 1957–1958. At that time, at the height of the cold war, there had been concerns over sovereignty and human activities on the continent, and the scientists of countries with an interest in Antarctica agreed to cooperate in the study of the continent. Twelve countries were active in Antarctica during the IGY, and these twelve became the original signatories of the treaty: Argentina, Australia, Belgium, Chile, France, Japan, New Zealand, Norway, South Africa, the Soviet Union, the United Kingdom, and the United States.

The treaty is open for signature by any member of the United Nations, but here are two distinctly different types of membership:

- Full, or "consultative," which is obtained by significant scientific activity and usually a base on the continent. These nations now number twenty-eight, and they have full voting rights.
- Non-Consultative (eighteen nations), which is obtained by simply signing the treaty. These eighteen nations can participate in meetings, but they do not vote on decision-making issues.

The principal provisions of the treaty are that Antarctica should be preserved for peaceful purposes (military personnel and equipment can be present, but there can be no engagement in military activity); there is freedom of scientific cooperation, with findings to be shared by all members of the treaty. The sticky issue of prior claims of sovereignty by seven nations

(Argentina, Australia, Chile, France, New Zealand, Norway, and the United Kingdom) was finessed by Article 4, which does not recognize any of the claims but also does not reject them; no new claims or extension of existing ones may be made for the duration of the treaty.

Over the years the consultative meetings have brought forth a number of recommendations and agreed measures on conservation, environmental issues, and mineral exploitation (prohibited by a 50-year protocol signed in 1991). This body of agreements, along with the periodic meetings, have led to what could be called an "Antarctic Treaty System," with a permanent secretariat in Buenos Aires, Argentina.

The two Latin American nations with the greatest interest and strongest presence in Antarctica are Argentina and Chile, both original consultative countries with claims in the area. Brazil also operates a permanent base, and a number of other Latin American nations have participated in Antarctic activities by establishing scientific bases and significant scientific activities: Ecuador, Uruguay, and Peru. Colombia, Cuba, Guatemala, and Venezuela have also signed the treaty. The United States has a significant presence, with three permanent stations and a comprehensive scientific program.

Besides protecting Antarctica from damaging economic, tourist, or military activities, the treaty stands as the first arms control agreement of the cold war and as a unique example of a political regime originally created by scientists of various nations who cooperated in the study of the area in the IGY.

See also *Antarctica, Argentine and Chilean claims to; Argentina, U.S. Relations with; Chile, U.S. Relations with; Beagle Channel Dispute (Argentina/Chile); Malvinas/Falkland Islands Controversy and War (Argentina/United Kingdom)*

JACK CHILD

REFERENCES AND FURTHER READING

Child, Jack. *Antarctica and South American Geopolitics: Frozen Lebensraum.* New York: Praeger, 1988.

Dodds, Klaus. *Geopolitics in Antarctica: Views from the Southern Oceanic Rim.* New York: Wiley, 1997.

Morris, Michael A. *Great Power Relations in Argentina, Chile and Antarctica.* New York: St. Martin's Press, 1990.

Anti-Americanism in Latin America

The phenomenon of anti-U.S. sentiment in Latin America is old and complex, but its scholarly treatment is still undeveloped. Only since the attacks of September 11, 2001, and the invasion of Iraq in 2003 has a rich scholarship responded to the rising tide of anti-Americanism in the western hemisphere and around the globe. From this work certain distinguishing features of *anti-yanquismo* in Latin America have emerged: its long pedigree, often foreshadowing hatred of the United States in other regions; U.S. economic and military domination as a cause; and its reflection of internal dynamics such as the rise of nationalism and class and ethnic tensions.

DEFINITIONS AND SCHOLARSHIP

As in other areas of the world, definitions of anti-Americanism in Latin America vary widely. The oldest definition has come from conservative observers, who have seen anti-Yankee sentiment as a rejection of the culture of the United States: its democracy and freedom, its materialism, its mechanized modernity, and its "loose" cultural norms. Such essentialism defines anti-Americanism as antipathy to what the United States *is*. In contrast, a second definition traces anti-Americanism as a reaction to what the United States *does*. This second group is largely made up of progressive observers who point to evidence of Washington's imperial and hegemonic behavior. Many in this second group prefer the term "anti-imperialism" rather than "anti-Americanism."

More recent approaches have become less politicized and more subtle. Some looked at Latin Americans' criticism of themselves as too eager to embrace U.S. norms and not sufficiently nationalistic. Others, less interested in a priori definitions of anti-Americanism, gravitated toward its processes: which social groups have produced it, who has controlled anti-U.S. policies, and what responses those policies have provoked in Washington. Others still emphasized the variability of anti-Americanism by country, region, and social group. New research has aimed at the popular and political articulations of anti-Americanism rather than reproducing the major speeches and works of literature by elite Latin Americans or revolutionaries.

The only point of agreement has been that "anti-Americans" express a consistently negative assessment of some aspect of the United States. At the same time, all have accepted that almost no Latin American individuals or groups have been comprehensive in their anti-Americanism. In fact, a defining feature of *anti-yanquismo* has been its ambivalence. For instance, even an enemy of Washington such as Cuba's Fidel Castro long admitted that he admired U.S. culture. Being of two minds is largely a sincere sentiment; for Castro it was also a rhetorical strategy for dividing the U.S. people from their government's policies.

The history of anti-Americanism in Latin America indicates that all scholars have a wealth of evidence from which to make their arguments. Anti-U.S. sentiment existed since the early nineteenth century and did not abate with the end of the cold war; instead, it peaked in the 2000s.

HISTORY OF ANTI-AMERICANISM IN LATIN AMERICA

The first generation of Latin Americans who expressed consistent suspicion of the United States were the leaders of movements of independence from Spain. Simón Bolívar and others had little to say about the culture of the United States other than to admire the liberal political institutions of the former British colonies, but Bolívar soon distrusted the Founding Fathers' hypocrisy: they had kind words of support for Latin American republican revolutions but not corresponding actions. In 1806 Venezuela's Francisco de Miranda, who participated in the American Revolution, organized raids against the Spanish, but U.S. Secretary of State James Madison failed to support them. John Adams also viewed

Latin Americans as priest-ridden, ungovernable, and corrupt Catholics. The Creole elite, of which Bolívar was a prominent member, believed as Bolívar did, that U.S. help would only come if self-interested. It was at this time that Mexicans began referring to U.S. citizens with the negative *gringos*. In 1825 Bolívar sought a military alliance with London rather than Washington, and the next year he kept U.S. diplomats away from an Inter-American conference. It is no surprise that Bolívar became the inspiration for Venezuela's Hugo Chávez.

Anti-Americanism became more widespread and visceral in the mid- to late-nineteenth century when more Latin Americans were exposed to the land hunger of U.S. investors and fire-breathing expansionists. In the 1840s white settlers in Texas demanded its separation from Mexico, and a war led by James Polk soon tore off Mexico's northern half. The 1850s was the age of Caribbean and Central American filibusters, the most serious of which was William Walker's takeover of Nicaragua from 1855 to 1857. In response, Latin Americans emphasized not the neglect of U.S. citizens but their unwanted attention: they called them eagles, snakes, and the like. They also feared U.S. social systems, which threatened either to impose slavery on free labor systems or else to encourage white male democracy in hierarchical societies. This period also saw the birth of anti-Americanism "from below" as small farmers and cattle ranchers opposed U.S. soldiers and plantation owners in Mexico and elsewhere. Latin American anti-Americanism was more widespread than ever when one Brazilian in 1893 claimed that "there is no Latin American nation that has not suffered in its relations with the United States" (Rubin and Rubin, 105).

Many suffered further from the War of 1898 to the end of U.S. military occupations in 1934. The U.S. government not only ejected Spain from the continent but installed a new hegemony in Central America and the Caribbean through massive land purchases and lowered tariffs, takeovers of customs receipts and new loans through Wall Street, and dozens of landings of U.S. Marines to control local politics and prop up puppet leaders, including long-term occupations of Haiti, the Dominican Republic, Nicaragua, and Cuba. In this period Latin Americans developed a more systematic and holistic anti-Americanism that no longer feared being absorbed into the continental United States but rather fought against being part of an informal empire.

Early century anti-Americanism blended cultural and policy grievances to both explain U.S. behavior and produce alternative identities for Latin Americans. In 1900 Uruguayan author José Enrique Rodó published *Ariel,* an essay that brought together educated elites around the notion that Latin America had a "spiritual," refined civilization that was superior to the materialistic, individualistic United States. "Arielism" influenced several writers such as Nicaragua's Rubén Darío and Argentina's Manuel Ugarte, who in 1923 published *The Destiny of a Continent*. Ugarte claimed not to be a "Yankee hater," preferring to criticize specific cultural traits and to warn against further U.S. expansion. In 1925 Mexico's José Vasconcelos made his own argument for Latin American superiority in *The Cosmic Race,* which argued that Latin Americans should take pride in racially mixed societies that contrasted with the racial divisions of U.S. civilization. Arielism, indigenism, and pan-Hispanism—a rapprochement with Spanish culture—spawned schools of thought, literary magazines, and political organizations, for example the American Popular Revolutionary Alliance (APRA) founded in Peru in 1924.

At the popular level, anti-Americanism was more pragmatic and violent—a rejection of U.S. military personnel. Everywhere the Marines landed, they met two kinds of opposition. One was urban and peaceful, operating through politicians, journalists, and diplomats who tried to end occupations through activism and rhetoric. The other was rural and violent, often led by local strongmen or young idealists who grew more nationalistic as occupations wore on. The best known are Charlemagne Péralte, who led Haiti's "Cacos" in 1918 and 1919 against the U.S. imposition of forced labor, and Augusto Sandino, who fought a six-year guerrilla war in Nicaragua that secured the departure of U.S. forces in 1933. Sandino was by far the most persistent and internationally supported. He also articulated almost every anti-U.S. idea of the time: anti-imperialism, nationalism, indigenism, Arielism, and Marxism. He even departed from the usual ambivalence to blame all U.S. citizens for electing imperialist presidents.

The period from 1933 to the late 1950s was relatively free of anti-Americanism because the U.S. government had a policy of no direct military intervention. Moreover, most of the Americas collaborated successfully during World War II. Certainly, some grievances over the war existed, and some feared as U.S. ploys the creation of a pan-American military alliance in 1947 and a corresponding diplomatic body, the Organization of American States in 1948. Argentina was most hostile to the United States: it remained close to the Axis during the war, and its leader Juan Perón decried "Yankee imperialism" in his 1946 electoral campaign.

Perhaps the most important source of anti-Americanism at midcentury was the rise of Marxism-Leninism. Peru's José Carlos Mariátegui founded the region's first Socialist party in the 1920s, and after World War II eminent Latin Americans such as Chile's Pablo Neruda turned to socialism to understand U.S.-Latin American relations. Communism and its myriad forms—and feuding political parties—offered clear anti-American explanations and prescriptions: it blamed Latin America's poverty on the rapaciousness of capitalism and argued for state-directed economies; it encouraged cross-border cooperation by workers and others; and it minimized racial and gender divisions in favor of class consciousness. Many even applied Marxist analysis to culture, imagining U.S. "cultural imperialism" to be a systematic assault against the values of Latin Americans through corporate media.

In 1958 physical attacks on Vice President Richard Nixon in South America punctuated the transition from good neighborliness to cold war anti-Americanism. Direct and sometimes successful assaults on U.S. power marked this fifth period of anti-Americanism. Reeling from the 1954 overthrow of reformist Jacobo Arbenz in Guatemala and U.S. support for dictators, revolutionary groups in the late 1950s and early 1960s proliferated. The Cuban Revolution inspired most of them.

Its improbable military victories, its anti-dictatorial rhetoric, and its rapid sweep of U.S. property and Cuban collaborators impressed many from Mexico to Brazil.

Revolutions took various forms. In Chile, elections secured the rise of Marxist Salvador Allende in 1970, who immediately moved against U.S. copper interests. In Nicaragua the Sandinista guerrillas overthrew a U.S.-supported dictator in 1979. In Bolivia in 1952 and Peru in 1968, movements nationalized U.S. properties, and in countless other countries state-directed import substitution industrialization aimed to undo the damage associated with "dependency." The backlash from Washington against Chile, Nicaragua, Cuba, and unsuccessful revolutions in Brazil (1964), the Dominican Republic (1965), and Grenada (1983) created still more anti-Americanism in the continent. Covert and overt interventions recalled the days of "gunboat diplomacy" from the early twentieth century.

ANTI-AMERICANISM TODAY

After the cold war, anti-Americanism subsided in the 1990s but then increased dramatically as Latin Americans sharply disagreed with the Bush administration's "war on terror." Polls indicated that majorities believed that the 9/11 attacks were a retribution for U.S. policies, with many feeling that it was "good for [the] U.S. to feel vulnerable." In January 2005 the Pew Global Attitudes project concluded that "anti-Americanism is deeper and broader now than at any time in modern history" (Pew Research Center 106, 109).

Some of this antipathy was owed to U.S. policies in the Middle East, but others opposed U.S. support for an anti-narcotics war in Colombia, encouragement of a coup against Hugo Chávez in 2002, and overall pressure on Latin America to open its trade without reciprocation by Washington. These "populist" and "anti-neoliberal" grievances emerged from two dominant tendencies of the political left. One was an openly anti-imperialist, mass-based, state-directed anti-Americanism armed with stinging rhetoric, mostly from leaders such as Chávez, Evo Morales of Bolivia, Daniel Ortega of Nicaragua, and Rafael Correa of Ecuador. The most anti-U.S. was clearly Chávez, who battled U.S. corporations, threatened to cut off oil to the United States, befriended Castro, and called Bush "the devil" at the United Nations in 2006.

The other tendency was a less confrontational, less authoritarian, free market, social democratic left embodied by Luiz Inácio Lula da Silva in Brazil, Christina Fernández de Kirchner in Argentina, and Michelle Bachelet of Chile. They mostly collaborated with U.S. policies and kept their rhetoric respectful but often defied Washington on trade and terrorism.

To be sure, anti-Americanism has not swept the entire continent. There are still key states where leaders are strongly pro-United States, such as in Colombia, or where anti-U.S. contenders lost elections, such as in Mexico. In 2005 the United States ratified a trade treaty with the Dominican Republic and Central America, confirming polls that show that anti-U.S. sentiment there is much weaker, perhaps due to the strong economic and migratory ties to the United States.

See also *Allende Gossens, Salvador; American Popular Revolutionary Alliance (APRA) (Peru); Bolívar, Simón; Brazil, Coup d'État, 1964; Bush, George W.; Castro Ruz, Fidel; Central America, Filibusters; Chávez Frías, Hugo; Cultural Imperialism; Darío, Rubén; Dominican Republic, U.S. Intervention, 1965–1966; Good Neighbor Policy; Grenada, U.S. Invasion of, 1983; Haya de la Torre, Víctor Raúl; Hispanidad; Import Substitution Industrialization (ISI); Lula da Silva, Luíz Inácio; Mariátegui, José Carlos; Morales Ayma, Juan Evo; Neruda, Pablo; Panama Riots, 1964; Rodó Piñeyro, José Enrique; Sandino, Augusto César*

. . . . ALAN MCPHERSON

REFERENCES AND FURTHER READING

Grandin, Greg. "Your Americanism and Mine: Americanism and Anti-Americanism in the Americas." *American Historical Review* 111, no. 4 (October 2006): 1042–1066.

McPherson, Alan. *Yankee No! Anti-Americanism in U.S.-Latin American Relations*. Cambridge, MA: Harvard University Press, 2003.

McPherson, Alan, ed. *Anti-Americanism in Latin America and the Caribbean*. New York: Berghahn Books, 2006.

Pew Research Center, "Global Opinion: The Spread of Anti-Americanism," January 24, 2005, http://people-press.org/2005/01/24/global-opinion-the-spread-of-anti-americanism/.

Rama, Carlos M. La imagen de los Estados Unidos en la América Latina: de Simón Bolívar a Allende. Mexico City: Secretaría de Educación Pública, 1975.

Reid, John. *Spanish American Images of the United States, 1790–1960*. Gainesville: University Press of Florida, 1977.

Rubin, Barry, and Judith Colp Rubin, eds. "Yankee Go Home!" In *Hating America*, 101–124. New York: Oxford University Press, 2004.

Anti-War Treaty of Non-Aggression and Conciliation, 1933

(**See** *Seventh International Conference of American States, Montevideo, 1933*)

Aranha, Oswaldo

Oswaldo Euclides de Souza Aranha (1894–1960), a politician and diplomat who served as Brazilian ambassador to the United States from 1934 to 1937, is a significant figure in U.S.-Brazilian relations for his ability to make Brazil an ally of the United States during World War II. Aranha appeared on the cover of the January 19, 1942, issue of *Time* magazine, accompanied by an article dedicated to the hemispheric initiatives to foster collective security against the Axis powers. The article described Aranha as a realist who saw that a close relationship with the United States was in the best interests of Brazil. Yet he is probably best known for his diplomatic activities at the first special session of the United Nations General Assembly held in 1947: first, as head of the Brazilian delegation, Aranha began a still-standing tradition that the first speaker at the opening of the UN General Assembly is always a Brazilian; second, at that same international forum he made a strong defense for the partition of Palestine to create the State of Israel, an initiative publicly recognized in 2007 when a street in Tel Aviv was named in his honor.

Aranha was a high-profile Brazilian politician during the first half of the twentieth century, with a long string of high-level government positions. A graduate from the Rio de Janeiro Military Academy (*Colégio Militar*), Aranha also obtained a law degree from the Rio de Janeiro Law School (*Faculdade de Direito*) and studied international law in France. Until 1923 he practiced law in the state of Rio Grande do Sul, where he was born; in 1925 he started his political career as mayor of his native town, Alegrete, and later he was elected to both the state and federal legislatures.

REVOLUTION

Aranha's ascension to national politics occurred in 1930 during the revolution led by Getúlio Vargas during the height of the Great Depression. From 1889, when a republican movement overthrew the Brazilian monarchy, and until 1930, the so-called "Old Republic" had been characterized by the dominance of the "coffee and milk politics" (*a política do café com leite*). In this period politicians of São Paulo and Minas Gerais alternated in occupying the country's presidency, an arrangement reflecting the political and economic power of the agricultural oligarchies (coffee in São Paulo; cattle in Minas Gerais). The world economic depression and the incipient yet increasingly restive urban workers' movement weakened the coffee barons and shook the alliance between the São Paulo and Minas Gerais states.

At the beginning of 1929 President Washington Luís, who was born in São Paulo, supported another politician of the same state, Júlio Prestes, to succeed him. Immediately, politicians from other states responded with the creation of a new political party, the Liberal Alliance (*Aliança Liberal*), which backed the presidential candidacy of Getúlio Vargas, born in Rio Grande do Sul. Prestes won the popular vote on March 1, 1930, a result that the Liberal Alliance rejected under the allegation of electoral fraud. In a climate of popular discontent due to the economic crisis and lack of political consensus, and with the approaching November 15 inauguration of Prestes, Vargas launched the revolution on October 3, and he took the presidency with "ample powers" (*amplos poderes*), conferred by a military junta, on November 3, 1930. Vargas inaugurated a new era of national politics, based on populism, corporativism, centralization of power, and harassment of opponents; his policies supporting industrialization set the basis of the modern Brazilian economy. Oswaldo Aranha, who for a brief time was occupying the post of governor of Rio Grande do Sul, allied himself to Vargas.

DIPLOMATIC MISSIONS

For his staunch support for Vargas and his revolution, Aranha was nominated minister of justice and later headed the Finance Ministry. After returning from his ambassadorial position in Washington, Aranha was designated minister of foreign affairs. It was in that capacity that Aranha, during the second World War, organized in Rio de Janeiro the third conference of American Foreign Ministers. The event brought to Brazil's capital at that time top diplomats of twenty-one nations of the Americas, including the U.S. undersecretary of state Sumner Wells and his forty-five-man delegation. The objective of the Franklin Delano Roosevelt administration in the 1942 Rio conference was to consolidate the work initiated in the previous summits—Panama in October 1939 and Havana in July 1940—toward Pan-American solidarity and hemispheric security, and now additionally, to secure the support of Latin American governments for the U.S. war effort against Germany and Japan. The Vargas administration, which at first had sympathized with Nazi Germany, shifted its position after the conference. Aranha was a supporter of the Pan-Americanism movement, which seeks to establish close relationships in the Americas for the protection of common interests. Following Aranha's recommendations, the Brazilian government in August 1942 declared war on Germany and Japan. In 1944 a Brazilian expeditionary force of 25,000 troops went to Europe and joined the allies in the Italian campaign.

With the end of the first Vargas administration in 1946, Aranha remained in government and was nominated by President Eurico Gaspar Dutra to head the Brazilian mission at the UN Multilingual. As one of the greatest supporters of the United Nations since its inception, Brazil also gave full support to the 1948 UN Universal Declaration of Human Rights, which was developed in great measure in response to the Holocaust. In the context of the indignation and repulsion produced by the World War II genocide, Brazil supported the creation of a Jewish state in Palestine. An eloquent public speaker, Aranha fought and lobbied for the creation of Israel. In 1953, during the second Vargas administration, he held ministerial positions in finance and agriculture. At the Itamaraty, as the Ministry of Foreign Relations of Brazil is known, Aranha is recognized as one of the architects of the Brazil-U.S. commercial relations. In the name of Brazilian interests, Aranha negotiated important U.S. loans to finance Brazil's plans of industrialization and national development.

See also *Brazil, U.S. Relations with; Vargas, Getúlio Dornelles; World War II, 1939–1945*

. . . . IVANI VASSOLER

REFERENCES AND FURTHER READING

"The Americas: United We Stand." *Time*, January 19, 1942, www.time.com/time/magazine/article/0,9171,766308,00.html.

The Avalon Project, "Havana Meeting of Ministers of Foreign Affairs of the American Republics," www.yale.edu/lawweb/avalon/decade/decad058.htm.

Copeland, Lewis, Lawrence Lamm, and Stephen J. McKenna, eds. *The World's Great Speeches*. Mineola, NY: Dover Publications, 1999.

Arbenz Guzmán, Jacobo

The government of Guatemalan Jacobo Arbenz (President 1951–1954) became the first government in Latin America to be a casualty of the cold war between the United States and the Soviet Union, regardless of whether that government was influenced by communism.

Jacobo Arbenz Guzmán (1913–1971), the offspring of a Swiss father and a Guatemalan mother, was born in Quetzaltenango, Guatemala, on September 14, 1913, and in 1932, he entered the Guatemalan Army Academy. As a captain, he formed part of a civilian-military junta which deposed Guatemalan dictator Jorge Ubico's puppet successor, Federico Ponce Valdés, in October 1944. Promoted to colonel, Arbenz served as defense minister during Juan José Arévalo's presidency (1945–1950), and he became a presidential candidate in the 1950 election. Backed by three leading political parties, as well as by organized labor, Arbenz won over 62 percent of the vote. The United States welcomed the change, for it regarded Arbenz as more moderate than his predecessor.

Although he admitted that he was not a Communist, the United States began to worry about Communist influence in his government after he took office in 1951. His wife, the Salvadoran-born María Vilanova, though heir to a family fortune, was a Marxist sympathizer. There was no denial that Communists began to occupy key posts in his administration. With the government's consent, Communist propaganda began to target American-owned enterprises and urged the nationalization of the United Fruit Company (UFCO), the International Railways of Central America, and the Empresa Eléctrica.

Relations between Washington and the Arbenz government deteriorated with the passage of the Agrarian Reform Law of 1952, whose purpose was to distribute idle privately owned lands to landless peasants. Owners were to be paid based on their own assessment of the land's tax value, and they were to be compensated over a thirty-year period. While the law applied to both foreign and national landowners, it was clear that it was principally aimed at UFCO. By 1953, over 400,000 UFCO-owned acres had been expropriated. UFCO claimed that it was owed more than $15 million in compensation, but the government was only willing to compensate $595,000 since UFCO had purposely undervalued its holdings in its tax declaration. UFCO was not the only entity whose land was expropriated, for another 800,000 acres were expropriated from Guatemalan nationals and some 55,000 landless peasants benefitted from Arbenz's agrarian reform program. As a result of the expropriations Arbenz's government incurred UFCO and the landowners' wrath.

Since the Agrarian Reform Law would not allow owners to appeal their land expropriation in Guatemalan courts, UFCO called on the Eisenhower administration for help. At the same time of UFCO's appeal, the Arbenz administration nationalized the International Railways of Central America and the Empresa Eléctrica.

Eisenhower's secretary of state, John Foster Dulles, whose family had close ties to UFCO, began to convince the administration that a response was needed in Guatemala. Dulles not only cited the expropriation of American-owned companies, but he pointed to Communist infiltration in Arbenz's government. Guatemalan foreign policy seemed to help Dulles's contention that it had fallen under the Soviet orbit, for at international forums Guatemala would side with Soviet proposals as well as condemnation of the United States.

At first, the United States attempted to convince the other Latin American nations that Guatemala's communist leanings represented a threat to them. At the meeting of the Organization of American States (OAS) held in Caracas in March, 1954, the U.S. delegation, hoping for a resolution authorizing military intervention to combat communism in the western hemisphere, only obtained a resolution condemning communist leaders from seizing power in the western hemisphere.

A Guatemalan exile army under CIA auspices began training in Honduras in 1953 and 1954 for a possible invasion of Guatemala under the command of Colonel Carlos Castillo Armas. On May 17, 1954, when the CIA received news that a shipment of Czech weapons was unloaded at Puerto Barrios, purportedly to arm popular militia, plans were accelerated for Castillo Armas's invasion. Ironically, the Guatemalan army, which was leery of the establishment of a rival force, intercepted the shipment and held it at its disposal.

Castillo Armas crossed the border into Guatemala on June 18, 1954, but it was the CIA-provided planes flying over Guatemalan skies which convinced the army to defect Arbenz. Abandoned and despondent, Arbenz sought refuge in the Mexican Embassy. He lived in exile in Mexico and later was a frequent visitor to Castro's Cuba. He died in Mexico City on January 27, 1971.

See also *Arévalo Bermejo, Juan José; Guatemala, U.S. Relations with; Guatemala, U.S. Invasion of, 1954; Puerifoy, John B.*

JOSÉ B. FERNÁNDEZ

REFERENCES AND FURTHER READING

Immerman, Richard H. *The CIA in Guatemala: The Foreign Policy of Intervention*. Austin: University of Texas Press, 1983.

LaFeber, Walter. *Inevitable Revolutions: The United States in Central America*. New York: Norton, 1984.

Schlesinger, Stephen, and Stephen Kinger. *Bitter Fruit: The Untold Story of the American Coup in Guatemala*. New York: Doubleday, 1982.

Arévalo Bermejo, Juan José

A self-proclaimed "spiritual socialist" intellectual who rejected Marxist class struggle and unbridled capitalism, Juan José Arévalo Bermejo was elected president of Guatemala in a free election held in December, 1944, after receiving 85 percent of the popular vote.

DOMESTIC CAREER

Born in Taxisco, Guatemala, on September 10, 1904, Juan José Arévalo was the son of a cattle rancher father and a schoolteacher mother. A precocious student, Arévalo received a bachelor's degree in education when he was only eighteen and later studied in Argentina where he received his doctorate in philosophy from the University of La Plata in 1931. After teaching at the University of Tucumán, Argentina, Arévalo returned to Guatemala. In 1944 he overwhelmingly won the 1944 elections and was inaugurated as president on March 15, 1945.

A reform-minded individual, Arévalo was instrumental in proclaiming the Constitution of 1945. It provided for individual freedoms, basic labor rights, free compulsory education, health care, and better housing conditions. The Constitution also granted the right to vote to illiterate males and literate females and contained a clause allowing for land expropriation with just compensation for the owners. Arévalo not only proclaimed the 1945 Constitution but put it into practice. In 1946, his administration established the Social Security Institute, providing social security for urban and rural workers. In an effort to provide labor reforms, his Labor Code of 1947 recognized labor unions, collective bargaining, and government arbitration in labor-management disputes.

In an effort to help small domestic manufacturers, his administration created the Production Development Institute. Through this entity, small domestic manufacturers received tax breaks and low interest loans.

Arévalo's government undertook an illiteracy-eradication campaign by bringing education to the Indian rural masses. In an effort to restructure Guatemalan society, his administration earmarked over one third of the national budget for education, housing, and health care. His government also began a public works program to improve communications in Guatemala and reduce unemployment. To offset these expenses, the Guatemalan armed forces' budget was reduced considerably.

U.S. RELATIONS

Although the Arévalo administration distributed a modest amount of German-owned coffee acres which had been expropriated during World War II, it decided not to expropriate the American-owned United Fruit Company (UFCO) holdings so as not to provoke the United States.

The Arévalo government did not recognize the Communist party, but undoubtedly the Guatemalan Central Labor Federation (CGT) was Communist-influenced and Communists dominated its higher echelons. This fact, together with Arévalo's left-of-center policies and his independent foreign policy, worried American policymakers. In 1946 the Arévalo government called on the United States to diplomatically isolate dictatorial regimes in Latin America. The United States, however, ignored this call. Arévalo, on the other hand, responded by supplying weapons to José "Pepe" Figueres's successful revolt against Costa Rican President Rafael Calderón Guardia, who attempted to perpetrate himself in power through a puppet president.

Relations between the United States and the Arévalo government deteriorated when the American ambassador to Guatemala, Richard Patterson, insinuated that Arévalo's reform program was Communist oriented. Arévalo interpreted Patterson's actions as interfering in Guatemalan internal affairs and virtually declared him persona non grata. As a result, the United States recalled Patterson, but upon his return, he continued to denounce Arévalo.

Arévalo not only had to contend with the U.S. displeasure but also faced staunch opposition from Guatemalan oligarchs who pointed out that his reforms were a violation against private ownership. Moreover, the Guatemalan armed forces viewed him with suspicion.

On March 15, 1951, Arévalo, after surviving twenty-two overthrow attempts, finished his term in office and handed the presidency to the democratically elected Jacobo Arbenz. Arbenz, however, was overthrown in 1954 as a result of an American-inspired invasion led by Colonel Carlos Castillo Armas. After the Arbenz overthrow, Arévalo wrote a book, *The Shark and the Sardines,* criticizing American imperialism in Latin America.

In 1963 elections were to be held in Guatemala, and when it became clear that Arévalo was going to be a candidate, the Guatemalan army overthrew President Miguel Ydígoras Fuentes, cancelled the elections, and replaced him with a junta headed by General Enrique Peralta Azurdia. Although the coup was a blow to President John F. Kennedy's Alliance for Progress and his quest for democracy in Latin America, the Kennedy administration believed that the junta would best protect American interests in Guatemala.

In 1966 elections were held in Guatemala, and Arévalo served as Guatemalan ambassador to several countries in the administration of democratically elected President Julio César Méndez Montenegro. Juan José Arévalo died in Guatemala City in October 1990.

See also *Arbenz Guzmán, Jacobo; Guatemala, U.S. Relations with; United Fruit Company (UFCO)*

. . . . JOSÉ B. FERNÁNDEZ

REFERENCES AND FURTHER READING

Arévalo, Juan José. *The Shark and the Sardines.* June Cobb, trans. New York: Lyle and Stuart, 1961.

Galich, Manuel. *¿Por qué lucha Guatemala? Arévalo y Arbenz: Dos hombres contra un imperio.* Ciudad Guatemala: Editorial Cultura, 1994.

Leonard, Thomas M. *The United States and Central America 1944–1949.* Tuscaloosa: University of Alabama Press, 1984.

Argentina, Financial Crisis, 2000–2002

The Argentine financial crisis of 2000–2002 had economic, social, and political dimensions. Over the course of two years between 2000 and 2002, output fell by more than 15 percent, the Argentine peso lost three-quarters of its value, and registered unemployment exceeded 25 percent while more than half of the population of the erstwhile rich country lived below the poverty line. The political and economic crisis reached its climax on December 20, 2001, when Fernando de la Rúa resigned from the presidency following severe riots, which had left more than twenty people dead and hundreds wounded. Shortly thereafter, Provisional President Adolfo Rodriguez Saá declared the default on close to $150 billion in foreign debt, the largest sovereign default in history. On January 6, 2002, Eduardo Duhalde, the fourth president since de la Rúa's resignation, devalued the peso and forcibly converted all dollar-denominated debts and deposits into pesos. This marked the end to more than a decade of the fixed exchange rate system known as convertibility.

The crisis needs to be understood in the context of the mixed performance of the fixed exchange rate system over the previous decade. On April 1, 1991, following two years of uncontrollable hyperinflation, President Carlos Menem and his new Minister of Economy Domingo Cavallo established parity between the U.S. dollar and the new, freely convertible peso, which was fully backed by international reserves. Initial skepticism on the part of domestic and international observers quickly gave way to exuberance as the fixed exchange rate system known as "convertibility" restored price stability and investors' confidence. By the end of 1992, inflation had fallen to single digits, Argentina once again enjoyed access to international financial markets, and economic growth had picked up strongly.

These early successes of convertibility obscured some of its severe flaws. Inflation remained substantially higher than in the United States, which led to an increasing overvaluation of the peso so that Argentine producers became uncompetitive on world markets. As a consequence, industrial production fell sharply as a share of gross domestic product (GDP), unemployment soared, and the balance of trade turned sharply negative. Low interest rates and the overvaluation of the peso also encouraged borrowing in dollars both by the government and by private corporations. Between 1991 and 1998, total external debt more than doubled from $65 billion to more than $140 billion.

As a string of financial crises in Asia in 1997 and in Russia and Brazil in 1998 rattled world financial markets, investors started to worry about Argentina's solvency and demanded higher interest rates to compensate for the risk. This added to the strain on the economy, which was already suffering under a severe recession. de la Rúa, who assumed the presidency in December 1999, had to simultaneously restore investors' confidence, eliminate the fiscal deficit, and stimulate the economy. However, this proved economically and politically impossible because efforts to reduce the fiscal deficit worsened the economic slump while simultaneously alienating important allies within the ruling coalition. Under these circumstances, Argentina asked for international help in late 2000. The IMF agreed to a $20 billion preemptive stabilization program, which was supposed to restore investors' confidence and help lift the economy. It failed on both counts.

By April 2001, after two ministers of economy had resigned in quick succession, de la Rúa called on Cavallo, the architect of the Convertibility Plan, to serve as minister of economy with exceptional powers. However, instead of saving the country, Cavallo's erratic measures made the crisis even worse. He modified the Convertibility Law, organized an ill-conceived voluntary debt restructuring, which left Argentina with an even higher debt burden, and tried to adjust government spending automatically to match tax receipts with the so-called "Zero Deficit Law." None of these measures helped to restore confidence, generate economic growth, or balance the budget, but instead they encouraged capital flight and contributed to an increasingly explosive social climate.

While the economy moved closer to economic collapse during the second half of 2001, only a large international rescue operation similar to the one the Clinton administration had orchestrated for Mexico in 1994 could have saved Argentina. However, the George W. Bush administration was opposed to what it perceived as "bailouts" of irresponsible investors and governments on ideological grounds. The IMF half-heartedly offered Argentina an additional (U.S.) $8 billion at the end of August even though Managing Director Horst Köhler and the IMF staff doubted that a collapse could be averted. However, the IMF finally cut off funding to Argentina on December 3, after a massive bank run had forced President de la Rúa to restrict withdrawals from banks to 250 pesos per week. This measure was the final spark, which lit the social powder keg and precipitated de la Rúa's downfall, Argentina's default on its external obligations, and the collapse of the fixed exchange rate system.

. . . . KLAUS VEIGEL

See also *Argentina: U.S. Relations with; Austral Plan, 1985 (Argentina); Debt Crisis, Latin America, 1870s, 1930s, 1980s; International Monetary Fund (IMF); Menem, Carlos Saúl; Tequila Effect, 1994*

REFERENCES AND FURTHER READING

Blustein, Paul. *And the Money Kept Rolling In (And Out): Wall Street, the IMF, and the Bankrupting of Argentina.* New York: Public Affairs, 2005.

International Monetary Fund, Independent Evaluation Office. *The IMF and Argentina, 1991–2001.* Washington, DC: International Monetary Fund Publication Services, 2004.

Mussa, Michael. *Argentina and the Fund: From Triumph to Tragedy.* Washington, DC: Institute for International Economics, 2002.

Argentina, U.S. Relations with

Over the past two centuries, the United States and Argentina have enjoyed generally cooperative relations. There has also been a rich history of bilateral cultural contact, characterized in the first instance by American literary, film, television, and musical influences in Argentina. Despite this, the public face of bilateral ties has frequently been one of conflict and antagonism. There are two explanations for this seeming contradiction. First, and most important, periods of sometimes explosive conflict have frequently overshadowed a long history of friendly relations. Far from having defined the history of United States-Argentine relations, conflict has never provoked a severe break in or violent ending to bilateral ties. Periods of hostility have never challenged or determined long-term patterns in cooperative economic and strategic relations. At times, as incomplete or fanciful political gestures, conflicts have in fact masked strong underlying bilateral ties.

A second explanation for the apparent contradiction lies in how both Argentines and Americans have interpreted tensions. While motivations have varied, there is a long history of Argentine political leaders, diplomats, scholars, and many others overstating the nature of Argentine conflict with the United States, while emphasizing and, at times, exaggerating the force of United States imperialism. In the United States, there has rarely been a popular interest in relations with Argentina. As a result, politicians have found little political capital to be gained from the politicization of bilateral relations. As in Argentina, though, but for different reasons, among American policy makers and academics there has frequently been an overestimation of crisis. In part, this has to do with an ideological rigidity among some Americans over what has constituted good and bad bilateral ties. After 1943, for example, some key American policy makers identified populist leader Juan Domingo Perón as a Nazi sympathizer and an antagonist of the United States. Once cast, that image was unshakable, despite Perón's efforts at improved ties, even though many U.S. officials were unconvinced by the negative image and worked behind the scenes to promote strong bilateral relations.

THE NINETEENTH CENTURY: COOPERATION AND CRITICISM

Before 1880 there was little controversy. Independence movements in both countries were primed by local capital interests hoping to end colonial trade restrictions and to increase their international markets. Between 1798 and 1810 a substantial bilateral commerce began as 125 American ships reached the Rio de la Plata, trading in slaves among dozens of other goods. The United States remained neutral in the warfare between Spain and its colonies, but American commercial contact with South America contributed to the Argentine independence struggle. Leaders of the American Revolution inspired Manuel Belgrano and other Argentine patriots in their writings and their politics; Belgrano cited George Washington's farewell address as a guide for his own thinking on nation building. The United States also served as a source of weapons for Argentine insurgents. In 1811 an Argentine delegation in the United States to purchase armaments for the struggle against Spain met with a supportive President James Madison.

In 1823 the United States and the United Provinces of La Plata (as Argentina was first named) established formal ties. During the 1820s and 1830s the Argentine government repeatedly cited the Monroe Doctrine in appealing for American support in a possible conflict with Brazil and over British claims to the Falklands/Malvinas Islands. Argentina's 1853 Constitution marked one of several steps toward the consolidation of central authority in Argentina through the mid-nineteenth century and provides an example of how Argentine views of the success of the early American republic came to influence Argentine nation building. The emphasis in the 1853 Constitution on the need for immigration as a motor for economic expansion drew directly on a sense among Argentine elites, including Juan Bautista Alberdi and Domingo F. Sarmiento, that the American model of success was one to emulate in South America.

Distance kept Argentina outside the core of U.S. activity in Latin America, though after 1850 American railroad builders in Argentina took business and ideological inspiration from Manifest Destiny-inspired expansion in the Caribbean. Also at midcentury, many prominent Argentines began to see the United States as both a model for political and economic expansion and an example of what Argentina might have been minus the long period of military struggles that marked the River Plate region in the four decades after independence. The mid-nineteenth century also marked the origins of a longstanding sore point in bilateral relations—U.S. trade restrictions on Argentine agricultural produce.

The first period of contradiction in U.S.-Argentine relations began around 1889 and continued until 1930. On the one hand, some Argentine leaders complemented explosive export-led growth in Argentina with strong support for U.S. business interests in the Americas. On the other hand, government leaders and others in Argentina became increasingly vocal in criticizing U. S. influence in the Americas and in Argentina in particular. During this period American policy toward Argentina was charted through the nascent Pan-American movement. As Americans sought expanded commercial and financial opportunities in the Americas, the U.S.-led Pan-American Union became the prime diplomatic forum for the exercise of objectives such as free trade in the Americas. Despite occasional and vociferous protest, the Argentine government was a longstanding backer of U.S. Pan-American goals.

A public posture critical of U.S. policy in Argentina and Latin America contradicted a more quiet face of Argentine policy that supported Washington's business and strategic objectives in the hemisphere. Beginning with the First Pan-American conference in 1889 and 1890, Argentine officials blasted U.S. imperial objectives in trying to normalize conditions of trade and finance in the hemisphere, but scholars have overestimated the strength of anti-Americanism in Argentine diplomacy. In 1902 Argentine Foreign Minister Luis María Drago protested against British coercion of Venezuela over loan defaults. What came to be known as the Drago Doctrine was read as an indictment of any foreign power intervening in the domestic affairs of a Latin American nation over loan defaults. Had Drago's views been accepted by the international community as law, they may well have limited U.S. intervention in the Caribbean basin in the three decades that followed, but Drago's comments drew on three decades of Argentine criticism of European, not American, filibustering. The foreign minister meant his stand not as an attack on the United States but as founded on the Monroe Doctrine.

THROUGH TWO WORLD WARS: SUSPICIONS ABOUT ARGENTINE NEUTRALITY

During the first World War, Hipólito Yrigoyen, president of Argentina, maintained his government's neutrality. Before U.S. entry into the war in 1917, this prompted concern in Washington over Yrigoyen's refusal to define Argentine neutrality in keeping with American strategic leadership in the hemisphere (that is to say, in a manner that favored Great Britain and its allies over Germany). After Washington declared war on Germany, American policy makers saw Argentine efforts to organize a group of Latin American neutrals as a risk to U.S. predominance in the region.

At the end of the first World War, the Red Scare in the United States spread to Argentina. In the months before the armistice and through early 1919, the United States Office of Naval Intelligence, the Military Intelligence Division of the United States Armed Forces, and State Department diplomats became increasingly suspicious, first of German espionage in Argentina, then of Communist agitation. Americans exaggerated the perceived menace but supported the Argentine government's shift toward a tougher, sometimes violent repressive policy against left-wing agitators. The end of a perceived Communist threat in the early 1920s coincided with a new spurt in American business interest in Argentina. Argentines had taken quickly to American automobiles and, as a related consequence, there was increased interest in oil production, for which Standard Oil of New Jersey won important new concessions.

Popular and negative perceptions of monopolistic American corporations drove a decade of debate in the Argentine media and in Congress over the possibility of controls and restrictions on the activities of U.S. business. Passed in 1921 by the House and a year later in the Senate, Argentina's anti trust legislation was directed primarily at American meatpacking corporations and oil companies. The law lacked the bite of more stark reforms in Mexico, but it gave impetus to the formation of the powerful state oil company, Yacimiento Petrolíferos Fiscales, in 1922 and to strong anti-American sentiment in the late 1920s over a U.S. Department of Agriculture (USDA) ban on the importation of Argentine beef. While the USDA issued its ban as a consequence of foot-and-mouth disease endemic in Argentina, cattle producers and political leaders in Argentina saw the measure as an extension of the United States Tariff Act of 1922 that had subjected Argentine exports to high protective duties.

While bilateral trade continued to grow in the late 1920s, diplomatic tensions came to a head in 1928 at the sixth Conference of American States in Havana. Argentine Ambassador to the United States Honório Pueyrredón led a public attack on U.S. intervention in Nicaragua and in the Americas more broadly. While American diplomats interpreted the criticism as Argentine government policy, Pueyrredón had, in fact, acted independently. The Argentine government reprimanded Pueyrredón, who had probably drafted his widely reported anti-American remarks as a domestic political tactic to wrest the leadership of the Argentine Radical party from President Hipólito Yrigoyen. Still, Americans remained suspicious. They linked Pueyrredón's initiative to earlier efforts by Yrigoyen to marshal an independent group of Latin American neutrals during the first World War. They would also tie it to later efforts by President Juan D. Perón to generate an Argentine-led Latin American bloc.

The Great Depression halted the rapid growth of bilateral economic ties during the 1920s. Argentine Foreign Minister Carlos Saavedra Lamas's leading diplomatic role in the negotiation of a peace between Paraguay and Bolivia at the conclusion of the Chaco War led to his winning the Nobel Peace Prize in 1936. The significance of the peace negotiations and the award in the context of U.S.-Argentine relations comes in the context of occasional contention between the two nations over U.S. intervention in Latin America. In this instance, with little at stake strategically for either nation, there was no contention between Argentina and the United States. Here, the United States was willing to cede a regional leadership role to Argentina.

During the second World War Argentina played a role not unlike what it had played during World War I, as a strong backer of the allied cause through the provision of foodstuffs and other goods. Despite this, as in the case of the first World War, American policy makers found Argentine neutrality threatening. On the outbreak of the second World War, Argentine and American strategic interests diverged. Over the next two years, Washington adopted a neutrality that allowed for increasing economic and strategic support for the allied cause. At the same time, the United States tried to set the terms for a pro-allied, Pan-American neutrality for other nations in the hemisphere. Argentina balked, maintaining a strict and more impartial neutrality. Argentine neutrality was formed in part as a consequence of domestic politics that most policymakers in Washington could not grasp.

In 1940, as competing pro-allied and pro-Axis political leaders vied for authority in Argentina, the weak, pro-allied government of president Roberto Ortiz urged Washington to understand Argentina's neutrality as pro-allied on the basis of strong commercial support for the allied cause. Ortiz pressed Americans further to understand that pro-allied neutrality would depend on increased commercial opportunities for Argentine goods in the United States and the survival of Ortiz's own shaky government. While some American policy makers responded sympathetically to Ortiz, the Argentine president's admonishments went unheeded. The fall of Ortiz's government in 1940 severely weakened Argentine democracy. More Argentines became disillusioned with Washington, believing (as many had during the first World War) that Americans were demanding too much of them. Americans wanted to shape Argentine neutrality and to force a break in Argentine-German relations, but at the same time they offered no prospect of more advantageous terms of trade for Argentine goods entering the United States.

After the United States entry into the War, Americans squandered opportunities generated by Argentine interest in and affection for American popular culture, principally Hollywood films. They became obsessed with an exaggerated Nazi menace in Argentina and a purported pro-Nazi tendency among Argentine political and military leaders, while ignoring the ongoing Argentine supply of the allies with raw materials and foodstuffs. When the Argentine military took control of the government in 1943, bilateral relations were further strained. United States Secretary of State Cordell Hull spearheaded a State Department faction that ascribed pro-Nazi tendencies to the new government. In late 1944, when Hull stepped down as secretary, some in the State Department, including Nelson D. Rockefeller, saw the opportunity for a rapprochement with Argentina, but the Hull vision of a pro-Nazi Argentina continued to win sway.

1945 TO 1955: THE PERÓN ERA

In May 1945 Spruille Braden arrived in Buenos Aires as United States ambassador. Braden pressed immediately and vociferously for Argentina to adopt a strong anti-Nazi position. His actions were seen as interventionist by most Argentines. Braden clashed with Juan Domingo Perón, a prominent member of the military government who had developed a broad base of populist support among Argentine workers. Rockefeller opposed Braden's hard public line against Perón as did the British government, which urged his recall. However, in the immediate aftermath of President Franklin D. Roosevelt's death in April, a power vacuum in the State Department favored Braden who won the backing of Hull-era government bureaucrats, political liberals, organized labor, and the national news media, all now convinced that Argentina had become a bastion of Nazism. In one of the most famous popular expressions of United States-Argentine

The Casa Rosada, or Pink House, in Buenos Aires houses the offices of the country's president and his executive staff. Built in the later nineteenth century, it bears bullet holes from a 1955 coup attempt against Juan Perón. The back balconies were made famous by the emotional speeches of Perón's wife Eva, but many other Argentine leaders have addressed the populace from there.

SOURCE: Thomas M. Leonard Collection

relations, *Time* magazine featured Braden on its front cover, taking on an Argentina infested with Nazis.

In August, Braden returned to Washington as assistant secretary of state. He remained undaunted in his campaign against Perón. When Perón announced his candidacy for the Argentine presidency in the 1946 national election, Braden became determined to block that possibility. Days before the election, the State Department released Braden's "Blue Book," an outline of purported links between Argentina and the Nazis during the war. The strategy to undermine Perón's credibility, as a member of the wartime military government, backfired. Argentines were incensed at what was perceived as Washington's intervention in their domestic affairs. Perón won the presidency in a landslide.

Between Juan Perón's election to the Argentine presidency in 1946 and his toppling by the military in 1955, U.S.-Argentine relations followed the contours of Perón's policies. In the late 1940s Perón maintained parallel policies toward the United States. The public face of Peronism included fierce anti-American and anti-imperial rhetoric and a "third position" diplomacy by which Perón tried to generate support in the developing world for a political project that opposed both United States and Soviet predominance. At the same time, behind the scenes, Argentine officials tried unsuccessfully to garner United States aid and new commercial bilateral commercial opportunities. When Washington pressed European nations (illicitly, by the terms of State Department regulations) to spend Marshall Plan dollars on American, but not Argentine, grain exports, Perón lobbied for a policy reversal. While the Department of State eventually identified thirty-three cases of discrimination related to the Marshall Plan against Argentina, the policy was never reversed.

Anti-American Argentine government rhetoric in the late 1940s and early 1950s was offset by the growing impact of American Cold War-era culture on Argentina, expressed most clearly in the arrival of the television set and American TV programming in Buenos Aires. Perón reversed his economic nationalism with a series of measures capped by a 1953 law reopening the country to foreign investment and the issuance of a new set of contracts to Standard Oil of California. American concerns over Argentina's claim (later disproved) to a controlled atomic reaction gave way to nuclear cooperation agreement in 1953 and the construction of a United States-designed Argonaut experimental reactor in Argentina in 1958.

1955 TO 1976: CLOSER TIES THROUGH RECURRING COUPS

The military government that followed Perón's ouster in 1955 established a pattern in relations with the United States followed by subsequent military governments between 1966 and 1971 and 1976 and 1983. The military adopted policies favoring American companies, more open international trade and finance, and Cold War anticommunism. Lingering Argentine government discord with private American firms was quickly resolved—in this case, an unfavorable contract Standard Oil of California had negotiated with Perón and restrictions on the remittance of profits by American firms in the United States. The United States Export-Import Bank and a handful of private New York-based banks, previously hesitant to loan Argentina money, immediately offered the new government $200 million in credits.

In the aftermath of the Cuban Revolution, young Argentine military officers, like their counterparts in other Latin American countries, became convinced of National Security Doctrine precepts that future warfare in their homeland would be nonconventional, would be fought against an internal Communist menace, and would imply widespread civilian casualties. The rise of General Juan Carlos Onganía, a strong national security doctrine proponent and Cold War warrior, within the Argentine military (and later, in 1966, to the Argentine presidency through a violent coup d'état), reflected the powerful influence of the U.S. military in Argentina and presaged the Dirty War of the 1970s. The John F. Kennedy administration rapidly expanded military cooperation programs with many Latin American countries, including Argentina, that led not only to a dramatic increase in military equipment sales but also to sales specifically earmarked for counterinsurgency warfare, like helicopters and light armored vehicles.

Elected in 1958 to the Argentine presidency, Arturo Frondizi initially reacted positively to the Kennedy administration's Alliance for Progress (AFP). This reflected both Frondizi's commitment to anticommunism through American economic assistance in Latin America and his confidence that the program offered the prospect of real change in Argentina. To the consternation of a wary and hawkish Argentine military high command, after Fidel Castro came to power in Cuba, Frondizi repeatedly offered Washington his good offices as a mediator of the emerging Cuban-American conflict. By late 1961, however, it became clear to Argentines that the level of funding they had hoped for through the AFP would not be forthcoming. During a visit to the White House, the first for an Argentine president, Frondizi indicated to Kennedy that the levels of economic assistance the United States was offering Argentina were inadequate to offset growing economic problems. Those problems, in turn, were destabilizing the democracy that Frondizi led.

Frondizi's admonishment of Kennedy proved prophetic. His ouster by the military in 1962 ushered in four years of unstable democratic rule. As the Argentine economy buckled under mounting inflation, declining industrial production, and growing instability, the United States government escalated criticisms of Argentina's inability and unwillingness to follow IMF prescriptions for economic success. This, in turn, weakened Arturo Illia's democratic government and contributed indirectly to General Onganía's 1966 coup d'état. Illia was also weakened by a split in his government over the 1965 Dominican invasion. While the Argentine military and a number of high ranking officials favored support of OAS-sanctioned United States military occupation of the Dominican Republic, Illia opposed it vehemently.

Despite some initial criticisms of the 1966 military takeover by Robert Kennedy, Jacob Javitz, and other members of the United States Congress, Washington quickly recognized the de facto regime in Argentina. Bilateral relations during Onganía's government were outstanding. The Argentine government renegotiated contracts with American oil companies allowing both their greater access to Argentine oil and potentially higher profits. Onganía subscribed to the national security doctrine in outlining his government's key foreign policy parameters and proved more willing than any government in the preceding decade to rigorously follow IMF economic directives.

During the brief presidency of Héctor Cámpora, when the Argentine government adopted strongly economic nationalist policies that were in evidence through much of Latin America at the time, U.S. policymakers and diplomats responded with a calm not evident a generation before when Juan Perón had come to power. Military sales from the United States to Argentina soared. Relations between the Confederación General de Trabajo (CGT), the Argentine central labor union, and the AFL–CIO were never stronger, based in part on ranking U.S. labor officials having identified the Peronist CGT as strongly anti-Communist.

When the military staged a coup d'état in March 1976, United States authorities played a role different to the one Americans played at the time of the Chilean coup three years earlier. Unlike Augusto Pinochet's takeover in Chile, there is no evidence that the U.S. participated in the planning or execution of the Argentine coup. At the same time, Secretary of State Henry Kissinger and other U.S. policymakers knew of the coup long in advance and sympathized both with its stated objective (the destruction of a largely invented Communist menace) and its methods, which included widespread torture and killing of thousands of civilians.

1977 TO 2001: CONVERGENCE ON HUMAN RIGHTS AND NEOLIBERAL ECONOMICS

During the 1970s, Argentine-U.S. relations suffered considerable strain as a result of United States President Jimmy Carter's emphasis on human rights in foreign policy. Carter's election signaled a sea change in U.S. policy, as he made human rights a policy priority, impacting both arms sales to Argentina and Argentina's place in the international community. Through the late 1970s the U.S. government registered hundreds of queries and complaints in Argentina over cases of torture and disappearances. While the Argentine military government found Carter's position an unfriendly aberration in the course of U.S. foreign policy, many Argentine opponents of the dictatorship, including future president Raúl Alfonsín, took heart in the human rights stance of many Americans. On the whole, economic and strategic relations remained strong. The United States supported a shift in Argentine economic policy opening Argentina to free trade and foreign investment. Argentina was generally supportive of American Cold War anticommunism. As had been the case in the past, however, there were points of misunderstanding and friction. While the Argentine generals had some sense of the debate within the Carter administration on the place of human rights in foreign relations, they overestimated the importance of some aspects of their own policy (including, for example, support for Carter administration policy on the Panama Canal) on U.S. policy. Some American policymakers were surprised and dismayed over Argentina's strong ties to Cuba, Yugoslavia, and other socialist nations through the nonaligned movement and equally disappointed over Argentina's decision to step up grain exports to the Soviet Union in the aftermath of the Afghanistan invasion.

The greatest source of bilateral tension during the period of military rule came at the time of the Falklands/Malvinas War in 1982. In anticipation of the Argentine invasion of Falklands/Malvinas in April, Argentine foreign minister Nicanor Costa Mendez convinced his nation's military leadership that the United States would side with Argentina in the conflict. It was a dramatic miscalculation. From the outset, the United States supported the British in a war that proved disastrous for the Argentine military and helped push the ruling junta from office a year later.

At the close of the dictatorship period in 1983, Argentines elected the human rights lawyer and Radical party leader Raúl Alfonsín to the presidency. Bilateral ties during the 1980s were influenced by ongoing Argentine economic problems including an escalating foreign debt, growing IMF pressures on Argentines, and animosity among many Argentines for a perceived U.S. influence in IMF-imposed restrictions. Argentina emerged as a leader in the nonaligned movement, voicing severe criticisms of U.S. and Soviet nuclear armaments production. In television, film, and music, there was a deluge of American cultural influences in Argentina. Trade grew slowly. Much of Alfonsín's energies—like those of Arturo Frondizi—were given over to trying to convince wary U.S. policymakers that democracy in Argentina would never be secured without a massive infusion of foreign aid from the United States and a U.S.-sponsored solution to perennial Argentine foreign indebtedness.

Shortly after his election to the Argentine presidency in 1989, Carlos Menem undertook a remarkable about-face in policy toward the United States. During his first three years in office Menem's government did away with two generations of irritants in bilateral relations. For the first time in its history, through its participation in the 1991 Gulf War, Argentina formally allied itself with the United States. The Menem administration all but cancelled Argentina's nuclear program, long a source of concern in Washington. Moreover, Argentina became a leader in what would come to be termed the Washington Consensus, rapidly selling off state-owned corporations to private investors and opening the country to foreign trade and investment. Perhaps most important, the Menem government stabilized the country's monetary situation by a Convertibility Law that tied the value of the Argentine peso to the United States dollar. As in other Latin American countries, evidence of burgeoning growth and a dynamic stock exchange through the 1990s gave way to mounting indicators of rampant child poverty, unprecedented government corruption, and the sacking of the national treasury by a generation of Argentine politicians in the name of free market reforms.

CONCLUSION: A NEW AUSTERITY

The Argentine economic crisis of December 2001 ushered in a surprising shift in U.S.-Argentine relations. For several months before what Argentines called the "crack," U.S. Treasury Secretary Paul O'Neill had publicly criticized Argentine authorities for their incompetent management of Argentina's economic policy. O'Neill and other George W. Bush administration officials had decided to make Argentina a test case for a new, tougher, U.S. stand toward what they viewed as reckless and corrupt borrowing practices among developing nations and the lax lending policies of banks and the IMF. When Argentina devalued its currency and defaulted on its loan repayments, and once it became clear that there would be no larger financial shock waves across the international community, Washington remained surprisingly silent on Argentine government actions. The Bush administration took the position that borrowers and lenders would have to work out their own financial problems. Washington would play no role in resolving the crisis. In the four years following the crack, there were signs of economic recovery in Argentina. Despite President Nestor Kirchner's left-of-center rhetoric and his close ties to Venezuela's Hugo Chávez, U.S.-Argentine relations remained strong in all regards.

See also *Antarctica, Argentine, and Chilean Claims to; Argentina, Financial Crisis 2000; Beagle Channel Dispute (Argentina/Chile); Braden, Spruille; "Disappeared Ones" (Desaparecidos), Argentina and Chile, 1970s–1980s; Drago, Luis M.; Malvinas/Falkland Islands Controversy and War (Argentina/United Kingdom); Frondizi, Arturo; Great Depression and Latin America; Operation Condor; Perón Sosa, Juan Domingo; Seventh International Conference of American States, Montevideo, 1933; Southern Common Market (MERCOSUR); World War II*

. . . . DAVID M. K. SHEININ

REFERENCES AND FURTHER READING

Cisneros, Andrés, and Carlos Escudé. *Historia general de las relaciones exteriores de la República Argentina.* Consejo Argentino de Relaciones Exteriores, 1998–2003.

Peterson, Harold F. *Argentina and the United States, 1810–1960.* Albany: State University of New York Press, 1964.

Sheinin, David. *Argentina and the United States: An Alliance Contained.* Athens: University of Georgia Press, 2006.

Tulchin, Joseph S. *Argentina and the United States: A Conflicted Relationship.* Boston: Twayne, 1990.

Arias Madrid, Arnulfo

Arnulfo Arias Madrid (1901–1988), brother of Harmodio Arias (former President 1932–1936), served three terms as Panama's president. He first won Panama's 1940 presidential election. Documents from the National Archives of Panama reveal the latter Arias as a Panamanian nationalist and a racist who resorted to undemocratic methods, but not an Axis sympathizer as he is often reputed to be.

FIRST PRESIDENCY (WORLD WAR II)

After Arias won Panama's 1940 presidential election, he immediately promulgated a constitution (which took effect the next year) that prohibited immigration by "people of the Negro race whose original language is not Spanish, the yellow race, and races originating from India, Asia Minor, and North Africa" (Arnulfo Arias Papers). More than racism was involved. "People of the Negro race whose original language [was] not Spanish" (Arnulfo Arias Papers) came from English-speaking Jamaica or Barbados and often had better jobs than other Panamanians in the Canal Zone. Chinese and Indian immigrants tended to become merchants in Panama City and Colón, and they also spoke English, the language of their customers (tourists and people from the Canal Zone). Barely two weeks into Arias's first presidency, Justice Minister Ricardo Adolfo de la Guardia ordered that commercial signs must appear in Spanish. If other languages appeared, the Spanish must appear first, and letters of the second language could be no more than half the size of the letters of the Spanish words. A business with a name like "Jimmy's Place" must find a Spanish name. There would be fines for noncompliance. Modern Quebec has similar laws to protect its French language.

Arias was also an anti-Semite. Indeed, on June 23, 1941, the head of Panama's secret police, Juan Ramón Ramírez, presented a list of forty-four "foreign Hebrews" living in Panama. The information included their names, identity numbers *cédulas*, addresses, family situations, employment information, and Panamanian bank accounts (including their size and location). No other group of foreigners merited such a list. Unfortunately, Arias's government was not uniquely anti-Semitic. Few allied or neutral governments wanted Jewish refugees.

Arias did not, publicly or privately, express admiration for Hitler, but he did admire Spanish leader Francisco Franco, who had attained office after winning a civil war with assistance from Hitler and Mussolini. Arias's wife, Ana Matilda Linares de Arias, was president of the Panamanian Red Cross. Early in 1941, Luis de la Barra Lastarría of Panama's delegation to the Fourth Inter-American Conference of the Red Cross, held in Santiago de Chile, proposed a resolution of special greetings to the Spanish Red Cross, expressing a wish for "the complete restoration of noble Spain, from which we inherit our blood" (Speech given by Luis de la Barra Lastarría, Arnulfo Arias Papers).

Arias was also less than fully cooperative with U.S. diplomacy. When U.S. Ambassador Edmund C. Wilson requested a list of German and Italian nationals in Panama, Arias replied only that he would provide a list of all foreign residents and U.S. authorities could guess which ones were German and which were Italian. The U.S. government requested military bases in Panama but outside the Canal Zone. It wanted leases of 999 years but offered 99 years as a compromise. Arias agreed that the 1936 treaty obliged the Republic of Panama to provide such a site in the event of a *conflagración internacional*. However, he successfully insisted that the occupation of any military base outside the Canal Zone should terminate when World War II ended and that the U.S. government should compensate those displaced or otherwise inconvenienced.

Arias's brother, Harmodio Arias, was publisher of the newspaper *Panama América*. When Harmodio refused to relinquish control of the newspaper to the president, Arias apparently ordered a reprisal on his brother's other business, cattle. Arias's quarrel with his brother became important for U.S.-Panamanian relations when Harmodio sided with conspirators who ousted Arnulfo Arias from the Panamanian presidency at a time most convenient to U.S. interests.

From April 1941 Harmodio and his coconspirators contemplated a coup d'état; they received their opportunity in the context of an undeclared naval war fought between the U.S. and German navies from September to December 1941. Many U.S.-based ship owners actually registered oceangoing ships in Panama, because its labor laws and safety standards were less rigorous than American ones. Arias refused, however, to allow these U.S.-owned vessels of Panamanian registry to arm. Edmund C. Wilson, U.S. ambassador to Panama, gave the green light. On October 9, 1941, the conspirators seized control and replaced Arias with Ricardo Adolfo de la Guardia, Arias's minister of justice. The new de la Guardia administration immediately granted permission for the arming of those ships.

SECOND AND THIRD PRESIDENCIES

Arnulfo Arias ran again in the 1948 presidential election and probably won the largest number of votes, but the national guard, the real power broker in Panama, favored his opponent, Domingo Díaz. Díaz was inaugurated but soon died. Daniel Chanis, the first vice president, became president. However, after quarrels with Chanis and Roberto Chiari, vice president of Panama, who held office for only four days, National Guard Comandante José Antonio Remón decided that Arias had won the election after all. Arias's second presidency lasted from November 24, 1949, to May 9, 1951, until Remón ousted him as well.

During Arnulfo's second presidency, an agreement with the U.S. government facilitated travel between Panama City, located east of the Canal Zone, and its hinterland, west of the Canal Zone. Previously, Panamanians had needed special drivers' licenses, ownership registration papers, and license plates to travel across the Canal Zone. On November 1, 1950, the U.S. State Department and the Panamanian Foreign Ministry announced that for a twelve-month trial period, Panamanian documents would suffice along a clearly specified route.

Arias won a third presidential term in 1968. During the election campaign, he and his opponent David Samudio each claimed to be more likely to regain the Canal Zone. Arias won, but immediately after his inauguration he quarreled with Bolívar Vallarino, head of the national guard, and eleven days into his presidency, the national guard ousted him. Arias spent the mid-1970s fighting unsuccessfully against the efforts of the Ford and Carter administrations to come to terms with President Omar Torrijos. He died in 1988.

See also *Caribbean, German U-boat Threat, World War II; Carter, Jimmy; Good Neighbor Policy; Hay–Bunau-Varilla Treaty, 1903; Hispanidad; Johnson, Lyndon B.; Nazi Activities in Latin America, World War II; Panama, Independence of, 1903 Panama Riots, 1964; Panama, U.S. Relations with; Reagan, Ronald W.*

GRAEME S. MOUNT

REFERENCES AND FURTHER READING

"Arnulfo Arias Papers for His First Presidency," from the Constitution of 1940, Box 10, File 1, housed at the Archivos Nacionales de Panamá in Panamá City.

Gunther, John. *Inside Latin America.* New York: Harper and Brothers, 1941.

LaFeber, Walter. *The Panama Canal: The Crisis in Historical Perspective.* Oxford, UK: Oxford University Press, 1979.

Major, John. *Prize Possession: The United States and the Panama Canal, 1903–1979.* Cambridge, UK: Cambridge University Press, 1993.

Mount, Graeme. *895 Days That Changed the World: The Presidency of Gerald R. Ford.* Montreal, Canada: Black Rose Press, 2006.

Arias Peace Plan

(**See** *Arias Sánchez, Oscar*)

Arias Sánchez, Oscar

Oscar Arias Sánchez (1940–) served as Costa Rica's president from 1986 to 1990 and 2006 to 2010. He was instrumental in the peace process in the civil wars of other Central American countries, drawing the ire of the United States but garnering him the 1987 Nobel Peace prize.

EARLY CAREER AND RISE TO POWER

Arias was born into a wealthy coffee family in Heredia, Costa Rica. He was educated at the University of Costa Rica and earned a PhD in political science from the University of Essex, in the United Kingdom. Upon his return from England, he was offered and accepted a position as an assistant to former president José Figueres Ferrer. In 1970 Figueres sought the nomination of the Partido Liberación Nacional, or National Liberation Party (PLN), and won a second presidential term (during his first term as head of state, after the civil war of 1948, he took the title of junta leader rather than president). Arias joined President Figueres's cabinet as minister of national planning (Planificación Nacional y Política Económica).

In 1978 Arias sought and was elected to a four-year term in the unicameral fifty-seven-member Asamblea Legislativa (legislative assembly) as a deputy for the PLN. He resigned in 1981 to help the PLN's presidential candidate, Luis Alberto Monge, campaign for the 1982 election. Arias became the PLN's presidential candidate himself for the general election of 1986. He won with over 52 percent of the popular vote; his party took a majority of the seats in the legislative assembly, marking the first time that the PLN had ever won back-to-back presidential elections.

Although the economic crisis was less severe than at the start of his predecessor's term in office and had been brought under control, it still required serious attention as well as long-term adjustments. Though Arias campaigned during the 1986 election on a traditional social democratic PLN platform, once in office, his government continued the gradual reorientation of the economy toward privatization with a series of economic reforms opening some state-controlled sectors of the economy to private companies.

THE PURSUIT OF PEACE AND HUMAN RIGHTS

Unlike the Monge administration, relations between the Arias administration and the United States quickly became strained. Arias refused to permit a continuation of Monge's compliance in the contra war in Nicaragua and pushed to close down the U.S.-proxy army, the contras, and its southern front that operated out of Costa Rica. Almost immediately upon taking office, Arias took it upon himself to reinvigorate the Contadora Group's (composed of Mexico, Venezuela, Colombia and Panama) peace process to end the fratricidal civil wars in Costa Rica's Central American sister republics (Nicaragua, El Salvador, and Guatemala). As Arias demonstrated his commitment to the Central American peace process, the Reagan administration in the United States showed its displeasure both diplomatically and financially. While U.S. aid to Costa Rica jumped significantly during Monge's administration, it declined sharply during the Arias administration. U.S. aid had soared from an average of just $7 million per year prior to 1982 to a stable rate of $214 million per year beginning in 1983. Once Oscar Arias's foreign policy intentions became clear, U.S. aid declined precipitously to less than $6 million by the mid-1990s. The sudden reduction in U.S. aid appeared to have been in retaliation for Arias's Central American peace accord, which was at odds with the U.S. policy for the region.

Undeterred, in 1987 Arias pushed a Central American peace plan involving only the Central American republics and excluded both the United States and the Contadora Group. In spite of the Reagan administration's open hostility toward Arias's peace initiative, all five Central American presidents signed the peace accords in August 1987. Arias's effort to initiate a peace process in the region was recognized with the 1987 Nobel Peace Prize, the award that helped establish the Arias Foundation for Peace and Human Progress (Fundación Arias Para la Paz y Progreso Humano). The foundation finds programs in three broad areas promoting women's equality in Central America, change-oriented philanthropy in Latin America, and demilitarization and conflict resolution in the developing world.

Aside for the peace program, Arias left a major mark on Costa Rica's polity by signing a constitutional amendment to create a constitutional chamber of the supreme court. This constitutional chamber became a major actor in Costa Rica's political and social life and has been central to the country's rights revolution of the last twenty years. Significantly, the court in 2003 overturned a 1967 constitutional amendment barring presidential reelection. This ruling allowed Arias

U.S. President Barack Obama (left) reaches out to Costa Rican President Oscar Arias (right) at the start of the opening ceremonies of the Fifth Summit of the Americas in Port of Spain, April 17, 2009.

SOURCE: DAVID DE LA PAZ/Xinhua/Landov

to seek a second presidential term in the general election of 2006. Although initial polling data showed Arias with a huge margin of popular support, he secured the presidency by only 1.2 percent (slightly more than 18,000 votes) over Ottón Solís.

RETURN TO THE PRESIDENCY

Unlike his first term in office when diplomatic ties to the United States were frequently strained, Arias's second term has been characterized by a close economic and political relationship. From Arias's perspective, the end of the Cold War and the advent of globalization changed the terms of the international debate for Costa Rica. Instead of returning to old issues, Arias campaigned on and pushed for legislative approval for the Central American-Dominican Republic Free Trade Agreement (CAFTA-DR). The treaty, he argued, was fundamentally important to the continued economic well-being of all Costa Ricans.

Although President Arias's political party did not have majority control in the fifty-seven-member, single chamber, legislative assembly, his goal of passing the CAFTA enabling laws did enjoy majority support of a multiparty block of deputies in the assembly. The considerable levels of popular dissatisfaction with the treaty, though, pushed Arias to request a national referendum on the issue. In October 2007 Costa Rica held its first ever referendum to resolve the CAFTA agreement issue. In the final tally, the pro-CAFTA block won a narrow victory of 52 percent to 48 percent. In the subsequent months, the legislative assembly slowly passed most of the enabling laws, but it had to request a deadline extension from the United States to complete the task.

In mid-2009 Arias was pushed back onto the international stage as a mediator in the crisis brought about by the overthrow of President Manuel Zelaya of Honduras in a coup d'état. Arias's negotiations (San José Accord) received U. S. support, but he ultimately failed to broker a resolution. The crisis was finally contained by the regularly scheduled presidential election of a new Honduran president in November.

See also *Central American Wars, 1980s; Central American-Dominican Republic Free Trade Agreement, 2004 (CAFTA-DR); Costa Rica, U.S. Relations with; Costa Rica-Nicaragua Boundary Dispute; Nicaraguan-Costa Rican Conflict, 1948; Reagan, Ronald W.; U.S. Agency for International Development (USAID)*

. . . . BRUCE M. WILSON

REFERENCES AND FURTHER READING

Abrams, Irwin. "Behind the Scenes: The Nobel Committee and Oscar Arias." *Antioch Review* 46, no. 3 (Summer 1988).

Arias Sánchez, Oscar. *Ten Years after Esquipulas: Looking toward the Future (Reports and Papers/Academic Council on the United Nations System).* Waterloo, Ontario, Canada: Academic Council on the United Nations System, 1997.

Arias Sánchez, Oscar. *Horizons of Peace: The Costa Rican Contribution to the Peace Process in Central America.* San José, Costa Rica: Fundación Arias para la Paz y el Progreso Humano, 1994.

Cox, Vicki. 2007. *Oscar Arias Sánchez.* New York: Chelsea House Publications, 2007.

Wilson, Bruce M. *Costa Rica: Politics, Economics, and Democracy.* Boulder, CO: Lynne Rienner, 1998.

Aristide, Jean-Bertrand

Haitian politician and former Catholic priest, Jean-Bertrand Aristide (1953–) was born on July 15, 1953, in a village along Haiti's southern coast. He served as Haitian president in 1991, 1994 to 1996, and 2001 to 2004. Aristide was orphaned as an infant and raised by the Society of St. Francis de Sales. With the society's support, he graduated from the State University of Haiti in 1979 and was ordained a priest in 1983. He earned a master's degree in psychology from the University of Montreal. He spoke Kreyol as well as French, Spanish, English, Hebrew, Italian, German, and Portuguese. He was an accomplished poet, composer, musician, and writer.

He became the parish priest in the La Saline slums of Port-au-Prince, acquiring the nickname "Titide" or "little priest." An exponent of liberation theology, he became a leader of the radical wing of the Haitian Roman Catholic Church and an opponent of the dictatorships of François "Papa Doc" and Jean-Claude "Baby Doc" Duvalier. Broadcasting from St. Jean Bosco Church on the national Catholic radio, he condemned their lack of concern for democracy and the poor. His efforts soon focused international attention on human rights violations in Haiti. They also led to persecution of his followers by Duvalier's henchmen known as "tonton macoutes."

Catholic authorities ordered Aristide to stop his "radical" preaching. Eventually, his efforts forced Baby Doc and his minions to flee Haiti for France. They were succeeded by the military regimes of General Prosper Avril and, later, General Henri Namphy, that did little to alleviate the poverty and corruption in Haiti. Aristide spoke against them too.

In 1988 thugs of the military junta attacked and killed thirteen members of Aristide's congregation. The Salesian authorities defrocked Aristide two weeks later, and the Roman Catholic Church ordered him to Rome. His departure was blocked by thousands of angry Haitians who shut down the airport. He remained in Port-au-Prince operating a medical clinic and halfway house for the homeless.

In 1990 the United States, supported by the United Nations and the Organization of American States (OAS), persuaded the Haitian military to hold elections. The front runner was Marc Bazin, an experienced civil servant. Just before the December elections, Aristide decided to run. The vast majority of voters were voting for the first time in a truly free election. While Aristide received 67.5 percent of the popular vote, his party, the Lavalas or "Avalanche" party, only won a few the seats in the Haitian parliament.

Aristide took office on February 7, 1991. He soon scared the elite commercial and military classes in Haiti by abolishing the military and replacing it with a police force and prosecuting people suspected of being Duvalierists. On September 30, 1991, he was ousted by General Raoul Cedras. Aristide first fled to Venezuela and then to the United States. Following his overthrow, thousands of boat people fled Haiti. The United States denied most of them refugee status. The United States, United Nations, and OAS placed an embargo on Haitian exports and their importation of petroleum and other essential products. These efforts proved only partially successful since the majority of people who suffered were poor.

In 1993, after several failed attempts, President William J. Clinton convinced Cedras and Aristide to meet in New York. Cedras agreed to let Aristide return as president for the final twenty-seven months of his single, nonrenewable term (October 15, 1994–February 1, 1996) and provide amnesty for the military. When Haitian elites reneged on the agreement, Clinton sent 23,000 U.S. troops to Haiti to reinstate Aristide. On December 17, 1995, Haiti held another presidential election, and René Préval succeeded Aristide in February 1996.

In the 1990s Aristide criticized the International Monetary Fund (IMF) for being "a tool of the rich." In 2000, Aristide's reorganized Lavalas party won control of Haiti's senate. On November 26 Aristide again ran for president, this time against four token candidates. The primary opposition parties accused Aristide's faction of election fraud and boycotted the election. Clinton agreed and pointed to delays in the distribution of voter ID cards as proof that Aristide had rigged the election.

Many Western nations suspended government-to-government aid to Haiti, which had not received help from the World Bank and the Inter-American Development Bank for years. In late January 2004, the Revolutionary Artibonite Resistance Front started a rebellion. On February 29 Aristide left Haiti. While President George W. Bush denied it, Aristide (Trinidad and Tobago agreed) claimed the United States kidnapped him and forced him out. Many Caribbean Community Common Market (CARICOM) states worried that Aristide's ouster prior to the end of his term was a dangerous precedent regarding external interference in the internal affairs of member states.

On May 31, 2004, Aristide and his family went to Johannesburg, South Africa. In 2006, Préval was elected president of Haiti and said he would consider allowing Aristide to return.

See also *Cedras, Raoul; Clinton, William J.; Duvalier, François; Duvalier, Jean-Claude; Haiti, U.S. Intervention under President Clinton, 1994; Inter-American Development Bank (IDB); Liberation Theology; Namphy, General Henri*

. . . . WILLIAM HEAD

REFERENCES AND FURTHER READING

Aristide, Jean-Bertrand and Flynn, Laura. *The Eyes of the Heart: Seeking a Path for the Poor in the Age of Globalization.* Monroe, ME: Common Courage Press, 2000.

Aristide, Jean-Betrand. *In the Parish of the Poor: Writings from Haiti by Jean-Bertrand Aristide.* Amy Wilentz, trans. Maryknoll, NY: Orbis, 1990.

Dupuy, Alex. *The Prophet and Power: Jean-Bertrand Aristide, Haiti and the International Community*. New York: Rowman and Littlefield, 2007.
Perusee, Rodney J. *Haitian Democracy Restored*. Lanham, MD: University Press of America, 1995.
Wilentz, Amy. *The Rainy Season: Haiti since Duvalier*. New York: Simon and Schuster, 1990.

Armed Forces of National Liberation (FALN) (Puerto Rico)

The Armed Forces of National Liberation (FALN) of Puerto Rico was a Cold-War-era paramilitary group that struggled to gain Puerto Rico's liberation as a nation independent of the U.S. government. Growing out of a 1950s student pro-independence organization and a tradition of pro-independence movements, the U.S.-based FALN called for a popular front of the Marxist-Leninist variety, rejecting support from non-Marxist countries and advocating a Socialist-Communist government for a fully independent Puerto Rico. A separatist movement, it used terror tactics in an attempt to gain these objectives. The movement was based on both nationalism and socialism and was spurred to growth in part by the economic difficulties facing Puerto Rico in the middle of the twentieth century. Setting itself against the U.S. government and military, it sent members to and recruited members within the United States to carry out bombings on U.S. soil, such as in New York and Chicago. Representatives of FALN then used the press interest in these actions to call attention to its cause and announce its intentions and motivations.

Since its territory came under U.S. control with the Spanish-American-Cuban War, Puerto Rican pro-independence movements had generally remained a minority of the island's population. Many within Puerto Rico have sought improvement and aid through the existing structures put in place by the U.S. government, and others—generally those among the elite—have often been pleased with the status quo that provided tax incentives and concessions that required Puerto Rico's continued status as a U.S. territory. Many, however, saw continued economic problems in Puerto Rico as a sign that the colonial status of the island was not working. The U.S. government had attempted to solve this problem by initiating reforms, making Puerto Rico a commonwealth in 1952 to promote industry and creating an Industrial Incentive Act in 1954. Nevertheless, industry stagnated and pro-independence movements continued. In the 1960s, during the height of U.S. preoccupations with the Cold War, the FALN arose to attempt to answer these problems and promote nationalism on the island. The extent and success of Puerto Rican terrorist organizations in this era were a clear indication of discontent among many Puerto Ricans on the island and within the continental United States.

Led by William Morales, the FALN was classified by the Federal Bureau of Investigation (FBI) as a terrorist organization, and its leaders and members were persecuted as criminals and were considered threatening to U.S. national security throughout the 1970s. The height of FALN actions took place through the second half of the 1970s, during which time it executed over one hundred terrorist bombings, and most acts were carried out on U.S. soil. During this time, the organization maintained a great deal of support from its members in the United States and from other organizations subversive to the U.S. government, such as the Weather Underground and other prominent Puerto Rican separatist groups such as the Macheteros, led by Filiberto Ojeda Rios. The FALN became a special target of the FBI Counter-Intelligence Program (COINTELPRO). Many of its members were arrested throughout these years, and others fled to other countries—especially to refuge from U.S. authorities in Cuba. In 1977 FALN leader William Morales was severely injured in a bombing action in Queens, New York, and he fled to Mexico. In 1983 he was arrested there, but the Mexican government declined to hand him over to U.S. authorities, and he went into exile in Cuba. The organization dissolved in 1983 with many of its members by then in FBI custody and leader Morales in Cuba. Other Puerto Rican separatist groups protested the detaining of FALN members in the continental United States and continued to call for an independent Puerto Rico.

Diplomatic and federal attempts to deal with the contentious issue of the Puerto Rican pro-independence movement have remained controversial. In 1999 U.S. President William Clinton commuted the sentences of sixteen FALN members; both their imprisonment and then their pardons caused widespread controversy, as did the 2005 death of Machetero leader Rios. Rios was killed in Puerto Rico in a confrontation with the FBI. FBI agents claimed that they entered his property with an arrest warrant and that he began shooting; Rios's wife, the only other eye witness, claims that the FBI agents began shooting first and that the 72-year-old Rios was only protecting himself. Criticism of FBI handling of the situation was widespread for many reasons, however. Among them was the fact that the FBI carried out the operation without first alerting local law officials.

See also *Puerto Rico, U.S. Relations with*

. . . . ELLEN D. TILLMAN

REFERENCES AND FURTHER READING

Gonzalez-Cruz, Michael. "The U.S. Invasion of Puerto Rico: Occupation and Resistance to the Colonial State, 1898 to the Present." *Latin American Perspectives* 25, no. 5 (Sep., 1998): 7–26.
Heine, Jorge. *A Time for Decision: The United States and Puerto Rico*. Lanham, MD: North-South, 1983.
Meléndez, Edwin, and Edgardo Meléndez, eds. *Colonial Dilemma: Critical Perspectives on Contemporary Puerto Rico*. Boston: South End Press, 1993.
Smith, Brent L. *Terrorism in America: Pipe Bombs and Pipe Dreams*. Albany: State University of New York Press, 1994.

Arms Industry in Latin America

The size and sophistication of Latin America's defense industries vary widely. Argentina, Chile, and Brazil are capable of manufacturing aircraft, armored vehicles, and naval hardware. Peru and Mexico have more modest defense industries devoted to the manufacture of light arms, ammunition, and navy patrol boats. Another group of countries including Honduras, Bolivia, Costa Rica, and Uruguay do not have significant arms industries.

CHALLENGING U.S. SUPREMACY IN ARMS DEALING

Prior to World War I, a handful of Latin American countries produced arms and ammunition, but all sophisticated weaponry—warships in particular—came from Europe or the United States. From World War II to 1967 the United States held a virtual monopoly on the supply of advanced defense technology to Latin America, but that position came to an abrupt end once other arms-exporting countries started selling defense technology to Latin America through coproduction and licensing agreements.

In the first two decades after World War II Washington offered Latin American nations military hardware under the terms of the Military Assistance Program. In the 1960s, however, Congress began to eliminate grant aid while simultaneously exercising greater control over the export of American military products, technologies, and services. Specifically, the United States refused to export supersonic fighter jets, deeming them inappropriate for the continent's militaries and likely to result in arms proliferation. This attitude generated resentment among South American governments, which saw such policies as insulting encroachments on their sovereignty.

A watershed moment came in 1967 when Peru decided to buy twelve Mirage 5 fighter jets from France in direct violation of Washington's wishes, making Peru the first Latin American nation (excluding Cuba) to possess supersonic combat aircraft and redefining South America's military environment. European defense firms aggressively challenged U.S. preeminence as the region's arms supplier and proved more willing to sell arms and technology to governments without political conditions. By the time the Carter administration decided to make weapons sales contingent on a yearly assessment of respect for human rights, many militaries had already come to view the United States as unreliable.

ARMS MANUFACTURE IN ARGENTINA, CHILE, AND BRAZIL

National leaders in Argentina—many of whom were military officers—had long viewed arms production as a path to industrial and technological development. In 1941 the Argentine state established the DGFM (Dirección General de Fabricaciones Militares) as a conglomerate to manage fourteen factories across the country producing a variety of arms, communication equipment, chemicals, and steel. In 1983 it employed an estimated 40,000 people.

In the 1960s Argentine leaders formulated *Plan Europa* to import European defense technology in response to U.S. Congressional restrictions. Contracts were signed with French, British, Swiss, and West German firms for licenses to manufacture everything from warships and tanks to machine guns and missiles. *Plan Europa* was designed to build on Argentina's existing production capabilities while importing advanced technology. For example, the Argentine Defense Ministry contracted with German engineers to help design a medium sized tank (Tanque Argentino Mediano) for domestic production in 1974. That year Argentina's aircraft industry (Fábrica Militar de Aviones) introduced its own counterinsurgency ground attack plane, the IA 58 Pucará, which saw action during the Dirty War (1976–1983) and the Falklands War (1982).

In 1975 U.S. legislation sponsored by Senator Ted Kennedy terminated all American military sales to Chile as a punishment for the Pinochet regime's human rights violations. Because the Chilean military had depended so heavily on U.S. defense technology, the air force, army, and navy were obliged to renovate antiquated hardware, locate new sources of supply, and acquire manufacturing licenses from other arms-exporting states.

Cardoen Industries, a Chilean firm that mostly manufactured explosives for the mining sector prior to 1975, took advantage of new opportunities to enter defense production and won contracts to supply the Chilean army with armored personnel carriers. By the 1980s Cardoen Industries was manufacturing armored vehicles, mines, rockets, grenades, and torpedoes. This entrepreneurial success led to exporting, and from 1984 to 1988 the industrial enterprise sold $200 million worth of cluster bombs to Iraq.

Chile's national aircraft industry ENAER (Empresa Nacional de Aeronáutica de Chile) reached a new level of development in the 1980s with the design, manufacture, and export of a military trainer, the T-35 Pillán. Assisted by Piper Aircraft, a private U.S. company unaffected by the arms embargo, ENAER successfully replaced Chile's outdated trainers, obtained under the Military Assistance Program, that had become difficult to repair following passage of the Kennedy Amendment.

Brazil is both Latin America's largest weapons producer and the only Latin American country to design and build a substantial portion of the jets, armored vehicles, and warships in its arsenal. National leaders began pursuing the goal of weapons self-sufficiency after the country initiated a process of industrialization in the 1930s. By the 1960s, Brazil's private sector had all the means to create economies of scale for the efficient manufacture and export of arms: advanced industrial infrastructure, low labor costs, and the capacity to fabricate all primary parts.

In 1964 Brazilian engineers founded the private aerospace firm Avibrás and received contracts from the Brazilian military to manufacture rockets. By the 1980s Avibrás began exporting multiple launch rocket systems. The firm also developed antitank and antiship missiles. At its peak during the Iran-Iraq War, Avibrás employed 6,000 people.

Brazil's largest aircraft manufacturer and top exporter EMBRAER (Empresa Brasileira de Aeronáutica) is the world's fourth largest civilian airplane maker and a testament to the strength of Brazil's aeronautical industry. In 1988, the company employed 12,000 workers. A quick survey of Latin America's air force fleets reveals that nearly every country in Latin America owns and operates EMBRAER military aircraft.

Brazilian tank production illustrates one way the United States has contributed to the development of Latin America's arms industry. In the 1950s Brazil received eighty aging M3A1 Stuart light tanks and three hundred M-41 Walker Bulldog light tanks through the U.S. Military Assistance Program. In the 1970s the Bernardini Company of São Paulo rebuilt those tanks with European components and some indigenous modifications before receiving a contract, in 1980, to build a Brazilian battle tank, the Tamoio, which relied on the American M-41 design.

CONCLUSION

In the 1980s critics described Latin America's bourgeoning defense industries as a misallocation of resources and a form of luxury production for a social minority (the military). Critics also feared that an emerging military industrial complex would politicize the armed forces and encourage them to meddle in civilian decision making about defense budgets. At the same time, arms exports represented one way to generate foreign exchange. Moreover, indigenous arms industries facilitated technological development and decreased political dependence on external suppliers, especially the United States.

The conclusion of the Iran-Iraq War, combined with the collapse of the Soviet Union, greatly reduced global demand for conventional weapons. The feasible production of Argentina's medium tank and Brazil's main battle tank effectively ended with Operation Desert Storm because both units depended on export markets in the Middle East, which dried up immediately after that conflict.

The impulse to produce weapons in Latin America has generally been part of a strategic vision to achieve industrial development and lessen dependence on foreign suppliers of military products. Countries that developed arms industry early—Argentina, Chile, Brazil—still have the best capabilities to make and repair arms, but the entire region still imports its most sophisticated military hardware. In this market, the United States must compete with western Europe, Israel, and Russia.

See also *Arms Transfers to Latin America; Chile, U. S. Relations with; Inter-American Conference for the Maintenance of Continental Peace and Security, Rio de Janeiro, 1947*

. . . . JOHN R. BAWDEN

REFERENCES AND FURTHER READING

Baek, Kwang-il, Ronald D. McLaurin, and Chung-in Moon, eds. *The Dilemma of Third World Defense Industries: Supplier Control or Recipient Autonomy?* Boulder, CO: Westview, 1989.

Brzoska, Michael, and Thomas Ohlson, eds. *Arms Production in the Third World.* London: Taylor & Francis, 1986.

Le Roy, François. "Mirages over the Andes: Peru, France, the United States, and Military Jet Procurement in the 1960s." *Pacific Historical Review* 71, no. 2 (2002): 269–300.

Varas, Augusto. *Militarization and the International Arms Race in Latin America.* Boulder, CO: Westview, 1985.

Arms Transfers to Latin America

The United States has used arms transfers to Latin America to bolster its allies, gain favor with the region's political elite, to further its hemispheric policy objectives. Arms transfers take place via government-to-government agreements, the transfer of excess defense articles from U.S. surplus inventories, commercial sales of military and dual-use items, clandestine operations, or through the black market. Arms transfers can be directed toward either governments or nonstate actors. Not all arms flowing to Latin America from the United States, however, has been sanctioned by the U.S. government—guerrillas, criminal gangs, and narcotraffickers have relied at least partly on the U.S. market to arm themselves.

SCOPE OF ARMS TRANSFERS

Tracking the totality of arms transfers, however, is difficult. Congress, by law, is notified when the Department of Defense proposes government-to-government foreign military sales of major defense items above a certain threshold, but many military items fall below this threshold. Commercial and black market sales of arms are even more difficult to monitor.

As a percentage of the total global arms trade, transfers to Latin America have been historically small when measured in dollar amounts. According to SIPRI Yearbook, in 2007 to 2008 the United States exported roughly $251 million worth of arms to Latin American countries. This equals just 1.7 percent of all U.S. arms exports during this period. Even during the height of U.S. interventionism in the region, the total percentage of U.S. exports was relatively low when compared to the global total. From 1981 to 1990, when the United States was supporting counterinsurgency operations in El Salvador, Guatemala, and Colombia, arms exports to Latin America totaled just under $3.5 billion or slightly more than 3.0 percent of total U.S. arms exports for that period. This low percentage, however, is a reflection of the fact that Latin American countries have generally received fewer advanced weapons system and have instead been a market for smaller arms intended for internal security.

Prior to World War II Latin American countries obtained most of their arms from Europe. This was due to historical ties between Latin American and European militaries as well as statutory restrictions in the United States on arms exports. Since the end of World War II the United States became the primary exporter of arms to Latin America. Throughout the Cold War and post-Cold War era, U.S. policy toward Latin America largely focused on bolstering "friendly" governments against internal threats and counternarcotic operations, thus the type of arms transferred to Latin America have generally reflected these policy goals. Consequently arms transfers have more often been in the form of smaller weapons systems that are more useful in internal counterinsurgency and counternarcotics operations. Thus, aircraft in Latin American militaries tend to be smaller and designed for precision ground attacks. For example, U.S.-made A-37 Dragonflies, small aircraft originally designed for counterinsurgency operations in Vietnam, are in the inventories of Chile, Colombia, Dominican Republic, Ecuador, El Salvador, Guatemala, Honduras, and Peru. Another U.S. aircraft designed for counterinsurgency, the AC-47T, was sent to Colombia and El Salvador during the height of their internal conflicts. Supporters of these arms transfers argue that they played an important part in keeping the hemisphere safe from Communist influence.

With the exception of Colombia, Latin American countries have received far lower levels of security assistance since the 2001 terrorist attacks, as Washington's attention has focused elsewhere. Throughout the 2000s military assistance has come mostly in the form of spare parts and training for systems already in a given country's arsenal. Weapons that have been transferred include Blackhawk UH-60 and Huey UH-1 helicopters; light weapons such as machine guns, rifles, pistols, grenades, and carbines; transport vehicles; and ammunition. In 2002 Chile ordered 10 new F-16 fighters, which began delivery in 2005.

CLANDESTINE AND BLACK MARKET SALES

The implications of U.S. arms transfers to Latin American countries have been the source of intense political debate and controversy, both in the United States and Latin America. During the Cold War arms transfers were used by the United States to bolster allied governments against possible Communist incursions into the region. However, increased documentation of human rights abuses and the turn toward military dictatorships within the region led the Carter presidency to impose a ban on the transfer of advanced U.S. weapons to Latin America. The ban was also largely driven by the concern that an arms race for advanced weaponry such as fighter aircrafts and armored fighting vehicles could have a potentially destabilizing effect. This ban was adhered to, with the exception of a sale of F-16 fighters to Venezuela in 1983, until President Clinton lifted it in 1997. In the 1980s the violation of a Congressional ban on arms transfers and other support for the Nicaraguan contras was a major part of the Iran-Contra scandal. Support given to governments fighting counterinsurgencies—such as El Salvador and Guatemala—was also criticized, as it was often unclear whether those arms were being used to target insurgents or were instead being used against legitimate members of civil society and nonviolent political opposition groups. Even countries without active insurgencies, but with questionable human rights records toward their own citizens, were recipients of U.S. arms transfers. For example, the United States exported $2.2 billion worth of arms to Brazil's military dictatorship during a period in which it is reported that 150,000 to 300,000 Brazilians disappeared.

THE LEGACY OF ARMS TRANSFERS

The legacy of internal conflict in Latin America has meant that arms transfers are not going solely to government forces. During the Cold War both the United States and the Soviet Union provided arms to insurgent groups, such as the contras in Nicaragua by the United States and the Farabundo Martí National Liberation Front (FMLN) in El Salvador by the Soviet Union. In addition to the clandestine transfer of arms by governments, Latin America has a large black market funneling small arms and light weapons to guerrillas, drug traffickers, street gangs, and other criminals. Many of these weapons originate from the United States. The total extent of this trade is unknown, but anecdotal evidence from available sources indicates that highly lethal weapons are widely available. In 1997, twenty-nine members of the Organization of American States signed the Inter-American Convention on Illicit Arms Trafficking, which commits its signatories to cooperate in combating illegal arms trafficking by strengthening export controls, sharing law enforcement information, requiring markings on firearms, and establishing a coordinated licensing system for exports and imports, among other provisions. The United States, which is a signatory, has not yet ratified the treaty, although President Obama has encouraged the Senate to do so.

The historical impact of arms transfers to Latin America, whether through legal or illegal means, has been costly. Armed actors, whether they be government forces, narcotraffickers, guerrillas, paramilitary forces, or gangs, have been responsible for considerable amounts of violence and disorder, including the forced displacement of large populations. With the end of the Cold War, the impact of these transfers has not completely dissipated. The armed insurgencies in Guatemala, El Salvador, and Nicaragua were peacefully negotiated; however, the region still suffers from the legacy of the weapons that flowed into the area during this period, with criminals having ready access to an ample supply of leftover stock. Human rights also remain an issue. Colombia, the largest recipient of U.S. arms transfers due to its cooperation in the "War on Drugs," has been highly criticized for its human rights record, with the U.S. State Department continuing to document instances of extrajudicial killings, forced disappearances, military collaboration with illegal armed groups, torture, and mistreatment of detainees. Nevertheless, the United States sees support for Colombian security forces as an important component of its foreign policy.

See also *Arms Industry in Latin America; Central American Wars, 1980s; Drug Trafficking; Guerrilla Warfare; Inter-American Conference for the Maintenance of Continental Peace and Security, Rio de Janeiro, 1947; Inter-American Defense Board (IADB); Military, Role in Politics; NSC-68 (U.S. National Security Council); Soviet Union, Latin American Policy; U.S. Military Assistance Program*

. . . . DAVID R. ANDERSEN

REFERENCES AND FURTHER READING

The Arms Sales Monitoring Project at Federation of American Scientists, www.fas.org/programs/ssp/asmp/index.html.

Betts, Richard K. "The Tragicomedy of Arms Trade Control." *International Security* 5, no. 1 (1980): 80–110.

Hartung, William D., and Frida Berrigan. "U.S. Weapons at War 2008," 2008, www.newamerica.net/publications/policy/u_s_weapons_war_2008_0.

Klare, Michael T., and David R. Andersen. *A Scourge of Guns: The Diffusion of Small Arms and Light Weapons in Latin America.* Washington, DC: Federation of American Scientists, 1996.

Stockholm International Peace Research Institute. *SIPRI Yearbook 2009: Armaments, Disarmament and International Security.* Oxford, UK: Oxford University Press, 2009.

Asia-Pacific Economic Cooperation (APEC)

The Asia-Pacific Economic Cooperation (APEC) forum, established in 1989, now has a membership of twenty-one "member economies," the majority of which border on the Pacific Ocean. It was set up at the end of the Cold War primarily to strengthen the linkages between the economies of

East Asia, Australia, Canada, and the United States. Mexico became the first Latin American member in 1993.

GENESIS AND MISSION

From the outset APEC was represented as an exercise in open regionalism, in contrast to the preferential trading practices that characterize the North American Free Trade Agreement (NAFTA) finalized in 1994 between Mexico, the United States, and Canada. Unlike many other regional economic or political organizations, the boundaries of APEC are particularly, even deliberately, elusive. Latin American governments have joined or sought to join, in part because trade and investment flows in Latin America have shifted over the past two decades toward other parts of the world besides the United States, especially Asia.

The founding members of APEC in 1989 were Australia, Brunei, Canada, Indonesia, Japan, Malaysia, New Zealand, the Philippines, Singapore, South Korea, Thailand, and the United States. China, Hong Kong, and Taiwan joined in 1991. The official term "member economy" was crucial to the complicated politics of these three members. Hong Kong became a Special Administrative Region (SAR) within the People's Republic of China in 1999 but has retained its position as a member economy of APEC.

Mexico and Papua New Guinea joined in 1993, followed by Chile in 1994, inclusion signaling the expansion of APEC into Latin America. At the same time as Latin American interest grew, APEC also expanded northwestward and southwestward. For example, while Peru became a member economy in 1998, so did Russia and Vietnam. The Indian government is currently seeking membership of APEC. Other current aspirants include Laos, Mongolia, and Pakistan, as well as Guam, Colombia, and Ecuador. There have been no members added in a decade, and some members are concerned that the larger potential entrants, especially India, could shift the center of gravity of the organization to Asia and away from the Asia-Pacific (however defined). In this context APEC would be carried even further away from its linkages to Latin America.

Latin American interest in APEC is tied to growing trade and financial connections across the Pacific. APEC also makes limited claims on member economies, in comparison to NAFTA for example. Since its establishment, APEC has clarified its aim as purely economic openness, not to be like the European Union (EU) in broader political terms that may threaten national sovereignty. APEC was viewed from the outset as a loose organization of "like minded economies" seeking to remove "barriers to economic exchange among members in the interest of all" (Bergsten 1994, 176), according to C. Fred Bergsten, former chair of the Eminent Persons Group (EPG), who facilitated the establishment of APEC. He also emphasized that APEC was eventually to serve as a "force for world-wide liberalization" (Bergsten 1994, 176).

EARLY MEETINGS

Despite the global agenda, the first APEC meetings (Seattle, late 1993, and Bogor, Indonesia, November 1994) attended by the official heads of the member governments—including Mexico and Chile—were concerned with trade liberalization within APEC. On the final day of the Bogor meeting, the leaders agreed in principle to the almost complete elimination of tariff barriers and obstacles to capital flows within the APEC region by the year 2020 for developing economies and 2010 for developed economies.

Nevertheless, the consensual character of agreements made at APEC meetings pointed to the organization's weak institutionalization. By the time of the fourth annual meeting in Vancouver in November 1997, the Asian financial crisis presented APEC leaders with a serious problem; in fact, in the view of some observers, APEC had become virtually irrelevant. In particular, the prominent role the International Monetary Fund (IMF) began to play in the management of the Asian financial crisis provided the United States (ambivalent about APEC from the outset) with the opportunity to encourage economic liberalization and deregulation in Asia, something that had occurred earlier in much of Latin America, particularly in the wake of the 1982 debt crisis. The IMF's intervention in Thailand, Indonesia, and South Korea directly challenged the nascent multilateral and consensual approach to regional economic issues embodied by APEC.

Still, since 1993, the annual meetings have all been attended by the heads of government, except for Taiwan (Chinese Taipei). APEC's deputy executive director is always an official drawn from the "member economy" that is in line to sponsor the rotating annual meeting (see Table 1).

RECENT ACTIVITY

In symbolic terms at least, the Latin American members had begun to make their presence felt in APEC by the first decade of the twenty-first century, including hosting three meetings. The growing Latin American presence also coincided with a rejuvenation of APEC in the wake of the 1997 Asian financial crisis. In 2001 the leaders laid the groundwork for a new set of trade negotiations and agreed to support trade capacity-building assistance efforts that facilitated the launching of the Doha Development Agenda at the end of 2001. They also signed off on the Shanghai Accord sponsored by the United States, which reinforced the need to further open markets and engage in capacity building and structural reform. They also included a commitment to implement APEC transparency standards, reduce the cost of trade transactions by five percent over five years in the Asia-Pacific, and strengthen trade liberalization in relation to goods and services and information technology. At the 2007 meeting the government leaders agreed to aspire to the goal of reducing energy use in economic development by 25 percent; however, the specifics of this commitment, like much about APEC, were left open. The annual meeting in mid-November 2009 in Singapore, followed a year later by the 2010 meeting in Yokohama, Japan, produced upbeat declarations and the reiteration and fine tuning of APEC's overall goal. In concrete terms the main item of note was the 10 percent drop in tariff barriers across the APEC region from the end of the 1990s to the present.

TABLE 1: ANNUAL MEETINGS OF THE ASIA-PACIFIC ECONOMIC COOPERATION

YEAR	HOST CITY, COUNTRY	YEAR	HOST CITY, COUNTRY
1993	Seattle, United States	2004	Santiago, Chile
1994	Bogor, Indonesia	2005	Busan, South Korea
1995	Osaka, Japan	2006	Hanoi, Vietnam
1996	Manila, the Philippines	2007	Sydney, Australia
1997	Vancouver, Canada	2008	Lima, Peru
1998	Kuala Lumpur, Malaysia	2009	Singapore, Singapore
1999	Auckland, New Zealand	2010	Yokohama, Japan
2000	Brunei Darussalem, Brunei	2011	Honolulu, United States
2001	Shanghai, China	2012 (planned)	Vladivostok, Russia
2002	Los Cabos, Baja California Sur, Mexico	2013 (planned)	Manado/Bali, Indonesia
2003	Bangkok, Thailand		

Sources: Asia-Pacific Economic Cooperation, "About APEC: History," 2011, www.apec.org/About-Us/About-APEC/History.aspx; APEC USA 2011 Hawaii Host Committee, www.apec2011hawaii.com/; Asia-Pacific Economic Cooperation Vladivostok–2012, http://vladivostok2012.com/; Asia-Pacific Economic Cooperation, "2008 Leaders' Declaration," 2008, www.apec.org/Meeting-Papers/Leaders-Declarations/2008/2008_aelm.aspx.

At this juncture it is unclear what the future holds for APEC. In fact, one trend, as already mentioned, is for it to move toward a more Asia-centered organization. Compared to NAFTA or other regional economic organizations in Latin America, not to mention the efforts to create a Free Trade Area of the Americas (FTAA), the future role of APEC in Latin America is unclear. On the one hand it is gaining Latin American members, but on the other hand, its possible expansion in other directions as well highlights its relative lack of a coherent vision beyond the founding notion of open regionalism.

In relation to free trade, APEC may be of secondary though continuing importance to the U.S. pursuit of a growing number of bilateral free-trade agreements (FTAs), many of them with countries in Latin America (Chile, El Salvador, Nicaragua, Honduras, Guatemala, the Dominican Republic, and Costa Rica, with Peru and Colombia pending), along with NAFTA. Meanwhile, there is a distinct lack of momentum for the creation of the FTAA, which would include upward of thirty-four countries. While FTAA has its supporters, it has languished in comparison to the bilateral FTAs and even in comparison to APEC.

See also *Central American-Dominican Republic Free Trade Agreement, 2004 (CAFTA-DR); North American Free Trade Agreement (NAFTA), 1992*

. . . . MARK T. BERGER

REFERENCES AND FURTHER READING

Berger, Mark T. *The Battle For Asia: from Decolonization to Globalization.* London: RoutledgeCurzon, 2004.

Berger, Mark T., and Mark Beeson. "APEC, ASEAN+3 and American Power: The Limits of the New Regionalism in the Asia-Pacific." In *The Political Economy of Regions and Regionalisms,* edited by Morten Bøås, Marianne H. Marchand, and Timothy M. Shaw, 58–72. Basingstoke, UK: Palgrave Macmillan, 2004.

Bergsten, Fred C. "APEC and the World Economy: A Force for Worldwide Liberalization." *Foreign Affairs* 73, no. 3 (1994): 176.

Nishijima, Shoji, and Peter H. Smith, eds. *Cooperation or Rivalry? Regional Integration in the Americas and the Pacific Rim.* Boulder, CO: Westview, 1996.

Ravenhill, John. *APEC and the Construction of Pacific Rim Regionalism.* Cambridge, UK: Cambridge University Press, 2001.

Roett, Riordan, and Guadalupe Paz, eds. *China's Expansion into the Western Hemisphere: Implications for Latin America and the United States.* Washington, DC: Brookings, 2008.

Aspinwall, William H.

William Henry Aspinwall (1807–1875) was a businessman remembered primarily for his role in establishing steamship navigation between Panama and U.S. ports on the Pacific Ocean and in construction of a railroad across the isthmus. Born in New York City, Aspinwall was the posthumous son of a merchant. As a youth he became a clerk in a firm headed by his maternal uncles, Gardiner Greene Howland and Samuel Shaw Howland, who were engaged in trade with Mexico and Europe. In 1832 he became a partner in the firm, and in 1837 the Howland brothers turned over the business to Aspinwall and his cousin William Edgar Howland.

The new firm prospered as a major export-import house with increased business in Latin America and was known for its clipper ships, such as the *Sea Witch,* which became famous itself for sailing from China to New York in the record time of seventy-four days in 1849. By the late 1840s, however, Aspinwall had become interested in improved communications with the Pacific ports of the United States. To this end, in November 1847 he reached an agreement with Secretary of the Navy John Y. Mason to provide mail service between Panama and Oregon (and later California as well). In 1848 the Pacific Mail Steamship Company was incorporated in New York, and Aspinwall was named president of the new enterprise. Three steamers—the *California,* the *Oregon,* and the *Panama*—were soon plying Pacific waters from Panama to U.S. ports to the north. In 1856 Aspinwall resigned as president of Pacific Mail.

During this period Aspinwall had also been contemplating construction of a railroad across Panama. While ships regularly brought passengers and cargo from eastern U.S. ports to the Atlantic coast of Panama, and Pacific Mail moved them north, the journey across the isthmus was time-consuming and difficult. In 1849 Aspinwall became a founder of the Panama Railroad Company, incorporated in New York that year. The following year a contract was signed with the Colombian government authorizing construction of the railroad. Construction began in 1850 and was completed in 1855.

In 1852 the settlement built at the Atlantic terminus of the railroad was named Aspinwall, supposedly at the urging of Victoriano de Diego Paredes, the Colombian foreign relations secretary who had signed the 1850 contract. In reality, it was railroad cofounder John Lloyd Stephens who suggested the name to Paredes. The Colombian government soon rejected the name, calling the town Colón instead. U.S. citizens persisted in using Aspinwall to designate the town until the late nineteenth century, but Colón eventually prevailed.

A strong Unionist during the U.S. Civil War, Aspinwall took part, with John M. Forbes, in a secret mission to England in the spring of 1863 to try to prevent the Confederacy from acquiring ironclads being built there that might be used for military purposes. The mission failed, but Aspinwall and Forbes were credited with improving Northern espionage in England and helping to sway public opinion in favor of the Union.

See also *Panama Railroad*

. . . . HELEN DELPAR

REFERENCES AND FURTHER READING

Kemble, John H. *The Panama Route, 1848–1869*. Berkeley: University of California Press, 1943.

Maynard, Douglas H. "The Forbes-Aspinwall Mission." *Mississippi Valley Historical Review* 45 (June 1958): 67–89.

McGuinness, Aims. *Paths of Empire: Panama and the California Gold Rush*. Ithaca, NY: Cornell University Press, 2008.

Association of Caribbean States (ACS)

The Association of Caribbean States (ACS), established in Cartagena, Colombia, on July 24, 1994, to promote social, political, and economic cooperation among the Caribbean nations, was a reaction to the North American Free Trade Agreement (NAFTA) between the United States, Canada, and Mexico, which went into effect on January 1, 1994. More generally, the ACS is a response to the challenges and opportunities presented by the globalization of the international economy and the liberalization of trade relations in the western hemisphere, and the organization is representative of the more assertive role that Caribbean states have attempted to play in the global economy in the post-Cold War period.

MEMBERSHIP

Notwithstanding the linguistic, ethnic, and political heterogeneity of the Caribbean, it has been viewed by scholars as a distinctive region within the western hemisphere since the advent of the Cold War. The United States, especially, defined the region geographically, in terms of national security interests, rather than culturally. Surprisingly, once the Cold War ended, Caribbean states have emphasized their mutual uniqueness, both at the regional and international level, and they have attempted to address local concerns through collective action based on geographic rather than cultural unity. In October 1992, at a special meeting of the Caribbean Community (CARICOM) in Trinidad and Tobago, representatives from Colombia, Cuba, the Dominican Republic, and Venezuela were invited to attend as observers. Plans were laid for the foundation of the ACS in Colombia in 1994.

The twenty-five member states in 2010 are Antigua and Barbuda; the Bahamas; Barbados; Belize; Colombia; Costa Rica; Cuba; Dominica; the Dominican Republic; El Salvador; Grenada; Guatemala; Guyana; Haiti; Honduras; Jamaica; Mexico; Nicaragua; Panama; St. Kitts and Nevis; St. Lucia; St. Vincent and the Grenadines; Suriname; Trinidad and Tobago; and Venezuela. Aruba, France (on behalf of French Guiana, Guadeloupe, and Martinique), the Netherlands Antilles, and Turks and Caicos are the four associate member states. Argentina, Brazil, Canada, Chile, Ecuador, Egypt, Finland, India, Italy, the Netherlands, South Korea, Morocco, Peru, Russia, Spain, Turkey, Ukrain, and the United Kingdom have observer status. The ACS headquarters is located in Port of Spain, Trinidad and Tobago. Dominican scholar Rubén Silié Valdez was the secretary general of the association from 2004 to 2008, when Guatemalan diplomat Luis Fernando Andrade Falla was elected to the post. Although the ministerial council meets annually, there have been four summits—Trinidad and Tobago (1995), the Dominican Republic (1999), Venezuela (2001), and Panama (2004)—attended by heads of state.

OPERATIONS

The ACS seeks to strengthen regional cooperation in cultural, economic, political, scientific, social, and technological relations. The members hope to build upon their geographic proximity and common historical experiences to create cultural, economic, and social development for the 250 million people they represent. The ACS strives to facilitate economic development in the region, with the ultimate goal of making member state economies more competitive in the international market. In addition to economic development, the ACS also seeks to promote social development and environmental protection. Funding for ACS programs and workshops comes from a variety of local and international donors as well as the member states.

Four special committees emphasize trade, transportation, tourism, and natural disasters. The ACS encourages economic cooperation to expand economic activities, especially trade and investment, in the Caribbean Basin. Efforts are made to enable small economies to penetrate the markets of larger trading partners, such as the United States and the European Union. ACS members have also tried to present a common agenda when dealing with the World Trade Organization (WTO). Given the importance of tourism to many Caribbean economies, the ACS seeks to increase the number of flights to the Caribbean. The ACS also encourages more direct air linkages between the member states, which has the potential to increase regional tourism and seeks the formation of language training classes to provide local workers with the skills necessary to handle the increased number of foreign tourists.

Notwithstanding the emphasis on increased tourism, the ACS realizes the potential threat to the natural environment. Given the importance of the Caribbean Sea to the future growth of tourism in the region, the member states have a vested interest in limiting pollution and monitoring waste disposal. In addition to supporting efforts to limit the transport of illegal drugs, in the aftermath of the tragic September 11, 2001, events, the ACS has focused on increasing security for air and sea travelers. The ACS has encouraged the cooperation of disaster planning and relief agencies in the Greater Caribbean, an area that has been subjected to hurricanes, earthquakes, and volcanic eruptions. It is especially concerned with the development of early warning systems that could limit the loss of life during natural disasters. A problem of global concern, the AIDS epidemic, is also of concern to the ACS. Health care and educational prevention programs have been sponsored by the ACS.

ASSESSMENT

Much to the chagrin of the U.S. government, which continues to impose an economic blockade on Cuba, Cuban membership in the ACS has provided Cuba with opportunities for economic growth and development. As a result, Cuban trade in the Caribbean has increased dramatically since the mid-1990s. Regardless, U.S. administrations, since the founding of the ACS, have expressed verbal support for addressing the special concerns of the small island states in the Caribbean. The tangible benefits of the ACS in the international economic arena, however, are debatable. ACS concerns, such as unifying responses to natural disasters, ending shipments of nuclear materials through the Panama Canal, and ending the U.S. economic embargo of Cuba, have been sidestepped by successive U.S. administrations. Scholars, therefore, are divided in their evaluation of the effectiveness of the ACS.

See also *Belize, U.S. Relations with; Caribbean Community Common Market (CARICOM); Colombia, U.S. Relations with; Costa Rica, U.S. Relations with; Cuba, U.S. Relations with; Dominican Republic, U.S. Relations with; El Salvador, U.S. Relations with; Guatemala, U.S. Relations with; Guyana, U.S. Relations with; Haiti, U.S. Relations with; Honduras, U.S. Relations with; Mexico, U.S. Relations with; Nicaragua, U.S. Relations with; North American Free Trade Agreement (NAFTA), 1992; Panama, U.S. Relations with; Suriname, U.S. Relations with; Venezuela, U.S. Relations with*

MICHAEL R. HALL

REFERENCES AND FURTHER READING

Girvan, Norman. *Cooperation in the Greater Caribbean: The Role of the Association of Caribbean States.* Kingston, Jamaica: Ian Randle, 2006.

Fischer, Thomas. *The United States, the European Union, and the "Globalization" of World Trade: Allies or Adversaries?* Westport, CT: Quorum Books, 2000.

Serbin, Andrés. *Sunset over the Islands: The Caribbean in the Age of Global and Regional Challenges.* New York: Palgrave MacMillan, 1999.

Atkins, Edwin F.

Edwin F. Atkins (1850–1926) was the son of Boston merchant Elisha Atkins, who began importing sugar from the Cuban port of Cienfuegos in 1838. The elder Atkins groomed his son for the sugar trade, and in the late 1860s and 1870s, young Edwin visited Cuba often, learning Spanish and establishing close ties to local officials and elites. These visits coincided with key changes in Cuba, including the Ten Years' War: an interracial insurgency that fought to end slavery and Spanish rule. Although put down in 1878, the rebellion accelerated the emancipation of Afro-Cubans and the financial collapse of the planter class.

This economic crisis spurred Edwin Atkins to move directly into sugar production. In 1884 he assumed ownership of a foreclosed estate named Soledad, near the port of Cienfuegos. From the beginning his efforts to revitalize the plantation were linked to changes in U.S. foreign policy. The same year Atkins obtained Soledad, the United States and Spain negotiated a commercial treaty that sparked a decade-long sugar boom in Cuba. With his vast lands, modernized sugar mill, and commercial ties to the Northeast, Atkins became one of the most influential businessmen in Cuba. Yet this rapid rise was built in part on racial domination. By the 1890s the managers of Atkins's estates had developed a system of labor control that aimed to divide and intimidate a workforce that consisted of Afro-Cuban ex-slaves, Spanish laborers, and Chinese immigrants.

By the mid-1890s Atkins faced a series of crises. In 1894 Washington hiked its tariffs on Spanish goods, bringing Cuba's sugar boom to a halt. The ensuing economic upheaval opened the way for Cuban nationalists to renew their war against Spain. As in the earlier conflict, Spanish officials warned that independence would lead to racial violence akin to that of the Haitian Revolution. Atkins shared these fears and drew attention to the racial characteristics of the rebels. After insurgents burned some of his cane fields in late 1895, he announced that "the damage was caused by colored men" (Atkins Family Papers). As the rebellion grew so did Atkins's fears. If Spain proved unable to halt the insurgency, he worried, Cuban society would collapse into racial chaos. As he warned Secretary of State Richard Olney in May 1896, although Cuban moderates favored autonomy from Spain and conservatives hoped for U.S. annexation, "the insurgent side, the negro element . . . are not inclined to settle the matter short of absolute independence" (Atkins 1926/1980, 235–236). The danger in his mind was that Spanish defeat, or ill-conceived U.S. intervention, might leave the black rebels in charge of an independent Cuba.

As a result, by 1897 he welcomed the rising prowar sentiment among Americans and hoped President William McKinley would act decisively to restore order and even annex Cuba. In January 1898 Atkins assured the U.S. consul in Havana that "the desire for annexation extends to all classes" (Atkins Family Papers). But he continued to warn that if Washington intervened, "it would have to hold the Island, or abandon it to a race war worse than the present one" (Atkins Family Papers). Atkins's anxieties only grew as the United States moved toward war with Spain. Not only was Washington informally allied to the predominantly black insurgents, but the passage of the Teller Amendment seemed to preclude American control over Cuba. During the ensuing U.S. occupation of the island, Atkins continued to lobby U.S. officials, and although he failed to secure annexation, he helped shape the commercial and labor policies of occupation authorities such as General Leonard Wood. When U.S. troops departed Cuba in 1902, Atkins declared himself largely satisfied with the imperial protectorate put in place by the Platt Amendment.

Over the following decade Atkins continued to wield influence over Cuban politics and U.S. policymakers. During a second U.S. occupation, from 1906 to 1909, he again worked with American officials, and in the summer of 1912 he helped prompt another brief intervention in response to fears of an Afro-Cuban rebellion. In a cable to now-Army Chief of Staff Leonard Wood in June 1912, he warned, "Only prompt action can prevent serious trouble. You know the Cuban negro quite as well as I do" (Atkins Family Papers). Soon after, marines arrived to guard Soledad. By the 1910s Atkins was no longer the preeminent American sugar planter in Cuba, for corporations such as the United Fruit Company had developed massive sugar enclaves in eastern Cuba, but he remained a formidable figure in the Cuban sugar industry until his death in 1926, and many of his holdings remained in his family until they were nationalized by the regime of Fidel Castro.

See also *Cuba, U.S. Relations with; Sugar, U.S. Policy; Ten Years' War, 1868–1878 (Cuba)*

. . . . JASON M. COLBY

REFERENCES AND FURTHER READING

Atkins, Edwin F. *Sixty Years in Cuba.* New York: Arno Press, 1980. (Originally published 1926)

Atkins Family Papers. Massachusetts Historical Society, E. F. Atkins to G. S. Turner, January 25, 1898. Vol. 2/18, letterbook 7.

Ayala, César A. American Sugar Kingdom: The Plantation Economy of the Spanish Caribbean. Chapel Hill: University of North Carolina Press, 1999.

Scott, Rebecca J. *Degrees of Freedom: Louisiana and Cuba after Slavery.* Cambridge: Ma: Harvard University Press, 2005.

Atlantic Community Development Group for Latin America

The political changes in Cuba in the late 1950s and early 1960s and Fidel Castro's alliance with the Soviet Union increased the fears of the spread of communism in other Latin American countries, the backyard of the United States. This new perceived threat shifted priorities for the U. S. government and western Europe toward finding viable policies to help Latin American countries prosper under capitalist economies and, by the same token, keep the Soviet Union at bay. For example, in 1961 President John F. Kennedy's administration launched the Alliance for Progress, a political initiative to foster aid and economic collaboration for Latin American countries and thereby protect U. S. interests from Soviet influence.

At the same time the private sector made its own effort to reach out to Latin American countries. A group of banks and other private organizations from the United States, western Europe, Japan, and Latin America founded, in the early 1960s, the Atlantic Community Development Group for Latin America (ADELA). By offering grants to private companies in "developed countries" that started joint ventures with companies in Latin American countries, ADELA sought to spur economic development by fostering technology transfers and the acquisition of know-how by Latin American companies. ADELA was formed in Luxembourg by 235 large banks and industrial companies. ADELA's first project was financed by the International Finance Corporation (IFC) in 1964, which joined ADELA in funding a new Colombian company, *Forjas de Colombia S.A.*, to begin producing steel in Colombia. Many others followed.

The participation of privately funded organizations like ADELA became very popular, and ADELA sought political and economic support from the United States and other developed countries. The popularity of this and similar initiatives was based on the perceived ability of the private sector in developed countries to provide support and know-how to developing countries' entrepreneurs in order to foster a strong and successful private sector throughout Latin America. By 1969, with a total capital of $187.3 million (one third in the hands of U.S. corporations), ADELA had participation in more than one hundred companies in Latin America. ADELA was successful in the 1960s in providing private support to Latin America and increased its working capital by 100 percent in the period from 1964 to 1969.

See also *Dependency Theory and Latin America; Import Substitution Industrialization (ISI)*

. . . . ANDRÉS GALLO

REFERENCES AND FURTHER READING

Corrado, Emilio. "Economic Development Through Private Enterprise." *Foreign Affairs* (June 1963): 708.

International Organization. *International Bank for Reconstruction and Development,* 18, no. 4 (Autumn 1964): 846–854.

Lowenthal, Abraham. Alliance Rhetoric versus Latin American reality." *Foreign Affairs* (April 1970): 494.

Martins, Luciano. "The Politics of U.S. Multinational Corporations in Latin America." In *Latin America and the United States: The Changing Political Realities,* edited by Julio Cotler and Richard Fagen. Stanford, CA: Stanford University Press, 1974.

Atocha, Alexander

A Spaniard by birth who naturalized as a citizen of the United States, Alexander J. Atocha served as a representative of Mexican power broker and intermittent president Antonio López de Santa Anna. Atocha played a significant and largely secret role in the Mexican-American War (1846–1848).

Hostilities between the United States and Mexico intensified during the middle decades of the nineteenth century. In

1836 the Republic of Texas seceded from Mexico and quickly attained recognition from the United States, France, and Belgium. When Texas and the United States agreed to annexation in 1845, Mexico challenged the claim and skirmishes broke out along disputed borders. The United States declared war against Mexico in May 1846. During the first year of the conflict, both sides engaged in a series of mostly secret negotiations. Alexander Atocha, who had first represented Santa Anna in talks with U.S. President James K. Polk and Secretary of State James Buchanan in February 1846, carried confidential messages in January 1847 from Santa Anna to Washington, D.C. The messages indicated that Santa Anna was willing to endorse the sale of California to the United States and the Rio Grande border between Texas and Mexico. Polk sent Atocha back to the former Mexican president with responses to particular provisions and an offer to continue secret negotiations with Santa Anna. At the same time Polk was pursuing another secret initiative. He had authorized a secret mission led by Moses Beach to Mexico City with directions to meet with and foment dissension among Catholic clerics. Polk privately wished that the Beach mission would result in a peace treaty. Meanwhile, General Winfield Scott was directing U.S. military troops as they occupied the port of Veracruz with intent to march toward Mexico City.

In an interesting twist, Mexican President Valentín Gómez Farías sought to discredit his political rival Santa Anna and made public Beach's plan to stir Catholic opposition, but he made it appear that it was Atocha's initiative. This meant that, for all appearances, Santa Anna was now associated with a conspiracy between the U.S. government and the Roman Catholic Church to bring an end to the war. Nonetheless, Santa Anna quickly returned to the presidency, overthrowing the Gómez Farías regime and quickly gaining official U.S. recognition. Atocha had succeeded in promoting Santa Anna as a legitimate power broker to the U.S. government.

Alexander Atocha had his own interests at stake in the negotiations, as he held significant financial claims against the Mexican government. A peace treaty, he thought, would facilitate pursuit of his claims, especially if the United States were to back such claims. Indeed, the U.S. Court of Claims ultimately ruled in favor of Atocha in 1873, with an award of the substantial sum of $207,852.60 for losses sustained as a result of his expulsion from Mexico in 1845. The ruling referenced a special act of relief for Atocha passed by the U.S. Congress in February 1865. By the time of the ruling, however, Atocha had died, and the award was distributed to the administratrix of his estate, Eliza J. Atocha.

See also *Beach, Moses Yale; Buchanan, James; Mexican-American War, 1846–1848; Polk, James K.; Santa Anna, Antonio López de; Scott, Winfield*

GREGORY S. CRIDER

SELECTED WORKS

United States Supreme Court, 84 U.S. 439, Ex parte Atocha.

REFERENCES AND FURTHER READING

Griswold del Castillo, Richard. *The Treaty of Guadalupe Hidalgo: A Legacy of Conflict.* Norman: University of Oklahoma Press, 1992.

Leonard, Thomas M. *James K. Polk: A Clear and Unquestionable Destiny.* Lanham, MD: Rowman and Littlefield, 2001.

Austin, Moses

As the first *empresario* to obtain permission to bring American settlers into Spanish Texas, Moses Austin (1761–1821) played an important role in the history of Texas even though he died before being able to carry out his plans. Austin was born in Durham, Connecticut, on October 4, 1761. As a young man, he was involved in business ventures in Philadelphia and in Richmond, Virginia. In the 1790s Moses and his brother Stephen gained control of rich lead deposits in Wythe County, Virginia. Moses Austin is often cited as a major leader in developing the American lead mining industry. Hearing of rich lead deposits in Missouri, which at that time was still Spanish territory, Austin visited there in 1796 and moved to Missouri in 1798, settling near the French settlement of Ste. Genevieve. He founded the town of Potosi, Missouri, near his mines. The mining venture prospered for several years, but uncertainties about business in the region created by the U.S. purchase of the Louisiana Territory from France, followed a few years later by the economic disruptions of the War of 1812, created financial troubles for Austin. He had been considering possible business ventures in Spanish Mexico since roughly 1813, perhaps at first thinking primarily of getting involved in the Santa Fe trade. After the Adams-Onís Treaty seemed to confirm Spanish control of Texas in 1819, Austin began considering the possibility of taking American settlers into Texas.

In December 1820 Austin went to Texas and met with the provincial governor, Antonio Mária Martínez, at San Antonio de Bexár. Spanish officials were concerned about illegal American settlement in Mexico and the filibustering expeditions led by American adventurers who sought to bring Texas under American control. It is estimated there were already three thousand Americans illegally living in east Texas. So Austin was at first rebuffed, and in fact Martínez told him to leave Texas and not to return. Before he left San Antonio, however, Austin encountered the Baron de Bastrop, whom he had met years earlier in New Orleans. Bastrop offered to speak to the governor on his behalf, and in January 1821 Austin was given official permission to bring three hundred American Catholic families into Texas and a large grant of land along the Brazos River for this purpose. Spanish officials hoped that these legally admitted settlers might help to provide a barrier to prevent further illegal U.S. entry into Texas and also help protect the area from Indian attacks. Martínez also hoped that these settlers might help to develop the region, as few Mexican citizens were willing to settle in Texas. There were only about 3,500 Mexicans living in Texas at this time.

Moses Austin contracted pneumonia on his way home from Texas and died within a few months. He told his wife of his wish that his son Stephen F. Austin go ahead with the colonization plan, which Stephen did, becoming heralded as one of the "founding fathers" of the American settlements in Texas. Moses Austin died at his daughter's home in Missouri on June 10, 1821.

See also *Austin, Stephen F.; Mexico, U.S. Relations with; Texas, U.S. Annexation of*

. . . . MARK S. JOY

REFERENCES AND FURTHER READING

Cantrell, Greg. *Stephen F. Austin: Empresario of Texas.* New Haven, CT: Yale University Press, 1999.

Gracy, David B. II. *Moses Austin: His Life.* San Antonio, TX: Trinity University Press, 1987.

Austin, Stephen F.

Stephen F. Austin (1793–1836) was born in 1793 in southeastern Virginia, where his family was involved in lead mining. In 1798 the family moved to southeastern Missouri to develop the rich lead deposits found there. Missouri was still under Spanish rule at this time, but it came under U.S. control with the Louisiana Purchase in 1803. After spending two years at Transylvania University in Kentucky, Austin joined his father in lead mining and other business ventures in Missouri. In 1813, at age 21, he was elected to the territorial legislature of Missouri. He served in this body until 1819, when he moved to Arkansas to pursue family business interests there. However, he stayed only briefly in Arkansas, and by December 1820 he had moved to New Orleans to study law.

AUSTIN LEADS THE *EMPRESARIOS* INTO TEXAS

In early 1821 Stephen's father, Moses Austin, had received permission to bring three hundred American Catholic families into Spanish Texas. Moses Austin died before he could proceed, and by the time Stephen began to pursue the colonization plan, Mexico had rebelled against Spanish rule and become the independent Republic of Mexico.

Stephen Austin traveled to San Antonio de Bexár in the summer of 1821 to make arrangements to carry out his father's colonization plans. He received permission to proceed and began recruiting potential settlers. The first of these settlers arrived in Texas in December 1821. However, Austin was then informed that the provisional government in Mexico City had not approved the transfer of his father's grant to him. He then went to Mexico City and negotiated an arrangement whereby agents to recruit settlers, called *empresarios,* would be given sizeable land grants to encourage settlement. Austin eventually brought in these original three hundred families, who became known in Texas folklore as "The Old Three Hundred" and are often considered the beginning of Anglo-American settlement in Texas (although a number of Americans had already been living there illegally). Over the next several years the revolutionary struggles and instability within the government of Mexico caused these colonization arrangements to be amended, rescinded, and reinstated several times. In 1825 the state legislature of Coahuila and Texas passed a law with provisions similar to Austin's original *empresario* agreement. Under the terms of this state legislation, he later brought in nine hundred more American families.

Because the Mexican government was not ready to fully exercise jurisdiction and control over these settlements in Texas, Austin initially had much of the civil and military authority over his colony in his own hands. In November 1827 the constitution of the state of Coahuila and Texas went into effect, after which Austin did not exercise as many official government responsibilities. But he continued to have considerable influence on relations between the Mexican government and the American settlers in Texas, and he gave much attention to developing orderly procedures for making land grants and recording title to lands.

FROM TENSIONS TO INDEPENDENCE

By the 1830s the rapid growth of the American settlements in Texas was alarming the Mexican government. There was continual friction and mutual suspicion between the settlers and the Mexican authorities. The settlers feared that the government would become more restrictive; the government feared the settlers would try to become independent or make Texas a part of the United States. Austin often served as a middleman, attempting to calm these disputes. New laws passed by the Mexican federal government in April 1830 blocked further American settlement in Texas. These laws also cancelled the *empresario* contracts then in effect. When the American settlers began to grow restive under Mexican rule in the early 1830s, Austin often counseled restraint, arguing that their grievances could be worked out within the Mexican legal system.

Austin took part in several conventions of Texas residents where such grievances were aired. In 1833 a convention at San Felipe drafted a new constitution for a separate state of Texas, breaking it away from Coahuila. Although Austin had initially counseled against this move, he was chosen to take the constitution and a petition concerning it to Mexico City. He succeeded in getting the Mexican government to lift some of the provisions of the 1830 law that had barred further American immigration into Texas. However, he believed that Antonio López de Santa Anna, who was in control in Mexico at this time, would never agree to a separate state for Texas. So, believing he had accomplished all that he could, he started home to Texas. However, in January 1834 he was arrested in Saltillo on suspicion of trying to foment a rebellion in Texas and taken back to Mexico City. Although he was never formally charged or convicted of any crime, he was imprisoned until December 1834 and not allowed to leave Mexico until July 1835.

His imprisonment soured Austin on the chance of Texans being able to work out their problems under Mexican rule. While he was away from Texas, the Americans there had begun to press for independence, and Austin came to agree with this sentiment. When fighting began in October 1835, Austin was briefly put in command of the Texas volunteer forces. However, in November 1835 he was chosen as one of three commissioners to go to the United States to try to enlist aid and raise funds for the war effort. While many Americans were sympathetic to the cause of the Texans, and some individuals did go to Texas to fight, the U.S. government under Andrew Jackson was reluctant to intervene. Jackson feared that if his administration showed interest in annexation, the question of slavery in Texas would reignite the sectional debate within the United States.

CONCLUSION

After the war for Texas independence ended, Austin agreed to stand for election for the presidency of the Republic of Texas. However, in the election held in September 1836, he was defeated by Sam Houston, largely because of Houston's popularity due to his role in the war with Mexico. Austin did agree to serve under Houston as secretary of state. He was confirmed in this office by the Texas Senate in late October 1836, but he served only briefly before he died of pneumonia on December 27, 1836.

See also *Austin, Moses; Mexico, U.S. Relations with; Texas (Lone Star Republic), U.S. Relations with, 1836–1846*

. . . . MARK S. JOY

REFERENCES AND FURTHER READING

"Austin, Stephen Fuller." In *Handbook of Texas Online*, www.tshaonline.org/handbook/online/articles/fau14.

Barker, Eugene C. *The Life of Stephen F. Austin*. Nashville, TN: Cokesbury Press, 1925; reprint, New York: AMS Press, 1970.

Cantrell, Greg. *Stephen F. Austin: Empresario of Texas*. New Haven, CT: Yale University Press, 1999.

Siegel, Stanley. *A Political History of the Texas Republic, 1836–1845*. Austin: University of Texas Press, 1956.

Austral Plan, 1985 (Argentina)

The Austral Plan was a set of economic measures adopted by the administration of Argentine President Raúl Alfonsín on June 14, 1985. Its goal was to stabilize the Argentine economy, which was suffering from high inflation and deep recession in the wake of the transition to democracy and the outbreak of the international debt crisis in 1982. It consisted of three main elements. The government sharply reduced its outlays and increased taxes in order to eliminate the fiscal deficit and the necessity to use inflationary financing. It froze prices and wages by decree and ordered financial contracts to be de-indexed in order to break with the inflationary inertia. Finally, it replaced old and severely devalued peso notes with new austral notes at a rate of 1,000:1. The austral was pegged to the dollar at 0.80 australes per dollar.

The architects of the Austral Plan were a group of Argentine economists under the leadership of Juan Vital Sourrouille, Alfonsín's minister of economy since February 1985. They espoused a structuralist theory of inflation, which rejected the focus on monetary policy proposed by Chicago School economists. They argued that orthodox anti-inflationary programs failed to address the political and economic costs of reducing inflation, which had resulted in the breakdown of previous stabilization programs. A "heterodox shock" program like the Austral Plan, by contrast, would eliminate inflationary expectations instantaneously and make stabilization economically and politically sustainable. The International Monetary Fund (IMF), the Federal Reserve, and the U.S. Treasury disagreed with the economic theory behind the Austral Plan and were skeptical with respect to the plan's likelihood of success. However, the grave risks an Argentine default posed for international financial markets in the context of the debt crisis convinced the IMF and the U.S. government to support the measures.

The initial results of the Austral Plan fully vindicated the hopes of Sourrouille and his team. Inflation virtually disappeared overnight and the fiscal deficit fell sharply. The results also created confidence among important business sectors and the international financial community and laid the groundwork for a rapid but fleeting economic recovery during the second half of 1985. The Austral Plan was also a political success because it created a positive economic and social climate in time for the midterm congressional elections in November 1985.

Shortly after the elections, however, the Austral Plan began to fall apart in the face of opposition from inside and outside of government. Peronists, members of the ruling Unión Cívica Radical (UCR), and the restive military attacked the Austral Plan for depressing real wages and demanded large wage increases. At the same time, the Alfonsín administration failed to eliminate the fiscal deficit and had to resort to inflationary financing. Inflation, therefore, quickly picked up again. While the annualized rate of inflation was 26 percent in October 1985, it increased to over 170 percent in August 1986. The subsequent years witnessed desperate attempts to resurrect the early success of the Austral Plan with the help of a series of new plans including the Australito (little Austral) in February 1987 and the Primavera (Spring) Plan in mid-1988. However, all the subsequent plans failed to stabilize the economy even in the short term and contributed to Argentina sliding into hyperinflation in early 1989.

See also *Argentina, U.S. Relations with; Debt Crisis, Latin America, 1870s, 1930s, 1980s; Economic Commission for Latin America and the Caribbean (CEPAL); International Monetary Fund (IMF)*

. . . . KLAUS VEIGEL

REFERENCES AND FURTHER READING

Dell'Aquila, Marco and Luigi Manzetti. "Economic Stabilization in Argentina: The Austral Plan." *Journal of Latin American Studies* 20, no. 1 (1988): 1–26.

Dornbusch, Rudiger and Mario Henrique Simonsen, eds. *Inflation Stabilization with Incomes Policy Support: A Review of the Experience in Argentina, Brazil and Israel*. Cambridge, MA: MIT and National Bureau of Econ Research, 1987.

Machinea, José Luis. "Stabilization under Alfonsín." In *Argentina in the Crisis Years, 1983–1990: from Alfonsín to Menem*, edited by Colin M. Lewis and Nissa Torrents, 124–143. London: Institute of Latin American Studies, 1993.

Ávila Camacho, Manuel

Manuel Ávila Camacho was president of Mexico from 1940 to 1946. He oversaw Mexico's entry into World War II and worked to improve relations between Mexico and the United States after the tumultuous years of the previous administration. Manuel Ávila Camacho was the last of the revolutionary generals to hold the Mexican presidency. His administration is considered to be a move away from revolutionary policies and toward an institutionalization of the Revolutionary party.

Manuel Ávila Camacho was born in Tezuitlán, Mexico, on April 24, 1897. As a young man he attended school, but he joined the army in 1914 to fight with the revolutionary forces of Venustiano Carranza. He rose quickly through the leadership ranks and made important alliances, particularly with Lázaro Cárdenas, who became president in 1934 and ousted the strongman Plutarco Elías Calles, architect of six years of puppet presidents known as the Maximato. Ávila Camacho eventually became minister of national defense under President Cárdenas. Because of his loyalty to Cárdenas and an extensive network of political supporters, Ávila Camacho was chosen by Cárdenas to be the Revolutionary party's presidential nominee in 1940. He easily won the election and was sworn into office in December of that year.

Ávila Camacho faced several international crises immediately upon assuming the presidency. In 1938 Cárdenas had expropriated and nationalized Mexico's oil industry. Powerful private oil interests in the United States and Europe had protested the move. U.S. oil companies, in particular, put enormous pressure on the administration of President Franklin Roosevelt to take action against the Mexican government and they had led a boycott of Mexican oil, which nearly bankrupted Mexico. Throughout 1941 Ávila Camacho negotiated with U.S. diplomats, and on the eve of the Japanese attack on Pearl Harbor, the two governments finally reached an agreement on a settlement of the oil issue.

World War II was the other international crisis that dominated Ávila Camacho's presidency. After two Mexican oil tankers were attacked by German submarines in the Gulf of Mexico in May 1942, the Mexican president declared a state of war and formally joined forces with the allied powers. Ávila Camacho committed Mexican resources in the form of raw materials and agricultural products for wartime production to assist in the war effort. Goods from Mexico provided a steady supply of critical war materials. A labor agreement between the Ávila Camacho and Roosevelt administrations created the Bracero Program—a temporary work permit program that allowed Mexicans to work in industry and agriculture in the United States. The Bracero Program was aimed at wartime labor shortages in the United States, but the program was so popular that it continued until the 1960s.

Ávila Camacho wanted to see Mexico play a larger direct role in the war effort and in 1945 he sent an air squadron to fight in the liberation of the Philippines. Mexico's Squadron 201 was the nation's only direct military contribution in World War II, but the squadron fought bravely and made real contributions to the success of the Philippines campaign. Because of his enthusiastic cooperation during World War II, Ávila Camacho played a prominent role in the postwar peace process. He participated in the planning of the United Nations and in 1944 he was one of the original signatories of the organization's charter. In 1945 Ávila Camacho hosted the Inter-American Conference on the Problems of War and Peace in Mexico City, which provided the foundation for the later formation of the Organization of American States (OAS).

Manuel Ávila Camacho oversaw a number of changes in domestic policy and he often brought his foreign and domestic policies together under the rubric of national unity. In the early months of his administration, Ávila Camacho boldly claimed "soy creyente" (I am a believer) in an attempt to reach out to the conservative and ultra-Catholic segments of the population that had been alienated by earlier revolutionary policies. He created a new system of social security in an attempt to expand benefits to the labor class. Ávila Camacho targeted educational reform as part of the nation's patriotic duty during wartime, creating a program to combat illiteracy that was widely publicized but only moderately successful. Finally, in 1946 he reorganized the Mexican Revolutionary Party (PRM), which had dominated politics since its formation in 1929. The new organization incorporated business and industrial interests and took the name Institutional Revolutionary Party (PRI). The party controlled the Mexican presidency until 2000.

Manuel Ávila Camacho retired from public life after leaving the presidency in 1946. He died on October 13, 1955.

See also *Bracero Program; Cárdenas del Rio, Lázaro; Defense Sites Agreements, World War II; Good Neighbor Policy; Inter-American Conference on the Problems of War and Peace, Mexico City, 1945; Lombardo Toledano, Vicente; Marshall Plan and Latin America; Mexico, U.S. Relations with; Messersmith, George S.; Nazi Activities in Latin America, World War II; Third Meeting of Consultation of the Ministers of Foreign Affairs of the American Republics, Rio de Janeiro, 1942*

. . . . MONICA RANKIN

REFERENCES AND FURTHER READING

Krauze, Enrique. *Mexico: Biography of Power.* New York: Harper Collins, 1997.

Niblo, Stephen R. *Mexico in the 1940s: Modernity, Politics, and Corruption.* Wilmington, DE: SR Books, 1999.

Rankin, Monica. *México, la patria! Propaganda and Production during World War II.* Lincoln: University of Nebraska Press, 2009.

Bacon, Robert

Robert Bacon (1860–1919), 39th U.S. secretary of state, graduated from Harvard, traveled internationally, became a successful businessman in Boston, working for such companies as J. P. Morgan and Company from 1894 to 1903, and became involved in the formation of U.S. Steel in 1901. At Harvard Bacon met future U.S. President Theodore Roosevelt, and from that social connection and those that he would make in his years as a prominent U.S. businessman, Bacon developed networks that would aid him later in building and carrying out a diplomatic career in official service to the U.S. government.

From late 1905 to 1909 Bacon served as assistant U.S. secretary of state under Secretary of State Elihu Root, during the second presidential term of Theodore Roosevelt. While in this position, he also briefly served as acting secretary of state in 1906. In 1906, when a revolt in Cuba broke out under the presidency of Tomás Estrada Palma, Roosevelt invoked Article 3 of the Platt Amendment, sending Bacon to Cuba with a commission headed by U.S. Secretary of War William Taft. The mission resulted in an occupation of Cuba that lasted from late 1906 to 1909. In January of 1909 Roosevelt appointed Bacon as secretary of state for the remainder of Roosevelt's last presidential term. In this short time as Secretary of State, Bacon worked toward and was influential in securing Senate consent for the 1909 Root-Cortés Treaty. This agreement, signed between the United States, Panama, and Colombia, smoothed over tense relations with Colombia by allowing the country free use of the canal. While the agreement had been arranged under previous Secretary of State Elihu Root, Bacon was highly influential in getting the agreement passed in the United States. He also used his brief term as secretary of state to push for the improvement of natural resource conservation in the Americas, a vital aspect of President Roosevelt's agenda.

After leaving service as secretary of state, Bacon continued his diplomatic service to the end of his life. His successor as secretary of state, Philander C. Knox, appointed Bacon as an ambassador to France before World War I. Shortly thereafter, the Carnegie Endowment for International Peace sponsored Bacon to undertake a trip to South America. At the Endowment's invitation, Bacon traveled to Brazil, Argentina, Uruguay, Chile, Peru, and Panama, giving speeches to explain the Endowment and its purpose of improving Inter-American relations. In 1915 he published a description of the events of his visits, entitled *For Better Relations with our Latin American Neighbors*. In his speeches and his interactions with officials of the countries he visited, Bacon used his diplomatic and Latin American experience to attempt to build diplomatic cooperation for the Carnegie Endowment.

In 1917 Bacon went on to serve in the U.S. Army in World War I, starting as a major, then a lieutenant colonel, and finally a colonel in the American Expeditionary forces in France, for which service he received the U.S. Distinguished Service medal. He died shortly after returning home for surgery in 1919.

See also *Knox, Philander C.; Platt, Orville; Roosevelt, Theodore; Root-Cortés Treaty, 1909; Root, Elihu; Taft-Bacon Mission to Cuba, 1905; Taft, William H.; United States, circum-Caribbean Interventions, 1900–1934: Cuba; United States, circum-Caribbean Interventions, 1900–1934: Panama*

. . . . ELLEN D. TILLMAN

REFERENCES AND FURTHER READING

Bacon, Robert. *For Better Relations with our Latin American Neighbors: A Journey to South America.* Washington, DC: Carnegie Endowment for International Peace, 1915.

Bemis, Samuel Flagg, ed. *The American Secretaries of State and Their Diplomacy* (two volumes). New York: Alfred A. Knopf, 1927.

Mihalkanin, Edward S., ed. *American Statesmen: Secretaries of State from John Jay to Colin Powell.* Westport, CT: Greenwood Press, 2004.

Scott, James Brown. Introduction by Elihu Root. *Robert Bacon: Life and Letters.* New York: Doubleday, 1923.

Baker, James A. III

James Addison Baker III (1930–) was White House chief of staff and secretary of the treasury under President Ronald Reagan and secretary of state under President George H. W. Bush. He was responsible for the ultimately unsuccessful "Baker Plan" to resolve debt problems for developing countries and for helping to resolve conflicts in Nicaragua and El Salvador.

Born to a wealthy Houston family in 1930, Baker attended a private prep school before enrolling at Princeton University, where he received a BA in History in 1952. After serving two years in the Marine Corps, he studied law at the University of Texas at Austin. Graduating in 1957, he began practicing corporate law with a Houston firm. In 1959 Baker met Bush, and the two forged a close friendship. Baker first became politically active as campaign chair for his friend's unsuccessful 1970 Senate campaign and then went on to serve in a variety of positions in the Republican party, including chairman of President Gerald Ford's 1976 reelection campaign and senior advisor to Ronald Reagan's 1980 presidential campaign. Over the years, Baker developed a reputation as a highly skilled politician.

In January 1981 Baker became Reagan's chief of staff. Over the next four years he ran the White House efficiently, minimizing the number of crises that emerged from the president's chaotic administration. From 1985 to 1988 Baker served as secretary of the treasury. Although he was a member of the National Security Council, he was not informed of plans to sell arms to Iran in exchange for the release of American hostages and for funds that could be channeled to the contras, rebels against Nicaragua's left-wing Sandinista government. In 1985 he developed the Baker Plan to deal with the debt crisis in the developing world. Over a three-year period, commercial and development banks would increase lending by $29 billion to the world's fifteen most-indebted countries, ten of which were in Latin America. The debtor countries would adopt market-oriented reforms, including deficit reduction and tight monetary policies. Some of the targeted countries did experience limited economic growth, but the plan was inadequate to meet the magnitude of the crisis. The subsequent Brady Plan, named after Baker's successor, Nicholas Brady, called for banks to write off some of the debt owed by developing countries. Before the end of Reagan's presidency, Baker left the Treasury to direct Bush's successful 1988 presidential campaign.

As secretary of state from January 25, 1989, to August 23, 1992, Baker was cautious, pragmatic, and tough minded. A series of dramatic events—including the reunification of Germany, the end of the Cold War, the collapse of the Soviet Union, and the 1990–1991 Gulf War—focused his attentions on Europe and the Middle East. Because of a backlash against the Reagan administration's illegal provision of funds to the Nicaraguan contras, Baker doubted he could win Congressional approval for hard-line policies in Central America. Instead, he brokered a bipartisan agreement that called for a negotiated settlement to the conflict in Nicaragua and provided $150 million in humanitarian (nonmilitary) aid to the contras. The United States stopped supporting the violent overthrow of the Sandinista government, instead calling for free elections in Nicaragua. Elections did take place in February 1990, with the Sandinistas being voted out of power. Baker pushed the government of El Salvador and the guerrillas of the Farabundo Martí National Liberation Front (*Frente Farabundo Martí para la Liberación Nacional* or FMLN) to negotiate an end to that country's civil war. In 1992 Baker joined Salvadoran government and FMLN leaders in signing peace accords that called for the reform of Salvadoran institutions and an end to twelve years of guerrilla warfare. Baker also tried negotiations to remove Panamanian strongman Manuel Noriega from power. When talks failed and Noriega became more aggressive toward the United States, Baker supported the use of force to depose the Panamanian leader. In December 1989 U.S. troops captured Noriega and took him to the United States, where he was tried on charges of drug trafficking and was convicted in 1992.

Near the end of Bush's term, Baker left the State Department to become White House chief of staff and to manage his friend's reelection campaign. After Bush's defeat, Baker returned to the practice of law in Houston as a senior partner in Baker Botts, a firm his great grandfather had founded, and he served as senior counselor to the Carlyle Group, a global investment firm. In 2000 he led the legal team for presidential candidate George W. Bush during the Florida recount, helping the younger Bush into the White House.

See also *Bush, George H. W.; Central American Wars, 1980s; Debt Crisis, Latin America, 1870s, 1930s, 1980s; Noriega Moreno, Manuel Antonio; Reagan; Ronald W.*

. . . . STEPHEN AZZI

REFERENCES AND FURTHER READING

Baker, James A. III. *Work Hard, Study . . . and Keep Out Of Politics! Adventures and Lessons from an Unexpected Public Life.* With Steve Fiffer. New York: G. P. Putnam's Sons, 2006.

Baker, James A. III. *The Politics of Diplomacy: Revolution, War and Peace, 1989–1992.* With Thomas M. DeFrank. New York: G. P. Putnam's Sons, 1995.

Coatsworth, John H. *Central America and the United States: The Clients and the Colossus.* New York: Twayne, 1994.

LaFeber, Walter. *Inevitable Revolutions: The United States in Central America,* 2nd ed. New York: Norton, 1993.

Baker Plan

(**See** *Baker III, James* A.)

Balaguer Ricardo, Joaquín

President of the Dominican Republic from 1960–1962, 1966–1978, and 1986–1996, Joaquín Balaguer Ricardo (1906–2002) was a strong supporter of U.S. Cold War policy. A protégé of dictator Rafael Trujillo, the diminutive, unmarried, soft-spoken intellectual was a crafty politician who eventually facilitated the transition from authoritarianism to democracy in the Dominican Republic. Balaguer was born on September 1, 1906, in Navarette to Joaquín Balaguer Lespier, a Catalan immigrant from Puerto Rico, and Carmen Celia Ricardo. The only boy in a family of several daughters, Balaguer had a strong attraction to literature in his youth and eventually wrote several books. In 1929 he earned a law degree from the Universidad Autónoma de Santo Domingo (UASD).

A prominent official during the Trujillo dictatorship (1930–1961), he held positions in both the Ministry of Education and the Ministry of Foreign Relations, serving in Spain, Colombia, Ecuador, and Mexico. From 1957 to 1960 he was the vice president of the Dominican Republic. He ascended to the presidency in 1960 when Trujillo's brother, Héctor, resigned, bowing to U.S. pressure for democratization in the aftermath of Fidel Castro's 1959 revolution. After Trujillo's assassination on May 30, 1961, Balaguer began the transition to democracy. A period of political turmoil led to a military coup on January 16, 1962; Balaguer went into exile in the United States. In April 1965 Francisco Caamaño Deñó led a leftist-inspired

U.S. Vice President Hubert H. Humphrey (right) congratulates Joaquín Balaguer on the occasion of the latter's return to the presidency of the Dominican Republic by popular vote on July 1, 1966.

SOURCE: National Archives

insurrection to bring former president Juan Bosch, who ruled for seven months in 1963, back to power. U.S. officials saw this effort as counterproductive to U.S. foreign policy goals. To forestall a potential "second Cuba," U.S. President Lyndon Johnson ordered 23,000 Marines to intervene militarily in the Dominican Republic. In 1966, in elections supervised by the Organization of American States (OAS), Balaguer, viewed as the candidate most likely to preserve order and protect U.S. hegemony, defeated Bosch.

From 1966 to 1978, Balaguer, who relied more on persuasion than force (notwithstanding the occasional political murder), maintained order and stability while simultaneously protecting U.S. interests in the Dominican Republic. Balaguer's political style can be described as popular caudilloism. Unlike most of his contemporaries, Balaguer did not use public office to enrich himself. A nature lover, Balaguer implemented the national parks system in the Dominican Republic. As the leader of the Partido Reformista Social Cristiano (PRSC), Balaguer was able to initiate economic growth and embarked on a massive public works campaign fueled by high sugar prices, a generous sugar quota from the United States, and the immigration of thousands of Dominicans to the United States, which alleviated social pressure at home. A successful manipulator, Balaguer was able to co-opt the military and appease foreign investors. By the end of the 1970s, however, the popularity of artificial sweeteners in the United States destabilized the sugar export-based Dominican economy. Following presidential elections in 1978, Balaguer relinquished power, albeit grudgingly, to Antonio Guzman, the leader of the Partido Revolucionario Dominicano (PRD).

Notwithstanding the PRD's attempts at political liberalization, economic pandemonium and excessive political corruption facilitated Balaguer's return to power in 1986. From 1986 to 1994 Balaguer attempted to revive the Dominican economy while simultaneously paying greater respect for political liberties and human rights. His administration tried to develop agricultural activities to replace sugar production and to invest in developing tourism, which has since become the largest income generator in the Dominican Republic. Remittances from the hundreds of thousands of Dominicans working in the United States became a substantial revenue generator. Notwithstanding massive infrastructure projects, civil unrest was fueled by fuel shortages, which resulted in frequent blackouts. The construction of the Columbus Lighthouse in 1992, which cost $200 million, greatly increased criticism of Balaguer's regime. Balaguer, virtually blind but still intellectually viable, won the 1994 presidential election, although most observers considered the elections fraudulent. To quell political tumult, Balaguer agreed to call for early elections in 1996. Promising not to run, and certain that his own PRSC could not beat the PRD candidate, a man of Haitian ancestry, Balaguer supported the ultimate victor Leonel Fernández, the leader of the Partido de Liberación Dominicana (PLD) and the protégé of his rival Bosch. Although blind, Balaguer unsuccessfully ran for president in the 2000 elections. He died of heart failure at the Clinica Abreu in Santo Domingo on July 14, 2002.

See also *Bosch Gaviño, Juan; Johnson, Lyndon B.; Sugar, U.S. Policy; Trujillo Molina, Rafael Leónidas*

. . . . MICHAEL R. HALL

REFERENCES AND FURTHER READING

Balaguer, Joaquín. *Memorias de un Cortesano de la "Era de Trujillo."* Santo Domingo, Dominican Republic: Editora Corripio, 1989.

Betances, Emelio. *State and Society in the Dominican Republic.* Boulder, CO: Westview Press, 1995.

Moya Pons, Frank. *The Dominican Republic: A National History.* Princeton, NJ: Markus Wiener, 1998.

Baltimore Affair, 1891

On October 16, 1891, 120 sailors from the USS *Baltimore* received shore leave in Valparaiso, Chile. Instead of a relaxing day in Chile's main port, they became involved in bar brawls and street violence that resulted in the death of two Americans, the wounding of seventeen, and the imprisonment of thirty-six. When the ship's captain, W. S. Schley, convened a board of inquiry and blamed the Chileans for the fights, the United States demanded a Chilean apology and reparations. The Chileans balked and conducted their own investigation that blamed drunken American sailors for provoking the fights and demanded that several sailors stand trial for their involvement while commending the police for their professional behavior.

In the days that followed the incident, the State Department complained to the Chilean government about its delay in acknowledging responsibility. In his annual message to Congress in December 1891, President Benjamin Harrison threatened to seek congressional approval for U.S. intervention if the matter was not quickly resolved. Harrison reflected the jingoistic American public that demanded the punishment of the responsible Chileans.

The Chileans were equally bellicose, and their emotions were further stirred when the U.S. minister to Chile, Patrick

Egan, withheld key information from the Chilean investigators. The infuriated Chilean foreign minister, Manuel Matta, described President Benjamin Harrison's statements about the events as erroneous and deliberately incorrect. Matta also demanded Egan's recall. The Chileans added insult to injury by staging mock torpedo attacks on the USS *Yorktown* anchored in Valparaiso harbor. Before the year's end the Chileans tried to defuse the situation by agreeing to submit the dispute to arbitration by a third party, but support within the Chilean government disappeared as most government officials left Santiago to escape the summer heat (December to March in the southern hemisphere).

When the attempts at arbitration failed, the United States prepared for war. On January 21, 1892, the State Department threatened to sever diplomatic relations with Chile unless it capitulated. And on January 25, President Harrison sent Congress a summation of the incident with the implication that he wanted the legislature to declare war on Chile. The U.S. Navy began stockpiling weapons, and U.S. officials sought the support of the Peruvians and Bolivians who wanted revenge for their defeat in the War of the Pacific (1879–1884).

Under such pressure, the Chileans caved in. They paid $75,000 in reparations to the wounded sailors and families of the deceased, refuted Matta's charges against Harrison, and withdrew the request for the recall of Egan. Urged on by the House Foreign Affairs Committee, President Harrison accepted the Chilean offer.

While most Americans soon forgot the incident to focus on emerging issues in Venezuela and Cuba, the *Baltimore* Affair caused much antipathy toward the United States among Chileans. In the broader context, the *Baltimore* Affair highlighted the continued American drive to challenge all competitors, both foreign and regional, in Latin America. The incident also stood as another in a long list of U.S. injustices to all Latin Americans.

See also *Chile, U.S. Relations with; Blaine, James G.; Harrison, Benjamin; War of the Pacific, 1879–1883*

. . . . KYLE LONGLEY

REFERENCES AND FURTHER READING

Armstrong, William M. *E. L. Godkin and American Foreign Policy, 1865–1900.* Santa Barbara, CA: Greenwood Press, 1977.

Eselle, Patricio. "La controversia chileno-americano de 1891 a 1892." *Estudios de la Historia de las Instituciónes Politicas y Sociales,* 1 (1967): 149–277.

Goldberg, Joyce. *The Baltimore Affair.* Lincoln: University of Nebraska Press, 1986.

Banco del Sur (Bank of the South)

On December 6, 2007, in Buenos Aires, Argentina, the presidents of Argentina, Bolivia, Brazil, Ecuador, Paraguay, and Venezuela signed an agreement that established the Banco del Sur, or the Bank of the South, for the purpose of lending money to its member nations for infrastructure and social projects. Banco del Sur was seen as an alternative to the World Bank and the International Monetary Fund (IMF), which, beginning in 2003 had demanded the deepening of neoliberal economic reforms as a condition for loans or in determining the amount of money loaned. These countries had become increasingly unwilling to accept these measures that produced further socioeconomic difficulties for their populations.

Venezuelan President Hugo Chávez remains the chief critic of the World Bank and the IMF, whom he alleges provide support based upon Western political interests. For example, the Latin America share of IMF loans dropped from 80 percent to 1 percent between 2003 and 2007, while during the same time period, Turkey became the major recipient of IMF aid, approximately 75 percent of the institution's total. Yet, according to United Nations statistics, slightly over 50 percent of Latin America's population remains in poverty.

Chávez proposed creating a Latin American bank in 2006 to serve the interests of the southern hemisphere, not the imperialistic-focused northern-based international institutions. Despite its existence, the Bank confronts several issues. For example, initial funding for the $7.4 billion Banco del Sur was to be evenly shared by the original six members, but recognizing the wealth disparity between them, the founding nations agreed on a sliding scale of contributions, based upon one's ability to contribute. It soon rose to $10 billion, with contributions assessed at $4 billion for Argentina, Brazil, and Venezuela; $400 million to come from Ecuador and Uruguay; $100 million from Bolivia and Paraguay; and the remaining $3 billion from Chile, Colombia, Guyana, and Suriname. This raises the following question: Shouldn't the larger contributors have a greater role in the decision-making process? Given Latin America's unfavorable trade balance and unbalanced budgets, just how and when these assessments will be made remains unanswered. Venezuela serves as a model in reverse. Analysts point to its $58 billion in oil revenues for 2007 for the state owned and operated oil industry, yet the government reports an operating deficit of $3.8 billion. And, if the bank's loans are to be made through state agencies at subsidized rates, Latin America's age-old issue of political corruption comes to the forefront.

At the moment, Banco del Sur stands as a Latin American response to the shortcoming of the neoliberal economic model and to U.S. attention being focused upon other global regions and issues rather than Latin American economic development.

See also *Chávez Frías, Hugo; Inter-American Development Bank (IADB); International Monetary Fund (IMF); World Bank*

. . . . THOMAS M. LEONARD

REFERENCES AND FURTHER READING

Artana, Daniel. "Why Banco del Sur Is a Bad Idea," February 25, 2010, www.americas-society.org/article.php?id=2184&nav=res&pid.

Mallen, Roberto. "Bank of the South: Another Step toward Latin American Integration." *The Panama News* 13, no. 23 (December 2007): 5–7.

McIvor, Paul, "Venezuela's Banco Del Sur: The End of the IMF in Latin America?" March 21, 2007, http://upsidedownworld.org/main/content/view/667/1/.

Swann, Christopher. "South America's New Piggy Bank: Chávez Uses His Country's Oil Wealth To Help Neighbors, Blunt U.S. Influence," *Toronto Star,* March 1, 2007, A19.

Banking, Offshore

Offshore banking is cross-border intermediation of funds and provision of services to nonresident individuals and corporate entities by banks located in offshore financial centers (International Monetary Fund or IMF). Offshore banking became an important part of the global circuity of capital because of several changes in the global financial system in the second half of the twentieth century. These changes include the breakdown of the Bretton Woods system of fixed exchange rates pegged to the U.S. dollar in the 1960s, recycling of petrodollars in the 1970s, improvements in electronic telecommunications, and the creation of the Eurodollar market ("Eurodollars" are U.S. currency held in banks located outside of the United States and "Eurocurrency" is any major currency held in banks outside of the country of issuance).

CHARACTERISTICS

Offshore financial centers—often labeled tax havens—are jurisdictions that "host financial activities that are separated from major regulating units (states) by geography and/or by legislation. This may be a physical separation, as in an island territory, or within a city such as London or the New York International Banking Facilities" (Hampton 1996, 4). Latin America has many offshore financial centers (OFCs), which can be classified literally as "offshore;" for example, small island nations such as the Cayman Islands or the Bahamas or those classified legislatively as "offshore" even though the jurisdiction is onshore, through the passage of laws attracting nonresident capital—for example, Panama in Central America or Uruguay in South America. The IMF recognizes sixteen OFCs in the Caribbean (Anguilla, Antigua, Aruba, Bahamas, Barbados, British Virgin Islands, Cayman Islands, Dominica, Grenada, Montserrat, Netherlands Antilles, Puerto Rico, St. Kitts and Nevis, St. Lucia, St. Vincent and Grenadines, Turks and Caicos Islands). Most are small island nations where offshore financial services and tourism are the major contributors to the economic base. Three jurisdictions providing offshore financial services are recognized in Central America (Belize, Costa Rica, Panama) and one in South America (Uruguay). In addition, Bermuda is classified as a western hemisphere OFC even though the island is not considered part of Latin America.

OFCs are jurisdictions that have large numbers of financial institutions engaged in business with nonresidents. They typically have external assets and liabilities out of proportion to domestic financial indicators. For example, in 2006, the Cayman Islands registered approximately 300 banks with total assets of over $500 billion. The jurisdiction's domestic economy of $2 billion gross domestic product (GDP) was much smaller than the offshore deposit base. According to Warf (2002) the Panamanian offshore banking sector employed more people than any other economic sector with a workforce of approximately 13,000. In addition, offshore banks generated 11 percent of the country's gross national product (GNP) with deposits of over $27 billion. Offshore banking is the most important financial service in many OFCs, but other financial services offered could be mutual funds, hedge funds, insurance, re-insurance, accountancy, trust and company formation and administration, ship registration, and ship management.

INCREASED SCRUTINY

Offshore banks are attractive to those wishing to protect assets, hide assets, or launder money gained from such activities as drugs, prostitution, or gambling. OFCs offer low or zero taxation, relatively little financial regulation, and—importantly—customer secrecy and anonymity. In 1989, in response to mounting concern over money laundering, the Financial Action Task Force (FATF) on money laundering was established by the G-7 economies. Money laundering is recognized by the FATF as the processing of illegal profits from a variety of activities including illegal arms sales, smuggling, drug trafficking, prostitution, and other activities of organized crime as well as such white collar crimes as embezzlement, insider trading, bribery, and computer fraud schemes. In addition, after the September 11th attacks, tensions between the onshore and offshore world have increased further due to the concerns related to the use of money laundering to fund terrorist groups.

According to FATF, criminals seek to launder illegal profits by disguising the sources or moving the funds to a place where they are less likely to attract attention. As one of the primary OFC and offshore banking marketing strategies is to provide confidentiality, offshore financial institutions have come under serious scrutiny by FATF, and many centers (and the banks located there) strive to establish anti-money laundering systems in compliance with FATF guidelines. OFCs work with FATF and other onshore organizations in order to remain in good standing and protect the reputation of the center. The baseline for offshore anti-money laundering policies emanates from the now widely accepted "know your customer" requirement that many offshore financial institutions and offshore banks currently use. Know your customer policies require official proof of identification using passport and other official documents and include monitoring and reporting of any suspicious transactional activity.

The Caribbean region has its own anti-money laundering organization called the Caribbean Financial Action Taskforce (CFATF–see www.cfatf.org) that includes thirty members located in the Caribbean basin. CFATF is a regional chapter of FATF and has the major goals of prevention and control of money laundering and eradication of terrorist financing.

Onshore jurisdictional pressures, whether addressing money laundering, unfair tax practices, or the opaque nature of offshore financial service provisions, are likely to create tensions as OFCs strive to maintain credible reputations in the global financial system. Many Caribbean OFCs are former colonies or dependent territories of European colonial powers such as the United Kingdom, France, and the Netherlands, and the concomitant onshore-offshore relations are more permissive and tolerant than relations with the United States and nearby OFCs. Great concern has been shown by the U.S. federal government and its agencies (particularly the Treasury Department and the Internal Revenue Service) over tax avoidance and/or evasion by U.S. citizens and corporations using offshore financial services in Latin American OFCs.

Because there is no colonial history or ties that bind offshore and onshore jurisdiction for U.S. and Latin American relations, the U.S. government is more aggressive in its stance toward OFCs and more vigilant in its pursuit of U.S. citizens and corporations seeking to use offshore financial services. For example, see the 2006 U.S. Department of State's report addressing issues in U.S. relations with Caribbean OFCs (http://fpc.state.gov/documents/organization/61637.pdf) and the International Narcotics Control Strategy Report addressing money laundering and evasion (www.state.gov/p/inl/rls/nrcrpt/2006/vol2/html/62140.htm).

See also *Caribbean Community Common Market (CARICOM); Central American Common Market (CACM)*

SHARON C. COBB

REFERENCES AND FURTHER READING

Errico, Luca, and Alberto Musalem, "Offshore Banking: An Analysis of Micro and Macro Prudential Issues," IMF Working Paper, WP/99/5, 1999.

Hampton, Mark *The Offshore Interface: Tax Havens in the Global Economy*. New York: St. Martin's Press, 1996.

OECD, Harmful Tax Competition: An Emerging Global Issue, 1998, www.oecd.org/dataoecd/33/0/1904176.pdf.

Roberts, S. "Fictitious Capital, Fictitious Places: The Geography of Offshore Financial Flows." In *Money, Power and Space,* edited by Stuart Corbridge, Ron Martin, and Nigel Thrift, 91–115. Oxford, UK: Blackwell, 1994.

Warf, Barney. "Tailored for Panama: Offshore Banking at the Crossroads of the Americas." *Geografiska Annaler* 84 (2002): 47–61.

Banzer Suárez, Hugo

Hugo Banzer Suárez (1926–2002) was born in a small town in the Santa Cruz region of Bolivia. He attended military schools in Bolivia, Argentina, Brazil, and the United States. He trained at the U.S. Army School of the Americas in the Panama Canal Zone and learned English. He also trained at the Fort Hood, Texas, Armored Cavalry School, and received the high honor of the Order of Military Merit from the U.S. government. In 1964, when René Barrientos Ortuño staged a coup (allegedly supported by the Central Intelligence Agency and the Pentagon), Banzer was named minister of education and subsequently served as Bolivian military attaché to Washington. Both his time in U.S. military training as well as military attaché strengthened his attachment to the United States and gained him many high-powered American military friends.

In 1971 the leftist government of Juan José Torres González exiled Banzer for staging a failed coup. From his exile in Argentina he staged a second and successful coup that same year. Subsequently, Banzer ruled as dictator for seven years, a period known as the Banzerato. Banzer had the support of many groups: the MNR (Movimiento Nacionalista Revolucionario), the party of the 1952 revolution; several former Bolivian presidents; the rightist political party, the Falange Socialista Boliviana (FSAB); and the United States. In order to bring together political factions, he created the Frente Popular Nacionalista (FPN), although the alliance crumbled during his tenure in office. During his regime there were thirteen attempted coups and he was finally overthrown in November 1978 by the left-leaning commander in chief of the Army, General David Padilla Aranciba.

Banzer's government was very repressive. In 1974 he staged an "autogolpe," or a coup against parts of his own government. He then closed the universities, censored the press, banned all political parties or any political activity, and sent many people into exile. Banzer's regime has been accused of one hundred "disappearances," thirty-nine political assassinations, more than four hundred deaths, and over three thousand politically related arrests. Over nineteen thousand Bolivians fled the country; almost seven hundred of these were political exiles. The worst massacre occurred in January 1974 when the army killed between eighty and two hundred indigenous peasant farmers because they protested rising prices. Finally, Banzer participated in the notorious Operation Condor, where South American dictators cooperated to assassinate each other's exiled political dissidents.

During the first years of the regime exports of natural gas increased, sales of oil increased, and tin prices skyrocketed. The United States purchased over one-third of Bolivia's legal exports and perhaps much of its illegal export of cocaine, of which Bolivia produced more than 30 percent of the world's supply. Many charged Banzer and his family with having strong drug connections. He did have a road built into the Chapare region in Bolivia, which then became the chief coca growing area in the country. Moreover, the drug mafia had a great deal of power during the Banzer dictatorship. When Banzer later became president in 1997, however, he vehemently denied any drug connections and became a staunch ally of the United States against the drug trade.

From the beginning of his coup and throughout his two regimes, Banzer enjoyed support from the United States, particularly the Nixon administration and the military. Many believe the United States provided aid for Banzer's 1971 coup, including all military supplies and Air Force radio communications. In fact, the American Green Berets trained the actual military battalion that started the uprising. Nine days after the coup, the United States recognized Banzer's government. Banzer repaid the United States by expelling 119 Soviet diplomats, devaluing the peso from 12 to 20 per dollar, and passing liberal investment laws to attract foreign capital, all of which garnered a substantial increase in foreign aid loans to Bolivia. USAID (U.S. Agency for International Development) gave $50 million and military aid rose 200 percent. The United States gave other large loans supporting strict austerity programs. These policies resulted in protests and a growing foreign debt.

In 1977, however, when President Jimmy Carter came into office, Banzer lost a great deal of support because of the serious accusations of human rights abuses. Carter pressured Banzer to call for elections in 1978, and Banzer was forced out of office that year. Banzer legally ran for president in 1979, 1980, 1989, and 1993, and finally in 1997 he won. During his presidency he worked with the United States to form a plan to stop the drug trafficking of cocaine from Bolivia to the United States. He resigned in 2001 because he became ill with lung cancer.

See also *Bolivia, U.S. Relations with; Carter, Jimmy; National Revolutionary Movement (MNR) (Bolivia); School of the Americas; U.S. Agency for International Development (USAID)*

. . . . GINA HAMES

REFERENCES AND FURTHER READING

Blum, William. *Killing Hope: U.S. Military and CIA Interventions since World War II.* Monroe, ME: Common Courage Press, 1995.

Klein, Herbert S. *A Concise History of Bolivia.* Cambridge, UK: Cambridge University Press, 2003.

Malloy, James M. and Eduardo Gamarra. *Revolution and Reaction: Bolivia, 1964–1985.* New Brunswick, NJ: Transaction Books, 1988.

Mitchell, Christopher. "The Politics of Military Conservatism: The Banzer Regime." In *The Legacy of Populism in Bolivia, from the MNR to Military Rule,* edited by Christopher Mitchell, 61–78. New York: Praeger, 1977.

Barco Vargas, Virgilio

Virgilio Barco Vargas (1921–1997) was president of Colombia from 1986–1990. A member of the Liberal party, Barco had a lengthy career in Colombian politics that started in the 1940s. He served at both the local and national levels of government before winning the presidency. In his home department of Norte de Santander, he held jobs that included secretary of public works and was an elected member of the municipal councils of both Durania and his hometown of Cúcuta. On the national level he served at different times as minister of agriculture, minister of public works, and minister of finance and was elected to both the Chamber of Representatives and the Senate. He was also ambassador to both the United Kingdom (twice) and the United States.

During the Barco administration, the war on drugs as we currently understand it became a major factor in Colombian politics. While there had been multiple declarations of war by Barco's own government, as well as that of the two prior Colombian presidents, the wave of violence that was unleashed in the later portion of his presidency took the conflict to a new level. During this period, the Medellín Cartel led by Pablo Escobar became a major international actor, and the Colombian state began to see a direct threat to its ability to function from such actors.

Extradition emerged as a major issue during the Barco administration in terms of relations with the United States. Colombia had ratified an extradition treaty with the United States in 1980 (which came into effect in 1982), and U.S. officials saw it as tool to fight drug traffickers. In Colombia the treaty was seen as damaging to Colombian sovereignty. Indeed, Barco's predecessor (Belisario Betancur, 1982–1986) initially did not utilize this tool for that exact reason. While the Colombian Supreme Court had ruled on June 25, 1987, that extradition of Colombian nationals was unconstitutional, the assassination of presidential candidate Luis Carlos Galán by the Medellín Cartel on August 18, 1989, prompted Barco to declare war on the cartels and to issue an emergency decree allowing for extraditions to the United States to resume. Twenty-four Colombian nationals were sent to the United States on drug charges between August 1989 and December 1990. These extraditions prompted a violent response from the cartels, including two hundred bombings against government and civilian targets between late August and October of 1989.

During the Barco administration, the administration of U.S. President George H. W. Bush implemented its Andean Initiative (in September 1989), which sought to combat the illicit drug industry by the three-pronged approach of military assistance, crop eradication, and alternative development.

Other noteworthy events during the Barco administration included the demobilization of the M-19 guerrilla group and the first steps in a process that would lead to the promulgation of a new constitution for Colombia in 1991.

Barco's last stint of public service came as ambassador to the United Kingdom (1990–1992). He suffered from Alzheimer's disease and died of stomach cancer.

See also *Colombia, U.S. Relations with; Drugs, U.S. War on; Escobar Gaviria, Pablo; Gaviria Trujillo, César; M-19: 19th of April Movement (Colombia)*

. . . . STEVEN L. TAYLOR

REFERENCES AND FURTHER READING

Bagley, Bruce Michael. "Dateline Drug Wars: Colombia: The Wrong Strategy." *Foreign Policy* 77 (Winter 1989–1990): 154–171.

Kline, Harvey F. *State Building and Conflict Resolution in Colombia,* 1986–1994. Tuscaloosa: The University of Alabama Press, 1999.

Barletta Vallarino, Nicolás Ardito

An economist who studied under future American Secretary of State George Shultz at the University of Chicago, Nicolas Barletta (1938–) served Panamanian military dictator Omar Torrijos as an adviser and cabinet minister for five years. In 1978, a year after the Panama Canal Treaty was signed, following negotiations that he participated in, Barletta resigned to become vice president of the World Bank.

With presidential elections looming in 1984, the first held during the sixteen years of military rule, the uncharismatic Barletta was handpicked by Noriega to run under the banner of the Torrijos-formed political entity, the *Partido Revolucionario Democratico* (Revolutionary Democratic Party—PRD). Barletta looked to be the loser in the balloting against former President (and longtime aspirant) Arnulfo Arias. Yet, as the official candidate, Barletta, a beneficiary of a government-funded campaign, government media coverage, and government-directed registration fraud, and with the Panamanian Defense Forces (PDF) members voting early and often, was declared the winner anyway, by all of 1,713 votes. The United States embassy in Panama City estimated that Arias actually won by more than 60,000 votes. Barletta's dubious victory earned him the nickname *"Fraudito."*

Yet, Secretary of State George Shultz attended Barletta's inauguration on October 11, 1984. In his memoir, *Turmoil and*

Triumph (1993), Shultz explained that his purpose in attending was to support the transition to democratic government from direct military rule.

Facing the world's highest per capita debt, President Barletta planned to increase taxes and reduce the budget deficit by cutting government services. His economic reform package quickly made enemies of Panamanians across the spectrum, including some of his supporters in the military who had relied on government spending to placate the Panamanian masses. Within ten days, Barletta, whose years at the World Bank left him with few political allies, felt compelled to withdraw his plan.

Another issue guaranteed to win no political favors that Barletta looked to tackle was bureaucratic reform. The president demanded a better work ethic from government employees who saw public service as an opportunity to help themselves. By taking on these two issues, Barletta's opponents began to question his political skill.

Barletta's relations with Noriega were formal, with the president frustrated about his relative lack of communication with the strongman. For his part, Noriega remarked that "I know everything the president does. I even know which moment he pees" (Buckley 1991, 21).

While Barletta was in New York City to deliver an address to the UN General Assembly, the outspoken Noriega opponent, Hugo Spadafora, was gruesomely murdered. Barletta's call for an independent commission to investigate Spadafora's murder resulted in the president being called back to Panama. Upon his arrival at PDF headquarters, Barletta was informed that his resignation was required unless he changed his mind about the investigation. When Barletta, a friend of Spadafora's father, declined, a PDF officer accused the him of being "too damn democratic." Barletta was left shivering under house arrest in Noriega's frigid PDF office without food for fourteen hours and fearing for the safety of his family. He then signed a letter of resignation and was stripped of the office given to him just eleven months earlier.

Upon Barletta's resignation, Vice President Eric Arturo Delvalle succeeded him. Yet, it was made clear to all that Noriega, who always preferred to work in the background, was now the open leader of Panama.

See also *Noriega Moreno, Manuel Antonio; Panama, U.S. Relations with*

. . . . GREG MURPHY

REFERENCES AND FURTHER READING

Buckley, Kevin. *Panama: The Whole Story*. New York: Simon and Schuster, 1991.

Kempe, Frederick. *Divorcing the Dictator: America's Bungled Affair with Noriega*. London: I. B. Tauris, 1990.

Koster, R. M., and Guillermo Sanchez. *In the Time of the Tyrants*. New York: Norton, 1990.

Shultz, George. *Turmoil and Triumph*. New York: Scribners, 1993.

Barrios, Justo Rufino

Called "The Reformer" by his fellow Guatemalans, Justo Rufino Barrios (1835–1885) is still revered by his countrymen. He arose from modest circumstances, ascended to the presidency of his homeland, and fatally overextended himself. As president, Barrios transformed his nation from a backwater Central American republic to a regional leader in the area's dealings with the United States.

Justo Rufino Barrios was born in the village of San Lorenzo, in the department of San Marcos. His above average intellect and energy were evident from an early age. Upon graduating from the local church academy, he went to Guatemala City to study law, receiving his law license in 1862.

By 1867 the residents of western Guatemala decided to reclaim the region's former status as the independent state of Los Altos. The residents of Quetzaltenango department joined the revolt against the central government. Barrios cast his lot with the rebels, proved a capable military leader, and quickly rose within the rebel army to the rank of general. In July 1871 Barrios joined with other rebel generals and dissidents and issued the Plan of the Fatherland, which favored the ouster of the Conservative regime. With the backing of Mexican President Benito Juárez, Barrios and his compatriots succeeded and installed General García Granados as president in August 1871. In reward for his service, Barrios was named commander of Guatemala's armed forces.

After installing García Granados as president, Barrios returned to Quetzaltenango, where he received word that the president had been overthrown. Barrios gathered his forces, led a successful march on the capital, and became Guatemala's new president. Not wishing to see a Liberal regime next door, the Conservative Honduran government gave its military backing to a group of Guatemalan Conservatives who wished to unseat Barrios. The new president responded by declaring war on Honduras, and with the President of El Salvador, announced his intention to reunite the old United Provinces of Central America. This prospect raised more eyebrows in Mexico City than in Washington, for Mexican president Porfirio Diaz saw more of a threat in a united Central America than did the United States.

Barrios politically dispatched his opponents and set about pushing his reform package through the Guatemalan Congress, a Liberal agenda, which sought to replicate a U. S.-style constitutional regime. Among the early reforms enacted were freedom of the press, disestablishment of the church, and freedom of religion. This brand of liberalism, however, was different from its predecessor of the 1820s and 1830s and adhered to Auguste Comte's theory of positivism, which placed economic development and progress ahead of constitutional norms. For Guatemala, that meant opening the economy up to German investors, who came to control the export side of the coffee trade, while leaving the growing to local landowners. It would be another two decades before U. S. investors, who bankrolled the nation's banana industry, entered the Guatemalan export economy.

In 1873 Barrios won a full six-year term as Guatemala's chief executive. He oversaw a complete overhaul of Guatemala's infrastructure, bringing railroads, a telegraph system, and a compulsory, publicly funded education system. He also established a new, accountable police force and embarked on a massive public works program that remodeled Guatemala City.

Because Barrios wanted to make his reforms permanent, he drew up Guatemala's first constitution, which was ratified in 1879. The following year, he was elected to another six-year term, on the claim that his work was not done. Two unresolved issues were an ongoing border dispute with Mexico and the reunification of Central America. Barrios had ostensibly enlisted the support of Honduras and El Salvador to accomplish this goal. Without warning, El Salvador's President Zaldivar withdrew from the Central American Union and sent envoys to Mexico to enlist that country's assistance in overthrowing Barrios. Mexican President Porfirio Díaz feared the prospect of a strong Central America and sent his troops to seize disputed territory in the department of Soconusco. Barrios personally led the Guatemalan Army on a preemptive strike into El Salvador, where it engaged the Salvadorans at Chalchuapa. While he was leading a cavalry charge, an enemy bullet hit Barrios in the chest, killing him instantly. Though the U. S. consul to Guatemala tried to dissuade him from this foray, Washington preferred to let events play out. Nevertheless, Barrios left a legacy of reform that enabled his country to enter into the North American trading economy as a full-fledged junior partner.

See also *Díaz Mori, Porfirio; Juárez García, Benito; United Provinces of Central America, 1823–1839*

PETER B. GUSHUE

REFERENCES AND FURTHER READING

Buchenau, Jurgen: *In the Shadow of the Giant: The Making of Mexico's Central American Policy, 1876–1930*. Tuscaloosa: University of Alabama Press, 1996.

Clegern, Wayne. *Origins of Liberal Dictatorship in Central America: Guatemala, 1865–1873*. Boulder: University of Colorado Press, 1994.

McCreery, D. J. *Development and the State in Reforma Guatemala*. Athens: Ohio University Press, 1983.

Baseball

Baseball, one of the most popular games in the United States, Canada, Cuba, Puerto Rico, Venezuela, Panama, Mexico, and the Dominican Republic, and arguably the national pastime in several of these countries, entered *La Era de Oro,* or the Golden Age, for Latin American born players in the 1990s. By 2006, 192 or 23.6 percent of all Major League Baseball players had been born in Latin America. The fact that, beginning in 2002, over 80 percent of foreign-born minor league players also originated in Latin America suggests that this trend will not be a short-term anomaly. With less acclaim, many professional players, Latin or not, now head to Latin America to hone their skills in extremely competitive Winter Leagues in the Dominican Republic, Venezuela, Puerto Rico, and Mexico, culminating with the *Serie del Caribe* in February.

ORIGINS

Baseball is one of many American bat and ball games that probably evolved from the British and Irish game of rounders. The first game resembling modern-day baseball was played in Beachville, Ontario, in 1834. The Knickerbocker Club hosted the first game of baseball in the United States in 1846 in Hoboken, New Jersey. By the 1860s baseball had arrived in the Caribbean. There are multiple stories of its origin in Latin America, but almost everyone agrees that after the adoption of the game in Cuba, it played a central role in the game's spread through the Caribbean. This is because baseball was just becoming popular in the United States around the time that Cubans were migrating to and from the United States in large numbers as a result of Cuba's Ten Years War (1868–1878), the Little War (1879–1880), and the Independence War (1895–1898). One story of baseball's origins in Cuba proposes that Cuban brothers Nemesio and Ernesto Guilló (or Guillót), upper-class teenagers returning from their studies in Mobile, Alabama, introduced baseball to locals in 1864. A more widespread story has it that in 1866, U.S. sailors anchored in Matanzas Bay introduced baseball to stevedores loading sugar onto ships bound for the United States.

By 1870 baseball had spread to the Dominican Republic, probably from Cubans fleeing the Ten Years War against Spanish colonial rule. In the Dominican Republic the game's popularity spread because of its promotion by sugar refinery managers, who saw it as a positive diversion for their workers during the slow time after the sugarcane harvest. Baseball would later provide one of the few positive means of interaction between Dominicans and occupying U.S. troops stationed on the island between 1916 and 1924. Cuba may have also played a central role in the spread of baseball to Venezuela when Cuban businessman Emilio Cramer visited that country in 1895. Others claim, however, that the Franklin brothers, Amenodoro, Emilio, Gustavo, and Augusto, from Caracas, established the first baseball team in Venezuela upon their return from studying in the United States that same year. Cuba also played a central role in the diffusion of baseball to Puerto Rico. Most argue that a year prior to the Spanish-Cuban-American War of 1898, the sons and nephews of a Spanish diplomat who had taken to baseball while stationed in Cuba introduced the game in Puerto Rico. After the war U.S. troops stationed on the island played against local ball teams. On the other hand, no one knows who originally spread the game to Nicaragua, but the game had arrived there by 1888 or 1889. Finally, there are conflicting reports about both the timing and location of the advent of baseball in Mexico. Some argue that baseball arrived when U.S. troops shared their passion for the game with locals during the U.S.-Mexican War (1846–1848) in 1847. Others argue that baseball did not enter Mexico until it reached the borderlands city of Nuevo Laredo in the 1870s. Still others argue that Colonel Joseph Robertson, a Tennessean who once served under General Robert E. Lee, introduced baseball to Mexicans along the Monterrey-Tampico railroad when he allowed his U.S. workers to play that game in celebration of the fourth of July in 1889. The latter case appears to be false given that the "Mexico Club" team came into existence in 1887 in Mexico City.

Latin players playing in the United States and U.S. players playing in Latin America served as an early form of intercultural exchange. Cuban-born Ésteban "Steve" Bellán was the first Latin American to play professional baseball in the United States when in 1871 he suited up for the Troy Haymakers of the National Association. Bellán would go on to play a leading role in the world's second oldest baseball league, Cuba's *Liga de Base Ball,* when he led his Havana team to the league's 1878–1879 inaugural championship. Major League Baseball officially banned African American players in 1895. In the first decade of the twentieth century, American League President Ban Johnson also banned major league clubs from competing against Cuban teams during the winter, fearing that they might lose against colored teams. This meant that while white (predominantly Cuban) players were still eligible to play in the United States, colored Latin players were forced to play in the Negro Leagues. For example, in 1911 Cubans Armando Marsans and Rafael Almeida became the first modern-day Latin Americans to play major league baseball when they played outfield for the Cincinnati Reds. Management responded to complaints about their dark skin by claiming that they were of Castilian descent. In 1919, Cuban Adolfo Luque, "The Pride of Havana," passed as white much more easily, pitching for the Cincinnati Reds against the Chicago "Black Sox." Luque would go on to win 27 games in 1923.

Race continued to be an issue into the 1940s as the Reds released Cuban pitcher Tommy de la Cruz after only one season because of complaints about his dark skin color. In Cuba, on the other hand, the Cuban League, first established in 1878, began accepting black players (from Cuba and the United States) in 1900. Many of the best Negro League players—including Oscar Charleston, Josh Gibson, and Satchel Paige—took advantage of the Cuban League or winter baseball. Meanwhile, many black Cubans like Martín Dihigo, José Méndez, and Alejandro Oms played on Negro League teams. In addition, integrated teams from the Cuban League went on barnstorming tours of the United States, competing primarily against Negro League teams. After Jackie Robinson broke the color line in 1946 (and prior to the flood of Latin American players beginning in the 1970s), players from Latin America, including Alfonso "Chico" Carrasquel, Luis Aparicio, Juan Marichal, Roberto Clemente, and Orlando Cepeda, began to take on an expanded role in Major League Baseball.

POLITICAL IMPACT

Political leaders also used baseball as a tool for diplomacy and building national identity. Between 1868 and 1898 Cuban *criollos* used their rejection of bullfighting and adoption of baseball as Cuba's national sport as a means of denying their political connection to Spain even as they tied themselves through both migration and economic ties more closely with the United States. Spanish officials took the adoption of baseball as a means of resisting their rule so seriously that they officially banned the game in 1895. In 1914 Venustiano Carranza, self-proclaimed first chief of the Mexican Revolution (1914–1917) and president of Mexico (1917–1920), tried a similar gambit when he outlawed bullfighting and named baseball as Mexico's national pastime. He hoped, incorrectly, that doing so would lead Woodrow Wilson to extend *de jure* recognition to Carranza's revolutionary faction as the official government of Mexico. A year later, Carranza sent a representative to the National Association of Professional Baseball meeting in San Francisco, an organization of minor league club owners from the United States and Canada, proposing that Mexico be admitted into the North American minor league baseball system with a division of its own composed of clubs from northern Mexico. The foundation of the Mexican League, however, would not come until the 1920s when Carranza was already dead.

Baseball also played a central role in the Cold War after Fidel Castro took power in Cuba in 1959. Only a year after Castro took power, the International League relocated the Cuban Sugar Kings from Havana to Jersey City, New Jersey. Shortly thereafter, Castro transformed the Cuban League into an amateur association. Cuba would quickly come to dominate most world tournaments, including the Olympics, Intercontinental Cup, the Pan-American Games, and the World Cup. Meanwhile, Cuban defectors, especially high profile players like "El Duque" Hernández and José Contreras, were celebrated as heroes in the U.S. press for their, sometimes fictionalized, daring escapes. The Cold War showdown reached its apogee in 1999 when the Baltimore Orioles split two games against Castro's Team Cuba.

FUTURE

In 1990 Latinos made up 13 percent of Major League Baseball players. By 1997, they had surpassed the number of African American players. This is explained, in part, by the Latin American economic dependence on the United States and disparities in wealth between the two regions. Major League Baseball has sponsored a series of exhibition games in Latin America (and Asia) in hopes of expanding into new consumer markets. More importantly, the rise and expansion of training academies in the Caribbean highlights Major League Baseball's attempts to control labor costs. Most Latin American players are purposely not eligible for the Major League draft, allowing Major League franchises to sign dozens of young Latin players for the cost of a single player from the United States.

See also *Clinton, William J.; Cuba, U.S. Relations with*

. . . . ANDRAE MARAK

REFERENCES AND FURTHER READING

Bjarkman, Peter C. *Diamonds around the Globe: The Encyclopedia of International Baseball.* Westport, CT: Greenwood Press, 2005.

Burgos Jr., Adrian. "Playing Ball in a Black and White 'Field of Dreams': Afro-Caribbean Ballplayers in the Negro Leagues, 1910–1950." *The Journal of Negro History* 82, no. 1 (Winter 1997): 67–104.

Fainaru, Steve, and Ray Sánchez. *The Duke of Havana: Baseball, Cuba, and the Search for the American Dream.* New York: Villard, 2001.

Marcano Guevara, Arturo J., and David P. Fidler. *Stealing Lives: The Globalization of Baseball and the Tragic Story of Alexis Quiroz.* Bloomington: Indiana University Press, 2002.

Perez Jr., Louis A. "Between Baseball and Bullfighting: The Quest for Nationality in Cuba, 1868–1898." *The Journal of American History* 81, no. 2 (September 1994): 493–517.

Regalado, Samuel O. *Viva Baseball! Latin Major Leaguers and Their Special Hunger.* Urbana: University of Illinois Press, 1998.

Batista y Zaldívar, Fulgencio

Prior to Fidel Castro's ascent to power on January 1, 1959, no other figure in twentieth century Cuban political history exercised so much influence as General Fulgencio Batista y Zaldívar (1901–1973). From 1933 until 1959 Batista was the "strong man" of Cuban politics.

BATISTA'S FIRST REIGN: 1933–1944

Born in Veguitas, a poverty-stricken *barrio* in Banes, Oriente Province, Batista, a Cuban mulatto, was educated at a Quaker missionary school. After holding a number of odd jobs, he joined the Cuban army where he became a stenographer.

After the fall of Dictator Gerardo Machado in August 1933, Batista, an army sergeant, rose to power by leading the "sergeants' revolt," which toppled the provisional government on September 4, 1933. Through a series of puppet presidents, Batista, who immediately promoted himself to colonel, would rule Cuba by the grace of the army, labor, middle class, and the United States.

A cunning individual, Batista took advantage of President Franklin D. Roosevelt's Good Neighbor policy, and as a result, the Platt Amendment, which had given the United States free rein to interfere in Cuban affairs, was abrogated in 1934. Additionally, his excellent relations with the United States helped mitigate the impact of the Great Depression on Cuba. Loans from the American Import-Export Bank helped stimulate the economy while the Jones-Cooligan Act (1934) and the Reciprocal Trade Agreement guaranteed Cuba a preferential sugar quota. In exchange, Cuba agreed to lower duties on American imports. By 1937 Cuban sugar accounted for 37 percent of American sugar imports. However, the Cuban sugar industry was largely in the hands of the Americans, for American-owned sugar mills produced 56 percent of Cuban sugar.

Realizing that by the end of the 1930s he had become the arbiter of Cuban politics, Batista opened the way for Cuban democracy by authorizing the drafting of a new constitution, which in 1940 became a reality. The Cuban Constitution of 1940 became one of the most progressive documents in Latin American history. It provided for all of the basic freedoms and individual rights and granted women the right to vote. Under the constitution, labor enjoyed a privileged position, for it provided for social security, recognition of labor unions, collective bargaining, minimum wage, health insurance, workers' compensation, unemployment compensation, and paid vacations. Additionally, it declared the state as the legal owner of subsoil rights. While the constitution recognized the right of private property, it justified the right of the state to expropriate property.

After building an impressive coalition of different segments of Cuban society, Batista was elected president in 1940, receiving 60 percent of the votes cast. Batista's presidency from 1940 until 1944 was a democratic one where Cubans, for the most part, enjoyed the basic freedoms. His presidency coincided with World War II and on December 9, 1941, Cuba became one of the first Latin American nations to declare war on Germany. This alliance with the United States paid dividends, for the United States agreed to buy millions of tons of sugar at prices ranging from 1.6 cents to 3 cents per pound. Moreover, the United States granted Cuba favorable terms on loans that were used to finance a myriad of public works projects. Cuba granted the United States the use of military installations and in exchange received much needed equipment for the armed forces. One group which benefited from the war was the Communist party. Not only did the Batista government recognize the Communist party and the Soviet Union in 1943, but it also appointed several communists to cabinet posts.

Since the 1940 constitution prohibited the immediate reelection of the president, Batista stepped down in 1944 and his nemesis Ramón Grau won the presidential election, marking the beginning of Auténtico Party rule, which continued with his successor, Carlos Prío Socarrás (1948–1952). In 1944 Batista moved to Daytona Beach, Florida. Over the next four years, he administered the millions of pilfered dollars that he had deposited in the United States.

BATISTA'S SECOND REIGN: 1952–1958

Batista returned to Cuba in 1948 and announced his candidacy for the presidential elections scheduled for June 1952. Aware that his popularity had ebbed and his presidential chances were minimal, he staged a coup on March 10, 1952, which deposed President Prío. Because of the general discontent with the corrupt Prío administration, reaction to the coup was mixed. The United States opted for "law and order" rather than the democratic process and granted the Batista government diplomatic recognition and economic and military aid.

Batista's coup resulted in the demise of Cuban democracy. Soon dissatisfaction broke out among different factions of Cuban society and on July 26, 1953, Fidel Castro, a young Cuban lawyer, launched an unsuccessful attack on the Moncada Barracks in Oriente Province.

In 1954 Batista was elected president in a fraudulent election. Despite his dictatorship, there was considerable economic progress. Largely through native and foreign investments, the Cuban economy ranked among the top five in Latin America and 59 percent of the Cuban population had achieved middle class standards of living. Under Batista's Social and Economic Development Plan, urban working conditions improved and there were gains in education, health, and housing standards. Additionally, modest attempts were made at economic diversification by granting tax breaks and other economic concessions.

In spite of the diversification attempts, sugar remained king in Cuba, for it accounted for 80 percent of exports. Although during Batista's rule, Cubans owned 113 of the 162 sugar mills on the island, accounting for 55 percent of the sugar production, the Cuban economy was extremely dependent on American purchases of Cuban sugar at a fixed price. Moreover, approximately 7 percent of the Cuban imports were from the United States and the island was the largest importer of American agricultural food products in Latin America.

In spite of the economic gains, Batista's seven-year dictatorship was marred by rampant corruption, graft, gangsterism, nepotism, and violence. As a result, Cubans yearned for a change. In 1956 their hopes were crystallized when Fidel Castro, who had been granted amnesty after the Moncada Barracks fiasco, landed on the coast of Oriente Province and began a guerrilla campaign in the Sierra Maestra mountains.

Batista's corrupt and ill-prepared army was no match for Castro's fighters. Additionally, in the cities, Castro sympathizers and other anti-Batista elements conducted an urban guerrilla campaign against his regime. Unable to neutralize his opponents, his government resorted to the use of repressive tactics, and thousands of Cubans—many of them innocent civilians—were imprisoned, tortured, or murdered.

Batista's regime suffered a severe setback when in May 1958, the American government, concerned about Batista's abuses, declared an arms sale embargo. Batista sent 10,000 soldiers to crush the rebels in the Sierra Maestra, but the two-month offensive ended in disaster because of his army commanders' ineptitude and the guerrillas' fighting tenacity. Desperate for soldiers, Batista's army resorted to the recruitment of poor, illiterate young men. Lacking training and discipline, they were quick to surrender.

In a last minute attempt to save his government, elections were held in November 1958. Batista's handpicked successor won the election, which was once again marred by fraud and voting irregularities. However, realizing that his rule was coming to an end, Batista fled Cuba on December 31, 1958, and sought asylum in the Dominican Republic. He later lived lavishly from millions of dollars extracted from the Cuban treasury in Madeira and Spain. In August 1973 he died in Spain.

See also *Castro Ruz, Fidel; Cuba, U.S. Relations with; Cuban Revolution, 1956-1959, U.S. Policy toward; Good Neighbor Policy; Grau San Martín, Ramón; Platt, Orville; Prío Socarrás, Carlos*

. . . . JOSÉ B. FERNÁNDEZ

REFERENCES AND FURTHER READING

Leonard, Thomas M. *Castro and the Cuban Revolution.* Westport, CT: Greenwood Press, 1999.

Pérez-Stable, Marefeli. *The Cuban Revolution: Origins, Course and Legacy.* New York: Oxford University Press, 1999.

Suchlicki, Jaime. *From Columbus to Castro.* Washington, DC: Brassey, 1997.

Thomas, Hugh. *Cuba: The Pursuit of Freedom.* New York: Harper and Row, 1971.

Vilaboy, José L. *Motivos y culpables de la destrucción de Cuba.* San Juan: Editora de Libros Puerto Rico, 1973.

Batlle y Ordóñez, José

Known as the "Founder of Modern Uruguay," José Batlle y Ordóñez (1856–1929) was the most influential figure in twentieth century Uruguayan political history. Plagued by a visceral rivalry between a Liberal political group known as the *Colorado* (reds), and a Conservative political group known as the *Blancos* (whites), Uruguay suffered from political instability, economic stagnation, and civil wars throughout the nineteenth century. Yet, one man, José Batlle, was able to transform his country into an oasis of peace, stability, and prosperity that endured for much of the twentieth century.

Born in Montevideo on May 21, 1856—his father, Lorenzo, was even president of Uruguay from 1868 until 1872—Batlle became a journalist and in 1886 founded the influential newspaper *El Día*. In 1903 the General Assembly elected him president of Uruguay. In March 1904 *Blanco* leader Aparicio Saravia led an uprising against Batlle which turned into a civil war. As the war progressed, Argentina's president Julio Roca began to supply Saravia's army with military equipment. Confronted with the situation, Batlle asked President Theodore Roosevelt's administration to send a naval squadron to enforce the La Plata River countries' neutrality. Secretary of State John Hay was not persuaded and informed the beleaguered Batlle that the United States would not guarantee Uruguay's sovereignty against the encroachments from any of its neighbors. Although the United States' refusal was a blow to Batlle, his forces emerged victorious at the Battle of Masoller, which ended the war on September 1, 1904.

After the war Batlle wanted to effect change through public education, a mixed economy, and labor legislation, but reconstruction efforts made the task impossible. He, was able, however, to leave budgetary surplus and reduce Uruguay's foreign debt. Because the United Kingdom remained the influential economic power in Uruguay, United States-Uruguayan diplomatic relations reflected Uruguay's insignificance to the State Department.

At the end of his presidential term in 1907, Batlle spent the next few years in Europe, studying European socioeconomic and political systems, particularly the Swiss Collegiate Executive System by which the nation's presidential powers were limited by a National Council. During his European stay, Batlle also headed the Uruguayan delegation to the Second Hague Peace Conference (1907). Unfortunately for Batlle, his proposal for establishing a multinational peacekeeping force to prevent war was rejected.

On February 12, 1911, he returned to Uruguay and began a one month campaign for the presidency. In March 1911 the General Assembly elected him president by a narrow margin. His administration created nearly thirty state-owned enterprises ranging from oil refineries to meat packing plants, along with a state insurance bank, a state mortgage bank, and the National Bank. All of them turned into profitable ventures because Batlle appointed managers based on their competency rather than party affiliation. His further domestic goals were educational and electoral reform.

During his second term Batlle found himself in a controversy between United States and French interests when he selected an American engineering firm over a French one to build waterworks and sewer systems in Uruguay. The American company because it offered better rates, but it also offered better conditions for Uruguayan workers. French diplomats alleged that the Americans had bribed Batlle to obtain the contract, but their allegations were never corroborated. In terms of trade relations, the fact that the United States had replaced the United Kingdom as the principal exports of manufactured goods to Uruguay by the end of Batlle's presidential term is noteworthy.

Batlle left office in 1915, but he continued to exercise influence through *El Día*. When the United States entered World War I in 1917, Batlle used his statesmanship to persuade the Uruguayan Foreign Ministry to conduct a policy of "friendly" neutrality toward the Allies to offset Argentine "friendly" neutrality toward the Central Powers. In 1917 he saw his dream come true with the ratification of a new constitution, effective in 1919. The constitution became a model for the rest of Latin America, providing for basic civil liberties, separation of church and state, compulsory free education, the right of labor to organize and strike, workers' compensation, minimum wage, and retirement benefits. It did not include agrarian reform, a goal of Batlles, but it did provide for universal suffrage and an Executive Branch divided between the president (elected by popular vote) and a nine-member National Council of Administration (based on proportional representation). The General Assembly remained a bicameral legislature, but membership was based on election of proportional representation. Batlle remained active in politics and in *El Día* until his death on October 20, 1929.

See also *Hay, John; Uruguay, U.S. Relations with; Wilson, Woodrow; World War I, 1914–1918*

. . . . JOSÉ B. FERNÁNDEZ

REFERENCES AND FURTHER READING

Pendle, George. *South America's First Welfare State.* London: Royal Institute of International Affairs, 1952.

Vanger, Milton. *José Batlle y Ordoñez of Uruguay: The Creation of His Time 1902–1907.* (Cambridge, MA: Harvard University Press, 1963.

Vanger, Milton. *The Model Country: José Battle y Ordoñez of Uruguay 1907–1915.* Hanover, NH: University Press of New England, 1980.

Vanger, Milton. *Uruguay's José Battle y Ordoñez: The Determined Visionary 1915–1917.* Boulder, CO: Lynne Rienner Publishers, 2010.

Bayard, Thomas F.

Born on October 29, 1828, in Wilmington, Delaware, Thomas Francis Bayard (1828–1898) was the fourth generation of his family to serve in the United States Senate, and he furthered his family's political reputation through his long career as a politician and diplomat. From 1853 to 1854 Bayard served as United States district attorney for Delaware, after which he served at a law firm in nearby Philadelphia. In 1858 he returned to Wilmington and became involved in state politics. When Civil War appeared imminent, Bayard stood with his fellow *Peace Democrats* in opposing Lincoln's policy of coercion to keep Southern states within the Union. Nevertheless, when the Delaware General Assembly considered secession in January 1861, Bayard was instrumental in convincing the body to vote against it.

After the Civil War, Bayard served for sixteen years in the U.S. Senate (1869–1885) and held such posts as chairman of the Senate Finance Committee and president pro tempore. Senator Bayard ran three presidential campaigns (1876, 1880, and 1884), finishing second to the eventual candidate each time.

After losing the Democratic presidential nomination in 1884 to Grover Cleveland, Bayard became Cleveland's secretary of state. In his four-year term, Bayard was best remembered for the number of disputes he settled. Among these were the "Samoan Question" with Great Britain and the Fishery Treaty with Canada, over fishing rights in the North Atlantic. However, he had no substantial dealings with Latin America. When Cleveland returned to the White House in 1893, Bayard became ambassador to the United Kingdom. The most contentious dispute of Bayard's diplomatic career occurred during his stay in London. Since 1876 Venezuela had been asking the United States to become involved on its behalf over a British-drawn boundary—the Schomburgk Line—between Venezuela and the colony of British Guiana. Washington expressed concern over the matter but did little else to facilitate a resolution of the border dispute.

Had the sitting secretary of state (Walter Q. Gresham) not died, the issue would have remained in obscurity. Gresham's successor, Richard Olney, decided to take up Venezuela's cause and make the Venezuelan Boundary Dispute a test case of the United States' right to assert the Monroe Doctrine in defense of its Latin neighbors vis-à-vis the European powers. The dispute erupted out of a letter Olney sent to British Prime Minister Lord Salisbury (in July 1895), which took a broad interpretation of the Monroe Doctrine. While Salisbury reacted to Olney's letter by inaction, his colonial security for British Guiana, Joseph Chamberlain, took umbrage. Ambassador Bayard's job in this dispute was to gently nudge the world's greatest colonial power to agree to submit its boundary dispute with Venezuela before international arbitration.

Complicating matters was Cleveland's Message to Congress (December 1895), which raised the possibility of war should the United Kingdom refuse to submit the dispute to arbitration. Within this explosive situation, Bayard had to soothe a bruised ego (Chamberlain's) and nudge Salisbury toward a peaceful resolution. By February 1896 Bayard's efforts bore fruit. Lord Salisbury announced that the British government agreed to submit the boundary dispute before a five judge panel (two British, two Americans, and one Russian), which would render a final decision. Even Secretary Chamberlain came around, agreeing to travel to Washington in the fall of 1896 to open negotiations with Secretary of State Olney.

Bayard's quiet diplomacy reaped benefits that extended beyond the boundary dispute, for it laid the groundwork for a wider partnership between the United States and Great Britain. What is more significant, however, is the fact that the Venezuelan Boundary Dispute marks the entrance of the United States onto the world stage as a major power.

See also *Cleveland, Grover; Olney, Richard; Venezuela-British Guiana Boundary Dispute, 1890s*

. . . . PETER B. GUSHUE

REFERENCES AND FURTHER READING

LaFeber, Walter. "The Background of Cleveland's Venezuelan Policy: A Reinterpretation." *American Historical Review* 66 (July 1961): 947–967.

Tansil, Charles Callan. *The Foreign Policy of Thomas F. Bayard.* New York: Fordham University Press, 1940.

Young, George B. "Intervention under the Monroe Doctrine: The Olney Corollary." *Political Science Quarterly* 57, no. 2 (June 1942): 247–280.

Bay of Pigs Invasion, 1961

On April 17, 1961, 1,511 anti-Communist Cuban exiles invaded or supported the invasion of Cuba at the Bathia de Cochines (Playa Giran), better known as the Bay of Pigs, in an attempt to overthrow the Marxist regime of Fidel Castro.

GENESIS

The invasion plan originated during the presidency of Dwight D. Eisenhower. U.S.-Cuban relations had degenerated since Castro deposed U.S.-backed dictator Fulgencio Batista on New Year's Eve 1958. The Central Intelligence Agency (CIA) told Eisenhower that Castro wanted closer relations with the USSR. The threat of a Soviet military base in an enemy client state just ninety miles from Florida led the president, on March 17, 1960, to approve CIA plans to establish a military training base for Cuban exiles to prepare for an invasion. The CIA secretly recruited troops and trained exiles at a hidden camp in the Sierra Madre Mountains on the Pacific coast of Guatemala. They designated the unit the 2506th Brigade. Most members of the administration, particularly Vice President Richard M. Nixon, favored the invasion and believed it would be supported by most Cubans.

The plan, code named "Operation Zapata," called for a landing near the old colonial city of Trinidad, located in the Escambray mountain foothills 252 miles southeast of Havana. Throughout 1960, brigade members trained and made mock landings along the Florida coast. When Nixon lost the November 1960 presidential election to Democrat John F. Kennedy, it appeared the operation was dead. Just before Kennedy's inauguration in January 1961, Eisenhower severed diplomatic relations with Cuba. On February 17, the CIA briefed the new president about Operation Zapata, and he approved it with some key changes. Kennedy wanted to make it appear the invasion had been planned by the exiles. The landing sites were moved to Giran and Zapatas Largo beaches in the Bay of Pigs on the southeastern coast of Cuba. While the CIA still expected thousands of local Cubans to support the rebellion, they failed to consider that the new landing positions were much further away from the location of the proposed indigenous uprising in the Escambray Mountains.

Among those Senators Kennedy confided in, Democrats like J. William Fulbright warned that the invasion was an act of hypocrisy—it was too similar to actions which the United States had often accused the Soviet Union of undertaking—and that it was both morally and legally wrong. Kennedy pressed on even though on April 12, 1961, he told a press conference that the United States had no intention of intervening in Cuban affairs.

The exiles were supported by twenty old B-26B *Invader* bomber/attack aircraft. As part of Kennedy's design to keep U.S. participation secret, these planes were marked with Fuerza Aerea Revolucionaria or Cuban Air Force (CAF) insignias. Theoretically, this would convince the public that these aircraft were flown by anti-Castro CAF pilots. Kennedy also decided to keep U.S. Naval and Marine air forces just off the Cuban coast.

In October 1960 Cuban leaders presented evidence to the United Nations that the United States was training mercenaries. Loose talk among the exiles in Miami fell into the hands of Soviet KGB agents who passed it on to Castro. While unclear of the full scope of the plot, Castro decided to round up thousands of potential opponents, summarily executing many of the leaders and effectively damaging internal support for the invasion. Even with this setback, anti-Castro units did execute several acts of sabotage including the bombing of El Encanto, a major department store in Havana.

AN UNSUCCESSFUL INVASION

Early on April 15, 1961, three squadrons of rebel B-26Bs took off from CIA air strips in Puerta Cabezas, Nicaragua, beginning "Operation Puma," the air phase of the invasion. They attacked Cuban air fields in Ciudad Libertad, San Antonio de Los Baños, and Antonio Maceo International Airport. Since Castro had done little to protect his aircraft, they proved easy targets. Still, the rebel planes had to fly a long distance and only had fuel enough to stay over the targets for a few minutes. Plans called for air strikes to continue for an additional forty-eight hours prior to the landings scheduled for just after midnight on April 17, 1961. This was important since the destruction of Castro's air forces, especially his T-33 jet aircraft, would provide the exiles air superiority.

While experts agree that Kennedy must be ultimately responsible for cancelling the second wave of air strikes, the specifics are still debated. The president originally approved the follow-up air attacks. However, on the first day, UN Ambassador Adlai Stevenson was totally surprised by the air attacks and vehemently denied them. When it became clear that the United States was part of the attacks, a humiliated Stevenson contacted the White House and reached presidential adviser McGeorge Bundy. Unaware of the vital nature of the air strikes, Bundy, supported by Secretary of State Dean Rusk, either acted unilaterally in the president's name or on Kennedy's orders and cancelled the second wave.

Even with the lack of air cover and the potential danger of changing landing sites, on April 17 the CIA initiated the invasion when four transport ships—the *Houston, Rio Escondido, Caribe,* and *Atlantico*—sailed to their rendezvous with two CIA-owned amphibious landing craft known as LCIs (*Blagard* and *Barbara J*) off the southeastern coast of Cuba. At the start some of the landing craft lodged on a reef eighty yards off shore since CIA over flights had misidentified them as seaweed. The invasion commander Colonel José Pérez San Román landed most of his men and two CIA agents.

While air strikes had severely damaged Cuban naval forces, Cuba's air forces were superior to the rebel aircraft and Castro's troops, led by Francisco Ciutat de Miguel, had already contained the indigenous revolt in Escambray. Nearly 20,000 Cuban regulars and militia met the invasion supported by Soviet tanks and artillery. Within minutes, loyalist T-33 jets heavily damaged all of the rebel ships, sinking the *Houston,* the primary supply ship. The T-33s also shot down or ran off rebel air cover.

By April 19 the invaders were defeated, even though the Cuban military officially continued operations until April 21. Subsequent evidence supports the belief that the president had approved one hour of U.S. air cover from the aircraft carrier *Essex* on April 19, in an effort to evacuate the rebels. The plan apparently failed because of a lack of coordination between the State Department and Pentagon.

Depending on the source, between 68 and 115 exiles were killed while the remainder surrendered and were tried for treason. The leaders were sentenced to death and the rest to thirty years in prison. Ten Cuban exiles, four U.S. pilots, and six of Castro's pilots were killed during air operations. Cuban deaths were at first, officially placed at 87, but in reality there were probably between 2,000 and 4,000 deaths, with 1,800 to 3,200 killed in bombing raids.

Captured members of the Cuban brigade that landed at the Bay of Pigs in April 1961 return to the United States in December 1962. President Kennedy chose not to appear at the airport to greet them.

SOURCE: National Archives

AFTERMATH

After twenty months of negotiations that lasted until after the Cuban Missile Crisis in October 1962, Castro released the surviving 1,113 rebels in exchange for $62 million in food, medicine, and equipment. On December 29, 1962, the president and the first lady, Jacqueline Kennedy, met the returning members of the 2506th Brigade in the Orange Bowl in Miami, Florida. In spite of this effort to demonstrate Kennedy's support for the exiles and his strong anti-Communist posture, they never forgave him.

The Bay of Pigs Invasion proved to be an embarrassment for the Kennedy administration. On April 22, 1961, Kennedy, who privately blamed the CIA for the failure, ordered special presidential military advisers General Maxwell Taylor, Chief of Naval Operations Admiral Arleigh Burke, CIA Director Allen Dulles, and Attorney General Robert Kennedy to conduct a thorough investigation. They submitted a report on June 13, 1961, but it did not become public until 1981. Based on the report, Kennedy asked CIA Director Allen Dulles, Deputy Director Charles Cabell, and Director of Operations Richard Bissell to resign.

The president's lack of understanding of the need for air cover and his half-hearted support of the plan in the first place both contributed to its failure. The CIA's willingness to continue operations in spite of intelligence that indicated it had no chance for success also contributed to the disaster. Some experts have suggested that Dulles was upset that Kennedy did not give the plan his total attention and decided that in the unlikely event the operation worked, he would take credit. If it failed, as it probably would, circumstances would force Kennedy to send in U.S. Marine ground and air forces to save the day, thus gaining the ouster of Castro in any case. Kennedy's refusal to take such a risk surprised Dulles and led to the disaster.

The U.S. military had little input in the operation. During the subsequent investigation, Burke reminded Dulles that the "actual conduct of the operation 'was all in one place and that was in CIA'" (Kornbluh 1998, 249).

Perhaps equally damning for Dulles and the CIA was the fact that at the very moment one of its most important operations began, Dulles was in Puerto Rico presenting a speech and was unavailable to immediately respond to the president. Some have suggested Dulles wanted to use this as an excuse for not briefing the president on the events.

There is also at least some evidence that the CIA never really wanted a true counterrevolution in Cuba. Colonel Ramon, the brigade commander, and many of the invasion leaders were old Batista men whom the CIA was convinced could never lead an indigenous revolution and would depend on U.S. air and ground forces for success.

Beyond the president's and the CIA's culpability, it is also important not to slight Cuba's abilities. It seems evident, in retrospect, that no one in authority in the United States at the time ever really understood that there was not as much opposition to Castro in Cuba as they expected and that the Cuban military was better than they thought. Castro's victory at the Bay of Pigs also made him a national hero and helped solidify his shaky regime in the eyes of rural and working-class Cubans. Many experts believe this single event raised Cuban nationalism to the point where Castro's leadership was guaranteed. At the beginning of 2011 Castro's brother Raoul led Cuba after decades of Fidel's rule.

The Bay of Pigs Invasion also led Castro into closer relations with the Soviet Union. Fearful of another U.S. invasion or attempt on his life (the latter of which was sought unsuccessfully by the CIA), he turned to a willing Nikita Khrushchev to place Russian military forces and missiles in Cuba not only to protect the island but to reorder the balance of the Cold War more in the favor of the Eastern Bloc. This change in Cuban-Soviet relations and policies soon led the world to the brink of nuclear war during the Cuban Missile Crisis in 1962.

See also *Castro Ruz, Fidel; Cuba, U.S. Relations with; Eisenhower, Dwight D.; Kennedy, John F.*

. . . . WILLIAM HEAD

REFERENCES AND FURTHER READING

Higgins, Trumbull. *The Perfect Failure: Kennedy, Eisenhower and the CIA at the Bay of Pigs.* New York: Norton, 1987.

Kornbluh, Peter, ed. *Bay of Pigs Declassified: The Secret CIA Report on the Invasion of Cuba.* New York: New Press, 1998.

Triay, Victor Andres. *The Bay of Pigs: An Oral History of Brigade 2506.* Gainesville: University Press of Florida, 2001.

Welch, David A., and James G. Blight, eds. *Politics of Illusion: The Bay of Pigs Invasion Reexamined.* Boulder, CO: Lynne Rienner, 1998.

Wyden, Peter. *Bay of Pigs: The Untold Story.* New York: Simon and Schuster, 1979.

Beach, Moses Yale

Moses Yale Beach (1800–1868) was best known in his time as an inventor and newspaper publisher, but he also played an important role representing the interests of United States President James K. Polk in the Mexican-American War (1846–1848). He was a special agent for the cause of U.S. expansionism in the 1840s.

Born to a modest household in rural Connecticut, Beach experienced various levels of success in different manufacturing enterprises, including several years running paper mills. But he achieved his most significant prominence after marrying the sister of the owner of *The New York Sun* and eventually buying the newspaper and serving as its editor in chief. During the Mexican-American War, Beach organized the Associated Press, originally a cooperative of five New York newspapers.

Moses Beach used his newspaper to advocate for U.S. expansionism and the concept of Manifest Destiny in particular. Manifest Destiny held that the United States, as a chosen nation, carried the moral duty to expand territorial claims throughout the North American continent. Beach wrote commentaries in *The New York Sun* arguing that Mexican rule was despotic and corrupt and that U.S. annexation of Mexican territory would "liberate" and improve Mexican lives. Beach, in fact, promoted the All Mexico Movement, which called for the incorporation of the entirety of the Mexican nation into the United States. As hostilities between the United States and Mexico mounted, first with U.S. recognition of the Republic of Texas in 1836 and again with U.S. annexation of Texas in 1845, Beach advocated more and more aggressive U.S. actions. After several border skirmishes, the United States declared war against Mexico in May 1846.

Beach became an active agent in the Mexican-American War when President Polk and Secretary of State James Buchanan assigned him and another journalist from *The New York Sun,* Jane McManus Storm, to an official mission to Mexico in 1846. The charge to Beach and Storm was to gather information and explore the possibilities of a peace settlement with the Mexican government. But they traveled to Mexico in November under other pretenses. Purported to have business interests south of the border, Beach traveled with a British passport obtained in Havana and then headed to Veracruz and afterward to Mexico City. Beach was accompanied by Storm and his daughter. In Veracruz, Mexican immigration officials arrested Beach as a spy, but they released him after Storm swore that he was a British subject. Once in Mexico City, Beach and Storm met with officials of the Roman Catholic Church and other political dissidents. Though records are scant, it appears that the pair of U.S. agents pushed the church to rise in opposition to the Mexican government's war effort. The government responded by quickly suppressing the uprising and running Beach and Storm back to Veracruz and then back to Havana.

Special agent Beach, however, continued operations in Mexico. He again began working to convince local and regional clerics to withdraw support for war efforts and to help clear the path for U.S. military advances. For instance, in May 1847 Beach successfully urged the bishop of Puebla to influence local officials and citizens to welcome the arrival of the U.S. Army, an effort that General Winfield Scott acknowledged to have facilitated his occupation of Puebla and his subsequent march to Mexico City. Scott's military occupation of the capital in September ultimately forced a resolution of the war. The 1848 Treaty of Guadalupe Hidalgo ceded to the United States nearly one million square miles of territory, including all or part of the present-day states of California, Nevada, Arizona, Utah, Wyoming, Colorado, New Mexico, Kansas, Oklahoma, and Texas.

Following the war, Beach remained involved in advocacy for U.S. expansionism. In 1848, when the Caste War had led the white elite of the Yucatán to invite foreign annexation for fear of a complete Maya takeover, Beach wrote in support of U.S. acquisition of the remote territory of Mexico. He argued that occupation of the peninsula would facilitate a railroad across the Isthmus of Tehuantepec and thus U.S. control of transoceanic transportation and commerce. Other advocates of U.S. annexation of Yucatán emphasized the threat of European occupation (especially by Britain or Spain), while some political proponents of slavery saw the opportunity to expand the number of slave states. When annexation of Yucatán proved impossible, many proponents, including Beach, then turned their attention to Cuba. Playing especially on fears of growing British influence in the Caribbean, Beach and others succeeded in convincing President Polk to make a bid on the island colony. In the end, however, Spain rejected Polk's offer.

In 1848 Moses Yale Beach turned control of *The New York Sun* over to his sons, Moses Sperry Beach and Alfred E. Beach, but he continued to write commentaries on Inter-American affairs and promote the cause of Manifest Destiny.

See also *All Mexico Movement (United States); Manifest Destiny; Mexican-American War, 1846–1848; Polk, James K.; Scott, Winfield*

. . . . GREGORY S. CRIDER

REFERENCES AND FURTHER READING

Eisenhower, John S. D. *So Far from God: The U.S. War with Mexico, 1846–1848.* Norman: University of Oklahoma Press, 2000.
Knott, Stephen. *Secret and Sanctioned: Covert Operations and the American Presidency.* New York: Oxford University Press, 1996.
Leonard, Thomas M. *James K. Polk: A Clear and Unquestionable Destiny.* Lanham, MD: Rowman and Littlefield, 2001.
O'Brien, Frank M. *The Story of The Sun.* New York: George H. Doran, 1918.
Zoraida Vázquez, Josefina, and Lorenzo Meyer. *The United States and Mexico.* Chicago: University of Chicago Press, 1987.

Beagle Channel Dispute (Argentina/Chile)

This long-standing territorial dispute between the neighboring countries of Argentina and Chile brought them to the brink of war in 1978 but has been resolved due to papal intervention and arbitration in 1984. At stake was the sovereignty of three uninhabited islands (Picton, Lennox, and Nueva) at the eastern mouth of the Beagle Channel (named after Darwin's ship), which connects the Atlantic and Pacific at the tip of South America. Although direct U.S. involvement in the dispute was minimal, there was concern that a military confrontation or conflict between these two countries would undermine the Inter-American system, affecting U.S. interests in the western hemisphere.

TO THE BRINK OF WAR

The roots of the conflict lie in the lack of precise boundaries at the time of independence of these nations (1810). In 1881 they agreed in principle that the border would run along the continental divide as defined by the highest peaks of the Andes and along the Beagle Channel to the south of Tierra del Fuego. However, the agreement did not precisely define the course of the Beagle Channel, and these three islands were claimed by both Chile and Argentina. Possession of these seemingly unimportant islands was significant from the geopolitical and economic standpoint because they were linked to notions of projection of power into the South Atlantic all the way to the Antarctic Peninsula, where Argentina and Chile (as well as the United Kingdom) have wedge-shaped sovereignty claims. If Argentina were to posses the islands, that nation could project a 200-mile economic sovereignty claim toward Antarctica 600 miles away across the Drake Passage. But if Chile were to posses the islands at the mouth of the Beagle then that would interrupt the continuity of tripartite Argentina and strengthen Chile's own claim to Antarctica.

Bilateral negotiations were carried on through to 1971, when the issue was submitted to the British Queen for arbitration. She in turn convoked a group of five judges from the International Court of Justice in The Hague. These judges examined the evidence supporting the rival claims and on May 2, 1977, they made the recommendation (approved by the Queen) to give sovereignty to the Chileans, who accepted the result. Argentina's de facto military government rejected the result on narrow legal terms, announcing its position on January 25, 1978. In Argentina right-wing nationalists and many military officers and geopolitical analysts vociferously attacked the result, hinting that it was the product of a long-standing unwritten alliance between the United Kingdom and Chile.

In Argentine politics it was argued that to accept the arbitration award was a sign of weakness which favored the Chilean claim unfairly. The issue strengthened the significance of hard-liners in the Argentine junta who—with considerable support—argued for rejecting the award and going to war with Chile, if necessary. Two ineffective bilateral border commissions were formed; Chile suggested going back to the International Court of Justice, where a legalistic approach favored them. Argentina, however, demanded continuing bilateral negotiations since its leaders felt that its military superiority could be used to threaten the Chileans.

Diplomatic relations became tense, and both sides prepared to mobilize their forces. In Argentina air and ground forces were deployed to the area and the navy sent patrol boats in support of "Operación Soberanía," which called for taking the islands by force, and if necessary, invading the Chilean mainland. As the seriousness of the situation became clear, Pope John Paul II sent personal messages to the two presidents calling for a peaceful solution to the dispute. Preparations for war continued, and Argentina began to put Operación Soberanía into action. Finally, on December 22, 1978, the two sides acceded to the Pope's pleas and pulled back from their confrontational postures.

PAPAL INTERVENTION AND THE FALKLAND/MALVINAS CONFLICT

The Pope named Cardinal Antonio Samoré as his special representative to act with his good offices to mediate the differences between the two countries. In a matter of a few weeks the Argentine and Chilean representatives signed the Act of Montevideo on January 9, 1979, which called for withdrawal of forces from the border area and urged Argentina and Chile to accept mediation under the guidance of Cardinal Samoré. They agreed and continued to negotiate despite further tension raised by detainees on both sides, the closing of the Argentine side of the border, and the formal Argentine repudiation of the 1977 General Treaty on the Judicial Settlement of Disputes in January 1982. In early 1982 Argentine forces began to deploy in another direction: the Argentine bases on the eastern (Atlantic) side of their territory in response to rising tensions with Britain, which led to the April 2, 1982,

Beagle Channel

The map above shows the area of territorial dispute between the countries of Argentina and Chile. Both countries claimed three uninhabited islands (Picton, Lennox, and Nueva) at the eastern mouth of the Beagle Channel, which, as shown by the map, connects the Atlantic and Pacific Oceans at the tip of South America. The three small but potentially strategic islands form a kind of triangle east of the much larger Isla Navarrino, which sits across the Channel from Argentine town of Puerto Harbeton. Isla Picton, the northernmost of the three, is nearest to Puerto Harbeton, Isla Nueva is to the south and east (at the easternmost point of the Channel), and Isla Lennox is to the west, almost due south of Picton and due west of Nueva, hugging close to Isla Navarrino.

"retaking" (the British would say "invasion") of the Falkland/Malvinas Islands.

Despite Argentine reservations, a negotiated solution mediated by the Vatican finally emerged with the January 23, 1984, Treaty of Peace and Friendship, ratified by Argentina in March and Chile in April 1985, which favored Chile by awarding it sovereignty of the Beagle Channel Islands, while Argentina was granted maritime and economic rights in what the agreement called "the Sea of Peace" in the South Atlantic. Argentine acceptance of the sovereignty decision—which the country had rejected in 1977—was made possible by the advent of elected civilian presidents after the 1982 Malvinas/

Falklands fiasco. Most notable among them was Raúl Alfonsín, who was anxious to solve a border problem which could be used by fervent nationalists and the military to enhance their internal political status.

In a sense the Beagle Channel dispute can be seen as a precursor of the South Atlantic conflict, a war which the Argentine military had long prepared for and which they felt would justify their existence, budget, and importance. The Argentine military government was fully prepared to fight Chile in 1978 over the Beagle Channel Islands, but the Pope's intervention at the last minute with two loyal Catholic South American nations made an Argentine-Chilean war impossible. The Argentine military, anxious to use nationalism and patriotism to its benefit, focused on the Malvinas/Falklands. As the war unfolded the Argentine military government became suspicious of Chilean cooperation with Britain because of gratitude for the Beagle Channel dispute favoring Chile. After the war it was learned that this Chilean-British cooperation was little more than occasional intelligence information and limited emergency access to Chilean military installations in the south.

See also *Antarctic Treaty, 1959; Antarctica, Argentine, and Chilean Claims to; Malvinas/Falkland Islands Controversy and War (Argentina/United Kingdom)*

. . . . JACK CHILD

REFERENCES AND FURTHER READING

Child, Jack. *Geopolitics and Conflict in South America: Frozen Lebensraum.* New York: Praeger, 1988.

Kelly, Philip. *Geopolitics of the Southern Cone and Antarctica.* Boulder, CO: Lynne Rienner, 1988.

Morris, Michael A. *Great Power Relationships in Argentina, Chile and Antarctica.* London: Macmillan, 1990.

Beals, Carleton

Carleton Beals (1893–1979) was one of the first journalists from the United States to specialize in Latin America. Born in Kansas, young Carleton moved with his family to California in 1897. He entered Mexico in 1918 and was soon caught up in the culture and politics of the Mexican Revolution. The U.S. reading public was interested in Mexico. U.S. armed forces had intervened in Mexico in 1914 and 1916. The continuation of revolutionary turmoil troubled U.S. government and business leaders, and there was a strong possibility of another intervention. Beals's first book on the revolution, *Mexico: An Interpretation* (1923), was a defense of the Mexican people, their revolutionary efforts, and the administration of President Alvaro Obregón. This book established Beals as a leftist commentator and placed him in opposition to the U.S. officials who pressured Mexico to abandon plans to transfer property and power from the owners of large agricultural estates and industries to peasants and workers.

Beals defended the Mexican government throughout the 1920s. A freelance journalist whose income came from his publications, Beals placed articles in *The Nation, The New Republic,* and other periodicals with a liberal to leftist orientation. These publications disturbed the U.S. State Department, which classified Beals as a socialist with connections to the Communist party in Mexico. U.S. Ambassador James Sheffield reported to Washington from Mexico City that Beals was one of a group to radical propagandists paid by the government of Mexican President Plutarco Elías Calles. Sheffield's accusation was inaccurate, but the leftist reporter did associate with two equally ardent defenders of Mexico: writer Ernest Gruening and academic Frank Tannenbaum. He also befriended Communist party organizers Bertram and Ella Wolfe, but he was not a member of the party. The culmination of Beals's work as an opponent of U.S. intervention came in 1927. He accused the administration of President Calvin Coolidge and Secretary of State Frank Kellogg of threatening to intervene to protect the property of U.S. investors. Mexico had become a controversial issue in the United States. Critics such as Beals contributed to the debate that led to Washington's decision to use diplomacy rather than military intervention.

Beals had good relationships with several outstanding figures in Mexican politics and culture. He interviewed Presidents Obregón and Calles, frequently met with educator Moisés Sáenz, writer Anita Brenner, and anthropologist Manuel Gamio. By contrast, Beals was openly critical of the corrupt practices of labor leader Luis Morones. He had an especially close relationship with mural artist Diego Rivera, who illustrated Beals's *Mexican Maze,* a 1931 book that emphasized current cultural and social trends in a crucial period in Mexico's history.

The United States did not intervene in Mexico in the 1920s, but U.S. Marines moved into Nicaragua in an attempt to defeat the nationalist rebel Augusto Sandino. This intervention was also controversial in the United States. Beals risked life and limb on jungle paths and mountain trails to enter Nicaragua secretly to interview Sandino. On February 3, 1928, the journalist met with the rebel leader while the Marines and the Nicaraguan guerrillas were involved in combat. Beals's account of this interview appeared in *The Nation,* and his expedition to Central America was a main topic in his 1932 book, *Banana Gold.* While dubious about Sandino's chances for victory, Beals concluded that he was a popular and capable leader who stood for the best interests of the Nicaraguan people. This dramatic interview and his writing on Mexico made Beals a prominent commentator on U.S. policy in Latin America, which continued into the 1960s.

Beals visited Cuba, Peru, Chile, and Argentina and wrote extensively on the region. In the late 1930s he warned that anti-U.S. feelings in Latin America furnished an opportunity for German and Italian fascism to expand into the western hemisphere. The fascist defeat in World War II removed this threat. The Cold War, however, saw the expansion of Soviet communism in the region. As in the 1920s, the U.S. government was concerned about the left in Latin America, and the Central Intelligence Agency (CIA) used clandestine operations to overthrow the leftist government in Guatemala in 1954. Beals was one of the few journalists who found evidence of this U.S. intervention, but he encountered great difficulty in finding a publisher for his writing on this subject during the McCarthy era. Beals made a comeback into print with Fidel Castro's revolution in Cuba in 1959. He continued to write on Latin American affairs until his death in 1979.

See also *Calles, Plutarco Elías; Coolidge, Calvin; Guatemala, U.S. Invasion of, 1954; Kellogg, Frank B.; Sandino, Augusto César; United States, circum-Caribbean Interventions, 1900–1934, Cuba; United States, circum-Caribbean Interventions, 1900–1934, Mexico; United States, circum-Caribbean Interventions, 1900–1934, Nicaragua*

. . . . JOHN A. BRITTON

References and Future Reading

Beals, Carleton. *The Coming Struggle for Latin America.* Philadelphia, PA: Lippincott, 1937.

Britton, John A. *Carleton Beals: A Radical Journalist in Latin America.* Albuquerque: University of New Mexico Press, 1986.

Meyer, Eugenia. *Conciencia histórica norteamericana sobre la Revolución de 1910.* Mexico City, Mexico: Instituto Nacional de Antropología e Historia, 1970.

Belaúnde, Víctor Andrés

Víctor Andrés Belaúnde Diez Canseco (1883–1966) was a Peruvian intellectual, diplomat, publisher, and educator who served as president of the fourteenth session of the General Assembly of the United Nations.

Born in Arequipa into a politically conservative and politically active upper class family, Belaúnde was a grandchild of General Pedro Diez Canseco, three-time interim president of Peru. Belaúnde studied law at the universities of San Agustin in Arequipa and San Marcos in Lima, where he graduated with a law degree. He later earned advanced degrees in law, political, science and the humanities. In 1903 Belaúnde joined the Peruvian foreign service. After participating in the Bolivian border negotiations (1905–1906), Belaúnde returned to the Foreign Affairs Ministry where he served as chief of the Boundaries Section (1907–1911). Subsequently, Belaúnde served in the Peruvian diplomatic missions in Spain, Argentina, Germany, and Bolivia.

In addition to his diplomatic activities, Belaúnde was part of the generation of 1900 that contributed to his deep interest in national affairs and led him to teach modern philosophy at San Marcos University and to publish his first three books on Peruvian history and society between 1908 and 1914. Leading a group of young intellectuals, in 1918 Belaúnde founded *Mercurio Peruano,* a journal of social science and literature that appeared, with several interruptions, until 1978.

Because of his opposition to President Augusto B. Leguía, in 1919 Belaúnde resigned his short-lived appointment as ambassador to Uruguay and spent the next ten years abroad, from where he leveled harsh criticism of the Leguía regime, including the assertion that Leguía accepted an almost servile position to the United States that adversely affected Peruvian diplomatic independence and national interests. Belaúnde also resided initially in France and then in the United States, where he lectured in Spanish and Florida. His efforts to promote interest in Latin America received support from the University of Miami, where he established a division of Spanish-American studies. In 1930 Johns Hopkins University appointed him the Albert Shaw Distinguished Chair in international relations. During those years Belaúnde wrote and published several essays that assembled together in his *Meditaciones Peruanas* (1932).

Returning to Peru in 1931, Belaúnde represented Arequipa in the Constituent Assembly, and shortly after he reassumed his diplomatic career. Belaúnde took part in the discussions that brought the Peruvian-Colombian boundary dispute to a conclusion in 1934. For his efforts Belaúnde was appointed ambassador to Colombia in 1934 and to Switzerland in 1936.

Belaúnde returned to Peruvian academic life in 1938 and joined the Universidad Católica (Catholic University), where he eventually became chair of the law department, vice president, interim president (1946), and emeritus president (1965). Founder and chairman of the Peruvian Society of Philosophy, he also chaired the Institute Riva-Agüero, devoted to high studies in the humanities, and the national academies of history and language.

Belaúnde led the Peruvian delegation to the United Nations in 1945 where he was thrust into the international limelight as president of the UN Security Council, a post he held three times in 1955 and 1956, and as president of the fourteenth session of the UN General Assembly in 1959 and the UN's fourth emergency special session in 1960, which considered the UN role in bringing the Congo civil war to its conclusion. Belaúnde also served as Peruvian minister of foreign affairs during a short time in 1957.

Belaúnde's most important book was *Peruanidad* (1943), where he proposed the need to change Peruvian disparate social and economic conditions through reconciliation of all Peruvians with their own past in order to create a strong national unity that would avoid the revolutionary changes proposed by Víctor Raúl Haya de la Torre and José Carlos Mariátegui. Rooted in strong Catholic beliefs, Belaúnde's ideas found expression in several political parties, including Acción Popular (Popular Action), led by his nephew Fernando Belaúnde Terry, and Democracia Cristiana (Christian Democracy) and Partido Popular Cristiano (Popular Christian Party), which were generally considered conservative in character.

See also *Belaúnde Terry, Fernando; Haya de la Torre, Víctor Raúl; Peru, U.S. Relations with*

. . . . JORGE ORTIZ-SOTELO

Selected Works

Belaúnde, Víctor Andrés. *Peruanidad.* Lima, Peru: Comisión Nacional del Centenario de Víctor Andrés Belaúnde, 1987.

References and Further Reading

García Belaúnde, Domingo, and Víctor Andrés Belaúnde. *Peruanidad, contorno y confín. Textos esenciales.* Lima, Peru: Fondo Editorial del Congreso, 2007.

Belaúnde Terry, Fernando

A trained architect and practicing politician, Fernando Belaúnde Terry (1912–2002) was twice president of Peru (1963–1968 and 1980–1985). His upper class family of politicians and intellectuals from Arequipa left the country in the 1920s. Belaúnde then attended school and began engineering studies in Paris. In 1930 he moved to the United States, graduating from the University of Texas in 1935 with a degree in architecture. After a short working experience in Mexico, Belaúnde returned to Lima, Peru, in 1936, where he enjoyed a successful academic career culminating in 1955 when he became the first dean of the civil engineering and architecture department at the Universidad Nacional de Ingeniería (National University of Engineering).

Belaúnde's political activism began in 1944 as one of the founders of the *Frente Democrático Nacional* (National Democratic Front, FDN), which brought together political independents and the Alianza Popular Revolucionaria Americana (American Popular Revolutionary Alliance, APRA). Together, the parties worked for the presidential election of APRA candidate José Luis Bustamante y Rivero in June 1945. The election also sent Belaúnde to the national congress where he served for three years until a military coup overthrew Bustamante in October 3, 1948. Belaúnde returned to academia and continued to be a critic of the Manuel Odría regime until 1956, when he unsuccessfully ran for the presidency as the candidate of the *Frente Nacional de Juventudes Democraticas* (Democratic Youth National Front, FNJD). In 1956 he founded Acción Popular (Popular Action Party, AP), which offered itself as a middle ground between the rightist conservative parties—especially the *Union Nacional Odriista* (Odriista National Union) —and the leftist APRA and Communist parties. For the next several years Belaúnde traversed extensively through the provinces and villages of Peru, during which he explained the party's ideology and sought voter support. Belaúnde's effort contributed significantly to his 1963 presidential election victory.

Belaúnde's victory came at the height of the Cold War and the popularity of Cuba's Fidel Castro among Latin America's working classes. Castro's regime appeared as a threat to Latin America's established order and, in Peru, as a danger to its historic elitist rule and its control of the economy in cooperation with foreign corporations. Belaúnde's promise to address these issues momentarily appeared as a middle ground between the elites and the growing number of revolutionary groups within Peru. For these reasons his government initially received U.S. socioeconomic assistance. But this changed by late 1963.

Belaúnde first focused upon agrarian reform and instituted measures to relocate urban and coastal peasants inland in order to become small, independent farmers, but the program did not achieve its goals. Potentially more important was the government's long-standing dispute with International Petroleum Company (IPC), a subsidiary of Standard Oil Corporation, over the ownership of the La Brea oil fields in northern Peru and its refusal to pay taxes for several years on its Peruvian operations. Belaúnde did not solve the problem within ninety days after taking office, as promised during his presidential campaign. The agreement reached in April 1968 failed to satisfy the demands of Peruvian nationalists who wanted nothing less than Peruvian ownership of the oil fields and refineries.

Throughout the crisis, the U.S. refusal to sell advanced military fighter planes to Peru further strained bilateral relations and reached a low point in late 1967 when France sold Mirage fighter planes to the Peruvian government. The failed agrarian reform program, the unsatisfactory IPC agreement, rampant inflation—along with the growing leftist movements and government corruption—led to a military coup on October 3, 1968, led by General Juan Velasco Alvarado. Belaúnde departed for the United States, where he spent the next twelve years teaching at Harvard, Columbia, and George Washington universities. Peru's military government was to rule the country until 1980, when democracy was restored and Belaúnde was reelected president.

Belaúnde's second presidency faced several problems, including a short war with Ecuador in 1981 and an excessive external debt that adversely affected the Peruvian economy by contributing to worker inspired slowdowns in production and concomitant unemployment and inflation. Leftist revolutionaries—the *Sendero Luminoso* (Shining Path) and *Movimiento Revolucionario Tupac Amaru* (Tupac Amaru Revolutionary Movement, MRTA)—began a terrorist campaign that lasted into the 1990s, with some minor focuses resisting even today. Belaúnde's failure to address these problems contributed to his rapid decline in popularity. Bilateral relations with the United States suffered because Belaúnde's government failed to address human rights violations in its struggle against the revolutionary groups. Further straining relations were Peru's restoration of diplomatic relations with the Soviet Union and Eastern European countries, Belaúnde's criticism of the United States for its support of the British during the Falkland/Malvinas War, and the president's further criticism of the U.S. invasion of Grenada on October 25, 1983.

After leaving the presidency in 1985, Belaúnde remained active in politics. He became senator for life, a privilege abolished by the 1993 constitution. In 1990 he supported the presidential candidacy of Mario Vargas Llosa against the victor, Alberto Fujimori. Until his death in 2002, Belaúnde was one of Fujimori's most outspoken critics.

See also *American Popular Revolutionary Alliance (APRA) (Peru); Grenada, U.S. Invasion, 1983; Guerrilla Warfare; Malvinas/Falkland Islands Controversy and War (Argentina/United Kingdom); Peru, U.S. Relations with*

. . . . JORGE ORTIZ-SOTELO

Selected Works

Belaúnde Terry, Fernando. *Peru's Own Conquest.* Lima, Peru: American Studies Press, 1965.

REFERENCES AND FURTHER READING

Zapata Velasco, Antonio. *El joven Belaúnde. Historia de la Revista El Arquitecto Peruano.* Lima, Peru: Editorial Minerva, 1995.

Belize, U.S. Relations with

Belize is a nation of about eight thousand square miles located on the Caribbean side of the Central American isthmus between Mexico and Guatemala. Its population is between 250,000 and 300,000 and is ethnically diverse, with mestizo and creole groups predominating. For centuries it was a British logwood and mahogany extraction settlement but became a colony in 1862. It gained internal self-government in 1964 and independence in 1981. The economy is diverse, including a growing tourist industry, sugar, citrus, and marine exports, and recently the discovery and export of petroleum. Belize currently does greater than 50 percent of its export trade with the United States and there is a very strong American cultural presence, particularly through the media. A great number of Belizeans regularly live in or visit the United States, with many sending considerable remittances to Belize, which help offset the country's imbalance of trade. It is popularly said that in Belize it is hard to find anyone who does not have a relative living in the United States.

COLONIAL PERIOD

Belize's relationship with the British North American territories, which would become the United States, dates from approximately the middle of the seventeenth century, when logwood (principally for use in dyeing woolens but also as inlay), and later mahogany, was shipped to the principal ports of those colonies, from Charleston to Boston. As many as four ships might arrive per month in Boston from Belize in the fall of any given year. This trade was an extension of the coastal trade of the colonies and was part of the famous triangular trade carried on by Yankee captains principally from New York and Boston. While the bulk of this timber was destined for sale in the United Kingdom, some was sold in the North American colonies as part of the expansion of the area's textile and cabinet industries. This trade suffered periodically during the frequent wars between Spain and its European rivals.

Until 1787 the settlement at Belize was dependent for legal and administrative oversight on the town of Black River, Honduras, which also had oversight of a string of agricultural and trading settlements along the coasts of Honduras and Nicaragua. The Moskito Coast or Shore, as the region from Black River to Bluefields was known, had a history of British settlement as old as that of Belize and had figured actively in the Anglo-Spanish struggle in the region. It seems never to have been regulated by international treaty and, unlike Belize, was not limited in what it could export or grow and settlement was not prohibited. Also unlike Belize, the Moskito Shore developed a more open and racially mixed society with only the highest posts being closed to persons of mixed race. Toward the middle of the eighteenth century, many planters saw in the area the potential for the development of an agricultural colony somewhat on the order of the mainland colonies. To this end they advertised widely for settlers and investors. With the loss of the North American colonies, however, Great Britain washed its hands of further settlement colonies, abandoning the Shore and transferring most of its inhabitants to Belize. Shipping in and out of Belize would stop at Black River for further local commodities. In return they brought textiles, construction materials, liquor, weapons, and other agricultural goods. Stops at Black River and Belize were often made to fill a ship's hold before returning north.

The wars of the American Revolution produced the dislocation of trade with occasionally severe hardship in Belize, the abandonment of the Belize settlement from 1779 until 1783, and the relocation of loyalists, particularly from South Carolina and Georgia, first at Black River and later at Belize. In addition, as part of the treaties of 1783 and 1787, which ended the American Revolution and redrew colonial boundaries, Great Britain transferred over two thousand persons from Black River to Belize in the summer of 1787. This transfer, and subsequent battles in 1798, virtually guaranteed Belize as a unique entity in Central America.

NINETEENTH CENTURY

The Napoleonic Wars and the War of 1812 again interrupted trade between Belize and the young United States. However, the expanding cabinet and furniture industries in the United States caused an increased demand for Honduras mahogany from Belize as the export of logwood declined. Belize continued to ship mahogany to the United States well into the twentieth century, but after the 1830s a slow decline in exports of the material set in.

Until the 1850s Belize was the dominant entrepôt for European trade with Central America. It was also the de facto transfer point for travelers to upper Central America, making Belize an obligatory stop for commercial and diplomatic personnel visiting the region. As the United States began to explore the possibilities of commercial and diplomatic relations with the new states of Central America, its diplomats spent time in Belize. Most famous of these was John Lloyd Stephens, first envoy plenipotentiary to the Central American Confederation, who, based in Belize, later revealed the ancient Maya to the modern world.

As the decline in forest product exports continued after 1830, discussion developed in Belize about the need for diversification of the economy. This discussion was also fostered by the introduction of large numbers of mestizos and Mayas from Yucatan into Belize as a result of the Caste Wars in that region which developed after midcentury and lasted intermittently until about 1900. These new settlers introduced sugar cane cultivation to the north of Belize and land owners saw in its development a chance to recoup losses in forest product sales. This new industry would see the introduction of a plantation-style economy into Belize and its staffing by the import of indentured laborers from a variety of sources but chiefly from India, China, and the West Indies. Early plans called for the introduction of freed American blacks, but the American consul at Belize opposed this move on the grounds that working conditions in Belize were too harsh.

While the United States was engaged in its Civil War, Great Britain turned its settlement at Belize into the colony of British Honduras with oversight from Jamaica. This produced no small amount of complaint from Washington, but the issue declined, and by 1871 Belize traded in its legislature for direct administration from London as a crown colony. During much of the time which followed, efforts were made to reverse the decision of 1871, leading first to universal adult suffrage in 1954 and internal self-government in 1964.

The U.S. Civil War and its aftermath were to strengthen ties between Belize and the American South. First, the Civil War interrupted, to a degree, trade with the United States, as had happened in prior wars. But the Confederacy's need for arms provided many opportunities for remedying these losses through contraband trade, a practice which Belize merchants were simultaneously developing with the warring factions in Yucatan. At the end of the Civil War many displaced southerners sought new homes in Central and South America, with many arriving in Belize. Although most spent but a short while in Belize, certain plantations in the north and south of Belize were their creation. In the south of the country settlers from Mississippi, refusing to work further with persons of African heritage, pressed for the importation of East Indian indentured laborers. Today the Confederate families are gone, but the East Indian community continues to live in roughly the same area as the old southern plantations. As a result of the increased commerce with the recovering south, and for reasons of speed, by the 1870s Belize altered the route used to transport its mail, replacing Jamaica with New Orleans, effectively tying itself closer to the American economy.

From the 1860s the great merchant houses of Belize began a gradual change in ownership and products were imported. From this period until about 1920 there was an increase in German-owned firms in the area. A number of these immigrants came to Belize after spending time in the Unites States, and some came as a result of the American destruction of Greytown, Nicaragua. By the 1880s the Germans had married into creole families and had begun a shift in imports, offering not only British and continental goods but an increasing quantity of American merchandise. By the first decades of the twentieth century advertisements in Belize newspapers regularly featured American products.

EARLY TWENTIETH CENTURY

Export trade to the United States increased, particularly with the southern ports of New Orleans and Mobile. The old timber trade continued but there were major shifts in agriculture. As American fruit companies expanded their interests in Central America, Belize developed a banana industry and experimented with the production of coffee, cacao, and citrus, as well as lesser tropical items such as cashews and coconuts. There was a boom in the production of sugar and rum, particularly in the Toledo district in the south of the country. Virtually all of this production was destined for the United States. As seeming proof of this, Belize took part in the agricultural exhibition at New Orleans in 1900. Belize also served as the point of export for chicle from its interior and from Guatemala, most of it bound for the Chicago-based Wrigley company, until the crash of that market in the 1940s. This pattern of attachment to the American economy has meant that the country's economic cycles tend to follow those of the United States.

The American experimentation with prohibition in the 1920s and 1930s gave a needed boost to the Belizean economy and helped it to survive the first years of the Great Depression. However, this temporary boom came to an end with the catastrophic hurricane of September 10, 1931, which destroyed both stocks of alcohol and the infrastructure which made it work. First response to this hurricane came from American warships in the area, which left only after British forces arrived. The extreme economic straits which followed eventually produced calls for greater local autonomy and a more just society, requests strongly supported by an increasing number of Roman Catholic teachers from the Unites States. The American government, through its consulate in Belize City, has played no small role in helping Belize toward independence.

Preceding and during the Second World War, the United States carried out the roundup of many German, Italian, and Japanese nationals living in Latin America. These individuals were sent to concentration camps throughout the Unites States but primarily in the American southeast. Part of this roundup was carried out in Belize with the agreement of the local government and the use of local police. During the roundups, both Germans and Jews with German names were gathered together and sent to camps in Texas and Georgia.

BELIZE AFTER INDEPENDENCE

Unlike many other British colonies, Belize could not attain independence in the 1960s due to border disputes with Guatemala. In 1859 Great Britain and Guatemala signed a treaty demarcating the western boundary of the territory, but disagreements arose concerning interpretation of parts of that treaty and the Guatemalan government never ratified it. Guatemala's claim to Belize was often asserted for internal political purposes, and maps everywhere in that country included Belize as a part of Guatemala, often with the phrase "Belize is ours" included. Guatemala's continuing claim, including offers of free education for Belizeans and the maintenance of empty seats in the national assembly for absent Belizean representatives, retarded the development of Belize by providing a level of insecurity unappealing to investors. The claim was arbitrated by an American representative in 1968, an arbitration rejected by both Belize and Guatemala. It would take another generation and the votes of other former colonies in the United Nations to allow Belize to gain independence in 1981 and to get at least tacit recognition from Guatemala in 1992.

There has been an increasingly strong U.S. presence in Belize from the 1960s. While some of this presence is due to increased economic expansion and trade, there has been an increased number of Belizeans living in the Unites States or traveling back and forth between the two countries. A second disastrous hurricane in 1961 sent many Belizeans north. The emigration of Belizeans to the United States became visible after the Second World War, but the post-1961 emigration began to affect the ethnic balance in the country as primary emigrants were creoles and Garifuna, both groups of African heritage. This ethnic balance was further aggravated by the wars in Central America during the Reagan administration. These wars caused increasing numbers of mestizos, primarily from El Salvador and Guatemala, to emigrate to Belize seeking a safer, more stable life. The resulting change in ratios of major ethnic groups remains a major topic of concern in Belize today.

With the introduction of television to Belize in the late 1970s, Belizeans had direct access to American media and presentations of lifestyles. Movies, sports, soap operas, and general television programming became daily fare for Belizeans, fuelling an increased exodus of creoles to the United States. The presence of the U.S. Agency for International Development (USAID) created, in effect, a shadow government in Belize, and American troops made occasional small-scale maneuvers in Belize. Throughout this time the Peace Corps sent increasing numbers of volunteers to Belize, furthering local familiarity with American ways of thinking and stimulating agricultural production destined for the American market. As a result of this increasing exposure, the number of Belizeans attending post-secondary institutions in the United States continues to grow.

In the decades following independence in 1981, American influence in Belize has become omnipresent, and Belize grows increasingly involved in issues affecting the United States. Increasing numbers of Americans visit and retire to Belize, take an active part in the tourist boom, and share in the nation's agricultural sector. The American consular staff has increased considerably due to an ever increasing desire for visas to the United States. Concurrent with these closer ties is an increasing immigration of Central Americans, Indians, and Chinese to Belize, many of whom are seen as using Belize as a stepping stone to the United States. Along with these issues Belize, which has long, open borders, has increasingly been reported as permitting human trafficking and the transshipment of drugs through its territory. Beginning in the 1990s, the U.S. Government has returned to Belize some of its nationals who had been involved in criminal activities in the United States. These returning former criminals introduced gang turf wars in Belize City, including the occasional drive-by shooting, and from about 1995 until about 2003, they were regularly involved in the robbery and occasional murder of recent Chinese immigrants. In the first few years of the twenty-first century the American government began the construction of a new embassy in Belmopan, the Belizean capital.

See also *Belize, Guatemalan Claims to; Central American Wars, 1980s; Clayton-Bulwer Treaty, 1850; Drug Trafficking; Greytown Incident, 1854; Stephens, John Lloyd; Ubico y Castañeda, Jorge*

ST. JOHN ROBINSON

REFERENCES AND FURTHER READING

Bolland, O. Nigel. *Belize, a New Nation in Central America.* Boulder, CO: Westview Press, 1986.

Clegern, Wayne. *British Honduras, Colonial Deadend: 1859–1900.* Baton Rouge: Louisiana State University Press, 1967.

Dobson, Narda. *A History of Belize.* London: Longman Caribbean, 1973.

Grant, Cedric. *The Making of Modern Belize: Politics, Society and British Colonialism in Central America.* Cambridge, UK: Cambridge University Press, 1976.

Kramer, Arnold. *Undue Process: The Untold Story of America's German Alien Internees.* New York: Rowan and Littlefield, 1997.

Pares, Richard. *Yankees and Creoles: The Trade between North America and the West Indies before the American Revolution.* Hamden, CT: Archon Books, 1968.

Winer, Jonathan M. "Alien Smuggling: Elements of the Problem and the U.S. Response." *Trends in Organized Crime* (Spring 1968): 3–13.

Belize, Guatemalan Claims to

Since the seventeenth century British woodcutters and buccaneers had been visiting what would become British Honduras (now Belize). In 1763, after its defeat in the Seven Years War, Spain formally agreed that British subjects could exploit forests in the region, and twenty years later, the Spanish government reaffirmed the rights of British subjects to cut and remove wood between the Hondo and Belize Rivers. A 1786 revision permitted British lumberjacks to work as far south as the Sibun River and specified that British subjects had the right to remove mahogany. In 1798, when Spain was temporarily allied with revolutionary France against Great Britain, there was a final but unsuccessful attempt to expel the British from the Central American mainland. However, at no point did the Spanish crown recognize British sovereignty in any part of mainland Central America; it only recognized the right of British subjects to be physically present and to exploit natural resources.

COMPETING BRITISH AND GUATEMALAN CLAIMS

In 1821 Spain lost its mainland colonies, and basing their claim on the treaty of 1786, British authorities insisted that British subjects could legally remain between the Hondo and Sibun Rivers. The governments of Spain's successor states, Mexico and Guatemala, disagreed. As heirs of Spain—they said—they inherited the sovereignty which Spain had never ceded to Great Britain (by this point, the United Kingdom). Twenty years later, the British government expanded even further southward, to the Sarstoon River.

An 1893 Anglo-Mexican treaty, ratified in 1897, settled the matter with Mexico; by that treaty, the government of Porfirio Díaz recognized British sovereignty in return for British assistance in pacifying rebellious Mexican Amerindians. Failure to settle with Guatemala would disrupt both the colony and Guatemala for another ninety years.

The United Kingdom and Guatemala *did* reach an agreement in 1859. Its terms were that Guatemala would renounce its claim to British Honduras (the land between the Hondo and Sarstoon Rivers) in exchange for a railroad from the Atlantic Coast to Guatemala City, construction of which the British government would finance. However, differences of interpretation and misunderstandings led to so many delays that the British withdrew their offer. Guatemala reasserted its claims, and Guatemalan maps depicted British Honduras as the Guatemalan province of Belize.

In 1972 the British government sent an aircraft carrier, two frigates, and a destroyer to the colony, by this time usually known in English as "Belize" rather than "British Honduras." It also doubled the size of the British garrison charged with defending the colony from a Guatemalan attack. The threat of a Guatemalan invasion to eradicate and absorb the colony (not simply to change the location of the border) delayed Belizean independence, although the colony did acquire internal self-government.

Demographically, Belize was (and remains) significantly different from Guatemala. As in Guatemala, there are Amerindians, descendants of the Maya. However, most of the European population is of British extraction, and there are two groups of black people: descendants of African slaves, most of whom are Protestants and have English as their first language; and Caribs, descendants of people whom the British deported from the Eastern Caribbean island of St. Vincent after a rebellion in 1797 to the Honduran island of Roatan (in the Republic of Honduras), most of them Roman Catholic, who intermarried with black Africans and subsequently migrated to British Honduras. There are also descendants of refugees from various Central American and Mexican conflicts; a significant East Indian and Arab population; and Mennonites, descendants of Canadians whose ancestors believed that they could withstand modernization in Central America better than in Manitoba. These people did not want to be Guatemalan.

INCREASED TENSIONS AND RESOLUTION

During the 1960s and 1970s there were two principal political parties: the People's United Party (PUP), largely Roman Catholic; and the United Democratic Party (UDP), largely Protestant. Until 1984 the PUP held office under Prime Minister George Price, who promoted a Belizean identity complete with flag and national anthem. Price and his associates did not want to become Guatemalans, but they anticipated that eventually Guatemala might accept an independent Belize. The UDP, by contrast, was more British than the British, opposing independence, flying the Union Jack, and singing *God Save the Queen*. UDP supporters feared that the only alternative to British colonial rule would be a Guatemalan takeover.

By 1978 tensions with Guatemala were so acute that British soldiers surrounded the international airport and assumed positions along the Guatemalan border. British marines staged amphibious landings at Punta Gorda, within sight of Guatemala. Guatemala had almost no international support for its claims. When the government of Kjell Laugerud (1974–1978) was actively claiming that Belize was Guatemalan territory and threatening war, U.S. Secretary of State Henry Kissinger and U.S. Ambassador Francis Meloy urged patience and responsible behavior. In November 1980 the United Nations unanimously (139:0) adopted a resolution in favor of Belizean independence in 1981.

Finally, in March 1981, the British, Guatemalan, and Belizean governments reached an agreement. The Guatemalan government renounced its claim to Belizean land in exchange for an adjustment of the maritime boundary in such a way that Guatemala could have better access to the Caribbean and control of the fish and petroleum reserves of the continental shelf. Guatemala also gained the following: permission to use Belizean ports as entrepôts, places to load and unload imports and exports from third countries without having to pay duties; the right to construct pipelines; and access to the highway between the border and the coast. Guatemalans could also operate on the Belizean islands of Ranguana and Sapodilla. Belize, with a population of 140,000, became independent September 21, 1981.

Even then, the United Kingdom and Guatemala did not have diplomatic relations, and they would not until 1986. The British government continued to spend twenty-five million pounds each year so that British forces could remain in Belize to resist any Guatemalan aggression. Happily, peace prevailed, and both sides benefited. Paved highways now link the Guatemalan province of Petén to the country's national grid, and tourists combine beach holidays in Belize with archeological visits to Tikal. Yet as late as 2004, Commonwealth Caribbean heads of government felt it necessary to issue a communiqué which "reiterated their total support for Belize's sovereignty and territorial integrity in the face of Guatemala's unfounded and anachronistic claim to Belizean territory." (The communiqué, issued at the end of the Commonwealth Heads of Government meeting in St. Kitts March 27, 2004, is available on LexisNexis.)

See also *Belize, U.S. Relations with; Buchanan, James; Clayton-Bulwer Treaty, 1850; Ford, Gerald R.; Guatemala, U.S. Relations with; Reagan, Ronald W.*

. . . . GRAEME S. MOUNT

REFERENCES AND FURTHER READING

Dopson, Darda. *A History of Belize.* Hong Kong: Longmans Caribbean, 1973.
Spinner, Thomas J. Jr. "Belize, Guatemala and the British Empire." *Revista/Review Interamericana* VI, no. 2 (Summer 1976): 282–290.
Thorndike, Tony. "The Conundrum of Belize: An Anatomy of a Dispute." *Revista/Review Interamericana* XI, no. 2 (Summer 1981): 159–182.
Wandell, D. A. G. *British Honduras: A Historical and Contemporary Survey.* London: Oxford University Press, 1961.

Benton, Thomas Hart

As a U. S. senator from Missouri between 1821 and 1851, Thomas Hart Benton (1782–1858) was extensively involved in the political debates over western expansion, the expansion of slave territory, and virtually every other major political issue that came before Congress. His advocacy of "hard money" as opposed to paper currency earned him the nickname "Old Bullion Benton." A major advocate of western expansion, Benton was a prominent figure in the debates over the Oregon question, the annexation of Texas, and the issues leading to the war between the United States and Mexico that began in 1846.

Benton was born in Hillsborough, North Carolina, on March 14, 1782. His father died in 1790 but had previously purchased a large tract of land near Franklin, Tennessee, and the family moved there around 1799. Benton briefly attended Chapel Hill College (the forerunner of the University of North Carolina). In 1806 he was admitted to the bar in Tennessee and began to practice law in Nashville. He served in the Tennessee state senate from 1809–1811. During the War of 1812, he served as an officer with a Tennessee regiment of volunteers and for a time as an aide-de-camp to General Andrew Jackson. As a young politician in Tennessee, Benton had formed an early friendship with Jackson. Troubles between Jackson and Benton over relationships with friends and family members brought an end to this friendship, and in 1813 the two men were involved in an armed brawl in which Jackson was wounded.

After the War of 1812, Benton moved to St. Louis, Missouri, where he edited the *Missouri Enquirer* newspaper and continued his law practice. When Missouri entered the Union in 1821, Benton was elected as one of the state's first U.S. senators, and he served in the Senate from August 1821 to March 1851. Benton was the first U.S. senator to serve for thirty years in that body.

When Jackson was elected president in 1828, Benton left the Democratic-Republican party to become a Jacksonian Democrat, and he eventually renewed his friendship with Jackson. This relationship made Benton a powerful force in the Senate during Jackson's administration, especially during Jackson's second term.

Although Benton was one of the leading advocates of the westward expansion of U.S. territory, his position on issues connected with expansionism was not always predictable. Early in his political career he advanced the theory that at least parts of Texas were originally included in the territory that the United States acquired from France in the Louisiana Purchase and that Secretary of State John Quincy Adams had foolishly signed away the U.S. claim to this territory in the Adams-Onís Treaty of 1819. In the debate over the Oregon country, Benton was one of the earliest advocates of the compromise that was finally adopted, which led to the United States giving up claims to any land north of the forty-ninth parallel. Benton believed that the argument that the United States had any legitimate claim to territory north of that line was an extremist position.

Benton also believed it was inevitable that Texas would eventually become part of the United States. However, when the annexation of Texas was first debated, he opposed the treaty because he believed the boundaries being claimed by Texas, including the lands clear to the Rio Grande River valley, were much greater than what had originally been considered Texas before the Adams-Onís Treaty. Like many in Congress, he was reluctant to see the United States go to war with Mexico in 1846. However, once the war began, he believed that politicians had to support the troops in the field, so he voted for funds to prosecute the war. During the war, President James K. Polk considered Benton one of his chief advisors on military matters. Although Benton at times called for greater respect for Mexican territorial rights, he also hoped that as the war ended, careful negotiations and purchases might bring such desirable areas as the California coast into the United States. In 1841 Benton's daughter Jesse married Captain John C. Frémont, who was an army officer prominently involved in the exploration of the west and in the army's occupation of California during the U.S.-Mexican War.

In 1850 Benton lost his Senate seat. Many of his political opponents in Missouri believed he had not pressed forcefully enough for the expansion of slavery into the territory ceded by Mexico. In 1852 he was elected to the House of Representatives from a district in the St. Louis area. He served one term in the House but lost his bid for reelection in 1854. In 1856 he ran for governor of Missouri but was defeated. He lived the remainder of his life in Washington, D.C., working on various literary projects. He died April 10, 1858.

See also *Mexico, U.S. Relations with, Texas, U.S. Annexation of*

MARK S. JOY

REFERENCES AND FURTHER READING

Benton, Thomas H. *Thirty Years' View: Or, a History of the Workings of the American Government for Thirty Years, from 1820 to 1850.* 2 vol. 1854–1856. Reprint, New York, Greenwood Press, 1968.

Smith, Elbert. *Magnificent Missourian: Thomas Hart Benton.* Philadelphia, PA: Lippincott, 1957.

Berenson, Lori

Lori Berenson (1969–) is an American political activist who was arrested, convicted, and imprisoned for supporting terrorist activities in Peru. Born on November 13, 1969, in New York City, she is the daughter of Mark Berenson and Rhoda Kobeloff Berenson, both university professors. Berenson attended the Massachusetts Institute of Technology but dropped out before graduation. From 1990–1991 she worked in Washington, D.C., and Managua, Nicaragua, as secretary and translator for Salvador Sánchez Cerán, a leader of the Farabundo Marti National Liberation Front (FMLN), a leftist guerrilla organization active in El Salvador. She was involved in negotiations that ended a long Salvadoran civil war. Berenson then moved to El Salvador in 1992, where she remained engaged in leftist politics.

By 1995 she had moved to Peru, where she rented a large home and took out press credentials, alleging that she was writing for *Modern Times* and *Third World Viewpoint,* two leftist journals published in New York. On the evening of November 30, 1995, members of DINCOTE, the Peruvian antiterrorist police, arrested Berenson and then later that night stormed her home. In the assault one person was killed, several were wounded, and twenty-one accused members of the Tupac Amaru Revolutionary Movement (MRTA) were arrested, including Miguel Rincón, a MRTA (Tupac Amaru Revolutionary Movement) leader. Police also discovered a large cache of weapons, including a hundred hand grenades and two thousand sticks of dynamite. Although Rincón was DINCOTE's main target, it was Berenson who generated the most international notoriety as the case unfolded.

Interrogated following her arrest, Berenson denied any knowledge of the more than a dozen MRTA members living on the fourth floor of the house on November 30. She admitted to knowing Rincón and that he was a member of MRTA but claimed MRTA was a revolutionary rather than a terrorist organization. In a defiant, even angry, appearance the police allowed her to make to the press on January 8, 1996, Berenson continued to differentiate between revolutionaries and terrorists. Her televised statements and appearance alienated Peruvians, who were tired of years of terrorism perpetrated by MRTA and the Shining Path movement.

Accused of treason against the fatherland, despite not being a Peruvian citizen, Berenson was tried by a military tribunal of judges hooded to conceal their identity against terrorist reprisals. The prosecutors argued that Berenson had gone to Peru to assist MRTA. Her press credentials were, they insisted, simply a ruse to gain entry to the Peruvian Congress and gain information for a MRTA plan to attack it and take the parliamentarians hostage. They noted that she had published no articles in either journal she claimed to represent. The tribunal found Berenson guilty and on January 11, 1996, sentenced her to life in prison.

Berenson's parents and Ramsey Clark, the former U.S. attorney general, launched a media campaign in the hope of liberating her. The U.S. government, during both the Bill Clinton and George W. Bush administrations, worked quietly to secure her release or a reduction in her sentence. International pressure brought about a new trial in a civilian court in 2001, in which she was convicted of a lesser charge of assisting a terrorist group and was sentenced to twenty years in prison. The following year the Inter-American Commission on Human Rights, a seven-member autonomous body elected by the Organization of American States, concluded that her trials were unjust but the Inter-American Court of Human Rights rejected the commission's findings, concluding that the civilian trial was legitimate. While imprisoned, she married her lawyer, Aníbal Apari, in 2003, and bore a son, Salvador, in 2009.

In May 2010 Berenson was released on parole by a Peruvian judge, on the condition that she remain in Peru until her twenty-year sentence was finished. Many Peruvians protested her parole, and in August a court ordered her sent back to prison. In November 2010 she was released once again, with the stipulation that she remain in Peru.

See also *Inter-American Commission on Human Rights; Inter-American Court of Human Rights; Shining Path (Sendero Luminoso) (Peru); Tupac Amaru Revolutionary Movement (MRTA) (Peru)*

KENDALL BROWN

REFERENCES AND FURTHER READING

"Committee to Free Lori Berenson: A Young Woman Held Political Prisoner in Perú," March 6, 2001, www.freelori.org/.

Levi, Jonathan, and Liz Mineo. "The Lori Berenson Papers," *The Nation*, August 24, 2000, www.thenation.com/article/lori-berenson-papers?page=0,1.

Berle, Adolf A. Jr.

Educator, diplomat, and presidential adviser, Adolf Augustus Berle Jr. (1895–1971), was a child prodigy who became an economic theorist and policymaker, helped craft the banking and securities laws of the New Deal, and shaped many twentieth-century ideas about property and power.

LAWYER AND ECONOMIC ADVISER

He was born in Boston, Massachusetts, on January 27, 1895. He received a BA in history in 1913, an MA in history in 1914 from Harvard College, and a law degree in 1916 from Harvard Law School. Berle spent a year in private practice in Boston before serving in World War I. Following the war he acted as a member of the American delegation to the Paris Peace Conference. Unhappy with the harsh terms of the Versailles Treaty, he resigned in protest. He prophetically decried the severe punishment of Germany and warned there would likely be dire consequences.

In late 1919 Berle moved to New York City to become a member of the law firm of Berle, Berle and Brunner, where he remained, taking frequent leaves to fulfill responsibilities as a public servant and diplomat. In 1927 Berle became a professor of corporate law at Columbia University and remained on the faculty until 1963. Berle was noted for his frankness and shrewd understanding of political and economic power.

As the U.S. economy teetered on collapse in the late 1920s and early 1930s, Berle began to make a convincing argument that the main reason for the financial decay of the nation was conservative and antiquated concepts from the "Robber Baron" era of the late nineteenth century. Franklin D. Roosevelt turned to Berle and other progressives during his 1932 campaign for what would become the "Brain Trust." This original group of advisers which included, among others, Berle, Gardiner Means, and Rexford Tugwell, played a major role in forging the New Deal, especially the "First Hundred Days." Following Roosevelt's inauguration in March 1933, Berle and the Brain Trust began to craft sweeping legislation that reshaped the basic banking and securities laws and policies of the United States from that time to this. While his official position from 1933 to 1938 was as special counsel to the Reconstruction Finance Corporation (RFC), he had a direct hand in the creation of numerous banking and finance agencies such as the Federal Deposit Insurance Corporation (FDIC) and, what eventually became known as the Securities and Exchange Commission (SEC).

Although he published several books during his lifetime, the first and, perhaps, the most important was a work he coauthored with Means in 1932, entitled *The Modern Corporation and Private Property*. In this seminal work, the authors examined the fabric of the U.S. economy, demonstrating that the basic means of production in America were concentrated in the hands of the largest two hundred corporations. This was something they believed stagnated the American economy. Berle and Means's publication was the first to examine the rift between the shareholders/owners of companies and the controlling corporate management. They argued that this rift subverted the American system of private property and seriously questioned both the legality and national benefit of this pre-1933 business/industrial system/model. Berle's later works emphasized the power of the management of large corporate enterprises to control the market, rendering obsolete the majority of the economic theories pertaining to how the free marketplace operated. Berle wrote several other legal textbooks and works on legal, social, and economic commentaries. These included *The 20th Century Capitalist Revolution* (1954), *Tides of Crisis* (1957), and *Power without Property* (1959).

ASSISTANT SECRETARY OF STATE

From 1938 to 1944 Berle served as Roosevelt's assistant secretary of state for Latin American affairs where he sought to extend his economic concepts to Latin America. He attended many Inter-American conferences and acted as spokesman for

Roosevelt's Good Neighbor policy. He was a U.S. delegate to the Inter-American Conference for Maintenance of Peace in Buenos Aires, 1936–1937, and two Pan-American conferences (Lima, Peru, 1938; Havana, Cuba, 1940).

From the outset both Berle and President Roosevelt realized that Central and South America were becoming hot beds of Axis intrigue and espionage. After discussing the issue with Federal Bureau of Investigation (FBI) chief J. Edgar Hoover, the president decided to make Berle the White House's liaison for hemispheric counterintelligence and formally established the Special Investigative Service (SIS), designed to root out enemy agents in Latin America. This new FBI/State Department arrangement officially began on July 1, 1940. Many in the administration doubted that two men of such divergent backgrounds and personalities could get along, much less make a success of such a difficult assignment. Instead Berle and Hoover not only worked effectively together, but they played a major role in keeping the states of Latin America out of fascist hands throughout the war. What had been a tradition of dysfunction between the State Department and the FBI was quickly wiped away. On the one side Berle did as much as anyone to implement the Good Neighbor policy in Central and South America, while Hoover and his agents rooted out any potential of an Axis base of operations in the western hemisphere (Webb 2007).

Ultimately the numbers suggest just how effective this relationship proved to be. Members of the SIS, working closely with State Department officials and embassy staff in Latin America, between July 1, 1940, and December 31, 1945, located 832 enemy agents and apprehended 336. While most either fled or were deported, 105 were convicted of espionage and collectively spent 1,340 years in prison. They also identified 222 "smugglers of strategic materials" in the western hemisphere and captured 75 of them. Operatives of the SIS conducted 641 separate investigations and shut down 24 clandestine radio stations used by Axis agents to communicate with their superiors and colleagues (Statistics from Tables 1 & 2, SIS Statistics; Section 10, File 64-4104, Administrative Records of the SIS, Record Group 65 [RG 65], National Archives at College Park, MD [NACP]).

Clearly, the Berle-Hoover relationship was very important in winning World War II. Their ability to place their egos on hold and focus on results kept the Axis at bay throughout this critical period in hemispheric history.

AMBASSADOR TO BRAZIL

In 1944 Berle acted as president of the International Conference on Civil Aviation and served as American ambassador to Brazil from 1945 to 1946. When Berle arrived in Rio de Janeiro on January 24, 1945, he entered a nation in marked transition from extreme dictatorship and economic stagnation to one attempting to find its way in the world of international capitalism. Berle soon became sympathetic to the general concerns of Latin American nations over their relationship with powerful foreign (especially U.S.) corporations that seemed focused only on reaping profits and not at all with the welfare of the people in the nations from which they took these profits.

He was caught on the horns of a dilemma—his position demanded that he support U.S. interests, but he agreed with Latin American leaders that private investments cost them more in foreign exchange than they received in capital investment. Berle frequently wrestled with big U.S. oil companies, which were soaking up these profits. Berle was also concerned that the greed of foreign capitalism was creating a backlash leading inevitably toward socialism. Little wonder that when he departed Brazil, he did so with good feelings from Brazil and not so good feelings from U.S. companies.

In 1952 he resumed his professorship at Columbia University and became a founder and chairman (1952–1955) of the Liberal party in New York. In 1961 Berle, at the insistence of President John F. Kennedy, assumed the chair of the Task Force on Latin America, which helped found the Alliance for Progress. Having experience in dealing with Latin America, in March 1961, President Kennedy sent him to Brazil to meet with President Jânío Quadros in an effort to establish a united front against Cuban dictator Fidel Castro. Quadros, wanting to remain neutral, rudely rebuffed the overture, sending Berle home with the concern that radicalism was spreading all over Latin America.

CONCLUSION

Berle remained active in his later years. He died in New York on February 17, 1971. Without question, his writing and support of government policy had a major impact on shaping America's post-Depression economy. As Berle's official biographer, Jordan Schwartz, writes, "Aspiring to be the Marx of the shareholding class, a great social critic who rallied people to corporate liberalism, he sought to transform the system rather than abolish it—a task he considered as revolutionary as uprooting capitalism itself" (1987, vii). He pursued this policy both in the United States and in Latin America.

See also *Alliance for Progress; Castro Ruz, Fidel; Good Neighbor Policy; Inter-American Conference for the Maintenance of Peace, Buenos Aires, 1936; Kennedy, John F.; Quadros da Silva, Jânio; Roosevelt, Franklin D.*

. . . . WILLIAM HEAD

REFERENCES AND FURTHER READING

Berle, Adolf Augustus Jr. *Latin America: Diplomacy and Reality*. New York: Published for the Council on Foreign Relations by Harper and Row, 1962.

Berle, Adolf Augustus Jr. *Power without Property: A New Development in American Political Economy*. New York: Harcourt, Brace, 1959.

Berle, Adolf Augustus Jr. *Tides of Crisis*. New York: Reynal and Hitchcock, 1957.

Berle, Adolf Augustus Jr. *The 20th Century Capitalist Revolution*. New York: Harcourt, Brace, 1954.

Berle, Adolf Augustus Jr., and Gardiner Means. *The Modern Corporation and Private Property*. New York: Macmillan, 1932.

Ronning, C. Neale, and Albert P. Vannucci. *Ambassadors in Foreign Policy: The Influence of Individuals on U.S.-Latin American Policy*. New York: Praeger, 1987.

Schwarz, Jordan A. *Liberal: Adolf A. Berle and the Vision of an American Era*. New York: Free Press, 1987.

Webb, G. Gregg. "Intelligence Liaison between the FBI and State, 1940–44: Effective Interagency Collaboration," April 15, 2007, https://www.cia.gov/library/center-for-the-study-of-intelligence/csi-publications/csi-studies/studies/vol49no3/ html_files/FBI_State_3.html.

Betancourt Bello, Rómulo

Rómulo Betancourt Bello (1908–1981), often called the father of Venezuelan democracy, was president of Venezuela from 1945 to 1948 and then again from 1959 to 1964. He consistently fought to institutionalize representative democracy in Venezuela and was seen by U.S. officials as a stalwart against communism. A powerful orator, he wrapped his political agenda in democratic and nationalist rhetoric. His efforts were facilitated by the tremendous revenues generated by Venezuela's petroleum industry, which provided the money needed to co-opt the various pillars of Venezuela's corporatist society. His main vehicle for political control was Acción Democrática (AD), a center-left political party established by Betancourt in 1941. Unlike most Venezuelan leaders who illegally enriched themselves while in office, Betancourt, a short, chunky, pipe smoker, left office with virtually the same amount of money he had when he entered it.

Betancourt was born in Guatire, Miranda, near the capital, Caracas, on February 22, 1908. While studying law at the Universidad Central de Venezuela, he participated in radical student groups protesting against the Juan Vicente Gómez dictatorship (1908–1935). For his protests against the dictatorship, in 1928 he was arrested, jailed, and exiled from 1929 to 1936. His contact with other Caribbean dictators convinced him that the whole system of personalistic authoritarian dictatorships had to be destroyed. Therefore, in 1931, along with other Venezuelan exiles, Betancourt issued the Plan of Barranquilla, which called for social revolution in Venezuela. Though Betancourt dabbled with Marxism, founding the Marxist-oriented Organización Venezolana (OV) in 1935, he was soon disillusioned with communism, and in 1937 communist members were expelled from the OV. It was transformed in 1941 into AD, a powerful center-left party with a strong power base among the labor unions, students, the growing urban middle class, and young military officers. In 1945 AD and a group of young military officers toppled the military government that succeeded Gómez. Betancourt was chosen to lead the civilian/military junta ruling Venezuela until the December 1947 presidential elections that brought AD leader Rómulo Gallegos to power in February 1948. Betancourt initiated universal suffrage, social reforms, and secured half the profits from the foreign oil companies operating in Venezuela. The 50/50 petroleum law with the foreign oil companies—Creole (Standard Oil of New Jersey), Gulf, Shell, Texaco, and Mobile—guaranteed the Venezuelan government 50 percent of all oil company profits in Venezuela. At the same time Betancourt built a lasting friendship with U.S. industrialist Nelson Rockefeller, the head of the Office of the Coordinator of Inter-American Affairs, during World War II. Rockefeller's family controlled the Creole Oil Company, the largest U.S. oil firm operating in Venezuela.

Numerous elites, generals, businessmen, and large landowners, however, were frightened by AD's populist rhetoric. Marcos Pérez Jiménez overthrew the AD government in 1948. Betancourt went into exile in New York City until Pérez Jiménez himself was overthrown in 1958. On October 31, 1958, members of Betancourt's AD, Jóvito Villalba's Democratic Republican Union (URD), and Christian Democrat Rafael Caldera's Independent Political Organizing Committee (COPEI), met at Caldera's home to sign the Pact of Punto Fijo, a civilian plan to avoid interparty conflicts, strengthen constitutional democracy, and establish a government of national unity to ensure that all political forces (excluding communists) were represented in the political system.

Betancourt won the December 7, 1959, presidential elections with 49 percent of the vote. He promulgated a new constitution in 1961 to institutionalize representative democracy, which lasted until the 1999 constitution unveiled by Hugo Chávez. His administration created the Corporación Venezolana de Petróleos (CVP), designed to oversee the Venezuelan petroleum industry, and cofounded the Organization of Petroleum Exporting Countries (OPEC), an international oil cartel, with Saudi Arabia, Iraq, Iran, and Kuwait. Land reform programs distributed undeveloped private property and state lands to increase agricultural production. Oil wealth allowed for compensation to the land owners who had their property confiscated.

Betancourt made enemies on both the left and the right. Fidel Castro's government armed members of the Armed Forces of National Liberation (FALN). Dominican dictator Rafael Trujillo supported plots by Venezuelan exiles to overthrow Betancourt. After Betancourt protested Trujillo's actions before the Organization of American States (OAS) and broke diplomatic relations with the Dominican Republic in 1960, Trujillo orchestrated an assassination attempt on June 24, 1960, that left Betancourt badly burned. Betancourt's foreign policy, known as the Betancourt Doctrine, was to deny recognition to any regime, left or right, that came to power through military force. U.S. President John F. Kennedy viewed Betancourt's government as the best defense against authoritarianism and communism. Betancourt died in Doctor's Hospital in New York City on September 28, 1981.

See also *Castro Ruz, Fidel; Chávez Frías, Hugo; Kennedy, John F.; Pérez Jiménez, Marcos; Trujillo Molina, Rafael Leónidas*

. . . . MICHAEL R. HALL

REFERENCES AND FURTHER READING

Alexander, Robert Jackson. *Rómulo Betancourt and the Transformation of Venezuela.* Somerset, NJ: Transaction Publishers, 1981.

Kelly, Janet, and Carlos A. Romero. *United States and Venezuela: Rethinking a Relationship.* New York: Routledge, 2001.

Rivas, Darlene. *Missionary Capitalist: Nelson Rockefeller in Venezuela.* Chapel Hill: University of North Carolina Press, 2002.

Bidlack-Mallarino Treaty, 1846

Formally known as General Treaty of Peace, Amity, Navigation, and Commerce, the Bidlack-Mallarino Treaty was signed on December 12, 1846, by Benjamin A. Bidlack, U.S. chargé d'affaires in Colombia (then called New Granada), and Manuel María Mallarino, Colombia's secretary of foreign affairs. Most provisions of the treaty dealt with mundane issues such as trade, but Article 35, which related to the then-Colombian province of Panama, would produce much controversy.

After Bidlack, a former Democratic representative from Pennsylvania, arrived in Bogotá, the Colombian capital, on December 1, 1845, the president of Colombia, Tomás Cipriano de Mosquera, proposed a treaty to settle long-standing differences. As drafted, the treaty adopted the most-favored-nation principle for trade and provided that neither signatory would impose discriminatory tariffs on the products or shipping of the other. Article 14 guaranteed that the citizens of each country would enjoy complete liberty of conscience and would be free to practice their religion in private homes or places of worship. In addition, cemeteries were to be established in Colombia for the burial of U.S. citizens who died there. This article represented a concession to non-Catholics by Colombia, where Roman Catholicism remained the official religion.

Although these and other provisions of the treaty conformed to U.S. goals, Article 35 was the result of apparent Colombian fears of European threats to Latin America. The Mosquera administration was especially alarmed by recent incursions by the British, who seemed bent on expanding the borders of the Moskito kingdom, over which they exercised a protectorate. In 1841 Colonel Alexander Macdonald, superintendent of the British colony of Belize (also known as British Honduras), had driven Nicaraguan forces from San Juan del Norte and had moved to Bocas del Toro, Panama, where he had raised the Moskito flag. Accordingly, Colombia now looked to the United States to be a counterweight to any British ambitions in Panama, already seen as a site for transisthmian communications. There was also concern in Bogotá about a projected (though ultimately aborted) invasion of Ecuador by its former president, Juan José Flores, with Spanish and British support.

Under Article 35 Colombia pledged that "the right of way or transit across the Isthmus of Panama, upon any modes of communication that now exist, or that may be, hereafter, constructed" would be "open and free to the Government and citizens of the United States." For its part the United States guaranteed "the perfect neutrality of the . . . Isthmus, with the view that the free transit from the one to the other sea, may not be interrupted or embarrassed in any future time . . . ." The United States also guaranteed "the rights of sovereignty and property" which Colombia possessed over Panama (Colombia Peace, Amity, Navigation, and Commerce Treaty).

The Colombian Congress ratified the treaty the following year, but it was greeted without enthusiasm in the United States. Not only had Bidlack lacked formal authorization to negotiate the treaty, but there was concern that Article 35 might involve the United States in an "entangling" foreign alliance. After President Mosquera sent his son-in-law and former president, Pedro Alcántara Herrán, as minister to Washington to expedite approval, the Senate ratified the treaty on June 3, 1848, by a vote of 29 to 7. The Clayton-Bulwer Treaty (1850), in which both the United States and Great Britain disavowed territorial ambitions in Central America, also calmed Colombian fears.

Despite its original goals, the Bidlack-Mallarino Treaty actually resulted in the erosion of Colombian authority in Panama, especially after the completion of the Panama Railroad in 1855. During periods of internal upheaval and on occasion at the request of Colombian or local officials, the United States landed troops on the isthmus at least twelve times between 1856 and 1902 to keep the transit route open. Finally, ignoring its guarantee of Colombian sovereignty over Panama, the United States played a decisive role in its successful separation from Colombia in 1903.

See also *Watermelon War, 1856*

. . . . HELEN DELPAR

REFERENCES AND FURTHER READING

Colombia Peace, Amity, Navigation, and Commerce Treaty: General treaty, with additional article, signed at Bogota, December 12, 1846, http://tcc.export.gov/Trade_Agreements/All_Trade_Agreements/exp_002803.asp.

Delpar, Helen. "Colombia: Troubled Friendship." In *United States-Latin American Relations, 1850–1903: Establishing a Relationship,* edited by Thomas M. Leonard, 58–80. Tuscaloosa: University of Alabama Press, 1999.

Lockey, Joseph B. "A Neglected Aspect of Isthmian Diplomacy." *American Historical Review* 41 (January 1936): 295–305.

Bishops' Conference, Medellín, 1968

"Bishops' Conference, Medellín" refers to the Latin American Episcopal Conference (CELAM) meeting held by Roman Catholic bishops in Medellín, Colombia, in August 1968. The objective of the Medellín conference was to interpret the principles of the Second Vatican Council (Vatican II, 1962–1965) within the Latin American context, for their eventual application in Latin America. Vatican II redefined the Catholic Church's role in the world and in the lives of its adherents, emphasizing that God's grace and salvation were to be found everywhere, not only in the Church. This translated into increased toleration of ecumenism and religious freedom. Vatican II also advocated a positive approach to the modern world and "human progress." This included pastoral innovations such as celebrating mass in local languages and promoting Bible study among laypeople.

COMMITMENT TO SOCIAL JUSTICE

Vatican II was a European invention dominated by European concerns. Its applicability to Latin America was not obvious: clergy were in short supply, vast sectors of the population were illiterate (making Bible study difficult), and clergy and pastoral workers saw more poverty and repression than they did modernity and progress. In addition, throughout its history the Church in Latin America had served the tiny yet powerful national elites and upheld the status quo, thereby implicating itself in the perpetuation of poverty and misery in the region. The 1968 CELAM called for the Church to promote and practice a "preferential option for the poor." This meant that pastoral workers would turn their attention to the poor and their plight, not to alleviate their most immediate needs with charity but to assist them in becoming the subjects of their own progress. This new pastoral orientation was predicated on the idea that a more just society would not be reached through merely integrating the poor into existing social, political, and economic structures, which were sources of oppression. Instead, the existing social, political, and economic structures—defined as sinful—would need to change, and the Church would work to change them. To this end, the hierarchy dedicated Church resources—including personnel—to work on behalf of the poor. Clergy, nuns, and laypeople were encouraged to involve themselves in social action work and to collaborate with people of common cause regardless of their religious affiliation, which marked a stark departure from the traditional policy of religious intolerance and avoidance of involvement in activities that could be construed as political.

In addition, Medellín committed the Latin American Church to denounce injustice. This decision gained only selective adherence. For example, many bishops neglected to speak out against, and some openly supported, repressive military regimes, even as others denounced the regimes' abuses. In many cases, groups of clergy and nuns spoke out more quickly and assertively than the bishops to denounce oppression and gross human rights violations. In response, authoritarian regimes and death squads throughout Latin America persecuted Catholic clergy, nuns, and laypeople associated with the "prophetic" Catholic Church.

NEW KINDS OF CHRISTIAN COMMUNITIES

One reason that clergy and nuns often responded more quickly to oppression than did the hierarchy was that they were closer to the victims and survivors of abuse and oppression. Medellín emphasized pastoral work in Christian Communities (also known as Christian Base Communities), which marked a break with traditional Catholic practice. Christian Communities were small groups of Catholics who met in neighborhood chapels and homes to discuss the Bible and their faith. In Christian Communities that followed the tenets of liberation theology, discussion often included analysis of congregants' daily lives and the immediate social, economic, and political context. Many clerics and nuns moved into urban slums, rural communities, and similarly marginalized areas of the countries in which they worked in order to serve and accompany the poor directly. There, they formed Christian Communities and supported the people among whom they lived in their efforts to form subsistence organizations, cooperatives, and so forth, which were often labeled "communist" or "subversive" by national elites and the right-wing authoritarian regimes.

At best the organizations were viewed with suspicion, and right-wing regimes and their supporters across Latin America took to calling the clergy "red priests" and targeting them for abuse (harassment, torture, expulsion, disappearance, execution). The U.S. government trained, funded, and backed regimes that actively persecuted, tortured, and killed priests, nuns, and laypeople who adhered to Medellín and those who followed liberation theology. Perhaps the most famous example is El Salvador. Assassins linked to the U.S.-backed Salvadoran government and security forces killed Archbishop Oscar Romero on March 24, 1980, while he said mass in San Salvador. In December 1980 Salvadoran national guardsmen abducted, interrogated, raped, and executed four U.S. churchwomen: Sisters Dorothy Kazel, Maura Clarke, and Ita Ford, and Catholic lay missionary Jean Donovan. The killings motivated widespread protest in the United States, but U.S. government aid to the Salvadoran regime continued—and eventually increased—under the Reagan administration, despite ongoing atrocities.

Pastoral workers' actions were guided by new religious ideas emerging from Vatican II and Medellín that upset traditional beliefs about salvation, God's grace, and sinfulness. Medellín emphasized collective rather than individual sin, especially the social, political, and economic structures that led to, and were caused by, the wealthy's domination of the poor. Medellín condemned this situation of "structural violence" and asserted that the wealthy were primarily responsible for its existence and continued enforcement. Sinfulness consisted of upholding this status quo; the wealthy and powerful were therefore guilty of sin. Salvation was to be found not in individual penance or sacraments but in the struggle to liberate the oppressed from the structures of inequality and violence. Christian love was defined as solidarity with the poor and oppressed, which included class confrontation and taking the side of the poor in conflicts with the wealthy and powerful. Christians were called upon to build the kingdom of God in this world, rather than stoically suffering and enduring oppression in the hopes of entering the "kingdom" after death. Therefore, faith must be translated into libratory action on behalf of the poor and oppressed.

The 1960s were an era of movements for freedom and equality that were not necessarily of Christian inspiration or of purely Christian membership. Medellín's answer to these movements was twofold: that salvation came from the struggle for liberation and that God's grace also resided in historical movements for freedom and equality. Christians could find both salvation and God's grace within these movements, and therefore Christians were called upon to work from *within* them to bring religious meaning to the libratory struggle.

See also *Colombia, U.S. Relations with; Conference of Latin American Bishops (CELAM); Liberation Theology; Roman Catholic Church in Latin America*

. . . . ALISON J. BRUEY

REFERENCES AND FURTHER READING

Berryman, Phillip. *Stubborn Hope: Religion, Politics, and Revolution in Central America.* Maryknoll, NY, and New York: Orbis Books and The New Press, 1994.

Berryman, Phillip. *The Religious Roots of Rebellion: Christians in Central American Revolutions.* Maryknoll, NY: Orbis Books, 1984.

Lernoux, Penny. *People of God: The Struggle for World Catholicism.* New York: Penguin, 1990.

Lernoux, Penny. *Cry of the People: United States Involvement in the Rise of Fascism, Torture and Murder and the Persecution of the Catholic Church in Latin America.* New York: Doubleday, 1980.

Bissell, Richard M. Jr.

Richard Mervin Bissell Jr. (1910–1994) was a central figure in the United States' early Cold War foreign policy and the development of the Central Intelligence Agency (CIA) and the chief architect of the failed Bay of Pigs invasion in 1962. His actions, and the covert operations they spawned, were central to the U.S. effort to keep communism out of Latin America during the 1950s and early 1960s.

Raised in privilege, Bissell was educated at Groton and Yale, where he distinguished himself amongst his graduating class in 1932 as an outsider, a risk-taker, and a man of exceptional intelligence. He briefly taught economics at Yale before leading the coordination of Allied shipping during the Second World War and then becoming postwar head of the Economic Cooperation Administration set up to administer the Marshall Plan for Europe. Following his successful involvement in the European recovery program, he briefly worked for the Ford Foundation, but he was appointed as a direct representative of CIA Director Allen Dulles during the Guatemalan coup of 1954. He thus witnessed firsthand the U.S. operation (PBSUCCESS) that led to the overthrow of reformist Guatemalan president Jacobo Arbenz Guzman, and he considered it a triumphant validation of a bold new strategy of deploying psychological and covert operations in the service of Cold War foreign policy. Inspired by this example, Bissell was later to lead efforts to oust Fidel Castro following the Cuban revolution of 1959.

Following his engagement in PBSUCCESS, Bissell went on to head the development of the U-2 spy plane in the mid-1950s. After delivering the U-2 in less than two years and substantially under the planned budget, he was appointed the CIA's director of plans in 1958. His job was to coordinate and oversee all of the CIA's covert operations worldwide.

Bissell was a representative member of the talented technocracy that led much of U.S. foreign policy in the early Cold War. He, like many others, had faith in the power of bold, ambitious, and intellectually rigorous enterprises—often centered around American technical ingenuity—to achieve U.S. foreign policy goals. These beliefs were soon directed toward Fidel Castro, who was, by 1960, seen as a primary threat to the interests of the United States in Latin America. Bissell thus led a series of increasingly disastrous efforts to destabilize the Castro regime.

Early plans focused on the humiliation, and eventually the assassination, of Castro personally, through a series of variously absurd and horrific plots that ranged from distributing chemicals that would make the Cuban leader's beard fall out (and thus supposedly emasculate him), to asking the Mafia to kill Castro on their behalf. Bissell was thus involved in some of the earliest efforts within the CIA to assassinate foreign heads of state. Nothing came of these early plots against Castro, however, and focus moved toward organizing an external invasion led by trained Cuban exiles.

The initial plan developed by Bissell's staff, mostly recruited directly from Operation PBSUCCESS, was to train Cuban exiles in preparation for an extended guerrilla operation in the Sierra Maestra. Over time this small operation expanded into a much larger scale plan for a seaborne invasion at Trinidad. In turn, as President Kennedy raised concerns over the plausibility of denying U.S. involvement in such major operations, Bissell relocated the invasion to the Bay of Pigs and scaled down some elements of the plan, including the number of U.S. bombing runs that would accompany the invasion in order to take out the Cuban military presence.

It is widely conceded that Bissell failed fully to explain the implications of these changes to the president: the virtual impossibility of a fall-back option of guerrilla operations in the new location, some eighty miles from the Sierra Maestra, and the significant likelihood that limited bombing runs would fail to eliminate the enemy air force. Some, including the historian Piero Gleijeses, have speculated that Dulles and Bissell knew the initial operation would not succeed and believed that this would oblige full-scale intervention by the U.S. Army to support the rebel force. They consciously intended to create a crisis which would force the president's hand. Either way, President Kennedy refused to intervene when the affair unfolded and the invasion was quickly quashed.

Bissell was held to be one of the primary responsible parties for the debacle. He and Dulles were quickly ousted from the CIA, and Bissell was offered a technical job developing the next generation of spy planes, which he refused. He worked in paragovernmental organizations during the 1960s and 1970s, including the Ford Foundation, but he would not again take a major role in the U.S. government. He died in 1994.

See also *Bay of Pigs Invasion, 1961; Castro Ruz, Fidel; Cuba, U.S. Relations with; Cuban Revolution, 1956-1959, U.S. Policy toward; Dulles, Allen M.; Eisenhower, Dwight D.; Guatemala, U.S. Invasion of, 1954; Kennedy, John F.*

ALEX GOODALL

REFERENCES AND FURTHER READING

Bissell, Richard M. *Reflections of a Cold Warrior: From Yalta to the Bay of Pigs.* New Haven, CT: Yale University Press, 1996.

Gleijeses, Piero. "Ships in the Night: The CIA, the White House and the Bay of Pigs." *Journal of Latin American Studies* 27, no. 1 (February 1995): 1–42.

Kornbluh, Peter, ed. *Bay of Pigs Declassified: The Secret CIA Report on the Invasion of Cuba.* New York: New Press, 1998.

Thomas, Evan. *The Very Best Men; Four Who Dared: The Early Years of the CIA.* New York: Simon and Schuster, 1995.

Black Warrior Incident, 1854

The Black Warrior Incident was an 1854 diplomatic dispute between the United States and Spain that resulted from the seizure by Spanish authorities of a U.S.-flagged steamer in Havana harbor. The incident threatened to lead to open conflict between the two countries, an outcome favored by some Americans who saw in the episode an opportunity to wrest Cuba from Spanish control. The U.S. minister to Spain, Pierre Soulé, was among those who advocated a forceful response to a perceived affront against the American flag, but conciliatory gestures by the Spanish government and shifts in U.S. politics and diplomatic strategy helped to defuse the crisis.

The dispute arose after Spanish officials in Cuba impounded the *Black Warrior* and arrested its captain for failing to declare the ship's New York-bound cargo of cotton when the vessel called at Havana en route from Mobile on February 28, 1854. Though Cuban regulations technically required all cargoes to be declared, the owners of the *Black Warrior* noted that Havana port officials had on many previous occasions accepted their practice of omitting goods in transit from the ship's manifest. In reporting on the incident, many U.S. newspapers stoked anti-Spanish feeling and called for renewed efforts to annex Cuba, professing outrage at the apparently arbitrary behavior of the port authorities and characterizing the incident as an insult to the United States.

In this charged atmosphere, President Franklin Pierce sent a bellicose message to Congress on March 15 in which he blamed Spain for the crisis and hinted that his administration would be willing to resort to force to secure a favorable settlement. On March 17 Secretary of State William Marcy sent instructions to Soulé directing him to demand an indemnity of $300,000 and to call upon the queen of Spain to "visit with her displeasure" the officials who were responsible for the seizure of the ship.

In Madrid, Soulé aggressively pressed U.S. claims over the following weeks. He presented Marcy's note on the Black Warrior Incident to the Spanish government on April 8, and when a response was not immediately forthcoming, he insisted upon payment of the indemnity and removal of the officials responsible within forty-eight hours. Even after word reached Spain that the *Black Warrior* had been returned to its owners upon payment of a fine, Soulé maintained that an indemnity was necessary to erase "the insult offered to the dignity of the nation whose colors it bore" (Chadwick 1909, 260). In a May 7 note to Soulé, Spanish Foreign Minister Angel Calderón de la Barca defended the actions taken by the Spanish authorities in Cuba but reported that the fine paid by the ship's owners would be returned. Believing that officials in Washington might be more inclined toward moderation than Soulé, the Spanish foreign minister simultaneously instructed his minister to the United States to present a conciliatory note to Marcy. Though Marcy continued to express dissatisfaction with the Spanish position, the release of the ship and the remission of the fine helped to diminish tensions. Under these circumstances, the Secretary of State told Soulé on June 22 that the "President is unwilling to resort to any extreme measures," adding that Pierce "does not therefore expect you will at present take any further steps in relation to the outrage in the case of the *Black Warrior*" (Ettinger 1932, 278). Though Soulé avoided sharing the revised U.S. position with the Spanish government until December 1854, the case was subsequently addressed as a matter for negotiation rather than as a potential casus belli. The Black Warrior Incident was formally resolved in August 1855, when Spain paid an indemnity of $53,000 to settle the dispute.

If the intensity of the initial U.S. reaction to the seizure of the *Black Warrior* can be interpreted as an illustration of the strong nationalist feeling of the period and as evidence of the enduring strength of expansionist interest in Cuba in the mid-1850s, the willingness of the Pierce administration to back away from its initial aggressive response can be understood as a reflection of an evolving U.S. diplomatic strategy and of shifting U.S. political realities. In April 1854, even as the U.S. government sought satisfaction from Spain in the Black Warrior Incident, Marcy empowered Soulé to offer the Spanish government up to $130 million for Cuba. It may be that the United States softened its position so as not to poison the atmosphere for a possible negotiated purchase of the island. Moreover, the Black Warrior crisis occurred at a moment of heightened sectional tension within the United States. The introduction of the Kansas-Nebraska Bill in January 1854 had reopened an acrimonious debate over the future of slavery. Many northerners became suspicious of annexationist interest in Cuba, fearing the consequences of incorporating another slaveholding territory into the union. It therefore would have been difficult for the Pierce administration to muster the national support necessary for a confrontation with Spain. These factors may help to account for the decision to pursue a negotiated solution to the Black Warrior Incident.

See also *Buchanan, James; Central America, Filibusters; Marcy, William L.; Ostend Manifesto, 1854; Pierce, Franklin; Soulé, Pierre*

. . . . HALBERT JONES

REFERENCES AND FURTHER READING

Chadwick, French Ensor. *The Relations of the United States and Spain: Diplomacy*. New York: Charles Scribner's Sons, 1909.

Ettinger, Amos Aschbach. *The Mission to Spain of Pierre Soulé, 1853–1855*. New Haven, CT: Yale University Press, 1932.

Janes, Henry Lorenzo. "The Black Warrior Affair." *American Historical Review* XII, no. 2 (January 1907): 280–298.

May, Robert E. *The Southern Dream of a Caribbean Empire, 1854–1861*. Baton Rouge: Louisiana State University Press, 1973.

Blaine, James G.

James G. Blaine (1830–1893) was a major political figure in late nineteenth-century U.S. politics. He led, and was supported by, a major faction of the Republican party and was instrumental in deciding the Republican presidential nominee in four different elections, 1876, 1880, 1884, and 1888. He was also secretary of state on two different occasions, in 1881 and then again from 1889–1892. In addition to serving as secretary of state, Blaine was also a U.S. representative, the speaker of the House of Representatives, and a senator. Aside from his various political careers, Blaine was, at various times, a newspaper editor and best-selling author.

In his two stints as secretary of state, Blaine took an active interest in Latin America and consistently pushed for greater American involvement in the region. He was firmly against the intervention of European powers in the area and, in particular, sought to counter what he saw as widespread British influence. He also attempted to persuade nations in the region to accept the principle of arbitration of disputes instead of resorting to armed conflict. His first period as secretary of state is generally seen as less than successful in terms of U.S.-Latin American relations. He attempted to mediate the Mexican-Guatemalan border dispute and the peace terms of the War of the Pacific. He also tried to change the Clayton-Bulwer Treaty which forbid either the United States or Great Britain from taking control of an isthmian canal. He accomplished none of these objectives. He enjoyed greater success in his second term when he called and chaired the Inter-American conference of 1889–90, and he handled the Baltimore Affair with Chile with tact and diplomacy.

FIRST TERM AS SECRETARY OF STATE

Blaine's support was important in getting James Garfield elected President in 1880 and his reward was the position of secretary of state in the new administration. The position came with the stipulation that Blaine would not run against Garfield for the 1884 Republican nomination. Blaine accepted this deal and had a close relationship with Garfield. He wielded a great deal of influence in the latter's cabinet and was largely given a free hand in shaping foreign policy. It was in this context that he began his first term as secretary of state, but this period was brief as the assassination of Garfield led to the assumption of Chester Arthur as president, followed shortly by Blaine's resignation.

During this brief period Blaine attempted to mediate two conflicts. The first was between Mexico and Guatemala and focused on an old border dispute. Blaine attempted to convince the Mexican government to accept a negotiated settlement. He overestimated, however, the U.S. influence on the Mexican government, which was unwilling to acquiesce to the Guatemalan and U.S.-supported demands. The Arthur administration withdrew the strong support of the Guatemalan claim that Blaine had articulated, and the dispute was settled in Mexico's favor.

The second dispute that Blaine attempted to mediate during his first period as secretary of state was the War of the Pacific. The War broke out over the issue of nitrate taxes and saw Peru and Bolivia in conflict with Chile. Chile achieved a complete military victory which culminated in the occupation of the Peruvian capital of Lima. There was little left except to negotiate a peace settlement; however, this proved elusive. Blaine attempted to prevent Chile from acquiring territory as part of the peace agreement. In the end his attempts only prolonged the impasse, and Chile eventually did acquire Peruvian and Bolivian territory as part of the settlement.

The other notable U.S.-Latin American issue of Blaine's first term as secretary of state was his attempt to renegotiate the Clayton-Bulwer Treaty. The treaty, signed in 1850 between the United States and Great Britain, stipulated that neither nation would control an interoceanic canal constructed across Central America. Blaine advanced a number of arguments to the British as to why the treaty was no longer valid, but he was repudiated time and again by the British and the treaty remained in force until 1902 when the Hay-Pauncefote Treaty replaced it.

SECOND TERM AS SECRETARY OF STATE

In contrast to his first term as secretary of state, his second term (1889–1892) featured a less ambitious and more diplomatic Blaine. His support having been crucial to the victory of Benjamin Harrison in the 1888 presidential election, Blaine was once again given the position of secretary of state, allowing him to follow up on a project that he had hoped to accomplish earlier, a Pan-American Conference.

The 1889–1890 Pan-American conference did not accomplish a great deal in terms of treaties signed or agreements reached, but it planted the seeds for greater integration of the nations of the western hemisphere. During the conference Blaine played an important role in reducing the various Latin American nations' suspicions of U.S. President Harrison, who later recalled that, "in the conference of the American Republics Mr. Blaine did a very hard, successful and brilliant work" (Healy 2001, 159).

Harrison and Blaine's relationship eventually soured at the same time that Blaine was struggling with ill health and personal tragedy (the deaths of his son and daughter within a span of three weeks). Blaine's influence on U.S. foreign policy was greatly diminished as a result, with Harrison taking on more and more of the responsibilities. It was in this situation that a number of American sailors from the USS Baltimore were attacked while on shore leave in the Chilean port of Valparaíso. The U.S. government demanded redress from the Chilean government. Blaine attempted to achieve a resolution through negotiation but Harrison overrode him and threatened war. Though Chile agreed to the U.S. demands, the manner in which Harrison achieved this poisoned American-Chilean relations for years.

The Blaine-Harrison relationship eventually broke down completely and Blaine resigned in 1892. His health greatly diminished, and the death of his third child later in that year broke him. He grew seriously ill and died in January 1893.

See also *Baltimore Affair, 1891; Garfield, James A.; Harrison, Benjamin; Inter-American Conference, Proposed, 1881; War of the Pacific, 1879–1883*

. . . . JASON ZORBAS

REFERENCES AND FURTHER READING

Crapol, Edward P. *James G. Blaine: Architect of Empire.* Wilmington, DE: Scholarly Resources Inc., 2000.

Healy, David. *James G. Blaine and Latin America.* Columbia: University of Missouri Press, 2001.

Sater, William F. *Chile and the United States: Empires in Conflict.* Athens: University of Georgia Press, 1986.

Tyler, Alice Felt. *The Foreign Policy of James G. Blaine.* Minneapolis: University of Minnesota Press, 1927.

Blue Book, Argentina

(**See** *Braden, Spruille*)

Bogotá, Act of, 1960

In the late 1950s the Eisenhower administration began directing more attention toward Latin America in response to a series of crises that arose in the region.

Problems had simmered for years as the productivity of Latin American economies lagged far behind those in the

United States and western Europe. Early in the Cold War the United States often chose to support military dictatorships such as those of Anastasio Somoza in Nicaragua, Rafael Trujillo in the Dominican Republic, and Marcos Pérez Jiménez in Venezuela. These authoritarian leaders provided stability and supported the anti-communist efforts of Washington. However, the riots against visiting Vice President Richard Nixon in Peru and Venezuela in 1958 and Fidel Castro's defeat of Fulgencio Batista that same year pressured the Eisenhower administration into taking a more active role in promoting democracy and economic development in Latin America. Believing in particular that economic deprivation and a lack of opportunity played into the hands of the communists, the administration decided to focus on those areas.

In the economic realm, the administration moved away from relying primarily on limited and conditional loans and private efforts and more toward active public financing of development. In September 1960 U.S. officials took their ideas and plans to Bogotá, Colombia, for a meeting of the Inter-American nations. Building on its work in founding the Inter-American Development Bank (IADB), the Eisenhower administration proposed the Social Progress Trust Fund (SPTF). Designed to fund programs in individual countries through the IADB, the president emphasized that this program would help stymie the spread of communism.

Working with other leaders from the region, the administration secured the Act of Bogotá on September 13, 1960. The document stressed that "the preservation and strengthening of free and democratic institutions in the American republics requires the acceleration of social and economic progress in Latin America adequate to meet the legitimate aspirations of the people of the Americas for a better life and to provide them the fullest opportunity to improve their status" ("Act of Bogotá"). It called for programs that improved educational opportunities and public health and provided new, equitable, and rational tax codes and the mobilization of domestic resources to accomplish change.

The Act of Bogotá also observed that "it is understood that the purpose of the special fund (SPTF) would be to contribute capital resources and technical assistance on flexible terms and conditions . . . to support the efforts of the Latin American countries that are prepared to initiate or expand effective institutional improvements and to adopt measures to employ efficiently their own resources to achieving greater social progress and more balanced economic growth." The final declaration concluded that the approval would "renew their faith in the essential values which lie at the base of Western civilization, and reaffirm their determination to assure the fullest measure of well-being to the people of the Americas under conditions of freedom and respect for the supreme dignity of the individual" (Act of Bogotá).

As the meetings ended, U.S. officials emphasized that unlike other meetings where the United States focused exclusively on security matters at the expense of economic ones, this time Americans would increasingly focus on economic and social development in the region. The United States immediately allotted almost $500 million to the IADB to begin funding programs.

Others walked away from the conference with different lessons. Assistant Secretary of State Roy Rubottom emphasized that the act and other policies existed to "make the leaders (of Latin America), especially the traditional elite groups, fully aware of the critical need to do something to meet the rising expectations of their peoples in order to avoid violent change brought on by over-long suppression of popular measures" (Rabe 1988, 143).

In many ways the Act of Bogotá served as a precursor to the more advanced and ambitious Alliance for Progress program of the administration of President John F. Kennedy. It marked a significant change in U.S. attitudes and policies toward Latin America that continued for nearly a decade until sidetracked by the Vietnam War.

See also *Alliance for Progress; Inter-American Development Bank (IADB); Kennedy, John F.*

. . . . KYLE LONGLEY

REFERENCES AND FURTHER READING

"Act of Bogotá; September 13, 1960," The Avalon Project, Yale Law School, 1972, www.yale.edu/lawweb/avalon/intdip/interam/intam08.htm.

Rabe, Stephen G. *Eisenhower and Latin America: The Foreign Policy of Anticommunism*. Chapel Hill: University of North Carolina Press, 1988.

Bogotá Conference

(**See** *Ninth International Conference of American States, Bogotá, 1948*)

Bogotazo, 1948 (Colombia)

Bogotazo refers to the rioting in Bogotá, Colombia, that erupted after the assassination of the popular Liberal party leader Jorge E. Gaitán on April 9, 1948. (In Colombia the term *Nueve de Abril,* or Ninth of April, is more commonly used to refer to the events that occurred that day not only in Bogotá but in other parts of the country as well.) Gaitán's outraged followers—convinced that the ruling Conservative party was behind the assassination—vented their fury on the Ministry of Justice and other government buildings, churches, and the Conservative newspaper *El Siglo*. Massive looting of shops in downtown Bogotá—especially those owned by Middle Easterners and Jews—also took place. More than 150 buildings in the downtown area, excluding government buildings and many churches, were seriously damaged, most of them a total loss. Estimates of the dead and injured ran into the thousands.

Meanwhile, leftists of various kinds, including communists, seized radio stations and encouraged rioters to overthrow the Conservative government. No group, however, proved capable of effectively channeling the anger of the rioters toward the goal of ousting the government. Workers heeded a call for a general strike intended to bring down the government, but according to Herbert Braun, it was counterproductive and was called off on April 15.

Among those who initially hoped for a revolutionary outcome was a young Fidel Castro, who had come to Bogotá to attend a gathering of Latin American students sponsored by the Argentine government, then headed by Juan Perón. Before the assassination he was seen dropping "anti-imperialist" leaflets from the balcony of the elegant Teatro Colón, while a gala performance was taking place below. Castro had already met Gaitán once and had an appointment to meet him again the afternoon of the assassination. During the rioting Castro took part in an assault on a police station, where he acquired a rifle and some ammunition. Afterward he went to another police station that had been seized by rebels, but dismayed by the looting and chaos, he decided to return to Cuba. He later said that events in Bogotá had had a great impact on him.

The Conservative president, Mariano Ospina Pérez, remained in the presidential palace, which also came under attack, and he refused to flee. The government retained the support of the armed forces, which eventually moved to curb the rioters. In addition, top Liberal leaders gave their support to Ospina Pérez, who formed a bipartisan government. The coalition lasted only about a year, however, as Colombia became engulfed in the mainly rural partisan conflict known as *La Violencia.*

The rioting disrupted the sessions of the Ninth International Conference of American States, which was meeting in Bogotá at the time. Foreign ministers of all the western hemisphere nations were in attendance, including U.S. Secretary of State George C. Marshall. Also present was U.S. Secretary of Commerce W. Averell Harriman, who likened Bogotá after the riot to a European city that had been bombed during World War II.

By April 12 order had been generally restored in Bogotá and in other parts of the country. Gaitán's assassin, who had been immediately killed by the mob, was shown to be a young drifter without strong political affiliations. Even so, Ospina Pérez blamed the assassination and the rioting on an international communist conspiracy and moved to sever diplomatic relations with the Soviet Union. In addition, twelve leaders of Colombia's Communist party were arrested and held for two weeks. On April 12 Secretary of State Marshall also expressed his belief that the Bogotazo was communist-inspired and drew parallels with recent events in France and Italy.

Although proposals were made to move the Inter-American conference to Panama or another site and many of the delegates left the city, deliberations resumed on April 14 at a location several miles from downtown Bogotá and continued until April 30. The principal achievement of the conference was the drafting of the charter of the Organization of American States, which created a formal structure for the Inter-American system that had developed since 1889. In addition, after some debate, the delegates unanimously adopted a resolution declaring international communism or any other totalitarian doctrine to be incompatible with western hemisphere freedom, which rested "on the dignity of man as an individual and the sovereignty of the nation as a state" ("Declaration" 86). The resolution also condemned "interference by any foreign power, or by any political organization serving the interests of a foreign power, in the public life" of the Americas ("Declaration" 86).

See also *Gaitán Ayala, Jorge Eliécer; Ninth International Conference of American States, Bogotá, 1948*

. . . . HELEN DELPAR

REFERENCES AND FURTHER READING

Braun, Herbert. *The Assassination of Gaitán: Public Life and Urban Violence in Colombia.* Madison: University of Wisconsin Press, 1985.

"Declaration on the Preservation and Defense of Democracy in America," adopted by the Ninth International Conference of American States, at Bogota, on 2 May 1948." In *Encyclopedia of the United Nations and International Agreements,* edited by Edmund Jan Osmańczyk, 86. New York: Routledge, 2003.

Szulc, Tad. *Fidel: A Critical Portrait.* New York: William Morrow and Company, 1986.

Boland Amendments (1982/1984)

(**See** *Central American Wars, 1980s*)

Bolívar, Simón

Simón José Antonio de la Santísima Trinidad Bolívar y Palacios (1783–1830) was born on July 24, 1783, in Spanish-owned Caracas, Venezuela. Inspired though not aided by the United States, he became known as the liberator of all South America.

A WARRIOR FOR FREEDOM

His family was of Basque origin and, in his early life, he enjoyed the best European neoclassical education, focusing on great French thinkers like Voltaire and Jean Jacques Rousseau. After losing both his parents (father at age three, mother at age nine), he was sent to Europe, where he married Maria Teresa Rodríguez del Toro y Alaysa in 1802. In 1803, they went to Venezuela, where Maria died of yellow fever. Bolívar never remarried. He returned to Spain in 1804, just before Napoleon Bonaparte made himself emperor of France. Bonaparte later placed his brother, Joseph, on the Spanish throne. Disillusioned by Napoleon's betrayal of the ideals of the French Revolution, Bolívar traveled across Europe seeking some sort of philosophical resolution. In Italy, he determined to return home and free all of South America.

On his way home, he stopped in the United States and was deeply impressed by the marked contrast of U.S. freedom and the oppression in his own homeland. In 1807 Bolívar arrived in Venezuela and soon became part of the juntas attempting to resist Spanish authority. In 1808 Venezuela declared its independence. In hopes of gaining support from the United Kingdom, the new regime sent Bolívar and Andres Bello Luis Lopez Mendez to London.

When Bolívar returned home in August 1811, he made a public speech advocating independence for all Spanish America. In March 1812 a massive earthquake destroyed Caracas and forced him and others to flee. Spanish troops took advantage of the situation to retake the country, forcing the surrender of junta leader Francisco de Miranda in July. While in exile in Cartagena de Indias, Bolívar wrote his independence declaration entitled *Manifesto de Cartagena.* In 1813 independence forces in New Grenada (today Colombia, Panama, and parts of Venezuela) established the Congress of Tunja and appointed Bolívar military commander. On May 14 his forces invaded Venezuela, which initiated what became known as the "Admirable Campaign." After several stunning victories Bolívar, now proclaimed *El Libertador,* marched into Caracas on August 6, 1813, and a second Venezuelan Republic was established. In his famous "Decree of War to the Death," he vowed to fight Spain until all South America was free.

His success was short lived. In 1814 José Tomás Boves rebelled and toppled the new republic, forcing Bolívar back to New Granada. In 1815 he was once again forced into exile, this time in Jamaica, where he wrote his powerful "Letter from Jamaica" seeking support for an independent Latin America. He soon received support from Haitian leader Alexandre Pétion. Returning to Venezuela in 1817, he became the head of a new army and captured first Angostura (today Ciudad Bolívar) and, by 1819, he was on the verge of victory.

DICTATOR OF GRAN COLOMBIA

Bolívar won a decisive victory at the Battle of Boyacá in 1819, completely freeing New Grenada. On September 7, 1821, Bolívar, supported by the Angostura Congress, joined the newly liberated areas of the north into Gran Colombia, a federation that included modern Venezuela, Colombia, Panama, Bolivia, and Ecuador. Bolívar became president and Francisco de Paula Santander vice president. Throughout this period Bolívar's primary lieutenant, Antonio José de Sucre, continued to free more lands from Spain, winning victories at Carabobo in 1821 and Pichincha in 1822. On July 26 and 27, 1822, Bolívar held a meeting in Guayaquil with General José de San Martin, who had liberated much of southern South America and received the title Protector of Peruvian Freedom for having freed much of Peru. Together they agreed to continue the liberation of all of Peru, which they completed in early 1824. On February 10, 1824, the Peruvian Congress named Bolívar dictator. Bolívar now began the complete reorganization of all the states freed from Spain. Simultaneously, Sucre decisively defeated the Spanish cavalry on August 6, 1824, at Junín and finished off the remnant Spanish forces at Ayacucho on December 9. Bolívar had freed South America and become the most powerful man on the continent.

On August 6, 1825, at Sucre's behest, the Congress of Upper Peru established the Republic of Bolivia to honor Bolívar. In 1826 Bolívar wrote their constitution, which was a product of his understanding of the classical Greek and Roman democracy, the European Enlightenment, and the American Revolution. It was never enacted. Throughout 1826 internal divisions fomented discord across South America. Regional revolts broke out in Venezuela, leaving the South American coalition on the verge of collapse. While Bolívar eventually arranged a compromise with the rebels in Venezuela, unrest continued to spread as regional jealousy grew. Every time he put out one fire another began.

In April 1828 he declared amnesty for all those in revolt and called for a constitutional convention to be held in Ocana. He envisioned a U.S.-style federation of independent states, with a government designed to protect individual rights. Instead, selfish interests led most representatives to reject Bolívar's model. Fearful of impending anarchy, Bolivar unilaterally created a strong central government in Gran Colombia that included many elements of the 1826 stillborn Bolivian constitution. To assure stability, he also called for a lifetime presidency that allowed the executive to pick his successor. The heavy-handed proposal met with strong opposition, and convention dissidents proposed a plan which called for a federalist government with weak central authority much like the U.S. Articles of Confederation. Bolívar's delegates walked out rather than discuss this proposal, and the convention collapsed. On August 28, 1828, with violent political winds swirling all across South America, Bolívar made himself dictator.

Bolívar intended this to be a temporary measure designed to restore order and save the republic. On September 25 a failed assassination attempt left him emotionally shaken. Throughout the next two years, discontent and upheaval were rampant. Suffering from tuberculosis, Bolívar resigned and withdrew from public life on April 27, 1830. On December 17 he died in Santa Marta, Colombia, despised by many of the people he had worked so hard to free.

In 1842 his body was exhumed and moved from Santa Marta to Caracas, where it was laid to rest under a grand new monument honoring his memory. Over the passage of time Simón Bolívar's reputation has been restored and, today, throughout Latin America, he is their greatest hero—*The Liberator.* Venezuela and Bolivia celebrate his birthday as a national holiday.

See also *Latin American Independence, 1803–1826, U.S. Policy toward; Miranda, Francisco de; Pan-Americanism*

. . . . WILLIAM HEAD

REFERENCES AND FURTHER READING

Boyd, William. *Bolivar: Liberator of a Continent.* Sterling, VA: Capital Books, 2000.

Masur, Gerhard. *Simon Bolivar.* Albuquerque: University of New Mexico Press, 1948.

Paine, Lauran. *Bolivar the Liberator.* New York: Roy Publishers, 1970.

Bolivarian Alliance for the Americas (ALBA)

Shortly after becoming president of Venezuela in 1999, Hugo Chávez commenced a verbal assault upon the United States for its historic imperialistic role, real or perceived, in Latin American affairs. Chávez asserted that the proposed Free Trade Association of the Americas (FTAA) was the latest U.S. effort to economically exploit Latin America and, in effect, continue to impoverish its people. As a countermeasure to the FTAA, Chávez offered the People's Trade Agreement (Tratado de Comercio de los Pueblos, TCP). The initial TCP, signed on December 14, 2004, by Chávez and Cuban President Fidel Castro, provided Cuba with 96,000 barrels of oil per day at specially discounted prices. In return, Cuba sent an estimated 20,000 medical, educational, and other professional personnel to labor in Venezuela's poorest provinces. Cuba also agreed to provide Venezuelans with specialized medical care free of charge. TCP agreements would be the stepping stone to the Bolivarian Alliance for the Americas (Alanza Bolivarian para los Pueblos de Nuestro América or ALBA). Chávez spearheaded the effort.

The 2004 TCP provided for the inclusion of other Latin America and the Caribbean socialist and social democratic states. Eventually, seven nations signed on: Bolivia (2006), Nicaragua (2007), Dominica (2008), Ecuador (2009), Saint Vincent and the Grenadines (2009), Antigua and Barbuda (2009). The left-leaning Honduran President Manuel Zelaya committed his country to TCP, only to have it withdrawn after his ouster from office in June 2009.

In addition to membership growth, TSP members have made other advances. In the economic domain, for example, the membership agreed at its 2007 summit meeting to introduce a common currency for use only in intra-TSP trade. The resultant SUCRE finally became effective in 2010 and used for the first time in an Ecuador-Venezuela trade agreement in January 2011. The SUCRE will not be used outside the TCP membership. In the area of "soft diplomacy," those areas designed to win the hearts and minds of people, ALBA purchased a Chinese satellite for $400 million and has established a handful of television stations in member states for the transmission of ALBA news from Venezuela-based TV studios. Furthermore, Cuba reportedly has performed over one million surgeries unavailable in other member states.

Despite its progress, the completion of ALBA faces many challenges. Several of the members belong to other regional organizations with competing or conflicting missions. For example, Bolivia holds membership in the Union of South American Nations (UNASUR) that seeks to integrate the Southern Cone Common Market (MERCOSUR) and the Andean Community of Nations (Andean Trade Pact) free trade agreements. Saint Vincent and the Grenadines are members of the Caribbean Community (CARICOM) and Nicaragua is part of the Central American-Dominican Republic Free Trade Agreement that links it to the United States.

ALBA also confronts many external challenges. It remains dependent upon Venezuela's oil wealth, at a time when its productivity has slipped to fifth place among the Organization of Petroleum Exporting Countries (OPEC), and it comes under increasing criticism and isolation for its place as a hemispheric drug trafficking center. At home Chávez's dictatorship is under constant political threat, while at the same time, his failure to satisfy the socioeconomic needs of his people at times erupts into street protests. Chávez's proposal that the TSP create its own army raises the scepter regarding intervention in fellow member states. It has also brought criticism from Brazil and Peru.

The United States has taken measures to exacerbate the situation. For example, it expelled Bolivia from the Andean Trade Pact, which diminishes its economic prosperity and Evo Morales's image as a strong populist leader, while sending a signal to other Andean Trade Pact members to distance themselves from Chávez. Because Daniel Ortega's November 2010 election in Nicaragua was allegedly fraudulent, the United States has reduced its economic assistance to this poverty-stricken nation.

What began in 2004 as a simple Cuban-Venezuelan trade agreement evolved by 2011 as part of the continuing confrontation between the United States and Venezuela.

See also *Caribbean Community Common Market (CARICOM); Cartagena, Agreement of, 1969); Central American-Dominican Republic Free Trade Agreement, 2004 (CAFTA-DR); Free Trade Association of the Americas (FTAA); Southern Common Market (MERCOSUR)*

. . . . THOMAS M. LEONARD

REFERENCES AND FURTHER READING

Arreaza, Teresa, "ALBA: Bolivarian Alternative for Latin America and the Caribbean," January 30, 2004, http://venezuelanalysis.com/analysis/339.

Dominguez, Francisco, "ALBA: Latin America's Anti-Imperialist Economic Project," August 10, 2006, http://21stcenturysocialism.com/article/alba_latin_americas_anti-imperialist_economic_project_01110.html.

Hirst, Joel D., "The Bolivarian Alliance of the Americas," *Council on Foreign Relations,* December 10, 2010, www.cfr.org/venezuela/bolivarian-alliance-americas/p23585.

Bolivia, U.S. Military Antidrug Program, 1986

A U.S. military antidrug program in Bolivia, also known as Operation Blast Furnace, lasted from July to November of 1986. The program was part of the gradual expansion of U.S. military involvement in domestic and overseas counternarcotics operations began during the last years of the Reagan administration. Blast Furnace set the tone for a close cooperation between U.S. and Bolivian government agencies in Bolivian antidrug operations that lasted until November 2008, when President Evo Morales expelled the U.S. Drug Enforcement Administration (DEA) from his country.

Bolivian cooperation in the U.S.-led war on drugs began in 1983, shortly after the return of civilian rule. Whereas the dictatorship of General Luis García Meza (1980–1981) had been complicit in drug trafficking activities, the new government of Hernán Siles Zuazo (1982–1985) sought to demonstrate cooperation with U.S. antidrug efforts. In 1983, Siles Zuazo signed a coca eradication agreement (4,000 hectares over three years) in exchange for $14.2 million in U.S. assistance. That agreement also saw the creation of UMOPAR (Unidad Móvil Policial para Áreas Rurales), the country's first police force tasked primarily with counternarcotics operations. Nevertheless, coca cultivation doubled between 1982 and 1985, leading Washington to threaten to decertify Bolivia for failing to comply with the antidrug provisions of the 1961 Foreign Assistance Act (a precursor to the 1991 Andean Trade Preference Act) and to suspend $7.1 million in economic assistance.

The election of Victor Paz Estenssoro in 1985 brought a change in U.S.-Bolivia relations. In the wake of a devastating economic crisis, Paz Estenssoro sought to demonstrate his country's full cooperation with the U.S. drug war. In July 1986 Bolivia's government authorized the presence of U.S. troops on Bolivian soil. That month, one hundred sixty U.S. Rangers, about fifteen DEA agents, and six Black Hawk helicopters arrived in Bolivia. Their mission was to provide training and logistical support for nearly one thousand Bolivian personnel in counternarcotics operations, including significant coca eradication efforts. During this period the Bolivian military began to take an active part in counternarcotics operations, including the creation of an operational control unit (Comando de Tareas Operativas, CTO) to coordinate military and police operations.

Viewed as a success in Washington, Blast Furnace set the tone for continued U.S.-Bolivia cooperation in the drug war. Between 1986 and 2008, U.S. Special Forces operatives and DEA agents regularly operated in Bolivian territory. Part of this cooperation included the creation of FELCN (Fuerza Especial de Lucha Contra el Narcotrafico), a new paramilitary police unit tasked exclusively with counternarcotics operations. FELCN was created in close cooperation with the United States, which provided $123 million in equipment.

Direct involvement of U.S. military forces and DEA agents was highly unpopular among many sectors in Bolivia and generated a number of antigovernment protests. The 1989 election saw Jaime Paz Zamora, a center-left candidate who campaigned under the slogan "coca is not cocaine," win the presidency. U.S.-Bolivia relations have since continued to revolve around the drug war issue, with U.S. economic assistance tied directly to Washington's assessments of the Bolivian government's antidrug efforts.

See also *Drugs, U.S. War on; Morales Ayma, Juan Evo; Paz Estenssoro, Á. Víctor; United States and Andean Trade Preference Act, 1991; United States-Bolivia Anti-Narcotics Agreement, 1990; U.S. Drug Enforcement Administration*

. . . . MIGUEL CENTELLAS

REFERENCES AND FURTHER READING

Abbott, Michael H. "The Army and the Drug War: Politics or National Security?" *Parameters* 18 (December 1988): 95–112.

Bagley, Bruce M. *Myths of Militarization: The Role of the Military in the War on Drugs in the Americas*. New Brunswick, NJ: Transaction, 1991.

Youngers, Coletta A., and Eileen Rosin, eds. *Drugs and Democracy in Latin America: The Impact of U.S. Policy*. Boulder, CO: Lynne Rienner, 2005.

Bolivia, U.S. Relations with

Bolivia and the United States have historically developed different perceptions of themselves. A string of Bolivian military defeats in the nineteenth and early twentieth centuries gave rise to a defeatist strain in the writing of Bolivian history; in the United States, it is the reverse. The United States, confident that its national trajectory represents a model for the world to emulate, has provided investment capital, industrialized goods, and government assistance to Bolivia. In return, Washington expected Bolivia to provide a propitious environment for foreign trade and investment. The result has been a patron-client relationship.

From the earliest reports published by U.S. visitors soon after Bolivia's independence in 1825, the United States sought to exploit Bolivia's considerable natural resources. However, the motives of U.S. policymakers went beyond simply desiring economic gain. The technically advanced United States viewed Bolivian society, where the nonelite majority is composed largely of "Indians" (indigenous people), as in need of economic and political "uplift." At times Bolivia has followed the U.S. prescription for development; at other times Bolivia has resisted, charting its own course.

U.S. MISSIONS AND BOLIVIAN NATIONALISM

Two early examples of U.S. attempts to reform Bolivian institutions include the missions of Edwin Kemmerer in 1927 and Merle Bohan in 1941 and 1942. Kemmerer, funded by large U.S. banks, focused on improving the Bolivian banking system and the government's administrative network. Bohan went further, calling for a greater diversification of the Bolivian economy. For its part, Bolivia wanted the United States to help protect it from foreign threats. After its loss to Paraguay in the 1932–1935 Chaco War, Bolivia desired U.S. help at the peace table. Instead, Washington, wanting to avoid foreign entanglements, stood aside as Bolivia lost about one-third of its territory.

Two major currents in Bolivian history affected U. S.-Bolivian relations in the mid-twentieth century: nationalism and communism. A strain of nationalism—economic nationalism—called for greater state control over natural resources and for the state to claim a larger share of the profits of the sale of such products. At times, Bolivian nationalism threatened U.S. investment. With wide support from Bolivia's citizenry, many of whom thought that large foreign-owned oil conglomerates instigated the Chaco War, President David Toro Ruilova nationalized the holdings of U.S.-based Standard Oil in 1937. For many Bolivians oil is a form a national patrimony, and they believe the state has a duty to ensure that the proceeds from its sale benefit the nation as a whole. Despite disagreement, the two nations—brought together in part by the darkening clouds of World War II in the Pacific and Europe—agreed in 1942 that in exchange for Bolivian compensation for Standard Oil, the U.S. government would provide technical assistance. This marked the first U.S. assistance program for Bolivia.

Communism proved a less significant force than nationalism. Although communism became popular with some sectors of the union movement, in particular the main miners' union—the Federación Sindical de Trabajadoes Mineros de Bolivia (FSTMB), founded in 1944—most Bolivian communists embraced Trotskyism and were therefore not connected to the Soviet Union. As World War II and the Korean War propelled the mining industry, the FSTMB grew along with it; the solidarity of the miners was reinforced by sometimes-lethal repression.

Bolivia Territorial Losses

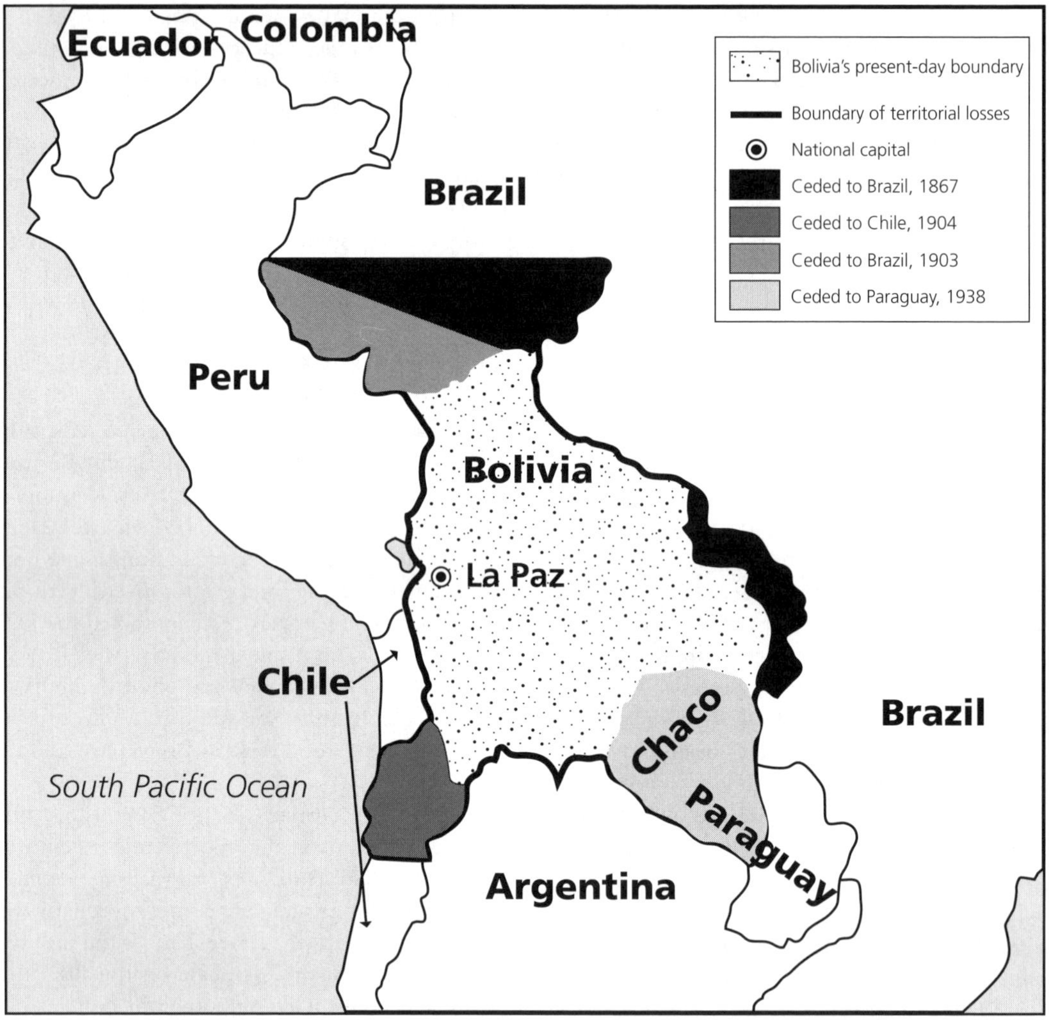

The map and key above show the Bolivian territorial losses to various nations from 1867 to 1938. These losses strained the U.S.-Bolivian relationship, because when Bolivia went to the peace table, the United States would not help, wanting to avoid foreign entanglements. As a result, Bolivia lost about one-third of its territory, including its coastline, as shown by the map.

THE ECONOMIC AND MILITARY ASSISTANCE NEXUS

Starting in the 1940s, U.S. interest in Bolivia's raw materials sharply increased. At the same time U.S. officials intensified their mission of promoting Latin American (including Bolivian) economic development. During World War II Latin America provided key resources to the Allies. Bolivia provided a sizable portion of the tin and other strategic minerals to aid in defeating the Axis powers. As the Cold War emerged, Washington leaders thought that Latin America again would provide important materials. In addition, U.S. policymakers concluded that Latin American economic development was necessary to lay the groundwork for stable, pro-U.S. governments. The Cold War coincided with the high tide of "modernization theory"—through modeling themselves after the industrialized nations and the judicious use of economic assistance, nonindustrialized nations could achieve economic "take off."

Although not apparent until the 1950s, the Movimiento Nacionalista Revolucionario (MNR) political party marked a turning point in Bolivian history, with important ramifications for U.S.-Bolivian relations. Appalled at the mistakes made by the nation's leadership during the Chaco War and the war's tragic outcome for Bolivia, a group of veterans formed a military lodge in 1934 to discuss reforming the Bolivian political and economic systems. In 1941 the lodge and a loose coalition, including the FSTMB and middle-class Bolivians, created the MNR, which quickly became the nation's most popular political party. There were two main visions of reform within the movement. The radical working class (mostly Indian) called for nationalization of key sectors of the economy and workers' representatives to sit on the boards of directors of the nationalized industries. For its part, the cautious middle class wanted only to nationalize the three largest, and all foreign-owned, mining companies. In the tempestuous government of Gualberto Villaroel López (1943–1946), three MNR leaders served in the cabinet. The first interaction between the MNR and the United States was not auspicious. Washington officials were wary of the MNR because its policies challenged free-market dictums. In addition, because of anti-Semitic remarks by its leadership, Washington feared the MNR was profascist. By withholding official diplomatic recognition until MNR officials were dismissed, Washington ensured their departure from the government.

After its 1951 election was thwarted by a preinaugural military coup, the MNR took power by force with few casualties in April of 1952. Militias of Indian miners formed the backbone of the MNR's military force, quickly defeating the Bolivian army. President Víctor Paz Estenssoro now presided over what came to be known as the Bolivian Revolution of 1952. Propelled by its left wing, the MNR moved quickly to give suffrage to Indians and women, implement agrarian reform, nationalize the three largest mining companies forming the Corporación Minera de Bolivia (COMIBOL), and greatly reduce the size of the Bolivian military. Together the MNR and the powerful Central Obrero Boliviana (Bolivian Workers' Union) formed and implemented domestic economic policy. The power-sharing arrangement was called *co-gobierno,* or co-government.

In some respects MNR policy reflected the late-nineteenth-century Latin American liberals' vision of an economically and socially integrated nation. By means of roads and railroads, the MNR wanted to physically integrate the fertile eastern portion of the country (the *Oriente*) into the rest of the country. The MNR promoted social integration through educational reform, including expanded efforts to teach the Indians Spanish (most of whom spoke only Quechua, Aymara, or other indigenous languages) and a Europeanized way of life.

After offering official diplomatic recognition to Bolivia in June of 1952, Washington positively responded to Paz's 1953 request for emergency assistance. In light of the radicalism of the revolution and McCarthyism gripping the United States, warming relations proved especially unusual. For its part, the U.S. government realized that there existed no other option but to support the MNR, even though some of the party's members were communist. U.S. policymakers thought the best way to contain the leftists and communists was to ensure that the cautious moderates in the party—who controlled nearly all of the leadership positions—would remain dominant. As such, the small initial program grew into one of the region's largest aid programs: During the 1950s the U.S. dispensed almost $200 million in support to Bolivia, assisted by the persistent lobbying of a very knowledgeable and savvy ambassador, Víctor Andrade Uzquiano. Bolivia, in a sense, traded its centuries-old dependency on mineral exports for dependency on economic assistance.

As low tin prices reduced foreign exchange, the Bolivian government printed money (in part to support a struggling COMIBOL), and inflation spiraled above 100 percent by the mid-1950s. In response Washington created the Monetary Stabilization Board in La Paz, its membership made up of Bolivian and U.S. officials. Although few realized it at the time of its 1956 founding, the board's actions would significantly reverberate through Bolivian history. To ensure swift enactment of controversial reforms, Washington informed La Paz that if it did not accept the board's stabilization plan, economic assistance would be cut. The MNR leadership decided to accept the set of reforms that cut the money supply and government budget while loosening up government restrictions on economic activity. Because the powerful head of the board, George Jackson Eder, viewed land reform as an impediment to agricultural productivity, the plan called for it to be curtailed. The plan cut COMIBOL's budget, mines were closed, miners were thrown out of work, strike violence increased, and the left of the MNR became increasingly unhappy.

DICTATORSHIP AND ANTI-U.S. SENTIMENT

The strain of complying with the stabilization plan exacerbated internal dissent within the MNR, leading to a political crisis. With the exit of the left-wing members in 1963, *co-gobierno* effectively came to an end. The next year a military coup easily toppled the government, sending Paz into exile. The United States, with the quiet acquiescence of the moderates of the MNR, began a small program of military assistance in the late 1950s. President John F. Kennedy, who took office in 1961 and announced a decade-long "Alliance for Progress" in Latin America, greatly increased both economic and military assistance for Latin America—including Bolivia. Even as U.S. leaders asserted the importance of democracy in the region, Washington's reliance on pro-U. S. dictatorships proved an important Cold War strategy.

During the era of military dictatorships, from the mid-1960s to the mid-1980s, Bolivia experienced political repression, economic growth, and growing anti-U.S. sentiment. Workers, campesinos, and students who protested government policies sometimes paid with their lives. The economic growth was first stimulated by higher prices for metals and petroleum and then by the increasing diversification of the Bolivian economy. The *Oriente's* fertile soil began to provide surplus agricultural products for export. By the 1970s revenues from oil and natural gas sales had significantly increased.

The late 1960s represented a period of rising anti-U. S. sentiment in Bolivia. As U.S. assistance to the Andean country increased, some Bolivians feared concomitant Yankee influence. In 1967 U.S.-trained Rangers in the Bolivian military proved instrumental in capturing Ernesto "Che" Guevara de la Serna, an Argentine revolutionary who aimed to foment a Cuban-style revolt in the Bolivian *Oriente.* (Bolivian troops later executed him.) Guevara's attempt at revolution was doomed from the beginning as the popular, Quechua-speaking President, René Barrientos Ortuño, who staged the 1964 coup but was elected with a solid majority in 1966, was implementing a land reform. Moreover, Guevara did not link up with Bolivia's divided leftist movement and received little help from the campesinos. Aside from giving the Bolivian military an important victory, Guevara's defeat highlighted U.S. counterinsurgency policy in the region.

Fears of Yankee influence heightened with the 1969 release of a popular, compelling, Bolivia-produced movie, *Blood of the Condor* (*Yawar Mallku* in Quechua). Portraying the U.S. Peace Corps ("Progress Corps" in the film) as sterilizing Indian women, the film was popular at art house theatres and universities not only in Latin America but in the United States and Europe. The powerful yet unproven accusation of sterilization focused anti-U.S. feeling on the Peace Corps, and leftist President Juan José Torres González abruptly ordered the Corps to leave the nation in 1971.

The year 1971 marked the beginning of two important trends that would eventually transform Bolivian politics. First, in August of 1971, Hugo Bánzer Suárez's regime came to power, initiating a string of repressive military regimes that proved so brutal that the revulsion against them created a consensus for change. Democracy reemerged in 1982. Reversing traditional U.S. Cold War policy of supporting stable anticommunist governments of any political tendency, Jimmy Carter's (President 1977–1981) concern with human rights violations compelled his administration to reduce assistance to dictatorships in the region. Second, in 1971, an ethnically based Indian movement in Bolivia—building on campesino movements going back to the early twentieth century—emerged and grew despite the repression of the military governments. These Indians asserted—in contrast to the MNR's policy of assimilation—that the Bolivian nation should recognize and accept Indian culture as equally valid as western culture. They called for an end to injustice against the Indians, the teaching of Indian languages in the country's schools, and other reforms.

Largely through the efforts of Paz, who returned to the presidency in 1985, Bolivia weathered a collapsing economy while maintaining the consensus for democracy. U.S. economic advisors and the MNR government agreed on a "shock treatment" to reduce inflation. Mirroring the experience of the Stabilization Board in the 1950s, the policy cut the money supply and reduced government spending—in this case including the partial privatization of an inefficient COMIBOL struggling to cope with lower tin prices. Layoffs of miners and widespread protest resulted. In addition, Paz and his associates increased the power of the office of the presidency. By the end of Paz's term in 1989, the economy had begun to improve.

NEOLIBERALISM AND THE "DRUG WAR"

By the early 1990s Bolivia had gone from economic turmoil to a model of neoliberal reform. Neoliberalism, an increasingly popular movement in Latin America at that time and pushed by Washington leaders, prescribed opening up the economy to international capital and the simultaneous implementation of reform (such as political decentralization, the privatization of state-run industries, and educational reform), theoretically providing for the majority to benefit more greatly from increased foreign economic activity. Embracing neoliberalism, President Gonzalo Sánchez de Lozada y Sánchez Bustamante (or "Goni"), serving from 1993 to 1997, implemented a package of reforms (the "Plan de Todo"). As Bolivia notched impressive gains in economic growth, the popularity of neoliberalism grew simultaneously.

However, one important area of conflict remained in U.S.-Bolivian relations: the "drug war." Unemployed miners migrated to the *Oriente* in search of a new livelihood, discovering it in an old crop with a new use: coca leaves. Coca had been grown in the Andes for centuries, used to suppress appetite and cure ailments; it was used even as a gift to deities and to divine the future. With the refinement of coca into cocaine, however, the market for the leaf became international. Although cocaine had been invented at the end of the nineteenth century, it did not become a widely used drug until the mid-twentieth century. When a concentrated form of cocaine known as "crack" became popular in the 1980s, demand pushed up the price of coca leaves. By planting multiple coca crops per season, and with low storage and transportation costs, *cocaleros* (coca farmers)—many of whom had mired in rural poverty—earned a comfortable living. As U.S. economic assistance fell in the early 1980s, Bolivia, in a sense, traded its dependency on U.S. assistance to a dependency on coca leaf exports.

Washington policymakers attempted to stem the social problems of drug addiction in the United States through reduced coca production and interdiction. In Bolivia, this effort proved controversial on many levels. Campesinos feared coca eradication meant a return to poverty. Banding together in resistance, some tangled with Bolivia's security forces. As part of the drug war, the United States mandated benchmarks for coca eradication and cocaine interdiction. If Bolivia did not meet such benchmarks, the U.S. government would not support loans from international financial institutions. In addition, Bolivians disliked the U.S. policy of tying a portion of U.S. assistance to a requirement that the nation set up special tribunals for suspected criminals in the drug trade. The drug war clearly exposed the disadvantages for the client in a patron-client relationship. Further, because some U.S. assistance went to Bolivian security forces, the nation's fragile democracy could be threatened. Many Bolivians maintained that efforts to constrict the production and supply of illegal drugs were futile, and they concluded that the only viable solution was for users of illegal drugs to stop using them.

THE INDIGENOUS MAJORITY ASSERTS POLITICAL POWER

When Bánzer—the former dictator—was elected president in 1997, he stepped up coca-eradication efforts, at a high cost to Bolivian society. Dwindling earnings from coca sales dampened growth in an economy that was running out of steam. As the neoliberal model unraveled, critics challenged it, among them Juan Evo Morales Ayma (known as "Evo"), an

Indian whose family hailed from the highlands around Oruro but had moved to the *Oriente*. Starting as an organizer of *cocaleros*, he led protests, including blockading roads as a way to pressure government officials. Morales later held political positions in Cochabamba, but his ambitions ran higher. He unsuccessfully ran for president in 2002, losing by about 2 percent to Goni (Sánchez de Lozada), despite an ill-timed comment by the U.S. ambassador that buoyed Evo's prospects in the campaign's closing stretches. The ambassador asserted that a Morales victory would necessarily cause Washington to cut assistance to Bolivia. Rejecting a U.S. attempt to interfere in its electoral process, some Bolivians shifted their support to Evo's diverse coalition of leftists—including, most prominently, indigenous peoples.

President Goni decided to transship Bolivian gas to Chilean ports and to increase taxes (the government was nearly bankrupt), which spurred significant popular protest and, in turn, a crackdown. Fearing he lacked enough support to effectively govern, Goni fled in October 2003 to exile in the United States, where he had lived as a young man. Goni's vice president, Carlos Mesa, served from 2003 to 2004, and Eduardo Rodriguez served from 2004 until January 2006. Capitalizing on the wide discontent of both the traditional political parties, which many viewed as corrupt and a failing faith in neoliberalism, Morales built support. Serving as the nation's first president of indigenous extraction, he won election in January 2006 with 54 percent of the vote, buoying the hopes of many Indians that his administration would promote a more just and egalitarian society.

Although some feared that Morales would join the anti-United States bloc of Venezuela and Cuba, Morales proved pragmatic in his foreign relations—including those with the United States. Even as Washington grumbled at some of his policies (such as increasing state control over Bolivia's resources), Morales has pledged to continue the drug war. Even as the Obama administration took over, Morales and Washington leaders have avoided open confrontation.

See also *Bolivia, U.S. Military Anti-Drug Program, 1986; Bolivian Revolution, 1952–1956, U.S. Policy toward; National Revolutionary Movement (MNR) (Bolivia); Paz Estenssoro, Á. Víctor; United States-Bolivia Anti-Narcotics Agreement, 1990*

. . . . JAMES F. SIEKMEIER

REFERENCES AND FURTHER READING

Blasier, Cole. *The Hovering Giant—U.S. Responses to Revolutionary Change in Latin America, 1910–1985*, 2nd ed. Pittsburgh, PA: University of Pittsburgh Press, 1985.

Grindle, Merilee S., and Pilar Domingo, eds. *Proclaiming Revolution: Bolivia in Comparative Perspective*. Cambridge, MA and London: Harvard University David Rockefeller Center for Latin American Studies and the Institute for Latin American Studies, 2003.

Klein, Herbert S. *A Concise History of Bolivia*. Cambridge, UK: Cambridge University Press, 2003.

Lehman, Kenneth D. *Bolivia and the United States: A Limited Partnership*. Athens: University of Georgia Press, 1999.

Siekmeier, James F. "Persistent Condor and Predatory Eagle: The Bolivian Revolution and the United States, 1952–1964." In *The Eisenhower Administration, the Third World, and the Globalization of the Cold War*, edited by Kathryn C. Statler and Andrew L. Johns, 197–221. Lanham, MD: Rowman and Littlefield 2006.

Zunes, Stephen. "The US and Bolivia: The Taming of a Revolution, 1952–1957." *Latin American Perspectives* 28 (September 2001): 33–49.

Bolivian Revolution, 1952–1956, U.S. Policy toward

The Movimiento Nacionalista Revolucionario (Nationalist Revolutionary Movement or MNR) was the most potent political force in Bolivia in the 1950s and early 1960s. The MNR and the United States forged a pragmatic relationship, both recognizing that it was in their best interests to work together.

FORMATION AND EARLY YEARS

The MNR formed after the 1932–1935 Chaco War with Paraguay, in which Bolivia lost thousands of soldiers and about one-third of its territory. Because Bolivia's elite held a vast economic, social, and political power, many urged reform to reduce or eliminate its power. In 1941 a military lodge, Razón de Patria (Duty to the Nation), in combination with middle-class reformers, workers, and campesinos (small farmers), banded together to create the MNR.

In part because the bulk of Bolivia's lucrative mines were owned by the elite, the nation's traditional dependence on the export of minerals proved an important focus of the MNR. It wanted to quickly eliminate the considerable influence of the three largest (and foreign-owned) mining companies that accounted for about 80 percent of Bolivia's foreign exchange. Moreover, only nationalization of the companies' assets into a state-run mining enterprise could earn sufficient income to pay for other necessary reforms: improved public services and infrastructure and diversification of the economy away from metals. Although U.S. policymakers viewed Bolivia's tin as an important, western-hemisphere source of the strategic material, after World War II the U.S. interest in Bolivian tin diminished as mines in Asia began producing significant amounts of tin with higher grade ore than Bolivia's.

The MNR first exerted influence in government when Gualberto Villaroel López successfully staged a coup in late 1943 and appointed three MNR leaders to his cabinet. The reformist Villaroel soon alienated the powerful oligarchy. For its part, the United States, fearing the party was profascist because of some anti-Semitic remarks by some MNR leaders, withheld official diplomatic recognition until Villaroel dismissed the MNR leaders from his cabinet. Washington ensured their hasty exit.

THE MNR IN POWER

After Bolivia returned to democracy, the MNR won the election in 1951. Although temporarily sidetracked by a preinaugural military coup, after less than a week of fighting between MNR militias and the Bolivian military (resulting in about six hundred deaths), the party took power. Its ascent became known as the Revolution of 1952. Headed by Víctor Paz Estenssoro, one of the MNR's founders and arguably one of Bolivia's preeminent statesmen of the twentieth century, the MNR quickly enacted deep reforms that transformed

Bolivia's economy, society, and politics. It nationalized (with compensation) the three largest mining companies, creating the state-run Corporación Minera de Bolivia (COMIBOL), but it emphasized there would be no further nationalizations. The party enacted one of Latin America's most profound agrarian reforms, transferring land from the landed *latifundios* to landless campesinos, many of them indigenous ("Indian"). In addition it enacted educational reforms to socially integrate the Indian majority. Because many of the Indians only spoke their native tongues, the MNR thought instruction in Spanish would facilitate their integration into the Hispanic, Europeanized culture of Bolivia's urban middle class. The MNR also extended suffrage to Indians and women. The party greatly reduced the size of the army (to make it less of a threat to its power). In a sense, the MNR's actions mirrored the wave of Asian and African decolonization in the late 1940s through the 1960s, except that the MNR did not need to achieve political independence from a colonial power. Instead, it called for a type of internal decolonization: it aimed to create a more egalitarian society with a more diversified economy independent of the power of the Bolivian elite.

The party's considerable accomplishments were tarnished by the marginalization and repression of some of its opposition. Additionally, divisions between the party's left-wing and moderate element emerged. The left called for state ownership of important sectors of the economy while the moderates wanted economic diversification and a working, if not close, relationship with the United States. The left was more numerous, but the moderates occupied most leadership positions.

During the height of the Cold War, Washington supported the MNR even though it contained communists, seeing the party's moderates as the only bulwark against a left-wing takeover. Moreover, Washington gave Bolivia $74 million in economic assistance (grants, loans, and food aid) between 1952 and 1956. Given that Bolivia central bordered all of South America's powerful Southern Cone nations, Washington thought that assistance could simultaneously maintain the MNR moderates in their leadership positions and bolster party unity. U.S. leaders wanted to prevent a breakup of the MNR, which could lead to a power vacuum in the center of South America which an extremely leftist or communist group might fill. Moreover, U.S. officials thought supporting a democratic, reformist regime in the third world would send a signal to citizens of developing world nations—who might be sympathetic to the communist movement—that Washington cared about their well-being.

Crucial in maintaining harmonious relations between the two nations was Ambassador Víctor Andrade Uzquiano, serving as ambassador from 1952 to 1958 and from 1960 to 1962. Echoing Paz Estenssoro's pro-U.S. stance, and tirelessly promoting Bolivian interests, he helped shaped U.S. policy toward Bolivia. He was one of the first Latin American representatives in Washington to affect Inter-American relations and a model for his successors.

MILITARY TAKEOVER

As tin prices and COMIBOL's revenues fell, the MNR attempted to shore up a shaky economy through increasing the money supply and stimulating high inflation, over 100 percent by 1956. The next year, Washington and the MNR forged a consensus initiating a dramatic change in policy: U.S. policymakers promised continued aid if—and only if—Bolivia accepted a package of austerity measures, including reducing COMIBOL's workforce. As unproductive mines were closed and miners lost their jobs, strike violence escalated. A large rift widened between the left and the centrists, threatening party cohesion. In response, moderates quietly coordinated U.S. military assistance to disarm the militias and strengthen the Bolivian military. With a November 1964 military coup, the U.S. government supported a succession of anticommunist military regimes as strategic Cold War allies.

See also *Bolivia, U.S. Military Anti-Drug Program, 1986; Bolivia, U.S. Relations with; National Revolutionary Movement (MNR) (Bolivia); Paz Estenssoro, Á. Víctor; United States-Bolivia Anti-Narcotics Agreement, 1990*

. . . . JAMES F. SIEKMEIER

REFERENCES AND FURTHER READING

Grindle, Merilee S., and Pilar, Domingo, eds. *Proclaiming Revolution—Bolivia in Comparative Perspective*. Cambridge, MA: David Rockefeller Center for Latin American Studies, Harvard University, 2003.

Lehman, Kenneth D. *Bolivia and the United States: A Limited Partnership*. Athens: University of Georgia Press, 1999.

Sanders, G. Earl. "The Quiet Experiment in American Diplomacy: An Interpretative Essay on U.S. Aid to the Bolivian Revolution." *The Americas* 33 (July 1976): 25–49.

Siekmeier, James F. "Persistent Condor and Predatory Eagle: The Bolivian Revolution and the United States, 1952–1964." In *The Eisenhower Administration, the Third World, and the Globalization of the Cold War*, edited by Kathryn C. Statler and Andrew L. Johns, 197–221. Lanham, MD: Rowman and Littlefield, 2006.

Siekmeier, James F. "Trailblazer Diplomat: Bolivian Ambassador Víctor Andrade Uzquiano's Efforts to Influence U.S. Policy, 1944–1962." *Diplomatic History* 28 (June 2004): 385–406.

Wilkie, James. *The Bolivian Revolution and U.S. Aid Since 1952—Financial Background and Context of Political Decisions*. Los Angeles: Latin American Center, University of California, 1969.

Zunes, Stephen. "The U.S. and Bolivia: The Taming of a Revolution, 1952–1957." *Latin American Perspectives* 28 (September 2001): 33–49.

Bonsal, Philip W.

A career diplomat from New York City who specialized in Latin American affairs, Philip Wilson Bonsal served as ambassador to Colombia in 1955–1957, Bolivia from 1957–1959, Cuba from 1959–1960, and Morocco from 1961–1962. After graduating from Yale University in 1924, he worked for AT&T in Cuba, Spain, and Chile, and for the Federal Communications Commission from 1935–1937. He entered the Foreign Service in 1938 and was first assigned to Havana, then to the Office of American Republics, becoming assistant chief and acting chief by 1943.

Bonsal is best remembered as the last U.S. ambassador to Cuba before the two countries broke relations. As an experienced bilingual diplomat with a good reputation in Latin America and no links to the Fulgencio Batista regime, the choice of

Bonsal was a sign of the Eisenhower administration's willingness to seek an accommodation with Fidel Castro. On arrival in Havana one month after the Cuban Revolution began, he congratulated the revolutionaries on their victory and sought a meeting with Castro. However, the Eisenhower administration soon decided that the Castro government was too radical and by the end of the year adopted a policy of regime change. As the Cuban government nationalized U.S. properties and the Eisenhower administration suspended Cuba's sugar quota, Bonsal, who advised that retaliation would only drive Cuba closer to the Soviets, was increasingly sidelined during the spiral of hostile actions. He was recalled to Washington against his wishes in October 1960 and the United States never again sent an ambassador to Havana.

A SERIES OF LOST ARGUMENTS

At an early stage in his career, Bonsal established himself as a member of the circle of State Department officials around Undersecretary of State Sumner Welles, who took seriously the principles of the Good Neighbor policy that called for treating Latin Americans as equals and ending U.S. intervention in their affairs. During World War II he sought, with limited success, to bring these principles to bear upon a number of wartime security measures. When the United States developed a blacklist for Axis nationals and their contacts in Latin America, the Proclaimed List of Certain Blocked Nationals, Bonsal argued that it should be converted from a unilateral measure into a cooperative venture with Latin American participation. At his urging, consultative commissions were created in Latin American capitals to help coordinate the blacklisting process. Rather than providing local governments with a veto over the blacklists, however, the commissions were tasked with enforcing economic warfare measures developed in Washington.

After Pearl Harbor, the State Department and Federal Bureau of Investigation began to identify potentially dangerous Axis nationals they sought to have expelled from Latin America and interned in the United States. Bonsal tried to ensure that Latin American laws and political sensitivities would not be violated in the process, but security concerns took precedence in the initial years of the war. In mid-1943 Bonsal argued that the internment program should be wound down because the Axis threat had receded and the intense pressures exerted upon Latin American governments to get them to deliver their own residents were causing more harm than good to U.S. interests in the region. The program continued until 1945.

When Bolivian army officers close to the neutralist government of Argentina overthrew the government of Enrique Peñaranda in a bloodless coup on December 20, 1943, the United States broke with a Good Neighbor-era policy and refused to recognize the new government. For the next six months Secretary of State Cordell Hull insisted that the Bolivian regime hand over some of its German residents for internment before the United States would grant it recognition. Bonsal strongly criticized this policy as a form of intervention that could only damage U.S. standing. During a tour of Latin American capitals, his assessment was confirmed by the many government officials with whom he met, but he lost that argument as well.

After leaving the Division of American Republics, Bonsal was sent to Madrid in 1944, where he was chargé d'affaires from 1946 to 1947. He served in The Hague and in Paris, the latter as embassy counselor advising W. Averell Harriman on the Marshall Plan. From 1952 to 1954 he was called back to Washington as director of the Office of Philippine and Southeast Asian Affairs and was present as an adviser at the Geneva Conference that ended French intervention in Indochina.

CONCLUSION

Bonsal's ambassadorial postings were marked by his efforts to maintain contact with a wide range of members of civil society, including opposition figures. This angered the Colombian dictator Gustavo Rojas Pinilla but helped Bonsal nurture good relations with the reformist Bolivian government of the Movimiento Nacional Revolucionario (MNR). He is often credited with having moderated the MNR government, and it was hoped that he would achieve the same result in Cuba. After retiring from the Foreign Service in 1965, he wrote a book in 1971 about his Cuban experience. He concluded that he never had the chance of bridging the gap between two hostile sides, and he was critical of Castro's repressive measures. But he also sought to refute the right-wing criticism of having been too soft on Castro by showing just how little influence he had over U.S.-Cuban relations during his tenure, and he insisted that even if the failed invasion at the Bay of Pigs had succeeded in overthrowing Castro, his reading of Cuban history told him that another Cuban leader would have come along to take his place and take up his goals. He also blamed U.S. intervention in general as counterproductive, an approach that must be considered "as dead as colonialism as an effective political method in today's world" (Bonsal 1971, 223).

See also *Bolivia, U.S. Relations with; Castro Ruz, Fidel; Cuba, Rapprochement with the United States, 1960s–1990s; Cuba, U.S. Embargo of; Cuba, U.S. Relations with; Good Neighbor Policy; Hull, Cordell; National Revolutionary Movement (MNR) (Bolivia)*

. . . . MAX PAUL FRIEDMAN

REFERENCES AND FURTHER READING

Bonsal, Philip W. *Cuba, Castro, and the United States*. Pittsburgh, PA: University of Pittsburgh Press, 1971.

Friedman, Max Paul. *Nazis and Good Neighbors: The United States Campaign against the Germans of Latin America in World War II*. New York: Cambridge University Press, 2003.

Wood, Bryce. *The Dismantling of the Good Neighbor Policy*. Austin: University of Texas Press, 1995.

Bosch Gaviño, Juan

Respected by followers and opponents alike and admired for his sincerity and honesty, Juan Bosch (1909–2001) was one of the most important figures in twentieth-century Dominican political history. A charismatic leader, Bosch is still regarded as the greatest prose writer in Dominican literature.

PROTEST AND EXILE

The son of a Catalan father and a Puerto Rican mother, he was born in La Vega, Dominican Republic, on June 30, 1909. After his high school graduation, he worked in the capital. Passionate about writing, he wrote his first collection of short stories in 1931, a year after Dominican dictator Rafael Leonidas Trujillo took power. A prolific writer, Bosch's works were characterized by his empathy for the poor.

In October 1937, taking advantage of the Dominicans' antipathy toward the Haitians—Haiti once occupied the Dominican Republic in the nineteenth century—Trujillo conducted the massacre of 15,000 Haitian migrants in the Dominican Republic. Bosch was one of the very few Dominicans who ventured to condemn the genocide. This gesture earned him the dictator's wrath. In 1938 he fled to Puerto Rico and a year later, he settled in Cuba.

In July 1939 he founded the Dominican Revolutionary Party (PRD), a left-of-center party committed to the overthrow of Trujillo and to bringing democracy and socioeconomic change to the Dominican Republic. He was also active in Cuban politics and became a confidant of Cuban President Carlos Prío Socarrás.

On March 10, 1952, General Fulgencio Batista overthrew the Prío regime and jailed Bosch. After his release he left for Costa Rica where he taught at the university. Shortly after the Central Intelligence Agency assisted assassination of Trujillo, on May 30, 1961, Bosch returned to the Dominican Republic after more than twenty years in exile. After a brief interim government, elections were scheduled for December 20, 1962. The Kennedy administration not only lent its full support to the election process, but when Trujillo sympathizers began to create unrest in the country, it sent a naval contingent as a warning to the *Trujillistas*.

PRESIDENCY

Bosch's presidential platform included more jobs, better working and housing conditions, and a plan to address the country's ills. Although there were eight candidates vying for the presidency, Bosch, supported by the urban poor and landless peasants, won the election with 62 percent of the vote. On February 27, 1963, Bosch became the first freely elected president of the Dominican Republic in thirty-three years. One of his first measures upon assuming the presidency was the drafting of a new constitution. Proclaimed on April 29, 1963, it contained provisions for civil and political rights, agrarian reform, collective bargaining, a mixed economy, and the right to own property.

With an overwhelming majority in Congress, Bosch started a reform agenda. He began an agrarian reform program through the distribution of formerly held Trujillo estates. Additionally, he started an industrialization plan by nationalizing Trujillo family industrial enterprises and granting workers profit-sharing incentives. Moreover, he undertook a war on bureaucratic corruption, followed a strict interpretation of the constitution's separation of church and state, and began a reorganization of the military.

U.S. Vice President Lyndon B. Johnson (right) congratulates renowned Dominican writer Juan Bosch (left) following the latter's election to the presidency of the Dominican Republic on February 27, 1963. Bosch's term was short-lived; a September 25, 1963, coup sent him into exile, and by December Johnson had become U.S. president and his administration recognized the military government in hopes of avoiding a communist takeover.

SOURCE: National Archives

While he was active in promulgating his reforms, the forces which would unseat him were gathering momentum. Businessmen wanted a share of the Trujillo-held enterprises. Landowners were concerned that he was moving too fast on his agrarian reform program and feared they would be next. Bureaucrats were angered by his anticorruption measures. The Roman Catholic Church adamantly opposed what it perceived to be an intentional secularization effort. Army officers were leery that his military reorganization would diminish their prestige and traditional role in Dominican political life. The United States, while proclaiming the Alliance for Progress's goals and commitment to democracy, only granted him token financial support for his socioeconomic program and believed Bosch was not being "tough" on perceived communists. His own supporters even chastised him for being cautious, indecisive, and not revolutionary enough.

OVERTHROW AND RETURN

On September 25, 1963, the Dominican armed forces overthrew Bosch, citing a communist presence in his government. His overthrow represented a challenge for the Kennedy administration's commitment to bring democracy to Latin America. While the administration had been disappointed at Bosch's "soft" stand on communism, it viewed the coup as a major blow to the Alliance for Progress. The Kennedy administration withheld recognition of the military government, but after Kennedy's assassination, the Johnson administration restored diplomatic relations with the Dominican Republic in December 1963, in exchange for a promise to hold future elections.

Bosch went to exile in Puerto Rico and a civilian junta replaced the military government. The junta scheduled elections for September 1965, but on April 25, 1965, a group of young army officers, commanded by Colonel Francisco Caamaño and numerous PRD followers, ousted the junta and demanded Bosch's return to the presidency. A civil war ensued when air force General Elías Wessin y Wessin struck at Bosch's supporters. President Johnson, fearful at the possible loss of American lives and concerned that the Dominican Republic could become another Cuba, sent over twenty thousand soldiers and later secured a peacekeeping force from the Organization of American States (OAS). The American response represented a change from the Alliance for Progress to the Johnson Doctrine, which sought to stop the spread of communism in Latin America by direct military action.

After an interlude, Bosch returned to the Dominican Republic and in June 1966, he lost the presidential election to Joaquín Balaguer. After deciding not to run in the 1970 presidential election, Bosch broke with the PRD in 1973 and formed the Dominican Liberation Party (PLD). The party's initial militant revolutionary orientation and Bosch's sympathy for Fidel Castro did not sit well with American policymakers and the Dominican electorate. Bosch unsuccessfully ran for the presidency in 1978, 1982, 1986, 1990, and 1994. Despite his losses, he still had a large following. After the 1994 election he retired from politics. He died on November 1, 2001. PRD President Hipólito Mejía ordered a state funeral for the venerable figure of Dominican politics.

See also *Balaguer Ricardo, Joaquín; Dominican Republic, Conflicts with Haiti; Dominican Republic, U.S. Intervention, 1965–1966; Dominican Republic, U.S. Relations with; Johnson, Lyndon B.; Kennedy, John F.; Trujillo Molina, Rafael Leónidas; Wessin y Wessin, Elías*

JOSÉ B. FERNÁNDEZ

REFERENCES AND FURTHER READING

Guerrero, Miguel. *El golpe de estado: Historia del derrocamiento de Juan Bosch.* Santo Domingo, Dominican Republic: Editora Corripio, 1993.

Hartlyn, Jonathan. *The Struggle for Democratic Politics in the Dominican Republic.* Chapel Hill: The University of North Carolina Press, 1998.

Molineau, Harold. *U.S. Policy toward Latin America: From Regionalism to Globalism.* Boulder, CO: Westview Press, 1990.

Wiarda, Howard, and Michael Kryzanek. *The Dominican Republic: A Caribbean Crucible.* Boulder, CO: Westview Press, 1982.

Wucker, Michele. *Why the Cocks Fight: Dominicans, Haitians and the Struggle for Hispaniola.* New York: Hill and Wang, 1999.

Boston Fruit Company

Boston Sea Captain Lorenzo Dow Baker (of the Boston Standard Steam Navigation Company) and Boston businessman Andrew Woodberry Preston brought ten other business partners together in 1885 to form the Boston Fruit Company, a banana-selling firm, located in Boston, Massachusetts. Lorenzo Baker served as president; Andrew Preston became the Boston manager. They made Jamaica their main source of supply, as Lorenzo Baker knew the island well and had made many contacts there before buying several banana farms on the island. The Boston Fruit Company would become the largest tropical farm and shipping company in the world, but it began as a small company with small capital investments from its twelve partners.

When the Boston Fruit Company was organized, the tropical fruit trade was a difficult and risky business. Many banana ships were lost at sea, late ships meant rotted fruit and lost profits, and hurricanes could wipe out entire crops. Because of good luck and cautious financial decisions on the part of Baker and Preston, the Boston Fruit Company became a successful company and on September 20, 1890, it was formally incorporated under the laws of Massachusetts with $531,000 in capital assets.

In 1892 Baker and Preston had purchased 3,100 acres of land in Jamaica for the Boston Fruit Company, and they were importing bananas to Boston eight months out of the year rather than four to five, like most of their competitors. In the decade of 1890s, as the Boston Fruit Company sold all it could to Bostonians, Baker and Preston purchased large shares of stock in competing banana firms, bought banana plantations in Cuba and the Dominican Republic, and invested in new, expensive steamships, operating eleven by the end of the decade. Baker referred to his ships as the "Great White Fleet." By 1899 the Boston Fruit Company had become the second largest banana firm in the United States, doubling its imports of bananas between 1890 and 1899.

On March 20, 1899, Baker and Preston joined forces with Minor Cooper Keith, the world's largest producer of bananas, who owned the Colombia Land Company, Ltd., the Tropical Trading and Transport Company, and vast banana plantations in Costa Rica and Colombia. Other bankers and executives joined the venture to form the United Fruit Company, a New Jersey corporation, which instantly became the largest banana monopoly in the world. Four of the original partners of the Boston Fruit Company became directors of the United Fruit Company, with Andrew Preston becoming the first president.

The Boston Fruit Company was a large monopolistic enterprise that would wield influence beyond the banana plantations. Leaders in the host countries were more than willing to grant concessions to the Boston Fruit Company, while giving up autonomy over their shipping and trade and losing vast tracks of land to a private, foreign-owned business. The Boston Fruit Company would set the stage for the larger monopoly, the United Fruit Company, which would dominate the banana trade in Central America and wield an unprecedented amount of political power in the region until 1970.

See also *Cuyamel Fruit Company; Keith, Minor C.; Meiggs, Henry; Preston, Andrew; United Fruit Company (UFCO)*

VIRGINIA S. WILLIAMS

REFERENCES AND FURTHER READING

Dosal, Paul J. *Doing Business with the Dictators: A Political History of United Fruit in Guatemala, 1899–1944.* Wilmington, DE: Scholarly Resources Books, 1993.

Wilson, Charles Morrow. *Empire in Green and Gold: The Story of the American Banana Trade.* New York: Greenwood Press, 1968.

Bowers, Claude G.

The journalist, orator, political advisor, and popular author, Claude G. Bowers (1878–1958) served as U.S. ambassador to Spain from 1933 to 1939 and U.S. ambassador to Chile from 1939 to 1953. Born in Indiana to a staunch Democratic family, Bowers became one of the most influential Democratic party spokespersons of the first half of the twentieth century. During the 1900 U.S. presidential campaign Bowers wrote editorials for the *Indianapolis Sentinel* and made stump speeches in an effort to drum up local support for William Jennings Bryan, the Democratic party's losing U.S. presidential candidate in 1896, 1900, and 1908. Bowers endorsed Bryan as a spokesperson of the common man while repudiating as acts of imperialism Republican President William McKinley's annexations of Puerto Rico and the Philippines and his establishment of a U.S. protectorate over Cuba following the Spanish American-Cuban War of 1898.

After a stint as the aide to progressive Indiana Senate Democrat John Worth Kern from 1910–1916, Bowers returned successfully to journalism, and his editorials in William Randolph Heart's *New York Evening Journal* helped Franklin D. Roosevelt win the U.S. presidential election in 1932. Roosevelt rewarded Bowers with an ambassadorial post in Spain. Unlike most U.S. embassy personnel and U.S. businessmen in Spain, Bowers was a strong supporter of the parliamentary democracy of the Second Spanish Republic, before and during the Spanish Civil War (1936–1939). Bowers left Europe after the Second Spanish Republic fell to General Francisco Franco's fascist and monarchist forces, which were aided by Adolf Hitler's Germany and Benito Mussolini's Italy.

The Second World War began in Europe following Germany's invasion of Poland in September 1939, six months after the fall of the Second Spanish Republic and only days after Bowers arrived in South America to serve as U.S. ambassador to Chile. In Chile Bowers carried out the Roosevelt administration's Good Neighbor policy, which served to solidify economic, military, and cultural links between the United States and Chile after the United States entered the war in December 1941. Bowers worked with Chilean groups and politicians who favored breaking relations with the Axis powers of Germany, Italy, and Japan. He sought Chilean support for the Allied powers' war effort amidst a large and influential German-Chilean population and largely indifferent Chilean public. During the war Chile followed a neutralist foreign policy while generally cooperating with the Allied powers by increasing Chile's vital wartime exports of copper, nitrate, and other raw materials to the United States. In return Chile was provided with a large amount of U.S. military equipment through Lend-Lease Program agreements. Chile finally broke diplomatic relations with the Axis powers in January 1943.

After the Second World War U.S. investment and aid became increasingly important to the Chilean economy. During the early years of the Cold War era Bowers oversaw Chile's continued receipt of U.S. loans through the Export-Import Bank and supervised Chile's participation in U.S. President Harry S. Truman's Point Four Program. A political appointee and Democratic party partisan, Bowers retired from his diplomatic career in August 1953 following the election of Dwight D. Eisenhower, a Republican, as president of the United States. Bowers lived out the rest of his life in New York City. In 1954 he published *My Mission to Spain: Watching the Rehearsal for World War II,* a memoir denouncing the rise of Franco and the noninterventionist policies of Britain, France, and the United States during the Spanish Civil War. Despite his years of experience as a diplomat in Spain and Chile, Bowers never learned conversational Spanish. A lifelong opponent of racial equality, he died on January 21, 1958. His memoir recounting the fourteen years he served as U.S. ambassador to Chile, *Chile through Embassy Windows, 1939–1953,* was published a month after his death. An autobiography, *My Life: The Memoirs of Claude Bowers,* was published posthumously by Bowers's daughter Patricia in 1962.

See also *Bryan, William Jennings; Chile, U.S. Relations with; Cuba, U.S. Relations with; Eisenhower, Dwight D.; Export-Import Bank (EXIM); Good Neighbor Policy; Lend-Lease Program, World War II; McKinley, William; Point Four Program; Puerto Rico, U.S. Relations with; Roosevelt, Franklin D.; Spanish-Cuban-American War 1895–1898; Truman, Harry S.; World War II, 1939–1945*

. . . . DAVID M. CARLETTA

REFERENCES AND FURTHER READING

Francis, Michael J. "The United States and Chile during the Second World War: The Diplomacy of Misunderstanding." *Journal of Latin American Studies* 9/1 (May 1977): 91–113.

Jessner, Sabine, and Peter J. Sehlinger. "Claude G. Bowers: A Partisan Hoosier." *Indiana Magazine of History* 83/3 (September 1987): 217–243.

Little, Douglas. "Claude Bowers and His Mission to Spain: The Diplomacy of a Jeffersonian Democrat." In *U.S. Diplomats in Europe, 1919–1941,* edited by Kenneth Paul Jones, 120–146. Santa Barbara, CA: ABC-Clio, 1981.

Sehlinger, Peter J., and Holman Hamilton. *Spokesman for Democracy: Claude G. Bowers, 1878–1958.* Indianapolis: Indiana Historical Society, 2000.

Bracero Program

The Bracero Program brought millions of Mexicans to the United States as contract workers, particularly in the southwest and Midwest. Although it originated during World War II, the program continued after the war concluded, lasting until 1964.

CREATION AND GROWTH

During the Second World War, the United States drafted millions of its citizens into the armed forces. At the same time, the unprecedented military mobilizations required increased agricultural and industrial production. Consequently, the nation experienced major labor shortages and encouraged females to enter the workforce as well as recruited foreigners as migrant workers to meet wartime workforce needs. The Bracero Program was one such recruiting effort.

In August 1942 the U.S. and Mexican governments came to terms over the Emergency Labor Program, although the U.S. Congress did not officially sanction the program until the following April as Public Law 45. This agreement established a minimum wage for recruited temporary Mexican workers (commonly called *braceros*), provided for the transportation and housing of braceros, and granted braceros the right to solicit termination of the employment at any time. However, employers issued contracts to braceros in English, which resulted in many workers being ignorant of their basic rights under the U.S.-Mexican accord. The Emergency Labor Program resulted in the recruitment of over two hundred thousand Mexican contract laborers between 1942 and 1947. Most braceros had prior experience with agricultural work, and most came from the provinces of Zacatecas, Michoacán, Guanajuato, Puebla, and Jalisco in central Mexico. The vast majority of braceros during World War II worked in California agriculture, although others found employment in the southwest railroad industries. Still other Mexican workers made their way to Washington and Oregon in the northwest and Midwestern states such as Illinois and Michigan.

The Mexican government was reluctant to allow its citizens to work as *braceros* in Texas due to the state's notorious reputation for anti-Mexican prejudice and discrimination. Despite assurances from Texas Governor Coke Stevenson that the state would enact antidiscrimination policies to protect Mexicans, the Mexican government did not officially grant permission for Mexicans to work in Texas until 1947. Nevertheless many Mexican nationals found employment in Texas during World War II as undocumented immigrants lured by lax border enforcement. The Mexican government's fears of racial discrimination in Jim Crow-era Texas proved correct, as reports circulated that Mexican migrants often lacked adequate running water and faced exclusion from many restaurants and movie theaters.

When it came time to renew the Bracero Agreement in 1947, the Mexican government found its bargaining power significantly weakened from its position in 1942. The temporary labor program had proven vital to the Mexican economy, as the country came to depend heavily on the braceros' remittances as a source of revenue. As a result the United States found itself in a relatively advantaged position to control the terms of the new labor agreement between the two nations. Despite Mexican opposition the new agreement decentralized regulations and allowed private employers to set the terms of employment contracts with their workers, with significantly less oversight from the U.S. federal government. Mexican officials feared that this stipulation, along with the large influx of undocumented Mexicans into the border region, would lead to the exploitation of Mexican workers. Most braceros between 1947 and 1951 consisted of undocumented Mexicans, already present in the United States, who had formally been issued labor contracts from their employers.

In the summer of 1951 Mexico and the United States reached a new contract labor agreement that significantly increased the number of Mexican workers entering the United States. The 1951 agreement served as the Bracero Program's regulatory statute until the program's termination in 1962, and during this time span, over four million Mexicans came to the United States as braceros. The vast majority of braceros continued to work in Texas and California agriculture. Despite the large volume of Mexicans securing employment as contract workers during the 1950s, the U.S. federal government also launched a massive deportation initiative, Operation Wetback, during the second half of the decade.

CESSATION AND LEGACY

A confluence of factors during the early 1960s led to the eventual end of the Bracero Program. Modern farm equipment and new machinery resulted in a need for fewer workers to cultivate and harvest crops. The American Federation of Labor and labor activists, such as César Chávez, organized opposition to the Bracero Program, claiming that the continual influx of large numbers of migrant workers served to depress wages and working conditions. At the same time religious-based and human rights organizations raised public awareness of the braceros' substandard living and working conditions. Finally, the large numbers of undocumented Mexicans already present in the southwest fulfilled many employers' needs for agricultural workers, rendering the contract labor program irrelevant to a significant degree. After twenty-two years of providing Mexican workers to American industries, the Bracero Program officially terminated on December 31, 1964.

The Bracero Program served as a catalyst for future waves of Mexican migration to the United States, both legal and illegal. The braceros themselves represented an important link between U.S. employers in need of additional workers and Mexican males in search of work. Upon returning to Mexico at the end of their employment term, braceros informed others of job opportunities in the United States, fostering patterns of migration that still continue to this day. At the same time many U.S. employers, particularly in Texas, preferred hiring undocumented Mexicans over braceros due to the additional expenses that braceros entailed, such as processing fees, minimum wages, room and board, and a temporary term of employment. The same Mexican provinces that provided most of the braceros are still the leading sources of Mexican emigration today.

See also *Ávila Camacho, Manuel; Immigration and Nationality Acts, 1952 and 1965 (United States); Immigration and Naturalization Service, United States; Immigration Policy: United States; Mexico, U.S. Relations with; North American Agreement on Labor Cooperation, 1992; Padilla Peñalosa, Ezequiel*

. . . . JUSTIN D. GARCÍA

REFERENCES AND FURTHER READING

Acuña, Rodolfo F. *Occupied America: A History of Chicanos*, 6th ed. New York: Pearson Longman, 2007.

Chavez, Leo R. *Shadowed Lives: Undocumented Immigrants in American Society*, 2nd ed. Orlando, FL: Harcourt Brace, 1998.

Meier, Matt S., and Feliciano Ribera. *Mexican Americans/American Mexicans: From Conquistadors to Chicanos*. Union Square West, NY: Hill and Wang, 1993.

Braden, Spruille

As ambassador to key Latin American countries during World War II and then as the top U.S. official for Latin American affairs, Spruille Braden (1894–1978) aggressively pursued U.S.

commercial and security interests with little patience for the principle of noninterference, thereby helping to bring the era of the Good Neighbor policy to an end.

EARLY LIFE AND CAREER

Born in a log cabin in Montana, Braden followed his father William into the mining industry and earned a degree in mining engineering at Yale in 1914. He spent nine years doing business in Chile on behalf of his family's Braden Copper Company and various financial and energy concerns. While in Chile he married Maria Humeres Solar, a descendant of Spanish royalty. Returning to the United States in 1925, he bought and ran companies such as the Monmouth Rug Company of New Jersey and the Rehabilitation Corporation, a real estate investment firm.

Braden first undertook government service as a delegate to the Seventh International Conference of American States at Montevideo in 1933 and the Pan-American Commercial Conference in 1935. From 1935–1938, he served as U.S. delegate with the rank of ambassador and chair of the Chaco Peace Conference, negotiating an end to the war between Bolivia and Paraguay. He was appointed ambassador to Colombia (1939–1941), Cuba (1942–1945), and Argentina (May through August 1945). President Harry Truman named him assistant secretary for American Republics Affairs from August 1945 to June 1947.

For an ambassador posted abroad, Braden exerted an unusual amount of influence in the development of wartime policy in Latin America, partly because his enormous self-confidence and force of will led him to initiate actions he deemed important without consulting Washington first. (Truman's Secretary of State Dean Acheson once remarked that Braden was the only bull to carry around his own china shop.) His influence also came from his initial wartime posting to Colombia, a country at the heart of U.S. concerns over Nazi influence in the region. Colombia's substantial German population and an active local branch of the Nazi Party, combined with its proximity to the Panama Canal, made it high on the list of security issues as the United States moved toward war.

ANTI-NAZI ESPIONAGE

Braden played an important early role in producing intelligence on the Nazi threat in Latin America. He claimed to have originated the idea of bringing the Federal Bureau of Investigation (FBI) to Latin America. His embassy was the first to begin collecting data on German commercial operations in preparation for blacklisting, well before Washington issued a general request for such information and developed a formal blacklisting program. In both Colombia and Cuba, he employed amateur spy networks to deliver information on Nazi activities at a time when U.S. intelligence services were in their infancy. The amateurs produced mixed results, with unconfirmed data passed to Washington and recirculated to diplomatic missions throughout Latin America. Braden's embassy became the source of some of the most inflated threat assessments that persuaded the Roosevelt administration to divert resources to the physical removal of Axis nationals from Latin American countries. Braden was the first U.S. diplomatic representative to lobby the government to which he was accredited to deport its German residents to the United States, helping to launch a deportation program later characterized by Justice Department officials as ineffective and probably illegal.

His effort to preempt any possible use of a German civilian airline against the Panama Canal was his most important contribution to western hemisphere security. In May 1940 Braden convinced Washington to move against Sociedad Colombo-Alemana de Transportes Aéreos (SCADTA), whose management and pilots were German although Pan American Airways (Pan Am) owned a majority financial interest. He persuaded the State Department of the potential danger of German pilots, some of them reserve officers in the *Luftwaffe* or members of the Nazi Party, flying aircraft in a country neighboring the canal. After protracted negotiations Braden and other officials persuaded Pan Am to fire SCADTA's German personnel and replace them with U.S. pilots, a task completed within a month. SCADTA became Avianca (Aerovías Nacionales de Colombia), with a Colombian president and Pan Am the principal stockholder, and no German company flew planes within range of the canal for the duration of the war.

Transferred to Cuba in 1942, Braden again hired an unofficial espionage network, this time turning to Ernest Hemingway because of the writer's connections among Cuba's Spanish exiles. Hemingway provided the embassy with reports on the assorted expatriate communities active in Havana, and in return he asked Braden to equip his fishing yacht, the *Pilar,* with a bazooka and machine guns for submarine hunting. According to Braden's memoirs, he skirted regulations and provided the weapons. Whether Hemingway's information was valuable or useless—Braden said both things at different times—the writer never caught a submarine.

Braden believed the amateur espionage groups were necessary because he disdained the work of U.S. military intelligence in Latin America. He was critical of many rival agencies and at various times tangled with the Office of the Coordinator of Inter-American Affairs, the Office of Naval Intelligence, the Military Intelligence Division, the Board of Economic Warfare, and the FBI. In many of his dealings with Latin Americans, Braden exhibited a kind of self-assurance that could be perceived as condescension or arrogance. He often expressed frustration at the inefficiency and dilatoriness he detected in Latin Americans, attributing it to their innate character. The Braden Copper Company took a paternalistic approach to its Chilean employees, enforcing a moral code that required the firing of unmarried women who became pregnant and involved company police searching workers' lodging at night. Braden blamed the difficult negotiations surrounding the Chaco War, which historians have understood as rooted in nationalism and competition for resources, on the Indian trickery of Paraguayans and Bolivians.

LATER CAREER: CONFRONTATION IN ARGENTINA

This frame of mind may have contributed to Braden's most infamous confrontation in Latin America, when after arriving in Buenos Aires as ambassador in May 1945, he waged a highly publicized campaign to prevent Juan Perón from being elected president of Argentina in elections planned for the following year. The ambassador gave public speeches and press conferences claiming that Perón would bring fascism to Argentina, and he continued his campaign after Truman brought him back to Washington in September to serve as assistant secretary for Latin America. From there he organized a report on Perón's alleged fascist connections known as the Blue Book. Perón responded by turning the election into a referendum on U.S. interference in Argentine politics, using the slogan *Braden o Perón,* and he won in a landslide. Ambassador George Messersmith suggested a rapprochement with Perón, and he and Braden clashed over the issue until Secretary Acheson eased them both out of the State Department. "Bradenism" entered the lexicon to describe undiplomatic treatment of Latin Americans.

As a private citizen Braden continued to argue on behalf of pursuing U.S. interests regardless of Latin American opinion, and he displayed a fierce anticommunism. In 1953 as a lobbyist for the United Fruit Company, he demanded armed intervention against the government of Jácobo Arbenz of Guatemala, provoking a formal protest from the Guatemalan Foreign Ministry. During the 1960s he chaired the anticommunist U.S. Citizens' Committee for a Free Cuba calling for the overthrow of Fidel Castro.

See also *Argentina, U.S. Relations with; Bolivia, U.S. Relations with; Colombia, U.S. Relations with; Cuba, U.S. Relations with; Good Neighbor Policy; Hull, Cordell; National Revolutionary Movement (MNR) (Bolivia); Perón Sosa, Juan Domingo*

. . . . MAX PAUL FRIEDMAN

REFERENCES AND FURTHER READING

Braden, Spruille. *Diplomats and Demagogues.* New Rochelle, NY: Arlington House, 1971.

Pike, Fredrick B. *FDR's Good Neighbor Policy: Sixty Years of Generally Gentle Chaos.* Austin: University of Texas Press, 1995.

Rawls, Shirley N. "Spruille Braden: A Political Biography." PhD diss., University of New Mexico, 1976.

Wood, Bryce. *The Dismantling of the Good Neighbor Policy.* Austin: University of Texas Press, 1985.

Woods, Randall Bennett. *The Roosevelt Foreign-Policy Establishment and the "Good Neighbor": The United States and Argentina, 1941–1945.* Lawrence: Regents Press of Kansas, 1979.

Brady Plan

(See *Debt Crisis, Latin America, 1870s, 1930s, 1980s)*

Brain Drain

Brain drain is a term used to describe the movement of highly skilled and educated migrants from one country to another, typically from a less developed to a more developed country that offers greater employment opportunities, higher wages, and/or greater political stability.

The phenomenon represents a net loss for the country of origin, which expends resources to educate and train the individual, who then does not contribute to the economy and to the country's overall development. Conversely the host country enjoys "brain gain" for the opposite reasons. With regard to Latin America the vast majority of this drain goes to the United States. Indeed the issue began to draw attention after World War II when the U.S. economy grew at a rapid rate. However many migrants are also attracted to Europe, Canada, or, less commonly, to other Latin American countries.

Brain drain from Latin America has at times been caused by political turmoil, generally when professionals feel threatened by authoritarian governments or civil war. Examples include the early years of the Cuban Revolution, the 1966 coup in Argentina (which prompted mass resignation of scientific faculty) as well as the 1976 Argentine coup, or the worst years of the insurgencies and drug wars in Colombia.

Once the Cold War ended and the number of democracies in Latin America grew, it became associated primarily with economic underdevelopment, which is accompanied by unemployment and relatively little investment in research and development. Persistent underdevelopment therefore fosters a vicious cycle, since a country loses the very citizens that it requires to spur growth. It is therefore even more challenging for the least developed countries to retain those workers. Individuals with university degrees are far more likely to emigrate from the poorest countries (particularly Central America and the Caribbean) than from the wealthier countries.

Nonetheless it can also be associated with economic shocks in relatively more developed countries. For example hyperinflation and macroeconomic instability in Brazil from 1986 to 1993 sparked skilled outmigration. There was also an exodus from Argentina in the wake of the economic crisis that exploded in 2001.

The intergovernmental International Organization for Migration has worked with Latin American governments to create highly targeted programs intended to accelerate "voluntary return." There are also nongovernmental "network diasporas" that link skilled emigrants back with their country of origin through hometown organizations and professional associations. Their goal is to encourage "brain circulation," whereby skilled workers may live abroad for long stretches but also invest their time and abilities back home.

Although Latin American policymakers have been aware of the problem for decades, they were slow to develop a coherent policy response. Brazil and Ecuador have led the way in promoting initiatives aimed at higher skilled (and wealthier) migrant communities or even convincing them not to leave in the first place.

The Brazilian government has increased spending on higher education and research, which has greatly reduced the number of Brazilians leaving the country to obtain college degrees. One unintended consequence, however, is that Brazil has also experienced "brain gain" at the expense of other Latin American countries.

Ecuador has focused more on making return of both people and money an attractive option through its "Plan Retorno" ("Return Plan"), which provides reductions or elimination of taxes on capital goods coming back into the country. Further it offers low interest loans to start up new businesses as a way to encourage productive investment. Unlike Brazil, however,

Ecuador has a weaker economic base that makes the overall project more difficult.

Any such effort also faces constant competition from the H-1B immigration program in the United States, which covers skilled foreign workers. It allows for a three-year stay, with the possibility of a three-year extension and eventual application for permanent residency. After September 11, 2001, the United States has accepted fewer petitions, but demand remains high. Although immigration is always a highly charged issue in the United States, accepting well-educated and skilled migrants is generally viewed in a positive light.

Thus, brain drain is a product both of strong "push" (the lack of opportunity at home) and "pull" (available visas for skilled workers) factors that are longstanding and change only slowly. The most effective long-term solution is for governments to provide material incentives for workers to remain in the country or at least to invest their resources back into the economy. Ultimately, however, that must occur in the context of economic growth and expansion.

See also *Immigration Policy, United States*

. . . . GREGORY WEEKS

REFERENCES AND FURTHER READING

"International Organization for Migration: Americas," www.iom.int/jahia/Jahia/pid/250.

Özden, Çağlar, "Brain Drain in Latin America," Expert Group Meeting on International Migration and Development in Latin America and the Caribbean, November 30–December 2, 2005, www.un.org/esa/population/meetings/IttMigLAC/P10_WB-DECRG.pdf.

Pellegrino, Adela. "Trends in Latin American Skilled Migration: 'Brain Drain' or 'Brain Exchange'?" *International Migration* 39, no. 5 (2001): 111–132.

Brazil, Coup d'État, 1964

The Brazilian Coup d'Etat of March 31, 1964, was perhaps the most important event in post-World War II Brazilian history. It ended Brazil's first attempt at democracy and instituted a military dictatorship that ruled for more than twenty years. Although the U.S. role of providing encouragement and offering assistance to the plotters—both before and after the coup—was indicative of U.S. policy during the Cold War, ultimately the coup did little to alter the dynamic of the relationship. U.S. and Brazilian interests continued to diverge and the close relations that characterized the first half of the twentieth century were not restored.

INSTABILITY GROWS IN BRAZIL

Despite the U.S. role, most of the causes of the coup were indigenous. Although the constitution of 1946 created a democratic government, there had been no experience with that form of government and the masses were susceptible to demagogic appeals. Party affiliation had more to do with one's opinion of longtime president Getulio Vargas (1930–1945, 1951–1954) than of ideology or policy differences. Brazil experienced enormous economic growth after 1945, but the political system was severely polarized, which the Cold War exacerbated. The Brazilian elite fought hard to preserve its privileges. Although the military had intervened less than in other Latin American nations, there was a pattern of increased intervention. Indeed the 1946 constitution granted the military the "moderating power" to replace governments that threatened the constitution, a power previously exercised by the emperor in the nineteenth century. There were several coups and failed attempts between 1945 and 1964.

Whatever the long-term and structural problems, the crises that led to the 1964 coup began to intensify after the success of the Cuban Revolution. Castro's success emboldened reformers and revolutionaries alike and raised the political stakes. Brazil had just experienced a period of enormous growth and optimism, including the construction of a new capital, Brasilia, under Juscelino Kubitschek. The economic boom also created high inflation and increased debt, which became major issues in the 1960 presidential campaign. The winner, Jânío Quadros, had been nominated by the anti-Vargas National Democratic Union (UDN), but he had never been a member of the party. Moreover, because the constitution allowed for split ticket voting, Vice President João Goulart of Vargas's Brazilian Workers Party (PTB) won reelection.

Quadros proved to be highly unstable and managed to alienate all sides of the political spectrum by attempting to weld a conservative economic policy of fiscal restraint with a radical foreign policy of neutralism in the Cold War. This "independent foreign policy" sought to make Brazil a leader in the developing world by increasing ties with the Soviet bloc and the newly emerging nations in Africa and Asia. This policy prompted Quadros to abandon Brazil's traditional role as mediator between the United States and Latin America, as Quadros sought to protect revolutionary Cuba.

The Cuban Revolution also prompted the United States to modify its policies of relying on private investment as the source of development, eventually leading to John F. Kennedy's Alliance for Progress. Ostensibly, Kennedy offered to underwrite massive reforms in Latin America in order to win the "race between evolution and revolution." But Kennedy also sought to isolate and liberate Cuba, and in addition to economic aid, the Kennedy administration drastically increased military assistance and training of soldiers and police, creating the School of the Americas in the Panama Canal Zone.

The Organization of American States (OAS) convened in Punta del Este, Uruguay, in July 1961 to inaugurate the Alliance for Progress. In the aftermath of the conference Quadros created a crisis by giving a medal to Cuban Finance Minister Ernesto "Che" Guevara. Faced with immediate and widespread protest, Quadros resigned abruptly. Goulart was in China on a trade mission. Top generals in the Brazilian army declared Goulart unacceptable, while others called on their colleagues to follow the constitution. Civil war appeared imminent, but it was averted by a compromise that allowed Goulart to assume the office of president, albeit with truncated powers.

Goulart spent the next eighteen months seeking to restore his powers by proving the compromise was unworkable. He also began to push for "basic reforms" that included land redistribution and the nationalization of the electric and telephone industries. Although he traveled to the United States in April

1962 to win support from the Kennedy administration and applaud the Alliance for Progress, he retained Quadros's independent foreign policy. At the second Punta del Este Conference in January 1962, called in response to Castro's "Declaration of Havana," Brazil joined with Argentina, Chile, and Mexico to oppose any harsh measures and instead engineered a compromise that merely kicked Cuba out of the OAS.

The Kennedy administration did not trust Goulart, especially after he proved unwilling to take strong measures against inflation or the balance of payments crisis because it would hurt his base. Through the Central Intelligence Agency (CIA), the United States began funding candidates hostile to Goulart, but the PTB actually increased its seats in the 1962 midterm elections.

THE COUP AND ITS CONSEQUENCES

Goulart's unwanted and unsuccessful effort to mediate the Cuban Missile Crisis so irritated U.S. officials that Kennedy sent his brother Robert to warn Goulart that he needed to fight communism at home more vigorously. A plebiscite in January 1963 restored his powers, but it did not improve relations. By 1963 U.S. officials were plotting to remove Goulart. This was accomplished by the adoption of an "islands of sanity" policy that bypassed the national government and sent economic assistance directly to state government in opposition to Goulart. Kennedy also sent Vernon Walters (future deputy director of the CIA), who had served with the Brazilian Expeditionary Force in Italy as military liaison.

These efforts continued after the death of Kennedy. Meanwhile the economic and political crises in Brazil continued unabated. By early 1964 there was open discussion of an imminent revolution or Goulart-led coup. On March 13, at a rally attended by thousands of supporters, Goulart signed decrees expropriating privately owned oil refineries and underutilized lands near federal projects. Just three days later the new assistant secretary of state for Inter-American affairs, Thomas Mann, announced that the United States would no longer oppose military coups but would recognize any government in effective control, a clear signal to Brazilian plotters to proceed.

In the final days prior to the coup, U.S. officials, especially Walters and Ambassador Lincoln Gordon, assisted the conspiracy that coalesced around the leadership of Walters's close friend and Army Chief of Staff General Humberto Castelo Branco. As the coup was being launched on March 31, the United States began "Operation Brother Sam," to provide military assistance in case of civil war. On April 1, while Goulart was still in Brazil attempting to mobilize resistance, President Lyndon B. Johnson congratulated the military for its "constitutional" change of government, making recognition unnecessary.

United States officials always expressed surprise and dismay at the turn of events after the coup, but their policies indicate otherwise. On April 9 the junta announced a state of siege and issued the first of several "Institutional Acts" that effectively destroyed the constitution and created a military dictatorship. Castelo Branco became the president and the military cancelled citizenship rights to fifty-five members of congress, six state governors, two supreme court justices, and three former presidents, as well as hundreds of former top officials. The Johnson administration showered the new regime with massive aid: in the 1964–1970 period only South Vietnam and India received more U.S. assistance dollars. Corporate investment likewise flowed into Brazil. Yet despite the largesse, subsequent general-presidents after Castelo Branco reverted back to the independent foreign policy. By 1970 Brazilian-American differences had emerged on issues such as nuclear proliferation, the Angolan civil war, Cuba, the Law of the Seas Treaty, and the Arab-Israeli conflict. For a short-term fix of a minor problem, the end of the Brazilian-American alliance was a high price to pay for the United States.

See also *Alliance for Progress; Brazil, U.S. Relations with; Furtado, Celso; Gordon, Lincoln; Goulart, João Belchior; Kennedy, John F.; Mann, Thomas C.; Quadros da Silva, Jânio*

. . . . W. MICHAEL WEIS

REFERENCES AND FURTHER READING

Black, Jan Knippers. *United States Penetration of Brazil.* Philadelphia: University of Pennsylvania Press, 1977.

Leacock, Ruth. *Requiem for Revolution: The United States and Brazil, 1961–1969.* Kent, OH: Kent State University Press, 1990.

Parker, Phyllis R. *Brazil and the Quiet Intervention, 1964.* Austin: University of Texas Press, 1979.

Skidmore, Thomas E. *Politics in Brazil, 1930–1964: An Experiment in Democracy.* New York: Oxford University Press, 1967.

Weis, W. Michael. *Cold Warriors and Coups d'Etat: Brazilian-American Relations, 1945–1964.* Albuquerque: University of New Mexico Press, 1993.

Brazil, U.S. Relations with

In terms of geographical area, natural resources, and size of population, Brazil and the United States share a similarity in that they are the two giant nations of the western hemisphere. Over the past two centuries, however, the United States has achieved more political stability and economic success than Brazil and has become the world's leading superpower. Although Brazil is credited with great economic potential and is often considered "a country of the future," it has been no more than a middle-level power in world affairs. Nevertheless, Brazil is an important regional power in South America. Moreover, as a former colony of Portugal, Brazil historically believed itself to be politically and culturally different and at times has felt alienated from the Spanish-speaking countries of South America. These nations historically observed Brazil's territorial expansion across the interior of the continent with suspicion.

In particular Brazil felt challenged by the rise of neighboring Argentina, and to counter this anxiety it looked for external diplomatic support especially from the Anglo-Saxon United States. Brazil has also regarded the United States as a valuable market for Brazilian exports, especially coffee, and in the twentieth century Brazil has seen the United States as the principal source of capital investment for industrial development. Consequently the United States has generally found diplomatic relations with Brazil to be friendly and cooperative, providing a welcome contrast to the often antagonistic relationship that has existed between the United States and most of the Spanish-American countries. Historians have referred to an "unwritten alliance" in which Brazil has acted as a link or intermediary in being actively involved in many of the policy initiatives undertaken by the United States in hemispheric affairs. Such occasions were the emergence of Pan-Americanism at the end of the nineteenth century, the decisions to join World War I and World War II, and measures to combat the communist threat in the Americas. However, there were areas of disagreement between Brazil and the United States. Perceived threats to national interests have provoked Brazilian criticism and, in some cases there has been retaliation, especially over controversial questions such as the freedom of trade and protection of the environment.

INDEPENDENCE TO THE MID-NINETEENTH CENTURY

During the colonial period when the North American colonies were ruled by Great Britain and Brazil was under the control of Portugal, geographical distance and mercantilist policies dictated that there was relatively little contact between the two peoples. At the end of the eighteenth century political differences were accentuated by the fact that the United States became a republic and adopted an antimonarchical tradition. The detached attitude of the Brazilian elite toward the United States changed, if only briefly, as a result of the declaration of Brazilian independence from Portugal in September 1822. A priority of Emperor Pedro I was to secure his formal diplomatic recognition from the great European powers. However the refusal of the Portuguese king to recognize Brazil's independence initially prevented the other European monarchs from establishing formal diplomatic relations with the new country. Even though it would mean recognizing a monarchy, President James Monroe saw an opportunity for American commercial advancement. Consequently, he acted ahead of the European governments and established formal diplomatic relations with the new Brazilian empire in 1824. As early as the 1820s the political and diplomatic elite of Brazil clearly recognized the leading influence of the United States in hemispheric affairs. This recognition was demonstrated when the Brazilian chargé d'affaires, José Silvestre Rebelo, was received by Monroe in Washington, and the chargé not only expressed his gratitude for American diplomatic recognition but also proposed a political-military alliance between the two countries based on the principles of the Monroe Doctrine. The idea of an alliance was intended to secure American support for Brazil's continental security while at the same time also providing a means of helping the newly independent state against the contingency of European political and economic interference. Brazil was to be disappointed because the Monroe administration was averse to acquiring overseas political or military entanglements. No special consideration was therefore given to Brazil, which was viewed as just one of several Latin American countries currently seeking to establish diplomatic relations with the United States.

For much of the nineteenth century Brazil and the United States had little in common and rarely impinged upon each other. The United States avoided diplomatic involvement in Brazil's local conflicts in the Cisplatine War (1825–1828) and the War of the Triple Alliance (1865–1870). In the American Civil War (1861–1865) Brazil granted belligerent rights to the Confederate states, but Emperor Pedro II privately favored the cause of the Union. The Civil War was influential in bringing about the emancipation of the slaves in the United States and this gave encouragement to the movement for the abolition of slavery in Brazil, which eventually materialized in 1888. It also resulted in a few thousand Confederate exiles choosing to emigrate to Brazil in what turned out to be an unsuccessful venture. The most frequent and ultimately enduring contact between Americans and Brazilians was through trade. A commercial treaty was signed in 1828 but lapsed in 1841, as Brazil adopted the policy of tariff protection. Despite initial American optimism, trade between the United States and Brazil turned out at first to be relatively modest. The economic reality was that both countries were primarily agrarian economies that produced very similar items and had therefore not a great deal to sell profitably to each other.

From the beginning of the nineteenth century the actual balance of trade was invariably in Brazil's favor, a trend that was increased by the growing demand for Brazilian coffee, which made the United States Brazil's largest and most lucrative export market. Nevertheless in terms of economic and cultural relations, the Brazilian elite was much closer to Europe than to the United States during the nineteenth century. The nation most admired was Great Britain. The British were the world's leading maritime power. They were also the biggest traders and investors in Brazil so that most Brazilian diplomatic efforts were directed at cultivating close relations with Great Britain. For much of the nineteenth century the United States was regarded as a much less significant power.

PAN-AMERICANISM

By the last quarter of the nineteenth century the United States had risen to become a leading industrial power. Moreover the visit of Emperor Pedro II to the Centennial Exhibition at Philadelphia in 1876 symbolically lifted the barriers of geography and history that had kept Brazil and the United States apart for so long. Relations signally improved during the period of Pan-Americanism which was marked by diplomatic initiatives of the United States to organize the Washington Pan-American conference (1889–1890) and develop a policy of promoting hemispheric trade by negotiating bilateral trade treaties. The timing of the initiatives was propitious on account of the overthrow of the Brazilian empire by a military coup in November 1889. The rulers of the new Brazilian republic felt insecure and desperately wanted U.S. diplomatic and military support. There was also a desire to increase trade by selling more sugar and coffee specifically to the United States. The Brazilian government was prepared, therefore, to respond positively to American proposals to negotiate a trade treaty, which would ensure that sugar and coffee were imported into the United States free of customs duty. In return Brazil reduced duties on imports of American manufactured goods. Brazil's pro-U.S. action was highly significant because it was the first Latin American country to sign such an agreement, and by doing so, it enabled the United States to implement the policy of concluding similar treaties with other countries.

Later, Brazilian politicians and merchants complained of American double-dealing when the United States negotiated a treaty with Spain that resulted in Cuban sugar being granted the same tariff benefits as Brazil. Anti-American sentiment was aroused, but it was reduced by President Grover Cleveland's very pleasing arbitration of Brazil's boundary dispute with Argentina over the Misiones territory in 1895. The United States was viewed as a friend of Brazil. In 1895 the Brazilian Senate sent Cleveland a note of congratulations for what was regarded as his successful handling of the Venezuelan Boundary Dispute between Venezuela and Great Britain. When the United States went to war with Spain in 1898 the Brazilian government, in marked contrast to the Spanish-American nations such as Argentina and Chile, was conspicuous in showing a sympathetic attitude in allowing American warships to take on fuel and to refit in Brazilian ports.

APPROXIMATION

The relationship between Brazil and the United States was visibly strengthened during the first decade of the twentieth century in a period that marked the emergence of "the unwritten alliance." The friendly feeling reflected a convergence of national interests. In the United States President Theodore Roosevelt and Secretary of State Elihu Root genuinely desired to improve relations with Latin America, while in Brazil Foreign Minister Baron do Rio Branco and the Brazilian ambassador in Washington, Joaquim Nabuco, were evolving a strategy that sought to switch attention away from the great European powers and "approximate" their country's foreign policy as closely as possible to that pursued by the United States. This strategy was exemplified by the upgrading of diplomatic relations between the United States and Brazil to ambassadorial level in 1905. Rio Branco's ambitions to make Brazil the leading power in South America were seemingly endorsed by Root's decision to attend the Pan-American conference held at Rio in 1906, the first time a serving American secretary of state had left the country on a diplomatic mission. Root even hinted at the possibility of an alliance between the two countries based on the Monroe Doctrine. The exact meaning of what such an alliance would constitute was unclear, but the idea of a special relationship with the United States excited Rio Branco and Nabuco.

Disillusionment, however, soon followed. For the United States the region of primary strategic concern was Mexico, Central America, and the islands of the Caribbean. By contrast Brazil and the South American nations were perceived as remote and peripheral to U.S. national security. This was made apparent by Root's unwillingness to aid Brazil against Argentina. Rio Branco was fearful of Argentine naval expansion and wanted American support to offset the perceived military threat posed by its powerful neighbor. The United States, however, did not want to take sides and thereby disturb the existing balance of power in the region. By its decision not to support Brazil against Argentina, the United States revealed the limited value of the strategy of approximation and exposed the precariousness of Brazil's pretensions to South American leadership.

WORLD WAR I

The United States and the nations of Latin America responded to the outbreak of war in Europe in 1914 with declarations of neutrality. However they could not escape the resulting severe dislocation of the normal channels of world trade and investment. For the United States this disruption presented a signal opportunity for increased trade and investment with Latin America. Brazil appeared as a particularly large and enticing economic market. American manufacturers and investment banks eagerly displaced the formerly dominant British commercial interests. From this point onward British economic influence in Brazil was in sharp decline and Wall Street replaced the City of London as the main source of Brazil's inward capital investment. Moreover Americans attached increased economic and diplomatic importance to Brazil after the United States declared war on Germany in April 1917. First and foremost Brazil was valued as a supplier of vital raw materials for the war effort. It also provided a means by which the United States could influence the foreign policies of the other South American countries. Just like the United States, Brazilian merchant shipping had been threatened by German submarine warfare. President Woodrow Wilson hoped that Brazil would join the war as a cobelligerent and that this would influence the other South American countries, especially Argentina, to follow suit. Brazil's decision to go to war against Germany in October 1917, however, was interpreted in Argentina as a deliberate Brazilian effort to revive the policy of approximation with the United States.

Argentine calculations were correct insofar that Brazilian officials expected that close wartime association with the United States would not only produce material economic benefits but also directly assist Brazil's long-standing aspiration to be the leading power in South America. Brazil also nursed a desire to become actively involved in world affairs. Although Brazilian military forces did not actually participate in wartime hostilities, the status of being a cobelligerent meant that Brazil was invited to attend the Versailles Peace conference (1919–1920), and with Wilson's support, Brazil was rewarded with a temporary seat on the council of the newly formed League of Nations. In the United States, however, the U.S. Senate rejected American membership of the league. As the United States subsequently repudiated Wilson's internationalist policies and withdrew into isolationism, the diplomatic ties with Brazil began to slacken. The "unwritten alliance" was consigned to the past as Brazil diverged from the United States and the Brazilian elite chose to embark upon a strategy designed to assert their country's influence not only in the western hemisphere but in the wider world. However Brazil's request for a permanent seat on the council was rejected by the great European powers and also by the Spanish-American nations who had never accepted the idea that Brazil should have a special status. Brazil's resort to a veto to prevent Germany gaining a permanent seat resulted in diplomatic humiliation and Brazil's decision to quit the league in 1926.

WORLD WAR II

After a period of relative neglect during the 1920s, American diplomatic interest in Brazil notably revived as part of the "Good Neighbor" policy espoused by President Franklin D. Roosevelt, who took office in 1933. Behind the uplifting rhetoric of acting as a good neighbor, there was a calculated desire to increase trade with Latin America in order to help the U.S. economy recover from the ravages of the Great Depression. Like the earlier policy of Pan-Americanism, this desire would be achieved by the negotiation of bilateral reciprocal trade agreements involving mutual tariff reductions. The Roosevelt administration similarly saw Brazil as one of the countries most likely to be willing to negotiate such an agreement. A draft treaty was duly agreed and signed in 1935, but commercial relations did not proceed smoothly.

The Roosevelt administration was disturbed by the perceived fascist sympathies of President Getúlio Vargas, who had come to power in Brazil in 1930 and went on to establish a fascist-style dictatorship in 1937 known as the "New State." During this period there was a marked increase in trade between Brazil and Nazi Germany. In fact Vargas sought to play off Germany against the United States in order to maximize the economic advantages for Brazil. While welcoming further contact with Germany, he continued to stress, through his pro-American ambassador in Washington, Osvaldo Aranha, a desire to maintain close and friendly relations with the United States. The relationship with the United States was significantly boosted in 1939 by the outbreak of war in Europe, which closed off trade links between Brazil and Germany and greatly enhanced the strategic significance of Brazil's long coastline bordering the Atlantic Ocean. Just as in World War I, Brazil was again highly regarded in the United States as a supplier of strategic minerals and raw materials. After the United States entered the war in 1941, northeast Brazil effectively became a large U.S. military base and "trampoline" for supplying the Allied campaign in North Africa and Italy. In return Brazil received massive quantities of U.S. Lend-Lease aid, amounting to almost 75 percent of total Lend-Lease aid assigned to Latin America for the whole wartime period.

Brazil officially joined the war against Germany in August 1942. Despite public pronouncements that an equal relationship existed, Brazil was essentially a subordinate of the United States throughout the war. The reward was substantial financial and material aid from the United States, some of which was used for economic development, especially the creation of national steel and petroleum industries. The sheer quantity of aid also meant that Brazil was able to surpass Argentina as the leading military power in South America. In addition Brazil acquired international prestige because it was the only South American country to take on an active combat role in the war. The participation of 25,000 soldiers of the Brazilian Expeditionary Force (FEB), who fought with success in the Italian campaign under U.S. military command, encouraged Brazil once again to aspire to the status of a world power, an aspiration which Roosevelt personally encouraged Vargas to pursue.

The pattern of events during and after World War I, however, was repeated because the success of Brazil's diplomatic ambitions was ultimately contingent on continued U.S. diplomatic support. The "unwritten alliance" in the shape of American preferential treatment for Brazil was effectively curtailed by Roosevelt's death in 1945. His successor, President Harry Truman, supported a continuance of friendly relations, but he did not want Brazil to become too militarily powerful and thereby upset the balance of power in South America. Although the Truman administration readily granted large-scale economic assistance to western Europe in the form of the Marshall Plan starting in 1947, it refused to give similar aid to help Latin American governments develop and modernize their economies. Brazilian diplomats contended that their country deserved special consideration on account of its loyal support of the United States during the war. When financial aid was not forthcoming, Brazil's annoyance was exemplified in its unwillingness to send a token military expeditionary force to join U.S. forces in the Korean War (1950–1953).

Discontent continued throughout the 1950s as the Eisenhower administration resisted requests for U.S. government loans and argued instead that Brazil should seek private capital investment to fund its ambitious plans for industrial development, which were symbolized by the building of a new federal capital at Brasília. In 1958 President Juscelino Kubitschek proposed "Operation Pan America," a major program of economic development for all the nations of the hemisphere. Although Kubitschek envisaged Brazil as playing an important part in the implementation of the scheme, he expected the United States to take the leading role in providing the funds. A negative response, however, was forthcoming from the Eisenhower administration, which saw the idea as a calculated ploy to extract U.S. money to finance extravagant expenditure. A separate scheme devised by the U.S. government eventually emerged when John F. Kennedy became president in 1961; it was known as the Alliance for Progress. Kennedy paid tribute to Kubitschek's work in directing attention to the need for a hemispheric aid program, but he stressed that the idea of the Alliance for Progress originated in the United States rather than Brazil.

COLD WAR

The American attitude of studied neglect toward Latin America in the years immediately following World War II sharply changed during the 1950s as a result of growing alarm over the perceived rise in the influence of international communism in the western hemisphere. In Brazil American anxiety focused on the danger of communist infiltration, especially in the poverty-stricken northeastern region, where it was feared that a Cuban-style guerrilla movement might emerge. There was also concern over the "independent" foreign policy pursued by President Jânio Quadros, which implied that Brazil would no longer automatically take the side of

Brazilian President Juscelino Kubitschek (left) and U.S. Vice President Richard M. Nixon (right) overlook Brazil's Gilherme Guinie Steel Plant at Volta Redando on February 5, 1956. The plant was built during World War II with U.S. financial and technical assistance. Post-war U.S. investment in Brazil fell short of Kubitschek's ambitions.

SOURCE: National Archives

the United States in the Cold War against the Soviet Union. When Quadros resigned in 1961 he was succeeded by the left-wing political leader, João Goulart. Despite pressure from the United States Goulart continued to maintain diplomatic relations with Cuba. Moreover he approved the expropriation of U.S.-owned companies and restrictions on their remittances of profits originally made in Brazil. The administrations of John F. Kennedy and Lyndon Johnson distrusted Goulart and believed that he intended to establish a dictatorship that would include communists. American policy sought to destabilize his regime by limiting financial aid.

At the same time covert assistance was given to Goulart's political opponents and close relations were maintained with senior military officers. Colonel Vernon Walters, who had served as U.S. liaison officer between the American and Brazilian forces in the Italian campaign, was sent to Brazil as U.S. military attaché in 1962. Walters was a personal friend of many Brazilian generals and had once shared a camp tent in Italy with General Humberto Castelo Branco, the leader of the military coup that overthrew Goulart in 1964. The circumstantial evidence appeared so compelling that the coup was widely interpreted as inspired, if not secretly directed, by the U.S. embassy in Brazil. While President Johnson enthusiastically welcomed the fall of Goulart in 1964, he categorically denied that the United States had played an active role either in planning or executing the coup. Nevertheless, in marked contrast to the unsympathetic attitude previously shown toward Goulart, Johnson proceeded to praise the new military government and provide it with diplomatic support and greatly increased financial aid and investment. The military junta was delighted to receive U.S. economic assistance, which it regarded as vital for its ambitious plans to develop and modernize the Brazilian economy. The generals also admired the achievements of the United States and considered that country as the leader of the free world in the battle against international communism. The ideological affinities were underscored by Brazilian diplomatic support for Johnson in his controversial military intervention in the Dominican Republic in 1965. Brazilian combat troops were sent to the island as part of the Inter-American Peace Force. Brazil's leading role was demonstrated by the appointment of a Brazilian general as commander of the Peace Force. The American public also became more aware of Brazil as a result of growing tourism and the popularity of Brazilian art, architecture, and music, especially the fusion of samba and jazz known as "bossa nova."

NATIONALIST FOREIGN POLICY

The convergence of American and Brazilian national interests did not persist for very long after the 1964 coup. The geopolitical reality had not altered in that the United States was much more directly concerned with the communist threat emanating from Fidel Castro's Cuba and the rise of the Sandinistas in Central America. By contrast Brazil was still too geographically distant and peripheral to U.S. national security. Moreover, the threat of communism in Brazil was effectively contained by authoritarian military rule.

At the same time Brazilian diplomacy began to demonstrate a different perspective on hemispheric and world affairs. General Artur Costa e Silva set the tone when he became president in 1967 and countered domestic criticism that Brazil was too subservient to the United States by implementing what was essentially a return to the "independent" foreign policy of Quadros and Goulart. To avoid being associated with the left-wing presidents, however, the military government preferred the policy to be described in public as "nationalist." Another change of emphasis was the importance attached to the growing divergence between the affluent nations of the "north" or "first world" and the less economically developed countries of the "south" or "third world." According to this north-south vantage point Brazil currently had more in common with the south, and its priority should be to use foreign policy as a tool for promoting the country's economic development so that it could develop as a world power and eventually join the nations of the north.

Brazil's north-south perspective also reflected the relative decline of the United States as the world's leading economic superpower, a development that temporarily undermined the importance of commercial links. During World War II the United States had absorbed more than 50 percent of Brazil's total exports. The proportion fell to less than 20 percent during the 1970s. Consequently Brazil looked beyond the

United States for alternative export markets and sources of inward capital investment, a strategy that was stimulated by the "oil shocks" in 1973 and 1979 and the resulting need to earn more foreign exchange from exports to pay for the rising cost of oil imports. Particular effort was directed by Brazilian diplomats to expanding trade with the affluent nations of western Europe. New markets were also developed and cultivated in Africa, the Middle East, Asia, and the Communist bloc. An opportunity to enter the vast Chinese market was presented when diplomatic relations were established with Communist China in 1974.

The decision to recognize Communist China predated by four years a similar action by President Jimmy Carter and illustrated Brazil's determination to exercise autonomy in its foreign policy, even if this diverged from the diplomacy of the United States. Indeed the pursuit of a "nationalist" policy that stressed export-led growth combined with protection for home industries frequently resulted in conflict with the United States. Brazilian exporters complained of American tariff barriers and discriminatory customs duties that seriously affected their sales in the United States of such products as instant coffee, shoes, and steel. American corporations responded by contending that Brazil maintained a strict protectionist policy designed to prevent foreign competition with Brazilian producers of computers and armaments. Nuclear power was a particularly divisive issue. While successive Brazilian governments denied any intention of ever acquiring nuclear weapons, they insisted on Brazil's right to develop atomic energy for peaceful industrial purposes and as an alternative source of power to oil. Consequently they resolutely resisted American pressure to sign the 1965 Nuclear Non-Proliferation Treaty. Moreover, much to American displeasure, Brazil signed an agreement with a west German consortium to supply nuclear reactors. Economic self-interest also influenced Brazilian policy toward the Middle East and resulted in disagreement with the United States over the Arab-Israeli issue. Dependent upon the Middle East for 80 percent of its oil imports, Brazilian governments visibly adopted a pro-Arab attitude. Further examples of Brazil's divergence from the United States were the rejection of President Carter's call for a boycott of the 1980 Moscow Olympic games and an unwillingness to give public support for the attempts of President Ronald Reagan to counter the communist threat in El Salvador and Nicaragua.

During the 1970s some members of the military government fondly predicted that Brazil would become a world power by the end of the twentieth century. This aspiration appeared increasingly unlikely as Brazil was afflicted by political instability, including the impeachment and removal of President Fernando de Collor from office in 1992, persistent hyperinflation, and the failure to maintain high levels of industrial growth. No longer so optimistic about achieving great power status, Brazilian governments were suspicious of what they regarded as calculated attempts by the United States and the great European powers to infringe the sovereignty of less powerful nations and to establish international institutions for their own economic benefit. Brazil was, therefore, extremely distrustful of proposals designed to regulate world trade, limit the growth of population, establish international ownership of the seabeds, and put restrictions on arms sales. Especially contentious was the issue of the environment and campaigns directed by foreign organizations to express their concern over the deforestation of the Amazon.

CONTEMPORARY U.S.-BRAZILIAN RELATIONS

Despite international criticism Brazil did not want to appear too confrontational. During the 1980s economic factors brought about a return to closer cooperation with the United States because Brazil needed American diplomatic and financial assistance in order to negotiate a satisfactory resolution of the debt crisis which required Brazil to raise billions of dollars to service the annual interest payments on its foreign loans. Moreover the decline in trade between the two countries during the 1970s proved to be only temporary. By the 1990s the United States was once again Brazil's largest single export market and trade between the two countries almost doubled during the decade. Both countries, however, were also economic competitors in regional and global markets. The United States diverged from Brazil by forming the North Atlantic Free Trade Agreement (NAFTA) with Canada and Mexico in 1992. In effect the United States showed that Mexico was its preferred economic partner in Latin America. Brazil opted instead to join with Argentina, Paraguay, and Uruguay in forming a separate customs union known as Mercosul. Brazilian diplomacy sought to promote the development of Mercosul not only for its economic benefits but also to provide a stronger bargaining position in trade negotiations with the new economic "megablocs" of the world such as NAFTA and the European Union. Indeed, NAFTA was seen as an obstacle to Brazil's desire to expand Mercosul. While Brazil proposed a broader South American Free Trade Area (SAFTA) as a logical next step in regional economic integration, the United States preferred the development of a Free Trade Area of the Americas (FTAA), stretching from Alaska to Cape Horn and ultimately leading to global free trade.

In addition to clashes in negotiations to liberalize world trade, the United States was disappointed by Brazil's disinclination to regard the war on terror after the 9/11 attacks as seriously as the Cold War struggle against international communism. The administration of President Luiz Inácio Lula da Silva, which took office in 2002, was also critical of the U.S.-led invasion and occupation of Iraq. As the senior partner in Mercosul, Brazil believed that it had finally become the leading power in South America if not in Latin America. Moreover, as a member of the "BRICS," Brazil was identified along with Russia, India, and China as one of the fastest-growing economies in the world. Conscious of its growing economic strength and diplomatic status, Brazil felt that it could pursue its own national interests independently and without any longer needing to approximate its foreign policy so closely to that of the United States.

See also *Brazil, Coup d'État, 1964; Kubitschek de Oliveira, Juscelino; Lula da Silva, Luiz Inácio; Monroe Doctrine; Nabuco, Joaquim; Pedro II, Emperor Dom; Rio Branco, Barão do; Roosevelt, Franklin D.; Root, Elihu; Third International Conference of American States, Rio de Janeiro, 1906; Vargas, Getúlio Dornelles; Wilson, Woodrow*

. . . . JOSEPH SMITH

REFERENCES AND FURTHER READING

Bandeira, Moniz. *Presença dos Estados Unidos no Brasil (Dois Séculos de História).* Rio de Janeiro, Brazil: Civilização Brasileira, 1978.

Burns, E. Bradford. *The Unwritten Alliance: Rio Branco and Brazilian-American Relations.* New York: Columbia University Press, 1966.

Hilton, Stanley E. *Brazil and the Great Powers, 1930–1939: The Politics of Trade Rivalry.* Austin: University of Texas Press, 1975.

Hirst, Monica. *The United States and Brazil: A Long Road of Unmet Expectations.* New York: Routledge, 2005.

McCann, Frank D. *The Brazilian-American Alliance, 1937–1945.* Princeton, NJ: Princeton University Press, 1973.

Smith, Joseph. *Brazil and the United States: Convergence and Divergence.* Athens: University of Georgia Press, 2010.

Smith, Joseph. *Unequal Giants: Diplomatic Relations between the United States and the Brazilian Republic, 1889–1930.* Pittsburgh, PA: University of Pittsburgh Press, 1991.

Weis, W. Michael. *Cold Warriors and Coups d'Etat: Brazilian-American Relations, 1945–1964.* Albuquerque: University of New Mexico Press, 1993.

Wesson, Robert. *The United States and Brazil: Limits of Influence.* New York: Praeger, 1981.

Briggs, Ellis O.

Ellis Ormsbee Briggs (1899–1976) graduated from Dartmouth College in 1921 and passed the Foreign Service Exam in 1925. His first assignment, as vice consul in Lima, Peru, served as the starting point for a career specialization in Latin America. For the next twenty years Briggs held posts in Latin America, as well as Asia and Washington, D.C. From 1933 to 1937 Briggs served in Cuba under Ambassador Jefferson Caffery. During this period the United States finally abrogated the Platt Amendment, which had been enacted in 1901 to ensure U.S. involvement in Cuban affairs after the end of the Spanish American War, and Colonel Fulgencio Batista consolidated power with U.S. support. In 1937 Briggs returned to Washington, D.C., to take over as assistant chief of the Division of American Republics. In this position Briggs professed support for an interpretation of the Good Neighbor policy that stressed mutual respect in Inter-American relations. Yet he was highly skeptical of the position that Washington should or could solve long-standing problems of economic inequality and exploitation in Latin America.

In 1944 Briggs was named U.S. ambassador to the Dominican Republic. As World War II was drawing to an end, as were European dictatorships, American policymakers encouraged the transition to democracy in Latin America. Briggs was especially critical of Rafael Trujillo's dictatorship in the Dominican Republic, which had been formally supported by the United States, especially as a friendly Caribbean outpost during the war. Briggs emphasized to the U.S. State Department his conclusion that continued military support for Trujillo and other Latin American dictatorships would only slow the transition to democracy in the region. He convinced Secretary of State James Byrnes to discontinue arms sales to Trujillo. Briggs also served briefly as chief of the Division of Caribbean and Central American Affairs in 1944.

In 1945 Briggs was briefly assigned to the American Embassy in China, but he returned before end of the year to serve as director of the Office of American Republic Affairs, where he was a close advisor to Assistant Secretary of State Spruille Braden. He and Braden helped to define U.S. postwar policy toward the region and worked to clarify the U.S. government's position on intervention in the internal affairs of American nations. Briggs concluded that a significant majority of nations should be required in order to approve any multilateral intervention. He also favored a policy of encouraging private enterprise in Latin America and consistently disapproved of aiding totalitarian governments in the region, but Cold War priorities prevented U.S. policymakers from implementing many of his recommendations. Briggs next served as ambassador to Uruguay from 1947 to 1949. This post was followed by three eventful years in Czechoslovakia, from 1949 to 1952. In 1952 he went to South Korea and remained there during armistice negotiations, before returning to Latin America to serve as ambassador to Peru from 1955 to 1956 and ambassador to Brazil from 1956 to 1959.

While in Brazil Briggs became the first U.S. ambassador to visit all twenty-two Brazilian states, and he shared President Juscelino Kubitschek's enthusiasm for the development of the vast interior region of Brazil. He helped arrange a loan from the Export-Import Bank for construction of the new capital city of Brasilia. Briggs was also instructed by Washington, D.C., in the aftermath of the Soviet Union's first successful launch of their satellite Sputnik, to obtain from Brazil rights to build a missile-tracking system on the remote island of Fernando de Noronha, two hundred miles off the Brazilian coast. Briggs also recognized the growing anti-U.S. sentiment in parts of Latin America, most notably evident in the violent anti-American crowds and riots that greeted Vice President Richard Nixon on his 1958 tour of Latin America.

Briggs received the Presidential Medal of Freedom in 1955. He retired from the Foreign Service in 1961. He wrote several memoirs about his diplomatic service before his death in 1976.

See also *Batista y Zaldívar, Fulgencio; Brazil, U.S. Relations with; Caffery, Jefferson; Cuba, U.S. Relations with; Dominican Republic, U.S. Relations with; Export-Import Bank (EXIM); Good Neighbor Policy; Kubitschek de Oliveira, Juscelino; Platt, Orville; Trujillo Molina, Rafael Leónidas*

. . . . MOLLY M. WOOD

SELECTED WORKS

Briggs, Ellis. *Farewell to Foggy Bottom.* New York: David McKay, 1964.

Briggs, Ellis. *Proud Servant.* Akron, OH: Kent State University Press, 1998.

REFERENCES AND FURTHER READING

Pike, Frederick B. *FDR's Good Neighbor Policy: Sixty Years of Generally Gentle Chaos*. Austin: University of Texas Press, 1995.

Brooke, General John R.

John R. Brooke (1838–1926) was a major general in the United States Army during the Civil War and the Spanish American War. He served as military governor of Puerto Rico and military governor of Cuba.

Brooke was born on July 21, 1838, in Pottstown, Pennsylvania, and he was educated in nearby Collegeville and West Chester. On April 20, 1861, at the outbreak of the Civil War, he joined the 4th Pennsylvania Infantry as a captain. Within a few months he was promoted to brevet colonel of the 53rd Pennsylvania Infantry and served in the 1862 Peninsula Campaign. Though twice critically wounded—once at Gettysburg and once at Cold Harbor—he recovered each time and finished the war with the rank of brigadier general. After the war he was granted a permanent rank of lieutenant colonel, but by 1888 he had again achieved the rank of brigadier general. In 1890 he and his 7th Cavalry supported General Nelson Miles in the campaign against Plains Tribes practicing the "Ghost Dance." The campaign ended in the infamous battle at Wounded Knee.

Not long after the Spanish-American-Cuban War began, on May 17, 1898, Brooke took command of the provisional Army Corps at Camp Thomas, Chickamauga National Military Park, near Oglethorpe, Georgia, where the I and III Corps were trained before they left for embarkation points in Tampa, Florida, on their way to Cuba. Overcrowding, inadequate clean water, poor sanitation, and insect borne disease caused a high rate of illness and death among the soldiers. Brooke desperately tried to repair this terrible situation, using his personal influence, to eventually get the quartermaster and medical departments to send help. While the problem slowly began to improve, the incident was one of the worst scandals in U.S. military history.

As U.S. forces moved to the Caribbean, Brooke accompanied General Miles to Puerto Rico where, on July 31, 1898, he commanded the invasion, landing at Arroyo and advancing to Guayama, where he engaged a significant Spanish force. Sweeping through the Spanish enemy, the Americans proceeded to Cayey, which Brooke was about to assault, when word came of the armistice. After the departure of the Spanish, Brooke was appointed military governor of Puerto Rico and served from August 30 (officially October 18) to December 5, 1898. It was in December that Spain, under the terms of the Treaty of Paris, ceded Puerto Rico to the United States. General Brooke was then appointed governor general of Cuba from December 28, 1898, to December 20, 1899, being replaced by General Leonard Wood.

While Puerto Rico began the twentieth century under U.S. military rule, with officials, including the governor, appointed by the U.S. president, the Foraker Act of 1900 gave Puerto Rico some autonomy, including a popularly elected House of Representatives.

Following his tour of duty in the Caribbean, Brooke returned to the United States as commander of the Department of the East headquartered in Philadelphia from May 10, 1900, to July 21, 1902. It was in July 1902 that he retired from the Army. Brooke remained in Philadelphia until his death at age 88 on September 5, 1926. He was buried at Arlington National Cemetery.

See also *Puerto Rico, U.S. Relations with; Spanish-Cuban-American War 1895–1898; Wood, General Leonard*

. . . . WILLIAM HEAD

REFERENCE AND FURTHER READING

"Department of Puerto Rico: Major General John R. Brooke to be Placed in Command," *The New York Times*, August 17, 1898.

"Gen. J. R. Brooke Comes to Atlanta," *Atlanta Constitution*, May 18, 1898.

Hendrickson, Kenneth E. Jr. *The Spanish-American War*. Westport, CT: Greenwood Press, 2003.

Morris, Nancy. *Puerto Rico: Culture, Politics, and Identity*. Westport CT: Praeger/Greenwood, 1995.

Spanish-American War, Foraker Act of 1990, General Leonard Wood and Treaty of Paris, 1898 (U.S.-Spain).

Brothers to the Rescue

Brothers to the Rescue (*Hermanos al Rescate*) is a small anti-Castro activist group that operates out of Florida. It briefly attained notoriety when the deaths of four of its staff at the hands of the Cuban air force created an international incident in February 1996.

The group was formed in May 1991 by an anti-Castro activist, José J. Basulto. Its initial goal was to search by plane for Cuban refugees who had gotten into difficulties while trying to escape Cuba across the Florida straits and inform the U.S. Coast Guard. The organization claims to have aided thousands of individuals in often life-threatening circumstances. However Basulto also had a long history of involvement in more aggressive attempts to destabilize the Castro regime. The Cuban government has repeatedly complained that Brothers to the Rescue airplanes had made provocative incursions into Cuban airspace.

This activism increased substantially after the *balsero* (rafters) crisis of 1994–1995. The mass emigration of Cubans, fleeing the hardship of the Special Period, resulted in the internment of thousands of migrants in Guantánamo Bay Naval Base. To resolve the crisis, the Clinton administration was forced to negotiate with Castro, and they eventually reached an agreement limiting future migration of Cubans to twenty thousand annually and for the return of *balseros* detained at sea to Cuba. Meanwhile the number of U.S. businesses investing in Cuba was increasing and the voices calling for constructive engagement were growing louder just as the immediate economic crisis of the Cuban Special Period seemed to be fading. A major breakthrough in U.S.-Cuban relations seemed possible, which produced a sense of crisis among many of the major exile organizations and an accompanying acceleration of anti-Castro efforts. The exile community stepped up the pressure on the government, strengthening their lobbying of legislative allies and launching provocative public campaigns such as anti-Castro flotillas and "civil disobedience" marches. Further Brothers to the Rescue flights followed in January 1996, with the planes dropping leaflets over Cuba containing the UN Declaration of Human Rights.

On February 24th, 1996, two Brothers to the Rescue planes were shot down by Cuban MiGs, killing four people (three of whom were U.S. citizens). Precise motivation is unclear, but it seems plausible that Castro sought to benefit from a renewed bout of hostility with the United States, securing his internal authority by generating external hostility to the "*Yanqui imperialists*." The Cuban government claimed that the planes had violated Cuban airspace; other groups, including the International Civil Aviation Organization, contested this. The attack was condemned by the UN Security Council. President Clinton abandoned his constructive engagement policies almost completely. He condemned the attacks, increased funding for the anti-Castro radio station Radio Martí, limited flights between the island and the mainland, and supported the embargo-tightening Cuban Liberty and Democratic Solidarity bill, better known as Helms-Burton.

The Brothers to the Rescue group continues its activities. Members allege that the Clinton administration colluded with the Cuban government over the incident. Basulto has been awarded damages against the Cuban government in a U.S. court. It appears unlikely that the group will again play such a critical role in U.S.-Latin American relations.

See also *Castro Ruz, Fidel; Clinton, William J.; Cuba, U.S. Embargo of; Cuba, U.S. Relations with; Cuban Americans; Cuban Liberty and Democratic Solidarity Act, 1996 (United States)*

. . . . ALEX GOODALL

REFERENCES AND FURTHER READING

Bardach, Ann Louise. *Cuba Confidential.* London: Penguin, 2004.

Mariño, Soraya M. Castro. "US-Cuban Relations during the Clinton Administration." *Latin American Perspectives* 29, no. 4 (July 2002): 47–76.

Brum Plan

(**See** *Brum Rodríguez, Baltsar*)

Brum Rodríguez, Baltasar

Baltasar Brum Rodríguez (1883–1933) was a Uruguayan politician and president from 1919 to 1923. He was born in Artigas, in the area of Cuaró, on June 18, 1883. His family came from the Azores islands of Portugal, but they had Flemish origins. José Batlle y Ordóñez, whom Brum met in Paysandú in September 1903, fascinated him. Brum was first a member and then director of the student association of Montevideo while attending law school there. He was part of the delegation that represented Uruguay at the First American Student conference held in January 1908 in Montevideo.

In December 1908 he graduated from law school. After travelling to Europe he returned to Salto in 1910 and started a law firm. Brum taught philosophy and literature in Salto's high school and represented Salto in the Colorado Party Convention. There Brum and Luis A. Thevenet, from the White party, debated the ideas of Batlle y Ordóñez. In 1913 President Batlle y Ordóñez appointed Brum to the position of minister of education. Brum was also the interim foreign minister in 1914, the interior minister in 1915–1916, the interim finance minister in 1915, and the minister of foreign affairs between 1916 and 1918. He was the author and promoter of important laws, such as one that established free education at all levels and another which created a nationwide public library system.

On April 2, 1916, Brum sustained serious injuries when a large cornice fell from a building and fractured his skull. The signs of mental imbalances at the end of his life were considered the result of this accident. In October 1917 Brum encouraged Uruguay to cut ties with Germany and ordered the confiscation of four German vessels that were anchored in the bay of Montevideo. He supported the formation of a North and South American Union within the League of Nations. On January 5, 1918, at the Colorado Party convention, Brum was proclaimed his party's candidate for president of Uruguay. He traveled to the United States by invitation of Woodrow Wilson's administration and maintained a series of diplomatic contacts in line with his affinity for the United States. Later, during his presidency, Brum ruled that the fourth of July, Independence Day in the United States, would be a national holiday in Uruguay, called the Day of Democracy.

Brum was elected president of Uruguay and he was sworn into office on March 1, 1919, at the age of 35. His powers of office were severely limited by the new constitution, which created the National Council of Administration. Brum ratified the Treaty of Versailles (1919) and governed with Batlle's reformist politics: a mandatory day of rest each week, minimum wages for rural workers, and so forth. He attempted other civil reforms, such as women's right to vote, but he was unsuccessful in his efforts.

When Brum finished his term in office he became the director of the daily newspaper *El Día* (1926–1927) and served as the president of the board of the *Banco Hipotecario* (Mortgage Bank). On November 26, 1929, Brum became president of the National Council of Administration. Upon the coup d'état of March 31, 1933, Brum barricaded himself in his house and made desperate attempts to put the government back in power. The next day, when the police surrounded his house, Brum, along with some of his friends, went to the door, defiant and armed. Then he stepped into the street and shot himself in the chest.

See also *Uruguay, U.S. Relations with*

. . . . LINCOLN MAIZTEGUI CASAS

REFERENCES AND FURTHER READING

Welker, Juan Carlos. *Baltasar Brum verbo y acción.* Montevideo, Uruguay: Imprenta Letras s.a, 1945.

Caetano, Gerardo. *La República Conservadora, 1916–1929 (tomo II).* Montevideo, Uruguay: Editorial Fin de Siglo, 1992.

Casas Maiztegui, Lincoln. *Orientales, una historia política del Uruguay (tomo II).* Montevideo, Uruguay: Planeta, 2006.

Martínez, José Luciano. *Gabriel Terra: el hombre, el político, el gobernante.* Montevideo, Uruguay: 1937.
Vanger, Milton I. *José Batlle y Ordóñez of Uruguay: The Creator of his Times.* Cambridge, MA: Harvard University Press, 1961.

Bryan, William Jennings

William Jennings Bryan (1860–1925) was an American attorney, statesman, and politician. He ran as the Democrat's candidate for president three times, but his largest impact on U.S.-Latin American relations came during his term as Woodrow Wilson's secretary of state.

PRESIDENTIAL NOMINEE

After attending law school at Union Law College in Chicago, Bryan taught high school. After practicing law in Jacksonville, Illinois, from 1883 to 1887, he moved to Lincoln, Nebraska.

Bryan became an outspoken prohibitionist and proponent of world peace and popular democracy. He was a lifelong critic of large banks, businesses, and railroads. In the 1890s he became a leader of the Populist party and the pro-Silver movement during the national currency debate.

In 1890 Bryan was elected to Congress in the Democrat's landslide. He was narrowly reelected in 1892 but lost a bid for the U.S. Senate in 1894. At a critical moment in the 1896 Democratic National Convention in Chicago, Bryan delivered his famous "Cross of Gold" speech that swept him to the nomination, but the issue split the party, and he lost to William McKinley.

During the Spanish-American War of 1898, Bryan supported America's war effort, volunteering to be an Army officer. Bryan spent the war in Florida. Afterward, Bryan opposed the acquisition of colonies like the Philippines. In 1900 the Democrats nominated Bryan again. Bryan abandoned the currency issue and emphasized anti-imperialism. McKinley won again but was assassinated in September 1901. Theodore Roosevelt became president and evolved into one of the most progressive reformers in U.S. history, with Bryan in a lesser national role. In 1908 Bryan ran for president again against Roosevelt's hand-picked successor, William Howard Taft, and lost one final time.

As Bryan's political fortunes declined, he turned to his Christian faith. Over the first quarter of the twentieth century Bryan made thousands of speeches to hundreds of fundamentalist congregations on what became known as the Chautauqua speaking circuit. Bryan espoused the Social Gospel which believed that Christianity should be the basis of human and social progress. Bryan opposed the evolutionary theories of Charles Darwin mainly because he believed that social Darwinism in the late nineteenth and early twentieth centuries had been the excuse for colonialism in the Americas, Asia, and Africa.

SECRETARY OF STATE

In 1912 Theodore Roosevelt's Progressive party candidacy attracted voters away from the Republican party and allowed Democrat Woodrow Wilson to be elected president. Bryan's decision to support Wilson played a major role in Wilson's nomination. While Wilson decided to run his own foreign policy, he appointed Bryan secretary of state out of deference to his long service to the Democratic party. Philosophically Bryan opposed neo-imperialism, especially in Latin America, even though he supported U.S. intervention in Mexico to capture revolutionary Pancho Villa.

Over the first two years of the Wilson administration, Bryan proved critical in maintaining party unity as they pushed through extensive reform legislation. Even though he had little experience in foreign affairs, he was able to negotiate thirty treaties with smaller nations calling for arbitration between each nation before declaring war. In Latin America, although Bryan advocated freedom for the Philippines and home rule for Puerto Rico, he also supported protection of U.S. business interests. He spent much of his time smoothing over the enmity that had been created by his predecessor, Philander C. Knox, and advocating a more benign financial intervention by the U.S. government in an effort to reduce European influence in the region. Perhaps his greatest demonstration of friendship toward Latin America was his conciliatory attitude to an aggrieved Colombia in the negotiation of a treaty between the two nations.

In spite of this conciliatory attitude, he also consistently supported the Platt Amendment that permitted open-ended U.S. interference in Cuban affairs and U.S. intervention in Mexico in an ultimately fruitless effort to capture Pancho Villa in 1914. In June 1915, after his departure from office, his policies facilitated the U.S. intervention in both Haiti and Santa Domingo.

Perhaps the most noteworthy Latin American issue to confront Bryan as secretary of state involved an attempt to build another transisthmian canal. Unable to convince the United States to build a canal in Nicaragua, by the end of 1904 Nicaraguan President José Santos Zelaya had begun seeking support from France, Germany, and Japan to build a canal to compete with the proposed American canal in Panama. Concerned about European influence in the area, in 1909 Knox unsuccessfully sought Nicaraguan concessions to allow the United States to send troops to protect U.S. property in Nicaragua. That same year the United States provided political support to Conservative-led forces rebelling against Zelaya and intervened militarily to protect American lives and property. From 1912 to 1933, with the exception of a nine-month period in 1925–1926, the United States maintained troops in Nicaragua.

On August 5, 1914, Secretary Bryan and Emiliano Chamorro Vargas signed the Chamorro-Bryan Treaty, a modification of the Castillo-Knox Treaty that had never been ratified. The earlier treaty allowed the United States to intervene in Nicaragua. The later treaty "only" gave the United States the exclusive right to build an interoceanic canal across the San Juan River for a period of ninety-nine years, with Nicaragua receiving three million dollars. The real motive for this treaty was to keep foreign powers out of Central America. The Chamorro-Bryan Treaty, which omitted the intervention clause, was ratified by the U.S. Senate in 1916. The treaty was terminated in July 1970.

While Bryan supported the U.S. intervention in the Mexican Revolution in 1914, when German submarine U-20 sank the RMS *Lusitania* in May 1915, killing 128 Americans, he publicly refused to deliver Wilson's harsh message to Germany fearing it would bring war. Although on June 9, 1915, Bryan resigned in protest, he supported Wilson's reelection and, when the U.S. declared war in April 1917, he gave Wilson his total support.

LEGACY

In 1925 Bryan responded to a request by the World Christian Fundamentals Association to help prosecute John T. Scopes for teaching evolution in a Tennessee public school. His eloquent opponent was defense attorney Clarence Darrow. Their presence created a national media frenzy. Bryan spent much of the trial defending a literal interpretation of the Bible. Though Scopes was found guilty and fined $100, the conviction was later overturned, and the trial became a symbol of the battle of fundamentalism versus modernism.

Bryan died in Dayton, Ohio, on July 26, 1925, and he was buried in Arlington National Cemetery. His tombstone reads, "He kept the Faith." While he was never elected president, he was one of the most influential Americans of his time.

With his attitudes toward Latin America, in one sense his seemingly contradictory attitude toward U.S. intervention in the region only adds to the complexity of his personality. In another way it makes him typical of Americans, even progressives of his day. While he denounced the imperialistic policies of past administrations, he was very much an interventionist who believed in the superiority of American political and economic institutions over their Latin American counterparts.

See also *Chamorro Vargas, Emiliano; Coolidge, Calvin; Knox, Philander C.; McKinley, William; Mexican Revolution, 1911–1917, U.S. Policy toward; Platt, Orville; Roosevelt, Theodore; Taft, William H.; Villa, Francisco "Pancho"; Wilson, Woodrow; Zelaya López, José Santos*

. . . . WILLIAM HEAD

REFERENCES AND FURTHER READING

Cherny, Robert W. *A Righteous Cause: The Life of William Jennings Bryan.* Norman: University of Oklahoma Press, 1994.

Coletta, Paolo E. *William Jennings Bryan* (three volumes). Lincoln: University of Nebraska Press, 1964.

Glad, Paul W. *The Trumpet Soundeth: William Jennings Bryan and His Democracy 1896–1912.* Lincoln: University of Nebraska Press, 1960.

Kaplan, Edward. *U.S. Imperialism in Latin America: Bryan's Challenges and Contributions, 1900–1920.* Westport, CT: Praeger, 1998.

Kazin, Michael. *A Godly Hero: The Life of William Jennings Bryan.* New York: Alfred A. Knopf, 2006.

Koenig, Louis W. Bryan. *A Political Biography of William Jennings Bryan.* New York: Putnam, 1971.

Bryan-Chamorro Treaty, 1915

In the early 1900s, despite having a concession for the Panama Canal, U.S. policymakers worried about the possible canal route through Nicaragua being sold to a foreign competitor. Problems intensified with Liberal nationalist Nicaraguan president José Santos Zelaya, who had ruled Nicaragua since 1893. He responded negatively when the United States chose the Panama route and increasingly reached out to foreign investors (including the Germans) and intensified efforts to reestablish the Central American Union.

In 1909 a rebellion against Zelaya began with Conservative forces led by Juan Estrada. U.S. officials took advantage of the opportunity to displace Zelaya and replace him with a more compliant Nicaraguan president. U.S. troops actively shaped the outcome by their direct actions to hinder the rebels and in 1911, Conservative leader Adolfo Díaz took the presidency. He negotiated loans that gave American businessmen control of Nicaragua's national bank, 51 percent of the railroads, and the receipts of customs houses. At the time he even proposed a parallel to the Platt Amendment in Cuba, an agreement that would allow the United States the perpetual right to intervene in Nicaraguan affairs.

Problems intensified when Nicaraguan nationalists, led by Minister of War Luis Mena, began a war against Díaz. As the rebels appeared near victory, President William Howard Taft ordered 2,700 Marines into Nicaragua. Their efforts stemmed the rebel tide and sustained Díaz in power. When the majority of Marines withdrew in November 1911, 130 remained in place as a "legation guard"—a reminder that the United States supported Díaz. As one Marine legend, Smedley Butler, observed later, "It is terrible that we should be losing so many men fighting . . . all because Brown Bros. [a New York banking house] have some money down there" (LaFeber 1993, 50). That reality remained a fact, however.

President Díaz and his allies badly managed the Nicaraguan national treasury and soon requested financial assistance from the United States. His greatest bargaining chip remained the possible canal route and the threat of negotiating a concession with the Germans or Japanese. As the United States neared its completion of the Panama Canal, President Woodrow Wilson took over in 1913 and inherited the turmoil in Nicaragua. Earlier, State Department official George Weitzel negotiated a treaty with Nicaraguan Foreign Minister Emiliano Chamorro Vargas, which granted the United States the exclusive rights to the Nicaraguan route, a naval base in the Gulf of Fonseca, and additional bases on the Great and Little Corn islands in the Caribbean, in exchange for $3 million.

Weitzel's efforts momentarily stalled until Wilson and Secretary of State William Jennings Bryan began pushing for negotiations, turning their back on their denunciations of the "Dollar Diplomacy" to secure such a prized strategic advantage. This led *The New York Times* to emphasize that Wilson and Bryan's policy was similar to 10 percent diplomacy, rather than the "dollar diplomacy" of Taft and Secretary of State Philander Knox. In subsequent talks Bryan proposed a very favorable loan by the U.S. government, but Wilson and others refused to put Washington into the business of banking. Not long after, Díaz submitted a revised version of the Weitzel-Chamorro Treaty that included a reiteration of earlier calls for a Nicaraguan Platt Amendment, believing that the mere threat of U.S. intervention helped sustain his presidency. Such a proposal met strong opposition in the Senate Foreign Relations Committee, whose members emphasized that they would not consider any treaty that contained such a clause.

For more than a year Wilson, Bryan, and other U.S. diplomats moved forward, as the outbreak of war in Europe further fueled fears of a foreign threat in Central America, where German immigrants had significant power. Ultimately the parties agreed to purchase the exclusive rights to a Nicaraguan canal for the United States and options for bases in the Gulf of Fonseca in return for $3 million (most of which went to U.S. and British bankers and bondholders, with only $836,000 reaching Nicaragua). The Wilson administration submitted the Bryan-Chamorro Treaty to the Senate in 1914.

Some significant opposition to the treaty developed. In Central America the Costa Ricans and Salvadorans protested and said that the Bryan-Chamorro Treaty violated existing agreements including the Cañas-Jérez Treaty of 1858 and other accords. They took their arguments to the recently established Central American Court, which sided with them. In turn, the Nicaraguans withdrew from the court, ultimately killing the organization. In the United States opponents of the treaty highlighted the dependency of Díaz, as one Minnesota senator, William Smith, observed that the Marines kept him in power despite the wishes of the Nicaraguan people.

Ultimately, in 1916 both parties accepted the Bryan-Chamorro Treaty (named despite the fact that Bryan left the Wilson administration in 1915). Colonel Clifford D. Ham, who had taken charge of the Nicaraguan customs houses during an earlier crisis, crowed that agreement had ended foreign countries from securing concessions from the Nicaraguans, including the Germans, and ensured the protection of U.S. national security and its investment in the Panama Canal Zone.

The Bryan-Chamorro Treaty remained in force until 1972. That year President Richard Nixon terminated the treaty to reward the loyalty of virulently anti-Communist Nicaraguan strongman, Anastasio Somoza Debayle. Nonetheless nationalist Nicaraguans reminded their countrymen of the symbolism of the treaty, and the groundswell of anti-Americanism erupted into full-scale conflict in 1979 with the rise to power of the Sandinistas.

See also *Bryan, William Jennings; Cañas-Jérez Treaty, 1858; Central American Court of Justice; Chamorro Vargas, Emiliano; Díaz Recinos, Adolfo; Dollar Diplomacy; Knox, Philander C.; Nixon, Richard M.; Panana Canal Treaties (Carter-Torrijos), 1977 Platt, Orville; Somoza Debayle, Anastasio; Taft, William H.; Wilson, Woodrow; Zelaya López, José Santos*

. . . . KYLE LONGLEY

REFERENCES AND FURTHER READING

Espino, Ovidio Diaz. *How Wall Street Created a Nation: J. P. Morgan, Teddy Roosevelt, and the Panama Canal.* New York: Basic Books, 2003.

LaFeber, Walter. *The Panama Canal: The Crisis in Historical Perspective.* Updated edition. New York: Oxford University Press, 1990.

LaFeber, Walter. *Inevitable Revolutions: The United States and Central America.* 2nd edition. New York: Norton, 1993.

Mack, Gerstle. *The Land Divided: A History of the Panama Canal and Other Isthmian Canal Projects.* London: Octagon Books, 1974.

McCullough, David. *The Path Between the Seas: The Creation of the Panama Canal, 1870–1914.* New York: Simon and Schuster, 1978.

Bucareli Agreements, 1923

The Bucareli Agreements, an arrangement comprised of the signing of the minutes of a conference by emissaries of U.S. President Warren G. Harding and Mexican President Alvaro Obregón, temporarily settled Mexican-U.S. difficulties arising from Mexico's constitutional provisions concerning agrarian reform and subsoil mineral rights. This arrangement led to American recognition of the Obregón government. It also represented a shift in emphasis away from armed intervention in U.S.-Latin American relations toward the use of diplomatic persuasion to promote hemispheric goodwill, thus pointing the way to the Good Neighbor policy.

U.S.-Mexican difficulties arising from the Mexican Revolution stemmed from provisions in the Mexican Constitution of 1917 promoting land reform and limiting foreign property rights. Article 27 stated that all land, water, and subsoil minerals belonged to Mexico. The U.S. government, trying to protect nearly $900 million of American investments in Mexico from expropriation and nationalization, argued that surface ownership conferred subsoil rights and defended the legality of concessions granted before the constitution took effect. When the Mexican government rejected these claims, U.S. President Woodrow Wilson adopted a constitutional legitimacy test to justify withholding diplomatic recognition and considered military intervention in Mexico.

Harding, Wilson's successor, tried to resolve the matter through confidential exchanges with Obregón, but Secretary of State Charles Evans Hughes, backed by Secretary of the Interior Albert Fall and the largest American oil companies operating in Mexico, insisted that Mexico must abandon Article 27 as the price for recognition. Mexican nationalism prevented Obregón from accepting this demand.

Between 1921 and 1923 the Mexican government, seeking U.S. recognition, demonstrated its willingness to fulfill its international obligations. Specifically the Mexican Supreme Court, in five separate rulings known collectively as the "Texas cases" (1921–1922), established the doctrine of "positive acts," which held that Article 27 would not be applied retroactively provided that oil companies had made some attempt before May 1917 to extract petroleum from the soil. Obregón also repealed petroleum tax laws aimed at reducing foreign oil influence in Mexico.

In early 1923 the Harding administration abandoned Wilson's nonrecognition policy toward Mexico. The postwar economic recession generated demands to expand U.S. trade with Mexico from the Department of Commerce, small oil companies, manufacturers, and significant individuals in industry (Henry Ford), the press (William Randolph Hearst), labor (Samuel Gompers), and Congress (William Borah). Meanwhile Fall and Hughes lost their influence over U.S.-Mexican relations. Fall, who favored intervention in Mexico, was removed from office due to his involvement in the Teapot Dome scandal. Hughes, seeing that the Mexican government had survived without American recognition, dropped his insistence for assurances to protect American property rights from confiscation. Instead he asked General James Ryan, a representative of the Texas Oil Company of Mexico who understood the aims of both sides, to persuade Harding and Obregón to appoint a joint commission to settle U.S.-Mexican difficulties.

Harding's appreciation of Mexican nationalistic sensitivities and Obregón's desire for reconciliation with the United States paved the way for a settlement.

Harding selected Charles Warren, a former ambassador to Japan, and John Burton, a former secretary of the interior, to meet with Ramón Ross, the director general of Public Charity, and Fernando González Roa, counsel for Mexico's national railways, at the Foreign Ministry Office in Mexico City. In protracted discussions that lasted from May 14 to August 15, 1923, the Mexican commissioners gained U.S. acceptance of the doctrine of "positive acts" regarding the implementation of Article 27. Adherence to this doctrine meant Mexican acknowledgement of pre-1917 oil concessions and no retroactive enforcement of Article 27. For landowners or those with leases who had failed to perform such "positive acts," the Mexican government promised to grant them preferential rights to extract petroleum from their lands. The commissioners also agreed that Americans who had their agricultural lands expropriated would receive compensation. If the claim involved less than 1,755 hectares, they would be paid with bonds that earned 5 percent interest over a twenty-five-year period; if more than 1,755 hectares had been seized, they would receive an immediate cash settlement. In addition, two joint U.S.-Mexican claims commissions were established, one to adjudicate government and individual claims since 1868 and the other to resolve claims arising from the Mexican Revolution (1910–1920).

The Bucareli Agreements improved Mexican-U.S. relations, albeit temporarily. By muting the oil controversy, they led to American recognition of the Mexican government (August 31, 1923) without Mexico being forced to modify its constitution. When the Mexican government faced a revolt a year later, the United States supported Obregón, supplying him with military aid while enforcing its neutrality laws to deny aid to rebel forces. This aid helped Obregón suppress the rebellion and ensured that Plutarco Elías Calles, Obregón's hand-picked successor, became Mexico's next president. But the agreement was not a formal treaty, allowing future Mexican governments to claim that this arrangement was non-binding. This became evident when Calles tried to implement Article 27 in 1925 by narrowing the definition of "positive acts" and increasing taxes on U.S.-owned oil production. This did not prevent the Mexican government from nationalizing its oil industry in 1938.

See also *Calles, Plutarco Elías; Good Neighbor Policy; Harding, Warren G.; Hearst, William Randolph; Hughes, Charles Evans; Mexican Revolution, 1911–1917, U.S. Policy toward; Mexico, U.S. Relations with; Oil, Expropriation of Foreign Companies; Wilson, Woodrow*

DEAN FAFOUTIS

REFERENCES AND FURTHER READING

Grieb, Kenneth J. *The Latin American Policy of Warren G. Harding.* Fort Worth: Texas Christian University Press, 1976.

Hall, Linda. *Oil, Banks, and Politics: The United States and Postrevolutionary Mexico, 1917–1924.* Austin: University of Texas Press, 1995.

Meyer, Lorenzo. *Mexico and the United States in the Oil Controversy, 1917–1942.* 2nd ed. Translated by Muriel Vasconcellos. Austin: University of Texas Press, 1972.

U.S. Department of State. *Proceedings of the United States-Mexican Commission Convened in Mexico City, May 14, 1923.* Washington, DC: United States Government Printing Office, 1925.

Buchanan, James

James Buchanan (1791–1868) was the fifteenth U.S. president, U.S. representative and senator from Pennsylvania, minister to the United Kingdom, and U.S. secretary of state. Buchanan was born on April 23, 1791, near Mercersburg, Pennsylvania. He graduated from Dickinson College in 1809 and moved to Lancaster, Pennsylvania, where he was admitted to the bar in 1812. During the War of 1812 he served in a volunteer light dragoon. Buchanan was elected to the Pennsylvania House of Representatives from 1814 to 1820. He was elected to the U.S. House of Representatives from 1821 to 1830 as a federalist. From 1832–1834 he served as minister to Russia. He changed his political affiliation to the Democratic party and won election as a U.S. senator in 1834. Buchanan served as a U.S. senator until 1845, when he resigned to become secretary of state for President James K. Polk.

SECRETARY OF STATE

As U.S. secretary of state, Buchanan negotiated the 1846 Oregon Treaty, which established the forty-ninth parallel as the northern boundary of the western United States. Buchanan worked to settle growing tensions with Mexico by advocating negotiations, seeking to convince Mexico to transfer the border of Texas to the United States and accept monetary compensation for the California and New Mexico territories. Buchanan's course of action was not supported by President Polk, who with others, pushed for the eventual war with Mexico. Even during the conflict, Buchanan sought ways to end the war with negotiation, and he pushed the Polk administration for specific goals for the war.

In his role as secretary of state, Buchanan also sought to purchase Cuba from the Spanish government. He presented an offer of $100 million for Cuba, which was rejected by Spain in 1848. Buchanan never advocated the overthrow of nations in the Caribbean and Latin America through intrigue and force, but he sought ways through negotiations and money. For example Buchanan helped to negotiate a treaty with Nicaragua in 1849 to ensure exclusive rights to U. S. companies to build a canal to link the Atlantic and Pacific oceans. He also sought to establish friendly ties with the United Kingdom as an avenue to deal with the growing presence of the Royal Navy and British businesses operating in Latin America.

In 1853 he returned as minister to the United Kingdom. A year later Buchanan and two other diplomats (John Y. Mason, Pierre Soulé) drafted a secret document known as the Ostend Manifesto in Ostend, Belgium. The document's purpose was the acquisition of Cuba by the United States. Proslavery southerners saw Cuba as a possible new slave state. Pierre Soulé, the U.S. minister to Spain and proslavery supporter, was responsible for writing the document. The three diplomats formulated a plan to offer $120 million for Cuba, and if the offer was refused, then the United States would be justified in taking the island to prevent abolition of Cuban slavery. The recent seizure of the *Black Warrior,* an American ship by Cuban authorities, increased the resolve of the proslavery faction. Information on the document leaked out to the newspapers and the public, and those in President Franklin Pierce's administration, especially U.S. Secretary of State William L. Marcy, were forced to announce their opposition to the proposal.

Despite his involvement in the manifesto, James Buchanan came out as the leading contender for the Democratic nomination for the 1856 presidential election. Since he was serving overseas, he was not tainted by the uproar over the Kansas-Nebraska debate. In addition much of the blame of the manifesto fell upon the Pierce administration and Pierre Soulé. Politically he was a northern Democrat who favored proslavery interests within the party. He was the candidate for office that offended the least number of Democrats, both abolitionist and proslave. Fortunately for Democrats the Know-Nothing party candidate, Millard Fillmore, took votes from the Republican party candidate, John C. Fremont, and ensured a Democratic victory in 1856.

PRESIDENT

At the time of Buchanan's inauguration in 1857, the slavery debate had spilled into violence in many regions of the country. Buchanan relied on the judicial branch of the U.S. government, specifically chief justice of the Supreme Court, Roger Taney, to settle the growing crisis by ruling in the Dred Scott case. Taney's ruling, that Dred Scott was not free even though his master moved him into free territory, was considered a victory for slavery supporters, but Taney's opinion also energized the abolitionist movement. For Buchanan, his attempt to sidestep the issue only backfired on him.

Buchanan's subsequent actions continued to move the nation on the path to a violent civil war over slavery. He threw the support of his administration behind the proslave Lecompton Constitution, despite the popular vote against it in Kansas. The U.S. Senate rejected the ill-advised constitution and forced the issue back to the Kansas voters.

Buchanan's policies to reduce national tariffs led to the Panic of 1857, which was fueled, in part, by the shortage of government revenues. The Republican party won enough seats in the U.S. Congress to block the passage of bills favoring the proslave faction. In 1860 the Democratic party finally split over the question of slavery, and a number of states began seceding from the Union. Buchanan argued that their actions were wrong, but executively he did nothing to stop the damage.

In his foreign policy Buchanan continued the pattern of his earlier efforts as secretary of state to use diplomacy to resolve any regional conflicts in Latin America. He followed the course of President Franklin Pierce in opposing American filibuster operations in Costa Rica, Honduras, and Nicaragua through the use of federal marshals and the U.S. Navy. After the signing of the Rivas Manifesto by Costa Rica and Nicaragua, Buchanan assured both nations that the United States would deal with filibusters so as to prevent both nations from calling upon European countries for protection. Buchanan continued to implore the U.S. Congress to allow him to forge stronger ties to the region, but the rise of sectionalism prevented enough of a congressional majority for approval for treaties and appointment of envoys. Southern congressmen did not want to allow the Buchanan administration to strengthen itself diplomatically in Latin America with the impending secession brewing in the United States.

Buchanan lived though the American Civil War, and afterward he attempted to clear his reputation by publishing a written defense of his actions as president. He died on June 1, 1868, and was buried in Lancaster, Pennsylvania.

See also *Black Warrior Incident, 1854; Cuba, U.S. Relations with; Manifest Destiny; Mexican-American War: Treaty of Guadalupe Hidalgo, 1848; Ostend Manifesto, 1854; Pierce, Franklin; Soulé, Pierre*

. . . . WILLIAM H. BROWN

REFERENCES AND FURTHER READING

Binder, Frederick Moore. *James Buchanan and the American Empire.* Selinsgrove, PA: Susquehanna University Press, 1996.
Buchanan, James. *Mr. Buchanan's Administration on the Eve of the Rebellion.* New York: Appleton, 1866.
Freehling, William W. *The Road to Disunion, Volume II: Secessionists Triumphant.* New York: Oxford University Press, 2006.
Klein, Philip Shriver. *President James Buchanan: A Biography.* University Park: Pennsylvania State University Press, 1962.
Potter, David. *Impending Crisis: 1848–1861.* New York: HarperTorch Books, 1976.
Smith, Elbert B. *The Presidency of James Buchanan.* Lawrence: University Press of Kansas, 1975.

Buenos Aires Conference

(**See** *Fourth International Conference of American States, Buenos Aires, 1910; Inter-American Conference for the Maintenance of Peace, Buenos Aires, 1936*)

Bunau-Varilla, Philippe J.

Philippe Jean Bunau-Varilla (1859–1940) was a French engineer known for his efforts to promote Panama as the site of a transisthmian canal and for his role as Panama's first minister to the United States. Bunau-Varilla was born in Paris, but scholars Gustavo Anguizola and David McCullough differ on the circumstances of his birth. Anguizola believes that Bunau-Varilla came from distinguished lineage, but McCullough believes he was born out of wedlock to an unknown father. Bunau-Varilla was trained as an engineer at the prestigious Ecole Polytechnique and the Ecole des Pontes et Chausées (Bridges and Highways). In 1884 he sailed to Panama to take part in the canal-building project of the French firm Compagnie Universelle du Canal Interocéanique. Within a year he was appointed general manager and chief engineer of the company. He later resigned but remained in Panama as a contractor.

After the bankruptcy of the French firm in 1889, Bunau-Varilla, like other contractors, was forced to become a "penalty stockholder" in its successor, the New Panama Canal Company. He purchased the newspaper *Le Matin,* which in 1896 scored a journalistic coup by publishing documents that demonstrated the innocence of accused spy Alfred Dreyfus. He remained committed to the ideas of a canal in Panama and, with William Nelson Cromwell, was effective in urging Congress to select Panama in preference to Nicaragua as the site for the canal. One of his best-known feats was persuading the U.S. Senate of the danger of volcanic activity in Nicaragua by placing on the desk of every senator a Nicaraguan stamp that showed an erupting volcano. Three days later the Senate voted in favor of Panama.

Bunau-Varilla also was active in advancing the plot that led to the secession of Panama, a Colombian province, in November 1903, and he had meetings with Assistant Secretary of State Francis B. Loomis, Secretary of State John Hay, and President Theodore Roosevelt, who indicated that the United States would block Colombian efforts to regain control of Panama.

Although Bunau-Varilla was a French citizen and had not visited Panama since 1888, he was named "envoy extraordinary and minister plenipotentiary" to the new republic. He immediately negotiated a treaty with Secretary Hay that allowed the United States to build a canal in Panama, made Panama a U.S. protectorate, and authorized the New Panama Canal Company to sell its assets to the U.S. government. Historians have differed on whether Bunau-Varilla served Panama well in signing the treaty and in pressing the Panamanian government to ratify it almost immediately. The U.S. Senate ratified the treaty on February 3, 1904; three days later Bunau-Varilla resigned as minister to Panama.

After the United States purchased the assets of the New Panama Canal Company for $40 million, Bunau-Varilla's firm received its original investment ($440,000) plus a profit of about 3 percent, or $13,200. He was in Panama for the opening of the canal in August 1914, but that event was overshadowed by the start of World War I. During the war Bunau-Varilla was assigned the task of providing clean water for the troops and determining the proper amount of chlorine to ensure safety. In 1916, at the battleground of Verdun, he was hit by a bomb and lost a leg. He was the author of several works, including *Panama: The Creation, Destruction and Resurrection* (1914) and *From Panama to Verdun: My Fight for France* (1940).

See also *Eisenhower-Remón Treaty, 1955; Hay–Bunau-Varilla Treaty, 1903; Isthmian Canal Commission (Walker Commission); Kellogg-Alfaro Treaty, 1926; New Panama Canal Company; Panama, Independence of, 1903; Panama Canal Treaties (Carter-Torrijos), 1977; Panama, Isthmian Canal Interests, Nineteenth Century; Spooner Act, 1902 (United States)*

. . . . HELEN DELPAR

REFERENCES AND FURTHER READING

Anguizola, Gustavo. *Philippe Bunau-Varilla: The Man behind the Panama Canal.* Chicago: Nelson-Hall, 1980.

McCullough, David. *The Path between the Seas: The Creation of the Panama Canal, 1870–1914.* New York: Simon and Schuster, 1977.

Bunker, Ellsworth

A U.S. diplomat during the Dominican Republic Crisis (1965) and ambassador to Vietnam (1967–1973) in the crucial years of the Vietnam War, Ellsworth Bunker (1894–1984) ended his distinguished career as chief negotiator of the 1977 Panama Canal Treaties.

Bunker was born to a prestigious New York family. A Yale graduate, he managed his family's sugar company that held investments in Mexico and Cuba. His friend and former Yale rowing coach, Secretary of State Dean Acheson, persuaded Bunker at the age of 57 to enter a career in diplomacy. His first assignment came in 1951 as U.S. ambassador to Argentina, where he helped Washington improve its formerly hostile relations with President Juan Perón, now viewed as an important Cold War ally. Bunker subsequently served as ambassador to Italy from 1952 to 1953, became head of the American Red Cross from 1953 to 1956, and returned to government service from 1956 to 1959 as ambassador to India and Nepal, where he played a key role in the clandestine U.S.-Indian alliance against an aggressive People's Republic of China. Subsequently President Kennedy awarded Bunker the Presidential Medal of Freedom for mediating the New York Agreement over Western New Guinea negotiating the Dutch relinquishment of that territory and its cession to Indonesia and for helping to resolve the dispute between U.S. ally Saudi Arabia and Nasser's Egypt over the newly independent Republic of Yemen.

Bunker next served as U.S. ambassador to the Organization of American States (OAS) from 1964 to 1966, a period of intense confrontation between the United States and what it perceive as a Castroite threat to the region. Bunker defended his nation's actions against charges of aggression in the 1964 Panama Canal riots during which twenty-one Panamanians and four U.S. soldiers died in the fighting. He also helped organize a delegation of Caribbean and Central American countries to supply troops for the 1965 U.S. invasion of the Dominican Republic, lending Washington diplomatic cover for its largely unilateral intervention. The Johnson administration feared "another Cuba" in the region and crushed the leftist rebels who sought to reinstall the democratically elected Juan Bosch to office. Bunker led the three-man delegation from the OAS that established a pro-U.S. government in the wake of the invasion. For maintaining a cool and deliberate course throughout these crises, Bunker earned the moniker "the Refrigerator" that in his later career would be replaced by "Sly Fox." For his accomplishments Bunker gained another Medal of Freedom in 1967 and his toughest assignment yet—ambassador to war-torn Saigon.

Bunker held this position for six years from 1967 until 1973, directing diplomatic policy through various debacles. He became most famous to the American people for his televised appearance on the U.S. embassy's lawn following the failed yet shocking Viet Cong sapper assault against the embassy compound during the 1968 Tet Offensive. Bunker recovered from that low point and helped implement Nixon's Vietnamization program before leaving his post following the January 1973 peace accords that ended major U.S. involvement in the war.

Next Bunker accepted the position of U.S. ambassador-at-large that brought him his final assignment—negotiating the U.S. transfer of control over the Panama Canal to the Republic of Panama. Like so many of his past positions this job was fraught with political perils. Bunker had to deal with conservative Congressional opposition to "surrendering" the strategic waterway, long regarded by many Americans as U.S. territory, following a period of American retreat from Southeast Asia. First appointed to heading the U.S. negotiating team by President Nixon in 1974, Bunker faced recalcitrance from U.S. workers in the Canal Zone, the so-called Zonians, over losing their well-paid jobs and privileged, colonial lifestyle. Bunker also encountered strong resistance from the U.S. military that strove to maintain its cushy base complex astride the Canal. Panamanian General Omar Torrijos's mercurial personality, as well as his threats of guerrilla warfare and demands for $1 billion from the U.S. government, added to the obstacles of obtaining a ratifiable agreement. A skillful manager of the key debates, Bunker worked his way around the deadlocked points of U.S. military base demands and Panamanian intransigence over a more drawn-out and compromised transfer of sovereignty to fashion the fundamentals of the successful 1977 treaty. Bunker and his associates, Sol Linowitz and Secretary of State Cyrus Vance, gained traction by dividing the negotiations into two distinct treaties, one regarding the joint U.S.-Panamanian operation of the canal until 2000 and the other dealing with the maintenance of a U.S. defense umbrella over the waterway until 2000, with guarantees for a neutral and open canal thereafter. Bunker's legendary reputation, risqué sense of humor, and unflappable determination all combined to gain concessions from the parties involved. His shepherding of the treaty over various hurdles marked the capstone to a long diplomatic career and served to improve U.S.-Latin American relations at a crucial historical juncture.

See also *Argentina, U.S. Relations with; Chiari Remón, Roberto Francisco; Dominican Republic, U.S. Relations with; Johnson Doctrine; Linowitz, Sol M.; Organization of American States (OAS); Panama Canal Treaties (Carter-Torrijos), 1977*

. . . . MICHAEL E. DONOGHUE

REFERENCES AND FURTHER READING

Jorden, William J. *Panama Odyssey.* Austin: University of Texas Press, 1984.

LaFeber, Walter. *The Panama Canal: The Crisis in Historical Perspective.* New York: Oxford University Press, 1989.

Schaffer, Howard B. *Ellsworth Bunker: Global Troubleshooter, Vietnam Hawk.* Chapel Hill: University of North Carolina Press, 2003.

Bureaucratic-Authoritarian Regimes

Bureaucratic-Authoritarianism, a concept developed by Brazilian political scientist Guillermo O'Donnell, is a dictatorship that uses coercion to respond to perceived threats to the capitalist system. The term "Bureaucratic-Authoritarianism" comes from the fact that the military keeps order through oppressive measures while leaving civilian technocrats (bureaucrats with highly technical training in American universities) to direct other policy.

EXPLAINING LATIN AMERICAN DICTATORSHIP

Bureaucratic-Authoritarianism is a political economic explanation that was designed to replace the modernization paradigm that had failed to explain the rise of authoritarian regimes in South American states such as Argentina (1946–1955) and Brazil (1930–1945 and 1950–1954). According to the modernization theory, capitalist industrialization would transform traditional authoritarian states into modern democracies. However when authoritarian regimes appeared in Brazil, Argentina, Chile, and Uruguay in the 1960s and 1970s after long periods of industrialization, O'Donnell concluded there were fatal flaws in the modernization theory. He suggested an alternative course of political development that helped explain South American cases.

Bureaucratic-Authoritarian theory recognizes an historical sequence of three political systems: oligarchic, populist, and bureaucratic-authoritarian. The three systems are distinguished by the structure of the political regime (particularly in terms of political competition and freedoms), the class makeup of the dominant political coalition, and types of public policies (particularly as they are related to resource distribution). In addition to recognizing and describing the political systems, Bureaucratic-Authoritarian theory seeks to explain the transition from one system to the next. The transitions are the result of tensions created as a result of industrialization, increasing political activation of the popular sector and the growth of technocratic roles in bureaucracy.

In the first stage, being generally primary product exporting countries, political elites make public policy to address their own needs. At this stage the mass public is not activated and political competition is limited. The government does not need to consider the needs of the rest of the population, so policy distributes resources to the elites.

As the country develops economically and politically, the urbanization and industrialization resulting from the policies provide the basis for a populist coalition between the industrial elites and the urban popular sector. Public policy tends to focus on industrialization and the expansion of the domestic market with an anti-export bias. There is a heavy reliance on importing intermediate and capital goods and no development of capital goods or technology. While the political system may not necessarily be electorally competitive, the demands of the public need to be considered as they are politically activated.

As countries continue to develop economically the demands of the masses increase as they become more politically mobilized. These demands soon threaten to overwhelm the ability of the government to provide the political and economic goods. Proponents of Bureaucratic-Authoritarianism believed that no democratically elected regime could afford to take the measures necessary to promote economic growth while reassuring foreign and domestic investors so that democracy could develop and persist. The result was the inevitable entrance of the military to impose the necessary and painful economic policies, as determined by technocrats, who would allow the country to pass through the middle level of economic development to a level where the economy was strong enough to meet the needs of the masses. It is at this point, at least in theory, that the military would return the country to popular control.

LINKAGE TO IMPORT SUBSTITUTION INDUSTRIALIZATION (ISI)

The concept of Bureaucratic-Authoritarianism is closely linked to Import-Substitution-Industrialization (ISI) policies aimed at economic and political development. According to O'Donnell, at the initial stage of industrialization, economic activities center around the production of consumer goods. To achieve ISI, the state offers protection and subsidies to domestic enterprises to produce for the local market previously supplied by imports. The protectionist measures reduce the degree of competition, thereby allowing industrialists to offer higher wages and benefits to workers. Also, industrialists are interested in expanding workers' income in order to increase the purchasing power of the domestic market. On the other hand, as workers realize that the ISI policy provides them with higher income and more consumer goods, they are willing to offer political support to industrialists. Hence, ISI policy is both beneficial to industrialists and workers. This forms the basis of an "incorporating" populist coalition, in which the industrialists give wages to workers and allow them to form unions, while workers provide markets and political support to industrialists in return. Such harmonious relations between industrialists and workers lead to declining costs of toleration.

However, ISI is relatively easy only during its initial phase, when the policy is applied mainly to consumer goods. After this the constraints from the external sector become more stringent, because the earlier ISI requires large imports of intermediate and capital goods, which leads to external deficits and inflation. Industrialists thus feel the need to "deepen" the industrialization process (i.e., start to produce the intermediate and capital goods themselves). There is then a push by the industrialists for public policy that focuses on protection and promotion of the production of the intermediate and capital goods that had been previously imported. The push for development-friendly policies conflicts with the populist policies that the civilian governments need to maintain their political control, opening the way for military involvement.

In trying to cater to both groups, public policy becomes confused and leads to an economic downturn. Military officials, who become disillusioned with the populist policies of the civilian government, decide that they are the experts and they can run the government better than the democratically elected civilians. Military officials view the country's problem as one of inefficiency caused by the populist policies of the civilian democratic regime, which allowed the masses to siphon off society's political and economic goods. The policy interests of the new military leaders, who prefer development policy, clash with the desires of the people, and repression and exclusion are the order of the day. Military officials take over and force their particular development program, created by technocrats, on the country.

See also *Argentina, U.S. Relations with; Brazil, U.S. Relations with; Chile, U.S. Relations with; Import Substitution Industrialization (ISI); Uruguay, U.S. Relations with*

. . . . SCOTT DITTLOFF

REFERENCES AND FURTHER READING

Collier, David, ed. *The New Authoritarianism in Latin America.* Princeton, NJ: Princeton University Press, 1979.

O'Donnell, Guillermo. "Reflections on the Patterns of Change in the Bureaucratic-Authoritarian State." *Latin American Research Review* 13, no. 1 (1978): 3–38.

O'Donnell, Guillermo. *Modernization and Bureaucratic-Authoritarianism: Studies in South American Politics.* Berkeley: Institute of International Studies, University of California, 1973.

Burnham, Forbes

Forbes Burnham (1923–1985), leader of British Guiana/ Guyana from 1964 until 1985, had a command of the English language which enabled him to enthrall an audience. He was also unscrupulous, manipulating elections and relying on U.S. support to keep a grip on both government and military power in Guyana for two decades.

Burnham served in the People's Progressive Party (PPP), government elected in 1953 and deposed six months later by British colonial authorities on account of its pro-Soviet orientation. Between then and the next parliamentary elections (1957), Burnham founded a new party, the People's National Congress (PNC). Most PNC supporters were, like Burnham, of black African descent, and for the rest of Burnham's life, most of the electorate voted along racial lines. Those whose ancestors came from the Indian subcontinent voted for the PPP. Those of African descent favored Burnham and the PNC.

As a majority of the electorate was of Indian extraction, the PPP won the parliamentary elections of 1957 and 1961. Successive British governments wanted to unload their Caribbean colonies, but U.S. governments opposed independence for British Guiana as long as the PPP held office. One Soviet-bloc country in the neighborhood (Cuba) was more than enough, and to placate its American ally, British authorities changed the rules. Uniquely among British possessions, British Guiana would no longer be divided geographically into constituencies with the candidate receiving the most votes representing that constituency in the Legislative Assembly. Rather the entire colony would be one single constituency, and each political party would receive a share of the seats proportionate to its share of the popular vote. In the first such election the PNC won fewer seats than the PPP, but by forming a coalition with smaller parties, Burnham was able to form a government. In 1966 British Guiana became independent Guyana, with Burnham as prime minister.

For the rest of Burnham's life, the PNC held office. Even PNC supporters admitted that elections were not honest and defended electoral manipulation on other grounds. Robert Moore, a history professor from the University of Guyana who became his country's high commissioner (ambassador) to Canada, explained to a Canadian audience in 1974 that if the PNC had not cheated, it would not have won the 1973 election. Yet for the sake of stability, the PNC simply *had* to win, said Moore. The United States, the people of Georgetown (Guyana's overwhelmingly Afro-Guyanese capital city), and members of the Guyana Defence Force (the country's army, most of whose members were of African descent) would not have tolerated a PPP victory.

Despite his supposedly anticommunist credentials, Burnham pursued a left-wing agenda. In 1971 he nationalized U.S.- and Canadian-owned bauxite companies. Despite assurances to the contrary, he then nationalized Booker Brothers, a British corporation which operated a chain of retail stores and manufactured sugar-related products for export. North American and European-owned banks and pharmaceutical factories became government property. With the eradication of the private sector, students had to depend upon government for scholarships. Those known to oppose the PNC or those who wanted to study irrelevant subjects (like history) need not apply. Before he became a general, Burnham wanted people to call him "comrade" rather than "sir." Burnham granted landing rights to Cuban aircraft carrying combat forces to Angola, and he visited North Korea. Indeed, Guyana became the only western hemisphere country other than Cuba to host a North Korean embassy during the Cold War. Burnham's government strengthened relations with Cuba, East Germany, and North Korea, as those with western countries unraveled.

Burnham opposed the 1983 U.S. military intervention in Grenada, and in response to a Brazilian charge that there were many Cuban soldiers in Guyana, the U.S. government ordered aerial surveillance of that country. Under Burnham the economy plummeted, and consumer goods became scarce. World Bank figures indicate a shrinkage of 6 percent of gross domestic product between 1980 and 1987. Rice production fell from 256,000 tons in 1980 to 236,000 tons in 1985. Sugar production fell from 3,831,000 to 3,270,000 during the same period. Trinidad and Tobago suspended sales of subsidized petroleum when Guyana could not pay even the reduced price.

Burnham also promoted a cult of personality. Guyana had become a republic in 1970, but in 1980 further constitutional changes transferred real power from the prime minister to the president. Burnham became the country's first president. He also became a general in the Guyana Defence Force and wore a military uniform. His intention was that when he died, his body would go to Moscow to be embalmed like the corpses of Lenin and Stalin. However it rotted in the Guyanese heat before it could leave the ground.

See also *Dulles, John Foster; Guyana, U.S. relations with; Jagan, Cheddi; Manley, Michael*

. . . . GRAEME S. MOUNT

REFERENCES AND FURTHER READING

Naipaul, V. S. *The Middle Passage: A Caribbean Journal.* Chatham, England: Picador, 2001.

Rabe, Stephen J. *U.S. Intervention in British Guiana: A Cold War Story.* Chapel Hill: University of North Carolina Press, 2005.

Bush, George H. W.

George Herbert Walker Bush (1924–) is a retired Republican politician who served as president of the United States from 1989 to 1993. During his prolific career Bush held a number of prominent national and international political positions, including vice president under President Ronald Reagan (1981–1989) and director of Central Intelligence (1976–1977) under President Gerald Ford. His presidential policies in Latin America largely continued those initiated by his predecessor, Ronald Reagan.

PRIOR TO THE PRESIDENCY

George Bush's background and early experiences prepared him for an influential life in international politics. Born to a New York banking family and son of a U.S. senator, Bush was educated in private schools in Connecticut and Massachusetts before joining the U.S. Navy in 1942. Earning decorations as a fighter pilot in the Pacific Theater during World War II, Bush returned to the United States, graduated from Yale University, and made a personal fortune in offshore oil drilling in Texas. The conservative Bush involved himself in electoral politics in the 1960s and experienced mixed results, losing two U.S. Senate races but winning two U.S. House campaigns. During the 1970s Bush served the Nixon and Ford administrations as ambassador to the United Nations (1971–1973), chair of the Republican National Committee (1973–1974), and chief of the U.S. Liaison Office to the People's Republic of China (1974–1975). In the aftermath of the Church Committee's findings that impugned the integrity of the Central Intelligence Agency (CIA), President Ford appointed Bush as director of Central Intelligence. Bush's presidential campaign in 1980 failed, but eventual victor Reagan appointed Bush as his running mate, seeking to strengthen the ticket's foreign policy credentials.

As vice president, George Bush maintained a low political profile, attending ceremonial events and advising the president on special issues, such as drug smuggling. Behind the scenes the vice president played his most significant role in Latin American affairs. Most notably he became deeply involved in the Reagan administration's efforts to topple the Sandinista government in Nicaragua. The Boland Amendments (1982–1984) prevented the U.S. government from directly supporting the contras, the counterrevolutionary military forces who sought to overthrow the left-wing Sandinistas. Subsequently the administration actively pressured private parties and other nations to provide military and financial support to the contras; nations that provided such support included Guatemala, Honduras, Panama, Israel, and Saudi Arabia. In 1986 the "Iran-Contra" scandal, in which top-ranking Reagan officials had secretly arranged arms sales to Iran (which was under an arms embargo at the time) in an attempt to win the release of six U.S. hostages held by Hezbollah, became widely known. Proceeds generated from the sales had been diverted to the contras in Nicaragua. Vice President Bush declared that he was "out of the loop" and had no direct involvement in these arrangements, but several records –including his own personal diary–later documented Bush's active presence in numerous meetings for planning and executing these affairs. Several Reagan officials were indicted for federal crimes in this scandal. In the final days of his presidency, Bush pardoned Caspar Weinberger (secretary of defense under Reagan), Elliott Abrams (assistant secretary of state under Reagan), Robert McFarlane (national security advisor under Reagan), and others charged with crimes in the Iran-Contra affair.

PRESIDENCY

George Bush won election to the presidency in 1988. Much of his foreign policy, including support for right-wing allies in Latin America, continued the strategies of the Reagan administration. As the Cold War ended with the collapse of the Soviet Union, President Bush projected a "new world order," in which the United States would lead in global cooperation and the rule of law. One of the Bush administration's first overseas initiatives was the military invasion of Panama in December 1989. The purpose of this mission, "Operation Just Cause," was to depose Panamanian leader Manuel Noriega, who was accused of drug trafficking, human rights abuses, and denial of democratic processes. Noriega, a Cold War ally, had a long relationship with the United States and with Bush. The Panamanian had been on the payroll of the CIA since the 1960s, having met Bush in 1976 in Panama when he was the director of Central Intelligence, who courted his continued favor with the United States. During the Reagan presidency Bush again visited Panama for the purpose of seeking Noriega's help in running guns and cash to the contras attacking Nicaragua. But the Iran-Contra scandal had revealed Noriega as a political liability to Bush. Noriega, essentially a double agent who had also maintained strong ties with the Castro government in Cuba, was not only exposed as deeply involved in drug trafficking and money laundering schemes and closely connected to Bush, but he also had proven unwilling to take all available measures to defeat the Sandinistas. To distance himself from his history with Noriega, Bush vilified the Panamanian leader during his presidential campaign and carried through his resolve to depose the dictator in the military invasion. In a swift action, involving the deaths of twenty-three U.S. troops and approximately 3,000–4,000 Panamanians, the U.S. military established control and captured Noriega within twenty-three days. The triumph clearly strengthened Bush's political stock domestically.

During his presidency George H. W. Bush also initiated talks with the governments of Mexico and Canada to advance the North American Free Trade Agreement (NAFTA), which

George H. W. Bush (third from left) with (from left to right) White House Chief of Staff John Sununu, Secretary of State James Baker, National Security Advisor Brent Snowcroft, Vice President Dan Quayle, Secretary of Defense Dick Cheney, Robert Gates, and General Colin Powell in the White House Oval Office viewing a videotape on Panamanian General Manuel Noriega, January 4, 1990, the day after Noriega surrendered himself to the U.S. military. The notorious strongman was later convicted on drug charges and sentenced to thirty years in prison.

SOURCE: Courtesy of the George H.W. Bush Presidential Library would reduce or eliminate most tariffs on products traded among the three nations. Proponents argued that free trade would broaden markets and increase economic opportunities for all parties. But the political left criticized the proposal for lacking provisions for environmental protections and labor rights and for promoting primarily the interests of an international investor class. Others complained that the treaty would only send U.S. jobs to Mexico and result in lower wages. Ultimately, though not completed during the Bush presidency, the treaty was signed in the early days of the administration of President William J. Clinton and represented a triumph of a neoliberal agenda.

Bush sought reelection in 1992 but lost to Democrat Clinton, whose campaign emphasized the economic recession and not issues of foreign policy. Although he has continued to participate in occasional public service efforts and voice his political opinions, George H. W. Bush effectively retired from politics after his 1992 electoral defeat. His eldest son, George W. Bush, succeeded Clinton as president in 2001 and proceeded to appoint many of Reagan's and his father's foreign policy advisors to his own cabinet and staff.

See also *Central American Wars, 1980s; Central Intelligence Agency (CIA); Church Committee; Neoliberal Economic Development Model; Nicaragua, U.S. Relations with; Noriega Moreno, Manuel Antonio; North American Free Trade Agreement (NAFTA), 1992; Panama, U.S. Relations with; Reagan, Ronald W.; Sandinista National Liberation Front (FSLN) (Nicaragua)*

. . . . GREGORY S. CRIDER

SELECTED WORKS

Bush, George. *All the Best, George Bush: My Life in Letters and Other Writings.* New York: Simon and Schuster, 1999.

REFERENCES AND FURTHER READING

Crandall, Russell. *Gunboat Democracy: U.S. Interventions in the Dominican Republic, Grenada, and Panama.* Lanham, MD: Rowman and Littlefield, 2006.

Kornbluh, Peter, and Malcolm Byrne, eds. *The Iran-Contra Scandal: The Declassified History.* New York: The New Press, 1993.

Walsh, Lawrence E. *Firewall: The Iran-Contra Conspiracy and Cover-Up.* New York: Norton, 1998.

Bush, George W.

George W. Bush (1946–) served as the forty-third president of the United States from 2001–2009. He began his first term with significant focus on Latin America and the stated goals of developing close cooperation and more equal relations with U.S. neighbors. The combination of the September 11th terrorist attacks, U.S. policy in Iraq, changing economic conditions, the rise of leftist leaders in Latin America, and other factors, however, helped push the Bush administration back to more familiar U.S. patterns of limited attention to Latin America and attempts at regional dominance. The Bush years were marked by the failure to complete negotiations for a Free Trade Area of the Americas (FTAA) and by numerous other regional policy disagreements. Bush was more successful negotiating bilateral trade agreements and addressing some specific security issues. After early regional support, Bush became a frequent target of negative comments from Latin American leaders and popular protests. For much of his presidency polls across Latin America showed that Bush was the least popular American president in history with support from less than one-quarter of Latin America's populace.

While running for president Bush spoke of building new ties to introduce a "Century of the Americas." His first major foreign trip as president was to the third Summit of the Americas held in Quebec in April 2001. There he stressed the region's moves to democracy and economic growth and pledged to move forward on numerous trade deals, including an FTAA by 2005. Coming from Texas, Bush was particularly interested in Mexico, and he had ties to President Vicente Fox. Fox made a state visit to Washington in September 2001. The two laid out a bold agenda on trade, drug enforcement, energy, and immigration issues, and Bush suggested U.S.-Mexican ties were the country's most important international relationship.

Days after Fox's visit, September 11th triggered a profound shift in Bush's priorities. No Latin American country was home to Al-Qaeda terrorists and, despite rhetorical support, none was prepared to make major military or economic contributions to the war on terrorism. Regional issues such as poverty and the environment now seemed less important and immigration was cast in light of protecting the homeland. Regional neglect turned to tension as Bush shifted focus to Iraq. Many in Latin America saw U.S. unilateral actions and stretching of international law on preemptive intervention as repeating U.S. history of intervention in Latin America. Leftist leaders in Brazil, Venezuela, and Cuba became increasingly vocal critics, but, more notably, key U.S. allies Mexico and Chile refused to support a UN Security Council resolution authorizing war against Iraq in spring 2003.

Changing economic conditions also affected Bush's relations with Latin America. Early in his administration several Latin American economies stumbled, and in his second term, the United States entered into a deep recession. Each set of events lowered regional trade and led to disputes over who should give economic advice. Many Latin Americans questioned the free market, neoliberal policies frequently praised by Bush. This contributed to the rise of more leftist leaders in Latin America. For Bush the greatest challenge came from Venezuelan President Hugo Chávez, who described U.S. policies as imperialist, referred to Bush as the devil, and personally shadowed Bush with protest events on his last trips to the region.

The centerpiece of Bush's cooperative initiatives was supposed to be the FTAA. Negotiations began under Clinton, but most of the details remained to be worked out before a completion target of 2005. Bush was a strong proponent of the FTAA, but U.S. desires to gain access to other markets while maintaining protective tariffs and subsidies for U.S. agriculture led to opposition. Talks largely ended unsuccessfully in 2003 and Bush was unable to restart the process at a 2005 summit. With regional efforts stymied, Bush focused on trade agreements with Chile, Central American countries and the Dominican Republic, Panama, Colombia, and Peru. Despite these agreements U.S. share of trade and investment in Latin

America declined, as Europe and China emerged as major competitors. Nominal U.S. aid to the region increased under Bush, but in constant dollars aid decreased and much of it went to just five countries involved in the drug war.

On security issues the United States retained regional dominance. Bush strongly backed Plan Colombia to address drug dealing and violence, encouraged the removal of Haitian leader Jean-Bertrand Aristide who was seen as corrupt, and increased sanctions on Castro's Cuba. Bush also was slow to condemn a 2002 coup attempt against Chávez, and across several countries administration officials spoke in favor of electing more conservative, pro-U.S. parties. Bush's lack of regional support contributed to the 2005 rejection of Washington's candidate for the general secretary of the Organization of American States and a 2006 dispute over Latin America's nomination for the UN Security Council, but on the whole, while U.S.-Latin American relations became cooler under Bush, there was no sharp break.

. . . . JOHN W. DIETRICH

See also *Chávez Frías, Hugo; Fox, Vicente; Free Trade Association of the Americas (FTAA)*

REFERENCES AND FURTHER READING

Castaneda, Jorge. "The Forgotten Relationship." *Foreign Affairs* 82, no. 3 (2003): 67–81.

Leogrande, William M. "A Poverty of Imagination: George W. Bush's Policy in Latin America." *Journal of Latin American Studies* 39 (2007): 355–385.

Reich, Otto J. "Good Neighbor: President Bush's Real Record in Latin America." *National Review* 59, no. 6 (2007): 30–33.

Butler, Anthony

The Butlers, originally from South Carolina, moved to Kentucky in 1790. When his father died in 1805, Anthony Butler (1787–1850) briefly became the ward of a distant family acquaintance, Andrew Jackson. Well-connected and ambitious, Butler married into the powerful Crittenden family and fought alongside Jackson at the Battle of New Orleans. After the War of 1812 he served in the Kentucky and Mississippi legislatures and concurrently rented slaves. The occupation compelled him to spend some months in Texas in 1828, collecting debts from Stephen F. Austin and gathering information about the rich potential of the province. In 1838, after his diplomatic career in Mexico, Butler moved to Texas and was elected to the legislature and as grand master of the Masons. He moved back north in 1848 and drowned following a steamboat explosion on Lake Erie in April 1850.

BUTLER'S ROLE IN U.S. FOREIGN POLICY

In August 1829 Butler journeyed to Washington to share his rationale for the annexation of Texas with the newly elected "Old Hickory" (President Jackson). They agreed that U.S. security and the inability and cost to Mexico of governing the distant and unruly territory provided compelling justification for a transfer of the property. John Quincy Adams had futilely offered $1 million for Texas; Jackson would increase the amount to $5 million. The president ignored Butler's lack of Spanish language skills and foreign policy credentials and dispatched him as chargé d'affaires to Mexico City. Arriving in December 1829 Butler encountered rumors of a Spanish invasion of Mexico and a new conservative government with General Anastasio Bustamente as president and pro-British, anti-American Luis Alamán in the foreign office. The foreign secretary developed a policy in 1830 that militarized the region, curbed new American colonization into Texas, and pressured existing settlers to exit the territory. Butler's efforts to discuss a transfer met with a firm rebuff.

The envoy remained naively optimistic. That confidence was fueled by Alamán's willingness to conclude a trade agreement (April 1831) granting most-favored nation status to the United States with no discriminatory duties and neutral rights in time of war. Butler also decided to sign the long-delayed treaty of 1828 that set the Sabine River as the border between Texas and the United States; Jackson sharply disapproved, but the treaty was endorsed by the Senate. Buoyed by these successes and strong pressure from the White House, Butler pleaded unsuccessfully for the annexation of Texas. The president had become increasingly concerned about British influence in the province and a potential uprising of the volatile Texans, which would complicate and hinder U.S. acquisition.

A window of opportunity opened in January 1833 when General Antonio López de Santa Anna engineered a coup that placed the liberal Valentín Gómez Farias in the presidency. Gómez Farias offered the best hope for the sale of Texas, but a cautious Butler never advanced his cause before the liberal government fell in the spring of 1834. Instead, in 1833, he promulgated three deceptive schemes to Washington: (1) loaning money to Mexico—with likely default—utilizing Texas as security, (2) occupying East Texas to the Nueces River—which the Americans had claimed—with the military to potentially provoke a war, and (3) bribing Mexican officials at a cost of perhaps $500,000 to guarantee the sale. Jackson rejected all three ploys as outrageous and irresponsible and ordered Butler to suspend negotiations for Texas and concentrate on a new boundary.

Anger, frustration, and betrayal enveloped Butler in 1834 as he viewed his personal and political future squelched by the resurgent Mexican conservatives led by Alamán and a president possessed of a self-righteous sense of morality. "What a scamp!" the now-savvy Jackson had scribbled on a Butler letter of March 7 (Gibson 1972). Butler pressed on, negotiating an agreement in April 1835 for a joint commission to survey the disputed territory between the Sabine and Neches Rivers. In Washington in June, he advanced new plans for bribing Mexican officials. While Jackson again balked, he imprudently sent Butler back to Mexico to offer the government an additional $500,000 for San Francisco Bay. The Texas Revolution had commenced and many Mexicans viewed the United States, and Butler personally, as conspiring with the rebels. The unpopular diplomat was recalled in January 1836, but he remained for an additional ten months, advancing his land interests before his expulsion over challenging the secretary of war, José Tornel, to a duel. Arrogant, deceptive, and self-seeking, Butler had some successes in treaty-making, but he failed in his primary objective. His appointment is widely regarded by historians as one of the most ill-advised of the Jackson administration.

See also *Jackson, Andrew; Mexican-American War, 1846–1848; Texas, U.S. Annexation of*

. . . . JOHN BELOHLAVEK

REFERENCES AND FURTHER READING

Belohlavek, John M. *Let the Eagle Soar! The Foreign Policy of Andrew Jackson*. Lincoln: University of Nebraska Press, 1985.

Gibson, Joe "A. Butler: What a Scamp!" *Journal of the West* XI (April 1972): 235–247.

Lamar, Quinton Curtius. "A Diplomatic Disaster: The Mexican Mission of Anthony Butler, 1829–1834." *Americas* XLV (August, 1988): 1–17.

Saxon, Gerald D. "Anthony Butler: A Flawed Diplomat." *East Texas Historical Journal* XXIV (1986): 3–14.

Butler, Smedley D.

Smedley D. Butler (1881–1940) was an American major general who fought in Latin America but later became famous for denouncing U.S. foreign policy. He was born in Chester County, Pennsylvania, and grew up in a Quaker family. His father, Thomas S. Butler, was a lawyer and a judge and served as a U.S. Congressman for many years, chairing the House Naval Affairs Committee during the Harding and Coolidge administrations. Smedley Butler attended The Haverford School but dropped out in 1898 at the age of sixteen to join the Marines. Butler lied about his age in order to secure a commission as a second lieutenant in the Spanish-American War already underway in Cuba.

After Cuba the Marines sent Butler to China to fight in the Boxer campaign, where he was twice wounded, and Butler was promoted to captain before turning nineteen. In 1903 Butler was sent to Honduras to protect the U.S. Consulate from rebels, in the beginning of a long series of U.S. interventions in Central America that would continue for the next two decades. As a major Butler became a respected field commander in the Nicaraguan intervention of 1912, going from there to Panama, and then to Veracruz, Mexico, where he received his first of two Medals of Honor. The U.S. occupation of Haiti (1915–1934) represented a high point for Major Butler's career, where he received his second Medal of Honor and the respect of Assistant Secretary of the Navy Franklin D. Roosevelt.

Butler left Haiti in 1918 as a lieutenant colonel to serve in France, where his leadership earned him the temporary rank of brigadier general, and at thirty-seven he became the youngest general ever in Marine history. In the early 1920s Butler commanded Quantico, the U.S. Marine headquarters located just outside of Washington, D.C., where he became somewhat of a political insider. In 1924 he was hired to run the Philadelphia police force for a year. From 1927 to 1929 Butler commanded the Marine Expeditionary Force in China. Upon returning to the United States in 1929, he was promoted to major general. After being denied a promotion in 1931, Butler retired as a major general in 1931 and set out on a new career path. He had grown weary of what he saw as injustices in U.S. foreign policy and his role as a "gangster for capitalism."

Butler is known for his life after retirement as a writer, lecturer, and critic of war and United States imperialism as much as he is known for his military career. In the 1930s, as many Americans were war-weary, Butler confessed that he had been a "racketeer for capitalism" all those years he served in the Marines. Although he remained loyal to the Marine Corps, he criticized U.S. foreign policy and equated overseas imperialism with domestic gangsterism, topics which mesmerized his audiences in the 1930s. He spoke often on behalf of the League against War and Fascism and he was the most recognizable leader of the veterans' antiwar movement. Butler tirelessly gave speeches against the horrors of war, the workings of the military-industrial complex, and the interests of big business, which he felt war fueled. In 1933 he gave a speech entitled "War is a Racket," which contemporary critics of war remember Butler for writing. One of the most poignant lines of "War is a Racket," which deals with Butler's years in Latin America, follows:

> I helped make Mexico safe for American oil interests in 1914. I helped make Haiti and Cuba a decent place for the National City Bank boys. I helped in the raping of half a dozen Central American republics for the benefits of Wall Street. I helped purify Nicaragua for the international banking house of Brown Brothers in 1090–1912. I brought light to the Dominican Republic for American sugar interests in 1916. (Butler 1933)

In 1934 Smedley Butler was involved in a controversy known as the "Business Plot" when he told a congressional committee that a group of wealthy industrialists had approached him to lead a military coup to overthrow President Franklin D. Roosevelt. The alleged individuals involved in the plot denied being involved and the charges were dropped. The media subsequently ridiculed Butler's allegations.

Butler wrote over thirty articles in the 1930s and two books. His most famous work was the book he wrote in 1935 entitled, *War is a Racket* (Butler 1935). Butler spoke about the economic and the geopolitical factors that motivated war. He was a critic of both mainstream political parties, and although he had worked closely with Franklin D. Roosevelt in the past, he spoke out against the Roosevelt administration in the 1930s, especially as Roosevelt showed interest in the growing European conflicts.

A pacifist when the Second World War broke out in Europe, Butler bemoaned the grumblings of war in the United States, beginning in the late 1930s. In early 1940 Butler set out on his last speaking tour while Germany launched its blitzkrieg in Europe. Butler died on June 21, 1940.

See also *Haiti, U.S. Relations with; Mexican Revolution, 1911–1917, U.S. Policy toward; Roosevelt, Franklin D.*

. . . . VIRGINIA S. WILLIAMS

REFERENCES AND FURTHER READING

Butler, Smedley D. *Old Gimlet Eye: The Adventures of Smedley D. Butler as Told to Lowell Thomas*. New York: 1933. Reprint edition. Quantico, VA: Marine Corps Association, 1981.

Butler, Smedley D. *War is a Racket*. New York: Round Table Press, 1935.

Schmidt, Hans. *Maverick Marine: General Smedley D. Butler and the Contradictions of American Military History*. Lexington: University Press of Kentucky, 1987.

Cabot, John M.

John Moors Cabot (1901–1981) graduated from Harvard University in 1923, earned a degree in history from Oxford University, and joined the U.S. Foreign Service in 1927. His early posts in Latin America led to his career specialization. He served first in Peru from 1926 to 1928, followed by posts in the Dominican Republic, Mexico, Brazil, Guatemala, and Argentina.

In 1942 Cabot was appointed assistant chief of the State Department's Division of American Republics, followed by an appointment in 1944 to chief of the Division of Caribbean and Central American Affairs. In this post he was instrumental in structuring post-World War II hemispheric relations, and he served as the Latin American area advisor to the Dumbarton Oaks conference, the international conference held in Washington, D.C, to set up the United Nations. Cabot also helped draft the charter of the Organization of American States in 1948. He first honed his anticommunist credentials when serving briefly as chargé d'affairs in Buenos Aires, Argentina, in 1945. U.S. policymakers were suspicious of the Populist President Juan Perón, but Cabot recognized the weaknesses of anti-Perónist forces in Argentina and advocated a more moderate approach to Perón in order to prevent Perón from aligning with the Soviet Union.

From 1950 to 1952 Cabot served as U.S. minister to Finland, before returning to Washington, D.C, in 1953 when Secretary of State John Foster Dulles appointed him assistant secretary of state for Inter-American affairs. In this capacity Cabot recommended that the Eisenhower administration should focus on economic reform in Latin America in order to counter internal communist influence in the region. In 1953 Cabot joined the U.S. delegation to the Inter-American Economic and Social conference in Caracas. He believed that a major source of resentment in Latin America against the United States was due to the lack of U.S. economic aid to the region. Cabot also disagreed with the Eisenhower administrations' views that communism in Latin America was directed from Moscow. Cabot consistently opposed leftist regimes in Latin America, including that of President Jacobo Arbenz in Guatemala, but he was convinced that communists in Latin America were native to the region and gained strength because of their attention to social and economic reforms.

In 1953 Cabot accompanied the president's brother and advisor, Milton Eisenhower, on an official mission to South America to gather information. Cabot endorsed Eisenhower's ensuing report, which urged that the United States assume some responsibility for Latin America's economic welfare. Furthermore Cabot questioned the assumption that private investment could solve Latin America's economic problems and concluded that foreign investment could not grow in Latin America due to an outdated infrastructure and a labor force with limited technical skills or education. He also recognized the inherent problems caused by disparities of wealth in Latin America and questioned the appeal of policies intended for wealth to "trickle down" to the masses. His recommendations to the Eisenhower administration were modest, but fundamental differences with Secretary of State John Foster Dulles remained.

Cabot was appointed U.S. ambassador to Sweden from 1954 to 1957. He returned to Latin America as U.S. ambassador to Colombia from 1957 to 1959 and U.S. ambassador to Brazil from 1959 to 1961. He continued to advance the view that U.S. policy in Latin America should emphasize economic aid and raised concerns about Eisenhower policies in the region. He repeated his concerns that private foreign investment could not be expected in countries lacking modern infrastructure. Cabot served as U.S. ambassador to Poland from 1962 to 1965. Upon his retirement from the Foreign Service in 1966, Cabot taught at the Fletcher School of Law and Diplomacy at Tufts University and consulted at the Edmund A. Walsh School of Foreign Service at Georgetown University. He is the author of several books, including *Toward Our Common Destiny* (1954) and *First Line of Defense: Forty Years' Experiences of a Career Diplomat* (1979). He died in 1981.

See also *Communism in Latin America; Dulles, John Foster; Eisenhower, Dwight D.; Eisenhower, Milton; Perón Sosa, Juan Domingo; Tenth International Conference of American States, Caracas, 1954); World War II, 1939–1945*

. . . . MOLLY M. WOOD

SELECTED WORKS

Cabot, John Moors. *Toward Our Common Destiny*. Boston, MA: Fletcher School of Law and Diplomacy, 1954.

REFERENCES AND FURTHER READING

"John Moore Cabot is Dead at 79; U.S. Ambassador to 5 Countries," *The New York Times*, February 25, 1981.

Rabe, Stephen. *Eisenhower and Latin America: The Foreign Policy of Anticommunism*. Chapel Hill: The University of North Carolina Press, 1988.

Caffery, Jefferson

Jefferson Caffery (1886–1974) passed the diplomatic service exam in 1911 and was assigned to the U.S. legation at Caracas, Venezuela. From there he rose through the professional diplomatic ranks, in a variety of posts in Latin America, Europe, and Asia, and eventually he served as U.S. ambassador to El Salvador (1926–1928), Colombia (1928–1933), Cuba (1933–1937), and Brazil (1937–1944). In 1933 Caffery returned to Washington, D.C., to accept the position of assistant secretary of state for Latin American affairs, under Secretary of State Cordell Hull. He worked primarily on the diplomatic problems surrounding the evolving U.S. relationship with Cuba after President Franklin Roosevelt indicated his desire to implement the Good Neighbor policy of nonintervention in Latin America. Cuba, in particular, had chafed under the Platt Amendment, which was integrated into the 1902 Cuban Constitution and ensured U.S. involvement in Cuban domestic and foreign affairs and severely restricted Cuban autonomy.

In 1933 U.S. warships patrolled the waters around Cuba, but the United States refused to intervene when a military faction led by Fulgencio Batista installed a new government under Ramón Grau San Martín, which the U.S. refused to recognize. A nationalist and a leftist, Grau implemented social and economic reforms and seized some American-owned sugar mills. Roosevelt sent Caffery to Cuba in late 1933 as his "special presidential representative." In this capacity Caffery sought to establish a working relationship with Batista, who had come to believe that Grau's policies would result in U.S. intervention, which he intended to avoid at all costs. Batista therefore arranged for Grau's resignation and installed his hand-picked choice, Colonel Carlos Mendieta, as president (though Batista remained in control). The United States promptly recognized the new government and officially abrogated the Platt Amendment in 1934. Caffery survived an assassination attempt at the U.S. Embassy on May 24, 1934, but nevertheless he remained in Cuba as U.S. ambassador until 1937, as Batista consolidated his power and the U.S. strengthened economic ties to his regime.

In 1937 Caffery accepted the position of U.S. ambassador to Brazil, one of the most important posts in Latin America. Shortly after Caffery arrived in Brazil, President Getúlio Vargas dismissed the Brazilian congress, took personal dictatorial powers, and proclaimed the formation of the *Estado Novo* (New State). He also purchased weapons from Germany. The United States had been growing more concerned through the decade with issues of hemispheric security and was alarmed at the way Vargas, who had signed trade agreements with both the United States and Germany in the past, carefully calculated how he could maintain and balance economic relationships with both countries. There was a significant German population in Brazil, and the Brazilian military was especially pro-German. When war did break out in Europe in 1939, Brazil declared neutrality. The U.S. responded with offers of defense assistance for Brazil, if needed, and economic assistance, which Caffery helped to negotiate. In 1940 the United States made a loan available to Brazil for the construction of an important steel mill. In the meantime Brazil agreed to sell certain strategic materials, such as bauxite and rubber, only to the United States, and thus Brazil fell more clearly into the U.S. economic sphere of influence. The United States also arranged to build air bases in the largely defenseless region known as the "bulge" on the northeastern coast of Brazil. Brazil finally severed diplomatic relations with Germany in January 1942 and declared war.

In January 1943 Vargas and President Roosevelt met personally aboard a U.S. destroyer off the northeast coast of Brazil. Caffery briefed Roosevelt privately on Vargas's positions and assured the president that Vargas would agree to adhere to the anti-Axis wartime alliance. He was not certain, however, that Vargas would respond positively to Roosevelt's suggestion that Brazilian troops be used to protect the Portuguese colonial possessions in the Atlantic, the Azores, and Madeira. Nothing, in fact, came from this particular suggestion, but Vargas did apparently convince Roosevelt of the opportunities for a Brazilian Expeditionary Force of combat troops, which eventually fought in Italy. In the meantime, there had been some criticism leveled against Caffery for cultivating too close a relationship with Vargas, especially as domestic opposition to Vargas grew. Caffery found himself in an impossible situation whereby the State Department made clear that he could not ignore growing leftist opposition to Vargas, but he could also not encourage this opposition without angering Vargas, with whom he had worked so hard to cultivate a relationship in order to promote the wartime alliance. Caffery therefore left Brazil in late 1944 and was sent to Paris and then to Cairo. He retired from the Foreign Service in 1955.

See also *Batista y Zaldívar, Fulgencio; Brazil, U.S. Relations with; Good Neighbor Policy; Grau San Martín, Ramón; Platt, Orville; Roosevelt, Franklin D.; Vargas, Getúlio Dornelles; World War II, 1939–1945*

. . . . MOLLY M. WOOD

References and Further Reading

Dur, Philip. *Jefferson Caffery of Louisiana: Ambassador of Revolutions*. Lafayette: University of Southwestern Louisiana Libraries, 1982.

Leonard, Thomas, and John Bratzel, eds. *Latin America during World War II*. New York: Rowman and Littlefield, 2007.

Calderón Guardia, Rafael

Costa Rica's president from 1940 until 1944, Rafael Angel Calderón Guardia (1900–1970) was one of the country's most important and controversial political figures. During the period from 1940 to 1948, he supported the United States in World War II, but he fought a civil war that marked the demise of his good relations with Washington.

Catholic social justice ideas shaped Calderón Guardia in his formative years. A physician who was popular with the poor, he joined the *Partido Republicano Nacional* (National Republican Party). By 1936 he had advanced from heading the municipality of San José to presiding over Congress, where he supported the conservative and authoritarian president León Cortés Castro. For the election of 1940 Cortés Castro sponsored Calderón Guardia, probably hoping to use him as a puppet, since the constitution prohibited presidents from serving a consecutive term.

As president, however, Calderón Guardia departed from the pro-German Cortés Castro and aligned Costa Rica with the United States in World War II. Relations between the two countries were attuned to the strategic interests of the United States, which deemed Costa Rica part of its sphere of defense. After the Pearl Harbor attack of December 7, 1941, the Costa Rican government preempted Washington by declaring war on Japan the following day. War was declared on Germany and Italy on December 11. Under United States pressure, Calderón Guardia targeted Costa Rica's German, Italian, and Japanese minorities, some of whom would experience internment, expulsion, and expropriation of property. A Lend-Lease agreement was signed on January 16, 1942, whereby the United States proposed to transfer armaments and munitions to Costa Rica. On July 9 the Export-Import Bank supplied a loan of $2,000,000 to stabilize Costa Rica's ailing economy. Costa Rica also cooperated in the construction of the Inter-American Highway and granted the United States-based Rubber Reserve Company exclusive purchasing rights to its exportable rubber. In 1943 Costa Rica supplied about 10,000 acres of land to plant cinchona trees for military-medical purposes.

Calderón Guardia was a popular but also controversial president. For his ambitious social reform agenda, he depended on the Roman Catholic Church and eventually on the communists as well. In 1941 compulsory social security was introduced. In 1942 he proposed to amend the constitution with the so-called *Garantías Sociales* (Social Guarantees). Together with the Labor Code of September 15, 1943, these were his most incisive social policies; however, they were accompanied by corruption in government, questionable electoral practices, and a friendship with the Nicaraguan dictator Anastasio Somoza García. Disenchanted conservative elites and other groups grew increasingly opposed to Calderón Guardia and his successor, Teodoro Picado Michalski.

In 1948 tensions culminated in a civil war of international dimensions. In an election marked by a climate of extraordinary hatred and violence, former president Calderón Guardia ran against the candidate of the United Opposition party, Otilio Ulate Blanco, who was declared the winner. However, the electoral tribunal did not declare a victor unanimously and deferred to Congress, where Calderón Guardia enjoyed majority support and the election was thus annulled on charges of fraud. Amid the evolving crisis, the government's most determined opponent, José Figueres Ferrer, who had been preparing a rebellion after effectively being exiled by Calderón Guardia in 1942, took up arms in March 1948. After over a month of fighting, the foreign diplomatic corps mediated a peace agreement. Calderón Guardia went into exile and a provisional junta under Figueres Ferrer soon replaced the agreed-upon interim government. While not intervening directly in the war, the United States did little to stop Figueres Ferrer from receiving support from Guatemala and hindered Somoza García from aiding the Costa Rican government. Historians Kyle Longley and Jacobo Schifter argue that the government's association with the communists contributed to this moderate stance. Both United States Ambassador Nathaniel Davis and the astute Figueres Ferrer were emphatically anticommunist. Published Department of State materials suggest the United States sought to prevent the conflict from destabilizing the rest of Central America.

Calderón Guardia's influence did not cease entirely after 1948. In vain he attempted to invade Costa Rica under Figueres Ferrer from Nicaragua in December 1948 and January 1955. This damaged Calderón Guardia's relationship with the United States further, while strengthening that of his nemesis. Until permitted to return to Costa Rica in 1958, he lived in Mexico. Calderón Guardia ran for president once more, in 1962, unsuccessfully, although he remained committed to Costa Rican politics until his death in 1970.

See also *Caribbean, German U-boat Threat, World War II; Caribbean Legion; Communism in Latin America; Eighth International Conference of American States, Lima, 1938; Figueres Ferrer, José; First Meeting of Consultation of the Ministers of Foreign Affairs of the American Republics, Panama, 1939; Lend-Lease Program, World War II; Nazi Activities in Latin America, World War II; Nicaraguan-Costa Rican Conflict, 1948; Pan American Highway; Roosevelt, Franklin D.; Second Meeting of Consultation of the Ministers of Foreign Affairs of the American Republics, Havana, 1940; Somoza García, Anastasio; Third Meeting of Consultation of the Ministers of Foreign Affairs of the American Republics, Rio de Janeiro, 1942; World War II, 1939–1945*

. . . . CARLOS MEISSNER

References and Further Reading

Bell, John Patrick. *Crisis in Costa Rica: The 1948 Revolution.* Austin: The University of Texas Press, 1971.

Calderón Guardia, Rafael Angel. *El gobernante y el hombre frente al problema social costarricense.* San José, Costa Rica: Com. Nacional de Conmemoraciones Históricas, 1995. (Originally published in 1942)

"Foreign Relations of the United States, Diplomatic Papers, 1940, Volume V, The American Republics." Washington, DC: United States Government Printing Office, 1961.

"Foreign Relations of the United States, Diplomatic Papers, 1941, Volume VI, The American Republics." Washington, DC: United States Government Printing Office, 1963.

"Foreign Relations of the United States, Diplomatic Papers, 1941, Volume VII, The American Republics." Washington, DC: United States Government Printing Office, 1962.

"Foreign Relations of the United States, Diplomatic Papers, 1942, Volume VI, The American Republics." Washington, DC: United States Government Printing Office, 1963.

"Foreign Relations of the United States, Diplomatic Papers, 1943, Volume VI, The American Republics." Washington, DC: United States Government Printing Office, 1965.

"Foreign Relations of the United States, 1947, Volume VIII, The American Republics." Washington, DC: United States Government Printing Office, 1972.

"Foreign Relations of the United States, 1948, Volume IX, The Western Hemisphere." Washington, DC: United States Government Printing Office, 1972.

Longley, Kyle. *The Sparrow and the Hawk: Costa Rica and the United States during the Rise of José Figueres.* Tuscaloosa: The University of Alabama Press, 1997.

Schifter, Jacobo. "Origins of the Cold War in Central America: A Study of Diplomatic Relations between Costa Rica and the United States (1940–1949)." PhD diss., Columbia University, 1983.

Calero, Adolfo

(See *Central American Wars, 1980s)*

Calhoun, John C.

John Caldwell Calhoun (1782–1850) was one of the most prominent United States politicians prior to the beginning of the American Civil War in 1861. Calhoun served as state representative, U.S. representative, U.S. secretary of state, U.S. secretary of war, U.S. vice president under President Andrew Jackson, and U.S. senator from South Carolina. During the Mexican-American War, Senator Calhoun remained a subdued critic of the war and believed that the invasion of Mexico and the admission of Texas was a step toward disharmony and discord with the American republic, but he also saw Texas as a bulwark against British antislavery influence.

Calhoun was born on March 18, 1792, near Abbeville, South Carolina. After a nominal education, he attended Yale College and read for the law at the Litchfield Law Academy. He soon was elected to state legislature and later served in the U.S. House of Representatives. While in Congress, Calhoun became identified with a number of young politicians who supported a strong nationalist agenda; they were identified as "War Hawks." In 1817 he was selected to serve as U.S. secretary of war under President James Monroe, and he succeeded reforming and strengthening the department after its mismanagement during the War of 1812.

After a losing bid to secure the soon to be called Democratic party's nomination as president, Calhoun was elected to serve as vice president under John Quincy Adams from 1824–1828 and under Andrew Jackson from 1828–1832. During this period Calhoun slowly began to transform himself from a strong nationalistic supporter to a strict states' rights advocate. He saw the internal political wrangling, which resulted in the election of John Quincy Adams as president, as harbinger of the dangerous growth of federal power. Calhoun saw this federal power as a direct threat to the rights of the southern states within the context of the American Union. The Cherokee Indian removal and the employment of a national tariff broke the final strands of support between Calhoun and Jackson. In 1832 Calhoun resigned as vice president and returned to Congress as a U.S. senator from South Carolina.

In 1825 Vice President Calhoun had organized resistance in the U.S. Senate against the appointment of U.S. delegates to the Panama Congress, which was a formal diplomatic conference of several recently created Latin American counties. Calhoun sought to blunt the influence of Henry Clay of Kentucky over American diplomacy in the region. Still harboring presidential aspirations, Calhoun did not want fellow congressmen to support his rival Clay's desire to foster a greater American commercial zone throughout the Americas. In addition, as Calhoun was becoming the national spokesperson for southern interests in the U.S. Congress, he sought to prevent any American recognition of the Latin American countries due to their antislavery positions. This was especially true with the island nation of Haiti, which was expected to attend the conference.

Calhoun continued to serve as a U.S. senator from his native state until 1843. During this period he became the leader of a number of proslavery politicians, who saw Calhoun as the moral and philosophical leader of their cause to thwart the abuses of federal power. He retired from the Senate in 1843 and attempted another run for the presidency in 1844. William Henry Harrison won the election as president but soon died after his inauguration, and Vice President John Tyler became President. President John Tyler appointed Calhoun as U.S. secretary of state upon the death of Aber Upshur in February 1844. As U.S. secretary of state, Calhoun was now the lead player in the efforts to admit the Texas Republic into the United States. During this effort, Great Britain was sending envoys to the Texan government to obtain influence to support the country's diplomatic efforts in Latin America, particularly with Honduras. Calhoun turned the issue of Texas annexation into a cause to prevent the influence of British antislavery from blunting proslavery westward expansion through the issuance of the "Pakenham Letter," addressed to Richard Pakenham, British minister to the United States. In 1845 Calhoun returned to the U.S. Senate and refused to endorse or condemn a declaration of war against Mexico. He hoped that Mexico, not the U.S. forces stationed in Texas, would punish those forces that had crossed over the Rio Grande River.

Calhoun continued to serve in the Senate until his death in 1850. His last efforts were directed to bring about a unified southern political effort as a defense to what he perceived as the growing tide of northern abolitionism embolden by the majority power of northern states. He wrote papers and gave speeches to focus the southern political establishment toward southern nationalism. His last speech, read by a fellow senator, warned of the future abuses of a northern majority over the southern states. After his death his thoughts regarding a dual American presidency were published to protect the minority status of the southern slave states.

See also *Clay, Henry; Great Britain, Nineteenth-Century Interests in Latin America; Jackson, Andrew; Latin American Independence, 1803–1826, U.S. Policy toward; Managua, Treaty of, 1860; Manifest Destiny; Mexican-American War, 1846–1848; Taylor, Zachary; Texas (Lone Star Republic), U.S. Relations with, 1836–1846; Tyler, John*

. . . . WILLIAM H. BROWN

References and Further Reading

Bartlett, Irving H. *John C. Calhoun: A Biography.* New York: Norton, 1993.

Calhoun, John C. *The Papers of John C. Calhoun* (28 volumes). Columbia: The University of South Carolina Press, 1995.

Cheek, H. Lee Jr., ed. *John C. Calhoun: Selected Writings and Speeches.* Lanham, MD: National Book Network, 2003.

Freehling, William W. *The Road to Disunion: Secessionists at Bay, 1776–1854.* New York: Oxford University Press, 1990.

Peterson, Merrill D. *The Great Triumvirate: Webster, Clay, and Calhoun.* New York: Oxford University, 1987.

Calles, Plutarco Elías

Plutarco Elías Calles (1877–1945), who served as president of Mexico from 1924 to 1928, was one of the most important leaders of revolutionary Mexico and a very significant figure in U.S.-Mexican relations. He hailed from the northwestern border state of Sonora and rose to political significance during the first decade of the Mexican Revolution (1910–1920). In February 1913 he joined the constitutionalist alliance of Venustiano Carranza, Alvaro Obregón, and Pancho Villa to fight against the dictatorship of Victoriano Huerta. His most significant contribution to that cause came in provisioning constitutionalist forces with arms, food, and money from the United States in violation of U.S. neutrality laws. After the disintegration of the constitutionalist coalition, he used his cross-border connections in Arizona to help Carranza and Obregón defeat Villa. In August 1915 First Chief Carranza named Calles governor of Sonora. At the height of World War I Calles antagonized the U.S. government by maintaining friendly relations with German agents and by levying production taxes on the U.S.-owned copper mining companies. At the same time, however, he continued to cultivate his relationship with U.S. supporters of the constitutionalists.

Beginning in September 1919 Calles enhanced his reputation as a nationalist reformer in successive positions in the national government. In particular, he forged a strategic alliance with labor leader Luis Napoleón Morones, who in turn enjoyed close ties to Samuel Gompers of the American Federation of Labor (AFL). With Morones and Gompers, Calles advertised the Mexican Revolution abroad as a socially progressive movement similar to European social democracy. He also helped the Obregón administration procure U.S. diplomatic recognition in August 1923. The following month he announced his presidential candidacy on a prolabor and nationalist platform. He won election in July 1924.

As president, Calles challenged the U.S. government over two issues: the privileges of the foreign-owned oil industry and U.S. military intervention in Nicaragua. In his quest to implement Article 27 of the 1917 revolutionary constitution, which stipulated that land and subsoil were the property of the Mexican nation, he attempted to force the oil companies and other foreign mining and land companies in Mexico to apply for confirmatory concessions that would have resulted in higher tax rates. In response U.S. Secretary of State Frank B. Kellogg strenuously objected to these attempts and, in June 1925, suggested that the Mexican government was "on trial before the world" for its nationalist policy. In January 1927 Kellogg's rhetoric intensified amidst Calles's support for a Nicaraguan faction opposed to U.S. intervention in that Central American country, causing Calles and his advisers to fear a U.S. invasion. Indeed U.S. military intelligence correspondence intercepted by a Mexican spy in the U.S. embassy appeared to confirm the validity of these fears. Shortly thereafter, however, Kellogg named the conciliatory Dwight Morrow as the new U.S. ambassador to Mexico, and Calles and Morrow succeeded in normalizing U.S.-Mexican relations. In the end Mexico's nationalist laws remained on the books but eluded enforcement, and the U.S. government imposed its preferred situation on Nicaragua. Nevertheless Calles's nationalist stance of the years 1924–1927 joins the 1938 oil expropriation under President Lázaro Cárdenas as the most significant Mexican challenge to U.S. interventionism and economic imperialism in the interwar period.

Following his presidency Calles remained involved in Mexican politics as the so-called "Jefe Máximo," or informal arbiter of political events, and he founded a ruling party that (albeit under three different names) would not be ousted from the presidency until 2000. The elder Calles was conciliatory toward the United States, and he frequently visited the country for medical and family reasons. Several of his children studied in the United States and from 1936 to 1941 Calles resided in San Diego following his flight to exile during the Cárdenas administration.

See also *Cárdenas del Río, Lázaro; Hughes, Charles Evans; Mexican Revolution, 1911–1917, U.S. Policy toward; Mexico, U.S. Relations with; Morrow, Dwight W.; Oil, Expropriation of Foreign Companies*

. . . . JÜRGEN BUCHENAU

References and Further Reading

Buchenau, Jurgen. *Plutarco Elías Calles and the Mexican Revolution.* Lanham, MD: Scholarly Resources, 2006.

Meyer, Lorenzo. *The United States and Mexico during the Oil Controversy.* Austin: University of Texas Press, 1971.

Smith, Robert F. The United States and Mexican Revolutionary Nationalism, 1916–1932. Chicago: University of Chicago Press, 1972.

Calvo, Carlos

Carlos Calvo is best remembered for a legal concept, the Calvo Clause, which has had a large influence on international business in the western hemisphere. Calvo was born in Buenos Aries, Argentina, and began his career as a consular agent and diplomat in 1852. He took a special interest in the laws that affected international businesses. He studied cases in which nations such as Argentina imposed legal regulations on international businesses. Calvo compiled a massive six-volume work published in French under the title *Le droit international the'orique et pratique* (*The Theory and Practice of International Law*). Much of his professional career was devoted to research and writing on the five editions of this treatise, which appeared from 1868 to 1896. This study was read by diplomats, lawyers, business leaders, and politicians in Latin America, the United States, and Europe and serves as the fundamental expression of Calvo's ideas.

DEVELOPING THE CALVO CLAUSE

Calvo began this study in the 1860s, a decade which marked several turning points in international affairs. There were innovations in the technologies of international communications and transportation. In 1866 submarine telegraph cables spanned the north Atlantic and soon reached the Caribbean, Mexico, Central America, and South America. In the next few decades wooden sailing ships gave way to steam-powered vessels of iron and steel. Businesses used the new technologies to expand trade with Latin America. In the same period an ominous event took place in Mexico. A French company was unable to collect the repayment of a loan extended to the Mexican government. The French government agreed to settle the matter and, with the aid of the United Kingdom and Italy, sent an armed force into Mexico to collect the debt in 1862. The French government used this intervention to attempt to impose the empire of Maximilian I on Mexico. Calvo saw this armed intervention as an abuse of power by the intervening nations. This situation was a threatening precedent because banks and businesses that made loans to Latin American countries could then appeal to their governments for an armed intervention when the borrower did not repay the loan on schedule. Calvo's homeland, Argentina, like Mexico and other Latin American countries, had entered a period in which European and U.S. companies would play a large role in their economic development. Calvo wanted to devise a legal means of reducing the opportunity for such interventions.

His solution was the Calvo Doctrine, which evolved into the Calvo Clause. The difference between the doctrine and the clause is important. The Calvo Doctrine was a promise of nonintervention that was supposed to be written into treaties between nations such as Mexico and the United States. The downfall of the Calvo Doctrine came when the governments of industrialized, capital-exporting nations such as the United States refused to include such provisions in treaties. The Calvo Clause, however, had a much larger impact. It was typically one of the articles in a contract between a private business and a Latin American government. The Calvo Clause appeared in a large number of contracts during the last decades of the nineteenth century and the early part of the twentieth century. The main point of the clause was that foreign businesses agreed to accept the jurisdiction of the local courts (such as those of Mexico or Argentina) and therefore, relinquished the right to appeal to their home government (such as the United States or France) for the collection of debts. The right to appeal to one's home country was generally referred to as the right of diplomatic protection. Under the Calvo Clause the legal grounds for diplomatic protection were eliminated, and the potential for armed intervention was reduced.

ADOPTION AND CONTINUING RELEVANCE OF THE CALVO CLAUSE

The Calvo Clause formed a part of many contracts, but one case stands out because it led to recognition of the broad applicability of this legal principle. The Mexican Claims Commission (MCC) was an international tribunal set up in 1923 by the United States and Mexico to settle claims arising from the violent phase of the Mexican Revolution (1910–1920). In 1926 the MCC rendered its judgment on the claims of the North American Dredging Company of Texas against the Mexican government. The dredging company had signed a contract with the administration of President Francisco Madero to clear the port of Salina Cruz. While the work was underway, President Madero's government fell as a result of a political revolt. The dredging company did not receive full payment for its work. Lawyers representing the company took their claims to the MCC. The MCC ruled against the dredging company mainly on the grounds that the 1912 contract included a Calvo Clause, which meant that the company had to rely on the Mexican courts and could not appeal to an international tribunal such as the MCC. Although critics questioned some aspects of the decision, the basic ruling that upheld the validity of the Calvo Clause gained wide recognition among lawyers, judges, and the international business community.

The Calvo Clause apparently lost much of its relevance in the 1990s in the surge of international investments and the promotion of international commerce through treaties such as the North American Free Trade Agreement. Many Latin American governments agreed to accept the international arbitration of business claims, a practice that invalidated the Calvo Clause. Some experts in international law, however, contended that the Calvo Clause remained relevant in the new millennium. Well-known Spanish lawyer and international arbiter Bernardo Cremades argued in 2004 that Calvo's emphasis on the primacy of national courts remained embedded in many international business agreements. He cited four of the larger Latin American nations as following this approach in their relations with multinational corporations: Brazil, Argentina, Mexico, and Venezuela.

Over a century before Cremades published his analysis, Carlos Calvo enjoyed the respect of his homeland and of diplomats and international lawyers in many nations. Calvo's voluminous writing and the ideas contained in them constituted one of the first significant systematic statements from a developing nation on both the problems of and solutions for the complex process of globalization.

See also *Argentina, U.S. Relations with; Debt Crisis, Latin America, 1870s, 1930s, 1980s; Drago, Luis M.; Madero, Francisco I.; Maximilian, Archduke Ferdinand, Emperor of Mexico; Mexican Revolution, 1911–1917, U.S. Policy toward; North American Free Trade Agreement (NAFTA), 1992*

. . . . JOHN A. BRITTON

REFERENCES AND FURTHER READING

Cremades, Bernardo. "Disputes Arising Out of Foreign Direct Investment in Latin America: A New Look at the Calvo Doctrine and Other Jurisdictional Issues." *Dispute Resolution Journal* (May, 2004).

Dugard, John. "The Calvo Clause. Third Report on Diplomatic Protection: Addendum, International Law Commission." 54th Session, 2002.

Dunn, Frederick S. *The Diplomatic Protection of Americans in Mexico.* New York: Columbia University Press, 1933.

Shea, Donald R. The Calvo Clause: A Problem of Inter-American and International Law and Diplomacy. Minneapolis: University of Minnesota Press, 1953.

Calvo Doctrine

(**See** *Calvo, Carlos*)

Camarena, Enrique

Enrique Camarena (1947–1985) was an agent in the U.S. Drug Enforcement Administration (DEA) who was kidnapped, tortured, and killed while investigating drug trafficking activities in Guadalajara, Mexico, in 1985. His death prompted a massive mobilization of investigators in the DEA, led to new legislation on drug crimes in the United States, and resulted in a brief diplomatic incident between the United States and Mexico.

Camarena was born on July 26, 1947, in Baja California and his family moved to Calexico, California, when he was a child. Camarena served in the U.S. Marine Corps before returning to Calexico to work in law enforcement. He joined the DEA as a special agent in 1974, shortly after its creation. In 1981 he was assigned to the Guadalajara resident office where he carried out local investigations and other field work. By all accounts, Camarena was an honest and hardworking law enforcement agent.

On February 7, 1985, Camarena was abducted by armed men along with Alfredo Zavala, a Mexican pilot who had supported local antidrug law enforcement officials. The DEA launched an extensive investigation into Camarena's disappearance. U.S. officials immediately suspected notorious drug bosses Rafael Caro-Quintero, Miguel Angel Félix Gallardo, and Ernesto Fonseca in the disappearance, and investigators quickly began to suspect that the drug lords were being aided by local law enforcement. The investigation stalled until the bodies of Camarena and Zavala, bound and gagged, were discovered near a rural road in early March. A forensic examination indicated that both men had been tortured for several days before dying from blunt-force wounds to the head and face.

One week later Mexican officials arrested five local Jalisco law enforcement officers on suspicion of their involvement in the Camarena abduction. Those officers eventually admitted their involvement in the kidnapping, and they implicated the suspected drug bosses in the agent's death. As the investigation progressed, DEA officials became convinced that high-ranking Mexican officials were involved either in the crime or in obstructing the investigation. The agency eventually launched Operation Leyenda, which was the largest murder investigation ever undertaken by the DEA, leading to the convictions of more than a dozen individuals, including a number of high-ranking drug bosses. But DEA officials also had evidence of the involvement of low-level accomplices, such as Humberto Alvarez Macháin, a doctor suspected of administering medical care to keep the agent alive during his days of torture. When Mexican officials failed to pursue charges against the doctor, DEA agents hired bounty hunters to kidnap the doctor and transport him to U.S. territory for arrest and prosecution. Macháin appealed his arrest on grounds that it violated the U.S.-Mexican extradition treaty, and Mexican officials objected on diplomatic grounds. In 1991 the U.S. Supreme Court ruled that Macháin could be tried in the United States. His case was eventually dropped for lack of evidence, but it set a legal precedent that is still cited by U.S. officials in detaining suspects in the war on terror.

Camarena's death inspired a national campaign known as Red Ribbon Week. During the annual October campaign, participants wear red ribbons to demonstrate their support for antidrug policies.

See also *Drug Trafficking; Mexico-U.S. Border and Drug Control; U.S. Drug Enforcement Administration*

MONICA RANKIN

References and Further Readings

Drug Enforcement Agency, "A Tradition of Excellence: The History of the DEA from 1973 to 2003," www.dea.gov/pubs/history/index.html.

Lowenfeld, Andreas S. "Kidnapping by Government Order: A Follow-Up." *American Society of International Law* 84, no. 3 (July 1990): 712–716.

Campos, Francisco Luiz da Silva

Francisco Luiz da Silva Campos (1891–1968) was recognized as a Brazilian presidential adviser. The son of Jacinto Alves da Silva Campos and Azejúla de Souza e Silva, Campos was born in Dores do Indaiá, Minas Gerais. He earned a law degree from Free Faculty of Law of Belo Horizonte and established himself as a lawyer in Belo Horizonte and Pitanqui. He was a supporter of authoritarianism who frequently clashed with U.S. interests and diplomats in the buildup to World War II but also participated in a later military government that had U.S. support.

As a professor he taught at the Faculty of Law in his home state and received tenure at the Federal University of Rio de Janeiro. He served in several political positions within the state of Minas Gerais, including state legislator, federal legislator, and secretary of the interior. Campos was also mayor of Belo Horizonte. In office he promoted a profound educational reform. Campos, as a leader of the Liberal Alliance, participated in the conspiracy that culminated the 1930 revolution, which ended the Old Republic and supported Getúlio Vargas.

In the interim government Campos was the first minister of health and education (1930–1932), where he reformed training procedures for primary school teachers to promote nationalist values and established a federal university educational system. He wrote several works related to education, including *Educação e cultura* (1940). In addition he authored several case studies and opinions for constitutional, administrative, and civil law texts. In December 1935 the mayor of the Federal District, Pedro Ernesto, appointed him secretary of education. Beginning with this post he established himself as one of the most important representatives of the right in Brazil, developing a sense of authoritarianism.

A turbulent course of events between 1930 and 1935 contributed to the coups d'état led by Vargas in November 1937. Campos played a central role in the coup of 1937. He was made general-counsel by Vargas and drafted the dictatorial constitution. Later that year Vargas appointed Campos as the new minister of justice. He wrote the Estado Nôvo (New State) program/constitution, which incorporated several corporatist features. Campos was inspired by the Polish constitution. In 1940 he published O Estado Nacional that emphasized a fascist outlook. The United States, in particular U.S. Ambassador Jefferson Caffery, indicated their skepticism toward the effectiveness of the democracy with Campos's constitution. The United States condemned the Estado Nôvo based on Campos's preference toward authoritarianism.

An advocate of authoritarianism, Campos in 1931 cofounded the "Mineiro Black Shirts," the fascist miners' union. He also attempted to establish a national youth organization similar to fascist paramilitary organizations in Germany, but he failed to receive approval from other ministers. In the events leading to World War II, Campos sought to strengthen relations with Germany rather than the United States. He worked against U.S. Ambassador Oswaldo Aranhas, who supported strong ties with the United States. Resistant to Brazil aligning with the Allied forces, Campos asked German Ambassador Karl Ritter if the Reich government would send an anti-Comintern exhibit to Brazil and worked alongside officials of the Reich government.

In a newspaper interview Campos promoted the Estado Nôvo and advocated that Brazil should be included in the list of corporative states. He compared the constitution's ability to strip parliaments of their powers with Franklin D. Roosevelt's legislative program. On November 30, 1937, U.S. Undersecretary Sumner Welles visited the Brazilian embassy to reject Campos's claims. Roosevelt faced a rebellious Congress and did not need Campos's description of his administration reaching the populace of the United States. Welles and Aranha accused Campos of attempting to break relations between Brazil and the United States.

In 1939 Campos also rejected the accords Aranha developed with the United States, which consisted of Brazil paying foreign debt. Despite Campos's contact with Reich officials, Brazil officially agreed to support the Allied forces. In 1942 Vargas forced the resignation of several officials formally tied to the Axis powers to establish stronger relations with the United States. On July 17, 1942, Vargas accepted the resignation of Justice Francisco Campos.

Campos continued engaging in Brazilian affairs as an appointed representative in the Inter-American Judicial Committee (1943–1955). In 1943 Campos signed, on behalf of Brazil, the 1948 Universal Declaration of Human Rights. After fifty years away from public office, he participated in the coup of 1964 against the government of President João Goulart. He wrote the institutional framework of the new military regime, supported by the United States, known as Institutional Act No.1 and No. 2. In 1968 he died in Belo Horizonte.

See also *Aranha, Oswaldo; Brazil, Coup d'État, 1964; Brazil, U.S. Relations with; Caffery, Jefferson; Goulart, João Belchior; Inter-American Judicial Committee; Vargas, Getúlio Dornelles; Welles, Sumner; World War II, 1939–1945*

. . . . .MIRIAM ELIZABETH VILLANUEVA

References and Further Reading

Levine, Robert M. *The Vargas Regime; The Critical Years, 1934–1938.* New York: Columbia University Press, 1970.

McCann, Frank D. *The Brazilian-American Alliance, 1937–1945.* Princeton, NJ: Princeton University Press, 1974.

Moraes, Maria Célia Marcondes de. *Reformas de ensino, modernização administrada: a experiência de Francisco Campos: anos vinte e trinta.* Florianópolis, Santa Catarina, Brazil: UFSC, Centro de Ciências da Educação, Núcleo de Publicações, 2000.

Nava, Carmen. "Lessons in Patriotism and Good Citizenship: National Identity and Nationalism in Public Schools during the Vargas Administration, 1937–1945." *Luso-Brazilian Review* 35, no. 1 (1998): 39–63.

Cañas-Jerez Treaty, 1858

The Cañas-Jerez Treaty, 1858, defined the Nicaraguan-Costa Rican boundary along the San Juan River and granted each nation jurisdictional rights over the river. The dispute dates to the 1785 Spanish order that determined the administrative divisions for its New World colonies. When Central America declared its independence from Spain in 1821, the five nations (Costa Rica, El Salvador, Guatemala, Honduras, and Nicaragua) defined their territorial sovereignty upon the principle of *uti possidetis juris,* meaning that the colonial boundaries of each province would become the territorial demarcations of each state. Because these colonial boundaries lacked detail, and owing to the lack of topographical knowledge at the time, a number of Central American boundary disputes arose after 1821. The Costa Rican-Nicaraguan border problem was further complicated by the former's annexation of Nicoya and Guanacaste Provinces during the early 1820s, which became permanent after the collapse of the United Provinces of Central America in 1839. Nicaragua lost and Costa Rica gained approximately 5,000 square miles.

During the next generation Nicaragua and Costa Rica preoccupied themselves with the establishment of governments and governmental institutions and economic development, leaving little time to focus on foreign policy issues. The lack of communication and transportation between the capitals further exacerbated diplomatic relations. Not until 1858, when foreign interest in a transisthmian canal appeared as a possible reality, did the two governments attempt to settle their boundary problem. The result was the signing of the Cañas-Jerez Treaty on April 15, 1858.

According to the treaty Nicaragua relinquished its claim to the Nicoya and Guanacaste territories in return for complete sovereignty over the San Juan River to its southern bank but granted Costa Rica free and perpetual use of the river for international and intrastate commerce. The treaty also bound Nicaragua to consult with Costa Rica over any future canal rights on the San Juan River. In effect each side claimed it had treaty rights over control of the river, a fact that the Nicaraguans in particular had difficulty accepting. In 1888 U.S. President Grover Cleveland served as arbiter in the dispute and ruled the treaty provisions valid. The provisions again were reaffirmed in the 1907 Central American Treaty of Friendship.

In 1914 the United States and Nicaragua completed the Bryan-Chamorro Treaty. For $3 million Nicaragua granted the United States canal rights, using the San Juan River, naval posts in the Gulf of Fonseca, and the Corn Islands for security of the eastern terminus of the anticipated canal. Costa Rica and El Salvador took the case to the Central American Court of Justice, which in 1916 ruled the Bryan-Chamorro Treaty inoperative because it violated the 1858 Cañas-Jerez Treaty.

The opening of the Panama Canal in 1914 and the anticipated addition of new locks in 2012 to accommodate modern freighters and tankers put to rest international questions about the use of the San Juan River but not boundary disputes between Costa Rica and Nicaragua. In 1998, for example, the Nicaraguan government prohibited Costa Rican civil guards from patrolling the river with arms, and in 2006 Nicaragua challenged the Costa Rican use of the river to supply arms to its civil guard on the river's southern bank. The International Court at The Hague agreed to hear the case. On July 19, 2009, the court ruled that the Costa Rican government has the right, under the Cañas-Jerez Treaty, to use the San Juan River for commercial and recreational purposes, but that the *Tico* government cannot use the river to transport arms and munitions, including to local police stations on its river banks. The court also ruled that, while Nicaragua has treaty rights to administer the river's navigation, it does not have the right to charge fees to Costa Rican vessels for such action.

Finally some 5,000 impoverished people residing in approximately 1,000 square miles of swamp-infested waters on Costa Rica's northern border want to declare their independence as a new nation. The residents claim that the stone markers that delineate the Nicaraguan-Costa Rican border, according to the 1858 Cañas-Jerez Treaty, were located too far south than the proper location, a fact verified by aerial photography. These people assert that Costa Rica, by its inaction, no longer can claim the territory, and that they have no desire to return to Nicaraguan control, giving them sufficient justification to form a new country. Costa Rica took the matter to the International Court of Justice in December 2010. On March 3, 2011, the court requested that each side refrain from sending military troops into the disrupted territory and that Costa Rica dispatch to protect the environment. A resolution of the territorial dispute remains in diplomatic limbo.

See also *Bryan-Chamorro Treaty, 1915; Costa Rica-Nicaragua Boundary Dispute; Panama, Isthmian Canal Interests, Nineteenth Century; San Juan River Canal Project; Vanderbilt, Cornelius*

. . . . THOMAS M. LEONARD

References and Further Reading

Hill, Howard H. "The Nicaraguan Canal Idea to 1913." *Hispanic American Historical Review* 28, no. 2 (May 1948): 197–211.

Hudson, M. O. "The Central American Court of Justice." *The American Journal of International Law* 26, no. 4 (October 1932): 759–786.

Rogers, Tim, "A New Nation?" *Inside Costa Rica,* July 24, 2003, http://insidecostarica.com/specialreports/costarica_a_new_nation.htm.

Caperton, Admiral William B.

William Banks Caperton (1855–1941), who retired as United States Navy rear admiral in 1921, was a prominent figure in U.S.-Latin American diplomacy in the first decades of the twentieth century, especially during the first World War. After serving in the Spanish-American War he was involved in U.S. naval actions from 1914 to 1919 in Mexico, Haiti, the Dominican Republic, Nicaragua, Brazil, Uruguay, and Argentina. His command was especially instrumental in the building of U.S. relations with Brazil and Uruguay during the period from 1917 to 1919, when close alliance with those countries was vital to U.S. war interests in the Atlantic.

Caperton graduated from the United States Naval Academy in 1875, whereupon he began a naval career that involved his first five years at sea in the Atlantic and then numerous posts within naval administration. Between posts Caperton also returned to the Naval War College for further instruction. His first involvement in Latin America came with his service on the USS *Marietta* during and after the Spanish-American War (1898). After having served in various posts within the United States and being promoted to rear admiral in 1913, Caperton began his naval command in Latin America in 1914 after assuming command of the Cruiser Squadron, Atlantic Fleet. Under this charge he commanded the U.S. naval forces of Vera Cruz, Mexico, in 1915 and then commanded the force that intervened in Haiti in 1915. There he was given power to erect a government under the supervision and control of U.S. Naval and Marine Corps personnel, and he served as acting ruler of that government for almost a year, despite the fact that he did not speak French. Due to his experience and successes in Haiti, Admiral Caperton was called to command the naval forces intervening in the neighboring country of Santo Domingo (current-day Dominican Republic) in mid-1916, where he briefly commanded the intervention before it was turned over to more permanent occupying forces. Upon being relieved of command in Santo Domingo, Caperton served as commander in chief of the Pacific Fleet and was called to Nicaragua in late 1916 when the U.S. minister there called for aid due to upcoming elections that threatened to overthrow the U.S.-backed government of Adolfo Díaz.

Caperton's most important contributions to U.S.-Latin American relations came with his service in the southern Atlantic. With official U.S. entry into World War I, Caperton commanded the fleet that patrolled the eastern coast of South America from aboard the flagship USS *Pittsburgh.* His mission there was twofold, both to seek out and deter German naval raiding forces and to build good will with South American countries. As a commanding officer who emphasized sensitivity to cultural differences and worked closely with civilian diplomats, he was highly influential in the shift of Brazilian diplomacy toward the United States. Caperton arrived in Brazil just after that country revoked its neutrality in World War I in 1917 under President Wenceslau Braz, after Germany's unrestricted submarine warfare had caused damage to Brazilian shipping. Based from Bahia and Rio de Janeiro in Brazil throughout 1917, where he oversaw cultural exchange missions including a Fourth of July celebration in Brazilian streets, Caperton also carried out diplomatic missions to Uruguay and Argentina. In addition to building friendly relations with Brazil and Uruguay, diplomacy to Argentina was considered vital due to Argentina's continued neutrality and unsure future under President Hipólito Irigoyen. Irigoyen was negotiating with the German government, but he was concerned about unrestricted submarine warfare. Caperton's diplomatic missions, meant to possibly influence Argentina, were also important in relieving Brazilian and Uruguayan fears of potential Argentine expansionism. Just before the war's end with the Treaty of Versailles in November of 1918, U.S. President Woodrow Wilson named Caperton special representative to attend the inauguration of the new Brazilian president, Rodrigues Alves. The next year he was sent as a special naval delegate to the inauguration of Uruguayan President Baltasar Brun, previous minister of foreign affairs and a close friend of Caperton's.

At the end of his active career Caperton served as a witness on the U.S. Senate inquiry into the occupation and administration of Haiti and Santo Domingo in 1920. He retired from active naval duty in November of 1921 heavily decorated and returned home to Rhode Island. Among his medals awarded by the U.S. Navy were the Order of the Bust of Bolívar (Third Class) by the government of Venezuela and the National Order of the Southern Cross by the government of Brazil. He died in December, 1941, at the naval hospital in Newport, Rhode Island.

See also *Guillaume Sam, Vilbrun; Mexican Revolution, 1911–1917, U.S. Policy toward; United States, circum-Caribbean Interventions, 1900–1934: Dominican Republic; United States, circum-Caribbean Interventions, 1900–1934: Haiti*

. . . . .ELLEN D. TILLMAN

References and Further Reading

Burns, E. Bradford. *The Unwritten Alliance: Rio-Branco and Brazilian-American Relations.* New York: Columbia University Press, 1966.

Healy, David. "Admiral William B. Caperton and United States Naval Diplomacy in South America, 1917–1919." *Journal of Latin American Studies* 8, no. 2 (November 1976): 297–323.

Heaton, Dean R. *Four Stars: The Super Stars of United States Military History.* Baltimore, MD: Gateway Press, 1995.

McCormick, Thomas J., and Walter LaFeber. *Behind the Throne: Servants of Power to Imperial Presidents, 1898–1968.* Madison: University of Wisconsin Press, 1993.

Caracas Conference

(**See** *Tenth International Conference of American States, Caracas, 1954)*

Cardenal Martínez, Reverend Ernesto

Renowned poet, revolutionary, and Sandinista spokesman, the Reverend Ernesto Cardenal Martínez (1925–) was born to upper-class parents in Granada, Nicaragua, in 1925. Educated at the Universidad Nacional Autónoma of Mexico (UNAM) in Mexico City (1942–1946) and Columbia University in New York City (1947–1949), Cardenal did not begin to publish poetry or become active politically until his early thirties. It was at that time that he also experienced a religious conversion and began to speak out against the U.S.-backed dictator of Nicaragua, Anastasio Somoza García.

His first canonical work, *Epigramas* (1961), which he began writing in the 1950s, conflates the extremes of ecstasy and pain associated with his love for two women with his political involvement. After his religious conversion in 1956 he gave up the search for a woman's love and entered the Trappist Monastery in Gethsemani, Kentucky, where he studied for two years under poet/monk Thomas Merton. During this period of study and meditation he adopted Merton's philosophy of nonviolence and kept a diary that formed the basis for a book of poems, *Gethsemaní, Ky.* (1960), as well as a book of reflections published some ten years later as *Vida en el amor* (Life in Love, 1970; translated as *To Live Is to Love,* 1972). He left the monastery in 1959 for health reasons but continued to train for the ministry in Mexico and later in Colombia. He was finally ordained as a priest in Granada, Nicaragua, in 1965. During this period he began one of his most famous poems, finally published in 1965, *Oración por Marilyn Monroe y otros poemas* (translated as *Marilyn Monroe, and Other Poems,* 1975), in which he decries the evils of capitalism using Marilyn Monroe as the symbolic victim of U.S. consumerism.

Cardenal has been prominent in promoting the controversial combination of political activism and Catholicism known as liberation theology. Based on the communist teachings of the early church and following the suggestion of his mentor Thomas Merton, he founded a utopian Christian commune in 1966 on an island in Lake Nicaragua named Our Lady of Solentiname, which later became an artists' colony. Cardenal's work, *El evangelio de Solentiname* (1975, 1977; translated as *The Gospel in Solentiname,* 1976–1982) is a product of this eleven-year experience. As Cardenal became increasingly involved with the Sandinista National Liberation Front (FSLN), he broke with Merton's philosophy of nonviolence, concluding that the fight against dictatorship in Nicaragua justified the use of force for self-defense. After 1976 his name became synonymous with the Sandinista guerrillas as he helped rouse popular support for the revolutionary army which ousted Somoza and claimed a victory for socialism in 1979.

For the following eight years until his resignation in 1988, Cardenal served as minister of culture under the Sandinista government. When Pope John Paul II visited Nicaragua in 1983, he openly scolded Cardenal for disobeying his directive to resign his governmental post in a now famous picture showing Cardenal kneeling before him. During his period in government Cardenal was active in promoting poetry workshops and other cultural initiatives throughout the country among all socioeconomic classes. Despite this work, which occupied most of his time, Cardenal continued to write essays, edit anthologies of Nicaraguan poetry, and publish his own poetic work. In fact, what some critics have referred to as his magnum opus, *Cántico cósmico* (1989; translated as *Cosmic Canticle,* 1993), was written during the postrevolutionary years. His aesthetic approach to poetry, known as "Exteriorism," was based on a type of linguistic collage that integrated quotations, newspaper clippings, historical excerpts, and cinematic cuts with the sharp and often ironic subjective commentaries of the poet himself. Cardenal's aesthetic views, however, became the focal point for increased tensions and controversy among the various factions within the Sandinista government, prefiguring the Sandinista defeat in the presidential elections of 1990.

With Cardenal's resignation, the ministry of culture was dissolved, and as the Sandinista government collapsed, Cardenal's dreams of a socialist society for Nicaragua were dashed. In January 1995 Cardenal renounced his membership in the FSLN, citing human rights violations and increasing internal corruption. His most recent publication is a selection of poems titled *Versos del pluriverso* (2005; translated as *Pluriverse: New and Selected Poems,* 2009). The text, edited by Jonathan Cohen, includes translations by Cardenal's Trappist mentor Thomas Merton. He has twice been nominated for the Nobel Prize in Literature, a testimony to the quality of his work.

Today Cardenal travels all over the world reading his poetry and serving as a kind of international ambassador for peace. American poet Robert Bly has commented that Cardenal's poetry "unites political ugliness and the beauty of imaginative vision" (Hartman 1998).

See also *Liberation Theology; Sandinista National Liberation Front (FSLN) (Nicaragua); Somoza Debayle, Anastasio; Somoza García, Anastasio*

. . . . ANN B. GONZÁLEZ

SELECTED WORKS

Cántico cósmico. Managua: Editorial Nueva Nicaragua, 1989. Translated by Jonathan Lyons as *Cosmic Canticle*. Willimantic, CT: Curbstone, 1993.

Epigramas. Mexico City: Universidad Nacional Autónoma de México, 1961.

Hartman, Steven. "Ernesto Cardenal." *Writer's Online Magazine* 3, no. 1 (Fall 1998). www.albany.edu/writers-inst/webpages4/archives/olv3n1.html#cardenal.

Oración por Marilyn Monroe y otros poemas. Medellín: La Tertulia, 1965. Translated by Robert Pring-Mill as *Marilyn Monroe, and Other Poems*. London: Search Press, 1975.

Versos del pluriverso. Madrid, Spain: Trotta, 2005. Edited by Jonathan Cohen and translated by Mireya Jaimes-Freyre, John Lyons, Thomas Merton, Robert Pring-Mill, Kenneth Rexroth, Donald D. Walsh, and the editor as *Pluriverse: New and Selected Poems*. New York: New Directions, 2009.

REFERENCES AND FURTHER READING

Dawes, Greg. "Ernesto Cardenal." In *Dictionary of Literary Biography, Volume 290: Modern Spanish American Poets, Second Series*. A Bruccoli Clark Layman Book. Edited by María A. Salgado, University of North Carolina at Chapel Hill, 42–55. Farmington Hills, MI: Gale, 2004.

Dawes, Greg. *Aesthetics and Revolution: Nicaraguan Poetry, 1979–1990*. Minneapolis: University of Minnesota Press, 1993, 64–108.

Cárdenas del Río, Lázaro

General Lázaro Cárdenas del Río (1895–1970) is widely seen as the personification of the Mexican Revolution. Born in Jiquilpán, Michoacán state, on May 21, 1895, he joined the Mexican revolutionaries in 1913 and in 1934 became president of Mexico.

Aware that the rural masses were dissatisfied with the slow progress of the revolution, he initiated a land redistribution program. During his presidency over 47 million acres were distributed, mostly in the form of *ejidos* (communal lands). He also concentrated on bringing progress to rural Mexico and as a result, "Indian" (indigenous) peasants became integrated into the national life of Mexico for the first time in history. Also concerned with workers' welfare, Cárdenas was instrumental in establishing the *Confederación de Trabajadores Mexicanos* (Confederation of Mexican Workers or CTM) in 1936. The CTM began a campaign for higher wages and better working conditions. Since labor unions always knew that they could count on Cárdenas's support, 18,000 oil workers struck for higher wages and a series of concessions against fourteen American and British-Dutch-owned oil companies in May 1937.

The Cárdenas administration turned over the dispute to the Industrial Arbitration Board. On December 18, 1937, the board ruled that the oil companies were to grant the workers an approximate 26,300,000 pesos as compensation. The oil companies charged the board with collusion and turned their case to the Mexican Supreme Court. On March 1, 1938, the Supreme Court ruled in favor of the workers and set March 7 as the date for the compensation payment. Cárdenas was hopeful that a compromise would be reached, but the oil companies refused. On March 18, 1938, Cárdenas—who already had expropriated foreign mining and railroad interests—decided to strike at the oil companies. Using Article 27 of the Mexican Constitution, which declared that all subsoil rights belong to the state, he expropriated the oil companies, overturning the compromise with the United States and the oil companies that had been negotiated when the constitution was first ratified.

Cárdenas's action made him a popular hero in Mexico, but the oil companies were not about to surrender. The British government not only broke diplomatic relations with Mexico, but it also asked the American government for military intervention. At first, President Franklin D. Roosevelt's administration engaged in a war of words with Mexico, and Treasury Secretary Henry Morgenthau refused to enter into an agreement for the purchase of Mexican silver.

Fortunately for Cárdenas and Roosevelt, their respective ambassadors played a prominent role in defusing the crisis. Mexican Ambassador Castillo Nágera kept reminding the American president of his much heralded Good Neighbor policy by which he pledged not to resort to military intervention in Latin America. He also stressed that Mexico had agreed to compensate the oil companies. American Ambassador Josephus Daniels, who ironically had been secretary of the Navy during the American occupation of Veracruz in 1913, assured Cárdenas that the United States intended to be a good neighbor and that a solution was imminent.

During negotiations the oil companies continued to demand American military intervention, but the Roosevelt administration ignored their pleas. Cárdenas, for his part, assured the United States that the oil companies would be compensated but at the amount established by his government. Although compensation did not occur during Cárdenas's presidency, his successor, Manuel Ávila Camacho, in 1942, paid $24,000,000 in compensation to the oil companies, much less than the $450,000,000 that they were seeking. Despite acceptance of the Mexican compensation, the oil companies were out to seek revenge, for they conducted a boycott of PEMEX, the Mexican state-owned oil company. The boycott—which lasted more than a quarter century—prevented Mexico from buying much-needed equipment and technology. Additionally the oil companies refused to buy and refine Mexican oil.

Cárdenas's foreign policy was consistent with his principles. He incurred the wrath of Soviet dictator Joseph Stalin for granting asylum to his nemesis, Leon Trotsky. Additionally he was an active supporter of the Spanish Republic during the Spanish Civil War. Mexico's delegation at the League of Nations was one of the first to condemn the Italian invasion of Ethiopia. Subsequently he condemned the Nazi invasion of the Low Countries and France.

Contrary to his detractors who claimed he would perpetuate himself in power, he left office when his term expired in 1940. After his presidency, he became a senior figure in

Mexico's ruling Partido Revolucionario Institucional (PRI), which controlled the country for the remainder of his lifetime. On October 19, 1970, Lázaro Cárdenas, one of the most beloved figures in Mexican modern history, died.

See also *Ávila Camacho, Manuel; Calles, Plutarco Elías; Daniels, Josephus; Mexico, U.S. Relations with; Oil, Expropriation of Foreign Companies*

. . . . JOSÉ B. FERNÁNDEZ

References and Further Reading

Grayson, George W. *The Politics of Mexican Oil.* Pittsburgh, PA: University of Pittsburgh Press, 1980.

Krauze, Enrique. *General misionero: Lázaro Cárdenas.* Ciudad México: Fondo de Cultura Económica, 1987.

Meyer, Michael C., and William L. Sherman. *The Course of Mexican History.* New York: Oxford University Press, 1991.

Cardoso, Fernando Henrique

Fernando Henrique Cardoso (1931–) was born in his grandmother's house in Rio de Janeiro on July 18, 1931, and grew up in São Paulo, Brazil. Cardoso served two terms as Brazil's president from January 1, 1995, to January 1, 2003, winning both elections with an absolute majority.

Cardoso received his PhD from the University of São Paulo in sociology and during the 1960s emerged as an influential intellectual in the analysis of social changes, especially in Latin America, international development, dependency, democracy, and state reform. With the publication of his seminal work, *Dependency and Development in Latin America* (1969), Cardoso established his reputation as a world-class sociologist. He was an ardent critic of Brazil's bureaucratic authoritarianism, which came to power after the Brazilian military ousted the democratically elected president João Goulart in 1964 and remained in power until democracy resumed in 1985. Although Cardoso is the son and grandson of Brazilian generals, his view of the authoritarian rule was shaped by his arrest and interrogation by Brazilian security forces in addition to the bombing of his research institute at the University of São Paulo. To escape his persecutors and the military's iron hand, Cardoso spent the 1970s and early 1980s living and teaching in the United States, France, and Chile, before returning to Brazil.

In 1979 Cardoso returned to Brazil after having received amnesty, which allowed the return of political exiles. Cardoso, one of the founding fathers of the Brazilian Social Democratic Party (PSDB), was then elected São Paulo's senator in 1982. As a senator Cardoso became a driving force behind the enactment of the 1988 constitution, which has been heralded as one of the most liberal constitutions in Brazilian history. In September of 1992 the Brazilian Chamber of Deputies overwhelmingly voted for the impeachment of Brazilian President Fernando Collor de Mello, the young and previously unknown former governor from the poor northeastern state of Alagoas, following allegations of corruption. Rather than face a full impeachment and the possibility of losing all of his political rights, Collor de Mello resigned and his vice president, Itamar Franco, assumed the presidency.

During the Franco administration inflation soared to an unprecedented annual rate of 2,490 percent in 1993. Franco recalled Cardoso from his post as Brazilian foreign minister to become, in 1994, his finance minister. Cardoso had served only six months as Brazilian foreign minister, from 1992 to 1993. During his short stay as the head of the Minister of Foreign Relations, Cardoso, the multicultural intellectual sociologist, was able to bring Brazil into the international spotlight through the formation of the Common Market of the South (MERCOSUR) and the easing of tensions between Argentina and Brazil, which had initiated under the government of José Sarney.

Upon assuming the position as minister of finance, Cardoso's first goal was to bring Brazil's rate of inflation under control. Cardoso launched the "Real Plan," an anti-inflation program which within two years brought Brazil's rampant rate of inflation under control. Riding on the coattail of his "Real Plan" success by taming Brazil's hyperinflation, Cardoso announced his intentions to run for the presidency of Brazil. Cardoso was elected president in 1994 in a landslide victory against his opponent, Luis Inacio "Lula" da Silva, Brazil's current leftist president. During his first term in office Cardoso was able to keep Brazil's inflation under control and the Brazilian *real,* Brazil's new currency introduced by Cardoso, remained stable. Cardoso also introduced a privatization program and economic modernization, both of which have been criticized for their unexpected manifestations of social exclusion.

Meanwhile, in the years since Cardoso's presidency, MERCOSUR (or MERCOSUL) has grown in strength. MERCOSUR is an economic association among Brazil, Argentina, Paraguay, and Uruguay, established in 1991 with the signing of the Treaty of Asuncion, which envisioned the creation of a free-trade zone that would eventually evolve into a full-fledged "common market" along the lines of the European Union. Under the MERCOSUL Treaty, Brazil's biggest rival in Latin America, Argentina, becomes an essential partner in Brazil's foreign policy to create a stronger Latin America vis-à-vis the United States and the rest of the world. In October 2003 Argentina and Brazil signed the "Buenos Aires Consensus." This important document signed between Presidents da Silva and Néstor Kirchner (Cardoso's successor) reflects the common aspiration for economic growth with social justice and manifests the determination to transform the MERCOSUL trading block into a catalyst for building a better future for Latin America. The "Buenos Aires Consensus," according to Greider and Rapoza (2003), is a "proposed alternative to the much-despised 'Washington Consensus,' which has straitjacketed developing economies with its harsh economic rules." Upon the end of his term as president, Fernando Henrique Cardoso has been appointed a special assistant to former UN Secretary Kofi Aman. Cardoso remains active in Brazil's politics.

See also *Dependency Theory and Latin America; Economic Commission for Latin America and the Caribbean (CEPAL); Southern Common Market (MERCOSUR)*

. . . . JOSÉ DE ARIMATÉIA DA CRUZ

REFERENCES AND FURTHER READING

Font, Mauricio A., ed. Charting A New Course: The Politics of Globalization and Social Transformation: Fernando Henrique Cardoso. New York: Rowman & Littlefield, 2001.

Goertzel, Ted G. Fernando Henrique Cardoso e a Reconstrução da Democracia no Brasil [Fernando Henrique Cardoso and the Reconstruction of Democracy in Brazil]. São Paulo, Brazil: Editora Saraiva.

Greider, William, and Kenneth Rapoza, "Lula Raises the Stakes," *The Nation*, December 1, 2003, www.thenation.com/article/lula-raises.

Smith, William C., and Nizar Messari. "Democracy and Reform in Cardoso's Brazil: Caught Between Clientelism and Global Markets?" *The North-South Agenda*. Papers, 33, September 1998.

Carías Andino, Tiburcio

Born in Tegucigalpa, the Honduran capital, Tiburcio Carias Andino (1876–1969) was raised in the small hamlet of Zambrano in the central part of the country. After a secondary school education he entered the Central University and earned a law degree. He soon became engaged in Liberal party politics following his father, General Calixto Carias' footsteps, in local conflicts. Joining a militia he fought on behalf of liberal causes, serving in several administrative posts throughout Honduras until 1903, when he joined Manuel Bonilla (President 1903-1907) and others to found the National party.

The new organization sought a more broadly based movement than the personalistic and factional groups common at the time. Its platform called for economic progress, building the country's infrastructure, and organizing segments of society—such as farmers, students, business groups—under the direction and supervision of the state. It would in time look similar to Mexico's revolutionary party, the PRI (Revolutionary Institutional Party), with several corporate entities forming its political base.

By 1923, as a National party leader, Carias organized an armed resistance to Rafael Lopez Guiterrez (President 1920–1924), who wanted to continue in office. Carias ran for president, winning a plurality but lacking a required majority. The armed conflict between liberals and nationalists prompted U.S. Secretary of State Charles Evans Hughes to dispatch an envoy and U. S. Marines to protect U.S. banana companies and to reach a settlement in the dispute. Carias accepted the creation of a provisional government led by Jose Vicente Tosta, thereby withdrawing as a presidential candidate.

Between 1924 and 1932 Carias devoted his time and effort organizing the National party in all parts of Honduras and serving in the national legislature. Running again for president in 1928, he was defeated by liberal Mejia Colindres. Later he defended incumbent Colindres (President 1928–1932) from dissident liberals to assure a fair election in 1932. Obtaining arms from El Salvador and hiring pilots to conduct tactical aerial operations throughout Honduras, he defeated liberal candidate Angel Zuñiga Huete by 20,000 votes and began the longest period of executive rule in Honduran history.

Carias's term as president started during a global depression. Banana exports from U.S.-owned companies in Honduras dropped dramatically. Further the Panama disease (a fungus in banana plantations) destroyed most of the crops. Carias tackled the country's economic woes with cuts in government salaries and a hefty loan of $300,000 from the New Orleans Bank and Trust Company, as well as a conservative fiscal program. He introduced exchange controls, pushed Congress to enact tariffs to regulate duties on imports, and negotiated a reciprocal trade agreement with the United States. The opposition Liberal party was intimidated by press censorship and the exile of its partisans. Overall, Carias's goal was peace for the country and order in the manner of governance.

In 1936, the end of his first term, Carias, like other Latin American presidents, sought *continuismo,* extending one's office beyond the legal time limit. He successfully called for a constituent assembly to repeal the constitution and to write a new constitution allowing him to run for president again. In effect Carias was allowed to run again in 1936 when his term was extended to 1943. The following year he promised not to run again in 1948.

Tiburcio Carias adhered to three basic foreign policy objectives throughout his long term in office. His first objective was to keep peace with his four Central American neighbors: Guatemala, El Salvador, Nicaragua, and Costa Rica. His second objective was to develop and carefully maintain close relations with the United States. His third objective was to participate in the international conference system in the Americas. Each of these goals reflected the realities Honduras faced at home and abroad. Carias needed political stability at home, assured by nonintervention from his neighbors and economic assistance from Washington. He became an unabashed U.S. ally during the second World War and early years of the Cold War. Moreover he maintained cordial relations throughout his term with neighboring dictators, Jorge Ubico of Guatemala, Maximiliano Hernandez Martinez of El Salvador, and Anastacio Somoza of Nicaragua.

The defeat of the Axis power in World War II discredited dictators in Latin America, and in 1944, Carias faced student and labor unrest demanding greater freedom. With the ouster of Guatemala's Jorge Ubico and El Salvador's Maximiliano Hernandez Martinez in 1944, Carias underwent increasing pressure to step down in 1948. Although Washington and Carias had particularly close ties, North American diplomats in Honduras urged him to bring his sixteen-year rule to an end. Mounting street demonstrations opposing the Carias dictatorship further convinced the president to depart, but he selected as the National party candidate his longtime friend and ally, Minister of Defense Manual Galvez (1949–1954), who defeated the liberal leader, Angel Zuniga Huete.

Although out of office, Carias retained his leadership of the National party until 1963. In 1954 Carias ran for president again as head of one two factions within the National party. The other, MNR (Nationalist Reformist Movement), was headed by Abraham Williams, Carias's longtime vice president. Although Carias won the most votes of the two National party contenders, he lost the election to the Liberal party candidate, Ramon Villeda Morales.

Tiburcio Carias remained visible as a political figure until his death in 1969. He was more respected than loved. His chief legacies were ending the country's long-standing civil wars and creating a stable government. By controlling a party and a professional military his dictatorial rule provided a very limited free press and little political freedom. He believed that his sixteen years as president was the embodiment of what the people wanted, namely peace and order.

See also *Amapala Agreement, 1923; Honduras, U.S. Relations with*

. . . . THOMAS J. DODD

References and Further Reading

Argueta, Mario. *Tiburcio Carias; Autonomia de Una Epoca, 1923–1948.* Tegucigalpa, Honduras: Editorial Guaymuras, 1989.
Dodd, Thomas. *Tiburcio Carias: Portrait of a Honduran Political Leader.* Baton Rouge: Louisiana State University Press, 2005.
Morris, James. *Caudillo Politics and Military Rulers.* Boulder, CO: Westview Press, 1984.
Rudolph, James, ed. *Honduras: A Country Study.* Washington, DC: Foreign Area Studies, 1984.
Stokes, William. *Honduras: An Area Study in Government.* Madison, University of Wisconsin Press, 1950.

Caribbean, German U-boat Threat, World War II

German U-boats never did irreparable damage to the Allied cause during World War II, but they were a powerful threat to the integrity of Allied shipping and communications, especially in the Caribbean in 1942. Continued U-boat attacks also meant the looming possibility of more devastating damage, the fear of which was amplified on the Allied side by memories of U-boat successes in World War I. Furthermore U-boat attacks on shipping in the Caribbean did real damage to ports and facilities in countries such as Trinidad and Tobago, Venezuela, and Panama, adding to the psychological threat they posed to Allied forces and morale.

Despite having concluded treaties with Great Britain in the 1930s that allowed German naval rebuilding, Germany began the war in 1939 with a navy much less powerful and much less technologically advanced than the British Royal Navy. At first believing that England would not join the war, Hitler did not authorize a rapid ship-building program until the late 1930s, when relations with England were clearly breaking down. The German navy therefore still lagged in development in September of 1939, when England declared war in response to the German offensive on the continent. German U-Boat Commander Admiral Karl Doenitz was directed to work with the German air force (Luftwaffe) to carry out a war of attrition against England—to break down the will of the people to fight by attacking merchant ships and communication lines. For this reason the German naval battle quickly focused on submarine warfare, the only realistic way to fight the superior British navy. This strategy was at first successful, heavily damaging English imports, until the United States entered the war in December of 1941, which brought with it the declaration of war against Germany by most Central American and Caribbean governments. With U.S. entry, the German navy—which had been instructed to avoid tension with neutral shipping—had to rapidly spread itself out to fight across the Atlantic.

Despite the fact that Doenitz at first found a vulnerable U.S. coastline unprepared for submarine warfare, the United States, strongly backed by its Latin American allies, was able to respond quickly. Within months German U-boat successes had dropped off. Great Britain and the United States responded to U-boat threats with improvements in convoys and technology, including radar advances for which Germany was not prepared. Admiral Doenitz shifted his U-boats from the northeast coast of the United States to the mid-Atlantic and then into the waters of the Caribbean and the Gulf of Mexico. In the Caribbean Doenitz found Allied forces that were much less prepared for submarine warfare and natural land features that were much more suitable to submarine warfare. The Caribbean was well beyond the efficient reach of some contemporary German U-boats, however, and the German navy had to develop innovative and extensive answers to the problem of distance. It did so by creating submarine refueling stations along the way to allow even the smaller—and therefore more maneuverable—U-boats longer duration in Caribbean waters. These efforts paid off in the short run, as the Allied reliance on oil shipping through the Caribbean gave German U-boats abundant targets, with predictable paths that were therefore easy to locate in strategic passages—including the Panama Canal, which was at the time unprepared for submarine warfare.

The result was near catastrophe for Allied shipping and morale in the spring of 1942, with Doenitz's U-boats sinking four hundred merchant ships to fewer than twenty U-boats lost. Damage was such that some merchant and supply ships' crews refused to leave port without strong convoy protection, ships were sunken within harbors throughout the Caribbean (one German U-boat captain was even so daring as to set fire to an oil refinery in Aruba after sinking a number of ships), and the U.S. government began to seriously consider alternate forms for transporting oil. But the high point of German U-boat attacks in the Caribbean lasted less than a year, and by 1943 they had ended. A number of factors contributed to this change: One was that, despite U-boat successes in sinking merchant ships, Germany could not replace lost ships at the rate the U.S. Navy was growing. Another was that U-boats were called to other theaters. The quick Allied response to the U-boat threat, however, was also instrumental. Even as early as 1940, the British and U.S. governments and militaries had begun to work closely together to combat the German U-boat threat, and as of 1942 they enjoyed increasing support from Caribbean-region governments, which allowed more bases for Allied naval forces. It was the result of this early cooperation and its effectiveness that had caused Doenitz to move his forces so far south in the first place. While German naval technology in the area of submarine warfare remained relatively stagnant, the Allies developed advances in sonar, radar, magnetic mines, and other areas during these years of naval struggle in the Atlantic and the Caribbean, giving them a growing advantage in individual battles that supplemented the larger size of the Allied naval forces.

U.S. technological cooperation with Great Britain in the development of antisubmarine technology even before it entered the war was part of negotiations that also gave the United States more bases for training in the Caribbean. From these and other U.S. bases throughout the Caribbean, the United States was able to carry out an effective antisubmarine campaign—including through the use of its own submarines—and halt the frequent sinking of Allied merchant ships and oil tankers. Even where Allied shipping lacked sufficient convoys to protect it from submarine attacks, by 1943 it had radar advanced enough to allow it to detect and avoid German U-boats. After the initial shock of lack of preparedness for battle against German U-boats, especially in the Caribbean, German attacks on Allied shipping in the area—and the protection that the U.S. could provide against them—actually led to a more anti-German sentiment in many Latin American countries that had not yet officially joined the Allied powers. When U-boats moved from the Caribbean to other areas in 1943, a similar effect was seen down the coast of South America, where German attacks on neutral shipping tilted some neutral Latin American countries to the side of the Allies.

See also *English-Speaking Caribbean, U.S. Relations with; Lend-Lease Program, World War II; Nazi Activities in Latin America, World War II*

. . . . .ELLEN D. TILLMAN

References and Further Reading

Blair, Clay. *Hitler's U-Boat War: The Hunters, 1939–1942*. New York: Random House, 1996.

Doenitz, Karl. *Memoirs: Ten Years and Twenty Days*. Bonn, Germany: Athenaum Verlag Junker and Duennhaupt, 1958.

Hoyt, Edwin P. *The Death of the U-Boats*. New York: McGraw-Hill, 1988.

Kelshall, Gaylord T. *The U-Boat War in the Caribbean*. Trinidad and Tobago: Paria, 1988.

Morison, Samuel Eliot. *History of United States Naval Operations in World War II*. Boston: Little, Brown, 1947.

Rohwer, Jurgen. *Axis Submarine Successes of World War Two: German, Italian and Japanese Submarine Successes, 1939–1945*. Translated by John A. Broadwin. Annapolis, MD: Naval Institute Press, 1999.

Caribbean Basin Initiative (CBI)

The Caribbean Basin Initiative (CBI) refers collectively to several U.S. legislative acts designed to tighten economic ties between America and selected nations in the region. The sequence to date has included the Caribbean Basin Economic Recovery Act of 1983 (CBERA), followed by the Caribbean Basin Economic Recovery Expansion Act of 1990 (CBERA Expansion Act), the U.S.-Caribbean Basin Trade Partnership Act of 2000 (CBTPA), certain provisions of the Trade Act of 2002, and the Hemispheric Opportunities through Partnership Encouragement Act of 2006 (HOPE).

GENESIS AND MEMBERSHIP

The concept of the CBI originated with Jamaican Prime Minister Edward Seaga, who argued that economic development and democratization in the region would best be fostered through enhanced economic opportunities. President Reagan seized on the idea after the 1983 invasion of Granada by the United States and Eastern Caribbean States (OECS). The prospect of regional destabilization in the aftermath of Maurice Bishop's assassination in Granada, Nicaragua's Sandinista regime, El Salvador's civil war, and the like, caused the Caribbean region to become a major U.S. policy concern. In particular the innovative structure of the CBI was a response to U.S. domestic concerns. The small-government rhetoric of the Reagan years made handouts, while never popular, even less so. By tying enhanced economic growth, stability, and democratization to greater opportunities for U.S. firms, the CBI offered a politically feasible delivery environment for foreign assistance. Fears of regional instability that could generate a large influx of refugees also played a role in the passage of the legislation.

The CBI provides for preferential access to the U.S. market for member countries. Although duty-free importation of many manufactured products had already existed through the Generalized System of Preferences, the CBI expanded that list and also increased the amount of products that could enter the United States duty-free. The CBI provided incentives for foreign direct investment (FDI) by U.S. corporations into the region. Although the CBI increased U.S. foreign aid to member nations, it also represented a departure from American aid-based foreign policy to the new "trade, not aid" perspective. Direct aid was targeted at long-term economic growth through programs designed to stimulate private-sector growth. The Caribbean Trade and Competitiveness Program, for example, funded private-sector growth and job creation in the hospitality, tourism, information, and communication technology sectors. New skills training programs and local chambers of commerce were created to provide a basis for competitiveness. Export financing assistance allowed regional firms to enter the export market. Trade missions were also supported, as were health programs, including HIV/AIDS treatment and prevention.

The CBI currently includes the following nineteen countries from Central America and the Caribbean: Antigua and Barbuda, Aruba, Bahamas, Barbados, Belize, British Virgin Islands, Costa Rica, Dominica, Grenada, Guyana, Haiti, Jamaica, Montserrat, the Netherlands Antilles, Panama, St. Kitts and Nevis, St. Lucia, St. Vincent and the Grenadines, and Trinidad and Tobago. Additional countries may be included in the agreement via U.S. presidential designation. However accession countries must have U.S. counternarcotics certification and must also meet criteria related to international standards for workers' rights, transparency, and nondiscrimination in government procurement, protection of intellectual property, and so forth. The president may remove a country from the CBI if that country no longer meets those criteria, which are reviewed annually by the Office of the U.S. Trade Representative.

IMPACT

The results of the CBI have been mixed. On the one hand industry growth has clearly been fostered. Not only have traditional export sectors benefited, but also new manufacturing facilities, notably for electronics and energy and related chemical products, have developed. Economic diversification has reduced the percentage of CBI exports to the United States that are traditional agricultural products from over 50 percent in 1983 to just 37 percent in 2006. Exports from CBI nations to the United States have tripled since the CBI's inception, although CBI members' share of U.S. imports continues to fall. On the other hand the benefits of the CBI do not appear to be evenly distributed across member countries, with larger economies—such as the Dominican Republic, Jamaica, and Trinidad and Tobago—having experienced the most impact.

The impact of the CBI has been diluted by more recent economic events. First among those is the North American Free Trade Agreement (NAFTA), which granted Mexico benefits on par with those enjoyed by the CBI countries. Mexico's sheer relative size provided its firms with economies of scale that CBI nations simply could not match. In addition the size and increasing prosperity of the Mexican market made it a substantially more desirable foreign direct investment opportunity for U.S. corporations than the CBI members. Second, decreasing U.S. quotas on agricultural imports, particularly sugar, have also hurt most CBI nations, while only a few have spawned new manufacturing jobs related to the CBI. Third, the rise of the Pacific Rim countries as competitors in traditional sectors such as textiles has hurt Caribbean nations considerably. Caribbean firms must find ways to use their geographic proximity to the U.S. market and the resultant delivery time advantages to leverage their exports. Even so the effects of the recent Central American-Dominican Republic Free Trade Agreement (CAFTA-DR), which provides duty-free access to the United States for countries whose exports match those of CBI countries quite closely, will also mitigate the benefits of the CBI. CBI countries that join CAFTA-DR will lose CBERA and CBTPA status, as happened to El Salvador, Guatemala, Honduras, and Nicaragua, which exited the CBI in 2006, and the Dominican Republic in 2007.

Perhaps the most enduring benefit to Caribbean nations from the CBI has been to raise the region's profile for U.S. policymakers, as the CBI provides both a reminder of the region's needs and a forum for periodic discussions with high-level U.S. officials. The CBI's knock-on effects are evident from the passage of the aforementioned acts of 1990 and 2000, preventing the original CBI legislation from being a one-shot enhancement. More surprisingly Caribbean nations also benefited from inclusion in the Africa Growth and Development Act of 2001, making them eligible for a large pool of assistance.

See also *Caribbean Basin Partnership Act, 2000 (United States); Caribbean Community Common Market (CARICOM); Central American-Dominican Republic Free Trade Agreement, 2004 (CAFTA-DR); Economic Commission for Latin America and Caribbean (CEPAL); Enterprise for the Americas Initiative; Offshore Assembly: "807 Industries"*

. . . . JEFFREY W. STEAGALL

References and Further Reading

Barry, Tom, Beth Wood, and Deb Preusch. *The Other Side of Paradise: Foreign Control in the Caribbean.* New York: Grove Press, 1984.

Deere, Carmen Diana, coord. *In the Shadow of the Sun: Caribbean Development Alternatives and U.S. Policy.* Boulder, CO: Westview Press, 1990.

Johnson, Peter. "Caribbean Basin Initiative: A Positive Departure." *Foreign Policy* 47 (Summer, 1982): 118–122.

Lowenthal, Abraham F. "The Caribbean Basin Initiative: Misplaced Emphasis." *Foreign Policy* 47 (Summer, 1982): 114–118.

Winetraub, Sidney. "The Caribbean Initiative: A Flawed Model." *Foreign Policy* 47 (Summer, 1982): 130–133.

Caribbean Basin Partnership Act, 2000 (United States)

The U.S.-Caribbean Basin Trade Partnership Act (CBTPA) was approved by the U.S. Congress on October 1, 2000, and President Clinton signed the proclamation to implement the act on October 2, 2000, as Title II of the Trade and Development Act. The CBTPA constituted an expansion on the 1983 Caribbean Basin Economic Recovery Act (CBERA), which was the initial form of the 1983 Caribbean Basin Initiative (CBI), and it sought to gain the advantage that had been lost with Mexico's entry into the North American Free Trade Agreement (NAFTA).

The CBI, established by a series of U.S. congressional actions in the 1980s, became the Reagan administration's Inter-American model development program to promote democracies and the creation of free markets in Central America and the Caribbean. In response to the proposal initiated by Jamaican Prime Minister Edward Seaga for a plan to fight communism in the region, this military and economic aid package was announced February 24, 1982, at the meeting of the Organization of American States (OAS). The CBI promised to give economic assistance to pro-U.S. countries to allow duty-free shipping of products to the United States; to quell political unrest in the region; to punish Soviet and Cuba-supported leftist revolt in El Salvador, Guatemala, and Grenada; and to isolate the pro-Castro Sandinista government in Nicaragua. The U.S. Congress, which deferred to the power of business and labor to block the preferences and incentives to investment in the member countries, did not approve the CBI until July 1983, and only with a much-narrowed duty-free list. Reagan, and after him, George H. W. Bush, failed to obtain approval to expand the program, but Clinton secured passage of the CBTPA in 2000.

The CBTPA assures trade preferences to the benefit of the twenty-four member countries of the CBI for duty-free exportation of products to the United States. (Because it brought those members into parity with Mexico, the CBTPA is referred to in the U.S. Congress as a "CBI-parity" or "NAFTA-parity" act). The act assigns responsibility to the United States Trade Representative to establish and publish other determinations concerning customs procedures, and it emphasizes the significance of the component of apparel products made of U.S.-knit yarns and cotton in its acceptance of exports to the United States under the new terms. Carrying over criteria from the CBERA, the CBTPA requires member countries to ensure standards of workers' rights, to respect international intellectual property rights, and to take steps against the narcotics trade and corruption.

Eight of the eighteen CBERA beneficiaries are also beneficiaries under CBTPA: Barbados, Belize, Guyana, Haiti, Jamaica, Panama, St. Lucia, and Trinidad and Tobago. Additional member countries, bringing the total to twenty-four, are Antigua and Barbuda, Aruba, Bahamas, Costa Rica, Dominica, the Dominican Republic, El Salvador, Grenada, Guatemala, Honduras, Montserrat, Netherlands Antilles, St. Kitts and Nevis, St. Lucia, St. Vincent and the Grenadines, and the British Virgin Islands. The CBTPA was set to expire on September 30, 2010, but the U.S. Congress approved continuation of the agreement until September 30, 2020, with the provision that it would be superseded in the case of any member country's entry into a free trade agreement with the United States.

The goal of the CBTPA has been to reduce economic dependency in the region through economic development and poverty reduction, which would contribute to reducing drug trafficking and illegal immigration. The CBTPA expansion of CBI and CBERA has helped to generate imports from CBI countries totaling $19.6 billion in 2008, an amount that exceeded the 2007 total by $56 million. Implementation of the CBTPA has also brought on denunciations by the American Federation of Labor–Congress of Industrial Organizations (AFL–CIO) of related workers' rights violations under the CBTPA dispensation in the maquiladora and banana sectors of the region, and those denunciations prompted governments to address some of the highly visible cases involving anti-union activity and violations of labor codes.

See also *Association of Caribbean States (ACS); Caribbean Basin Initiative (CBI); Caribbean Community Common Market (CARICOM); Economic Commission for Latin America and the Caribbean (CEPAL); North American Free Trade Agreement (NAFTA), 1992; Organization of Eastern Caribbean States (OECS)*

. . . . EUGENIO MATIBAG

References and Further Reading

Caribbean Basin Trade Partnership Act (CBTPA), H.R. 984, title II. 106th Congress, 1999; 106 H.R. 984.

Office of the United States Trade Representative, Executive Office of the President, "Caribbean Basin Initiative (CBI)," December 31, 2009, www.ustr.gov/trade-topics/trade-development/preference-programs/caribbean-basin-initiative-cbi.

Office of the United States Trade Representative, Executive Office of the President, "Statement by Timothy Reif before the House Committee on Ways and Means Subcommittee on Trade," November 17, 2009, www.ustr.gov/about-us/congressional-affairs/congressional-hearings-and-testimony/2009/november/statement-timothy-.

U.S. Labor Education in the Americas Project (USLEAP), "Caribbean Trade Programs (CBI and CBTPA)," http://usleap.org/caribbean-trade-programs-cbi-and-cbtpa.

Caribbean Community Common Market (CARICOM)

The Caribbean Community Common Market (CARICOM) is an economic free trade zone that developed naturally out of the Caribbean Free Trade Area (CARIFTA), which had previously been established among former island colonies of the United Kingdom. Its interest in protecting its small agricultural industries led to a dispute between the United States and the European Union in the 1990s.

GENESIS

It was initially expected that the former British Caribbean territories would become independent as an internally self-governing federal state, for their mutual support and protection from external powers. The British Caribbean Federation Act, 1956, established the necessary structures. However rivalries between the states soon brought about its collapse, and the various states then became independent separately. In 1965, under the Dickenson Bay Agreement, the newly independent Antigua and Barbuda, Barbados, Guyana, and Trinidad and Tobago created CARIFTA. Its purpose was to give the states a joint international presence in trade negotiations, particularly in dealing with their former colonial power, Great Britain, and their most powerful neighbor, the United States. In 1968 the founding states were joined by Dominica, Grenada, Saint Christopher (or St. Kitts)-Nevis-Anguilla, Saint Lucia, and Saint Vincent and the Grenadines, followed by Montserrat (which did not proceed to independence) and Jamaica. Anguilla rebelled against rule from St. Kitts-Nevis and eventually returned to British rule, but in 1971 British Honduras joined CARIFTA, although it did not gain independence until 1981.

At the Seventh Heads of Government conference of CARIFTA in 1972, Commonwealth Caribbean leaders took the decision to transform the organization into a "Common Market," providing for the free movement of labor and capital between member states and their eventual economic integration. The treaty (which established the Caribbean Community, with a population of some 5.5 million) and the agreement (which established the Common Market) were signed by representatives of Barbados, Guyana, Jamaica, and Trinidad and Tobago on July 4, 1973, at Chaguaramas, Trinidad and Tobago. The agreement was subsequently annexed to the treaty of Chaguaramas under the name of the Common Market Annex. The dual structure was intended to allow states to join either organization separately, but in practice all the original members joined both, though the Bahamas (which was closely associated with the United States) chose only to join the community. Associate members are Anguilla, Bermuda, the British Virgin Islands, the Cayman Islands, and the Turks and Caicos Islands.

GROWTH AND DEVELOPMENT

The process of integration made little progress at first, however, being hampered by political disputes and by the maintenance of import restrictions in each state. However the U.S. intervention in Grenada in 1982 was not universally welcomed, and the impact of other regional and global developments, in particular the creation of the North American Free Trade Agreement (NAFTA, 1994) and the formation of the World Trade Organization (WTO, 1995), threatened the stability of the small and often fragile economies of the island states. Between 1993 and 2000 the Inter-Governmental Task Force (IGTF) produced nine protocols to amend the treaty, and subsequently these were incorporated in a single document now in force, known formally as "The Revised Treaty of Chaguaramas Establishing the Caribbean Community, including the CARICOM Single Market and Economy." The purpose of the revisions was to strengthen the integration process with the ultimate objective of creating a single market and economy. Additionally, with the accession of Suriname in 1985 and Haiti in 2002, membership was extended beyond the commonwealth countries and the organization became, in practice, multilingual.

Externally the first big challenge was to try to maintain some form of preferential access of bananas to the European Union (EU). Belize, Jamaica, and the Windward Islands had, hitherto, enjoyed a guaranteed British market, but the advent of the European single market (1992) threatened this, as without protection small producers on family-run farms in the Caribbean could not compete against the large U.S.-owned corporations producing bananas in Central America and Ecuador. However in September 1995, the U.S. Government filed a complaint with the WTO against the EU's banana regime on behalf of Chiquita Brands. In June 1998 the EU approved a reform of the regime which was supported by CARICOM, but the Clinton administration claimed that the reform was still discriminatory and hence incompatible with WTO provisions and imposed sanctions on EU products. It was not until April 2001 that the trade negotiator for the U.S. government, Robert Zoellick, concluded an agreement to end the nine-year dispute, but at a heavy cost to the economies of the Windward Islands.

STRUCTURE

The principal organ of the community is the Heads of Government conference which meets annually, with additional meetings if required. The conference determines policy, concludes treaties on behalf of the community, and is responsible for the external relations of the community. Individual Heads of Government additionally hold regional portfolios with responsibility for specific areas. The conference is assisted by a small bureau which has the capacity to initiate proposals and the responsibility for ensuring that decisions are carried out. The Community Council of Ministers consists principally of the ministers responsible for community affairs and is responsible for strategic planning and coordination. Four other ministerial councils deal with trade and economic development, foreign and community relations, human and social development, and finance and planning, respectively. The Caribbean Court of Justice, established in 2005, settles disputes between member states and has replaced the judicial committee of the British Privy Council as the final court of appeal for Barbados and Guyana.

The secretariat provides administrative support for the decision-making organs of the community and is based at Georgetown, Guyana. The current secretary general (acting) is H. E. Lolita Applewhaite of Barbados, who served as deputy secretary general from 2003 to 2011, when Sir Edwin Carrington of Trinidad and Tobago stood down. Institutions established within the CARICOM framework include the Caribbean Agricultural Research and Development Institute (CARDI), the Caribbean Meteorological Organization (CMO), and the Caribbean Disaster Emergency Response Agency (CDERA). A number of separate regional organizations are also associated with CARICOM. Among these is the Caribbean Development Bank, which was founded in 1969 to promote economic growth in the Caribbean region. The United States is not an associate member, although Canada, Mexico, and Colombia are.

See also *Association of Caribbean States (ACS); Caribbean Basin Initiative (CBI); Chiquita Brands International; English-Speaking Caribbean, U.S. Relations with; Organization of Eastern Caribbean States (OECS)*

. . . . PETER CALVERT

REFERENCES AND FURTHER READING

Axline, Andrew. Caribbean Integration: The Politics of Regionalism. London: Frances Pinter, 1979.
Braveboy-Wagner, and Jacqueline Anne. Small States in Global Affairs: The Foreign Policies of the Caribbean Community. London: Palgrave Macmillan, 2008.
Caribbean Community (CARICOM) Secretariat, www.caricom.org/index.jsp.

Caribbean Legion

The Caribbean Legion, a term first coined by U.S. journalists in November 1948, refers to a loose, fluid, and somewhat clandestine group of Latin Americans around the Caribbean basin, who sought to aid the establishment of democracies in the region during the post-World War II era. Though U.S. policymakers were initially somewhat accepting of calls for regional democracy, as the Cold War progressed the Caribbean Legion became a symbol of unacceptably destabilizing radicalism.

RISE AND FALL OF DEMOCRATIC HOPES

The Caribbean Legion comprised disparate and autonomous figures from across the region—from national leaders and political exiles to militants and mercenaries—who drew on a postwar peak of democratic idealism. During the war U.S. leaders proclaimed a desire for the establishment of freedom and democracy in their vision of a new, postwar world order. Many Latin Americans looked to the Atlantic Charter, a document signed by the United States and Great Britain in 1941, setting forth the need for national self-determination, global social and economic advancements, and the end of empire building by the west. In a region that felt it had been alternatively exploited, abused, and ignored by its powerful northern neighbor, the charter inspired some hope among these democracy advocates that the United States would disengage from imperialism and focus instead on promoting regional economic and social progress. With the defeat of European and Japanese fascism in 1945, these advocates felt their time had come, evidenced by the emergence of fledgling democracies in Cuba under Ramón Grau San Martin (1944), Guatemala under Juan José Arévalo (1944), and Venezuela under Rómulo Ernesto Betancourt Bello (1945).

The formation of democracies based on these ideals was to be brought about by ousting or assassinating some of the region's most notorious and entrenched symbols of oligarchy and dictatorship: men like Rafael Leonidas Trujillo in the Dominican Republic and Anastasio Somoza Garcia in Nicaragua. Though the various figures with affinities to democratic ideals were often spread across the continent, pursuing their own independent agendas, some of them were at times able to coordinate plans of action, giving rise to the symbolic label of the Caribbean Legion. A 1947 attempt to overthrow Trujillo through a sea invasion of the Dominican Republic by around 1,200 Cuban and Dominican exiles became widely publicized before it had a chance to embark. After Trujillo's strenuous complaints the revolutionaries were quickly dissuaded by a Cuban government that was wary of tempting the ire of the United States. However, President Juan José Arévalo of Guatemala welcomed the chastened exiles and their weapons into Guatemala to train and plot further operations. In doing so, he made Guatemala the "mecca" for the Caribbean Legion. Arévalo advocated wider regional democratization and was the mastermind behind the *Pacto del Caribe* of December 17, 1947, which called for the liberation of the Dominican Republic, Nicaragua, and Costa Rica.

Of greater success for the Caribbean Legion's image was the effort to oust President Teodoro Picado of Costa Rica, headed by former exile José Figueres. After the government's electoral fraud in March 1948, Figueres instigated his plans for revolution, receiving important military supplies from the Guatemalan government (from the failed Dominican invasion of 1947). The legion's role was given significant attention by the press and U.S. policymakers, which seemed to bode well for efforts to overthrow Somoza in neighboring Nicaragua. However, after the Organization of American States (OAS) demanded a cessation of tensions between Nicaragua and Costa Rica, and Figueres fell out with General Juan Rodriguez, the military commander of the legion, democratic exiles turned their attention back to Trujillo.

The Dominican Republic was invaded by air from Guatemala on June 19, 1949, in what became known as the Luperón Affair. Again, the attempt was easily dealt with by Trujillo's military, spelling the end of the legion in practical terms. Of the new or potential democracies in the second half of the 1940s, by 1954 only Costa Rica remained a democracy, having renounced the *Pacto del Caribe's* pledges of solidarity by voting with sixteen other OAS members against Guatemala at the Caracas conference of 1954. Despite this collapse the legion's name continued to be invoked by supporters and detractors alike, including U.S. policymakers, during the 1950s.

U.S. RELATIONSHIP TO THE CARIBBEAN LEGION

The United States had broadly supported, albeit cautiously and somewhat unenthusiastically, calls for Latin American democracy immediately after World War II. A November 1945 proposal of Uruguayan Foreign Minister Eduardo Rodriguez Laretta called for collective regional action against dictatorships, and it met with the initial approval of the United States, notably the U.S. Assistant Secretary of State for Inter-American Affairs Spruille Braden. Braden thought that liberal democracies were the most natural allies of the United States in the fight against communism. Nevertheless the United States quickly distanced itself from the Caribbean Legion. As the 1950s approached Cold War concerns intensified, leading to greater support for anticommunist dictatorships. Trujillo and Somoza eagerly demonstrated their anticommunist credentials while repeatedly invoking the legion's violations of OAS guarantees of nonintervention between American states. The dictators also appealed to their traditionally strong relationship with the United States, playing on a theme epitomized by a statement famously attributed to Franklin Roosevelt: Somoza "might be a son of a bitch, but he's *our* son of a bitch."

Though the U.S. relationship with dictatorships in Nicaragua and the Dominican Republic was not unproblematic, they were traditional allies that policymakers felt could be relied upon to support U.S. efforts toward regional stability and the furthering of the Cold War agenda. The challenges posed to these dictators by high profile figures in the Caribbean Legion, like Arévalo and Figueres, was clear and increasingly worrying to the United States. A 1954 State Department memorandum from regional policy heads charged Figueres with possessing both a "Messiah complex" and "great unpredictability" (U.S. Department of State 1983, 375).

Estrangement from the United States spelled the end for the Caribbean Legion, but despite prominent defeats and minimal lasting impact on hemispheric relations, the image of the legion resonated as potentially destabilizing for its detractors across the hemisphere. The legion's image and demise also helped shape the views of its supporters and subsequent leftist nationalist movements.

See also *Arévalo Bermejo, Juan José; Betancourt Bello, Rómulo; Figueres Ferrer, José; Grau San Martín, Ramón; Somoza García, Anastasio; Tenth International Conference of American States, Caracas, 1954; Trujillo Molina, Rafael Leónidas*

. . . . OLIVER MURPHEY

References and Further Reading

Ameringer, Charles D. *The Caribbean Legion: Patriots, Politicians, Soldiers of Fortune, 1946–1950.* University Park, PA: Pennsylvania University Press, 1996.

Gleijeses, Piero. "Juan Jose Arevalo and the Caribbean Legion." *Journal of Latin American Studies* 21, no. 1 (February 1989): 133–145.

Longley, Kyle. *The Sparrow and the Hawk: Costa Rica and the United States during the Rise of José Figueres.* Tuscaloosa: University of Alabama Press, 1997.

Rabe, Stephen G. *Eisenhower and Latin America: The Foreign Policy of Anticommunism.* Chapel Hill: University of North Carolina Press, 1988.

Schwartzberg, Steven. "Romulo Betancourt: From a Communist Anti-Imperialist to a Social Democrat with US Support." *Journal of Latin American Studies* 29, no. 3 (October 1997): 613–665.

United States Department of State. *Foreign Relations of the United States, 1952–54, Vol. 4, The Americas.* Washington, DC: United States Government Press, 1983.

Carnegie, Andrew

An American industrialist who rose from poverty to immense wealth in the latter half of the nineteenth century through his investments in the steel industry, Andrew Carnegie (1835–1919) also had a strong interest in U.S.-Latin American relations. He was born in Dunfermline, Scotland, and immigrated with his family to the Pittsburgh, Pennsylvania, area in 1848 at age thirteen. He soon found work as a bobbin boy in a textile plant, earning $1.20 a week. Carnegie next worked as a messenger and later became the manager of a telegraph office. Carnegie advanced to the position of general superintendent of the Pennsylvania Railroad. During the U.S. Civil War (1861–1865) Carnegie expertly organized the War Department's telegraph operations.

Carnegie saw the opportunity for industrial growth in the United States in the postwar period. As a railroad man he forecast the rapid expansion of the system which would drive the demand for iron and steel. He founded the Keystone Bridge Company in Pittsburgh and built or purchased seven steel mills, the most famous of which was the Homestead Steel Works, site of the violent Homestead Strike of 1892. In 1901 he sold Carnegie Steel to the newly formed U.S. Steel Corporation, headed by the financier J. P. Morgan, for $450 million. Andrew Carnegie then devoted the rest of his life to philanthropy, funding a vast library system, endowing the Carnegie Institute of Technology (today's Carnegie Mellon University) and creating the Carnegie Endowment for International Peace.

Carnegie's interest in U.S.-Latin American relations began with his appointment by President Benjamin Harrison as a delegate to the 1889 Pan-American Congress. It was Carnegie's only political appointment, and the meeting made a great impression on the industrialist. His attitude toward Latin America was shaped by this experience and he subsequently wrote the following:

> I found the South American representatives rather suspicious of their big brother's intentions. A sensitive spirit of independence was manifest, which became our duty to recognize. In this I think we succeeded, but it will behoove subsequent governments to scrupulously respect the national feeling of our Southern neighbors. It is not control, but friendly cooperation upon terms of perfect equality we should seek. (Carnegie 1948, 48)

He would steadfastly adhere to this view of Latin America. Carnegie also formed a friendship with Manuel Quintana, the Argentine delegate who later became president of that republic.

On October 16, 1891, a group of American sailors from the USS *Baltimore* were involved in a brawl while on shore leave in Valparaiso, Chile. Two of the sailors died of knife wounds and seventeen were incarcerated by Chilean police. American President Benjamin Harrison demanded an apology, sought compensation for the dead sailors, and threatened war. Carnegie was concerned that President Harrison had overreacted to the situation. In an informal meeting with the president, Carnegie urged caution. He reiterated the policy formulated at the Pan-American Congress that all disputes would be settled through peaceful arbitration. Carnegie also advised Harrison that the image of the United States would be tarnished if he resorted to war. He recommended that Harrison take action against the captain of the *Baltimore* for his indiscretion in granting shore leave when there was rioting in Valparaiso. Carnegie's protest was to no avail, as Harrison persisted with his bellicose policy. The dispute was resolved when Chile, lacking international support, backed down and agreed to the U.S. demands.

Carnegie's close friendship with Elihu Root, (U.S. secretary of state 1905–1909) resulted in his most significant contributions to improving relations with Latin America. Root asked Carnegie if he would consider funding the construction of a building to house the Bureau of American Republics (later the Pan-American Union, today the Organization of American States or OAS). Carnegie enthusiastically agreed and stated, "I am happy in stating that it will be one of the pleasures of my life to furnish to the Union of all the Republics of this hemisphere, the necessary funds . . . for the construction of an international home in Washington" (Wall 1970, 910). The white, marble Pan-American Union building was built at a cost of $850,000 and remains the headquarters for the OAS. Root also encouraged Carnegie to support the building of the Central American Court of Justice. The court was the result of Root's and of other diplomats' efforts at the Central American Peace conference held in Washington in 1908. Carnegie agreed to contribute $100,000 to the court building, which was dedicated in 1910 at Cartago, Costa Rica.

See also *Baltimore Affair, 1891; Central American Conference, Washington, 1907; Central American Court of Justice; First International Conference of American States, Washington, 1889; Harrison, Benjamin; Organization of American States (OAS); Root, Elihu*

. . . . GEORGE M. LAUDERBAUGH

References and Further Reading

Carnegie, Andrew. *The Autobiography of Andrew Carnegie.* Boston: Houghton Mifflin Company, 1948.

Krass, Peter. *Carnegie.* Hoboken, NJ: Wiley, 2002.

Wall, Joseph. *Andrew Carnegie.* New York: Oxford University Press, 1970.

Carranza Garza, Venustiano

Venustiano Carranza Garza (1859–1920) proved to be a most unlikely leader of the Mexican Revolution against the aging, corrupt regime of Porfirio Díaz. He first rose to prominence as a firm supporter of Díaz but later participated in the successful overthrow of his former patron and emerged as the first president of the Mexican Republic under the constitution of 1917. In doing so, he also clashed with the foreign policy of Woodrow Wilson.

Carranza was born in the small farming town of Cuatro Ciénegas—one of fifteen children born to a relatively prosperous ranching family. As was typical of a scion of the landed elite in the late nineteenth century, Carranza entered state and local politics. Carranza first served two terms as the mayor of Cuatro Ciénegas, followed by terms as state legislator, two terms in the national congress, and one term as provisional governor of Coahuila.

Carranza's national political aspirations were possible only because of his support of Porfirio Díaz, who enjoyed an iron grip on Mexican politics from 1884 to 1911—a close association that would later cause him trouble. Carranza first opposed Madero, but in a move motivated more by pragmatism than philosophy, he moved to the rebel's side in 1911. Madero named Carranza to be his minister of war, although Carranza's political ambitions were for higher office. Carranza burnished his revolutionary credentials when he emerged as a leader in the effort to overthrow Victoriano Huerta's counterrevolutionary government in 1913. The Wilson administration in Washington, D.C, considered Huerta's violent rise to power as illegitimate and sought to undermine his government. In April 1914 Wilson authorized the military occupation ofVeracruz by U.S. Marines to prevent the landing of the German ship *Ypiranga,* which was loaded with weapons for the Huertista forces. More than two hundred Mexicans died in the effort to repel the invaders. While Carranza tried to distance himself from this assault on Mexican sovereignty, he did benefit from Huerta's decision to divert troops to face down the Americans, thereby allowing the Carrancista constitutionalist forces to seize the initiative in northern Mexico. The combination of the constitutionalist victories in the north and the loss of customs revenues that resulted from the American occupation of Mexico's most important port ultimately led to Huerta's downfall in July 1914.

The several years following Carranza's rise as provisional president were by far the most chaotic of the entire revolution. The chaos was a result of the civil war as revolutionaries, who had allied together to bring down Huerta, turned against one another. After Carranza assumed power, Alvaro Obregón, who was most committed to legitimacy of the government, chose to stand by his side. Pancho Villa and Emiliano Zapata distrusted Carranza's old ties to the Díaz regime, doubted his dedication to fundamental social reform, and soon declared themselves to be in rebellion. Villa tried to get the United States involved in the civil war by launching a raid on Columbus, New Mexico, in March 1916. Woodrow Wilson ordered General John J. Pershing to pursue Villa into Mexico to capture him. Carranza ordered Pershing out of Mexico and sent troops to see to it that the Americans recognized Mexican sovereignty. After Pershing spent months wandering in northern Mexico without catching sight of Villa, Wilson recalled his expedition. Before he returned to the United States in January 1917, however, his troops clashed with Carranza's federal forces.

In order to consolidate his power and legitimize the revolution, Carranza called for a constitutional convention to replace the outdated constitution of 1857. A radical faction seized control of the convention and forced through a series of radically anticlerical provisions, which Carranza felt obliged to accept. With the new constitution in place, Carranza handily won new presidential elections. On his inauguration day Obregón retired to Sonora, leaving Carranza to forge a new government under the constitution. While the constitution provided Carranza's government new legitimacy, he was uncomfortable with its radical nature.

Carranza chose to delay the constitution's full enforcement until he could deal with Mexico's deep economic problems. Compounding his difficulties, Zapata and Villa once again declared themselves in rebellion.

In 1920 Carranza tried to retain his power by fixing the upcoming presidential elections. Instead of surrendering to a fair and free election, Carranza tried to name a successor which he himself could control. His former minister of war, Alvaro Obregón, had already announced his candidacy for the election. In retaliation of Carranza's violation of the constitution he himself had promulgated, Obregón joined with other powerful Sonorans, Adolfo de la Huerta and Plutarco Elías Calles, to overthrow Carranza and replace him with a provisional president until new elections could be held.

Faced with the powerful personality of Obregón, and with an equally powerful rebel army marching on Mexico City, Carranza was forced to flee. Before he could reach safe exile, he was assassinated by one of his own bodyguards.

See also *Calles, Plutarco Elías; Díaz Mori, Porfirio; Doheny, Edward L.; Madero, Francisco I.*

. . . . MATTHEW A. REDINGER

References and Further Reading

Gilly, Adolfo. *The Mexican Revolution.* New York: The New Press, 2005.

Richmond, Douglas W. *Venustiano Carranza's Nationalist Struggle, 1893–1920.* Lincoln: University of Nebraska Press, 1983.

Ruíz, Ramón Eduardo. *The Great Rebellion: Mexico, 1905–1924.* New York: Norton, 1980.

Carrera Turcios, José Rafael

Though he was Guatemala's ruler from 1839 to 1865, Rafael Carrera (1814–1865) was the least likely candidate for the job. Unlike the scions of Central America's elite, Carrera had no formal education and was illiterate. At age 12 he joined the army as a drummer boy. Following his stint in the army, Carrera worked as an itinerant agricultural laborer until around age nineteen, when he established a successful pig-raising business in the small town of Mataquescuintla in eastern Guatemala and soon secured a marriage to the daughter of one of the town's landowners.

By 1837 Carrera spoke openly against the centralized government of the United Provinces of Central America (UPCA) and its taxing system, which he believed to be exorbitant. He also opposed the authority of the central government at the expense of the individual five states. Carrera's anger turned into action. UPCA President Francisco Morazán instituted draconian measures to contain the 1837 cholera epidemic, including quarantining entire towns. A detachment of federal troops, including some former convicts, was sent to forcibly evict Carrera and his family from their home. Carrera decided to stand and fight. In the ensuing shootout a federal soldier shot and killed his wife. Carrera held President Morazán and his government responsible for his wife's death. Ironically

Carrera had come to the government's attention only months before when he managed to dissuade an angry mob from lynching a government official who had been sent to administer the quarantine. His leadership skills had so impressed the local governor that he had been offered a captaincy in the local militia.

Carrera used his wife's demise as a cause to draw those who had become frustrated with the overreaching policies of the United Provinces. From a core of thirteen ragtag irregulars Carrera's cause and charisma built an armed movement that the government could not stop. Much of his support came from Guatemala's indigenous population, who were incensed at the government's confiscation of their communal lands, despite the fact that Carrera spoke only Spanish. By 1838 the United Provinces had disintegrated, their leader retreating into his native Honduras. Carrera and his army were warmly received in the streets of Guatemala City as Carrera himself took control of Guatemala. In 1840 the federal army finally surrendered to Carrera's superior force. President Morazán went into a self-imposed exile in Colombia, making one last futile attempt to regain power before being tried and executed for treason.

One of Rafael Carrera's first actions as ruler of Guatemala was to rescind Morazán's anticlerical reforms and invite back those religious orders that had been expelled, putting priests in charge of public education while signing a concordat with the Vatican in 1852. Carrera also proved a friend to Guatemala's landowners, for he protected their property rights and managed to keep the indigenous population in check. For the next twenty-five years Carrera served as Guatemala's caudillo, either serving as president in his own right or supervising those who did.

If Carrera had any weakness it was in the area of foreign relations. Because Guatemala was the largest and most populous of the Central American states, Carrera often meddled in the affairs of Guatemala's neighbors, replacing liberal regimes with conservative leaders. Carrera also proved ineffective against the European powers. When Great Britain asked him to sign a border treaty, Carrera made his mark on the document, not realizing that he was legitimizing a British colony on Guatemala's eastern flank. As the first president of an independent Guatemala, Carrera conducted a cordial relationship with the United States, despite the occasional flare-ups (e.g., the Walker Affair) that impacted relations between the two nations.

The Walker Affair is an incident that directly involved Rafael Carrera in the defense of not only Guatemala but also of all of Central America. By 1856 William Walker, a dynamic yet diminutive American adventurer, had succeeded in elevating himself to the presidency of Nicaragua. Ostensibly he and his band of mercenaries had come to the aid of Nicaragua's conservative government in its ongoing civil war with the nation's liberals. Carrera's role in this incident was to lead—along with Costa Rican president José Mora—a national army, composed of troops from the four other Central American republics against Walker in an effort to oust him from power. In the end Carrera and Mora led a successful campaign against the American usurper, sending him back to the United States.

See also *Guatemala, U. S. Relations with; Morazán Quesada, José Francisco; United Provinces of Central America, 1823–1839*

. . . . PETER B. GUSHUE

References and Further Reading

Smith, Carol, ed. *Guatemalan Indians and the State, 1540–1988.* Austin: University of Texas Press, 1990.

Sullivan-González, Douglas. *Piety, Power and Politics: Religion and Nation Formation in Guatemala, 1821–1871.* Pittsburgh, PA: University of Pittsburgh Press, 1998.

Woodward, Ralph L. *Carrera and the Emergence of the Republic of Guatemala.* Athens: University of Georgia Press, 1990.

Cartagena, Agreement of, 1969 (Andean Pact)

The Andean Pact, or Andean Community (ANCOM), was formed in 1969 with the Agreement of Cartagena to create a regional common economic market. The older Latin American Free Trade Association (LAFTA) had benefited the larger countries of Mexico, Brazil, and Argentina. Therefore, five smaller nations signed the original agreement: Bolivia, Colombia, Chile, Ecuador, and Peru. In 1973 Venezuela joined. A decrease in U.S. dominance during the 1970s helped create a viable context within which to start such a community.

The goals of ANCOM were to create employment and trade cooperation and promote industrial, agricultural, and social development. Several aspects of the agreement were to help regional and international trade: tariff-reduction programs, a joint external tariff, coordination of financial policies, jointly planned industrial development, and preferential treatment for Bolivia and Ecuador as the least developed members. To administer the pact an Andean Tribunal and an Andean Parliament were established, along with the Andean Presidential Council, a Court of Justice, the Latin American Reserve Fund, the Andean Development Corporation, the Commission (legislative branch), and Junta (executive branch). The decisions by the Commission required national legislation for implementation, however.

The pact has had continuing problems. Chile withdrew in 1976. The pact has lacked national support from member governments. In addition transport and communications barriers, difficulties in reconciling internal and external economic policies, problems implementing a common external tariff, and equal distribution of benefits to nations at different levels of development remain issues. Little significant industrial investment has occurred, so the area continues to rely upon import substitution. Some critics argue that the policies of the program were well thought out and viable, but they were not carried through by member nations for reasons such as individual nationalism.

In the 1980s things began to change. With the signing of the Quito Protocol in 1987 and the Trujillo Protocol in 1996, the Andean nations sought to revitalize the Andean Community and become a common market by 2000. One of the important changes was that Andean laws (decisions) would be binding on the member countries and require no national action to become effective and that countries could not use domestic law as an excuse for noncompliance with community law. Results have been mixed. In countries such as Colombia, Ecuador, and Peru, intraregional trading has increased, while in Bolivia and Venezuela, it has not. All five nations have increased their intra-Andean exports. By the 1990s a free trade area was provisionally created as well as a common external tariff (CET). Venezuela withdrew its membership in 2006 over discussions of trade between the United States and Peru and Colombia. Venezuela argued that if Peru and Colombia signed separate bilateral trade agreements with the United States than this would cause a flooding of U.S. goods into the market. Bolivia's president Evo Morales agreed with Venezuela's president Hugo Chávez, although Bolivia did not resign from the pact. In December of 2007 a free trade agreement between Peru and the United States was ratified and came into force in January 2009.

See also *Bolivia, U.S. Relations with; Bush, George H. W.; Chávez Frías, Hugo; Chile, U.S. Relations with; Columbia, U.S. Relations with; Free Trade Association of the Americas (FTAA); Latin American Free Trade Association (LAFTA); Morales Ayma, Juan Evo; United States and Andean Trade Preference Act, 1991; Venezuela, U.S. Relations with*

GINA HAMES

References and Further Reading

Adkisson, Richard V. "The Andean Group: Institutional Evolution, Intraregional Trade, and Economic Development." *Journal of Economic Issues* 37, no. 2 (June 2003): 371–379.

Mace, Gordon. "Consensus-Building in the Andean Integration System: 1968–1985." In *The Political Economy of Regional Cooperation: Comparative Case Studies,* edited by W. Andrew Axline, 34–71. London: Pinter, 1994.

"Treaties and Protocols: Andean Subregional Integration Agreement 'Cartagena Agreement,'" www.comunidadandina.org/ingles/normativa/ande_trie1.htm.

Carter, Jimmy

Jimmy Carter (1924–) was the thirty-ninth president of the United States, serving from 1977–1981. He sought to begin a "new era" in relations between the United States and Latin America. Elements of the new era were identified in an April 1977 speech to the Organization of American States (OAS) and included greater emphasis on human rights and efforts to resolve lingering problems, including relations with Cuba and the Panama Canal. With these initiatives Carter hoped to move the United States beyond the Cold War, to improve its relations with the countries of this hemisphere, and to emphasize diplomatic solutions to outstanding problems. The next four years would demonstrate, however, that the Cold War had not ended, that the human rights emphasis harmed relations with some governments, and that efforts to solve problems diplomatically were undermined by domestic politics in the United States.

HUMAN RIGHTS AND THE PANAMA CANAL

Carter's signature policy was human rights. While the administration hoped to utilize quiet diplomacy to advance its human rights goals, it also used public mechanisms, such as withholding military aid from a number of pro-American Latin American dictatorships, including Argentina, Brazil, and Guatemala, and voting against loans in international financial institutions. These policies undoubtedly heartened those in Latin America who were persecuted by their governments, but at the cost of alienating traditional allies and the American business community. Carter later acknowledged that he had not "fully grasp[ed] all the ramifications" of the human rights policy, noting in his memoirs that the "promotion of human rights . . . cut across our relations" with many types of countries, "even some of our longtime Western allies." (Carter 1982, 144)

The complications of the human rights policy became most apparent during Nicaragua's civil war. There, a human rights emphasis would call for pressure on the rightist, anticommunist, but brutal dictator, Anastasio Somoza to leave office, while a traditional anticommunist emphasis would call for support for Somoza against the Sandinista opposition that was leftist and, in some cases, pro-Cuban. Carter hedged, sometimes supporting Somoza and at other times calling on him to leave office. The administration belatedly proposed a transition to a government that included neither Somoza nor the Sandinistas, but by then the Sandinistas were on the verge of victory. American indecision contributed not only to an unfortunate outcome but also left it with only limited influence upon the new government.

Cold War considerations and domestic politics also undermined Carter's effort to improve ties with Cuba, a country with which the United States had had hostile relations since Fidel Castro came to power in the late 1950s. In his first six weeks in office Carter halted reconnaissance flights over Cuba and cancelled the bans on travel by Americans and on expenditures in Cuba. Soon the two governments had signed boundary and fisheries agreements and opened interest sections in each other's capital. Yet lingering suspicions and Cold War realities meant little ultimately came of this initiative. Cuba's dispatch of thousands of troops to Africa and the later "discovery" of a Soviet brigade in Cuba—which had been there for more than a decade—became domestic issues in the United States. The Soviet invasion of Afghanistan further undermined efforts to improve ties with Cuba. The final straw occurred in 1980 when, frustrated by an inability to develop an orderly emigration process with the United States, the Cuban government allowed more than one hundred thousand people, including criminals, to leave for the United States.

Carter's most enduring legacy in Latin America was the Panama Canal Treaties (Carter-Torrijos), 1977. While negotiations between the United States and Panama began in the mid-1960s, only during the Carter administration were the treaties finalized and ratified. These treaties initiated a gradual transfer of authority over the canal to Panama, allowed American forces to defend the canal before and after the transfer, and insured the canal's permanent neutrality. These agreements were very controversial in the United States, as Carter noted in his memoirs. While the treaties did advance U.S. ties with Latin America, their positive impact was mitigated to a certain extent by the tone of the congressional debate.

CARTER'S POSTPRESIDENTIAL YEARS

Carter continued his efforts in support of human rights, social justice, and peaceful resolution of conflicts after leaving office. Many of his efforts were done through the Carter Center, a unique institution that links a public center with a presidential library. The center's efforts in Latin America took many forms, from fighting disease and working for a moratorium on arms sales to promoting peaceful settlement of disputes.

One common political activity is election monitoring. Several examples illustrate the types of influence the center, and Carter, has had. In Panama Manuel Noriega, the military strongman, clearly favored one candidate in the May 1989 elections. In an effort to prevent a fraudulent election, Carter pressured Noriega to allow an election observer mission. When initial returns showed Noriega's candidate losing, Panamanian election officials intervened to alter the results. A witness to the fraud, Carter sought to persuade Noriega to honor the results and leave the country. When the Panamanian leader refused, Carter held a press conference to denounce the election publicly. Although his mission had been unable to insure a fair election, Carter was able to draw international attention to the fraud.

A similar course of events might have happened in Nicaragua after its February 1990 election. The outcome of the election, a surprise to many, was a victory for opposition forces. To prevent a repetition of the Panama experience, Carter met with President Daniel Ortega and persuaded him to leave office, telling him that leaving office could be his greatest contribution to Nicaraguan democracy and that he, Carter, had learned that life went on after losing. Once Ortega agreed, Carter worked with opposition parties to guide the transition to a new government.

Carter also led an election observer mission to Haiti in December 1990. While the election was free and fair, the victor, Jean-Bertrand Aristide, was overthrown seven months later by the Haitian military. In the aftermath of the coup Carter criticized the Bush administration for its indifference to the reversal of democracy in Haiti and then the Clinton administration for contemplating military action to restore democracy. Carter believed negotiations to be the best approach. In an effort to avoid an invasion, Clinton authorized Carter, Senator Sam Nunn, and Colin Powell, former chairman of the Joint Chiefs of Staff, to go to Haiti to work out a diplomatic solution. Using creative diplomacy, inducements, and threats, the delegation was able to get an agreement in which the military left power and Aristide was allowed to return to power.

While Carter was rejected by the American public in the 1980 presidential election, his efforts since leaving office have been recognized by many. The most important recognition came in December 2002 when he won the Nobel Peace Prize for, in the words of the Nobel Committee, "his decades of untiring effort to find peaceful solutions to international conflicts, to advance democracy and human rights, and to promote economic and social development" (http://nobelprize.org/nobel_prizes/peace/laureates/2002/press.html).

See also *Cédras, Raoul; Cuba, Rapprochement with the United States, 1960s–1990s; Human Rights; Noriega Moreno, Manuel Antonio; Panama Canal Treaties (Carter-Torrijos), 1977; Sandinista National Liberation Front (FSLN) (Nicaragua); Somoza Debayle, Anastasio*

. . . . DAVID JERVIS

REFERENCES AND FURTHER READING

Brinkley, Douglas. *The Unfinished Presidency: Jimmy Carter's Journey beyond the White House*. New York: Viking, 1998.

Carter, Jimmy. *Keeping Faith: Memoirs of a President*. New York: Bantam, 1982.

Newson, David D. *The Diplomacy of Human Rights*. Lanham, MD: University Press of America, 1986.

Pastor, Robert A. *Condemned to Repetition: The United States and Nicaragua*. Princeton, NJ: Princeton, 1987.

Smith, Wayne. *The Closest of Enemies: A Personal and Diplomatic Account of U.S.-Cuban Relations since 1957*. New York: Norton, 1987.

Castillo Armas, Carlos

In 1953 President Dwight Eisenhower's administration decided to topple the allegedly communist-riddled government of Guatemalan President Jacobo Arbenz. It found a willing collaborator in the figure of Colonel Carlos Castillo Armas (1914–1957).

Born in Santa Lucía Cotzumalguapa, Guatemala, on November 4, 1914, Castillo Armas entered the Guatemalan Army Academy in 1933 and graduated as an officer in 1936. In 1950 he led an unsuccessful coup attempt against the democratically elected reformist government of President Juan José Arévalo. Wounded and captured in the attempt, he was imprisoned but sought asylum in the Colombian embassy.

By 1953 Castillo Armas had gathered a group of Guatemalan exiles in Honduras with the purpose of ousting the Arbenz regime. As relations between Guatemala and the United States deteriorated over the expropriation of the United Fruit Company holdings (UFCO), President Eisenhower authorized the Central Intelligence Agency (CIA) to provide covert training and military support for Armas's group and devise a plan of action for his projected invasion of Guatemala. The plan was accelerated when the CIA learned that on May 17, 1954, the Arbenz regime had received a weapons shipment from Czechoslovakia, a Soviet satellite. According to the CIA plan Castillo Armas was to cross into Guatemala. At the same time his American-supplied planes were to drop leaflets over military installations urging the Guatemalan army to defect, while a massive radio transmitter campaign would call for a popular uprising.

On June 18, 1954, Castillo Armas crossed the border from Honduras into Guatemalan territory. It is not clear what the size of his army was, for estimates range from one hundred fifty to four hundred men. The invasion, however, did not go as planned. His planes experienced mechanical failure and could not depart from their base in Honduras. Additionally, after driving twenty-five miles into Guatemalan territory, he became ill and his offensive stalled. Furthermore, in spite of the propaganda, the Guatemalan army confined itself to the army's barracks and no popular uprising materialized.

As the situation deteriorated for Castillo Armas, the Eisenhower administration decided to send several fighters piloted by American soldiers of fortune to bomb Guatemalan cities. The planes' appearance was enough for the Guatemalan army to abandon the president, while Arbenz and his supporters panicked. On June 27, 1954, Arbenz resigned, collected large sums of money from the treasury, and sought refuge in the Mexican Embassy. On July 3, 1954, a triumphant Castillo Armas made his entry into Guatemala City.

On September 1, 1954, Castillo Armas was "elected" president through a plebiscite. Upon assuming power he abolished the 1945 constitution, revoked the Arbenz administration's 1952 Agrarian Reform Law and returned the expropriated UFCO holdings. Additionally he banned the Communist party and numerous Arbenz sympathizers were jailed. The Eisenhower administration supported his regime by granting it $80 million in economic aid.

Although in 1956 Castillo Armas allowed a new constitution and the election of a new congress, discontent with his administration erupted in 1957. On July 26, 1957, presidential guard Romeo Vázquez Sánchez assassinated Castillo Armas. To this day his motives for the assassination remain unknown.

See also *Arbenz Guzmán, Jacobo; Arévalo Bermejo, Juan José; Eisenhower, Dwight D.; Guatemala, U.S. Invasion of, 1954; Guatemala, U.S. Relations with; Puerifoy, John B.; United Fruit Company (UFCO)*

. . . . JOSÉ B. FERNÁNDEZ

References and Further Reading

Immerman, R. H. *The CIA in Guatemala*. Austin: University of Texas Press, 1982.

Schlesiger, Stephen, and Stephen Kinger. *Bitter Fruit: The Untold Story of the American Coup in Guatemala*. New York: Doubleday, 1982.

Castro Ruz, Fidel

Fidel Castro (1926–) led the successful guerrilla movement that ousted Dictator Fulgencio Batista in 1959 and then set in motion the Cuban Revolution. From then until February 2008 Castro led Cuba as president, chief of the armed forces, first secretary of the Communist party, and finally as "maximum leader." He transformed Cuba into a socialist nation and until its collapse in 1991, aligned himself with the Soviet Union.

1960S

During the first decade of the Cuban Revolution, Castro faced a confrontational United States. The U.S. efforts to topple the regime—including an economic embargo, sponsorship of the Bay of Pigs invasion in April 1961, Cuba's expulsion from the Organization of American States (OAS) in January 1962, "Operation Mongoose" designed to assassinate Castro, and other sabotage schemes—all ended in failure. During the same time period his relations with the Soviet Union were not cordial. The Soviet Union established trade relations with Cuba in 1960 and placed missiles in Cuba in 1962 but was forced to remove them because of U.S. pressure, not with Castro's consent, a factor that exacerbated the relationship. Castro thought that the missiles were placed in Cuba to defend the island against a U.S. invasion. The Soviets never trusted Castro and were disenchanted with his adventures in Latin America during the 1960s. At the time, Soviet policy advocated local communist parties to come to power through existing political apparatus, not violence.

Neither the Soviet dissatisfaction nor the U.S. pressure prevented Castro from attempting to export revolution to Latin America during the 1960s. In the second Declaration of Havana on February 5, 1962, Castro called on all revolutionaries to fan the flame of liberation across Latin America and supported such movements in Bolivia, Colombia, Guatemala, Peru, and Venezuela. As a result of these policies Castro and Cuba stood alone, isolated from the United States, ostracized by all of Latin America, save Mexico, and was increasingly frowned upon by the Soviet Union.

By contrast, ten years later Castro and Cuba enjoyed international status out of proportion to the country's size, force, and economy. Some argue that Castro's success came because the Soviet Union bailed out the defunct Cuban economy starting in 1968. Others argued that Castro gambled that the Soviets could not afford to cut him off without suffering a tremendous loss of international prestige, particularly in the underdeveloped world. Thus Castro was free to pursue his own international policies.

1970S

Certainly Castro supported Soviet foreign policy. Before the 1972 meeting of the Non-Aligned Movement in Algiers, Castro defended the Soviet Union as a nonimperialist state. During a 1971 visit to Marxist Chilean president, Salvadore Allende, Castro publically noted that the ballot box was an acceptable road to a socialist revolution. In return, when the Soviet premier, Leonid Brezhnev, visited Cuba in 1974, he applauded the country for being a model for other developing nations to follow. Brezhnev, however, did not mean for Castro to pursue an independent foreign policy.

Castro, however, did just that. He pursued a more temperate policy toward Latin America and gained Cuba's admission to a number of Latin American economic associations, including its most important at the time, SELA (the Latin American Economic System). Castro openly supported Jamaica's socialist president, Michael Manley, by supplying construction workers, doctors, teachers, buses, tractors, and prefabricated housing. He applauded Panama's strongman, Omar Torrijos, for standing up to the United States without provoking a response and completing the 1977 Panama Canal Treaties that provided for Panama's control of the canal in 2000. A sign of Castro's hemispheric standing by the end of the 1970s can be measured by the fact that ten Latin American countries extended recognition to Cuba.

His incipient globalism began in the spring and summer of 1972 when he visited ten African and East European countries and participated in the Non-Aligned Movement summit conference in Algiers, where he sought to unite the underdeveloped world in its effort to receive greater assistance from the industrialized nations. Cuba's forays into global affairs were intended to strengthen the country's international image,

The military garb of Cuban leader Fidel Castro (left) contrasts with the civilian clothes of his host, Chilean President Salvatore Allende (right). Castro visited the recently elected socialist president for almost a month, from November to December, 1971. Castro's efforts on behalf of Marxism, revolutionary or elected, were of great concern to U.S. diplomats. U.S. anticommunist intrigues led to Allende's death during a military coup on September 11, 1973, that put in power repressive right-wing dictator Augusto Pinochet.

SOURCE: Prensa Latina-TASS/SOURCE/NEWSCOM

but each instance produced the opposite impact. In the 1970s Castro focused upon Africa's wars of national liberation, most notably the Angolan Civil War, but across Africa, from 1974 to 1977, Cuban soldiers served Soviet interests. Cuban military units appeared in Syria during the 1973 Yom Kippur War, but their role has never been fully revealed. However, in so doing, they appeared to side with the Arab world in its conflict with Israel. Castro also undertook a modest program of development assistance by sending some eight thousand doctors, agronomists, teachers, and other specialists to Africa, the Caribbean, and southeast Asia. The peak of Castro's world standing came in 1979 when Cuba hosted the sixth conference of the Non-Aligned Movement, and he was elected its president. Within a year Castro's international prestige began to decline markedly. To the consternation of the non-aligned nations, Castro defended the Soviet invasion of Afghanistan and, at the same time, he became the focal point of U.S. President Ronald Reagan's policy in Grenada. The ineptitude of Cuban military forces in Grenada during Operation Fury in 1983 weakened Cuba's prestige in the socialist world.

On two occasions the United States dealt directly with the Soviet Union to solve the crisis. In 1970 Secretary of State Henry Kissinger successfully challenged the Soviet construction of a submarine base at Cienfuegos, and in the 1980s the United States again negotiated an end to Soviet aid to the Nicaraguan Sandinistas, including Cuban military advisors, doctors, and other support personnel.

1980S TO PRESENT DAY

The 1980s brought several changes. On the one hand Castro benefited from his pro-Argentine stance on the Falklands/Malvinas War that found the United States siding with Great Britain. In addition an increase in world demand for sugar brought a new degree of prosperity to Cuba, including the opportunity to diversify its economy. Trade and diplomatic relations were established with nearly all hemispheric nations and significant trade relations with Britain, Canada, Japan, Mexico, and Spain, in particular. In contrast relations with the Soviet Union worsened as the 1980s progressed. The changes ushered in by Premier Mikhail Gorbachev opened the floodgates to the downfall of the Soviet Union and its East Bloc satellite states by 1991. As early as 1986 Gorbachev signaled a new economic relationship was in the making, but with the collapse of the Soviet Union, Cuba lost its economic benefactor. Cuba appeared on the verge of collapse.

Thanks to the largesse of western European investors, Japan, China, and the UN Historic Preservation Program, Castro and his economic advisors deftly steered Cuba through its "special period" in the early 1990s to a period of economic recovery in the late 2000s. Castro capitalized upon the expansion of U.S. agricultural trade to Cuba, despite the opposition of President George W. Bush. From 2001 through 2007, the bilateral trade climbed from $127,000 to nearly $1 million annually. But it also revealed the weakness in the Cuban economy, a slack that was picked up by Venezuelan President and U.S. nemesis, Hugo Chávez. However Castro's 2010 declaration that the communist economic model does not work is antithetical to the socialist Chávez's beliefs and his connections with the Iranian regime. How this contradiction will play out remains unclear at this writing.

See also *Batista y Zaldívar, Fulgencio; Bay of Pigs Invasion, 1961; Cuba, Rapprochement with the United States, 1960s–1990s; Cuba,*

U.S. Embargo of; Cuba, U.S. Relations with; Cuban Democracy Act, 1992 (United States); Cuban Liberty and Democratic Solidarity Act, 1996 (United States); Cuban Missile Crisis, 1962; Cuban Revolution, 1956-1959, U.S. Policy toward

. . . . THOMAS M. LEONARD

REFERENCES AND FURTHER READING

Brenner, Philip. *From Confrontation to Negotiation: U.S. Relations with Cuba.* Boulder, CO: Westview Press, 1988.

Dominguez, Jorge. *Castro and International Affairs.* Beverly Hills, CA: Sage, 1988.

Erisman, H. Michael. *Cuba's Foreign Relations in a Post Soviet World.* Gainesville: University Press of Florida, 2000.

Gleijeses, Piero. *Conflicting Missions: Havana, Washington and Africa, 1959–1976.* Chapel Hill: University of North Carolina Press, 1982.

Ignacio, Raymont. *Fidel Castro: My Life: A Spoken Autobiography.* Translated by Andrew Hurley. New York: Scribner's, 2008.

Kaplowitz, Donna. *Anatomy of a Filed Embargo: U.S. Sanctions Against Cuba.* Boulder, CO: Lynne Reiner, 1998.

LeGrand, Geoff, and Alexandra Reed. "Castro's Change of Heart: The Implications for Cuba, Venezuela, and the United States." Report of the Council on Hemispheric Affairs, September 17, 2010.

Leonard, Thomas M. *Fidel Castro: A Biography.* Westport, CT: Greenwood Press, 2004.

Morley, Morris H. *Imperial State and Revolution: The United States and Cuba, 1952–1986.* Cambridge, UK: Cambridge University Press, 1987.

Morley, Morris H., and Chris McGillion. *Unfinished Business: America and Cuba after the Cold War, 1989–2002.* Cambridge, UK: Cambridge University Press, 2002.

Peréz, Louis A. *The United States and Cuba: Ties of Singular Intimacy.* Athens: University of Georgia Press, 1990.

Sullivan, Mark P. "Cuba: Issues for the 111th Congress." Washington, DC: Congressional Research Service, 2010.

Castro Ruz, Raúl

(**See** *Castro Ruz, Fidel; Cuba, U.S. Relations with; Cuban Revolution, 1956–1959, U.S. Policy toward*)

Cédras, Raoul

Born in Jérémie, Haiti, on July 9, 1949, Raoul Cédras was the leader of the military junta that ruled Haiti from 1991 to 1994. Although he did not initiate the September coup d'état that toppled President Jean-Bertrand Aristide (Major Michel François, head of the military in Port-au-Prince, gets that credit), Cédras quickly became the face of what Haitians derisively referred to as "the de facto regime." A lieutenant general in the Forces Armées d'Haïti, Cédras was responsible for the murder of more than a thousand Haitians when the country was essentially occupied by its own army.

While Cédras's army and paramilitary forces were slaughtering his supporters, Aristide lived mostly in the United States, negotiating for his return with the U.S. government, the Organization of American States (OAS), the United Nations, and various power brokers in Haiti. In October 1991 U.S. President George H. W. Bush met with Aristide and pledged support for the ouster of Cédras and the return to democracy. The OAS called for all members to cut trade, financial, military, and diplomatic ties with Haiti. Only the Vatican recognized the Cédras regime as a legitimate government. In November the United States (along with thirty-three other nations) imposed a trade embargo on Haiti, and by the end of December Haiti's economy appeared to grind to a halt.

In February 1992 the OAS-brokered Protocole d'Accord à Washington was signed by Aristide and Haitian parliamentary leaders, paving the way for Aristide's return, but the protocol was blocked by Cédras and never ratified.

The brutality of the Cédras regime resulted in thousands of "boat people" fleeing Haiti, and in May 1992 President Bush signed the "Kennebunkport Order," under which all Haitian refugee boats were interdicted and their passengers returned to Port-au-Prince with no opportunity for asylum. Bill Clinton (President 1993–2001) continued the Bush administration's restrictive policy on Haitian refugees, and the crisis with the Cédras regime escalated.

In July 1993 on Governor's Island, New York, Cédras and Aristide signed an internationally backed agreement to restore democracy and return Aristide to office on October 30. On that very date, however, Cédras reneged. Under international pressure the United States was left with little choice but to intervene with its military in Haiti, which it did with no opposition after the diplomatic trio of former President Jimmy Carter, Senator Sam Nunn, and former Chairman of the Joint Chiefs of Staff Colin Powell successfully persuaded Cédras to relinquish power. Beginning on September 26, 1994, Operation Uphold Democracy, initially using more than twenty thousand U.S. military personnel and about two thousand personnel from several other countries, effectively controlled Haiti. On October 4 Major François fled to the Dominican Republic, and on October 13 Cédras and other military leaders departed for Panama. On October 15, 1994, Aristide returned to a jubilant welcome from the Haitian masses as their rightful president.

On November 16, 2000, a Haitian trial court convicted Cédras of murder in absentia. Cédras was last reported living in comfort in Panama City, Panama.

See also *Aristide, Jean-Bertrand; Clinton, William J.; Haiti, Refugees from; Haiti, U.S. Intervention under President Clinton, 1994; Haiti, U.S. Relations with*

. . . . ROBERT LAWLESS

REFERENCES AND FURTHER READING

Jean-François, Hérold. *Le coup de Cédras.* Port-au-Prince, Haiti: Mediatek, 1995.

Malone, David. *Decision-Making in the UN Security Council: The Case of Haiti, 1990–1997.* Oxford, UK: Clarendon, 1998.

Pezzullo, Ralph. *Plunging into Haiti: Clinton, Aristide, and the Defeat of Diplomacy.* Jackson: University Press of Mississippi, 2006.

Central America, Filibusters

Filibusters were American citizens who used armed force to procure economic and political influence beyond the borders of the United States from 1848–1861. Their efforts were directed mainly southward toward Cuba, Mexico, and the Central American republics. These illegal excursions disrupted diplomatic relations of the United States within its own hemisphere by damaging relationships with Latin American counties and the United Kingdom.

MAKEUP OF THE FILIBUSTER EXPEDITIONS

The majority of the filibusters were young, unmarried fortune seekers and adventurers. In Narciso Lopez's Cuban expedition, the greater majority of the eighty-five men were under the age of twenty-five. These filibusters also recruited runaway teenage boys with stories of power and wealth south of the U.S. border. Many of the Americans were veterans of the late war with Mexico or the gold rush to California in 1848 and 1849. Most of these men were inspired by profit, but there was also a desire to expand the influence of proslavery out of the United States into the Latin American countries. The preponderance of these proslavery southerners saw opportunity in the Spanish-speaking lands, where they could obtain economic power and political influence in a new slave-owning empire.

Many filibuster groups used the notion of colonization or immigration to disguise their true intentions. A number of American politicians secretly supported filibuster groups as a method to increase the size of the Union through the introduction of new slave states. One example was Senator John A. Quitman of Mississippi, who unsuccessfully attempted to raise a filibuster army to take Cuba in the early 1850s. The diplomatic problems caused by filibusters impeded the efforts of several U.S. presidents to purchase Cuba and the northern areas of Mexico prior to the U.S. Civil War.

Along with the Americans were numbers of Europeans who saw filibustering as a way to find adventure and fortune. Many filibuster military organizations consisted of veterans of past conflicts and the 1848 revolutionary movements in Europe. Immigrants also made up a large number of recruits to filibuster organizations, especially in William Walker's filibuster army in Nicaragua. The register of Walker's army recorded roughly 287 Europeans. In the Battle of Santa Rosa in March 1856, the filibuster force consisted of a French battalion, a German battalion, and two American battalions.

Most of the filibuster groups were organized in loose military companies. Walker's filibuster army followed an organizational scheme typical of the mid-nineteenth century armies with artillery, cavalry, infantry (both light and regular), and rangers. The battlefield success of filibusters was due in part to their combat experience and the use of modern weapons, such as revolvers and percussion rifles. Walker's army remained unique among the filibusting expeditions, because it possessed its own naval support, which consisted of an armed schooner captured from the Costa Rican navy.

Despite their modern weapons and military experience, the filibusters were hampered by inefficient supply. Many expeditions to Cuba and Central America were forced to use unreliable ships to ferry men and equipment. One of the main reasons for the failure of the Lopez expeditions to Cuba was the inability to procure enough shipping to supply and reinforce the filibusters. Walker's army was finally defeated in the field in 1857, when Cornelius Vanderbilt supplied military advisors and modern weapons to the Central American nations fighting the filibusters.

U.S. GOVERNMENT RESPONSE

According to U.S. law, filibustering was a violation of the Neutrality Law of 1818, which prohibited the organization within the United States of any armed force that intended to attack a friendly foreign power. The American government attempted, through the enforcement of this law, to prevent its citizens from filibustering, mostly by preventing potential filibustering groups from organizing and collecting arms for future operations. U.S. Marshals watched for expeditions in ports like San Francisco and New Orleans, while the U.S. Navy stood ready to intercept any filibuster vessels.

In February 1854 the Spanish governor-general, Marques de la Pezuela, seized the American Merchant ship *Black Warrior* in the harbor in Havana, Cuba. The seizure was based on the charge that the *Black Warrior's* manifest did not match the cargo in its hold. Pezuela refused to allow the American captain to contact the American Consul within the city. This action became a diplomatic tug of war between Spanish authorities attempting to control American intrigue in Cuba and southern U.S. proslavery leaders looking for an excuse to seize the island. The American minister to Spain, Pierre Soulé, attempted to use the incident to bring about a war between the two nations. The American uproar drew the support of President Franklin Pierce and other congressional leaders looking to punish Spain for the outrage. Senator Quitman delayed in exploiting the political anger to mount an expedition to Cuba or even assisting in political efforts to change the Neutrality Law of 1818. Eventually the incident was resolved diplomatically with the release of the ship and payment of a fine.

In 1855 President Pierce issued a proclamation against filibustering and ordered federal district attorneys to stop any ships that might be carrying recruits and equipment for filibustering operations. In doing so the president reaffirmed efforts to obtain Cuba through purchase, not military action. These enforcement efforts played a role in preventing filibusters from gathering men and supplies prior to expeditions, such as Senator Quitman's repeated attempts to raise a force to invade Cuba. In 1857 the U.S. Navy joined the Royal Navy in blockading a Nicaraguan port that was being used to supply William Walker's filibuster army, which spelled the beginning of the end to Walker's excursions in Central America.

AREAS OF MAIN FILIBUSTER OPERATIONS

Mexico was the initial focus of filibuster activity after its defeat in the Mexican War. Americans saw the defeated nation as a fruit ripe for the picking by enterprising young men. Mexico could also be seen as a place for the expansion of slavery out of the southern United States. Claims of gold deposits in the Sonora region in western Mexico drew the attention of Americans and foreigners living in California.

One of the most famous of the filibusters, William Walker, was the leader of the first filibuster expeditions to western Mexico. He occupied Baja California in November 1853 and declared the Republic of Sonora. This first attempt by Walker failed, and by 1854 he was back in the United States. A sizable contingent of French immigrants attempted to move into Sonora, but local forces defeated them. The last filibuster scheme in western Mexico was the Henry Crabb expedition that was captured and executed in Caborca, Mexico, in 1857. In addition, there were other filibuster groups operating in areas south of the Rio Grande River.

Filibusters also focused their attention toward the island of Cuba, which was a logical extension of Manifest Destiny southward from the southern United States. In Cuba Southerners saw a perfect location for new slave states that might serve as a counterweight to the creation of free states. They viewed Spain, Cuba's colonial ruler, as a declining European power that would offer little serious defense of the island. Also Cuba's tropical climate was a perfect environment for the introduction of cash crops from the southern United States, where cotton and tobacco occupied a majority of acreage. Narciso López conducted two major expeditions against the Spanish authorities on Cuba in 1850 and 1851. Many of his filibusters were Southerners from the United States, such as Roberdeau Wheat and William L. Crittenden, and wealthy southerners provided the funds for military equipment. Lopez and his men were eventually defeated by the Spanish garrison during their last foray to Cuba and were put to death. A number of his followers did escape back to the United States and later participated in the U.S. Civil War.

William Walker's filibuster army in Nicaragua drew the most press attention and came the closest to success in Central America. Large profits were being made in the transcontinental route though Nicaragua to the Pacific Ocean, due to the California Gold Rush. Cornelius Vanderbilt and others purchased companies to move people and supplies through Nicaragua. Internal Nicaraguan politics and British diplomacy began to affect the profits from this endeavor. Through the influence of Byron Cole and Henry Crabb, William Walker became interested in the economic opportunities presented by Nicaraguan agriculture and transportation routes. Vanderbilt's competitors initially financed Walker's men into Nicaragua to control and protect their transportation companies, while Walker believed that he was taking the first steps to create a new republic.

From 1855 to 1857 William Walker was the dominant power in Nicaragua. His initial group of 58 men grew into a small army of 1,200. Walker assisted the Nicaraguan Democrats in taking over the country and by defeating their domestic opponents, the Legitimist faction. Soon Walker became embroiled in a brutal war with surrounding Central American republics. Walker took over the presidency of Nicaragua and legalized slavery within the country. He also threatened to take over the transportation companies operating in Nicaragua. To stop Walker, Vanderbilt directed his financial resources to the countries surrounding Nicaragua. Eventually Walker's force was defeated by the growing power of Costa Rica and other neighboring countries and his dwindling supplies. Walker and his small band of survivors returned to the United States in 1857. Walker attempted to return to Nicaragua later that year but was stopped by a U.S. Navy squadron. In 1860 he attempted to assist in a possible revolt in Honduras but was captured by the Royal Navy. Walker was handed over to the Honduran government, which executed him on September 12, 1860.

See also *Central America, Filibusters; Costa Rica, U.S. Relations with; Cuba, U.S. Relations with; Guatemala, U.S. Relations with; Honduras, U.S. Relations with; López, Narciso; Manifest Destiny; Mexican-American War, 1846–1848; Mexico, U.S. Relations with; Nicaragua, U.S. Relations with; Pierce, Franklin; Vanderbilt, Cornelius*

. . . . WILLIAM H. BROWN

REFERENCES AND FURTHER READING

Brown, Charles H. *Agents of Manifest Destiny: The Life and Times of the Filibusters*. Chapel Hill: The University of North Carolina Press, 1980.
Carr, Albert Z. *The World and William Walker*. New York: Harper & Row, 1963.
Greene, Laurence. *The Filibuster: The Career of William Walker*. Indianapolis, IN: Bobbs-Merrill, 1937.
May, Robert E. *The Southern Dream of a Caribbean Empire, 1854–1861*. Baton Rouge: Louisiana State University Press, 1973.
May, Robert E. *Manifest Destiny's Underworld: Filibustering in Antebellum America*. Chapel Hill: The University of North Carolina Press, 2002.
Potter, David M. *The Impending Crisis, 1848–1861*. New York: Harper Torchbooks, 1976.
Rosengarten, Frederic Jr. *Freebooters Must Die: The Life and Death of William Walker, the Most Notorious Filibuster of the Nineteenth Century*. Wayne, PA: Haverford House, 1976.
Scroggs, William O. *Filibusters and Financiers: The Story of William Walker and His Associates*. New York: McMillan, 1916.
Walker, William. *The War in Nicaragua*. Detroit, MI: Ethridge, 1971. (originally published 1860)

Central America: Unification Efforts since 1840

Historically the five Central American republics (Costa Rica, El Salvador, Guatemala, Honduras, and Nicaragua) have been portrayed as one geographic unit, best illustrated by Hubert Howe Bancroft's 1886 three-volume classic, *History of Central America,* and Ralph Lee Woodward's seminal work, *Central America: A Nation Divided* (3rd ed., 1999). The unity impression stems from the region's Spanish colonial experience when it was unified as the *Audiencia de Guatemala* and part of the larger Viceroyalty of Mexico. The Central Americans unsuccessfully attempted to recreate the *audiencia* with the United Provinces of Central America that lasted from 1823 to 1840. Motivated by external events on four subsequent occasions in the nineteenth century, the Central Americans momentarily attempted unification.

The first came in May 1855 when the U.S. filibusterer, William Walker, and his small mercenary army, arrived in Nicaragua at the behest of the country's liberals, who sought to wrest political control from the ruling conservatives. Walker accomplished that objective within five months of his arrival, but he also had his own ambitions: impose a Central American Union under his direction. The conservatives in the other four Central American republics formed a military alliance that ousted Walker in a battle at La Virgin on March 1, 1856. Following Walker's defeat, the five Central American Republics returned to their individual machinations.

Beginning in the 1860s liberals returned to political power across Central America. At the same time President Ulysses S. Grant rekindled U.S. interest in a transisthmian canal. The two forces—the liberal vision of Central American unity and U.S. canal interests—came together in 1880, one year after the Frenchman Ferdinand de Lesseps commenced construction of a canal route at Panama. The U.S. minister to Central America, Cornelius A. Logan, found Guatemalan President Justo Rufino Barrios receptive to the idea of a Central American Union under his leadership that would secure the region from foreign penetration under the terms of the Monroe Doctrine but also provide the United States the opportunity to build and secure a transisthmian canal. The idea passed into history when Barrios sent a special negotiator scurrying off to Washington, D.C., where it was rebuffed by the Rutherford B. Hayes administration.

Still the U.S. canal euphoria continued. In 1884 Secretary of State Frederick T. Frelinghuysen completed a treaty with the Nicaraguan minister to the United States, Joaquín Zavala, that provided for a U.S. constructed and operated canal through Nicaragua in return for a U.S. guarantee of Nicaraguan territorial integrity. Fearful that the Guatemalan leader might force a Central American Union to get Nicaraguan treaty approval, the Nicaraguan legislature rapidly approved the Frelinghuysen-Zavala Treaty but, not anxious to become embroiled in Central American political affairs, U.S. President Grover Cleveland refused to submit the treaty to the Senate for its consideration. Again plans for both the canal and Central American unity efforts collapsed.

In 1895 El Salvador, Honduras, and Nicaragua, prompted by nationalistic Hondurans who threatened to engulf the region in conflict and suspicious of the growing presence of U.S. entrepreneurs, formed a loose federation, the Greater Republic of Central America. None of the governments were willing to surrender their autonomy to a central government. In 1898 El Salvador withdrew from the republic, bringing the venture to an end. This final nineteenth-century attempt at Central American unity confirmed the century-long U.S. impression that the region's ruling elite only talked about the vision of isthmian unity but were unwilling to take any measures to implement it. U.S. policy became evident at the 1907 and 1923 Central American conferences where U.S. policymakers refused to include the unity question on the conference agendas. The Central Americans finally came together in 1960 with the formation of the Central American Common Market (CACM). Subsequently other intraregional agencies were formed, including the Central American Defense Council (CONDECA) and the Central American Bank for Economic Integration (CABEI). In 2004 the five republics joined with the Dominican Republic to complete the Central American-Dominican Republic Free Trade Agreement (CAFTA-DR).

See also *Central American Bank for Economic Integration (CABEI); Central American Common Market (CACM); Central American Conference, Washington, 1907; Central American Conference, Washington, 1923; Central American Defense Council (CONDECA); Central American-Dominican Republic Free Trade Agreement, 2004 (CAFTA-DR); United Provinces of Central America, 1823–1839*

. . . . THOMAS M. LEONARD

REFERENCES AND FURTHER READING

Karnes, Thomas L. *The Failure of Union: Central America, 1824–1960.* Chapel Hill: University of North Carolina Press, 1961.

Stansifer, Charles L. "United States-Central American Relations, 1824–1850." In *United States-Latin American Relations, 1800–1850: The Formative Generations,* edited by T. Ray Shurbutt, 25–45. Tuscaloosa: University of Alabama Press, 1991.

Woodward, Ralph Lee. *Central America: A Nation Divided,* 3rd ed. New York: Oxford University Press, 1999).

Central American Arms Limitation Agreement, 1923

(**See** *Central American Conference, Washington, 1923*)

Central American Bank for Economic Integration (CABEI)

The Central American Bank for Economic Integration (CABEI) was established by El Salvador, Guatemala, Honduras, and Nicaragua in December 1960, culminating from the 1951 Organization of Central American States (ODECA) 1958 Multilateral Treaty of Free Trade and Integration, and the 1959 Treaty of Uniform Import Tariffs, among other initiatives of the same countries. Costa Rica joined as a founding member in 1963, while Argentina, Colombia, the Dominican Republic, Mexico, Panama, Spain, and Taiwan entered as nonregional members, and Belize entered as a beneficiary member. Headquartered in Tegucigalpa, Honduras, CABEI's strategic goal of balancing economic integration and social development traditionally emphasized three pillars: poverty reduction, regional integration, and globalization.

Poverty reduction attracted $1.09 billion since 2005, allocated to education (El Salvador), hospital construction (Nicaragua), replacement of the 1932 national identity card (Guatemala), rural electrification (Guatemala), rural financing (Belize), and social security infrastructure development (Costa Rica), among others. Targeting micro, small, and medium enterprises, CABEI also funded border zones, created social transformation of Central America, and established financing for the majorities department to help marginal entrepreneurs.

CABEI pioneered western hemisphere regional economic integration when the closely aligned Central American Common Market (CACM) was established in 1960. CACM's bold experimentation with the Central American Common Fund (1981) and the common external tariff (1985) disguised the difficulties it faced amid the 1980s conflicts and the $11 billion debt the region owed in 1984 (which further lowered living standards by 25 percent). Buoyed by the United States, the region persisted with economic integration, concluding the Central American Free Trade Agreement (CAFTA) with it and the complementary Plan Puebla Panama (PPP, renamed Mesoamericana Project) with Mexico in the early twenty-first century. CABEI provided $9 million in 2009 for the Central American Electrical Interconnection System, for example, and up to $1.86 billion until then to develop transportation (Inter-American Highway Network) and energy supply (hydroelectric plants).

Country-specific regional infrastructural projects, such as Costa Rica's 3G mobile telephone system, Guatemala's La Aurora International Airport modernization, and Port Cortés in Honduras, also received CABEI funds, while CABEI also initiated the Central American Mezzanine Infrastructure Fund, Regional Stock Market, and the Regional Securities Settlement System, to consolidate a regional identity. CABEI supports the Central American Integration System, streamlining not just U.S. interests but also Spanish—evident in its participation in, and contributions to, the Summit of the Americas and Iberoamericana summits.

As one of the world's sixteen largest multilateral banks, CABEI promotes globalization and competitiveness, encouraging and enhancing private entrepreneurs (about 40 percent of CABEI loans went to this sector). It funded outsourcing projects (such as the Contact Center in Nicaragua), tourism (through Costa Rica's *Monte del Barco* Property Development Investment Fund), highways (helping Costa Rica's *Concesionaria Autopistas del Sol, S.A.*, build the "Highway to the Sun"), and technical projects (like establishing EARTH University in Costa Rica with its signature components, the Technological Innovation Center and the Green Conference Center). Additionally CABEI actively seeks a European Union free trade agreement, while its alliances with the World Bank Group, the Inter-American Investment Corporation, the Inter-American Development Bank, the Andean Development Bank, and the Caribbean Development Bank further demonstrate policy congruency with the United States.

During the 2007–2009 recession, CABEI actually expanded capitalization from $2 billion to $5 billion—a far cry from the $16 million authorized capital it began with in the 1960s. CABEI's board of governors, representing either the economic minister or the central bank chief of each founding member, sits at the top, followed by a nine-member board of directors (one for each member country) and a competitively elected executive president with a five-year term, renewable once only. Harmony at each level extends its future viability.

CABEI's total assets expansion from $3.4 billion in 2004 to $5.4 billion in 2008, loan extensions from $2.7 billion in 2004 to $4.3 billion in 2008, and income growth increases from $56.2 billion in 2004 to $83.29 in 2009, suggests, even with liabilities mounting from $2.08 billion in 2004 to $3.74 billion in 2008 and equities rising to $1.7 billion from $1.37 billion in 2004, the organization is deepening. How it has survived both political and financial turmoil in the past while registering growth makes its progress toward fulfilling its three pillars increasingly irreversible.

See also *Central American Common Market (CACM); Central American-Dominican Republic Free Trade Agreement, 2004 (CAFTA-DR)*

. . . . IMTIAZ HUSSAIN

REFERENCES AND FURTHER READING

Central American Bank for Economic Integration (CABEI). *Annual Report, 2009*. Tegucigalpa, Honduras: Author, 2009.

Central American Bank for Economic Integration (CABEI). *Fostering Development: CABEI, 1961–2001*. Tegucigalpa, Honduras: Author, 2001.

Large, William R., ed. *An Enduring Partnership for Development: Central America and the IDB since 1990*. Washington, DC: IDB, 2004.

Central American Common Market (CACM)

During the 1950s the UN Economic Commission on Latin America and the Caribbean (ECLAC) advocated regional integration as a development scheme for Latin America. It was argued that integration, along with Import Substitution Industrialization (ISI), would stimulate industrial development and economic growth in small-to-medium economies, such as those in Central America. Central American countries had a history of integration, beginning with the Central American Federation (1823–1838). Renewed integration efforts began in October 1951 with the establishment of the Organization of Central American States (ODECA), comprised of Costa Rica, El Salvador, Guatemala, Honduras and Nicaragua, which established the regional commitment to greater economic cooperation. In 1952 the Committee of Economic Cooperation began consultation on economic integration with the aid of ECLAC.

GENESIS AND OPERATIONS

The Multilateral Treaty on Free Trade and Integration was signed in 1958, calling for the gradual liberalization of regional trade with the ultimate goal of free trade among member states over a ten-year period. In 1959 the Central American Agreement of Tariff Equalization created a common external tariff by averaging the existing tariffs of individual members. In April 1960 Guatemala, El Salvador, and Honduras signed the tripartite Treaty of Economic Association which established, with few exceptions, the free trade of goods and the reduction of the time period on excluded goods from ten to five years. On June 3, 1961, El Salvador, Guatemala, and Nicaragua ratified the General Treaty of Central American Economic Integration, creating the Central American Common Market (CACM). They were joined by Honduras in April 1962 and Costa Rica in September 1963. The treaty's goals were to establish free trade among members, to create a common external tariff, to harmonize industrial policies, to promote regional industry, and to facilitate the free movement of products throughout the region. While the countries achieved relative success in trade liberalization and the establishment of a common external tariff, the

CACM functioned as more of a customs union than common market. The United States supported the new trade scheme, which coincided with regional objectives in promoting trade and development. The United States provided almost $200 million to the Central American Bank in the 1960s, although most of the funds favored U.S. corporations.

The structure of the CACM consisted of five main governing institutions. The Central American Economic Council, consisting of the ministers of economy of the five member states, was responsible for the coordination of economic policy. The Executive Council, comprised of vice ministers of the economy, was responsible for the execution of the treaty and dispute resolution. The Permanent Secretariat (SIECA), headed by the secretary general appointed by the Economic Council for a three-year term, was the main administrator, acting as the judicial body for the Executive and Economic Councils. The Central American Bank for Economic Integration (CABEI), comprised of the ministers of the economy and presidents of their respective central banks, was responsible for funding CACM projects. The Central American Clearing House oversaw monetary transactions between member states.

The early years of the CACM were characterized by significant increases in intraregional trade, foreign trade, and the promotion of industry. Between 1960 and 1969 interregional trade grew from $32.7 million to $263.2 million, an increase of 800 percent. However, the benefits of integration and industrialization were uneven among different sectors and different countries. Additional investment and competition from U.S.-owned companies increased significantly during this period, limiting the development of new regional industries. Costa Rica, the most developed of the five countries, was wary of full participation in the CACM due to cheaper labor in other, less-developed member states. El Salvador and Guatemala, two of the more developed countries in the region, were the primary beneficiaries of industrial development and interregional trade. Industrial development occurred at the expense of the agricultural sector, which resulted in increases in unemployment. By the late 1960s Honduras and Nicaragua, the less-developed members, began to experience deteriorating trade conditions. By 1970 Honduras's trade deficit was $51 million, of which $37 million was with its CACM trading partners. The dispute over benefits resulted in tensions between member states. The 1969 Soccer War between El Salvador and Honduras was the result of land reforms in Honduras meant to halt the influx of Salvadoran migrant laborers, which had been facilitated by Salvadoran land tenure patterns and the loss of jobs to industrialization and declining agricultural production. Honduras ultimately imposed protective tariffs, effectively withdrawing from the CACM in 1970. Costa Rica, which had become dependent on trade with Honduras, followed suit, although it lifted the imposition of tariffs the following year. Interregional trade slowed significantly by the mid-1970s as economic and political crises loomed in member states. Intraregional exports declined from 26.1 percent in 1970 to 13.7 percent in 1984, with most members experiencing negative growth by 1979. Moreover the region's economies had become more dependent on trade with the United States than they had been two decades prior. The CACM effectively collapsed in 1979 amid economic and political crisis in the region, although a common external tariff remained in effect until 1986.

REVIVING THE CACM

Attempts at resuscitating the CACM began in the early 1980s, but no real progress occurred until the mid-1980s with the Central American peace process. The revitalization of the CACM began during the Esquipulas meetings in 1986 and 1987, as leaders linked regional peace with regional prosperity. In June 1990 the five Central American presidents met to discuss plans for regional integration. The Antigua Declaration provided for an Economic Action Plan for Central America (PAECA) to promote regional integration, which served as the basis for renewing the CACM. Subsequent meetings with the economy ministers in Guatemala City and vice presidents in San Salvador culminated in an agreement to reorganize the CACM and its institutions to be more inclusive and supportive of equitable development. The General Treaty was adapted to reflect current conditions, including a shift in the dominant economic model from ISI to export-led growth. Some original institutions, such as ODECA and SIECA, were reinstated in concert with the formation of new structures to oversee the integration process. The Central American Integration System (SICA) was established in 1991 with the signing of the Protocol of Tegucigalpa. SICA is composed of three governing bodies: the Central American Parliament (PARLACEN), the Central American Court of Justice, and the Secretariat General of the Central American Integration System (SG-SICA). In 1993 the five CACM countries signed the Central American Economic Integration Protocol to the General Treaty on Central American Economic Integration with the goal of creating a customs union, a monetary union, and the free movement of labor and capital, although the latter two appear unlikely. In 2004 CACM members signed the Central American Free Trade Agreement (CAFTA) with the United States.

See also *Central American Bank for Economic Integration (CABEI); Central American-Dominican Republic Free Trade Agreement, 2004 (CAFTA-DR); Central American Wars, 1980s; Central American Common Market (CACM); Economic Commission for Latin America and the Caribbean (CEPAL); Export-Based Economies; Import Substitution Industrialization (ISI); Organization of Central American States (ODECA); Soccer War, 1969; United Nations Observer Group in Central America (ONUCA), 1989–1992*

. . . . CHRISTINE J. WADE

References and Further Reading

Bulmer-Thomas, Victor. "The Central American Common Market: From Closed to Open Regionalism." *World Development* 26, no. 2 (1998): 313–322.

Holbrik, Karel, and Philip Swan. *Trade and Industrialization in the Central American Common Market: The First Decade.* Austin: University of Texas Press, 1972.

Hufbauer, Gary C., and Jeffrey Schott. *Western Hemispheric Economic Integration.* Washington, DC: Institute for International Economics, 1994.

McClelland, Donald. *The Central American Common Market.* New York: Praeger, 1972.
Rodriguez, Ennio. "Central America: Common Market, Trade Liberalization and Trade Agreements." In *Economic Integration in the Western Hemisphere,* edited by Roberto Bouzas and Jaime Ros, 146–170. Notre Dame, IN: University of Notre Dame Press, 1994.
Walter, Ingo. *The Central American Common Market: A Case Study in Economic Integration in Developing Regions.* New York: New York University Press, 1967.

Central American Conference, Washington, 1907

The Central American Conference, held in 1907, fell within the context of the U.S. circum-Caribbean policy designed to bring political and financial stability to the region as a means to secure the Panama Canal from foreign interlopers and from the political turmoil that plagued the region and might possibly spill into Panama. The conference can be viewed as an extension of the 1902 Platt Amendment to the Cuban constitution, the 1903 Hay–Bunau-Varilla Treaty with Panama, and President Theodore Roosevelt's 1904 declaration on the Monroe Doctrine, popularly known as the "Roosevelt Corollary." The immediate causes of the conference can be credited to Nicaraguan President José Santos Zelaya's continued anger at the United States for choosing Panama as the site of the transisthmian canal and his ambition to dominate Central America (defined to include Costa Rica, El Salvador, Guatemala, Honduras, and Nicaragua).

President Roosevelt set the tone in 1901 when he observed that every failure on Central America's part would not only bring calamity to the region but also misfortune to the United States, by inviting European intervention that violated the 1823 Monroe Doctrine. Eighty years after its independence in 1821, Central America continued to be plagued by the legacies of Spanish colonial rule that contributed to continued political instability that pitted land owning elites against each other and demonstrated a lack of maturity in managing its fiscal affairs that left the region indebted to Europe. Costa Rica was an exception, a fact that contributed to its aloofness from regional affairs. Although the coffee barons remained in control of the national government, Costa Rican politics were more tranquil and its debt manageable.

Recognizing that Panama was the favored route for a U.S. transisthmian canal route, Zelaya set out to establish himself as the leader of a Central American union. He convened a conference of his counterparts at Corinto, Nicaragua, in January 1902 that produced a declaration to submit all interstate debts to arbitration and a promise not to aid revolutionary movements within the neighboring republics. The Corinto Conference enhanced Zelaya's prestige and contributed to four years of regional peace. The calm shattered in May 1906 when a group of Guatemalan exiles, with Salvadoran assistance, invaded their homeland in an unsuccessful effort to oust President Manuel Estrada Cabrera. Subsequently the regional presidents, except for Zelaya, agreed to a regional peace conference at San José. Zelaya went further by ordering his troops to invade Honduras with the objective of bringing it under his control. Washington policymakers' worst nightmare appeared on the verge of reality: a political/military conflagration that could spill over into Panama. In response to the crisis the U.S. State Department quickly arranged a conference that was held in Washington, D.C., between November 14 and December 20, 1907. The conference produced several treaties, three of which were central to U.S. policy objectives.

The General Treaty of Peace and Amity provided for the nonrecognition of governments that came to power by *coup d'état.* Further, the treaty banned Central American governments from intervening in each other's internal affairs. Honduras, the weakest and most vulnerable to outside interference in its domestic politics, was declared neutral. Another accord established the Central American Court of Justice that was envisioned as a nonpolitical instrument for settling disputes among the five nations. These treaties satisfied the U.S. objective of achieving regional political stability through a guaranteed treaty system. The Central Americans, on the other hand, were satisfied with those agreements that pointed toward union and considered the Central American Bureau as the most important accomplishment because it intended to increase cooperation among the Central American nations by introducing modern education facilities; developing trade, agriculture, and industry; and reforming legal institutions. While the treaties brought momentary tranquility to the region, they also illustrated the different objectives of the United States and the Central American states.

The treaty system fell apart when on March 28, 1911, revolutionary groups ousted Honduran President Miguel B. Dávila. The Costa Rican government took the matter to the Central American Court of Justice, whose judges reflected their national interests rather than the facts of the case. The court proved ineffective, a fact driven home in its 1918 ruling on the Bryan-Chamorro Treaty that granted the United States the right to construct a canal across Nicaragua. The Managua government complied with U.S. instructions to ignore the court. And while the treaty sought to prevent intrastate conflicts in Central America, it said nothing about U.S. intervention. By the end of World War I, the United States interfered in Central American internal affairs nineteen times.

. . . . THOMAS M. LEONARD

See also *Bryan-Chamorro Treaty, 1915; Central American Conference, Washington, 1923; Hay–Bunau-Varilla Treaty, 1903; Platt, Orville; Roosevelt Corollary to the Monroe Doctrine*

References and Further Reading

Langley, Lester D. *The Banana Wars: An Inner History of American Empire, 1900–1934.* Lexington: University of Kentucky Press, 1983.
Martínez Moreno, A. *La conferencia de Washington de 1907 y la corte de justicia de central Americana.* San Salvador, El Salvador: Rodríguez Hermanos, 1957.
Munro, Dana G. *Intervention and Dollar Diplomacy in the Caribbean, 1900–1921.* Princeton, NJ: Princeton University Press, 1964.
United States Department of State. *Papers Relating to the Foreign Relations of the United States, 1907.* Washington, DC: Government Printing Office, 1910.

Central American Conference, Washington, 1923

The Central American Conference, 1923, stands as a high-water mark of the U.S. effort to bring political stability to Central America during the first half of the twentieth century. Save Costa Rica, the history of the other four regional countries (El Salvador, Guatemala, Honduras, and Nicaragua) had been marred by constant political strife. To end the continuing political crisis, U.S. policymakers determined that the imposition of constitutional government upon the Central American republics would correct that deficiency. The first effort came with the 1907 Washington conference, but its treaty system fell into total disarray by the end of World War I. U.S. State Department officials placed responsibility upon the Central Americans without recognizing the adverse impact that U.S. policies and actions had upon that same treaty structure.

The immediate causes of the 1923 conference are traced to the ascendency of five new presidents in 1919 and 1920: General Rafael López Guitérrez in Honduras, Diego Manuel Chamorro in Nicaragua, Carlos Meléndez in El Salvador, Carlos Herrera in Guatemala, and Julio Acosta Guardia in Costa Rica. All but Acosta were considered weak political leaders. Over the next two years each fell victim to political intrigue and, in varying degrees, each new president supported the idea of a Central American union. Toward that end delegates from the five nations convened in San José, Costa Rica, from December 4, 1920, to January 19, 1921, and produced a federal constitution. The governments of El Salvador, Guatemala, and Honduras approved the document and promulgated a federation in October 1921. Prodded by the United States, Nicaragua subsequently approved the pact. Costa Rica, in which President Acosta returned the *Ticos* to their traditional aloofness from regional affairs, did not consider ratification of the treaty. While the U.S. State Department optimistically believed that the agreement would bring regional political stability, facilitate U.S. investments, and limit Mexican influence in the area, it withheld recognition of the federation until it demonstrated that it could function effectively.

The federation fell apart beginning in January 13, 1921, when Guatemalan General José Manuel Orellana ousted Herrera and joined forces with Honduran Liberal President Guitérrez against their conservative political enemies. This placed the governments in Tegucigalpa and Guatemala City against the governments in Managua and San Salvador. Border skirmishes soon followed. To avoid a regional war, in August 1922 the United States summoned the presidents of El Salvador, Honduras, and Nicaragua to a conference upon the cruiser *Tacoma* in the Gulf of Fonseca, where they agreed to a U.S.-sponsored peace conference. At the same time of the *Tacoma* conclave, Francis G. White, head of the State Department's Latin American division, convinced Secretary of State Charles Evans Hughes to host a Central American Conference to bring about a more durable regional peace.

When the conference convened on December 4, 1922, divergent interests quickly surfaced. Hughes, as conference chairman, clearly indicated that the United States had only two major objectives: better political relations among the Central American states and an arms limitation agreement that would assist in achieving that goal. However the Honduran delegate Alberto Uclés changed the meeting's tenor when he declared that the question of union should not only be on the conference agenda but it also should be settled first, before any other issues were discussed. El Salvador's delegate, Francisco Martínez Suárez, agreed. Hughes did not and promptly adjourned the meeting. When it reconvened on December 18, Uclés and Martínez stood alone in a vote that defeated their motion. The conference moved on. At its concluding session on February 7, 1923, the conference delegates signed twelve agreements. Five treaties fell within the purview of the U.S. objective to bring political peace and stability to Central America.

According to the General Treaty of Peace and Amity the five republics agreed to oppose all actions that threatened their constitutional governments. This included the nonrecognition of governments that came to power through a *coup d'état* or revolution, unless legitimized by free elections. The treaty further stipulated that the free elections must not sanction a revolutionary regime, a revolutionary leader, or a close relative or high ranking civilian or military official who had been in power six months before or after the event. Governments were not to assist exiles or contending parties anywhere in Central America or interfere in each others' internal affairs, and they were to prevent revolutionary activities within their own borders. A newly established Central American tribunal and commissions of inquiry were designed to settle disputes between the nations. Tribunals would be appointed on an ad hoc basis as crisis arose, while the commissions of inquiry were to objectively investigate disputes and report their findings to the tribunal. Finally, the Central Americans agreed to implement an Electoral Projects Program that would codify voting procedures, establish equal protection for electoral boards, and verify voting results. These four treaties were to be in effect until February 22, 1934. They satisfied the U.S. objective of achieving constitutional order and political stability.

The Central American militaries long served the interests of the political elite, interests not always compatible with those of the nation. At times the military acted in its own interests. As a result of this privileged position, military budgets consumed the majority of national expenditures, placing limitations on other government functions. To correct this imbalance, and spurred on by the success of the 1921–1922 Washington Disarmament conference, the United States set out to reduce the size of Central American militaries to that needed only for national defense. Although the five Central American nations agreed in principle to arms reduction, each expressed its own concerns with regard to its population, area, current military strength, internal order, and border defense. While the United States favored replacing national armies with national guards or constabularies, not all Central Americans agreed, particularly El Salvador. In the end a treaty provided for the following size of national armies, including national guards: Guatemala, 5,200 men; El Salvador, 4,200; Honduras and Nicaragua, 2,500 each; and Costa Rica, 2,000 for a five-year period. The treaty also called upon the

Central American nations to utilize the expertise of a military that already engaged in the building of national guards, an indirect reference to the United States, which had done so in the Dominican Republic and Haiti. The arms limitation agreement had a five-year life span following the last ratification.

Although not noted as such, the seven other agreements, with a ten-year life span, addressed Central American economic and social problems that fell within the purview of the region's traditional desire for union, such as customs, currency and banking reform, agricultural development, communications and transportation facilitation among the republics and control of federal expenditures. Both sides left Washington satisfied that their objectives had been met: political stability for the United States and the path to union for the Central Americans. Ratification of the twelve treaties did not go smoothly throughout Central America. Only the General Treaty and the Arms Limitation conventions and only three of the seven agreements dealing with a regional union were ratified by all Central American states.

Central American political turmoil soon followed the conference. El Salvador, Guatemala, Honduras, and Nicaragua became embroiled in internal political conflict and the United States military found itself involved in the latter two countries. Central America's continued political intrigue prompted State Department official Stokely W. Morgan to observe in 1927 that revolutions were a way of life in Central America and that there was nothing the United States could do about it. Central American arms expenditures did not decrease by 1930, when military budgets differed little from those in 1924. Two countries—El Salvador and Nicaragua—capitalized on the 1923 treaty that provided for U.S. military training of a national guard, but without reducing the size of the national army.

Beyond the frustration with Central America, other pressures led to a change in U.S. policy. Europe's condition after World War I removed it as a threat to the circum-Caribbean region; the larger Latin American nations became increasingly vocal against U.S. interventions, an outcry paralleled in the United States as Marine body bags came home from the chase of Augusto César Sandino. The "Roosevelt Corollary" to the Monroe Doctrine that sanctified U.S. preemptive action in Central America was declared nonoperational by Under Secretary of State J. Reuben Clark in 1929. By the time President Franklin D. Roosevelt announced his Good Neighbor policy in 1933, the Central American governments were under military leaders: Tiburcio Carías (Honduras), Maximiliano Hernández Martínez (El Salvador), Anastasio Somoza de García (Nicaragua), and Jorge Ubico (Guatemala). They had no interest in adhering to a treaty that militated against them and neither did Costa Rica, which viewed the treaty as an act of U.S. heavy-handedness. Delegates from the five republics gathered in Guatemala City on February 15, 1934, not to renew the treaty, but to let it lapse. The United States did the same a year later.

See also *Bryan-Chamorro Treaty, 1915; Central American Conference, Washington, 1907; Central American Court of Justice*

.... THOMAS M. LEONARD

References and Further Reading

Langley, Lester D. *The Banana Wars: An Inner History of American Empire, 1900–1934.* Lexington: University of Kentucky Press, 1983.

Leonard, Thomas M. *U.S. Policy and Arms Limitation in Central America: The Washington Conference of 1923.* Los Angeles: Center for the Study of Armament and Disarmament, California State University, 1982.

Munro, Dana G. *The United States and the Caribbean Republics, 1921–1933.* Princeton, NJ: Princeton University Press, 1974.

Central American Court of Justice

After decades of instability, the post–Cold War era offered Central American republics the opportunity to reinvigorate their long-desired regional integration. With this objective, on December 13, 1991, Costa Rica, El Salvador, Guatemala, Honduras, Nicaragua, and Panama signed the Tegucigalpa Protocol, which founded the new Central American Integration System (*Sistema de la Integración Centro Americana* or SICA). Understanding that SICA would require a judicial frame in which to settle disputes among its members, Article 12 of the Tegucigalpa Protocol created the Central American Court of Justice.

FIRST CENTRAL AMERICAN COURT OF JUSTICE

Similar to regional integration the Central American Court of Justice was not a new idea and its antecedents can be traced to the early twentieth century. Beginning in the late 1890s both José Santos Zelaya and Manuel Estrada Cabrera (the Nicaraguan and Guatemalan leaders, respectively) developed an increasing competition to control the region. Such animosity reached its apex in 1906, when Nicaragua and Guatemala initiated an open military confrontation. Knowing that a long war would eventually affect American interests in the region, the United States called on the Central American republics to settle their differences in a conference in Washington, D.C.

Gathered in Washington in 1907 Central American representatives not only settled some of their disputes but also created a Central American Court of Justice to prevent future wars. Being the first international court of justice in history, the new institution created high expectations both within and outside of the region. Outside of the region, Americans were among the most enthusiastic, as the international court represented a triumph of the progressive ideas. An expression of this passionate response came from Andrew Carnegie, who donated $100,000 for the court's building.

Despite the original excitement the court progressively lost legitimacy, especially after the dispute around the Bryan-Chamorro Treaty. In 1914 leaders from Washington and Managua signed this treaty, which gave the United States the exclusive rights to build a canal in Nicaragua. In exchange Adolfo Díaz, the Nicaraguan dictator, would receive American protection in case of domestic instability.

The establishment of this new American protectorate quickly alerted nearby Central American republics, especially Costa Rica and El Salvador. Both republics filed a case in the Central American Court of Justice, questioning the legitimacy of the treaty and arguing that the treaty infringed upon

Nicaraguan territorial sovereignty. While the court accepted the Costa Rican and Salvadorian arguments and mandated that Nicaragua abrogate the treaty, the United States encouraged Díaz to ignore the Court's decision.

By doing this, the United States and Díaz removed the court's legitimacy, because they showed how powerless the institution was in enforcing its decisions. Being useless for conflict resolution, the Central American republics showed no willingness to pursue a renovation of the protocols that would have extended the existence of the court. As a result the first Central American Court of Justice ceased to exist in 1917.

SECOND CENTRAL AMERICAN COURT OF JUSTICE

Despite attempts to reinstate a Central American court, only the end of the Cold War created the conditions necessary to establish a new regional organization. Without Soviet menace, jingoistic anticommunist dictators became a liability for the United States. Therefore the State Department progressively reduced its support of those regimes, encouraging the rise of democratic forces.

Different from classical dictators, Central American democracies encouraged regional, rather than national, approaches to face the challenges of globalization. According to these leaders regional integration was the only way to guarantee development and democracy. Under this spirit Central American presidents signed the Tegucigalpa Protocol, creating SICA as a regional bureaucracy and the Central American Court of Justice as the guarantor and executor of the protocol.

Located in Managua the Central American Court of Justice mandates over several matters, including disputes among member states and disagreements about the interpretation of the Tegucigalpa Protocol. Additionally the court determines the necessary measures to achieve legal standardization across the region. However the court's authority is limited in two ways. First it cannot rule over territorial or maritime disputes among its members. Second it cannot rule over human rights cases, as those are exclusively in the jurisdiction of the Inter-American Court of Human Rights.

Although the new Central American Court of Justice has not yet faced major challenges, especially since Costa Rica is not a full member, it is expected to play a major role in providing a legal framework for fighting currents threats against democracy such as Maras and military coups. More important the Central American Court of Justice represents the rise of a novel Central American consciousness that places the respect for and enforcement of laws as the corner stone of the "Great Fatherland."

See also *Bryan-Chamorro Treaty, 1915; Bryan, William Jennings; Central American Conference, Washington, 1907; Díaz Recinos, Adolfo; Estrada Cabrera, Manuel; Wilson, Woodrow; Zelaya López, José Santos*

. . . . CRISTÓBAL ZÚÑIGA ESPINOZA

REFERENCES AND FURTHER READINGS

Central American Court of Justice, http://portal.ccj.org.ni/ccj2/.

Central American Integration System, www.sica.int/sica.int/index_en.aspx.

Lafeber, Walter. *Inevitable Revolutions. The United States in Central America.* 3rd ed. New York: Norton, 1993.

Central American Defense Council (CONDECA)

The Central American Defense Council (*Consejo de Defensa Centroamericana,* CONDECA) was established in December 1963, when the defense ministers of Guatemala, Honduras, and Nicaragua agreed to coordinate their military planning and joint defense operations to repel internal communist subversion. CONDECA met officially for the first time in June 1964. El Salvador and Costa Rica joined in 1965 and 1966, respectively, while Panama cooperated in joint exercises as an observer, although not as a full member.

The political and economic unification of Central America had long been a goal of regional states. On October 14, 1951, the heads-of-state of Guatemala, Nicaragua, El Salvador, Honduras, Costa Rica, and Panama met and agreed to form the Organization of Central American States (*Organización de Estados Centroamericanos,* ODECA) to facilitate economic cooperation. That same year the United States began an ultimately fruitless effort to negotiate military assistance treaties with Central American nations individually. To coordinate a regional response to the deepening Cold War, the United States asked ODECA member states to begin planning for military cooperation in 1956, leading ultimately to CONDECA.

By the early 1960s interstate tensions and internal political unrest had eased, clearing the way for ODECA to pursue deeper international cooperation. In 1960 ODECA established the Central American Common Market (CACM) to oversee member states' economic integration. Then ODECA members again considered military cooperation. The mechanism for joint defense had already been established under U.S. auspices in the 1947 Rio Pact. Through the early 1960s plans for CONDECA emerged in talks between U.S. officials and member states' foreign ministers and ministers of defense. On June 6, 1963, U.S. President John F. Kennedy reorganized the U.S. military operations center in Panama as the U.S. Southern Command. With this demonstration of the U.S. commitment to security in the region, the defense ministers of Guatemala, Honduras, and Nicaragua established CONDECA on December 14, 1963, leading to the organization's first official meeting in Guatemala City in June 1964.

Within the context of the Cold War, particularly as U.S. concerns in Central America centered on the Soviet Union's efforts to build beachheads in the region, a U.S.-led system of unified military operations among Central American states was most attractive. To maximize the cooperation between CONDECA and the United States, member states worked closely with the U.S. Central Intelligence Agency and officers of the U.S. armed services. While military chiefs of the member countries originally comprised CONDECA's staff, the United States urged CONDECA to expand its charter to include internal security officers so that Costa Rica and Panama, which had no conventional military, could join the council.

The primary intended target of CONDECA was internal communist subversion. To insure the member states were most effective in responding to internal pressures, they coordinated and standardized their intelligence operations, military training protocols, and their common goals and objectives. The U.S. Department of Defense noted in 1964 that long-standing military rivalries among Central American countries made an organized response to communist insurgencies difficult, but CONDECA provided a mechanism for reducing these traditional rivalries. Ultimately coordination and standardization, from U.S.-supplied equipment to training in intelligence gathering, logistical support, and the military were central elements of CONDECA. By 1968 most member countries standardized their military insignia, uniforms, and ranks modeled after the U.S. armed forces.

To prepare CONDECA member states to fight insurgencies, the armed forces of Guatemala, El Salvador, Honduras, and Nicaragua joined the U.S. Southern Command forces in joint military maneuvers in the 1960s. These operations demonstrated that CONDECA could coordinate with the United States and that member states, for the first time, were capable of successfully cooperating in planning and carrying out tactical operations. These operations allowed CONDECA members to devise standard procedures and objectives for dealing with insurgents and to demonstrate their growing abilities to coordinate their militaries from the top command staffs to the soldiers on the ground. This coordination proved more apparent than real, however, and little evidence points to CONDECA's involvement in putting down Central American insurgencies in the 1960s, 1970s, and 1980s.

In spite of these outward signs of cooperation, internal tensions ultimately resulted in the disbandment of CONDECA. The 1969 Soccer War between Honduras and El Salvador caused the former to withdraw from the organization, after which CONDECA fell into quiescence. The administrations of Richard Nixon and Ronald Reagan tried to resurrect CONDECA in the 1970s and 1980s, but both attempts proved ineffective. The Reagan administration proved temporarily more successful and briefly revived CONDECA in 1983 in its war against the Nicaraguan government. The United States staged major military maneuvers in Honduras to threaten the Sandinistas. But Costa Rica, Panama, and Guatemala demonstrated little interest in the Reagan initiative, and the revivification of CONDECA proved short-lived. In the end member states' military chiefs proved more concerned with their own domestic power than regional cooperation, and CONDECA ultimately failed to live up to the U.S. government's hopes.

See also *Central American Common Market (CACM); Costa Rica, U.S. Relations with; El Salvador, U.S. Relations with; Guatemala, U.S. Relations with; Honduras, U.S. Relations with; Nicaragua, U.S. Relations with; Organization of Central American States (ODECA); Panama, U.S. Relations with; Ríos Montt, Efraín; Soccer War, 1969 (Honduras/El Salvador)*

. . . . MATTHEW A. REDINGER

References and Further Reading

Dixon, Marlene, and Susanne Jonas, eds. *Nicaragua under Siege.* New York: Synthesis Publications, 1984.

Horowitz, Irving Louis, John Gerassi, and Josue de Castro, eds. *Latin American Radicalism: A Documentary Report on Left and Nationalist Movements.* New York: Random House, 1969.

Woodward, Ralph Lee Jr. *Central America: A Nation Divided.* New York: Oxford University Press, 1999.

Central American-Dominican Republic Free Trade Agreement, 2004 (CAFTA-DR)

The Central American-Dominican Republic Free Trade Agreement (CAFTA-DR) is an agreement that was signed between the United States, El Salvador, Guatemala, Honduras, Nicaragua, Panama, and the Dominican Republic in 2004. The U.S. House of Representatives narrowly approved CAFTA-DR with a vote of 217–215 on July 28, 2005. As President George W. Bush lobbied members of the Republican party on Capitol Hill in an effort to pass the controversial bill, he said that trade would expand to lift people out of poverty and that CAFTA-DR would address the problem of illegal immigration into the United States because families would have more opportunities to stay at home. The Central American-Dominican Republic Free Trade Agreement was passed ten years after the North American Free Trade Agreement (NAFTA), and many people in the western hemisphere were growing wary of the effects of free trade. NAFTA has had a deleterious impact on the poor and the agricultural sector of Mexico, giving U.S. agricultural products an advantage due to heavy U.S. government subsidies to farmers (not free trade) and destroying the livelihood of over 15 million Mexicans who depend on agricultural exports. As a result one of the consequences of NAFTA has been an increase in Mexican immigration to the United States.

President George W. Bush announced the following at the Third Summit of the Americas: "We have a great vision before us: a fully democratic hemisphere, bound together by good will and free trade" (Bush 2001). His administration hoped to pass the Free Trade Area of the Americas (FTAA), which would expand NAFTA to every country in Central America, South America, and the Caribbean, except Cuba. Negotiations began right after the completion of NAFTA in 1994 and were supposed to have been finished by early 2005. The FTAA was met with popular protests all over the hemisphere, and the South American countries of Argentina, Bolivia, and Brazil led the opposition. With so much opposition in South America, the Bush administration put the FTAA on hold and instead took a piecemeal approach to a hemispheric free trade plan. CAFTA-DR, however controversial, represents one more step in linking the Americas by free trade agreements.

CAFTA-DR allows the partial exemption of the most viable product in each country; it considers long terms for tariff reductions for sensitive products. The fiscal realities of Central American countries and the Dominican Republic, however, have a limited capacity to implement programs to direct income support programs for farmers who are negatively affected and need to transition to growing different crops. At the same time most of the support is tariff protection, which will disappear in time.

Just two years into the CAFTA-DR, Central Americans began experiencing some of the same effects that Mexicans have experienced for more than a decade. Central Americans have begun migrating at a higher rate than they did during the wars of the 1980s. Central American immigrants cross through multiple borders before making their way into the United States, and this has caused Mexico to add more soldiers to its border with Guatemala, as well as more immigration and military checkpoints throughout southern Mexico.

Another problematic issue regarding CAFTA-DR, and other free trade agreements in the Americas, is what critics claim as the undemocratic nature of them, which has led to political protests throughout the hemisphere. Costa Ricans just narrowly approved joining CAFTA in an October 2007 referendum vote shrouded in controversy. Costa Rica was the last country to sign on to CAFTA-DR and the only country to have a referendum vote on the agreement. In the United States, during a controversial war and an active hurricane season, when most Americans' attention was elsewhere, there was still an active debate in Congress over CAFTA-DR, where it passed the House of Representatives by only two votes. The Senate passed the agreement 54–45. On the day of the House vote, President Bush and Vice President Dick Cheney both made appearances on Capitol Hill to rally members.

In Guatemala, where tens of thousands of protesters crowded around the National Congress to demand that CAFTA-DR be put to a national referendum, the military was called to break up the protest in violation of the 1996 peace accords. Guatemalan Bishop Monsignor Alvara Ramazzini stated, "DR-CAFTA was negotiated behind peoples' backs" (Ricker and Stansbury 2006, 21). In all the countries involved, including the United States, the ratification of CAFTA-DR is one that critics condemn as antidemocratic. Throughout Central America and the United States, people took to the streets in protest, for fair trade and in support of economic policies that put people first over global capital.

See also *Central American Wars, 1980s; Free Trade Association of the Americas (FTAA); Immigration Policy, United States; Mexico, U.S. Relations with; North American Free Trade Agreement (NAFTA), 1992*

. . . . VIRGINIA S. WILLIAMS

References and Further Reading

Angel, Amy. "Transition Policies for the Agricultural Sector in CAFTA-DR." Paper presented at the first annual workshop of the CAFTA-DR Agrifood Market Integration Consortium (CAMIC), November 2008, San José, Costa Rica. http://.camic.tamu.edu/sanjose/angel_english.pdf.

Bush, George W. Address to the Third Summit of the Americas, Quebec, Canada, April 21, 2001.

Ricker, Tom, and Burke Stansbury. "The CAFTA Chronicles: Strong-Arming Central America, Mocking Democracy." *Multinational Monitor* 27, no. 1 (January 2006): 21.

Central American Wars, 1980s

Widespread violence took the lives of hundreds of thousands of Central Americans in the late 1970s and early 1980s as several countries in the region became sites of extreme government repression, leftist insurgency, and civil war. In the name of anticommunism, state forces, most notably in El Salvador and Guatemala, waged war against a broad spectrum of the population, from leftist guerrilla combatants to civilians—unionists, peasants, students and intellectuals—as well as Roman Catholic priests and lay workers. The region's conflicts were rooted in long histories of exploitation and inequality, a stranglehold on power by elite sectors and military forces, and the vehement resistance of these groups to even moderate reform. Though they grew from such internal problems, the conflicts were prolonged and intensified by U.S. government alliances with and support for antireformist sectors in the region. Despite resistance from some members of Congress, the U.S. government supported the region's often brutal regimes (along with the anti-Sandinista "*Contras*" in Nicaragua) because they were judged to be crucial partners in the struggle to contain communism.

The Central American wars were formally ended through negotiated settlements and elections in the 1990s, after several of the conflicts had reached a stalemate. It is worth noting that the fall of the Soviet Union fundamentally changed U.S. perceptions of the struggles in Central America, which helped bring them to a close.

NICARAGUA

U.S. preoccupation with Central America in the 1980s had much to do with events in Nicaragua, where an opposition movement led by a leftist revolutionary army called the Sandinista National Liberation Front (FSLN) took power in 1979. After more than four decades of dictatorial rule by three different members of the Somoza family, the Sandinistas toppled the last of the Somoza rulers—Anastasio Somoza Debayle—in July 1979.

Multiclass opposition to the dictatorship had developed over the previous decade, and Anastasio Somoza responded with violence and a state of siege. The labor movement, prompted by sharply falling wages and living standards in the 1970s, sponsored widespread work stoppages and strikes, and peasants and plantation workers supported by the Roman Catholic Church demanded better wages and working conditions. The Nicaraguan business sector became increasingly critical of the corrupt Somoza government by the late 1970s, and U.S. president Jimmy Carter officially withdrew U.S. support for the dictatorship in 1979, withholding new military aid.

While Carter did not want—and tried to prevent—a Sandinista victory following the 1979 fall of Somoza, his administration nonetheless recognized the Sandinista government when it came to power and reinstated some U.S. aid. At the same time, however, the U.S. developed links to ex-Somoza national guardsmen operating as an anti-Sandinista opposition force in neighboring Honduras.

The Sandinista Revolution brought a socialist-leaning government to power in Central America, a region long tied to the U.S. economically and politically. Though the Sandinistas aimed for political pluralism and a mixed economy (with elements of capitalism and socialism), they did move to fundamentally alter a system they viewed as exploitative and unjust. They undertook land reform, raised wages, and put food subsidies in place. They nationalized the import-export sector, a move vehemently opposed by Nicaraguan and foreign business interests. At times they curtailed the civil liberties of opposition figures, though such freedoms were usually respected and they did not engage in the kinds of repression practiced by military regimes elsewhere in the region.

Despite the willingness of the Sandinistas to moderate their revolutionary goals (and to service the large foreign debt inherited from Somoza), the regime change was viewed with alarm in conservative U.S. policy circles. When Ronald Reagan campaigned for president in 1980 he held Carter responsible for a general loss of U.S. influence in the region and for the Sandinista victory in Nicaragua in particular. He described the Carter administration's foreign policy, with its emphasis on human rights, as a "foreign policy bordering on appeasement." The American people, Reagan said in his campaign stump speech (reproduced in *The New York Times,* February 29, 1980), were "prepared for large and definite purpose," part of which involved a retooling of U.S. foreign policy to "begin the moral and military rearmament of the United States for the difficult, dangerous decade ahead."

That rearmament would profoundly shape Central American politics, beginning in Nicaragua. When Reagan won the presidency, he pursued aggressive U.S. actions to undermine the Sandinista government, using various tools at his disposal including antigovernment propaganda, the elimination of military aid to the country, pressure on international lenders to cut credit to the government, and beginning in 1985, a U.S. trade embargo. Most importantly, in his first year in office Reagan began covert funding to the armed contra opposition exiles in Honduras, sending nearly $20 million in aid via the Central Intelligence Agency (CIA).

The U.S. supported the contras throughout the 1980s with additional money, intelligence, and training. The exile opposition force, staging almost daily raids into Nicaraguan territory, engaged in sabotage aimed at destroying the economy. The CIA in turn mined Nicaraguan shipping harbors to further disrupt trade. Contra forces attacked pro-Sandinista civilians, and by 1985 they had killed an estimated thirteen thousand people. When the U.S. Congress blocked further U.S. aid to the contras, the Reagan administration resorted to raising funds secretly through illegal arms sales to Iran. By 1989 U.S. support to the contras had amounted to some $400 million.

To bolster support for its Central America policy, the Reagan administration continually accused the Sandinista government of sending arms and other forms of support to guerrilla revolutionaries active in neighboring El Salvador. Given the dire economic circumstances in Nicaragua and the government's own struggle against the contras, it is unlikely that such support amounted to much, but it is clear that the Sandinista victory gave a psychological boost to leftist opposition movements throughout the region, including those in El Salvador. It was a modeling effect the U.S. went to great lengths to diminish.

The U.S.-funded contra war continued until 1990, and all told, over thirty thousand Nicaraguans were killed in the fighting. Ultimately, however, the Sandinistas were voted out of office rather than overthrown. In elections held in February 1990 the Sandinistas were defeated by the National Opposition Union (UNO) presidential candidate, Violeta Barrios de Chamorro.

EL SALVADOR

The war in neighboring El Salvador, lasting thirteen years, took the lives of an estimated seventy thousand Salvadorans, a great majority of them civilians killed at the hands of state forces. In addition to the dead and disappeared, vast numbers of Salvadorans were displaced during the violence, and one in six people fled into exile.

El Salvador, too, had suffered a long history of repressive dictatorships prior to the 1980s. The regime of General Maximiliano Hernández Martínez began a pattern of extraordinarily violent official responses to demands for reform, when uprisings against the Salvadoran oligarchy in 1932 were met by army massacres of some thirty thousand peasants. The peasant uprising was cast as a communist threat, and El Salvador's military government won the support of U.S. President Herbert Hoover. It would be one in a long line of repressive regimes supported by the United States as allies in the fight against communism.

For four decades after the 1932 massacre the oligarchy maintained near total control of Salvadoran society, but widespread popular mobilization and demands for reform resurfaced in the 1970s. The state again met them with bloody repression. Death squads closely linked to the Salvadoran military assassinated opposition politicians, peasant leaders, unionists, and Roman Catholic Church activists. Several leftist guerrilla groups emerged in the 1970s and called for the overthrow of the state. In alliance with worker and student groups, they gained support as other means of political protest evaporated in the repression.

Government-sponsored violence prompted Jimmy Carter to cut U.S. military assistance to El Salvador in March 1977, although that did little to lessen the brutality of the Salvadoran military. Despite a move to joint military/civilian rule in 1980, state terror continued unabated and included the assassination of Archbishop Oscar Romero on March 24, 1980, a day after his public condemnation of state violence. In the increasingly repressive context, opposition groups united in a military/political alliance: political parties founded the Democratic Revolutionary Front (FDR), in league with a new guerrilla umbrella group, the Farabundo Martí National Liberation Front (FMLN).

In the face of strengthening opposition Carter resumed military aid to the Salvadoran government during his final days in office. Levels of aid then increased dramatically under Ronald Reagan. (In military aid alone, average levels of U.S. support went from $1.6 million per year from 1977 to 1980 to nearly

$99 million per year from 1981 to 1984, and it rose even higher in Reagan's second term.) Reagan viewed the Salvadoran conflict as a crucial test for U.S. anticommunist policy in the region and engaged in a public relations campaign to win American support for the war against the guerrillas. Members of the U.S. Congress continually resisted renewed support for the Salvadoran military and attempted to tie aid to improvement in human rights, yet aid—and repression—continued. In one of the war's most dramatic acts of terror, the U.S.-trained Atlacatl Battalion in January 1982 massacred over seven hundred peasants at El Mozote. The Reagan administration's response was to obfuscate, to claim that no compelling evidence tied Salvadoran state forces to the massacre, and to blame the FMLN guerrillas. Total U.S. aid to the Salvadoran government amounted to $6 billion over the course of the war.

Even with U.S. funding the Salvadoran military was unable to defeat the FMLN and the conflict reached a stalemate by the mid-1980s, although civilian deaths continued to mount. The FMLN pushed for a negotiated settlement, while Salvadoran security forces and their U.S. sponsors resisted. The FMLN escalated attacks on military targets in the capital in 1989, a move that was met with increased army assassinations of civilians deemed sympathetic to the opposition, including the murder of six Jesuit priests (and their housekeeper and her daughter) at the Central American University in November of that year.

Following the assassinations of the Jesuits, the United States finally put pressure on the Salvadoran government to negotiate with the FMLN, a lengthy and ultimately successful process mediated by the United Nations. A peace accord was signed between the government and guerrilla forces in 1992, and a UN-sponsored Truth Commission was established to investigate atrocities committed during the conflict.

GUATEMALA

The devastation of war was even more severe in Guatemala, where several revolutionary guerrilla armies battled successive governments, mostly military regimes, on and off for thirty-six years. A UN-sponsored Truth Commission investigating the war estimated that more than two hundred thousand Guatemalans died in the conflict, 93 percent of them at the hands of state forces. Over 80 percent of the dead and disappeared were Mayas. In the early 1980s the army defined Guatemala's highland Mayas as natural sympathizers of the guerrillas and thus enemies in the war against "subversion." Soldiers in "scorched-earth" raids completely destroyed over six hundred Mayan communities, killing men, women, and children, destroying homes, crops, and sacred sites. The UN Truth Commission in 1998 determined that these army counterinsurgency practices constituted acts of genocide.

Like the other conflicts in the region, the Guatemalan civil war had deep roots. Since the growth of the coffee industry in the late nineteenth century, the Guatemalan state had been at the service of the oligarchy, facilitating vast land acquisitions and ensuring a cheap and repressed (and increasingly landless) labor force. During a singular period of reform, from 1944 to 1954, the governments of Arévalo and Arbenz began expanding social services and worker rights, and in 1952 they passed sweeping land reform. That experiment in democratic reform was ended and reversed with a CIA-sponsored coup in 1954. From that point forward the military, with U.S. funding, would grow to dominate Guatemalan politics, responding to popular mobilization with an iron fist. The first opposition guerrilla groups, founded by junior army officers rebelling at the lack of reform and democracy in the country, emerged in eastern Guatemala in the 1960s. They were soon defeated but regrouped and reappeared in the 1970s in the western highlands. With army repression of almost all forms of opposition in the late 1970s, the guerrilla armies, especially the Guerrilla Army of the Poor (EGP) and the Revolutionary Organization of People in Arms (ORPA), attracted the support of growing numbers of students, unionists, and Ladino and Maya peasants.

Over the course of the late 1970s and early 1980s widespread mobilization (armed and unarmed) was met with unmitigated army terror—assassinations of community leaders, their disappearance and torture, and massacres of dozens and then hundreds at once. Bodies of massacre victims were dumped in clandestine mass graves, many of which are now being exhumed by the Guatemalan Forensic Anthropology Foundation (Fundación de Antropología Forense de Guatemala, FAFG).

The Guatemalan military became so extreme in its use of terror that it received relatively little financial support from the United States during the Carter administration and during Reagan's first term, when Congress managed to block most aid requests. Technical assistance and equipment nonetheless made their way to Guatemala via the CIA and U.S. allies such as Israel.

Extreme state terror brought the opposition to its knees, with most of the leadership of the guerrilla umbrella Guatemalan National Revolutionary Unity (URNG) pushed into exile by 1983. The war continued, however, with the state unable to wholly defeat the guerrilla insurgency.

By the early 1990s pressures mounted on the Guatemalan state to negotiate a settlement. A long and halting peace process, mediated by the United Nations, finally culminated in peace accords between the government and URNG in 1996, although political violence continued and included the assassination in 1998 of Bishop Juan Gerardi just after his release of a Truth Commission report by the Human Rights Office of the Archdiocese of Guatemala (ODHAG).

HONDURAS

Honduras, which shares borders with Guatemala, El Salvador, and Nicaragua, became involved in the Central American wars of the 1980s mostly due to its geographic location. It had several small guerrilla groups of its own (with combatants numbering in the hundreds), including the Morazan Front for the Liberation of Honduras (FMLH), the Cinchoneros Popular Liberation Movement (MPLC), and the Lorenzo Zelaya Popular Revolutionary Forces (FPR-LZ), but these did not have much popular support and never posed a threat to the government. More critically from the perspective of the United States, Honduras was a place where guerrillas from El Salvador and Guatemala congregated, and thus a buildup of the Honduran military was viewed as strategically crucial to the anticommunist struggle. During the Reagan administration, Honduras served as the base of the Nicaraguan antiSandinista contra forces and the staging ground for their attacks into Nicaragua.

Honduras managed to maintain procedural democracy while civil wars raged elsewhere in the region, but the country was increasingly militarized over the course of the 1980s. U.S. military aid grew from under $4 million in 1980 to nearly $60 million per year by 1985, and it included technical assistance, training, and infrastructure. Despite a high level of militarization the Honduran armed forces did not engage in the same extreme levels of repression as their counterparts in El Salvador and Guatemala, although they did kill an estimated one thousand people during the 1980s.

See also *Counterinsurgency; Farabundo Martí National Liberation Front (FMLN) (El Salvador); Guatemalan United Revolutionary Front (URNG); Guerrilla Warfare; Kissinger Commission; La Matanza (El Salvador); Menchú Tum, Rigoberta; Reagan, Ronald W.; Sandinista National Liberation Front (FSLN) (Nicaragua); United Nations Observer Group in Central America (ONUCA), 1989–1992*

. . . . BETSY KONEFAL

References and Further Reading

Booth, John A., Christine J. Wade, and Tomas W. Walker. *Understanding Central America: Global Forces, Rebellion, and Change*. 4th ed. Boulder, CO: Westview Press, 2006.

Danner, Mark. *The Massacre at El Mozote: A Parable of the Cold War*. New York: Vintage Books, 1994.

Goldman, Francisco. *The Art of Political Murder: Who Killed the Bishop?* New York: Grove Press, 2008.

Human Rights Office of the Archdiocese of Guatemala (ODHAG). *Guatemala: Never Again!: The Official Report of the Human Rights Office, Archdiocese of Guatemala,* abridged English translation. Maryknoll, NY: Orbis Books, 1999.

Schmitz, David F. *The United States and Right-Wing Dictatorships*. New York: Cambridge University Press, 2006.

Walker, Thomas W., and Ariel C. Armony, eds. *Repression, Resistance, and Democratic Transition in Central America*. Wilmington, DE: Scholarly Resources, 2000.

Wickham-Crowley, Timothy P. *Guerrillas and Revolution in Latin America: A Comparative Study of Insurgents and Regimes since 1956*. Princeton, NJ: Princeton University Press, 1992.

Central Intelligence Agency (CIA)

The Central Intelligence Agency (CIA), created in 1947, is the primary agency in the United States to collect, analyze, and distribute foreign intelligence. It shaped U.S.-Latin American relations throughout the Cold War by mounting or supporting numerous military coups against left-leaning governments, a record that ultimately turned the agency into *the* symbol of U.S. imperialism in Latin America.

EARLY YEARS

The roots of the CIA go back to the Office of Strategic Services (OSS), one of several U.S. intelligence services during World War II. The experience of working closely with British intelligence convinced William J. Donavan, head of the OSS, and Allen Dulles, his star officer, that the United States needed a centralized intelligence service after the war. Opposition from the military and the Federal Bureau of Investigation (FBI), as well as President Harry S. Truman's fear that the OSS might become a GESTAPO-like organization, led him to abolish it in September 1945. George F. Kennan and other foreign policy experts urged Truman to strengthen U.S. intelligence capabilities, however. In early 1946 he created the Central Intelligence Group (CIG), which drew on the expertise of experienced intelligence officers to produce reliable information about the Soviet Union and its plans for Eastern Europe, but a lack of legal standing and a budget limited its reach.

On July 26, 1947, Congress passed the National Security Act creating the CIA. It defined the agency's basic duties and also authorized it to perform other functions and duties as they relate to national security, a provision that came to be interpreted as permission to conduct secret operations. In December 1947 the National Security Council issued a top secret order that authorized the CIA to conduct covert psychological operations in order to keep an eye on Soviet activities. But the CIA still competed with other U.S. intelligence agencies and had to finance its earliest operations in Europe with money secretly diverted from the Marshall Plan. On May 27, 1949, Congress passed the CIA Act to remedy that legal and financial uncertainty. The act gave the agency the widest conceivable powers and a generous and secret budget, and it limited oversight to a small congressional committee.

The CIA preserved the spirit of the OSS. Allen Dulles had advised Truman on its creation, and former OSS analysts such as Frank Wisner, James Angleton, Richard Helms, William E. Colby, and William J. Casey soon joined the agency. In Europe the CIA took over operations to develop anticommunist assets that had begun as OSS projects at the end of World War II. Anticommunism trumped all other concerns: the CIA secured former Nazis and Nazi-sympathizers as operatives and assets and, if necessary, provided them with new identities to facilitate their escape from prosecution. U.S. army intelligence, the Vatican, the Italian Mafia, and the CIA cooperated to create rat lines for notorious war criminals to make their way to Italian ports and from there to safety in South America. In the decades to come the CIA employed these assets to fight the radical left in Latin America. Klaus Barbie, for example, fled to Bolivia, where he instructed army units in the use of torture and helped organize several military coups.

By the early 1950s the CIA had the presence in Latin America to carry out all of its functions. The Agency's Office of Policy Coordination (OPC) mounted one of its first major covert operations in Guatemala, where a left-leaning government under Colonel Jacobo Arbenz had been in power since 1951. Executives of the United Fruit Company (UFCO) alerted the U.S. government to Arbenz's progressive land reform threatening the expropriation of some of the company's extensive holdings. The CIA saw communist influence at work and planned a covert operation to overthrow Arbenz.

The Truman administration balked, but the plan came back to life under President Eisenhower. In late 1953 the new Secretary of State John Foster Dulles and the new Director of Central Intelligence (DCI), his brother Allen, convinced Eisenhower to authorize the covert operation. Code-named PBSuccess, it combined funding for Guatemala's internal opposition, recruitment of disaffected military members, sabotage against port facilities, and radio propaganda to undermine Arbenz's popular support. The CIA-funded rebel army seized power despite security breaches and embarrassing military defeats, but only after Guatemala's military high command—fearful of a full-blown U.S. invasion—convinced Arbenz to resign. The CIA presented PBSuccess as a successful blueprint for future interventions, but its fallout came to haunt the Guatemalan people, the CIA, and the United States. Mass arrests of Arbenz-supporters ordered by Colonel Carlos Castillo-Armas, Guatemala's new leader, unleashed a spiral of violence that held Guatemala in its grip for decades. Latin Americans saw the operation as definitive proof that the United States had abandoned the Good Neighbor policy and would rely on covert and overt force to impose its Cold War policies on the western hemisphere.

CUBA AND "PREVENTING A SECOND CUBA"

The Cuban Revolution defined the CIA's role in Latin America for the remainder of the Cold War. After Fidel Castro and his rebel army had overthrown Fulgencio Batista, on January 1, 1959, they began building a Cuba without a powerful political or economic role for the United States. In the fall of 1959 the CIA stepped up its operations to undermine the Castro regime. Its Miami station became the largest in the world as the CIA tried to build a credible exile-Cuban opposition to Castro. By March 1960, as Cuba began nationalizing U.S. companies and strengthening ties with the Soviet Union, the CIA presented a "Program of Action against the Castro Regime." Its core was a two-thousand-strong paramilitary force of Cuban exiles, the Brigade 2506, with a mission to invade Cuba. As for PBSuccess, the agency prepared the ground with radio propaganda, sabotage, economic warfare, and support for internal opposition. President John F. Kennedy approved the CIA-planned invasion shortly after taking office. The exiled Cubans landed in the Bay of Pigs on April 17, 1961, and Castro's forces routed them in less than three days. The failure cemented Castro's power at home and his status as an anti-imperialist hero in Latin America. The CIA, on the other hand, became *the* symbol of U.S. imperialism.

Ironically the fiasco at the Bay of Pigs strengthened ties between the CIA and the hard-line anti-Castro exiles. The agency retained many of them as operatives for covert missions in Cuba and against Cuban allies in Latin America and beyond, doing the CIA's dirty work and often using their positions and contacts to pursue an anti-Castro agenda even without explicit orders. Former members of Brigade 2506 participated in Operation Mongoose, a series of covert operations launched in January 1962 to eliminate Fidel Castro and overthrow the Cuban regime. These included various far-fetched schemes to assassinate Castro or, alternatively, to embarrass him in front of the Cuban public. President Lyndon B. Johnson phased out Operation Mongoose after Kennedy's assassination. In 1965 the CIA sent Cuban exiles as pilots to the Congo, where they fought against the Simba rebellion that received support from a column of Cuban military advisers led by Che Guevara. The CIA also dispatched exile Cubans to Bolivia in 1967 to help the national army track down, arrest, and kill Guevara on his latest mission to export the Cuban Revolution. In 1976 two Brigade 2506 veterans and former CIA operatives—Luis Posada Carriles and Orlando Bosch—participated in the bombing of a Cuban airliner that killed all seventy-three people on board.

Over the course of the 1960s the CIA greatly expanded its operations throughout Latin America to prevent a "second Cuba." The effort went hand-in-hand with Kennedy's Alliance for Progress policy, designed to strengthen U.S.-Latin American cooperation on economic development, democratic institutions, and cultural exchange. An early victim of Kennedy's new policy was Rafael Trujillo, the Dominican Republic's military dictator and a longtime U.S. ally in the Cold War. As the United States stepped up its criticism of strongman rule in Cuba, a right-wing dictator such as Trujillo was no longer an expedient ally. The CIA lent support to his assassination by a group of Dominican dissidents on May 30, 1961. In Brazil the CIA initiated covert operations against the leftist government of President João Goulart in 1962 with the goal to defeat him in the next elections or, if necessary, to push him out by assisting domestic coup plotters. Often, agencies used to implement Alliance for Progress policies, such as the American Institute for Free Labor Development, provided cover for CIA operatives.

The CIA mounted a political action program in Chile to prevent the popular socialist politician Salvador Allende from winning the presidency. In 1964 CIA funds helped the Christian Democrat Eduardo Frei defeat Allende, but ahead of the 1970 presidential election the socialist appeared set for victory. Henry Kissinger, then national security advisor under President Nixon, further expanded CIA covert operations, funding conservative groups and the anti-Allende press. He even had the CIA inquire with trusted Chilean officers about a preemptive military coup. Allende won nevertheless, secured the loyalty of the military leadership, and assumed power in a peaceful transition. The CIA continued its political and economic warfare, either directly or through opposition groups and allied businesses, such as the multinational company ITT. One result was an extensive transport strike that undermined Allende's popular and military support. The U.S. government welcomed the violent military coup that overthrew Allende on September 11, 1973. The CIA celebrated it as an operational success.

When reports in the U.S. press suggested that covert operations had helped overthrow a democratically elected president, Congress opened an investigation. The Select Committee to Study Governmental Operations with Respect to Intelligence Activities, headed by Idaho Senator Frank Church, produced a report titled, "Covert Action in Chile 1963–1973" that revealed CIA actions in great detail and demanded more extensive oversight. Even as Congress called for reform, the

CIA continued to pursue its legally questionable and morally condemnable course in South America. In the mid-1970s, the CIA provided financial and logistical support for the Chilean military regime's secret police, the Directorate of National Intelligence (DINA). Not only did DINA play a central role in the arrest, torture, and disappearance of hundreds, if not thousands, of former Allende supporters, but it also spearheaded Operation Condor, a transnational cooperation of intelligence, police, and military officers that extended counterinsurgency warfare beyond national borders. At the very least, the CIA provided technical support for Condor's information exchange and thereby facilitated assassinations, such as the 1976 car bombing of Orlando Letelier, a Chilean exile, in Washington, D.C.

President Jimmy Carter's DCI, Admiral Stansfield Turner, overhauled the CIA to repair its damaged reputation, but excessive secrecy returned in 1981 with President Ronald Reagan and Vice President George H. W. Bush, himself a former DCI. Reagan appointed William Casey, an OSS veteran, as new DCI and asked him to develop a plan for the containment of perceived Cuban influence in Central America. The CIA justified its financial and material support for the contras, paramilitary forces waging war on Nicaragua's Sandinista government, with the need to curtail arms shipments to leftist guerillas in El Salvador. The true objective, however, was the overthrow of a government that enjoyed Cuban support. Panama's military strongman Manuel Noriega, a CIA asset since the 1960s, supplied pilots to smuggle weapons to the contras, used his influence with regional military leaders, and supported CIA sabotage missions in Nicaragua. When the CIA-orchestrated mining of the Nicaraguan coast caused an international outrage, Congress cut off funds for the contras. Undeterred, Casey and Colonel Oliver North—the key figure on the National Security Council—continued the secret war on Nicaragua with funds raised from allied governments, private donors, and illegal arms deals with Iran. The scheme supplied the contras with arms, but when a supply plane went down over Nicaraguan territory, Congress demanded explanations from the White House. The subsequent Iran-Contra investigation disgraced the administration, exposed illegal CIA covert operations, and ended an era of secretive OSS veterans in charge of the CIA.

AFTER THE COLD WAR

The demise of the Soviet Union and the end of the Cold War forced a rethinking of the CIA's role. In the 1990s and 2000s the CIA retained its presence in Latin America, but it was no longer engaged in the large-scale covert operations that had defined U.S.-Latin American relations during the Cold War. Its own actions and the indiscriminate brutality of some of its favored regimes earned the CIA a lasting place in the Latin American popular political imagination, however. Whenever critics accuse the United States of interfering in the domestic affairs of their country—for example after the coups against Venezuela's President Hugo Chávez in 2002 or Haitian President Jean-Bertrand Aristide in 2004—they suspect a CIA covert operation, probably greatly exaggerating the agency's role. Recent CIA operations remain clouded in secrecy, and we still know surprisingly little even about operations in the more distant past due to a declassification practice that puts the CIA's own assessment of the proper level of secrecy above the public's right to know. For now historians rely on often heavily redacted documentation released under the Freedom of Information Act to tell the agency's history.

See also *Agee, Philip; Bay of Pigs Invasion, 1961; Castro Ruz, Fidel; Central American Wars, 1980s; Dulles, Allen M.; Guatemala, U.S. Invasion of, 1954; Operation Condor; Operation Mongoose*

. . . . OLIVER J. DINIUS

REFERENCES AND FURTHER READING

Agee, Philip. *Inside the Company: CIA Diary*. New York: Stonehill, 1975.

Cullather, Nick. *Secret History: The CIA's Classified Account of its Operations in Guatemala, 1952–54*. 2nd ed. Stanford, CA: Stanford University Press, 2006.

Prados, John. *Safe for Democracy: The Secret Wars of the CIA*. Chicago: Ivan R. Dee, 2006.

Scott, Peter Dale, and Jonathan Marshall. *Cocaine Politics: Drugs, Armies, and the CIA in Central America*. Updated ed. Berkeley: University of California Press, 1998.

U.S. Senate, Select Committee to Study Governmental Operations with Respect to Intelligence Activities. *Church Report: Covert Action in Chile 1963–1973*. Washington, DC: U.S. Government Printing Office, 1975. http://foia.state.gov/Reports/ChurchReport.asp.

Weiner, Tim. *Legacy of Ashes: The History of the CIA*. New York: Doubleday, 2007.

Chaco War, 1932–1935

The Chaco War (1932–1935) was a bitter struggle between Paraguay and Bolivia over disputed territory that caused massive casualties and proved the failure of international peacekeeping mechanisms, including U.S. mediation. Since their independence in the early nineteenth century, Paraguay and Bolivia had been unable to agree over the boundary that separated the two countries, in part because it stretched through the Gran Chaco or Chaco Boreal, a vast, poorly explored, harsh wilderness. The Chaco was bounded on the southwest by the Pilcamayo River and along its eastern edge by the Paraguay River.

BUILDUP TO CONFLICT

Nonetheless by the 1920s, interest in the region mounted. Territorial claims dating back several decades fueled the tensions. Both countries sensed their lack of international prestige and believed they could enhance their status by expanding into the Chaco. Paraguay had been devastated by its war against Brazil, Uruguay, and Argentina from 1864 to 1870, having lost most of its adult male population in the conflict. Chile humiliated Bolivia in the War of the Pacific (1879–1883), seizing its Pacific province of Litoral and cutting off Bolivia's access to the sea. To compensate Bolivia laid claim to lands in the Chaco, over which Paraguay also declared itself sovereign. Some Bolivians hoped to expand their territory to the Paraguay River and build a port there, as the Paraguay was navigable out to the Atlantic. In contrast the Pilcamayo River, a major tributary of the Paraguay which had its origin in Bolivia, was not suitable for shipping due to the swift current in its upper stretches. The two nations also competed over the Chaco in the belief that it held valuable natural resources, including petroleum. Royal Shell and Standard Oil both showed interest in potential Chaco oil fields.

Thus several factors pushed Paraguay and Bolivia into conflict over the Chaco Boreal. In 1921–1923 Bolivia tried to negotiate rights to a corridor through which it could build an oil pipeline across the Chaco, but governmental instability in Paraguay made it impossible for the two countries to reach an agreement. By the mid-1920s both nations began sending military parties into the Chaco and set up fortified outposts there. These incursions heightened tensions, yet neither nation was prepared for a major war. Each rushed to arm itself with the most modern weapons available. Meanwhile mediation attempts by Argentina, the Pan-American Union, and the Commission of Neutrals between 1927 and 1932 failed to reconcile the two countries. U.S. president Herbert Hoover took a hands-off approach, naively asserting that in the Americas, public opinion would block the outbreak of war.

Chaco War 1932–1935

The map and key above show the land that was disputed between Paraguay and Bolivia in the Chaco War, 1932–1935. These countries were unable to agree on the boundary that separated the two countries because it stretched through the Gran Chao, which includes the Chaco Boreal. This map shows the present-day boundaries of these countries as a result of the war. The Chaco Central south and west of the Rio Pilcomayo is part of Argentina (the river forms part of the border between the two countries).

A COSTLY WAR TO BOTH SIDES

The war began in July 1932, when a Bolivian patrol attacked a Paraguayan garrison, Carlos Antonio López, on the eastern shore of Lake Chuquisaca. Bolivia initially denied the attack and claimed that its forces had only defended themselves, although Bolivian president Daniel Salamanca Urey admitted a year later that his forces had fired the first shots. Such an admission earlier might have facilitated attempts to mediate an end to the conflict, but by the time Salamanca spoke, the war was underway.

With a population of 3,000,000 compared to 800,000 for Paraguay, Bolivia confidently entered the conflict, sure its superior numbers would overwhelm the Paraguayans. Bolivian forces attacked and captured several small Paraguayan forts in the north-central Chaco, but President Salamanca then ordered a halt to the offensive, fearing that Argentina might enter the war on Paraguay's side. Paraguay soon seized the initiative, and in a bloody battle that cost each side nearly three thousand dead and wounded, retook Fortín Boquerón, the most important of the garrisons that it had lost earlier. This touched off a round of recriminations in Bolivia, whose population had expected an easy victory.

Bolivia had great difficulty supplying its forces in the field. It bought weapons from Britain, but Chile, Argentina, and Peru blocked or hindered their importation. Even when the armaments reached Bolivia via Brazil, primitive road and rail systems made it arduous to ship them to the areas of the Chaco where they were needed. Paraguay, on the other hand, received help from Argentina, both in the shipping of goods from foreign suppliers, in the provision of war matériel, and even in military personnel. Some Argentine air force pilots retired temporarily and flew planes for the Paraguayan military.

While Bolivia's Salamanca feuded with his military leaders, Paraguayan President Eusebio Ayala and General Enrique Peñaranda worked more harmoniously. Paraguayan forces drove westward across the Chaco, capturing many enemy fortifications and Bolivian soldiers. Between late 1932 and mid-1934 Paraguay occupied nearly all the contested territory. In December 1934 the Paraguayans captured most of a Bolivian army after enticing it into the middle of the Chaco. Nonetheless Paraguay faced growing logistical challenges in supplying its forces in the Chaco wilderness. The desperate Bolivian government finally ordered a general mobilization of the population, bringing its demographic superiority into the conflict.

By 1935 neither country could sustain the war effort. Their governments were nearly bankrupt, and their casualties had reached per capita levels similar to those suffered by the European nations in World War I. Bolivia and Paraguay agreed to a cease-fire mediated by several Latin American nations and the United States, which took effect on June 14, 1935. Due to lengthy negotiations the war did not formally end until three years later. Paraguay retained most of the Chaco, but the conflict was disastrous for it as well as Bolivia. Bolivia lost nearly 60,000 dead or nearly 2 percent of its population, and Paraguay suffered 36,000 dead or 4.5 percent of the population. By discrediting its political system Bolivia's defeat contributed to the political radicalism that led to the revolution of 1952. Despite his successful prosecution of the war, Paraguay's President, Ayala, was removed in 1936, with his nation struggling to recover financially and demographically from the conflict.

THE FAILURE OF FOREIGN INTERVENTION

International peace organizations and countries that tried to mediate in the conflict failed miserably. Neither the League of Nations nor the Pan-American Union had the mechanisms or the prestige to prevent two of Latin America's poorest nations from going to war. As for the United States, the Roosevelt administration at first avoided direct intervention, in part because its Good Neighbor policy proscribed heavy-handed involvement. Both sides purchased war matériel in the United States, but the U.S. Congress eventually passed an arms embargo in May 1934. Paraguay criticized the United States for permitting Standard Oil Company of New Jersey to aid Bolivia, where the firm had petroleum operations, but Standard Oil denied the accusations. Although both belligerents were part of the League of Nations, it struggled to mediate an end to the war because both the United States and Brazil insisted that American nations should resolve the conflict. Sponsored by Argentina, Brazil, Uruguay, Peru, and Chile, the Chaco Peace conference eventually negotiated the peace treaty of July 21, 1938, which ended the war. But the efforts by American nations to mediate were beset by hemispheric rivalries, as between Argentina (which had provided the earliest and most aggressive intervention) and that nation's rivals, Brazil, Chile, and the United States. Indeed Argentina and the United States both ended up competing for hemispherical leadership as much as resolving the crisis.

See also *Bolivia, U.S. Relations with; League of Nations; Pan-American Union; Paraguay, U.S. Relations with*

. . . . KENDALL BROWN

REFERENCES AND FURTHER READING

Farcau, Bruce W. *The Chaco War: Bolivia and Paraguay, 1932–1935*. Westport, CT: Praeger, 1996.

Hughes, Matthew. "Logistics and the Chaco War: Bolivia versus Paraguay, 1932–1935." *Journal of Military History* 69 (April 2005): 411–437.

Rout, Leslie B. Jr. *Politics of the Chaco Peace Conference: 1935–1939*. Austin: University of Texas, Institute of Latin American Studies, 1970.

Wood, Bryce. *The United States and Latin American Wars, 1932–1942*. New York: Columbia University Press, 1966.

Chamizal Boundary Dispute, 1864–1964

The Chamizal Boundary Dispute (1864–1964) was a conflict regarding the U.S.-Mexico border in El Paso, Texas, and Ciudad Juárez, Chihuahua. Prior to 1864 the 640-acre Chamizal tract was part of Juárez, south of the Rio Grande. After a violent flood, however, the Chamizal became part of El Paso, north of the river. From 1864 on, the issue of Chamizal ownership drew persistent attention from both nations.

The eastern boundary between the nations, delineated by the deepest channel within the Rio Grande, was established in the 1848 Treaty of Guadalupe-Hidalgo. Natural alterations of the river and their impact on the international boundary were not taken into consideration fully in 1848. Following surveys of the boundary in the 1850s, United States Attorney General Caleb Cushing determined that natural erosion and accretion would not demand legal alteration in the boundary. However, Cushing noted that should the river change course abruptly, the midpoint of the deserted channel would remain the boundary.

Following the 1864 flood and subsequent shift of the Rio Grande's course, Mexico raised issues of title in Chamizal, although when the issue rose again in 1867 both nations seemed in agreement with Cushing's earlier assessment. In the 1870s Mexico pushed to establish a fixed-line boundary to permit indisputable land titles, and in 1884 the two nations signed a treaty establishing the location of the deepest channel, as surveyed in 1848 and 1853, as the international boundary and abiding by Cushing's tenets.

Nevertheless, several issues plagued this 1884 agreement. In 1889 the International Boundary Commission (IBC) was established to litigate these issues. The IBC was comprised of one representative from each nation, which effectively made it incapable of solving disputes until a Canadian representative was added in 1911. Although a 1910 convention calling for arbitration stipulated that Chamizal be awarded solely to either the United States or Mexico, the IBC's 1911 arbitration decided the tract should be split. For the ensuing two decades the United States refused to abide by the decision, claiming the IBC had no authority to divide the tract and further refused, from 1925 to 1932, to agree to Mexico's desire to seek resolution at The Hague.

In 1933, at the start of the Good Neighbor policy, the two nations agreed on river rectification as a solution, establishing what would become a fixed-line boundary and including recognition of Mexico's title to part of Chamizal. However this solution was not implemented for another three decades, when, during the Cold War, U.S. ambassador to Mexico, Thomas C. Mann, was determined to settle the Chamizal dispute and heal its detrimental effect on hemispheric relations. On January 14, 1963, to help strengthen the Alliance for Progress, Presidents John F. Kennedy and Adolfo López Mateos ratified the Chamizal Treaty based on the original 1911 arbitration. The settlement featured thirteen points, including 437 acres awarded to Mexico and 197 acres to the United States and channelization of the Rio Grande between El Paso and Juárez. Compensation to relocate Chamizal residents was expensive for the United States; however the settlement removed a major moral and emotional irritant from the nations' relationship. The Chamizal Settlement Treaty was passed quickly in Mexico and unanimously by the United States Senate Foreign Relations Committee. In 1967 Presidents Lyndon B. Johnson and

Gustavo Díaz Ordaz met in the Chamizal to formally proclaim settlement of the Chamizal boundary dispute.

See also *Good Neighbor Policy; Johnson, Lyndon B.; Kennedy, John F.; Mann, Thomas C.; Mexican-American War: Treaty of Guadalupe Hidalgo, 1848; Mexico, U.S. Relations with*

. . . . MARTIN CHRISTIANSEN

REFERENCES AND FURTHER READING

The Chamizal Settlement. Washington, DC: U.S. Department of State, 1963.

Lamborn, Alan C., and Stephen P. Mumme. *Statecraft, Domestic Politics, and Foreign Policy Making: The El Chamizal Dispute.* Boulder, CO: Westview Press, 1988.

Liss, Sheldon B. *A Century of Disagreement: The Chamizal Conflict, 1864–1964.* University Press of Washington, DC, 1965.

Chamorro, Violeta

Violeta Barrios Torres de Chamorro (1929–) is a Nicaraguan publisher, politician, and former president. She was born in Rivas, Nicaragua, to a wealthy family who educated her in private Catholic schools and in the United States. She married Pedro Joaquín Chamorro in 1950 and they had five children. In 1952 Pedro took over the anti-Somoza newspaper, *La Prensa,* and was frequently jailed for its content. On January 10, 1978, Pedro was assassinated and Violeta took over the newspaper.

Initially Chamorro supported the Sandinista rebels who, led by Daniel Ortega, overthrew the Somozas' long and bloody regime. Chamorro joined the Sandinista First Coalition Junta, but she soon resigned because of their socialist ideology. Since the only real opposition was the contras, she briefly supported them, causing the Sandinistas to temporarily shut down the paper. The paper remained popular since it opposed the Sandinista's socialist program and called for an end to the civil war.

Chamorro's family split. Her son Pedro and daughter Cristiana worked at *La Prensa.* In 1984 Pedro joined the contras. Her daughter Claudia became Sandanista ambassador to Costa Rica and her son Carlos became the editor of the Sandinista National Liberation Front (FSLN) newspaper, *Barricada.*

During the 1980s the Reagan administration covertly supported the contras. In 1989 President George H.W. Bush called on the Sandinistas to allow free elections. Isolated and fearful of U.S. intervention, they relented and elections were held in 1990. The elections were deemed fair by UN observers, including former U.S. President Jimmy Carter. The fourteen major opposition parties created an anti-Sandinista coalition called the Union Nacional Opositora (UNO), selecting Chamorro as their presidential candidate. In spite of starting far behind against the charismatic Ortega, she ran a vigorous grassroots campaign that appealed to a wide range of Nicaraguans, including the Roman Catholic Church. She won, receiving 55 percent of the vote. The UNO won fifty-one of ninety-two seats in the legislature. The Sandinistas received only 41 percent and thirty-nine seats. She was sworn in on April 25, 1990.

Ortega allowed the results to stand and helped assure a smooth transition. Chamorro ended the war in Nicaragua by dismantling the contras. To maintain the peace she reduced the power of the military and granted unconditional amnesties to all political factions. She kept the Sandinista land redistribution programs and even kept Ortega's brother Humberto as a military leader.

In 1994 the contras rose again but were quickly suppressed through a peace agreement among all the parties. To symbolize this peace the government bought nearly every weapon in the nation and had them buried in concrete in a park in the heart of Managua, declaring "never again."

Chamorro stabilized the war-torn economy. She curbed hyperinflation by cutting government spending. She attempted to create a free market system through the Mayorga Plan that sought to integrate Nicaragua into the world market and increase foreign investment. The plan proved unpopular because government cuts led to increased unemployment and eliminated many social programs, particularly for women. Chamorro was also criticized for not supporting reforms to prohibit nepotism, legislative approval to tax, reduction of the presidential term from six to five years, and expansion of constitutional liberties.

The United States had contributed $9 million to Chamorro's campaign, and relations grew strong. Bush removed the embargo that dated to Sandinista days and provided $300 million in economic aid in 1990 and $241 million in 1991. The aid did not solve Nicaragua's economic problems.

In 1992, even though Chamorro led a moderate government, conservative Republican Senator Jesse Helms of North Carolina orchistrated $104 million in financial aid to Nicaragua because many Sandinistas were still part of the Nicaraguan government.

In 1996 Chamorro decided not to run for reelection. The UNO candidate, Arnoldo Aleman, won the October 1996 election and on January 10, 1997, Chamorro left office. Aleman inherited a nation with a 5 percent annual growth rate, a relatively stable economy, and a peaceful society, even though unemployment was at 17 percent and inflation at 11 percent annually. The best example of Chamorro's success is that her former rival, Daniel Ortega, was elected president in 2006 without violence.

See also *Central American Wars, 1980s; Chamorro Cardenal, Pedro Joaquín; Ortega Saavedra, José Daniel; Sandinista National Liberation Front (FSLN) (Nicaragua)*

. . . . WILLIAM HEAD

SELECTED WORKS

Chamorro, Violeta. *Dreams of the Heart.* New York: Simon and Schuster, 1996.

REFERENCES AND FURTHER READING

Close, David. *Nicaragua: The Chamorro Years.* Boulder, CO: Lynne Rienner, 1999.

LeoGrande, William M. *Our Own Backyard: The United States in Central America, 1977–1992.* Chapel Hill: University of North Carolina Press, 1998.

Walker, Thomas W., ed. *Nicaragua without Illusions.* Wilmington, DE: Scholarly Resources Inc., 1997.

Chamorro Cardenal, Pedro Joaquín

The publisher of the newspaper, *La Prensa,* journalist and crusader of democracy in Nicaragua, Pedro Joaquín Chamorro Cardenal (1924–1978) was born to Pedro Joaquín Chamorro Zelaya and Margarita Cardenal Argüello. Chamorro's father was the editor of prestigious daily, *La Prensa,* which became the mouthpiece of the opposition Conservative party. The paper bore the wrath of the brutal regime of Anastasio Somoza García (Dictator 1936–1956) and both father and son Chamorro were at the receiving end for the regime.

As a student of law in 1940s Chamorro became one of the opponents of Somoza and was imprisoned. Afterward he moved to Mexico to study journalism and came back to Nicaragua in 1948. After four years he was named the editor of *La Prensa* in 1952. He was imprisoned in 1954 on charges of rebellion and later released, only to be arrested again. After Somoza's assassination in 1957 Chamorro was sent off to the distant northern town of San Carlos. In 1959 he escaped to Costa Rica with wife Violeta Barrios de Chamorro, the future president of Nicaragua. Chamorro did not remain idle and continued in antigovernment activities in the year 1959. Along with his cohorts, he was captured and faced a trial by the military court for the third time. He was sentenced to nine years for plotting against the state. He was freed in 1969 and continued his editorials for *La Prensa,* attacking the policies of the government.

The United States had been deeply involved in the affairs of Nicaragua from the beginning of the twentieth century by dollar diplomacy, sending Marines and propping up the government. From the 1930s the Somoza family had become an invaluable ally of the United States. The family dominated the political landscape of Nicaragua. Anastasio Somoza Debayle (President 1967–1979) became a trustworthy ally of the United States, supporting the country in various international forums. His oppressive and authoritarian regime was being supported by the second most populated democracy of the world. Somoza was reelected president in September 1974, and he ruthlessly suppressed any form of dissent.

In the strict censorship of the press, the main target was Chamorro's *La Prensa.* The social condition in Nicaragua was deteriorating. The political, economic, and social establishments of Nicaragua were growing restive, and the conservative leader Chamorro began to rally against Somoza. In December 1974 he formed the broad-based *Unión Democrática de Liberación* (UDEL, Democratic Union of Liberation), comprised of conservatives, liberals, civic groups, Christian Democrats, and business organizations. He campaigned vigorously for the restoration of civil rights, free elections, political pluralism, and human rights. However the United States continued to support Somoza in spite of his blatant violation of human rights, policy of repression, and pocketing of million dollars' worth of aid.

The politics in Nicaragua were fast changing, and the left-leaning Sandinista National Liberation Front (FSLN) was expanding its clout. In June 1977 the U.S. Congress gave assent to continuation of military assistance for Somoza's government. In the same month Chamorro joined hands with the FSLN. In a meeting held at San José in Costa Rica, UDEL and FSNL formed the *El Grupo de los Doce* or Group of Twelve, with the avowed aim of ending the Somoza regime. It was comprised of church personnel, notable attorneys, architects, business persons, plantation owners, architects, and others. Chamorro's days were numbered as the regime wanted to get rid of its most vocal opponent. A *La Prensa* editorial criticizing the exploitative practices of the Somoza-owned Nicaraguan blood industry may have been the last straw. On January 10, 1978, Chamorro was assassinated by Domingo Acevedo Chavarria, who, along with four accomplices, was pardoned by Chamorro's widow, Violeta Barrios de Chamorro, when she became president.

It was believed that Somoza was behind the killing. After the killing, about thirty thousand people took to the streets of the capital city of Managua, with much torching of vehicles. Property belonging to the dictator's family was destroyed. After a call of a general strike, unrest spread throughout the country. The government harshly suppressed the riots. The *La Prensa* office came under violent attacks by the government. The death of Chamorro started a chain of events leading to Somoza's ouster. The Carter administration (1977–1981), which prized human rights, suspended all military assistance by February 1978. In spite of a strong lobby in Washington, the dictator had to flee from Nicaragua to Miami on July 17, 1979. While alive, Chamorro fought tirelessly against an oppressive regime upholding the cause of democracy and human values. His death was not in vain, as it unleashed a series of events leading to suspension of American military assistance, the final ouster of Somoza, and eventually his wife's term as president.

See also *Chamorro, Violeta; Nicaragua, U.S. Relations with; Sandinista National Liberation Front (FSLN) (Nicaragua); Somoza Debayle, Anastasio*

. . . . PATIT PABAN MISHRA

REFERENCES AND FURTHER READING

Chamorro, Violeta Barrios de. *Dreams of the Heart: The Autobiography of President Violeta Barrios de Chamorro of Nicaragua.* New York: Simon and Schuster, 1996.

Edmisten, Patricia Taylor. *Nicaragua Divided: La Prensa and the Chamorro Legacy.* Pensacola: University of West Florida Press, 1990.

Chamorro Vargas, Emiliano

Emiliano Chamorro Vargas (1871–1966), son of Salvador Chamorro Oreamuno and Gregoria Vargas Báezwas, was a prominent politician, diplomat, and army chief of Nicaragua. He played an important role in U.S.-Latin American relations as Conservative party member, Nicaraguan minister to the United States, and president of the country.

The United States was reinvigorated with successes after war with Spain and access to new markets created by the Open Door policy. Theodore Roosevelt (President 1901–1909) and his successor, William H. Taft (President 1909–1913), sought a greater role for the United States in Latin America, particularly the Caribbean. The Roosevelt Corollary enhanced the scope of the Monroe Doctrine by proclaiming that the United States not only had a right to check European intervention but also to interfere in domestic affairs of Latin American countries. The Roosevelt Corollary of the Monroe Doctrine as well as dollar diplomacy witnessed an increasingly greater role for the United States. His phrase. "speak softly and carry a big stick," aptly described U.S. imperialism. In the wake of the imminent completion of the Panama Canal, U.S. influence was increasing in countries like Honduras, Guatemala, Haiti, and Nicaragua.

The United States began to interfere in Nicaraguan affairs by supporting the conservative army chief, Chamorro, and politicians like Adolfo Díaz and against José Santos Zelaya the president. Zelaya executed two Americans accused of bomb blasts as well as some revolutionaries, and on November 18, 1909, U.S. warships were dispatched in retaliation. The Marines occupied Nicaragua until 1933 with an interregnum of some months in 1926 and 1927.

Chamorro was the leader of the Conservative party of Nicaragua as well as chairperson of the constituent assembly. Afterward he became the country's representative in the United States. Taft's successor, Woodrow Wilson (President 1913–1921), continued the same U.S. policy in Nicaragua by giving final shape to a draft treaty initiated by Taft. U.S. Secretary of State William Jennings Bryan and Chamorro signed the Bryan-Chamorro Treaty on August 5, 1914. By paying a meager $3 million, the United States received the exclusive right to construct a canal across the country, as well as the right for ninety-nine years to establish a naval base at Corn Island in the Caribbean and on the Gulf of Formosa. The treaty also included a clause authorizing American intervention in Nicaragua. Costa Rica, El Salvador, and Honduras claimed that the treaty was an infringement on their rights, a claim vindicated by a ruling of the Central American Court of Justice, but the United States and Nicaragua did not accept the verdict. The U.S. Senate approved the treaty in 1916. Chamorro returned from Washington after making Nicaragua virtually a U.S. protectorate. No foreign power could dare act against U.S. interests. Only in July 1970 was the treaty abrogated.

Chamorro was elected as the fifty-fifth president and remained in office from 1917 to 1921. There was no change in American policy toward Nicaragua as long as U.S. interests were served. Chamorro was defeated in his reelection bid by Carlos José Solorzano. Calvin Coolidge (President 1923–1929) decided to recall the Marines from Nicaragua as the successive pro-American governments in capital Managua were safe from any violent political upheaval. But there were contests for power among rival politicians, and the liberals resented the conservatives, who were long entrenched in power. Chamorro returned to power again in 1926 after deposing Solorzano, becoming president for a second time on March 14, 1926. But his second tenure was short lived due to lack of U.S. support and he had to resign on November 11, 1926. Adolfo Díaz, a long-time U.S. ally, became president, and the Marines were sent back to Nicaragua again in early 1927.

Chamorro was a very ambitious politician from the time he took part in a conspiracy to oust President Zelaya in 1893. A successful diplomat, he represented his country not only in the United States but also in several European capitals after his second term as president was over. Chamorro was at loggerheads with Anastasio Somoza García (President 1937–1957), but they reached an understanding in 1950. Although it cost him support of a few members of his party, eventually the conservatives received some seats in the Nicaraguan congress. Chamorro died on February 26, 1966, in Managua.

See also *Bryan, William Jennings; Bryan-Chamorro Treaty, 1915; Roosevelt Corollary to the Monroe Doctrine; Roosevelt, Theodore; Zelaya López, José Santos*

. . . . PATIT PABAN MISHRA

REFERENCES AND FURTHER READING

LaFeber, Walter. *Inevitable Revolutions: The United States in Central America.* 2nd ed. New York: Norton, 1993.

Kammen, William. *A Search for Stability: United States Diplomacy toward Nicaragua, 1925–1933.* Notre Dame, IN: University of Notre Dame Press, 1968.

Walker, Thomas W. *Nicaragua: Living in the Shadow of the Eagle.* 4th ed. Boulder, CO: Westview Press, 2003.

Chapultepec Conference

(**See** *Inter-American Conference on the Problems of War and Peace, Mexico City, 1945*)

Chatfield, Frederick

Fredrick Chatfield (1801–1872) was born into a middle class London family, the youngest son of elderly parents. Little is known about Chatfield's early years, including his education in military matters. For sure the socially ambitious Chatfield lived a pampered life that left him financially irresponsible. Finally in 1826, his father, a veteran sea captain for the East India Company, used his connections at the foreign office to have his son first assigned to the consular service at Memel, Russia, and subsequently to Aix-la-Chapelle at the time of Belgian independence in 1830. There he impressed other foreign diplomats who reported such to the British ambassador. When offered the assignment to Central America in 1834, Chatfield saw it as a stepping stone to advance his own career.

CHATFIELD IN GUATEMALA

Chatfield arrived in Guatemala City in 1834 as Great Britain's minister to the United Provinces of Central America (UPCA) with instructions from the foreign office to enhance British commercial opportunities throughout the region and to insure the Central American government's repayment of loans to private British bondholders that dated to the early 1820s. Subsequently Chatfield pursued territorial interests that demonstrated British interests in a transisthmian canal and resulted in a diplomatic confrontation with the United States.

Chatfield quickly negotiated a commercial treaty with UPCA similar to the U.S. 1825 Treaty of Amity and Commerce. However little commerce followed. As with the United States, Central Americahad little to offer the world beyond cochineal and indigo and lacked the financial capability to purchase British goods. In fact the Central American elite continued to prefer Spanish manufactures over others. With Spain refusing to trade with independent Central America, British and Dutch ships carried the goods westward. Chatfield did not help the British standing with the region's ruling elite when he openly opposed the construction of new or the enhancement of existing ports on Central America's Pacific coast. Chatfield correctly understood that these ports would not facilitate trade with Europe, an opinion not shared by Central America's ruling elite, who viewed Chatfield's opinion as another example of his interference in local matters, a characteristic of his eighteen-year stay in Central America. With the collapse of UPCA in 1839 and 1840, trade came to a temporary standstill.

Chatfield's second assignment was to insure the repayment of loans made by British private sector lenders immediately after Central America's independence in 1821. The British reasoned that repayment remained contingent upon the survival of the UPCA, as it would be easier to collect funds from one government rather than five. For this reason Chatfield publicly supported Central American unity, including Francisco Morazán's efforts to revive the union after its 1840 collapse.

Shortly after his arrival in Guatemala City in 1834, Chatfield traveled to the Moskito Coast and to Belize, where English settlers who arrived in the seventeenth century bequeathed to the king's government a protectorate. When Chatfield refused to discuss Guatemala's claims to Belize with Juan Galindo, the latter departed for Washington, D.C., to seek U.S. assistance under the terms of the Monroe Doctrine. President Andrew Jackson demurred, preoccupied with expansion into Texas and the extension of the National Bank's charter. Galindo then sailed to London, where he met a similar response.

With the UPCA's collapse by 1840, Chatfield continued to push British interests with the individual five nations. In addition to seeking commercial opportunities and offering the locals free advice on taxes and government, Chatfield's efforts contributed to the superintendent at Belize extending British control over the Bay Islands, located off the Honduran coast, in 1841. Already having declared a protectorate over the Miskito Indians, British authorities extended their protectorate to the town of San Juan del Norte on the Costa Rican border, recognizing that it was the most likely Caribbean terminus for a transisthmian water and land crossing to the Pacific Ocean.

BRITISH-U.S. TENSION OVER TIGRE ISLAND

Until the Treaty of Guadalupe Hidalgo in 1848 that ended the Mexican-American War, the United States in the 1840s ignored pleas from Central American governments and from its own consular agents in the area—William S. Murphy and Henry Savage—to thwart continued British expansion. During this time period the United States looked west, not south, for expansion. As the war drew to its close, U.S. attention turned to a transportation route across the Central American isthmus. To meet the British challenge that included the June 1, 1848, seizure of San Juan del Norte and renaming it Greytown, President James K. Polk dispatched Elijah Hise to Nicaragua, where he concluded a commercial treaty that also granted the United States the right to construct a canal through its territory. But Hise returned to Washington, D.C., in September 1849, where a new secretary of state, John M. Clayton, wanted to put his own stamp on any solution. Hence Clayton did not submit the treaty to the Senate for its consideration but instead dispatched Ephraim George Squier to Central America to secure a canal treaty without a U.S. guarantee. Squier violated his instructions. The treaty bearing his name paralleled that of his predecessor, Hise. Squier then descended upon Honduras to gain U.S. control over Tigre Island in the Gulf of Fonseca, long considered the western terminus of any canal across Nicaragua.

Squier believed that Chatfield was too timid to do anything but accept the *fait accompli*. Squier misjudged his colleague. Chatfield viewed the seizure of Tigre island as a prelude to the establishment of a protectorate. He quickly boarded the *HMS Gorgon* and directed it to the Gulf of Fonseca, where British troops seized the island. Chatfield justified the action on the Honduran failure to pay its unsettled debts with British bondholders. Cooler heads prevailed in London, where the foreign office rescinded Chatfield's occupation order.

Neither Great Britain nor the United States were anxious to go to war over Central America. Problems in Europe, and the question of slavery in the territories gained from the Mexican-American War, were more pressing. These problems significantly contributed to the subsequent British withdrawal from Central America and the United States postponing its interest in the region for a generation. Amidst these policy changes, Chatfield returned to London in 1852.

See also *Clayton-Bulwer Treaty, 1850; Hise-Selva Treaty; Polk, James K.; Squier, Ephraim G.*

. . . . THOMAS M. LEONARD

REFERENCES AND FURTHER READING

Kortge, Dean. "The Central American Policy of Lord Palmerston." PhD diss., University of Kansas, 1973.

Rodriguez, Mario. *A Palmerstonian Diplomat in Central America: Frederick Chatfield*. Tucson: University of Arizona Press, 1964.

Williams, Mary W. *Anglo-American Isthmian Diplomacy, 1815–1915*. Washington, DC: American Historical Association, 1916.

Chávez Frías, Hugo

Hugo Rafael Chávez Frías (1954–) is the current president of Venezuela and one of the most polarizing political figures in Latin America in recent years. Widely known for his advocacy of revolutionary transformation in Venezuela and his aggressive anti-U.S. rhetoric, his supporters claim him as the voice of a new Latin American movement of "twenty-first century socialism" and independence from *yanqui* imperialism, while his opponents attack him as a *caudillo*, a dictator, and a megalomaniac.

Chávez spent his early career in the army, including at least ten years planning a military coup against Venezuela's ruling elite. In seeing the military as a source of revolutionary change, he followed in a long-standing Latin American tradition, exemplified most vividly during Chávez's youth by Panama's General Omar Torrijos. Chávez has tended to be ambiguous about the changing substance of his revolutionary thinking, but he has identified himself most closely and consistently with nineteenth-century peasant leader Ezequiel Zamora, revolutionary thinker Simón Rodríguez, and, above all, the hero of Latin American independence, Simón Bolívar.

The long-planned Chávez coup was launched in 1992, during the second presidency of Carlos Andrés Pérez, but it lacked a mass civilian uprising or widespread support within the military. As with Fidel Castro's famous assault on the Moncada Barracks, though, this initial defeat propelled Chávez onto the national stage. He became widely known as a populist "antipolitician" and, after a short period of imprisonment, successfully ran for election as president in 1998.

In office Chávez has used his position to rewrite the Venezuelan constitution, reformulate the constituent assembly, weaken the powers of the Supreme Court, put allies in charge of the nation's major industries and infrastructure, purge the army of disloyal elements, tighten his grip over the media, and expand public spending on social programs both within Venezuela and elsewhere in the world. He has successfully resisted fierce opposition from the old elite, as well as the middle classes and some organized labour groups, although he only narrowly avoided being deposed in a coup in April 2002. Supporters point out that, after some years of crisis, unemployment and infant mortality rates declined under the first term of Chávez's presidency, while literacy rates, life expectancy, and average incomes went up. Ambitious *misiones* were also established to wage war on poverty, unemployment, ill health, and poor education. Opponents note that, despite munificent oil bounties, Chávez has enlarged the national debt, failed to control endemic inflation (it was around 30 percent in 2002 and 2003), not stemmed violence on the streets that has grown exponentially, and achieved little in terms of rooting out corruption. The old oligarchy was instead replaced by a class of *nouveaux riches,* commonly known in Venezuela as the *boliburguesia* ("Bolivarian bourgeoisie"), built from patronage dispensed by the president.

In promoting his revolutionary agenda Chávez was undoubtedly aided by consistently rising oil prices, which allowed Venezuela to project its power far beyond what would otherwise have been possible. But he was also able to take advantage of his tremendous personal popularity within Venezuela, especially among the poorest segments of society. Internationally Chávez also benefited from his opposition to a very unpopular U.S. president, aligning himself with the most vocal critics of President George W. Bush's foreign policy, particularly Fidel Castro, and regularly launching *ad hominem* attacks upon Bush, calling him, among other things, a donkey, an alcoholic, the devil, and *un pendejo* (roughly equivalent in tone to "asshole" or "dumbass").

Compared to the positions adopted by left-of-center leaders in Argentina, Brazil, and elsewhere, then, Chávez consciously chose to provoke and exacerbate tensions between the Venezuelan and U.S. governments in order to reinforce his revolutionary credentials. His hostility was reciprocated by the U.S. government, which was undoubtedly aware of and (some speculate) perhaps even involved in, the anti-Chávez coup of 2002. Some right-wing commentators in the United States regularly included Chávez alongside the "Axis of Evil" countries and advocated his overthrow or assassination, while Chávez has justified major arms purchases for the Venezuelan army as preparations for a potential U.S. invasion. Nevertheless, the United States remains a major purchaser of Venezuelan oil, and both sides seem to have preferred vocal criticism and fractious diplomacy to more open or violent confrontation that might substantially affect ongoing trade relations.

Chávez thus established himself as the central figure in a supposed pan-continental movement to the left in the early years of the twenty-first century and a return to the hostile anti-Americanism common to Latin American politics during the Cold War. He vocally rejected the "Washington Consensus," and sought to promote ideas and allies that would weaken the influence of the United States throughout the region and the world, even going so far as to put forward policies—such as providing cheap oil to poor U.S. citizens and offering aid to victims of Hurricane Katrina—that implicitly challenged Washington's authority within the U.S. territory itself. After a prolonged period in which U.S.-Venezuelan tensions manifested in multiple ways, including through clashes between Chávez and the pro-U.S. government of neighboring Colombia, Venezuela's relations with the United States reached their lowest point at the end of Bush's presidency. In September 2008 Chávez expelled U.S. Ambassador Patrick Duddy, alleging he had been involved in plots to overthrow the Venezuelan government. In 2009 Chávez also launched investigations into Duddy's replacement, chargé d'affairs John Caulfield, for allegedly meeting anti-Chávez activists during a trip to Puerto Rico.

The election of President Obama, the collapse of global oil prices following the global recession of 2008, and growing opposition to Chávez's rule at home seem to have contributed to a relaxation of tensions between the two powers. Formal diplomatic relations were restored in June 2009. Nevertheless Chávez continues to voice his plans for the revolutionary transformation of Latin America, while many on the U.S. right continue to express their hostility to Chávez both personally and politically. As such the final impact of Chávez for U.S.-Venezuelan relations has yet to be fully revealed. Chavez was diagnosed with cancer.

See also *Bolívar, Simón; Bush, George W.; Castro Ruz, Fidel; Pérez Rodríguez, Carlos Andrés; Torrijos Herrera, Omar; Venezuela, U.S. Relations with*

ALEX GOODALL

REFERENCES AND FURTHER READING

Kozloff, Nikolas. *Hugo Chávez: Oil, Politics, and the Challenge to the U.S.* New York: Palgrave Macmillan, 2006.

Marcano, Cristina, and Alberto Barrera Tyszka. *Hugo Chávez.* New York: Random House, 2004.

Wilpert, Greg. *Changing Venezuela by Taking Power: The History and Policies of the Chávez Government.* New York: Verso, 2007.

Chiari Remón, Roberto Francisco

Two-time president of the Republic of Panama (1949; 1960–1964) who led his nation through the crisis of the 1964 Panama riots, Roberto Chiari (1905–1981) was born to a prominent isthmian family that had extensive holdings in the sugar industry.

From 1924–1928 Roberto's father Rodolfo Chiari served as president of Panama. Roberto was educated at the Colegio de La Salle in the capital where he earned a degree in business. From 1924 to 1931 he worked as a presidential aide first for his father and later for Harmodio Arosemena (President 1928–1931). Chiari was elected to a five-year-term as a Liberal party deputy to the national assembly from 1940–1945. Ricardo Adolfo de la Guardia (President 1941–1945) appointed Chiari minister of health and public works in 1945, positioning him as a possible successor. But that same year Chiari was defeated in his first bid for the presidency. In 1948 he was elected second vice president of Panama and served briefly as president for a five-day period in November 1948 during a political crisis in which National Police strongman José Antonio Remón forced President Daniel Chanís to resign from office. In 1960 Chiari forged a political comeback, winning a four-year term as president.

President Chiari immediately confronted an economic downturn and a growing political crisis with the United States over the issue of Panamanian sovereignty in the Canal Zone. Since the 1956 Suez Crisis, local students, activists, and intellectuals increased their agitation over what they viewed as the unfair treatment of Panama vis-à-vis the United States over canal profits, the right to fly the Panamanian flag in the Canal Zone, and the perpetuity clause of the 1903 treaty. The prosperous U.S. enclave and its zonian residents made many Panamanians feel like second-class citizens in their own country. These grievances culminated in the November 1959 flag riots. The Chiari administration moved aggressively to address these concerns. In the fall of 1961 Chiari wrote President John F. Kennedy asking for a comprehensive revision of U.S.-Panamanian relations with regard to the canal operations and U.S. rights in the Canal Zone. In June 1962 Kennedy invited Chiari to the White House to discuss these issues. While Kennedy was willing to make substantial concessions, he still strove to maintain the U.S. supreme position in the zone. In 1963 Chiari and Kennedy signed a symbolically important accord that gave Panama the right to fly its flag jointly alongside the U.S. flag in fifteen sites in the Canal Zone. Other concessions, including a larger annuity for canal use and an end to the perpetuity clause, would presumably follow.

But the flag accommodation ironically touched off the gravest crisis in the history of U.S-Panamanian relations. In early January 1964 during Christmas break, U.S. students from Balboa High School in the zone, angered over the flag accord and goaded by their chauvinistic parents, ran the U.S. colors up the lone flag pole in violation of the Chiari-Kennedy agreement (a second pole at the school for the Panamanian flag had not yet been erected). Outraged Panamanian students at the nearby *Instituto Nacional* entered the zone, confronted the U.S. students, and attempted to fly their own banner on the pole. A scuffle ensued in which U.S. students reportedly tore the Panamanian flag. News of the event touched off massive riots in which twenty-one Panamanian and four U.S. soldiers lost their lives. When the fighting first erupted, Chiari moved to call out the Panamanian National Guard to end the violence but was wisely dissuaded from this action by his foreign minister Galileo Solís, who noted that if the president did so, *he* and not the Americans would incur the wrath of the Panamanian people.

Instead Chiari protested the U.S. militarization of the crisis in the Organization of American States (OAS) and the United Nations (UN) and broke off relations with Washington as the casualties mounted. The Johnson administration brought enormous pressure to bear against Chiari to relent and seek a diplomatic solution to the crisis. Bereft of U.S. loans Chiari petitioned Franco's Spain for a $5 million loan to keep his government afloat. In April 1964 Chiari and Johnson restored relations which led to a December 1964 decision to negotiate an entirely new treaty to replace the 1903 accords. After thirteen years of often frustrating negotiations involving successor governments to the Chiari administration and four U.S. presidents, the Panama Canal Treaties (Carter-Torrijos), 1977 emerged to resolve the seventy-four-year-old dispute over the canal. Chiari was also noted in his term for his expansion of health, housing, and hydro-electrical projects in Panama for which he utilized the large increase in U.S. Alliance for Progress funding under President Kennedy.

See also *Johnson, Lyndon B.; Organization of American States (OAS); Panama Canal Treaties (Carter-Torrijos), 1977; Panama, U.S. Relations with; Remón Cantera, José A.*

. . . . MICHAEL E. DONOGHUE

REFERENCES AND FURTHER READING

Conniff, Michael L. *Panama and the United States: The Forced Alliance.* Athens: University of Georgia Press, 2001.
Jorden, William J. *Panama Odyssey.* Austin: University of Texas Press, 1984.
LaFeber, Walter. *The Panama Canal: The Crisis in Historical Perspective.* New York: Oxford University Press, 1989.

Chicago Boys

The Chicago Boys were a group of Chilean neoliberal economists who implemented the neoliberal free market theories of Milton Friedman and Arnold Harberger who were faculty members in the economics department at the University of Chicago. When right-wing General Augusto Pinochet came to power in Chile in a 1973 military coup, the Chicago Boys introduced policies that drew heavily on the theories promoted at the Chicago School of Economics. The policies focused on economic liberalization, privatization of state-owned companies, and stabilization of inflation.

The Chicago Boys were immediately criticized for going against the economically orthodox policies of centralized government command and control and for agreeing to work for

General Pinochet, who ruthlessly and brutally crushed any political opposition to the policies.

The legacy of the Chicago Boys is unsettled. Some claim that the willingness of the Chicago Boys to work for a cruel dictator and start a different economic approach was one of the best things that happened to Chile, while others claim that the reforms did little to help the economy. Neoliberal proponents claim the policies helped Chile attain its economic success. Opponents dispute the neoliberal success claims, charging that the economic benefits Chile has experienced came from a general improvement in the world economy and not the neoliberal policies. While Chile is a leader in many economic indicators in South America, the neoliberal policies also led to a high level of income inequality.

The name Chicago Boys comes from their participation in a collaborative program between Universidad Católica in Chile and the economics department of the University of Chicago. The program included University of Chicago professors teaching at the Universidad Católica in Chile, book donations, and scholarships to Chilean students. Some of the undergraduates who participated in the program continued their studies in graduate economics at the University of Chicago, but the whole group was heavily influenced by the Chicago School of Economics.

The neoliberal economic reforms were embraced in the wake of runaway inflation under President Salvador Allende. In 1972 inflation was running at 150 percent, helping lead to shortages of many food and consumer items. The economic problems, which had been manipulated to create a favorable environment for a coup, set the stage for a complete overhaul of the economic system.

The day after the 1973 coup, General Pinochet was briefed on a confidential economic plan known as *El Ladrillo* (the brick). The report, which was as thick as a brick (hence the name), had been prepared by opponents of President Allende's government. *El Ladrillo* contained the core elements of what would become the Chilean neoliberal economic policy. Pinochet's government privatized almost every nationalized industry, encouraged foreign investment, and eliminated protectionist trade barriers. The policies forced domestic businesses to compete with imports on their own merits or go out of business. The reforms eliminated the right-wing industrial oligarchy, which depended on protections and subsidies in order to maintain their economic and political power. As a result of the neoliberal policies, by late 1982 Chile was mired in a severe recession that lasted over two years.

See also *Chile, U.S. Relations with; Pinochet Ugarte, Augusto*

SCOTT DITTLOFF

REFERENCES AND FURTHER READING

Gabriel Valdes, Juan. *Pinochet's Economists: The Chicago School of Economics in Chile*. Historical Perspectives on Modern Economics. New York: Cambridge University Press, 1995.

O'Brien, Phil, and Jackie Roddick. *Chile: The Pinochet Decade: The Rise and Fall of the Chicago Boys*. Latin American Bureau special brief. New York: Monthly Review Press, 1983.

Chile, U.S. Relations with

A glance at a map of the western hemisphere reveals that Chile and the United States are separated by a great distance. Chile's capital, Santiago, is over five thousand miles south of Washington, D.C. Such a large distance might imply a distant relationship between the two nations characterized by polite but infrequent interaction. Such is not the case. Chile and the United States, from the mid-nineteenth century through most of the twentieth century, have experienced periods of misunderstanding, tension, and hostility. The two nations even veered close to war in the early 1890s, and the United States intervened deeply into Chilean domestic politics in the early 1970s. The history of the troubled relationship between these two distant but closely connected nations deserves closer inspection.

The opportunity for quick riches overcame distance to make the California gold rush of the 1850s an important and fractious event in U.S.-Chilean relations. One often-used route from the Atlantic coast of the United States to the gold fields in the period before the transcontinental railroad was around South America's Cape Horn. The Chilean port of Valparaíso was a major rest stop on this ten-thousand-mile voyage. The 49ers who visited Chile were an eager, aggressive lot whose bumptious, brawling behavior left a negative impression with the host country. News of the gold strike spread throughout South America, and a sizeable number of Chileans embarked on the adventure of seeking their fortunes alongside the 49ers from the eastern United States. The presence of the Chileans—over 5,500 according to the U.S. Census of 1852—in a competitive quest for riches, led to expressions of resentment by U.S. citizens. Resentment boiled over into an antiforeigner riot in San Francisco as early as 1849, in which a mob directed much of its hostility at Chileans. This anti-Chilean sentiment continued for several years with the Californians formally expelling Chileans from the gold fields in 1850. Although these events involved personal and social interaction more than formal diplomacy, U.S.-Chilean relations were off to a difficult start.

Another crisis emerged in 1866 and, in the course of this event, the actions of U.S. diplomats and the inaction of the U.S. navy angered Chile. Spain, Chile's colonial mother country, decided to reassert its imperial pride by deploying a fleet of warships under the command of Admiral José Pareja to the west coast of South America. Pareja's expeditionary force posed a genuine threat to the financially troubled Peruvian government. Chilean leaders, sensing their nation might be next on Admiral Pareja's list for intervention, denounced Spain's actions in Peru. As expected, Pareja's vessels turned south to blockade Valparaíso and thereby punish the Chileans. Alarmed by the Spanish intervention, Chilean journalist Benjamín Vicuña Mackenna launched a publicity campaign in the United States to stimulate public support and to nudge Washington to enforce the Monroe Doctrine (which included a commitment to fend off European territorial ambitions in the Americas). Although the eloquent Mackenna received an enthusiastic response from several leading public figures in the

United States, Secretary of State William H. Seward chose to ignore the Monroe Doctrine and give Chile a low priority on his agenda. Instead Seward curried favor with the Spanish government, in part to gain approval for the construction of a submarine cable in Spain's Caribbean possessions for the benefit of New Yorker James Scrymser's international telegraph company. This diplomatic tilt toward Spain was a disappointment in Santiago, but the decision of the U.S. Navy to withdraw its warships from Valparaíso harbor to make way for the Spanish navy's bombardment of the port city was seen as an outrage. Pareja's warships pummeled Valparaíso, leaving fifteen million pesos in damage. The Spanish blockade and the attack on Valparaíso left the Chileans incensed, and their anger was directed at the United States as well as Spain. In their view the government in Washington had refused to enforce its own hemispheric policy—the Monroe Doctrine—at the expense of Chile.

THE WAR OF THE PACIFIC AND ITS AFTERMATH

The strained relationship between the two countries worsened during the War of the Pacific (1879–1884). The Atacama Desert and its rich deposits of nitrate were the focus of a dispute that involved Chile and its neighbors to the north, Bolivia and Peru. The boundaries in this valuable but lightly populated region had been in doubt since the colonial era. Chile gave up its claim to the disputed area in 1874 by signing an agreement with Bolivia which promised not to increase taxes on the thriving Chilean nitrate mining enterprises. In 1879, however, Bolivia broke the agreement by raising taxes. The Chilean government responded by ordering its armed forces to occupy the disputed area. Several years earlier Bolivia had formed an anti-Chilean alliance with Peru so that Chile faced a war with two opponents. The Chilean navy defeated the Peruvian fleet to clear the way for the invasion of the disputed province of Tarapacá. After victories at sea and on land, Chile prepared to take Lima. At this point the United States stepped in to find a peaceful settlement in October 1880. U.S. Secretary of State William Evarts arranged a meeting of the belligerents on board the U.S. Navy's *Lackawana,* but the U.S. diplomats bungled the negotiations. The *Lackawana* conference collapsed. The Chileans carried out their invasion plans and by January 1881 controlled Lima. Chile had defeated both Bolivia and Peru.

The role of the United States escalated in the aftermath of the War of the Pacific. Evart's successor as secretary of state, James G. Blaine, took a much more active part in the peace negotiations. The new secretary of state had a sensitivity to what he saw as the larger geopolitical dimensions of the war. He argued that Chile's victory was a triumph for Great Britain, the country that, Blaine pointed out, had extensive investments in nitrate mining and other business enterprises in Chile. By supporting the cause of Peru, Blaine hoped to stymie the expansion of the British commercial interests on the Pacific coast of South America and open the way for U.S. interests. But Blaine's policy was awkward and poorly coordinated. The U.S. minister in Santiago, former Civil War General Judson Kilpatrick, was sympathetic to Chile, a position that found reinforcement in his marriage to a Chilean woman. Kilpatrick's ill health limited his effectiveness, however, and left much of the impetus for policy implementation in the hands of the secretary of state.

Blaine took a transparently anti-Chilean approach in line with the interests of U.S. corporations that held investments in Peru. In particular, the Peruvian Corporation, based in the United States under the direction of Jacob Shipherd, lobbied vigorously for the U.S. government to block Chile's annexation of the nitrate provinces of Tarapacá, Arica, and Tacna, in order to protect his company's investments. Chilean leaders suspected that this combination of business and political interests in the United States had set a course to dominate nitrate mining on the Pacific coast of South America by depriving Chile of its hard-won control of the nitrate region. Chile's diplomatic representative in Washington, Martínez, found Blaine to be unreliable in their discussions and the U.S. public and politicians to be misinformed on the origins of Chile's dispute with Peru. Blaine and Shipherd fed U.S. newspapers stories slanted to favor Peru. Martínez initiated a public relations campaign in the U.S. press that explained the Chilean position on the War of the Pacific and the intrusion of U.S. politicians and businesspersons in the postwar settlement. Martínez contributed to the defeat of the secretary of state's efforts to block Chile's retention of Tarapacá.

Chile's relations with the United States continued to have unexpected twists even after the departure of Blaine from the State Department following the assassination of President James Garfield. Chester Arthur (President 1881–1885) appointed Frederick Frelinghuysen as secretary of state. Frelinghuysen soon announced a more moderate policy toward Chile. Blaine, however, had dispatched two diplomats to Chile just before his tenure ended. Veteran diplomat William Trescot and Blaine's son Walker were already on their way to Chile with instructions to undo Chile's annexation of the disputed territory. At this point Martínez again took the initiative to foil Blaine's directives. Chile's man in Washington telegraphed news of Frelinghuysen's change in policy to Santiago where Foreign Minister José Manuel Balmaceda was preparing to receive the Trescot-Blaine mission. The U.S. State Department sent notification of the moderation in policy by ship so that when the two U.S. delegates reached Santiago, they were unaware of Frelinghuysen's recent directives. Balmaceda had the pleasure of informing the two befuddled diplomats of the current U.S. policy. He then announced that Chile would retain Tarapacá according to its own plans and would hold Arica and Tacna until a plebiscite would decide their future. Foreign Minister Balmaceda and Domingo Santa María (President 1880–1886) held the upper hand in dealing with President Chester Arthur's State Department. The Martínez-Balmaceda collaboration had defeated the United States at the negotiating table just as the Chilean army and navy had defeated the Peru-Bolivia alliance on the field of war.

CONTINUED TENSIONS AND THE THREAT OF WAR

By the 1880s the relationship between the United States and Chile had become one of mutual suspicion and resentment. The Chilean view of the United States had broadened from the unfortunate experiences of the gold rush and the Spanish bombardment of Valparaíso to a more pervasive concern about imperial ambitions. Chile had come to see the U.S. aggression in the war with Mexico (1846–1848) and the subsequent taking of California as considerably different from Chile's provocations and territorial compensation in the War of the Pacific. Also the expansion of U.S. businesses in Mexico and the Caribbean, and the U.S. armed intervention in Panama in 1885 to protect the property and lives of U.S. citizens on the isthmus, seemed to be harbingers of more assertive actions. Officials in Washington had their own concerns about Chile. At the center of the U.S. analysis of the role of Chile in the hemisphere was the impressive capability of the Chilean navy. That nation's warships had not only defeated Peru's navy but also captured its best iron-clad warship, the *Huascar,* to add it to Chile's growing fleet of even more modern steel-hulled, heavily armed ships. With its acquisition of Tarapacá and other nitrate-rich provinces, Chile enhanced its material wealth, and the government had a larger tax base. The Chilean navy revealed its range of operations with the dispatch of the *Esmeralda* to patrol the Pacific waters off Panama during the U.S. intervention there in 1885. Three years later Santiago annexed Easter Island, a symbolic and perhaps strategic gesture to show that Chile had stepped into the imperial geopolitics of the late nineteenth century.

Into the uncertainties of U.S.-Chilean relations, New York entrepreneur James Scrymser thrust his new international cable firm, the Central and South American Telegraph Company. Chile was crucial to Scrymser's plans to outmaneuver his chief rivals, the British cable companies under the guiding hand of John Pender. Scrymser used his connections with Santiago to gain control of Chile's international communications and thereby undercut Pender and the British. In the process, however, Scrymser had to rely on the U.S. Navy and State Department at the same time that he curried favor with Chile. He also had to deal with divisions in Chilean politics. In an especially risky venture in the late 1880s he collaborated with Balmaceda who, by that time, was president of Chile. Balmaceda was embroiled in a bitter controversy with the Chilean national congress, which eventually resulted in a bloody civil war. Balmaceda lost the war, and Scrymser had to scramble to establish a working relationship with the new government. In spite of these obstacles, by 1891 Scrymser dominated international communications on the Pacific coast of South America.

Balmaceda was a resourceful strategist in his dealings with U.S. businesspeople and diplomats, but his political skills failed in his relations with the Chilean congress. The president planned to use the national budget for extensive internal improvements such as roads and bridges and the expansion of the school system, but he became entangled in a bitter quarrel with his political opposition. The congress refused to approve the annual budget in 1891, and Balmaceda decided to run the government by presidential decree. This impasse resulted in a civil war between the congress with the support of the navy and the president who had the allegiance of the army. The United States tended to favor Balmaceda. For example, when congressional agents purchased arms in the United States and attempted to ship them from California on a Chilean transport, the *Itata,* the administration of President Benjamin Harrison termed this shipment illegal and sent the U.S. cruiser *Charleston* to capture the *Itata.* The congressional rebels were forced to surrender the *Itata* to the U.S. Navy. The U.S. minister to Santiago, Patrick Egan, claimed there was a British conspiracy behind the congressional revolt. In spite of Harrison and Egan's support of Balmaceda, the congressional forces soon defeated the president's army. Santiago descended into chaotic conditions, and the deposed president committed suicide in September 1891. The victorious congress saw the United States as Balmaceda's most important ally and resented its interference in Chilean affairs.

The tensions between Washington and Santiago worsened to the point that the two countries seemed to be headed for war. The U.S. cruiser *Baltimore,* stationed off Chile during the recent civil war, gave its crew shore leave in Valparaíso in October of 1891. Rest and recreation turned into diplomatic disaster. The stridently anti-U.S. sentiment among the Chilean people and the undisciplined behavior of the *Baltimore's* sailors resulted in a riot at the True Blue Saloon in Valparaíso's harbor district and the deaths of two of the crew. The Harrison administration demanded prompt justice. The Chilean courts moved at a deliberate pace that was too slow for Washington. Harrison exchanged hostile cables with Chilean Foreign Minister Manuel Matta. The newspapers in both countries were filled with editorials and news coverage that depicted the issue as a nationalistic cause célèbre. Both journalists and diplomats reported on the growing likelihood of war.

By 1891–1892 the balance of naval/military power had shifted to favor the United States. The U.S. Navy had added several modern warships while Chile had been weakened by the recent civil war. President Harrison understood this advantage, and he and other political leaders were aware of the increasing bellicosity of the popular press in the United States. Harrison abandoned traditional diplomatic practice and pushed Chile into a corner. Either Santiago agreed to U.S. demands regarding the deaths of the *Baltimore* crewmen, or he would turn the matter over to the aroused U.S. Congress, presumably for a declaration of war. The president informed Foreign Minister Matta that the Chilean government had only two days to decide, a dramatic move unprecedented in diplomatic practice that demanded reliance on the cable system and required an exceptionally short time for the decision. The Chilean government gave in. It admitted that law enforcement was inadequate in the True Blue Saloon incident and paid compensation to the deceased sailors' families.

AN ASYMMETRICAL RELATIONSHIP: CHILE CONFRONTS A NEW WORLD POWER

Chileans resented the outcome of the dispute of 1891–1892 and regarded the United States as an immature nation with aggressive designs in Latin America and elsewhere in the world. Subsequent events seemed to confirm these conclusions. Chilean diplomats were disturbed by Washington's assertion of its claim for hegemony in the 1895–1896 Venezuela-British Guiana boundary dispute. The quick defeat of Spain in the war of 1898, the subsequent U.S. annexation of Puerto Rico and the Philippines, and the U.S. economic domination of and frequent interventions in Cuba provided further confirmations. The Panama affair of 1903—in which President Theodore Roosevelt supported the dismemberment of Colombia in order to secure U.S. control over the future canal—offered further evidence. This resentment simmered for years, but it boiled over in 1913 during the visit of by then ex-President Theodore Roosevelt to Santiago. The occasion was Roosevelt's address at the University of Chile. The ostensibly friendly atmosphere was broken when eighty-year-old Martínez launched an unexpected attack on the Monroe Doctrine and U.S. policy in general in a provocative introduction for the visiting dignitary. This attack, delivered by a younger university colleague, was a reminder of the legacy of animosity between the two countries that dated back to the Blaine-Martínez confrontations of the 1880s and the Spanish bombardment of Valparaíso in 1866.

World War I supplied the next test for this strained relationship. The United States declared war on Germany in 1917 and expected the other American nations to follow suit. Chile, however, refused to do so in spite of pressure from the administration of President Woodrow Wilson. Chilean leaders offered Wilson little support to a large extent because of his idealistic statements on the virtues of Pan-American unity and representative government on one hand and his military interventions in Mexico and several Caribbean nations on the other. Chilean Luis Sanfuentes (President 1915–1920) also had to reckon with the political influence of his nation's large German immigrant population and its cultural and business ties to Germany that had endured for several decades. Some Chileans saw Germany as a counterweight to U.S. expansionism in southern South America. President Sanfuentes maintained neutrality throughout the war, a position that found reinforcement from neighboring Argentina which also refused to declare war on Germany.

While diplomatic relations between Chile and the United States remained cool during the early years of the twentieth century, business activity increased substantially. Britain and Germany, two of Chile's main sources of trade and investment, were severely weakened by the war whereas the U.S. corporations enjoyed an extended period of growth. The Central and South American Telegraph. Company prospered and, after some reorganization, emerged in the 1920s as International Telephone and Telegraph U.S. mining companies also expanded operations, especially Anaconda and Kennecott in copper and Bethlehem Steel in iron ore. First National City Bank of New York established offices in Chile during World War I and expanded operations thereafter. The growth of U.S. investment served as a timely stimulus for the Chilean economy, which had to find alternatives to nitrate exports because German scientists had devised a method of extracting nitrogen from the atmosphere and thereby developed a readily available substitute for Chilean nitrates. U.S. investments in communications, banking, copper, and iron ore compensated for this loss. The Tacna-Arica question was an issue between Chile and Peru that, from its beginnings, had involved the United States. Chile controlled the provinces but only temporarily. By the 1920s this arrangement had been in place forty years. U.S. officials including President Calvin Coolidge and General John J. Pershing had attempted to resolve the issue with no success. Pressure from Washington revived old antagonisms and, by the late 1920s, the Tacna-Arica question seemed almost insoluble. In 1928, almost by accident, a breakthrough occurred. The Chilean and Peruvian delegations to the Inter-American conference in Havana sailed on the same ship. Informal conversations were congenial and soon the representatives of the two nations had opened an informal path to resolution. To make matters official, they asked U.S. Secretary of State Frank Kellogg to intercede. Kellogg urged the diplomats of the two countries to renew official negotiations and, with the reestablishment of diplomatic relations, Chile and Peru finally solved their differences. Peru regained Tacna, and Chile held Arica. A major cause of difficult relations in the aftermath of the War of the Pacific had been removed in 1929 after forty-six years.

Chile's deeply rooted skepticism about the United States and Chileans' traditional ties to Germany emerged as important factors during World War II. President Franklin Roosevelt's Good Neighbor policy made only marginal gains in improving relations with Chile so that Washington's push for hemispheric unity against the Axis threat met a lukewarm response. The rise of left-wing nationalism in Chile in the late 1930s brought on another confrontation with the United States. The administration of Pedro Aguirre Cerda (President 1939–1941) and a Popular Front coalition that included socialists and communists created CORFO (Corporation for Development) in 1939 that imposed taxes and restrictions on foreign-owned corporations, most of which were headquartered in the United States. Chile decided to remain neutral even after the Japanese attack on Pearl Harbor. The United States was concerned about Chile's large pro-German population and the activities of German espionage agents in that nation. President Aguirre Cerda died in 1941, but his successor, the moderate Juan Antonio Rios (President 1942–1946), continued the neutrality policy. Even after Santiago severed relations with Berlin in 1943, the government refused to make a formal declaration of war until February of 1945. The U.S. Department of State was frustrated by Chile's reluctant support for the war effort.

THE COLD WAR

The early years of the Cold War saw an improvement in U.S.-Chilean relations. From the late 1940s to the 1960s both governments were disturbed by the spread of communism and cooperated on projects to strengthen representative government and free enterprise in the Americas. Fidel Castro's 1959 revolution in Cuba added to this mutual resolve. John F. Kennedy (President 1961–1963) inaugurated the Alliance for Progress to stimulate moderate social and economic reforms as buttresses against another communist revolution in Latin America. Chilean Eduardo Frei Montalva (President 1964–1970) epitomized both the hopes and ultimately, the failings of Kennedy's liberal approach to the region. The leader of the moderately liberal Christian Democratic party, Frei Montalva, promised to expand public education, to speed up the pace of agrarian reform to benefit peasant farmers, and to create a more equitable arrangement for the Chilean workers in the employ of the two U.S. copper companies—Anaconda and Kennecott. Montalva's efforts fell short. He did oversee the expansion of public schools, but his policies in land reform and copper mining failed to reach public expectations. Land reform moved slowly, held back by requirements for increased food productivity. The government negotiated a complex deal with Kennecott that provided for 51 percent ownership of its operations in Chile by the government, but this package deal tied both Kennecott and the government to U.S. banks and international credit institutions. Neither copper miners nor peasant farmers saw substantial gains in their daily lives after much optimistic discussion.

The outcome of the 1970 presidential election in Chile became a measure of the Cold War competition between capitalism and communism in the hemisphere. The United States had argued that communism could achieve power only by violent revolution, the means employed by Castro. In Chile, however, socialist Salvador Allende led the presidential election by a narrow margin with 36 percent of the vote. The congress confirmed his victory because he was clearly the leader in terms of votes cast. Allende headed the Popular Unity party, a coalition of leftist groups that included both socialists and communists. The new president had participated in national electoral politics since the 1930s and finished second in the 1964 presidential race. The United States, however, saw Allende's victory as a serious threat to its anticommunist strategy because it indicated that the far left—including communists as well as socialists—could gain power not only by revolution but also at the polls. The Central Intelligence Agency (CIA) had funneled as much as $21,000,000 into the campaign to defeat Allende. The narrow Popular Unity triumph was seen as a defeat in Washington.

Allende's administration had monumental challenges both at home and abroad. Expectations were high for improvements in the lives of peasants, miners, and other working class people. In the international arena Allende faced opposition from Richard Nixon (President 1969–1974) and his national security advisor, Henry Kissinger. Allende moved ahead rapidly on his domestic agenda. He accelerated land reform by expropriating large agricultural holdings and turning them over to poor farmers. The government nationalized the properties of several major international corporations including Kennecott, Anaconda, International Telephone and Telegraph, and General Motors. Complications quickly followed. Foreign investment left Chile and the resulting decline in private sector productivity of basic consumer items led to shortages and inflation. The large landowners who had lost their estates, and the middle class, battered by inflation, became outspoken opponents of the government. The Nixon administration saw an opportunity to exploit the unrest. The CIA provided the funds and the expertise for an anti-Allende propaganda campaign in the Chilean media and also supported professional organizations of rural landowners, industrialists, and truck drivers to undermine the fragile economy. To further weaken Allende, the United States blocked the normal channels of credit, which meant that the Chilean government had difficulty in borrowing funds for routine budgetary shortfalls. The Allende administration, while it actually increased its voting support in municipal elections to 51 percent in 1971, faced a deepening economic crisis.

The Chilean military overthrew the Allende government on September 11, 1973. The coup was well-coordinated, with the key cities of Valparaíso and Concepción falling under the control of the armed forces as well as Santiago. Allende died during combat in Santiago, victim of an apparent suicide, although he may have died in the fighting. The United States participated in destabilizing his government, but its role in the overthrow continues to be the subject of controversy. There is no doubt, however, that Washington moved quickly to establish diplomatic relations with the new military regime headed by General Augusto Pinochet. This close relationship between the military dictatorship and the U.S. government constitutes one of the darkest chapters in U.S.-Chilean relations. The Pinochet government imposed extreme measures to root out what it judged to be centers of radical influence. It immediately seized thousands of suspected leftists and confined them to the National Stadium where a large number were tortured and executed without trial. Military and law enforcement personnel sacked and burned the offices of the Socialist and Communist parties and also raided the homes of members of the Allende administration. The Pinochet government conducted summary trials of suspected leftists followed by prompt executions. The number of persons victimized by this reign of terror has been difficult to determine, but there is substantial evidence to support these figures: at least three thousand executions and over thirty thousand cases of torture. An estimated two hundred thousand people fled Chile during this time. The U.S. recognition of the Pinochet regime established ties between Santiago and Washington during this period of massive human rights violations, leaving a stain on the historical record of both countries.

Pinochet's brutal repression became a larger issue in the United States in 1976 when agents of Chile's DINA (Directorate of National Intelligence) assassinated Orlando Letelier, a diplomat during the Allende administration, on the streets of Washington, D.C. The agents planted a bomb in Letelier's car, which exploded, killing its intended victim and also Ronni Moffitt, a U.S. citizen. The Federal Bureau of Investigation

(FBI) identified Michael Townley and three other culprits in the assassination and, after considerable resistance from Pinochet, these four were extradited to the United States. A federal court found them guilty of murder. The information made public during the investigation and trial linked the assassins to DINA, a severe blow to the already tarnished reputation of the Pinochet government. By the late 1970s the State Department warned Pinochet that his repressive methods were too extreme. Jimmy Carter (President 1977–1981) roundly condemned the Chilean dictator and reduced U.S. foreign aid to Chile. In defiance Pinochet ignored these pressures and continued his dictatorial government until 1989.

The United States and Chile established another close linkage in the Cold War years in the area of political economy. Pinochet welcomed a team of economists from the University of Chicago (known as the "Chicago Boys"), which provided guidelines on the establishment of policies that favored unfettered free enterprise—ideologically in contrast to Allende's government-directed reforms. This policy led to the privatization of government-owned enterprises and constituted one of the first major applications of neoliberalism in Latin America. Chile attracted foreign private investment, especially from the United States. With an increase in copper prices on the international market, the Chilean people prospered in the late 1970s, but the hemispheric economic downturn of the early 1980s reversed this trend and hit Chilean consumers hard.

A NEW RELATIONSHIP

The United States continued to be an important factor in Chilean politics through the 1980s. Aware of his critics, Pinochet attempted to improve his image with the U.S. public and particularly among politicians and policymakers in Washington. On the other hand many Chilean leftist exiles took refuge in the United States and explained their case against Pinochet in the U.S. media and academic institutions. With growing pressure in Chile and from the United States, Pinochet agreed to hold a plebiscite on the continuation of his regime. Much to the dictator's surprise, the vote in October of 1988 was 55 percent against him, which brought about a relatively quiet end to the violent dictatorship.

Chile and the United States entered a new period in the history of their relations in 1990 with the inauguration of democratically elected President Patricio Aylwin. He was the first of four consecutive presidents from a coalition known as the Concertación. Aylwin (President 1990–1994) and Eduardo Frei Ruiz Tagle (President 1994–2000) were Christian Democrats, and Ricardo Lagos (President 2000–2006) was a socialist succeeded by fellow socialist Michelle Bachelet in 2006. All four were victorious in open presidential elections. The liberal/leftist inclination of the Concertación offered a marked contrast to the conservative character of the United States government under President George W. Bush (President 2001–2009). In spite of these differences Chile and the United States signed a free trade agreement on June 6, 2003, with very little controversy or fanfare. In this period of relative calm the two nations experienced no direct confrontations that could compare with the crises that involved Pinochet and his human rights violations, Allende and his opposition from the Nixon administration, or the late nineteenth-century animosities involving the territorial settlement of the War of the Pacific and the war scare associated with the *Baltimore* affair. U.S.-Chilean relations weathered the storms of more than a century and a half of controversy and confrontation to enter a period of apparent harmony.

See also *Anti-Americanism in Latin America; Baltimore Affair, 1891; Blaine, James G.; "Chileanization" of Foreign Properties; Dictators, U.S. Policy toward; "Disappeared Ones" (Desaparecidos), Argentina and Chile, 1970s–1980s; Frelinghuysen, Frederick; Monroe Doctrine; Pinochet Ugarte, Augusto; Scrymser, James; Tacna-Arica Dispute, 1883–1929; Trescot, William H.; War of the Pacific, 1879–1883; World War I, 1914–1918; World War II, 1939–1945*

. . . . JOHN A. BRITTON

REFERENCES AND FURTHER READING

Britton, John A. "'The Confusion Provoked by Instantaneous Discussion': The New International Communications Network and the Chilean Crisis of 1891–1892 in the United States." *Technology and Culture* 48 (October, 2007): 729–757.

Britton, John A., and Jorma Ahvenainen. "Showdown in South America: James Scrymser, John Pender, and the United States-British Cable Competition," *Business History Review* 78 (Spring, 2004): 1–27.

Drake, Paul W., and Ivan Jakšić, eds. *The Struggle for Democracy in Chile.* Lincoln: University of Nebraska Press, 1995.

Ensalaco, Mark. *Chile under Pinochet: Recovering the Truth.* Philadelphia: University of Pennsylvania Press, 2000.

Goldberg, Joyce. *The* Baltimore *Affair.* Lincoln: University of Nebraska Press, 1986.

Kornbluh, Peter. *The Pinochet File: A Declassified Dossier on Atrocity and Accountability.* New York: New Press, 2003.

Pike, Frederick. *Chile and the United States, 1880–1962.* Notre Dame, IN: University of Notre Dame Press, 1963.

Sater, William F. "Chile: Clash of Global Visions II." In *United States-Latin American Relations, 1850–1903,* edited by Thomas Leonard, 169–196. Tuscaloosa: University of Alabama Press, 1999.

Sater, William F. *Chile and the United States: Empires in Conflict.* Athens: University of Georgia Press, 1990.

Sigmund, Paul E. *The United States and Democracy in Chile.* Baltimore, MD: Johns Hopkins University, 1993.

Chilean Development Corporation (CORFO)

On April 29, 1939, Chile's newly elected Popular Front President Pedro Aguirre Cerda created the Production Development Corporation (CORFO) (Corporación de Fomento de la Producción de Chile). The government organization's most immediate objective was reconstructing the cities Concepción and Chillán, which had been devastated by a powerful earthquake on January 24, 1939. Rebuilding the territories would require a strong government response. More generally the organization aimed to expand domestic industry—import substitution industrialization—and create new sources of urban employment.

To get CORFO off the ground the Aguirre administration needed external financing and the most likely source of funds, in one way or another, was the United States. U.S. ambassador to Chile, Norman Armour, urged Washington to provide generous credits for Chile's development plans through the Export-Import Bank. He was eager to build good will at a time when the Roosevelt administration wanted to lessen German influence in South America. At the same time Congress was not eager to fund Chilean plans for economic development beyond earthquake relief. U.S. investment in Chile was concentrated in extractive industries and the State Department's priorities lay with protecting those investments.

During preliminary exchanges, Ambassador Armour warned Eduardo Wacholtz, Chile's minister of hacienda, that any drastic action against American companies in the form of higher taxes could hurt Chile's chance of receiving Export-Import Bank credits. President Aguirre then informed Armour that if external loans were not secured, Chile would obtain funds for reconstruction from taxation on private companies, including U.S.-owned companies. Chilean officials also made it known that they had credit offers from Germany.

In August 1939 the United States extended Chile $5 million over a six-month period with the expectation that the loan would be used to purchase imports from the United States. The following year, 1940, CORFO opened an office in New York City to negotiate for Export-Import Bank credits. In June bank officials announced the provision of a $12 million credit to CORFO for the acquisition of industrial machinery from the United States.

In the 1940s CORFO created public oil, power, steel, and transportation industries. Empresa Nacional de Electricidad, founded in 1944, constructed hydroelectric plants and carried out a national electrification plan. Four years later CORFO created the Compañía de Acero del Pacífico, which developed Chile's iron and steel industry. CORFO also gave domestic producers credit and technical assistance. Initially CORFO had four departments: agriculture, commerce and transport, energy and combustibles, mining and industry. Later it was expanded to include new areas such as research and development, finance, accounting, and a focus on promoting competitiveness and innovation among Chile's private enterprises.

CORFO is significant for increasing the role of state planning in Chile's economy during the 1940s and 1950s. Chile lacked a private sector capable of mobilizing the capital for major industrial projects and so the government took the lead promoting national industry. However the organization's establishment required the Chilean government to secure financing for an organization intended, in the long run, to lessen Chile's dependence on imports, mostly from the United States. Santiago acquired credits for CORFO in part because of the 1939 earthquake but also because of its shrewd negotiations with Washington at a time the United States government sought to curb German influence in Chile and strengthen its ties to South American countries.

See also *Chile, U.S. Relations with; Export-Import Bank (EXIM); Import Substitution Industrialization (ISI)*

. . . . JOHN R. BAWDEN

References and Further Reading

Francis, Michael J. *The Limits of Hegemony: United States Relations with Argentina and Chile during World War II.* Notre Dame, IN: University of Notre Dame Press, 1977.

Corporación de Fomento de la Producción: 50 años de realizaciones 1939–1989. Santiago, Chile: USACH, 1989.

"Chileanization" of Foreign Properties

"Chileanization" refers to the Eduardo Frei Montalva (1964–1970) administration's program to acquire 51 percent ownership in the Chilean mining industries. Iron, which accounted for 7.7 percent of mining exports, was not subject to Chileanization. Nitrates only accounted for 2.5 percent of Chile's mining exports, and Chileanization of the remaining foreign-controlled operations was achieved in 1968 through SOQUIMICH (Chemical and Mineral Society of Chile). Copper, the most important of Chile's mining industries, was the primary focus of the Chileanization program. Throughout the 1960s the United States backed the Frei administration financially and politically in an attempt to keep the left from coming to power. Chile was one of Latin America's leading recipients of Alliance for Progress funding, which was meant to promote reforms to demonstrate that living conditions for the poor and working classes could improve significantly without turning to socialism or communism. The United States supported the expansion of copper mining in Chile in part because of rising demand for copper generated by escalating U.S. military involvement in Vietnam. The United States also viewed the Chileanization program favorably. The influx of copper profits into fiscal coffers would be useful in sustaining and furthering reforms of the type that the United States thought would keep Marxists at bay; and greater Chilean control of the copper mines would partially address the left's calls for economic independence from foreign-run capitalist interests, thereby contributing to political stability.

In 1964 copper constituted 61 percent of Chile's total exports, and 85 percent of all Chilean copper production was controlled by the U.S. transnationals Kennecott and Anaconda. Kennecott, through its subsidiary Braden, ran the El Teniente mine in central Chile. Anaconda, through its subsidiaries Chile Exploración and the Andes Mining Company, ran the Chuquicamata and Salvador mines in northern Chile. The Chileanization program had two primary objectives: to double copper production by 1970 and to increase the amount of copper processed and refined in Chile. The state would reinvest the profits in the expansion of mining facilities, especially processing plants.

In December 1964 President Frei sent the Chileanization bill to parliament, and it became law in January 1966. The state proposal included acquisition of 51 percent ownership according to the estimated December 31, 1969, net book value, with semestrial payments at 6 percent interest. Anaconda did not accept the proposal but agreed to form mixed companies with

25 percent state ownership. This resulted in the formation of the Explotadora Cordillera, which took over mining operations at Exótica, and the Socieded Minera Andina, which was formed with Corporación Cerro and 25 percent state capital. Kennecott's Chilean holdings made up only a small portion of its international operations, and the company pressed for a deal before the passage of the law. The Chilean government, eager to prove that the program could succeed, entered into negotiations with Kennecott to acquire a 51 percent share of Braden's El Teniente operations. Kennecott achieved a favorable deal that included payment far higher than the book value (US $160 million vs. the US $66 million book value), reduced sales tax, underestimated copper prices, and retention of management control.

A view of a copper strip mine in Chile. In the 1960s copper represented a majority of Chile's mineral exports and the focus of a "Chileanization" program that partially nationalized the copper industry. Chile's Socialist President Salvador Allende Gossens oversaw the complete nationalization of the industry in 1971.

SOURCE: National Archives

Anaconda's Chilean operations formed a larger part of the company's overall holdings, and Anaconda resisted Chileanization until June 1969. Anaconda then requested nationalization with compensation under what became known as "pacted nationalization," with immediate Chileanization leading to a gradual nationalization over the course of three years. The 1969 shift to pacted nationalization with Anaconda marked a broader shift toward nationalization of copper mining in general. The Chileanization agreements were meant to last for twenty years, but they were not producing the desired results. The foreign-run mine administrations failed to meet production goals; by 1970 copper production had only increased 10 percent, although the favorable terms and rising world copper prices meant that Kennecott in particular reaped large profits in 1967 and 1968.

The Chileanization program had several important effects on the Chilean mining industry: copper production increased and plans were made for expansion, Chileans gained more prominence in management-level positions, and more copper was processed and refined in Chile. The government also priced Chilean copper at London Metal Exchange rates, which were nearly double the price at which U.S. copper companies had sold Chilean copper. Although production only increased 10 percent by 1970, Chilean export earnings doubled due to rising copper prices and international demand.

Critics lambasted the Chileanization program for being too timid and for granting the foreign companies, especially Kennecott, much too favorable contract terms. In 1971 during the Allende Gossens administration (1970–1973), the Chilean Congress voted unanimously to nationalize the copper industry, thereby granting the Chilean state absolute and exclusive dominion over all the copper mines.

See also *Allende Gossens, Salvador; Chile, U.S. Relations with; Chilean Development Corporation (CORFO); Frei Montalva, Eduardo*

. . . . ALISON J. BRUEY

REFERENCES AND FURTHER READING

Salazar, Gabriel, and Julio Pinto. *Historia contemporánea de Chile III: La economía: mercados, empresarios y trabajadores.* Santiago, Chile: LOM, 2002.

Taffet, Jeffrey F. *Foreign Aid as Foreign Policy: The Alliance for Progress in Latin America.* New York: Routledge, 2007.

Traslaviña, Hugo, Richard Vera, Leonardo Cáceres, and Rubén Andino. *Nuestro cobre. Nosotros los chilenos #7.* Santiago, Chile: LOM, n.d.

Vitale, Luis. "El Primer Gobierno DC: Eduardo Frei Montalva." In *Para recuperar la memoria histórica: Frei, Allende y Pinochet,* edited by Luis Vitale, Luis Moulian, Luis Cruz, Sandra Palestro, Octavio Avendaño, Verónica Salas, and Gonzalo Piwonka. Santiago, Chile: CESOC, 1999.

China, People's Republic of, Relations with Latin America

The People's Republic of China (PRC) and Latin America have intensified business and diplomatic relations over the past two decades. The PRC has looked to Latin America as a source of raw materials and foodstuffs, as a place to sell its manufactured products, and as a geostrategic asset in its competition with the United States. Latin American countries have looked to the PRC as a market for their raw materials and foodstuffs, as a source of direct foreign investment, and as a potential ally to diminish the influence of the United States within the hemisphere. The complementary nature of these interests indicates that the relationship between the Latin American states and the PRC will become a factor of growing significance for the political, economic, and social conditions of the western hemisphere.

China and Latin America had trading relations on a small scale since the sixteenth century and some Chinese emigrated to Peru and Mexico as laborers during the nineteenth century. Nevertheless relations between China and the region remained limited due to the tremendous political challenges facing a fragmented and war-torn China. The victory of the communists in the Chinese civil war (1946–1950) brought about a situation where China had begun its path to becoming a functional nation-state, although that state's roots in Marxism and Leninism made it sympathetic to workers and peasants in developing parts of the world, including Latin America. Despite the PRC's foreign policy oriented toward solidarity with the developing world, American dominance over the western hemisphere, the Sino-Soviet split during the heat of the Cold War (1961), and an inwardly focused development policy during the Cultural Revolution (1965–1976) contributed to the its limited engagement with the region prior to the 1990s. In fact until the 1970s, many Latin American countries—with the exception of Communist Cuba in 1960—continued to recognize the Republic of China (Taiwan) instead of the PRC as the legitimate government of China. By 2011 only a handful of Latin American countries in the Caribbean, Central America, and Paraguay do not recognize the PRC as the legitimate government of China. Nonrecognition of Taiwan and acceptance of Chinese rule in Tibet are two core state interests central to PRC diplomacy within the region.

Li Changchun (front), a member of the Standing Committee of the Political Bureau of the Communist Party of China (CPC) Central Committee, visits the former residence of Simón Bolívar, the Caracas-born, Latin American independence hero, in Caracas, capital of Venezuela, March 26, 2006. A mural behind Li's group depicts the encounter of Christian missionaries and the indigenous population.

SOURCE: Xinhua/Landov

TRADE AND FOREIGN DIRECT INVESTMENT

Besides these diplomatic interests the PRC has aggressively pursued its economic interests in the region. Total trade between Latin America and the PRC has grown from $10 billion in 2000 to $100 billion in 2010. This amount is roughly one-fifth of the volume of trade the United States conducts with the region. China's imports include copper (Chile and Peru), iron (Brazil and Peru), petroleum (Venezuela and Brazil), nickel (Cuba), zinc (Peru), soybean products (Argentina and Brazil), and a variety of other raw materials and foodstuffs as well as some manufactured items from countries such as Costa Rica (integrated circuits).

In general Latin America has run a trade surplus with the PRC, although Mexico has run a persistent trade deficit. The PRC exports toys, textiles, footwear, cell phones, computers, household appliances, motorcycles, and cars to the region. Concerns about the PRC's trade practices have led to disputes over the "dumping" of goods that have made their way to the World Trade Organization on several occasions. These perceived assaults on Latin American manufacturers fit into a broader narrative of the PRC replicating the relationship of dependency and neocolonialism that is understood by some to be the dynamic behind the failure of Latin American economies to grow as fast as more developed states. Others view the PRC as bidding up the value of the region's commodities and contributing to export-led growth of the economy as well as offering consumers access to a wider range of less expensive consumer goods.

The great recession of 2008 shrunk direct foreign investment in Latin America by 40 percent to 50 percent by 2009. The need for capital to develop important income-generating assets has increased interest in the PRC as a source of direct foreign investment. From 2005 to 2010 the PRC has invested $23.437 billion in the region, roughly $4 billion a year, focusing investments in the mining (Brazil, Chile, Ecuador, Peru), hydrocarbon (Argentina, Brazil, Colombia, and Venezuela), and agricultural sectors (Argentina and Brazil), though also including some investments in the low and middle end of the manufacturing sector (Mexico and Uruguay). In the near future the PRC has promised to increase investment in the region by $100 billion, although concerns about ethnic tensions, labor unrest, and the potential for nationalization have made PRC investors cautious in pursuing Latin American assets. Disappointments about the trickle of Chinese funds into the region and the qualitative nature of the investments have made some Latin Americans skeptical about the benefits of such investments for the long-term development of the region.

GEOSTRATEGIC CONCERNS

Though the PRC's involvement in Latin America has been largely business-centered, left-leaning populist regimes such as Argentina, Bolivia, Brazil, Chile, Cuba, Ecuador, and Venezuela have welcomed the PRC into the region's affairs as an ideologically sympathetic counterweight to the United States. The PRC offers a model of development that differs from the Washington consensus that has been forcefully rejected by Latin American populists such as Hugo Chávez and Evo Morales. Nevertheless the PRC has been cautious in its involvement in regional affairs not to offend the United States while capitalizing on its strategic partnerships to gain access to markets and resources essential to its continued economic development.

Despite this caution the presence of the PRC in Latin America has offered capital to regimes hostile to the United States that otherwise would have limited access to international capital markets and has thereby contributed to the survival of these anti-American regimes. PRC business interests also compete for raw materials that could fuel the growth of the American economy, facilitate the introduction of Chinese criminal gangs that complicate law enforcement efforts to control human and drug trafficking, and create networks that enhance Chinese intelligence-gathering capabilities near the United States. These capabilities augment PRC intelligence-gathering capabilities in Cuba, as well as those capabilities that have been developed by extensive military exchanges within the region. All of these factors complicate U.S. relations with the PRC as well as Latin America and have the long-run potential, if present trends continue, to threaten the dominant role held by the United States in the region. Yet, this new complexity also holds within it the potential for more just and sustainable relationships as the balancing of competing interests could lead to more effective rules, norms, and international regimes.

See also *Dependency Theory and Latin America; Export Based Economies; Taiwan, Relations with Latin America; U.S. Economic Investments in Latin America*

. . . . TODD MYERS

References and Further Reading

Eisenman, Joushua, Eric Heginbotham, and Derek Mitchell, eds. *China and the Developing World: Beijing's Strategy for the Twenty-First Century*. London: M.E. Sharpe, 2007.

Ellis, R. Evan. *China in Latin America: The Whats and Wherefores*. Boulder, CO: Lynn Rienner, 2009.

Gallagher, Kevin, and Roberto Porzecanski. *The Dragon in the Room: China and the Future of Latin American Industrialization*. Stanford, CA: Stanford University Press, 2010.

Lederman, David, Marcelo Olarreaga, and Guillermo Perry, eds. *China's and India's Challenge to Latin America*. Washington, DC: The World Bank, 2008.

Roett, Riordan, and Guadalupe Paz, eds. *China's Expansion into the Western Hemisphere: Implications for Latin America and the United States*. Washington, DC: The Brookings Institution Press, 2008.

Chiquita Brands International

Chiquita Brands International, headquartered in Cincinnati, Ohio, is one of the world's top banana producers and the leading banana distributor in the United States. Its products are sold in about seventy countries worldwide. Although it produces many other fruits and processed food items, it is famous in the United States for Chiquita bananas.

Chiquita Brands International Inc. was founded in 1871 by U.S. railroad entrepreneur Henry Meiggs. The company has undergone three name changes, originating as the United Fruit Company (UFCO). In 1970 when Eli Black purchased the company, he renamed it United Brands Company. United Brands again changed names to Chiquita Brands International in 1985 to take advantage of the name recognition of the Chiquita banana. The Chiquita name was created in 1944 to brand United Fruit's bananas and distinguish them from other company's bananas—a first in the banana industry. "Miss Chiquita," appearing as an animated banana, sang the *Chiquita Banana Song* to help teach consumers about the nutritional value of bananas and how to ripen them. The song jingle became a big hit in its own right and increased the visibility of United Fruit's bananas. In 2002 Chiquita Brands International underwent Chapter 11 reorganization and now operates under the name Chiquita Brands.

The company has had a deep and abiding impact on the politics and development of the countries in which it worked, especially in Latin American countries such as Guatemala, Honduras, Nicaragua, Ecuador, and Panama. United Fruit/Chiquita has been accused of exploitation and colonialism and is often viewed as the archetype of multinational corporate influence on the so-called "banana republics." While its influence has lessened in recent years, the company still plays a significant role in the region.

A 1998 *Cincinnati Enquirer* investigative report detailed human rights abuses and the creation of shell companies to get around laws limiting land ownership and labor rights. While Chiquita sued the newspaper and received a front page apology and a $14 million payment, the company did not challenge the veracity of the allegations, just how the information was obtained (much of it through illegal hacking into company voicemail systems).

In 1997 the United States, in a filing with Guatemala, Mexico, and Honduras, to the World Trade Organization (WTO), won a victory in the "banana trade wars." The WTO ruled that the European Union's (EU) trade policy giving preferential treatment to bananas from former European colonies was illegal. The WTO filing was prompted by former Chiquita CEO Carl Lindner, a large campaign contributor to both Democrats and Republicans.

In 2007 Chiquita Brands was fined $25 million as part of a settlement with the U.S. Justice Department for having ties to three Colombian paramilitary groups that are on the U.S. State Department's list of foreign terrorist organizations. Between 1989 and 2004 Chiquita subsidiaries paid millions of dollars to the United Self-Defense Forces of Colombia, Revolutionary Armed Forces of Colombia, and the National Liberation Army in exchange for local, employee protection in Colombia.

More recently Chiquita has begun to clean up its image by working with the Rainforest Alliance to improve its environmental policies. Improvements in working conditions, such as allowing Latin American employees to join unions, are also occurring, but at a much slower pace.

See also *Boston Fruit Company; Cuyamel Fruit Company; European Economic Community and Latin America; European Union and Latin America; Guatemala, U.S. Invasion of, 1954; Standard Fruit and Shipping Company; United Fruit Company (UFCO); Vaccaro Brothers Fruit Company*

. . . . SCOTT DITTLOFF

References and Further Reading

Chapman, Peter. *Bananas!: How The United Fruit Company Shaped the World.* New York: Canongate, 2008.

Jenkins, Virginia Scott. *Bananas: An American History.* Washington, DC: Smithsonian Institution Press, 2000.

Koeppel, Dan. *Banana: The Fate of the Fruit That Changed the World.* New York: Penguin Group, 2007.

Christmas, Lee

The life and career of Lee Christmas (1863–1924), an American-born soldier of fortune, are a blending of fact and legend. His date of birth is listed as 1863, but there is no fixed date of birth. What is known is his place of birth: Livingston Parish, Louisiana. Christmas resurfaces in the historical record when he appears on the payroll of a New Orleans based railroad from 1892 to 1894 as a brakeman, fireman, and engineer, until he was fired due to color blindness. In November 1894 he moved to Puerto Cortes, Honduras, where he found work as a railroad engineer.

Christmas's decision to immigrate to Honduras took his life on an unexpected trajectory. In Laguna Trestle on April 14, 1897, his train was captured by forces rebelling against Honduran President Terencio Sierra. Instead of becoming a captive Christmas joined the rebels. In 1899 he defected to President Sierra's side. His service to the government was rewarded in 1902, when he was appointed colonel and chief of police of the capital, Tegucigalpa. As President Sierra's grip on power loosened, Christmas defected again in 1903, becoming an *aide de camp* to rebel General Manuel Bonilla. When Bonilla assumed power he promoted Christmas to the rank of general, which he retained for the entirety of Bonilla's first term as Honduras's chief executive, from April 13, 1903, to February 25, 1907, which was long by Honduran standards at the time. It began and ended at the behest of the usual sponsor of regime changes during this period, the U.S.-based United Fruit Company (UFCO). Upon Bonilla's ouster, General Christmas exiled himself to Guatemala.

In 1910 Bonilla and Christmas tried to reclaim the Honduran government and failed, due to a lack of sufficient arms. A year later, however, Bonilla and Christmas resupplied and rearmed themselves—this time with U. S. Army surplus Colt Model 1895 machine guns—and recaptured the government. U. S. government involvement in this civil war was tangential at best, for it was New Orleans-based Cuyamel Fruit Company that purchased the surplus armaments for Bonilla's army. Following a decisive victory over governmental forces at the Battle of La Ceiba on January 25, 1911, Christmas was once again in charge of Honduras's military. His use of machine guns for fire support of infantry—the first recorded use of this tactic—was quickly adopted by the Allied and Central powers in World War I (1914–1918).

By 1913, due to Bonilla's health, Honduras had another president, and General Lee Christmas was forced to go into exile once again. Some reports have General Christmas returning to Guatemala; others place him in a variety of Latin American republics, such as an *aide de camp* for Emiliano Zapata in the Mexican Revolution. Like many other episodes in Christmas's career, the Zapata story is difficult to confirm.

Around 1921 Christmas, with his wife Ida Culotta, a Honduran national, returned to Louisiana, taking up residence in New Orleans. Years of jungle combat in Central America's damp climate took their toll on his health, for he had contracted tuberculosis by the time he returned home. On January 24, 1924, one day short of the thirteenth anniversary of his victory at La Ceiba, Christmas died.

See also *Cuyamel Fruit Company; Standard Fruit and Shipping Company*

. . . . PETER B. GUSHUE

References and Further Reading

Euraque, Dario. *Reinterpreting the Banana Republic: Region and State in Honduras, 1870–1972.* Chapel Hill: University of North Carolina Press, 1996.

Langley, Lester, and Thomas Schoonover. *The Banana Men: American Mercenaries and Entrepreneurs in Central America, 1880–1930.* Lexington: University of Kentucky Press, 1995.

Wilson, Charles. *Empire in Green and Gold; the Story of the American Banana Trade.* New York: Holt, 1947.

Christopher, Warren

Warren Minor Christopher (1925–2011) was an attorney and diplomat from the United States and served in many prominent public roles, frequently representing Democratic presidential administrations. In international politics Christopher worked as deputy secretary of state under President Jimmy Carter and as secretary of state under President William J. Clinton.

After serving in the U.S. Naval Reserve with active duty in the Pacific Theater during World War II, Christopher graduated from Stanford Law School in 1949. In the 1950s and 1960s he held a number of attorney positions in private firms and government agencies, including a term as deputy attorney general (1967–1969) during the Lyndon B. Johnson administration.

In the Carter administration Christopher shaped U.S. policy with Latin America by advancing the new president's controversial human rights initiative. Christopher's appointment as deputy secretary of state—a position he held through the entire term of the Carter presidency (1977–1981)—was his first public work in foreign relations, and he drew attention for his efforts in gaining the release of U.S. hostages in Iran, settling the Algiers Accords, and negotiating with the People's Republic of China. But Christopher also took the lead in implementing President Carter's human rights policy. In his inaugural address Carter declared human rights as his top priority in foreign relations. The president appointed Christopher to chair the Interagency Committee on Human Rights and to execute a new policy that linked continuation of U.S. aid to foreign nations to the improvement of human rights practices in those nations. In Latin America the policy challenged established alliances with several military governments, including those in Argentina, Bolivia, Uruguay, Paraguay, and El Salvador. Citing ongoing violations of human rights standards, Christopher oversaw the limitation or complete denial of military assistance to these regimes. Critics asserted that the policy was applied unevenly, that it led to indecision, and that it even limited options for leveraging improvements in abusive regimes.

Christopher led efforts to weaken a longstanding ally of the United States, Nicaraguan dictator Anastasio Somoza Debayle. Reversing pro-Somoza policies of the Richard Nixon and Gerald Ford presidencies, the Carter administration denounced abuses by the Nicaraguan regime and effectively suspended all U.S. military and economic aid to the dictatorship in 1977. But as the identity of a potential successor government was not clear, and the Carter administration was not eager to embrace the mass-based nationalist movement of the Sandinista National Liberation Front (FSLN), Christopher appeared reluctant to call for Somoza's outright removal. After widespread popular uprisings toppled the Somoza government in July 1979, Christopher sought to limit the influence of Sandinistas in the post-Somoza government and threw his support to political forces that favored private property and strong ties with the United States.

When the Democrats returned to the White House in 1993, President Clinton's appointment of Warren Christopher as secretary of state surprised many observers. It appeared that Clinton, relatively inexperienced in foreign policy himself, had appointed a political moderate whose views on international relations were largely unknown. During his tenure of service, which spanned the entire first term of Clinton's presidency (1993–1997), Secretary Christopher pursued goals of expanding the North Atlantic Treaty Organization (NATO) and advancing peace negotiations in the Middle East. Christopher advocated withholding low-tariff trading privileges to pressure China to improve human rights practices, but President Clinton rejected the idea. Further the Clinton presidency—and Christopher's State Department, in particular—were criticized for failing to respond more promptly to the upheaval in Rwanda that led to the massacre of more than half a million people.

By all appearances Latin America was not a priority region for Secretary of State Christopher. He did not make a multination tour of Latin America until more than three years after starting the position. In 1994 Christopher did support the U.S.-led coalition that returned democratically elected President Jean-Bertrand Aristide to power in Haiti after a military coup, but by Christopher's own telling, retired chair of the Joint Chiefs of Staff, General Colin Powell, and former President Carter, played the most significant roles in this effort.

Secretary Christopher's most important foreign policy goal in Latin America was to expand trade, and the lynchpin was the implementation of the North American Free Trade Agreement (NAFTA). Though brokered by the Bush administration in December 1992, Christopher backed President Clinton's endorsement of the pact that was intended to reduce trade barriers and ease the flow of capital among the United States, Canada, and Mexico. Christopher had little to do with the legislative strategy or the drafting of labor and environmental supplements to the agreement, but he did deliver a speech in Los Angeles in November 1993 arguing that NAFTA would strengthen both foreign and domestic U.S. policy. Christopher further posited that passage of NAFTA would allow advances both in negotiations to expand trade with Asian economies and in the Uruguay round of talks on the General Agreement on Tariffs and Trade (GATT). Congress ultimately passed approval of NAFTA.

See also *Bush, George H. W.; Carter, Jimmy; Clinton, William J.; Haiti, U.S. Relations with; Nicaragua, U.S. Relations with; North American Free Trade Agreement (NAFTA), 1992; Powell, Colin L.; Sandinista National Liberation Front (FSLN) (Nicaragua); Somoza Debayle, Anastasio*

. . . . GREGORY S. CRIDER

SELECTED WORKS

Christopher, Warren. *In the Stream of History: Shaping Foreign Policy for a New Era.* Palo Alto, CA: Stanford University Press, 1998.

REFERENCES AND FURTHER READING

Lake, Anthony. *Somoza Falling.* Boston, MA: Houghton Mifflin Harcourt, 1989.

Morley, Morris H. *Washington, Somoza, and the Sandinistas: State and Regime in U.S. Policy toward Nicaragua, 1969–1981.* Cambridge, UK: Cambridge University Press, 1994.

Church Committee

Senator Frank Church (Democrat from Idaho) was chairman of the Senate Select Committee to Study Government Operations with Respect to Intelligence Activities (1975–1976). The Church Committee investigations represented the most thorough examination of U.S. intelligence services' activities undertaken at that time and began an ongoing debate over the proper balance between national security requirements and the founding principles of the republic.

OVERVIEW

During the Cold War covert operations run by the Central Intelligence Agency (CIA) provided presidents with a seemingly inexpensive and politically viable means of combating the menace of global communism. However, from the time of its creation with the National Security Act of 1947, domestic critics have pointed out the challenges that an intelligence service with broad powers presents to constitutional government. Rumors of CIA excesses abroad that began with the botched Bay of Pigs invasion and culminated with the Watergate scandal provoked public indignation and Congressional investigations into the abuses of U.S. intelligence services.

The Church Committee sought to balance the needs of national security and secret intelligence operations with the rule of law and traditional American principals. Executive authority and accountability for the actions of the CIA provided one of the focal points of Church Committee investigations. Carrying forward the work of the Rockefeller Commission, the Church Committee investigated CIA coup and assassination plots against leaders in Africa, Asia, and Latin America during the 1950s, 1960s, and 1970s. The Church Committee found that in the early 1960s the CIA developed a general assassination capability and targeted Cuba's Fidel Castro and Congo's Patrice Lumumba. CIA-sponsored coup attempts occasionally led to the death of the head of state or other governing officials. Such was the case with the Dominican Republic's Rafael Trujillo in 1961, South Vietnam's Ngo Diem in 1963, and Chile's General Rene Schneider in 1970. The Committee unreservedly condemned the peacetime assassination of foreign leaders as un-American and made a compelling case for increased Congressional oversight of the intelligence operations of the United States government.

IMPORTANT INSTANCES OF CIA INVOLVEMENT

The Cuban revolution set an ominous precedent for communist takeovers in developing nations. The Eisenhower administration interpreted Fidel Castro's revolution in 1959 as Moscow-directed and ordered the CIA to begin planning his overthrow in late 1959. The Church Committee found that the CIA ran at least eight assassination operations against Fidel and Raul Castro from 1960 to 1965. The Committee found that CIA Director Allen Dulles, believing that he had "circumlocutious" authorization from Eisenhower and Kennedy, most likely authorized the plots. These operations, which were designated "Operation Mongoose" under the Kennedy administration, included bizarre schemes such as poisoned cigars, an exploding seashell, a botulism-laced diving suit, poison pills, and professional hit contracts with seedy organized crime figures. Some of these plots never advanced beyond the planning stage. None were successful.

The Eisenhower administration, concerned about improving its image in Latin America, responded to the ideological threat that Castro's revolution represented by withdrawing support for notorious dictators like the Dominican Republic's Rafael Trujillo. The Church Committee found that both Presidents Eisenhower and Kennedy authorized the CIA to assist a Dominican dissident group that intended to overthrow Trujillo from the period of February 1960 to May 1961. President Kennedy, Dulles, and the assistant secretary of state for Inter-American affairs knew that the dissidents carrying out the coup intended to kill Trujillo. Concerned about the possibility of a communist takeover after the overthrow of Trujillo, Kennedy rescinded the coup plot in mid-May of 1961. Nevertheless Dominican dissidents assassinated Trujillo on May 30, 1961.

The Church Committee discovered that the CIA had been running covert operations to influence Chilean electoral politics since the early 1960s. Under the Johnson administration the CIA spent over $3 million ensuring that the Marxist candidate Salvador Allende did not win the presidency in 1964. On September 15, 1970, President Richard Nixon ordered the CIA to execute a two-track operation to prevent Allende from assuming the presidency. Track I called for a propaganda campaign to prevent Allende from winning the election, which was not successful. Track II, which Nixon authorized through his national security advisor, Henry Kissinger, thus bypassing normal bureaucratic channels, called for the removal of the constitutionally minded General René Schneider from his position as the head of the Chilean military as part of an elaborate scheme to constitutionally prevent Allende from taking office. Track II was a preparatory phase for a Chilean military takeover and included a vigorous campaign of propaganda and economic pressure. The Committee concluded that the CIA, and probably the White House, knew that the dissidents executing the CIA-sponsored coup to prevent Allende from assuming office planned to kidnap General Schneider but did not expressly authorize his assassination. Allende was overthrown in a military coup in 1973, during which he allegedly took his own life.

CONCLUSION

Church was concerned that the CIA had been behaving badly, and Church's critics claimed that the Church Committee investigations compromised ongoing intelligence, collection operations, and national security. The Committee's report indicates that a significant command and control communication problem existed in the Executive Branch due to the doctrine of "plausible deniability." The Committee's evidence suggests that when assassination operations began under the Eisenhower administration, Dulles interpreted strongly worded statements by Eisenhower concerning the need for regime change in Cuba and the Congo as "circumlocutious" authorization for assassination. Thus assassinations were never forthrightly discussed in the presence of the president. While this does not remove the possibility that Presidents Eisenhower, Kennedy, Johnson, and Nixon authorized or knew about assassination operations, plausible deniability acted as a legal shield to presidential culpability. Church's concern was that plausible deniability also acted as a blank check for officers within the CIA to operate outside of the bounds of accountability. Church Committee recommendations led to the creation of the Foreign Intelligence Surveillance Act (FISA), the Foreign Intelligence Surveillance Court (FISC), and Gerald Ford's executive order in 1976 to ban U.S.-sanctioned assassinations of foreign leaders.

See also *Allende Gossens, Salvador; Bissell, Richard M. Jr.; Communism in Latin America; Cuba, U.S. Embargo of; Cuban Revolution, 1956-1959, U.S. Policy toward; Dulles, Allen M.; Eisenhower, Dwight D.; Good Neighbor Policy; International Telephone & Telegraph (ITT) Corporation; Kennedy, John F.; Kissinger, Henry A.; Nixon, Richard M.; Pinochet Ugarte, Augusto; Rockefeller, Nelson A.*

. . . . JAMES A. HOLEMAN

References and Further Reading

Alleged Assassination Plots Involving Foreign Leaders: An Interim Report of the Select Committee to Study Government Operations with Respect to Intelligence Activities, United States Senate: Together with Additional, Supplemental, and Separate Views. New York: Norton, 1976.

Ashby, Leroy, and Rod Gramer. *Fighting the Odds: The Life of Senator Frank Church*. Pullman: Washington State University Press, 1994.

CIA Targets Fidel: Secret 1967 CIA Inspector General's Report on Plots to Assassinate Fidel Castro. New York: Ocean Press, 1996.

Johnson, Loch K. *A Season of Inquiry, Congress and Intelligence*. Chicago, IL: Dorsey Press, 1988.

Miller, Russel A., ed. *US National Security, Intelligence and Democracy: From the Church Committee to the War on Terror*. New York: Routledge, 2008.

Rabe, Stephen G. *Eisenhower and Latin America: The Foreign Policy of Anticommunism*. Chapel Hill: The University of North Carolina Press, 1988.

Ranelagh, John. *CIA, a History*. London: BBC Books, 1992.

Smist, Frank J. Jr. *Congress Oversees the United States Intelligence Community, 1947–1989*. Knoxville: University of Tennessee Press, 1990.

U.S. Covert Actions by the Central Intelligence Agency (CIA) in Chile (Including the "Assassination" of Salvador Allende) 1963–1973: The Church Committee Report and the Hinchey Report as Presented to the U.S. Congress. Rockville, MD: Arc Manor, 2008.

Weiner, Tim. *Legacy of Ashes: The History of the CIA*. New York: Anchor Books, 2007.

Cipriano Castro Ruiz, José

Strongman José Cipriano Castro Ruiz "the Lion of the Andes," was the thirty-seventh president of Venezuela (1899–1908). He was born in Capacho, Tachira, Venezuela, on October 12, 1858, into a middle-class landholding family who, like most in this region, had close ties to Colombia. He was educated at a seminary school in nearby San Cristóbal.

In 1876 Cipriano Castro managed an antigovernment newspaper, *El Album*. In 1878 he joined a group of separatists who tried to seize San Cristóbal and failed. While Cipriano Castro escaped, in 1884 his public conflict with a local churchman, Juan Ramon Cardenas, landed him in prison. After six months he escaped and hid in Cucuta, where he met his future wife, Rosa Zoila Martinez, best known as *Doña Zoila*.

In June 1886 Cipriano Castro returned to Tachira as part of an army that defeated the government forces of General Espíritu Santo Morales. Promoted to general, Cipriano Castro met Juan Vicente Gómez , and together they began to climb the ladder of power. In 1890 Cipriano Castro was elected governor of Tachira but fled to exile in Colombia when the government in Caracas, which supported him, was overthrown in 1892. Over the next seven years Cipriano Castro criminally appropriated thousands of cattle which he sold for a large profit, money he used to recruit a private army.

On October 20, 1899, he seized power as the nation's supreme military commander. He became the first Andino (someone from the mountain region of Venezuela) to rule. His nine years were unusually corrupt and despotic. Cipriano Castro changed the constitution, making him president and his ally Gómez vice president. His regime featured the execution, murder, or exile of his opponents, numerous rebellions, his own ostentatious lifestyle, and foreign conflicts. Contemporaries and historians alike believed him to be the worst dictator in Venezuelan history. Cipriano Castro's actions angered nearly every major government in Europe, causing U.S. President Theodore Roosevelt to fear they might intervene and establish new colonies in the western hemisphere.

In 1902 Cipriano Castro, who owed millions to European bankers, refused to repay these debts. Great Britain, Italy, and Germany set up a blockade along the Venezuelan coast and even fired on Venezuelan coastal fortifications. Roosevelt especially feared German ambitions. In 1903 he warned the Germans that Admiral Dewey's Caribbean squadron would stop any effort to establish new colonies.

While the Europeans backed down, Roosevelt feared that South American nations might try to use the Monroe Doctrine to justify deliberately defaulting on European loans. He also realized the European powers might use such fiscal irresponsibility to demand access to customs port revenues and seize ports like they had in China, where the leases lasted ninety-nine years. Not only would this be a violation of the Monroe Doctrine, but European port occupation in the circum-Caribbean region threatened the security of the Panama Canal.

On December 6, 1904, in his annual message to Congress, Roosevelt proclaimed his famous "corollary" to the Monroe Doctrine, declaring that the United States had the right not only to oppose European intervention in the western hemisphere but to intervene in the domestic affairs of Latin America if it could not protect U.S. investments. Tying this policy to the Monroe Doctrine won public acceptance in the United States and, when Roosevelt sent warships to the region, it convinced Cipriano Castro to settle with the foreign investors.

Five years later the dictator again provoked foreign intervention. This time the Dutch navy destroyed part of Venezuela's tiny navy. Again the United States arbitrated a settlement that favored European investors. The mediation was confirmed by the Permanent Court of Arbitration at The Hague.

In 1908 Cipriano Castro went to Paris seeking treatment for syphilis. He left the government with Gómez, who seized power. Cipriano Castro remained in Puerto Rico for the last sixteen years of his life plotting an unsuccessful return. He died on December 4, 1924. His Restoration Liberal party remained in power for a total of fifty-nine years, almost uninterrupted.

See also *Monroe Doctrine; Roosevelt Corollary to the Monroe Doctrine; Roosevelt, Theodore; Venezuelan, U.S. Relations with*

. . . . WILLIAM HEAD

REFERENCES AND FURTHER READING

McBeth, Brian S. *Gunboats, Corruption, and Claims: Foreign Intervention in Venezuela, 1899–1908.* Westport, CT: Greenwood Press, 2001.

Perkins, Dexter. *Evolution of American Foreign Policy.* New York: Oxford University Press, 1966.

Vesser, Cyrus. *A World Safe for Capitalism: Dollar Diplomacy and America's Rise to Global Power.* New York: Columbia University Press, 2002.

Civic Action Programs

In the aftermath of the Cuban Revolution (1959) the United States sought to transform social conditions in Latin America and to increase security to prevent and/or eliminate communist insurgencies in the region. Civic action programs formed a central component of U.S.-sponsored counterinsurgency measures. Civic action programs called upon Latin American militaries to become an arm of social transformation by engaging them in projects in the fields of education, training, public works, agriculture, road construction, communications, health, and sanitation. By directing civic action programs, the Latin American military, with U.S. training and economic support, was to improve both its image and social conditions. The United States viewed the Latin American military as a stabilizing force and a vehicle for modernization in the region.

ORIGINS AND DEVELOPMENT OF CIVIC ACTION

In 1961 President John F. Kennedy introduced the Alliance for Progress with the goal of dramatically increasing U.S. aid to Latin America as a means of transforming social and economic conditions and promoting democracy. In the same year the United States Joint Chiefs of Staff provided President Kennedy with twenty-seven recommendations for how the military could support the goals of the Alliance for Progress. The military's plan was to expand military, police, psychological, and intelligence assistance to Latin America while at the same time encouraging Latin American militaries to engage in civic action programs. Kennedy persuaded the U. S. Congress to rescind bans on providing counterinsurgency training and equipment to Latin America, setting the stage for a distinct form of U.S. military engagement in the region. He looked to Samuel P. Huntington, Morriss Janowits, and John L. Johnson as sources of support for this new approach to U.S. military engagement in the region. In addition to providing aid and training, the administration promoted the Kennedy Doctrine, which identified an internal enemy as the principle threat to Latin American security, thereby justifying counterinsurgency training and aid.

Between 1950 and 1975 the United States trained over 28,000 Latin American military personnel in the United States and at the U.S. Army School of the Americas in the Panama Canal Zone. Seventy percent of the training provided to Latin American military personnel at this School of the Americas was devoted to counterinsurgency training, which included an emphasis on civic action programs. At the same time U.S. officials believed that training Latin American military personnel in the United States would introduce them to a democratic ideal in which military authority was subordinated to that of elected civilian officials. Between 1962 and 1973, the key years of U.S.-sponsored counterinsurgency training and support for civic action programs, no fewer than sixteen military coups took place in Latin America.

Civic action programs called upon both the military and development agencies to act in capacities distinct from the norm. It mandated coordination between and among U.S. and Latin American military officials, the U.S. Agency for International Development (USAID), and private voluntary organizations. USAID established the Office of Public Safety to train police forces throughout Latin America. At the same time it oversaw development projects in troubled rural areas identified as potential sites for communist insurgency, transforming the agency into an active participant in a U.S.-initiated counterinsurgency campaign in the region.

Civic action programs in Latin America followed models established by the United States in Vietnam, where President Eisenhower authorized the concept and initiated programs in 1960. The military provided basic services including literacy training, medical assistance, and infrastructure development as a means of winning "hearts and minds," thereby diminishing the appeal of communism. While Vietnam represented the most recent experiment in civic action, the United States had a longer history of engaging in programs of this type in Latin America. When U.S. Marines occupied Haiti (1915–1934), the Dominican Republic (1916–1924), and Nicaragua (1912–1932, off and on), and the U.S. Army intervened in Cuba and Panama, the U.S. military also promoted civic action programs, including public works projects directed by the U.S. military and the training of local military and police organizations to engage in armed control and to carry out civil projects.

CIVIC ACTION IN LATIN AMERICA HISTORY AND MODELS

Most Latin American countries had a history of civic action that preceded the U.S. support for it as part of a counterinsurgency program initiated by the Kennedy administration. The military in many Latin American countries played a crucial role in building roads, providing medical services and education, and even directing mail distribution.

Guatemala was the first country in Latin America to accept a U.S. Army civic action advisory team in 1960 with a full-time civic action adviser following in 1962. Guatemala's leading counterinsurgency commander, Colonel Carlos Arana Osorio (Guatemala's president from 1970 to 1974), attributed 70 percent of his success to civic action programs that won the support of local peasants by building roads and feeding school children hot lunches. Arana Osorio oversaw a counterinsurgency campaign in northeastern Guatemala from 1966–1968 that killed some six thousand to eight thousand people to defeat a few hundred guerrillas. The United Nations declared the Guatemalan military's counterinsurgency campaign, which killed two hundred thousand people between 1960 and 1996, a genocide for its targeting of Maya people and determined that the military and related paramilitary groups were responsible for 93 percent of the massacres and disappearances.

In 1962, after three years of support for a counterinsurgency campaign in Colombia, the United States initiated Plan Lazo, a comprehensive three-year plan designed to eliminate guerrilla forces and enhance the power and image of Colombia's military and government. The plan called for coordinated control over all public security forces, improved intelligence operations, and expansion of civic action and psychological operations to gain popular support for the military. Plan Lazo established mobile intelligence groups that integrated military, police, and civilian intelligence activities at the local level and special hunter-killer teams that used the information obtained to kill or capture insurgent leaders. At the same time it promoted civic action projects to enhance popular support for the Colombian military and government.

Similar programs were initiated in Bolivia, Ecuador, and Venezuela. By 1965 thirteen Latin American countries participated in U.S.-sponsored civic action programs. In the 1960s roughly 15 percent of U.S. military aid to Latin America was allocated to civic action, with a total for all of Latin America in 1964 being about $14 million. U.S. Army officials in the early 1960s offered statistics about pamphlets distributed, roads built, teeth cleaned, and medicine distributed to declare civic action "unquestionably successful." U.S. emphasis on civic action in Latin America ended in the 1970s, when the threat of insurgency in the region seemed to have dissipated. The U.S.-sponsored civic action programs strengthened the military position in Latin American governments and, in fact, military dictatorships were entrenched across the region during the 1970s. By 1976 only three nations in the region could be considered democratic.

See also *Bureaucratic-Authoritarian Regimes; Counterinsurgency; Cuban Revolution, 1956–1959, U.S. Policy toward; School of the Americas*

. . . . SUSAN FITZPATRICK BEHRENS

References and Further Reading

Birtle, Andrew J. *U.S. Army Counterinsurgency and Contingency Operations Doctrine, 1942–1976.* Washington DC: Center of Military History, United States Army, 2006.

Blaufarb, Douglas S. *The Counterinsurgency Era: U.S. Doctrine and Performance 1950 to the Present.* New York: The Free Press, 1970.

Grandin, Greg. *The Last Colonial Massacre: Latin America in the Cold War.* Chicago, IL: University of Chicago Press, 2004.

Lieuwen, Edwin. *Generals vs. Presidents: Neomilitarism in Latin America.* London: Pall Mall Press, 1964.

Rabe, Stephen R. *The Most Dangerous Area in the World: John F. Kennedy Confronts Communist Revolution in Latin America.* Chapel Hill: The University of North Carolina Press, 1989.

Wright, Thomas C. *Latin America in the Era of the Cuban Revolution.* Westport, CT: Praeger, 1991.

Clark, J. Reuben

Joshua Reuben Clark Jr. (1871–1961), trained as a lawyer at Columbia University, served in the State Department from 1906 until 1913 and then again from 1928 to 1933, his last two and one-half years as the U.S. ambassador to Mexico. He is perhaps best known as the author of the 1928 Clark Memorandum, a reinterpretation of the Monroe Doctrine that emphasized the European focus of the 1823 policy statement, specifically excluded the Roosevelt corollary of 1904 and ostensibly served as an outline for the less interventionist Good Neighbor policies of Herbert Hoover and Franklin Delano Roosevelt.

EARLY CAREER AND WORLD WAR I

J. Reuben Clark was born just outside Salt Lake City and began his formal education at the University of Utah, earning his high school diploma and bachelor's degree within four years and graduating first in his class. He attended law school at Columbia University in New York, compiling a remarkable academic record that saw him named to the editorial board of the Columbia Law Review as a first-year student and being admitted to the New York Bar at the end of his second year. Upon completion of his law degree in 1906 Clark was chosen by Secretary of State Elihu Root to become assistant solicitor of the State Department.

In 1910 President Taft named Clark as solicitor for the State Department. Clark was involved in resolution of the long-outstanding Alsop Claim, which involved damages an American company suffered in the Bolivia-Chile-Peru "War of the Pacific" from 1879 to 1884. The claim, which was arbitrated by the King of England, resulted in a favorable judgment for the United States for close to $1 million. In 1912 he wrote *Memorandum on the Right to Protect Citizens in Foreign Countries by Landing Forces,* a justification of U.S. intervention, citing forty-seven previous uses of military force.

In 1913 Clark left the State Department to open a private law practice in Washington, D.C., serving business and international clients such as J. P. Morgan and Company, the Cuban legation, and the Guatemalan ministry. During World War I he became a major in the Judge Advocate General's Officer's Reserve Corps and was instrumental in developing regulations for the newly instituted selective service. Serving in the attorney general's office during the war, Clark also authored a legal opinion with the ponderous title, *Emergency Legislation Passed Prior to December 1917 Dealing with the Control and Taking of Private Property for the Public Use, Benefit, or Welfare, Presidential Proclamations and Executive Orders Thereunder, to and Including January 31, 1918, to Which Is Added a Reprint of Analogous Legislation Since 1775,* justifying Woodrow Wilson's presidential war powers. He was awarded the Distinguished Service Medal for his wartime contributions.

THE CLARK MEMORANDUM

Clark returned to the State Department as under secretary of state in 1928. His return to the department coincided with growing domestic and hemispheric criticism of U.S. interventions in Latin America. The Monroe Doctrine, and its "corollary" articulated by Theodore Roosevelt in 1904, was oftentimes perceived as the official rationale for U.S. actions, which led to specific hostility toward that doctrine. Secretary of State Frank Kellogg, in the midst of a successful negotiation of his treaty renouncing war and anticipating a Senate debate that might include discussion of the Monroe Doctrine, asked Clark in the fall of 1928 to provide him with a memorandum on the issue. Finished in December 1928, the *Memorandum on the Monroe Doctrine* combined a summary of the doctrine's past history and interpretation with Clark's opinion of its scope and significance. It remained an internal document until its publication in March of 1930.

In essence the Clark Memorandum emphasized that the doctrine, as articulated in 1823, was directed toward Europe and was not intended as a guide to relations between the United States and the nations of Latin America. The doctrine was based on the principle of self-preservation that Clark acknowledged but only a narrow aspect of that principle—the threat of European intervention in, or attacks on, the republics of Latin America. Given this constrained definition, the Roosevelt corollary, which authorized U.S. intervention in the internal affairs of Latin American nations to prevent fiscal, political, and/or social disorder, could not be justified as a part of the Monroe Doctrine and therefore could not be its corollary. This legalistic renunciation of the Roosevelt Corollary as having sanction under the Monroe Doctrine has often been interpreted as a wholesale repudiation of the Roosevelt Corollary, as well as the principle of intervention in general. The Good Neighbor policies of Hoover and Franklin Delano Roosevelt that followed were characterized by a movement away from intervention; this policy shift, together with the publication of Clark's memorandum in 1930, seemed evidence of its influence in shaping policy. In fact the memorandum's influence is often overstated, as are its anti-interventionist sentiments.

In the memorandum Clark clearly states that intervention by the United States in Latin America to protect its interests and security, as articulated and practiced through the Roosevelt corollary, is justified under the broader principle of self-preservation. He simply disassociated it from the Monroe Doctrine. Contemporary members of the State Department, such as Dana Gardner Munro and Francis White, who were quite influential in U.S. Latin American policy, did not see the memorandum as signaling a shift in guiding principles. Most historians credit the U.S. shift away from interventionism in the 1930s as a pragmatic response to failed policies and poor hemispheric relations.

CONCLUSION

On November 28, 1930, Herbert Hoover named Clark as the U.S. ambassador to Mexico. He resigned in February 1933 just before Franklin Delano Roosevelt took office. Immediately after leaving the State Department, Clark briefly served as president of the newly created Foreign Bondholders Protective Council, a private entity with official sanction designed to assess and evaluate foreign bond offerings and informally arbitrate bond defaults. In April 1933 Clark, a life-long Mormon, opted to devote the remainder of his life to the service of his church, publishing numerous theological texts and eventually becoming first counselor to the seventh president of the Church of Jesus Christ of Latter-day Saints. Clark died on October 6, 1961, at age ninety.

See also *Good Neighbor Policy; Hoover, Herbert; Kellogg, Frank B.; Monroe Doctrine; Roosevelt, Theodore*

. . . . DAVID B. CASTLE

REFERENCES AND FURTHER READING

J. Reuben Clark Law Society, "J. Reuben Clark's Biography," www.lclark.edu/law/student_groups/j_reuben_clark_law_society/biography.php.

Munro, Dana G. *The United States and the Caribbean Republics, 1921–1933.* Princeton, NJ: Princeton University Press, 1974.

Perkins, Dexter. *A History of the Monroe Doctrine.* Boston, MA: Little, Brown, 1963.

Sessions, Gene A. "The Clark Memorandum Myth." *The Americas* 34, no. 1 (July 1977): 40–58.

Clark Memorandum on the Monroe Doctrine

(**See** *Clark, J. Reuben*)

Clay, Henry

Henry Clay (1777–1852) played a remarkable role in fostering early U.S.–Latin American relations and made a contribution in the development of the Monroe Doctrine. As speaker of the House of Representatives (1811–1820, 1823–1825), he launched, in the late 1810s, a campaign for the recognition of Latin American nations, consistently opposing the pre-1822 moderate course of Monroe-Adams. In U.S. public opinion Henry Clay was widely perceived as the main supporter of the Spanish-American revolutions; he was also praised for his activities by rebels in the New World.

HOUSE ADVOCATE OF EXPANSION AND RECOGNITION

An avid expansionist, in late 1810 Clay advocated in the Senate the occupation of East Florida. He first mentioned his interest in South America and a possible all-American union against monarchic Europe in January, 1813. In January 1816 Clay spoke in favor of supporting South American revolutions and thus of counteracting the rise of British influence in the New World. From January 1817 Clay started active agitation for Spanish-American revolutions. Up to March 1818 this campaign centered on revision of neutrality laws and thus on recognizing rebellious Spanish colonies as legal belligerent parties. Opposing the usual Anglo-Saxon criticism of Spanish American culture and civic traditions, Clay stressed that public vices of Spanish colonies were not inherent but were results of the Spanish tyranny. Thus he anticipated the inevitable rapid progress of Spanish American nations after they achieved independence.

From March 1818 Henry Clay started an open campaign in support of recognition of independence, first, of Rio de la Plata. Clay rightly believed that the Holy Alliance would not intervene in the New World in support of Spain—a view not shared by the majority of U.S. decision makers. He started to elaborate his ambitious plan of creating a Pan-American system as the balance of its European antagonist. This Pan-American Union should have counteracted the European involvement in the New World but not have interfered in the Old World affairs. Such a plan was first proposed by Henry M. Brackenridge in his published letter to James Monroe in mid-1817. Though Clay's motions were defeated they were noted in Europe and troubled British Prime Minister Viscount Castlereagh.

A delay with the Transcontinental Treaty ratification allowed Clay, at the height of his influence and popularity, to put relations with Spain and its rebellious American colonies on the congressional agenda. From early 1820 he advocated the recognition of Spanish-American nations, with the incentive of the annexation of Texas (claiming it as part of the Louisiana Purchase) and also the control of Florida. Clay had first stated that the United States borders should have reached the Pacific and Rio Grande (Texas) back in March 1818.

He formally proposed the motion to recognize the independence of any Spanish American nation chosen by the administration on May, 20, 1820. This resolution was adopted (80–75) and was the first victory of the speaker's cause. In early February 1821, Clay again reiterated his proposal to appoint a minister in one of the South American nations but lost with margins of 73–76 and 79–86.

Later in February 1821, the Transcontinental Treaty was finally ratified. A conversation with John Quincy Adams soon after confirmed to Clay that the ratification of the Transcontinental Treaty cleared all obstacles to the recognition of the Spanish-American nations in mid-1822.

On May 19, 1821, in Lexington, Kentucky, Clay made his most radical speech on foreign policies, proposing the Pan-American Union as a counterpart to the Holy Alliance to make this new united North and South America a rallying point and asylum of liberty. It is thus important to note that Clay's famous American system included not only the program of internal improvements (first proposed also in March 1818) but also a foreign dimension aimed at putting the United States at the head of the emerging New World nations. Developing with the help of internal improvements, U.S. industries could have found outlet not only inside the nation but also within this newly independent American domain.

SECRETARY OF STATE

After the so-called "corrupt bargain" brought John Quincy Adams to the presidency, Clay was appointed Adams' secretary of state (1825–1829). During that time Clay apparently tempered his grand hemispheric schemes and became an instrument of John Quincy Adams' policies. On December 5, 1825, the United States signed and ratified a treaty with the Federation of Central America which later served as a model free trade agreement of perfect equality and reciprocity and a most-favored-nation treaty with Brazil (December 12, 1828).

Clay also attempted to organize a settlement of Spain with its former colonies through the Russian mediation (May 1825–mid-1826). His plan implied the preservation of the colonial status quo of Cuba and Puerto Rico; it failed because of the unwillingness of the Spanish to discuss the topic. In the relations with Mexico Clay developed his expansionist course, making overtures to the possibility of shifting the border set by the Transcontinental Treaty. In 1827 he instructed Minister Poinsett to suggest selling the whole Texas or its half (with the border on the Colorado River) for $1 million or half that amount, respectively. These aggressive proposals were never seriously considered by the Mexican government.

Clay supported the participation of the United States in the Inter-American Panama Congress of 1826—a measure which lead to his harmless duel with John Randolph in April of 1826. In his instructions to the appointed U.S. representatives at the Panama Congress, Clay elaborated a wide program of U.S.-Latin American policy. The United States would remain neutral politically and focus first of all on the development of commercial connections through free trade principles. The neutrality dictated the noninterference in the relations among American nations and the United States declining to join continental unions. The United States favored the peaceful settlement of Spain with its former possessions and the colonial status quo of Cuba and Puerto Rico. Though Clay's instructions were never implemented—the U.S. representatives never reached Panama—its main principles (neutrality, liberalization of commerce and navigation, defense of status quo in the Caribbean), along with southward expansion, defined the Latin American policies of the United States almost until the end of the nineteenth century.

CONCLUSION

Later the threat to the Union posed by the slavery issue transformed Clay's expansionism. In 1844 as a presidential candidate he opposed the annexation of Texas—a step which possibly cost him the election. During the Mexican War Clay and John Quincy Adams headed the opposing Conscience Whigs faction. Clay collaborated with Daniel Webster on the Compromise of 1850 which left colonists to decide on slavery in New Mexico but declared California a free state; it forestalled the Civil War, but only for a decade.

See also *Adams, John Quincy; Bolívar, Simón; Calhoun, John C.; Carrera Turcios, José Rafael; Latin American Independence, 1803–1826, U.S. Policy toward; Mexican-American War, 1846–1848; Monroe Doctrine; Panama Conference, 1826; Poinsett, Joel R.; Transcontinental Treaty, 1819; Texas, U.S. Annexation of*

. . . . ANDREY ISÉROV

References and Further Reading

Clay, Henry. *The Papers of Henry Clay*, edited by James F. Hopkins, Mary W. M. Hargreaves et al., 11 vols. University Press of Kentucky, Lexington, 1959–1992.

Peterson, Merrill D. *The Great Triumvirate Webster, Clay, and Calhoun*. New York: Oxford University Press, 1987.

Remini, Robert V. *Henry Clay: Statesman for the Union*. New York: Norton, 1991.

Van Deusen, Glyndon G. *The Life of Henry Clay*. Westport, CT: Greenwood Press, 1979. First published 1937 by Little, Brown.

Clayton, John M.

(**See** *Clayton-Bulwer Treaty, 1850*)

Clayton-Bulwer Treaty, 1850

The Clayton-Bulwer Treaty, concluded between U.S. Secretary of State John M. Clayton and the British Minister at Washington Henry Lytton Bulwer on April 19, 1850, tried to settle Anglo-American differences in Central America. Both sides recognized the commercial importance of a proposed canal across Nicaragua and agreed to joint ownership, operation, and protection of it. But they failed to adjust Anglo-American political differences on the isthmus, which prevented the construction of the contemplated waterway until the early twentieth century.

GENESIS

After acquiring Oregon and California in the late 1840s, the United States sought a transit route across Central America to link its Atlantic and Pacific territories, to provide security for its new possessions, and to promote trade with East Asian markets. These objectives clashed with Britain's Moskito protectorate and its settlement in Belize. Moreover Britain sought control of the Bay Islands, which commanded the Atlantic approach to the proposed waterway. Wary of recent signs of American ascendancy in the region (i.e., the Bidlack-Mallarino Treaty and the Treaty of Guadalupe Hidalgo), Britain moved to protect its maritime control of the Caribbean and its holdings in Central America by seizing San Juan del Norte, the projected eastern terminal of a canal across Nicaragua, in January 1848 on behalf of the Moskito king and renaming it Greytown. The United States, increasingly aware of the need for a transit route across Central America due to the California Gold Rush, feared that Britain would use the Moskito protectorate to monopolize control over the proposed canal. To make matters worse Ephraim George Squier, the American chargé d'affaires in Central America, and Frederick Chatfield, the British consul-general in the region, engaged in a personal rivalry to advance the interests of their respective governments. Squier secured an unauthorized treaty from Nicaragua that gave the United States exclusive transit rights across that country, promised the Central American states that the United States would uphold the Monroe Doctrine against British encroachments on the isthmus, and seized Tigre Island to prevent Britain from gaining control of the western terminal of the projected waterway. Meanwhile Chatfield had bolstered British influence on the isthmus by enforcing payment of British claims through the use of naval blockades.

In negotiating the Clayton-Bulwer Treaty, Bulwer sought to remove Anglo-American tensions arising from the Squier-Chatfield feud and to prevent American annexation of the Central American states. He hoped to facilitate the construction of a canal across Nicaragua without abandoning the Moskito protectorate, a point of British honor. He therefore focused on the commercial objective of the treaty, trying to sidestep the Monroe Doctrine by not addressing any territorial questions in Central America. Clayton sought British acceptance of a nonexclusive canal policy which necessitated the abandonment of the Moskito protectorate.

AN AMBIGUOUS AGREEMENT AND ITS AFTERMATH

The conflicting aims of the negotiators produced the confused language in Article 1 of the convention as they tried to conceal their differences on the Moskito protectorate in the interests of promoting the canal project. Both parties pledged not to "occupy or fortify, or colonize, or assume or exercise any dominion over Nicaragua, Costa Rica, the Moskito Coast or any part of Central America" (Bevans 1974, 105–108). They also disavowed the use of any "alliance, connection or influence that either possesses with any [Central American] State or Government through whose territory the said canal shall pass . . . for the purpose of occupying or holding, directly or indirectly, exclusive control of the proposed canal . . ." (Bevans 1974, 105–108). To Clayton the prohibition on occupying or establishing dominion throughout the region denied the Moskito protectorate and British colonization rights to the Bay Islands and restricted Britain's presence in Belize to specific log-cutting rights acquired from Spain in 1786. Bulwer, however, held that the provision recognized existing protectorates, alliances, and dominions as long as they were not used to gain exclusive control over the projected canal and only forbade future colonization in the region.

To protect Britain's presence in Central America, Bulwer, in a declaration that preceded the exchange of ratifications of the treaty, managed to exempt Belize and the Bay Islands from the agreement. He also argued that the Moskito Coast and Greytown were excluded from the convention because they were not new possessions. The weakness of the Taylor administration and congressional Whigs, as well as the ongoing debate over the extension of slavery, prevented Clayton from convincing Bulwer to accept the American interpretation of the agreement, which would remove Britain from the isthmus.

The ambiguities of Article 1 produced several problems in Anglo-American isthmian relations throughout the 1850s and nearly provoked a third Anglo-American war. The Prometheus Affair, the establishment of the Bay Islands as a British colony, the demands of the Young America faction of the Democratic party to enforce the Monroe Doctrine in Central America, the inability to resolve the Costa Rica-Nicaragua boundary dispute, and the bombardment of Greytown aggravated Anglo-American differences in Central America. Then, in 1856, American filibuster activities in Nicaragua became entangled with presidential politics and British violations of American neutrality laws during the Crimean War, resulting in a war scare. Acknowledging that distance, an indifferent public, and the need to protect its commercial interests made it difficult for Britain to resist the American interpretation of the Clayton-Bulwer Treaty, the British government negotiated the Clarendon-Dallas Treaty (1856), agreeing to abandon the Bay Islands and Moskito protectorate. But references to slavery in the agreement led the U.S. Senate to add a number of amendments to the treaty that made it unacceptable to the British government.

LEGACY

The British government unilaterally resolved the Central American Question in 1859–1860 through treaties with Guatemala, Honduras, and Nicaragua. In these agreements Britain accepted the American interpretation of the Clayton-Bulwer Treaty—the boundaries of Belize were fixed, the Bay Islands were ceded to Honduras, and Britain relinquished the Moskito protectorate in return for a ten-year annuity to the Indians and recognition of Greytown as a free port.

Despite American approval of the treaties, the Clayton-Bulwer Treaty remained a constant source of friction In Anglo-American relations as every late-nineteenth-century U.S. administration, beginning with that of Grant, insisted that America should unilaterally construct and control any canal across

Central America. The convention, one of the most unpopular treaties in American history because it blocked American expansion and violated the Monroe Doctrine, was superseded by the second Hay-Pauncefote Treaty in 1901, which granted the United States the exclusive right to construct and operate an isthmian canal. Such recognition of U.S. supremacy in the western hemisphere contributed to the Anglo-American rapprochement of the early twentieth century.

See also *Belize, U.S. Relations with; Bidlack-Mallarino Treaty, 1846; Central America, Filibusters; Chatfield, Frederick; Costa Rica-Nicaragua Boundary Dispute; Grant, Ulysses S.; Great Britain, Nineteenth-Century Interests in Latin America; Greytown Incident, 1854; Hay-Pauncefote Treaty, 1901; Honduras, U.S. Relations with; Managua, Treaty of, 1860; Mexican-American War: Treaty of Guadalupe Hidalgo, 1848; Monroe Doctrine; Nicaragua, U.S. Relations with; Squier, Ephraim G.; Taylor, Zachary*

. . . . DEAN FAFOUTIS

References and Further Reading

Bevans, Charles I., comp., *Treaties and Other International Agreements of the United States of America, 1776–1949,* vol. 12: United Kingdom-Zanzibar. Washington, DC: U.S. Government Printing Office, 1974.

Jones, Wilbur Devereux. *The American Problem in British Diplomacy, 1841–1861.* Athens: University of Georgia Press, 1974.

Van Alstyne, Richard W. "British Diplomacy and the Clayton-Bulwer Treaty, 1850–1860," *Journal of Modern History* 11, no. 2 (June 1939): 149–183.

Williams, Mary Wilhelmine. *Anglo-American Isthmian Diplomacy, 1815–1915.* Washington, DC: American Historical Association, 1916.

Cleveland, Grover

Stephen Grover Cleveland was the twenty-second and twenty-fourth president of the United States.

Son of a Presbyterian minister, conservative Democrat, and a lawyer by vocation, Grover Cleveland (1837–1908) enjoyed a meteoric political rise. Elected Mayor of Buffalo in 1881, Cleveland won the New York governorship the following year and the White House two years after that. He arrived in Washington, D.C., in March 1885 with a reputation for honesty. Cleveland lost his bid for reelection in 1888 to Republican Benjamin Harrison, but he won the office back in 1892, becoming the only U.S. president to serve two nonconsecutive terms.

Cleveland opposed any form of territorial expansion into Latin America. In 1885 he withdrew the Frelinghuysen-Zavala Treaty from consideration by the Senate because it would have given the United States control of a canal across Nicaragua. On trade, Cleveland preferred a general reduction in tariff rates and steadfastly opposed the Republican party strategy of maintaining a high protective tariff that allowed for the importation of certain items from targeted countries at lower rates through reciprocity agreements. When he took office in 1885 Cleveland withdrew pending reciprocity agreements with Latin American nations that the outgoing Arthur administration had submitted to the Senate and abruptly ended other reciprocity discussions that were in progress.

Two issues dominated U.S. relations with Latin America during Cleveland's first presidency: the Venezuela boundary crisis and the Cuban insurrection against Spanish rule.

In the summer of 1895 Cleveland sent a stern note to Great Britain demanding that the queen's government moderate its claims in a boundary dispute between British Guyana and Venezuela. Cleveland followed his diplomatic note with a public warning in his annual address to Congress in December. Ultimately Great Britain accepted the arbitration proposal, and the Paris Tribunal delivered its judgment in 1897. Cleveland was less concerned about the location of the boundary or the interests of Venezuela than in promoting the principle that the United States would not tolerate any European power acting in the western hemisphere without its consent. This position significantly expanded the scope of the Monroe Doctrine but was consistent with Cleveland's own policy toward territorial expansion. Several nations, including Mexico and Chile, voiced their discontent with this revision in U.S. policy.

When Cubans revolted against Spanish rule in 1895, Cleveland issued a proclamation of neutrality. He had no interest in intervention and had little sympathy for the rebels whom he considered lawless thugs. Cleveland believed that the best solution to the crisis was for Spain to grant some liberal reforms. Under this premise Cleveland offered his offices for arbitration and negotiation, but Spain rejected the appeal. Throughout his term Cleveland steadfastly resisted bellicose calls for more active involvement.

Despite Cleveland's opposition to territorial acquisition or forcing open markets in Latin America, he was not disinterested in regional affairs. He dispatched U. S. armed forces to help suppress revolts in Panama in 1885 and Brazil in 1893, and Cleveland successfully mediated a boundary dispute between Argentina and Brazil during his second term.

See also *Bayard, Thomas F.; Frelinghuysen-Zavala Treaty, 1884; Great Britain, Nineteenth-Century Interests in Latin America; Monroe Doctrine; Olney, Richard; Spanish-Cuban-American War 1895–1898; Venezuela-British Guiana Boundary Dispute, 1890s*

. . . . GREGORY J. DEHLER

References and Further Readings

Kagan, Robert. *Dangerous Nation: America's Place in the World from its Earliest Days to the Dawn of the Twentieth Century.* New York: Knopf, 2006.

Welch, Robert E. Jr. *The Presidencies of Grover Cleveland.* Lawrence: University Press of Kansas, 1988.

Clinton, Hillary Rodham

Hillary Diane Rodham Clinton (1947–) is a Democratic politician in the United States, currently serving as secretary of state in the Barack Obama administration. In this position Clinton has declared her intention to distinguish a foreign policy of the Democratic administration from that of the Republican Bush presidency (2001–2009), but some practices and initiatives in Latin America suggest continuities from prior administrations.

FIRST LADY, SENATOR, AND PRESIDENTIAL CANDIDATE

Hillary Rodham's early training and education prepared her for a prominent public life. Born to a family of modest means and Republican politics in Chicago, Rodham earned degrees from Wellesley College and Yale Law School. Though already involved in numerous political campaigns and causes, Rodham cast an even more prominent political profile after her marriage to fellow Yale law graduate and future U.S. President William J. Clinton in 1975. The marriage and the success of Bill Clinton's political pursuits probably resulted in Hillary Clinton curtailing or delaying some of her own electoral aspirations, but she took full advantage of her positions as "first lady" of Arkansas and later as "first lady" of the United States to advance a number of political concerns. While her husband was governor of Arkansas (1983–1992), Hillary Clinton continued to practice law and political advocacy, focusing foremost on domestic issues of children's law and family policy. As the spouse of the president of the United States (1993–2001), she suspended her legal career but played a central if unofficial role in White House policymaking, advocating most prominently for a measure that ultimately failed passage: national health care reform. Though she worked primarily on U.S. domestic issues, Clinton did travel to 79 countries during these eight years as spouse to the president, including most of the nations of Latin America. For instance in October 1995, on her way to a meeting of western hemisphere first ladies in Asunción, Paraguay, Clinton toured Nicaragua and Brazil, meeting with national political leaders and observing social and economic conditions. Clinton later referred to the five-day trip as "a blueprint for future travels."

As the second term of her husband's presidency came to a close, Hillary Clinton won election to a U.S. Senate seat in New York, a position she served from 2001 to 2009. Although she served on the Armed Services Committee (2003–2009), Senator Clinton prioritized domestic rather than international issues. In key foreign policy votes Clinton supported initiatives of the George W. Bush presidency such as the Patriot Act (2001), U.S. military action in Afghanistan (2001), and the Iraq War Resolution (2002). As Senator Clinton did not take high-profile positions on policy issues in Latin America.

In 2008 Senator Clinton sought the Democratic nomination for the U.S. presidency and received widespread financial and popular support, but Senator Barack Obama defeated her in the primaries and won the general election in November. Clinton spoke critically of the North American Free Trade Agreement (NAFTA) during the primary campaign in Ohio, but she generally did not feature issues involving Latin America in her campaign. In a political effort to restore unity within the Democratic party, Obama appointed Clinton as secretary of state.

SECRETARY OF STATE

As the principal administrator and representative of U.S. foreign policy in the Obama administration, Clinton led efforts to restore the global reputation of the United States, which many world leaders questioned after President Bush's unpopular policies on the Iraq War and global climate change. While continuing many policies initiated by the prior administration, including the wars in Iraq and Afghanistan, the Obama administration also declared commitment to diplomacy and development. For her part Clinton addressed issues of global climate and promoted women's empowerment. Attention to events in Iraq, Afghanistan, Egypt, and the Middle East has led Clinton's State Department to pay less notice to affairs in Latin America.

Yet Secretary Clinton played a prominent role in at least two instances in Latin America during her first two years in the position. The first was the political controversy surrounding the coup d'état in Honduras in June 2009. Under orders from the Honduran supreme court, soldiers stormed the home of President Manuel Zelaya, forcing him out of office and out of Honduras. The court had ruled that Zelaya's decision to hold a nonbinding poll on constitutional reform was illegal; the national congress voted for the ouster of the leftist president and approved succession to the presidency by the speaker of congress, the conservative Roberto Micheletti. Micheletti immediately declared a "state of exception" and suspended civil liberties. International human rights organizations reported numerous abuses by the military government, including repression of political opposition, interference with independent news reporting, and widespread police and paramilitary violence throughout the countryside and urban areas. International organizations, including the United Nations and the Organization of American States (OAS), broadly condemned the coup and denounced the Micheletti government. Though the U.S. ambassador to Honduras noted that the coup was illegal and unconstitutional, Secretary Clinton was more reserved in her criticism and refrained from referring to the action as a military coup. Clinton supported peace talks between Zelaya and Micheletti, overseen by Costa Rican President Oscar Arias, but many Latin Americans criticized her and the Obama administration for legitimizing the Micheletti regime and for overlooking human rights abuses. Few were convinced by Secretary Clinton's declaration in Buenos Aires in March 2010 that the Honduran crisis had been resolved successfully and nonviolently. Even after previously scheduled elections were completed in November 2010, many Latin American leaders judged them illegitimate, as civil liberties and political rights had not yet been fully restored to Honduras. These events, and the construction of two new U.S. military bases in Honduras after the coup, eroded the credibility of Secretary Clinton among many in Latin America.

The second event in Latin America to draw attention to Clinton was the earthquake in Haiti in January 2010. The massive quake resulted in more than 200,000 deaths and millions of dislocated and impoverished Haitians. As governments from around the globe and nongovernmental organizations responded to the disaster, Secretary Clinton arrived in Port-au-Prince quickly to announce full U.S. support for relief efforts while respecting the sovereignty of the Haitian government. Initially her presence and statements were well received. One year after the quake, however, complaints about delays in promised relief funds and exclusion of Haitian participation in directing reconstruction efforts soured the image of foreign agencies, including the U.S. State Department.

Clinton has indicated the importance of curtailing the drug trade, strengthening U.S. relations with Mexico, and promoting free trade initiatives in the Americas, and these issues are likely to be emphasized as she moves forward with her political career. Although Secretary Clinton has denied having any electoral aspirations for the future, speculation about her presidential ambitions persist as she retains significant popularity among the U.S. voting public.

See also *Clinton, William J.; Honduras, U.S. Relations with; North American Free Trade Agreement (NAFTA), 1992; Obama, Barack H.; Organization of American States (OAS); Drugs, U.S. War on*

. . . . GREGORY S. CRIDER

Selected Works

Clinton, Hillary Rodham. *Living History*. New York: Oxford University Press, 2003.

References and Further Reading

Bernstein, Carl. *A Woman in Charge: The Life of Hillary Rodham Clinton*. New York: Knopf, 2007.

Human Rights Watch. *After the Coup: Ongoing Violence, Intimidation, and Impunity in Honduras*. New York: Author, 2010.

Clinton, William J.

In 1992 William Jefferson "Bill" Clinton (1946–) defeated President George H.W. Bush, and he was inaugurated in 1993 as the forty-second president of the United States. The former governor of Arkansas, he brought very little foreign policy experience to the office, although he did deal with the Mariel Boatlift when Cuban refugees rioted in several Arkansas centers in 1980. Early on the new president focused primarily on domestic affairs, especially in the wake of the end of the Cold War. He admitted to wanting to avoid foreign policy issues and for a two-term U.S. president, he did remarkably little in regard to Latin America. In dealing with the region he rejected for the most part the "gunboat diplomacy" that had characterized Ronald Reagan and George H. W. Bush, but he provided few substantive changes in U.S.-Latin American relations, focusing instead on domestic issues and other parts of the world.

NAFTA AND MEXICO

Despite initially having little interest in U.S.-Latin American relations, Clinton made several "experienced" appointments in the State Department and National Security Council. These included Secretary of State Warren Christopher and Anthony Lake as national security adviser. Both had significant experience dating back to the Johnson administration. Both chose a course of caution and proceeded with a deliberate and meticulous course that promoted democracy among many of the fragile governments in the region evolving from twenty or more years of dictatorial rule.

Clinton's first area of engagement in U.S.-Latin American relations was the North American Free Trade Agreement (NAFTA), which Clinton backed despite strong opposition from his party. He inherited the agreement, signed in October 1992 by President Bush along with Mexican President Carlos Salinas de Gortari and Canadian Prime Minister Brian Mulroney, which sought to better integrate the economies of Mexico, the United States, and Canada by reducing, then eliminating, many tariffs and economic restrictions. The legislatures of Canada and Mexico approved NAFTA with only limited opposition, both wanting to spark economic growth. In the United States, however, labor unions, environmentalists, and others (including Texas billionaire and third-party presidential candidate H. Ross Perot) denounced the agreement and warned of economic losses that would develop as American jobs went south.

President Clinton firmly supported free trade with Latin America, a traditional position among Southern U.S. politicians, and vigorously campaigned for the legislation. The tide was turned when the largest audience ever to view a cable program watched Clinton's Vice President Al Gore dismantle Perot and his arguments on "Larry King Live." Within a short time public support swung in favor of NAFTA. The House approved the treaty 234–200 and the Senate by a vote of 61–38 in November 1993. NAFTA went into effect January 1, 1994.

Mexican relations came to the forefront again in December 1994 when the Mexican peso began a free fall. Overvalued and undergirded by questionable government spending policies, the peso lost value quickly. The Clinton administration reacted rapidly, securing a $50 billion loan from various groups including the U.S. Treasury. The peso stabilized and three years later the Mexican government paid off the loans ahead of schedule. Other countries including Brazil followed suit in what one person characterized as a "tequila effect," or a hangover, although the economies never faced the same problems as Mexico and international monetary assistance also helped prevent severe dislocations.

CARIBBEAN CHALLENGES

Despite his efforts to avoid foreign policy issues, Clinton encountered numerous challenges in the Caribbean, especially early in his presidency. A refugee problem developed in Haiti as much of the international community rallied against the military government of General Rauol Cédras, which took power in late 1990 in a coup from the short-lived democratic government of a young priest, President Jean-Bertrand Aristide. The Organization of American States (OAS) almost immediately imposed a trade embargo that further worsened economic conditions on the island. The United States originally took in some of those fleeing Haiti, putting them in camps at Guantánamo Bay, Cuba, but then it began ordering the return of all those leaving, many in makeshift rafts, continuing a policy of deportation dating to the Carter administration and the Jean-Claude Duvalier government in Haiti. Soon after Clinton took office in January 1993, reports surfaced that two hundred thousand people planned to flee Haiti.

Problems worsened as the Clinton administration continued the policy of deporting Haitians. In July 1993 the OAS and United Nations continued pressuring Cédras to resign and allow Aristide to return to power. In October U.S. and Canadian peacekeepers arrived to try to help with an agreement that provided such a scenario. Cédras' allies met them at the docks and threatened to turn Haiti into another ungovernable Somalia, where American troops had died during a recent humanitarian intervention. The troops withdrew and for nearly a year, the Clinton administration sought an alternative. Under pressure from the Congressional Black Caucus and human rights activists, Clinton pressed Cédras to leave voluntarily, threatening invasion and taking steps to prepare for one.

Last minute negotiations by Jimmy Carter, Colin Powell, and Sam Nunn in September 1994 prevented significant bloodshed as the military junta agreed to leave Haiti and allow Aristide to return to power. Nonetheless fifteen thousand American troops landed in Operation Uphold Democracy. They encountered little resistance and one journalist dubbed the event "the Immaculate Invasion." For nearly a year U.S. troops stayed in place, serving as police officers, medics, and engineers. As promised they withdrew in April 1995. Critics continued to skewer Clinton, as one emphasized the president took the action not to promote human rights but rather to stop a massive influx of poor refugees into Florida.

In addition to Haiti Cuba perplexed Clinton, just as it had caused problems for every president since Eisenhower. The economic situation in Cuba had deteriorated significantly with the end of subsidies provided by the former Soviet Union. President George H. W. Bush had tightened the embargo on Cuba with the signing of the Cuban Democracy Act in 1992. In response more Cubans began trying to leave for the United States, where historically if they touched American soil, they received asylum.

In August and early September 1994 an estimated thirty-six thousand Cubans escaped from the island, headed toward the United States, in *balseros,* rafts, or anything that would float. The Clinton administration attempted to stem the flow by directing the *balseros* to its naval base at Guantánamo, Cuba, and then to Panama. Castro ended the outmigration following an agreement reached on September 9 that permitted twenty thousand Cubans per year to leave for the United States but with the appropriate paperwork provided by the U.S. Interests Section in Havana. And henceforth, Cubans would be granted admission to the United States if they reached U.S. land ("dryfoot"), while those caught at sea ("wetfoot") would be returned to Cuba.

However in February 1996, Cuban MiG jets shot down two planes (killing four people) of a Cuban exile group, Brothers to the Rescue, that routinely made flights from the United States over the island to drop propaganda leaflets, despite warnings from Castro. Immediately denunciations arose from the United States, including from Secretary of State Madeline Albright, who publicly charged the Cubans with cowardice. Clinton himself gave life to otherwise languishing legislation initially introduced by Senator Jesse Helms (R-NC) and Representative Dan Burton (R-IN). The president announced that he would sign, if passed, the Helms-Burton bill that would allow U.S. citizens to sue foreign companies doing business in Cuba on confiscated lands as well as tighten economic and cultural restrictions on Cuba. After Clinton's announcement Congress passed the sponsored bill, and Clinton indeed signed it.

Over time the Clinton administration softened some of the provisions of the Helms-Burton Act, in part to ease tensions with the European Union regarding trade issues, in particular the bill's provisos that attempted to punish foreign-owned companies that utilized U.S. nationalized properties in Cuba and to deny U.S. entry visas to executives of those countries. It allowed more American flights to Cuba and in 1999 began allowing the transfer of modest sums of $1,200 a year from Cuban Americans to their families.

Under Clinton's People-to-People program the Baltimore Orioles baseball team split a two-game home series, with the Cuban national all-star team. It marked the first time since 1959 that U.S. and Cuban baseball teams played games in each other's country. Nearly one hundred thousand people attended the games. The Cuban American community protested that the series provided an air of legitimacy to Castro; Roman Catholic officials nixed the proposal that all proceeds from the games go to the church's charity in Cuba, *Caritas.* Negotiators finally agreed to divide the money between youth athletic programs in both countries. And following the game in Baltimore two Cuban players defected to the United States.

Still, tensions remained high and intensified in 2000 when U.S. officials found a young boy, Elián González, floating in the Gulf of Mexico, brought him to the United States, and placed him in the custody of family members. Some people called for Elián's return to his father in Cuba because of the child's relationship with his sole remaining parent. In response hardline, anti-Castro Cuban exiles exploited the episode to inflame passions. A standoff ensued, culminated by a raid by federal agents to take the boy and return him to Cuba with his father. Cuban Americans loudly denounced the Clinton administration, and the incident likely contributed to a decrease in support for Vice President Al Gore in Florida in the disputed 2000 presidential election.

As Clinton left office in 2001 he left a mixed legacy in Latin America, one that laid the groundwork for future successes, such as the U.S. efforts in fighting the violence in Colombia via the Plan Colombia, where the United States increased military and humanitarian assistance to battle narco-terrorists. In other areas such as Cuba, substantial challenges remained. Nonetheless he would continue to work in the region as a private citizen, such as his efforts to raise money, together with George H. W. Bush, for the Haitian earthquake victims in 2010.

. . . . KYLE LONGLEY

References and Further Reading

Berman, William C. *From the Center to the Edge: The Politics and Policies of the Clinton Presidency.* Lanham, MD: Rowman and Littlefield, 2001.

Hyland, William G. *Clinton's World: Remaking American Foreign Policy.* New York: Praeger, 1999.

Morely, Michael, and Chris McGillion. *Unfinished Business: America and Cuba after the Cold War, 1986–2001.* Cambridge, UK: Cambridge University Press, 2002.

Coffee as an Export Crop

In a region that depends heavily on agricultural export, coffee figures prominently in the export history of a significant number of Latin American economies. The countries of Latin America currently produce approximately double the amount of coffee of the rest of the world combined. Due to this, coffee represents a very significant portion of economic activity in several Latin American countries, although this dominance has faded somewhat over time.

NINETEENTH CENTURY TO THE GREAT DEPRESSION

Coffee was introduced into Latin America by the French, who began coffee cultivation in their Caribbean colony of Martinique. From there coffee cultivation spread throughout the Caribbean and Latin America. The cultivation and exportation of coffee fit nicely with the colonial structure of Latin America due to the centralization of land into large estates that could easily transform into large agricultural operations.

The concentration of wealth into the hands of the few, coupled with the huge profits coffee could earn, meant that the export and profitability of coffee increased steadily throughout the nineteenth century. The growth of coffee had three primary ramifications during this period. First the reliance on an agricultural crop for such a large portion of the state's economy meant that Latin America occupied a peripheral position to the large industrial states of North America and Europe, from whom Latin America also imported a wide variety of finished goods. Second it meant that coffee growers shifted from engaging in subsistence agriculture to being aggressive entrepreneurs since there was so much money to be made in the coffee trade. Third the growth of Latin American elite also helped to usher in the rule of the military, with a military strongman at the helm, loyal to the interests of the elite.

By the late nineteenth century coffee growers dominated the politics of many countries in Latin America, especially those in Central America. For instance in El Salvador, a coffee grower was president from 1898–1931, in Costa Rica from 1870–1948, and in Nicaragua from 1893–1909. The seizure of power by coffee growers meant that coffee exportation often helped to finance the takeover of government and facilitate the coffee growers' use of the state apparatus to further aid coffee exportation and profitability.

During this period coffee also contributed to the changing landscape of labor and the demographics of Latin America. Coffee production required high labor intensity, and after slavery was outlawed, the countries of Latin America turned to other sources of labor, primarily European immigrants—even at a time in which many Latin Americans were unemployed. In Brazil for instance, the government even paid for the passage of millions of Europeans to Brazil on the assumption they would be better workers.

The time from the middle of the nineteenth century until the Great Depression represented the zenith of power for the Latin American coffee-growing elite. Similarly to most countries of the world, the Great Depression represented a seismic shift in the world economy. The plight of many of the agricultural export countries of Latin America was even more pronounced, due not only to the nature of agricultural exports and their price volatility but also the very heavy reliance on foreign markets. For instance in Colombia approximately 90 percent of coffee exports were going to the United States.

A young Costa Rican woman examines coffee beans ready for harvest. Coffee provided a huge economic boom for many Latin American countries in the latter half of the nineteenth century, although the benefits were largely confined to the elite. Continually falling prices since that time led to the formation of the International Coffee Organization in 1963 to establish quotas and other controls.

SOURCE: National Archives

IMPORT SUBSTITUTION INDUSTRIALIZATION AND THE INTERNATIONAL COFFEE ORGANIZATION

In response many countries of Latin America embarked on a policy of Import Substitution Industrialization (ISI) in order to lessen the reliance on volatile agricultural export markets. While this strategy of ISI worked in many countries for the short term, for the coffee growers ISI represented a shift away from their own preeminence in the economy. It also put into motion a wave of industrialization that eroded the role of coffee as a percentage of economic output in many Latin American countries. While certainly an important export in many countries, throughout the twentieth century coffee would represent a smaller and smaller part of a country's gross domestic product (GDP). For instance in Colombia coffee was about 10 percent of GDP in the early 1950s, but it represented about 2 percent by the 1990s. As a total percentage of exports, coffee dropped from about 80 percent in the 1950s to about 10 percent by the end of the 1990s, due not only to the diversification of the economy but also to the rise of coffee production in Africa and Asia.

The continual fall of coffee prices since the 1950s led the world's coffee-producing countries to form the International Coffee Organization (ICO) in 1963. Unlike many agricultural products, coffee prices tend to rely heavily on supply, as demand is relatively constant. Therefore if supply is low, the price is high, and if supply is high, the price is low. This supply-based profitability means that coffee producers would benefit greatly from coordinating their efforts. The ICO, among other measures, seeks to equalize supply and demand through export quotas in order to stabilize prices. Prior to the ICO coffee producers would often resort to such measures as destroying a portion of their crop in order to reduce supply. For instance between 1931 and 1940, Brazil destroyed 78 million sacks of coffee.

The falling price of coffee and the impact on workers and many small producers who live at the subsistence level has also helped to initiate a move toward "Fair Trade" coffee in which farmers are guaranteed a price floor as well as a number of labor- and community-related benefits. This movement has done little, however, to stem the growing crisis among coffee-growing countries, as the price of coffee in real terms is lower than it has been in one hundred years, affecting the estimated 125 million people worldwide who are dependent on coffee production for their livelihood.

See also *Export Based Economies; Great Depression, Impact on Latin America; Import Substitution Industrialization (ISI); Inter-American Coffee Agreement, 1940; International Coffee Agreement, 1962; International Organization of Banana Exporters*

. . . . ANDREW P. MILLER

References and Further Reading

Blake, Charles H. *Politics in Latin America.* Boston, MA: Houghton Mifflin, 2008.
International Coffee Organization, www.ico.org.
Johnson, David Conrad. "Confronting a Catch-22: The Guatemalan Coffee Economy in the Era of the International Coffee Agreement, 1962–1989." PhD diss., Texas Christian University, 2005.
McGreevy, William. *An Economic History of Colombia: 1845–1930.* Cambridge, UK: Cambridge University Press, 1971.
Paige, Jeffrey M. *Coffee and Power: Revolution and the Rise of Democracy in Central America.* Cambridge, MA: Harvard University Press, 1997.
Skidmore, Thomas E., and Peter H. Smith. *Modern Latin America.* New York: Oxford University Press, 2005.

Colombia, U.S. Relations with

Colombia and the United States have a long history of mutually beneficial relations. Although not immune from controversy—particularly in connection with the separation of Panama (1903)—the bilateral relationship has served the national and international interests of both countries. Since independence Colombians looked to the United States to advance their internal state-building agenda, economic development, and national security goals. American objectives focused on encouraging stability, security, and prosperity in Colombia, strategically located in northwest South America. Increasingly interdependent entities, Colombia and the United States have formed meaningful cultural, economic, military, and political ties.

COLONIAL AND POSTINDEPENDENCE PERIODS

During the colonial period European powers limited relations between North and South America. Indeed colonists in present-day Colombia and the United States had few formal interactions. Yet during the Age of Revolution North American political philosophers inspired many South American revolutionaries. While European thinkers most heavily influenced the revolution in Spanish America, copies of the U.S. Constitution and related literature circulated among Spanish American elite. South American agents traveled in the United States to raise support for the war against Spain. Some U.S. merchants smuggled supplies to Latin American armies; a few U.S. volunteers served with revolutionary units in northern South America.

These contacts aside, the U.S. government, for many years, maintained a position of strict neutrality. It feared that overt U.S. support for South American independence would endanger the United States. Then, in 1819, Simón Bolívar led anti-royalist forces into Bogotá—effectively clearing northern South America of Spanish military units. James Monroe (President 1817–1825) and Secretary of State John Quincy Adams subsequently announced their commitment to South American independence. In 1820 they dispatched an unofficial U.S. representative, Charles S. Todd, to Bogotá. He concentrated on establishing bilateral commercial relations and curtailing piracy in the Caribbean. In the United States Colombian diplomat Manuel Torres established relations with the Monroe administration. He also collected data on the U.S. system of government and education, which he sought to apply in Colombia.

In 1822, after Spain accepted the Adams-Onís Treaty, resolving the status of Florida, the U.S. government formally recognized Gran Colombia, comprising modern Colombia, Ecuador, Panama, and Venezuela. It was the first Latin American republic recognized by the United States, an indication of the perceived importance of Colombia. At that time U.S. and Colombian officials anticipated that Gran Colombia and the United States would be the principal economic and political powers in the western hemisphere.

In December 1823 the first official U.S. representative to Colombia, Richard C. Anderson (1823–1826), carrying the title minister plenipotentiary, presented his credentials to the Bolívar government in Bogotá. Two years later U.S. and Colombian officials signed their first bilateral commercial treaty. Still, Great Britain dominated Latin American markets during the nineteenth century; the U.S. and Colombian economies were oriented toward the export of raw materials, limiting early trade relations. Even so U.S. commerce with Colombia exceeded expectations in both countries. Among all Latin American republics, Mexico alone accounted for more U.S. commerce during the decade after independence.

In Bogotá, after independence, Colombian leaders differed on some foreign policy matters. In particular Bolívar

(President 1819–1830) sought an alliance with Great Britain, the most capable guarantor of Latin American independence. Several influential Colombians, who supported the president, wanted to work with Great Britain to eliminate the international slave trade, which placed them at odds with politicians from the U.S. south. Vice President Francisco José de Paula Santander, on the other hand, wanted to establish a formal partnership with the United States. By way of geographic proximity and republican principles, he believed, the United States was a natural ally of Colombia. This debate affected planning for the Colombian-sponsored Panama Congress of 1826. Bolívar, at first, did not want to invite the United States; Santander compelled the president to acquiesce.

In Washington the invitation to attend the Panama meeting raised questions about U.S.-Latin American relations. As for U.S. policy toward Colombia, Americans were keen on preventing Bolívar from attacking Spanish forces in Cuba and Puerto Rico, actions U.S. officials thought would disrupt hemispheric tranquility. They also wanted to encourage the growth of democratic institutions—and religious freedom—in South America. The conversation exposed certain cultural and racial stereotypes, as some U.S. officials opposed partnering with Latin Americans. Still in 1826, the U.S. Congress appointed Anderson, who had established an excellent rapport with the Colombian government, to represent the United States at the Panama conference. Yet Anderson died (in Cartagena) while traveling to the meeting. A second U.S. representative, Pennsylvania politician John Sergeant, arrived in Panama after the meeting adjourned. In the end the Panama congress produced agreements only Bogotá ratified.

Following Anderson's death Andrew Jackson (President 1829–1837) appointed William Henry Harrison (1829) as minister to Colombia. Harrison clashed with Colombian officials. Unhappy with Colombian political developments, he purportedly lectured Bolívar on the meaning of democracy. President Jackson soon withdrew Harrison from Colombia. U.S. Minister Thomas P. Moore restored good relations with Gran Colombia. Yet internal problems consumed Colombia's attention during Moore's tenure. In 1830 Ecuador and Venezuela seceded from Gran Colombia. In Bogotá officials adopted a new constitution and name—New Granada.

NEW GRANADA

The geography of northwest South America, which contributed to the collapse of Gran Colombia, hindered communications, economic development, and the spread of national sentiment. The three cordilleras of the Andean range isolated many Colombian communities; the landscape challenged road and railway engineers. Colombian terrain likewise limited economic development and the growth of international commerce. Colombia exported gold, cotton, tobacco, coffee, and other raw materials. But the lack of mature internal transportation systems and the relative isolation of key markets curtailed economic development. The compartmentalization also affected internal political affairs, particularly the intense and highly localized liberal-conservative rivalry that developed during the mid-1800s.

In New Grenada Santander (President 1832–1837) presided over a period of political stability, government restructuring, and educational reform. U.S. chargé d'affaires Robert McAfee supported Santander, although some U.S. officials disliked New Granadan economic policy and the prominent domestic role of the Roman Catholic Church. The New Granadan civil war, 1837 to 1841, also troubled U.S. policymakers, particularly the secessionist movement in the Department of Panama, the main point bilateral contact—and focus of relations over the decades to come.

From the early nineteenth century U.S. policymakers, entrepreneurs, and business people showed great interest in Panama. The isthmus, they believed, held potential as an Inter-American commercial center, location for an overland transit route between the Pacific and Atlantic Oceans, and possible site for an interoceanic canal. In 1841 U.S. authorities decided to recognize the independence of Panama, much as they had Venezuela and Ecuador a decade before. Bogotá, they concluded, had lost total control of the isthmus. U.S. diplomats, however, did not implement the policy before the civil war ended, allowing New Granada to retain Panama.

In the aftermath of the conflict political stability returned to northwest South America. The John Tyler (President 1841–1845) and James K. Polk (President 1845–1849) administrations worked to invigorate bilateral relations, especially commerce, and negotiate a formal agreement governing U.S. access to Panama. In the early 1840s New Granadan officials had invited Britain and France into an international project to develop Panama. When the diplomatic overture failed, Bogotá turned to the United States.

In 1845 the new U.S. chargé d'affaires to New Granada, Benjamin Bidlack explored the possibility of a bilateral treaty with President Tomás Cipriano de Mosquera y Arboleda (President 1845–1849) and Foreign Minister Manuel María Mallarino. Mosquera insisted that Bidlack and Mallarino negotiate a comprehensive treaty covering a wide array of bilateral issues. The U.S. government soon agreed. Bidlack and Mallarino opened formal discussions in mid-1846.

By the end of year the two diplomats had produced the Bidlack-Mallarino Treaty, which both governments ratified in 1848. The bilateral agreement covered trade relations, religious matters, U.S. access to Panama, and foreign investment in New Granada—all key issues to U.S. policymakers. In return the United States guaranteed New Granadan sovereignty over Panama, a U.S. position that would survive until 1903. The bilateral treaty was the most comprehensive international agreement ratified by the U.S. Senate until the end of the nineteenth century.

U.S. expansion following the Mexican-American War (1848) heightened U.S. involvement in Panama. In the 1850s U.S. entrepreneurs built a major railroad across the isthmus to shorten the trip to the west coast of the United States. The influx of Americans became great sources of revenue for New Granada. At the same time it spawned cultural tensions. The 1856 Panama City riot confirmed U.S. fears of Panamanian lawlessness and heightened New Granada's suspicion of foreigners.

ROAD TO PANAMANIAN INDEPENDENCE

The pace of bilateral contact slowed during the 1860s. Both countries experienced major internal conflicts. In the United States the federal government suppressed southern secessionism and outlawed slavery—to the great satisfaction of people across Latin America. In 1861 a liberal revolution in New Granada toppled the central government. Liberals subsequently adopted a new constitution; they renamed the country the United States of Colombia. Civil conflict returned to Colombia, again, in the 1880s. Nationalist Rafael Núñez (President 1880–1882, 1884–1886, and 1887–1894) defeated the rebellion, rewrote the constitution, and created the Republic of Colombia.

Toward the end of the century the pace of Colombian-American interaction accelerated. Colombian diplomats, led by Carlos Martinez Silva, participated in the First International American conference (1889–1890) in Washington, D.C. They became principal supporters of the Pan-American Union as a forum for Inter-American cooperation. Several major U.S. companies, including United Fruit Company (UFCO), established operations in Colombia. In 1894 American capitalists completed a sixty-mile railroad linking Cartagena and Calamar, on the Magdalena River. Around the same time Colombians began, for the first time, studying and traveling in the United States in significant numbers.

By the late nineteenth century, however, the expectations of early U.S. and Colombian officials had gone unfulfilled. While the United States had emerged as a major industrial power—and increasingly important internal actor—Colombia, for various reasons, did not develop into an economic or military leader in the Americas. The separation of Panama exemplified the disparity in strength between the two countries.

For many years U.S. officials sought access to Panama for the construction of an interoceanic waterway. In 1869 the Colombian congress rejected a treaty that would have allowed the United States to build a canal across the isthmus. In 1870 the U.S. Senate failed to act on a second agreement. Colombians, thereafter, brought French canal builder Ferdinand de Lesseps to Panama. Construction crews began cutting a sea-level waterway across the isthmus in 1881. By the end of the decade, however, the French project had collapsed, reopening the possibility of a Colombian-American project.

As a result of the Spanish-American War (1898), the United States acquired colonies in the Caribbean and Pacific—and a new sense of national purpose. The U.S. Navy wanted a canal in Panama to shorten the trip between the Atlantic and Pacific Oceans. In addition many Americans wanted easier access to Asian markets, upon which they believed the economic health of the United States relied. The U.S. government therefore refocused its attention on building a canal in Panama, a goal soon entangled with Colombian internal affairs.

During the Thousand Days War (1899–1902), liberal and conservative armies fought to control the republic. Panamanian separatists, unhappy with the government in Bogotá, sought independence. In 1901 Bogotá asked the United States to land troops in Panama—as the United States had done on several occasions during the nineteenth century. Recognizing Colombian sovereignty over Panama, as described in the Bidlack-Mallarino Treaty, the U.S. government reluctantly agreed to send U.S. Marines to support Colombian authorities. Around the same time U.S. officials pushed for an internal Colombian political settlement. Liberal and conservative leaders signed a peace agreement aboard the USS *Wisconsin* in November 1902.

In the months thereafter policymakers believed the two countries would soon launch a canal project in Panama. During the war U.S. and Colombian diplomats negotiated the Hay-Herrán Treaty, authorizing the United States to build a canal across the isthmus. In March 1903 the U.S. Senate ratified the treaty. Yet reservations soon surfaced in Bogotá, where the ratification process became entangled in domestic political disagreements. In August the Colombian Senate rejected the treaty, which some senators believed comprised Colombian sovereignty in Panama.

Angered by the Colombian move Theodore Roosevelt (President 1901–1909) reversed U.S. policy toward Colombia. If another revolt erupted on the isthmus, the United States would seek to maintain stability in Panama, not Colombian control. The new U.S. position encouraged Panamanian separatists. In November 1903 Manuel Amador Guerrero and his followers revolted against Colombia. The U.S. government quickly recognized the Panamanian independence, signed a canal accord, and began the construction of an interoceanic passageway.

U.S. support for Panamanian independence damaged U.S. relations with Colombia. Anti-American sentiment was rampant in Colombia during the early 1900s. Colombian citizens harassed Americans working in Colombia. Public officials denounced the United States in various public settings. While many constructive, private Colombian-American activities continued, the formal relationship suffered.

Attempting to restore good relations, U.S. and Colombian diplomats negotiated the Thomson-Urrutia Treaty in 1914. The Colombia government recognized the independence of Panama; the U.S. government agreed to pay $25 million to Colombia for its territorial loss. The treaty also settled the border between Colombia and Panama. The Colombian senate quickly ratified the agreement. The U.S. Congress approved the treaty after World War I. The agreement contributed to the resolution of U.S.-Colombian differences, as did economic and political contacts during World War I.

RENEWED INTERRELATIONSHIP THROUGH TWO WORLD WARS

During the First World War Colombia remained neutral but expressed sympathies with the Allied powers. Global ideological divisions highlighted U.S.-Colombian compatibility. At the same time the war had a significant impact on the Colombian economy, which until then relied on exports to Europe. After 1915 the United States emerged as the principal market for Colombian exports. Indeed by the end of the decade, nearly 73 percent of Colombian imports came from the United States. Looking for outlets for U.S. capital, American investors also began supporting projects in Colombia. The wartime period likewise began a period of beneficial bilateral interaction on health and development initiatives, such as an antimalaria campaign.

Around the same time Marco Fidel Suárez (President 1918–1921) theorized on the nature of Colombian-American relations. The South American republic, he observed, could not escape contact with the United States. Therefore Colombians should use the relationship to the country's advantage. The Suárez Doctrine dominated Colombian foreign policy through the early twenty-first century.

The pace of Colombian-American commercial interaction continued to expand during the 1920s. U.S. oil companies, which first entered Colombia during World War I, enlarged their holdings. Other firms invested in manufacturing, agriculture, mining, and utilities. By the end of the decade Americans held over $300 million in government bonds and direct investments in Colombia. Public health projects, supported in part by the Rockefeller Foundation International Health Board, likewise grew after World War I. The United Fruit Company's subsidiary in Colombia, the Magdalena Fruit Company, controlled vast resources on the Caribbean coast, the location of major unrest in 1928.

The Good Neighbor policy, launched by Herbert Hoover (President 1929–1933), furthered Colombian-American reconciliation. In 1933 Secretary of State Cordell Hull renounced intervention as an instrument of U.S. power in the western hemisphere. The following year, in July 1934, Franklin D. Roosevelt (President 1933–1945) visited Cartagena. He was the first sitting U.S. president to visit the republic. In various diplomatic settings Colombian and U.S. officials established outstanding working relations. In fact a series of liberal politicians, from 1930 to 1946, established warm personal relationships with their American counterparts—a partnership between Colombian liberals and U.S. Democrats rooted in compatible political philosophies.

In 1938 Eduardo Santos (President 1938–1942) suggested that the two countries elevate their diplomatic missions to embassy status. Convinced that turbulence in Europe and Asia required greater Colombian-American cooperation, Santos wanted embassies in each other's capitals to improve bilateral communication and coordination. The Roosevelt administration, sharing Santos' concerns, dispatched Spruille Braden to serve as the first U.S. ambassador to Colombia. In February 1939 Miguel López Pumarejo became the first Colombian ambassador in Washington, D.C., Gabriel Turbay replaced López in November. The diplomatic move symbolized the beginning of a period of intense U.S.-Colombian interaction.

Colombia and the United States worked together to defend the western hemisphere during World War II. In December 1941 the Santos administration broke relations with Japan, Germany, and Italy. Later, in 1944, Bogotá declared a state of belligerency with the Axis powers, a political move linked to a German submarine attack on a Colombian warship in the Caribbean. Colombian and American diplomats cooperated at various wartime meetings to enhance hemispheric political solidarity. The Colombian government increased its shipments of raw materials to the United States; U.S. economic assistance helped mitigate wartime economic instability in Colombia.

The two countries established important military ties between 1939 and 1945. The first U.S. military advisors arrived in Colombian in 1939. Colombian servicemen gained access to U.S. military schools. Colombia received U.S. military equipment under the provisions of the Lend Lease Act (1941). Colombian forces, in turn, undertook some regional security missions, such as antisubmarine and counterespionage operations. The Colombian government did not send troops overseas, like Brazil and Mexico, but it did contribute to regional stability, including the defense of the Panama Canal.

After the war Colombian and American officials collaborated in the formation of new international organizations. Colombian diplomat Alberto Lleras Camargo was the principal representative of Latin American interests at the San Francisco conference (1945). He successfully advocated for the rights of regional organizations, such as the Pan-American Union, under the new UN structure. Two years later, in Rio de Janeiro, Brazil, Colombian and U.S. representatives brokered an Inter-American defense pact providing for a regional response to any attack on an American state by an extracontinental aggressor. Then, at the Bogotá conference (1948), they worked together to create the Organization of American States (OAS), a strong international body to replace the Pan-American Union. Alberto Lleras served as the first OAS director general.

LA VIOLENCIA AND THE EARLY COLD WAR

Internally a political, religious, and economic conflict, known as *la Violencia* (1946–1958), erupted in Colombia. It began as a political dispute during the 1946 presidential election. *La Violencia* accelerated following the assassination of Liberal party leader Jorge Eliécer Gaitán in April 1948. The following year Mariano Ospina Pérez (President 1946–1950) declared a state of siege, ruling Colombia by executive decree.

Aspects of *la Violencia* troubled the Harry S. Truman (1945–1953) administration. U.S. policymakers wanted to support democracies in Latin America. The conservative governments of Ospina and Laureano Gómez (President 1950–1953), they concluded, exhibited characteristics of authoritarian regimes. In particular U.S. officials objected to the treatment of U.S. protestants in Colombia, many of whom were targets of religious violence. Yet Colombia's international position in the cold war against communism kept the two countries linked in mutually beneficial ways.

In 1950 President Gómez, a strong anticommunist, decided to join the U.S.-led UN command in Korea. A Colombian infantry battalion and warship arrived in the western Pacific in 1951. That same year in Washington, Colombian diplomats were key agents of hemispheric unity at the Fourth Meeting of Foreign Ministers of American States. The conference produced recommendations for the creation of the Military Assistance Program, which included grant funds to support Latin American military units for hemisphere defense.

In Korea the Colombian armed forces made a meaningful contribution to the UN effort. The Colombian battalion engaged in heavy combat during the Kumsong offensive (October 1951) and at Old Baldy (March 1953). The Colombian frigate ARC *Almirante Padilla* performed escort, blockade, and bombardment missions in Yellow Sea and Sea of

At Washington, D.C.'s, National Airport in April 1960, U.S. President Dwight D. Eisenhower (front left) greets Colombian President Alberto Lleras Camargo (front middle), who came to the United States to seek additional security assistance. U.S.-Colombian collaboration on the anticommunist Cold War has since given way to joint military action against illegal drugs and terrorism.

SOURCE: Photography by Abbie Rowe, Courtesy of the National Park Service, NARA

Japan. When the ship returned to South America in 1952, the Colombian Navy purchased two additional frigates to continue its work with the UN armada.

The United States provided economic and military assistance to Colombia during the early Cold War. Between 1945 and 1950 the U.S. government provided little direct aid to Latin America. After 1950, however, Latin American countries, including Colombia, received greater attention. U.S. authorities provided economic assistance for health, infrastructure, and educational projects in Colombia. As for military aid, before 1953 U.S. officials refused to deliver certain types of material to Colombia. The Ospina and Gómez administrations, they feared, would employ U.S. equipment against Colombians during *la Violencia*. Still Colombia's involvement in the Korean War ensured the delivery of significant U.S. foreign assistance, including military aid through the Military Assistance Program.

In June 1953, a few weeks before the Korean War ended, the Colombian armed forces toppled the Gómez regime. Upon taking power the military government of Gustavo Rojas Pinilla (President 1953–1957) made good progress on a variety of domestic issues, including lowering the levels of internal violence. At first the Dwight D. Eisenhower (President 1953–1961) administration, keen on stability in Latin America, supported the Colombian military experiment in Colombia. In addition Colombia's military contribution to the UN Emergency Force during the Suez Crisis (1956) gratified U.S. officials. It marked the beginning of Colombia's long-term involvement in Middle East peacekeeping.

Yet as the Colombian internal situation deteriorated, the Eisenhower administration expressed its preference for civilian government in Colombia. U.S. Ambassador Philip W. Bonsal clashed with General Rojas over the military's handling of the Colombian press and other internal issues. In early 1957 the Rojas regime, in poor financial condition, requested a financial bailout package from Washington. Not wanting Rojas to continue in power, the Eisenhower administration balked while a liberal and conservative political coalition took action. In 1958 the National Front Coalition, led by Alberto Lleras, restored civil government to Colombia.

Between 1958 and 1960 the Eisenhower administration, determined to support democracies in Latin America, provided the Alberto Lleras government (President 1958–1962) with significant economic assistance. Vice President Richard Nixon's tumultuous tour of South America (1958) and the Cuban Revolution (1959) suggested that friendly regional governments might succumb to communist insurgencies.

The administration decided to increase direct U.S. economic aid to Latin America, including an expansion of the Inter-American Development Bank and creation of the Social Progress Trust Fund, both benefiting Colombia. With the National Front government, U.S. policymakers, including influential U.S. Ambassador John Moors Cabot, worked to address the conditions (poverty, inequality) that gave rise to communist government through U.S.-supported education, health, and development programs.

Then in 1960, responding to the Colombian president's request for internal security assistance, Eisenhower agreed to convert the Colombian-American security relationship into an alliance designed to promote Colombian domestic tranquility. During World War II and the early Cold War, U.S. and Colombian military officers concentrated on creating compatible military units to defend the Americans against conventional threats. Beginning in 1961 the United States provided direct U.S. military aid to Colombian forces involved in internal security operations, a program later expanded by John F. Kennedy (President 1961–1963).

COOPERATION AND EXCHANGE IN THE MID-TWENTIETH CENTURY

In 1961 President Kennedy announced the Alliance for Progress. In the years thereafter, Colombia became a major recipient of U.S. aid. In December 1961 Kennedy visited Bogotá to advertise Inter-American cooperation—and discuss with President Lleras issues of mutual concern. Carlos Lleras Restrepo (President 1966–1970) criticized aspects of the Alliance for Progress and U.S. international lending practices. The two countries, however, remained closely aligned in pursuit of shared interests. By 1968 Colombia had received $833 million in U.S. economic assistance through the Alliance for Progress.

At the same time the U.S. military supported the Colombian civic action program known as Plan Lazo, designed to promote domestic stability and development. In Colombia the Alliance for Progress failed to achieve its stated objectives; major socioeconomic problems remained. Yet by the end of the decade the Colombian government, with U.S. support, had addressed some major internal problems and largely eliminated antigovernment guerrilla groups, formed during the early 1960s, including the Revolutionary Armed Forces of Colombia (FARC).

The Colombian-American cultural exchange deepened during the mid-twentieth century. In the early 1900s Colombian students and travelers carried U.S. culture to Colombia. A few years later American film became popular in major Colombian cities. The gradual growth in bilateral contact during the 1930s and 1940s influenced both countries; government-sponsored programs exposed citizens in both countries to music, art, and literature. The Fulbright Program, established in 1946, supported the educational exchange of Colombian and American scholars. U.S. Peace Corps volunteers began living and working in Colombia in 1962.

While European influences remained strong in Colombia, American culture gained widespread acceptance among Colombian citizens. Conversely Colombian musicians, painters, and writers began touring the United States. Major exhibits in Washington, Miami, and elsewhere exposed thousands of U.S. citizens to Colombian culture; Colombian writers, such as Nobel Prize winner Gabriel García Márquez, attracted large audiences in the United States.

Colombia entered a period of impressive economic growth during the 1970s, deepening commercial and trade relations between the two republics. Indeed the level of direct U.S. foreign investment in Colombia doubled between 1970 and 1975. The stability of Colombian democratic institutions, in contrast to the regional trend toward dictatorship, attracted many U.S. businesses. At an official level, however, the size and scope of bilateral projects declined during mid-decade. Indeed U.S. economic aid to Latin America dipped for domestic political and economic reasons. The United States also trimmed its foreign military assistance program after the Vietnam War.

In Colombia Alfonso López Michelsen (President 1974–1978) broke with the United States on several key diplomatic issues. He supported the reintegration of Cuba into the Inter-American system and Panamanian demands during the Panama Canal Treaties negotiations. Julio César Turbay Ayala (President 1978–1982) later reversed Colombia's position on some contentious matters. Throughout Colombian-American officials remained connected on other key issues, an indication of the ongoing compatibility of U.S.-Colombian interests.

DRUG WAR

By the end of the decade the international drug trade concerned U.S. and Colombian policymakers—as did the deterioration of Colombia's domestic security situation. When demand for cocaine exploded, Colombian cartels started moving cocaine from South America to the United States and beyond. In Colombia the narco-traffickers corrupted public institutions through bribery, intimidation, and violence. The growth of the drug trade and related developments invigorated several antigovernment guerrilla groups, notably FARC. In many areas right-wing paramilitary units appeared to combat the guerrillas.

In 1978 Colombian and American officials launched the first major counterdrug operation in South America. The two governments signed a comprehensive extradition treaty (1979) and the Jimmy Carter (President 1977–1981) and Ronald Reagan (President 1981–1989) administrations provided Bogotá with significant counternarcotics assistance. In December 1982 President Reagan met Colombian Belisario Betancur Cuartas (President 1982–1986) in Bogotá to discuss, among other things, Colombian-American counterdrug cooperation. Although Reagan and Betancur disagreed on some matters, such as the best way to handle the Central American crisis, they partnered on other key international projects, including the effort against transnational crime. After the Medellín cartel assassinated Justice Minister Rodrigo Lara Bonilla (1984), President Betancur declared war on the cartel. By the end of the decade the United States was supporting, with direct U.S. assistance, a full range of counterdrug activities in Colombia.

Each year, between 1988 and 1992, the United States sent approximately $100 million in counternarcotics aid to Colombia. In February 1990 George H. W. Bush (President 1989–1993) attended an international meeting on the control of illicit trafficking in Cartagena. Colombian authorities extradited some traffickers to the United States; U.S. government contractors worked on crop eradication projects. American agents played an important part in bringing down Medellín drug kingpin Pablo Escobar Gaviria (1993). By 1994 Colombian-American cooperation had damaged the cartels. Still the drug trade flourished among small traffickers and, increasingly, armed groups such as FARC.

For Colombia and the United States, certain bilateral problems arose after the election of Ernesto Samper Pizano (President 1994–1998). In Colombia allegations surrounding Sampar's link to the Cali cartel created problems for U.S. officials. The U.S. government eventually revoked Samper's visa, barring him from visiting the United States. On the ground Colombian military human rights abuses—and connections to rightwing paramilitary organizations—raised moral issues for the Bill Clinton (President 1993–2001) administration.

In 1996 the U.S. Congress decertified Colombia as a partner in the war on drugs, rendering the republic ineligible for U.S. security assistance. Without U.S. aid, the Colombian government struggled to defend major population centers against the guerrilla armies, funded with profits from the drug trade. The Colombian economy contracted; U.S. business in Colombia, considered by many too risky, rapidly declined. Colombia appeared on the verge of complete collapse—an imploding, failed state at the geographic center of the western hemisphere.

Amid the internal chaos tens of thousands of Colombians migrated to the United States during the late twentieth century. In doing so expatriates spread Colombian culture to major U.S. cities. Grammy Award winning singer-songwriter Shakira became a popular sensation in the United States following the release of her 1998 album, *¿Dónde Están Los Ladrones?* Later the American television series, *Ugly Betty*, based on the Fernando Gaitán Salom's telenovela *Yo soy Betty, la fea*, captivated U.S. viewers and won numerous awards, including three Emmys and two Golden Globes.

Meanwhile, in Colombia, Andrés Pastrana Arango (President 1998–2002) developed a state-building program called Plan Colombia. The plan called for the development of counterdrug forces, supported by the United States, to break the drug trade, thereby weakening the FARC. The U.S. government supported the plan, recertified Colombia, and promised to deliver significant U.S. assistance to the country. By design the United States would provide security assistance; European countries would back Pastrana with economic aid. The U.S. Congress limited U.S. aid to combating the drug trade in Colombia—the Colombian security forces could not engage the FARC with Plan Colombia military equipment.

In August 2000 President Clinton traveled to Cartagena to discuss Plan Colombia implementation with President Pastrana. By the end of the Pastrana presidency, the two countries had achieved some important bilateral goals. However the Colombian government's negotiation with the FARC had collapsed, and the economic component had failed to materialize. The two countries were nonetheless poised to make significant progress over the years ahead.

Working within the Plan Colombia framework, Álvaro Uribe Vélez (President 2002–2010) developed and implemented a multidimensional internal security strategy. The Uribe initiative included major economic and judicial reforms. The George W. Bush (President 2001–2009) administration strongly supported the Colombian initiative. In 2002, after the terrorist al-Qaeda attacks, the U.S. government lifted restrictions on U.S. assistance, allowing Colombians to employ Plan Colombia material against illegally armed groups, including FARC, classified as terrorist organizations by the U.S. Department of State. Throughout, the capabilities of Colombian security forces increased—evident during the dramatic 2008 recovery of U.S. and Colombian hostages held by FARC. Overall the U.S. government invested more than $6 billion in Plan Colombia between 1999 and 2009.

In a region increasingly hostile toward the United States, Colombia emerged as the key U.S. ally in South America during the early twenty-first century. With U.S. assistance the Colombian internal security, economic, and social situation improved dramatically. Although focused on the Middle East and Central Asia, Barack Obama (President 2009–) administration pursued a series of bilateral agreements to strengthen Colombia, consolidate recent gains, and further Colombian-American objectives. In June 2009 officials signed a bilateral agreement to accelerate scientific and technological cooperation. A short time later Colombia and U.S. diplomats concluded negotiations on a Defense Cooperation Agreement to enhance security cooperation. A Free Trade Agreement initiated by the Bush administration, however, encountered opposition in the U.S. Congress, where it still awaits passage. Even so the nature of the contemporary Colombian-American alliance suggests that close bilateral relations will continue into the foreseeable future—advancing the national and international interests of both countries.

See also *Bidlack-Mallarino Treaty, 1846; Bolívar, Simón; Bonsal, Philip W.; Braden, Spruille; Cabot, John M.; Clayton-Bulwer Treaty, 1850; Clinton, William J.; Colombia, U.S. Relations with; Communism in Latin America; Convention Against Illicit Traffic in Narcotic Drugs and Psychotropic Substances, 1988; de Lesseps, Ferdinand Marie; Escobar Gaviria, Pablo; Good Neighbor Policy; Hay-Herrán Treaty, 1903; Hull, Cordell; Inter-American Coffee Agreement, 1940; Korean War, 1950–1953; Lehder Rivas, Carlos; Lleras Camargo, Alberto; Mutual Security Act, 1951 (United States); Ninth International Conference of American States, Bogotá, 1948; Organization of American States (OAS); Pan American Airways; Pan-American Union; Panama Railroad; Protestantism in Latin America; Roosevelt, Franklin D.; Roosevelt, Theodore; Root-Cortés Treaty, 1909; Social Progress Trust Fund; Thomson-Urruita Treaty, 1914; United Fruit Company (UFCO); U.S. Military Assistance Program; Watermelon War, 1856; World War I, 1914–1918; World War II, 1939–1945*

. . . . BRADLEY LYNN COLEMAN

REFERENCES AND FURTHER READING

Coleman, Bradley Lynn. *Colombia and the United States: The Making of an Inter-American Alliance, 1939–1960.* Kent, OH: Kent State University Press, 2008.

DeShazo, Peter, Tanya Primiani, and Phillip McLean. *Back from the Brink: Evaluating Progress in Colombia, 1999–2007.* Washington, DC: Center for Strategic and International Studies Press, 2007.

Park, E. Taylor. *Colombia and the United States, 1765–1934.* Durham, NC: Duke University Press, 1935.

Randall, Stephen J. *Colombia and the United States: Hegemony and Interdependence.* Athens: University of Georgia Press, 1992.

Commercial Bureau of the American Republics

(**See** *First International Conference of American States, Washington, 1889*)

Committee For Political Defense

(**See** *World War II, 1939–1945*)

Communism in Latin America

Communism in Latin America has two forms, distinct, yet not unrelated: orthodox communist ideology, and local communist ideology. The important distinction is that the former is primarily externally based, drawing its support and ideological positions from the more institutional/governmental activities of Communist political parties, whether in power or in opposition. The latter is more local in its ideology, manifest in less formally constituted groups and deviating somewhat from the traditional Marxist/Leninist framework. However these forms are not mutually exclusive and can overlap into hybrid forms, as they have done in the past. Indeed it may be more accurate to refer to these local ideologies as leftist rather than communist, but their positions on redistribution and social justice, and their tendency toward anti-Americanism, are similar enough to be considered communist movements.

LOCAL COMMUNIST IDEOLOGY

José Carlos Mariátegui (1894–1930) has been claimed by both camps of Latin American communism, the institutional PCP (Communist Party of Peru) and Sendero Luminoso (the Shining Path). Mariátegui is often cited within Latin America as among the first, and perhaps the most influential, Marxists of that region. Other, more nationally known, leftist revolutionaries during this time included Ricardo Flores Magon, founder of the anarchist Mexican Liberal party, and Luiz Carlos Prestes, leader of the Brazilian Communist party in the early 1900's.

Mariátegui's most famous work, *Seven Essays of Interpretation of Peruvian Reality,* is a materialist analysis of Peruvian society. In this work he identifies the working class as being important in any form of revolutionary movement, but he also argues for a revolutionary strategy that includes the Indian population as a force for socialism. Land is the foundation of the struggle, and the communal connection the Indians retain with the land makes them the cornerstone of any economic change. Mariátegui emphasizes the role of indigenous cultures, stating that at the base of Incan civilization was an "agrarian communism" that yielded economic results superior to those of colonial Peru.

Mariátegui's work has influenced many, including Che Guevara. Both men are considered Marxists, yet their interpretation of Marxism in the Latin American context allows for the dominance of agrarian issues over urban industrial relations and the possibility that the indigenous, rural population could have a strong role in the revolution, although such was not the case in the Cuban Revolution. For Guevara (and Castro, as well) Marxist theory was a guide to action, but the road differed according to context; after the Cuban Revolution, Guevara moved from a proletariat-based economic analysis to one more centered on the latifundian relationship between land owner and peasant, and he developed Foquismo, a peasant-centered guerrilla strategy.

Subcomandante Marcos, of the Zapatista movement in southern Mexico, supports the indigenous role and the unique context mentioned by both Guevara and Mariátegui. He also speaks to the important function of translation, not solely in terms of language but also in terms of culture and cosmology. When the Zapatista Army of National Liberation (EZLN) "crashed" (Marcos calls it the *"choque"*) into the indigenous culture, the organization learned that success would hinge on it being less a vanguard and more a representative of indigenous communities, with indigenous goals and values. The need for a translation of indigenous cultures into the movement is vital to its (the movement's) success.

Indigenous communist movements are anchored in land distribution issues, but they reflect numerous areas of exclusion and oppression. Lack of access to social, health, and market services, displacement of communities in favor of economic development, and little or no political recognition within their countries facilitate the connection to a Marxist/Leninist ideology. Yet their philosophical treatment of "the Other" as being a focal point of identity and resistance is more related to anarchy-communism than it is the Marxist-Leninist vanguard strategies. The complete and continuous rejection of the formalization of authority and the use of voluntarism and consensus practiced by the Zapatistas parallel the earlier ideas of Flores Magon.

The Brazilian Communist party office in Rio de Janeiro, 1965, appears to be celebrating the party's forty-second anniversary. After a coup orchestrated by General Humberto Castelo Branco in 1964, any movement toward communism in Brazil was effectively suppressed and did not play a leading role in U.S.-Brazilian relations, in contrast to U.S. interactions with other Latin American nations.

SOURCE: National Archives

TRADITIONAL MARXIST PARTIES

Parties with formal ties (actual or ideological) to international Marxism emerged in Latin America in the early twentieth century. The oldest is commonly identified as the *Partido Comunista de Chile,* which was founded as *Partido Obrero Socialista* in 1912. During the Cold War Communist parties existed in all countries in the region.

Imported from Europe, many of these parties were traditional Soviet Marxist bureaucratic party liners, with the Chilean example noted earlier being an obvious exception, since it predated the Soviet Union by about five years. These parties favored the proletarian approach in that their core, their strength, was in urban workers. They also favored an institutional approach with an emphasis on a vanguard party made up of some workers, but also intellectuals and party elite, who would lead the workers. The parties had difficulty turning into a true force, since the development process of Latin American countries had not progressed to the point where the urban proletariat was a large or coherent group. Indeed using a historical argument, it has been argued that any assumption that the Latin American countries would develop along similar lines as those in Europe was a fatal error of the Communist parties. The composition of their supporters was simply not broad enough to change the system and was not likely to achieve that degree of breadth in the future. Historically, then, Latin America Communist parties have followed a fairly pacific approach to their cause, waiting for the right time. Their time may have passed, without them really being aware of it. Jorge Castañeda, in *Utopia Unarmed,* describes them as tribunal parties, defending the interests of an increasingly incoherent constituency, but ceasing their struggle to win power over the system.

Some Communist parties that are part of the World Communist Movement are grouped around the Communist Party of the Soviet Union (CPSU) model and still adhere to Marxism/Leninism. These parties include the Communist party of Argentina, the Communist party of Chile, the Colombian Communist party, the Communist party of Cuba (*Fuerza de la Revolución*), the Peruvian Communist party, and the Communist party of Venezuela. As parties based on Marxist ideology, they stress the priority of distribution over accumulation and/or the exploitation of the working class (similar to the indigenous philosophy discussed earlier). Further, they advocate a strong role for the state to correct social and economic injustices. The indigenous movements are not quite as committed to working within the state system.

Based on work done by Michael Coppedge, the following table reflects the presence of identified Marxist/Leninist parties for selected periods of the twentieth century.

Overall, the presence of Marxist-Leninist parties declined in the 1990's from the previous decade, but otherwise represents a consistent increase across the board.

SIGNIFICANT COMMUNIST STRUGGLES

The following is a brief overview of four countries where both indigenous and institutional party structures have formed the basis for communist struggles. Bolivia and Mexico are countries where the indigenous influence is very strong, and Nicaragua and Cuba represent countries where more traditional Communist parties have spearheaded revolutions.

BOLIVIA

Bolivia remains primarily rural with very little possibility of an urban proletariat, and there is still a close to sharecropping relationship between the *hacendados* and the Indians. As the poorest nation on the continent, Bolivia is an example of both types of communist struggle, party driven and movement driven. In 1952 the National Revolutionary Movement (NRM), headed by Víctor Paz Estenssoro, took power. The Paz government redistributed political and economic opportunities in ways favorable to the Indians—reorganization of the latifundia system, nationalization of the tin companies, and abolishment of the literacy requirement for voting. After 1952 a major organization with a traditional leftist approach composed of both miners and urban workers, the *Central Obrera de Bolivia* (COB), was formed. Though the group had achieved some land reform, COB was by and large rejected by the indigenous and ignored by the government, and it did not participate with traditional political parties. The group continued participation in local governance, where members instituted and maintained communal land use.

The COB is an example of the general practice of the isolation of communist movements on the part of the government, the movements, and the indigenous. This isolation has resulted in the formation of social capital and indigenous identity outside the political frame. Since then communist ideologies have been promulgated primarily through social movements, some more formal than others. There has been a rise in Indian left movements, for example, the Guerrilla Army of Tupac Katari (EGTK, or *Kataristas*), but most influence has been wielded through the social movement structure.

At the beginning of the twenty-first century popular social movements pressured the government for redistribution. In 2000 the first Water War occurred in Bolivia's third largest city, Cochabamba. After five months of public revolt the people of Cochabamba regained control of their water system from U.S. giant Bechtel and its water-privatizing partners. The second Water War occurred in El Alto, where privatization of water and sewer services had caused an increase in prices to $445 a year, in a country where the average minimum wage is about $66 a month.

The Gas War reached its nexus in 2003, with strikes, road blocks, and mass protests led by both indigenous and labor groups (including the COB). The fight was based on a distributional issue, with the social movement protesting the international exploitation and exportation of the gas resources, without providing for domestic consumption.

The social movement option, uniting indigenous and traditional groups, has in recent times been bolstered by the election of Evo Morales in 2006, leader of the Socialist Movement (MAS), a left political party that was active in the water and gas wars.

MEXICO

The Mexican Revolution (1910–1920) demonstrates the difficulty of classifying left movements as being traditionally Marxist or representative of local communist ideology. Although Adolfo Gilly identifies the revolution as a commodity war brought on by inherent contradictions of expansionary capitalism, he also emphasizes the complexity of the struggle—from bourgeoisie to peasant and from north (Pancho Villa) to south (Emiliano Zapata). In the 1920s both the United States and the Soviet Union interpreted it as being a Bolshevik revolution, the former fearing communism in its sphere of influence and the latter hoping to use Mexico as a base to build Communist parties throughout the region. Both

TABLE 1: NUMBER OF MARXIST PARTIES IN SELECT COUNTRIES DURING THE TWENTIETH CENTURY

		1912–1939	1940–1959	1960s	1970s	1980s	1990s
Argentina	(1912–1995)	6	2	5	4	7	11
Bolivia	(1956–1993)		2	3	2	13	3
Brasil	(1945–1994)		5			4	6
Chile	(1915–1993)	5	9	6	5	5	5
Colombia	(1931–1994)		2		2	2	5
Costa Rica	(1948–1994)		1	1	6	2	5
Ecuador	(1947–1994)		4	1	3	3	4
México	(1961–1994)			1	2	3	2
Perú	(1931–1995)			3	6	10	3
Uruguay	(1917–1994)	2	2	3	1	1	1
Venezuela	(1947–1993)		3	1	6	8	2
Total		13	30	24	37	58	4

Source: Adapted from Coppedge, Michael. "A Classification of Latin American Political Parties." Working Paper #244 http://nd.edu/~kellogg/publications/workingpapers/WPS/244.pdf (November 1977). Calculations by the author.

the United States and the Soviet Union underestimated the local character of the revolution and overestimated the results.

Zapata's social programs in the south did have a lasting legacy, emerging in the 1990s. In 1994 on the eve of Mexico signing the North American Free Trade Agreement (NAFTA), a guerrilla rebellion in Chiapas led by the EZLN attempted to overthrow the government, but it was quickly suppressed by government troops. Marcos describes the struggle of the indigenous against neoliberalism as one where the very cultural, physical, and historical identity of the indigenous is threatened.

Since then a parallel group has formed, with more civic and cultural objectives than the more militant EZLN—the Zapatista community. The Zapatistas continue their struggle for the redistribution of land, and in 2001 they declared thirty-two autonomous communities in Chiapas. Each community member contributes through participation in one or more institutions: the three member Good Government Juntas, the political decision makers for the Caracoles (government centers for the communities); the social process (currently, most evident in health care); and the economic process (autonomous centers of distribution and new agricultural mechanisms of production). Yet the Zapatistas move beyond traditional revolutionary approaches. Rather than bring more people into old spaces of participation, they have introduced new spaces into the existing power network. The resistance is not merely reactionary, working against the Mexican government's increasingly neoliberal agenda; it is a positive and creative act.

CUBA

Castro communism runs directly counter to the traditional tactics of Marxist/Leninist Communist parties, even though Cuba represents the strongest tie to Soviet influence in the twentieth century. Che Guevara, in *Guerilla Warfare,* states that the Cuban Revolution contributed three fundamental lessons to the conduct of movements in Latin America. First, popular forces can win against the enemy. Second, it is not necessary to wait until all conditions for revolutions exist; they can be created. Finally, in underdeveloped Latin America, the countryside is the basic area for armed fighting.

Fidel Castro's overthrow of Cuban leader Fulgencio Batista on New Year's Day 1959 is the center-point of most discussions on communism in Latin America. Castro, with two influential companions—Che Guevara and Camilo Cienfuegos—led a successful two-year guerrilla campaign called the 26th of July movement (the date of the guerrilla capture of the Moncada Barracks in 1953, when Castro was captured by government troops). The collapse of the Batista government came sooner than perhaps even Castro had anticipated, and it opened the way to an institutionalization of the five revolutionary laws Castro had referred to in his 1953 court appearance after his arrest. In his speech titled, "History Will Absolve Me" (1968), Castro outlined these objectives: the assumption of political power by the people (represented through the revolutionary movement), agrarian reform, 30 percent share of industrial enterprises, 55 percent share of sugar production, and the confiscation of fraudulent holdings.

There was no mention of communism in this speech, nor was any formal declaration of communist ideology ever mentioned during the guerrilla campaign. The guerrilla fighters were primarily students and middle class, with limited involvement of peasants or of any organized labor. Only late in the movement did the Communist party offer its support. It was not until 1965 that the Cuban Communist party was formed and established formal ties with the international structure. The Soviet relationship, which was to become an economic lifeline to Cuba after the 1961 U.S. trade embargo, was not established until 1960.

Castro's form of communism did involve the redistribution of land, the establishment of universal education and health care, and a complete overhaul of the political system. The smallest political units are the Committees in Defense of the Revolution organized at the community level. They have various functions, including monitoring activities within the neighborhoods, organizing political and social events, mobilizing support, and so forth. Interpretations of the functions vary; some may see it as a form of local control, whereas others see it as a way to actively involve the population in civic activities. On the national level there is a Council of Ministers (the president is a member of the council), a National Assembly of People's Power, and a People's Supreme Court. Cuba faced a number of challenges to its communist regime when the Soviet Union collapsed. In order to bolster a flagging economy after 1991, Cuba opened its doors to limited tourism and foreign direct investment. In addition to initiating more porous borders, Cuba also needed to introduce economic reforms to attract foreign investment, such as the licensing of small businesses and entrepreneurial activities, the legalization of the U.S. dollar, and the reduction of the state role in agricultural production and consumption. These efforts have been moderately successful, but the United States continues its attempts to isolate Cuba, with the Torricelli Act (1992) and the Helms-Burton Act (1996), which contain language that punishes firms investing in Cuba. Even though President Barack Obama relaxed the embargo in April 2009 by permitting remittances and some limited travel, there continues to be a strained relation between the two countries.

NICARAGUA

The Nicaraguan Revolution in 1979 established a left government, focused on redistribution of land and benefits and the establishment of a socialist political and economic system. The Sandinistas (formally the FSLN, Sandinista National Liberation Front) had formed in 1961 under Carlos Fonseca, with no formal ties to communist ideology or Communist party structures. The FSLN represented a broad spectrum of revolutionary groups, divided into three factions: 1) the Proletarian tendency, committed to organize workers and youth as a precondition to action; 2) the Prolonged popular war tendency, focused on the mobilization of the peasantry to fight a long-term conflict; and 3) the insurrectional tendency (*terceristas*), emphasizing broad class alliances and a rapid overthrow through simultaneous rural and urban struggle. Prior to the FSLN victory, Fonseca was killed, succeeded by Daniel Ortega.

The Sandinista political ideology set it apart from the Soviet style of communism in that it believed that revolution could be improvised and that subjective conditions could create objective conditions. This is very much like Guevara's comments on the Cuban Revolution, stating it is possible to change consciousness. The flexibility within the movement found in the three factions of the FSLN was required due to the many faces of dependency in the twentieth and the twenty-first centuries. Whereas traditional Marxism states that the only group that really had consciousness was the working class and that the capitalists were a clearly defined group, even when they became the global finance capitalists identified by Lenin, a neoliberalist interpretation of globalization creates an enemy much less specific than that envisioned by either Marx or Lenin, an actor that is internal and external.

The Sandinistas held power from 1979 to 1990. Their political and social structure was similar to Cuba's, although the variety of interests encompassed by the FSLN resulted in more complex power arrangements, and the economic program and approach to land reform was slightly more market oriented than what was in place in Cuba. Land redistribution was primarily targeted on *Somocista* holdings, and nationalization of industries was limited to approximately 30 percent. Relations with the United States were strained and the international embargo, coupled with U.S. support for opposition forces (the contras, for example), resulted in the electoral removal of the FSLN in 1984.

COMMUNISM IN THE TWENTY-FIRST CENTURY

The left has seen great advancements in Latin America in the last decade, both in electoral politics and in the success of indigenous or broader social movements. As of 2010 over half the governments in Latin America are to the left of the political spectrum, many of which are on their second or third term of office. These governments have attained legitimacy due to successful economic programs and moderate ideological stances. Yet these political parties are increasingly divergent from the more radical and socially minded movements. Indigenous groups and social movements, such as those in Bolivia and southern Mexico, focus on a larger international foe—neoliberalism—while the left political parties concentrate on a more national agenda. The future does not promise any compromise between the two forces, and it is likely that the communist ideology in Latin America and the world will be significantly altered by their struggle.

See also *Bolivia, U.S. Relations with; Council of Mutual Economic Assistance (COMECON); Cuba, U.S. Relations with; Dulles, John Foster; Farabundo Martí National Liberation Front (FMLN) (El Salvador); Grenada, U.S. Invasion of, 1983; Guevara de la Serna, Ernesto "Che"; Johnson Doctrine; Khrushchev, Nikita; Mexico, U.S. Relations with; Nicaragua, U.S. Relations with; Soviet Union, Latin American Policy*

. . . . PEGGY ANN JAMES

References and Further Reading

Carr, Barry. *Marxism and Communism in Twentieth Century Mexico*. Lincoln: University of Nebraska Press, 1992.

Castañeda, Jorge G. *Utopia Unarmed*. New York: Vintage Books, 1993.

Castro, Fidel. "History Will Absolve Me." New York: The Viking Press, 1968.

Cavaluzzi, Todd, Morris Morley, James Petras, and Steve Vieux. *The Left Strikes Back: Class Conflict in Latin America in the Age of Neoliberalism*. Boulder, CO: Westview Press, 1999.

Coppedge, Michael. "A Classification of Latin American Political Parties." Working Paper no. 244, http://nd.edu/~kellogg/publications/workingpapers/WPS/244.pdf, November 1997.

Gilly, Adolfo. *The Mexican Revolution*. New York: The New Press, 2005.

Guevara, Che, Brian Loveman, and Thomas Davies. *Guerrilla Warfare*, 3rd ed. Lanham, MD: Rowman and Littlefield, 1997.

Mariátegui, Jose Carlos. *Seven Interpretive Essays on Peruvian Reality*. Austin: University of Texas Press, 1988.

Mudimbe-boyi, Elisabeth. *Beyond Dichotomies: Histories, Identities, Cultures, and the Challenge of Globalization*. Albany, NY: SUNY Press, 2002.

Spenser, Daniela. *The Impossible Triangle: Mexico, Soviet Russia, and the United States in the 1920s*. Durham, NC: Duke University Press, 1999.

Weyland, Kurt, Raúl L. Madrid, and Wendy Hunter, eds. *Leftist Governments in Latin America*. New York: Cambridge University Press, 2010.

Confederation of Central American States (1823–1839)

(**See** *United Provinces of Central America, 1823–1839*)

Confederation of Latin American Workers (CTAL)

The Confederation of Latin American Workers (CTAL) was founded on September 8, 1938, in Mexico City by delegations from thirteen Latin American countries. Vicente Lombardo Toledano, then the general secretary of the

Confederation of Mexican Workers (CTM), had the support of President Lázaro Cárdenas to create a workers' organization of hemispheric reach to bolster Mexico's anti-imperial economic policies. CTAL became the hemisphere's preeminent international labor organization for the decade from 1938 to 1948.

Nominally Marxist, CTAL adopted a reformist agenda that stressed anti-imperialism and adhered to the Communist International's antifascist Popular Front strategy. This enhanced CTAL's appeal to nationalist unions in Latin America and even to unions with close government ties. The North American Congress of Industrial Workers (CIO) supported CTAL, while the American Federation of Labor (AFL) rejected it as a communist organization. The administration of Franklin Delano Roosevelt compelled the AFL to take a more conciliatory line in the interest of hemispheric solidarity, however, not least because Toledano enthusiastically supported the idea of the Good Neighbor policy.

In 1941 CTAL called on its members to support the Allied cause and stressed Pan-Americanism over anti-imperialism. The commitment to the joint war effort led CTAL to adopt a no-strike policy, which severely restricted labor's ability to take advantage of its strong bargaining position and triggered accusations by leftist critics of a sell-out to the bourgeoisie. Toledano continued to pursue a Popular-National Front-Unity policy to form broad alliances, both with progressive governments and amongst different sectors of the labor movement, in order to prepare the ground for the founding of a worldwide labor federation. CTAL's Calí Congress in 1944 established the agenda for the immediate postwar period: democratic national unity governments, comprehensive economic development programs to reduce dependence on U.S. capital, and regional integration to counteract imperialism.

CTAL began to face powerful opposition from the United States. Starting in 1943 the Office of the Coordinator of Inter-American Affairs (OIAA) cooperated with the AFL and the International Labor Organization (ILO) to diminish CTAL's influence in the hemisphere. The AFL's emissary, Serafino Romuladi, worked to divide the labor movement in Latin America by supporting anti-CTAL groups and unions that welcomed foreign capital and labor-management cooperation. When the U.S. delegation unveiled the Clayton Plan at the Chapultepec conference in 1945, CTAL denounced it as a return to imperialist economic policies and called instead for state-led economic development throughout Latin America. Its Soviet connections, the affiliation with the World Federation of Trade Unions (WFTU), and opposition to U.S. postwar foreign policy made CTAL a prime target of Cold War repression by U.S.-friendly Latin American governments. The crackdown on its affiliates greatly diminished CTAL's influence by 1948; many former members adopted a nationalist position and some sided with AFL-sponsored organizations. The founding of the AFL-friendly Inter-American Federation of Workers (CIT) in 1948 and of the International Confederation of Free Trade Unions (ICFTU) sealed CTAL's fate. It existed as a phantom organization throughout the 1950s and dissolved officially in January 1964.

See also *Coordinator of Inter-American Affairs, Office of, World War II; Inter-American Federation of Labor (CIT); International Confederation of Free Trade Unions (ICFTU); Lombardo Toledano, Vicente*

. . . . OLIVER J. DINIUS

REFERENCES AND FURTHER READING

Kofas, Jon V. *The Struggle for Legitimacy: Latin American Labor and the United States, 1930–1960*. Tempe: Arizona State University Press, 1992.

Toledano, Vicente Lombardo. *The C.T.A.L., the War and the Postwar*. Mexico City: Universidad Obrera de Mexico, 1945.

Conference of American States on Conciliation and Arbitration, Washington, 1928–1929

The 1923 endorsement of the Gondra Treaty during the Fifth International Conference of American States had stopped short of mandating binding arbitration in all disputes between hemispheric powers. The Inter-American Commission of Jurists inserted into its provisional code of rights and duties of American states language that outlawed any intervention by one state in the internal affairs of another. This led to even stronger debates and disagreements during the Sixth International Conference, when Latin American delegations pushed for a resolution that banned interference of any sort by one American state in affairs of another. Charles Evans Hughes, the head of the U.S. delegation, asserted that a move to protect the rights of property or of citizens made temporary "interpositions" allowable under international law. In the wake of bitter discussions relating to resolutions that banned war and military force in Inter-American disputes, the conferees called for a meeting that would design institutions and procedures that would promote conciliation and arbitration in such cases. Shifts in thinking, highlighted by Hughes' public endorsements of a proposal made by Panamanian delegate Ricardo Alfaro, appeared to open the way for a broad agreement.

CONTENTS OF THE TREATIES

The U.S. government, following Secretary of State Frank B. Kellogg's lead, invited representatives from the American states to meet in Washington, D.C., for the purposes of producing resolutions that condemned war and that established a system of arbitration and conflict resolution for international disputes involving American countries. With the exception of Argentina, which failed to officially authorize and fund its delegation, all states sent representatives.

After four weeks of negotiations and debate, the conference presented two compacts: the General Convention on Inter-American Conciliation and the General Treaty of Inter-American Arbitration, which included the Additional Protocol of Progressive Arbitration. The first treaty expanded the authority of the conciliation commissions that had been put into place by the Gondra Treaty and the agreements made at the Fifth International Conference of American Republics. It gave these commissions new authority to investigate all disputes involving two or more states. It also allowed a commission, based upon the findings of its investigations, to facilitate negotiations between states involved in disputes. Further the commissions could take a conciliatory role leading to resolution of disputes without having first obtained permission from one or more of the parties involved.

Following the convention guidelines, disputes not resolved through negotiation would move forward for investigation and arbitration. A separate Arbitration Treaty defined the process that would apply to all states that ratified the agreement. This commitment to mandatory arbitration of disputes pertained to all disputes except those that fit entirely within the domestic jurisdiction of one of the parties involved, with no element or issue subject to international law and those involving one or more states that had not ratified the agreement.

The Additional Protocol allowed states to clear the exceptions or qualifications that left certain issues or disputes outside the jurisdiction of the Arbitration Treaty. In theory this would expand the role of arbitration in conflict resolution as time passed and as states voluntarily subjected an expanding range of issues and disputes to the process.

IMPACT AND LEGACY OF THE CONFERENCE

The treaty was more impressive on paper than in fact. Although it was the first treaty to establish a hemispheric system to settle major disputes between American states drafted since the Second International Conference of the American States in Mexico City (1901–1902), its design limited its power. The treaty established no standing committee or body that would start the arbitration process. It required all states involved to submit to the process, and it provided no recourse in a circumstance where one or more parties involved resisted the decision of the arbitration panel. Critics asserted that the treaty represented an acceptance of arbitration as a concept but not as an obligation.

The positive and constructive international sentiments that produced the Conciliation and Arbitration treaties evaporated with the close of the 1920s. The Great Depression affected every American state. In Latin America a wave of military coups transformed the political and diplomatic scene. Many of the new dictatorships openly rejected international bodies and agreements that limited their authority and freedom of action.

Eighteen states ratified the Conciliation Treaty. By 1933, however, only ten had ratified the Arbitration Treaty and the Additional Protocol. The U.S. Senate approved the Conciliation Treaty quickly. In contrast it required the Executive Branch to negotiate distinct agreements each time a specific case came up for discussion. Each agreement would require Senate approval. The Senate also stipulated that disputes that first developed prior to the ratification of the treaty were not subject to its stipulations. These restrictions made the State Department drop its support for the treaty. Without ratification from the U.S. government the Arbitration Treaty had little impact on Latin American affairs. The exceptions and qualifications that other American states stipulated in their ratifications made the treaty completely ineffective.

See also *Fifth International Conference of American States, Santiago, 1923; Sixth International Conference of American States, Havana, 1928*

. . . . DANIEL K. LEWIS

REFERENCES AND FURTHER READING

Connell-Smith, Gordon. *The Inter-American System.* New York: Oxford University Press, 1966.

Inman, Samuel Guy. *Inter-American Conferences 1826–1954: History and Problems.* Washington, DC: The University Press of Washington DC, 1965.

Scott, James Brown. "The Pan American Conference on Conciliation and Arbitration." *The American Journal of International Law* 23, no. 1 (January 1929): 143–152.

Smith, Peter. *Talons of the Eagle: Dynamics of U.S.-Latin American Relations.* 3rd ed. New York: Oxford University Press, 2007.

Conference of Latin American Bishops (CELAM)

The Conference of Latin American Bishops (*El Consejo Episcopal Latinoamericano* or CELAM), is an organization that seeks to promote dialogue and the exchange of ideas among the various national branches of the Roman Catholic Church in Latin America, between Latin America and the "developed" world, and between Latin America and the Vatican. Headquartered in Bogotá, Colombia, its intermittent general conferences have, over the years, developed into a central venue for dispute between the conservative and radical wings of the Roman Catholic Church.

BUILDUP TO MEDELLÍN CONFERENCE

The first general conference of CELAM was held in Rio de Janeiro, Brazil, in 1955, amidst a growing sense of crisis among the Catholic laity in Latin America and some of its hierarchy. In most Latin American countries the Roman Catholic Church had traditionally been closely allied with ruling political elites and the military and supported pro-U.S., anticommunist, Christian Democratic parties. However a gulf was opening between the middle- and upper-class supporters of the church and the Catholic masses who were primarily concerned with poverty, violence, and domestic inequity. Progressive forces within the church looked on in horror as conservatives supported the massive repression of *la Violencia* in Colombia and the dictatorial regime of General Alfredo Stroessner in Paraguay.

During the 1960s, under the influence of the interpretations of Catholic doctrine that came to be known as liberation theology, and sometimes supported financially by churches in Europe and the United States, the progressive wing of the Roman Catholic Church in Latin America grew much more active and vocal. It identified poverty as the central challenge facing the church, began to organize grassroots lay groups, experimented with dependency theory as an explanation of U.S.-Latin American relations, and sometimes even endorsed revolutionary and anticapitalist challenges to dictatorial regimes. Ironically the church's formerly quietist position often meant that it retained a position of power from which to criticize unpleasant regimes when other nongovernmental and reformist actors were destroyed. These concerns were in agreement with the reforms of the Second Vatican Council (1962–1965), but the reforms were often criticized as insufficient when dealing with Latin American realities. The growing influence of the left in the Church set the scene for the dramatic events of the 1968 general conference, held in Medellín, Colombia.

At the Medellín conference, the progressive wing was able to gain emphatic declarations of the need to change the church's focus. In the conceptual framework of the Medellín report, the promotion of human life was prioritized over both growth in the faith and the formal structures of the church. This provided a powerful message to the churches in Latin America in favor of social activism and support for reforms in the political sphere and allowed for a semipolitical role for church activists in raising consciousness, particularly among *campesinos*. During the 1970s the Chilean church was notable in aligning with the Marxist regime of Salvador Allende, and elsewhere national churches were among the foremost campaigners for human rights, agrarian reform, and movement to democratic rule, especially in Brazil, El Salvador, and Chile after 1973.

AFTER MEDELLÍN

The Medellín conference also gave impetus to opponents of change, and many national churches were reluctant to endorse the Medellín report, feeling that it departed from the church's focus on eternal verities in favor of secular strategies. A major victory for the conservative camp came with the election of the Colombian bishop, Alfonso Cardinal López Trujillo, as general secretary of CELAM in 1972. The Colombian church was widely considered to be one of the most traditional in Latin America. Nevertheless liberation theology continued to gain influence during the 1970s through the semiautonomous activities of Christian-based organizations, and many outside observers anticipated another confrontation at the next general conference, planned for Puebla, Mexico, in 1979.

Efforts to end the official support for radical applications of Catholicism were unsuccessful at Puebla. Despite withholding a formal endorsement of liberation theology per se, and stressing the importance of evangelization far more than Medellín had, bishops expressed a continuing belief that the church should adopt a "preferential option for the poor." The spirit of Puebla continued to reaffirm a spirit of social action and resistance over traditional principles of resignation and charity in the face of injustice.

Radical doctrinal interpretations implemented in parts of the Latin American church after Medellín and Puebla tended to highlight differences between the "third world" institutions and the "first world" churches of Europe and North America, many of which saw poverty and right-wing dictatorship as important issues but not necessarily preeminent during the Cold War. The Vatican opposed the radical direction prevalent in the Latin American church, not only for doctrinal reasons but also because of its challenge to ecclesiastic authority. This challenge became particularly acute as the church's role in fomenting protests against the military regime of El Salvador and in support of the Sandinista revolution in Nicaragua brought elements into direct opposition with the foreign policy of the United States. Though the Vatican adopted "the preferential option for the poor" as part of its official social teaching, under the papacy of John Paul II (1978–2005), it vigorously condemned liberation theology and used its monopoly over the process of episcopal appointments to ensure that orthodox Catholic priests replaced insurgents and radicals as bishops. Cardinal Joseph Ratzinger, who became Pope Benedict XVI in 2005, was chief "enforcer" of this policy. By the turn of the century some 90 percent of Latin American bishops had been appointed by John Paul II and the authority of the Vatican was firmly reestablished.

Since Puebla CELAM has attempted to retain the earlier conferences' emphasis on evangelization while downplaying the more radical implications of its message. The fourth and fifth general conferences, held in Santo Domingo, Dominican Republic, in 1992, and Aparecida, Brazil, in 2007, attempted to grapple instead with the challenge posed by rapidly expanding Protestant evangelical churches in Central America. Critics complain that the truly original contribution of Latin America to Catholicism has been lost in a quest for hierarchy and orthodoxy, while supporters argue that CELAM continues to make an invaluable contribution in developing the institutional structure of the church in Latin America and reinvigorating a sense of mission and activism among Catholics throughout the continent.

See also *Bishops' Conference, Medellín, 1968; Liberation Theology; Roman Catholic Church in Latin America*

. . . . ALEX GOODALL

REFERENCES AND FURTHER READING

Cleary, Edward L., ed. *Born of the Poor: The Latin American Church since Medellín.* Notre Dame, IN: University of Notre Dame Press, 1990.

Crahan, Margaret E. "Religion: Reconstituting Church and Pursuing Change." In *Americas: New Interpretive Essays*, edited by Alfred Stepan, 152–171. Oxford, UK: Oxford University Press, 1992.

Fleet, Michael. "Religion in Latin America." In *Understanding Contemporary Latin America,* edited by Richard S. Hillman, 322–335. Boulder, CO: Lynne Rienner, 2001.

Poblete, Renato. "From Medellín to Puebla: Notes for Reflection." *Journal of Interamerican Studies and World Affairs* 21, no. 1 (February 1979): 31–44.

Contadora Peace Process

(**See** *Central American Wars, 1980s*)

Continental Treaty, 1856

When the United States annexed much of Mexico's northern territory after the Mexican-American War, many Latin America nations came to fear the expansionist tendencies of their North American neighbor. Besides the official actions of the American government and its military, Latin American nations also feared "filibusters" from the United States—adventurers who often tried to provoke uprisings or rebellions within nations, with the goal of eventually bringing about U.S. intervention and possibly annexation. The filibustering expeditions of William Walker, who struggled to take control of Nicaragua beginning in 1854, had especially aroused concerns.

In response to these anxieties Chilean diplomats invited all nations of Latin America to send representatives to a meeting in Santiago, Chile, in September 1856. This meeting was known as the Congress of Santiago, and it met for one day of deliberations on September 15, 1856. Only Chile, Ecuador, and Peru sent delegations. An additional cause of concern immediately preceding the meeting was a decision by Ecuador to grant the United States a concession to mine guano (bird droppings, which were valuable for use as fertilizer) on the Galapagos Islands. Other nations along the Pacific coast of South America feared that this might ignite U.S. interest in annexing territory in their region. The Continental Treaty, which came out of the Congress of Santiago, proposed a confederation of Latin American nations to deal with external threats, with each nation agreeing to come to the aid of any other ally that was attacked by "expeditions or aggressions with land or naval forces proceeding from abroad." The treaty, which is also known as the Treaty of Alliance and Reciprocal Assistance, also outlined measures for dealing with "piratical expeditions" or filibusters and other exiles from foreign countries that sought to stir up trouble in Latin America. Whereas at earlier Pan-American conferences, Spain, France, or other European nations were understood to be the potential predators that were feared, in this case it was clearly the United States that inspired the concern of those signing the treaty. Nicaragua later signed the Continental Treaty, and several other Latin American nations expressed interest in it, but it was never fully implemented.

In November 1856 the diplomatic ministers posted to the United States from Costa Rica, Guatemala, Mexico, New Granada, Peru, El Salvador, and Venezuela met together in Washington, D.C., and negotiated a similar treaty known as the Treaty of Washington. Like many similar conferences both previously and afterward, the Congress of Santiago and the resulting Continental Treaty met with little success. However it is considered an important step away from the acceptance of the "right of conquest" in international law and the move toward requiring some type of genuine consultative process before territorial acquisitions would be recognized by the international community. It is also a part of the series of Inter-American conferences from 1826 to 1889 that eventually led to the creation of the Pan-American Union in 1890.

See also *Central America, Filibusters; Pan-Americanism*

MARK S. JOY

References and Further Reading

Alvarez, Alejandro. "Latin America and International Law." *The American Journal of International Law* 3, no. 2 (April 1909): 265–353.

Atkins, G. Pope, *Latin America and the Caribbean in the International System*, 4th ed. Boulder, CO: Westview Press, 1999.

Contras

(**See** *Central American Wars, 1980s*)

Contreras Sepúlveda, Manuel

Lieutenant Colonel Manuel Contreras Sepúlveda (1929–) played a crucial role in Chile's Dirty War in the mid-1970s, which, according to the state's official human rights report, killed 3,197 people. Little is known about Contreras' biography or early career, but officers who worked with him describe him as a fervent Roman Catholic. They highlight his competence and command, the bond he had with his men, and his engineering mind. He became a close confidant of his former teacher General Augusto Pinochet, who showed his friendship by serving as godfather to one of Contreras' children. As major Contreras spent two years (1967–1969) at the Army Career Officers School in Fort Belvoir, Virginia.

After the military coup against the government of Salvador Allende on September 11, 1973, Pinochet used Contreras to consolidate his power within the military junta. Contreras had demonstrated his repressive efficiency when he transformed the Military Engineering School in Tejas Verdas into a prototype for Chile's detention and torture centers. In November 1973 Pinochet ordered Contreras to create the Directorate of National Intelligence (DINA) to centralize the regime's intelligence gathering and repressive operations. Contreras commandeered officers and hired civilians to fill the ranks of DINA. Many of the bright young officers he recruited had studied intelligence with Contreras at the War Academy.

Contreras took advantage of generous budgets allocations and the Central Intelligence Agency's (CIA) technical assistance to transform DINA into a state-within-the-state so powerful that observers compared it variously to the gestapo and the KGB. Even before DINA's official creation by Decree 521 in June 1974, its methods dominated the junta's repression. DINA agents specialized in raids leading to mass arrests and built a network of secret detention and torture centers, where they extracted information from "internal enemies" before they killed and "disappeared" them. DINA ran the Villa Grimaldi, Chile's single most notorious torture center. By Contreras's explicit orders DINA operated extrajudicially, ignoring the law and circumventing the courts. Contreras symbolized the violent excesses of the Pinochet regime: U.S. intelligence analysts described him as the number one obstacle to the improvement of human rights in Chile.

Under Contreras DINA took the lead in Operation Condor, a network of intelligence, military, and police forces from Argentina, Bolivia, Brazil, Chile, Paraguay, and Uruguay that kidnapped, transferred, and eliminated "subversives" living outside their country of origin. Operation Condor's most infamous hit, the assassination of Chilean dissident Orlando Letelier in Washington D.C., in September 1976, ultimately led to Contreras' downfall. The Federal Bureau of Investigation (FBI) investigation of the car bombing implicated Contreras, which led Pinochet to dissolve DINA in 1977 and to ask for Contreras' resignation in 1978, but not before promoting him to general and guaranteeing impunity by passing an amnesty law. The United States unsuccessfully requested Contreras' extradition. In 1995 a Chilean court sentenced him to seven years in prison for the Letelier killing. He has remained in custody and currently serves multiple life sentences for other crimes committed as part of Operation Condor.

See also *Central Intelligence Agency (CIA); Counterinsurgency; Letelier de Solar, Orlando; Operation Condor; Pinochet Ugarte, Augusto*

. . . . OLIVER J. DINIUS

REFERENCES AND FURTHER READING

Dingis, John. *The Condor Years: How Pinochet and his Allies brought Terrorism to Three Continents.* New York: New Press, 2004.
Kornbluh, Peter. *The Pinochet File: A Declassified Dossier on Atrocity and Accountability.* A National Security Archive Book. New York: The New Press, 2003.

Convention Against Illicit Traffic in Narcotic Drugs and Psychotropic Substances, 1988

The United Nations Convention Against Illicit Traffic in Narcotic Drugs and Psychotropic Substances is a multilateral treaty designed to establish a comprehensive set of laws and guidelines to prohibit the production, distribution, and consumption of narcotics. The purpose of the convention was to reinforce and supplement the 1961 Single Convention on Narcotic Drugs as amended and the 1971 Convention on Psychotropic Substances. It was adopted in December 1988 and entered into force in November 1990. Guillermo Gedrega Gutierrez of Bolivia served as president of the conference that drafted the convention. Representatives from Argentina, Bahamas, Mexico, the United States, and Venezuela served as vice presidents, in addition to representatives from other regions.

The primary emphasis of the convention was to develop a set of guidelines for legislatures to adopt a uniform set of laws regarding all aspects of the production, distribution, and consumption of narcotics. The convention places a strong focus on punitive measures that states should use against those who participate in drug trafficking, including incarceration, treatment, education, aftercare, and social reintegration. The convention establishes jurisdiction for enforcement (Article 4), rules for confiscation (Article 5) and extradition (Article 6), standards for mutual cooperation between countries' law enforcement and judicial bodies (Articles 7, 8, 9, 10, and 11), mechanisms for monitoring dual-use items that could be used in the manufacture of illicit drugs (Articles 12 and 13), methods of crop eradication (Article 14), and control of traffickers' transportation methods (Articles 15, 16, 17, 18, and 19).

All countries in the western hemisphere are signatories to the convention. However some signed with reservations that reflected either their national culture or political power, and many Latin American countries have been highly critical of the convention. Because of the cultural and historical nature of coca to its indigenous population, Bolivia, for instance, objects to Article 3, Paragraph 2, which calls for national governments to make the personal "use, consumption, possession, purchase or cultivation" (United Nations, 1988) of the coca leaf illegal. Peru has also been critical of language that seeks to criminalize the traditional uses of coca.

Many of the criticisms associated with the treaty are a reflection of the power imbalance between the United States and the rest of the hemisphere. The United States, for instance, claims in a reservation to the convention that it is not obligated to provide assistance to countries whose leaders, it suspects, are benefiting from the drug trade. Mexico, however, counters that the U.S. declaration regarding legal assistance is a unilateral claim that runs counter to the purpose of the convention. Some Latin American states make reservations that reflect apprehension of how the United States might use the convention to justify further intervention in the region. For example Venezuela declares that the convention cannot be considered as a legal basis for the extradition of Venezuelan citizens. The United States did use the convention to justify inspecting the Cuban merchant ship *Hermann,* which was suspected of smuggling drugs, in international waters in January 1990. Mexico also has been critical of unilateral counterdrug operations in which the United States has crossed into Mexican territory.

Other key criticisms of the original convention is that it does not address the use of alternative development programs to provide incentives for coca, cannabis, or poppy growers—who often come from the most impoverished sectors of society—to switch to licit crops. In subsequent review conferences Latin American countries have argued for increased funds for alternative development programs. In addition many countries are critical of the convention's supply-side focus and have challenged its punitive recommendations and prohibitionist assumptions. They argue that source crop eradication efforts are the least effective way of limiting illegal drug use. These criticisms were strongly reflected in a 1993 letter written to the UN secretary-general by Mexico, which noted that despite international efforts to control supply, consumption was increasing and criminal organizations were expanding. The letter recommended that more attention be given to demand issues. Demand issues, including suggestions to decriminalize some narcotic use, have become more common areas of discussion at meetings of the Commission of Narcotic Drugs, which oversees the UN's antidrug conventions. Still there has been no successful effort to amend these treaties to reflect these criticisms. In the preface to its 2009 report the UN Office on Drug Control and Crime strongly rejected arguments for decriminalization. Nevertheless some countries are moving away from the prohibitionist norms of the convention in their own domestic laws by legalizing personal possession of some narcotics. Argentina, Mexico, Uruguay, Colombia, Chile, and Peru all have some legal leniency for the personal possession of some narcotics.

See also *Bolivia, U.S. Military Antidrug Program, 1986; Colombia, U.S. Relations with; Drug Trafficking; Drugs, U.S. War on; Escobar Gaviria, Pablo; Federal Bureau of Narcotics; Inter-American Drug Abuse Control Commission (CICAD); Mexico-U.S. Border and Drug Control; United States-Bolivia Anti Narcotics Agreement, 1990; U.S. Drug Enforcement Administration*

. . . . DAVID R. ANDERSEN

REFERENCES AND FURTHER READING

Jelsma, Martin. "Drugs in the UN System: The Unwritten History of the 1998 United Nations General Assembly Special Session on Drugs." *International Journal of Drug Policy* 14, no. 2 (2003): 181–195.

United Nations, "The United Nations Convention Against Illicit Traffic in Narcotic Drugs and Psychotropic Substances, 1988," http://www.unodc.org/unodc/en/treaties/illicit-trafficking.html.
United Nations Office on Drugs and Crime. *World Drug Report 2009*. New York: United Nations, 2009.

Convention for the Maintenance, Preservation, and Reestablishment of Peace, 1936

(**See** *Inter-American Conference for the Maintenance of Peace, Buenos Aires, 1936*)

Coolidge, Calvin

Calvin Coolidge (1872–1933) was the thirtieth president of the United States. He assumed that office after the death of Warren G. Harding in 1923 and subsequently won the presidential election of 1924. Coolidge, a lawyer from Vermont and former governor of Massachusetts, advocated a conservative, probusiness, small-government approach during his presidency that in many ways continued the orientation of his Republican predecessor in the White House.

In his policies and approach toward Inter-American relations, Coolidge favored continuing the Harding administration's tendency toward a gradual retreat from the overt intervention in Latin American affairs that had characterized U.S. actions during earlier administrations. A more conciliatory approach to Inter-American relations could be detected in the good offices he provided to Chile and Peru to help them solve their intractable Tacna-Arica dispute. Coolidge, acting as arbiter, ruled in 1925 that a plebiscite should decide outstanding border controversies, and his actions helped the two countries inch closer to ending the dispute than ever before. In the Caribbean the withdrawal of U.S. troops from the Dominican Republic took place under the Coolidge administration in 1924, even though the occupation of Haiti would continue until 1934. In relations with Mexico Coolidge attempted to steer a cautious path regarding the subsoil rights of the U.S. oil companies. Worried that their concessions might not be confirmed by the government of Plutarco Elias Calles, many oil companies supported the more aggressive posture of Secretary of State Frank B. Kellogg, who stated publicly that the United States would not countenance the failure of the Calles government to protect U.S. property rights and citizens. Ultimately Coolidge's appointment of his capable personal friend, Dwight Morrow, as ambassador to Mexico in 1927, facilitated compromise and a lessening of international tension.

Relations with Nicaragua proved more difficult. U.S. Marines had been stationed in Nicaragua since 1912, and U.S.-supervised elections returned a Conservative party candidate to the presidency every four years, much to the approval of U.S. administrators. In 1925, with the Nicaraguan economic and political situation stabilized, U.S. forces withdrew, only to have civil war break out between rival conservative and liberal factions. U.S. Marines returned in late 1926, supported the return of Adolfo Díaz (long a U.S. favorite) to the presidency, and helped to fight off a continuing rebellion by liberals Juan Sacasa and José María Moncada. Coolidge sent Henry L. Stimson to Nicaragua to negotiate an end to the hostilities; the resultant Tipitapa Accords kept Díaz in place, disbanded Nicaragua's army and replaced it with a National Guard supervised by U.S. Marines, and stated the intention of the United States to supervise elections in 1928. Almost all liberal commanders accepted the accords except Augusto César Sandino, who kept up his fight against foreign intervention in his country. Coolidge increased troop strength to over five thousand in an ultimately unsuccessful attempt to defeat the nationalist Sandino's guerrilla insurgency, a policy of escalation that found criticism throughout the United States. Elections took place in 1928 and the United States managed to withdraw its last remaining troops in 1933, but not until turning over the National Guard to Anastasio Somoza García.

Coolidge's record in relations with Latin America remained mixed. Mediation and compromise characterized his approach in some cases, and his attendance at the opening ceremonies of the Sixth International Conference of American States in Havana (1928) reflected his desire to improve Inter-American relations. But his administration's continued intervention in Nicaragua left a legacy of distrust and helped pave the way for the Somoza family's dominance of that country until 1979.

See also *Kellogg, Frank B.; Morrow, Dwight W.; Sixth International Conference of American States, Havana, 1928; Tacna-Arica Dispute, 1883–1929; Tipitapa, Peace Treaty, 1927 (Nicaragua); United States, circum-Caribbean Interventions, 1900-1934: Nicaragua*

. . . . WILLIAM E. SKUBAN

References and Further Reading

Coolidge, Calvin: *The Autobiography of Calvin Coolidge*. New York: Cosmopolitan Book Corporation, 1929.
Langley, Lester D., ed. "The Second Nicaraguan Civil War, 1925–1927" and "The Sandino Chase." In *The Banana Wars: United States Intervention in the Caribbean, 1898–1934*, 181–203. Wilmington, DE: Scholarly Resources, 2002.
Schoultz, Lars, ed. "Removing the Marines, Installing the Puppets" and "Establishing the Foundations." In *Beneath the United States: A History of U.S. Policy toward Latin America*, 255–289. Cambridge, MA: Harvard University Press, 1998.

Coordinator of Inter-American Affairs, Office of, World War II

This U.S. government agency was established by Council of National Defense Order on August 16, 1940, as the Office for Coordination of Commercial and Cultural Relations Between the American Republics (OCCCRBAR). During most of the time of its existence, however, it was called the Office of the Coordinator of Inter-American Affairs (OCIAA). In 1945, it was renamed the Office of Inter-American Affairs (OIAA). On April 10, 1946, it was abolished by executive order.

Among the hemisphere-wide projects of the Office of Inter-American Affairs—headed by Nelson Rockefeller during World War II—was the teaching of English, as in this Guatemala City elementary school. One sentence reads, "Vegetables are good for children."

SOURCE: National Archives

GENESIS

The immediate background for the establishment of the OCIAA was the success of Nazi aggression. If the coming of war had produced mixed reactions in the United States, dividing the country into fervent isolationists and interventionists, it triggered deep security concerns on both sides of the divide with regard to Latin America. The region was home to millions of German, Italian, and (to a lesser degree) Japanese descent, and many observers in the United States feared that these might turn into active agents of the Axis. By mid-1940, moreover, Latin America's vulnerable export economies seemed to be headed toward a severe downturn due to war-related disruptions of international trade and capital flows. Economic turmoil was expected to produce political destabilization which, in turn, was feared to provide a fertile ground for Axis intrusions and "Fifth Column" activities. Since U.S. observers tended to view Latin America's governments and state institutions as incapable or unwilling to deal effectively with the Nazi threat and subversive activities, many feared a political, cultural, and economic penetration, or even invasion, by Nazi Germany.

The OCIAA was established to respond to such threat perceptions by preparing and coordinating policies to stabilize Latin America's economies, secure and deepen U.S. influence in the region, and combat Axis inroads into the hemisphere, particularly in the commercial and cultural spheres. More precisely the OCIAA was to assist such objectives by establishing liaisons between various entities of government and civil society, thereby involving private interests in the preparation and implementation of policy initiatives. Toward this end the OCIAA engaged, as advisors or members of staff, representative and influential citizens from a wide variety of spheres, including finance, commerce, industry, communications and mass media, culture and education. Headed by businessman and philanthropist Nelson A. Rockefeller who served as the coordinator of Inter-American affairs, the OCIAA conducted massive programs both north and south of the Rio Grande, but its main activities were directed at Latin America.

The early history of the OCIAA was marked by considerable bureaucratic friction with other government agencies and particularly with the Department of State. In April 1941 the latter moved to assert its authority on all issues related to foreign policy. Thereafter most of the OCIAA's activities were subject to the Department of State's oversight and approval, but relations between the two entities evolved rather well.

OPERATIONS

In comparison to other war agencies and in terms of staff size, the "Rockefeller Shop" remained a relatively small entity. At its height it had some 1,100 employees in the United States and 300 technicians and field experts stationed throughout Central and South America. However the OCIAA relied to a significant degree on other public entities as well as private organizations and networks to carry out its mission. Thus in the United States it cooperated with a large number of business organizations, civic associations, and other "key groups" in a vast publicity effort to instill a positive perception of Latin America's peoples and civilization. In Latin America it created a network of volunteers, the so-called "Coordination Committees." With a total of 59 committees employing some 690 aides and assistants, the OCIAA came to be present in all major Latin American population centers. Operating under the supervision of U.S. embassies and legations, the Coordination Committees comprised influential members of the local American communities: executives of large U.S. corporations yet also independent long-time residents, professionals, journalists, and others. Not only did the committees serve as distribution centers for information and propaganda materials, they also provided local expertise in the formulation, implementation, and evaluation of OCIAA programs.

The OCIAA, moreover, established five subsidiary corporations to carry out its mission in the other American Republics: the Institute of Inter-American Affairs, the Institute of Inter-American Transportation, the Inter-American Navigation Corporation, the Inter-American Educational Foundation, and Prencinradio. The most important of these corporations, the Institute of Inter-American Affairs, engaged in large-scale public health and sanitation projects throughout Latin America and came to outlive the OCIAA. Prencinradio, a much smaller entity, was established to influence Latin America's press (*prensa*), cinema (*cine*), and broadcasting ("radio"), and served as a screen for covert operations that the U.S. government did not wish to be officially associated with.

To summarize the OCIAA's major operational fields is somewhat difficult. It engaged in a vast variety of activities, many of which remain to be studied. The OCIAA, moreover, was reorganized at various stages. It soon lost some of its earlier assignments to other, more specialized war agencies and gained new responsibilities as wartime demands changed. Thus the compilation of information on Latin American businesses with Axis ties as well as the updating of the "Black Lists" came to be handled by the Board of Economic Warfare. As the U.S. war economy demanded a steep increase in the shipment of strategic materials from Latin America, the OCIAA was called upon to help boost supply by implementing public health and sanitation programs in the areas concerned and by taking care of transportation problems. Hence the OCIAA's Institute of Inter-American Affairs initiated vast health programs, for example, in the rubber production zones of the Amazon, while other subsidiary corporations set out to assist ailing transportation systems in order to secure shipments. The OCIAA also helped to mitigate negative externalities brought about by increasing demands on Latin American economies and societies. Thus as the war-induced expansion of regional economies and the establishment of large U.S. military bases in Brazil and elsewhere in the region threatened to upset the local food supply, the OCIAA moved in to provide agricultural assistance.

Throughout the war the OCIAA engaged in massive programs in both the United States and in Latin America that were supposed to instill or reinforce good-neighborly attitudes toward the "hemispheric other." It produced and exhibited a wide variety of materials, which, disseminated through the radio, movie cinemas, the press, museums and art galleries, schools, civic centers, and other channels, reached millions of people from all walks of life. The OCIAA sought to evoke a unifying spirit and identity of the Americas by dwelling on imaginary Pan-American heroes, symbols, and rituals, and a shared history of emancipatory struggles. It sought to destabilize negative preconceptions on both sides of the continental divide, by reminding U.S. citizens, for example, of the strategic importance of Latin America for the Allied war effort and its previous and current contributions to world civilization. Latin Americans, in turn, were taught to have faith in the military and industrial capacity of the United States, to believe in the inevitability of an Allied victory, and to trust in U.S. institutions, science, and technology as agents for a better future. Apart from bombarding North and South Americans with a vast array of information and propaganda materials, the OCIAA also, and despite highly adverse wartime conditions, helped to bring about a considerable increase in cultural and educational interchange.

As World War II drew to its close, funding for the OCIAA was gradually reduced, and the remaining functions were integrated into other federal agencies, primarily the Department of State.

See also *En Guardia; Institute of Inter-American Affairs (IIAA); Walt Disney Studios and Latin America; World War II, 1939–1945*

. . . . GISELA CRAMER

References and Further Reading

Cramer, Gisela, and Ursula Prutsch. "Nelson A. Rockefeller's Office of Inter-American Affairs (1940–1946) and Record Group 229." *Hispanic American Historical Review* 86, no. 4 (2006): 785–806.

Office of Inter-American Affairs. *History of the Office of the Coordinator of Inter-American Affairs*. Washington, DC: Government Printing Office, 1947.

Costa Rica, U.S. Relations with

During its early years of independence, Costa Rica had limited contact with the United States. As a small and sparsely populated member of the defunct Central American Federation, the nation drew little interest from U.S. officials, merchants, and travelers. One of the few American visitors was U.S. diplomat John L. Stephens, who, in a widely read 1841 travel account, observed that Costa Rica "was not like the rest of Central America, retrograding and going to ruin, but smiling as the reward of industry" (Stephens 1969, 353). It was one of the earliest formulations of Costa Rican exceptionalism: the notion that Costa Rica was free from the backwardness and bloodshed that afflicted the other Central American nations. In later years Costa Ricans and U.S. visitors alike would claim that Costa Rica's supposed "whiteness," owing to a small indigenous population, was the key to its stability. But this earlier version of exceptionalism hinged largely upon the industriousness evident in the country's expanding coffee sector. By the 1840s coffee farming had become the central factor in the nation's relative prosperity, and it would play an important role in future relations with the United States, particularly after the U.S.-Mexican War and the ensuing California Gold Rush.

1840S TO 1900S: UNDER THE SHADOW OF MANIFEST DESTINY

The gold rush brought both opportunity and peril for Costa Rica. California's sudden population boom created new markets and commercial connections, enabling Costa Rican planters to export some of their coffee north to San Francisco. But the Gold Rush also placed Central America in the crosshairs of U.S. expansion. As thousands of Americans streamed across the isthmus on their way to California, many called for the conquest of Central America. Although Costa Rica remained free from foreign aggression, both of its neighbors fell under forms of American domination. In the Colombian province of Panama a U.S. company completed a transoceanic railway in 1855, thereby gaining control of much of the region's commerce and transportation. That same year U.S. adventurers led by William Walker conquered Nicaragua in the name of Manifest Destiny. Hoping to gain support from white southerners in the United States, they then reinstituted slavery. Central American fears only grew when Washington recognized the new regime. Convinced these "filibusters" would soon target his nation, Costa Rican President Juan Rafael Mora led an army north into Nicaragua. Supported by Great Britain the Costa Ricans defeated Walker's men at the Battle of Rivas. Although an outbreak of cholera forced the Costa Rican army to retreat, its victory weakened the filibusters, who fell from power in 1857. The crusade against Walker fostered national pride and unity among the Costa Ricans, who had not fought a war for independence against Spain. Over the following decades this *Campaña Nacional* ("National Campaign") became a rallying symbol of the nation's heroic defense of Central America against U.S. aggression and slavery.

The perceived threats from the United States were not limited to Walker, however. By the time of the filibuster war, interest in an interoceanic canal through Nicaragua had grown, and several American entrepreneurs sought concessions for its construction. Because the canal's projected Caribbean entryway, the San Juan River, formed Costa Rica's northeastern border with Nicaragua, Costa Rican leaders were determined to be included in any discussion of canal construction. Using its leverage over a weakened Nicaragua, Costa Rica negotiated the Cañas-Jerez Treaty in 1858, which required Nicaragua to consult Costa Rica before extending transit or canal concessions to American or other foreign interests. In the early 1860s the U.S. Civil War brought new perils. Like other Central American nations, Costa Rica sympathized with the Union, fearing that southern secession would lead to further slave expansion, but Costa Rican officials also refused Washington's requests to settle free African Americans in Costa Rican territory.

By the late 1860s and 1870s Costa Rican leaders were focused on their nation's development and looked to the United States as a source of expertise and entrepreneurs. The central figure in this period was General Tomás Guardia, who dominated Costa Rican politics from 1870 until his death in 1882. A quintessential liberal dictator, Guardia promoted a series of economic and political reforms. At the heart of his program was an Atlantic Railroad, which would run from the capital of San José to the Caribbean coast, thereby enabling Costa Rica to ship coffee directly to the eastern United States and Europe rather than depending on the long Pacific route around Cape Horn. At the same time he hoped the rail line would promote settlement of the lowlands around its Caribbean terminus of Limón. Costa Rica initially awarded the contract to U.S. entrepreneur Henry Meiggs, but it soon passed to his nephew, Brooklyn-born Minor Cooper Keith, who would play a pivotal role in Costa Rican life until his death in 1929.

From the beginning the railroad construction suffered from chronic shortages of labor and capital. Unable to attract Hispanic Costa Ricans to the malarial lowlands, Keith experimented with a variety of foreign labor sources, including criminals from New Orleans and Chinese contract labor. By the 1880s, however, he had settled upon British West Indians as the solution. Financing proved equally challenging, for Costa Rica had defaulted on its national debt and had no way to fund the construction. In 1884 Keith signed a contract with President Bernardo Soto. In return for renegotiating Costa Rica's debt and finishing the railroad, Keith would receive a 99-year lease on the rail line and 800,000 acres of land near Limón. Two years later he reached an accord with Costa Rica's British creditors, and by 1890 his West Indian workforce had completed the railroad.

In these same years Keith laid the foundation for the Costa Rican banana industry. In addition to establishing plantations of his own, he encouraged black immigrants to grow bananas and sell them exclusively to his Tropical Trading and Transport Company. By the time of the railroad's completion the company was exporting over one million stems of bananas annually, mostly to New Orleans. Yet even as he consolidated his hold over the Atlantic Railroad and banana sector, Keith faced fierce competition from other commercial interests, especially the much larger Boston Fruit Company. In 1889 when the collapse of Keith's New Orleans creditors threatened the ruination of his Central American operation, Costa Rican President Rafael Yglesias Castro extended him a government loan, keeping him financially afloat. Months later Keith decided to combine his interests with Boston Fruit. The result was the 1899 founding of United Fruit Company (UFCO), a transnational corporation that would dominate Costa Rica for years to come.

This same period witnessed an unprecedented wave of U.S. imperial expansion. Following the War of 1898, which left the United States with colonial possessions in both the Caribbean and Pacific, Washington grew determined to construct a Central American canal. Although Nicaragua remained the likeliest candidate, the resistance of its dictator, José Santos Zelaya, along with Costa Rican demands to be included in negotiations, diminished U.S. enthusiasm. To the surprise of both Nicaragua and Costa Rica, Washington chose Panama. In 1903 President Theodore Roosevelt severed the province from Colombia and commenced a decade-long construction of the canal. Partly to protect its canal monopoly, the United States then toppled Zelaya in 1909, initiating a long period of intervention in Nicaragua. Although Costa Rica remained free from Washington's control, the occupation of its neighbors raised fears of American domination. Indeed it was no coincidence that as U.S. imperial action and racial rhetoric grew more overt, Costa Ricans increasingly emphasized their whiteness and homogeneity in an effort to set themselves apart from the other nations of Central America and the Caribbean.

1910S TO WORLD WAR II: THE POWER OF UNITED FRUIT COMPANY

By the 1910s, however, Costa Rican anxieties centered primarily on UFCO. In addition to controlling the nation's railway and banana industry, the firm held a virtual monopoly over its external commerce, with UFCO's fleet shaping the country's trade patterns. Although nationalists and labor leaders proved the most vocal critics of the company, some American diplomats also voiced concern. In 1914 the U.S.

consul in Limón observed that UFCO managers were "using their powerful influence and great wealth to prevent other legitimate enterprises from entering the field" (Donaldson 1914). Equally troubling in the eyes of many Costa Rican elites, the company employed thousands of West Indian immigrants in its enclave around Limón. For a nation determined to safeguard its sovereignty and homogeneity, UFCO's power and labor policies raised many concerns.

During World War I Costa Rica experienced strained relations with both UFCO and the U.S. government. The conflict brought a steep drop in coffee and banana exports, and as unemployment grew so did resentment toward UFCO. Nationalists accused the company of using the crisis as a pretext to raise rail and shipping rates. At the same time President Alfredo González openly criticized the Bryan-Chamorro Treaty, which granted Washington exclusive rights to build a Nicaraguan canal. Claiming the agreement violated Costa Rican sovereignty, San José took the issue to the Central American Court of Justice, which the United States had helped to found. When the judges ruled in Costa Rica's favor, however, Washington ignored it, effectively destroying the court. Soon after, in early 1917, González was overthrown by his Minister of War Federico Tinoco, a close ally of UFCO. Both the company and Tinoco likely assumed that Washington would approve of the coup, but despite the efforts of UFCO's U.S. supporters, including the young lawyer John Foster Dulles, the Wilson administration adhered to its policy of refusing recognition to regimes that came to power undemocratically. This U.S. stance contributed to Tinoco's 1919 resignation and Costa Rica's return to constitutional government.

In the 1920s nationalism swept the countries of Latin America, and Costa Rica was no exception. With its free press and open political system, the nation became a center for anti-imperialist agitation. Much of this focused on Nicaragua, which was reoccupied by U.S. marines in late 1926. Costa Rican nationalists denounced the intervention and openly supported Nicaraguan insurgent Augusto Sandino in his struggle against U.S. occupation, but Costa Ricans also aimed their barbs at UFCO. In addition to accusing the company of "economic imperialism," many continued to criticize it for employing British West Indians. Among the most outspoken were the growing number of Hispanic laborers who had migrated to the banana enclave and resented the presence and competition of black immigrants. By the late 1920s these controversies threatened to derail efforts by Costa Rican and UFCO officials to negotiate a new banana contract.

The onset of the Great Depression brought another shift in U.S.-Costa Rican relations. Like other agrarian nations, Costa Rica was hit particularly hard by the economic crisis. Although Costa Rican officials cooperated with Washington's efforts to boost Inter-American trade, unemployment and economic anxiety continued to grow by the mid-1930s, as did calls for radical reform. Leading the push for change was the Costa Rican Communist party, which drew much of its strength from the banana workers in the Atlantic Zone. When the party launched a strike in August 1934, however, tensions between Hispanics and West Indians undermined worker solidarity. Pressured by the company Costa Rican President Ricardo Jiménez deported union leaders and broke the strike. Shortly after, UFCO and the Costa Rican government agreed to a new banana contract that enabled the company to shift its operations to the Pacific coast in an effort to escape banana disease and worker militancy around Limón. In return for this concession, the firm agreed to exclude blacks from employment in its new division.

With the coming of World War II, the U.S. government promoted economic and strategic solidarity with Latin America. Although Costa Rica did not figure prominently in U.S. military strategy, it cooperated with Washington's efforts both to defend the Panama Canal and to develop local sources of crucial war materials, such as Manila hemp, which had previously come from Southeast Asia. Yet political radicalism in Costa Rica continued to raise concerns among U.S. officials. Despite the defeat of the 1934 strike, the Communist party enjoyed growing public support, and during the war years Rafael Calderón (President 1940–1944) opened his government to communist advisers. Although this popular coalition proved acceptable during World War II, with the coming of the Cold War, Costa Rican conservatives and U.S. officials would become determined to prevent further communist inroads.

1948 TO 1980S: JOSÉ FIGUERES TO OSCAR ARIAS

This political tension came to a head in 1948, when Calderón and his communist allies seemed poised to take power again. In response, an opposition movement led by the charismatic José Figueres fielded an army and threw Costa Rica into civil war. After six weeks of fighting the rebels ousted the elected government and created a provisional junta. With Figueres at its head the junta drafted a new constitution, nationalized the banking industry, granted suffrage to women, and abolished the Costa Rican army. Although he returned the nation to democratic rule in 1949, Figueres remained a towering figure in Costa Rican politics and served twice more as president (1953–1958, 1970–1974). Throughout his career he proved not only a champion of social democracy at home but also a fierce opponent of dictators, many of whom had close ties to the United States. During the 1950s he supported the efforts of the Caribbean Legion, an international paramilitary force, to overthrow pro-U.S. dictators such as Rafael Trujillo in the Dominican Republic, Anastasio Somoza in Nicaragua, and Fulgencio Batista in Cuba. Yet his stern anticommunist stance at home and close cooperation with U.S. agencies such as the Central Intelligence Agency (CIA) enabled Figueres to avoid the fate of other nationalist reformers, such as Guatemala's Jacobo Arbenz.

Figueres' moderate approach set the course for Costa Rica's subsequent relations with Washington. Although San José continued to expand its social programs and even limit the power of UFCO, it remained a firm Cold War ally of the United States. Throughout the 1950s and 1960s Costa Rica enjoyed steady economic growth, due in large part to U.S. trade and economic aid. Changes in Washington's Cold War policies in the early 1970s brought unexpected opportunities for the tiny

U.S. President Harry S. Truman (left) and three-time Costa Rican president José Figueres Ferrer (right) looking at a globe. In 1958 Figueres testified before the U.S. Congress that socioeconomic divisions and U.S. support of dictators caused the attacks on Vice President Richard Nixon during a goodwill trip to Latin America.

SOURCE: Courtesy of the Harry S Truman Presidential Library

country. In 1972 Costa Rica followed the American lead in recognizing the Soviet Union, in the process securing a vast new coffee market. Conversely, after the U.S. transfer of recognition from Taiwan to China in 1979, the Costa Rican government arranged to maintain relations with Taiwan in return for economic aid.

The 1980s brought new tensions between Costa Rica and the United States. In Washington the administration of Ronald Reagan was determined to stem the radical tide that seemed to be sweeping Central America. In addition to supporting bloody counterinsurgency wars in El Salvador and Guatemala, it pushed for the overthrow of the leftist Sandinista government that had come to power in Nicaragua. Throughout the decade U.S. officials conducted a covert war against the Sandinistas using counterrevolutionaries, or contras, based in Costa Rica, as well as Honduras. For their part many Costa Rican leaders shared Washington's fears of communism but worried that Reagan's policies might spark a regional war. By the mid-1980s, as the contra war became increasingly controversial in the United States, Costa Rica began to limit the contras' activities in its territory and call for peace negotiations.

These efforts expanded during the first presidency of Oscar Arias (1986–1990). Throughout his term Arias promoted a regional peace settlement, despite fierce U.S. attempts to block his efforts. At the same time Costa Rica confronted growing economic pressures. In order to maintain its economic aid while defying Washington's policies, the Arias administration agreed to economic reforms recommended by the U.S. Agency for International Development (USAID) that threatened its fragile manufacturing base and cherished social welfare system. Meanwhile Arias' peace initiative received a boost in 1987 when he was awarded the Nobel Peace Prize. That same year the Iran-Contra scandal dealt a heavy blow to the Reagan administration's policies in Central America, making it more difficult to oppose the Costa Rican peace plan. By the time Arias left office in 1990, most of the Central American nations had agreed to negotiations, and his efforts contributed to the ending of conflicts in Nicaragua (1990), El Salvador (1992), and Guatemala (1996).

1990S TO 2010: A HAVEN OF ECOTOURISM

In the 1990s Costa Rica enjoyed steady economic growth and warm relations with Washington. Contributing to both was an unprecedented boom in the travel industry, which surpassed coffee and bananas as the largest sector of the economy. Drawing upon its exceptionalist image as the safest, most stable nation in the region, Costa Rica attracted large numbers of American tourists, exchange students, and retirees. Although racial rhetoric had become more muted by this time, it was still common for Costa Ricans and foreign visitors alike to attribute the nation's success (and implicitly its appeal) to whiteness. Equally important, the nation capitalized on the growing enthusiasm for "ecotourism" by billing itself as the most environmentally progressive nation in Latin America. Yet these same years witnessed a further neoliberal turn in government policies. As San José loosened its financial regulations and trade restrictions, Costa Rican businesses faced stiff foreign competition. By the late 1990s U.S. corporations had opened a variety of tax havens, pharmaceutical plants, and casinos in the Costa Rican capital.

Following the U.S. proclamation of the war on terror in 2001, Costa Rican officials sought to accommodate a shifting U.S. foreign policy while safeguarding their nation's image as a champion of democracy and human rights, particularly in Latin America. Despite its symbolic membership in the "coalition of the willing" during the 2003 U.S. invasion of Iraq, for example, Costa Rica opposed efforts by George W. Bush's administration to undermine Hugo Chávez's populist regime in Venezuela. As anger toward U.S. foreign policy grew, however, many Costa Ricans criticized their government's cooperation with Washington as well as its neoliberal policies. These debates resulted in a hotly contested 2006 election, which saw Arias win a second term as president. Although Arias supports free trade and maintains close relations with Washington, he continues to assert the independence from U.S. policy that has made Costa Rica a global leader in human rights and environmental policy despite its small size.

See also *American Convention on Human Rights, 1969 (Pact of San José); Arias Sánchez, Oscar; Boston Fruit Company; Bryan-Chamorro Treaty, 1915; Cañas-Jerez Treaty, 1858; Caribbean Legion;*

Central America, Filibusters; Central American Common Market (CACM); Central American Court of Justice; Central American Wars, 1980s; Coffee as an Export Crop; Costa Rica-Nicaragua Boundary Dispute; Figueres Ferrer, José; Keith, Minor C.; Manifest Destiny; Meiggs, Henry; Nicaraguan-Costa Rican Conflict, 1948; North, Oliver L.; Organization of Central American States (ODECA); Pastora Gómez, Edén; Reagan, Ronald W.; San José Agreement, Declaration of, 1960; Sandinista National Liberation Front (FSLN) (Nicaragua); San Juan River Canal Project; Stephens, John Lloyd; Taiwan, Relations with Latin America; United Fruit Company (UFCO); United Provinces of Central America, 1823–1839; United States, circum-Caribbean Interventions, 1900–1934: Costa Rica

. . . . JASON M. COLBY

REFERENCES AND FURTHER READING

Chomsky, Aviva. *West Indian Workers and the United Fruit Company in Costa Rica, 1870–1940.* Baton Rouge: Louisiana State University Press, 1996.

Donaldson, Chester. *Chester Donaldson to William Jennings Bryan, National Archives and Records Administration.* College Park, MD, May 12, 1914.

Edelman, Marc, and Joanne Kenen. *The Costa Rica Reader.* New York: Grove Weidenfeld, 1898.

Honey, Martha. *Hostile Acts: U.S. Policy in Costa Rica in the 1980s.* Gainesville: University Press of Florida, 1994.

Longley, Kyle. *The Sparrow and the Hawk: Costa Rica and the United States during the Rise of José Figueres.* Tuscaloosa: University of Alabama Press, 1997.

Stephens, John L. *Incidents of Travel in Central America, Chiapas and Yucatan.* New York: Dover, 1969. First published 1841.

Stewart, Watt. *Keith and Costa Rica: The Biography of Minor Cooper Keith, American Entrepreneur.* Albuquerque: University of New Mexico Press, 1964.

Yashar, Deborah J. *Demanding Democracy: Reform and Reaction in Costa Rica and Guatemala, 1870s–1950s.* Stanford, CA: Stanford University Press, 1997.

Costa Rica-Nicaragua Boundary Dispute

Before 1858 there was no clear line between Costa Rica and Nicaragua. Indeed until 1838 there had been no need for one. Both Costa Rica and Nicaragua had been part of the Spanish Viceroyalty of New Spain, then briefly part of Mexico, and finally part of the Central American Federation. The federation's disintegration in 1838 made boundary clarification essential.

In 1858 Nicaragua's Máximo Jerez and Costa Rica's José María Cañas signed the Cañas-Jerez Treaty, the basis of subsequent boundary claims. That treaty assigned the entire San Juan River to Nicaragua, even the lower two-thirds where the river forms the boundary. There the right bank would belong to Costa Rica, but Costa Rican sovereignty would end at the water's edge. Yet Costa Ricans could forever use the river for commercial purposes, *con objectos de comercio* in the Spanish original. Those words would prove contentious. Nicaragua could not impose tariffs or other charges upon Costa Ricans engaged in peaceful commerce without mutual consent.

The first major crisis arose late in the nineteenth century when U.S. authorities were contemplating an interoceanic canal route. The San Juan River was a plausible location. The Nicaragua route would have required dredging as well as digging from Lake Nicaragua through the height of land to the Pacific coast, but it might have been less costly than a canal built from scratch through the jungles of Panama. Both Nicaraguan and Costa Rican authorities wanted clarification of their rights under the Cañas-Jerez Treaty if such a canal were to materialize, and they took the dispute to U.S. President Grover Cleveland for arbitration. Cleveland interpreted *con objectos de comercio* as meaning, "with purposes of commerce." While President Cleveland confirmed the right of Costa Ricans to use the waterway for commercial purposes, the 1888 arbitration confirmed that Costa Rican "vessels of war" could not use the San Juan River without Nicaraguan consent. In 1913, after the U.S. and Nicaragua had signed draft canal treaties without Costa Rican authorization, the Central American Court of Justice confirmed that interpretation.

Tensions along the boundary continued throughout the twentieth century and into the twenty-first. Illegal immigration from Nicaragua into Costa Rica was a serious problem. Costa Rica enjoyed greater prosperity and political stability, and impoverished and oppressed Nicaraguans smuggled themselves across the international border. By 2010 per capita gross domestic product (GDP) was $10,900 in Costa Rica and $2,800 in Nicaragua. Throughout the 1970s and 1980s Nicaragua was a battle zone as Sandinista rebels fought the government led by Anastasio Somoza and, after the Sandinista victory, as the Reagan administration financed and provided weaponry to Nicaraguan rebels, the contras. Costa Ricans did not welcome the uninvited, often desperate, Nicaraguans.

In 1998 after Costa Rican police began patrols in boats along the San Juan River, Nicaragua's post-Sandinista government accused Costa Rican authorities of violating the Cañas-Jerez Treaty. As a reprisal Nicaragua imposed a fee of $25 per vessel and a visa requirement upon Costa Rican tourists who entered the river. It could do this, Nicaraguan authorities said, because *con objectos de comercio* meant, "with articles of commerce," and tourists were not articles. Costa Rican lawyers said that *con objectos de comercio* meant, "with purposes of commerce." The Costa Rican government took the matter to the International Court of Justice (ICJ) in The Hague, which in 2009 rendered a split decision. The ICJ agreed with the Costa Rican position on the meaning of *con objectos de comercio* and identified commercial tourism as a form of commerce. At the same time the ICJ also ruled that armed Costa Rican police could not use patrol boats in the San Juan River.

In November 2010, after Google posted a map which identified occupied Isla Calero in the Caribbean Sea as Nicaraguan territory, Nicaraguan forces occupied the island. The Costa Rican government of President Laura Chinchilla, who had assumed office earlier that year, declared that Google had erred and that Nicaragua had invaded Costa Rica. (Google admitted its mistake and changed the map.) Members of the Organization of American States (OAS) supported Costa Rica by a margin of 22:2, with Hugo Chávez's Venezuela representing Nicaragua's sole ally. José Manuel Insulza, secretary-general of the OAS, urged both sides to exercise restraint and resume talks. The Nicaraguan government of Sandinista President Daniel Ortega, who had returned to office in 2007, threatened to defy—even to withdraw from—the OAS, and President Chinchilla then took the issue to the ICJ.

See also *Cleveland, Grover; Costa Rica, U.S. Relations with; Honduras-Nicaragua Boundary Dispute; Nicaragua, U.S. Relations with; Nicaraguan-Costa Rican Conflict, 1948; San Juan River Canal Project*

. . . . WILLIAM HEAD

References and Further Reading

Department of State. *Papers Relating to the Foreign Relations of the United States of America, 1887*. Washington, DC: Government Printing Office, 1888.

Hayden, Bridgett. *Salvadorans in Costa Rica,* Tucson: University of Arizona Press, 2003.

Herzog, Lawrence A., ed. *Changing Boundaries in the Americas*. San Diego: University of California Press, 1993.

Kacowicz, Arie M. *Zones of Peace in the Third World. South America and West Africa in Comparative Perspective*. New York: State University of New York Press, 1998.

Cotonou Agreement, 2000

The ACP-EU Partnership Agreement, commonly referred to as the Cotonou Agreement, is a treaty between the European Union (EU) and the African, Caribbean, and Pacific Group (ACP), designed to help reduce poverty, promote sustainable development in the member states of the ACP, and facilitate the gradual integration of the ACP member states into the world economy. The Latin American members of the ACP are all of the sovereign islands of the Caribbean as well as Belize, Suriname, and Guyana. The treaty, signed in Cotonou, Benin, on June 23, 2000, is designed to last for twenty years, from March 2000 to February 2020. The agreement also contains a clause allowing it to be revised every five years.

The treaty is the latest in a series of agreements between the EU and the ACP. Its predecessor, the Lomé Convention, first signed in 1975 and then renewed in 1980, 1985, 1991, and 1996, was a continuation of the Yaoundé agreements between the EU member countries (primarily France) and their former colonies. Negotiations for an agreement to replace the Lomé Convention started in 1998.

Cotonou, in part, grew out of the so-called "banana trade wars," where the United States claimed that preferential trade benefits to the ACP countries violated the Most Favored Nation (MFN) clause under the General Agreement on Tariffs and Trade (GATT) by discriminating against imports from Latin American banana producers. When the World Trade Organization (WTO) replaced GATT in 1994, adopting most of its rules, it authorized sanctions against the EU to force compliance with WTO rules. Cotonou ended the sanctions.

Cotonou negotiations were full of obstacles, taking place during a period of global economic regime change where the "Uruguay Round" trade talks resulted in the setting up of the WTO as a multilateral agency to foster free trade. This, in conjunction with economic globalization since the late 1980s, challenged the fundamental relationship of the ACP and the EU.

While the Lomé Agreement was based on aid to the newly independent states of the ACP, as well as preferential trade agreements, the Cotonou Agreement is based on the creation of trade agreements between the ACP and the EU, in line with the WTO economic regime. The WTO demands free trade and discourages any preferential trade relationships. With the focus, then, on development, mainstays of the Lomé Agreement such as the SYSMIN and STABEX systems are eliminated, and development funds are based on performance on issues such as human rights and the development of democracy.

The Cotonou Agreement was signed by seventy-seven ACP countries, with Cuba, a candidate to the agreement, unable to sign it. Cuba was still included in the hope that the problems which prevented its signing would be resolved. The primary issue preventing Cuba's signature was the EU's insistence on Cuba making political changes that would promote democracy and guarantee human rights. The changes demanded by the EU come from a 1996 EU resolution entitled, "Common Position," which supports U.S. policy changes in Cuba even as the EU condemned the Helms-Burton Act.

In a 1998 agreement between the United States and the EU, the United States pledged not to enforce a provision in the Helms-Burton Act that would punish EU companies that do business in Cuba using expropriated properties. Since the 1998 agreement on Helms-Burton, the United States has refrained from enforcing the law against EU members and the EU has continued its policy of demanding democracy in Cuba, while at the same time carrying on with trade and investment deals there. The agreement freed EU members to continue investing in Cuba, but it also had the effect of internationalizing the U.S. sanctions strategy against investment in expropriated properties.

The Cotonou Agreement provides for the abolition of nonreciprocal trade preferences after a transition period of ACP-EU trade cooperation. The Economic Partnership Agreements (EPAs) must comply with WTO rules as well as take into account the differences in social and economic development levels between the ACP states and the EU. The Cotonou Agreement set in place a transitional phase of ACP-EU trade cooperation up through 2007, which required WTO approval. In November 2001 the ACP obtained a WTO waiver for the transitional trading arrangements of the Cotonou Agreement. From September 2002 to the end of 2007, EPAs were negotiated between the EU and ACP states. Starting in 2008 the nonreciprocal trade preferences were replaced with the new EPAs that were negotiated. The objectives of the EPAs are sustainable development of ACP states, the integration of ACP states into the global economy, and the eradication of poverty. The EPAs must furthermore support regional integration initiatives existing within the ACP and not undermine them.

See also *European Union and Latin America; Lomé Conventions, 1975–1994; World Trade Organization (WTO)*

. . . . SCOTT DITTLOFF

References and Further Reading

CONCORD Cotonou Working Group (Aid). "ACP-EU Relations: Will the EU Deliver on Its Promises? Challenges of the 10th EDF Programming Process." Report of the Seminar on the 9th and 10th EDF, Brussels, Belgium, February 27–28, 2007.

De la Rocha, Manuel. "The Cotonou Agreement and Its Implications for the Regional Trade Agenda in Eastern and Southern Africa." World Bank Policy Research Working Paper No. 3090, June 20, 2003, http://ssrn.com/abstract=636452.

Goodisman, Paul, Paulina M. Elago, and Roman Grynberg, eds. *The Cotonou Agreement: A User's Guide.* London: Commonwealth Secretariat, 2005.

Council on Hemispheric Affairs (COHA)

The Council on Hemispheric Affairs (COHA) is an informational, research, and advocacy organization promoting human rights and democratic institutions throughout Latin America. It emerged in 1975 in the aftermath of the 1973 Pinochet coup in Chile that overthrew the constitutional government of President Salvador Allende. As a result of the later revelations of White House complicity in that coup, as well as in Washington's subsequent interventionist backing of military-led juntas elsewhere in Latin America, a group of U.S.-area specialists, coming from diverse academic, diplomatic, religious, and civic backgrounds, gathered at the Ford Foundation in 1975 to create COHA.

The participants at its founding meeting—most of whom later became COHA's original trustees—included Professor Kalman Silvert of the Ford Foundation and New York University; Covey Oliver, former assistant secretary of state for Latin America under President Johnson; Professor Larry Birns of the New School and New York University; Rabbi Morton Rosenthal of B'nai B'rith; Thomas Quigley of the U.S. Catholic Conference; and Ernest Chanes, a prominent New York City civic leader. They all played a plenary role in building up the institution that almost immediately became relevant to the U.S.-Latin American policy debates that were taking place at that time. Because its trustees came from important public sectors of U.S. national life, including from national trade unions and professional organizations, COHA's credibility was enhanced by a string of illustrious chairpersons, including its second chair, Chuck A. Perlik, the president of The Newspaper Guild, whose organization represented tens of thousands of U.S. and Canadian journalists. Within a relative brief period COHA was routinely being cited by the national and world press and was looked upon as one of the largest and most active of such organizations in the United States and an important source for information and analysis on hemispheric issues by prestigious publications, TV networks, and academia.

The centerpiece of COHA's methodology has been the enormously important role played by COHA's interns (also known as research associates). Over the years more than one thousand interns, intentionally chosen from across the country and the world, who were carefully selected from small and modest institutions as well as from elite east coast institutions, who were selected in a highly competitive process. These people then worked in COHA's offices conducting a wide spectrum of activities. COHA's interns research, write about, and give interviews on such topics as the war against drugs, crime and sovereignty, U.S.-Cuba relations, corruption, free trade, and the status of the observance of social justice. This is done along with comprehending the struggle against dependency, alarm over the increasing concentration of wealth, and the creation of a Latin America that often does not serve the basic needs of its citizens. COHA's high standards have been maintained despite staff turnovers, each semester in part through the tireless efforts of its long-time director, Larry Birns, who for 35 years has guided the organization, since its founding in 1975.

COHA's goals are to advance human rights, to be an advocate for social values and economic justice, and to scrutinize the genuine efforts of Latin American governments to adhere to the principles of domestic and foreign institutions and their respectful and enlightened policies toward nations of the region. Although COHA has been described as "liberal," "eclectic" may be a more satisfactory description. For example COHA persistently has pressed for normalization of relations between Cuba and the United States, and it repeatedly cited Venezuela's left-leaning Venezuelan President Hugo Chávez as violating the spirit of the Venezuelan constitution, if not its letter. COHA's founding principles are meant to support open societies and the right of dissent and to buttress pluralistic political environments.

COHA therefore has opposed repressive regimes, both U.S.-friendly human rights violators like Colombia as well as left-leaning regimes like that of Nicaragua's Daniel Ortega. Because its support of the right of self-determination regarding individuals as well as countries, including democratically elected regimes that have chosen a different compass to direct their political and economic development than that of Washington, COHA's research as well as the democratic elements guiding it has sometimes been unwelcome to many U.S. allies, like the military juntas that ruled much of the region during the 1980s, although it has been appreciated by others, like the governments of Bolivia and Ecuador.

COHA at first enthusiastically supported the Obama administration's regional policies because it felt that the new administration would focus on constructive solutions in contrast to its predecessor and that the United States would treat Latin American states as co-equals. Unfortunately this did not turn out to be the case, as U.S. self-interests continue to dominate the White House agenda.

See also *Ford Foundation; Inter-American Dialogue; Washington Office on Latin America (WOLA); Woodrow Wilson Center, Latin American Program*

. . . . LARRY BIRNS

References and Further Reading

Council of Hemispheric Affairs. *Washington Report on the Hemisphere* (bimonthly publication), 1980.

Stanford University Finding Aids. *Records of the Council on Hemispheric Affairs, 1975–2002.* Palo Alto, CA: Stanford University Press.

Council of Mutual Economic Assistance (COMECON)

The Council of Mutual Economic Assistance (COMECON) dates from January 1949, at which point there were six founding members: Bulgaria, Czechoslovakia, Hungary, Poland, Romania, and the Soviet Union. Other countries joined: Albania, which adhered one month after the others but withdrew in 1961; the German Democratic Republic (East Germany) in 1950; Mongolia in 1962; Cuba in 1972; and Vietnam in 1978. Five countries gained Nonsocialist Cooperant Status: Finland in 1973, Iraq and Mexico in 1975, Nicaragua in 1984, and Mozambique in 1985. Yugoslavia had Associate Status, and in 1986, five countries with leftist governments attended COMECON's forty-second session: Afghanistan, Ethiopia, Laos, Nicaragua, and South Yemen. The Soviet Union dominated COMECON. At one point it had an estimated 90 percent of the land, 70 percent of the population, 65 percent of the income, and unquestioned military superiority over any combination of other members. Moscow was the site of COMECON's headquarters. Not surprisingly then, COMECON reflected Soviet priorities.

Although the Soviets did at times use trade through COMECON for political ends, Soviet interest in Latin America waxed and waned. In 1954 weapons manufactured in landlocked Czechoslovakia and shipped to Guatemala via Poland provided a pretext for the Eisenhower administration to instruct the Central Intelligence Agency (CIA) to overthrow the incumbent Guatemalan government. The Cuban revolution of 1959 provided new opportunities, commercial as well as military. However the Cuban Missile Crisis of 1962 led Soviet leaders to question their degree of involvement in the backyard of the United States, and COMECON interest declined, especially after the deposition of Nikita Khrushchev as Soviet leader in 1964. The Nicaraguan revolution of 1979 provided a new opportunity, but after 1985, when Mikhail Gorbachev became the Soviet leader, relaxation of tensions became the Soviets' highest priority.

For various reasons it is difficult to determine the extent of COMECON trade with Latin American countries. Soviet-bloc countries did not consistently publish reliable statistics. Often suppliers and customers bartered rather than using currency. COMECON countries suffered shortages of consumer goods for use at home, let alone for export. Latin Americans had limited money to spend on imports from any source, especially shoddy goods from COMECON countries, and the debt crises in the region in the 1980s only exacerbated this problem. Salvador Allende's leftist government, which held office in a highly developed Latin American country, lasted only three years (1970–1973). Shipments of weapons—to Guatemala, Cuba, or Nicaragua—damaged relations with the United States, a source of investment capital and desirable consumer goods. The best available statistics suggest that COMECON never gained even a 5 percent share of Latin American imports or exports.

COMECON dissolved in 1991, by which time most of its members no longer had communist governments and the Soviet Union was disintegrating.

See also *Communism in Latin America; European Economic Community and Latin America; Soviet Union, Latin American Policy*

. . . . GRAEME S. MOUNT

References and Further Reading

Curtis, Glenn E., ed. *Czechoslovakia: A Country Study*. Washington, DC: Federal Research Division of the Library of Congress, 1992.

Mujal-Leon, Eusebio. "Eastern Europe and Latin America." In *Europe and Latin America in the World Economy*, edited by Susan Kaufman Purcell and Francoise Simon, 139–172. Boulder, CO: Lynne Rienner, 1995.

Radu, Michael. "Eastern Europe and Latin America." In The USSR and Latin America, edited by Eusebio Mujal-Leon. Boston: Unwin Hyman, 1989.

Counterinsurgency

Following World War II and with the development of the Cold War, there was a significant increase in the number of insurgencies, especially in Europe's African and Asian colonies. Anti-colonial wars for national liberation and self-defined struggles for social justice prompted global powers to sharpen counterinsurgency practices. The United States applied and developed counterinsurgency in Vietnam and Latin America, where military planners worked to prevent a repeat of the 1959 Cuban Revolution. Counterinsurgency became the core strategy of the "dirty wars" of the 1970s and 1980s and reached a climax during the civil wars in Central America, especially Guatemala and El Salvador. After the Cold War it became a core element to the "war on drugs" in the Andean region and has played a central role in the prolonged Colombian civil war. It was also part of the Mexican government's response to the Zapatista rebellion. Counterinsurgency is a central strategy in the "global war on terrorism."

Military doctrine defines "insurgency" as the attempt to overthrow a government by illegal or irregular methods. Counterinsurgency, also known as COIN, is a strategy for defeating insurgencies. Its objective is to gain control over territory and population lost or contested by an insurgency. COIN defines "control" as returning a field of operations to a state of social, political, and economic normalcy. COIN strategists identify popular support as the key resource for insurgencies. They devise programs to address the larger political and economic context driving populations into rebel hands, while providing strong and clear incentives and sanctions to targeted populations. The goal is to take away popular support from the insurgents while also building legitimacy for the government. Counterinsurgency is a battle for the "hearts and minds" of the civilian population, a political battle ground instead of the traditional military battle between armies.

COIN uses multiple tactics to separate insurgents from their base of support. Incentives known as "civic action" may include offering communities development aid, such as new agricultural machinery, health clinics, schools, improved roads, potable water, or electricity. COIN in Latin America thus became closely associated with modernization projects, such as those promoted by the Alliance for Progress, and they have been coordinated with U.S. Aid for International Development (USAID) programs. These efforts are bolstered by aggressive public relations campaigns that put forward propaganda discrediting insurgents and promoting the government. In Guatemala, for example, the state distributed flyers to indigenous communities that represented Che Guevara as the devil who was being beaten by a soldier with a cross. Offering jobs, cash payments, and bureaucratic posts to key community members is used to gain loyalty. Amnesty programs also serve to pull individuals from the side of insurgents.

COIN deploys sanctions aimed at discouraging civilians from collaborating with the insurgents. Incentives given to compliant communities are denied to those supporting or suspected of supporting the insurgents. Serious punishments are issued for those known to work with the insurgents. These have included the removal of suspects from positions of power, their exclusion from work, harassment of individuals and communities by security forces, as well as imprisonment, torture, disappearances, and assassination. These sanctions are carried out in public fashion so they send a clear message to the population about the cost of collaborating with the insurgency. When sanctions become pervasive, COIN can appear to be a war against the people. A cycle of violence can result, as guerrilla armies apply similar sanctions to their target populations, especially those known or suspected of collaborating with the government. Sendero Luminoso's ruthless revolutionary campaign in Peru stands as the strongest example of an insurgency's use of terror against a population. Violence occurs as COIN tactics reach extreme levels of human rights violations and atrocities, such as the El Mozote massacre in December 1981, when the Atlacatl Battalion, an elite COIN unit of the El Salvadorian military, killed an estimated one thousand people.

More so than conventional war, COIN has a holistic perspective. According to the U. S. Army's COIN manual, "successful conduct of COIN operations depends on thoroughly understanding the society and culture within which they are being conducted" (Department of the Army 2006, 1–22). In the Army's view, insurgencies happen because of flaws in society and culture. COIN attempts to repair it by social engineering and nation-state building. COIN is closely associated with the "doctrine of national security," which perceives threats as coming from within society as against an external enemy. An obsession with subversion often results, which blurs the distinction between innocent civilians and legitimate threats to society. COIN runs the risk of identifying every member of society as a threat to the established order.

To distance themselves from the negative consequences of repression, governments frequently pursue COIN through covert measures. Deliberate misinformation and disinformation campaigns are used to mislead, confuse, or disorientate insurgents and their supporters. These "psychological operations" (psych ops) also include the use of rumors and media smear campaigns to generate uncertainty or a climate of intimidation within targeted populations. Coupled with death squad activities, psych ops can generate a culture of terror that encourages populations to support a return to "normalcy" through stringent "law and order" initiatives. Clandestine tactics, such as Operation Condor's intelligence gathering and elimination of "subversives" throughout the Southern Cone, have been directly connected to the United States. In some cases, such as El Salvador's Major Roberto D'Aubuisson Arrieta, individuals in charge of death squads and paramilitaries were linked to the Central Intelligence Agency. The United States teaches Latin American militaries counterinsurgency strategy at the School of the Americas and assists them in fighting insurgencies by sending Special Forces as field advisors.

See also *Alliance for Progress; Cuban Revolution, 1956–1959; El Salvador, U.S. Relations with; Guatemala, U.S. Relations with; School of the Americas*

. . . . GLEN DAVID KUECKER

References and Further Reading

Department of the Army, "Counterinsurgency," *Field Manual 3–24*, December 2006, www.fas.org/irp/doddir/army/fm3-24.pdf.

Galula, David. *Counterinsurgency Warfare: Theory and Practice*. Westport, CT: Praeger, 2006.

Greentree, Todd. *Crossroads of Intervention: Insurgency and Counterinsurgency Lessons from Central America*. Westport, CT: Praeger, 2008.

Joes, Anthony James. *Resisting Rebellion: The History and Politics of Counterinsurgency*. Lexington: University Press of Kentucky, 2004.

Kilcullen, David. "Three Pillars of Counterinsurgency." Remarks delivered at the U.S. Government Counterinsurgency Conference, Washington, DC, September 28, 2006.

Nagl, John. *Learning to Eat Soup with a Knife: Counterinsurgency Lessons from Malaya and Vietnam*. Westport, CT: Praeger, 2002.

Creole Affair, 1841

On November 7, 1841, a slave revolt took place aboard the *Creole*, a U.S.-based brig en route from Virginia to New Orleans. Near the Bahamas a group of slaves, led by Madison Washington, escaped the hold and took control of the ship, killing one crewman in the skirmish. Of the 135 slaves aboard the *Creole*, only nineteen participated in the uprising. After assuming control of the vessel, the slaves forced the crew to steer toward Nassau. Once in port at Nassau, authorities imprisoned the nineteen mutineers, while the rest of the slaves remained aboard the *Creole*. Local citizens, protesting the Nassau authority's decision to force slaves that had not participated in the revolt to remain on the ship, sailed to the *Creole* and set the captives free.

International law stated that a mutiny fell to the local jurisdiction associated with the physical location of the crime. Slavery was illegal in Nassau, a British possession, which under the British Emancipation Act of 1833 had ended slavery. As a result Nassau officials eventually allowed all the slaves, including the mutineers, to go free. U.S. slave owners, however, were not pleased with this decision and pressured President John Tyler to press for the slave's extradition. The slave owners argued that they had legally purchased the slaves, but the British government maintained that local law applied and since slavery was illegal in the Bahamas, so was slavery aboard any vessel that sailed its waters. This division led to increased tension between the United States and Britain.

As a result of the *Creole* incident, anti-British fervor ran high in the United States, especially among southern slave owners who had paid little attention to international affairs with Britain prior to the incident. Some southerners suspected that the *Creole* matter was a British attempt to promote an antislavery movement in the United States. At the same time northern abolitionists branded the mutineers, especially the leader Madison Washington, as heroes. For the British and U.S. governments, the incident brought issues to the forefront which neither side could easily resolve.

Daniel Webster, the secretary of state under Tyler, requested the return of the *Creole* slaves; the British prime minister, Robert Peel, failed to reciprocate in order to avoid a backlash from abolitionists. As no diplomatic solution presented itself, Webster attempted to downplay the *Creole* affair, fearing it would impact a resolution to the northeast boundary dispute that he hoped to resolve amicably with Britain. To maintain relations, he decided to concede the British decision that the mutineers would not go to trial as murderers. Webster also confirmed that extradition was not a possibility since such agreements between the two nations had expired along with Jay's Treaty in 1807. Webster maintained that the slave owners should receive some form of compensation for their loss; however British officials refuted this position. As a result authorities in Nassau freed the former slaves accused of the mutiny and the *Creole* returned to New Orleans without its human cargo.

The British foreign secretary, Lord Ashburton (Alexander Baring), arrived in the United States to work alongside Webster to negotiate a successful resolution to the northeast boundary dispute. The Webster-Ashburton Treaty, signed August 9, 1842, resolved the boundary issue between the United States and Britain by establishing the eastern U.S. boarder with Canada. Webster and Ashburton also, though not mentioned in the treaty, settled the matter of the *Creole*. Ashburton worried that the *Creole* incident would continue to plague and eventually undermine the completion of a successful treaty negotiation. As a result Lord Ashburton promised Webster that Nassau would avoid "officious interference" with U.S. ships and that he would take up the matter of restitution for the slave owners. As part of the treaty Webster secured extradition concessions from Britain in the case of certain crimes such as murder, piracy, and robbery; the clause did not extend to slave revolts or mutiny. In1853 a joint Anglo-American claims commission finally determined that authorities in Nassau had violated international law by interfering with legal slave trade. The claims commission ordered Britain to make financial restitution in the amount of $110,330 to the United States.

See also *English-Speaking Caribbean, U.S. Relations with; Jay's Treaty, 1794; Webster, Daniel*

MELVIN D. DAVIS

References and Further Reading

Jervey, Edward D., and C. Harold Huber. "The Creole Affair." *Journal of Negro History* 65, no. 3 (Summer 1980): 196–211.

Jones, Howard. *To the Webster-Ashburton Treaty: A Study in Anglo-American Relations, 1783–1843.* Chapel Hill: University of North Carolina Press, 1977.

Jones, Howard. *Crucible of Power: A History of American Foreign Relations to 1913.* Wilmington, DE: Scholarly Resources, 2002.

Jones, Howard, and Donald Rakestraw. Prologue to *Manifest Destiny, Anglo-American Relations in the 1840s.* Wilmington, DE: Scholarly Resources, 1997.

Wish, Harvey. "American Slave Insurrections before 1861." *Journal of Negro History* 22 (1937): 299–320.

Cristiani Burkard, Alfredo

Alfredo Cristiani Burkard (1947–) was born in San Salvador into a wealthy agricultural family, with some members interned in the United States during World War II for their pro-Mussolini sympathies and activities. Joining the family business after receiving a degree from Georgetown, Cristiani later became politicized with his disgust over Farabundi Martí National Liberation Front (*Frente farabundo Marti para la Liberacion Nacional,* FMLN) rebels and their followers squatting on farms. Following his kidnapping in 1980, Cristiani joined the Nationalist Republican Alliance (ARENA) party.

Following the presidential election defeat of party leader Roberto D'Aubuisson in 1984, ARENA, seeking to broaden its base of support, turned to the more conciliatory Cristiani as the new party leader. Cristiani was elected to El Salvador's National Assembly in 1988. Cristiani's decisive victory (53 percent to 36 percent) in the 1989 presidential elections over ruling party candidate Fidel Chavez Mena was also a victory of the moderate, probusiness faction of ARENA against the hard-line policies of D'Aubuisson.

Inaugurated on June 1, 1989, the new president entered office facing a nasty civil war and a Salvadoran economy in serious condition. Needing American help to resolve both difficulties, Cristiani found himself walking a fine line. With the FMLN pursuing an urban terror strategy in 1989, beginning with the assassination of close presidential adviser, Jose Rodriguez Porth, Cristiani aggressively pursued a crackdown on subversive groups within San Salvador, upsetting congressional leftists in the United States.

A major FMLN offensive into San Salvador in November 1989 spelled defeat but El Salvador's (and Cristiani's) reputation was severely tarnished when security forces murdered six Jesuit priests, as well as their maid and her daughter. Among the dead was the country's leading Jesuit, the FMLN-sympathizing Father Ignacio Ellacuria. Yet the apparently war-weary Ellacuria had displayed a surprisingly favorable disposition toward the new president. In return Ellacuria was seen by Cristiani as the only loyal opposition from the Salvadoran left.

While the George H.W. Bush administration saw Cristiani as pragmatic, liberal American congressmen brought pressure upon the Salvadoran president. There were no shortage of Capitol Hill visitors to Cristiani, telling "the president how to do his job," that is, demanding that Cristiani engage in dialogue, negotiations, and a cease-fire with the rebels. He was threatened with the termination of American aid and coffee boycotts if he did not meet these demands. Yet FMLN and congressional calls for a cease-fire were resisted by Cristiani, who feared that the rebels would use such a pause to resupply their fighters.

A consensus-builder known for his ability to focus on major goals and to move past occasional setbacks, such as the November 1989 FMLN urban offensive and brutal army reprisals, President Cristiani succeeded in presiding over the end of the civil war in January 1992. A border dispute with Honduras was also settled later that year.

One of Cristiani's accomplishments in improving the country's economic situation was to reorient El Salvador toward the private sector as opposed to the statist economic policies of his Christian Democratic predecessor. Lower tariffs were enacted and incentives, through free trade zones, were created for foreign investment. These moves helped pave the way for El Salvador to diversify its economy.

The resultant improvement of Salvadoran life during Cristiani's administration helped ARENA to retain the presidency and legislative control in the 1994 elections. Constitutionally barred from seeking a successive term, Cristiani returned to the private sector, opening a brokerage firm. Cristiani was unharmed in an apparent assassination attempt in 1996 when a bomb exploded outside the business.

See also *Central American Wars, 1980s; D'Aubuisson Arrieta, Roberto; El Salvador, U.S. Relations with; Farabundo Martí National Liberation Front (FMLN) (El Salvador)*

. . . . GREG MURPHY

References and Further Readings

"From Duarte to Cristiani: Where Is El Salvador Headed?" Hearings Before the Subcommittee on Western Hemispheric Affairs of the Committee on Foreign Affairs, House of Representatives, 101st Congress, 1st Session, July 13, 1989.

Haggerty, Richard A., ed. *El Salvador: A Country Study*. Washington, DC: Library of Congress, 1990.

Storrs, Larry K. *El Salvador under Cristiani, U.S. Foreign Assistance Decisions*. Washington, DC: Congressional Research Service, 1992.

Ulloa, Felix. *El Salvador: Electiones, 1997*. San Salvador: Fundación Guillermo Manuel Ungo, 1997.

Useem, Michael. *The Leadership Moment: Nine True Stories of Triumph and Disaster and Their Lessons for Us All*. New York: Crown Business, 1999.

Cromwell, William N.

A prominent New York attorney, William Nelson Cromwell (1854–1948) is remembered especially for his successful campaign to persuade the U.S. government to select Panama instead of Nicaragua as the site of an interoceanic canal.

Cromwell was born in Brooklyn, New York, but was taken to Peoria, Illinois, at an early age. After his father was killed during the Civil War, he returned to Brooklyn with his mother and brother. Because of the family's strained financial circumstances, he went to work as an accountant after graduating from high school. While employed by the firm of Sullivan, Kobbe & Fowler, he attended Columbia Law School through the generosity of Algernon Sydney Sullivan, the senior partner. Cromwell completed the course in two years and in 1879 formed a partnership with his benefactor in a new firm, Sullivan & Cromwell. After Sullivan's death in 1887, Cromwell became the leading figure in the firm, which later included John Foster Dulles and Allen W. Dulles among its partners. Cromwell himself became noted for his work in corporate reorganizations and consolidations.

In 1893 Cromwell became general counsel for the Panama Railroad Company, which was controlled by the New Panama Canal Company. The latter was the successor to the bankrupt French enterprise that had failed in its attempt to build a sea-level canal in Panama. In 1896 the New Panama Canal Company also retained Cromwell as its counsel. His main task, at a time when enthusiasm for construction of a canal gripped the United States, was to secure the adoption of the Panama route and to arrange for the sale of the company's assets to the U.S. government. In the 1890s, however, Nicaragua remained the preferred U.S. option. In addition the president of the New Panama Canal Company initially refused to name a price for its assets and was so indignant over Cromwell's insistence that he do so that he dismissed the attorney in July 1901. Cromwell was reinstated the following January, largely through the efforts of Philippe J. Bunau-Varilla, another Panama promoter.

Cromwell claimed credit for swaying the influential Ohio senator, Marcus A. Hanna, to the cause of Panama and for arranging for the establishment of the Isthmian Canal Commission (Walker Commission), which in 1902 selected the Panama route over Nicaragua once the New Panama Canal Company had set its price at $40 million.

Cromwell and Bunau-Varilla's lobbying of Congress bore fruit with the passage of the Spooner Act (1902), which provided for construction of the canal in Panama and for the sale of the company's property to the U.S. government for $40 million. Cromwell also played a role in negotiations with Colombia, whose consent was necessary for the transfer of the company's assets. When the resulting Hay–Herrán treaty failed to be ratified in the Colombian senate, Cromwell supported the separatist movement in Panama. The Hay–Bunau-Varilla Treaty, signed with the new republic in 1903, also provided for the sale of the New Panama Canal Company's property for $40 million. Cromwell billed the New Panama Canal Company more than $800,000 for his services and expenses, but in 1907 French arbitrators reduced that sum to $228,282.71.

In 1905 Cromwell was named fiscal agent for the republic of Panama, supervising its investments in the United States. He resigned this post in 1937 because by then he was living mainly in France. Long an admirer of that country, he supported numerous philanthropies there during and after World War I, such as assistance to the blind and to the hard-hit Valenciennes hand-lace industry and support for the construction of a memorial to the U.S. aviators of the Lafayette Escadrille. In 1936 the French Legion of Honor conferred upon him its highest award. On the occasion of his ninetieth birthday Helen Keller presented him with a gold medal in recognition of his work on behalf of the blind in the United States.

See also *Bunau-Varilla, Philippe J; Hay–Bunau-Varilla Treaty, 1903; Hay-Herrán Treaty, 1903; New Panama Canal Company; Panama, Independence of, 1903; Spooner Act, 1902 (United States)*

. . . . HELEN DELPAR

References and Further Reading

Dean, Arthur H. *William Nelson Cromwell, 1854–1948: An American Pioneer in Corporation, Comparative and International Law*. New York: Ad Press, 1957.
McCullough, David. *The Path between the Seas: The Creation of the Panama Canal, 1870–1914*. New York: Simon and Schuster, 1977.

Crowder, Enoch H.

Enoch Herbert Crowder (1859–1932) graduated from the U.S. Military Academy in 1881 and earned a law degree from the University of Missouri in 1886. He rose through the ranks of the military and was promoted to lieutenant colonel at the beginning of the Spanish-American War. Serving in the Philippines, Crowder held important posts in the military government, where he specialized in military law. In 1906 Crowder first went to Cuba as a legal advisor to the provisional government of Cuba, operating under the Platt Amendment. He supervised the Departments of State and Justice and helped to oversee elections in 1908. In 1910 Crowder represented the United States at the Fourth Pan-American conference in Buenos Aires. While in South America he also visited Chile, Peru, Ecuador, Colombia, and Panama. He served as Judge Advocate General of the United States from 1911 to 1923, when he retired from the Army and was appointed the first U.S. ambassador to Cuba.

Crowder had returned to Cuba after the end of World War I, in 1919, to supervise efforts at political reorganization, still ongoing under the Platt Amendment. He conducted an exhaustive study of all Cuban elections since 1908, essentially rewrote the electoral code, and promoted additional voter registration reforms. In spite of these efforts, results from the Cuban election of 1920 were disputed, resulting in violence, upheaval, and fears of civil war. Crowder returned to Cuba as a special representative of President Wilson in 1920, with the message that American troops were sure to follow unless the Cuban government followed Crowder's recommendations. He set up headquarters on the battleship Minnesota in the Havana harbor. This strategy and appointment reflected Wilson's tendency to rely on "special emissaries" to conduct foreign policy and his desire to avoid military intervention in Cuba if at all possible. Crowder's presence in Cuba also reflected the persistent U.S. belief that a more efficient administration of the system, new election codes, balloting and registration procedures, and other attempts to ensure honest elections, could provide stability and an end to chronic violence without U.S. military intervention. Crowder also assumed direction of the government's budget and helped to arrange an American loan.

Because of his experience drafting a new electoral code in Cuba, Crowder was approached by the State Department in 1920 to examine electoral law in Nicaragua, where President Chamorro was indicating that he would run for reelection in 1920, in violation of the Nicaraguan constitution. Crowder found the electoral law insufficient, and the State Department suggested that Chamorro invite Crowder to Nicaragua to study the law in greater detail and suggest practical changes. Not surprisingly Chamorro did not pursue this course of action.

While in Cuba for eight years Crowder asserted unprecedented authority, exercising control over President Alfredo Zayas and working mostly through hand-picked Cuban personnel. He sought to address problems of corruption through what he referred to as a "Moralization Program," which called for the removal of dishonest officials, and he attacked the ingrained problem of political patronage. In 1922 Crowder issued fifteen memorandums intended to virtually reorganize every part of the Cuban government, from the municipal to the provincial to the federal level. He demanded certain members of the Zayas government be removed and selected new ministers to replace them. He continued to emphasize the need for budget cuts and for finding methods of increasing revenue. In 1923 Crowder was named the first U.S. ambassador to Cuba. In this position he helped orchestrate the 1924 election of the favored U.S. candidate, the authoritarian Gerardo Machado, who obtained loans from U.S. bankers which improved the financial situation on the island. Crowder served as U.S. ambassador until 1927, when he returned to the United States to practice law.

After Crowder left Cuba, Machado suspended constitutional guarantees in order to suppress the growing opposition to his presidency. Violence spread and in 1933 Machado was forced into exile. New President Ramon Grau San Martin initiated widespread social reforms that the new U.S. ambassador, Sumner Welles, described as "irresponsible."

See also *Machado y Morales, Gerardo; Platt, Orville; Spanish-Cuban-American War 1895–1898; United States, circum-Caribbean Interventions, 1900–1934: Cuba; Wilson, Woodrow*

. . . . MOLLY M. WOOD

References and Further Reading

Perez, Louis. *Cuba and the United States: Ties of Singular Intimacy*. 2nd ed. Athens: University of Georgia Press, 1997.
Perez, Louis. *Cuba under the Platt Amendment, 1902–1934*. Pittsburgh, PA: University of Pittsburgh Press, 1986.

Cruzado Plan, 1985 (Brazil)

In Brazil President José Sarney faced a rising inflation rate, which was getting closer to 300 percent by 1986, and introduced a new economic plan to stop inflation. It was called the Cruzado Plan. The 1980s has been called the "lost decade" in Latin America economic performance. The Mexican default in the early 1980s started a domino effect on the rest of Latin American markets and international capital withdrew from the region. The lack of financing caused fiscal problems, especially due to the need of resources to sustain import substitution programs. Furthermore government activities extended into large parts of the economy through large public enterprises and other government programs. As a result most countries started to implement stabilization programs to contain inflation and restore macroeconomic order.

The Cruzado Plan, along with the Austral Plan in Argentina, was the most ambitious heterodox anti-inflationary attempt in the region. These plans followed the Latin American neostructuralist approach, which contends that the causes of inflation are not due to monetary policy mismanagement but to the economic structure that regulates transactions and payments in the economy. As a result this plan combined a set of economic measures for freezing goods prices, wages, rents, and mortgage payments, in an attempt to stop price escalation, as well as a prohibition of indexation clauses in contracts, designed to protect businesses from inflation, and the creation of a system of programmed wage rises. Finally the government introduced a new currency, the Cruzado (Cz$), which replaced the Cruzeiro (Cr$), at the rate of 1 Cz$ = 1,000 Cr$. The main goal of this plan was to stop "inertial" inflation by removing the indexation mechanisms in the economy through general price freezes. This approach differed from more orthodox stabilization plans that focus on the misalignment of aggregate demand and supply. To solve these other inflationary pressures the government needed to focus on the fiscal and monetary policies. However there were no attempts to control either government expenditures or monetary policy.

The initial results of the Cruzado Plan were impressive; inflation decreased sharply and economic activity boomed. However economic growth and the adjustment of real wages that took place in the following months created pressures on the demand side. Initially inflation was maintained thanks to the price freeze, but it could not be sustained any longer. President Sarney and his advisors did not listen to several people that recommended abandoning the price freeze in the first months and continued to sustain the program as it was established. After the elections in November 1986 the government realized the inflationary problems and implemented a second economic plan, Plan Cruzado II, in an attempt to reduce the pressures on the system. Utilities' tariffs and other prices were increased and a crawling-peg exchange rate was implemented. These measures, an attempt to reduce aggregate demand, backfired and inflation returned as strong as before the Cruzado Plan. In 1987 the country approached a hyperinflationary stage. The early success of the Cruzado Plan was history, but its failure was evident. Most economists argue that the heterodox plan could not work without restraint on the demand side, especially with respect to fiscal and monetary policies.

See also *Debt Crisis, Latin America, 1870s, 1930s, 1980s; Neoliberal Economic Development Model*

. . . . ANDRÉS GALLO

References and Further Reading

Baer, Werner, *The Brazilian Economy, Growth and Development.* 6th ed. Boulder, CO: Lynne Rienner, 2008.

Cardoso, Eliana. "From Inertia to Megainflation: Brazil in the 1980s." *In Lessons of Economic Stabilization and Its Aftermath,* edited by Michael Bruno, Stanley Fisher, Elhanan Helpman, and Nissan Liviatan, with Leora (Rubin) Meridor, 143–189. Cambridge, MA: The MIT Press, 1991.

Nazmi, Nader. *Economic Policy and Stabilization in Latin America.* New York: M. E. Sharpe, 1996.

Cuba, 26th of July Movement

The Movimiento 26 de Julio, or 26th of July Movement, was the revolutionary organization created by Fidel Castro to topple the Cuban government of Fulgencio Batista y Zaldivar. The name was born July 26, 1953, after a failed attack by Cuban rebels on the army's Moncada Barracks in Santiago de Cuba, which marked the beginning of the struggle against the Batista regime.

On March 10, 1952, Batista had seized power in a bloodless coup. In response to what many Cubans saw as a usurpation of their constitution, on July 26, 1953, Castro led a 160-man assault on the Moncada Barracks. The attackers picked that date because it was the one hundredth anniversary of the birth of Cuban patriot José Martí. After Batista's forces suppressed the uprising, they massacred sixty-eight of the captives in retaliation for the loss of twenty-two soldiers. Although Fidel and his brother Raúl initially escaped, they eventually surrendered in order to stop Batista's police from persecuting innocent people in Santiago. Fidel, a trained lawyer, defended his action in court with the argument that Batista's government, not *his* movement, was in violation of the law. After all, Batista had seized power illegally and then committed atrocities against defenseless prisoners. Fidel promised to lead a revolution which would promote land reform, economic modernization, employment opportunities, and expanded health and welfare services. The speech made him a hero to Cuba's youth and common people.

The tribunal sentenced Fidel to fifteen years in prison on the Isle of Pines, but Batista's government pardoned him after only eleven months. He and eighty-one other rebels then went to Mexico, where they reestablished the movement, which included a young Argentine named Ernesto "Che" Guevara. However Mexico proved no safe haven. The rebels received harassment from Mexican authorities, the FBI, and Batista agents. At one point, a Mexican police unit bribed by Batista imprisoned the movement leaders. After their release they decided to leave for Cuba.

They prepared their yacht *Granma,* and early on November 25, 1956, they sailed from the port of Tuxpan. On November 30 a radio broadcast informed them that Frank País had launched an uprising in Santiago de Cuba. On December 2, following a rough passage during which they exhausted their provisions, the sick and motley band reached the beach at Las Colorados. The stormy seas forced a daylight landing, and a ship spotted them. Fleeing the Cuban Air Force and then the Cuban Army, they finally regrouped in the Sierra Maestra mountain range, but only twelve of the eighty-one remained.

The remaining movement members formed a small guerrilla base from which Castro organized raids against military installations, where he seized weapons. They subsequently worked closely with local peasants. Fidel invited *New York*

Times reporter Herbert Matthews to his camp, and Matthews' reports created such international attention that new recruits joined. Urban guerrilla groups also became auxiliaries.

Early in 1958 as the movement grew, the U.S. State Department misread Cuban disaffection with Batista and reported that the dictator had the situation under control. Reality soon caused a change in direction. The Eisenhower administration demanded that Batista schedule free elections, and to increase the pressure it withheld arms shipments. In March 1958 forty-five civic organizations signed an open letter supporting Castro. One month later a general strike began to spread.

In April the movement divided into two units—the military group centered in the mountains and plains and the underground, urban wing led by Frank País. On May 24 Batista's army launched Operation Verano, an assault on Castro's stronghold in the Sierra Maestra. During the Battle of Jigue in July, more than ten thousand government soldiers failed to dislodge Castro's men. In late August the rebel army commenced conventional attacks. Cementing their friendly relationship with peasants, on October 10, 1958, movement rebels granted tenant farmers, squatters, and sharecroppers ownership of the land which they worked if it was less than sixty-seven acres.

In December 1958 rebel forces won a bloody battle for control of the city of Santa Clara. Batista and his closest advisers secretly boarded a flight to the Dominican Republic. A military junta opposed to the movement formed a provisional government, but on January 2, 1959, Cuban workers responded to Fidel's call for a general strike. Within twenty-four hours Guevara led a contingent into Havana. On January 6 the movement leadership appointed Manuel Urrutia acting president, and two days later, greeted by thousands of supporters, Fidel arrived in Havana.

During the following months disagreements among the rebel leadership culminated in acquisition of almost total power under Castro. In 1961 the movement was integrated into the *Organizaciones Revolucionarias Integradas,* and in 1965 it became the heart of the United party of the Cuban Socialist Revolution, later the Communist party of Cuba. Today the movement's flag is ubiquitous, and the 26th of July remains the single most important day on the Cuban calendar.

See also *Castro Ruz, Fidel; Cuban Revolution, 1956–1959, U.S. Policy toward*

. . . . WILLIAM HEAD

References and Further Reading

Chomsky, Aviva, and Pamela Maria Smorkaloff, eds. *The Cuba Reader: History, Culture, Politics*. Durham, NC: Duke University Press, 2003.

Guevara, Ernesto. *Che Guevara and the Cuban Revolution: Episodes in the Revolutionary War, 1956–1958*, edited by Mary-Alice Waters. New York: Pathfinder Books, 1996.

Leonard, Thomas M. *Castro and the Cuban Revolution*. Westport, CT: Greenwood Press, 1999.

Quirk, Robert E. *Fidel Castro*. New York: Norton, 1993.

Szulc, Tad. *Fidel: A Critical Portrait*. New York: Harper Collins, 2000.

Cuba, Permanent Treaty with the United States, 1903

The Cuban Permanent Treaty with the United States was a 1903 treaty between the two nations following the Spanish-American War, which granted Cuba full independence and defined the relationship between the two nations for the next thirty-one years. On December 10, 1898, Spain and the United States signed the Treaty of Paris, by which Spain renounced all rights to Cuba. It basically ended the Spanish Empire in the Americas and marked the beginning of U.S. expansion and political hegemony in the western hemisphere. The U.S. protectorate over Cuba lasted from 1899 to 1902, when the Permanent Treaty was concluded.

While Cubans believed that independence meant complete freedom from foreign presence, they did not know that the treaty was being constructed by Republican Senator Orville Platt (R-CT) and would include the Platt Amendment as a rider to an Army appropriations bill. While the amendment was named for Platt, it was actually drafted by Secretary of War Elihu Root. The treaty allowed America to end its occupation of Cuba once it was signed and "leave the government and control of the island of Cuba to its people." However the Platt Amendment established eight conditions to which the Cuban government had to agree before the U.S. forces withdrew.

It prohibited Cuba from entering into any international arrangement that might compromise Cuban independence or allow foreign powers to use the island for military purposes. America also reserved the right to intervene in Cuban affairs in order to defend Cuban independence and to maintain "a government adequate for the protection of life, property, and individual liberty" (Text of the Platt Amendment). It forced the Cubans to initiate plans to improve sanitary conditions on the island, relinquish claims on the Isle of Pines (today *Isla de la Juventud*), and agree to sell or lease territory for coaling and naval stations to the United States. This provision eventually gave the United States lease rights over Guantánamo Bay. Finally it made the Cuban government conclude a treaty with the United States that made the Platt Amendment legally binding and part of the Cuban constitution.

The basic motivation for this high-handed action was U.S. desire to protect its commercial business interests in Cuba. This amendment, which became part of the Permanent Treaty, circumvented the 1898 Teller Amendment, introduced by Senator Henry Teller of Nebraska, which committed the United States to granting Cuba full independence after Spanish forces left. By incorporating the Platt Amendment into the Cuban constitution, the United States was able to shape Cuban affairs without technically violating the Teller Amendment.

The Cubans in the meantime completed work on their constitution in early 1901 and prepared for free elections and the birth of a new democratic regime run by the Cubans themselves. They were shocked by the provisions of the treaty, and many protested the addition of the Platt

Amendment. While the Cubans loathed the terms, they had no alternative but to accept the terms and on June 12, 1902, in a highly contentious vote, the Cuban congress agreed to the treaty.

On May 22, 1903, Herbert G. Squires, envoy extraordinary and minister plenipotentiary, representing President Theodore Roosevelt and Cuban President Carlos de Zaldo y Beurmann, signed the treaty in Havana, thus initiating formal relations between the countries. Even though some members of the U.S. Senate opposed the treaty because it committed the United States to potential foreign interventions, in the end they ratified it on March 22, 1904. The Cuban legislature ratified it on June 20, 1904, and it was exchanged between the two nations in Washington, D.C., on July 1, 1904. The next day, President Theodore Roosevelt proclaimed the treaty to be enacted.

Over the next three decades the United States exercised its right to intervene in Cuban political affairs on eight occasions. By 1926 U.S companies owned 60 percent of the Cuban sugar industry and dominated not only the economy but often exercised a direct influence on the sociopolitical structure of Cuba.

Soon after his inauguration in March 1933, Franklin D. Roosevelt introduced the Good Neighbor policy. Even though the president did send Marines and warships to intervene in an upheaval in 1933, by the next year things in Cuba were sufficiently stable for the U.S. president to propose a change in U.S.-Cuban relations.

On May 22, after a brief exchange of notes and series of friendly negotiations, Secretary of State Cordell Hull, Assistant Secretary of State Sumner Welles, and Dr. Manuel Márquez Sterling, Cuban ambassador in Washington, met in Washington to conclude the Treaty of Relations, 1934. A week later they formally signed the treaty and the U.S. Senate ratified it on May 31, 1934. President Roosevelt acknowledged it on June 5, 1934, a day after the Cuban Congress ratified it. The treaty was exchanged on June 9, the same day Franklin D. Roosevelt publicly proclaimed it. Of note was the fact that the Treaty of Relations rejected the Platt Amendment but did not formally return control of Guantánamo Bay to Cuba.

This treaty replaced the Permanent Treaty of 1903 and defined the official diplomatic relationship between the United States and Cuba until Fidel Castro's 1959 Revolution, which took control of Cuba and still rules the island nation to the present day.

See also *Carter, Jimmy; Castro Ruz, Fidel; Cuba, U.S. Embargo of; Good Neighbor Policy; Guantanamo Naval Base; Hull, Cordell; Paris, Treaty of, 1898; Platt, Orville; Roosevelt, Franklin D.; Roosevelt, Theodore; Root, Elihu; Spanish-Cuban-American War 1895–1898; Teller, Henry M.; Welles, Sumner*

. . . . WILLIAM HEAD

References and Further Reading

Hernández, José M. *Cuba and the United States: Intervention and Militarism, 1868–1933*. Austin: University of Texas Press, 1993.

Perez, Louis A. *Cuba and the United States: Ties of Singular Intimacy*. Athens: University of Georgia Press, 2003.

Tegnell, Geoffrey, and Thomas Ladenburg. *Revolution and Intervention: U.S.-Cuban Relations in the Twentieth Century*. Boulder, CO: Social Science Education Consortium, 1991.

Text of the Platt Amendment, www.historyofcuba.com/history/platt.htm.

Thomas, Hugh. *Cuba: The Pursuit for Freedom*. New York: Da Capo Press. Revised editions published 1998 and 2002 in New York by MacMillian. First published 1971.

Cuba, Rapprochement with the United States, 1960s–1990s

On five occasions between 1963 and 1984, high-level and secret talks were held at the United Nations, Washington, D.C., and in Havana, Cuba, between U.S. presidential emissaries and Fidel Castro representatives regarding improvement of relations between the two countries.

The first meeting came in the fall of 1963 when delegates from each country met to discuss a possible secret meeting in Cuba that might include Fidel Castro. The Cuban suggestion came at a time when Castro had been burned by the Soviets in not coming to his rescue during the 1962 missile crisis, Moscow's lack of support for spreading revolution throughout Latin America, and the need for spare parts for U.S.-made machinery that permeated the Cuban economy. U.S. President John F. Kennedy accepted his advisors' suggestion that French journalist Jean Daniel be dispatched to Cuba for secret talks. Daniel's trip was scheduled for November 22, 1963, but the meetings were cancelled following the president's assassination the next day. New president Lyndon B. Johnson did not pursue the matter or two other gestures Castro put forward: in a July 6, 1964 *New York Times* interview and in his speech marking the fifth anniversary of the Cuban Revolution, July 26, 1964. Johnson was more interested in expelling Cuba from the Organization of American States (OAS) and having the organization help tighten the economic embargo on the island.

The third initiative came in June 1974 from Henry A. Kissinger, secretary of state and national security advisor to President Richard M. Nixon. Kissinger was motivated by the U.S. congressional opposition to continuing the U.S. embargo on Cuba, the fact that many European and Latin American nations opened trade relations with Cuba, and that improved relations fit into the larger administration policy of rapprochement with the Soviet Union and China. For the next 18 months several secret meetings were held in Havana, New York, and Washington, D.C., between advisors to Kissinger and Castro. Although the embargo issue dominated the conversation, a wide range of topics were also discussed, including human rights and compensation for nationalized U.S. properties in Cuba. The United States abruptly ended the discussions in February 1976, allegedly because of Cuban support for Puerto Rican independence and its commitment of troops to the Angolan Civil War.

Jimmy Carter came to the White House in January 1977 with a greater interest in Latin America than his two immediate predecessors and desirous of improving relations with Cuba. While calibrated steps were taken on both sides, including the establishment of "Interests Sections" in each nation's capital, the U.S. embargo and Cuban troops in Africa remained stumbling blocks to significant progress. In early 1978 Castro signaled his willingness to seek further accommodation. The first set of private talks began in May 1978 and led to the release and deportation of 2,500 political prisoners in Cuba to the United States that November. Several subsequent discussions were held throughout 1980 in Havana and Cuernavaca, Mexico, but nothing materialized. U.S. policymakers stiffened their position because of Castro's support of Maurice Bishop in Grenada and Sandinistas in Nicaragua and Cuba's continuing military role in Angola.

The final rapprochement proffer came in 1981 from Castro. Although not publicly known at the time, Soviet economic support of Cuba was beginning to weaken. Castro also understood that, in President Ronald Reagan, he faced an ardent anticommunist who would be pleased to topple the Cuban regime. Reagan set as a precondition for reaching any understanding that Cuba must sever its relationship with the Soviet Union, something no one expected in 1981. Given this, the discussions were meaningless when Secretary of State Alexander Haig met with Cuban Vice President Carlos Rafael Rodríguez in Mexico City in November 1981 and Special Ambassador Vernon Walters with Castro in Havana in March 1982. Castro made one more appeal in December 1984, but Reagan rejected it.

Cuban-U.S. relations reached their lowest ebb in nearly a generation when Reagan left office in 1989 and remained so through the late 1990s as the U.S. Congress tightened the embargo with the Torricelli and Helms-Burton bills. Despite President Bill Clinton's efforts to ease tensions just prior to leaving office, beginning in 2001 President George W. Bush changed direction when he tightened trade restrictions and presented a long list of demands that stripped the Castro brothers and their followers of all government positions and he introduced democratic practices that Cuba needed to meet in order to begin discussions on the normalization of relations with the United States.

United States policy again shifted direction with the presidential election of Barack Obama in November 2008. Three months into his administration, in April 2009, Obama delivered on his campaign promise to improve Cuban relations by lifting his predecessor's restrictions on Cuban-U.S. travel to the island and the restrictions on their financial remittances to Cuban relatives. Following Obama's initiative, numerous U.S. congresspeople who supported rapprochement with Cuba visited the island. Several of them met with Fidel or Raúl Castro. Although President Obama's representatives met on three separate occasions with Cuban government officials in Havana during the 2009 summer, analysts suggest that a rift between the Castro brothers dampens the opportunity for further rapprochement. Reportedly Fidel Castro does not share his brother's desire for warmer relations with the United States.

See also *Castro Ruz, Fidel; Cuba, U.S. Embargo of; Cuba, U.S. Relations with*

. . . . THOMAS M. LEONARD

References and Further Reading

Leonard, Thomas M., *Castro and the Cuban Revolution*. Westport, Ct: Greenwood Press, 1999.

"United States–Cuban Relations," www.latinamericanstudies.org/us-cuba.htm

Cuba, U.S. Embargo of

The Cuban Embargo, called the Blockade in Cuba, is not just one law; rather it consists of many presidential orders as well as laws that prohibit trade, travel, and political relations between the United States and Cuba. The basis for the presidential powers behind the embargo lies with the Trading with the Enemy Act of 1917. The act has been amended many times since 1917 and provides the president the power to restrict trade between the United States and its enemies in times of emergency. The goal of the embargo has been to bring about a democratically elected government in Cuba, one without the leadership of Fidel or Raúl Castro. In addition it has had the goal of bringing capitalism to the island. The embargo has been in place in one form or another since 1960. Virtually every president in the United States since 1960 has altered the embargo in some way. The embargo is a part of U.S. foreign policy and it became codified into law in 1992.

ESCALATING TENSION TO FULL EMBARGO

Castro and his revolutionary government came to power in January 1959. U.S. concerns about Cuba grew when the Cuban government enacted the Land Reform Law on May 17, 1959, which confiscated property for the state, including property owned by U.S. citizens. The U.S. government did not agree with the measure of compensation offered to the previous owners.

The next act that sparked U.S. reaction was a trade agreement in February 1960 between Cuba and the Soviet Union in which Cuba purchased crude oil from the Soviet Union, and the Soviet Union bought sugar from Cuba, sold raw materials to Cuba, and provided $100 million in credit. Consequently, with the encouragement of the U.S. government, U.S. and British oil companies refused to refine the oil. Castro responded by nationalizing the oil companies. In retaliation, in July 1960, the U.S. government cut the Cuban sugar quota. Castro countered by nationalizing U.S. companies in Cuba, including U.S. banks. The U.S. reaction was strong. On October 19, 1960, President Dwight D. Eisenhower stopped virtually all trade with Cuba except food and medicine. On January 3, 1961, the United States broke off all diplomatic relations with Cuba.

In April 1961 relations between Cuba and the United States spiraled downward as a result of an invasion in Cuba by American-trained, anti-Castro Cuban exiles. This invasion, called the Bay of Pigs, was specifically supposed to bring down the Cuban government; it was easily thwarted, however, by the Cuban military. Castro became incensed, and on May 1, 1961, he announced that Cuba would become a socialist republic. Aid from the Soviet Union rose substantially.

A paladore or home restaurant permitted to operate in public following Cuba's economic meltdown in the wake of the collapse of the Soviet Union and the loss of its economic assistance in 1991. The U.S. embargo on Cuba only intensified following the fall of the Iron Curtain.

SOURCE: Thomas M. Leonard Collection

The United States did not stand idly by. On September 4, 1961, Congress passed the Foreign Assistance Act that prohibited aid to Cuba and authorized the president to establish and maintain a total embargo on all trade between the two countries. In addition, on February 7, 1962, President John F. Kennedy stopped all trade with Cuba, including the reexport of Cuban goods from other countries. Finally, on August 1, 1962, Congress prohibited any aid to countries that assisted the Cuban government.

Unilateral sanctions by the United States had effectively closed relations with Cuba, but the U.S. government began to push for multilateral sanctions as well. In response to this pressure, the Organization of American States (OAS) excluded the Cuban government in 1962. By 1964 the OAS had imposed a commercial embargo on Cuba as well.

In 1962 the United States and Cuba became embroiled in the most intense standoff to date, and one that had global ramifications. The Cuban government had begun building missile bases on the island. The United States already had missile bases in Turkey, within range of the Soviet Union. Therefore the Cuban bases were seen as a prelude to war between the United States and the Soviet Union. After negotiations, however, the missile bases were dismantled. Relations continued to worsen, however. In 1963 Kennedy expanded the embargo by banning any travel to Cuba by U.S. citizens and any U.S. citizen from engaging in any financial or commercial transactions with Cuba. Moreover the Department of Commerce tightened restrictions on exports of food and medicine to Cuba and Congress restricted aid to any country that traded with Cuba.

1975–1982: A BRIEF THAW

In contrast to the 1960s, the years between 1975 and 1982 witnessed a reduction of restrictions against Cuba, both multilaterally and unilaterally. On July 28, 1975, the OAS voted to end its sanctions against Cuba. By this time many countries in the organization had already begun trading with Cuba again. In addition, Gerald Ford began to reduce some of the restrictions on U.S. trade with Cuba. For example he eased limitations on exports to Cuba by foreign subsidiaries of U.S. companies. Subsequently President Carter used his presidential prerogative not to renew earlier regulations. For example he did not renew the regulations on U.S. citizens traveling to Cuba and did not renew the regulation against spending U.S. dollars in Cuba. By 1978 Cubans could send money to their families, and by 1979 they were allowed to visit their families in Cuba.

1982–1996: RENEWED RESTRICTIONS

After the lenient Ford and Carter years, the next presidents, Ronald Reagan and George H. W. Bush, began tightening the restrictions again. Reagan strengthened the trade embargo by imposing more travel restrictions. In April 1982 he stopped all charter flights from Miami to Cuba.

President George H. W. Bush tightened the embargo more than it had been in decades. The U.S. government believed that because of the fall of the Soviet Union in 1991, and therefore the end of substantial aid to Cuba from the Soviet Union, increased sanctions against Cuba would cause Cuba's communist government to fall. Therefore in 1992 he signed the Cuban Democracy Act or the Torricelli Act. The Torricelli Act forbade U.S. companies, including subsidiaries abroad, from engaging in any trade with Cuba. The most controversial part of the act was a stipulation that any ships that had entered Cuban ports would not be allowed to enter U.S. ports for a period of 180 days. It also prohibited foreign-based subsidiaries of U.S. companies from trading with Cuba. Any company that did not adhere to these measures could be fined up to

$50,000. Moreover it decreased aid to countries that traded with or provided aid to Cuba, travel to Cuba by U.S. citizens was again tightened, and it severely restricted remittances to Cuba, including food and medicine.

The next momentous change in the embargo came in 1996. On February 24, 1996, two U.S. planes in Cuban territory that carried members of Brothers to the Rescue were shot down. As a result, on March 12, 1996, President Clinton signed the Helms-Burton Act or the Cuban Liberty and Democratic Solidarity Act. It finally made into law the sanctions against Cuba. It tightened sanctions against Cuba in several ways; in particular the Legislature was now able to override the Executive Branch in some cases regarding the embargo. It barred any foreign company from any business with confiscated Cuban property. Ships docking at Cuban ports were not allowed to dock at U.S. ports for six months. The bill also allowed U.S. nationals to file suit in U.S. courts against persons "trafficking" in their confiscated property. In addition foreign companies that invested in Cuba, especially property that the Cuban government had seized, could be sued in the United States. Other countries reacted strongly against the Helms-Burton Act. For example both Mexico and Canada passed laws that prohibited the Helms-Burton Act in their countries.

1998–2010: THE SLOW LOOSENING OF THE EMBARGO

Perhaps in response to Pope John Paul II's visit to Cuba in January 1998, sanctions began to loosen. By March of that year U.S. citizens were allowed to send up to $1,200 annually to relatives in Cuba, and direct flights between Cuba and the United States were permitted. Travel was still banned, however, if it was not for humanitarian purposes or professional research or sale of pharmaceutical goods.

In response in part to lobbying by agriculturalists in the United States, the Trade Sanctions Reform and Export Enhancement Act was passed by Congress in October 2000. The act allowed the sale of agricultural goods and medicine to Cuba for humanitarian reasons. Cuba did not accept this overture until after Hurricane Michelle in November 2001. President Bill Clinton allowed students to visit Cuba to study and people to send remittances to their families, but he also tightened the laws regarding Cuban immigrants. They now had to prove that they were political exiles. After the turn of the century, partly as a result of anti-embargo lobbying, many aspects of the embargo were lifted. By 2007 the United States was the largest food supplier of Cuba and its sixth largest trading partner.

In 2009 President Obama eased restrictions on travel to and from Cuba by Cuban Americans. In addition he allowed for more money to be sent to Cubans from Cuban American family members. In August 2010 the Obama administration hinted that it would again ease restrictions on travel to Cuba, especially for cultural, educational, and sporting purposes. After the November midterm elections, however, where the Democrats lost seats in the house and senate, any official move by the Obama administration toward opening travel stopped. Obama did make it easier to obtain licenses for travel under the existing regulations, however.

In its fifty-year history the embargo has not succeeded in its primary goal: to end the communist government in Cuba. As of 2010 there were several congressional members, especially from agricultural states, that were against the embargo because they wanted to trade with Cuba. Moreover many other countries believed the laws to be illegal under international law and had their own trading and political relations with Cuba.

See also *Bay of Pigs Invasion, 1961; Bush, George H. W.; Carter, Jimmy; Castro Ruz, Fidel; Clinton, William J.; Communism in Latin America; Cuba, U.S. Relations with; Cuban Democracy Act, 1992 (United States); Cuban Liberty and Democratic Solidarity Act, 1996 (United States); Cuban Missile Crisis, 1962; Cuban Revolution, 1956–1959, U.S. Policy toward; Dictators, U.S. Policy toward; Ford, Gerald R.; Helms, Jesse; Obama, Barack H.; Reagan, Ronald W.*

. . . . GINA HAMES

References and Further Reading

Kaplowitz, Donna Rich. *Anatomy of a Failed Embargo: U.S. Sanctions against Cuba.* London: Lynne Rienner, 1998.

Kaufman, Susan, and David Rothkopf, eds. *Cuba: The Contours of Change.* London: Lynne Rienner, 2000.

Roy, Joaquin. *Cuba, the United States, and the Helms-Burton Doctrine.* Gainesville: University Press of Florida, 2000.

Schwab, Peter. *Cuba: Confronting the U.S. Embargo.* New York: St. Martin's Press, 1999.

Smith, Wayne S., and Esteban Morales Dominguez, eds. *Subject to Solution: Problems in Cuban-U.S. Relations.* London: Lynne Rienner, 1988.

Cuba, U.S. Relations with

In the early twenty-first century, with its focus upon global terrorism and economic globalization, Cuba appears as a secondary issue to U.S. people and policymakers alike. The exceptions would be largely among the elder members of the Cuban American communities in south Florida, northern New Jersey, and northwest Indiana. To these people the aged Castro brothers who govern the island deserve nothing less than a vengeful retribution for forcing them to leave the homeland with the advent of Castro's revolution in 1959. For thirty-two years of the forty-six years of the Cold War, Cuban Americans received a sympathetic ear among U.S. policymakers. But with the collapse of the Soviet Union, the threat of communism dissipated and North American interest in Cuba's geopolitical importance waned.

Long before Fidel Castro's 1959 revolution, however, Cuba occupied an important place in U.S. policy. A 745-mile-long island, Cuba is located in the northern Caribbean Sea, with the Atlantic Ocean to its north. It is separated from the United States by ninety miles of waters known as the Florida Straits that provide direct passage into the Gulf of Mexico and washes ashore from the southern tip of the Florida peninsula westward past Alabama, Mississippi, Louisiana at Texas, and again southward to Mexico's Yucatán Peninsula. Between

The map and key above show the Soviet missile sites in Cuba that nearly sparked a nuclear war in 1962. The map also shows the U.S. Naval base in Guantanamo Bay, the Isle of Pines (a source of dispute after Cuban independence), and Mariel, the originating point from which approximately 125,000 refugees were allowed to leave, by Cuban leader Fidel Castro in 1980.

Cuba's most eastern point and Haiti's most western point is the Windward Passage that connects the Atlantic Ocean to the Caribbean Sea, a body of water that borders the southern shores of the Yucatán Peninsula southward along the coast of all Central American states, except El Salvador, then east to Colombia and Venezuela, then north and westward back to Cuba. The Windward Passage is in the direct path of shipping between the Panama Canal the eastern seaboard of the United States. Strategically located, Cuba is important to the flow of U.S. commerce, to its circum-Caribbean security interests, and to the movement of its naval ships between the Atlantic and Pacific Oceans.

COLONIAL PERIOD

On his first voyage to the New World, Christopher Columbus waded upon the Cuban shore on October 28, 1492, sailed along its southern shore during his second visit in 1494, and reported it to be a peninsula of the Asian mainland. Only after his son Diego conquered the territory in 1509 was Cuba recognized as an island. Over the next two centuries Cuba became an important piece of its New World empire. Its tobacco and sugar made their way into the European markets and the latter in the North American colonies. The city at Havana developed into a major port of call as the last stop for ship supplies for those vessels sailing back to Europe, just as the Windward Passage that sat between eastern Cuba and Haiti served as a major entry point for ships entering the Caribbean Sea from the Atlantic Ocean.

Because Cuba remained a Spanish colony and in theory closed to trade with the outside world, the value of its clandestine trade with the United States is unknown. From these contacts North Americans came to understand that Spain tightly controlled local government through Spanish-born (*peninsulares*) administrators appointed by the government in Madrid at the expense of Cuban-born whites (*criollos*), who operated most of the agricultural land, the merchant houses, and small businesses that contributed to the vibrancy of Havana and smaller towns across the island. At the bottom of the socioeconomic pyramid were the African slaves, free blacks and their descendents, who not only lacked civil and political rights, but with few exceptions, personal freedom. In addition to these colonial traits, informed North Americans and Cubans understood that their relationship was impacted oftentimes by events beyond their control, such as the British occupation of Havana in 1762 and 1763, the American Revolution from 1776 until 1783, and Toussaint L'Ouverture's successful 1791 revolt in Haiti.

Cuba remained impervious to the winds of revolution that swept across Central and South America in the early part of the nineteenth century. The *peninsulare* administrators and military remained loyal to the Spanish system. Despite their differences with the *peninsulare* class, the *criollo* sugar growers and refiners still benefitted from the Spanish mercantile system. Both groups had a special interest in maintaining the rigid social structure. As their counterparts from the mainland flocked to Havana during Latin America's independence movements in the early nineteenth century, and brought with them stories of violence, destruction, economic ruin, and the calamity caused in ending lower class restraints, this only reinforced island residents' belief that life was better under the Spanish flag. When Latin America completed its independence in 1826, only Cuba and Puerto Rico remained under Spanish control. The legacies from three hundred years of colonial experiences would have a long-lasting effect on the United States-Cuban relationship.

PRECARIOUS BEGINNINGS: THE EARLY NINETEENTH CENTURY

Thomas Jefferson, who maintained that the United States would someday acquire Cuba, instructed U.S. consuls in

Havana to watch for political events that might indicate a Cuban desire for a union. In 1809 he dispatched General James Wilkerson to Cuba to sound out Spanish authorities and others opposed to Joseph Bonaparte sitting on the Spanish throne about linking Cuba to the United States. Yet in October 1808, Jefferson's cabinet refused a proposal from a Cuban delegation to Washington requesting annexation to the United States. Jefferson recognized that the *peninsulares* and *criollos* were badly split over their loyalty to Spain and that it was best not to inject the United States into the argument. Before leaving office Jefferson advised incoming President James Madison to grant Napoleon a free hand in all the colonies of Spanish America in return for ceding Cuba to the United States. Madison rejected the advice.

Madison did fear, however, that the British-French conflict raging at the time might spread to the Caribbean and leave one of these powers in control of Cuba. Rumors in 1817 and 1818 asserted that Britain intended to occupy the island, and this increased pressure upon the new president, James Monroe, to annex Cuba. On the advice of his cabinet, the president begged off because the effort would jeopardize negotiations with Spain over the U.S. acquisition of Florida. Still, like his predecessor, Monroe dispatched an emissary to Cuba, New England businessman William Shaler, who reported that the *criollos* were widely split regarding their loyalty to Spain. And like his predecessor, Monroe rejected a secret proposal for the U.S. annexation of the island from a group of dissident Cuban *criollo* planters.

U.S. policy took a definitive stance following an 1821 *criollo* uprising against Spanish authority that threatened to escalate into a racial war with blacks, both free and slave. The uprising prompted a debate within Monroe's administration. Secretary of War and South Carolinian John C. Calhoun favored annexation on the grounds that a black Cuba would prevent any future U.S. annexation and that it would incite black uprisings across the U.S. south. Secretary of State John Quincy Adams argued otherwise. He claimed that the *criollo* leadership would be equally inept and result in constant racial conflict that would prompt British and/or French intervention to protect their Caribbean interests. Furthermore any British intervention could translate into a threat against U.S. security. Adams concluded that Spain's archaic rule over Cuba, rather than Cuba's independence, better served U.S. interests. The secretary prevailed and Adams' reasoning became the basis of U.S. policy toward Cuba until the century's end. British Foreign Minister Lord George Canning shared Adams' opinions, and in 1825, he wanted to form a tripartite pact to guarantee Spain's control over Cuba. Adams, then president, deferred to the policies of Washington and Jefferson of no permanent or entangling alliances. For the moment the Monroe Doctrine that declared the western hemisphere off limits to European colonization sufficed.

Over the next generation domestic issues on both sides of the Florida Straits contributed to little more than the usual discussions about Spanish imposed taxes and other fees on commerce between the United States and Cuba. With a high degree of nationalistic rhetoric, the North Americans argued about the merits and demerits of continuing the National Bank, the building of roads with federal monies, and the panic (recession) of 1837. In Cuba Spain continued to tighten its administrative control much to the dislike of the *criollos,* while the tobacco and sugar plantations continued to prosper. In both places, however, the slavery issue continued to simmer, more open in Cuba than the United States. Slave revolts were more common in the former, while testy rhetoric on the immorality of slavery and the underground railroad characterized the latter.

Between 1800 and 1840 Cuba became a sugar monoculture. That year it accounted for nearly 60 percent of Cuba's export earnings, with the United States the largest importer. The number of U.S. ships arriving in Cuba rose from 150 in 1796 to slightly over 1,500 in 1840. In turn the Cubans imported staves, barrels, hoops, nails, textiles, fish, salt, corn, flour, and rice from the United States. U.S. manufactures, such as iron-based products, provided the essential equipment for the ever expanding number of sugar refining mills. The expansion of sugar production also required a drastic increase in the labor force. It came in the form of African slaves. The number of slaves in Cuba rose from 85,000 in 1792 to 287,000 in 1827 to 436,000 in 1840, or approximately 45 percent of the Cuban population. A second demographic change fostered by the sugar expansion was the emergence of an entire new class of *criollo* landowners, who were at odds with the *peninsulare* government class and Madrid's rules of trade that they were sent to enforce. These economic and demographic changes would continue to intensify and eventually have serious repercussions in Cuban-U.S. relations.

Long before coming to the presidency in 1845, Democrat James K. Polk supported John Quincy Adams' "hands off" policy toward Cuba, but President Polk confronted an ever increasing southern demand for the annexation of Cuba, an intensity that deepened when the southerners learned that the land acquired from Mexico in the 1848 Treaty of Guadalupe Hidalgo would not support a slave-based economy. This in turn would have an adverse impact upon the south's representation in the national Congress. Polk, who was committed to purchasing Cuba, took the issue up with his cabinet in May and June 1848. In the end Polk's offer of $100 million to Spain was quickly rejected. The Madrid government informed the president that it would rather see Cuba sink into the sea than in North American hands.

After a four-year interlude the expansionist Democrats returned to the White House with the election of Franklin Pierce, who quickly set out to purchase Cuba. For that purpose southerner Pierre Soulé was dispatched to Madrid, but before arriving there, he met secretly with the U.S. ministers to London and Paris, James Buchanan and John Mason, respectively, in Ostend, Belgium, to discuss the matter and report back to Secretary of State William L. Marcy. They agreed that the United States should offer up to $120 million for Cuba and, if the Madrid government refused, take every measure necessary to gain control of the island from Spain. The Ostend Manifesto, though really a diplomatic dispatch and not a manifesto, became public before it reached Secretary Marcy in Washington in November 1854. The clamorous and critical public reaction in Europe and the United States stymied the initiative to acquire Cuba.

The Pierce administration also faced a potential filibuster expedition from the United States. John A. Quitman, former governor of Mississippi, planned an invasion of Cuba that would coincide with a *criollo* uprising and result in the island's annexation to the United States. Quitman, however, aborted the plan after Pierce announced that his administration would strictly enforce the nation's neutrality laws and the Spanish crushed the *criollo* uprising in February 1855.

During the time the United States maneuvered to acquire Cuba, a Cuban insurrectionist, Narciso López, led three attempts between 1848 and 1851, to drive the Spanish from Cuba. Lopez was a one-time, Spanish-appointed official in Cuba who amassed a variety of landholdings and mining interests. Initially López aligned himself with *criollos* in Havana and New York, who favored annexation to the United States in hopes of preserving Cuba's orderly social and economic structures without the Spaniards. On his last expedition in April 1851, López and his forces fell before the Spanish troops and López and one hundred of his surviving men were taken to Havana for summary trials and executions.

CUBAN WARS FOR INDEPENDENCE

Subsequently the Cuban issue became secondary to the domestic problems the United States confronted over slavery in the western territories and its four-year Civil War (1861–1865). But not so in Cuba where the *criollos,* mostly associated with sugar and its refining and ancillary businesses, became increasingly disgruntled with Spanish discriminations and the fear of a potentially free slave population. The disconnect with Spain finally erupted into the Ten Years' War (1868 to 1878). The war cost an estimated two hundred thousand lives and property damages estimated at $700 million. In the Treaty of Zanjón that ended the conflict, Spain promised administrative reforms, amnesty for the rebels, and emancipation of all slaves. Although slavery ended in Cuba in 1886, the Afro-Cubans remained tied to the plantation economy. Spain failed to deliver on the other reforms, causing continued Cuban *criollo* discontent with Spanish authority.

The war had other far-reaching effects on the development of Cuban society. It not only decimated the *criollo* class, but it opened the door to U.S. entrepreneurs. They filled the vacuum created by the ruin of the *criollo* aristocracy and the bankruptcy of Spanish interests. In the 1880s thousands of North Americans accompanied their investment dollars to the island to run the sugar plantations, mills and refineries, and merchant houses. By the mid-1880s an estimated $50 million was poured into Cuba by U.S. private investors. These trends contributed to Cuba's increased economic dependence on the United States. By 1895 Cuba ranked third behind Britain and Germany in exports to the United States. The U.S. market accounted for 87 percent of the Cuban exports. During this same time period, from 1878 to 1895, Cuban intellectuals, at home and abroad, increasingly blamed Spain for their poverty and the island's underdevelopment and unrest.

By the latter part of the 1880s many North American leaders throughout society accepted the "large policy" advocated by expansionists. The policy called for the need for markets, raw materials, and strategic ports, the need to improve the quality of life of "backward" peoples, and in anticipation of a transisthmian canal, the need to secure entrances into the Gulf of Mexico and the Caribbean Sea. Cuba fell into the purview of the "large policy." Its ample ports provided jump-off points for trade throughout the Caribbean and on to South America. Having endured nearly four hundred years of Spanish mismanagement, Cuba could become an object lesson for the implementation of U.S.-styled democracy in the underdeveloped world. These factors converged in the North American mindset by the time the Cuban War for Independence began on March 25, 1895.

The lack of leadership stymied the Cuban effort for independence during the 1880s. That changed in 1892 when José Martí founded the Cuban Revolutionary Party (CRP). With generous financial support from Cuban exiles, Martí prepared to liberate Cuba from Spanish authority. The conflict began on March 25, 1895. Despite Martí's death on May 19, 1895, his generals continued the fight. By the end of 1895 the rebels were at the gates of Havana and the Spanish army had a new general, Valierano Weyler, who soon found himself engaged in a guerrilla war against the rebels. Weyler's brutal tactics included *reconcentrados,* camps where entire villages were placed. Camp conditions were atrocious. Inadequate facilities, insufficient food supplies, and poor sanitation and medical conditions brought death to thousands of camp inhabitants. The cost to Spain in lives and money prompted an outcry to end the war in late 1897, but the Cubans rejected the offer of home rule within the empire.

Weyler's tactics also contributed to a popular moral crusade across North America, advanced by the "yellow press," to rid the island of brutal Spanish authority and replace it with a U.S.-style democracy. Advocates of the "large policy," who recognized Cuba's geostrategic importance, and defense strategists, who anticipated the American constructed and owned transisthmian canal, were soon joined by business groups, who anticipated opportunities on the island. Racists stood in opposition, arguing that the Afro-Cubans, *mestizos,* mulattos, and other mixed bloods were incompatible with North American society and values and could not be uplifted. Isolationists protested against any venture into the larger world, fearful of a European reaction.

Amidst this emotional and public debate, in the early evening of February 16, 1898, the USS *Maine* exploded in Havana harbor, killing 266 men. Only years later did a naval commission confirm that an explosion in the ship's engine room, not a torch by either loyalist or rebel forces, caused the tragedy. It mattered little; the United States marched toward war. On April 11, 1898, President McKinley asked for authorization to use military force to bring the Cuban situation to a conclusion. Congress obliged on April 19. When the president signed the declaration of war on April 25, war was declared to have existed since April 21. The declaration included the Teller Amendment that prevented the United States from annexing Cuba and sanctified its occupation only for the time necessary to put a functioning government in place. Any U.S. economic designs upon Cuba were checked by the Foraker Amendment that denied the occupying U.S. military government from granting any concessions for any business, mining, or infrastructure pursuits during the period of occupation. From all appearances the United States embarked on a moral crusade.

The U.S. portion of the war was short, technically four months. Hostilities officially ended in a White House ceremony on August 12, 1898. The U.S. suffered more casualties from yellow fever than in battle. Peace negotiations began in Paris on October 1 and the final accord, signed on December 10, 1898, granted to the United States the Philippine Islands, Guam, Puerto Rico, and Cuba, but the latter for only long enough to prepare it for independence. In addition Spain absorbed Cuba's $400 million debt, giving the new nation the opportunity to start with a clean slate.

The U.S. military occupation of Cuba began January 1, 1899, and lasted until May 20, 1902. First under the direction of General John R. Brooke and subsequently General Leonard Wood, the U.S. military directed sweeping infrastructure, and sanitation and health programs, including the containment of the deadly yellow fever disease. U.S.-based education and judicial systems were introduced. But when it came to implementing a democratic government, Wood, his advisors, and Washington, D.C., policymakers concluded that the legacies of four hundred years of Spanish occupation left the masses of Cubans, meaning Afro-Cubans, incapable of understanding, much less practicing, the principles of democratic government. While the *criollos* were capable, they would need long-term supervision, a conclusion that led Wood to insure that the "better classes" controlled government and for U.S. policymakers to grant Cuba its independence in 1902 only if the Platt Amendment became part of the Cuban constitution. The Cuban ruling class paid a heavy price. It reluctantly accepted the Platt Amendment that granted the United States control over its fiscal and monetary matters and foreign policy, limited its international debt, and granted the right to intervene when political stability was threatened.

FROM INDEPENDENCE TO REVOLUTION: 1902–1959

U.S. policy toward Cuba paralleled its circum-Caribbean policy for the first thirty years of the twentieth century. It sought to bring democratic government to countries plagued by the legacies of Spanish colonialism. Government instability in one country could spill over into another; fiscal irresponsibility made possible foreign intervention to collect debts. In both instances the security of the Panama Canal was at stake. Despite the work of Charles Magoon and Enoch Crowder, the United States achieved little in Cuba by 1920. And like other U.S. interventions in the Caribbean—the Dominican Republic, Haiti, Guatemala, Honduras, and Nicaragua—the U.S. search for political and fiscal stability provoked a sense of anti-American nationalism. Economic investments were one area where the North Americans did succeed. By the mid-1920s in Cuba, not only did the United States consume the majority of Cuban sugar and supply the island with almost all of its consumer goods, U.S. investors poured nearly $150 million into Cuban infrastructure: railroads, ports, warehouses, communications, water and sewerage, and tourism.

So pervasive was the U.S. presence in the Cuban economy that historian Leland Jenks entitled his 1928 book *Our Cuban Colony*. Clearly, on the eve of the Great Depression, Cuba had become economically dependent upon the United States, which, for all intents and purposes, appeared to support Cuba's established order. Cuban President Gerardo Machado acknowledged as much, when, at the 1928 Inter-American conference meeting in Havana, he spoke about the good that U.S. presence had done for Cuban development. Machado stood alone, however.

Other Latin American states spoke against U.S. interventionist policy at three other Inter-American conferences during the 1920s. A new generation of Cubans came of age during the 1920s, questioning not only the island's elite rulers but also the U.S. relationship. Their protests permeated Machado's presidency and contributed to his ouster in 1933. The call for withdrawal was equally widespread in the United States. The State Department recognized its failure to democratize the Caribbean nations. The Commerce Department argued that withdrawal from the region would contribute to an increase in hemispheric trade.

The lack of a European threat and the Democratic party's critique of intervention, together with these failures, contributed to President-elect Herbert Hoover's 1928 goodwill trip to Latin America and J. Rueben Clark's *Memorandum on the Monroe Doctrine* that denounced the Doctrine's Roosevelt Corollary. All of this led to the Good Neighbor policy enunciated by Secretary of State Cordell Hull at the Seventh International Conference of American States, meeting in Montevideo, Uruguay, in December 1933. Ironically the new U.S. policy was announced between the military's installation of socialist Ramón Grau Martín on September 10, 1933, and his ouster by the military on January 14, 1934. Army Sergeant Fulgencio Batista installed the socialist Grau Martín in Cuba's presidential palace, and with encouragement and approval from Franklin Delano Roosevelt's special emissary, Sumner Welles, and minister, Jefferson Caffrey, removed Grau Martín from office. From 1934 until his own election in 1940, Batista manipulated the presidency to his own advantage. He oversaw the writing of a new constitution in 1940, considered the most progressive in Latin America at the time. Batista curried favor with the United States, signing a Reciprocal Trade Treaty and agreeing to abrogate the Platt Amendment in 1934 and being one of the few to support the U.S. search for prewar hemispheric defense. When war erupted on December 7, 1941, Batista became an ardent supporter of the Allied cause and gave the United States free use of its territory for defense purposes. Economically the Cuban sugar growers benefitted immensely. With other sources of raw sugar—Eastern Europe, the Ukraine, and Southeast Asia were lost to the battlefield—the United States annually purchased the entire Cuban sugar crop for distribution to the Allied countries.

But all was not well in Cuba. As world sugar supplies returned to the global market in 1947 and 1948, the global demand for Cuban sugar significantly dropped. Rather than accept a series of U.S. grants and loans to diversify the Cuban economy, the sugar growers, refiners, and those in ancillary enterprises joined with communist national representatives to reject the U.S. largesse with assertions that it was just another way for the United States to assert its control over Cuba. The ever growing middle sector that benefitted from U.S. economic presence increasingly demanded honest elections, a free and democratic government and justice system, and an end to corruption, all legitimate. After 1948 the public outcry against the self-serving elitist government intensified. Fearing government collapse and possible anarchy, a group of army officers persuaded Batista to return to Cuba from Daytona Beach, Florida, where he had gone following the 1944 presidential contest. When Batista recognized that he could not win the 1954 presidential election, he engineered a coup d'état on March 10, 1952. He instituted six years of autocratic and brutal rule that sent Cuba down the road to revolution. The U.S. embassy in Havana reported on these events, but little more.

THE ERA OF THE CUBAN REVOLUTION, 1959-PRESENT

When the Eisenhower administration began in January 1953, Cuba was no more than a distant concern. The administration sought only to maintain Cuba's share of the sugar quota as a means to stave off political instability. Arthur Gardner, a political appointee, served as U.S. ambassador to Cuba during Eisenhower's first presidential term. He established a close and friendly relationship with Batista and ignored the State Department's instructions to establish contacts with his opponents. Gardner and his embassy staff consistently underestimated Fidel Castro's significance and the extent of the opposition to Batista. Others shared Gardner's positive view of Batista, including Vice President Richard M. Nixon, who, during his visit to Havana in February 1955, publically compared Batista to Abraham Lincoln and reported to Eisenhower that Castro was a remarkable man interested solely in Cuba's development. A Wall Street banker with no international experience, Earl E. T. Smith replaced Gardner in June 1957. He mistrusted the embassy staff and, fearing a public rebuke from Secretary of State John Foster Dulles, prevented critical analysis of Batista from reaching the State Department.

Meanwhile Castro continued to make strides and appeared to have a large and vibrant fighting force, as his interviews in February 1958 with *New York Times* reporter Herbert Matthews revealed. The Cuban response to the Matthews' interviews startled the unprepared Washington policymakers. Eisenhower responded by cutting Cuba from the U.S. Military Assistance Program (MAP). But Smith refused the State Department's instructions to establish contact with moderate opposition groups and, until his resignation in January 1959, he continued to identify Castro as a communist. After March 1958 opposition to Batista intensified and became violent, particularly Batista's punishment of dissidents, real or imagined. By December 1958 Batista's demise was apparent, but Eisenhower hoped to save the country from Castro when he dispatched William Pawley on a secret mission to Havana. When Batista refused to compromise, the United States stepped away. Isolated and devoid of support, in the early morning hours of January 1, 1959, Batista, along with several close advisors, fled to the Dominican Republic.

During the two remaining years of the Eisenhower administration, events on both sides of the Florida Straits led U.S. policymakers to conclude that Castro was indeed a communist and that he stood as a threat to western hemispheric security. This premise became the basis of U.S. policy toward Cuba for the next 50 years.

During his visit to the United States in April 1959, Castro announced that Cuba would be open to all and not reliant upon one country; he promised democracy with opportunity for all, along with economic and social development. Castro met privately with Vice President Nixon, who could not determine if Castro was a communist but said that he was naïve enough to fall victim to it. For sure Castro's actions on the island defied his rhetoric. *Batistianos* and other members of the Cuban elite were immediately executed after mock trials; elections were postponed, Castro consolidated his political power, rents and salaries came under government control, and agricultural lands were confiscated. For sure Castro established a brutal dictatorship, but events in 1960 made him a communist in the eyes of U.S. policymakers. On February 4, 1960, Soviet Deputy Premier Anastas Mikoyan arrived in Havana to open an exposition of Soviet consumer goods, but in reality he came to conclude a trade agreement with the Cuban government. The agreement provided Cuba with a twelve-year $100 million credit to purchase Soviet-made consumer items, construction materials, and machinery. In return the Soviets agreed to purchase five million tons of Cuban sugar for five years.

U.S. policymakers and the public recoiled at the Soviet presence. In the spring of 1960 U.S. policy response hardened. In March Eisenhower gave the Central Intelligence Agency (CIA) permission to plan for training a Cuban-exile brigade to invade the island. The belief was that a popular uprising against Castro would follow. John F. Kennedy learned of the plan following his November 1960 presidential election. He hesitantly approved the plan only a month before the April 1961 invasion and when it took place, he failed to approve the necessary protective air cover; without it, the invasion quickly collapsed. The international prestige that the Bay of Pigs fiasco cost Kennedy in 1961 was regained as a result of the October 1962 missile crisis. The Soviets placed intermediate range missiles in Cuba beginning in June 1962, not to defend Cuba as Castro believed, but to gain a sense of geopolitical balance with the United States. Premier Nikita Khrushchev reasoned that Soviet missiles within striking range of major U.S. east coast cities counterbalanced the U.S. missiles in western Europe aimed at the Soviet Union. Castro learned a harsh lesson when the Soviet missiles were withdrawn. Cuba was little more than a pawn between the Cold War superpowers. As a result Castro distanced himself from Moscow until the near collapse of the Cuban economy in 1968. Kennedy, however, remained fixated on the Cuban leader and sought his removal through attempting assassination, the undermining of his authority, destroying his public image, and attempting to destroy the Cuban economy under Operation Mongoose, a CIA-implemented operation. President Lyndon B. Johnson cancelled the operation in 1964.

Eisenhower's second policy initiative took place in public—the Congress—during the spring of 1960. Congressional representatives expressed vehement opposition to Castro and, like members of the administration, argued that the island's economic strangulation would bring the desired political change. Toward that end congress approved the Sugar Act of 1960 that continued to secure a special place in the U.S. sugar market for another year, but with the proviso that the president could adjust the quota as the situation demanded. That "situation" came on June 29, 1960, when Castro, as he promised if the Sugar Act became U.S. law, nationalized U.S.-owned oil companies. A week later, on July 6, Eisenhower embargoed Cuban sugar for the remainder of the year. In turn Castro continued the nationalization of U.S. businesses. In response Eisenhower imposed a total embargo, except for food and medicine, on October 19, 1960. And before leaving office on January 20, 1961, Eisenhower severed U.S. diplomatic relations with Cuba. President Kennedy tightened the embargo with restrictions on travel and monetary remittances to the island. Responding to an anti-Castro public groundswell, Congress cooperated with legislation on September 4, 1960, that imposed a total trade embargo. Kennedy persuaded western European allies to curtail their shipping to Cuba and for Japan to find other sources to satisfy its demand for sugar. Finally, as a Marxist or Communist state, Kennedy made Cuba ineligible for assistance under the Alliance for Progress. President Lyndon B. Johnson continued the hard line when, in July 1964, he persuaded the Organization of American States (OAS) to expel Cuba and shut down trade with the island. He was not as successful in persuading western European allies to further curtail their shipping to Cuba. Still the measures had their cumulative effect, and when combined with Ernesto "Che" Guevara's failed economic policy, the Cuban economy faced total collapse by 1970.

Other factors contributed to a changing global policy toward Cuba. It's economic weakness spoke for itself and contributed to international criticism of the U.S. embargo. The war in Vietnam not only resulted in criticism of U.S. involvement both home and abroad but opened the debate about the righteousness of wars of national liberation, including Cuba. President Richard M. Nixon's visits to China and the Soviet Union in 1972, coupled with his disinterest in Latin America, contributed to changes in policy toward Cuba. The western Europeans expanded their trade; Japan, India, and Southeast Asian nations soon followed. Between 1971 and 1975 several Latin American nations ended their Cuban embargo and welcomed Cuba into Latin American economic organizations. Finally, at the 1975 OAS meeting in San José, Costa Rica, the hemispheric trade ban on Cuba was lifted, leaving each nation free to pursue its own course. Although the United States approved the measure, it continued its own embargo that remains in effect today. In fact George W. Bush further tightened the embargo in 2004, only to have restrictions on U.S. travel and remittances to Cuba loosened by President Barack Obama in 2010 and 2011.

Other significant bilateral issues included the migration of Cuban people to the United States. Initially the outmigration was dominated by the Cuban elite and middle sectors, who opposed the revolution. But Castro controlled the escape valve. Following the exodus of an estimated five thousand people by boat from the port city of Camarioca, Castro closed the door to the mass exodus of these people, whose professions were important economic assets, and instead agreed to regularly scheduled plane flights from Havana to Miami. Between 1965 and 1973 250,564 people escaped Cuba on these freedom flights. The 1980 Mariel Boatlift and the *balseros* in 1994 totaled 150,000 people who reached the United States. The exodus of these nonelites, largely people of color, was used by the U.S. press to illustrate the serious plight of socioeconomic conditions in Cuba.

Cuba's forays into global affairs were intended to strengthen Cuba's international image, but each instance produced the opposite impact. Clearly Cuban soldiers served Soviet interests in Africa from 1974 to 1977. Having just extricated itself from Vietnam, the United States could do little but protest. The ineptitude of Cuban military forces in Grenada during Operation Fury in 1983 weakened Cuba's prestige in the socialist world. And on two occasions the United States dealt directly with the Soviet Union to solve the crisis. In 1970 Secretary of State Henry Kissinger successfully challenged the Soviet construction of a submarine base at Cienfuegos, and in the 1980s the North Americans again negotiated an end to Soviet aid to the Nicaraguan Sandinistas, including Cuban military advisors, doctors, and other support personnel.

While Castro orchestrated a vociferous public outcry in the 1999–2000 crisis over Elián González, it was the United States that determined his fate. Found drifting alone at sea by Miami fishermen, the five-year-old Cuban boy was brought to Miami. According to U.S. policy at the time, he was entitled to U.S. citizenship, but the Clinton administration determined that the boy was better served by being returned to his father in Cuba. Castro claimed victory, but few outside Cuba believed him.

The collapse of the Soviet Union in 1991 brought new economic investors to Cuba and not the United States, but those investments slowed dramatically after September 11, 2001, and the subsequent global war on terror. The Cuban economy worsened to the degree that the government imported U.S. foodstuffs, beginning in 2002. Retired president and father of the Cuban Revolution, Fidel Castro admitted publicly in late 2010 that the communist model does not work. Castro also issued a rebuke of the Iranian regime and its Middle East policies that antagonize the United States. These statements, accompanied by President Raúl Castro's announcement that the one million state jobs would be eliminated and trade reforms would be pursued, suggested to many analysts that Cuba is reaching out to the United States as it had in 1963, 1964, 1977, 1981, and at various times in the 1990s. With the exception of Jimmy Carter, the previous efforts at rapprochement stumbled on issues dating to the 1959 Cuban Revolution. In the changed world of 2011, would they do so again?

See also *Adams, John Quincy; Batista y Zaldívar, Fulgencio; Bay of Pigs Invasion, 1961; Castro Ruz, Fidel; Cuba, Rapprochement with the United States, 1960s–1990s; Cuba, U.S. Embargo of; Cuban Americans; Cuban Democracy Act, 1992 (United States); Cuban Liberty and Democratic Solidarity Act, 1996 (United States); Cuban Missile Crisis, 1962; Cuban Revolution, 1956–1959, U.S. Policy toward; Dance of the Millions; Grau San Martín, Ramón; López, Narciso; Jefferson, Thomas; Louisiana Purchase, 1803; Monroe Doctrine; Platt, Orville; Soulé, Pierre; Spanish-Cuban-American War 1895–1898; U.S. circum-Caribbean Interventions, 1900–1934: Cuba*

. . . . THOMAS M. LEONARD

References and Further Readings

Brenner, Philip. From Confrontation to Negotiation: U.S. Relations with Cuba. Boulder, CO: Westview Press, 1988.

"Castro's Change of Heart: The Implications for Cuba, Venezuela and the United States." Report on the Hemisphere, Council on Hemispheric Affairs, Washington, DC, Vol. 30, no. 17, September 28, 2010, 1+.

Erisman, H. Michael. *Cuba's Foreign Relations in a Post Soviet World.* Gainesville: University Press of Florida, 2000.

Foner, Philip S. *A History of Cuba and Its Relations with the United States*, 2 vols. New York: New York International Publishers, 1965.

Gellman, Irwin F. *Roosevelt and Batista: Good Neighbor Diplomacy in Cuba, 1933–1945.* Albuquerque: University of New Mexico Press, 1973.

Gleijeses, Piero. *Conflicting Missions: Havana, Washington and Africa, 1959–1976.* Chapel Hill: University of North Carolina Press, 1982.

Jules, Benjamin. *The United States and the Origins of the Cuban Revolution.* Princeton, NJ: University of Princeton Press, 1990.

Jules, Benjamin. *The United States and Cuba: Hegemony and Dependent Development*, 1880–1934. Pittsburgh, PA: University of Pittsburgh Press, 1977.

Kaplowitz, Donna. *Anatomy of a Filed Embargo: U.S. Sanctions against Cuba.* Boulder, CO: Lynne Reiner, 1998.

Levine, Robert M. *Secret Missions to Cuba: Fidel, Bernardo Benes and Cuban Miami.* New York: Palgrave, 2002.

May, Robert E. *Southern Dream of a Caribbean Empire, 1854–1861.* Baton Rouge: Louisiana State University Press, 1973.

Morely, Morris H. *Imperial State and Revolution: The United States and Cuba, 1952–1986.* Cambridge, UK: Cambridge University Press, 1987.

Morely, Morris H., and Chris McGillion. *Unfinished Business: America and Cuba after the Cold War, 1989–2002.* Cambridge, UK: Cambridge University Press, 2002.

Offner, John T. *The Unwanted War: The Diplomacy of the United States and Spain over Cuba, 1895–1898.* Chapel Hill: University of North Carolina Press, 1992.

Peréz, Louis A. *The United States and Cuba: Ties of Singular Intimacy.* Athens: University of Georgia Press, 1990.

Peréz, Louis A. *Cuba between Empires, 1878–1902.* Pittsburgh, PA: University of Pittsburgh Press, 1983.

Peréz, Louis A. *Cuba under the Platt Amendment, 1902–1934.* Pittsburgh, PA: University of Pittsburgh Press, 1983.

Sullivan, Mark P. *Cuba: Issues for the 111th Congress.* Washington, DC: Congressional Research Service, 2010.

Cuban American National Foundation

The Cuban American National Foundation (CANF) is the largest and most influential Cuban exile organization in the United States. The organization is headquartered in Miami and maintains field offices in Chicago, Jacksonville, Los Angeles, New Orleans, Tampa, San Juan, Puerto Rico, and West New York, New Jersey. The CANF worked to bring about the removal of Fidel Castro from power and now seeks the removal of Raúl Castro, the end of communism in Cuba, and the transition of Cuba toward a democratic, capitalist society. Its website describes its work as efforts to "advance human rights in Cuba, educate public opinion on the plight of the Cuban people, dispel prejudice and intolerance against Cubans in exile and promote Cuban culture and creative achievements" (www.canf.org/).

FOUNDING AND EARLY YEARS

Jorge Mas Canosa, a Cuban exile who escaped to Florida in 1960 and participated in the failed Bay of Pigs invasion during April 1961, and Raúl Masvidal, a banker, founded CANF in 1981. Since then the organization has worked tirelessly to marshal a hard-line anti-Castro and anticommunist stance among U.S. policymakers toward Cuba. One of CANF's major successes in its early years occurred in 1983 when it successfully lobbied President Ronald W. Reagan to establish Radio Martí, Spanish-language radio programming transmitted from the United States into Cuba. Reagan and CANF intended Radio Martí to operate similarly to that of Radio Free Europe, which was broadcast from the 1950s to the 1980s and contained programming that aimed to increase public opposition toward communist regimes. Under Jorge Mas Canosa's leadership, CANF secured millions of dollars in funding for the programming from the U.S. government. The first broadcast of Radio Martí aired on May 20, 1985, and programming continues to this day. In 1990 CANF led successful efforts to launch TV Martí, which carried televised anti-Castro programming, news, and entertainment to the Caribbean island. During the 1990s, CANF established and funded its own radio station, *La Voz de la Fundación* (The Voice of the Foundation), to transmit programming into Cuba.

1990S AND 2000S

With the collapse of the Soviet Union during the summer of 1991 and during the subsequent presidency of William Jefferson Clinton, the U.S. government devoted significantly less attention toward communism than it had throughout the Cold War in prior decades. Nevertheless CANF continued to lobby political figures of both major parties to adopt or maintain anti-Castro positions. The foundation also participated in charitable causes resulting from natural disasters. In the aftermath of Hurricane Andrew's devastation of southern Florida in August 1992, CANF took an active role in the relief and recovery efforts by donating funds and supplies such as food and clothing. Throughout the 1990s the organization's cofounder and spirited leader, Jorge Mas Canosa, visited anti-communist political figures from around the world to draw attention to his organization's cause and to foster international anti-Castro sentiments. Mas Canosa met with Russian President Boris Yeltsin, Spanish Prime Minister José María Aznar, and Argentine President Carlos Saúl Menem.

The foundation scored legislative victories with the passage of the Cuban Democracy Act (also known as the Torricelli Act after its sponsor, Democratic New Jersey Congressman Robert Torricelli) and the Cuban Liberty and Democratic Solidarity Act, commonly referred to as the Helms-Burton Act for its sponsors, Republican North Carolina Senator Jesse Helms and Republican Indiana Congressman Dan Burton. President George Herbert Walker Bush signed the Torricelli Act into law on October 23, 1992, which tightened the U.S. trade embargo on Cuba by further restricting American companies from engaging in trade with Cuba and prohibiting U.S. citizens and residents from sending money to persons in Cuba. The Helms-Burton Act of 1996 contained a variety of provisions that maintained and strengthened the trade embargo and intensified U.S. opposition to the Castro regime. However CANF suffered a major setback on November 23, 1997, when Mas Canosa died of lung cancer and respiratory failure at the age of fifty-eight in his southern Florida home.

During the ongoing political saga regarding the fate of Elián González, a six-year-old Cuban citizen rescued at sea in November 1999, CANF took an active role in the campaign to keep González in the United States with his extended family rather than return the boy to his father in Cuba. Ultimately, however, federal agents removed González from a cousin's house in Miami, and he was subsequently returned to Cuba and reunited with his father despite widespread outrage among the Cuban American community. The failed attempt to keep González with his U.S.-based relatives represented a major public relations embarrassment for the anti-Castro CANF, which had been one of the most powerful and successful lobbying organizations in the United States over the previous two decades.

CANF has been vocal about the need for social, political, and economic reforms within Cuba since Fidel Castro turned over presidential authority to his younger brother Rául in the summer of 2006. Since Cuba's change in leadership, CANF has advocated that the U.S. government take a more active role in pressing for postcommunist, prodemocracy policies within Cuba.

See also *Cuba, U.S. Relations with; Cuban Americans; Cuban Liberty and Democratic Solidarity Act, 1996 (United States); González, Elián; Helms, Jesse; Latinos and U.S. Policy; Radio and TV Martí*

JUSTIN D. GARCÍA

REFERENCES AND FURTHER READING

Bardach, Ann Louise. *Cuba Confidential: Love and Vengeance in Miami and Havana.* New York: Vintage Books, 2003.

Levine, Robert M., and Moises Asis. *Cuban Miami.* Piscataway, NJ: Rutgers University Press, 2000.

Cuban Americans

Cuban Americans constitute the third-largest nationality of Latinos in the United States, after Mexican Americans and Puerto Ricans. According to the 2000 Census, approximately 1.225 million persons of Cuban ancestry lived in the United States. Cuban Americans comprise between 3 and 4 percent of the total U.S. Latino population. Although the majority of Cuban Americans live in southern Florida, other Cuban communities exist in New Jersey, New York, and Pennsylvania. Cuban Americans, as a group, are quite distinct from other Latino national-origin groups in terms of socioeconomic status, manner of entry into American society, and political affiliation. Cuban Americans, on average, have higher levels of education than either Mexican Americans or Puerto Ricans and a higher per capita income than either group. While Mexican Americans and Puerto Ricans tend to vote for the Democratic party in elections, Cuban Americans have traditionally staunchly supported the Republican party until very recent years when a generation of younger, U.S.-born Cuban American voters have come of age. For example in 2008, Democratic Presidential candidate Barack Obama won a larger portion of Florida's Cuban American vote than any Democratic presidential candidate since the 1980s, as Obama won 57 percent of Florida's Latino vote. Political scientists noted that a generational divide is shifting the Cuban American vote in Florida, with older, first-generation voters still supportive of Republican policies, while younger, American born and raised Cubans increasingly support the Democratic party.

AFTER THE CASTRO REVOLUTION

The vast majority of first-generation Cubans entered the United States as political refugees after Fidel Castro overthrew Fulgencio Batista in 1959 and declared Cuba a communist nation. This time period corresponded with the height of the Cold War, and the U.S. government provided political and financial support to Cubans fleeing the island to undermine Castro's regime. The first waves of Cuban refugees in the early 1960s consisted of the island nation's displaced government officials and upper- and middle-class professionals. The U.S. government provided the early refugees with a generous array of social and financial benefits, including free transportation to the United States, small business loans, and professional job recertification. No prior or later immigrant group had ever been entitled to such extensive benefits. In 1963 schools in Miami-Dade County adopted bilingual education programs for Cuban children, and in 1973 the country officially declared itself bilingual. In the mid-1970s a Spanish-language version of the *Miami Herald* began circulation. Although some Cuban refugees encountered hardships upon arrival, most eventually overcame them. In less than two decades a thriving Cuban American ethnic economic enclave emerged in Miami with numerous Cuban-owned businesses, banks, construction, and other service companies. This ethnic enclave facilitated the incorporation of later-arriving Cuban refugees into

Miami by providing co-nationals with jobs, loans, and a social support network.

A major wave of Cuban refugees entered the United States during the spring and summer of 1980 during the Mariel Boatlift. During this time Castro permitted Cubans who wished to leave the island to do so, and approximately 125,000 refugees entered the United States in less than six months. This large, sudden influx caught southern Florida off guard and led to overcrowding and increased unemployment. The Mariel Boatlift marked a significant shift in public perception of Cubans and led to a stigmatization of the community. While the early waves of Cuban refugees were primarily white professionals and elites, *marielitos* consisted largely of poorer, darker complected individuals. The media reported that several marielitos had criminal records and that the influx also included homosexuals and mentally disabled persons. Even Miami's established Cuban American community expressed some unease with the influx of marielitos.

The rapid growth of the Cuban American population, the growth of Cuban-owned businesses and economic power in Miami, the Mariel Boatlift, and the growing presence of the Spanish language in public life alarmed many Floridians. In 1980 voters in Miami-Dade County approved an "English-Only" language policy referendum that repealed the county's status as officially bilingual and bicultural. A grassroots organization, Citizens of Dade United, sponsored the referendum. Exit polls revealed that white, working-class and middle-class voters were the strongest supporters of the legislation.

Miami's Cuban American community perceived the English-Only referendum as an expression of anti-Cuban hostility, and ironically, the antibilingual ordinance ultimately backfired by prompting greater Cuban participation in Miami-Dade County's political and cultural affairs. For example, Xavier Suarez, an early Cuban refugee, became mayor of Miami in 1985. The growing political power of the Cuban American community enabled Joe Carollo and Manny Diaz, both born in Cuba, to win election as mayor of Miami in 1989 and 2001, respectively. Voters elected Ileana Ros-Lehtinen to the U.S. House of Representatives in 1989 and Lincoln Diaz-Balart in 1992. Both were born in Havana. In the early 1990s, following the election of several Cuban Americans to political office, Miami-Dade County repealed the English-Only policy implemented in 1980.

THE RECENT YEARS

In November 1999 members of the Coast Guard rescued a six-year-old Cuban boy, Elián González, off the Florida coast. González's mother and most of the others on board their boat had drowned at sea trying to reach the United States. González's situation sparked an emotional dilemma as to the whether the boy should be allowed to remain with his uncle in Miami or returned to his father in Cuba. Eventually the federal government decided that González would be returned to Cuba and placed into the custody of his father. When González's relatives in Miami refused to comply with the Department of Justice on handing the boy over for repatriation, federal agents stormed the home on April 22, 2000, and forcibly removed Elián. This incident prompted massive protests from the Cuban American community and a citywide strike against President Clinton, Attorney General Janet Reno, and the U.S. government in general. In response Miami's non-Cuban residents launched counterdemonstrations criticizing Cuban Americans and supporting the U.S. government. The Elián González saga illustrated the divisions between Miami's Cuban and non-Cuban populations. Although Cuban Americans in New Jersey and a dozen other states held rallies expressing support for González to remain in the United States, the rallies outside of Miami did not trigger massive counterprotests.

Several high-profile Cuban American celebrities have had a significant impact on American culture in recent decades. Popular Cuban American actors and actresses include Steven Bauer, Cameron Diaz, Eva Mendes, Andy García, and the late Desi Arnaz. Emilio Estefan is a respected music producer, while Gloria Estefan, Jon Secada, and the late Celia Cruz are world-famous recording artists. Vida Guerra and Daisy Fuentes are popular models. In the world of sports, José Canseco helped the Oakland Athletics reach the World Series from 1988–1990, while pitcher Livan Hernandez led the Florida Marlins to victory in the 1997 World Series and Pablo Morales won gold medals in swimming at the 1984 and 1992 Summer Olympics.

See also *Castro Ruz, Fidel; Cuba, U.S. Relations with; Cuban American National Foundation; Cuban Revolution, 1956–1959, U.S. Policy toward; González, Elián; Latinos and U.S. Policy; Mariel Boatlift, 1980*

. . . . JUSTIN D. GARCÍA

REFERENCES AND FURTHER READING

Grenier, Guillermo J., and Lisandro Pérez. *The Legacy of Exile: Cubans in the United States*. Boston, MA: Allyn and Bacon, 2002.

Portes, Alejandro, and Alex Stepick. *City on the Edge: The Transformation of Miami*. Berkeley: University of California Press, 1993.

Rieff, David. *The Exile: Cuba in the Heart of Miami*. New York: Touchstone, 1993.

Stepick, Alex, Guillermo Grenier, Max Castro, and Marvin Dunn. *This Land Is Our Land: Immigrants and Power in Miami*. Berkeley: University of California Press, 2003.

Cuban Democracy Act, 1992 (United States)

The Cuban Democracy Act, often known by the name of its primary sponsor, Representative Robert G. Torricelli, was a measure passed in 1992 that sought to strengthen and broaden the sanctions on Cuba that had been in place since 1962.

The act's stated goal was to bring about a peaceful transition to democracy and encourage respect for human rights and individual freedoms in Cuba. It sought to achieve this end by developing a two track policy. On the one hand it strengthened the thirty-year embargo on Cuba. It prohibited foreign subsidiaries of U.S. companies from trading with the Cuban government. On the other hand democracy was to be promoted by the development of new communications networks, a relaxation of travel restrictions to the island and the provision of humanitarian aid (though the scope of this latter element was drastically undermined by being made conditional upon on-site inspections). The president was instructed to repeal the measures contained within the bill only when Castro had made demonstrable steps toward free and fair elections and protecting human rights in Cuba.

The bill came before Congress at a time of considerable optimism for anti-Castro activists in the United States. Cuban Americans had been increasingly vocal in Washington during the Reagan years. Moreover, following the collapse of the Soviet Union in 1991, Cuba's primary source of external financial support was removed. Severe fuel shortages in Cuba led to the so-called "Special Period," characterized by a massive loss of industrial and agricultural productivity and endemic unemployment and food shortages. Believing that the collapse of Castro's regime was imminent, supporters of the Torricelli Bill concluded that it would provide the necessary impetus for transforming Cuba into a pro-U.S., liberal and democratic state.

As the bill proceeded through Congress in 1992, the presidential contest between President George H.W. Bush and his Democratic challenger William Jefferson Clinton was underway. Bush initially opposed the bill, arguing that it was unnecessary, likely to damage U.S. relations with third-party nations, and constitutionally problematic. However Clinton quickly moved to support the bill, believing that he could win both short-term campaign benefits and make longer-term inroads into the Cub American vote in Miami. More than a million dollars in campaign contributions from Miami Cubans followed in the subsequent months, and some Cuban Americans eventually shifted support to Clinton in the election. Following Clinton's endorsement President Bush backtracked on his initial opposition and ultimately signed the bill into law. However it was left to his successor to enforce.

The Cuban Democracy Act was controversial from the outset. While supporters considered it to be a necessary step in isolating the Castro regime, opponents of the bill attacked it as a vindictive act of Cold War triumphalism. They tended to argue that economic crisis would not be sufficient to unseat Castro; indeed the anti-American hostility generated by a tightening sanctions regime would provide Castro an opportunity to entrench his rule still further by demonstrating his nationalist credentials. Critics also claimed that the act was more about U.S. domestic political posturing than it was about reforming Cuba. Castro's regime did indeed survive the Special Period. Nevertheless supporters of the act insist that it continues to contribute to the package of U.S. measures that create pressure on Cuba toward regime change.

It is unclear exactly how much aid and business to Cuba have been deterred by the first track component of the Cuban Democracy Act. The European Union unanimously declared its opposition to coercive measures against Cuba shortly following the act's passage. Several European countries continued to provide aid to Cuba, but they were not in receipt of U.S. aid and were therefore unaffected by the act's provisions. Other countries that stopped conducting favorable trade deals in the early 1990s (such as Mexico) were primarily influenced by Cuba's failure to pay prior debts rather than the effect of U.S. laws. And there is little evidence of a major impact on U.S. business subsidiaries. Meanwhile, while President Clinton used the second track component of the law to put forward a series of relaxations on communications and travel during his first term, the crisis of Cuban American relations in 1995 after the shooting down of the Brothers to the Rescue flights significantly narrowed the opportunity for constructive engagement.

The bill's sponsor, Robert Torricelli, went on to be a U.S. senator. His period of office was dominated by a political scandal, and in 2002 he decided not to seek reelection.

See also *Brothers to the Rescue; Bush, George H. W.; Castro Ruz, Fidel; Clinton, William J.; Cuba, U.S. Embargo of; Cuba, U.S. Relations with; Cuban Americans*

. . . . ALEX GOODALL

References and Further Reading

Bardach, Ann Louise. *Cuba Confidential.* London: Penguin, 2004.
Mariño, Soraya M. Castro. "US-Cuban Relations during the Clinton Administration." *Latin American Perspectives* 29, no. 4 (July 2002): 47–76.
Vanderbush, Walt, and Patrick J. Haney. "Policy toward Cuba in the Clinton Administration," *Political Science Quarterly* 114, no. 3 (Autumn 1999): 387–408.

Cuban Liberty and Democratic Solidarity Act, 1996 (United States)

The Cuban Liberty and Democratic Solidarity (LIBERTAD) Act, most commonly known by the surnames of its primary sponsors, Jesse Helms and Dan Burton, was an act passed in 1996 that tightened the thirty-year U.S. embargo on Cuba and transferred substantial authority over it from the presidency to Congress. It marks one of the most notable examples of derogation of presidential authority over foreign policy in recent years, and it resulted in the institutionalization of Cold War policies toward Cuba in the post-Cold War era.

The Helms-Burton Act began its passage through congress in early 1995, following the Republican victories in the congressional elections of 1994 and the raising of Senator Jesse Helms to chair of the Senate Foreign Relations Committee. Helms was a well-known leader among the Republican right, noted for his vocal anticommunism approach in foreign policy and his conservative approach to social issues at home. Its other main sponsor, Dan Burton, was elected in the early 1980s and had an equally strong record for voting with the conservative wing of the Republican party. By 1995 he had established his reputation in the House through repeated attacks on President Clinton's alleged corruption.

The bill proposed a number of measures for tightening the U.S. embargo on Cuba, including restrictions on Cuban accession to international trade bodies like the International Monetary Fund, World Trade Organization (WTO), and North American Free Trade Agreement. However the most significant component was Title III, which was designed to limit Castro's effort to integrate Cuba into the world economy without making an accompanying political transformation. Title

III allowed U.S. citizens to sue corporations that had profited from assets taken by the Cuban regime during or immediately after the Cuban revolution. Since anti-Castro activists considered these assets to be stolen property, the logic of suing the beneficiaries was relatively straightforward. However critics complained that it was unrealistic to invalidate all Cuban government nationalization since 1959 by declaring it to be theft, while many lawyers argued that the law's extraterritoriality was a violation of U.S. international agreements. Radical critics declared that Helms-Burton was simply a continuation of the Monroe Doctrine and Roosevelt Corollary. Opposition was particularly vocal in the international community, where the European Union, Mexico, and Canada all condemned the law.

Following the success of the election-year Cuban Democracy Act in 1992, supporters of the bill, both inside and outside Congress, believed that political pressure in the run-up to the presidential election of 1996 would generate support for the bill and force the administration to adopt it. Initially the State Department opposed the bill, and it appeared that it would fail in the Senate. Clinton's staff considered the existing Cuban Democracy Act of 1992 to be a solid and sufficient basis for U.S.-Cuban relations in the post-Cold War period and lobbied to undermine support for Helms-Burton. In particular they opposed clauses within the bill that sought to punish U.S. businesspeople who sought to develop new market relationships with Cuba. Nevertheless the administration's opposition rapidly fell away following the February 1996 shooting down (by the Cuban air force) of two planes run by the anti-Castro group, Brothers to the Rescue. In the weeks that followed Clinton's administrators not only agreed to support the bill but also acquiesced in the addition of an extra clause which required the president to seek congressional approval for any future relaxation of the embargo. From this point onward the central feature of U.S. relations with Cuba—the sanctions regime—would no longer be left to Executive Branch control. This was particularly significant given the Clinton foreign policy team's clear preference for constructive engagement and free trade policies toward former Cold War rivals, as shown by the president's policy toward Russia, Eastern Europe, China, and the unilateral ending of the Vietnamese embargo a year earlier.

Under sizeable international pressure applied through the WTO, President Clinton suspended the application of Title III of the act in 1997 and meanwhile continued his earlier efforts to increase nongovernmental links among U.S. citizens, U.S. organizations, and the Cuban regime. The measure seems to have failed to deter international business from Cuba: some 180 companies invested in Cuba between the bill's passage and 2000. However analysts have noted that by ensuring that the embargo would only be fully lifted following a vote in Congress, the Cold War framework of relations was institutionalized at a time when other Cold War tensions disappeared. A change in leadership on the Cuban side now seems more likely to significantly alter bilateral relations than changing leadership in the United States. Needless to say this was exactly the outcome that the supporters of Helms-Burton sought to achieve.

See also *Brothers to the Rescue; Castro Ruz, Fidel; Clinton, William J.; Cuba, U.S. Embargo of; Cuba, U.S. Relations with; Cuban Americans; Cuban Democracy Act, 1992 (United States); Helms, Jesse*

. . . . ALEX GOODALL

References and Further Reading

LeoGrande, William M. "Enemies Evermore: U.S. Policy toward Cuba After Helms-Burton." *Journal of Latin American Studies* 29, no 1 (February 1997): 211–221.

Roy, Joaquín. *Cuba, the United States, and the Helms-Burton Doctrine: International Reactions*. Gainesville: University Press of Florida, 2000.

Vanderbush, Walt, and Patrick J. Haney. "Policy toward Cuba in the Clinton Administration." *Political Science Quarterly* 114, no, 3 (Autumn 1999): 387–408.

Cuban Missile Crisis, 1962

On October 14, 1962, a U.S. U-2 reconnaissance plane's photographs confirmed that Soviet missile sites were being constructed in Cuba. President John F. Kennedy immediately formed a fifteen-man executive committee (EXCOM) to advise him on policy options. For the next two weeks the world stood on the brink of nuclear war while EXCOM convened daily meetings and Soviet Premier Nikita Khrushchev huddled with his advisors at the Kremlin in Moscow. The missile crisis ended on October 28 when, in a public radio address, Khrushchev announced that Soviet missiles would be withdrawn from Cuba.

GENESIS

Several theories have been given to explain Khrushchev's decision to place missiles in Cuba. The Soviet leader perceived Kennedy to be weak and indecisive, given his failed leadership during the April 1961 U.S.-sponsored Bay of Pigs invasion and the manner in which he handled the affair in its aftermath. Two months later, during their Vienna summit conference in June 1961, Kennedy's behavior convinced Khrushchev of his hesitancy. Khrushchev wanted to exploit Kennedy's shortcomings. Against the recommendation from his military advisors, who distrusted Castro, Khrushchev placed the missiles in Cuba for the announced purpose of counterbalancing the fifteen U.S. Jupiter missiles in Turkey that were aimed at Soviet cities. U.S. policymakers also understood the wider geopolitical implications: Soviet missiles in Cuba would negate the leverage the United States gained when it placed missiles in western Europe. Fidel Castro was deeply disappointed to learn that Khrushchev did not intend to use the missiles for the defense of Cuba against an American invasion, despite his year-long public clamor to defend the island against a U.S. attack.

Kennedy's reaction is most often placed within the historical context of the Monroe Doctrine and Secretary of State John Quincy Adams' Cuban policy. The first declared the western hemisphere off limits to foreign encroachments, and Adams declared that U.S. security was threatened should Cuba fall into a third party's hands, other than Spain. These 1823 statements remained policy guidelines and were re-enforced by a September 1960 congressional resolution that authorized the president to direct military intervention in Cuba to rid it

October 29, 1962. Meeting of the Executive Committee of the National Security Council (EXCOMM) regarding Cuba, in the Cabinet Room, White House, Washington, D.C. Clockwise from top right side of table: Under Secretary of State George Ball, Secretary of State Dean Rusk, President John F. Kennedy, Secretary of Defense Robert S. McNamara, Deputy Secretary of Defense Roswell Gilpatric, Chairman of the Joint Chiefs of Staff General Maxwell Taylor, Assistant Secretary of Defense Paul Nitze, Deputy United States Information Agency (USIA) Director Donald Wilson, Special Counsel to the President Theodore Sorensen, Special Assistant to the President for National Security McGeorge Bundy, Secretary of the Treasury C. Douglas Dillon, Vice President Lyndon B. Johnson (mostly hidden behind Dillon), Attorney General Robert F. Kennedy, former Ambassador to the Soviet Union Llewellyn Thompson, Arms Control and Disarmament Agency Director William C. Foster, Central Intelligence Agency (CIA) Director John McCone (mostly hidden behind Thompson and Foster).

SOURCE: Cecil W. Stoughton, Courtesy of the John F. Kennedy Presidential Library

of communism. Kennedy's image had been further badgered by Soviet aggressiveness in eastern Europe and its construction of the Berlin Wall in August 1961. Almost unnoticed by public policy analysts at the time was Kennedy's response to the building of the wall, with the airlifting of troops into Berlin as a symbolic warning for the Soviets not to advance into the city's western sector and, by implication, elsewhere, including Cuba. Subsequently some analysts suggested that Khrushchev should have at least paused in Cuba in response to Kennedy's action; domestically political pundits quickly drew a relationship between Kennedy's response to missiles in Cuba and the forthcoming November 1962 congressional elections.

In June 1962 reports within the Cuban communities in Miami and New York City indicated that the Soviets were preparing to construct medium and intermediate range missile sites in Cuba. Through that summer the chatter increased and made its way into Washington's congressional circles, which in turn reported it to the administration. Recalling the failed intelligence by the same communities prior to the 1961 Bay of Pigs invasion, Kennedy administration officials publicly dismissed the reports' validity. In reality, between May and October 1962, the Soviets dispatched to Cuba 47,000 troops, including five missile regiments, twenty-four launching pads, forty-two rockets, forty-two bombers, forty MiG-21 jet fighter planes, two anti-aircraft defense units, and thirty-six nuclear warheads. Subsequently the Russians shipped Intermediate Range Ballistic Missiles (IRBMs) capable of carrying the nuclear warheads. The first U.S. suspicion came from an August U-2 flight, but Soviet ambassador to the United States, Anatoly Dobrynin, consistently denied the missile presence in his conversations with the president's brother and attorney general, Robert F. Kennedy. On September 11 Khrushchev reassured Kennedy that no offensive missiles were shipped to Cuba.

RESOLUTION OF THE CRISIS

The Soviet cover story was blown with the October 14 U-2 flight that showed the construction of SS-4 sites in San Cristobal in western Cuba. Kennedy quickly formed EXCOM, which convened for the first time on October 16 to consider five potential courses of action: (a) do nothing, (b) undertake secret backdoor diplomacy, (c) initiate an air strike to destroy the missiles, (d) launch an invasion, or (e) establish a naval blockade. For the next five days EXCOM reviewed the options and determined a course of action.

Given the congressional resolution that authorized U.S. military action against Cuba and the forthcoming congressional elections, doing nothing was not an option. Secret diplomacy would provide the Soviets sufficient time to complete the missiles' installation and present the United States with a *fait accompli*. Kennedy dismissed the joint chiefs of staff recommendation for a land invasion of the island and Air Force Chief of Staff Curtis Lemay's call for an airstrike to eliminate the missile sites. Because each would cause heavy casualties, including Russian, the president worried that the Soviets might retaliate in Turkey or Berlin, where the United States could not act quickly, and each crisis had the potential to spiral into a wider confrontation. That left a naval blockade as the most reasonable option, but international law considered it an act of war, which Kennedy wanted to avoid at all costs.

Secretary of State Dean Rusk struck a compromise with his proposal for a "defensive quarantine" against the shipment to Cuba of offensive missiles only. Kennedy accepted the State Department's legal consul's advice that a quarantine was legal within the parameters of international law. As such it met U.S. security needs in the circum-Caribbean region, weakened Castro, and gave Premier Khrushchev a way to back out. The Monroe Doctrine and Adams' policy statements were alive and well in 1962. Kennedy accepted the National Security Council's plan of action on October 17. Emissaries were dispatched to inform western European allies, appeals for support were prepared for the United Nations and Organization of American States (OAS), Khrushchev would be asked to withdraw his missiles, and a U.S. naval flotilla would be placed in the Atlantic Ocean five hundred miles north of Cuba. At 5 p.m. on October 18, Kennedy spoke with Soviet Foreign Minister Andrei Gromyko, who reassured him that there were no offensive weapons in Cuba. Kennedy knew better. The next day reconnaissance flights discovered four more operational sites. U.S. ground and air forces were put on full alert, with B-52s of the Strategic Air Command ready to attack on a moment's notice.

October 22 and October 23 became the fateful days. On the morning of October 22, Kennedy authorized the "quarantine." He notified Khrushchev and sent special emissaries to the western European governments to do the same. Secretary Rusk secured OAS approval. At 5 p.m. he informed congressional leaders and called them to the White House. At 7 p.m. he delivered a seventeen-minute national television address revealing the presence of missiles and demanding their removal. He also announced that he was creating a "quarantine" to prevent any more missiles from entering Cuba. He proclaimed that the United States "regarded any nuclear missile launched from Cuba against any nation in the Western Hemisphere as an attack by the Soviet Union on the United States, requiring a full retaliatory response" (Radio and Television Report 1964, 485). Finally Kennedy declared that any Soviet ships entering Cuban waters would be stopped and searched, and if they tried to run the blockade, he would order U.S. ships to fire on them. On October 23 U.S. Ambassador Adlai Stevenson exposed the Soviet missiles before the UN Security Council.

On October 27 and 28 a deal was worked out whereby the Soviet missiles would be removed from Cuba under UN supervision, the Soviet Union would not reintroduce offensive military material to Cuba in return for U.S. promises to secretly withdraw its Jupiter missiles from Turkey, and it would not invade Cuba. Castro was infuriated by the U.S.-Soviet deal in which he played no part, making him little more than a pawn between the Cold War superpowers. Given the embarrassment, in November 1962 Castro refused to permit UN inspectors on to the island to oversee the withdrawal of the Soviet missiles. The United States relied on its own air and sea reconnaissance to verify the withdrawal. Castro henceforth isolated himself from the Soviets until the near collapse of the Cuban economy in 1970.

AFTERMATH

Kennedy was lauded at home and in Latin America for his bold action during the missile crisis. Most of the European allies also applauded the president, but with some hesitancy. They argued that if war erupted between the superpowers, it would be fought on the ground in Europe and not the hurling of missiles between the United States and the Soviet Union.

A subsequent consequence of Castro's refusal to permit UN supervision of the missile withdrawal came in 1970 when the Soviets commenced construction of a submarine base at Cienfuegos. U.S. Secretary of State Henry Kissinger was quick to point out that because of Castro's action, the United States was free to take military action in Cuba, a position that prompted the Soviets to halt construction.

Release of new documents and revelations made at conferences in Washington, D.C., Moscow, and Havana in the early 1990s revealed how close the world came to nuclear war. In October 1962 the Pentagon estimated that 180,000 troops, with a 10 percent casualty rate, would be needed for a successful Cuban invasion. While the Pentagon had germ warfare plans for pre-invasion use, there is no evidence that the discussion reached the highest levels of policymakers. At the same time U.S. intelligence did not know that the Soviets placed 42,000 combat troops in Cuba and that if the U.S. invasion took place, Soviet army commanders in Cuba claimed that they would have used the short-range tactical nuclear warheads at their disposal. One positive result of the whole incident was the establishment of the "hotline" or "red telephone," which afforded U.S. and Soviet leaders with direct communications to avoid a future nuclear crisis.

See also *Castro Ruz, Fidel; Cuba, U.S. Relations with; Kennedy, John F.; Soviet Union, Latin American Policy*

. . . . WILLIAM HEAD

References and Further Reading

Blight, James G., and Philip D. Zelikow, eds. *The Kennedy Tapes: Inside the White House During the Cuban Missile Crisis.* Cambridge, MA: Harvard University Press, 1997.

Brugioni, Dino A. *Eyeball to Eyeball: The Inside Story of the Cuban Missile Crisis.* New York: Random House, 1991.

Brune, Lester H. *The Cuba-Caribbean Missile Crisis of October 1962: A Review of Issues and References.* Claremont, CA: Regina Books, 1996.

Frankel, Max. *High Noon in the Cold War.* New York: Ballantine Books, 2004.

Fursenko, Aleksandr, and Timothy Naftali. "One Hell of a Gamble:" The Secret History of the Cuban Missile Crisis. New York: Norton, 1997.

Hilsman, Roger. *The Cuban Missile Crisis: The Struggle over Policy.* Westport, CT: Greenwood Press, 1996.

"Radio and Television Report to the American People on the Soviet Arms Buildup in Cuba, October 22, 1962." The Public Papers of President John F. Kennedy, 1962. Washington, DC: Government Printing Office, 1964, 485.

Utz, Curtis. *Cordon of Steel: The U.S. Navy and the Cuban Missile Crisis.* Washington, DC: Naval Historical Center, 1993.

Cuban Revolution, 1956–1959, U.S. Policy toward

U.S. policy toward the Cuban Revolution before the flight of dictator Fulgencio Batista on December 31, 1958, vacillated dramatically between support for the dictatorship and support for democratic alternatives. Though it identified high stakes on the neighboring island, President Dwight Eisenhower's administration never found an alternative to Batista on the right and Fidel Castro on the left. The inability to pin down Castro's true intentions confused U.S. policy further. The result was a near paralysis in U.S. policy that allowed Castro to free Cuba from U.S. influence. By late 1959 Washington prepared to overthrow the revolution.

INITIAL RESPONSE

In the first year after Castro and eighty-two other revolutionaries headed out of Mexico on a yacht called *Granma* and ran aground Cuba's shores on December 2, 1956, U.S. policymakers treated this antidictatorial struggle no differently from any other. Castro became ensconced in the southeastern Sierra Maestra with as little as a few dozen men—among them his brother Raúl Castro, Camilo Cienfuegos, and

In the wake of the Cuban revolution, foreign industries and businesses were brought under state control. The Havana Hilton, a symbol of U.S. economic influence on the island, is renamed the "Havana Libre" after the revolution, to emphasize Cuba's break with the United States.

SOURCE: Thomas M. Leonard Collection

Ernesto Che Guevara—and stood little chance of winning. He also controlled only the mountain-dwelling faction of the 26th of July Movement, and his *barbudos* (bearded ones) were only one of several groups fighting Batista. And Cuba, with one of the highest per capita incomes in Latin America, did not seem ripe for revolution.

The U.S. government first responded by increasing its support to Batista. From 1956 to 1957 military aid grew from $1.7 to $2 million and then to $3 million in 1958. This aid was to be used for "hemispheric defense," but its real purpose was to repress internal opponents. Central Intelligence Agency (CIA) Director Allen Dulles also helped found the Communist Activities Repression Bureau (BRAC in Spanish). And in 1956–1958, while the Export-Import Bank approved ten loans to Cuba, the island's sugar exports to the United States increased every year, favored by the U.S. sugar quota. All the while the U.S. Information Service, the Embassy, the American Federation of Labor–Congress of Industrial Organizations (AFL–CIO) union, the thousands of sailors who visited yearly, and the eight thousand U.S. citizens living in Cuba, helped spread U.S. dollars, cultural values, and labor practices.

There was, however, rising interest in Castro in the U.S. media. Most famously, Herbert Matthews of *The New York Times* met with the guerrilla in his mountain hideout on February 17, 1957. Castro charmed Matthews, fooled him into thinking his forces were larger than they were, and convinced him he was not a communist. Matthews' articles showed the world that the 26th of July was alive and well.

GROWING UNEASE AS CASTRO TAKES POWER

A turn in policy began when U.S. officials became frustrated that Batista was unable to end the insurrection even with U.S.-supplied Sherman tanks and B-26 aircraft. Rebels now also attacked U.S. corporations and kidnapped U.S. citizens. In June 1957 Secretary of State John Foster Dulles forced Ambassador Arthur Gardner to resign for his excessive praise of Batista and replaced him with Earl E. T. Smith, who condemned police brutality. In the following months U.S. officials, hoping to improve their intelligence, even developed links with insurrectionists. Washington wondered whether to continue supporting Batista, woo the rebels, or do nothing.

In January 1958 the choice was made to ostracize Castro but ease Batista out in favor of moderates in the June elections. However instead of creating favorable conditions for the elections, Batista increased his red-baiting, suspended political freedoms, and renewed censorship. So on March 14, 1958, the State Department placed an arms embargo on his government. However, immediately under pressure from Smith and the joint chiefs of staff, the State Department eased the embargo in April and May.

Castro's final offensive in fall 1958 caught the U.S. government without solutions. Batista hung on and Castro remained unacceptable to Washington but also more powerful than moderates. The State Department never obtained any evidence of Castro links to communism. The National Security Council met twenty-six times between April and December 1958, yet Cuba was never on the agenda.

In the first week of 1959, the 26th of July rode into Cuban towns triumphantly. Castro then further confused Washington with his two-faced style. Sometimes the Cuban assured foreign corporations that he would not nationalize them and told foreign journalists that he would be free from communist influence. Yet he executed hundreds of *batistianos* in show trials, dismissed elections, and slashed rents and utility rates. U.S. officials had few allies left as Castro edged out moderates and tens of thousands of wealthy and middle-class Cubans emigrated.

In April 1959 Castro visited the United States and Canada and drew huge crowds. The Cuban defied traditional images of the unpopular strongman *and* of the subservient democrat when he refused to accept any economic aid from Washington. For most of 1959 the U.S. media, even anticommunist publications such as *Time* and *Business Week,* welcomed him with cautious optimism. Leftist publications such as *The Nation* and *The New Republic* praised the Cuban's early reforms while rightists such as the *National Review* and most television networks feared his hidden communism.

LOSING CUBA

After May 17, 1959, when Havana unveiled its secretly drafted, radical agrarian reform, U.S. confusion turned to panic. Businessmen stormed the White House, the State Department, and new Ambassador Phillip Bonsal demanding intervention. Losing Cuba most hurt U.S. capital, which, on the eve of the revolution, owned 36 of 161 sugar mills, 2 of 3 oil refineries, 90 percent of public utilities, and half the railroads and mines. Yet for U.S. officials Cuba had broken no law since it promised compensation, and Castro contravened no Inter-American agreement since he still was not aligned with Moscow. They also feared making a martyr out of Castro if they intervened. Their only response, a few formal letters of protest, went unanswered.

In October 1959 Castro exaggerated a dropping of leaflets by a defector in order to consolidate his rule inside Cuba. He also sided with radicals such as Guevara and his brother and jailed *barbudos* such as Húber Matos, who now questioned his independence from communists. These political moves prompted a definitive revision of U.S. policy. On November 5th Herter wrote to the president that he now supported a policy to bring about Castro's downfall. In early 1960 that policy turned into concrete plans to create anti-Castro propaganda, bolster what opposition remained, and prepare an invasion by exiles.

. . . . ALAN MCPHERSON

See also *Bay of Pigs Invasion, 1961; Bonsal, Philip W.; Castro Ruz, Fidel; Central Intelligence Agency (CIA); Cuba, 26th of July Movement; Cuba, U.S. Relations with; Dulles, Allen M.; Dulles, John Foster; Guerrilla Warfare; Guevara de la Serna, Ernesto "Che"; Herter, Christian A.; Matthews, Herbert L.*

References and Further Reading

Bonsal, Philip. *Cuba, Castro, and the United States*. Pittsburgh, PA: University of Pittsburgh Press, 1971.

Paterson, Thomas. *Contesting Castro: The United States and the Triumph of the Cuban Revolution*. New York: Oxford University Press, 1994.

Smith, Wayne. *The Closest of Enemies: A Personal and Diplomatic Account of U.S.-Cuban Relations since 1957*. New York: Norton, 1987.

Welch, Richard Jr. *Response to Revolution: The United States and the Cuban Revolution, 1959–1961*. Chapel Hill: The University of North Carolina, 1985.

Cultural Imperialism

Cultural imperialism can be thought of as the process whereby powerful countries attempt to penetrate and dominate the cultural life of weaker countries by imposing their values, attitudes, and beliefs on them. Commonly identified agents of this domination are the mass media, corporations, voluntary organizations such as missionary groups, and governmental or nongovernmental development agencies. In Latin America the term cultural imperialism has most often been applied to the activities of the United States. Though the United States has never been an imperial power in the classical or formal sense, since the nineteenth century it has made Latin America the object of territorial and economic expansion.

NINETEENTH CENTURY

Nineteenth-century Latin America was marked by a desire to forge an intellectual, cultural, and political path independent of both Europe and the United States. It was during this period that Latin American intellectuals first denounced U.S. cultural imperialism. Uruguayan essayist José Enrique Rodó is best known for his essay, *Ariel* (1900), which is organized as a debate between two characters from Shakespeare's *The Tempest*, Ariel and Caliban, who stood for the United States and Latin America, respectively. In that essay and in other writings, Rodó rejected U.S. utilitarianism and warned Latin American youth against nordomania, the lionization of North American values and culture, urging them to look to Europe and western literary and artistic traditions for their inspiration, rather than to the business-minded United States. This position was informed by the writings of José Martí, who advocated intellectual and cultural independence from both the United States and Europe for all of Latin America, though he admired republican democracy as it was practiced in the United States and the "Protestant work ethic."

At the end of the nineteenth century most Americans believed that Latin America desperately needed to be exposed to the civilizing influence of American culture. As Emily Rosenberg has amply documented, corporations; voluntary associations, such as the Young Men's Christian Association (YMCA); and Protestant missionaries undertook concerted campaigns to spread the values of thrift and the work ethic, modern communication and transportation structures, and ideas about free market capitalism. Corporations sought special concessions to operate telegraph, trolley, and electricity concerns in the region or expand their distribution networks to include major Latin American cities.

EARLY TWENTIETH CENTURY

During World War I the U.S. government took a more active role in spreading American culture in Latin America. For example the Committee on Public Information opened reading rooms in Mexico that made available North American magazines, fiction, and newspapers and offered English classes. Likewise the government worked doggedly in collaboration with private corporations to expand American cable, radio, and news services in Latin America, ensuring multiple outlets for positive stories about American politics and society. Perhaps the single most important vehicle for spreading the American dream, beginning in the 1920s, was motion pictures. Film producers touted the movies' universal values and potential as an instrument of peace, while critics and cultural nationalists decried the way that films spread the values of mass consumption and new forms of sexuality. All agreed that motion pictures had become the best advertisement in Latin America for American mass-produced goods, ranging from clothing to automobiles.

In the 1930s President Franklin D. Roosevelt articulated a new orientation toward Latin America: the Good Neighbor policy. Before the U.S. entered World War II, the Division of Cultural Relations focused on scholarly and cultural exchange. Other government offices worked on information campaigns to counter Nazi influence in Latin America. During the war the Office of the Coordinator for Inter-American Affairs (later the Office of Inter-American Affairs), headed by Nelson Rockefeller, focused on further expanding U.S. control of and access to communications channels and providing technical assistance to Latin America. The film division routinely censored movies destined for Latin American screens, made Spanish-language newsreels, and worked with studios to produce films, such as Walt Disney Studio's animated feature, *Saludos Amigos* (1945), which would foster hemispheric understanding. Once the United States entered the war, the Office of War Information (OWI) continued much of the work of spreading pro-American information. After the war's end the State Department's cultural apparatus shrunk in size. Some of its functions were relocated to specific agencies. The U.S. Information Agency (USIA) was formed to provide an information bulwark—in the form of radio shows, news, and so forth—against communism, while the Fulbright program was designed for the use of intercultural and scholarly exchange to foster understanding and cooperation.

LATER TWENTIETH CENTURY

Many Latin Americans perceived these programs as evidence of the United States's ongoing quest to exert political, economic, and cultural control over the region. In the 1950s media imperialism became the dominant paradigm for thinking about U.S. cultural imperialism in the region. Latin American media and communications scholars examined the structure of the media industries in Latin America using dependency theory, which proposed that asymmetrical relations of power had stunted the development of Latin American countries. Scholars and critics were especially sensitive to the power of the mass media to disseminate values and ways of life considered foreign.

The most well-known example of this school of thought is perhaps Ariel Dorfman and Armand Mattelart's *Como leer al Pato Donald* [*How to Read Donald Duck: Imperialist Ideology in the Disney Comic*]. Written in the aftermath of the Central Intelligence Agency-backed overthrow of Salvador Allende's socialist government, the book offers a reading of Disney comics as an instrument of cultural imperialism, designed to habituate Latin American readers to capitalism. In many countries a growing discontent about the dominance of U.S. culture blossomed into new forms of cultural production such as the *tercer cine* movement.

Scholars have divided theories of cultural imperialism into those that focus on nationalism, critiques of capitalism, and critiques of modernity. In everyday life it is harder to make such distinctions. Anti-American sentiment and arguments against cultural imperialism continue to be mobilized to protest larger sociopolitical processes of economic globalization, industrialization, and modernization that generate high levels of inequality. While it is difficult to define the concept of cultural imperialism, it is clear that many Latin Americans, particularly those not reaping the benefits promised by bilateral or multinational trade agreements such as the North American Free Trade Agreement (NAFTA), perceive U.S. culture as a powerful and negative force.

See also *Good Neighbor Policy; Hispanidad; Martí y Pérez, José Julián; North American Free Trade Agreement (NAFTA), 1992; Rodó Piñeyro, José Enrique; World War II, 1939–1945*

. . . . LAURA ISABEL SERNA

References and Further Reading

Dorfman, Ariel, and Armand Mattelart. *Como leer al Pato Donald.* Valparaiso, Chile: Ediciones Universitarias Valparaiso, 1971.

O'Brien, Thomas F. *Making the Americas: The United States and Latin America from the Age of Revolutions to the Era of Globalization.* Albuquerque: University of New Mexico Press, 2007.

Rosenberg, Emily. *Spreading the American Dream: American Economic and Cultural Expansion 1890–1945.* New York: Hill and Wang, 1982.

Schilling, Herbert I. *Communication and Cultural Domination.* White Plains, NY: International Arts and Sciences Press, 1976.

Tomlinson, John. *Cultural Imperialism: A Critical Introduction.* Baltimore, MD: The John Hopkins University Press, 1991.

Cuyamel Fruit Company

Founded by Samuel Zemurray in 1912, Cuyamel Fruit Company was a successful U.S.-based banana company operating in Honduras during the first half of the twentieth century. Zemurray, who earned the nickname Sam the Banana Man, was a Bessarabian immigrant who began his career as a produce vendor in 1899 selling bananas from a cart in Mobile, Alabama. He eventually relocated to New Orleans and contracted with United Fruit Company (UFCO), the largest U.S.-based fruit company operating out of Central America, to sell bananas that were on the verge of ruin to local dealers. He eventually partnered with Ashbell Hubbard, who had his own UFCO contract in Mobile, to form Hubbard-Zemurray Company in 1903. The partners acquired a couple of steamers and purchased bananas directly from Honduran sources to resale in Mobile and New Orleans. As part of his venture Zemurray secured a concession from the Honduran government to build a railroad between Cuyamel and Veracruz. From the outset UFCO owned 60 percent of Hubbard-Zemurray Company's stock. In 1911, however, Zemurray reformed his company as Cuyamel Fruit, with a goal of outpositioning Vaccaro Brothers and Company (later Standard Fruit and Steamship Company) as the dominant banana exporter in Honduras.

Cuyamel established a successful business in Honduras, especially the La Lima Division. By 1920 Cuyamel secured concessions amounting to railway control from the Honduran government. Zemurray continued to run Cuyamel, and he was not above strong-arm tactics to acquire government concessions or squelch dissent. In 1912, when threatened by export taxes, he practically handpicked and armed General Manuel Bonilla in order to have a president in power who could provide Cuyamel favored status. At the same time Cuyamel grew its market share and assets making it a serious, though minor, rival to UFCO. Its growth and success, however, intensified the rivalry with UFCO, culminating in a series of manipulative efforts as both sides sought to control the situation on the Nicaraguan-Honduran border. A dispute over territory along the Montagua River led Nicaragua and Honduras to the doorstep of war in 1917. Meanwhile Cuyamel and UFCO were in competition for control over the same territory. Although the boundary dispute did not initially lead to war, the quarrel reemerged in 1928 when violence broke out over the disputed territory, with Cuyamel and UFCO leaders undoubtedly pulling the strings.

Seeking to snuff out competition and end an escalating price war, UFCO acquired Cuyamel in 1929 for $32 million. UFCO acquired all of Cuyamel's assets, including its Honduran banana plantations, company steamships, and railroad concessions. Samuel Zemurray, Cuyamel's founder, fared well in the sale. With the sale of Cuyamel he became a large shareholder in UFCO and joined its board of directors. As UFCO struggled during the protracted depression era of the 1930s, Zemurray took over as the company's chairman. In order to reestablish the company he undertook a reorganization, which included replacing UFCO workers with his old Cuyamel workers. UFCO later changed its name to United Brands and in the 1970s, Del Monte purchased UFCO.

See also *Honduras, U.S. Relations with; Standard Fruit and Shipping Company; United Fruit Company (UFCO); Vaccaro Brothers Fruit Company*

. . . . MELVIN D. DAVIS

References and Further Reading

Argueta, Mario. *Bananos y politicía: Samuel Zemurry y la Cuyamel Fruit Company en Honduras.* (Tegucigalpa, Honduras. Editorial Universitaria, 1989.

Karnes, Thomas L. *Tropical Enterprise: The Standard Fruit and Steamship Company in Latin America.* Baton Rouge: Louisiana State University Press, 1978.

Striffler, Steve, and Mark Moberg, eds. *Banana Wars: Power, Production, and History in the Americas.* Durham, NC: Duke University Press, 2003.

Woodward, Ralph Lee Jr. *Central America: A Nation Divided.* New York: Oxford University Press, 1999.

D'Aubuisson Arrieta, Roberto

Roberto D'Aubuisson Arrieta (1944–1992) was a Salvadoran political and military figure. Educated at both the Salvadoran Military Academy (Class of 1963) and the controversial School of the Americas (Class of 1972), D'Aubuisson was a fervent critic of communism and sought to expunge it from El Salvador by any means necessary. His extreme views and actions led the Reagan administration to keep him at arm's length and to support his presidential rival in 1984.

D'Aubuisson was a veteran of the 1969 Soccer War with Honduras, where he distinguished himself as a battlefield commander of a National Guard rifle company. D'Aubuisson achieved the rank of major and spent the majority of his career in the intelligence service. His position as an intelligence officer provided him with a unique opportunity to monitor his enemies. This surveillance, coupled with his attempts to set up an extensive national security network, led to the emergence of the infamous Salvadoran death squads that operated during the country's civil war. D'Aubuisson relied on death squads in part because, as an intelligence officer, he did not command a company of regular Salvadoran troops. He also had some difficulty recruiting supporters from the military establishment due to his political views, which were extremist even by Salvadoran military standards.

During the civil war, D'Aubuisson represented the extreme right wing of Salvadoran society. Despite some misgivings, the military, along with the Salvadoran coffee-growing elite, represented D'Aubuisson's main base of support. He delivered many speeches to promote his anticommunist, pro-military ideology, in which he accused those on the left of harboring anti-military attitudes, and he would often end his speeches by saying, "Long live the armed forces!"

D'Aubuisson's support of brutal counterinsurgency tactics put him into direct conflict with the Roman Catholic Archbishop of San Salvador, Oscar Arnulfo Romero, who had become a leading campaigner for human rights in El Salvador. Romero was assassinated in 1980, purportedly on the order of D'Aubuisson himself. D'Aubuisson's death squad activity, as well as his brutality against political opponents, led to the nickname "Blowtorch Bob," a reference to his preferred means of torture. Throughout his career, D'Aubuisson was implicated in a number of coups, murders, and assassinations.

In 1981, D'Aubuisson founded the Nationalist Republican Alliance (ARENA) in opposition to the ruling revolutionary governing junta, which ruled El Salvador from 1979 to 1982. Founding ARENA represented a concerted effort by D'Aubuisson and his allies to remove the junta from power. Financed primarily by the military and wealthy oligarchs seeking a return of order, D'Aubuisson worked to roll back the reforms that the junta had put in place, especially agrarian reforms. He was also upset by his arrest in the assassination of Archbishop Romero, although he was released without trial.

In 1982 ARENA triumphed in legislative elections by winning nineteen of sixty seats and negotiating a coalition government that put them into power. When the D'Aubuisson-led party won the elections, U.S. officials sought to undermine his administration by tying military aid to a decrease in human rights abuses, among other things. Although D'Aubuisson had long mistrusted Washington, this measure in particular caused estrangement between D'Aubuisson and the United States.

In 1984 D'Aubuisson ran for president of El Salvador against José Napoleón Duarte Fuentes but was defeated. U.S. support for Duarte was key to his victory. Despite D'Aubuisson's staunch anticommunist credentials, the Reagan administration supported Duarte in the presidential election for several reasons. First, D'Aubuisson was seen as an extremist, and his involvement in several high-profile plots, including the assassination of Archbishop Romero, was troubling, even to an administration that placed a lower priority on human rights. Second, because D'Aubuisson was a staunch Salvadoran nationalist, Washington was concerned that U.S. leaders might not have the type of influence over D'Aubuisson that they could have over Duarte. Third, the United States thought that Duarte had the best chance to unite El Salvador, defeat the rebels, and end the civil war.

The 1984 presidential election represented the zenith of D'Aubuisson's career. In 1985, ARENA lost in legislative elections, and in 1988, ARENA chose Alfredo Cristiani, rather than D'Aubuisson, as its presidential candidate. D'Aubuisson never stood trial for any of the crimes to which he was linked, although the United Nations Truth Commission report written at the conclusion of the civil war reported strong evidence of his involvement in the murder of Archbishop Romero. After a lengthy illness, D'Aubuisson died of throat cancer on February 20, 1992.

See also *Cristiani Burkard, Alfredo; Counterinsurgency; Duarte Fuentes, José Napoleón; El Salvador, U.S. Relations with; Soccer War 1969 (Honduras/El Salvador)*

. . . . ANDREW P. MILLER

REFERENCES AND FURTHER READING

Bosch, Brian J. *The Salvadoran Military Officer Corps and the Final Offensive of 1981*. Jefferson, NC: McFarland, 1999.

Lafeber, Walter. "The Reagan Administration and Revolutions in Central America." *Political Science Quarterly* 99, no. 1 (1984): 1–25.

Williams, Philip J., and Knut Walter. *Militarization and Demilitarization in El Salvador's Transition to Democracy*. Pittsburgh: University of Pittsburgh Press, 1997.

Dance of the Millions

The Dance of the Millions describes the speculative cycle that struck the Cuban sugar industry in 1920 and 1921, leading to the collapse of sugar prices, the crash of the national banking industry, and the takeover of sugar property by U.S. financial institutions. Internal political turmoil exacerbated the economic and financial crisis, prompting U.S. intervention in Cuban affairs.

Sugarcane was the backbone of the Cuban economy. Between 1902 and 1913, annual Cuban sugar output rose from 850,000 tons to 2.4 million tons. In 1913, Cuba accounted for 13 percent of the world production of sugar, up from seven percent in 1902. Sugar led Cuba's export-oriented economy, representing 72 percent of Cuban total export value in 1913. Fueling this expansion were the inflow of U.S. investments into the Cuban sugar sector and the privileging of Cuban sugar exports in the U.S. market, which had been facilitated by the Reciprocity Treaty of 1902.

World War I (1914–1918) transformed the patterns of speculative investment and further expanded the Cuban sugar sector. Disruption of the European beet sugar industry by war created shortages that led to greater demand for alternative sources of sugar. Beet sugar production dropped nearly 50 percent, from 8.3 million tons in 1914 to 4.42 million tons in 1918. Cuba picked up the slack, stimulated by market demand that drove sugar prices to unprecedented levels. In 1919, Cuba produced four million tons of sugar, the equivalent of 26 percent of the global supply. The average price of sugar rose steadily from 1.9 cents per pound in 1914 to 4.6 cents in 1918, when the agencies that regulated the sugar supply to the Allies introduced price controls. Whereas the annual value of Cuban sugar hovered around $100 million before the war, the war-induced sugar price boom contributed more than $300 million a year to the Cuban economy in the years 1916 through 1918. This prosperity continued unabated after price controls were lifted in late 1919. Prices that had surged to 9.2 cents per pound in 1919 continued to soar until reaching the historical peak of 22.5 cents in May of 1920. The value of the 1920 sugar crop surpassed $1 billion, when sugar accounted for 92 percent of total exports from Cuba, compared to 72 percent in 1913.

The wartime price boom mobilized large land, labor, and capital resources into the Cuban sugar industry. Cane cultivation expanded into virgin lands in the eastern provinces of Camagüey and Oriente. Thousands of laborers from Haiti, Jamaica, and China were hired to work in the cane fields of eastern Cuba. Large new sugar mills were established in the eastern regions, and existing mills in the traditional cane-growing regions of western and central Cuba were modernized. Although local and other foreign entrepreneurs participated in the sugar boom, U.S. banking and business firms played a very prominent role. These investments involved not only U.S. sugar-refining companies, but also the manufacturers of soft-drink and candy products such as E. Atkins & Company, which had links to the American Sugar Refining Company, and Milton Hershey, the chocolate manufacturer magnate. These firms sought to control all of the stages of the production process through vertical integration. The Coca-Cola Company also sought to secure direct supplies of raw sugar from Cuba.

Cuban and U.S. banks provided the capital that underwrote the Cuban sugar boom. The lucrative Cuban sugar market spurred expanded credit for sugar properties and crops. Beyond mortgaged mills and property, standing and future crops as well as warehoused sugar served as collateral for the loans. After price controls were abolished in late 1919, speculative investments proliferated, property became overvalued, and debt accumulated. Between 1919 and 1920, nearly one quarter of the 200 active sugar mills were sold, often at inflated prices. In late summer of 1920, loans amounting to as much as $80 million had been contracted based on sugar prices as high as 15 to 22 cents per pound. Violent price fluctuations in the second half of 1920 disrupted the speculative foundations of this financial system.

Global sugar prices plummeted when European beet sugar producers resumed exports, reaching a low of 3.8 cents per pound in December of 1920. As a result of a market glut, demand for Cuban sugar shrank, resulting in precariously high levels of debt among sugar producers in Cuba. The National City Bank took over as many as 60 bankrupt sugar mills in 1921. The sugar price crisis also provoked the crash of the Cuban financial system. The Cuban government declared a moratorium on bank withdrawals in order to protect undercapitalized Cuban financial institutions from ruin.

The sugar crisis created serious social and political consequences for Cuba. The population faced shortages of foodstuffs and a steep increase in the cost of living. Unemployment increased in rural and urban areas. The drop in sugar exports depleted government revenue, which in turn affected payments to teachers and public service employees. Discontent caused strikes and widespread public demonstrations.

The rigged presidential elections of November 1920 added a grave twist to the political turmoil. Determined to secure a victory for his Conservative Party, President Mario García Menocal intimidated candidates of the Liberal opposition during the campaign and engaged in electoral fraud. These actions upended the electoral reforms introduced by special U.S. envoy General Enoch H. Crowder in 1919. Appointed by the U.S. Department of State, General Crowder returned to Cuba in late 1921 to resolve the disputed elections. He also received broad instructions to introduce sweeping fiscal and administrative reforms in Cuba.

See also *Crowder, Enoch H.; Cuba, U.S. Relations with; World War I (1914–1917); Export-Based Economies; United States, circum-Caribbean Interventions, 1900–1934: Cuba*

. . . . LUIS A. GONZÁLEZ

REFERENCES AND FURTHER READING

Ayala, César J. *American Sugar Kingdom: The Plantation Economy of the Spanish Caribbean*, 1898–1934. Chapel Hill: University of North Carolina Press, 1999.

Jenks, Leland Hamilton. *Our Cuban Colony: A Study in Sugar*. New York: Vanguard Press, 1928.

Pérez, Louis A., Jr. *Cuba: Between Reform and Revolution*. 2nd ed. New York: Oxford University Press, 1995.

Thomas, Hugh. *Cuba: The Pursuit of Freedom*. New York: Harper & Row, 1971.

Daniels, Josephus

Josephus Daniels (1862–1948) was U.S. ambassador to Mexico from 1933 to 1941, one of the most difficult periods in the history of relations between these two countries. On the surface, Daniels seemed to be ill-suited for this role. A newspaper editor from Raleigh, North Carolina, he lacked diplomatic experience and his informal, folksy style seemed inappropriate. Also, as secretary of the Navy under President Woodrow Wilson, Daniels oversaw the U.S. armed intervention in Veracruz in 1914. Mexicans had bitter memories of this intervention, a problem that brought into question President Franklin D. Roosevelt's choice of Daniels to represent his administration in Mexico City.

Daniels's warm, open personality helped him overcome these difficulties, and he built a friendly working relationship with Mexican government officials. Like many nations during the Depression, Mexico initiated several programs to benefit the general public, and education was at the top of the list. On July 26, 1934, Daniels spoke approvingly of former President Plutarco Elías Calles' call for a revitalization of Mexico public schools. Daniels used a translation of Calles' words that, in essence, endorsed a government program that would "enter and take possession of the mind of childhood." The use of these words proved to be a blunder. Calles had also attacked the Roman Catholic Church in the same speech. Daniels did not mention this aspect of Calles' presentation, but Catholics and conservatives in the United States were offended by Daniels's positive reference to this speech and called for his resignation. The U.S. State Department received more than 10,000 letters and telegrams regarding this controversy, and about two-thirds of them condemned Daniels. The ambassador's tenure was threatened. Nevertheless, Roosevelt stood by Daniels, who continued in his Mexico City post.

The most serious controversy arose in 1938. At issue was the decision of Mexican President Lázaro Cárdenas del Río to expropriate foreign-owned oil properties in the culmination of a dispute between Mexican oil workers and multinational oil companies such as Standard Oil. Daniels had worked closely with Cárdenas and admired the political methods and policy goals of the young president. However, the oil companies, U.S. Secretary of State Cordell Hull, and many leading politicians and newspaper editors in the United States called for an aggressive opposition to the expropriation. Some even demanded military intervention. Daniels opposed this confrontational approach and openly supported Cárdenas. The ambassador used his close relationship with President Roosevelt to advocate a policy of moderation with the ultimate goal of a negotiated settlement. After some dramatic sessions involving oil company executives, diplomats, and financial experts, the negotiation process concluded in 1942. The oil companies accepted the transfer of property, and the Mexican government agreed to compensate the companies but with an amount lower than the companies wanted. The oil companies had originally demanded $200 million, but the final agreement provided a $24 million settlement. While Daniels was not a direct participant in these negotiations, his support of the Mexican government and his persistent calm in the face of controversy contributed greatly to the resolution of the conflict. Daniels stepped down as ambassador in November 1941 and continued to be a popular figure in Mexico.

See also *Calles, Plutarco Elías; Cárdenas del Río, Lázaro; Hull, Cordell; Mexican Revolution, 1911–1917, U.S. Policy toward; Oil, Expropriation of Foreign Companies; Roosevelt, Franklin D.; United States, circum-Caribbean Interventions, 1900–1934: Mexico*

. . . . JOHN A. BRITTON

REFERENCES AND FURTHER READING

Cronon, E. David. *Josephus Daniels in Mexico*. Madison: University of Wisconsin Press, 1960.

Schuler, Friedrich. *Mexico Between Hitler and Roosevelt: Mexican Foreign Relations in the Age of Lazaro Cardenas*, 1934–1940. Albuquerque: University of New Mexico Press, 1998.

Danish West Indies, U.S. Acquisition of

As part of a defensive strategy to maintain hegemony in the Caribbean and protect access to the Panama Canal during World War I, the United States purchased the islands of St. Thomas, St. John, and St. Croix—the Danish West Indies [Dansk Vestindien]—from Denmark for $25 million in August 1916. On March 31, 1917, at 4 p.m., the United States officially took possession of the three islands, and they became known as the U.S. Virgin Islands since the Danish geographic name for the islands had been Jomfruøerne [Virgin Islands]. March 31 is celebrated on the islands as Transfer Day as well as Danish Heritage Day, in tribute to the Danish cultural traditions instilled on the islands during over two centuries of Danish colonial rule.

The Danish West India and Guinea Company first colonized St. Thomas in 1672. The Danes subsequently colonized St. John in 1683. They established lucrative sugar plantations on the islands, which became dependent on slavery. In 1691 the main town on St. Thomas was renamed Charlotte Amalie in honor of the wife of Danish King Christian V. The Danish West India and Guinea Company purchased St. Croix from the French West Indies Company in 1733. All three of the islands were sold to King Frederick V in 1754, thus making them royal colonies. During the Napoleonic Wars, the British occupied the islands from 1801 to 1802 and 1807 to 1815, then returned them to Denmark. Following the abolition of slavery in 1848, the islands became an economic liability for the Danish government.

During the U.S. Civil War, Admiral David Dixon Porter convinced Secretary of State William Seward of the importance of acquiring the Danish West Indies. On October 24, 1867, the United States and Denmark negotiated a treaty for the sale of St. Thomas and St. John for $7.5 million, $300,000 more than the United States paid Russia for Alaska. Senator Charles Sumner, the chair of the Senate Foreign Relations Committee, an ardent foe of both Presidents Andrew Johnson and Ulysses S. Grant, successfully opposed the ratification of the treaty. Negotiations were reopened in 1892, but no steps were taken. In the aftermath of the Spanish–American War and the U.S. acquisition of Puerto Rico, U.S. government officials once again entertained the possibility of acquiring the Danish West Indies. The signing of the Hay-Pauncefote Treaty on November 18, 1901 between the United States and the United Kingdom gave the United States permission unilaterally to build a canal through Central America connecting the Atlantic and Pacific Oceans, renewing U.S. interest in the Danish West Indies. On January 24, 1902, therefore, following two years of negotiations, the Danes agreed to sell the islands for five million dollars. Although the U.S. Senate ratified the treaty, the Danish Rigsdag rejected it. U.S. officials believed that German manipulation of Danish politicians was the reason for the rejection of the treaty. Nevertheless, no documentation exists to support that claim.

With the opening of the Panama Canal on May 18, 1914, U.S. interest in acquiring the Danish West Indies was reinvigorated. U.S. interest in the islands had always been more strategic than commercial, and the desire to protect the vital sea lanes of communication leading to the Panama Canal convinced U.S. officials of the need to obtain the islands. Following the outbreak of World War I in 1914, U.S. officials were determined to acquire the islands to forestall the possibility of German acquisition of the islands, which might be used as a German submarine base. On August 4, 1916, U.S. Secretary of State Robert Lansing negotiated the sale of the Danish West Indies with Danish Ambassador Constantin Brun for $25 million. In addition, the treaty stipulated Denmark's uncontested control of Greenland. The U.S. Senate approved the treaty on September 7, 1916, and the Danish Rigsdag approved the treaty on December 21, 1916. Formal approval of the treaty came on January 17, 1917. Danish administration of the islands officially ended on March 31, 1917, one week before the United States declared war on Germany. At the time of U.S. acquisition, 33,000 people inhabited the islands, which occupy roughly 133 square miles of territory. The majority of the people, more than 30,000, were of African ancestry. U.S. citizenship was granted to the people of the U.S. Virgin Islands in 1927.

See also *Hay-Pauncefote Treaty, 1901; Lansing, Robert; Panama Canal, Administration of*

. . . . MICHAEL R. HALL

REFERENCES AND FURTHER READING

Dookhan, Isaac. *A History of the Virgin Islands of the United States*. Kingston, Jamaica: University Press of the West Indies, 2000.

Scott, James Brown. "The Purchase of the Danish West Indies by the United States of America." *The American Journal of International Law* 10, no. 4 (October 1916): 853–859.

Tansill, Charles Callan. *The Purchase of the Danish West Indies*. Baltimore, MD: The Johns Hopkins Press, 1932.

Darío, Rubén

Félix Rubén Garcia Sarmiento (1867–1916), more commonly known as Rubén Darío, was the leading poet of the Spanish language from 1888 to 1916; his subjects included U.S.–Latin American relations.

Born in Nicaragua in Metapa (now Ciudad Darío), Darío was a child prodigy; he learned to read by the age of three and published poetry by twelve. He received a thorough education grounded in the classics, studying with the Jesuits and at the National Institute. His career as a writer, newspaper correspondent, and diplomat led to a life of frequent travel throughout Latin America and Europe, where he interacted with many of the leading literary figures of the day. Darío is credited with nothing less than the transformation of Castilian Spanish; his poetry and prose took Spanish to new heights of expression and caused the center of literary creativity in the language to shift from Spain to Latin America. In fact, many claim that Darío's work divides Hispanic literary history into a "before" and "after." An admirer of several authors, from the Spaniard Miguel de Cervantes to the Americans Walt Whitman and Edgar Allen Poe, Darío was particularly influenced by French schools, including the romantics, Parnassians, and symbolists. His *Azul* (1888), a compilation of short stories and verse, is thought to be a key text in modernism, a broad literary movement aimed at the renewal of the Spanish language. While Darío's early works were characterized by fantasy, cosmopolitanism, and exoticism, his writings around the turn of the century—a period that saw the defeat of Spain in the Spanish-American War (1898) and heightened U.S. intervention in Latin America—expressed the sociopolitical concerns that earned him the reputation as the poetic spokesman for the Hispanic world.

Like many in the Hispanic world, Darío was alarmed by Spain's loss of its overseas empire and by U.S. expansionism. As a result, his writings turned to concerns about the future of both Hispanic culture and Latin America. His *España contemporánea: crónicas y retratos literarios* (1901), a collection of chronicles he wrote while living as a journalist in Spain, expresses sympathy toward the Spanish nation and a confidence in its revival. Soon after, Darío penned what would become his most famous critique of the United States, "A Roosevelt," a poem in *Cantos de vida y esperanza* (1905), the collection considered to be his masterpiece. U.S. intervention had led to the creation of Panama in 1903. The following year, President Theodore Roosevelt, the figure most representative of U.S. imperialism, proclaimed his corollary to the Monroe Doctrine, which justified the use of the U.S. military to police Latin America. Darío's "A Roosevelt" challenges the United States, "the future invader of our naïve America with its Indian blood, an America that still prays to Christ and still speaks Spanish." It extols Latin America's religious, moral, and aesthetic heritage, which it pits against a soulless but powerful United States. In referring to Latin America as "our own America," Darío's poem also expresses a pan–Latin American sentiment common to many other of the region's writers and intellectuals at the time, including José Martí of Cuba, Rufino Blanco-Fombona of Venezuela, and José Enrique Rodó of Uruguay.

But Darío was not always critical of the United States. In 1906, he took a much more favorable stance in his "Salutación al águila," a poem inspired by his participation in the Third Pan-American Conference, where he served as the secretary of the Nicaraguan delegation. The poem praises the virtues of the United States, a country personified by the eagle, and welcomes its influence: "Come magic eagle," it invites, and extend your "great strong wings" over the southern continent. In fact, Darío's sense of admiration toward the colossus to the north is even found in his more critical "A Roosevelt." This ambivalent stance toward the United States was typical of the many Latin Americans, who both admired the progress and inventiveness of the nation yet feared its imperialism. In his later years, Darío's writings were marked by an anguish about death, old age, and the human condition in general. He suffered psychological and physical problems, a result of the alcoholism that had plagued him throughout his life. While on a lecture tour of the United States, he contracted pneumonia in New York and died soon after that in his homeland in 1916. Today Darío's poetry still has a freshness to it, and his ambivalent sentiment toward the United States continues to have much currency.

See also *Martí y Pérez, José Julián; Panama, Independence of, 1903; Rodó Piñeyro, José Enrique; Roosevelt, Theodore; Spanish-Cuban-American War, 1895–1898*

. . . . CHRISTINA BUENO

SELECTED WORKS

Darío, Rubén. *Azul.* 1888.

———. *Prosas profanas y otros poemas.* 1896.

———. *España contemporánea: crónicas y retratos literarios.* 1901.

———. *Cantos de vida y esperanza.* 1905.

———. *Selected Poems of Rubén Darío.* Translated by Lynsander Kemp. Prologue by Octavio Paz. Austin: University of Texas Press, 1988.

REFERENCES AND FURTHER READING

Jrade, Cathy Logan. "Socio-Political Concerns in the Poetry of Rubén Darío." *Latin American Literary Review* 18, no. 36 (1990): 36–49.

Salgado, María A. "Rubén Darío." In *Encyclopedia of Latin American History and Culture,* edited by Barbara A. Tenenbaum, 353–355, New York: C. Scribner's Sons, 1996.

Watland, Charles Dunton. *Poet-Errant: A Biography of Ruben Darío.* New York: Philosophical Library, 1965.

Dartiguenave, Philippe Sudré

Philippe Sudré Dartiguenave (1863–1926) was president of Haiti from 1915 to 1922, at the beginning of the first U.S. occupation of that island nation.

In the early twentieth century, Haiti's traditionally volatile political life took a turn for the worse as many short-lived heads of states, known as the *présidents éphémères,* were overthrown in rapid succession. The last of the list was Jean Vilbrun Guillaume Sam, whose four-month presidency ended in July 1915, when he was dismembered by a mob in Port-au-Prince. Eager to institute some political stability, but also to prevent a possible German takeover and to secure a major sea lane to the Panama Canal, U.S. President Woodrow Wilson ordered an immediate invasion of Haiti, and the country remained under U.S. occupation until Franklin D. Roosevelt brought the occupation to an end in 1934 as part of his Good Neighbor policy.

Haiti was a de facto U.S. protectorate throughout this period, but given its traditional reluctance to see itself as an imperial power, the United States tried to maintain some semblance of Haitian self-governance. Occupation authorities asked the Haitian Senate to select Dartiguenave as the new president of Haiti in 1915 (as befitted contemporary racial attitudes, he and his immediate successors were all light-skinned *mulâtres* in a country that was ninety percent black).

Although Dartiguenave was nominally president of a sovereign country, his tenure was marked by important U.S. interference in Haitian affairs. In exchange for U.S. backing, Dartiguenave had to sign a treaty that legalized the U.S. military presence in Haiti and gave occupation authorities the right of customs receivership, which they then used to control tax receipts and budget decisions and to cow unruly Haitian senators by threatening to withhold their salaries. Dartiguenave's limited authority was further underscored when the United States appointed a pro-consul in 1922.

In 1917, Dartiguenave introduced a new constitution, which at the insistence of occupation authorities allowed foreigners to own land on Haitian soil (the ban on foreign ownership had been a staple of Haitian law since the 1804 declaration of independence). The constitution was ratified in a popular vote in 1918. Despite investments in sugar and sisal, U.S. economic interests in Haiti remained limited thereafter, and the main economic benefit to the United States was that control of Haitian finances allowed the prompt repayment of Haitian debts to U.S. banks.

Dartiguenave's political authority was also constrained by his country's precarious military situation. In the immediate aftermath of the invasion, the United States imposed martial law and disbanded what remained of Haiti's armed forces. It then created a constabulary captained by U.S. officers, the *gendarmerie*. Between 1918 and 1920, popular opposition to the *corvée* (forced labor) and the U.S. occupation led to the *caco* uprising, which the gendarmerie and U.S. Marines subdued by force.

Dartiguenave's presidency ended in 1922, when the United States brokered a peaceful political transition—a rare event in Haiti's political history—to another Haitian *mulâtre*, Louis Borno.

See also *Haiti, U.S. Relations with; United States, circum-Caribbean Interventions, 1900–1934: Haiti*

. . . . PHILIPPE R. GIRARD

REFERENCES AND FURTHER READING

Renda, Mary. *Taking Haiti: Military Occupation and the Culture of U.S. Imperialism, 1915–1940*. Chapel Hill: University of North Carolina Press, 2000.

Schmidt, Hans. *The United States Occupation of Haiti, 1915–1934*. New Brunswick, NJ: Rutgers, 1971.

Dawson, Thomas C.

Thomas Cleland Dawson (1865–1912) became a career U.S. diplomat, serving extensively in Latin America from 1897 to 1912. A lawyer, Dawson entered diplomatic service with an appointment as a secretary in the U.S. legation in Brazil. Later, he served as U.S. minister to a number of countries and as a special diplomatic representative. A highly respected diplomat within the U.S. government during a formative period in U.S. policy toward Latin America, Dawson was involved in many high-profile diplomatic situations. He prided himself on his knowledge of Latin American countries, but his general approach was common to U.S. attitudes of his time: He believed that Latin Americans on the whole were unprepared to manage economies or self-govern, working on the assumption that many Latin American revolutions were products of individual greed and power struggles lacking true ideology. He therefore tended to side with U.S. companies in disputes. This general U.S. attitude toward Latin America in those years, personified in Dawson as a diplomat, was one of the reasons for longer-term failures in U.S. diplomacy in Central America. Dawson was a proponent of U.S. economic control in the development and politics of Latin America.

After seven years in the U.S. legation in Brazil, Dawson was appointed U.S. minister resident and consul general to the Dominican Republic in 1904. There Dawson wrote his two-volume work about the histories of South American nations. His service in the Dominican Republic (1904–1907) coincided with an economic crisis there that brought European representatives demanding debt repayment and threatening intervention. Dawson worked with the Dominican government to design and implement the Dominican-American Convention of 1905 (ratified 1907). Under this document, U.S. banks provided loans to repay Dominican debts, and U.S. representatives controlled Dominican customs revenues to guarantee stable repayment. In 1907 Dawson was reassigned as a resident diplomatic officer in the U.S. State Department, in which position he served as a traveling specialist for diplomatic missions to Latin American countries.

Dawson was sent in 1907 to Honduras, where U.S. banana interests were concerned about and directly involved in a Honduran Revolution. A country whose economy was heavily dominated by U.S. financial interests, Honduras was undergoing a period of political instability. When a 1907 Honduran Revolution overthrew Manuel Bonilla's U.S.-friendly government, U.S. banana magnate Samuel Zemurray funded and aided an effort to restore Bonilla to power. Hoping to deter violence, the U.S. government carried out a standard mission of the time: It sent the U.S. Navy to halt immediate violence and a diplomatic representative to mediate. The Navy set up a neutral zone, which served as a safe refuge for revolutionary forces. Dawson took control of the political situation, requesting that each side in the conflict choose its preferred provisional president; the choice of which was fit to rule fell to him as the U.S. consul. Dawson then began the process of setting up presidential elections, which would soon bring Bonilla back to power.

Dawson went on to serve as U.S. ambassador to Colombia during the tense years of 1907 to 1909, when relations between the United States and that country were still strained due to U.S. actions involving Panamanian independence. In 1909, Dawson was sent to Chile to mediate a complicated dispute between the Chilean government and U.S. Alsop & Co. The Chilean government charged the company with unfair dealings, including that the U.S. government was intervening on its behalf illegally and unethically. Dawson sided with the company, threatening nonrecognition of Chile and removal of U.S. diplomatic representatives if the Chilean government did not agree. With such threats, he gained the acquiescence of Chile's government, effectively ending the dispute.

Dawson was sent as a special U.S. envoy to Nicaragua in 1910. As elsewhere throughout the Caribbean region at this time, the U.S. government emphasized retaining a U.S.-friendly government and stopping the intervention of European creditor nations that were demanding debt repayment. Dawson used his experience in the Dominican Republic to author the Dawson Pact, which made Nicaragua a virtual U.S. protectorate, temporarily suspending elections and giving U.S. representatives control of the bulk of Nicaraguan finances. As in the Dominican Republic, U.S. military occupation of the country soon followed. In late 1910, Dawson was sent as U.S. envoy extraordinary and minister plenipotentiary to Panama, where efforts to speed construction of the Panama Canal were under way. Dawson soon became ill and battled illness until his death in 1912.

See also *United Fruit Company (UFCO); United States circum-Caribbean Interventions, 1900–1934: Dominican Republic; United States circumum-Caribbean Interventions, 1900–1934:*

Honduras; United States circum-Caribbean Interventions, 1900–1934: Nicaragua

. . . . ELLEN D. TILLMAN

SELECTED WORKS

Dawson, Thomas Cleland. *The South American Republics*. 2 vols. New York: G. P. Putnam's Sons, 1910.

REFERENCES AND FURTHER READING

Acker, Alison. *Honduras: The Making of a Banana Republic*. New York: South End Press, 1989.
Herring, Hubert. *A History of Latin America from the Beginnings to the Present*. New York: Alfred A. Knopf, 1962.
LaFeber, Walter. *Inevitable Revolutions: The United States in Central America*. New York: W.W. Norton, 1984.

De la Madrid Hurtado, Miguel

Miguel de la Madrid Hurtado was born December 12, 1934, in the city of Colima, capital of the Mexican state of the same name. He was educated at the Universidad Nacional Autónoma de México (UNAM) in Mexico City and graduated with a law degree. He received a master's degree in public policy from the John F. Kennedy School of Government at Harvard University. He joined José López Portillo's cabinet on May 19, 1979, as the minister of planning and budget. On September 25, 1981, he was nominated by the Partido de la Revolución Institucional (Institutional Revolutionary Party, PRI) as its candidate for president. On July 4, 1982, he was elected the fifty-second president of Mexico. He was inaugurated on December 1, 1982.

When de la Madrid took office, he inherited a country in severe economic decline. He first moved to control inflation through top-down measures. He made several constitutional changes that reinforced the idea of state-led economic planning while protecting "strategic" economic sectors, including petroleum, petro-chemicals, telecommunications, electric and nuclear energy concerns, railroads, and banking. Afterward he pursued economic stabilization and an austerity program. He eliminated subsidies and price controls, reduced barriers to imports, and closed or privatized bankrupt state enterprises. The de la Madrid administration privatized 743 state-owned firms, public trusts, and decentralized agencies, which caught the attention of the International Monetary Fund (IMF). De la Madrid's liberalization program meant that by the end of 1985, less than half of all manufactured imports were subject to import permits. Mexico joined the General Agreement on Tariffs and Trade (GATT) in 1986, which committed the nation to further reductions in trade protection. However foreign investors did not trust the PRI, which meant that the anticipated investment boom failed to happen. In 1987 the stock market collapsed, causing further economic chaos.

De la Madrid deliberately charted a path away from the United States, in terms of foreign and domestic policy. On September 19, 1985, Mexico City was devastated by a series of earthquakes, and the PRI failed to respond adequately. Although the government was caught off-guard by the earthquakes, the minister of foreign affairs announced that Mexico did not need any aid, least of all from the United States. Similarly de la Madrid distanced himself from the United States in the aftermath of fraudulent elections in 1986 in Chihuahua. Anticipating a victory by the conservative Partido Acción Nacional (National Action Party, PAN), the PRI rigged the election to ensure that its own candidate would win. At a meeting with dissidents, de la Madrid's minister of the interior, Manuel Bartlett, explained that a PAN victory would give three historical enemies of Mexico—the Roman Catholic Church, the United States, and the business class—access to political power. Over the course of his presidency de la Madrid reminded the United States that Mexico's foreign policy, especially regarding the ongoing conflicts in Central America, would not be dictated from the north. Although closer economic ties were sought with the United States, de la Madrid wanted an independent foreign policy.

De la Madrid is seen as a transitional president. He bridged the gap between the economic tumult of the 1970s and the coming era of globalization. De la Madrid made a series of reforms, though few were successful. His economic reforms, for example, did not result in the anticipated boom. He is perceived as a classical liberal, but he did not hesitate to use fraud to maintain the PRI's dominant political position.

See also *General Agreement on Tariffs and Trade (GATT); Mexico, U.S. relations with; Reagan, Ronald W.; Salinas de Gortari, Carlos*

. . . . WILLIAM C. KELLY

REFERENCES AND FURTHER READING

Castañeda, Jorge G. *Perpetuating Power: How Mexican Presidents Were Chosen*. Translated by Padraig Arthur Smithies. New York: The New Press, 2000.
Cothran, Dan A. *Political Stability and Democracy in Mexico: The 'Perfect Dictatorship'?* Westport, CT: Praeger, 1994.
Haber, Stephen, Herbert S. Klein, Noel Maurer, and Kevin J. Middlebrook. *Mexico since 1980*. New York: Cambridge University Press, 2008.
Krauze, Enrique. *Mexico, Biography of Power: A History of Modern Mexico, 1810–1996*. Translated by Hank Heifetz. New York: HarperPerennial, 1997.

de Lesseps, Ferdinand Marie

Ferdinand de Lesseps (1805–1894) was the builder of the Suez Canal and the failed architect of the Panama Canal during the French construction period (1879–1889). Born in Versailles to a family of career diplomats, young de Lesseps spent his early years in Italy, where his father was the French consul general. He was educated at the Lycée Henri IV in Paris and held his first diplomatic post as the assistant vice consul to Lisbon. In 1828 he held a similar position in Tunis under his father and had his first experience working in the Arab world. After participating in the French conquest of Algeria, de Lesseps accepted a position as vice consul to Alexandria, where he first considered the idea of building a canal at Suez that would link the Red Sea with the Mediterranean, a project he discovered written in books from the Napoleonic expedition to Egypt. De Lesseps fostered important political connections in Egypt where, as consul general to Cairo, he gained the confidence of the Egyptian viceroy, Muhammad Ali, and formed a close friendship with the viceroy's son, Said Pasha.In 1837 de Lesseps returned to France. His role in important negotiations in Rome to bring Pope Pius IX back to the Vatican under French protection following the revolutionary upheavals of 1848 and 1849 led to de Lesseps's recall to Paris, investigation before a Council of State, and ultimate retirement from the foreign service, simultaneously with the deaths of his wife and daughter from disease.

But the ascension of his old friend Pasha Said to the viceroyalty of Egypt afforded de Lesseps the opportunity to accomplish his dream, the building of the Suez Canal. De Lesseps landed in Alexandria on the November 7, 1854. By the end of the month, the viceroy had signed the concession that allowed de Lesseps to begin this monumental construction project. De Lesseps confronted numerous obstacles: competing engineering schemes, initial British opposition to an endeavor that might threaten their commercial interests, and Ottoman concerns. But once he had the final plan in hand and the support of Emperor Napoleon III, he pushed the operation through with characteristic determination. A master of publicity, de Lesseps aroused the patriotism of the French people and through a subscription raised some 280 million francs from them to form a company. Actual digging began in April of 1859, and in November 1869, the canal was completed as one of the most celebrated engineering feats of the positivist age.

With his reputation at the heights, de Lesseps considered a number of larger engineering projects: a railroad from Peking to Bombay to Europe and an inland sea in French Algeria to increase rainfall in the Sahara. But in 1879, he finally settled upon a project large enough to encompass his reputation: the excavation of the Panama Canal. First proposed to Charles V in the sixteenth century, this project had captured the imagination of engineers and businessmen around the world, as it had the potential, like Suez, to transform commercial shipping rates overnight and greatly increase global trade. De Lesseps's project faced some diplomatic hurdles, however. During an 1880 tour of the United States to promote his canal enterprise, de Lesseps met with President Rutherford B. Hayes at the White House and assured the president that his was a private venture that did not violate the Monroe Doctrine. The nation of France would play no direct role in the construction. Hayes came to view de Lesseps's plans otherwise and in a March 8, 1880, address to Congress, he stated that any canal on the isthmus should be under U.S. and not European control. Hayes's statement aligned with thirty-four years of U.S. policy on the issue, beginning with the 1846 Bidlack Treaty, in which New Granada (Colombia and Panama today) granted Washington exclusive transit rights over the isthmus of Panama, and the 1850 Clayton-Bulwer Treaty, in which the United States and Great Britain agreed not to build any transoceanic canal in Central America unilaterally. Hayes sent a squadron of U.S. naval vessels to the coast of Panama in the summer of 1880 to punctuate his dissent.

Even without these U.S. concerns, de Lesseps's canal project proved a disaster. Neither he nor his engineers took into account the enormous problems of constructing the canal in Panama. The thick impenetrable jungle, mountainous terrain, torrential rains, and mudslides frustrated all efforts toward success. The ravages of malaria and yellow fever claimed 22,000 workers' lives. De Lesseps's insistence on a sea level canal instead of a lock system waterway also fatally damaged the French effort. De Lesseps used his genius reputation to raise some 400 million francs from French investors, but his canal company collapsed into bankruptcy in 1889, touching off a financial crisis in France. Having regarded the French effort as a violation of both the Monroe Doctrine and the 1850 Clayton-Bulwer Treaty, Washington viewed the project's collapse with satisfaction. Eventually, the United States would buy the remaining assets of the French company and in 1914 bring the excavation to fruition, after encouraging Panamanian independence from Colombia. In 1894, however, de Lesseps died in disgrace, his spirit broken, his reputation ruined.

See also *Clayton-Bulwer Treaty, 1850; France, Nineteenth-Century Interests in Latin America; Hayes, Rutherford B.; Panama Canal Treaties (Carter-Torrijos), 1977; Panama, Isthmian Canal Interests, Nineteenth Century*

. . . . MICHAEL E. DONOGHUE

REFERENCES AND FURTHER READING

Karabell, Zachary. *Parting the Desert: The Creation of the Suez Canal*. New York: Knopf, 2004.

LaFeber, Walter. *The Panama Canal: The Crisis in Historical Perspective*. New York: Oxford University Press, 1989.

McCullough, David. *The Path Between the Seas: The Creation of the Panama Canal 1879–1914*. New York: Simon and Schuster, 1977.

Death Squads

(**See** *Central American Wars, 1980s*)

Debt Crisis, Latin America, 1870s, 1930s, 1980s

Since independence from Spain and Portugal, Latin American countries have repeatedly suffered from debt crises—most notably in the 1870s, 1930s, and 1980s—that followed periods of speculative lending booms. Reasons for the lending booms varied considerably between countries and periods, but they started when investors believed that the region's economic prospects had dramatically improved. When the high expectations were disappointed, international lending stopped abruptly and left countries with a high debt burden, which they found impossible to service. This excessive debt led to prolonged periods of economic crisis during which Latin American countries were excluded from international financial markets. Lending resumed only several years later, after the international economic environment had become more favorable and debtor countries had restored financial stability. Scholars have attributed these boom and bust cycles to the irrationality of international financial markets, which tend to oscillate between manias and depressions, or to the profligacy of Latin American governments, which take advantage of the occasional availability of cheap credit to buy political support or fund politically expedient public works projects of dubious economic value.

BOOM AND BUST CYCLES DURING THE BELLE ÉPOQUE AND THE INTERWAR YEARS

Despite some obvious similarities, debt crises during the nineteenth and twentieth centuries were also significantly different. Before World War I, most foreign loans to Latin America were government-guaranteed bonds, often linked to a specific infrastructure project, such as the railroads or municipal waterworks. During boom phases, European investors bought these bonds in large quantities because they promised above-average returns. The explicit or implicit government guarantee also made them appear relatively safe. However, investors repeatedly learned the painful lesson that a government guarantee amounted to little when the government itself became insolvent, as in the 1870s, when a large number of Latin American countries defaulted on their foreign obligations, and again in 1890 and 1891 during the so-called Baring crisis, which started in Argentina but affected sovereign borrowers across Latin America. Resolving debt crises was difficult and time consuming so that Latin American countries remained excluded from international capital markets for long periods. Individual bondholders often pressured their own governments to help them assert their rights diplomatically or even militarily.

Lending to Latin American countries during the 1920s differed considerably from the period before World War I. The war ruined Europe economically and left its investors unable to supply Latin America with capital. The United States became Latin America's largest creditor. During the 1920s, Latin American governments received more than $2 billion in loans from U.S. investors, most of it in bonds floated in New York. This lending boom came to an abrupt end with the crash on Wall Street in the fall of 1929. Latin American countries suffered under the Great Depression in two ways. Credit dried up as banks in the United States and Europe struggled with a series of bank runs. At the same time, the economic crisis depressed prices for Latin America's traditional exports, and the United States and many European countries enacted protectionist measures that cut off vital export markets. Consequently, Latin American countries were unable to meet their external obligations. Except for Argentina, every Latin American country suspended its debt payments during the 1930s.

LATIN AMERICA DURING THE POSTWAR DECADES

While Latin American countries were able to repay their debt with exports during World War II, international financial markets remained essentially closed to them for a generation because the postwar economic system severely restricted international capital flows. Only with the gradual liberalization of capital markets in the late 1960s and early 1970s did Latin American countries once again receive foreign loans. The lending boom, which started in the early 1970s, was partially fueled by genuine optimism with respect to Latin America's growth prospects. The primary impetus, however, was the first oil shock in 1973. Oil-exporting countries in the Middle East made large profits, which they deposited with banks operating in offshore Eurodollar markets. These banks, in turn, looked for profitable investment opportunities in a process known as petrodollar recycling. Between 1972 and 1975, international banks extended almost $40 billion in new loans to Latin American countries. By the time the debt crisis broke out in August 1982, Latin American foreign debt had grown more than six-fold and surpassed $260 billion. In most cases, capital was invested not only in profitable ventures but also in massive construction projects; it also fueled consumption booms and capital flight.

The easy phase of petrodollar recycling ended in 1979, when the second oil shock in the wake of the Iranian Revolution caused oil prices to spike and precipitated another worldwide recession. In a second blow, the new chairman of the U.S. Federal Reserve, Paul Volcker, decided to tighten monetary policy to combat inflation. Debtor countries suddenly faced much higher interest charges on their foreign debt, most of which had been contracted at adjustable rates. The crisis first manifested itself in Eastern Europe in early 1981. Around the same time, Latin American countries also started to suffer from severe balance of payment crises. Argentina devalued the peso repeatedly amid growing political and economic crisis starting in mid 1981. Mexico followed with a series of large devaluations in early 1982. Argentina was the first Latin American country to suspend debt payments in the wake of the ill-fated invasion of the British-controlled Malvinas/Falkland Islands in April 1982.

THE OUTBREAK OF THE DEBT CRISIS

The financial crises remained largely localized until Wednesday, August 11, 1982, when the Mexican minister of finance, Jesús Silva Herzog, approached the International Monetary Fund (IMF) and the U.S. Treasury for emergency aid to avoid a default on its external obligations. While the origins and the nature of the Mexican crisis were not radically different from similar crises in Eastern Europe and Argentina, the political and economic consequences were more far-reaching. With a total foreign debt of $86 billion, Mexico had larger external liabilities than the countries that had experienced a similar crisis during the previous year. More important, Mexico's financial crisis raised the question whether developing countries would be able to service the large foreign debt. A default of one or more big countries would endanger the stability of the international financial system as a whole.

As a response to this threat, the IMF and the U.S. government, under the leadership of the Federal Reserve, took an active role in managing the Latin American debt crisis. Over the course of the next few years, they worked closely with commercial banks and Latin American debtor countries to reschedule existing debt and organize new loans to avoid a cessation of payments by any large Latin American country. The IMF-sponsored loans required the borrowing country to adopt austerity measures, which Latin American governments, many of which were in the process of transition from dictatorship to democracy, found hard to accept and even harder to implement. The result was a growing frustration on both sides. Latin American countries increasingly suffered from "adjustment fatigue" while commercial banks grew weary of sinking yet more money into a seemingly bottomless pit.

RESOLVING THE DEBT CRISIS AND SETTING THE SCENE FOR THE NEXT ONE

The Baker plan was the first comprehensive effort to overcome the debt crisis. On October 8, 1985, U.S. Secretary of the Treasury James A. Baker III proposed that heavily indebted developing countries should receive additional loans from commercial banks and multilateral development agencies in exchange for sweeping pro-market economic reforms, which would integrate them more tightly into the world economy. This plan received only a lukewarm reception. Latin American governments were deeply suspicious of the obligation to implement market-oriented reform as a precondition to these loans. Banks were enthusiastic about economic liberalization in Latin American countries but did not want to increase their exposure to troubled Latin American loans. The Baker plan collapsed in 1987 when Brazil declared a moratorium on paying interest on $87 billion it owed to commercial banks, and John Reed, chairman of Citicorp, sharply increased his bank's bad debt reserves to provide for possible losses from lending to heavily indebted developing countries. These events made it clear that heavily indebted Latin American countries would not grow out of their debt and that commercial banks were no longer willing to continue extending new loans.

With the collapse of the Baker plan, a new consensus slowly emerged that a solution to the debt crisis required substantial debt reduction. George H. W. Bush's secretary of the treasury, Nicholas F. Brady, proposed a voluntary and market-based debt reduction plan on March 10, 1989. It offered a variety of different collateralized bonds, called Brady bonds, in exchange for the old bank loans. All options offered significant concessions to debtor countries, either in terms of reduced principal and interest rates or in the extension of new credit lines. Commercial banks also benefited from the plan because they could reduce their exposure to developing countries' debt and realize losses, which were tax deductible. Mexico was the first Latin American country to implement the Brady plan in 1989. It was followed by Costa Rica (also in 1989), Venezuela (1990), Uruguay (1991), Argentina, and Brazil (1992). The conversion of old debt into tradable Brady bonds, together with far-reaching economic reform under the banner of the "Washington consensus," finally helped Latin American countries to overcome the debt crisis and set the stage for a new lending boom to so-called emerging markets in the 1990s.

See also *Baker, James A. III; International Monetary Fund (IMF); Oil Shocks Since 1970, Impact on Latin America; U.S. Economic Investments in Latin America*

. . . . KLAUS VEIGEL

REFERENCES AND FURTHER READING

Coatsworth, John H., and Alan M. Taylor. *Latin America and the World Economy since 1800*. Cambridge, MA: David Rockefeller Center for Latin American Studies, 1998.

Eichengreen, Barry J., and Peter H. Lindert. *The International Debt Crisis in Historical Perspective*. Cambridge, MA: MIT Press, 1989.

Kindleberger, Charles Poor. *Manias, Panics, and Crashes: A History of Financial Crises*. 3rd ed. New York: Wiley, 1996.

Lissakers, Karin. *Banks, Borrowers, and the Establishment: A Revisionist Account of the International Debt Crisis*. New York: Basic Books, 1991.

Declaration of Reciprocal Assistance, 1940

(**See** *Second Meeting of Consultation of the Ministers of Foreign Affairs of the American Republics, Havana, 1940*)

Defense Sites Agreements, World War II

During World War II, the leaders of the United States and Latin America entered into a number of bilateral agreements on hemispheric defense. Those agreements allowed the United States to establish military facilities in strategic locations in several Latin American countries. Most of the military sites were airfields, which provided vital logistical support to ongoing U.S. military wartime operations. The defense sites agreements are representative of the wartime collaboration between the United States and Latin America in the 1940s.

BUILD-UP TO WORLD WAR II

The U.S. military presence in Latin America was a sensitive issue. U.S. leaders had responded to or provoked internal Latin American crises in the 1910s and 1920s by sending military forces to intervene in Mexico, Central America, and the Caribbean. Growing resentment toward and suspicion of the United States resulted. The diplomatic efforts of the Franklin D. Roosevelt administration in the 1930s, dubbed the Good Neighbor policy, gradually lessened antagonism toward the United States by the late 1930s. In place of unilateral action, Roosevelt began working to foster military cooperation in the region. He started with bilateral military mission agreements with Brazil and Guatemala and later expanded the program to include other nations. Under those agreements, the United States set up training missions in an effort to supplant Italian and German military advisers in the region. The military missions agreements were considered a success, largely because they included provisions that prohibited Latin American nations from simultaneously allowing military missions from any other foreign government. By 1941 the United States was operating military missions in nearly every Latin American country, while the German and Italian missions had effectively been shut down.

Meanwhile, the United States wanted to expand its military presence in the region, particularly as the conflict escalated overseas. Through a series of Inter-American conferences, U.S. and Latin American leaders pledged greater cooperation on matters of hemispheric security. To improve military defense capabilities, Latin American leaders in many countries sought new equipment and supplies from the United States. Roosevelt's Lend-Lease program, initiated in 1941, provided a mechanism for supplying military equipment to U.S. allies. In exchange for weapons and other military equipment, U.S. defense leaders pushed Latin American governments to allow U.S. military bases on their soil. They justified such an action by pointing to areas of the Western Hemisphere that were most vulnerable to external attack. Latin American leaders nevertheless remained reluctant to permit such a direct military presence in their territory. Their reluctance was fueled by internal dissent over the validity of the U.S. presence. Fear and suspicion of the United States and its motives were often fostered by political opponents of Latin American leaders or by Nazi agents. As a result, to finalize defense sites agreements, U.S. leaders carried out intense negotiations for many months and even supported propaganda campaigns.

AREAS OF U.S. CONCERN

The northeastern coastal region of Brazil was an area of great concern to U.S. leaders. The Brazilian "hump" is geographically closer to Europe than it is to the United States, and German naval vessels threatened to encroach on this vulnerable coastal area. U.S. and Brazilian leaders began to negotiate the development of military bases in the region as early as 1939. To expedite the construction of vital airfields, the U.S. government solicited the involvement of Pan American Airways, believing that a private enterprise would seem less threatening and ease Latin American concerns. Despite reluctance on the part of Pan American executives and delays throughout the negotiation and construction process, the program was generally seen as a success. By the end of 1941, construction was under way at several sites in Brazil, and the U.S. military was already using many airfields. The model used for the Brazilian defense sites was also applied to other regions of Latin America. Pan American eventually built new airfields or improved existing sites in twenty-one locations throughout Latin America.

Another area of concern for the United States was the Panama Canal, and U.S. leaders carried out harried negotiations with Panamanian leaders over defense of the Canal Zone. A 1936 treaty had ended the U.S. protectorate over Panama and established joint responsibility between the two nations for protecting the canal. U.S. leaders urgently wanted new military bases in the region, but they met significant resistance from Panamanian leaders. While negotiations were still ongoing, the U.S. military began operating in strategic locations and building the necessary facilities. An agreement was finally reached for formalizing the arrangement in May 1942.

Mexico was the third major Latin American target of U.S. military attention during World War II. Its proximity to the United States and the potential vulnerability of both its coastlines made Mexico a strategic priority for hemispheric defense policies. In 1940 U.S. and Mexican leaders formed the Joint Mexican-United States Defense Commission, but because of domestic political pressures, the Mexican government stalled the negotiation process. After German submarines attacked Mexican oil tankers in the Gulf of Mexico in 1942, Mexico officially declared war, and military collaboration with the United States took on a new sense of urgency. In a strategy that replicated the efforts under way in Brazil, Pan American Airways secured contracts to build new airfields in Mexico or to improve existing ones. The efforts of the defense commission produced agreements that allowed the U.S. military to operate on eight sites throughout Mexico.

CONCLUSION

The United States eventually reached agreements that allowed the U.S. military to operate at strategic sites in Mexico and all of Central America as well as in Brazil and all of the countries along the west coast of South America. U.S. sites also operated in Venezuela, in Uruguay, and on most of the Caribbean islands, including some British Caribbean colonies. In exchange for the defense sites agreements, nearly every Latin American nation received Lend-Lease aid to update military equipment in the interest of hemispheric defense. But the Lend-Lease program in Latin America often took a backseat to the military priorities of U.S. allies in Europe and Asia. As a result, most Latin American nations received far less equipment and military aid than they had anticipated.

At the end of World War II, the U.S. military pulled out of most defense sites throughout Latin America. Exceptions included areas where the United States already had a long-standing tradition of military presence, such as Cuba and Panama.

See also *Caribbean, German U-boat Threat, World War II; Hull, Cordell; Lend-Lease Program, World War II; Marshall Plan and Latin America; Nazi Activities in Latin America, World War II; Pan American-Grace Airways; Roosevelt, Franklin D.; Third Meeting of Consultation of the Ministers of Foreign Affairs of the American Republics, Rio de Janeiro, 1942*

MONICA RANKIN

REFERENCES AND FURTHER READING

Chester, Edward. *The United States and Six Atlantic Outposts.* Port Washington, NY: Kennikat Press, 1980.

Conn, Stetson, and Byron Fairchild. *The Framework of Hemisphere Defense.* Honolulu: University Press of the Pacific, 2002.

Taylor, Philip B., Jr. "Hemisphere Defense in World War II." *Current History* 56, no. 334 (June 1969): 333–339.

Democratic Revolutionary Front (El Salvador)

The Democratic Revolutionary Front (FDR) emerged in the early 1980s as El Salvador's reformist social democratic political force. The FDR called for a comprehensive, yet nonrevolutionary set of reforms to overhaul the country's backward socioeconomic and political schemes whereby the state would play a larger role in the economy while preserving a healthy scope of liberal democracy and respect for human rights.

In April 1980, several social and political organizations, including left-of-center political parties, trade unions, and student organizations, came together to create the FDR as a last-ditch effort to find a political solution to the imminent eruption of civil war in El Salvador. The FDR's platform revolved around the need to dismantle, through nonviolent means, the pillars of the country's underdevelopment: the military dictatorship and the oligarchic economic system. The FDR emphasized the need to undertake comprehensive reforms within the context of a "democratic revolution" that would open the door to much-needed land reform, the dismantling of the state's repressive apparatus, and the guarantee of free elections, among other initiatives.

The military and the right-wing oligarchy did not welcome the FDR's program for change, however, equating its calls for reforms with the more radical and revolutionary project of the Farabundo Marti National Liberation Front (FMLN). By the time the FDR was advancing its agenda, the FMLN was already engaged in a guerrilla campaign to overthrow the government. As a result, the government's response was brutal: In November 1980, government-sponsored death squads kidnapped and assassinated the five-member FDR National Executive Committee, a crime documented by the UN-sponsored Truth Commission report in 1993. A generalized repression against other members of the FDR followed.

In light of these events, and seeing no other feasible avenues to bring about change, the FDR formed an alliance with the FMLN by becoming its political wing. As a result, several of the FDR's leaders, such as Guillermo Ungo and Rubén Zamora, had to go into exile and could not return to El Salvador until the mid-1980s. The FDR played a pivotal role in the ill-fated peace dialogue rounds between the FMLN and the Salvadoran government in 1984 and 1985. The Reagan administration considered the FDR an enemy because of its alliance with the FMLN and because of its left-leaning tendencies, and as such Washington viewed the FDR as on the "wrong side" of the Cold War divide. As the civil war intensified, the FDR disbanded, loosened its ties with the FMLN, and concentrated its political efforts within the electoral arena with a restructured political party called the Democratic Convergence (CD).

After very poor electoral performances in the late 1980s, and with the signing of the 1992 peace accords that ended the civil war, many of the former members of the FDR rejoined the FMLN in its new status as a legal political party. Ideological differences between social democrats and Marxists led many former FDR members to break away from the FMLN and reconstitute the FDR as a social democratic party, albeit small in size and influence, leaning toward the center of the political spectrum.

See also *Central American Wars, 1980s; El Salvador, U.S. Relations with; Farabundo Marti National Liberation Front (FMLN) (El Salvador); Rubén Zamora*

. . . . CARLOS VELÁSQUEZ CARRILLO

REFERENCES AND FURTHER READING

Baloyra, Enrique. *El Salvador in Transition.* Chapel Hill: University of North Carolina Press, 1982.

Dunkerley, James. *The Long War: Dictatorship and Revolution in El Salvador.* 2nd ed. New York: Verso, 1985.

López Vallecillos, Ítalo, and Víctor Antonio Orellana. "La Unidad Popular y el Surgimiento del Frente Democrático Revolucionario." *Estudios Centroamericanos* 35, no. 377–378 (1980): 183–206.

Montgomery, Tommy Sue. *Revolution in El Salvador: From Civil Strife to Civil Peace.* 2nd ed. Boulder, CO: Westview Press.

Stanley, William. *The Protection Racket State: Elite Politics, Military Extortion, and Civil War in El Salvador.* Philadelphia: Temple University Press, 1996.

Dependency Theory and Latin America

Dependency theory is a model of social and economic development that explicitly acknowledges global inequality between nations. Earlier theories of modernization argued that each nation-state developed through a series of economic stages, ultimately achieving industrialization and economic development. In contrast, dependency theorists argue that high-income countries have systematically impoverished low- and middle-income countries through historical processes of colonization and exploitation, leading to modern-day trade agreements. The result is that development cannot be achieved by low- and middle-income countries while they remain a part of the global capitalist system. In other words, the overdevelopment of some countries is structurally related to the underdevelopment of others. A variety of perspectives on dependency theory exist, including those espoused by Raúl Prebisch, André Gunder Frank, Fernando Henrique Cardoso, and Immanuel Wallerstein.

CONTRAST TO MODERNIZATION THEORY

Modernization theories frame development as a series of stages. This perspective was most clearly developed in the writings of Walt W. Rostow, whose 1960 book, *The Stages of Economic Growth: A Non-Communist Manifesto,* posited that development followed five distinct steps: (1) traditional, (2) the take-off, (3) the drive to maturity, (4) mass consumption, and (5) post-mass consumption. Gross domestic product per capita would be expected to increase in each stage, and a country's standard of living would improve in a unidimensional path toward development. Dependency theorists in Latin America criticized this model of economic development on the grounds that it did not reflect their empirical realities and that it displayed Eurocentric and pro-capitalist ideological bias. According to dependency theorists, modernization theory ignored the historical and political factors associated with development and inappropriately assumed that development was primarily a function of factors internal to each country. Instead, factors external to each country, including its relation to the world economic system, were seen to be crucial factors that shaped development trajectories.

ROOTS OF DEPENDENCY THEORY IN LA COMISIÓN ECONÓMICA PARA AMÉRICA LATINA Y EL CARIBE

Dependency theory grew out of contributions from a variety of perspectives. Economists, including Argentina's Raúl Prebisch, recognized in the 1950s that the terms of trade between raw commodities and manufactured goods deteriorated over time. This deterioration implied that countries whose economies focused on the export of raw commodities would, over time, lose their ability to import manufactured goods. Prebisch's work was highly influential within the *Comisión Económica para América Latina y el Caribe* (ECLAC) and affected its move toward import-substituting-industrialization (ISI) policies.

CENTRAL THEORISTS

Frank was a noted proponent of dependency theory, and argued that the economic position of high-income industrialized countries is inextricably tied to the position of low-income countries. In the context of Latin America, this perspective held that the region's economies were too dependent on their roles as exporters of raw commodities; in the 1960s, this thinking supported the region's ISI policies. Frank's contributions to dependency theory were central to its development; however, concerns have been raised in the literature about a tendency (particularly evident among English-language authors) to rely excessively on his writings at the expense of other authors, including Cardoso and a host of other reformist writers, including Osvaldo Sunkel, Celso Furtado, and Helio Jaguaribe. In addition, a neo-Marxist literature on dependency theory in Latin America features the writings of a diverse set of authors, including Frank and Ruy Mauro Marini, Theotonio Dos Santos, Oscar Braun, and Vania Bambirra; this literature is also often neglected by commentators who reduce dependency theory to the writings of Frank.

Cardoso's contribution to the dependency approach included a renewed integration of social and political factors to the existing economic frame of analysis used by dependency theorists. This synthesis allowed for a far more nuanced view of the role of internal and external factors, with the former no longer seen as a mere reflection of the latter. Cardoso's analysis also emphasized that dependency and development were not contradictory terms; in that respect, his analysis differed from Frank's and ultimately led to different perspectives regarding the viability of a transition to socialism in the region.

Wallerstein's refinement of dependency theory led to world systems theory. Under this model, the countries of the world are identified as forming part of the core, the semiperiphery, and the periphery. The core includes rich nations at the center of the capitalist world economy; these are countries that primarily import raw materials and commodities from other countries. Low-income countries form the periphery. Many of these countries were colonized in earlier periods and continue to exist in quasi-colonial relationships with the core; they provide inexpensive and dispensable labor markets, raw materials, and in some cases markets for finished industrial and commercial products. Semiperiphery countries have closer ties to the core. Wallerstein argued that the world economy shapes this state of dependency by imposing particular characteristics onto low- and middle-income countries: (a) a narrow, export-oriented economy tailored to the production of raw commodities and foodstuffs; (b) a lack of industrial capacity, which forces low- and middle-income countries to purchase expensive goods from the core; and (c) high levels of foreign debt, which provide leverage by which core countries can control trade agreements.

CRITIQUES OF DEPENDENCY THEORY

Concern has been raised about the extent to which dependency theorists ignore within-country factors that have blocked economic development in Latin America, with corruption typically cited as the most important overlooked factor. Critiques of dependency theory have also centered on the notion that wealth generation is not necessarily a zero-sum game; that is, wealth can be created without being destroyed elsewhere. Commentators have also raised concern that dependency theory, with its macro focus, detracts attention from more fundamental issues of class struggle within each society. From this perspective, development has much to do not only with a country's balance of trade but also with its internal political economy: how it distributes income and how it develops its welfare state. Along these lines, analyses that rest on nations as the unit of analysis may ultimately underestimate the importance of class and class struggle.

See also *Frank, Andre Gunder; Import Substitution Industrialization (ISI); Prebisch, Raúl*

. . . . FERNANDO G. DE MAIO

REFERENCES AND FURTHER READING

Cardoso, Fernando Henrique. "Dependency and Development in Latin America." *New Left Review* 74 (1972): 83–95.

Frank, André Gunder. *Latin America: Underdevelopment or Revolution*. New York: Monthly Review Press, *1969*.

Kay, Cristóbal. "Reflections on the Latin American Contribution to Development Theory." *Development and Change* 22, no. 1 (1991): 31–68.

Wallerstein, Immanuel. *The Capitalist World-Economy*. New York: Cambridge University Press, 1979.

Dessalines, Jean-Jacques

(**See** *Panama, Isthmian Canal Interests, Nineteenth Century*)

Destroyers for Bases Agreement, 1940

In the late 1930s, President Franklin D. Roosevelt played a game in which he publicly preached nonintervention in international affairs, while privately planning to rearm the U.S. in case of a foreign war. When the Germans invaded Poland in September 1939, World War II began in Europe. The Germans quickly swept across Europe, defeating France in June 1940.

Following the evacuation at Dunkirk in which 300,000 British and French troops escaped Nazi encirclement, the British were the only European nation left to stop Hitler. The German Luftwaffe began the Battle of Britain, and German U-boats began the battle of the Atlantic designed to terrorize and starve the British population into submission. Led by Prime Minister Winston Churchill, the United Kingdom resisted.

While sympathetic, Roosevelt refused to act because of isolationist U.S. public opinion. In 1936, 1937, and 1939, Congress had passed neutrality acts that banned the shipment of arms to combatant nations, unless paid for in cash. On May 15, 1940, Churchill sent Roosevelt a message requesting forty or fifty destroyers to protect convoys bringing vital supplies to the United Kingdom until that nation completed building its own destroyers. Initially, Roosevelt was reluctant to help because doing so required congressional approval, and Congress was unlikely to repeal the neutrality acts. When Roosevelt was nominated for a third term in July 1940, Churchill asked again. Now more confident of reelection, he assured Churchill that he would find a way to help.

Throughout, Roosevelt searched for a plan that would not require congressional approval. He bypassed the neutrality acts by declaring millions of rounds of U.S. ammunition and thousands of guns surplus, then shipping them to the United Kingdom.

In August 1940, as the Battle of Britain unfolded, U.S. intelligence warned that the British had only a fifty-fifty chance of preventing a successful German invasion. U.S. Ambassador Joseph P. Kennedy reported that a British surrender was inevitable. He urged Roosevelt to send the destroyers: As Churchill had warned, if the United Kingdom were vanquished, its colonial islands close to United States would fall into German hands.

Roosevelt persuaded a reluctant chief of naval operations, Admiral Harold R. Stark, to certify, as required by law, that the destroyers were no longer essential to national defense. Roosevelt also circumvented Congress by carrying out the exchange through an executive agreement. Isolationists challenged the action, but Attorney General Robert Jackson declared it a legal arrangement.

On September 2, 1940, British Ambassador Lord Lothian exchanged letters with U.S. Secretary of State Cordell Hull that laid the groundwork for an agreement. Hull concluded his letter by saying, "In consideration of the declarations above quoted, the Government of the United States will immediately transfer to His Majesty's Government fifty United States Navy destroyers generally referred to as the twelve hundred-ton type" (*Private Laws,* 1941, pp. 2406–2408). The British granted the United States 99-year leases on bases in the British West Indies, specifically the Bahamas, Jamaica, St. Lucia, Trinidad, Antigua, and British Guiana. They were leased two more, in Newfoundland and Bermuda. The final terms of the leases were settled in March 1941. By late 1940, the United States had transferred nine of the fifty destroyers to the Royal Navy.

Technically America accepted the "generous action [of making the bases available] to enhance the national security of the United States" and immediately transferred the fifty destroyers, also referred to as "flush-deck" destroyers or the "four-pipers." (*Private Laws,* 1941, 2406–2408.) The United States sent forty-three destroyers to the Royal Navy and seven to the Royal Canadian Navy. In the U.S. Navy they were of the Caldwell class, Wickes class, and Clemson-class. Once in the British Navy, the ships were renamed after towns and became the Town class. Royal Norwegian Navy crews manned five of destroyers, while HMS *Campbeltown* was crewed by Royal Netherlands Navy sailors and went down in the St. Nazaire Raid. Nine destroyers were eventually transferred to the Soviet Navy. Six of the fifty destroyers were sunk by U-boats, and three were lost to other enemy actions. Those that survived the war were scuttled in 1945 or 1947 by the British or later by the Soviet Navy.

Destroyer for Bases

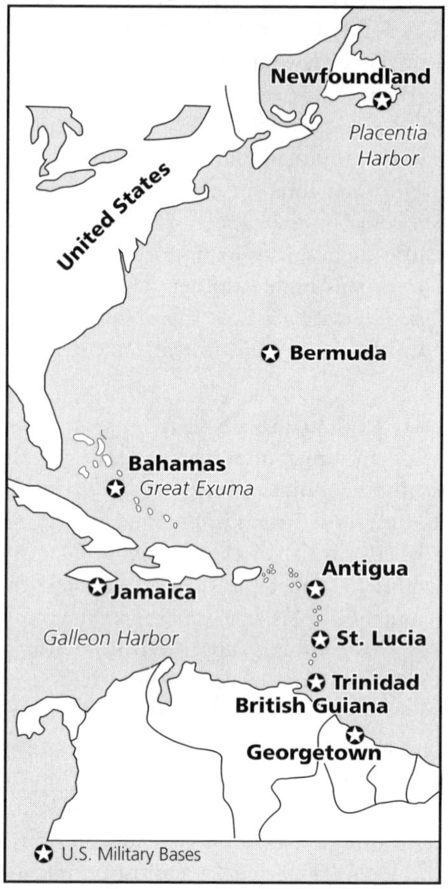

The map and key above show the military bases granted by the British to the United States in the British West Indies on the eve of World War II. By late 1940 the United States had transferred nine of the fifty destroyers to the Royal Navy. Despite formal U.S. neutrality, U.S. Ambassador Joseph P. Kennedy urged Franklin D. Roosevelt to send the destroyers, because otherwise a British surrender was "inevitable," and it was believed that if Britain was vanquished, its colonial islands would be controlled by the Germans and closed to the United States.

On September 3, 1940, during the Labor Day weekend, Roosevelt publicly announced the agreement. To assure public support, private organizations like the Committee to Defend America worked to convince Americans that supporting the United Kingdom was in their best interest.

Most of the destroyers needed extensive repairs and refitting and were, in fact, of little military value. What proved most important were the diplomatic implications. The president called the arrangement the most important "reinforcement of our defense . . . since the Louisiana Purchase" (Message of President Roosevelt to the Congress, September 3, 1940). Churchill considered it "a decidedly un-neutral act" that inaugurated the Anglo-American alliance of World War II. Most historians believe it was a critical first step in the Nazi defeat.

See also *Hull, Cordell; Roosevelt, Franklin D.; World War II, 1939–1945*

. . . . WILLIAM HEAD

REFERENCES AND FURTHER READING

Conn, Stetson, Rose C. Engelman, and Byron Fairchild. *Guarding the United States and Its Outposts.* Revised edition. Washington, DC: U.S. Army, Center of Military History, 2000.

Martin, Gilbert. *Churchill and America.* New York: Simon and Schuster, 2005.

Private Laws, Concurrent Resolutions, Treaties, International Agreements Other Than Treaties, and Proclamations. Part 2: U. S. Statutes at Large Containing the Laws and Concurrent Resolutions Enacted During the 2nd and 3rd Sessions, 76th Congress, 1939–1941, and Treaties, International Agreements Other Than Treaties, Proclamations, and Reorganization Plans. Volume 54. Washington, DC: Government Printing Office, 1941.

Reynolds, David. *The Creation of the Anglo-American Alliance, 1937–1941: A Study in Competitive Co-operation.* Chapel Hill: University of North Carolina Press, 1981.

Shogan, Robert. *Hard Bargain: How FDR Twisted Churchill's Arm, Evaded the Law and Changed the Role of the American Presidency.* New York: Scribner, 1995.

Díaz Mori, Porfirio

Porfirio Díaz (1830–1915) was one of the most notorious dictators in modern Latin America. As the president responsible for the modernization and industrialization of Mexico at the end of the nineteenth century, he earned praise from high-level U.S. officials and growing scorn from his own people. His commitment to Mexican modernization had important implications for U.S.-Mexican relations.

Following forays into the priesthood and the law, Díaz eventually settled on a military career as the quickest route to prestige and respectability. His most famous military exploit arises out of his defense of Puebla on May 5, 1862, when Mexican forces repelled French invaders. While his direct involvement remains a point of some controversy, his service in defense of Mexican sovereignty made him a hero of the people.

In 1870 Díaz entered politics, driven by his dedication to constitutional limits on presidential tenure. Following what he considered fraudulent elections in 1870 and 1876, Díaz declared himself in rebellion against the electoral victors. His devotion to the constitution proved to be an ironic justification for involvement in presidential politics since by the end of 1876, Díaz had orchestrated his own rise to power, beginning the *Porfiriato.* Except for four years from 1880 to 1884, during which his handpicked successor held the presidency, Díaz ruled Mexico from 1876 until 1911.

Díaz's highest priority as president—and the issue that brought a flood of foreign capital to Mexico—was the modernization of Mexico's infrastructure and industrial capacity. To attract the capital needed for modernization, Díaz used his power over the government to make Mexico attractive to foreign investors by modifying land ownership and taxation laws. Railroads, mines, factories, and port facilities were built throughout Mexico using foreign capital, and Mexico entered the modern industrial age.

MEXICAN MODERNIZATION

Amazing economic progress and industrial development were possible only because Díaz enjoyed total political and military control of Mexico. Politically, Díaz oversaw notoriously fraudulent elections through which he fashioned the government into his own tool. Electoral fraud was possible only through Díaz's iron-fisted military control of Mexico. Officers, chosen not so much for their skill as for their loyalty to Díaz himself, made the military weak as a tool of national defense but formidable in the suppression of internal dissent.

Díaz's political and military heavy-handedness sparked numerous insurrections, which he quelled with uncompromising harshness. To Díaz, opponents of his policies were no less than opponents of Mexican progress and therefore deserved no mercy. Díaz's control of the military also proved useful in foreign relations; he used the military to help the United States deal with recalcitrant Apache and Yaqui tribes in the Sonoran Desert at the end of the nineteenth century. This Native American pacification campaign, in fact, facilitated the deepening economic relations between the United States and Mexico as both nations sought to expand railroad, mining, and industrial interests at the expense of native populations.

The most immediate beneficiaries of Díaz's modernization schemes were foreign investors. Diaz catered to them through legislative manipulation that effectively seized land held communally by Native American communities, concentrated land in the investors' hands, and liberalized subsoil mineral rights to make investment in Mexico more attractive. Capitalists from the United States invested heavily in Mexican modernization. Díaz recognized that the investment in railroads, mining, and oil was essential for industrial development and modernization, and the United States was the single largest source of investment capital in those sectors. Mining and railroads benefited from nearly eighty percent of the total U.S. investment stream to Mexico. U.S. corporations controlled the vast majority of mines and more than seventy percent of the Mexican metals industry by the end of the *Porfiriato.* Likewise, early Mexican oil development was largely funded by U.S. sources. By the end of the nineteenth century, Díaz began to grow leery of making Mexico overly dependent on the United States and feared a loss of national sovereignty—long a complaint among the Mexican people. To counterbalance this U.S. dominance, he began working to improve Mexico's relations with European investors, particularly those from Britain, France, and Germany, much to the dismay of U.S. industrialists, who had grown used to controlling Mexico's industrial destiny.

LIBERAL OPPOSITION

Díaz's modernization efforts came at a heavy cost for working-class Mexicans. These common folk believed that Díaz had sold out the Mexican legal system to see that laws worked for the benefit of foreigners rather than Mexicans themselves. Increasingly, peasants found themselves trapped in a spiral of landlessness, poverty, debt, and virtual slavery. Most members of the liberal middle class were satisfied with the economic benefits of Porfirian modernization. As progress became secure, however, many liberals maintained that it was time for the restoration of political liberties citizens had lost in the government's effort to achieve that progress. Late in the nineteenth century, a new generation of liberals arose in opposition to the Díaz regime and called for social and political reform.

These liberal opponents complicated a relationship between Díaz and the United States already strained by his decision to increase European investment at the expense of U.S. capital. Díaz was particularly frustrated at an apparent unwillingness of the U.S. government to prosecute violations of international neutrality laws by Díaz's liberal opponents. In much the same way that Texans' donations of money, arms, and manpower facilitated Díaz's rise to power in 1876, U.S. supporters were providing significant aid to his own opponents in 1909 and 1910. While there is little evidence of complicity by Washington, the political ramifications of Díaz's decisions to favor European firms over well-connected U.S. capitalists were apparent.

Liberal opponents found reason to hope for change in an interview Díaz provided to the New York journal, *Pearson's*, in 1908, in which he announced his retirement from politics. He said he would not put forth his name for re-election in 1910 and would instead allow legitimate electoral competition to select his successor—pledges he no intention of honoring. Once the news that Díaz planned to step down reached Mexico, liberals scrambled to fill the void. Soon, a number of reform-minded individuals began publishing tracts condemning Porfirian corruption, and political parties arose to present candidates for the upcoming election. Díaz's most significant challenge came from a wealthy *hacendado* named Francisco I. Madero. At the beginning of Madero's presidential campaign, Díaz did not consider him a threat, but as Madero's crowds became larger and larger and more and more vocal in their calls for reform, Díaz decided that it was time to nip the Maderista movement in the bud. In June 1910, Díaz had Madero and other political opponents arrested and thrown in prison on trumped-up charges.

Díaz had little reason to fear defeat as the June 1910 elections neared. Mexico was still under his control, as it had been since 1876. When officials announced the electoral results, few were surprised. Madero won only 197 votes, while Díaz tallied more than one million. In a demonstration of magnanimity, Díaz released Madero from prison. Madero fled to the United States and issued a call for revolution against the Díaz regime, thus beginning the Mexican Revolution of 1910. By mid-1911, revolutionary forces controlled Mexico, and eighty-year-old Díaz decided to retire. As he was leaving for exile in Europe, he quipped, "Madero has unleashed a tiger. Now let's see if he can ride it." Shortly before his death in Paris in July 1915, Mexico was in the throes of revolutionary chaos. Although Díaz died virtually alone, he lived to see the revolution that overthrew him collapse under the weight of forces his own autocracy had controlled.

See also *Doheny, Edward L.; France, Intervention in Mexico, 1862–1867; Hayes, Rutherford B; Hearst, William Randolph; Huerta, Victoriano; Madero, Francisco Indalecio; Mexican Revolution, 1911–1917, U.S. Policy toward; Mexico, U.S. Relations with*

. . . . MATTHEW A. REDINGER

REFERENCES AND FURTHER READING

Beals, Carlton. *Porfirio Díaz: Dictator of Mexico.* Westport, CT: Greenwood Press, 1971, 1932.

Beezley, William. *Judas at the Jockey Club and Other Episodes of Porfirian Mexico.* 2nd ed. Lincoln: University of Nebraska Press, 2001, 1987.

Garner, Paul. *Porfirio Díaz.* London: Pearson Education, 2001.

Godoy, José F. *Porfirio Díaz, President of Mexico: The Master Builder of a Great Commonwealth.* New York: G. P. Putnam's Sons, 1910.

Hannay, David. *Díaz.* Port Washington, NY: Kennikat Press, 1970.

Díaz Recinos, Adolfo

Born in 1875 to Nicaraguan parents who lived in Costa Rica, Adolfo Díaz (1875–1964) rose to become president of Nicaragua on two occasions during the turbulent early decades of the twentieth century (May 9, 1911, to January 1, 1917, and November 14, 1926, to January 1, 1929), a period when civil war and U.S. military intervention shaped much of the political turmoil in Nicaragua.

Díaz worked as an engineer for the La Luz y Los Angeles Mining Company, an U.S. firm that operated gold mines on the eastern coast of Nicaragua at La Siuna. Conspiring with the U.S. government and U.S. business interests, Díaz helped channel funds for the October 1909 revolt to overthrow Liberal José Santos Zelaya (President 1893–1909). The authoritarian Zelaya had welcomed and worked with U.S. investors early in his rule, but the U.S. decision in 1903 to build a transoceanic canal in Panama, not Nicaragua, soured the dictator on any further cooperation with the *yanquis*. Instead, Zelaya sought loans from Great Britain and German or Japanese financing for a Nicaraguan canal as a counterbalance to the growing U.S. hegemony in Central America. This challenge provoked the United States and various U.S. companies with investments in the region to fund and support a rebellion that encompassed all of Zelaya's domestic enemies.

Díaz, who earned only $80 per month as an engineer, funneled some $600,000 toward the rebels. The United Fruit Company and U.S. banks were the main contributors. U.S. volunteers and soldiers of fortune also played a role in the revolt. Conservative Díaz soon emerged, along with liberal General Juan José Estrada and conservative Emiliano Chamorro, as the triumvirate of insurgent leaders who brought down Zelaya's 17-year-old regime. The United States broke diplomatic relations with Zelaya and landed Marines at the Nicaraguan port of Bluefields to guarantee the revolution's success. In December 1909, Zelaya handed over the reins of his flagging government to his foreign minister, José Madriz, then resigned and fled the country. Madriz proved incapable of defeating the rebellion and soon fell, followed by a series of short-term presidents, José Dolores Estrada, Luís Mena, and Juan José Estrada, none of whom held power for more than a few months or, in some cases, a few days.

With the support of Washington and Nicaraguan conservatives, Adolfo Díaz assumed the presidency in May of 1911 and brought a period of relative stability to Nicaragua for the next five years. He was forced, however, to rely on the U.S. Marines, whom he invited into Nicaragua in 1912 to put down a liberal revolt by Mena against his government. The Marines remained for the next decade, protecting conservative rule and U.S. investments. During his protectorate government, Díaz signed the unpopular 1914 Bryan-Chamorro Treaty, which guaranteed the United States exclusive rights in perpetuity for any Nicaraguan interoceanic canal as well as rights to naval bases in the Gulf of Fonseca and the Corn Islands. Díaz stepped down from his first presidency after the 1916 election, which put his former foreign minister, Chamorro, into the presidential palace.

Díaz returned to politics in 1926 when Chamorro, by then out of office, organized a coup to seize power from the elected president, Carlos José Solórzano Gutiérrez. The coup faltered following the brief withdrawal of the U.S. Marines. Washington regarded Díaz as more reliable than either Chamorro or Solórzano and showed its support for him by redeploying the Marines to Nicaragua to crush another liberal revolt led by former Vice President Juan Sacasa against Díaz. Secretary of State Frank B. Kellogg sent Henry L. Stimson to Nicaragua to mediate this confusing civil war. After meeting with Díaz, General José María Moncada, military leader of the liberal rebels, and Sacasa, who made conflicting claims on the office of presidency, Stimson hammered out an agreement among the three: Díaz would finish out Solórzano's term and then step aside after U.S.-supervised 1928 elections, and the Marine garrison would also withdraw from the country. The rebels would lay down their arms, and a U.S.-trained nonpartisan military force would be established to maintain political peace. This agreement became known as the Pact of Espino Negro. Notably, one liberal general, Augusto César Sandino, refused to sign the pact and continued to fight on against the Marines.

General Moncada won the 1928 elections and succeeded Díaz as president in January 1929. Díaz ran again for president on the conservative ticket in 1932 but was defeated by Juan Sacasa. Marked for arrest in 1936 when Anastasio Somoza García seized power, Díaz fled Nicaragua for the United States. He lived in New York, Miami, and New Orleans before moving to Costa Rica, where his parents had lived as exiles from the Zelaya regime. He died there in 1964 at the age of 88.

See also *Bryan-Chamorro Treaty, 1916; Kellogg, Frank B.; Knox, Philander; Nicaragua, U.S. Relations with; Sandino, Augusto César; United Fruit Company (UFCO); Zelaya López, José Santos*

. . . . MICHAEL E. DONOGHUE

REFERENCES AND FURTHER READING

Gobat, Michel. *Confronting the American Dream: Nicaragua Under U.S. Imperial Rule.* Durham, SC: Duke University Press, 2006.

LaFeber, Walter. *Inevitable Revolutions: The United States and Central America.* New York: W. W. Norton, 1993.

Langley, Lestor D., and Thomas C. Schoonover. *The Banana Men: American Mercenaries and Entrepreneurs in Central America 1880–1930.* Lexington: University Press of Kentucky, 1995.

Woodward, Ralph Lee, Jr. *Central America: A Nation Divided.* New York: Oxford University Press, 1999.

Dickinson-Ayón Treaty, 1867

Formally called a treaty of friendship, commerce, and navigation, the Dickinson-Ayón Treaty was signed on June 21, 1867, by A. B. Dickinson, U.S. minister to Nicaragua, and Tomás Ayón, Nicaragua's minister of foreign affairs. In several of the treaty's articles, each signatory extended commercial privileges to the other, such as most favored nation status. Nationals of each country were also guaranteed certain rights in the other regarding religious observance and burial, should they die there.

The most important articles pertained to communication between the Atlantic and Pacific oceans. Because of its closeness to the United States and its system of lakes and rivers, Nicaragua had long been viewed as a possible site for an interoceanic canal. U.S. interest rose after the Mexican War and the discovery of gold in California, and several entrepreneurs, among them Cornelius Vanderbilt, contemplated canal projects. Meanwhile, U.S. ambitions in Central America clashed with those of Great Britain, which seemed intent on territorial acquisition there. In 1849 U.S. emissaries to Nicaragua Elijah Hise and E. George Squier signed treaties with that government providing for construction of a canal and guaranteeing Nicaraguan sovereignty over the canal route. The United States did not ratify either treaty because both men had acted without authorization. However, Squier's aggressive actions in Nicaragua and Honduras helped bring about negotiations with Great Britain that led to the signing of the Clayton-Bulwer Treaty (1850), in which the two parties disavowed territorial aims in Central America and pledged that neither would seek exclusive control of any canal that might be built there.

Under the Dickinson-Ayón Treaty, the United States was granted the right of transit across Nicaragua "on any route of communication, natural or artificial, whether by land or by water which may now or hereafter exist." The United States guaranteed the neutrality and "innocent use" of the transit route and promised to protect it if Nicaragua was unable to do so. Nicaragua, however, reserved its sovereignty rights over the route. The United States also agreed to try to induce other nations to adhere to the treaty. The U.S. Senate ratified the treaty on January 20, 1868.

According to Thomas M. Leonard, the Dickinson-Ayón Treaty reflected early U.S. support for unilateral U.S. construction of a Nicaraguan canal despite the Clayton-Bulwer Treaty. In later years, sentiment grew even stronger in favor of sole U.S. control and construction by the U.S. government rather than by private interests. The Frelinghuysen-Zavala Treaty (1884) embodied this position, but it failed to be ratified in the U.S. Senate and was withdrawn in 1885 by President Grover Cleveland. Nicaragua renounced the Dickinson-Ayón Treaty in 1902.

See also *Clayton-Bulwer Treaty, 1850; Cleveland, Grover; Frelinghuysen-Zavala Treaty, 1884; Vanderbilt, Cornelius*

. . . . HELEN DELPAR

REFERENCES AND FURTHER READING

Hill, Roscoe R. "The Nicaraguan Canal Idea to 1913." *Hispanic American Historical Review* 28 (1948): 197–211.

Leonard, Thomas M. "Central America: The Search for Economic Development." In *United-States-Latin American Relations, 1850–1903: Establishing a Relationship*, edited by Thomas M. Leonard, 81–106. Tuscaloosa: University of Alabama Press, 1999.

Mack, Gerstle. *The Land Divided: A History of the Panama Canal and Other Canal Projects*. New York: Knopf, 1944.

Stansifer, Charles L. "United States-Central American Relations, 1824–1850." In *United States-Latin American Relations, 1800–1850: The Formative Generations*, edited by T. Ray Shurbutt, 25–45. Tuscaloosa: University of Alabama Press, 1991.

Dictators, U.S. Policy toward

The U.S. government adopted an ambivalent position regarding Latin American dictatorships in the twentieth century. While claiming to support the development of democracy in the region, the United States tolerated or supported antidemocratic and often abusive dictators and military juntas when policymakers deemed it economically or politically expedient to do so.

In the first half of the century, powerful business entities such as the United Fruit Company helped shape friendly U.S. policies toward reliably capitalist dictators in the Caribbean and Central America. Later, the perceived need to contain the spread of Communism in Latin America prompted the United States to throw its support behind anti-reformist military figures during the long decades of the Cold War. U.S. policymakers looked away as allies suspended constitutional rule and due process, governed by decree, and imprisoned, tortured, and executed political opponents. The list of Latin American dictatorships supported by the United States is lengthy. Among repressive allies in the first half of the twentieth century were rulers of the Dominican Republic, Guatemala, El Salvador, Nicaragua, and pre-revolutionary Cuba. As the Cold War turned Latin America—like much of the third world—into an arena of conflict between East and West, the United States supported repressive military dictatorships including those in Argentina, Brazil, Chile, Uruguay, and Paraguay, and again in El Salvador and Guatemala. In several cases, such as Guatemala in 1954 and Chile in 1973, the United States contributed directly to the overthrow of constitutionally elected democratic presidents and to the installation of military rule, albeit in the name of democracy.

STABILITY AND THE NATIONAL SECURITY DOCTRINE

In crafting policy toward the region, democratic niceties were sacrificed in a quest to ensure order, both in the 1920s when labor unionism in Latin America threatened U.S. economic investments and in the post–World War II period when widespread movements for reform and revolution were viewed by U.S. policy intellectuals as opening the region to Communist influence. Political reformers in the region were frequently suspect, and anti-Communist leaders, even those with records of repression, were viewed as allies and friends of the United States.

A pivotal moment for U.S. Latin America policy came in 1954, when the U.S. Central Intelligence Agency organized an exile invasion to oust the democratically elected reformer, Jacobo Arbenz of Guatemala, installing in his place a military regime headed by Colonel Carlos Castillo Armas. Vice president Richard M. Nixon commented on the possibilities brought about by the CIA-sponsored coup, noting that Guatemala's new ruler pledged "to do more for the people in two years than the Communists [*sic*] were able to do in ten" (*Los Angeles Times*, August 7, 1955). Post–1954 Guatemala was to be a showcase for anticommunist stability and development in the region. In fact, the U.S.-sponsored overthrow of Arbenz brought Guatemala's ten-year experiment in democracy to a standstill and ushered in a period marked by militarization and death squad violence. The elimination of the political center and virtually all democratic possibilities for change produced what U.S. policymakers had most feared: the rise of an armed leftist insurrection. The violence that was unleashed to defeat it reached the level of genocide. In a civil war that raged for the next three decades, some 200,000 Guatemalans were killed or disappeared, mostly at the hands of state security forces.

A few years after the overthrow of Arbenz, Cuba's Fidel Castro (unlike the ousted leader of Guatemala) embraced communism. Following the 1959 Cuban Revolution, the determination of U.S. policymakers to contain communism's spread in the western hemisphere led to strengthened alliances with militaries across the region. Support for anticommunist allies was unequivocal. President John F. Kennedy pledged in his inaugural address that in the battle against communism, the United States would "support any friend, oppose any foe." The National Security Doctrine, a U.S. policy formulation and blueprint for fighting communism, proclaimed that the United States would assume the task of protecting the hemisphere from external threats, while supporting Latin American militaries as they kept watch over threats of "internal subversion." U.S. military and technical assistance poured into Latin America in an effort to professionalize the region's armed forces, and the U.S.-run School of the Americas offered training to Latin American military officers.

The region's militaries—larger and better equipped, with a new sense of mission—stepped into positions of authority in the 1960s and 1970s as bureaucratic authoritarianism swept the region. In 1964 the U.S. government looked on with approval as Brazil's military ousted civilian president João Goulart. In 1973 the CIA supported the military overthrow of Chilean president Salvador Allende, and General Augusto Pinochet Ugarte stepped into what became a seventeen-year dictatorial rule. The United States gave its blessing to the new military rulers who took control of Uruguay and Argentina and looked favorably on the creation of a regional intelligence network among Latin American militaries called Operation Condor, even though the group coordinated transborder kidnappings and assassinations. Across militarized Latin America, with tacit U.S. approval and financial support, order and stability reigned as opposition and dissent were met by institutionalized terror.

THE U.S. EXECUTIVE VERSUS CONGRESS

In the 1970s, Congress repeatedly tried to reduce or end U.S. support for abusive Latin American dictatorships, despite determined executive branch commitment to allies in the anticommunist struggle. Senator Edward M. Kennedy convened hearings on Chile and pushed for limits on military aid; in 1976 an amendment passed that required ending aid to the Pinochet regime because of human rights abuses. In the House of Representatives, Tom Harkin sponsored legislation linking U.S. economic assistance to foreign governments' human rights records. The Nixon and Ford administrations, however, circumvented these restrictions when possible, and tacit U.S. approval of the ends, if not the means, sought by the region's military rulers was justified as vital to national security. The Carter administration was at times critical of governments with poor human rights records but due to security calculations, fell short of applying real pressure or tying U.S. assistance to changes in behavior. The region's anticommunist dictatorships were again embraced when Ronald Reagan was elected president. But partly due to Reagan's desire to win congressional cooperation for his anticommunist efforts in Central America (where military leaders diplomatically handed official power to civilians while retaining de facto authority), the Reagan administration finally started moving away from leaders such as Pinochet in the mid 1980s.

The debt crisis of the 1980s also contributed to the end of bureaucratic authoritarianism and, with it, U.S. support for Latin American dictators. One after another, the military dictators and juntas lost power. The civilians elected in their places inherited not just crippling economic problems but also the legacies of decades of brutality, torture, and impunity.

See also *"Disappeared Ones" (Desaparecidos), Argentina and Chile, 1970s–1980s; Guatemala, U.S. Invasion of, 1954; Human Rights; Operation Condor; Pinochet Ugarte, Augusto; School of the Americas*

. . . . BETSY KONEFAL

REFERENCES AND FURTHER READING

Dosal, Paul J. *Doing Business with the Dictators: A Political History of United Fruit in Guatemala, 1899–1944.* New York: SR Books, 2005.

Schmitz, David. *Thank God They're on Our Side: The United States and Right-Wing Dictatorships, 1921–1965.* Chapel Hill: University of North Carolina Press, 1999.

———. *The United States and Right-Wing Dictatorships, 1965–1989.* New York: Cambridge University Press, 2006.

Smith, Peter H. Talons of the *Eagle: Latin America, the United States, and the World.* 3rd ed. New York: Oxford University Press, 2008.

Dillon, C. Douglas

Clarence Douglas Dillon (1909–2003) was a prominent official in both the Eisenhower and Kennedy administrations. Although he was a member of the Executive Committee of the National Security Council (ExComm) during the Cuban missile crisis, he is best known for his role in creating the Social Progress Fund and the Alliance for Progress. As a key figure in both of those initiatives, he represents the continuity between the two administrations in terms of aid and development policy.

Dillon was the son of Clarence Dillon, a wealthy businessman and cofounder of Dillon, Read & Co. He studied at Groton and Harvard and entered the family business. After a stint in the Navy during World War II, he became chairman of Dillon, Read. In 1953 Eisenhower named him ambassador to France. He became assistant secretary of state for economic affairs in 1958 and, in June 1959, replaced Christian Herter as undersecretary of state.

As Dillon returned to Washington, relations with Latin America were in a state of flux following Vice President Richard Nixon's ill-fated goodwill tour. The related riots prompted Brazilian President Juscelino Kubitschek to propose an Operation Pan America, to which Eisenhower responded positively. Dillon championed a new policy, and over the next two years, hemispheric representatives laid the groundwork for a more liberal aid policy, culminating in the creation of the Inter-American Development Bank and the Social Progress Fund, which provided assistance for schools and hospitals. Dillon also persuaded U.S. leaders to modify their opposition to commodity agreements and the Latin American Free Trade Association (LAFTA).

Although a Republican, Dillon was named secretary of the treasury by President Kennedy in 1961. In that role, he led the U.S. delegation to Punta del Este, Uruguay, in August 1961, for the creation of the Alliance for Progress. Dillon was the star of the conference, holding his own in a famous exchange with Cuban Finance Minister Ernesto "Che" Guevara. At the key moment at Punta del Este, Dillon exceeded his instructions and without authority personally pledged that the United States would provide $20 billion to fund the alliance. That moment proved to be the high point of the Alliance for Progress.

Dillon served as treasury secretary until April 1965. He later chaired the Rockefeller Foundation and became a noted philanthropist.

See also *Alliance for Progress; Eisenhower, Dwight D.; Nixon, Richard M.; Quadros, Janio; Social Progress Trust Fund*

. . . . W. MICHAEL WEIS

REFERENCES AND FURTHER READING

Paterson, Thomas G., ed. *Kennedy's Quest for Victory, 1961–1963.* New York: Oxford University Press, 1989.

Rabe, Stephen G. *Eisenhower and Latin America: The Foreign Policy of Anticommunism.* Chapel Hill: University of North Carolina Press, 1988.

_______. *The Most Dangerous Area in the World: John F. Kennedy Confronts Communist Revolution in Latin America.* Chapel Hill: University of North Carolina Press, 1999.

Taffet, Jeffrey F. *Foreign Aid as Foreign Policy: The Alliance for Progress in Latin America.* New York: Routledge, 2007.

"Disappeared Ones" (Desaparecidos), Argentina and Chile, 1970s–1980s

Armed forces in numerous Latin American countries have adopted the tactic of "disappearing" political opponents to eliminate opposition and instill terror in the general population, a method of repression especially common during dictatorships in the 1970s and 1980s. The term is a euphemism for what generally involves illegal detention, torture, murder, and the dumping of bodies into undisclosed locations such as clandestine cemeteries or the sea. Security forces typically claim to have no knowledge of a disappeared person's whereabouts since no public record of arrest or detention exists. Victims were stripped of their basic right to protection under the law, including access to legal representation and due process. It was a tactic that mirrored the Nazi concept of "night and fog," where prisoners taken by state forces would "vanish" without a trace. In both the German and Latin American contexts, this practice has functioned as a method of repression and terror that goes beyond the abuses meted out to political prisoners since family and friends of the disappeared also experience fear and uncertainty.

Such tactics were routinely employed by Cold War allies of the United States, including military governments in Brazil, Uruguay, Paraguay, El Salvador, and Guatemala. The "Disappeared Ones" in Argentina and Chile number in the tens of thousands. Most of their cases remain unresolved. Secretary of State Henry Kissinger consistently sought to turn a blind eye to these violations, although the U.S. government did pressure military regimes--sometimes successfully—for information about disappearances of U.S. citizens or other high-profile missing person, such as Argentine journalist Jacobo Timerman.

ARGENTINA

Argentina stands out as one of the Latin American countries where state forces have used the tactic of forced disappearance most extensively. Thousands of prisoners in the 1970s and 1980s, after being kidnapped, tortured, and interrogated, were drugged and transported by naval officers in what are known as death flights. Forced aboard airplanes, prisoners were dumped, naked and alive, into the Rio de la Plata or the Atlantic Ocean. The famous Mothers of the Plaza de Mayo began demanding information on their disappeared sons and daughters in 1977, soon after an Argentine military junta (1976–1983) seized power, and they continue to march weekly in the Plaza de Mayo with the names of the missing embroidered into their signature white headscarves.

The Argentine military has admitted that some 9,000 of its former prisoners are unaccounted for. The Argentine National Commission on the Disappeared, a truth commission established by President Raul Alfonsín in 1986 to document abuses during the last dictatorship, determined the number of disappeared to be at least 11,000. Human rights groups set the figure much higher, at 30,000. Although details remain elusive, significant information on these crimes has been gathered, especially the high-profile confession regarding death flights (later retracted) by former Argentine naval officer Adolfo Scilingo and the scathing truth commission report, which contained detailed testimony of torture survivors, *Argentina: Never Again!* Recently declassified government documents from multiple sources—the U.S. government, the Paraguayan secret police, and Argentine intelligence police—are also being used in ongoing trials in Argentine courts of police and military officials accused of human rights crimes.

It appears that repressive forces in Argentina (and elsewhere) may not have wholly abandoned the practice of disappearance: In Argentina, demands are being made for security forces to disclose the whereabouts of Julio Jorge López, a key witness in the human rights trial of former police official Miguel Etchecolatz. López, who is in his late seventies, went missing just before his final testimony in the trial, September 18, 2006. (Etchecolatz, charged with murder, kidnapping, and torture, was sentenced to life in prison for his role in dictatorship-era repression.)

CHILE

Chilean officials during the dictatorship of Augusto Pinochet (1973–1990) also adopted the practice of "disappearing" political opponents and critics of the government beginning shortly after the 1973 coup. The official Chilean Truth and Reconciliation Commission, established in 1990 specifically to investigate the fate of the missing, classified more than 1,000 people as "disappeared," although few details have emerged on the whereabouts of victims. In 2001 the armed forces pledged cooperation with ongoing inquiries, but it revealed information on only 180 persons, 150 of whose bodies they admitted to disposing of in rivers and the sea. Since Pinochet left office in 1990, human rights cases involving the disappeared have proceeded slowly through the courts, despite amnesty protection that has been in place since 1978. Today more than 400 former military and police personnel are facing charges of forced disappearance, torture, or extrajudicial killings, and more than 150 have been convicted. At the time of Pinochet's death (due to a heart attack) in December 2006, he was under house arrest on charges of forced disappearance and torture, along with financial crimes.

Chilean military officials and General Pinochet himself were instrumental in creating an international military intelligence network, Operation Condor, which led to transnational disappearance of political opponents. Condor, which linked military officials in Chile and Argentina, as well as in Uruguay, Paraguay, and Brazil, facilitated abductions and disappearances across borders, with intelligence forces in member countries coordinating joint efforts to track down and capture people targeted by the dictatorships.

DISAPPEARANCE AND INTERNATIONAL HUMAN RIGHTS LAW

Disappearance is defined in international human rights law as a crime against humanity, and as such it is considered illegal, even in times of national emergency or martial law. Universal jurisdiction has been asserted in cases of disappearance, and it has been argued successfully in courts that an amnesty cannot be applied to such crimes. In Chilean courts, human rights advocates have also asserted that a statute of limitations cannot prevent prosecutions for disappearance since victims can be assumed—however unlikely it may be—to be alive, and thus the kidnappings are considered to be ongoing.

The crime of disappearance is the subject of a regional treaty, the Inter-American Convention on Forced Disappearance of Persons, and a treaty adopted by the UN General Assembly, the International Convention for the Protection of All Persons from Enforced Disappearance. The UN convention, opened for signature in 2006, entered into force in 2010. As of early 2011, it has 88 signatories, among them most Latin American countries.

August 30 has been named the International Day of the Disappeared, a commemoration begun by the nongovernmental Latin American Federation of Associations for Relatives of Detained-Disappeared, FEDEFAM. The office of the UN High Commissioner for Human Rights maintains a strong focus on the problem, with its Working Group on Enforced or Involuntary Disappearances registering some 50,000 cases of disappearance worldwide.

See also *Argentina, U.S. Relations with; Church Committee; Dictators, U.S. Policy toward; Human Rights; Operation Condor; Pinochet Ugarte, Augusto; Timerman, Jacobo*

. . . . BETSY KONEFAL

REFERENCES AND FURTHER READING

Comisión Nacional sobre la Desaparición de Personas (CONADEP). *Argentina, Never Again: A Report by Argentina's National Commission on Disappeared People.* 1986. www.desaparecidos.org/nuncamas/web/english/library/nevagain/nevagain_001.htm.

Dinges, John. *The Condor Years: How Pinochet and His Allies Brought Terrorism to Three Continents.* New York: New Press, 2004.

Feitlowitz, Marguerite. *A Lexicon of Terror: Argentina and the Legacies of Torture.* Revised and updated. New York: Oxford University Press, 2011.

Office of the United Nations High Commissioner for Human Rights. *International Convention for the Protection of All Persons from Enforced Disappearance.* www2.ohchr.org/english/law/disappearance-convention.htm.

Organization of American States, Department of International Law. *Inter-American Convention on Forced Disappearance of Persons.* www.oas.org/juridico/English/Treaties/a-60.html.

Verbitsky, Horacio, Juan Mendez, Gabriel Cavallo, and Esther Allen. *Confessions of an Argentine Dirty Warrior: A Firsthand Account of Atrocity.* New York: New Press, 2005.

Dodds, Harold W.

Harold W. Dodds (1889–1980) was a political scientist and university administrator in the United States who also worked as a technical adviser on political matters in Latin America in the 1920s. Known most prominently as president of Princeton University (1933–1957), Dodds became involved in reforming election laws in Nicaragua in the 1920s.

After World War I, the Republican administration of President Warren G. Harding (1921–1923) sought to move away from U.S. military occupation of Central American and Caribbean nations. In Nicaragua, U.S. Marines had been present since 1912, and elections had long been manipulated. Each of the presidential elections of 1912, 1916, and 1920 had resulted in victory for the conservative candidate, and each election was widely recognized as rigged. After pressuring the Nicaraguan government to establish free elections by 1924, U.S. Secretary of State Charles Evans Hughes arranged in 1922 for Dodds to study local election practices and propose appropriate reforms. The Nicaraguan Congress approved Dodds's proposals and enacted into law a new electoral code in March 1923. Reforms included voter registration and verification, antibribery measures, and ultimate electoral oversight by the Nicaraguan Congress.

The October 1924 elections resulted in victory for conservative Carlos Solórzano as president and liberal Juan Sacasa as vice president, but political problems followed. Incumbent President Bartolomé Martínez, initially a conservative presidential contender, withdrew from the race when the U.S. State Department threatened to refuse him official recognition because of constitutional prohibition of re-election. Martínez's subsequent efforts to disrupt the electoral process caused most local and international observers to call the election unfair. The new president was inaugurated in January 1925, and the U.S. Marines left Nicaragua by August. But a rebellion led by losing conservative candidate Emiliano Chamorro caused widespread political turmoil and armed conflict—forcing both Solórzano and Sacasa to vacate their elected posts, prompting liberal counterrebellions, and leading to a return by the Marines. In April 1927, former U.S. Secretary of War Henry Stimson presented liberal military leader José María Moncada a plan to disarm the country, to reform election laws again, and to allow U.S. supervision of the 1928 elections. Dodds again oversaw revisions of electoral procedures.

Dodds's new reforms featured U.S. supervision of both national and local electoral boards. Other measures included provisions for a two-party system, ballots for the illiterate, an appeals process, and controls over the supply of alcoholic beverages (which could be used for bribery purposes), but the most controversial measure was empowering U.S. Marines to chair each of the 432 three-member precinct election boards. Dodds argued that appointing U.S. civilians to these positions would prove expensive and logistically problematic and that Marines were disciplined, impartial, and knowledgeable of "Latin psychology." General Frank McCoy oversaw the national board. The reforms also designated the U.S. Marines and the recently formed *Guardia Nacional* to protect public order throughout the campaign. Dodds declared the 1928 elections a success, noting that they were "peaceful" and "fair and just." President Moncada, the liberal candidate, was inaugurated in January 1929.

Augusto César Sandino and his followers were most vocal in their criticisms of the 1928 elections. Sandino, the only Moncada lieutenant to reject Stimson's plan, led a rebellion to oust all U.S. Marines from Nicaragua. Sandino and his followers argued that as long as Marines supervised elections and occupied the nation, Nicaragua would never enjoy national sovereignty and freedom. Dodds dismissed Sandino as a "bandit," but the nationalist uprising continued for several years. Soon after the Marines transferred constabulary authority to the *Guardia* and left Nicaragua in 1933, the new police forces assassinated Sandino. Free elections were not established in Nicaragua until more than a half century later.

Dodds served the U.S. government in other Latin American affairs, including as technical adviser to General John J. Pershing in the Tacna-Arica negotiations between Peru and Chile in 1925.

See also *Chamorro Vargas, Emiliano; Harding, Warren G.; Hughes, Charles Evans; Nicaragua, U.S. Relations with; Sacasa, Juan B.; Sandino, Augusto César; Stimson, Henry L.*

. . . . GREGORY S. CRIDER

SELECTED WORKS

Dodds, Harold W. "American Supervision of the Nicaraguan Election." *Foreign Affairs* 7, no. 3 (April 1929): 488–496.

REFERENCES AND FURTHER READING

Dodd, Thomas J. *Managing Democracy in Central America: A Case Study, United States Election Supervision in Nicaragua, 1927–1933*. Piscataway, NJ: Transaction, 1992.

Schoultz, Lars. *Beneath the United States: A History of Policy Toward Latin America*. Cambridge, MA: Harvard University Press, 1998.

Doheny, Edward L.

Edward Laurence Doheny (1856–1935) rose from humble immigrant stock to become one of the most important oil industrialists in Mexico.

Doheny, born in Fond du Lac, Wisconsin, on August 10, 1856, to Patrick and Eleanor Doheny, showed great aptitude for mathematics in school and graduated at the top of his class in 1872. After a stint with the U.S. Geological Survey, during which he learned the details of the mining business, Doheny dived into mining himself. After a few failures, he acquired a partner, Charles Canfield, whose financial recourses allowed him to obtain oil leases near downtown Los Angeles in 1891. Within five years, the partners had productive wells across Southern California. Doheny considered himself a successful oilman and quickly sought to expand his operations.

In 1900, Doheny accepted an invitation to survey potential oil properties in Mexico. Near Tampico, Doheny found attractive prospects. His subsequent meeting with President Porfirio Díaz Mori brought together kindred souls: Díaz was eager to attract U.S. capital to modernize Mexico, and Doheny had financial connections ready to invest in Mexican oil properties. By 1901, Doheny had bought several leases and had incorporated the Mexican Petroleum Company. Over the next several years, Doheny worked to expand both his oil properties and his friendships with several governors in central Mexico. These relationships resulted in lucrative concessions and tax breaks for his oil company. These financial deals, combined with spectacular gushers in 1910 and 1911, made Doheny's company the largest oil interest in Mexico, with plans to market his oil globally.

Doheny's close partnership with Díaz was transformed from asset to liability as the Mexican dictator was thrown from power in 1911. Doheny's interests were caught up in the chaos of the early revolutionary period. By 1915, Venustiano Carranza had proven hostile to U.S. financial interests in Mexico. Doheny had good reason to fear: Carranza's new Mexican Constitution of 1917 included Article 27, which established Mexican control of all subsoil mineral rights. Doheny and other corporate giants worked on both sides of the border to mobilize public support of U.S. military intervention against the revolution. The fears of Doheny and other oilmen were laid to rest in 1927, when the Mexican supreme court decided that the constitution could not be enforced retroactively. Doheny quietly began divesting himself of Mexican oil, fearing that the government would eventually nationalize oil, which it did under President Lázaro Cárdenas in 1938.

For Doheny, the 1927 decision was not a time for celebration, for he was caught in the infamous Teapot Dome scandal involving in the influence of oil money in U.S. politics. He was tried on charges of bribery of government officials, and while he was acquitted, his reputation suffered nonetheless. At the time of his death on September 8, 1935, Edward Doheny had accomplished a great deal as a philanthropist and an industrialist. He developed extensive oil interests in the United States and Mexico. His reputation has, however, been inextricably linked to one of the most infamous scandals of the 1920s.

See also *Cárdenas del Río, Lázaro; Carranza Garza, Venustiano; Díaz Mori, Porfirio*

. . . . MATTHEW A. REDINGER

REFERENCES AND FURTHER READING

Davis, Margaret Leslie. *Dark Side of Fortune: Triumph and Scandal in the Life of Oil Tycoon Edward L. Doheny*. Berkeley: University of California Press, 1998.

Hall, Linda B. Oil, *Banks and Politics: The United States and Postrevolutionary Mexico, 1917–1924*. Austin: University of Texas Press, 1995.

Dollar Diplomacy

The term *dollar diplomacy* describes the U.S. foreign policy in Latin America and East Asia under Secretary of State Philander C. Knox and President William Howard Taft. It focused on extending U.S. economic power by providing loans to insolvent foreign countries. It was Taft who first coined the term during an address on December 7, 1909.

Dollar diplomacy allowed bankrupt foreign governments to obtain loans from private U.S. banks in return for direct U.S. financial supervision. Often private U.S. banking managers became the administrators of the loan, forcing the client nation to reorganize its financial system by imposing U.S.-style fiscal reforms, making them adopt the gold standard and implement western tax reforms.

In the developing world, especially the states of Latin America, the term has been used to denounce the role the U.S. government and U.S. corporations have played in using economic, diplomatic, and military power to open up foreign markets. While Taft may have introduced this new form of economic imperialism, its greatest exponent was Secretary Knox, who was a corporate attorney and one of the main founders of the massive U.S. Steel conglomerate. According to the Taft-Knox policy, U.S. loans or multinational loans in which U.S. business participated not only facilitated debt repayment but also assured prosperity for both sides. Knox's favorite slogan was "every diplomat a salesman."

Proponents believed this arrangement would protect the United States from overproduction and supply poorer nations with much needed manufactured products. They believed this would afford economic progress, political stability, and spread U.S. civilization throughout the hemisphere. They argued that while the policy involved competition with Europe and Japan in terms of buying bonds, floating loans, building railroads, and establishing banks, it was a symbiotic relationship that was good for everyone.

In 1904 Theodore Roosevelt, Taft's predecessor, had sown the seeds for this policy with the Roosevelt Corollary to the Monroe Doctrine. Roosevelt, fearful of European intervention in insolvent Latin American states, stated that the United States had the "right and obligation" to intervene if Latin American nations could not stabilize their own economic affairs in the face of international debts. Roosevelt reckoned that a lack of U.S. action would open the door to European, especially British or German, intervention. Germany's belligerence during the Venezuela affair of 1902 and 1903 spurred Roosevelt to action.

Taft expanded the policy, using it as a justification for protecting the Panama Canal, purchasing Honduras's debt to British bankers, and intervening in Nicaragua by helping overthrow one government and providing military support for another. In one of the most brazen examples of dollar diplomacy, Taft sent troops to seize customs houses in support of Nicaraguan insurgents during their revolt of 1912. Once the rebels had won, Knox urged U.S. bankers to offer loans to the new regime in order to increase U.S. financial influence. Within two years, the pro-U.S. regime was also confronted by a rebellion. This time a different president had to send U.S. forces to Nicaragua. These troops remained in Nicaragua for more than a decade.

Another trouble spot was the Caribbean state of Haiti, where the State Department had encouraged U.S. investment. Several financial crises and revolts led to U.S. intervention to prevent European intervention; the U.S. government was concerned about its strategic interests in protecting the ongoing construction of the Panama Canal. Throughout the Taft years, the Caribbean and Central America remained a hot spot that required U.S. commitment of its military resources. Apparently, neither Knox nor Taft realized that along with financial investments came the need to protect them from anti-U.S. agents in Latin America and Europe.

Latin America was not the only region affected by dollar diplomacy. East Asia, specifically a weakened and splintered China, was also in theory a fertile ground for dollar diplomacy. In China, Knox secured the entry of a U.S. financial syndicate, headed by J. P. Morgan, into a European consortium paying for the construction of a railway from Beijing to Guangzhou. In the case of Asia, Knox once again misunderstood the value of dollar diplomacy. He saw four hundred million customers. In fact, almost none of these millions had the money or the desire to purchase U.S. products. As a result, the seeming success of dollar diplomacy failed to counter economic instability or the tide of revolution in places like Mexico, the Dominican Republic, Nicaragua, and China. Instead it dragged U.S. military forces into one quagmire after another.

Even though the basic Taft-Knox approach to foreign policy was formally ended by President Woodrow Wilson, the pattern of intervention continued throughout the century and became the excuse for numerous U.S. interventions in places like Cuba, Nicaragua, Haiti, and the Dominican Republic between 1909 and 1934, when the Good Neighbor policy of Franklin D. Roosevelt began to end the U.S.'s heavy-handed policies in Latin America. Some would argue, however, that the pattern did not truly end until free elections were held in Nicaragua on February 25, 1990.

See also *Good Neighbor Policy; Knox, Philander; Roosevelt Corollary to the Monroe Doctrine; Roosevelt, Theodore; Taft, William H.; United States, circum-Caribbean Interventions, 1900–1934: Nicaragua; Wilson, Woodrow*

. . . . WILLIAM HEAD

REFERENCES AND FURTHER READING

Mulhollan, Page Elliott. *Philander C. Knox and Dollar Diplomacy, 1909–1913.* Austin: University of Texas Press, 1966.

Munro, Dana Gardner. *Intervention and Dollar Diplomacy in the Caribbean, 1900–1921.* Princeton, NJ: Princeton University Press, 1964.

Rosenberg, Emily S. "Revisiting Dollar Diplomacy: Narratives of Money and Manliness." *Diplomatic History* 22, no. 2 (Spring 1998): 155–176.

Scholes, Walter V., and Marie V. Scholes. *The Foreign Policies of the Taft Administration.* Columbia: University of Missouri Press, 1970.

Dominican Republic, Conflicts with Haiti

Relations between the Dominican Republic and Haiti have been plagued with conflict for almost two centuries. The generally tense relations between the two nations have frequently erupted into violence since 1821, when the

Dominican Republic first declared its independence. At the root of Dominican-Haitian conflict is the vast cultural divide between people who share a small Caribbean island. These cultural differences stem from the colonial period, when France established a colony on the western third of the island of Hispaniola and Spain established a colony on the eastern two-thirds of the island. The French established a lucrative sugar-producing colony based on slavery whereas the Spanish, who found virtually no gold on the island, allowed their colony to languish as a peripheral component of the Spanish empire in the New World. By the end of the eighteenth century, the French colony was populated primarily by black African slaves who spoke Kreyòl, a language derived from West African languages, and practiced voodoo, a religion influenced by West African spirituality. The people living in the Spanish colony, however, who represented less than one-fifth of the French colony's population, were primarily white and mulatto Spanish-speaking Roman Catholics who emphasized their European cultural traditions.

In 1795, following the Treaty of Basle, Spain surrendered the most westerly third of the island to France. Toussaint Louverture, a black leader of the Haitian Revolution, was convinced that the island should be united under one government and therefore invaded the eastern portion of the island in 1801. The invasion force withdrew in 1802 to return to Haiti to fight troops sent by Napoleon Bonaparte to subdue the uprising. Following Haiti's declaration of independence in 1804, Haitian leaders contended that the continued French presence in the eastern part of the island was a threat to Haitian independence and unsuccessfully invaded the eastern part of the island in 1805.

Spanish settlers were able to expel the French in 1808 and restore Spanish colonial rule, only to declare independence on November 30, 1821. Within weeks, Haitian troops invaded, and the militarily occupied the Dominican Republic from 1822 to 1844. To change the racial composition in the Dominican Republic, the Haitians encouraged the emigration of thousands of freed blacks from the United States to the eastern section of the island. Much Dominican hostility toward Haitians stems from this period. Following the second Dominican declaration of independence in 1844, Haiti made frequent attempts to reconquer the Dominican Republic under its leader Faustin Soulouque (1847–1859). Fear of Haitian military power convinced many political leaders in the Dominican Republic that the solution to the Haitian threat was annexation to a more powerful power, such as France, Great Britain, Spain, or the United States. This fear led to re-annexation to Spain (1861–1865). President Ulysses S. Grant submitted a draft treaty that would have annexed the Dominican Republic to the United States, but it did not get the required two-thirds approval by the U.S. Senate in 1870.

During the 1870s, the Dominicans began to develop a liberal export-led economy based on sugar production. Haitians were recruited to work on the Dominican sugar plantations, many of which became U.S.-owned during the U.S. military occupation of the Dominican Republic (1916–1924). The presence of large numbers of Haitians in the Dominican Republic was viewed as a necessary evil economically since Dominicans refused to cut sugar cane. During the Great Depression, however, the need for Haitian cane cutters diminished, and the Dominican government, led by Rafael Trujillo y Molina (1930–1961), unleashed a wave of terror against Haitians in the western sector of the Dominican Republic. Fearful of the Haitianization of the Dominican Republic, Trujillo, using the excuse that the Haitians were engaging in illicit activities, orchestrated the death by machete of more than 15,000 Haitians. Eager to mollify international critics, at the 1938 Évian Conference in France, Trujillo agreed to accept Jewish refugees from Nazi Germany, which resulted in a permanent Jewish settlement at Sosúa.

Following Trujillo's assassination in 1961, relations with Haiti did not improve. Dominican President Juan Bosch Gaviño, who ruled for only seven months in 1963, threatened to invade Haiti and overthrow brutal authoritarian Haitian dictator Francois Duvalier. Haitian cane cutters, however, continued to play an important role in the Dominican economy. Nevertheless, during the 1970s, Dominican President Joaquín Balaguer repeatedly warned that the Haitian presence in the Dominican Republic threatened Dominican national identity. Notwithstanding the decline of the Dominican sugar industry during the 1980s, Haitians continued to seek employment in the Dominican Republic. Following the overthrow of the Duvalier dictatorship in 1986, frequent political and economic chaos in Haiti convinced the Dominican government to close the border between the two nations. During the first decade of the twenty-first century, massive Haitian immigration to the Dominican Republic has resulted in the presence of more than 500,000 Haitians in the Dominican Republic. Accusations by human rights agencies that Haitians in the Dominican Republic are mistreated have increased tension between the two nations.

See also *Balaguer, Joaquín; Bosch Gaviño, Juan; Dominican Republic, U.S. Relations with; Haiti, U.S. Relations with; Trujillo y Molina, Rafael; United States, circum-Caribbean Interventions, 1900–1934: Haiti*

. . . . MICHAEL R. HALL

REFERENCES AND FURTHER READING

Danticat, Edwidge. *The Farming of Bones*. New York: Penguin, 1999.

Roorda, Eric Paul. *The Dictator Next Door: The Good Neighbor Policy and the Trujillo Regime in the Dominican Republic, 1930–1945*. Durham, NC: Duke University Press, 1998.

Vega, Bernardo. *Trujillo y Haiti: Volumen I (1930–1937)*. Santo Domingo: Fundacion Cultural Dominicana, 1985.

Dominican Republic, U.S. Intervention, 1965–1966

In April 1965, the U.S. government sent the first of more than 42,000 troops to prevent what it considered to be an imminent communist takeover in the Dominican Republic.

The intervention was successful in that the U.S. forces, soon backed by an Inter-American force, forced a peaceful settlement. Most historians judge that the fear of "another Cuba" in the hemisphere was exaggerated. The troops stayed until the summer of 1966.

FRAGMENTATION AND REVOLT

U.S. policies toward the Dominican Republic in early 1965 reflected the rapidly shifting priorities of John F. Kennedy, Lyndon B. Johnson, and their administrations toward dictatorship and democracy. After Dominicans assassinated dictator Rafael Trujillo y Molina in May 1961, Kennedy expressed a preference for democracy in the country but would settle for more dictatorship in order to avoid another Castro regime. Until 1963, Kennedy intimidated the Trujillo family away from power and showered the presidency of Juan Bosch Gaviño with Alliance for Progress funding. Soon, however, Washington viewed Bosch as an incompetent at best and an agent of communist infiltration at worst. Kennedy publicly lambasted the military coup against Bosch on September 25, 1963, but Johnson's administration soon embraced the military against what it considered encroaching Castroism. Donald Reid Cabral rose to the top of a junta that ruled a deeply fragmented Dominican society.

That fragmentation caused the revolt of April 24, 1965. Calling themselves Constitutionalists and soon led by Colonel Francisco Caamaño Deñó, junior officers rose up to force Reid's resignation and the flight of hundreds of police in the Colonial Zone—downtown Santo Domingo. Yet within days the semi-independent right-wing forces of General Elías Wessin y Wessin, encamped at San Isidro air base outside the city and calling themselves Loyalists, fought the rebels to a draw at the outskirts of the city. The Dominican air force and navy bombarded the capital, and as many as three thousand civilians died in the first few days. The Constitutionalists held their positions, and the Loyalists cabled Washington for help.

Officially, the initial landing of four hundred U.S. Marines on April 27 was only to protect U.S. citizens and other foreigners by evacuating them out of the Hotel Embajador. Within days, however, thousands more troops followed, this time placing themselves between the forces of Wessin and Caamaño. By early May, Operation Power Pack under General Bruce Palmer's command had deployed more than 42,000 U.S. troops, including more than 13,000 offshore.

FORESTALLING "ANOTHER CUBA"

President Johnson ordered the additional force to forestall what he saw as an international communist takeover of the Dominican Republic. He feared "another Cuba," in which a few guerrillas had taken over an antidictatorial struggle. The Central Intelligence Agency pointed to eight, then about fifty "Castro-trained, Castro-operated" rebels assuming command in the Colonial Zone, while the U.S. embassy fed Washington rumors about savagery in the streets. On April 30, after being warned by advisers—including his secretaries of state and defense—that there was no hard evidence of an external conspiracy, Johnson publicly declared that he saw "signs that people trained outside the Dominican Republic are seeking to gain control." On May 2, he openly accused international communists of having "seized" the revolt. Johnson also expressed the importance of securing his own political survival. "The worst domestic political disaster we could suffer would be for Castro to take over," he said. The president also later said he was "misled" while also taking the blame for his misjudgment (McPherson, 142, 137, 127).

On May 6 the Organization of American States created its first-ever multinational force, eventually called the Inter-American Peace Force, to legitimate the U.S. action. Fifteen member countries, a bare two-thirds majority approved it, largely with dictatorships in favor and democracies opposed. Only six nations contributed troops, however, Brazil leading with over 1,130 troops led by General Hugo Penasco Alvim. By mid-May, the foreign forces established the International Security Zone, a corridor of checkpoints separating the Loyalists from the Constitutionalists. To be sure, the cordon stopped the bloodshed. Yet its true purpose was to surround the Constitutionalists in the Colonial Zone and slowly press them to surrender.

Johnson first tried a political solution through backchannel diplomacy by sending his friend Abe Fortas to meet with the exiled Bosch in Puerto Rico. The various compromises reached, however, never earned the support of both Caamaño and Antonio Imbert, who now led the Loyalists. By late May, the White House handed over negotiations to U.S. Ambassador to the Organization of American States Ellsworth Bunker. While U.S. agencies bombarded Dominicans with three million pieces of propaganda and almost two hundred flights equipped with loudspeakers, Bunker pursued "a Latin approach to a Latin problem." On August 30, 1965, the signing of the Institutional Act and the Act of Reconciliation ended the showdown and handed interim power to Hector García-Godoy.

The intervention generated massive opposition. Almost every embassy in Latin America witnessed demonstrations, as did many others around the world. Latin Americans feared the return of gunboat diplomacy and decried the subservient role of the Organization of American States. In the United States, the press exposed many White House schemes, and the most potent criticism came from Senator William Fulbright, chair of the Senate Foreign Relations Committee, in a September 15, 1965, speech on the floor of the Senate. Polls, however, showed that U.S. citizens supported the intervention 3 to 1 and that Dominicans also did, 6 to 1.

Washington moved ahead with the presidential election scheduled for June 1, 1966. The CIA had secret polls showing former *trujillista* Joaquín Balaguer handily defeating Juan Bosch Gaviño. Still, the administration secretly created the 303 Committee to coordinate U.S. support for Balaguer. The exact amount of that support is still obscure, but it consisted of advice, men, and money. CIA assistant director Richard Helms confirmed that Johnson ordered his agency to win the election for Balaguer. Balaguer won with 57 percent of the vote, U.S. troops left soon thereafter, and U.S. officials regarded the episode as a victory over an attempted communist takeover.

See also *Balaguer, Joaquín; Bosch Gaviño, Juan; Bunker, Ellsworth; Fulbright, J. William; Inter-American Peace Force; Johnson Doctrine; Johnson, Lyndon B.; Trujillo y Molina, Rafael; Wessin y Wessin, Elías*

ALAN MCPHERSON

REFERENCES AND FURTHER READING

Gleijeses, Piero. *The Dominican Crisis: The 1965 Constitutionalist Revolt and American Intervention*. Translated by Lawrence Lipson. Baltimore, MD: The Johns Hopkins University Press, 1978.

Lowenthal, Abraham F. *The Dominican Intervention*. Baltimore, MD: The Johns Hopkins University Press, 1972.

McPherson, Alan. "Misled by Himself: What the Johnson Tapes Reveal about the Dominican Intervention of 1965." *Latin American Research Review* 38, no. 2 (June 2003): 127–146.

Palmer, Bruce, Jr. *Intervention in the Caribbean: The Dominican Crisis of 1965*. Lexington: The University Press of Kentucky, 1989.

Slater, Jerome. *Intervention and Negotiation: The United States and the Dominican Revolution*. New York: Harper & Row, 1970.

Dominican Republic, U.S. Relations with

The Dominican Republic is dependent on the United States in many ways, a fact symbolized by the fact that the most important Dominican diplomatic post is Washington, D.C., and the largest embassy in Santo Domingo is that of the United States. Although Dominicans sometimes resent the powerful U.S. presence in their country—especially the 1965 U.S.-led military intervention—and the patronizing attitudes of some Americans, most Dominicans have reconciled themselves to the influence of the United States in their country. At times, however, Dominican elites have skillfully engaged in reciprocal manipulation with U.S. policymakers and businessmen to their advantage.

For the United States, the Dominican Republic is an important partner in hemispheric affairs. The Dominican Republic, the second-largest Caribbean nation in terms of population and size, is the largest economy in the Caribbean. To counterbalance the influence of Fidel Castro's Cuba, since 1959 the U.S. government has sought to foster a stable, democratic, economically sound government in the Dominican Republic. The Dominican government has supported many U.S. initiatives in the United Nations and the Organization of American States. The Dominican government has facilitated U.S. efforts to curb illegal migration and curtail drug trafficking. The United States, in turn, supports Dominican efforts at economic diversification and encourages U.S. private investment in the Dominican Republic.

In recent years, the relationship of dependence has transformed into one of bilateral interdependence. An important component of this relationship is the presence of more than one million Dominicans in the United States. Culture has significantly affected the political and economic relations between the United States and the Dominican Republic. Although formal intergovernmental cultural exchanges and programs are important, the rapidly increasing transnational relations between the two nations, especially nongovernmental transactions, are significantly more important. The result is a North Americanization of the Dominican Republic and a countervailing Dominicanization of the United States. To counteract U.S. cultural penetration in Dominican society, President Joaquín Balaguer (1966–1978, 1986–1996) actively pursued a policy of Dominicanization of Dominican society, which stressed *hispanidad* (the Spanish cultural legacy). Balaguer's policy replicated that of General Rafael Trujillo (1930–1961), which sought to curtail Haitian cultural influences.

EARLY U.S.–DOMINICAN REPUBLIC FOREIGN RELATIONS

U.S. commercial interest in the Dominican Republic began during the eighteenth century when the Dominican Republic, which occupies the eastern two-thirds of the island of Hispaniola, was still a Spanish colony. U.S. trading vessels periodically called at Dominican ports. Although the entire island of Hispaniola was initially a Spanish colony, in 1697 the Spanish signed the Treaty of Ryswick, which ceded the western third of the island to France. The French colony, Saint Domingue (Haiti), became a lucrative sugar-producing colony, while the Spanish colony languished as an ignored colonial outpost. Following thirteen years of violent insurrection, Haitian slaves declared their independence in 1804. Because of the slavery question at home, the United States refused to grant Haiti diplomatic recognition. Although Dominican elites declared their independence in late 1821, the Haitians took control of the Dominican Republic in early 1822. While the United States was establishing diplomatic relations with other Spanish-speaking nations in Latin America during the 1820s and 1830s, the Dominican Republic was under Haitian occupation, which lasted until 1844.

In 1844, white elites orchestrated Dominican independence for the second time in the nineteenth century. Although the United States initially supported Latin American independence struggles during the 1820s, by the 1840s, U.S. policymakers, pointing out the religious, cultural, and racial differences between Latin Americans and North Americans, adopted an attitude of cultural superiority toward Latin America. Since the majority of Dominicans were black and mulatto, Hispanic, and Roman Catholic, the United States, plagued by the divisive institution of slavery at home, refused to grant diplomatic recognition to the Dominican Republic. Ironically, white elites in the Dominican Republic were just as dismissive and critical of the Dominican Republic's blacks and mulattos. In 1844, upon his arrival in Washington, D.C., to petition for diplomatic recognition, Dominican special envoy José M. Caminero told U.S. Secretary of State John C. Calhoun that half of the nation's 200,000 people were white, a gross exaggeration. Responding to the Dominican initiative, in 1846 President James K. Polk sent special agent Lieutenant David O. Porter to the Dominican Republic to investigate the situation.

Although Porter presented a favorable report that emphasized the potential of a U.S. naval base at Samaná Bay, Polk, preoccupied with the Mexican War, merely appointed a commercial agent to the Dominican Republic.

Between 1844 and 1860, Dominican leaders, fearful of Haitian military aggression, repeatedly sought annexation to the United States, Great Britain, France, or Spain. Imbued with the ideals of manifest destiny, in 1853, U.S. Secretary of State William L. Marcy sent special agent General William A. Cazneau to investigate the situation in the Dominican Republic. Cazneau was accompanied by his wife, Jane McManus Storm Cazneau, and cohort Colonel Joseph W. Fabens. Marcy instructed his agents to offer the Dominicans diplomatic recognition in return for a naval base at Samaná Bay. Opposed to the acquisition, Charles Sumner led the resistance in the U.S. Senate that stymied Marcy's initiative. In 1861, frustrated by their negotiations with the United States, which was preoccupied with the Civil War, the Dominican elites arranged the republic's re-annexation to Spain. This arrangement, however, proved to be mutually unrewarding and ended in 1865.

In the aftermath of the Dominican Republic's third declaration of independence, Dominican politicians, still fearful of Haitian military aggression, sought to annex their nation to the United States. By then, the U.S. Civil War had settled the issue of slavery at home. On September 17, 1866, guided by Secretary of State William H. Seward, the United States granted the Dominican Republic diplomatic recognition. President Andrew Johnson nominated General Cazneau as the first minister in the Dominican Republic. Sumner, the chair of the Senate Foreign Relations Committee, opposed Cazneau's nomination, and Johnson withdrew it. The United States sent a commercial agent to Santo Domingo, but diplomatic affairs were conducted through the U.S. mission in Port-au-Prince, Haiti. In 1867 Seward sent Assistant Secretary of State Frederick W. Seward (his son) and Porter to the Dominican Republic to investigate the possibility of purchasing or leasing land for a naval base at Samaná Bay. The government in power, led by General José María Cabral, however, was unwilling to engage in negotiations concerning land concessions. In 1868, after Buenaventura Báez, a confidant of Cazneau and Fabens, took power, a deal was developed for the annexation of the Dominican Republic to the United States, but the U.S. House of Representatives overwhelmingly rejected the embattled Johnson administration's proposal. The House action did not deter President Ulysses S. Grant, who actively sought to annex the Dominican Republic. In 1869 Grant sent his private secretary, Orville Babcock, as U.S. commissioner to the Dominican Republic. Assisted by Cazneau and Fabens, Babcock concluded an annexation treaty with Báez. On June 30, 1870, opposition in the U.S. Senate, once again led by Sumner, defeated the annexation treaty.

During the last quarter of the nineteenth century, the Dominican Republic pursued a liberal export-led economy based on sugar cultivation. Initiated by Cubans fleeing the Ten Years' War (1868–1878) at home, the sugar industry became the major industry of the Dominican Republic. U.S., Italian, Canadian, and Spanish investors quickly joined in the development of the nascent sugar industry. Generous concessions were awarded to foreign investors. In his search for foreign loans to develop the Dominican Republic's infrastructure, President Ulises Heureaux skillfully played the United States and European nations against each other. In 1889 the United States, which had maintained dual Dominican-Haitian diplomatic representation since 1866 from its mission in Port-au-Prince, agreed to the Dominican demand for separate representation. In 1891, the United States and the Dominican Republic signed a reciprocity treaty that removed tariffs from goods traded between the two nations. Angry European nations, which threatened to impose restrictive tariffs on Dominican exports, convinced Heureaux to abrogate the treaty in 1892. Between 1892 and 1912, Cuban and Spanish interests in sugar mills were purchased by U.S. and Canadian investors. Political and economic chaos returned to the Dominican Republic following Heureaux's assassination in 1899.

THE U.S. MILITARY OCCUPATION

The financial chaos and political turmoil following Heureaux's assassination coincided with a period in which the United States began to exert greater influence over the Caribbean region. In 1905, as the Dominican Republic plunged into deeper financial and political chaos, U.S. Secretary of State John Hay announced that the newly unveiled Roosevelt Corollary to the Monroe Doctrine would be applied to the Dominican Republic. In 1905 the Dominican government accepted a U.S.-implemented customs receivership, which collected Dominican export and import taxes. The United States allocated 55 percent of the revenue to pay the Dominican foreign debt and 45 percent to the Dominican government. At the same time, the United States attempted to persuade the Dominican government to carry out various fiscal and political reforms. Many Dominican elites wantonly facilitated the extension of U.S. hegemony for their own self-interest.

The groundwork for U.S. military intervention in the Dominican Republic was laid on May 13, 1916, when the United States sent 700 U.S. Marines to the Dominican Republic to restore order and stability. Political and economic chaos, which directly threatened U.S. investment in the sugar industry, in conjunction with the threat of European intervention and the desire to protect access to the Panama Canal, convinced the United States to intervene militarily in the Dominican Republic. On August 16, 1916, the U.S. government suspended payments to the Dominican government after President Francisco Henríquez y Carvajal refused to accept a U.S. government official as his financial adviser. The cessation of funds caused further economic chaos and resulted in President Woodrow Wilson sending more Marines to the Dominican Republic in November. The U.S. military government attempted to implement fundamental changes in the nation's political, economic, and social life in the hope of creating a stable neighbor that would safeguard U.S. strategic and economic interests. The Marines disarmed the Dominican population and created a theoretically apolitical national guard. The U.S. military government also facilitated the expansion of U.S. investment in the sugar industry.

In 1922 U.S. Secretary of State Charles Evans Hughes and former Dominican Minister of Finance Francisco J. Peynado announced the Hughes-Peynado Plan, which paved the way for presidential elections in the Dominican Republic and the withdrawal of U.S. Marines. In 1924, after the Dominicans ratified the Dominican-American agreement, which guaranteed the customs receivership until the foreign debt was paid to U.S. banks, the U.S. Marines left the Dominican Republic.

THE TRUJILLO DICTATORSHIP

During the dictatorship of Rafael Trujillo y Molina (1930–1961), successive U.S. presidential administrations overlooked the authoritarian nature of the Dominican government. Trujillo exploited U.S. fears of Nazism during the 1930s and communism during the Cold War to garner U.S. economic and military aid. Trujillo proclaimed himself the most ardent anticommunist in the western hemisphere and closely aligned his foreign policy with that of the United States. His voting record in the United Nations was parallel to that of the United States.

In 1930 Trujillo, the leader of the U.S.-created national guard, overthrew the government and established an authoritarian dictatorship. During the Great Depression, Trujillo was faced with governing a poverty-stricken nation with an empty treasury, a huge foreign debt, and a capital city destroyed by a hurricane. Within two decades, Trujillo had paid off the nation's foreign debts, developed a national infrastructure, and laid the groundwork for economic development by promoting industrialization. The tax on sugar exports accounted for most government revenue. In the process, Trujillo accumulated a personal fortune worth almost $1 billion. The cost of fiscal solvency was the complete loss of personal freedom of the Dominican people. Trujillo's seven intelligence agencies enabled the dictator to establish one of Latin America's most brutal authoritarian dictatorships.

One of Trujillo's most notorious acts was the massacre of 12,000 Haitians in the northern border region in 1937. To deflect criticism of his regime, Trujillo offered sanctuary to 100,000 Jewish refugees from Europe. By the end of the 1950s, Trujillo had managed to lose the support of the nation's elites, the Roman Catholic Church, and the U.S. government. In 1956 Trujillo's henchmen kidnapped dissident writer Jesús Galíndez from New York City. Following Castro's 1959 revolution in Cuba, U.S. policymakers were concerned that Trujillo's authoritarian excesses might lead to the establishment of a second communist regime in the Caribbean. Trujillo's failed attempt to assassinate Venezuelan President Rómulo Betancourt in 1960 convinced the United States that continued support of the Trujillo dictatorship could damage U.S. hegemony in the Caribbean region. The murder of three elite sisters—Minerva, Patria, and María Teresa Mirabal—on November 25, 1960, motivated the Dominican population to increase anti-Trujillo activities. On the evening of May 30, 1961, Trujillo was assassinated by a group of conspirators who had been both accomplices and victims of the dictatorship. The conspirators, armed with weapons provided by the United States, assassinated Trujillo as he was returning from a visit to one of his numerous mistresses. Attempts by Trujillo's son Ramfis to continue the dictatorship were futile, and the entire Trujillo family fled the island by the end of 1961.

Rafael Trujillo in 1930 as the general commandant of the Dominican Republic's national police force. His thirty-one year dictatorship was one of the most repressive in the Caribbean, but his anti-Nazi and later anticommunist policies garnered U.S. support.

SOURCE: National Archives

CONTEMPORARY U.S.-DOMINICAN FOREIGN RELATIONS

In December 1962, the Dominican people began their first experiment with democratic government. In U.S.-supervised elections, Juan Bosch Gaviño, who had lived in exile for most of the Trujillo dictatorship, was elected president with 60 percent of the vote. Initially hailed by the Kennedy administration as a potential showcase for democracy, the Bosch administration soon lost the support of the Dominican military and the United States. Even U.S. Ambassador John Bartlow Martin, who initially believed that the democratic experiment could work, became disillusioned with Bosch. U.S. officials were disturbed by Bosch's rhetoric, which was interpreted as being soft on communism. When Bosch attempted to limit the power of the Dominican military, General Elías Wessin y

Wessin orchestrated a military coup that removed Bosch from office on September 25, 1963. Bosch left the country, and the United States severed diplomatic relations and suspended all economic and military assistance.

In December 1963, President Lyndon B. Johnson recognized the governing junta led by Donald Reid Cabral and appointed W. Tapley Bennett Jr. to serve as U.S. ambassador. Reid Cabral's government, which implemented austerity measures, received extensive support from the U.S. government. In April 1965, a group of pro-Bosch military officers, known as Constitutionalists, led by Francisco Caamaño Deñó, staged a revolt to return the exiled Bosch to power. Loyalists within the army, who were supported by the nation's elites, rallied around General Antonio Imbert, one of Trujillo's assassins. Civilians stole weapons from the national police and began to kill police officers. The counterrevolution, launched on April 24, 1965, which took Ambassador Bennett by surprise, resulted in a civil war.

On April 28, the United States sent 400 Marines to restore order. Johnson, under the initial pretense of humanitarian concerns (the protection of U.S. citizens), eventually sent 23,000 U.S. troops, led by General Bruce Palmer, to restore order and stability. Although the Organization of American States quickly sanctioned the intervention, this was the first overt use of U.S. military forces in Latin America since the Marines were withdrawn from Haiti in 1934. Johnson, however, rationalized his decision to intervene as an attempt to prevent the spread of communism in the western hemisphere. His decision to intervene, however, was also based on domestic political concerns as well as Dominican elite manipulation of U.S. government officials. On August 31, 1966, the United States implemented the Act of Dominican Reconciliation with prominent Constitutionalists and Loyalists. Héctor García Godoy, who had been Bosch's foreign minister and was acceptable to both sides in the conflict, was chosen as president of a provisional government until elections could be held. To restore order and stability, both Wessin y Wessin and Caamaño Deñó were sent into exile.

In U.S.-supervised elections in 1966, Balaguer won, and he closely aligned the Dominican Republic politically and economically with the United States. All subsequent Dominican governments have pursued a foreign policy closely tied to that of the United States. In return for his pro-U.S. foreign policy, Balaguer was rewarded with generous sugar quotas and increased economic aid. To alleviate economic and social pressures on Balaguer's government, the United States relaxed its immigration policy. The result was a massive influx of Dominicans to the United States. Remittances from the more than one million Dominicans living in the United States contributed substantially to the Dominican economy. During Balaguer's administration, the Dominican Republic experienced the most spectacular growth of any Latin American nation during the 1970s. The nation's economic boom was made possible by political stability and a revitalized sugar industry.

High inflation and unemployment, along with a decrease in sugar consumption in the United States during the 1970s, however, undermined Balaguer's hold on power during his third term. In 1978 Balaguer lost the presidential election to Antonio Guzmán. Although Guzmán's administration implemented numerous health and education projects, by 1980 the Dominican economy had fallen into a recession. Plagued by the rising cost of oil imports, a sharp decline in the profits from sugar exports, and accusations that his daughter Sonia was involved in corrupt activities, Guzmán decided not to run for re-election in 1982. The 1982 elections were won by Salvador Jorge Blanco. Jorge Blanco's administration experienced a tremendous loss of popularity and legitimacy when it implemented U.S.-supported International Monetary Fund (IMF) austerity measures in May 1984. A series of violent riots broke out, which led to the death of dozens of Dominican citizens. Balaguer returned to office in 1986 and began economic diversification programs.

President Leonel Fernández (1996–2000, 2004–), who grew up in New York City, initiated a series of reforms designed to modernize the political economy and infrastructure. Sugar exports no longer represented a substantial component of Dominican revenue. Instead, tourism, mining (especially nickel), and remittances from Dominicans living abroad, primarily in the United States, accounted for most Dominican revenue. Fernández's government has been supportive of most U.S. government initiatives, including the war on terrorism.

See also *Balaguer, Joaquín; Betancourt Bello, Rómulo; Bosch Gaviño, Juan; Dependency Theory and Latin America; Dictators, U.S. Policy toward; Dollar Diplomacy; Dominican Republic, Conflicts with Haiti; Haiti, U.S. Relations with; Hispanidad; Samaná Bay, U.S. Interest in; Sugar, U.S. Policy; Trujillo y Molina, Rafael; United States, circum-Caribbean Interventions, 1900–1934, Dominican Republic*

. . . . MICHAEL R. HALL

REFERENCES AND FURTHER READING

Atkins, G. Pope, and Larman C. Wilson. *The Dominican Republic and the United States: From Imperialism to Transnationalism.* Athens: The University of Georgia Press, 1998.

Hall, Michael R. *Sugar and Power in the Dominican Republic: Eisenhower, Kennedy, and the Trujillos.* Santa Barbara, CA: Greenwood, 2000.

Roorda, Eric Paul. *The Dictator Next Door: The Good Neighbor Policy and The Trujillo Regime in the Dominican Republic, 1930–1945.* Durham, NC: Duke University Press, 1998.

Turits, Richard Lee. *Foundations of Despotism: Peasants, the Trujillo Regime, and Modernity in Dominican History.* Stanford, CA: Stanford University Press, 2003.

Vesser, Cyrus. *A World Safe for Capitalism: Dollar Diplomacy and America's Rise to Global Power.* New York: Columbia University Press, 2002.

Drago, Luis M.

Luis M. Drago (1859–1921) trained as a journalist and an expert in finance and law in his early years and gained recognition as a statesman and an innovative commentator on international affairs in the last two decades of his life. He was from a Buenos Aires family that was prominent in both politics and journalism. The high point of his career came when he served as foreign minister in the second presidency of Julio Roca (1898–1904). Argentina had emerged as one of the world's leading exporters of wheat and meat with close commercial ties to the United Kingdom and other European nations. Drago contributed some exceptional insights to the discussion of the often troubled financial and diplomatic relations between the European powers such as the United Kingdom, on one hand, and developing nations such as Argentina, on the other. In formulating his position in defense of the interests of Argentina, Drago turned to the United States and its Monroe Doctrine for support.

RESPONSE TO EUROPEAN INTERVENTION IN VENEZUELA

Foreign Minister Drago followed events in Venezuela very closely in the last months of 1902. The government of that country was deeply in debt to bankers and other creditors in Europe. When it appeared that Venezuela would not make its debt payments on time, Great Britain and Germany sent warships to force payment. The use of force to collect foreign debts was of great concern in Argentina. The government had borrowed heavily from European bankers to finance railroad construction, port improvements, and other types of economic development. These debts reminded Drago of the financial crisis of the early 1890s, when Argentina had to deal with a large debt owed mainly to British banks. This crisis was resolved without British naval or military intervention, but there was considerable discussion of such action in both London and Buenos Aires at that time.

In response to the intervention in Venezuela, the Argentine foreign minister composed a diplomatic memorandum that Argentina's representative, Martín García Merou, delivered to the U.S. State Department. In this document, Drago explained his objections to the use of force to collect debts. He argued that the use of force was, in effect, an invasion that violated a nation's sovereignty, and sovereignty was a fundamental concept that underlay international law. Such a use of force placed the rights of private corporations (banks and other businesses) over the rights of nations such as Venezuela and, by implication, Argentina. Also, the lenders understood that risks were involved in such loans before the loans were made. Furthermore, the Monroe Doctrine asserted that the United States was opposed to the occupation of the territory of a western hemisphere nation by a European power. The British-German naval intervention in Venezuela was, according to Drago, a violation of the Monroe Doctrine. Drago then urged that the United States support the views expressed in his memorandum.

Drago's statement of principles had a significant impact in the United States, Latin America, and Europe, but it did not contribute directly to the settlement of the Venezuela intervention controversy. Instead, U.S. President Theodore Roosevelt arranged for international arbitration of the debt crisis. Nevertheless, the Drago Doctrine was of major importance because it constituted the first widely recognized protest of a debtor nation against the use of force by industrialized nations to collect international debts. Prior to Drago's statement, the European powers had routinely intervened in Latin America, Africa, and Asia to collect debts and to impose their version of political order. The Drago Doctrine served notice to the imperial nations that such interventions violated the widely held norms of international behavior regarding sovereignty.

LEGACY OF THE DRAGO DOCTRINE

Although written in the form of a memorandum addressed to the U.S. State Department, Drago's statement had extensive circulation among diplomats, the press, and business leaders. Newspapers in Argentina and elsewhere in Latin America applauded the Drago Doctrine and, in the United States, press editorials from New York to San Francisco praised the Argentine foreign minister for his staunch defense of his nation's sovereignty and for his respectful appeal to the Monroe Doctrine. Of equal importance was the interest in the Drago Doctrine within the growing corps of experts in international law. The convening of international peace conferences at The Hague in the Netherlands and the expansion of international commerce and banking drew attention to the role of international lawyers. Drago enunciated his doctrine at a time when this new group of legal professionals was beginning to play a larger role in international affairs.

In spite of President Roosevelt's initiative to settle the Venezuelan debt issue and his pronouncement of his corollary to the Monroe Doctrine in 1904 (which endorsed the use of force and compulsory arbitration in debt disputes and thereby contradicted of some of the main points in the Drago Doctrine), the president continued to speak respectfully of Drago's contributions to the international discussion of such disputes. Roosevelt quoted Drago's writings in his 1906 message to the U.S. Congress. In response, Drago sent a personal message of gratitude to the president. Drago had established the point that debtor nations should have a voice in the debates regarding international debts and that the sovereignty of less developed nations deserved respect in the world arena. He gained lasting recognition on these points, even though the United States and other world powers did not follow all of the principles spelled out in the Drago Doctrine.

Drago continued to participate in international conferences and to speak and to write about international issues in his later years. He attended the 1907 Hague Peace Conference, where a revised and weakened version of his doctrine was the subject of discussion. Drago was a consistent opponent of the use of armed intervention as a means of collecting debts and defended the original intent of his doctrine on this point. Although his defense was not entirely successful at The Hague meeting, the veteran Argentine diplomat faced a respectful audience, and his views carried considerable weight. Many of his essays were translated into English and French in professional publications dealing with foreign policy and international law.

See also *Argentina, U.S. Relations with; Calvo, Carlos; Debt Crisis, Latin America 1870s; 1930s; 1980s; Monroe Doctrine;*

Roosevelt Corollary to the Monroe Doctrine; Roosevelt, Theodore; United States, circum-Caribbean Interventions, 1900–1934: Dominican Republic; Venezuelan Crisis, 1902

. . . . JOHN A. BRITTON

REFERENCES AND FURTHER READING

Drago, Luis M. "'Monroe Doctrine' and Diplomatic Claims of European Powers." *Papers Relating to the Foreign Relations of the United States.* Washington, DC: Government Printing Office, 1904, pp. 1–5.

———. "State Loans and Their Relation to International Policy." *American Journal of International Law* 1 (July and October, 1907): 692–726.

Finnemore, Martha. *The Purpose of Intervention: Changing Beliefs about the Use of Force.* Ithaca, NY: Cornell University Press, 2003.

Nettles, H. Edward. "The Drago Doctrine and International Law and Politics." *Hispanic American Historical Review* 8 (May 1928): 204–223.

Drago Doctrine

(**See** *Drago, Luis M.*)

Dreier, John C.

John Caspar Dreier (December 27, 1906–March 10, 1994) was a Cold War–era diplomat for the United States.

EARLY LIFE AND EDUCATION

Dreier was born in Brooklyn, New York, and educated at Harvard College, from which he graduated in 1928. He joined the State Department's Latin American Division in 1941 and later became the director of the Office of Regional American Affairs. In 1950 President Harry S. Truman appointed him U.S. representative to the Organization of American States (OAS). He was the chairman of the Council of the Organization of American States from 1952 to 1953. In his time at the OAS, he was also a member of the Inter-American Peace Committee and took part in numerous conferences. In 1961 he was appointed visiting professor of Latin American Affairs and the director of the Inter-American Center at the School of Advanced International Studies at Johns Hopkins University, Baltimore, Maryland. After retiring from full-time teaching in 1972, he became a trustee and teacher at the College of the Atlantic in Bar Harbor, Maine. At the same time, he involved himself in a number of conservation projects.

Dreier is the author or editor of two books, both published in 1962. The first is a monograph entitled *The Organization of American States and the Hemispheric Crisis.* The second is an edited volume called *The Alliance for Progress: Problems and Perspectives.*

PROFESSIONAL LIFE

While he was at the OAS, Dreier was involved in formulating and executing U.S. policy toward Latin America. In his published works, he acknowledged some of the mistakes that were made while glossing over others. Dreier saw U.S. policy toward Latin America through the prism of communism. For Dreier, international communism, represented outside the Americas by the Soviet Union and inside the Americas by Castro's Cuba, presented the most important threat to the United States and, by extension, the OAS. In Dreier's analysis, both the United States and the OAS made a mistake in dealing with Latin America solely through money, rather than making an honest effort to understand the hearts and minds of Latin Americans.

Dreier simultaneously conceived of the OAS as an instrument to extend the official U.S. policy of anticommunism in the Americas. In *The Organization of American States and the Hemispheric Crisis*, Dreier described the OAS as a "stabilizing influence" within the region and in the larger international community. But he did not hesitate to use the organization to sow dissent, as when he condemned Mexico, Argentina, and Brazil for their opposition to a U.S.-sponsored resolution to expel Cuba from the OAS. For Dreier, anticommunism was the litmus test because it represented the great post–World War II ideological struggle. Anticommunism defined how Dreier saw, and related to, Latin America.

The two major events of Dreier's time at the OAS were the 1954 Guatemala invasion and the 1959 Cuban Revolution, both of which were justified by anticommunism. Dreier framed the U.S.-led intervention to remove Guatemalan President Jacobo Arbenz as a continent-wide defense against Soviet-led communism. In Dreier's view, enunciated in *The Organization of American States and the Hemispheric Crisis*, Colonel Carlos Castillo Armas was the leader of a successful counterrevolution in the name of republicanism. Dreier's role in the incident was framed by his involvement with the council of the OAS. In a speech to the council, reprinted in *Latin America and the United States: A Documentary History*, Dreier reaffirmed the U.S.'s anticommunist position and stressed the domino theory. If Guatemala fell to communism, surely other American states would follow, he thought.

In analyzing the Cuban Revolution, Dreier saw the OAS as a forum to air anticommunist grievances. In this vein, he saw the OAS as an extension of U.S. Cold War policy. He was at a loss to explain the Mexican, Brazilian, and Argentine abstentions in the vote to expel Cuba from the OAS precisely because he viewed communism as a menace to American republics. In his mind, the OAS was a vehicle for hemisphere-wide anticommunism, which relegated economic issues, social issues, and even other political issues to the backburner. Part of this went to his vision for the OAS, which was a forum for all American nations to cooperate regarding hemispheric policies. For Dreier, the OAS served a noble purpose that went far beyond its initial administrative limits. In the Cold War world, the OAS was to be the front line of hemispheric anticommunism.

The Alliance for Progress, President Kennedy's Latin American aid program launched in March 1961, was adopted as an Inter-American program by the OAS at its conference in Punta del Este, Uruguay, in August 1961. Dreier saw the Alliance for Progress as an extension of the OAS's role in hemispheric relations: that is, to share responsibility among the hemisphere's nations and to achieve peace, security, political liberty, and economic and social progress. It was, as he wrote in *The Alliance for Progress: Problems and Perspectives*, "a broadly-conceived set of objectives and methods." Dreier advocated patience and pointed out the long-term investments needed in terms of economic, social, and political improvements. Still, he viewed communism as a pervasive threat; thus the Alliance for Progress was not just a cooperative agreement in terms of material improvement, but also an implicit defensive agreement against the international communist menace, symbolized by Moscow and Havana.

Dreier was a Cold Warrior, and his ideas about Latin America reflected that stance. He primarily saw the OAS as a way to protect Latin America from communism. In that interpretation, the OAS was an extension of U.S. policies.

See also *Alliance for Progress; Communism in Latin America; Guatemala, U.S. Invasion of, 1954; Kennedy, John F.; Organization of American States (OAS); Second Meeting of American Presidents, Punta del Este, 1967*

. . . . WILLIAM C. KELLY

SELECTED WORKS

Dreier, John C., ed. *The Alliance for Progress: Problems and Perspectives.* Baltimore, MD: The Johns Hopkins University Press, 1962.

Dreier, John C. *The Organization of American States and the Hemispheric Crisis.* New York: Harper and Row/Council on Foreign Relations, 1962.

———. "The Council of the OAS: Performance and Potential." *Journal of Inter-American Studies* 5, no. 3 (July 1963): 297–312.

REFERENCES AND FURTHER READING

Holden, Robert H., and Eric Zolov, eds. *Latin America and the United States: A Documentary History.* 2nd ed. New York: Oxford University Press, 2011.

Drugs, U.S. War on

Despite a long history of struggle against drug trafficking and addiction in the western hemisphere, the War on Drugs officially began in the 1970s under President Richard M. Nixon. Currently, the cost of the war is widely believed to exceed $500 billion. The Nixon administration grew concerned about the potential return of addicts from Vietnam. While campaigning for the presidency, Nixon had pledged to the American people to deal with the problem. Although his fear of addicts returning from Vietnam never materialized, Nixon took the steps to control the potential drug problem with new initiatives and agencies. He organized the Special Task Force Relating to Narcotics, Marijuana, and Dangerous Drugs, and he formed the Drug Enforcement Agency (DEA) to address the growing issue of illegal narcotics and set aside federal funds for prosecutors and police to prosecute drug offenders.

TIGHTENING THE U.S.-MEXICAN BORDER

The task force highlighted that the U.S.-Mexico border demanded greater control to stem the flow of drugs. The task force recommended that Americans should be persuaded to walk across the border rather than use their cars and that the border cities should be off limits to military personnel. Moreover, the task force made a series of spending recommendations asking for more detection devices, such as dogs and sensors, and increased expenditures for items such as planes and personnel for customs, the Border Patrol, and the Bureau of Narcotics and Dangerous Drugs.

White House adviser John Ehrlichman encouraged Nixon to make the unilateral decision to force Mexico to defoliate fields and implement stricter enforcement on the Mexican side of the border (White House, memorandum, June 18, 1969, White House Central Files: Subject Files FG 221, Box 5, National Archives, see also National Security Archive). With Ehrlichman's encouragement, Nixon promised to do everything possible to prevent narcotics from crossing the Mexican border into the United States.

That frontal attack came in the form of Operation Intercept, which started on September 21, 1969. Two thousand customs agents working around the clock stopped cars and people for inspection at thirty-one border crossings. Motorists, pedestrians, business owners, and even customs agents vented their frustrations as businesses lost money, and people waited six to eight hours to cross the border. Mexican journalists argued that Operation Intercept would only contribute to further mistrust of the United States. The intense searches on the border caused havoc, and businessmen protested loudly to local politicians and their national representatives. Inspectors on both sides of the border grew frustrated with the clogged border crossings. Their inspections turned up very little dope, but resentment grew from commuters, customs officials, and government officials. Eventually, Nixon negotiated certain shifts with President Gustavo Díaz Ordaz, offering Mexico greater military aid in the form of helicopters for crop eradication.

Recognizing that Operation Intercept had been ineffective, the United States and Mexico negotiated a policy of joint coordination. In 1970 Mexican and U.S. agents worked together to arrest Roberto Hernandez; his wife, Helen; his brother, Juan; and Mercedes Coleman in a raid that took place in Tijuana. A spokesperson for the Bureau of Narcotics and Dangerous Drugs described the operation as the most sophisticated and efficient of all clandestine drug trafficking operations. The bureau went on to argue that the Hernandez group had supplied much of the illicit drugs to the United States, smuggling more than twenty kilograms of heroin per week through Tijuana into San Diego and beyond. The transnational cooperation and arrest made national news in the United States and Canada. Reports claimed that Hernandez resisted arrest and had to be pulled from the home. Four years later, the DEA and Mexican authorities reunited to break up the prison trafficking ring that the Mendozas ran from La Mesa Penitentiary in Tijuana.

THE COCAINE EPIDEMIC

During the 1970s, police and prosecutors focused on marijuana, LSD, and heroin while cocaine poured into south Florida and made its way into New York, Los Angeles, and other major cities. To combat the rise in drug abuse, New York Governor Nelson Rockefeller proposed and the state legislature adopted some of the strictest penalties to

Heavily armed Bolivian troops search for illegal coca plants outside the hamlet of Tamboral in the tropical Chapare region, February 3, 2004. The war on drugs is no metaphor in Latin America, where the U.S. allies employ military personnel to battle drug lords and anti-drug efforts have replaced anticommunism as a central focus of U.S.–Latin American relations. Some allies, including César Augusto Gaviria Trujillo, president of Colombia from 1990 to 1994, have tried to move anti-drug efforts away from a military endeavor, with varying success.

SOURCE: DIEGO GUIDICE/KRT/Newscom

deter people from selling drugs. The Rockefeller drug laws demanded judges impose a fifteen-year sentence for anyone caught in possession of four or more ounces or selling two or more ounces of a controlled substance. Rockefeller and his supporters argued that treatment and rehabilitation were inadequate measures to combat drug abuse, so stricter laws regarding the sale and usage of narcotics had to be passed.

The DEA and police agencies celebrated the arrests of Timothy Leary and other counterculture figures and conducted major busts in New York, while south Florida became the central port of entry of cocaine with dramatic consequences. The DEA garnered extensive press coverage for Mendoza case as journalists reported that the Mendozas had replaced the French Connection in the heroin trade. Of course, by the mid 1970s, cocaine changed much of drug-fighting policies and tactics. Initially, many of the traffickers were entrepreneurs who stumbled into the trade through family connections, like Max Mermelstein who developed a sophisticated network to distribute Colombian cocaine for the Medillín cartel out of south Florida. Mermelstein hired pilots as well as other distributors in the United States. Working closely with the Colombians, Mermelstein and his colleagues introduced thousands of tons of cocaine into the market. With the flow of coke money, Miami's economy and building boomed in the 1970s.

To combat men such as Mermelstein and his crew and the growing cocaine epidemic, the U.S. government began to use the Coast Guard for drug interdiction and the military to scan the skies and the seas. The 1980s brought a new battle and along with it a new rhetoric. Many states began to model their drug laws on the Rockefeller drug laws, which guaranteed lengthy sentences that sent thousands of people to jail for minor drug charges. As they had during the Nixon administration, many scholars and politicians questioned the effectiveness of the struggle on demand. Despite those questions, the federal government was less likely than the media to address the treatment of addicts. While Nancy Reagan's campaign, Just Say No was portrayed as focusing on the demand side, the real money went to controlling the supply of drugs. This focus meant that the United States exported its war on drugs to all of Latin America rather than focusing mostly on Mexico. The first battles against supply and production took place in the Andes, using crop eradication in Bolivia and invading labs in Colombia. Prior to the establishment of the DEA, the Bureau of Narcotics and Dangerous Drugs (BNDD) had nine overseas offices. With the formation of the DEA, numerous overseas offices were added, and the war on drugs spread to all corners of the globe.

With the 1980s, the United States experienced a profound increase in drug cases with the introduction of crack. Thus, the drug war took on a more political and military battle. In 1988 President George H. W. Bush named William Bennett the first director of national drug control policy or the "drug czar." Bennett, a conservative, supported the war on drugs and oversaw its escalation by introducing the military as a tool to fight the supply lines. The military provided jets and submarines to monitor the Gulf of Mexico and the Atlantic. The Coast Guard's focus shifted to interdiction of drug trafficking, capturing boats and ships involved in transporting cocaine. As the direct lines to south Florida began to become more treacherous for traffickers, they shifted to the land border along the U.S. border with Mexico. As war on drugs expenses continued to mount in the 1980s, policing agencies and the DEA embarked on programs of demand reduction by developing education and prevention programs. These programs took place in schools. In addition, police and the DEA agency fought legalization in states such as California and Arizona.

In the 1990s, the DEA, working with U.S. customs as well as foreign agencies, established Operation Kingpin, which led to the arrests of many prominent Colombian drug traffickers in Colombia and the United States. A shift was taking place. By the mid 1990s, methamphetamine trafficking from Mexico and domestic production was growing. In turn, the DEA put pressure on store chains to limit sales of those products used in clandestine methamphetamine production. These efforts led to a shift of cocaine flows by air and sea into Florida to a land passage through Mexico. In turn, the war on drugs continues to the present, with the U.S.–Mexico border becoming the site of greater and greater focus for its central role in marijuana, heroin, methamphetamine, and cocaine trafficking. With Mexican drug traffickers gaining control of and access to much of the U.S. market, competition emerged from competing cartels in Mexico. That competition led to increased violence in the Mexican states that border the United States. In certain cities, local government officials have fled to the United States, while other cities have implemented curfews to attempt to control the violence.

See also *Bolivia, U.S. Military Anti-Drug Program, 1986; Convention Against Illicit Traffic in Narcotic Drugs and Psychotropic Substances, 1988; Drug Trafficking; Federal Bureau of Narcotics; Inter-American Drug Abuse Control Commission (CICAD); Mexico-U.S. Border and Drug Control; U.S. Drug Enforcement Administration; United States-Bolivia Anti Narcotics Agreement, 1990*

. . . . ELAINE CAREY

REFERENCE AND FURTHER READING

Doyle, Kate. "Operation Intercept: The Perils of Unilateralism." *National Security Archive*. April 2003. www.gwu.edu/~nsarchiv/NSAEBB/NSAEBB86/.

Gooberman, Lawrence A. *Operation Intercept: The Multiple Consequences of Public Policy*. New York: Pergamon Press, 1974.

Mermelstein, Max, with Robin Moore and Richard Smitten. *The Man Who Made It Snow: By the American Mastermind Inside the Colombia Cartel*. New York: Simon & Schuster, 1990.

Walker, William, III. *Drugs in the Western Hemisphere: An Odyssey of Cultures in Conflict*. Wilmington, DE: Scholarly Resources Press, 1996.

_____. *Drug Control in the Americas*. Albuquerque: University of New Mexico Press, 1989.

U.S. Drug Enforcement Administration. *DEA History*. www.usdoj.gov/dea/history.htm.

Drug Trafficking

In Latin America, drug trafficking has emerged as a significant complication in its relations with the United States. Beginning in the 1800s, cocaine became a tool of development in Peru. In Mexico, Chinese immigrants introduced poppy for personal use. In both Mexico and Peru, European pharmaceutical companies began to use the local supplies of coca and poppy for medicines and tonics that were sold in the hemisphere. From the licit sources, illegal cocaine and heroin were smuggled across borders to avoid customs. Prior to the 1930s and after the passage of the Harrison Narcotics Act of 1914, drug trafficking and addiction lagged behind alcoholism as social issues. Customs officials recognized quite early that narcotics and cocaine were smuggled across the border as well as alcohol, as drug traffickers used the early routes and ports that served alcohol to move heroin and cocaine. Initially, counter-narcotics enforcement remained a fringe element of the secretary of treasury under the U.S. Department of Customs, but in the 1930s the drug war was formalized.

FIRST HALF OF THE TWENTIETH CENTURY

Beginning in the early 1900s, State Department officials in Latin America became concerned about the shipment of opium from Asia to Latin American ports, where it was later transported to ports in the United States and Canada. Customs officials along the U.S.-Mexican border recognized in the 1910s that men and women smuggled alcohol as well as narcotics across the border. With the passage of the Blaine Amendment and the establishment of the Federal Bureau of Narcotics (FBN) in 1930, the Latin American drug trade drew greater attention. Moreover, the bureau's director, Harry J. Anslinger, brought attention to the perils of drugs and drug trafficking. Cocaine from Peru and Bolivia and opiate derivatives and marijuana from Mexico entered the United States by land along the U.S.-Mexican border or by ship and plane. Latin America also served as a trans-shipment site for Asian and European drugs destined for the North American illegal drug markets.

Beginning in the 1920s, several Latin American countries controlled the importation of Asian opium and cocaine production. They also ratified many of the international agreements on opium and cocaine trafficking. In the 1930s, the growing concern about addiction to marijuana, opiate derivatives, and cocaine, mostly from Latin America, led to the first diplomatic relations between Latin American countries and the United States with regard to drugs.

In the 1940s, Mexican heroin and South American cocaine continued to flow into the United States and Canada. Although Anslinger, the director of the Federal Bureau of Narcotics, as well as contemporary scholars noted that the amount of Asian opium had declined, Mexican traffickers had their own supply. In the late 1940s, G. H. L. Shermann, chief of the Narcotics Division for the Canadian Department of National Health and Welfare, noted that Italian crime syndicates sold brown Mexican heroin. Thus, Mexican traffickers easily filled the loss of Asian heroin with their own domestic supply. With these concerns, Mexican, Peruvian, and other Latin American governments began to share information on drug traffickers with the United States.

Beginning in the 1930s, the United States became increasingly concerned about the ties Latin American politicians and police had to drug trafficking. By the 1920s, U.S. State Department and Customs Enforcement officials complained about the low salaries for police officers in Latin America, arguing that this could led to corruption. Moreover, concerns of corruption and ties to drug trafficking grew in the 1940s and 1950s. In Mexico in 1947, Alejandro Araiza Lacy, a Mexican attorney, for senator from the Party of the Institution Revolution (PRI), along with Angel del Castillo, another prominent PRI party activist, were arrested while processing opium with their chemist, Estorgio Espinosa de Monteros. Working with two other prominent politicians in Sonora, Araiza and his crew employed fishing boats that went up the Sonoran coast to ports in the United States. Ironically, it was with the late President Plutarco Calles who hailed from Sonora that the United States entered into its first diplomatic agreement over narcotics trafficking. In 1950, Peruvian newspapers published a report regarding FBN officials' concerns about the ties of naturalized U.S. citizen and drug trafficker Eduardo Balarezo to prominent politicians. That leak, which was never verified, led to a formal apology from the FBN.

SECOND HALF OF THE TWENTIETH CENTURY

By the 1960s, the United States began to demand greater accountability from Latin American governments regarding drug trafficking. In turn, many Latin American leaders blamed the growing U.S. demand for fueling the drug trade. In the early 1960s, Latin Americans became more open to sharing information about their arrests and working transnationally with U.S. agencies. In turn, U.S. policing agencies began to offer training to Latin American officials. In 1973, the Drug Enforcement Administration (DEA) established bureaus across the globe. DEA agents could not carry firearms or arrest suspects; thus, they relied heavily on their Latin American hosts for information as well as contacts. The DEA has worked jointly with police agencies and the offices of the attorney general in many Latin American countries, resulting in the arrest of many prominent drug traffickers.

Despite increasing pressure from law enforcement agencies, drug traffickers have proven their ability to employ new forms of technology to further their businesses since the 1930s. Using airplanes, speedboats, and cell phones, drug traffickers have responded to police pressure. The fluidity with which trafficking enterprises adopt and employ new forms of technology, whether for transport, communication, or protection, reveals an expanding knowledge base. These abilities work in their favor against less nimble bureaucracies. Moreover, the ability of such enterprises to purchase political and police protection as well as excellent attorneys continues to undermine transnational investigations.

Since the late 1960s, drug traffickers have steadily exhibited their ability to change with market demand and further policing. In 1969, Operation Intercept's purpose was to disrupt the marijuana and heroin trade; however, it impeded the legal economic flows between the United States and Mexico when every car had to undergo inspection. Operation Intercept has little impact on the marijuana trade. With heightened security on the U.S.-Mexico border, Colombian traffickers and their U.S. colleagues introduced kilos of cocaine.

Beginning in the early 1970s, Colombian traffickers, who had moved human cargo in the wake of the violence in Colombia, turned to the lucrative cocaine trade as the demand grew in the United States. As heroin consumption declined, cocaine increased. In turn, the drug war escalated in the 1980s due to the rising consumption of cocaine. With greater patrols of the Florida coastline, greater security at major airports, and greater vigilance of shipping, cocaine traffickers moved from water transport to land. The DEA made a series of successful arrests of cocaine traffickers, disrupting the Cali and Medillín cartels. However, cocaine as well as other controlled substances continued to flow into the United States. Traffickers shifted to land crossings along the U.S.-Mexico border, which now serves as the main port of entry for cocaine, heroin, marijuana, and methamphetamines. As Colombian trafficking decreased, the Mexican drug war escalated, erupting along the U.S.-Mexico border, where different cartels struggle to control the central ports of entry into the lucrative U.S. market. The war on drugs continues to the present, with the U.S.-Mexico border becoming the site of greater and greater focus for its central role in marijuana, heroin, methamphetamine, and cocaine trafficking.

See also *Convention Against Illicit Traffic in Narcotic Drugs and Psychotropic Substances, 1988; Drugs, U.S. War on; Federal Bureau of Narcotics; Mexico-U.S. Border and Drug Control; U.S. Drug Enforcement Administration*

. . . . ELAINE CAREY

REFERENCES AND FURTHER READING

Anslinger, H. J., and William F. Tomkins. *The Traffic in Narcotics.* New York: Funk and Wagnalls Company, 1953.

Kenney, Michael. *From Pablo to Osama: Trafficking and Terrorist Networks, Government Bureaucracies, and Competitive Adaptation.* University Park: Pennsylvania State University Press, 2007.

Gootenberg, Paul. "The Pre-Colombia Era of Drug Trafficking in the Americas, Cocaine, 1945–1965." *The Americas* 64, no. 2 (October 2007): 133–176.
_____. *Andean Cocaine: The Making of a Global Drug*. Chapel Hill: The University of North Carolina Press, 2009.

Duarte Fuentes, José Napoleón

José Napoleón Duarte Fuentes (1925–1990), educated at Notre Dame University, was a joiner and a booster of the Boy Scouts, the Anti-Tuberculosis Society, and the Red Cross and a volunteer fireman. Those community activities led him into politics. Duarte was a strong believer in neighborhood organizations carrying out self-help projects and published a book on the subject.

Broad-shouldered and barrel-chested, the dynamic Duarte headed the Christian Democratic Party (PDC; *Partido Democrata Cristiano*), which sought to break the traditional stranglehold of one-party politics in El Salvador, where, no matter what the party label, the army was in firm control. Modeled after reformist capitalist parties in Western Europe, Chile, and Venezuela, Duarte's PDC was inspired by the social doctrines of the Roman Catholic Church. As mayor of San Salvador from 1964 to 1970, Duarte enforced tax collection from some of the nation's wealthiest families, some who had not paid municipal taxes in thirty years. The mayor sometimes personally went around collecting the taxes himself.

In the 1972 elections, Duarte headed an opposition coalition ticket to contest the presidency against the ruling National Conciliation Party (PCN, *Partido de Conciliacion Nacional*). The energetic Duarte campaigned throughout the country and was subject to harassment by government operatives. El Salvador's National Electoral Commission declared Duarte victorious, but the PCN-led government conducted a recount in which their candidate, Arturo Molina, was declared the winner.

Duarte initially counseled against an imminent uprising by his followers, but a general strike that he supported failed. When a coup did materialize from some opposition supporters in the military, President Sanchez was seized, and Duarte came out in support. The coup soon fizzled, however, and an enraged Sanchez had Duarte dragged out of the home of a Venezuelan diplomat, arrested, and beaten into unconsciousness with fists, blackjacks, brass knuckles, and pistol butts. International pressure forced Sanchez to release Duarte into exile in Venezuela. Duarte's facial injuries required plastic surgery.

Following a coup against the PCN-led government in October 1979, Duarte joined the junta in March 1980. He became its leader in December 1980, following the murders of four North American churchwomen as El Salvador teetered on the brink of civil war. There was strong evidence that Nicaragua was arming Soviet advisers within El Salvador's borders and assisting Salvadoran rebels.

Two rounds of 1984 presidential elections in El Salvador were marked with guerrilla armed attacks, assassinations, bombs, and thefts of election materials. The voters returned Duarte to power, yet critics on the left portrayed the Salvadoran patriot as a tool of the extreme right wing and the military as well as a pawn of the United States. U.S. presidential candidate Jesse Jackson referred to the Salvadoran elections as a "sham" and dismissed the winner, the U.S. ally, Duarte, as a "puppet."

With El Salvador's economy in shambles due to the war and his administration's policies, Duarte was forced to turn to Washington for a financial lifeline. Despite calls from liberal congressmen in the United States for a coalition government with the communist rebels, who had refused to participate in elections, Duarte was largely successful in arranging U.S. aid for his country. That aid was often tied to the continuing improvement in the Salvadoran human rights situation and the inefficient land reform schemes zealously championed by Duarte. As a result, by 1987, U.S. aid to El Salvador exceeded El Salvador's own contribution to its budget.

Duarte also struggled to maintain control over a military that had no recent history of obedience to civilian authority. Supported by his defense minister and chief of staff, Duarte was initially able to transfer army field officers suspected of political intrigue and human rights abuses. The 1985 kidnapping by the Farabundo Marti National Liberation Front (FMLN) of Duarte's daughter, Inez, undermined the military's confidence in the president, however, when Duarte insisted on taking the lead in the negotiations and was considered to be too generous in meeting the Film's demands in prisoner releases, including a rebel commander.

The FMLN accused the Salvadoran air force of indiscriminately bombing villages in and around the war zone, charges that were usually highly exaggerated. Still, Duarte used presidential discretionary funds to quietly compensate any victims, even though this effort was difficult, given how easily guerrillas easily mixed in with ordinary citizens.

Duarte was diagnosed with terminal liver cancer in 1988. While he did not live to see the end of the war, he was able to transfer power to another democratically elected president.

See Also *Central American Wars, 1980s; D'Aubuisson Arrieta, Roberto; El Salvador, U.S. Relations with; Farabundo Martí National Liberation Front (FMLN) (El Salvador); Reagan, Ronald W.; Romero, Archbishop Oscar Arnulfo*

. . . . GREG MURPHY

SELECTED WORKS

Duarte, José Napoleon Duarte. *My Story*. New York: Putnam, 1986.

REFERENCES AND FURTHER READING

Buckley, Tom. *Violent Neighbors: El Salvador, Central America, and the United States*. New York: Times Books, 1984.
U.S. Congress. House Committee on Foreign Affairs. Subcommittee on Western Hemisphere Affairs. *From Duarte to Cristiani: Where Is El Salvador Headed? Hearings Before the Subcommittee on Western Hemispheric Affairs of the Committee on Foreign Affairs*. 101st Congress, 1st sess., July 13, 1989.
U.S. Department of State, Electronic Reading Room. www.state.gov/m/a/ips/c22790.htm.
Webre, Stephen. José *Napoleon Duarte and the Christian Democratic Party in Salvadoran Politics, 1960–1972*. Baton Rouge: Louisiana State University Press, 1979.

Duggan, Laurence

Laurence Duggan (1905–1948) was a top State Department official on Latin American affairs during the administration of Franklin D. Roosevelt and enjoyed an excellent reputation as a dedicated public servant until the revelation that he had spied for the Soviet Union was followed by his mysterious death.

Duggan was born in New York City in 1905. After graduating from Phillips Exeter Academy cum laude in 1923 and from Harvard University with distinction in 1927, he worked for two years for the publisher Harper & Brothers. In 1929 his father, Stephen Duggan, who directed the Institute of International Education (IIE), sent his son on an extensive tour of Latin America to organize scholarly and professional exchange programs as secretary of the IIE's Latin American Division. Fluent in Spanish, widely traveled, and personally dedicated to improving hemispheric relations, Duggan advanced quickly after joining the State Department in 1930, becoming chief of the Division of American Republics in 1935, political adviser responsible for Latin America in 1941, and director of the Office of American Republics Affairs in 1944. After a brief service as assistant diplomatic adviser to the United Nations Relief and Rehabilitation Administration and work as a private consultant, he was chosen in October 1946 to succeed his father as director of IIE by a committee that included CBS Vice President Edward R. Murrow. In that year, IIE brought a thousand foreign students to universities in the United States, promoting Inter-American understanding just as Duggan had sought to do while at the State Department.

Duggan's influence on relations with Latin America was substantial; some people consider him to be the third architect of the Good Neighbor policy (in addition to Undersecretary Sumner Welles and Secretary of State Cordell Hull). As Welles's closest aide, Duggan persuaded him to instruct U.S. diplomats in Latin America to remain completely neutral on all internal affairs, even to the extent of declining to offer advice on domestic questions. During World War II, Duggan sought to strike a balance between necessary security practices that would reduce the Axis threat and blatant interference in Latin American affairs.

Duggan disagreed with Hull over the secretary's decision to return to the pre-Good Neighbor practice of withholding recognition from revolutionary governments.

On December 20, 1943, Bolivian army officers close to the neutralist government of Argentina overthrew the government of Enrique Peñaranda in a bloodless coup, and Hull refused to recognize the new government for six months. Duggan, credited by Bolivian diplomat Victor Andrade as one of the first U.S. officials to understand that what had taken place was not a Nazi coup, tried to dissuade Hull from this most direct violation of the Good Neighbor policy, noting that the new regime's cooperation with the Allied war effort was an improvement over Peñaranda's performance; it had increased deliveries of quinine and rubber and expropriated major Axis-owned businesses. Hull refused until the Bolivians agreed to hand over German residents who appeared on lists of suspect enemy aliens drawn up by U.S. intelligence, a quid pro quo Duggan recognized was damaging to the Roosevelt administration's standing in Latin America.

Within a month of recognition, Duggan followed Welles in being forced out of government, accused by Hull of passing secrets to Welles for Welles's newspaper column. Hull might also have known of a far more serious breach: Duggan had given secrets to the Soviet Union. Duggan was, for a time, one of the most cherished contacts of Soviet intelligence. Motivated by a romantic idealism and his anti-fascist convictions, Duggan passed documents to Soviet contacts from 1937 until his distaste for Stalin's purges and fear of exposure led him to try to distance himself from the Soviets in 1939. The Soviets repeatedly tried to re-enlist his services after the war was over despite his refusal. In December 1948, he was questioned about these contacts by the Federal Bureau of Investigation (FBI) and then days later approached again by Soviet agents demanding his assistance. On December 20, 1948, he fell to his death from the IIE's headquarters in a Manhattan office tower. Liberals such as Morrow argued at the time that red baiters in the House Un-American Activities Committee and the FBI had driven a decent man to suicide, but intercepted Soviet cables confirm Duggan's role in delivering classified documents dealing with Latin American and European affairs between 1937 and 1939. The betrayal inevitably overshadowed his legacy of working for improved Inter-American relations during his abbreviated lifetime.

See also *Bolivia, U.S. Relations with; Good Neighbor Policy; Soviet Union, Latin American Policy; Welles, Sumner*

. . . . MAX PAUL FRIEDMAN

REFERENCES AND FURTHER READING

Gellman, Irwin F. *Good Neighbor Diplomacy: United States Policies in Latin America, 1933–1945.* Baltimore: The Johns Hopkins University Press, 1979.

Weinstein, Allen, and Alexander Vassiliev. *The Haunted Wood: Soviet Espionage in America—the Stalin Era.* New York: Random House, 1999.

Welles, Sumner. *Laurence Duggan, 1905–1948: In Memoriam.* Stamford, CT: Overbrook Press, 1949.

Wood, Bryce. *The Making of the Good Neighbor Policy.* New York: Columbia University Press, 1961.

Dulles, Allen M.

Allen Macy Dulles (1893–1968), the eldest son of a Presbyterian minister from upstate New York, was part of an extended family that included three secretaries of state and several international lawyers. The Princeton-educated Dulles also earned a law degree at George Washington University. He was a celebrated intelligence officer in Europe during the two world wars and, during the 1920s and 1930s, pursued a career in corporate law with the powerful Sullivan and Cromwell firm, where he amassed a small fortune through acquisitions of shares in companies like United Fruit (UFCO). Dulles's roles as corporate lawyer and intelligence officer frequently overlapped. As Sullivan and Cromwell's representative to the State Department in the late 1920s, Dulles facilitated loans to several Latin American governments. In 1941 Dulles, travelling as a private businessman, orchestrated the transference of control of the Bolivian national airlines from German to U.S. hands.

President Dwight D. Eisenhower appointed Dulles to head the Central Intelligence Agency (CIA), and he served from 1953 to 1961, a time period that marked the shift from the noninterventionist Good Neighbor policy to covert intervention against a perceived global communist conspiracy, but without the budgetary constraints or political fallout of direct military intervention. The Dulles CIA worked closely with the State Department, which his brother John Foster Dulles headed. Dulles held overall operational responsibility of the CIA's overthrow of Guatemala's Jacobo Arbenz Guzman regime in 1954 and its failed attempt to overthrow Cuba's Fidel Castro regime in 1961. His day-to-day management of these operations was limited to high-level meetings and presidential briefings.

In Guatemala, the governments of Juan José Arévalo (1944–1951) and Arbenz (1951–1954) implemented land reform that threatened the United Fruit Company's extensive land holdings. United Fruit reacted to this threat to its privileged contractual position in Guatemala by portraying the reforms as Soviet inspired. The Truman and Eisenhower administrations shared that analysis. When Secretary of State John Foster Dulles's diplomatic pressure failed to restore the status quo, Eisenhower ordered the CIA to covertly overthrow Arbenz. Operation PBSUCCESS began in 1953 and led to the overthrow of the Guatemalan government, ending the threat to United Fruit but leading to decades of internal violence. Dulles hailed the operation as a great success, and his family resumed trips to its favorite vacation spot.

Cuba proved more troublesome. In 1959, Fidel Castro overthrew the corrupt Cuban oligarchy and nationalized North American businesses. Eisenhower interpreted Castro's actions as evidence of Soviet meddling and ordered CIA to begin planning his overthrow in late 1959. John Kennedy's narrow victory in the 1960 presidential election resulted in part from his aggressive posture toward Cuba during the presidential debates. Richard Nixon suspected that Dulles's classified briefing of Kennedy on Cuba gave Kennedy the edge during the debates.

Dulles gave Operation ZAPATA top priority but delegated most of the planning and oversight to his deputy director of plans, Richard Bissell. The CIA trained and equipped a guerilla force in Guatemala to lead a revolt in the Escambray Mountains in Cuba, which, it assumed, would provoke a general uprising. Kennedy, concerned that direct action against Cuba might provoke a Soviet invasion of Berlin, reluctantly approved the operation to proceed on the morning of April 17, 1961, but pressed the CIA to reduce the visibility of U.S. government support. This lowered visibility included the cancellation of crucial air support missions. Dulles kept a speaking engagement in Puerto Rico and was conspicuously absent during the operation. Kennedy publicly accepted responsibility for the failed Bay of Pigs fiasco but privately blamed CIA leaders for profound mismanagement and for attempting to force him into an overt military commitment. Kennedy quietly forced Dulles into retirement on November 29, 1961. Dulles held Kennedy personally responsible for the operation's failure, which he attributed to the cancelled airstrikes and Kennedy's reluctance to overtly commit the U.S. military. Not surprisingly, Kennedy did not seek Dulles's counsel during the Cuban missile crisis in 1962.

Ironically, President Lyndon Johnson, determined to quash rumors of a Soviet or Cuban hand in Kennedy's assassination, appointed Dulles in 1964 as liaison between the CIA and the Warren Commission, which was investigating the assassination. Dulles used this position to safeguard the secrecy of ongoing anti-Castro operations. In 1975 and 1976, the separate Church Committee investigation found that the CIA developed several plots to assassinate Castro between 1960 and 1965. Although Dulles never confirmed his role in the assassination plots on Castro or other leaders, such as the Dominican Republic's Rafael Trujillo y Molina, Bissell's Church Committee testimony left little doubt about Dulles's culpability. Until his death from pneumonia in 1969, Dulles used public speaking engagements to defend the agency, refute Kennedy loyalists' accusations of Dulles's betrayal during the Bay of Pigs, and deny conspiratorial allegations concerning his role on the Warren Commission.

See also *Bay of Pigs Invasion, 1961; Bissell, Richard; Church Committee; Cuban Revolution, 1956–1959, U.S. Policy toward; Dulles, John Foster; Guatemala, U.S. Invasion of, 1954; Operation Mongoose; United Fruit Company (UFCO)*

. . . . JAMES A. HOLEMAN

REFERENCES AND FURTHER READING

Cullather, Nick. *Secret History: The CIA's Classified Account of Its Operations in Guatemala, 1952–1954*. 2nd ed. Stanford, CA: Stanford University Press, 2006.

Grose, Peter. *Gentleman Spy: The Life of Allen Dulles*. New York: Houghton Mifflin Company, 1994.

Immerman, Richard H. *The CIA in Guatemala: The Foreign Policy of Intervention*. Austin: University of Texas Press, 1982.

Kaiser, David. *The Road to Dallas: The Assassination of John F Kennedy*. Cambridge, MA: Harvard University Press, 2008.

Kornbluh, Peter, ed. *Bay of Pigs Declassified: The Secret CIA Report on the Invasion of Cuba*. New York: The New Press, 1998.

Rabe, Stephen G. *Eisenhower and Latin America: The Foreign Policy of Anticommunism*. Chapel Hill: The University of North Carolina Press, 1988.

Schlesinger, Stephen, and Stephen Kinzer. *Bitter Fruit: The Story of the American Coup in Guatemala*. 2nd ed. Cambridge, MA: Harvard University Press, 2005.

Wyden, Peter. *Bay of Pigs: The Untold Story*. New York: Simon and Schuster, 1979.

Dulles, John Foster

John Foster Dulles (1888–1959) hailed from upstate New York. He studied philosophy at Princeton and the Sorbonne and acquired a law degree from George Washington University,

Washington, D.C. Although he was the eldest son of a Presbyterian minister, Dulles followed in the footsteps of his grandfather, John Watson Foster, a former secretary of state. He became a specialist in international finance, corporate law, and international diplomacy, bringing the faith of a Wilsonian internationalist to this situation. For Dulles, U.S. exceptionalism, moral duty, and financial benefit harmoniously coexisted. As both a corporate lawyer and diplomat, Dulles played an important role in shaping U.S.–Latin American relations in the first half of the twentieth century.

LAWYER AND LOBBYIST FOR DICTATORSHIPS

After a personal appeal by John Watson Foster to William Nelson Cromwell, the Sullivan and Cromwell firm hired Dulles in 1911. His work in Latin America for Sullivan and Cromwell prior to World War I included providing legal representation for an array of international investors in Panama, Brazil, Peru, Nicaragua, and Cuba. In 1916, Dulles contacted his uncle, Robert Lansing, who was President Woodrow Wilson's secretary of state, to encourage State Department support for Emiliano Chamorro's bid for the Nicaraguan presidency, an early indication of Dulles's penchant for promoting dictatorial government in exchange for stability and pro-U.S. policies. Again he used his relationship with Lansing at State to lobby for U.S. protection of North American property rights during a period of political upheaval in Cuba in 1917.

On the eve of U.S. entry into World War I, Lansing sent Dulles on a successful secret mission to Nicaragua, Costa Rica, Cuba, and Panama to ensure those countries sided with the United States. While in those countries, Dulles also conducted business on behalf of his international clients at Sullivan and Cromwell. During the war, Dulles entered the Army and worked for military intelligence and the War Trade Board. He also served as a legal adviser during the reparations negotiations at the Paris Peace Conference in 1919.

During the interwar period, Dulles returned to Sullivan and Cromwell as a full partner and provided representation for some of the firm's most important clients. In this context, Dulles worked on behalf of the Carib Syndicate's oil investments in Colombia, the Cuban Cane Sugar Corporation, the National Railroad Company of Haiti, Electric Bond and Share, the American and Foreign Power Company, United Railways of Central America, and the United Fruit Company. He also worked on behalf of international bankers and participated in an array of transactions involving loans and the sale of bonds and securities in Latin America during the 1920s. During the 1930s, Dulles helped negotiate the United Fruit contract with Guatemalan dictator Jorge Ubico.

COLD WAR

During World War II, Dulles worked through the Council on Foreign Relations and a variety of Protestant church organizations to promote the idea that the United States had a moral obligation to provide global leadership in the postwar world. With increasing Cold War tensions under the Truman and Eisenhower administrations, Dulles viewed the poverty-stricken areas of Africa, Asia, and Latin America as fertile ground for communist recruitment and subversion. Like many of his contemporaries, Dulles often interpreted postwar nationalist reform movements, particularly those that threatened North American investments, as part of a Kremlin-directed international communist conspiracy.

Dulles became secretary of state in 1953, serving until shortly before his death from cancer in 1959. Despite the appeals of Latin American leaders for a Marshall Plan for Latin America's economic recovery, Dulles treated the communist threat to Latin America as a political problem. He responded by encouraging Latin American governments to create the conditions conducive to attracting private investment, by providing limited military and economic aid to stable anticommunist regimes, and by authorizing a host of State Department programs designed to undermine leftist organizations. In the case of Guatemala, Dulles interpreted the labor and land reforms of the Jacobo Guzman Arbenz regime as evidence of Soviet meddling in the western hemisphere. Dulles provided the diplomatic groundwork for the CIA's overthrow of Arbenz in 1954. At the Inter-American Conference held in Caracas, Venezuela, in March 1954, Dulles produced an anticommunist declaration that Organization of American States (OAS) members, with the exception of Guatemala, Argentina, and Mexico, endorsed. When the Guatemalan government appealed to the United Nations (UN) to investigate Carlos Castillo Armas's armed incursion into Guatemalan territory, Dulles instructed the U.S. delegation to avoid a UN inquiry by insisting that this was an issue best resolved by the regional OAS. Mindful of the potential charge of Yankee imperialism, Dulles credited the "loyal citizens of Guatemala" for their successful resistance of an "alien despotism." Despite the dearth of evidence to tie Arbenz to international communism, Dulles privately hailed the CIA's operation as a great success.

The overthrow of Arbenz marked a decisive shift away from the Good Neighbor policy of nonintervention. To the consternation of Dulles's critics, the Eisenhower administration supported dictatorships in Latin America as preferable to political instability and social upheaval. Thus Dulles's State Department supported the repressive regimes of Anastasio Somoza of Nicaragua, Manuel Odria in Peru, Marcos Perez Jiménez in Venezuela, Rafael Trujillo y Molina in the Dominican Republic, and Fulgencio Batista in Cuba. Not surprisingly, these policies generated a significant amount of anti-Yankee sentiment, and in the late 1950s, a wave of revolution and social upheaval challenged the rule of dictators in the region.

See also *Arbenz Guzmán, Jacobo; Bissell, Richard; Cabot, John M.; Castro Ruz, Fidel; Cuban Revolution, 1956–1959, U.S. Policy toward; Dictators, U.S. Policy toward; Dulles, Allen M.; Eisenhower, Dwight D.; Foster, John W.; Good Neighbor Policy; NSC-68 (U.S. National Security Council); Guatemala, U.S. Invasion of, 1954; Ubico y Castañeda, Jorge; United Fruit Company (UFCO); U.S. Economic Investments in Latin America*

. . . . JAMES A. HOLEMAN

REFERENCES AND FURTHER READING

Gambone, Michael D. *Eisenhower, Somoza, and the Cold War in Nicaragua 1953–1961*. Westport, CT: Praeger, 1997.

Immerman, Richard H., ed. *John Foster Dulles and the Diplomacy of the Cold War*. Princeton: Princeton University Press, 1990.

______. *John Foster Dulles: Piety, Pragmatism, and Power in U.S. Foreign Policy*. Wilmington, DE: SR Books, 1999.

Pruessen, Ronald W. *John Foster Dulles: The Road to Power*. New York: The Free Press, 1982.

Rabe, Stephen G. *Eisenhower and Latin America: The Foreign Policy of Anticommunism*. Chapel Hill: The University of North Carolina Press, 1988.

Dumbarton Oaks Proposals

The Dumbarton Oaks proposals were issued to design and to plan the operation of a new international organization in the post–World War II world. The Big Four powers of Great Britain, United States, China, and the Soviet Union met at Dumbarton Oaks in Washington, D.C., between August 23 and October 7, 1944. This conference was preceded by almost two years of planning by an Informal Political Agenda Group formed by Secretary of State Cordell Hull and led by Leo Pasvolsky, U.S. State Department official and economist. The meeting was significant, among other things, because it brought to the forefront the attitude of the Big Four toward Latin America, the status of the Latin American countries, and issues of regionalism and U.S.–Latin American relations.

Proposals were drawn up for four principal bodies to constitute what came to be known as the United Nations Organization: the General Assembly, composed of all members; the Security Council, consisting of five permanent and six nonpermanent members chosen by the General Assembly to serve for a period of two years; the International Court of Justice; and the Secretariat. The proposals also sketched an Economic and Social Council under the General Assembly and agreed on an armed force under the Security Council to address matters of war and acts of aggression.

The Dumbarton Oaks proposals were received and agreed on amid much controversy. It was expected that the Latin American nations would be members. Aware of Latin America's dissatisfaction with its minimalistic role in the new world order, Hull proposed and began to lobby for the acceptance of Brazil as the sixth permanent member of the Security Council. The proposal fell apart on the question of Brazil's doubtful international role as well as issues of regional representation. Furthermore, inclusion of Portuguese-speaking Brazil would antagonize Spanish-speaking nations in the region, especially Argentina, which was pro-Nazi. President Franklin D. Roosevelt kept the issue open and hoped to convince Winston Churchill and Joseph Stalin. It was later decided that the Latin American countries would always occupy one of the elected seats on the council.

The U.S. delegates also envisioned Latin American resistance to the Soviet Union's demand of veto power for permanent members in the Security Council. The assumption was that the Latin American countries would never accept an unqualified veto as it would make them a mere "rubber stamp" in decisions of the great powers. Thus, a number of issues were left undecided: the veto, the composition of the membership, and whether the purview of the organization should include social and economic issues as well as security considerations (the British and U.S. position) or only security (the Soviet position).

The role of regional organizations became the focal point of Latin American concerns. To them, the historical record illustrated the dominance of external influence in affairs considered regional or internal. Latin America's twentieth-century political objective was to curtail U.S. influence throughout the region, particularly around the Caribbean, as seen at the four inter-U.S. conferences in the 1920s and at the 1936 Buenos Aires conference. The possibility of using the League of Nations to limit U.S. hemispheric influence had provided sufficient reason for the Latin American states to join, but the U.S. refusal of membership had served as the death knell for Latin American participation in the international organization.

Despite the promises of noninterference found in the U.S. Good Neighbor policy, the Latin Americans still mistrusted the Americans and feared that the new United Nations would serve the interests of the superpowers in dealing with regional matters. To reach their objectives, at both the 1945 Mexico City and San Francisco conferences, the Latin American countries endorsed the Dumbarton Oaks plan but also proposed greater representation and security for smaller nations and sought some legal check on the great powers by a code of international justice.

The Latin American countries found solace in Article 51 of the UN charter, which prevents UN interference in regional matters unless its involvement is requested by a regional organization. The Latin Americans anticipated that the Organization of American States, founded in 1948, would provide that protection. Thus, the Latin American actions in 1944 and 1945 gave rise to the Inter-American system that redefined Latin America's relations with the United States from the onset of the Cold War. Since 1950, Latin American governments have increasingly resisted U.S. policy and acted with greater independence in international affairs.

See also *Conference of American States on Conciliation and Arbitration, Washington, 1928–1929; Fifth International Conference of American States, Santiago, 1923; Good Neighbor Policy; Inter-American Conference for the Maintenance of Peace, Buenos Aires, 1936; League of Nations; Ninth International Conference of American States, Bogotá, 1948; Organization of American States (OAS); Seventh International Conference of American States, Montevideo, 1933; Sixth International Conference of American States, Havana, 1928*

LOPITA NATH

REFERENCES AND FURTHER READING

Hilderbrand, Robert. *Dumbarton Oaks: The Origins of the United Nations and the Search for Post War Security*. Chapel Hill: University of North Carolina Press, 2001.

O'Sullivan, Christopher D. *The United Nations: A Concise History*. Florida: Kreiger, 2005.

Dupuy de Lôme, Enrique

Enrique Dupuy de Lôme (1851–1904) was Spain's minister to the United States in the critical period immediately before the Spanish-Cuban-American War. He wrote a personal letter that criticized U.S. President William McKinley to his friend, Spanish politician José Canalejas y Méndez, who was touring Cuba. Cuban revolutionaries intercepted the letter in the Havana post office and turned it over to representatives of the Hearst publishing empire. Published in the *New York Journal* on February 9, 1898, the letter played a large role in expanding U.S. public support for war against Spain. Dupuy de Lôme's unflattering remarks about McKinley fueled an aggressive, warlike foreign policy that was exacerbated when the battleship *Maine* exploded in Havana's harbor nearly one week later. Dupuy de Lôme's letter directly contributed to McKinley's decision to declare war against Spain in April 1898.

Dupuy de Lôme was born on August 23, 1851, in Valencia, Spain. After the young man completed his early education, his father sent him to Paris to continue his studies and perfect his French. In admiration of his French uncle, Dupuy de Lôme, whose family had used only the Dupuy surname since the sixteenth century, re-established the full French surname. In 1868, Dupuy de Lôme returned to Spain to study law in Madrid. Simultaneously, he served as an orderly in the foreign ministry, the first step in a diplomatic career. After completing his legal studies at the Universidad de Madrid in 1872, he joined the diplomatic corps. Dupuy de Lôme subsequently served in Japan, Uruguay, Argentina, France, the United States, and Germany. In 1888 he was promoted to the rank of minister and posted as Spain's ambassador to Uruguay.

In 1892 Dupuy de Lôme was appointed Spain's ambassador to the United States. His posting lasted only a few months: Dupuy de Lôme submitted his resignation after the liberals took control of the Spanish government later in the year. Nevertheless, in 1895, following the outbreak of the Cuban Revolution, Dupuy de Lôme was re-appointed Spain's ambassador to the United States. He attempted to improve the negative public opinion of Spain in the U.S. press after yellow journalism unveiled the horrors of the *Reconcentrados* (Cuban detention centers) implemented by General Valeriano Weyler. Although U.S. President Grover Cleveland attempted to maintain a policy of neutrality toward the Cuban Revolution, McKinley, who took office in March 1897, supported an expansionist foreign policy, making Dupuy de Lôme's task of maintaining cordial U.S.-Spanish relations more difficult.

Although undated, Dupuy de Lôme's infamous handwritten letter was most likely written in mid-December 1897 and did not represent official Spanish policy. Regardless, sending the letter through the postal system and committing his personal views to paper was a diplomatic faux pas. Following the publication of the letter, Dupuy de Lôme resigned his post, although he continued to work for the Spanish foreign ministry. He died while working in Paris on June 30, 1904.

See also *Hearst, William Randolph; McKinley, William; Weyler y Nicolau, Valeriano*

. . . . MICHAEL R. HALL

REFERENCES AND FURTHER READING

Bechloss, Michael. *Our Documents: 100 Milestone Documents from the National Archives.* Oxford, UK: Oxford University Press, 2003.

Garcia Barron, Carlos. "Enrique Dupuy de Lôme and the Spanish American War." *The Americas* 36, no. 1 (July 1979): 39–58.

O'Toole, G. J. A. *The Spanish American War: An American Epic, 1898.* New York: W. W. Norton, 1986.

Trask, David. *The War with Spain in 1898.* Lincoln: University of Nebraska Press, 1996.

Dutch-Speaking Caribbean, U.S. Relations with

The Netherlands Antilles and Aruba make up two different sets of islands in the Caribbean. Aruba is west of Curaçao and Bonaire, also Dutch-speaking islands that lie north of Venezuela; Sint Eustatius, Saba, and Sint Maarten are south of the Virgin Islands. Spain colonized Aruba in 1499, but the Dutch took over the island in 1636. The Dutch also colonized the other islands in the seventeenth century. In 1956 the islands gained autonomy from the Dutch and became responsible for their internal affairs. In 1986 Aruba broke away from the other five islands to become an autonomous Dutch territory.

The six islands cover almost 780 miles in area. The population of the Netherlands Antilles, which is around 198,000, consists of almost 85 percent mixed black, with 15 percent of mixed white, Latin American, and East Asian. Aruba's population, which is almost 107,000, is composed of almost 80 percent white or Amerindian with the other 20 percent of mixed origins. The islands have relied on a few main industries. In the nineteenth century, Aruba successfully mined gold, and in the early twentieth century, it became a center of petroleum processing for companies in the United States as well as those in other countries. In the late twentieth century, after its oil refinery was closed in 1985, tourism dominated Aruba's economy. The other islands have similar economies. For example, almost four hundred thousand tourists came to Curaçao in 1995. About 15 percent of those were from the United States. The islands must import most of their capital goods, primarily from Venezuela, the United States, and Mexico. An international incident in Aruba in 2005 hurt Aruba's tourist industry dramatically. A U.S. high school student disappeared while on vacation in Aruba. As a result, the island spent more than $200 million to renovate hotels and resorts, as well as the airport and the cruise ship terminal, hoping to stimulate renewed tourist interest.

DRUG TRAFFICKING AND MONEY LAUNDERING

Drug trafficking has been one of the major issues between the Dutch-speaking Caribbean and the United States. Several events have characterized this relationship. In 2001 a large drug seizure in Aruba supported the idea that Aruba as an important stopping-over place for drugs coming into the United States and Europe from Colombia. Thirty-two people were arrested, and officers seized more than six kilograms of heroin, nearly one kilogram of crack, and $1,230,000 in U.S. currency. In addition, five more people were arrested in October of that year, caught with nearly three kilograms of heroin stashed inside their bodies in latex balloons. In addition to direct drug trafficking through travelers, baggage handlers were caught in a 1999 sting, smuggling cocaine into the United States on Air Aruba, Bahamas Air, and Ecuatoriana.

In addition to drug trafficking, offshore money laundering (often involving drug money), is also an issue of contention between the United States and the Dutch-speaking Caribbean. In 2000 the Organization for Economic Cooperation and Development named thirty-five areas that had tax laws attractive to companies and people who wished to avoid income, corporate, and capital gains taxes. The Netherlands Antilles and Aruba were among those thirty-five. In 2002 tighter restrictions on banking were put in place in the Netherlands Antilles. A later solution to this problem came into effect in 2004 between Aruba and the United States, the Tax Information Exchange Agreement (TIEA). U.S. taxpayers could now claim deductions for meetings, seminars, and conventions held in Aruba. The signers hoped this agreement would bring business to the island and open up communication regarding taxes. In addition, Aruba guaranteed that it would not be a safe haven for terrorism, money laundering, and tax evasion.

MILITARY BASES

Drug issues brought U.S. military bases to the islands, although military relations between the Dutch islands and the United States go as far back as the U.S. War for Independence. During that period, the Netherlands signed a secret treaty with the United States and the islands of the Dutch Antilles. Sint Eustatius became the main supply stopover for the Americans during the war. For example, Baltimore merchants brought 4,900 tons of goods to the Dutch Antilles in 1780 for transit to European or American buyers.

During World War II, Aruba and Curaçao used their oil refineries to supply English, French, and U.S. planes. In the later twentieth century, after the closing of bases in Panama, the United States decided to create a number of smaller bases in the Caribbean. Two of these smaller bases are on Aruba and Curaçao. The United States has ten-year renewable leases in these bases, which were created to monitor drug trafficking. One of the problems with these overseas bases, from the perspectives of the island governments, is the possibly negative environmental impact left behind by the United States when they leave. Moreover, the local governments have no jurisdiction on the military bases and no way to monitor their activities.

In 1999 a State Department official said that the bases were also used to monitor the Colombian guerrillas--in other words expanding their job of monitoring drug trafficking. These bases are known as forward operating locations or cooperative security locations. The military has spent more than $100 million for renovation of facilities in Aruba, Curaçao, and Ecuador. The bases have garnered some negative responses. For example, the president of Venezuela, Hugo Chávez, argued in December 2009 that the United States was putting a base on Aruba as place from which to attack Venezuela since relations between Venezuela and the United States were strained.

See also *Chávez Frías, Hugo; Drug Trafficking; Drugs, U.S. War on; U.S. Revolution (1776–1783) and Latin America; Venezuela, U.S. Relations with; World War II (1939–1945)*

. . . . GINA HAMES

REFERENCES AND FURTHER READING

Bryan, Anthony T. Working Paper "Caribbean Tourism: Igniting the Engines of Sustainable Growth." Agenda Paper no. 52. The North-South Center, University of Miami. November 2001 www.ciaonet.org/wps/bra03/bra03.html.

Lindsay-Poland, John. "U.S. Military Bases in Latin America and the Caribbean." *Foreign Policy in Focus* 9, no. 3 (August 2004).

Oostindie, Gert. *Paradise Overseas: The Dutch Caribbean: Colonialism and Its Transatlantic Legacies*. Leiden, The Netherlands: Macmillian, 2005.

Duvalier, François

Born on April 14, 1907, François Duvalier (1907–1971) was president of Haiti from 1957 to 1971. His father was a minor jurist, teacher, and journalist, and his mother was a baker. One of his early teachers was Dumarsais Estimé, who was a champion of the underprivileged black majority and a model for Duvalier's political career. Another of his teachers was Jean Price-Mars, the amateur ethnographer whose writings romanticized voodoo and the Haitian peasantry.

THE RISE OF "PAPA DOC"

In 1934 Duvalier graduated in medicine from the University of Haiti. In the 1940s, he attended the University of Michigan for a year, taking courses in public health. Back in Haiti, he participated in the U.S.-sponsored campaign against malaria and yaws, practicing primarily in the village of Gressier, just south of Port-au-Prince. Duvalier later claimed that his identification with rural Haitians was based on his work there. He also claimed that his patients there gave him the nickname "Papa Doc," by which he became widely known during his political career. In 1939 Duvalier married a nurse, Simone Ovide, and they had four children, three daughters and a son, the youngest.

In addition to absorbing Estimé's and Price-Mars's concepts of the ideological progressiveness of the black peasantry and the countering conservatism of the mulatto elite, Duvalier's political thinking was shaped by the occupation of Haiti by the U.S. Marines from 1915 through 1934. In 1938 Duvalier helped start the journal *Les Griots*, which published articles promoting Haiti's African identity.

In August 1946, Duvalier's former teacher Estimé was elected president and began what some historians have labeled the social revolution of 1946, which emphasized the African content of Haitian society and saw the emergence of a politically powerful urban middle class. The Estimé regime also displaced U.S.-oriented politicians and repudiated the imitative French culture of the elite.

Under Estimé, Duvalier became director general of the National Public Health Service in 1946, and in 1949, he began serving as minister of both health and labor. In May 1950, however, the army ousted Estimé, and in December, Paul Eugène Magloire, a former colonel in the army, was installed as president. An opponent of Magloire, Duvalier went into hiding in 1954 until an amnesty was declared in 1956 when Magloire fled into exile in the wake of widespread strikes and demonstrations.

Several provisional governments rose and fell, and in September 1957, Duvalier emerged as the self-proclaimed heir to the Estimé social revolution. He won the presidency with a decisive margin in an election closely supervised—and perhaps fixed—by the army. When he was inaugurated on October 22, some saw him as a tool of the army and others as a lackey of the U.S. embassy. Instead he began a father-son dynasty that lasted twenty-nine years despite at least five attempted coups and invasions from 1958 through 1968 and several bombings, protests, and riots.

FRANÇOIS DUVALIER IN POWER

An attempt in April 1963 to kill his children led Duvalier to become obsessive about his safety and to implement a campaign of oppression culminating in April 1964 in the declaration of himself as president-for-life and in August 1964 in the suspension of all rights. During his fourteen years as president, he never traveled outside Haiti, and, in fact, he rarely left the presidential palace.

To control the military, which was a potential challenge to his authority, Duvalier constantly rotated and changed the army's upper echelons, reduced the military budget, and created his own palace guard. He also developed an alternative volunteer militia loyal only to him, the notorious *tonton-makout*.

In addition, Duvalier spent considerable effort creating a personality cult. For example, he often dressed and spoke like the voodoo spirit of the dead, Baron Samdi, thereby interjecting himself into the voodoo pantheon to complete his identification with Haitian beliefs about supernatural spirits. One widely distributed poster showed him seated with Jesus Christ standing behind him, one hand on his shoulder, with the caption "I have chosen Him." Haitian radio became filled with his endless harangues.

Duvalier showed considerable finesse in handling Haiti's international neighbors. Early in his presidency, he practiced outright flattery in dealing with the Dominican Republic's Rafael Trujillo y Molina and Cuba's Fulgencio Batista. In fact, in 1958 he awarded Batista Haiti's highest medal of honor (created for the occasion) in exchange for a four million-dollar loan, which apparently was never repaid since Batista was overthrown the next year. Duvalier almost immediately sent his congratulations to Batista's replacement, Fidel Castro.

Trujillo was assassinated in 1961, only a few years after Duvalier took office, but Duvalier did not fare so well with Juan Bosch Gaviño, who was president of the Dominican Republic for seven months in 1963 and who gave asylum and support to anti-Duvalier Haitian exiles. At one point, Bosch threatened to invade Haiti, but he lacked the support of the Dominican military and eventually backed down. Duvalier got along better with the military governments that overthrew Bosch.

Duvalier's dealings with the United States generally focused on his promises to be a bulwark against the spread of communism in the Caribbean, and he often let Washington know that he needed more aid money to help depose Castro. When he deemed the aid money insufficient, Duvalier spent more time flattering Castro. Eventually Duvalier's brutal and corrupt rule caught the attention of U.S. President John F. Kennedy. The information that Duvalier was misappropriating aid monies led Washington to suspend aid in mid 1962 and to demand strict accounting procedures as a condition for the renewal of aid. In response, Duvalier renounced all aid from the United States, portraying himself as a nationalist. When Kennedy was assassinated in November 1963, Duvalier claimed that Kennedy's death was a result of a voodoo curse that Duvalier had imposed. Kennedy's successor, Lyndon B. Johnson, was distracted by the war in Vietnam, and Haiti became a minor player in world politics, although eventually aid to Haiti was resumed.

In January 1971, the constitution was amended to permit Duvalier to name his son as his successor. During the night of April 21, 1971, Papa Doc Duvalier died, and nineteen-year-old Jean-Claude Duvalier was proclaimed president-for-life the next day.

See also *Duvalier, Jean-Claude; Haiti, U.S. Relations with*

. . . . ROBERT LAWLESS

REFERENCES AND FURTHER READING

Abbott, Elizabeth. *Haiti: The Duvaliers and Their Legacy.* New York: McGraw-Hill, 1988.

Ferguson, James. *Papa Doc, Baby Doc: Haiti and the Duvaliers.* Oxford, UK: Basil Blackwell, 1987.

Lawless, Robert. *Haiti's Bad Press.* Rochester, VT: Schenkman, 1992.

Trouillot, Michael-Rolph. *Haiti, State Against Nation: The Origins and Legacy of Duvalierism.* New York: Monthly Review Press, 1990.

Duvalier, Jean-Claude

Jean-Claude Duvalier (1951–) is the son of François Duvalier, the longtime dictator of Haiti, who announced on January 22, 1971, that his son would succeed him as president-for-life. The elder Duvalier died on April 21, 1971, and, indeed, the nineteen-year-old Jean-Claude then became dictator of Haiti and remained in that position until he fled the country on February 7, 1986. Apparently the transition from father to son was worked out between François Duvalier and the U.S. administration of President Richard Nixon during the 1970 visit to Haiti of Nixon's special envoy, Nelson Rockefeller. The United States would support the political continuation of the Duvalier dynasty, and the new regime would support a

The Duvaliers, father François (back) and son Jean-Claude (front), controlled Haiti from 1957 to 1986. François, nicknamed "Papa Doc" from his time as a health worker, built up a strong base of popular support that Jean-Claude, "Baby Doc," gradually eroded with a combination of repressive actions and personal indulgences. Jean-Claude Duvalier fled to France in 1986 but returned unexpectedly in 2011.

SOURCE: AFP/NEWSCOM

U.S.-controlled economic program that benefitted U.S. companies but did little for the average Haitian.

During the first several years of his rule, the young Duvalier remained interested primarily in fast cars and fast women, and what little governance the second Duvalier regime practiced was largely carried out by his mother, Simone Duvalier, and his father's remaining colleagues. The shift to actual rule by Duvalier, as well as the beginning of his downfall, might conveniently be dated from the May 27, 1980, marriage between Duvalier and Michèle Bennett, the light-skinned daughter of a Haitian businessman; she encouraged him to take control of the regime from his mother. The new black middle class, however, felt betrayed, as did most dark-skinned Haitians whom François Duvalier had so carefully cultivated. The fact that the elaborate wedding apparently cost millions of dollars was perceived as a particularly insensitive insult by the poverty-stricken Haitians. And several years into the marriage, the shopping excesses of Michèle became highly publicized.

U.S. government aid continued to flow into Haiti, although most of the monies went directly into the pockets of Haitian government officials, and the Nixon administration paid little attention to the gross violations of human rights in Haiti. The first couple of years of U.S. President Jimmy Carter's administration emphasized human rights, and Duvalier made some progressive changes. Correctly reading the lack of interest in human rights of the incoming administration of U.S. President Ronald Reagan, the Haitian government arrested, tortured, killed, and deported several hundred progressive Haitian activists in early 1981, almost immediately after the installation of the Reagan administration.

During the tenure of the Reagan administration, the Duvalier dictatorship received about five times as much military aid as it had had from Carter, and the army in Haiti finally regained the power it had lost under François Duvalier. Also during these years, Haiti joined the ranks of debtor nations for the first time in its history, and the countryside was impoverished. The U.S.-sponsored eradication of the pig population in Haiti from May 1982 to June 1983 under the dubious claim of combating swine fever probably severely tested the endurance of Haitian peasants. In addition, erroneous reports in the early 1980s that Haitians were carriers of AIDS caused an injurious decline in tourism. By the mid 1980s, the numbers of refugees fleeing Haiti had grown dramatically.

On March 9, 1983, Pope John Paul II visited Port-au-Prince and declared that "something has to change here." Unrest increased and broke out into rioting the following year, with the most serious being in Cap-Haitien, Haiti's second-largest city. November 1985 saw several days of anti-Duvalier rioting in Gonaïves, the historic city where Haitian independence was declared on January 1, 1804. The following month, Duvalier closed two church radio stations in Port-au-Prince, which had been broadcasting anti-Duvalier stories. In January 1986, the United States cut back aid as reports of human rights abuses were publicized, and in the same month, anti-government demonstrations occurred in at least seven cities.

On February 7, Duvalier fled to France on a U.S. jet brought in from the U.S. base at Guantánamo, Cuba. The people celebrated the fall of the twenty-nine–year father-son dynasty by destroying everything associated with the Duvaliers, including François Duvalier's elaborate mausoleum. (His corpse, however, had already been removed and has yet to be found.) A Conseil National du Gouvernement (National Council of Government) headed by Lieutenant General Henri Namphy took control.

Jean-Claude Duvalier retired to France with little access to the wealth his family stole from Haiti, much of which was apparently taken by Michèle Bennett when she divorced Duvalier in 1989. Ironically Duvalier's live-in girlfriend is Véronique Roy, the granddaughter of Paul Magloire, an adversary and predecessor of his father as president of Haiti.

In the aftermath of the devastating earthquake, suddenly and without explanation, Jean-Claude returned to Haiti on January 19, 2011. While large crowds provided a hero's welcome to the former dictator, civil and human rights groups pressed for his arrest and trial for his ill deeds of the past. Some political analysts suggest that Duvalier is biding his time to capitalize upon Haiti's fluid and tumultuous political arena.

See also *Duvalier, François; Haiti, Refugees from; Haiti, U.S. Intervention under President Clinton, 1994*

. . . . ROBERT LAWLESS

REFERENCES AND FURTHER READING

Abbott, Elizabeth. *Haiti: The Duvaliers and Their Legacy*. New York: McGraw-Hill, 1988.

Ferguson, James. *Papa Doc, Baby Doc: Haiti and the Duvaliers*. Oxford, UK: Basil Blackwell, 1987.

Lawless, Robert. *Haiti's Bad Press*. Rochester, VT: Schenkman, 1992.

Prince, Rod. *Haiti: Family Business*. London: Latin American Bureau, 1985.

Echeverría Álvarez, Luis

Luis Echeverría Álvarez (1922–) was president of Mexico from 1970 to 1976. He was a lifelong politician and high-ranking member of the Institutional Revolutionary Party (PRI), Mexico's dominant political party. Echeverría is known for his role in the government repression of the 1968 student movement. He is also remembered for moving his administration to the left and instituting populist policies that contributed to an economic crisis in 1976. He was frequently a source of opposition to U.S. policy in the region, particularly regarding Cuba.

Echeverría was born January 17, 1922, in Mexico City. He was raised there and attended the National Autonomous University of Mexico (UNAM) to study law. Beginning in 1946, Echeverría worked his way up through the PRI ranks, holding a senior leadership position in the Ministry of the Interior by 1958. In 1964 he was named secretary of the interior by President Gustavo Díaz Ordaz. Echeverría was in that position when student protests erupted throughout Mexico City in the months before the 1968 Olympic Games. Just weeks before the opening ceremonies, military and law enforcement officials killed several hundred high school and university student protestors. Echeverría's role in the incident and the subsequent suppression of its details have been the source of much controversy, particularly in recent years. It is widely believed that, as secretary of the interior, he gave the order for military troops to open fire on the demonstration. He is also believed to have played a role in the government repression that followed, including an incident that became known as the Corpus Christi Massacre in 1971, after he became president. After the PRI lost the presidency in 2000, a special prosecutor placed Echeverría under arrest and prepared to charge him with war crimes and genocide for his role in the tragedies. The case met several legal obstacles, and to date, Echeverría has not been tried.

As president, Echeverría worked to build a populist coalition of support, and his six years in office were marked by large amounts of government spending. He increased funding for education and other social services. Echeverría also devoted government resources to expanding and modernizing the nation's infrastructure. Mexico's large oil reserves gave the president considerable negotiating power when it came to Mexico's relations with the United States. Echeverría defied the United States by establishing close relations with Chile's leftist president, Salvador Allende Gossens. He also spoke out in opposition to the U.S. embargo against the revolutionary government of Fidel Castro in Cuba; and under his leadership, diplomatic relations between Mexico and Cuba strengthened. Echeverría envisioned himself as a leader among Latin Americans and worked to transform the region's relationship with the United States. He led an effort in the Organization of American States (OAS) to temper its harsh stance toward Cuba, and he supported new regional blocs that united Latin American governments. One of the most notable of these was the Latin America Economic System (SELA) formed in 1975.

As Echeverría left office in 1976, Mexico was on the brink of a financial crisis. Overspending and poor fiscal planning in the preceding years had weakened the economy, and many observers blamed Echeverría for setting up a long period of economic stagnation in the 1980s that became known as "the lost decade."

See also *Latin American Economic System (SELA); Mexico City Olympics, 1968; Oil Shocks Since 1970, Impact on Latin America*

MONICA RANKIN

REFERENCES AND FURTHER READING

Krauze, Enrique. *Mexico: Biography of Power.* New York: Harper Collins, 1997.

Schmidt, Samuel. *The Deterioration of the Mexican Presidency.* Tucson: University of Arizona Press, 1991.

Economic Commission for Latin America and the Caribbean (CEPAL)

The Economic Commission for Latin America and the Caribbean, or the *Comisión Económica para América Latina* (CEPAL) as it is was first known in Spanish, was established in 1948. Its regional headquarters are in Santiago, Chile, and it was established under the overall auspices of the United Nations. Although CEPAL was inspired primarily by the United Nations and by key economists and government officials in Latin America and therefore was not a conduit for U.S. influence, its relative moderation was often in keeping with the developmentalist thinking that prevailed in the United States prior to the rise of neo-liberalism.

The first executive secretary of CEPAL was Gustavo Martínez Cabañas (Mexico), who served from December 1948 to April 1950.

Originally named the Economic Commission for Latin America (ECLA) or the *Comisión Económica para América Latina*, in 1984 it was renamed the Economic Commission for Latin America and the Caribbean (ECLAC), or the *Comisión Económica para América Latina y el Caribe*. However, in Spanish, it continues to be known by its original acronym: CEPAL.

DEVELOPMENT AND DEPENDENCY THEORY

The influential Argentine development economist, Raúl Prebisch, had been a key proponent of the need for an organization such as CEPAL. Prebisch articulated a conservative vision of dependency theory in the context of the overall post–1945 shift to an import-substitution industrialization policy in Latin America. He started his career with CEPAL in 1949 as Director of Research, a year after the organization was first established. He subsequently served as CEPAL's Executive Secretary from May 1950 to July 1963.

As an organization CEPAL directly sponsored or indirectly facilitated moderate development-oriented intellectual and policy work in the 1940s and 1950s. By the early 1960s, despite the efforts of Prebisch and CEPAL, many economists had become disillusioned with the import substitution strategy at the heart of CEPAL's theory and practice of development.

The increasingly radical forms of dependency theory that emerged in the 1960s and 1970s flowed directly out of the work done by CEPAL in the preceding decades. Critics increasingly pointed to the deeply entrenched, externally dependent character of the political economies of Latin America, which in their view undermined the effective application of import substitution to the region. They emphasized the continued existence of highly unequal land ownership patterns, the privileged position of foreign investment, and the profoundly narrow character of the export economies in the region. As a result, a number of influential economists directly or indirectly connected to CEPAL were gradually drawn toward an approach to development that was far more focused on the external relations of economic dependency across the region.

At the beginning of the 1960s, the regional CEPAL headquarters in Santiago, Chile, had become a major center for the emerging radical dependency approach. In fact, the Chilean economy appeared to be a particularly good example of the socioeconomic and political crisis that developed when the limits of the import substitution industrialization were reached. In 1970, the Chilean electorate voted for a Marxist government dedicated to the radical reform of the country's social and economic structures.

INFLUENCE OF ANDRÉ GUNDER FRANK

An economist whose work reflected the radicalization of economic development theory was André Gunder Frank. After 1959, he voiced support for both Chile under Allende and the Cuban Revolution, at the same time as he paid homage to Prebisch and CEPAL. Frank emerged in the second half of the 1960s as the most prominent proponent of radical dependency theory. In *Capitalism and Underdevelopment in Latin America*, published in 1967, Frank outlined the concept of "the development of underdevelopment." He articulated a model that directly linked underdevelopment and economic stagnation in the periphery (Latin America) to the extraction of an economic surplus by the metropolitan powers (Europe and the United States).

Despite the popularity of Frank's version of dependency theory, by the late 1960s, the vast majority of CEPAL's economists and policymakers were much more concerned with the internal structures that impeded economic development. Although they continued to call for moderate reform to the international terms of trade, they had no time for the revolutionary agenda and the call for a break from capitalism as such that went with radical dependency theory. For example, see Fernando Henrique Cardoso and Enzo Falleto, *Dependencia y desarrollo en América Latina* (1969). Cardoso, of course, went on to become finance minister and then president of Brazil at the end of the twentieth century.

To summarize, dependency theory was committed to revolution, while CEPAL remained focused on moderate reform. In the latter case, the agenda lived on in Latin America and beyond into the 1970s in the form of the call for the new international economic order (NIEO) at the United Nations. With the rise of neo-liberalism, however, even the moderate reforms articulated by CEPAL were marginalized.

RECENT HISTORY

At the same time, CEPAL continues to operate out of its regional headquarters in Santiago, Chile. After more than ten years as head of CEPAL, Prebisch was succeeded in August 1963 by José Antonio Mayobre ofVenezuela. The latter served as the organization's executive director until December 1966. Carlos Quintana (Mexico) directed the organization from January 1967 to March 1972, followed by Enrique V. Iglesias (Uruguay), who led the organization for more than twelve years, from April 1972 until February 1985.

Norberto González (Argentina) took over from March 1985 until December 1987, while Gert Rosenthal (Guatemala) directed the organization for almost ten years from January 1988 to December 1997. José Antonio Ocampo (Colombia) was executive secretary of the organization from January 1998 to August 2003, while José Luis Machinea (Argentina) has been in charge from December 2003 to the present.

CEPAL's current membership includes forty-four nation-states and eight territorial dependencies. It is one of five regional economic commissions established and operated under the United Nations. CEPAL is responsible directly to the UN's Economic and Social Council (ECOSOC). Furthermore, its membership extends beyond the formal boundaries of Latin America and the Caribbean to include Canada, France, Germany, Japan, the Netherlands, Portugal,

Spain, South Korea, and the United Kingdom, as well as the United States.

See also *Cardoso, Fernando Henrique; Frank, André Gunder*

MARK T. BERGER

REFERENCES AND FURTHER READING

Berger, Mark T. *Under Northern Eyes: Latin American Studies and U.S. Hegemony in the Americas, 1898–1990*. Bloomington: Indiana University Press, 1995.

Cardoso, Fernando Henrique. "The Consumption of Dependency Theory in the United States." *Latin American Research Review* 12, no. 3 (1977).

Cardoso, Fernando Henrique, and Enzo Falleto. *Dependencia y desarrollo en América Latina*. México: Siglo XXI, 1969.

Frank, André Gunder. "The Development of Underdevelopment." *Monthly Review* (September 1966).

Frank, André Gunder, Sing C. Chew, and Robert Allen Denemark. *The Underdevelopment of Development: Essays in Honor of Andre Gunder Frank*. Thousand Oaks, CA: Sage, 1996.

Love, Joseph L. "The Origins of Dependency Analysis." *Journal of Latin American Studies* 22, no. 1 (1990).

Prebisch, Raúl. "Five Stages in My Thinking on Development." In *Pioneers in Development*, edited by G. M. Meier and Dudley Seers. New York: Oxford University Press for the World Bank, 1984.

Prebisch, Raúl et al. *The Economic Development of Latin America and Its Principal Problems*. New York: United Nations, 1949.

Ecuador, U.S. Relations with

The official relationship between the United States and Ecuador began on January 13, 1832, when Ecuador's first president, Juan José Flores, wrote to U.S. President Andrew Jackson, announcing that Ecuador had declared its independence from Gran Colombia. Ecuador had declared its independence on May 13, 1830, and the fact that it took twenty months for the Flores government to inform the United States of its existence is an indication of the low priority of establishing diplomatic ties. Despite the slow start, the United States and Ecuador established a remarkably friendly relationship. Since 1832, the two nations have developed important security, development, and commercial ties that, on the whole, have resulted in a convergence of objectives that has superseded serious conflicts.

THE ROLE OF THE UNITED STATES IN ECUADOR'S TERRITORIAL DISPUTE WITH PERU

Ecuador's dispute with Peru over a vast area of the remote upper Amazon region has been the small nation's most persistent and vexing international problem. The dispute originated out of the imprecision of Spanish colonial borders and the lack of accurate mapping due to the remoteness of the region. Attempts at bilateral negotiations in the nineteenth century met with failure, as did a mediation effort by King Alfonso XIII of Spain in 1910. In 1924 Peru and Ecuador agreed to use the United States as the principal mediator of the dispute.

In July 1936, the United States hosted the Washington conference in an effort to resolve the dispute. President Franklin D. Roosevelt addressed the opening session on September 30, 1936, and urged the two parties to reach an agreement that would be welcomed throughout the hemisphere. However, the talks soon stalled, and the two sides made no progress toward a settlement. The U.S. effort to resolve the dispute was a diplomatic failure.

On July 5, 1941, hostilities broke out along the Zarumilla River. On July 12, Argentina, Brazil, and the United States arranged a cease-fire. On July 22, Peru opened a major offensive, citing Ecuadorian encroachments as justification. The Ecuadorians, outnumbered four to one, with no armor or air support, were quickly overwhelmed. The Peruvian army poured into Ecuador's El Oro Province, while its navy blockaded Guayaquil. On July 31, Ecuador, realizing that future resistance was impossible, accepted Peruvian demands. It was Ecuador's most humiliating moment. The Ecuadorian foreign minister, Julio Tobar-Donoso, summarized: "Disarmed and annihilated, Ecuador resigned herself to this measure which constituted the amputation of her sovereignty."

The brief war was an obvious disaster for Ecuador, but it had broader implications as it imperiled the hemispheric unity that Roosevelt and Sumner Welles had sought. The problem was further complicated by Japan's surprise attack on Pearl Harbor on December 7, 1941.

The U.S. government decided to support the efforts of Dr. Oswaldo Aranha, Brazil's foreign minister, to resolve the dispute at the Third Consultative Meeting of the Ministers of Foreign Affairs of the American Republics in Río de Janeiro in January 1945. Welles and Aranha manipulated the meeting agenda to preclude Ecuador from presenting the dispute during the plenary session. Their objective was to produce a settlement between the two nations without involving the other attending states. Aranha bluntly informed the Ecuadorian delegation that it had little choice but to agree to a permanent settlement without preconditions, telling Tobar-Donoso, "A country that doesn't have borders is like a man without skin. If you don't settle now Peru will continue the invasion. It is not possible to have preliminary terms; it is better to lose a limb than the whole body."

On January 29, Tobar-Donoso and his Peruvian counterparts signed the Protocol of Peace, Friendship, and Boundaries, which became known simply as the Río Protocol. Ecuador ceded the area east of the 1936 status quo line along with an additional 13,481 square kilometers of territory. The United States, Argentina, Brazil, and Chile agreed to be guarantors of the agreement. However, precise demarcation of one sector, known as *Cordillera del Condor,* proved to be difficult because of the extremely rugged terrain. Another complication stemmed from aerial mapping by the United States, which revealed geographical features, particularly the exact location of the Cenepa River and its watershed, that were contrary to descriptions contained in the Rio Protocol. Thus the dispute was not fully resolved, and the United States would be involved in the controversy for another five decades.

In 1950 Ecuador declared that the boundary demarcation in the Cordillera del Condor region could no longer be executed and withdrew from participation. In 1960 Ecuador's president, José María Velasco Ibarra, nullified the Rio Protocol, an action that the United States and the three other guarantor nations rejected. Nevertheless, Ecuador persisted in rejecting the protocol, and the lingering dispute resulted in armed clashes with Peru in 1981 and 1984. War broke out again in 1995, with Ecuador gaining a military advantage for the first time in the 153 years of the dispute. A cease-fire arranged by the four guarantors in Brasilia created a demilitarized zone.

The dispute was finally resolved in a 1998 treaty brokered by the United States, Brazil, Argentina, and Chile. The boundary was demarcated, Ecuador was granted access to five kilometers of the Marañón and private ownership but not sovereignty over the town of Tiwintza. In addition, a demilitarized zone that is also an ecological protection area was established on both sides of the border.

STRATEGIC CONCERNS OF THE UNITED STATES

The strategic interests of the United States regarding Ecuador intensified in 1904 with the construction of the Panama Canal. There were two central concerns. First was the threat of disease in the newly established U.S. Canal Zone. The second involved the defense of the Panama Canal. American sanitation officials, led by Dr. William Crawford Gorgas, wanted to rid Panama of tropical disease so that construction of the waterway could go forward. By 1906 that goal was accomplished. However, there was concern that ships transiting the Canal would reintroduce yellow fever, bubonic plaque, and other. diseases Ecuador's main port, Guayaquil, had the reputation of being one of the most pestilent places on the planet. The United States wanted it cleaned up, as did the Ecuadorian government. Despite the mutual objective, problems soon developed between Ecuador and the United States over the sanitation of Guayaquil.

The main problem was who would be in charge of the eradication effort. The United States wanted a U.S. expert to head the sanitary commission established by the Ecuadorian government. Ecuador, on the other hand, saw this demand as intrusion on its sovereignty. Despite the ill feelings, Dr. Gorgas was invited on several occasions to inspect conditions at Guayaquil and to provide recommendations to the Ecuadorian government. Gorgas inspected Guayaquil in 1913 and estimated that $900 million were needed to provided a central water and sewage system. He returned in 1916 as head of a commission organized by the International Health Board of the Rockefeller Foundation. Gorgas reported that Guayaquil was the last remaining endemic center in South America. His frank assessment set off a torrent of popular protests, and agitated mobs burned Dr. Gorgas in effigy.

In 1918 another American doctor, Michael E. Conner, was sent by the International Board of Health to Guayaquil to head a yellow fever eradication campaign. His personality and performance achieved spectacular results. Conner discovered a fish that would eat mosquito larvae in open water receptacles. This, combined with the oiling or draining of standing water, resulted in a dramatic decrease in yellow fever cases. By 1920, Guayaquil was rid of the dreaded killer. In the end, both the United States and Ecuador achieved their goals in the sanitation of Guayaquil, but they often chose tortuous paths to reach what appeared to be common objectives.

The defense of the Panama Canal was another U.S. objective that would involve Ecuador because of its possession of the Galapagos Islands. The Galapagos, which are situated in the Pacific about eight hundred miles west of the canal, offered an excellent location for the forward defense of the strategic waterway. U.S. policy was to prevent the transfer of the Galapagos to any non-American power.

War games in the 1920s revealed that the canal was vulnerable to air attacks, and the United States renewed its interest in the Galapagos. In addition to the Galapagos, the United States was worried about German aviation ventures, intelligence networks, and political influence in Ecuador. Ultimately, Ecuador saw an opportunity to enhance its security vis-à-vis Peru by cooperating with the United States.

Negotiations for air bases in Ecuador began as early as 1930, when a U.S. Army team was allowed to reconnoiter the Galapagos. In September and October 1940, a conference was held between military representatives of the two nations to establish a basis for hemispheric defense. A comprehensive policy statement outlined a plan of military cooperation that provided for the exchange of intelligence, contingency plans for reinforcement of Ecuador's armed forces in the event of an attack by a non-U.S. power, aerial mapping, and exchange of technical data. A military aviation mission was established, and President Franklin Roosevelt allotted $275,000 from his emergency fund for the development of aviation training facilities at Salinas and Quito.

The Roosevelt administration considered the German-controlled airline, *Sociedad Ecuatoriana de Transportes Aéreos* (SEDTA), to be a thinly disguised front for German agents. The United States supported Pan American Grace Airlines (Panagra) to compete with SEDTA and at the same time pressured Ecuador to restrict SEDTA routes. In the end, Ecuador nationalized SEDTA in September 1941.

After Pearl Harbor, Ecuador immediately offered the use of its coast for the establishment of bases. Naval and aviation bases were soon constructed at Salinas. The air base included a paved eight thousand–foot runway, barracks, repair shops, docking facilities, water system, hospital, and other support facilities. The cost for initial construction was around three million dollars. Its mission was to patrol a route covering the Galapagos, Guatemala, Panama, and return. Ecuador also granted the use of remote and uninhabited Baltra Island in the Galapagos for construction of an air base. In a matter of months, a complete base, including roads, two hundred buildings, runways, and desalinization plants were built at a cost of more than nine million dollars.

The wartime cooperation experienced by the United States and Ecuador represents the apogee of the relationship. Both parties benefited. The United States was able to defend the western approaches to the Panama Canal, and Ecuador received an infusion of cash and ultimately was granted control of the bases.

There were problems following the war as the United States sought to retain the Galapagos base. The United States rejected the demand of Ecuadorian President Velasco Ibarra for a payment of $100 million to retain the base. Instead, the United States turned over the Salinas base, hoping that this generous act would induce Ecuador to lease the Galapagos base at lower cost. The United States also offered to support a $3 million loan through the Import Export Bank in exchange for continued basing rights. As negotiations dragged on, U.S. interest in the Galapagos waned. The United States vacated the Galapagos base in 1946, leaving only the runway and two hundred empty buildings. Unlike the turnover of the Salinas base, this incident created considerable rancor in Ecuador.

After World War II, the U.S. strategic concern for Ecuador was to ensure that the Soviet Union or one of its surrogates did not establish a pro-Soviet, or even a nonaligned regime. Ecuador was not particularly concerned about a Soviet threat and viewed Peru as the primary threat to its territorial integrity. Ecuador also sought development aid from the United States and soon realized that the key to obtaining aid for modernization and defense projects was to support the U.S. anticommunist stance. Ecuador joined the Rio Pact and generally supported the United States in the Organization of American States, the United Nations, and other international organizations. In exchange, the United States increased military assistance and development aid to Ecuador throughout the Cold War.

DEVELOPMENT

Prior to World War II, U.S. participation in Ecuadorian modernization projects came largely from the private sector with only tacit encouragement from the U.S. government. During the administrations of Gabriel García Moreno (1860–1865 and 1869–1875), Arthur Rogers headed the effort to rebuild the city of Ibarra after the 1859 earthquake. Henry G. McClellan conducted surveys for roads and was involved in the construction of the national observatory, the second to be completed in South America and one of the most modern facilities in all the Americas. McClellan, along with John Curtis and Francis Merrill, started construction of the first railroad in Ecuador in July 1873.

American private enterprise projects increased dramatically after the liberal revolution of 1895 that brought Eloy Alfaro to the presidency (1895–1901 and 1905–1911). Alfaro revived the project to complete a railroad linking Guayaquil with Quito, which had started in 1873. In 1898 Alfaro contracted with Archer Harman, a U.S. railroad entrepreneur, to complete construction of the Guayaquil and Quito Railway. It was finished in June 1908.

The completion of the railroad brought dramatic changes to Ecuador. A national market evolved; for the first time, coastal and sierra products could be traded in a timely manner and with much lower transportation costs. Alfaro's vision of a united country was partially fulfilled, but regional conflicts remained. Perhaps the most controversial aspect of the project was its cost, around $18 million, which consumed a huge portion of Ecuador's national budget and contributed to its expanding international debt. The United States often sided with the railway company in its disputes with the Ecuadorian government and applied pressure to have bond holders properly paid. Ecuador, on the other hand, accused the company of faulty accounting, which hid profits and exaggerated losses. In the end, while the railroad brought progress to Ecuador, it did not alleviate all economic and social ills, and at times it strained relations with the United States.

In October 1926, Ecuador invited the famed Princeton University economist, Dr. Edwin Kemmerer, to inspect Ecuador's financial system and to make recommendations for reform. After five months, the Kemmerer mission issued a two thousand–page report, and most of its recommendations were quickly implemented by the government of Isidro Ayora Cueva.

The Kemmerer laws created the *Banco Central del Ecuador* and placed it on a sound financial footing, with deposits of gold from the national treasury, a minimum 50 percent cash reserve, and subscriptions of 15 percent of the deposits of member banks. Kemmerer's team implemented other reforms, which improved tax collection, increased customs receipts, and introduced modern accounting procedures. The government was to balance its budget and to use the gold standard for all fiscal transactions. The reforms were designed to improve Ecuador's abysmal international credit rating.

During World War II, the U.S. government began to provide Ecuador with development aid to rehabilitate El Oro Province in the aftermath of the Peruvian invasion. In addition, funding was provided to produce products needed for the war effort such as balsa wood, rubber, oil, and chinchona bark from which quinine is extracted. Public health programs were initiated, and an agricultural research center was established at Hacienda Pichilingue.

Under President Harry Truman's Point Four program, funding was increased in the form of loans from the U.S. Export-Import Bank. Infrastructure improvements included highway construction, water systems, new port facilities, airports, railroad expansion, agricultural development, fishing industry development, and other public works projects.

Aid to Ecuador and the rest of Latin America increased dramatically under President John F. Kennedy's Alliance for Progress, launched in 1961. Funding was expanded for infrastructure improvements, malaria eradication, rural electric projects, literacy campaigns, housing for the impoverished, public health clinics, and industrial and agricultural projects. The Peace Corps dispatched thousands of volunteers from 1961 until the present to work with Ecuador's poor. Under the direction of the U.S. Agency for International Development (USAID) agricultural, industrial, and public health projects have been sustained until the present.

COMMERCIAL RELATIONS

The most controversial commercial issue between the two nations involved fishing rights and led to the "tuna wars." In 1952 Ecuador, Chile, and Peru declared a two hundred–mile territorial limit from their coasts out to sea. This was rejected by the United States, which, like most countries, recognized a twelve-mile limit. Ecuador soon seized two fishing vessels, assessed heavy fines, and announced that all foreign ships that desired to fish in Ecuadorian waters would have to pay a fee. The United States refused to allow its commercial fishing fleets to pay the fee. Periodic seizures led to tension, and in 1963 the United States and the military government reached a secret gentlemen's agreement. The United States agreed not to press for a formal denouncement of the two hundred–mile limit, and Ecuador agreed not to enforce it. There was a four-year respite in seizures, but in 1971 Ecuador impounded fifty-one U.S. tuna trawlers. More than a hundred more incidents followed throughout the decade and into the 1980s. The U.S. response to the seizures was to withdraw aid. In 1982 the United Nations Convention on the Laws of the Sea established a twelve-mile territorial limit and a 188-mile exclusive economic zone. The convention provided a way for Ecuador and the United States to resolve the controversy, and when President Ronald Reagan accepted the accord, the tuna wars ended.

CURRENT ISSUES

When Dr. Rafael Correa, a U.S.-educated economist from Alianza País, a leftist political coalition, won the presidential runoff on November 26, 2006, relations with the United States began to sour. Correa campaigned on ending the neo-liberal economic policies of his predecessors, which the United States had favored. He also talked of no longer using the U.S. dollar as Ecuador's currency and became cozy with Hugo Chávez, the Venezuelan president and a major nemesis of the United States. In his first year in office, Correa consolidated power by calling a constituent assembly, which wrote a new constitution expanding his powers. This constitution was adopted in 2008, much to the chagrin of the United States. Correa suspended negotiations for a free trade agreement with the United States and announced that Ecuador would not renew the lease on the U.S. drug surveillance operation at the Manta Air Base, which expired in November 2009. Correa recently ordered a U.S. diplomat expelled from Ecuador, accusing him of meddling in the appointment of antismuggling police and suspending $340,000 in aid. While this downturn in the normally cooperative and friendly relationship between Ecuador and the United States is troubling, it is most likely temporary.

See also *Alfaro Delgado, Eloy; Alliance for Progress; Aranha, Oswaldo; Defense Site Agreements, World War II; Ecuador, U.S. Relations with; Ecuador-Peru Boundary Dispute; Guayaquil and Quito Railroad; Organization of American States (OAS); Pan American Airways Airport Development Program; Reagan, Ronald W.; Third Meeting of Consultation of the Ministers of Foreign Affairs of the American Republics, Rio de Janeiro, 1942; Tobar Donoso, Julio; Tuna War, 1963–1975 (Ecuador/United States)*

. . . . GEORGE M. LAUDERBAUGH

REFERENCES AND FURTHER READING

Drake, Paul W. *The Money Doctor of the Andes: The Kemmerer Missions, 1923–1933.* Durham, NC: Duke University Press, 1989.
Hey, Jeanne A. K. *Theories of Dependent Foreign Policy and the Case of Ecuador in the 1980s.* Athens: Ohio University Center for International Studies, 1995.
Lauderbaugh, George M. "The United States and Ecuador: Conflict and Convergence 1830–1946." Ph.D. diss., University of Alabama, 1997.
Pineo, Ronn. *Ecuador and the United States: Useful Strangers.* Athens: University of Georgia Press, 2007.
Zook, David H., Jr. *Zarumilla-Marañón: The Peru Ecuador Dispute.* New York: Bookman, 1964.

Ecuador-Peru Boundary Dispute

Many Latin American nations have been plagued by border controversies since achieving independence. Perhaps the most protracted of these was the dispute over Peru's common border with Ecuador, which resulted largely from the transfer of the territories from the Viceroyalty of New Granada to the Viceroyalty of Peru by the end of Spanish rule. The rugged terrain, which severely limited human habitation, also contributed to the problem.

PERUVIAN MILITARY BUILDUP LEADS TO CONFLICT

Both nations had disagreed over their common border since independence. In the 1880s, the two nations finally negotiated the García-Herran Treaty, but the Peruvian congress failed to ratify the agreement. During the opening decades of the twentieth century, both nations sent small detachments of troops to the disputed border area along the Napo River northwest of the river town of Iquitos. Even while Peru was having border differences with Colombia in the east, King Alfonso XIII of Spain still attempted to arbitrate the continuing border controversy between Ecuador and Peru. Peru's position hardened dramatically in the aftermath of the settlement of the Tacna-Arica border controversy with Chile in 1929, which resulted in a further loss of territory. Led by President Oscar Benavides, an army general who admired Mussolini, Peru rearmed during the lingering years of the Depression. The Peruvian military purchased arms and equipment from the United States, Italy, and Germany. The army grew from 8,000 men in 1933 to 25,000 in 1941. By comparison, Ecuador's army numbered only 4,000 and was not nearly as well equipped as Peru's.

Reflecting the type of rampant nationalism then common in Europe and Asia, the Peruvian army leadership was determined to resolve the border dispute on its own terms. The thinking was that in mid-1941, Washington would not be inclined to allow a military conflict among Pacific coast nations in South America to become protracted and to endanger the defenses of the Panama Canal. The Peruvian leaders were correct in this assumption.

When new border incidents in May 1941 were not calmed by multilateral talks held in Washington, Peruvian forces in the

Ecuador-Peru Boundary Dispute

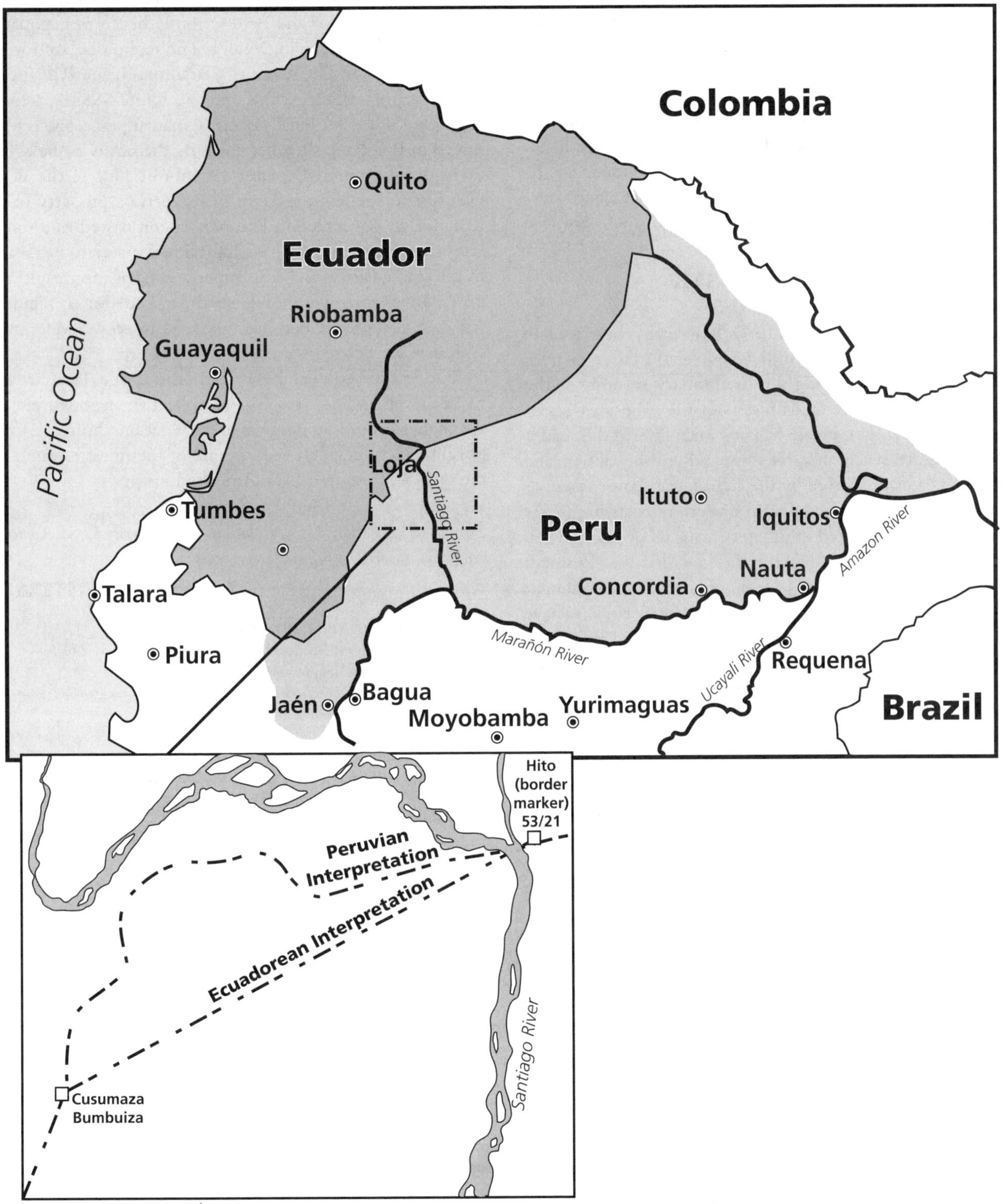

The map above shows the large border area over which Peru and Ecuador have disputed; much of the area is highly mountainous. The area of light shading encompasses the territories of Mainas and Jaén, while the dark shaded area shows the present-day boundary of Peru. The small box shows the area of later dispute, after the rest of the border was settled. Major fighting has erupted over the border in 1941 and in 1995, leading to U.S. involvement in peace agreements each time.

Zarumilla-Marañon region along the Ecuador frontier were placed on ready status. On July 5, fighting between Ecuadorian and Peruvian forces erupted in the border area as a prelude to a major Peruvian air, land, and sea campaign, which was initiated on July 22. Fighting occurred on the coast and in the eastern jungle, with the Peruvian army and air force employing paratroops and the navy sending its river craft and heavy cruisers to coastal and inland marine operations. Ecuadorian forces were simply outmanned and outgunned by the better-equipped and well-led Peruvians. Peruvian troops were occupying Ecuadorian territory when the Japanese bombed Pearl Harbor on December 7, 1941.

THE RIO PROTOCOL AND THE RENEWAL OF HOSTILITIES

The administration of Franklin D. Roosevelt thus became desperate to resolve the conflict and secure bases in both Ecuador and Peru. During the preliminary sessions of the Third Meeting of Foreign Ministers of the American States, held at Rio de Janeiro in late January 1942, Peru and Ecuador were pressed to reach an agreement and end hostilities. The settlement, later disavowed by the Ecuadorian government as coerced, called for the withdrawal of Peru's occupying forces as much as one hundred kilometers from its position when the fighting stopped. In the end, the so-called Rio Protocol left Ecuador claiming a net loss of 13,500 square kilometers. Feeling validated by the Rio Protocol, the Peruvians have claimed that the territorial dispute was at an end by reason of international law. Ecuador, on the other hand, consistently maintained that the Rio Protocol was unjust, being a product of higher World War II priorities by the guarantors, including Argentina, Brazil, Chile, and the United States.

After the war, the common border between Peru and Ecuador was mapped with the help of a U.S. Air Force and an expert geographical team headed by George McBride. The work of this team was laborious and dangerous, with some members of the team becoming casualties to the treacherous flying conditions in the Andes. By 1960, the entire border was marked, with the exception of a seventy-eight kilometers in the mountainous region known as the *Cordillera del Condor*. That year, the government of Ecuador disavowed the Rio Protocol, and the border issue acquired new connotations. Brief hostilities erupted in this area in 1981, but a major military confrontation involving some of the most sophisticated aircraft in the world drew international attention in January 1995.

Scaling down activities after their long counterinsurgency war with the Shining Path, the Peruvian armed forces were not prepared for a carefully planned show of force in the Alta Cenepa region. Using newly purchased shoulder-fired antiaircraft missiles to knock down Peruvian helicopters and some Soviet-made Peruvian attack aircraft, Ecuadorian ground troops held the high ground, using mortars and small arms fire effectively. In the air, Ecuadorian pilots flew Israeli-made Kifir fighters against the Peruvian Sukhoi-22 fighter bombers in some of the most technically advanced dog fights yet flown, at least until the 2003 Iraq war.

RESOLUTION

Perhaps motivated by economic considerations more than nationalism, Ecuador and Peru seriously began to negotiate a conclusion to the seemingly never-ending border controversy in the late 1990s. The original guarantors to the Rio Protocol, Argentina, Brazil, Chile, and the United States, actively supported the talks. Finally, an imaginative peace process was signed in Brasilia in October 1998. By the terms of the agreement, Peru granted Ecuador a symbolic plot in the Peruvian territory known as Tiwinza as a private property of the Ecuadorian government. The plot encompassed one square kilometer (247 acres). Two ecological parks were to be created in the immediate area. Most important, navigation rights and port concessions were established for Ecuador to facilitate Amazon commerce. Peru also pledged to seek development assistance for Ecuador's enterprises in the area.

The border conflict between Ecuador and Peru seemed to be never ending. Imaginative collective negotiations and the higher economic interests of both nations, however, made possible what is widely seen as one of the finest examples of diplomacy in modern Latin American history.

See also *Ecuador, U.S. Relations with; Peru, U.S. Relations with; Tacna-Arica Dispute, 1883–1929*

. . . . DANIEL M. MASTERSON

REFERENCES AND FURTHER READING

Cooper, Tom. "Peru vs Ecuador: Alto Cenepa War, 1995." *Air Combat Information Journal* (September 2003).

Masterson, Daniel M. *Fuerza armada y sociedad en el Peru modern, 1930–2000.* Lima, Peru: IEPE, 2001.

Scheina, Robert L. *Latin American Wars: The Age of the Professional Soldier.* Vol. 2. Washington, DC: Brassey's, 2003.

Simmons, Beth A. "Territorial Disputes and Their Resolution: The Case of Ecuador and Peru." *Peaceworks* (United States Institute of Peace), no. 27 (1999): 16–34.

Eighth International Conference of American States, Lima, 1938

The Eighth International Conference of American States, held in Lima, Peru, from December 9 to 27, 1938, was remarkable in at least two ways: (1) it was the shortest in the history of the Pan-American movement; (2) it negotiated not a single treaty or convention, although it approved 112 declarations, resolutions, and agreements, and paid repeated lip service to democratic principles. The flag-bedecked streets leading to the Peruvian legislative chamber, where the conference convened, included the flags and banners of more than the American republics; next to the Peruvian flag were those of Germany, Italy, and Japan, an odd occurrence at a solely Inter-American conference. But it did symbolize the extent of these nations' newfound economic presence in the western hemisphere since 1933.

U.S. economic strategies since 1933, including the reciprocal trade agreements, failed to provide significant gains for U.S.

products in Europe-oriented Latin American trade patterns. Moreover, the Good Neighbor policy, announced at the 1933 Montevideo Conference, delighted the Latin Americans, but it also hampered U.S. efforts to gain their cooperation regarding the rising war clouds in Asia and Europe, as seen at Buenos Aires in the 1936 conference.

THE LIMA CONFERENCE

By December 1938, German defiance of the 1919 Treaty of Versailles had reached a new high-water mark with the September Munich conference, which allowed Germany to annex Czechoslovakia's Sudetenland. Alarm bells went off in Washington, D.C., where the War and Navy Departments began considering various military measures—as eventually defined in the rainbow plans—that placed emphasis on securing the Panama Canal and Venezuelan oil supplies. In the meantime, U.S. policymakers sought to form Latin America into a bloc to confront Fascism. In many respects, the December 1938 Lima conference mirrored the 1936 Buenos Aires meeting, with the difference being that the level of urgency was considerably higher.

Secretary of State Cordell Hull headed the U.S. delegation to Lima. A handsome man, with flowing white hair and a top hat, Hull was the personification of a diplomat. His nemesis was José Cantilo, the chancellor or foreign minister of Argentina. Cantilo was not officially representing his country at the conference; officially, he was on a state visit to Peru. In fact, he was the leader of the Argentina delegation but decided to leave the conference ostensibly for health reasons; this meant all agreements had to be submitted to him at a distance. In this way, he could be both central to the negotiations and above them at the same time. This tactic did not endear him to the other delegates.

The goal of the U.S. delegation, the largest delegation that it had ever sent to a Pan-American meeting, was to organize Latin America against Fascist influence, both overt and covert, and to build the basis for alliances that would allow for coordinated military efforts. This later point was dropped by the United States early in the planning process since it was evident that it would never be adopted. Along with these goals, Hull wanted to advocate for liberalized multilateral trade agreements with most favored nation status, which would allow for much easier trade. Finally, Hull wanted to create a positive attitude in Latin America toward the United States.

The various countries of Latin America had their own goals. Latin American leaders agreed that U.S. intervention in the style practiced for decades in the Caribbean and Central America should be ended. They saw this conference as yet another opportunity to reaffirm the agreements against intervention reached in Montevideo five years earlier. As regards military concerns, some nations, including Venezuela and Brazil, where it was assumed military action was possible, were disposed to build stronger and closer relations with the United States. Other nations did not want to surrender any of their sovereignty and did not want to join a U.S.-led bloc. Argentina and Chile, in particular, talked in terms of working together as a hemisphere but, at the same time, maintaining sovereignty in their relationship with the world. This view was also held regarding economic relations. Nations with strong economic ties with Europe saw little benefit in giving up their established trading partnerships for new, uncertain ones with the United States.

At the meeting itself, the hemisphere was well represented with full delegations from most nations. Despite this, the Lima conference was notable for not producing a single treaty, only a declaration. The United States had hoped for more, but treaties require ratification. This often takes considerable time, and a declaration was more immediate.

A major change from the 1936 Buenos Aires meeting was that Germany and Italy, in particular, made considerable efforts in Lima to persuade the delegates not to abandon their trade pacts with Europe. They emphasized the checkered past of U.S.–Latin American relations, including the Mexican War, the seizure of the Panama Canal, and other U.S. incursions into Latin America. Germany and Italy might have also been behind the rumors of economic reprisals against any nation preferring the United States.

RESULTS OF THE LIMA CONFERENCE

As at previous meetings, the final declarations were fairly predictable. The conference adopted a statement about hemispheric unity and continental solidarity, emphasizing the historic relationship of the nations of the New World. The conference also concluded that each nation was sovereign and that this sovereignty should not be abridged.

In the area of confronting the fascist threat from Europe, the conference produced no binding alliance. Led by Argentina and Chile, the nations of Latin America could agree only on a statement that if the hemisphere was threatened, "they would coordinate their respective sovereign wills by means of consultation." The statement went on to indicate that "the governments of the American Republics will act independently in their individual capacities, recognizing fully their juridical equality as sovereign states." Finally, the declaration indicated that any of the foreign ministers could call a meeting to facilitate consultation about peace.

It is not strange then that economic and trade issues underlay many of the positions and decisions at this conference. U.S. economic proposals, although well meaning, tended to have a negative rather than a positive effect. In many respects, Argentina is a good example. That nation sold its beef and crops to Europe. The United States did not import Argentine beef—except for canned corned beef—contending Argentine beef could transfer hoof and mouth disease to U.S. cattle. This was particularly upsetting to Argentines, who considered their beef the finest in the world. In reality, the restriction on Argentine beef was to avoid competition with U.S. beef; it was enacted by U.S. senators—especially those from beef-producing states—during the Great Depression. The same was true for crops such as flax, where North Dakota farmers made sure that their representatives stopped Argentine flax.

Hull's solution was his earlier reciprocal trade proposals in which bilateral trade agreements would be generalized to the other Latin American states through "most favored nation" agreements. Many of the larger Latin American states had strong bilateral agreements with European states and were unwilling to jeopardize them. Germany, for example, had a series of agreements in Latin America based on blocked German currency, which required that foreign exchange from the sale of goods to a particular Latin American nation be used to buy only German products. These policies meant that trade was always equal, and there would be an even exchange that would not tax the foreign exchange of the receiving nation. Agreeing to the U.S. proposal would halt these trade arrangements at a time when the United States could not ensure that it would replace Europe as a needed customer for Latin American products.

Among many other issues discussed—such as trade issues governing postal regulations and sanitary conventions—was international interference in property seizures by Latin America states. When a Latin American state seized U.S. properties, the Latin America state in question argued that the resulting legal and economic questions should be adjudicated in its own courts and that foreign pressure was illegitimate. Because of its nitrate industry, Chile was particularly animated in this area. Ultimately, no final conclusion was taken, and the issue was sent off to a commission to examine the question.

To many observers, the Eighth International Conference of American States was a success. The delegates discussed the issues and produced a declaration that could be used as the basis for further meeting. The goal of the United States—to unify Latin America and to blunt fascist influence—was not achieved, but realistically, it had never had much chance of success. The basic issues were joined, however, and this conference would ultimately serve well as the predicate for future meetings.

See also *Good Neighbor Policy; Inter-American Conference for the Maintenance of Peace, Buenos Aires, 1936; Seventh International Conference of American States, Montevideo, 1933*

. . . . W. MICHAEL WEIS

REFERENCES AND FURTHER READING

Bemis, Samuel Flagg. *The Latin American Policy of the United States: An Historical Interpretation.* New York: Harcourt, Brace and World, 1943.

Haglund, David G. *Latin America and the Transformation of U.S. Strategic Thought, 1936–1940.* Albuquerque: University of New Mexico Press, 1984.

Inman, Samuel Guy. "The Lima Conference and the Totalitarian Issue." *Annals of the American Academy of Political and Social Science* 204 (July 1939): 1–14.

Mecham, J. Lloyd. *The United States and Inter-American Security, 1889–1960.* Austin: University of Texas Press, 1961.

Steward, Dick. *Trade and Hemisphere: The Good Neighbor Policy and Reciprocal Trade.* Columbia: University of Missouri Press, 1975.

Varg, Paul A. "The Economic Side of the Good Neighbor Policy: The Reciprocal Trade Program and South America." *Pacific Historical Review* 45 (February 1976): 47–71.

Eisenhower, Dwight D.

Dwight D. Eisenhower (1890–1969), as a boy in Abilene, Kansas, dreamt about living in Argentina as a gaucho. As candidate for president, he criticized President Harry Truman's Latin American policy for being a bad neighbor by "drift and neglect" and pledged more attention to the region's problems. As one of the greatest generals in U.S. history, one would have expected him to have a clear understanding of the region's strategic importance and the will to improve hemispheric relations. Unfortunately, this was not the case. U.S.–Latin American relations in the Eisenhower years were marked by adherence to Cold War dogma and private enterprise formulas, by missed opportunities, and by a penchant for crafting policies addressing secondary concerns. Thus, the many good things the Eisenhower administration did were often a case of too little, too late, and relations were actually much worse at the end of his term than in the beginning.

EMPHASIS ON FREE MARKET AND ANTICOMMUNISM

For the most part, the top foreign policymakers in the Eisenhower administration did not consider Latin America to be a priority. Preoccupied with Korea, Iran, Vietnam, strengthening NATO, and integrating Germany and Japan into the Western alliance, they had little time or money left for Inter-American concerns. Lower level officials and confidants, the most notable being the president's brother, Milton, handled hemispheric policy. Although he pledged to return to Franklin D. Roosevelt's Good Neighbor policy, Eisenhower was less tolerant of economic nationalism, government-owned corporations, and economic assistance than FDR, while being more supportive of military assistance, dictatorship, and interference or intervention.

These attitudes could be seen clearly in the biggest events of Eisenhower's first term: the Bolivian Revolution, the Tenth Inter-American Conference held in Caracas, Venezuela, in March 1954, and the overthrow of Jacobo Arbenz Guzmán in Guatemala in June 1954. In Bolivia, once it was determined that the revolutionaries had no ties with Moscow, Eisenhower proved largely indifferent to the course of the conflict. Indeed, Latin leaders who supported the broad outlines of U.S. policy often received enormous latitude to do whatever they wanted. At Caracas, the Eisenhower administration dashed the hopes of Latin Americans who had wanted the conference to address economic concerns and instead focused attention on the Cold War. The resulting Declaration of Caracas, which stated that communism was unacceptable in the western hemisphere, paved the way for the Central Intelligence Agency's (CIA's) subsequent overthrow of Arbenz. Although a wealthy landowner and capitalist, in 1952, Arbenz had supported a land reform act that expropriated several hundred thousand acres of land owned by the United Fruit Company. The Truman administration had flatly refused to intervene in the situation, but United Fruit had many close ties to the Republicans, including Secretary of State John Foster Dulles and CIA Director Allen Dulles. (The Dulles brothers were partners at Sullivan and Cromwell law firm, which represented United Fruit.) Unable to change the law, Eisenhower approved plans to remove Arbenz, who was replaced by the U.S.-supported

Carlos Castillo Armas. For the remainder of his term, Eisenhower worked diligently to enable the new regime to succeed, but to no avail.

Eisenhower claimed that the reason he wished to rely almost exclusively on trade and private U.S. corporate investment to meet Latin American development needs was his wish to make the region full partners and not merely sycophants. Unfortunately, opportunities for U.S. capital were global, and with the tax breaks demanded and the profits remitted back to U.S. stockholders, U.S. corporations proved inadequate to meet Latin American development needs or demand. Moreover, as the decade progressed, the prices Latin Americans received for their agricultural and mineral commodities decreased, while the price of manufactured imports increased, creating severe balance of payment difficulties throughout the hemisphere. This, in turn, fed discontent, anti-Americanism, and the feeling of neglect.

THE ACT OF BOGOTÁ AND THE RISE OF CASTRO

These feelings came to the forefront in early 1958 as Vice President Richard Nixon embarked on a "goodwill proof" tour. At each stop, Nixon confronted progressively angry crowds or embraced repressive dictators. When the tour reached its final destination, Caracas, Venezuela, a mob stormed the motorcade and nearly killed Nixon. While U.S. sources were quick to blame the events on communists, the fiasco prompted a reassessment in U.S. policy. Previously, Eisenhower had been unwilling to fund financial agreements or social projects that did not increase foreign exchange. After the Nixon trip, Eisenhower accepted the proposal of Brazil's Juscelino Kubitschek to create a high-level Operation Pan America and began to reverse previous opposition to join in commodity agreements, an Inter-American development bank, and a Latin American Free Trade Association. But even these modifications did not lead to an increase in U.S. economic aid. These efforts and the president's change of direction reached their apex in July 1960, when Eisenhower accepted the Act of Bogotá, which created the Social Progress Trust Fund, a forerunner to the Alliance for Progress. The Social Progress Trust Fund allowed for economic assistance for things that did not create additional foreign exchange but were deemed essential for the well-being of the region, such as hospitals, schools, and public housing.

By this time, the Cold War had come to the Americas. Throughout 1957 and 1958, Eisenhower officials had tried to gauge the likelihood of success of the insurgency launched against the Fulgencio Batista regime by Fidel Castro's July 26 Movement, as well as to determine the best way to influence the rebels. Knowing that Moscow did not back the insurgents, Eisenhower finally had cut aid to Batista in mid-1958, but he had been slow to realize the determination of the Cuban Revolution to sever ties to the United States and had reacted clumsily to Castro's radical restructuring of society. It is difficult not to come to the conclusion that Castro outsmarted Eisenhower. Although Eisenhower had avoided Castro when the latter visited the United States in 1959, he sent Nixon to gauge Castro's intentions. Nixon had returned uncertain about whether to offer carrots or sticks or whether Castro was a communist. Throughout 1959 and 1960, a dialectic of hostility emerged that played into Castro's hands, and traditional U.S. policies, such as demanding prompt compensation of seized property and cutting Cuba's sugar quota, all failed. In his final year in office, Eisenhower approved the training of Cuban dissidents, an action that would eventually result in the Bay of Pigs fiasco, and by the time he left office, the United States and Cuba had severed relations.

At the end of his second term in 1961, Eisenhower had traveled more miles and visited more countries than any sitting president in U.S. history. It is revealing that his first major trip to South America came in 1960, his last full year in office. While he presented his regional policy as the "good partner," Latin America remained off the main screen, and thus its problems and resentments toward the United States were allowed to fester.

See also *Bolivian Revolution, 1952–1956, U.S. Policy toward; Bonsal, Philip W.; Castro Ruz, Fidel; Cuban Revolution, 1956–1959, U.S. Policy toward; Eisenhower-Remón Treaty, 1955; First Meeting of American Presidents, Panama, 1956; Guatemala, U.S. Invasion of, 1954; Inter-American Development Bank (IADB); Kubitschek de Oliveira, Juscelino; Latin American Free Trade Association (LAFTA); Nixon, Richard M.; Tenth International Conference of American States, Caracas, 1954*

. . . . W. MICHAEL WEIS

REFERENCES AND FURTHER READING

Coleman, Bradley Lynn. *Colombia and the United States: The Making of an Inter-American Alliance, 1939–1960.* Kent, OH: Kent State University Press, 2008.

Gambone, Michael D. *Eisenhower, Somoza, and the Cold War in Nicaragua, 1953–1961.* Westport, CT: Praeger, 1997.

Immerman, Richard H. *The CIA in Guatemala: The Foreign Policy of Intervention.* Austin: University of Texas Press, 1982.

Paterson, Thomas G. *Contesting Castro: The United States and the Triumph of the Cuban Revolution.* New York: Oxford University Press, 1994.

Rabe, Stephen G. *Eisenhower and Latin America: The Foreign Policy of Anticommunism.* Chapel Hill: University of North Carolina Press, 1988.

Siekmeier, James F. *Aid, Nationalism and Inter-American Relations: Guatemala, Bolivia, and the United States, 1945–1961.* Lewiston, NY: Edwin Mellen Press, 1999.

Streeter, Stephen M. *Managing the Counterrevolution: The United States and Guatemala, 1954–1961.* Athens: Ohio University Press, 2000.

Weis, W. Michael. *Cold Warriors and Coups d'Etat: Brazilian-American Relations, 1945–1964.* Albuquerque: University of New Mexico Press, 1993.

Zahniser, Marvin R., and W. Michael Weis. "A Diplomatic Pearl Harbor? Richard Nixon's Goodwill Mission to Latin America in 1958." *Diplomatic History* 13, no. 2 (Spring 1989): 163–190.

Eisenhower, Milton

Milton Stover Eisenhower was brother to President Dwight D. Eisenhower. Although he never held an official Cabinet post, Dr. Eisenhower was a close and influential confidant and adviser to the president. A native of Abilene, Kansas, Eisenhower graduated from Kansas State University and served as vice consul in Edinburgh, Scotland. He began his domestic political career as director of information at the Department of Agriculture in 1928, where he remained until 1941. During World War II, he was an architect of the Office of War Information and the relocation of Japanese Americans on the West Coast to internment camps. While occupying these political posts, Dr. Eisenhower also served as president of Kansas State, then Pennsylvania State, and finally Johns Hopkins University.

FACT-FINDING MISSION

On two occasions, Dr. Eisenhower undertook high-profile diplomatic missions to Latin America for the Eisenhower administration. The first was a trip to ten South American nations in the summer of 1953, in which Dr. Eisenhower was sent as a special envoy on a "fact finding mission," designed to assuage fears that the United States was neglecting Latin American concerns over economic development and social progress and to promote hemispheric cooperation. The visit also put the administration's mark on the region. The Eisenhower campaign had characterized Latin America policy under Truman as the "poor neighbor policy." During the visit, Eisenhower met with Latin American leaders, who were often critical of the United States and insistent on the need for further aid.

His contemporaries and the president himself thought of Milton Eisenhower as a more liberal-minded counterpoint to those in the Republican Party and Eisenhower's Cabinet, like Vice President Richard Nixon or Secretary of the Treasury George Humphrey, who possessed stronger conservative or anticommunist reputations. In *The Wine Is Bitter,* Dr. Eisenhower wrote that Latin American reformers were sometimes mistakenly or maliciously labeled communist by business and political leaders and that economic and political reform was necessary, given the alternative of regional dictatorships and oligarchies. He believed these oligarchic hierarchies to be a form of feudalism, and as such, they were closer to communism than Latin American reformers, who appeared dangerously leftist to some Americans. Given his reputation and opinions, Dr. Eisenhower was a somewhat more conciliatory figure to send to Latin America, as he himself noted when (fruitlessly) opposing the choice of Humphrey to represent the United States at the November 1954 Rio Conference on economic issues.

Eisenhower filed his report on the findings of his South American mission in November 1953, concluding that there was a need for greater regional cooperation in economic, diplomatic, and military terms. The report advocated the establishment of an Inter-American bank, which eventually came to fruition at the close of the decade. Central to the development of Latin America in Eisenhower's view was greater investment by private capital, but his proposal also included programs of direct aid and technical assistance designed to improve Latin American agriculture, health, and education. Some scholars, like Stanley Hilton and Stephen Rabe, feel that the exhortations to self-help and private enterprise were the dominant themes of the report and Eisenhower's general thinking. Dr. Eisenhower did find it deeply worrying that Latin Americans were unwilling to provide much of the money for development themselves through higher taxes. Others, like Fredrick Pike, view Eisenhower's call for increased aid and assistance to Latin American nations as anticipating both the establishment of the Alliance for Progress under the Kennedy administration and the increase of direct governmental assistance to Latin America in the later years of the Eisenhower administration.

Eisenhower chose Bolivia in particular as in need of considerable aid. Although the decision to provide economic and moral support to Bolivia had been formulated before his June 1953 visit, Eisenhower's appearance there can be viewed, according to Stephen Zunes, as a turning point in U.S. Bolivia policy. The personal relationships forged by Dr. Eisenhower contributed to a significant program of aid that, by the late 1950s, was underwriting around a third of the Bolivian budget. Per capita assistance to Bolivia under President Eisenhower was rivaled by only two Latin American recipient nations: Guatemala and Haiti.

SECOND VISIT TO LATIN AMERICA

After the violence and anger engendered by the visit of Vice President Nixon to the region in 1958, Dr. Eisenhower's second Latin American visit was delayed for fear of an embarrassing repeat of events. When Dr. Eisenhower's trip to Central America did take place, he was keen to demonstrate how welcoming and nonconfrontational the crowds were. The Nixon visit ultimately served to give added impetus to Dr. Eisenhower's recommendations for greater economic aid and investment in Latin America and for more attention to its underlying social tensions. Eisenhower was also selected to sit on the Inter-American Committee of Presidential Representatives, giving further voice to his policy ideas. However, many of his ideas were not adopted, such as flying the Panamanian flag in the Canal Zone (this would only happen after a major incident in 1959) or the payment of equal wages for U.S. and Panamanian workers by the Panama Canal Company.

Eisenhower continued to be considered a Latin American expert by U.S. policymakers in the 1960s, and officials in the subsequent Kennedy and Johnson administrations occasionally consulted him. He was notably involved in the initial fallout from the Bay of Pigs invasion and was drafted by President Kennedy into the Tractors for Freedom Committee, a body designed to raise privately the funds necessary to buy tractors in exchange for the release of the 1,214 captured militants who had attempted Fidel Castro's overthrow on April 17, 1961. The effort ultimately broke down: Castro proved unwilling to part with his powerful bargaining chip and source of domestic political capital. The Kennedy administration was also compelled to distance itself from the committee due to increased domestic opposition to the committee's work on constitutional and moral grounds.

Dr. Eisenhower's influence on the administration and his brother the president was significant and helped to contribute toward wider aid to Latin America and greater attention to regional economic and social problems. However, his influence remains somewhat overlooked and unexciting when contrasted with the significant turmoil caused by the Nixon visit and the rise of leftist nationalism in Cuba at the decade's close.

See also *Alliance for Progress; Bay of Pigs Invasion, 1961; Bolivia, U.S. Relations with; Eisenhower, Dwight D.; Inter-American Development Bank (IADB); Kubitschek de Oliveira, Juscelino; Nixon, Richard M.; Panama Canal, Administration of; U.S. Economic Investments in Latin America*

. . . . OLIVER MURPHEY

REFERENCES AND FURTHER READING

Eisenhower, Milton S. *The Wine Is Bitter: The United States and Latin America.* Garden City, NY: Doubleday, 1963.

Hilton, Stanley E. "The United States, Brazil, and the Cold War, 1945–1960: End of the Special Relationship." *Journal of American History* 68, no. 3 (December 1981): 599–624.

Melady, Thomas Patrick. "A Review of Inter-American Economic Relations." *The Americas* 12, no. 3 (January 1956): 285–298.

Pike, Fredrick B. "Corporatism and Latin American-United States Relations." *Review of Politics* 36, no. 1 (January 1974): 132–170.

Rabe, Stephen G. *Eisenhower and Latin America: The Foreign Policy of Anticommunism.* Chapel Hill: University of North Carolina Press, 1988.

Zunes, Stephen. "The United States and Bolivia: The Taming of a Revolution, 1952–1957." *Latin American Perspectives* 28, no. 5 (September 2001): 33–49.

Eisenhower-Remón Treaty, 1955

The Eisenhower-Remón Treaty, signed in 1955, modified U.S.-Panamanian relations, particularly regarding the U.S.-controlled Canal Zone. Most Panamanians clearly disliked the Hay–Bunau-Varilla Treaty (1903), which had been only slightly modified by the Hull-Alfaro Treaty (1936). Panama's José Antonio Remón (President 1952–1955) demanded negotiations, and President Eisenhower acquiesced to avoid violence.

The Eisenhower-Remón Treaty was implemented early in 1957. U.S. authorities closed Canal Zone commissaries to Panamanian citizens, even those who worked for the Panama Canal Company. The ban was an advantage to Panama's merchants but a burden to impoverished Panamanian consumers, who would have to pay higher prices to Panamanian merchants. The Panama Canal Company estimated the treaty would deprive commissaries of half their business.

The treaty also permitted Panamanian inspectors to board ships of Panamanian registry, many of them U.S.-owned, while they were in Canal Zone waters, to investigate compliance with Panamanian maritime and labor laws. However, such boardings were to be only for purposes of investigation, not of enforcement, and they were not to interfere with the expeditious transit of any such vessel through the canal. Canal Zone authorities would determine the conditions of such inspections and could even prevent them if they saw fit.

The very terms of the Eisenhower-Remón Treaty illustrate the U.S. desire for Panamanian goodwill, along with U.S. determination to retain control of the Canal Zone. To enrich the Panamanian treasury, the United States would increase its annual rental payment for the Canal Zone from $430,000 to $1,930,000 and would annul the clause in the Hay–Bunau-Varilla Treaty that forbade the Panamanian government from levying an income tax on its own citizens if they worked for the Panama Canal Company. As a goodwill gesture, the U.S. government would cancel its provision forbidding Panama to build additional railroads or highways across its territory. At the same time, the Republic of Panama had to promise that no party from a third country could build a coast-to-coast railroad or highway without U.S. permission. The U.S. government also renounced its right to prescribe and enforce health standards within Panama City and Colón, and it agreed to transfer large sections of Cristóbal (in the Canal Zone) to Colón.

The Republic of Panama also made concessions. It would continue to allow a U.S. military base on its territory at Río Hato for at least fifteen years. Members of the U.S. armed forces would be able to travel without restriction between Río Hato and the Canal Zone, and they would not have to pay any Panamanian taxes. Moreover, officials of the Republic of Panama would renounce their right, under Article XIX of the Hay–Bunau-Varilla Treaty, to free rides on the Panama Railroad.

U.S. Ambassador to Panama Selden Chapin and Panamanian Foreign Minister Octavio Fabrega also signed a Memorandum of Understandings. In the memorandum, the U.S. government promised to seek legislation guaranteeing Panamanian workers equal pay for equal work with U.S. workers. At the same time, the U.S. government would grant Panamanians equal access to all positions in the Canal Zone whenever lack of qualifications or reasons of security did not necessitate a U.S. worker. The Eisenhower administration would ask Congress to transfer much military and other U.S. government–owned property located on Panamanian soil to the Republic of Panama and to withdraw the Panama Railroad entirely out of Panama City and Colón and into the Canal Zone. Former railroad property in Panama would become the property of the Panamanian government.

Panamanian newspapers showed differing degrees of approval. *Estrella de Panamá* praised anyone who had anything to do with the Eisenhower-Remón Treaty. In its issue of January 25, 1955, the newspaper said the treaty demonstrated "the high motives which guide [U.S.] relations with all other countries." *Panamá América* was more restrained. That same day, it editorialized that the new treaty was an improvement but that its terms "have not satisfied all the just aspirations of Panama." The U.S. Senate approved the treaty 72 to 14, despite objections from shippers, who feared higher tolls, and Canal Zone residents, who feared Panamanians would take their jobs.

Panamá América came closer than *Estrella de Panamá* in reflecting Panamanian opinion. Within three years, Ernesto de la Guardia Navarro (President 1956–1960) declared that he considered the treaty inadequate. Repeated statements of U.S. government officials indicate that despite the memorandum, Panamanians were not receiving the same pay as U.S. workers for the same jobs. Dissatisfaction with the Eisenhower-Remón

Treaty—combined with Egyptian success in taking control of the Suez Canal and its environs—paved the way for the riots that erupted on January 9, 1964.

See also *Dulles, John Foster; Eisenhower, Dwight D.; Hay–Bunau-Varilla Treaty, 1903; Hull-Alfaro Treaty, 1936; Remón Cantera, José A.*

. . . . GRAEME S. MOUNT

REFERENCES AND FURTHER READING

Ambrose, Stephen. *Eisenhower, the President.* New York: Simon and Schuster, 1984.

Finer, Herman. *Dulles over Suez: The Theory and Practice of His Diplomacy.* London: Heinemann, 1964.

King, Thelma. *El problems de la soberanía en las relaciones entre Panamá y los Estados Unidos.* Panama City, 1964.

LaFeber, Walter. *The Panama Canal: The Crisis in Historical Perspective.* Oxford, UK: Oxford University Press, 1979.

Major, John. *Prize Possession: The United States and the Panama Canal, 1903–1979.* Cambridge, UK: Cambridge University Press, 1993.

El Salvador, U.S. Relations with

A 1524 expedition led by Pedro de Alvarado began Spain's conquest of Cuscatlan, a land inhabited by Pipil Indians descendant from the Aztecs. Named El Salvador, "The Savior" in English, the colony, along with other provinces in Central America, declared its independence from Spain in 1821, achieving it without difficulty. However, these provinces immediately found themselves part of Mexico. El Salvador, the smallest of the five, soon resisted and severed its ties with Mexico. Its proximity to the United States has resulted in close economic ties and typically friendly diplomatic relations.

EARLY YEARS

In 1823, the United Provinces of Central America was formed under Manuel Jose Arce, with the capital located in San Salvador. With the dissolution of the federation in 1838, El Salvador initially sought to become part of the United States. General Francisco Morazon, the leader of his country and army for many years, was elected president in 1839. Instability and turbulence set in over the next sixty-seven years as domestic uprisings, frequent revolutions, and disputes with Guatemala and Honduras bedeviled the young nation.

Legal decrees in the 1880s prohibited Native American communities in El Salvador from collective ownership of the land, paving the way for eventual control by a small aristocracy, *las coatorce*, the fourteen families, which would later expand in size and number. Coffee became the major export crop.

As commercial ties deepened between El Salvador and the United States in the early years of the twentieth century, the Americans opened a consulate in the port city of Acajutla. A peace treaty between El Salvador and Guatemala was signed aboard the USS *Marblehead* in 1906 as President Theodore Roosevelt sought to halt their war from spreading throughout the region. This led to relative stability for the next twenty-five years, as the Meléndez clan became the political kingmakers. The Meléndez family backed Pio Romero Bosque in the 1927 presidential election to succeed Alfonso Quiñonez.

Romero Bosque, however, proved to be independent of the Meléndez machine, preferring to conduct the political affairs of the country himself. Romero Bosque ended the martial law imposed years earlier and relaxed press restrictions. In the surprisingly free election of 1931, Arturo Araujo of the Salvadoran Labor Party was elected president. But the Depression hit El Salvador hard, and discontent bubbled to the surface. By permitting the Salvadoran Communist Party to run in the December 1931 municipal elections, Araujo alarmed the armed forces. The communists had already flexed their muscles in 1930 at a May Day demonstration in downtown San Salvador that drew 80,000 people. But, perhaps the biggest factor in spurring the armed forces to move against the president was Araujo's inability to pay the military during the economic crisis.

MILITARY RULE

A December 2, 1931, army coup turned power over to Vice President Maximiliano Hernández Martínez, a move that ushered in military rule as a substitute for oligarchy rule. A January 1932 revolt in northwestern El Salvador, led by dedicated communist Faribundo Martí, resulted in the deaths of a number of landlords. President Martínez responded with a fury. The United States, under the provisions of a 1923 Central American treaty designed to discourage coups, did not recognize the Martínez government, offered to intervene to restore political stability. Martínez rejected the offer, and thousands were killed in the government counterattack (*La Matanza*), a disproportionate number of them Indians.

Organized communism in El Salvador was virtually destroyed. The surviving remnants went underground or to Mexican exile, not to emerge for years. The United States, following the lead of other Central American nations, finally recognized Martínez in January 1934.

As World War II approached, the totalitarian Martínez threw his lot in with the United States, the dominant trading partner, against the Axis powers, which included Germany, El Salvador's second-leading trade partner. The German consul, a former head of El Salvador's national mortgage bank, was expelled in 1940. The United States then extended Lend-Lease assistance to El Salvador.

During World War II, Salvadoran diplomats José Castellanos and George Mantello in Geneva issued nationality certificates (believed subject to less scrutiny than passports) to European Jews. The certificates were smuggled by other diplomats, primarily into Hungary, where they were filled out with the individual's personal information. The consulate acted initially without authority from the Salvadoran government, and the United States pressed El Salvador to honor the actions. In July 1944, Foreign Minister Julio Enrique entered into a bilateral agreement with Switzerland whereby the Swiss legation in Budapest would request full protection for the new Salvadoran citizens. El Salvador was the only nation to undertake such actions, and an estimated 30,000 European Jews were saved.

Meanwhile, Martínez's popularity began to seriously erode. He survived an April 1944 coup by Colonel Tito Tomás Calvo, but popular discontent was so great that Martínez stepped down in early May.

Following Martínez's departure, Andres Menéndez, a general with a reputation for honesty, formed a provisional government. As scheduled elections loomed, Menéndez showed no signs of rigging them in favor of the army's candidate against the civilian opposition; a military faction led by the reactionary chief of police, Colonel Osmin Aguirre, removed Menéndez from office in October 1944.

Aguirre's autocratic regime was unpopular but short. After repulsing an ill-conceived uprising led by liberal opposition leader Dr. Arturo Romero, the Aguirre regime allowed tightly controlled elections once again to become the norm. Thus, General Salvador Castañeda's general unpopularity was offset by the fact he was the official and sole candidate in the presidential election of January 1945.

Castañeda, considered a weak president and possessing low prestige, nevertheless sought to cancel 1949 elections that featured five candidates (including former President Aguirre and General Peña Trejo, who was financed by Nicaraguan dictator Anastasio Somoza and was reputedly so desperate for the job that he would seize the presidency by force if he had only ten supporters) and remain in power through *continuismo*. Instead, Castañeda did not even finish his term as he was ousted and jailed in December 1948 by a group of young officers led by Colonel Manuel Cordova and Major Oscar Osorio, an ambitious officer who had spent the better part of the previous four years bouncing between El Salvador and exile. The Castañeda regime was considered to be so corrupt that there was fear the freezing of assets of its government officials would have a terrible effect on the economic life of the nation.

The new junta was somewhat centrist, and Osorio formed a new political party, the Revolutionary Party of Democratic Union (PRUD), running for president in the next scheduled election. Despite a lackluster campaign where he focused on visiting military installations to ensure military support rather than making speeches to the people, Osorio was elected president in 1950. Under Osorio's rule, a new stability was achieved in Salvadoran life as public health programs, social security, and women's suffrage were provided. Osorio advocated reforms without threatening the basic capitalist structure of the country.

With only the most token opposition, Osorio's handpicked successor, José Maria Lemus, was elected president in 1956. The two soon had a falling out, however, as Lemus proved to be too independent for the former president, seeking to "cut the Gordian knot" with his predecessor and selecting his cabinet with little or no consultation with Osorio or PRUD. The Eisenhower administration considered Lemus to be "somewhat of a prima donna," but someone with a pro-U.S. orientation who could be counted on "to eliminate some of the graft of the Osorio administration" (U.S. Department of State, 1955–1957, p. 42). The Lemus administration ran into trouble, however, when coffee prices bottomed out in 1958 and El Salvador's budget deficit ballooned.

As part of its effort to strengthen its relations with Latin America, the United States invited Lemus for an official visit in March 1959. Washington saw El Salvador as a "happy contrast" to the dictatorships and political instability in other nations in the hemisphere. Lemus and President Dwight D. Eisenhower discussed the coffee situation, pending Central American economic integration, and proposals to establish an Inter-American Development Bank. Lemus also addressed a joint session of Congress and was feted with a ticker-tape parade in New York City.

Further difficulties ensued for Lemus following Fidel Castro's rise to power in Cuba in 1959. *Fidelismo* propagated by Cuban agents in association with domestic communist groups began to spread like wildfire, especially among university students. Lemus's "inept" efforts to treat the disorder—initially attempted to avoid using repressive measures, then lumping of all his opposition as communistic (National Archives and Records Administration, 1960a)—combined with his political isolation, left him vulnerable to the bloodless coup that took place on October 26, 1960.

POLITICAL GROWING PAINS

The coup, masterminded by Osorio, ushered in a left-of-center civilian-military junta. The United Sates recognized the new junta almost six weeks later "so that we would be in a position to attempt to influence the course of this government in every way possible and attempt to guide it towards a basically pro-Western orientation while bringing about badly needed social evolution" (National Archives and Records Administration, 1960b).

Osorio's plan to dominate the junta behind the scenes fell apart, however. A January 1961 coup by conservative military officers installed a junta that soon broke relations with the communist regime in Cuba.

A new political vehicle was formed for the government, the National Conciliation Party (PCN), and Julio Rivera became president. Rivera was one of President John F. Kennedy's regional favorites as the Salvadoran executive asked for relatively little from Kennedy's new aid program, the Alliance for Progress. The PCN, dominated by senior army officers with faithful support from the rural poor, loomed large in Salvadoran political life for the next eighteen years, winning presidential elections by whatever means were necessary.

In 1960 El Salvador helped form the Central American Common Market. As El Salvador's export-driven economy began to take off, El Salvador's small but emerging middle class began to seek a greater voice in government. José Napoleón Duarte Fuentes's liberal but anticommunist Christian Democratic Party (PDC) began to make gains, with Duarte being elected mayor of San Salvador in 1964.

The 1969 Soccer War erupted following the expulsion of some 25,000 Salvadoran immigrants from less populated Honduras. A border dispute had been simmering for two years. Riots in Honduras following a soccer match between the two countries frightened the Salvadorans living there, and the Salvadoran army invaded. The fighting lasted one hundred hours before its termination was mediated by ammunition and fuel shortages as well as the diplomatic efforts of the Organization of American States (OAS).

The Christian Democratic idea of peaceful reform through electoral means was severely tested in 1972 when its candidate for president, Duarte, was initially declared the winner only to come up short in a recount sponsored by the PCN-led government he was seeking to replace. The beneficiary of the creative count was Colonel Arturo Molina. A coup attempt was immediately launched by Colonel Benjamín Mejía and belatedly supported by Duarte. President Fidel Sánchez was arrested, but the uprising ended in failure as reinforcements poured in to assist pro-government forces in turning the tide.

The 1972 election results convinced even moderate leftists that democratic elections were not a viable path in El Salvador. Violence and kidnappings thus became a regular staple in the country. Allegations of fraud surfaced in the February 1977 presidential elections, in which the Christian Democrats ran retired Colonel Ernesto Claramount. The beneficiary this time was General Carlos Humberto Romero, who was declared the winner by a 2 to 1 margin. Claramount and his supporters staged a large demonstration in the capital. ORDEN, a government-sponsored *campesino* paramilitary organization, and other security forces attacked the protesters, leaving an estimated two hundred dead. It was the spark that began to set El Salvador ablaze. Two months later, the Marxist-inspired Faribundo Marti Popular Liberation Front (FMLN) kidnapped and killed Foreign Minister Mauricio Borgonono. A group called the White Warriors responded by killing a priest and threatened to kill fifty more Roman Catholic clergy unless they left the country. In July 1977, the Carter administration began restricting arms sales to El Salvador; in that same month, former President Aguirre was shot and killed in front of his home.

Under pressure from the Carter administration, Romero's last budget devoted a greater portion to education and health (34 percent) than any other Latin American country except Costa Rica. But, as the country continued its slide into chaos, Romero was ousted in October 1979 in a bloodless coup that Washington welcomed.

The left-of-center junta that replaced Romero soon fell apart as its left-wing members split and went into armed opposition. Enrique Álvarez, a cabinet minister in the junta, headed the Democratic Revolutionary Front. Álvarez accused the new, more moderate junta of having support only from the United States, a statement that found ready support from the Soviet Union, Cuba, and a delegation headed by Rep. Robert Drinan (D-MA), who called for an end to American military aid. In November 1980, security forces assassinated Álvarez and five associates.

More an article of faith than of reason, as grower cooperatives (as opposed to marketing cooperatives) had a poor economic track record, land reform in El Salvador was pushed by the Carter administration (and continued under Reagan with a shove from Congress, which threatened to hold up military aid without it). Although the urban-based Christian Democrats are most associated with the concept of land reform, the idea actually had its roots under Martínez in the immediate post-*Matanza* aftermath. The PCN, through President Fidel Sánchez and the Assembly, began picking up the mantle in the early 1970s, fixing maximum limits on land holdings and allowing expropriation. However, the largest landholders then divided their properties into smaller lots.

CIVIL WAR

Salvadoran security forces in 1980 engaged in ruthless counterterrorism measures, which included the killings of four American churchwomen. This drew criticism from U.S. Ambassador Robert White, appointed to be more a proconsul than a diplomat. White saw such tactics as counterproductive, but Salvadorans saw that the rebel support network in San Salvador was literally dying.

Attempting to present the incoming Reagan administration with a *fait accompli*, the FMLN launched a final offensive in January 1981. The lame-duck Carter administration reversed course and rushed military aid, but its effect was mostly psychological as the Salvadoran military beat back the rebels who, although heavily aided by the communist world, lacked the logistical network to fully use their arms cache. The guerrillas retreated into the countryside to regroup and continue the war there.

Although the Christian Democrats won the largest share of votes in the 1982 constituent assembly elections, they failed to gain a majority, and ARENA, led by the right-wing extremist coup-plotter, Roberto d'Aubuisson Arrieta, cobbled together a coalition with other right-wing parties. The real losers were the guerrillas, who were defeated in elections in which they did not participate because 83 percent of Salvadorans braved their threats to vote. U.S. pressure, however, prevented d'Aubuisson from assuming the provisional presidency. Instead, Álvaro Magana, an apolitical economist, took the post.

During a December 1983 visit to El Salvador, Vice President George H. W. Bush gave an ultimatum to Salvadorans that extrajudicial killings by security forces had to be curbed in return for continued aid. The human rights situation in El Salvador improved significantly.

Following Duarte's election to the presidency in 1984, El Salvador's military fortunes improved. Following exhortations from U.S. military advisers, Salvadorans started getting "rid of the dead wood" in the military theater. Search-and-destroy tactics urged by the United States were implemented by an initially reluctant Salvadoran military. The FMLN responded by gunning down a group of U.S. Marines at an outdoor café in San Salvador in 1985.

The cash-strapped Duarte administration became dependent on U.S. assistance to remain afloat. Without the hundreds of millions of dollars of American aid (economic and military), El Salvador was in real danger of collapsing and falling to Nicaraguan-supported communists. By 1987, U.S. aid totaled more than the entire Salvadoran contribution to its own budget. Former President Magana credited the United States with saving his country.

U.S. President Barack Obama (second from left) looks at a limited edition print of images of Archbishop Oscar Romero, who was assassinated in 1980, given to him by President Mauricio Funes of El Salvador (right). Monsignor José Luis Escobar Alas, Archbishop of San Salvador, stands next to Obama (left). The gift was presented during a tour of the Metropolitan Cathedral in San Salvador, El Salvador, on March 22, 2011. Romero's increasingly outspoken criticisms of the repressive actions of the U.S.-backed Salvadoran government led to his murder during the celebration of the Roman Catholic Mass.

SOURCE: SAUL LOEB/AFP/Getty Images/Newscom

As a result of major FMLN attack on San Salvador in November 1989, many secret FMLN members in the capital lost their covers and, thus, their lives. Reprisals from government forces included the notorious killings of Jesuit priests at the University of Central America.

POSTWAR EL SALVADOR

Peace accords were finally signed in 1992, ending the conflict that had claimed 75,000 lives. The FMLN demobilized and became an official opposition party, while the formerly powerful Christian Democrats soon slipped into virtual obscurity. Combatants from both sides joined the new National Civilian Police (PNC).

A United Nations–sponsored Truth Commission was established to investigate the most serious human rights abuse cases. The commission recommended that all those identified as violators of human rights be removed from government and military positions. The Legislative Assembly then granted amnesty for political crimes committed by security forces and the FMLN during the civil war.

The postwar improvement in the Salvadoran economy helped ARENA roll to victories in the 1994 legislative and presidential elections, with San Salvador's mayor, Armando Calderón Sol, winning the presidency. Despite FMLN gains in the 1997 legislative elections, ARENA's candidate in the 1999 presidential elections, Francisco Flores, was elected. Flores's agenda was twofold: further to increase Salvadoran economic gains and to strengthen bilateral ties with the United States. Under Flores, the dollar, already heavily in circulation in El Salvador due to remittances from immigrants in the United States, was made the official currency. The dollarization, opposed by the FMLN, resulted in higher prices for Salvadoran consumers but gradually stabilized the monetary system. Flores also committed El Salvador to free trade through opening up the country to foreign investment and through CAFTA (Central American Free Trade Agreement). Free trade zones helped diversify El Salvador's coffee-oriented economy while providing about 70,000 jobs in the textile and apparel industry.

El Salvador sent troops to participate in Operation Iraqi Freedom. Salvadoran troops participated in education, electricity, health care, and water treatment projects. Five Salvadoran soldiers were killed during the country's five-year deployment in Iraq, the longest stint of any Latin American nation. El Salvador's last troops departed in February 2009.

In 2004, ARENA once again retained the presidency, with Tony Saca handily defeating FMLN stalwart Shafik Handal.

Handal's defeat led the FMLN to pursue (at least publicly) a more moderate image. The FMLN's losing streak was broken in March 2009 with the election of Mauricio Funes. U.S.-Salvadoran ties, forged in war, remained close and strong. Salvadoran governments sided with the United States.

See also *Central American-Dominican Republic Free Trade Agreement, 2004 (CAFTA-DR); Central American Wars, 1980s; Coffee as an Export Crop; D'Aubuisson Arrieta, Roberto; Democratic Revolutionary Front (El Salvador); Duarte Fuentes, José Napoleón; Farabundo Martí National Liberation Front (FMLN) (El Salvador); Human Rights; La Matanza (El Salvador); Romero, Archbishop Oscar Arnulfo; Zamora Rivas, Rubén Ignacio*

GREG MURPHY

REFERENCES AND FURTHER READING

Leiken, Robert D. *Central America: Anatomy of Conflict.* New York: Pergamon, 1984.

National Archives and Records Administration. Central Decimal Files, 816.00 series. College Park, MD: Author, 1940–1944, 1945–1949, 1950–1954, 1955–1959.

National Archives and Records Administration. Confidential Files, Entry 3051B, Box 211. College Park, MD: Author.

National Archives and Records Administration. "Correspondence—Donald P. Downs, El Salvador" (RG 59, Lot 64D016, Box 1). College Park, MD: Author, 1960a.

National Archives and Records Administration. "FBI Survey of El Salvador" (RG 165, Entry 79, "P" File). College Park, MD: Author, April 1943.

National Archives and Records Administration. "United States Agencies—Exim Bank, El Salvador" (RG 59, Lot 64D016, Box 2). College Park, MD: Author, 1960b.

Skidmore, Thomas E., and Peter H. Smith. *Modern Latin America.* New York: Oxford University Press, 1984.

U.S. Department of State. *Foreign Relations of the United States, 1955–1957.* Vol. 7. Washington, DC: Author.

Wesson, Robert. *Communism in the Central America and the Caribbean.* Stanford, CA: Hoover Institution Press, 1982.

Whelan, James R., and Franklin Jaeckle. *The Soviet Assault on America's Southern Flank.* Washington, DC: Regnery Gateway, 1988.

Woodward, Ralph Lee, Jr. *Central America.* New York: Oxford University Press, 1976.

El Salvador–Honduras War

(**See** *Soccer War, 1969*)

Emergency Advisory Committee for Political Defense, World War II

Efforts to combat the danger of subversion from Axis agents in Latin America during World War II, coupled with the Franklin D. Roosevelt administration's desire to foster Inter-American cooperation, led to the creation of the Emergency Advisory Committee for Political Defense (CPD), sometimes called the Inter-American Committee for Political Defense. The CPD was established at a meeting of foreign ministers held in Rio de Janeiro from January 15 to 28, 1942, as the principal Inter-American organization responsible for responding to the internal Axis threat. Based in Montevideo, the CPD consisted of seven representatives: one each from Argentina, Brazil, Chile, Mexico, the United States, Uruguay, and Venezuela. The committee, headed by Uruguay Foreign Minister Alberto Guani, was responsible for coordinating Inter-American policy on Axis subversion, thereby fulfilling the Good Neighbor policy's promise of consultation and mutuality rather than the unilateral actions that had often characterized U.S. policy in the past.

The CPD's most successful program was to collect and publicize evidence of Nazi activities in South America, especially in Chile and Argentina, which did not join all other Latin American countries in breaking relations with the Axis powers in January 1942. The CPD also assembled reports on the state of internal security in each country, including registration and surveillance of aliens, entry and exit of aliens, control of foreign organizations and propaganda, protection of ports and facilities, and control of international communications. In the United States, this work was coordinated by Lawrence A. Knapp, head of the Liaison Office to the CPD at the Justice Department, and Assistant Chief Miguel A. de Capriles.

U.S. PRESSURE ON THE CPD

The main mission of the CPD, however, was to encourage reluctant Latin American governments to comply with a U.S.-initiated program of expelling Axis nationals for internment in the United States, begun immediately after the bombing of Pearl Harbor. Secretary of State Cordell Hull had expressed frustration with the reluctance of many governments in the region to follow Washington's guidance on the matter of deporting those Germans, Japanese, and Italians identified by U.S intelligence agencies as potential subversives. As the U.S. delegate, he chose Carl B. Spaeth, formerly head of the Western Hemisphere Division of the Board of Economic Warfare. Unlike some long-serving Latin American hands in the State Department, Spaeth placed a greater emphasis on achieving U.S. policy goals than on avoiding interference in Latin American affairs. Assistant Secretary of State Adolf Berle worried that if the CPD became known as a creature of the United States, it would lose its effectiveness, but Spaeth responded that the only danger was inaction. In correspondence with the department, he reported his practice of using cooperative delegates from other countries as fronts to present his proposals, so that these would not seem to have originated with the United States, while trying to prevent the introduction of original Latin American proposals to the CPD. In this fashion, a multilateral organization created for the purpose of mutual consultation became a vehicle for the pursuit of U.S. goals.

Thus, Spaeth spent much of his first year at the CPD sidetracking proposals supported by other governments, such as calls for enacting intelligence-sharing arrangements, which the State Department had promised at the Rio conference but which U.S. intelligence agencies did not want. He earned praise from Washington-based officials for successfully suppressing Latin American proposals for more than a year while pushing through measures calling for actions the United States already had been carrying out for some time.

The key CPD declaration on combating Axis subversion, Resolution XX, called for the internment of dangerous Axis nationals in neighboring countries where local facilities were inadequate. It was drafted in the State Department and presented by Spaeth himself. The timing of Resolution XX made it a retroactive endorsement of U.S. policies already under way. It was officially approved by the Montevideo committee and circulated to all governments in the western hemisphere in June 1943, eighteen months after the first deported Axis nationals arrived in the United States.

The CPD's resolution put a multilateral label on the regional deportation efforts, but officials in Washington knew that the program had been running at their initiative. In a memorandum sent to all diplomatic posts in Latin America in May 1943, the State Department acknowledged that Resolution XX had been designed to overcome statutory regulations and political objections in many Latin American countries, preventing the deportation of their legally resident Axis nationals. Once the CPD endorsed Resolution XX, U.S. diplomats received instructions to use the Inter-American call for action against subversion as a source of pressure on those governments that still declined to hand over their Axis nationals sought by the United States. Concurrently, members of the CPD visited several Latin American capitals to urge compliance with U.S. requests for deportations. This was notably successful in Ecuador, whose government agreed to continue deportations it had begun a year earlier. Altogether, fifteen nations participated in the deportation program. Most countries in the western hemisphere placed their German residents under financial restrictions and tracked their movements (neutralist Argentina was one notable exception). Community institutions such as German schools and clubs that had fallen under the influence of local Nazi Party organizations were closed.

The CPD's transmission of lists of individuals suspected of subversive activities drew the attention of the director of the Federal Bureau of Investigation (FBI), J. Edgar Hoover. President Roosevelt had assigned the task of intelligence collection in the western hemisphere to the FBI, and Hoover fought running bureaucratic battles with other agencies to retain this jurisdiction. In August 1943, he complained that the CPD was encroaching on his field, but CPD officials defended their work as not involving actual intelligence collection.

On December 20, 1943, Bolivian army officers close to the neutralist government of Argentina overthrew the government of Enrique Peñaranda in a bloodless coup. Fearful that the new regime might be under Axis influence, the United States refused to recognize it, and the CPD passed a resolution introduced by Chairman Guani recommending that the other American nations consult among themselves before granting recognition to a government established by force. This became known as the Guani Doctrine.

In May 1944, the CPD passed Resolution XXIV, urging Latin American governments to cooperate in receiving Jewish concentration camp inmates holding Latin American citizenship papers. The Nazis were willing to exchange them for German nationals in the western hemisphere, but this proposal came too late to meet Nazi demands, and the exchanges never took place.

AFTER WORLD WAR II

In the aftermath of the war, the deportation program was called into question by evidence that most of the internees taken from Latin America had not actually been dangerous. The FBI identified only eight individuals out of 4,058 German internees from Latin America against whom there was credible evidence of espionage or sabotage. At Washington's urging, the CPD passed Resolution XXVI on April 12, 1946, calling for the expulsion of dangerous Axis nationals remaining in the hemisphere. This time there was almost no compliance, as Latin American governments of various political stripes declined to credit the intelligence reports that had proved wrong before and decided that their residents did not pose any risk, now that the war was over.

In subsequent years, Uruguay sought to turn the CPD into an instrument for encouraging the spread of democracy and human rights, but the Cold War and the decline of democratic governments in the region worked against this proposal. The CPD was dissolved on November 3, 1948, by a resolution of the Council of the Organization of American States (OAS).

See also *Guani Doctrine; Nazi Activities in Latin America, World War II; Organization of American States (OAS); Uruguay, U.S. Relations with; World War II, 1939–1945*

. . . . MAX PAUL FRIEDMAN

REFERENCES AND FURTHER READING

Ball, Margaret. *The OAS in Transition.* Durham, NC: Duke University Press, 1969.

Friedman, Max Paul. *Nazis and Good Neighbors: The United States Campaign against the Germans of Latin America in World War II.* New York: Cambridge University Press, 2003.

Mecham, J. Lloyd. *The United States and Inter-American Security, 1889–1960.* Austin: University of Texas Press, 1961.

Spaeth, Carl B., and William Sanders. "The Emergency Advisory Committee for Political Defense." *American Journal of International Law* 38, no. 2 (April 1944): 218–241.

En Guardia

En Guardia was the Spanish-language magazine published by the U.S. Department of State under the direction of the Office of Coordinator of Inter-American Affairs (OCIAA) during World War II. The magazine was also published in Portuguese as *Em Guarda* and in English as *On Guard*. *En Guardia* used a photojournalism format similar to the popular *Life* and *Look* magazines of the period. The magazine targeted the middle and upper classes of Latin America and the English-speaking areas of the Caribbean and presented the U.S. view of World War II. OCIAA was originally established in 1940 as the Office for Coordination of Commercial and Cultural Relations between the American Republics, and Nelson Rockefeller was appointed head of the organization. OCIAA's mission was to counter the German economic, cultural, psychological, and subversive threat to the Americas by overseeing a hemisphere-wide program of economic cooperation and "vigorous educational and cultural programs." Rockefeller and his team at OCIAA were determined to win the hearts and minds of Latin Americans and gain support for U.S. objectives before and during the war.

By 1945 more than 300,000 copies of *En Guardia* were distributed monthly in the Spanish-speaking countries of Latin America, while an additional 24,000 were sent to Spain. *Em Guarda* was delivered to about 121,000 readers in Brazil, and an additional 24,000 copies were distributed in Portugal. The magazine emphasized the need to maintain the unity of the hemisphere against the Axis threat and highlighted the contributions of the Latin American nations to the war effort. For example, a 1943 edition of *En Guardia* featured Chile's wartime contributions. One article praised Chile for its copper output, which was critical to U.S. war industries. The magazine also lauded the Chilean government and people for supporting the United Nations in its battle against the Axis and noted that Chile had severed relations with the Axis powers and their satellites, including Vichy France.

En Guardia accentuated the traditional ties between the United States and Latin America with frequent references to the great liberators, Símon Bolívar and José de San Martín and their contributions to democracy. Feature articles portrayed Latin American presidents as democratic and provided extensive coverage of their visits to Washington. Latinos who served with distinction in the U.S. armed forces were often the subject of *En Guardia* human interest stories.

Another aim of *En Guardia* was to convince the readership of the military superiority of the Allies. Photographs of the latest planes, tanks, and ships were prominently featured, as were articles about the Latin American military personnel receiving training in the new weapons systems. The message was clear: Latin America would receive military assistance to modernize its armed forces to assist in thwarting attacks on the hemisphere by the Axis forces. Military equipment articles were also designed to counter magazines published by Germany such as *Signal* and *Ejercito Marina Aviacion*.

In addition to *En Guardia*, the OCIAA conducted other propaganda campaigns, using pamphlets, posters, newspaper articles, comic books, educational materials, radio news, and movies. In the end, Rockefeller's successful propaganda campaign, along with economic and military assistance programs and the offer of charter membership in the United Nations, resulted in all of the Latin American nations declaring war on Germany or Japan.

See also *Coordinator of Inter-American Affairs, Office of, World War II; Rockefeller, Nelson A.; World War II, 1939–1945*

. . . . GEORGE M. LAUDERBAUGH

REFERENCES AND FURTHER READING

Anthony, Edwin D. *Records of the Office of Inter-American Affairs.* Washington, DC: National Archives and Records Services Administration, 1973.

Bratzel, John, and Thomas Leonard, eds. *Latin America during World War II.* Boulder, CO: Rowman and Littlefield, 2007.

English-Speaking Caribbean, U.S. Relations with: Anguilla; Antigua and Barbuda; Bahamas; Barbados; British Virgin Islands; Cayman Islands; Dominica; Grenada; Jamaica; Montserrat; St. Kitts and St. Nevis; St. Lucia; St. Vincent; The Grenadines; Trinidad and Tobago, Turks and Caicos Islands

U.S. and English Caribbean relations began with the trade between Britain's North American and West Indian colonies from the end of the seventeenth century. It was an import and export trade dominated by the colonies that would become the United States, which exported more than they imported. Exports consisted principally of provisions, lumber, and livestock with the different U.S. colonies specializing in different products. From the West Indies, the U.S. colonies imported rum, molasses, sugar, and other minor tropical produce.

So valuable was the trade that when it was progressively reduced from 1783 to 1804 following American independence, many enslaved people died, the rum trade declined, and there was a general downturn in the West Indian economy. The trade was also important to the United States, which gained markets for surplus produce and stimulus for its shipping industry.

NINETEENTH TO EARLY TWENTIETH CENTURIES: BAHAMAS AND THE VIRGIN ISLANDS

One place where U.S. impact remained high, however, was the Bahamas. From 1782 to 1789, the Bahamas had been the recipient of what became known as the loyalist migration. As many as eight thousand people from the southern colonies migrated to the Bahamas, refusing to participate in the American Revolution out of loyalty to the British crown. The consequences of the migration were far reaching. Population trebled, cotton plantations were established, political reform occurred, the *Bahamas Gazette* was launched, and several new buildings were constructed. The period marked the end of the old regime and the beginning of modern times.

During the U.S. Civil War, 1861 to 1865, the Bahamas became for the second time an economic benefactor of events unfolding on the mainland. The islands, due to their ideal location less than fifty miles away from the southern U.S. boundary, became bases that challenged the blockade imposed by President Abraham Lincoln on the southern Confederacy. European and U.S. merchants purchased stores in the Bahamas, which were then resold in southern cities like Richmond. Blockade runners bought cotton cheaply in the United States and sold it in the Bahamas to Europeans at huge profits. More southern refugees flocked to the Bahamas, and wages in the islands almost doubled. Not all the runners, however, were fortunate enough to escape. Federal vessels captured as many as forty-two ships leaving Nassau to participate in the trade while twenty-two were sunk. The real misfortune, nevertheless, was the fact that the economic adventure was short-lived, coming to an end with the close of the war in 1865.

The Eighteenth Amendment to the U.S. Constitution provided yet another opportunity for U.S. activity in the Bahamas. The Volstead Act of December 1919 prohibited the manufacture, import, or sale of intoxicating liquors. Prohibition led to a thriving but illegal trade in alcohol, popularly known as bootlegging, in which the Bahamas had a considerable stake. Between 1920 and 1933, the Bahamas developed a liquor industry that manufactured and smuggled the illegal substance through the neighboring southern states. Speed boats and sometimes even airplanes brought cargoes of liquor from Grand Bahama and Bimini to Florida and the northeastern states. Even the Bahamian government, which refused to cooperate with the U.S. Excise Service in enforcing the ban, profited from Prohibition through the increased collection of customs duties on the alcohol trade. The stimulus to the Bahamian economy provided by the illegal liquor trade was evident in myriad aspects of Bahamian life. By 1932, however, the trade dried up when the Twenty-First Amendment to the U.S. Constitution repealed Prohibition. U.S. citizens were also involved in the land speculation frenzy that swept over the Bahamas following the 1920s crash of land speculation in Florida. Many rich U.S. investors bought land and constructed houses and hotels.

Meanwhile, the dawn of the twentieth century brought new interest in the English-speaking Caribbean by the U.S. government. In 1917 the U.S. government purchased from the Danes the three Virgin Islands of St. Thomas, St. John, and St. Croix. The strategic exigencies of a European world at war from 1914 to 1918 dictated the purchase. The Virgin Islands, located just forty miles west of the U.S. protectorate of Puerto Rico, were not far from southern U.S. borders. The Virgins were part of the area that the United States had begun to cordon off as its sphere of unilateral influence since the 1898 Spanish-Cuban-American War.

In the long run, the Virgin Islands became politically and economically dependent on the United States. The U.S. president appointed the governor of the Virgin Islands. In 1948 President Harry Truman held a referendum to determine the people's will for political independence. The majority rejected the offer. Economically, the islands are poor, with some trade in Port Charlotte Amalie in St. Thomas, tourism in St. John, and vegetable cultivation and export in St. Croix. The relative poverty of the islands meant that they looked forward to the financial benefits to which they were entitled as a U.S. outpost.

WORLD WAR II: DESTROYERS FOR BASES AGREEMENT

On September 2, 1940, the United States and Britain signed the "destroyers for bases" agreement. In exchange for fifty World War I destroyers, Britain would lease to the United States for ninety-nine years spaces in Trinidad, Antigua, St Lucia, Jamaica, and the Bahamas for the overall strategic defense of the region. The local governments and people of the targeted territories were not consulted.

By 1940, Britain and the Commonwealth were left standing alone in World War II against Nazi Germany and its allies. As early as 1935, the United States had vowed neutrality in the event of any European war and had imposed a strict ban on the shipment of weapons unless the same were exchanged for cash. Britain desperately needed a strong ally to bolster its war efforts. While the U.S.-initiated 1940 agreement did not as yet make Britain and America official World War II allies, the deal weakened America's neutrality, released Britain of the necessity of protecting its Caribbean colonies, and, as Anthony Maingot (1994) has pointed out, acknowledged that the United States was "the undisputed military power in the whole Caribbean" (p. 52).

TRINIDAD

U.S. leaders identified Trinidad as vital to the strategic defense of the western hemisphere. Its location just off the coast of Venezuela made it a vulnerable approach to the Panama Canal and the South American trade routes. Trinidad also had oil, which was important to wartime Britain. In December 1942, one of two lease agreements was signed to construct bases in Trinidad, covering the four northwestern bays of Chaguaramas, Carenage, Teteron, and Scotland and the two valleys of Chaguaramas and Tucker. The initial plan was to construct military air and sea bases, but as the war progressed, U.S. forces also built roads, developed quarries, and undertook extensive clearing operations.

The U.S. bases in Trinidad were invaluable both in defending against and attacking German U-boats operating in the region. From about December 1941 through the end of 1943, the Germans had engaged in the battle of the Caribbean. British and U.S. forces suffered significant losses until June 1942. In a war strategy referred to as Operation Tonnage, the Germans deployed a minimum of five U-boats and sank about 220 vessels in Caribbean waters without losing a single submarine through the first half of 1942. Half of the German hits were valuable oil tankers. The frequency of German attacks in Trinidad waters led locals to refer in dry jest to the northwestern bays as "torpedo junction." Bold attacks also occurred in the broad light of day right inside the Port-of-Spain harbor, where the Germans sank two ships in February 1942.

In the long run, nevertheless, U.S. servicemen in Chaguaramas, Trinidad, triumphed. By June 1943, the Germans suffered their first reverses in the Caribbean, largely owing to a secret intelligence called Ultra, which broke the secret code of the U-boats, and to sonar and radar technology. By the end of 1943, the Germans had withdrawn from the region.

In the immediate post–World War II period, however, the U.S. base in Chaguaramas, Trinidad, was a great source of contention. Locals perceived Chaguaramas as a clash between U.S. imperialism and West Indian nationalism. On April 22, 1960, Dr. Eric Williams, chief minister of Trinidad and Tobago at the time, opened the campaign to reclaim Chaguaramas by leading a march in the rain to Woodford Square; his followers carried placards saying, "Uncle Sam, we want back we land!" From about 1960 to 1977, Williams highlighted all the injuries that locals suffered on account of the U.S. presence at the base. The base dispossessed and dislocated residents, created friction between foreigners and locals, violated the country's currency regulations, increased the incidence of prostitution, denied locals access to the most picturesque beaches, and even threatened to undermine Trinidad's production and sale of citrus fruits on the international market. Chaguaramas was a colony within a colony. Williams insisted that the Yankees had to go.

Successive U.S. governments tried to pacify and delay Williams. By 1960, however, matters had come to a head. Three-state talks between November 28 and December 9 culminated in the decision for a phased withdrawal of U.S. forces from Trinidad, to be completed by the end of 1977. The withdrawal was accompanied by a developmental project including construction of the College of Arts and Sciences at the University College of the West Indies.

Despite Eric Williams's complaints, the U.S. base brought multiple advantages in the areas of infrastructural development, elimination of mosquito-related diseases, and employment. The U.S. presence in Trinidad, most observers agree, did more good than harm. It even inadvertently contributed to forging national identity, which culminated in independence.

ANTIGUA

The lease to build two American bases in Antigua, the Naval Air Station at Crabbs, and the more extensive Army Air Base at Coolidge was signed on March 27, 1941. These bases were used eventually as convalescent centers for survivors of torpedoed merchant ships.

The U.S. presence in Antigua was more memorable for causing the shameful relocation of the independent farmers of Winthorpes Village, which lay within the boundary that the U.S. government claimed for the Army Air Base at Coolidge. U.S. forces fenced around the entire area and installed four gates, issuing the villagers passes to enter and exit. They were virtually prisoners in their own land. The U.S. forces later used bulldozers and threatened to run through the villagers' houses and gardens if they did not leave. By April 1942, the villagers were in a new location west of Barnes Hill, which they now called New Winthorpes. However, the basic amenities that the United States promised in the new village were either inadequate and unsatisfactory or very slow in coming.

Locals also blamed the United States for reintroducing into Antigua racial tensions, increasing prostitution, and changing the expectations between the sexes by tempting and spoiling their females with gifts and money that islanders could not afford. Economically, the arrival of U.S. forces was fortuitous, for by the beginning of the twentieth century, Antigua's sugar-based economy was in shambles. A budget of four million dollars was allotted for the bases. Thousands of skilled and unskilled construction workers in Antigua and neighboring islands found jobs on the bases at wages that were less than they had anticipated but steadier and higher than were customary.

ST. LUCIA

St. Lucia was another of the British islands where, although the United States had constructed bases, military action was secondary to the economic and social consequences of this development. Gros Islet was selected for a small seaplane naval base. The larger concern was the St. Lucian Base Command in the south, adjacent to the town of Vieux Fort. The two popular centers of operation were called Beane Field and Cantonement.

One major military action took place on the island on March 9, 1942, at 10:52 p.m. in Castries harbor, when German submarines torpedoed two ships: *Lady Nelson* and *Umata*. Twenty people were killed and nineteen injured. One other ship, the *Alcoa*, narrowly escaped being torpedoed. Apart from this event, from 1941 to 1949, the St. Lucian bases were reduced to caretaker status. In 1955 U.S. forces returned to the island to build two radar stations.

For locals, the greatest benefit of the U.S. presence was financial relief. Upward of six thousand locals found employment at relatively high wages on the bases. The relief, however, fluctuated, eventually diminished, and was short-lived. By the end of 1945, there was no more work for locals on the bases.

U.S. drainage work in St. Lucia eliminated mosquitoes and the diseases they spread, but it also destroyed some of the mangrove. Equally devastating were the unsanitary conditions and the ill health that overtook settlements adjacent to the bases. Rapid urbanization in and around Vieux Fort town contributed to severe overcrowding, inadequate garbage disposal, a poor sewage system, and a contaminated water supply. Pulmonary tuberculosis and typhoid became widespread.

U.S.-style nightlife and other aspects of the alien culture were introduced to St. Lucia. The number of bars serving U.S. beers and playing U.S. music increased, along with spending on entertainment, women wearing slacks, prostitution, and sexually transmitted diseases.

JAMAICA

U.S. forces were not involved in heavy military action in the space that they acquired from the British in Jamaica, where a naval air station and a seaplane base were constructed. The bases were used to patrol the approaches to the Caribbean via the Windward Passage. By April 4, 1941, the air station was commissioned and was located on Little Goat Island on the southern side of Jamaica in Portland Bight, just thirty miles from the capital city of Kingston. By the summer of 1942, the work was completed, and by September 1944, the U.S. air station in Jamaica was reduced to caretaker status.

THE BAHAMAS

The Bahamas was another of the British colonies targeted for U.S. bases during World War II. Securing the Bahamas was crucial since they lay less than fifty miles away from the

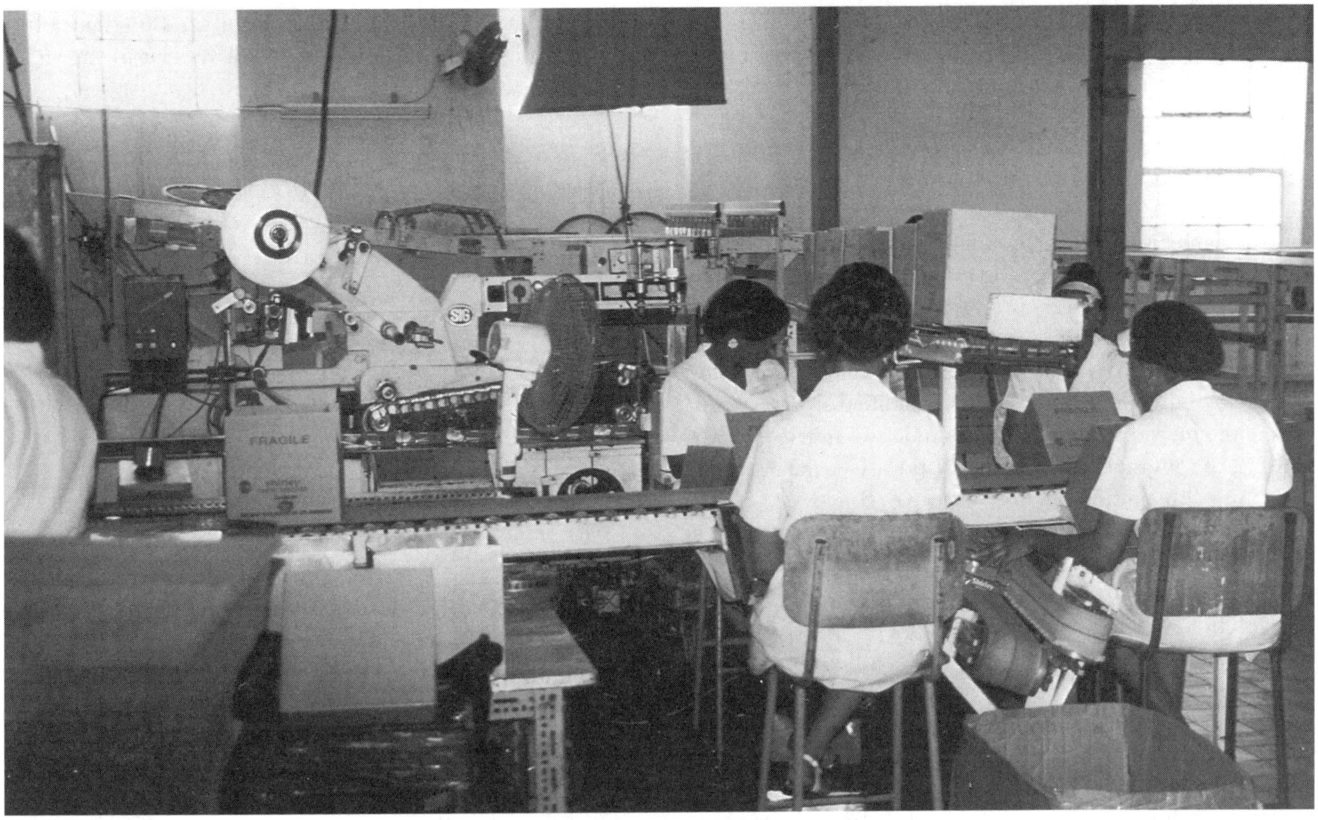

A biscuit (cookie) factory in Bridgetown, Barbados. Barbados was an original signatory of the Treaty of Chaguaramas, which established the Caribbean Community Common Market (CARICOM) on August 1, 1973. The other three were Jamaica, Guyana, and Trinidad and Tobago.

SOURCE: Thomas M. Leonard Collection

southern boundary of the United States. Little military action, however, was played out in Georgetown, Exuma, where the most substantial U.S. base on the islands was located.

Bahamians welcomed the U.S. presence, which, not for the first time in Bahamian history, brought temporary relief to the island's economy. Pleasantville Incorporated contracted to construct the U.S. bases in the Bahamas, projecting that an estimated 2,400 workers from Nassau and the Out Islands would gain employment on the base.

As it turned out, the U.S. bases were the immediate cause of the Nassau riot of 1942. Inequality of wages on the bases raised the ire of the local workers, who were paid less than U.S. workers. Workers rioted for nine days from May 31 to June 8, 1942. Five persons lost their lives, and forty were treated for minor injuries. In terms of property losses, the riot was devastating. The rising did reinforce the labor union movement of the island, and wages doubled from 4s to 8s a day. In addition, in the immediate post–World War II period, the Bahamas tourism industry witnessed a great boost based mainly on U.S. investments.

COLD WAR INTERVENTION IN GRENADA

The relative tranquility of U.S. relations in the postwar period was broken by the U.S. intervention in Grenada on October 25, 1983, which can be regarded as the most aggressive foreign policy action of Washington in the region. The intervention took place in collaboration with neighboring island of Dominica. It was part of the larger post–World War II Cold War politics between the United States and the Soviet Union.

On March 13, 1979, in Grenada, the People's Revolutionary Government (PRG) led by Maurice Bishop overthrew Eric Gairy and his Grenada Union Labor Party (GULP). Bishop tried to establish a welfare state by nationalizing the economy and sharing power with the people. He made strong anti-imperialist speeches such as "In Nobody's Backyard" delivered on April 13, 1979. Bishop also formed alliances with Cuba, North Korea, Libya, Iraq, and the Soviet Union. U.S. officials frowned on these developments. In addition, Grenadians began construction of a 10,000-foot runway on the southern tip of the island, crucial to the development of their airport and tourism. To the discomfort of U.S. observers, Cuban technical volunteers were performing most of the work. As early as 1981, U.S. spy planes over Grenada took satellite photos of the airport operations. U.S. Pentagon officials concluded that the extended runway would serve as a takeoff point for Soviet war jets, thus constituting a threat to the United States.

Despite U.S. misgivings about Bishop and the PRG, a suitable pretext to attack Grenada did not arise until the terrorist bombing in Beirut in 1983 that killed 241 U.S. Marines. President Ronald Reagan insisted that it was necessary to deploy 1,900 U.S. troops in Grenada to protect the 700 students and the staff at the St. George's University Medical School, most of whom were U.S. citizens and whose lives were threatened by the revolution.

The overwhelming majority of the casualties of the invasion were Cubans. Just eighteen U.S. soldiers died, and the U.S. press depicted them as martyrs for the cause of democracy. In addition, the invasion was seen as a rescue mission from Bishop's socialist experimentation. U.S. journalists strongly emphasized pictures of university students kissing the ground of Charleston Airport, South Carolina, having been airlifted from Grenada during the invasion. International opinion was much less favorable to the invasion: The United Nations General Assembly condemned the invasion by 108 votes to 9.

The intervention dealt a great blow to the first attempt at social revolution in the English-speaking Caribbean. The U.S. press wrote derogatorily of the new political order claiming, "Revolution is a large idea and Grenada a small island. Of such incongruities comedy is made. It becomes more empty of meaning, more powerful a tool, and thus more attractive to the next gang of thugs, posturers and dreamers" (Black 1988, 156). Bishop was murdered two days before the invasion, which ousted his successor, Hudson Austin, bringing to power the political conservative Herbert Blaize, who had been Grenada's premier during the period of Grenada's Associated Statehood as a British colony. Grenada regressed with the disintegration of the four-year-old People's Revolutionary Government; that is, politically, it lost the independence of action that it had begun to demonstrate under Bishop and the NJM. In the immediate aftermath of the 1983 invasion, the island was under U.S. control.

As was the custom, the U.S. invasion of Grenada was accompanied by economic aid to the island. Following the 1984 evacuation, the U.S. government gave Grenada about $110 million, which was spent on improving agriculture and transportation. The Point Salines Airport, which had previously generated much anti-American sentiment, received allocations from this aid and was by late 1988 a key to the island's booming tourism industry.

CONCLUSION

U.S. relations with the English-speaking Caribbean were largely facilitated by the fact that by the late nineteenth century, Britain was ready to surrender responsibility for the region to the rising superpower. The United States assumed this responsibility mainly because it coincided with strategic tactics of the mid-twentieth century, driven largely by virulent anticommunism. Ironically, the U.S. involvement in the region became part of the larger framework of the decolonization process, which eventually led most of the British Caribbean territories to the road of independence by the second half of the twentieth century. The proximity of the English-speaking Caribbean to the United States, which had wide implications for the U.S. economy and foreign policy, was generally responsible for their involvement in the affairs of the region by the end of the twentieth century.

See also *Association of Caribbean States (ACS); Caribbean Community Common Market (CARICOM); Caribbean, German U-boat Threat, World War II; Grenada, U.S. Invasion of, 1983*

. . . . GELIEN MATTHEWS

REFERENCES AND FURTHER READING

Bell, Herbert C. "The West India Trade before the American Revolution." *American Historical Review* 22 (January 1917): 272–282.

Black, George. *The Good Neighbour: How the USA Wrote the History of Central America and the Caribbean.* New York: Pantheon Books, 1988.

Chester, Edward W. *The United States and Six Atlantic Outposts.* Port Washington, NY: Kennikat Press, 1980.

Craton, Michael. *A History of the Bahamas.* 3rd ed. Waterloo: San Salvador Press, 1986.

Harmsen, Jolien. *Sugar, Slavery and Settlement: A Social History of Vieux Fort St Lucia from the Amerindians to the Present.* Castries, St. Lucia: St. Lucia National Trust, 1999.

Heine, Jorge. "Grenada: A Revolution Aborted." In *Caribbean Freedom Economy and Society from Emancipation to the Present,* edited by Hilary Beckles and Verene Shepherd, 557–565. Kingston, Jamaica: Ian Randle, 1996.

Lowes, Susan. "The U. S. Bases in Antigua and the New Winthorpes Story." www.projects.ilt.columbia.edu/antigua/base.

Maingot, Anthony. *The United States and the Caribbean.* Warwick University Caribbean Studies. London and Basingstoke: Macmillan Caribbean, 1994.

Maurice, St. Bernard. "The Chaguaramas Affair in Trinidad and Tobago: An Intellectual Reassessment." *Journal of Caribbean History* 40, no. 1 (2006): 92–116.

Morison, Samuel Eliot. *The Atlantic Battle Won. May 1943–May 1945.* Vol. 1. Boston: Little Brown, 1956.

Noguera, Pedro. "The Limits of Charisma Grenada's Eric Gairy (1922–1997) and Maurice Bishop (1944–1983)." In *Caribbean Charisma Reflections on Leadership, Legitimacy and Populist Politics,* edited by Anton Allahar, 72–89. Kingston and London: Ian Randle, 2001.

Palmer, Colin. *Eric Williams and The Making of the Modern Caribbean.* Kingston, Jamaica: Ian Randle, 2006.

Private Laws, Concurrent Resolutions, Treaties, International Agreements Other than Treaties, and Proclamations. Part 2 of *United States Statutes at Large Containing the Laws and Concurrent Resolutions Enacted during the Second and Third Sessions of the Seventy-Sixth Congress of the United States of America, 1939–1941 and Treaties, International Agreements Other than Treaties, Proclamations, and Reorganization Plans,* Vol. 54, 2406–2408. Washington, DC: Government Printing Office, 1941.

Proudfoot, Mary. *Britain and the USA in the Caribbean.* New York: Praeger, 1953.

Richardson, Bonham. *The Caribbean in the Wider World 1492 to 1992: A Regional Geography.* Cambridge, UK: Cambridge University Press, 1992.

Saunders, Gail. *Bahamian Loyalists and Their Slaves.* London: Macmillan, 1983.

———. "The 1942 Riot in Nassau: A Demand for Change?" *Journal of Caribbean History* 20, no. 2 (1985–1986): 117–146.

———. "The Social History of the Bahamas, 1890–1953." Ph.D. diss., University of Waterloo, 1985.

Taylor, Thomas. *Running the Blockade.* London, 1896.

Thompson, Alvin, ed. *Journal of Caribbean History,* Vol. 40, no. 1 (2006).

U.S. Department of State. Message of President Roosevelt to the Congress, September 3, 1940. *Bulletin,* Vol. 3, p. 201.

Enterprise for the Americas Initiative

In 1990, the world had just emerged from the Cold War and was entering a new phase. Liberal democratic ideals had triumphed in much of the world, and Latin America was no exception. Since World War II, most countries in the region had jettisoned authoritarian regimes and inward-oriented economic policies. Most were emerging from a decade of stagnant economic growth caused by political instability and economic mismanagement, and there were hopeful signs for free trade and development. Governments had managed to stabilize their economies and defeat rampant inflation; they began to live within their means; and they were opening their markets to promote economic growth.

GENESIS

Against this backdrop, President George H.W. Bush unveiled his Enterprise for the Americas Initiative (EAI). On June 27, 1990, in a meeting with administration officials, members of the diplomatic corps, and business leaders, the president made his pitch. He argued that the EAI would provide "incentives to reinforce Latin America's growing recognition that free-market reform is the key to sustained growth and political stability" (Bush, 1990). He cited the transition to democracy and free markets in the region and signaled via the EAI the U.S. willingness to support this change. Since President Kennedy's Alliance for Progress, the Cold War and national security prerogatives had guided U.S.–Latin American relations. The EAI marked a shift in U.S. foreign policy toward the region. Thereafter, the United States would emphasize trade and investment to support democratization and political stability.

Without committing to specific details or proposing significant financial support, the EAI sought to promote trade, foreign investment, and official debt reduction. The proposals to boost foreign investment and debt reduction were modest at best. Debt initiatives would deal with only a portion of about $12 billion in official debt to the United States. In 1990 Latin America's foreign obligations totaled more than $400 billion. With respect to foreign investment, the first Bush administration eventually proposed establishing an investment fund that would be managed by the Inter-American Development Bank, with contributions from the United States and other advanced industrialized nations. The long-term goal was to raise about $1.5 billion. The Bush Administration proposed to provide technical advice and financial support to aid privatization, the liberalization of investment regimes, and other sundry activities designed to bolster investment flows to the region. The limited scope of these two pillars, together with meager financial commitments, guaranteed that they would fail to match the President's ambitious rhetoric. In any event, many countries in the region were swiftly making progress on these fronts without much support from the EAI.

With respect to trade promotion, however, the lofty language of the EAI proposal fit the emerging policy consensus in the region. By June 1990, the Uruguay Round of the General Agreement on Tariffs and Trade (GATT) and the North American Free Trade Agreement (NAFTA) were being negotiated. Moreover, several countries in the region had already taken strides toward reducing trade and investment barriers. Chile and Mexico had done so, and others would quickly follow suit. Even in light of these positive trends, President Bush's rhetoric was bold if not quixotic: "We look forward to the day when not only are the Americas the first fully free, democratic hemisphere but when all are equal partners in a free trade zone stretching from the port of Anchorage to the Tierra del Fuego." (Bush 1990)

It is not surprising, therefore, that the notion of expanding free trade from Alaska to Tierra del Fuego was enthusiastically received in Latin America. In light of political constraints, in both the United States and other nations, a hemispheric free trade area was certainly a long-term objective. About two years after President Bush proposed the EAI, the United States had signed framework agreements with MERCOSUR and CARICOM as well as fourteen individual states. It was Bush's successor, President William J. Clinton, who proposed that a Free Trade Area of the Americas (FTAA) should be implemented by 2005. Serious discussions began in late 1994 at the Summit of the Americas in Miami, where leaders agreed to attempt to complete negotiations for an FTAA by 2005.

A HEMISPHERICAL FREE TRADE AGREEMENT FALLS THROUGH

The 1994 Miami summit and its successors failed to deliver a hemispheric free trade agreement as envisioned by the EAI. In the first decade of the twenty-first century, moreover, powerful leftist leaders returned to power in a few nations, not through coups or revolutions but via the ballot box. As of 2011, not only Cuba but also Venezuela, Bolivia, Nicaragua, and Ecuador continue to oppose an FTAA ideologically and politically. They are not alone in viewing it as an economic threat. Brazil, a potent competitor to U.S. agricultural producers, has taken the lead in standing up to the United States in negotiations. It is pressing on agricultural subsidies, which are a de facto form of protection that shields U.S. markets from Latin America. This tough bargaining between the United States, which is protective of agriculture and seeks concessions in property rights protection, and Brazil, which possesses a comparative advantage in raw materials, mirrors the conflict between developed and developing nations that is occurring in international multilateral trade negotiations under the Doha Round. It is difficult to see that a comprehensive FTAA will be achieved anytime soon. Nevertheless, since the early 1990s, nations in the hemisphere have signed a plethora of subregional trade agreements, including the colorfully named leftist Bolivarian Alternative for the Americas and the Caribbean or ALBA.

The United States continues to negotiate and deal with Latin American countries on economic and other issues. It also squabbles regularly with Cuba and Venezuela. Many leaders in the region complain that the United States pays insufficient attention to Latin America. Others complain that it remains an imperialist power bent on domination and should leave the region alone. Most would agree that U.S. policy toward the region is markedly different from what it was during the Cold War. Although the original program of the EAI did not add up to much, it does mark a turning point in U.S.–Latin American relations that endures into the twenty-first century.

See also *Bush, George H. W.; Free Trade Area of the Americas (FTAA); Inter-American Development Bank (IADB); North American Free Trade Agreement (NAFTA), 1992*

. . . . GABRIEL AGUILERA

REFERENCES AND FURTHER READING

Bush, George H. W. "Remarks Announcing the Enterprise for the Americas Initiative, June 27, 1990." In *The American Presidency Project* [online], edited by John T. Woolley and Gerhard Peters. www.presidency.ucsb.edu/ws/?pid=18644.

Carranza, Mario Esteban, *South American Free Trade Area or Free Trade Area of the Americas? Open Regionalism and the Future of Regional Economic Integration in South America*. Burlington, VT: Ashgate, 2000.

Green, Roy E., ed. *The Enterprise for the Americas Initiative: Issues and Prospects for a Free Trade Agreement in the Western Hemisphere*. Westport, CT: Praeger, 1993.

Mace, Gordon, and Hugo Loiseau. "Cooperative Hegemony and Summitry in the Americas." *Latin American Politics and Society* 47, no. 4 (2005): 107–134.

Vizentini, Paulo, and Marianne Wiesebron, eds. *Free Trade for the Americas? The United States' Push for the FTAA Agreement*. New York: Zed Books, 2004.

Environmental Protection, U.S. Influence on Latin American Policy

Due to factors such as high population growth, poverty, industrialization, certain trade and agricultural practices, and climate change, Latin America has been experiencing serious environmental problems that call for urgent and effective environmental protection measures. Environmental degradation observed in this region is a serious concern not only for Latin American nations but for all countries, especially since a large portion of tropical rainforests (which are extremely vital for Earth's ecological balance) are found in Latin America. Rapid depletion of natural resources also disrupts the already fragile social, political, and economic balances of the developing countries in this region, which in turn affect the United States and other countries within the interdependent global system. In response, given its position as a superpower, a leading international lender, and trade partner, the United States has actively sought to influence the environmental policies of Latin American countries.

DEBT-FOR-NATURE SWAPS FOR LATIN AMERICAN COUNTRIES AND THE ROLE OF THE UNITED STATES

Foreign debt is generally considered a major cause of environmental degradation in Latin America. The pressure to pay off external debts forces developing countries to increase their exports of natural resources, such as tropical timber, to the detriment of the environment. The tropical rainforests were being cleared in Latin America at such a high rate in the 1980s that some scientists predicted the large-scale disappearance of the tropical forests in this region by the year 2000. Initially, developed countries including the United States did not pay much attention to the environmental consequences of pressuring the heavily indebted countries to service their debts at any cost. However, as scientific research gradually exposed the dangers of environmental degradation and as environmental activists increasingly pressed for developed countries to take action, the United States and other industrialized nations began to consider possible remedies and alternatives. Subsequently, the "debt-for-nature swaps" initiative was developed, which generally involved restructuring, reducing, or buying a portion of a developing country's debt and then using a portion of proceeds to fund conservation projects within the debtor country.

Despite the later repudiation of the Kyoto Accord on climate change by President George W. Bush at the beginning of his presidency, the United States has led reform efforts regarding debt-for-nature swaps by being the first nation to implement important legislation to facilitate these environmental initiatives and the principal country for financing such exchanges. In 1989, as an initial legislative step in this process, the U.S. Congress authorized the U.S. Agency for International Development (USAID) to provide assistance to nongovernmental organizations for purchasing the commercial debt of foreign countries as part of a debt-for-nature agreement. A year later, the 1990 Enterprise for the Americas Initiative (EAI) authorized the exchange of bilateral debt for environmental protection. Under the EAI, the United States agreed to reduce the debt of eligible countries following their entrance into an environmental framework agreement with the United States, thus providing for the establishment of an environmental trust fund. For instance, in 1992, the United States reduced 10 percent of a $310 million debt Colombia owed in exchange for the transfer of $41.6 million in local currency into an environmental fund over a ten-year period. Argentina, Bolivia, Chile, El Salvador, Jamaica, Peru, and Uruguay have also participated in debt-for-nature transactions under the EAI program, which allowed for the funding of a wide range of activities in these countries, such as coastal zone marine management projects in Jamaica, environmental development projects in the Peruvian Andes, and community production grants in Bolivia.

Modeled after the EAI, the next U.S. legislative initiative to promote debt-for-nature exchanges was the Tropical Forest Conservation Act of 1998 (TFCA). As summarized by a congressional research service analyst, eligible conservation projects to be funded via this program contain "(1) the establishment, maintenance, and restoration of parks, protected reserves, and natural areas, and the plant and animal life within them; (2) training programs to increase the capacity of personnel to manage parks; (3) development and support for communities residing near or within tropical forests;

On islands in the Beagle Channel, which connects the Atlantic and Pacific at the tip of South America, cormorants (birds) and sea lions coexist. The Channel is named after the vessel famous for bringing Charles Darwin to explore the area. The governments of Argentina and Chile long disputed the territory until a 1984 treaty.

SOURCE: Graeme S. Mount Collection

(4) development of sustainable ecosystem and land management systems; and (5) research to identify the medicinal uses of tropical forest plants and their products." The Latin American countries that have participated in this newer program include Belize, Colombia, Costa Rica, El Salvador, Guatemala, Jamaica, Panama, Paraguay, and Peru. In addition, while the EAI was restricted to Latin American and Caribbean countries, the TFCA also expanded the EAI authorization to other countries with tropical forests, including Botswana, Indonesia, and the Philippines.

IMPACT OF ECONOMIC VENTURES WITH THE UNITED STATES ON ENVIRONMENTAL POLICIES

The United States also exerts influence on the environmental policies of Latin American countries through certain economic partnerships and trade agreements. For scholars, whether such influence is constructive or detrimental to environmental protection in this region is open to debate. As scholars Bryan Husted and Jeanne Logsdon (1997) note, the proponents of free trade argue that trade liberalization instigates economic growth and higher per capita incomes, which in turn (1) generate the resources to invest in pollution control; (2) allow for the importation of pollution control technologies; and (3) arouse greater public concern and awareness about environmental hazards. However, free trade critics assert that trade liberalization poses a serious threat to the environment in developing nations since (1) developed countries locate their high-polluting industries in poorer countries that are in dire need of investment; (2) environmental policies are set at low levels or are not effectively enforced in order to attract such industrial relocations; (3) local businesses limit spending on pollution control equipment to keep their costs low as a means to be competitive; and (4) higher consumption instigated by economic growth and higher incomes lead to more environmental degradation. Given this debate, a review of the economic ventures between Latin American countries and the United States may provide partial credence to both sides of the argument. For instance, some suggest that the North American Free Trade Agreement (NAFTA) has induced a progressive leap in Mexico's environmental policies. On the other hand, critics have drawn attention to severe environmental degradation and pollution in the region, which has been caused by the rapid growth of *maquiladoras* (export assembly plants), insufficient environmental protection, and mismanagement of hazardous industrial waste.

To conclude, the United States has displayed a significant influence—both positive and negative—on Latin American environmental policies. On the one hand, the United States has taken the lead among developed countries in funding debt-for-nature exchanges, thus enabling the conservation of vital natural resources in Latin American countries. On the other hand, the United States has been outsourcing most of its environmentally hazardous industries to developing Latin American countries because of their lower environmental standards, thereby implicitly promoting the maintenance of weak environmental regulations for capitalist purposes and contributing to environmental damage and pollution in the region. Given these clashing foreign influences along with domestic factors, policy reform for Latin America's environmental protection continues to be an arduous endeavor.

See also *Debt Crisis, Latin America, 1870s, 1930s, 1980s; Enterprise for the Americas Initiative; North American Agreement on Environmental Cooperation, 1992; North American Free Trade Agreement (NAFTA), 1992; United Nations Conference on Environment and Development, Rio de Janeiro, 1992; U.S. Agency for International Development (USAID)*

. . . . CIGDEM V. SIRIN

REFERENCES AND FURTHER READING

Freeland, Steven, and Ross P. Buckley. "Debt-for-Development Exchanges: Using External Debt to Mitigate Environmental Damage in Developing Countries." *West Northwest Journal of Environmental Law* 16 (2010): 77–101.

Hopkins, Jack W. *Policymaking for Conservation in Latin America: National Parks, Reserves, and the Environment.* Westport, CT: Praeger, 1995.

Husted, Bryan W., and Jeanne M. Logsdon. "The Impact of NAFTA on Mexico's Environmental Policy." *Growth and Change* 28, no. 1 (1997): 24–48.

MacDonald, Gordon J., Daniel L. Nielson, and Marc A. Stern. *Latin American Environmental Policy in International Perspective.* Boulder, CO: Westview Press, 1997.

Sheikh, Pervaze A. "Debt-for-Nature Initiatives and the Tropical Forest Conservation Act: Status and Implementation." *Congressional Research Service (CRS) Report for Congress*, 2010.

Tulchin, Joseph S., and Andrew I. Rudman. *Economic Development and Environmental Protection in Latin America.* Woodrow Wilson International Center for Scholars. Boulder, CO: Lynne Rienner, 1991.

Escobar Gaviria, Pablo

Pablo Emilio Escobar Gaviria (1949–1993) was one of the largest Colombian exporters of cocaine in the 1970s and 1980s, one of the richest men in the world, and the most important U.S. target in the war on drugs during the early 1990s. Escobar was born in Antioquia, Colombia. He proceeded in his youth from petty crime to murder and kidnapping, before becoming involved in the burgeoning business of marijuana exportation during the 1970s. From this, he moved into the cocaine industry when U.S. demand for the drug accelerated massively in the middle to later part of the decade. By the early 1980s, he was one of the leaders of the cocaine cartel centered in Medellín, Colombia.

COCAINE IN COLOMBIA

Cocaine, manufactured from coca leaves generally brought in from Peru and Bolivia, quickly grew to become the largest export commodity in Colombia. With the massive supply of foreign exchange dollars that accompanied it, as well as the extensive bribes and threats dispensed to occupants of the seats of power, it came to dominate Colombian politics as well as its society. Escobar painted himself as a Robin Hood figure, comparing himself to the Mexican outlaw-turned-revolutionary Francisco Pancho Villa and Argentinean guerrilla Ernesto "Che" Guevara de la Serna. He dispensed large sums of money for improvements, job creation, and other social projects in and around his native city. This, combined with a notoriously excessive personal life, quickly established his mythic reputation. He was linked to the murder of numerous rivals and both police and governmental figures who attacked him. Most notoriously, he was almost certainly responsible for the murders of two agents of the *Departamento Administrativo de Seguridad* (DAS), who had arrested him in March 1977 after finding thirty-nine kilos of cocaine in a truck he was bringing back from Ecuador.

At the time, the Colombian government was arguably more concerned about its conflict with the major Marxist guerrilla organizations, the *Fuerzas Armadas Revolucionarias de Colombia* (FARC), *Ejército de Liberación Nacional* (ELN), and M-19, than with the social disruption attendant on the growing drugs trade. While some evidence suggested the cartels had occasionally reached temporary accords with guerrillas for mutual interest, attempts to associate the two groups were undermined by violence between them. After some *narcos* were kidnapped in 1981, Escobar was involved in the organization of a group called *Muerte a Secuestradores* (Death to Kidnappers), which conducted open warfare with the guerrilla groups, often in tacit cooperation with Colombian army units.

In 1982 Escobar ran for office and was elected as a substitute to congress, but he was quickly ejected from both it and the New Liberal Party of which he was a member after the reformist Justice Minister Rodrigo Lara denounced him as a drug baron. He withdrew from formal politics in 1984; shortly afterward, Lara was assassinated.

THE U.S. WAR ON DRUGS

The Republican administration of Ronald Reagan was increasingly concerned with the social impact of cocaine on U.S. society, especially with the rise of crack cocaine, which conservative politicians implicitly associated with inner-city disorder, poverty, and ethnic minorities. Having little faith in the Colombian government or judicial system, the United States began to push for the extradition of the major narcotraffickers to face prosecution in the United States. Following a raid on a cocaine factory called Tranquilandia in March 1984, in which the United States was involved, Escobar and others naturally sought to present North American pressure as a challenge to Colombian sovereignty and paint themselves as nationalist heroes.

Escobar spent significant time away from Colombia between 1983 and 1985, searching but failing to find more secure places to live, including Panama and Nicaragua. On his return, he began a long, highly public process of negotiation with the Colombian government, in which he offered to turn himself in and provide various financial incentives to the state in exchange for immunity from extradition. To apply pressure on the government, the cartel launched massive bombing and assassination campaigns. This culminated in 1989 with the killing of presidential candidate and outspoken opponent of Escobar, Luis Galán and the attempted assassination of his successor, César Gaviria Trujillo. The latter failed, but drug traffickers succeeded in blowing up an Avianca airplane, killing 110 people on board.

President Reagan's successor in the White House, George H. W. Bush, was more concerned about the drugs issue than his predecessor. He had been instrumental in the war on drugs as vice president under Reagan and now consciously sought to shift the focus from enforcing border security to dealing with the production of cocaine at the source. Hostility to the Medellín cartel thus appeared to be growing in both the U.S. and Colombian governments. Between 1989 and 1991, the Colombian police and army conducted a massive manhunt for Escobar, supported by U.S. funds and personnel. Dozens of senior associates in the Medellín cartel were extradited, arrested, or summarily executed by the army. In response, Escobar and the other "extraditables" began kidnapping senior government officers and their families.

Ultimately, the new president of Colombia, César Gaviria, was more concerned about narco-terrorism than narco-trafficking. As such, he struck a deal with Escobar for his surrender in exchange for immunity from extradition to the United States. Once the Colombian congress passed a law in June 1991 prohibiting extradition, Escobar surrendered, taking up residence in a prison he had built himself on land he owned in Antioquia. The decision to end extraditions generated great frustration in the United States and contributed to the decision to decertify Colombia during the Clinton administration. This led to the curtailment of some U.S. economic aid to Colombia, although the impact was more symbolic than material.

Escobar used his enforced residence to rebuild his cocaine business, but within a year, he fled the prison when he came to believe he was to be transferred and potentially assassinated. The public humiliation associated with Escobar's escape forced the Gaviria government to intensify its efforts and accede to the deployment of U.S. Special Forces and advanced surveillance technology in Colombian territory. Despite the anger this decision caused in the press and congress, in the end, it was a joint U.S.-Colombian effort that tracked down Escobar in late 1993 and killed him.

Despite his involvement in the deaths of thousands of people, Escobar's funeral was attended by masses of local citizens. Many in Colombian society resented the role the United States had played in the manhunt and considered cocaine to be a *gringo* problem. Meanwhile, Escobar's death badly damaged the Medellín cartel but had no appreciable effect on the volume of cocaine being exported to the United States. In the end, the hunt for Escobar had become a punitive exercise rather than a strategy of supply reduction, and his enemies were satisfied with the exemplary role his death offered to others.

See also *Bush, George H. W.; Colombia, U.S. Relations with; Drugs, U.S. War on; Drug Trafficking; Gaviria Trujillo, César; Lehder, Carlos; Reagan, Ronald W.; Revolutionary Armed Forces of Colombia (FARC); U.S. Drug Enforcement Administration*

. . . . ALEX GOODALL

REFERENCES AND FURTHER READING

Bowden, Mark. *Killing Pablo: The Hunt for the Richest, Most Powerful Criminal in History*. London: Atlantic, 2001.

García Márquez, Gabriel. *News of a Kidnapping*. London: Penguin, 1998.

Strong, Simon. *Whitewash: Pablo Escobar and the Cocaine Wars*. London: Pan Books, 1996.

Escudé, Carlos

Carlos Escudé (1948–), Argentine political scientist and government adviser, obtained his doctorate with the support of a Fulbright Fellowship at Yale University in 1981 and won a Guggenheim Fellowship in 1984. During the 1990s, he served as special adviser to Argentina's foreign minister, Guido de Tella, under the presidency of Carlos Menem (1989–1999). Escudé is therefore not only the explicator but also the agent of a notable transformation of Argentina's foreign policy in its relations with the world's more powerful nations, especially the United States.

Escudé is most noted for his theory of *peripheral realism,* which is the pragmatic philosophy that advocates adaptation to the restrictive conditions experienced by the more vulnerable members of the interstate system. Promoting a "realism of the weak states," Escudé classifies international actors into three types: rule makers, rule takers, and the rogue nations: in other words, states that command, obey, or push back. In the case of Argentina, taking a realistic approach has meant leaving behind previous regimes' policies of territorial nationalism vis-à-vis the country's neighbors and confrontationalism vis-à-vis the United States and Great Britain in favor of improved relations with these two nations. Guided by his theory, the Menem government moved to deprioritize military might and state security, align diplomatically with the United States and the Euro-zone nations, and accept measures prescribed by the International Monetary Fund.

Escudé's historical analysis of the foundations of peripheral realism serves to explain his theory on Argentina's post–World War II economic decline. After a previous period of advantageous if neocolonial trade relations with Great Britain, Argentina, he writes, experienced the "miracle of Argentine underdevelopment," a period of less than satisfactory commercial relations with the United States as the new hegemonic power. The international factor in this miracle, argues Escudé, must be accounted for in a complete analysis of the restrictions on the national economy and its consequent stagnation. Argentina learned the hard lesson, during the 1940s, of North American boycotts, pushed into practice by U.S. liberals and imposed to punish Argentina for its stance of neutrality during World War II and to discourage Anglo-Argentine trade relations, especially with regard to the building of railroads and the sale of meat. Within this framework of strained triangular relations, a policy of industrialization under Juan Perón (President 1946–1955; 1973–1974), linked with import substitution, succeeded in developing the economy. Heavy protectionism and a small internal demand, together with a strong syndicalism and an independent anti-Peronist middle class, hampered economic growth and provoked the regime to intensify its authoritarian methods, thus heating up the cycle of political instability.

Escudé has traced the diplomatic history of an Argentina that challenged U.S. hegemony, as occurred during the Falklands/Malvinas crisis in 1982, bringing on negative consequences for the citizenry. The crisis of hyperinflation in 1989 and 1990 reoriented thinking in the Argentine government of Raúl Alfonsín (President 1983–1989) toward a search for monetary stability, economic development, and a pro-Western foreign policy that would not lead the country into conflict with the major world powers. During the Menem government, Argentina thus became aligned with the United States, raised its visibility in international forums, abandoned the Condor II missile project, and strengthened its political ties with Chile and economic ties with Brazil.

Realism of the periphery holds out the possibility of building international as well as domestic peace through participation in UN missions. Such participation, argues Escudé, could also steer military endeavors in the direction of conflict resolution as an alternative to answering perceived or potential threats from other countries. For Argentina, alliance building has meant withdrawing from the nonaligned movement and distancing itself from that movement's anti-U.S. positioning. The realignment with U.S. interests entailed future compliance with the United Nations Security Council and with the majority of the Western nations in their peace-keeping efforts. Indeed, with the scaling down of its military profile since the Falklands War of 1982, Argentina has renewed ties of cooperation with both the United States and Great Britain, conforming all the more to the model of the trading state. Escudé came out in support of President Cristina Fernández's foreign policy in the year of her election, 2010.

See also *Argentina, U.S. Relations with; Malvinas/Falkland Islands Controversy and War; Menem, Carlos Saúl; Non-Aligned Movement (NAM); Perón Sosa, Juan Domingo*

. . . . EUGENIO MATIBAG

REFERENCES AND FURTHER READING

Dominguez, Jorge I. "Security, Peace, and Democracy in Latin America and the Caribbean: Challenges for the Post-Cold War Era." In *International Security and Democracy: Latin America and the Caribbean in the Post-Cold War Era,* edited by Jorge I. Dominguez, 3–28. Pittsburgh, PA: University of Pittsburgh Press, 1998.

Escudé, Carlos. *Foreign Policy Theory in Menem's Argentina.* Gainesville: University Press of Florida, 1997.

Escudé, Carlos, and Andrés Fontana. "Argentina's Security Policies: Their Rationale and Regional Context." In *International Security and Democracy: Latin America and the Caribbean in the Post-Cold War Era,* edited by Jorge I. Dominguez, 51–79, Pittsburgh, PA: University of Pittsburgh Press, 1998.

Vas, Aldo C. "Review of *Foreign Policy Theory in Menem's Argentina,* by Carlos Escudé." *Journal of Interamerican Studies and World Affairs* 40, no. 1 (Spring 1998): 97–100.

Estrada Cabrera, Manuel

Born to Francisco and Imelda Cabrera in Quetzaltenango, Guatemala, Manuel Estrada Cabrera (1857–1924) rose to become the country's longest-serving president (February 8, 1898–April 15, 1920). He received his early education from the Roman Catholic Church, then studied to become a lawyer. After passing his bar exam, Estrada Cabrera practiced law in Quetzaltenango and Retalhuleu, western Guatemala's two major metropolises. As his reputation grew, Estrada Cabrera increased his involvement with Guatemala's Liberal Party, rising within its ranks.

Estrada Cabrera was not an especially charismatic individual. Nevertheless, his administrative skills won him an appointment to the cabinet of José Maria Reyna Barrios (President 1891–1898). When Reyna Barrios ran for reelection in 1896, he tapped Estrada Cabrera as his vice president. On February 8, 1898, President Reyna Barrios was assassinated, elevating Estrada Cabrera to the presidency. Being the first civilian to assume Guatemala's presidency in fifty years, Estrada Cabrera had to surmount some objections from within the officer corps. By August 1898, Estrada Cabrera overcame the objections and called for September elections, which legitimized his power. Subsequent rigged elections in 1904, 1910, and 1916 helped Estrada Cabrera maintain power until April 1920, when a popular uprising forced his generals to ask for his resignation. In all, Estrada Cabrera served for twenty-two uninterrupted years as Guatemala's chief executive, a record that is unlikely to be broken.

Although his regime was increasingly despotic, Estrada Cabrera did bring order and stability to Guatemala. In addition, he brought improvements in Guatemala's infrastructure, such as carriage roads and a railroad that linked Guatemala City with the country's main Caribbean port, Puerto Barrios. He also negotiated land ownership contracts with U.S.-based banana producer United Fruit Company, making Guatemala a major supplier of the yellow fruit to North America. Public education was also a major interest of Estrada Cabrera's, and he professed support for students and teachers during the early years of his reign.

Two other issues were also important to Estrada Cabrera: internal security and foreign affairs. In a sense, the two issues were inexorably linked, especially in relation to Guatemala's relations with its neighbors. Internal security was of utmost importance to Estrada Cabrera, for he saw plots against him in every corner and used a network of paid informants to uncover them. Those who dared speak out against his tyranny either rotted in his jails or left the country.

Guatemalan exiles living in Mexico and Central America were another source of Estrada Cabrera's paranoia, for he was convinced they were plotting to overthrow him. To neutralize these threats, Estrada Cabrera launched attacks into El Salvador, Honduras, and Mexico. Sometimes, his fears were warranted, as Honduras and El Salvador did harbor unfriendly Guatemalan refugees. By 1905, Honduras became a pawn, caught in a struggle for control between Estrada Cabrera and Nicaraguan strongman José Santos Zelaya. The struggle for Honduras became so destabilizing that it attracted the notice of Mexican President Porfirio Díaz, who convinced President Theodore Roosevelt to hold two peace conferences. The Marblehead Conference (1906) and Washington Conference (1907) established institutions that enabled Central America's states to peacefully settle their disputes. Despite assurances to the contrary, Estrada Cabrera soon reverted to his old ways.

Despite his unsavory image, Estrada Cabrera constantly curried Washington's favor. Rather than excoriate President Roosevelt for his role in the Panamanian revolt of 1903, Estrada Cabrera broke rank with his colleagues and expressed his support. He remained silent when a U.S.-supported revolt unseated his nemesis, José Santos Zelaya, in 1909. When the United States entered World War I on the side of the Allies, Guatemala also entered the fray, in support of the Allied cause. Instead of rewarding him for his pro-American stance, Washington began to put pressure on Estrada Cabrera to institute reforms. It took two earthquakes (in 1917 and 1918) to loosen Estrada Cabrera's grip on Guatemala. The corruption of his regime was laid bare after the earthquakes, when it was revealed that all of the relief money ended up in the pocket of the president and his cronies. Popular discontent built to the point that the country's military chiefs forced Estrada Cabrera to resign from office in April 1920.

See also *Central American Conference, Washington, 1907; Díaz Mori, Porfirio; Guatemala, U.S. Relations with; Roosevelt, Theodore; United Fruit Company (UFCO); Zelaya López, José Santos*

. . . . PETER B. GUSHUE

REFERENCES AND FURTHER READING

Asturias, Miguel Angel. *The President*. Translated by Frances Partridge. Prospect Heights, IL: Waveland Press, 1997.

Dosal, Paul. *Doing Business with the Dictators: A Political History of United Fruit in Guatemala, 1899–1944*. Wilmington, DE: Greenwood Press, 1993.

Munro, Dana G. *Intervention and Dollar Diplomacy, 1900–1921*. Princeton, NJ: Princeton University Press, 1964.

Estrada Doctrine

(**See** *Estrada Félix, Genaro*)

Estrada Félix, Genaro

Mexican diplomat, professor, and author, Genaro Estrada Félix (1887–1937) was born in Mazatlán, Sinaloa, on June 2, 1887. On moving to Mexico City, he taught at the Escuela Nacional Preparatoria and the Universidad Nacional Autónoma de México, and he wrote numerous essays and books of fiction, biography, history, and poetry. In 1923 he joined Mexico's foreign service and served in various posts, including subsecretary and secretary of foreign relations, Mexico's representative to the League of Nations from 1930 to 1931, ambassador to Spain from 1932 to 1935, and special representative to Turkey in 1933. Estrada died in Mexico City on September 29, 1937.

In 1930 Estrada drafted a new policy regarding recognition of foreign powers. Later known as the Estrada Doctrine, the policy espoused automatic recognition of a foreign government, regardless of how the regime came to power. Recent revolutions in Central America and South America precipitated debate in the western hemisphere about how to recognize a number of de facto regimes. No doubt an important influence on Estrada and the Mexican government was the difficulty experienced by the Mexican government in obtaining diplomatic recognition from foreign powers, most notably the United States, after coming to power after Mexico's revolution in 1917.

Estrada's policy of nonintervention and self-determination challenged the Tobar Doctrine of 1907. The earlier doctrine called on American states to deny recognition to regimes that toppled governments through unconstitutional means. Underlying the Tobar Doctrine was the belief that governments could inhibit revolutions in the region by refusing formal recognition.

The Estrada Doctrine formulated part of a distinct postrevolutionary Mexican foreign policy. Prior to Estrada, Mexico's president, Venustiano Carranza (1917–1920), formulated one of the first statements on foreign policy by the nascent revolutionary state. The Carranza Doctrine demanded, among other things, the rejection of the U.S. Monroe Doctrine and, instead, premised Mexican solidarity with other Latin American nations on mutual respect and absolute nonintervention. Thus, Estrada's Doctrine strengthened the spirit of Inter-American relations based on continuous diplomacy through a policy of automatic recognition of new governments.

Mexico forcibly pressed for its acceptance in the Inter-American system. Many Latin American countries embraced the Estrada Doctrine in reaction to the indiscriminate policies of large powers like the United States toward regime recognition. The United States, however, continued to apply national and political interests as the basis of recognizing new governments. At the Seventh International Conference of American States in 1933, participating governments adopted the Convention of Rights and Duties of States, which embodied broad nonintervention principles.

Throughout the twentieth century, the Mexican government strongly adhered to the Estrada Doctrine, with the notable exception of the refusal to recognize the regime of Francisco Franco in Spain. During the Cold War era, the Mexican government applied the Estrada Doctrine when it formally recognized the revolutionary governments of Cuba, Grenada, Guatemala, and Nicaragua. In addition, Mexico maintained ties with Cuba after 1964 when the Organization of American States (OAS) formally broke relations with Cuba as part of sanctions against the regime of Fidel Castro.

See also *Mexican Revolution, 1911–1917, U.S. Policy toward; Monroe Doctrine; Organization of American States (OAS); Tobar Donoso, Julio*

. . . . SUSANNE EINEIGEL

REFERENCES AND FURTHER READING

Dulles, John W. F. *Yesterday in Mexico: A Chronicle of the Revolution, 1919–1936.* Austin: University of Texas Press, 1961.

Ronning, C. Neale, ed. *Intervention in Latin America.* New York: Knopf, 1970.

Estrada Palma, Tomás

On May 20, 1902, after nearly four years of U.S. occupation, Tomás Estrada Palma (1835–1908) became the first elected president of Cuba. Born in Bayamo, Oriente Province, in 1835, he studied law at the universities of Havana and Seville but never graduated. During the Ten Years' War (1868–1878), he joined the Cuban patriots and was elected president of the Republic in Arms in March 1876. On October 19, 1877, Spanish troops captured him, but he was set free in 1878. He left Cuba and lived in Honduras, where he married President Santos Guardiola's daughter.

After Guardiola's death, Estrada Palma settled in the United States, where he served as schoolmaster at Central Valley School in New York. He also became a U.S. citizen and a Quaker. In 1887, José Martí, the Cuban patriot, asked him to join the Cuban independence cause.

When Martí was killed in Cuba on May 19, 1895, Estrada Palma became Martí's successor as leader of the Cuban Revolutionary Party. Although he never set foot in Cuba during its war for independence (1895–1898), he was instrumental in securing economic support from Cuban immigrants for the patriots' cause.

On June 12, 1901, the United States forced Cuba to incorporate the Platt Amendment to the Cuban Constitution. The amendment restricted Cuban independence. Following the adoption, elections were scheduled for December 31, 1901.

The overwhelming majority of Cubans favored war hero Máximo Gómez Báez for president. Gómez, however, declined, and traveled to New York to convince Estrada Palma to become a candidate. On November 26, 1901, Estrada Palma surrendered his U.S. citizenship and became a candidate against Bartolomé Masó. The United States favored Estrada Palma because he had no objections to the Platt Amendment, while Masó had vigorously opposed the amendment.

Estrada Palma was virtually unknown to eligible Cuban voters because he had not been on the island since 1878 and was living in the United States when the elections were held. Yet, he won the elections largely due to Gómez's unconditional support. He arrived in Cuba on April 20, 1902, and assumed the presidency on May 20, 1902.

Because of the Platt Amendment, the Estrada Palma administration was hampered in its relations with the United States. One of the clauses stipulated that Cuba was to lease coaling stations for the U.S. Navy. In 1903, he negotiated the permanent treaty with the United States, granting the coaling stations. The United States demanded four such stations, but Estrada Palma convinced the Roosevelt administration in 1903 to accept only two: Guantánamo and Bahía Honda, which was never used.

In terms of trade relations, his administration signed the Treaty of Commercial Reciprocity on December 11, 1902. Ratified by both Cuba and the United States, it granted Cuban sugar imports a 20 percent preferential tariff. In exchange, certain enumerated U.S. exports to Cuba received a 20 to 40 percent preferential tariff treatment. While the treaty brought about a financial bonanza to Cuba, it led to Cuban dependency on sugar and the United States. In addition, it opened the door for U.S. ownership of the majority of the Cuban sugar industry.

One of the problems faced by Estrada Palma's administration was that of paying retirement benefits to 40,000 independence war veterans. Estrada Palma secured a $35 million loan from the Speyer Bank. U.S. Secretary of War Elihu Root, who was an adviser to the bank, used his influence to ensure that the bank would be the granting agency.

In 1905, Don Tomás—as Cubans called him—decided to run for reelection. A number of his former supporters decried his candidacy, citing the electoral fraud perpetrated by his followers in the 1904 congressional elections. His opponent, General José Miguel Gómez of the Liberal Party, withdrew, charging that Don Tomás's followers were intimidating voters. As expected, Don Tomás was reelected in an election riddled with fraud on December 1, 1905.

In August 1906, Gómez revolted, and chaos ensued. Don Tomás, invoking a Platt Amendment article that authorized the United States to militarily intervene in Cuba, called on the Theodore Roosevelt administration to intervene to prevent a civil war. Roosevelt sent Secretary of War William Taft to Havana as envoy to meet with Estrada Palma and the rebels. When Taft informed Don Tomás that he was being intransigent, the president felt insulted and resigned on September 27, 1906. Two days later, two thousand Marines landed in Cuba to restore order.

After his resignation, Estrada Palma returned to his estate near Bayamo. He was proud of having left a $27 million surplus in the treasury but dejected at how the U.S. government had treated him. He died on November 4, 1908.

See also *Cuba, U.S. Relations with; Gómez Báez, Máximo; Platt, Orville; Roosevelt, Theodore; Root, Elihu; Spanish-Cuban-American War, 1895–1898; Taft, William H.*

. . . . JOSÉ B. FERNÁNDEZ

REFERENCES AND FURTHER READING

Costa, Octavio R. *Imagen y trayectoria del cubano en la historia.* Miami: Ediciones Universal, 1998.

Duarte Oropesa, José. *Historiología cubana: Desde 1898 hasta 1944.* Miami: Ediciones Universal, 1974.

Leonard, Thomas M. *Castro and the Cuban Revolution.* Westport, CT: Greenwood Press, 1999.

European Economic Community and Latin America

The European Economic Community (EEC) was created in 1957 with six participating countries: Germany, France, Belgium, Luxemburg, Italy, and the Netherlands. The European Community (EC) was formed in 1967 by unifying the EEC, the European Atomic Energy Commission, and the European Coal and Steel Community. In the next three decades, other countries were added to the EC, which reached twelve members in 1993. At that time, it was replaced by the European Union, a stronger type of economic integration that included a common monetary and fiscal policy, including a common currency, introduced in 2002, the euro. Since its beginning, the main goal of the EEC and later the EC was to foster trade and economic integration among the member nations and to extend the agreement to other European countries. The EEC also tried to create ties with developing nations, including Latin American countries. As a result, there were direct attempts to establish both economic and political relationships between the European bloc and Latin American countries.

Initially, the integration efforts of the EEC countries distracted from a great interest in increasing the relationship with Latin America, despite the historical ties with many of its countries. However, as time went on, the EC tried to reach out to Latin American countries by providing foreign direct investment, trade relationships, and economic aid. Furthermore, the EC served as an example for Latin American countries attempting regional integration.

In the case of foreign direct investment, European countries had an interest in establishing multinational companies. After World War II, Latin American countries attempted to replace imports with goods manufactured domestically, the import substitution strategy. With most Latin American markets closed to imports of industrialized goods, European countries had to invest in overseas branches as a way to produce and sell their products in Latin America. Since the governments in Latin American countries had a very important role in resource allocation and regulation of the economy, international agreements of cooperation and investment had to be negotiated. As a consequence, the presence of European companies in Latin America grew in the second part of the twentieth century, competing with companies from the United States. One of the goals of Latin American countries was to foster the adoption and transfer of new technologies through multinational corporations. Nonetheless, these companies usually provided outdated technology and exploited market advantages provided by the local government without providing general advantages for industrial development.

With respect to trade, the relationship between the EC and Latin American countries was difficult. The EC signed several trade agreements with some Latin American countries in the 1970s, which allowed for an increasing flow of goods and services in both directions. As a result, trade in both regions grew strongly for the period after World War II and through the 1980s. However, Latin American countries protested the EEC's adoption of generalized subsidies to agriculture, as well as the many restrictions on importing agricultural goods to the European markets. This became a traditional point of disagreement in the trade relationships between both regions. The EC was able to exert its economic power in dealing with specific agreements for agricultural goods not produced in the EEC, like bananas and coffee, as well as for some raw materials needed for the industrial sector. However, more general trade agreements for other agricultural products were not reached, and this was a recurrent issue in diverse meetings and forums. The lack of resolution of this issue led to the limited economic relationship and integration between the two regions, and it has undermined the advance of agreement in other economic areas.

Despite the disagreements on agricultural policy, and the importance for developing countries of being able to sell in developed markets, the EC was very active in providing foreign aid and technical assistance to Latin American countries. For example, in the 1970s, the EC provided nonpreferential trade agreements to Argentina, Mexico, Brazil, and Uruguay, as well as integration assistance to the Central American Common Market and the Latin American Free Trade Association; the latter included cooperation with and support of programs fighting poverty in Latin American countries, as well as general policy advice and collaboration. Most of these activities are performed through international organizations like the World Bank, the International Monetary Fund, and the Inter-American Development Bank, which were strongly influenced by Europe and the United States.

The creation of the European Union in 1993 and the subsequent addition of numerous countries have not significantly changed the challenges and opportunities for collaboration with Latin America. Furthermore, the creation of the World Trade Organization in 1994 has added a new forum where both regions can discuss their disagreements in terms of trade policy. Furthermore, the example of the European Union has become a recurrent instrument of debate when Latin American countries discuss integration projects.

See also *Atlantic Community Development Group for Latin America; Caribbean Community Common Market (CARICOM); European Union and Latin America; Institute for European-Latin American Relations (IRELA)*

. . . . ANDRÉS GALLO

REFERENCES AND FURTHER READING

Lietaer, Bernard A. *Europe + Latin America + the Multinationals: A Positive Sum Game for the Exchange of Raw Materials and Technology in the 1980s*. New York: Praeger, 1980.

Masoni, Vittorio, and Joris Voorhoeve. "The European Community's Development Program." *Finance and Development* 13 (September 1976): 36.

Mower, A. Glenn. *The European Community and Latin America: A Case Study in Global Role Expansion*. Westport, CT: Greenwood Press, 1982.

Smith, Peter H., ed. *The Challenge of Integration: Europe and the Americas*. New Brunswick, NJ: Transaction Publishers, North-South Center, University of Miami, 1993.

European Union and Latin America

The European Union was created in 1993 from the former European Economic Community (EEC), which had been established in 1957 with six initial member countries: Germany, France, Belgium, Luxemburg, Italy, and the Netherlands. In the next three decades, other countries were added to the organization: Denmark, the United Kingdom, Greece, Portugal, and Spain. There were twelve members in 1993, when the organization became the European Union, a stronger type of economic integration that included a common monetary and fiscal policy, including a common currency, introduced in 2002, the euro. Austria, Sweden, Finland, Estonia, Lithuania, Latvia, Poland, Czech Republic, Slovakia, Hungary, Slovenia, Malta, and Cyprus have joined the European Union since its creation in 1993; the total is now twenty-five member countries. Since its beginning, the main goal of the European Union was to foster trade and economic integration among the members and to extend the agreement to other European countries. The European Union established strong ties with Latin American countries, fostering economic relationships and integration. It also served as example for Latin American attempts at integration, which is the case with the MERCOSUR (Mercado del Cono Sur), the integration attempt joining Argentina, Brazil, Paraguay, and Uruguay and later Bolivia and Chile.

LIMITED RELATIONSHIP WITH LATIN AMERICA

The European Union symbolizes the ultimate success in regional economic integration worldwide. The adoption of common macroeconomic policies, starting in 1993, and the successive steps to establish a common currency have served as examples of successful integration for Latin American and other developing countries. In that respect, Latin American countries have looked at the European Union as a source of advice and guidance on how to foster their own integration programs. In particular, the MERCOSUR has tried to follow the steps of the European Union, although without much success. However, the relationship between the European Union and the MERCOSUR has been the most successful relationship developed in the region to date.

Despite the interest in the European integration movement and the strong historical, cultural, and religious ties, the European Union has not developed a strong trade relationship with Latin America as it has with other regions, like Africa and Asia. This could be linked to the strong colonial ties of Europe with Africa, whose economic relationship with Europe grew strongly after the independence movement in several African countries. Furthermore, European interests in Latin America have faced the opposition of and competition from U.S. economic interests. As a result, trade relationships between both regions have been less than optimal. Another important issue that defines economic relationships with Latin America is the trade barriers the European Union imposes on agricultural exports from Latin America. The generous subsidies the European Union provides to its own farmers—together with other barriers to free trade—harm agricultural producers in Latin America, whose countries have complained constantly in the World Trade Organization (WTO) and other international forums. Some of these problems with subsidies and barriers, as for example the banana trade with Ecuador, have involved a single country; in other cases, such as the broader range of agricultural products, a larger number of countries have brought their case to the WTO. Tariffs on the import of bananas from Ecuador have created several problems between the European Union and Ecuador. These unresolved trade issues make difficult other economic relationships between the regions. However, any long-term economic agreement between these two regions requires a successful solution to the issue of agricultural subsidies. The lack of success of the WTO Doha round of negotiations (2001–2008) hinders the chances for such an agreement in the near future.

POINTS OF CONTACT

Despite the disagreements on agricultural policy and the importance for developing countries of being able to sell in developed markets, the European Union is very active in providing foreign aid to Latin American countries. There are numerous examples of cooperation and support of programs fighting poverty in Latin American countries, as well as general policy advice and collaboration. Most of these activities are performed through international organizations like the World Bank, the International Monetary Fund, and the Inter-American Development Bank, which are strongly influenced by Europe and the United States.

Another area of strong cooperation among the regions is foreign direct investment. Following World War II, most Latin American countries adopted import substitution strategies of economic development, looking to close markets to foreign manufacturers and industrialize their own economies. Thus, European countries had an interest in establishing multinational companies as a way to produce and sell their products in Latin America. Such companies had to negotiate international agreements of cooperation and investment with the governments in Latin American countries, which play an important role in resource allocation and regulation of the economy. As a consequence, the number of European companies in Latin America grew in the second part of the twentieth century, competing with U.S. companies. One of the goals of Latin American countries was to foster the adoption and transfer of new technologies through multinational corporations. In the 1990s, European countries, especially Spain, Germany, France, the United Kingdom, and Italy, took part in the privatization process and market reforms in the region. A strong inflow of European capital to the region helped to modernize and improve the performance of formerly government-owned companies. These productive relationships, even though they declined in the 2000s, are still strong forces of economic integration among the regions. The inflow of foreign investment and the growing opportunities for European companies renewed the interest of the European Union in Latin America and increased the efforts to reach long-term sustainable economic agreements.

Latin American countries and the European Union have held a summit in Peru and met again in Madrid in May 2010 to discuss issues related to economic development, investment, integration, and trade (for additional information, see http://ec.europa.eu/external_relations/lac/index_en.htm). Nonetheless, these meetings have not been able to solve any of the outstanding trade issues between the two regions. As a result, although there could be mutual economic benefits from increasing economic relations, the divisive nature of the international trade issues slows the advance of such relations.

See also *Atlantic Community Development Group for Latin America; Caribbean Community Common Market (CARICOM); European Economic Community and Latin America; French-Speaking Caribbean: Guadeloupe, Martinique, U.S. Relations with; Institute for European-Latin American Relations (IRELA)*

. . . . ANDRÉS GALLO

REFERENCES AND FURTHER READING

Giustino, David de. *A Reader in European Integration.* London: Longman, 1996.

Holland, Martin. *The European Union and the Third World.* New York: Palgrave, 2002.

Kaufman Purcell, Susan, and Simon Francoise, eds. *Europe and Latin America in the World Economy.* London: Lynne Rienner, 1995.

Mower, A. Glenn. *The European Community and Latin America: A Case Study in Global Role Expansion.* Westport, CT: Greenwood Press, 1982.

Smith, Peter, ed. *The Challenge of Integration: Europe and the Americas.* New Brunswick, NJ: Transaction Publishers, 1993.

Evarts, William

William Evarts (1818–1901) was U.S. secretary of state during the administration of Rutherford Hayes (President 1877–1881). In that role, Evarts dealt with a number of diplomatic issues relating to Latin America: recognition of the Porfirio Díaz Mori-led Mexican government; the War of the Pacific between Peru, Bolivia, and Chile; and the pursuit of a transoceanic canal.

Evarts came from a distinguished New England background and achieved renown as a lawyer before his appointment. He was perhaps best known for his defense of President Andrew Johnson at the latter's impeachment trial. He was also known as an avid reformer and a New York Republican who was not part of the New York political machine of Roscoe Conkling. His nomination to the highest post in the Cabinet was a blow to Conkling and was thus based on both external and domestic concerns.

Shortly after he assumed his position, Evarts was forced to deal with a conflict along the Mexican-American border. In November 1876, Porfirio Díaz succeeded in driving Mexican President Sebastian Lerdo from Mexico's capital and established himself as president. President Ulysses Grant and Secretary of State Hamilton Fish decided to withhold formal recognition of the Díaz government until the new regime had established de facto control of the nation. This stance was consistent with previous U.S. policy but resulted in Evarts and Hayes inheriting the problem when they assumed office in 1877. The issue of recognition then became more complex when border raids increased along the Rio Grande. The raids led to the dispatch of U.S. forces along the Mexican border and a subsequent authorization to send U.S. forces into Mexico in pursuit of raiders who crossed the border. This order greatly alarmed the new Mexican government and precipitated a crisis in relations between the two nations. The crisis passed when the Díaz government began to exert its authority over the borderlands, and the number of cross border raids diminished. The United States then officially recognized the new Mexican government.

Shortly after the Mexican-border crisis ended, the War of the Pacific (1879–1883) began. Peru, Bolivia, and Chile fought over a nitrate rich area of the Atacama Desert, which bordered all three nations. In the end, Chile defeated the combined forces of Peru and Bolivia and annexed the region, leaving Bolivia a landlocked nation. Evarts supported an attempted mediation organized by the U.S. ambassadors to the belligerent nations, but the resulting Arica Conference was a failure. A series of miscommunications and personal conflicts between the U.S. representatives undermined the conference before it began, and the military conflict resumed shortly thereafter.

Evarts was also instrumental in shaping the view of the U.S. government toward the construction of a canal in Central America linking the Atlantic and Pacific. In 1880, French developer Ferdinand de Lesseps, who had been instrumental in the construction of the Suez Canal, began construction of the Panama Canal. Evarts declared that any canal of this sort in the western hemisphere would have to be controlled by the United States. This statement became the official policy of the United States and would govern the actions of subsequent administrations that were faced with the issue. Evarts later served in the U.S. Senate from 1885 to 1891.

See also *Díaz Mori, Porfirio; Hayes, Rutherford B.; War of the Pacific, 1879–1883*

. . . . JASON ZORBAS

REFERENCES AND FURTHER READING

Dyer, Brainerd. *The Public Career of William M. Evarts.* Berkeley: University of California Press, 1933.

Sater, William. *Chile and the United States.* Athens: University of Georgia Press, 1990.

Evarts Doctrine

(**See** *Evarts, William*)

Everett, Edward

Edward Everett (1794–1865) was born in Dorchester, Massachusetts. The son of an Episcopalian priest, he was educated at

Harvard and ordained a Unitarian pastor in 1814 but decided to pursue an academic career. Everett became a professor of Greek literature and then went to receive a Ph.D. at Goettingen (1817) and traveled in Europe and Asia Minor. Returning home in 1819, he became an editor of *North American Review* (1819–1823) and resumed a professorship at Harvard (1819–1825).

His political career began when he was elected as a member of Congress (1825–1835) and later Massachusetts governor (1836–1839). He served as a minister in Great Britain from November 1841 to August 1845. Opposed to the Mexican War, as were all the New England Whigs, Everett retired from politics to become the president of Harvard (1846–1849). After the death of Daniel Webster, Everett was appointed secretary of state and served in this capacity about four months, until the end of the President Millard Fillmore Whig administration (November 6, 1852–March 3, 1853). He concluded his political career as a senator from Massachusetts in 1853 and1854 and the vice presidential candidate for the Constitutional Union Party in the 1860 election.

Everett's role in early U.S.–Latin American relations was not significant, but his views on this subject were typical for one side of U.S. public opinion. In spite of his well-known enthusiasm for Greek revolutions and contrary to Jared Sparks, who succeeded him as an editor of the *North American Review*, Everett remained skeptical concerning the prospects of "Southern brethren." He stated that former Spanish and Portuguese colonies were not able to construct a stable political regime and that "South America will be for North America . . . what Asia and Africa are to Europe" (*North American Review*, April 1821, p. 435). In his famous Fourth of July oration, *The History of Liberty* (Charlestown, 1828), Everett proclaimed the role of the United States as a guide of *regulated liberty* for other nations, including those in Latin America.

As a secretary of state, Everett made a widely publicized application of the Polk Doctrine when in December 1852 he rejected an Anglo-French proposal of a tripartite convention guaranteeing to Spain the possession of Cuba. He declared that the United States had a special interest in this neighboring island and that it might have been potentially acquired by the United States as part of the purchases of Louisiana or Florida. This note served as a step to the Ostend Manifesto (August 16, 1854), a quickly discredited document stipulating that the United States would seize Cuba by force if Spain refused to sell the island.

Everett's elder brother, Alexander Hill Everett (1790–1857), a minister to Spain from 1825 to 1829, supported his younger brother Edward's skeptical views of Latin American self-governance in his *America; or a General Survey of the Political Situation of the Several Powers of the Western Continent* (1827). Everett visited Cuba and corresponded with Cuban liberal writer, historian, and abolitionist Domingo del Monte y Aponte (1804–1853). His nephew and namesake Edward Everett fought in the Mexican War and left numerous valuable drawings and maps of Texas.

See also *Mexican-American War; Ostend Manifesto, 1854; Polk, James K.*

. . . . ANDREY ISÉROV

REFERENCES AND FURTHER READING

Everett, Edward. *Orations and Speeches on Various Occasions*. 4 vols. 1853–1868.
Frothingham, Paul Revere. *Edward Everett, Orator and Statesman*. Boston: Houghton Mifflin, 1925. Reprint. Port Washington, NY: Kennikat Press, 1971.
Reid, Ronald F. *Edward Everett: Unionist Orator*. New York: Greenwood Press, 1990.
Varg, Paul A. *Edward Everett: The Intellectual in the Turmoil of Politics*. Selingsrove, PA: Susqehanna University Press, 1992.

Export-Based Economies

Export-based economies are those whose main source of hard currency and economic activity is their ability to sell the goods and services they produce, either in the international market or in the context of bilateral commercial agreements. There are two main kinds of export-based economies: first, the economies that rely on traditional primary export goods, such as coffee and bananas; and second, the economies that have diversified their export industries into more technologically based secondary production and now export manufactured and electronic goods. Latin American countries have traditionally depended on primary goods, as the historical role of Cuban sugar, Ecuadorian bananas, and Salvadoran coffee show. However, several countries have engaged in secondary production for many decades, especially Mexico, Brazil, and Argentina. The role of U.S.-based multinational corporations (MNCs) has been pivotal in the development of both forms of export-based economies in Latin America, producing mixed results in the process.

POST-INDEPENDENCE EXPORTS AND THE ROLE OF MNCs

Post-independence Latin America entered the dynamics of the nineteenth-century international market exclusively as a provider of primary goods and raw materials, continuing the role it had during colonial times. Taking advantage of Spain's weakened status in the aftermath of independence, Great Britain used its imperial power at the time to forge strategic alliances with governments of the new republican nations and invested in the production of raw materials to continue fueling its industrial growth. In this context, Chilean copper and Bolivian tin and silver, among other products, found a revitalized international market that allowed for substantial economic growth and the replenishment of national treasuries.

By the latter part of the nineteenth century and beginning of the twentieth century, U.S. MNCs, such as the United Fruit Company and the Chaparra Sugar Company, had already taken over the export economies in the Caribbean basin, especially the banana industries of Guatemala and Costa Rica, as well as the sugar sectors of Cuba and other Caribbean countries. The roles of these MNCs went beyond the economic realm, and in fact, they influenced the political evolution of these countries insofar as any threats to their interests were met with brutal responses (as was the case with Nicaragua in the early 1930s and with Guatemala in 1954) and the systems of governance and political economy that prevailed were designed to serve these MNCs' business priorities. In the same vein, U.S. government administrations have historically sought to bring about regime change in Latin America by imposing trade sanctions on unfriendly regimes, such as Castro's Cuba and Sandinista Nicaragua.

IMPORT SUBSTITUTION INDUSTRIALIZATION AND EXPORT SUBSTITUTION INDUSTRIALIZATION

The economic crash of 1929 and the Great Depression had a devastating impact on the primary export industries of Latin American countries, as the prices for these goods collapsed in the international market. As a result, many countries of the region moved from an emphasis on exporting primary goods and into import substitution industrialization. This move was undertaken to expand the countries' economic base and decrease their dependence on unreliable primary goods, as well as their dependence on industrialized countries for finished goods. The import substitution strategy sought to make Latin American countries producers of industrial goods, allowing them to become self-sufficient by increasing the purchasing power of the middle and working classes. This strategy required massive government involvement, but when ill-fated management and run-away foreign borrowing impaired its long-term success, countries like Mexico and Brazil adopted a mixed approach to maintain a degree of import substitution that would be combined with export substitution industrialization.

Export substitution attempted to diversify the primary export sectors by introducing technological innovations to increase their competitiveness and to make them more reflective of the changing demands in international commercial patterns. This shift in model of production welcomed the participation of transnationally based MNCs both in terms of investment and of technological expertise. In Mexico, for example, the oil-based export economy was complemented by an agribusiness sector that de-emphasized traditional products, like coffee and sugar, and concentrated on more lucrative cash crops, like palm oil and frozen fruits and vegetables. U.S.-based MNCs, such as Campbell's and Green Giant, have played a major role in the development of these agribusiness ventures. Moreover, Mexico also focused on the development of the manufacturing and assembling sectors, which produce clothes and automobiles mainly for North American markets; Fruit of the Loom and General Motors have played pivotal roles in these subsectors. Brazil and to a lesser extent Argentina have followed similar export-based models.

As the swing in export priorities took place, the worldwide shift in political economy, beginning in the early 1990s, has played an important role in the adoption of these strategies. Following the lead of the Washington Consensus principles, which upheld the need for free market economics, liberalized trade, and less central involvement in the economy, the International Monetary Fund (IMF) and the World Bank pushed for the revitalization of export industries in Latin America as a way to deal with the lingering effects of the 1980s debt crisis, especially in terms of transforming technologically advanced exports into stable sources of hard currency that would enable the servicing of foreign debts.

CONCLUSION

The performance of U.S.-based MNCs in the export industries of Latin American countries has been mixed. On the one hand, they have provided capital, investment, and technology for the development of these sectors, as well as markets for the goods and services they produce. On the other hand, the operations of MNCs have generated social conflicts as their massive use of land and resources has contributed to the inequitable distribution of these factors of production. MNCs have generated a technological and capital dependence that has grown exponentially through the years, and their political influence has encroached on internal dynamics in a detrimental way. Overall, and although they remain important sectors, Latin American export-based strategies in both their primary and secondary dimensions continue to face instability and unreliable conditions in international markets insofar as the products they sell, no matter how diversified or sophisticated, still depend on the business cycles of industrialized economies and remain vulnerable to shifts in demand.

See also *Arbenz Guzmán, Jacobo; Dependency Theory and Latin America; Frank, André Gunder; Guatemala, U.S. Invasion of, 1954; United Fruit Company (UFCO); U.S. Economic Investments in Latin America*

. . . . CARLOS VELÁSQUEZ CARRILLO

REFERENCES AND FURTHER READING

Alschuler, Lawrence. *Multinationals and Maldevelopment: Alternative Development Strategies in Argentina, the Ivory Coast and Korea.* Houndmills, UK: Macmillan Press, 1988.

Bethell, Leslie, ed. *Central America since Independence.* Cambridge, UK: Cambridge University Press, 1991.

Bulmer-Thomas, Victor. *The Economic History of Latin America since Independence.* 2nd ed. Cambridge, UK: Cambridge University Press, 2003.

Frank, Andre Gunder. *Capitalism and Underdevelopment in Latin America: Historical Studies of Chile and Brazil.* New York: Monthly Review Press, 1969.

Furtado, Celso. *Economic Development of Latin America: A Survey from Colonial Times to the Cuban Revolution.* London: Cambridge University Press, 1970.

Export-Import Bank (EXIM)

In February 1934, President Franklin D. Roosevelt established the first Export-Import Bank (EXIM) to facilitate trade with the Soviet Union after that country's recognition by the United States. A second Export-Import Bank, founded in March 1934, was to finance Cuban purchases of silver bullion to be coined into pesos at the U.S. Mint in Philadelphia.

Failed debt negotiations soon undermined the prospects for expanded U.S.-Soviet trade and prompted the merger of the two Export-Import banks in June 1935. EXIM's charter described its mission as extending credit to "aid in financing and to facilitate exports and imports and the exchange of commodities between the United States and other nations." In practice, the bank's lending focused almost exclusively on U.S. exports and contributed little to stimulating imports of foreign goods.

EXIM's mandate restricted loans to foreign borrowers that had no access to commercial credit in the United States or were subject to governmental restrictions on foreign currency reserves. EXIM extended credit (a) for agricultural exports that required extended repayment schedules, (b) for industrial exports, above all capital goods, on application by the exporter, and (c) as relief to exporters affected by foreign currency shortages in the importing countries. Early EXIM credits to Latin America financed the export of rails, locomotives, road-building equipment, machine tools, cotton gins, cast iron pipe, water meters, trucks, and pumps. In 1935 and 1939, Brazil received EXIM loans to meet its dollar obligations to U.S. exporters. In 1939, Nicaragua, Paraguay, and Uruguay also opened revolving credit lines to relieve temporary exchange shortages.

EXIM AND U.S. FOREIGN POLICY IN LATIN AMERICA

For U.S.–Latin American relations, EXIM mattered most in the first twenty years of its existence. Of the fifty-six countries that received loans between 1934 and 1953, nineteen were Latin American. In those years, EXIM lent more money to borrowers from Brazil and Mexico, respectively, than from any other country, if one excludes two exceptional Lend-Lease termination credits to the French government. In 1938, EXIM granted a pioneering development loan to the government of Haiti, which it used to contract U.S. engineering firms for a series of infrastructure projects to benefit the overall economy and foreign trade. The terms of the loan set a precedent in that they permitted the Haitian government to spend some of the money domestically rather than only on U.S. exports and services. In 1939 EXIM extended similar loans to the government of Nicaragua to build a segment of the Inter-American highway and to Paraguay for the construction of a highway connecting a major agricultural region with the capital Asunción.

EXIM's lending decisions closely reflected U.S. foreign policy priorities. With Europe at war starting in 1939, the United States focused on hemispheric cooperation. In 1940 Congress extended EXIM's charter to 1947 and granted Roosevelt's request to increase its lending authority to $700 million. The legislation stated EXIM's mission: "to assist in the development of the resources, the stabilization of the economies, and the orderly marketing of the products of the countries of the Western Hemisphere." EXIM established credit lines for the central banks of Argentina, Brazil, Uruguay, and Peru and financed public works programs in Cuba, Mexico, and Panama. In 1940 the bank authorized its first credit for an industrial development project: Brazil's National Steel Company received a $45 million loan to build an integrated steel mill in Volta Redonda. Many EXIM development loans during World War II aimed at increasing the production of strategic raw materials.

EXIM became more tightly integrated into the U.S. postwar foreign economic policy apparatus after World War II. Between late 1945 and 1948, the Truman administration used the bank to help the recovery effort in Western Europe; EXIM loans bridged the gap between the wartime Lend-Lease agreements and the inception of the Marshall Plan in 1948. That year, Latin America accounted for only 14 percent of EXIM's lending activity. With the Marshall Plan and the newly created International Bank for Reconstruction and Development (IBRD) in place to serve Europe's needs, EXIM again turned its attention to Latin America. By 1951, the region received 63 percent of the bank's disbursements. Driven by Cold War rationale, EXIM promoted development in the western hemisphere that would increase the supply of strategic raw materials and expand markets for U.S. goods.

EXIM'S DECLINING IMPORTANCE FOR LATIN AMERICA

The Dwight D. Eisenhower administration (1953–1961) curtailed EXIM's development lending to avoid competition with the World Bank, which had been founded in 1944. U.S. industrial exporters lobbied successfully, however, to preserve EXIM's role in financing U.S. international trade throughout the 1950s. Cuba's refusal in 1960 to repay EXIM loans contracted by the prerevolutionary government prompted the bank to reduce its exposure in Latin America. EXIM's focus shifted to parts of the third world where the United States competed directly with the Soviet Union for allegiance: South Asia, the Middle East, and sub-Saharan Africa. Development loans to Latin America became the territory of the Inter-American Development Bank (IABD), founded in 1959, and of the World Bank. EXIM remained an instrument of U.S. anticommunist foreign policy, however. In the mid-1960s, the bank extended loans to Brazil's military government and to Chile's Christian Democratic government, which used the funds for a partial nationalization of copper mines to counter the rising popularity of the left.

New economic circumstances in the 1970s again changed the role of EXIM. Competition from European and Japanese exports increased demand for assistance, but the end of the Bretton Woods system, the oil crisis, and the availability of petrodollar loans restricted EXIM's role in the 1970s. The Latin American debt crisis of the early 1980s brought EXIM back into play in its role as reinsurer of commercial coverage. As Latin American governments deferred payments on foreign currency–denominated debt, insurance claims by U.S. exporters mounted. In 1982 and 1983, EXIM established an insurance facility as part of the rescue packages for two of the worst-hit countries: Mexico and Brazil. The lack of big projects, little support in the Ronald Reagan administration, and financial losses in the decade after the debt crisis again marginalized EXIM. It provided emergency loans in the financial crises of the mid-and late 1990s, but it never returned to the prominent role it had played for U.S.–Latin American relations in its early years.

See also *Good Neighbor Policy; Inter-American Development Bank (IADB); International Bank for Reconstruction and Development (World Bank); Marshall Plan and Latin America; Roosevelt, Franklin D.; World War II, 1939–1945*

. . . . OLIVER J. DINIUS

REFERENCES AND FURTHER READING

Adams, Frederick C. *Economic Diplomacy: The Export-Import Bank and American Foreign Policy, 1934–1939*. Columbia: University of Missouri Press, 1976.

Arey, Hawthorne. *History of Operations and Policies of Export-Import Bank of Washington*. Washington, DC: Export-Import Bank, 1953.

Becker, William H., and William M. McClenahan Jr. *The Market, the State, and the Export-Import Bank of the United States, 1934–2000*. Cambridge, UK: Cambridge University Press, 2003.

Rodriguez, Rita M., ed. *The Export-Import Bank at Fifty: The International Environment and the Institution's Role*. Lexington, MA: Lexington Books, 1987.

Index

Page numbers and topics in bold type indicate principal treatment of topics. Illustrations and photos are indicated with italic page references. Alphabetization is letter-by-letter (e.g., Longley precedes Long Telegram).